D0126979

SECOND EDITION

The Language of Composition
Reading • Writing • Rhetoric

Renée H. Shea
Bowie State University, Maryland

Lawrence Scanlon
Brewster High School, New York

Robin Dissin Aufses
Lycée Français de New York

Bedford/St. Martin's
Boston • New York

For Bedford/St. Martin's
Senior Developmental Editor: Nathan Odell
Senior Production Editor: Bill Imbornoni
Senior Production Supervisor: Nancy J. Myers
Senior Marketing Manager: Daniel McDonough
Editorial Assistant: Emily Wunderlich
Copy Editor: Alice Vigliani
Indexer: Kirsten Kite
Photo Researcher: Julie Tesser
Permissions Manager: Kalina H. Ingham
Art Director: Lucy Krikorian
Text Design: Linda M. Robertson
Cover Design: Donna Lee Dennison
Cover Photo: Panoramic Images/Getty Images (US), Inc.
Composition: Jouve
Printing and Binding: LSC Communications

President, Bedford/St. Martin's: Denise B. Wydra
Presidents, Macmillan Higher Education: Joan E. Feinberg and Tom Scotty
Editor in Chief: Karen S. Henry
Director of Development: Erica T. Appel
Director of Marketing: Karen R. Soeltz
Production Director: Susan W. Brown
Associate Production Director: Elise S. Kaiser
Managing Editor: Shuli Traub

Library of Congress Control Number: 2012937280

Manufactured in the United States of America.

9   18

For information, write: Bedford/St. Martin's, 75 Arlington Street, Boston, MA 02116
(617-399-4000)

ISBN 978-0-312-67650-6

Acknowledgments
Acknowledgments and copyrights are included at the back of the book on pages 1153–1160, which constitute an extension of the copyright page.

To Michael Shea, William and Mary Scanlon,
and Arthur Aufses

About the Authors

Renée H. Shea was professor of English and Modern Languages at Bowie State University and former Director of Composition. She is coauthor of *Literature & Composition: Reading • Writing • Thinking* and two titles in the NCTE High School Literature series on Amy Tan and Zora Neale Hurston. She has been a reader and question leader for both AP Language and Literature readings.

Lawrence Scanlon taught at Brewster High School for more than thirty years. Over the past fifteen years he has been a reader and question leader for the AP Language exam. As a College Board consultant in the United States and abroad, he has conducted AP workshops in both Language and Literature, as well as serving on the AP Language Development Committee. Larry is coauthor of *Literature & Composition: Reading • Writing • Thinking* and has published articles for the College Board and elsewhere on composition and curriculum.

Robin Dissin Aufses is director of English Studies at Lycée Français de New York. She is coauthor of *Literature & Composition: Reading • Writing • Thinking*. Robin also has published articles for the College Board on the novelist Chang Rae Lee and the novel *All the King's Men*.

Preface

We designed *The Language of Composition: Reading • Writing • Rhetoric* to be the first college-level textbook intended for upper-level high school English courses, in particular the Advanced Placement* English Language and Composition course. Its goal is to help high school students read, analyze, and write with the same level of skill and sophistication of thought as they would in a first-year composition course in college. *The Language of Composition* offers a diverse collection of more than 150 college-level selections—including nonfiction, fiction, poetry, and visual texts—that are both interesting and suitable for a high school audience; practical advice on rhetoric, argument, reading, and writing; and special attention to synthesis and visual analysis skills in keeping with the content of the AP English Language and Composition course and exam.

The Language of Composition is the product of years of experience and collaboration. The three of us met through workshops where we were learning how to incorporate the theory and practice of rhetoric into high school curricula. The conversation that began in summer workshops extended to years of discussions about what worked with eleventh- and twelfth-graders and how to prepare students to succeed in or place out of first-year composition. The more we taught our students and worked with teachers, the more we came to appreciate the interrelationship among the three main components of this book: rhetoric, reading, and writing.

Sometimes we get lucky and life gives us second chances—as it has with *The Language of Composition*. Because of the excitement of teachers and students who have been using the book and the insights they have so generously shared, we learned what was working well, what needed more work, and what work was yet to be done.

What's New in the Opening Chapters?

A Chapter on Argument At conferences, at workshops, and in reviews, we heard many teachers asking for more information on argument—how to help students

---

*AP and Advanced Placement Program are registered trademarks of the College Entrance Examination Board, which was not involved in the publication of and does not endorse this product.

analyze arguments as well as write their own. Chapter 3, "Analyzing Arguments: From Reading to Writing," introduces the essential elements of argument—such as claims, evidence, fallacies, and arrangement—in an approachable and practical way. In this chapter, we take students through the process of constructing an argument on a topic of their own choice—from exploring ideas to crafting an arguable claim to developing evidence and structuring the overall essay.

Activity-Driven Opening Chapters   The opening chapters now give students many more opportunities to practice individual skills with brief, approachable texts. We believe that students learn by doing; we also acknowledge that teachers need more opportunities to scaffold and differentiate instruction in a challenging course such as AP English Language. In addition, each of the opening chapters concludes with a culminating activity on a series of brief texts and visual texts that allows students to demonstrate what they've learned in their work with single texts. This is yet another layer of scaffolding designed to help students of all levels reach proficiency.

Chapter Glossaries   The glossary of stylistic terms in Chapter 2 of the first edition was so popular with teachers and students as a handy reference, vocabulary list, and chapter summary that we decided to include similar glossaries in other opening chapters. Now Chapter 1 includes a brief Glossary of Rhetorical Terms, and Chapter 3 includes a brief Glossary of Argument Terms and Fallacies.

What's New in the Thematic Chapters?

Let's start with what's not new: the Central and Classic Essays that anchor the book. While we wanted this new edition to be much more than a cosmetic update, we recognized the importance of maintaining continuity in the core texts. So, while a few essays have moved and some new ones are enjoying the spotlight, every Central and Classic Essay from the first edition has been retained in this edition.

New Authors, Fresh Perspectives   This edition includes more than 80 new pieces of nonfiction, and we think that is very exciting. Voices new to this edition include classic writers such as Benjamin Franklin, Walt Whitman, and Andrew Carnegie, along with a host of influential contemporary thinkers, commentators, and humorists: Wendell Berry, Firoozeh Dumas, Jonathan Safran Foer, Thomas Friedman, Malcolm Gladwell, Chuck Klosterman, Michael Lewis, Dinaw Mengestu, Michael Pollan, Marjane Satrapi, Eric Schlosser, David Sedaris, Brent Staples, David Foster Wallace, Sarah Vowell, and Fareed Zakaria.

Two New Chapters   In this edition, we have shifted the focus of two chapters. The chapter on Work has become a chapter on The Economy. Particularly timely, this chapter focuses on personal and social issues surrounding the economy, as opposed to technical or political matters. The chapter on Nature has evolved into a chapter on The Environment. This shift in focus recognizes that the AP Language course is moving away from lyrical essays and nature writing and toward issue-driven arguments.

New Conversation Topics   To keep the book up-to-date and to give you fresh material for class, we have changed many of the topics of conversation in this edition. Paying College Athletes, for instance, and Sustainable Eating are topics at the forefront of our national conversation; they are issues that students can become quickly well-versed in without specialized or technical knowledge. In the Language chapter, the Conversation on American Politics and the English Language is a natural extension of Orwell's essay, and a topic that goes to the heart of the AP Language course's civic purpose. In the Popular Culture chapter, the Conversation on Exporting American Pop Culture shows that pop culture is about more than frothy celebrity gossip; it is a serious cultural and political force.

New Making Connections Questions   In this edition, we've added Making Connections questions to the Conversations to help students compare and contrast the various arguments in the Conversations, a key intermediary step in moving from analysis toward synthesis.

More Visual Texts   So much of the information our students access is visual, and with that comes an increasing need for visual literacy. This edition includes even more visual texts than the last—at least three per chapter, and many more in the opening chapters. From advertisements, to political cartoons, to fine art, to magazine covers, the visual texts in this edition pack a powerful rhetorical punch.

New Color Insert   It is hard to truly analyze a visual text if you cannot talk about color. This is why, in the new edition, we have included a 24-page color insert that reproduces every piece of color art in the book.

What Features Haven't Changed?

Opening Chapters on Key AP Language Skills   In the four opening chapters of *The Language of Composition*, we introduce students to the principles and language of rhetoric and argument that they will use throughout the book.

- Chapter 1, "An Introduction to Rhetoric: Using the 'Available Means,'" provides instruction in key rhetorical concepts, including the rhetorical situation, appeals, visual rhetoric, and more.

- Chapter 2, "Close Reading: The Art and Craft of Analysis," guides students through the close analysis of diction and syntax with an emphasis on their rhetorical effects.

- Chapter 3, "Analyzing Arguments: From Reading to Writing," helps students master the essential elements of argument and put them to use in their own writing.
- Chapter 4, "Synthesizing Sources: Entering the Conversation," introduces students to the use of sources to develop and enhance their own viewpoints.

Thematic Chapters with Essential Questions   The thematic organization, focused by essential questions, encourages students to explore the complexities of a single issue and synthesize the different viewpoints represented. We chose the nine chapter themes—Education, Community, The Economy, Gender, Sports, Language, Popular Culture, The Environment, and Politics—because they are ones that students will find interesting and relevant and that teachers can easily supplement with literary works or with materials from current events.

Diverse and Engaging Readings   We selected readings for *The Language of Composition* that exemplify excellent writing. Whether a text is narrative, expository, or argumentative, we believe that students benefit from reading and analyzing exceptional rhetoric from contemporary and classic authors. We also selected readings that are important and relevant to students because we believe that interesting, provocative topics promote active, critical reading.

Each thematic chapter is anchored by a Central Essay and a Classic Essay:

- The Central Essays are rich rhetorical and stylistic models, ideally suited to the AP English Language course, such as Martin Luther King Jr.'s "Letter from Birmingham Jail," Stephen Jay Gould's "Women's Brains," and Jamaica Kincaid's "On Seeing England for the First Time."
- The Classic Essays are canonical works written between the eighteenth century and the early twentieth century, giving students experience analyzing writing styles from different periods. Among the classic essays are Ralph Waldo Emerson's "Education," Virginia Woolf's "Professions for Women," Mark Twain's "Corn-Pone Opinions," and Jonathan Swift's "A Modest Proposal."

Knowing how important visuals have become as rhetorical texts in college study and in our society as a whole, we feature visual texts in every chapter. Among these are political cartoons, photographs, advertisements, tables or graphs, and paintings. We approach these visual texts, as we do the written ones, rhetorically, encouraging students to read them closely and ask questions about the ways artists and designers achieve their purposes.

In-Depth Questions and Writing Prompts   In *The Language of Composition*, we have worked to enable students to read with a writer's eye—that is, to see how they can use the techniques of professional and published writers in their own writing. Thus, we intend the questions that accompany the selections to link reading with writing. Always promoting active reading, the questions guide students from understanding what a text is about to how the content is presented as it is and why—the rhetorical strategies. Most readings in the book are followed by Exploring the Text questions, which are a mixture of questions that prompt for discussion and those that ask for a close analysis of rhetoric and style.

For the Central and Classic Essays, the questions are more extensive and grouped into more discrete categories:

- **Questions for Discussion** probe content and connections and support students' careful reading to help them to comprehend ideas, understand cultural and historical context, and make connections to compelling contemporary issues or influences.

- **Questions on Rhetoric and Style** address the *how* and *why* of a text by examining the choices the writer makes and the effect those choices have. On the micro level, these questions address such features as diction and syntax; on the macro level, they consider a text's patterns of organization. While Questions for Discussion are generally open-ended, Questions on Rhetoric and Style are close reading inquiries requiring precise answers similar to analytical essay or multiple-choice responses.

- **Suggestions for Writing** guide students toward written responses that extend the conversation from the reading and suggest ways that students might practice some of the strategies that the writer uses.

Conversations   Because students' ability to synthesize multiple sources is a primary concern of college composition courses—as well as a skill that must be demonstrated on the AP Language exam—the Conversation section in each chapter provides source material and guiding questions to help students use the words and ideas of others to support their own arguments. After synthesizing the written and visual texts provided, students are ready to develop their own voices and positions.

Student Writing   The Student Writing sections use high-quality papers by high school students and college freshmen to model the types of writing essential to success in the AP English Language course and in college. They range from timed writings to longer out-of-class assignments, from rhetorical analyses to essays that incorporate sources in support of an argument. These essays demonstrate the students' skill and creativity, yet they are all in-process, and the accompanying questions encourage revision and expansion, not mere editing or proofreading. We have found that such student work is more accessible than the work of professionals and often provokes suggestions and comments that students would be reluctant to make about a published author's work or even a peer's work if he or she is sitting at the next desk.

Grammar as Rhetoric and Style   These sections use examples from the chapter's readings to reinforce students' understanding of grammar and show how to use grammar and syntax to achieve a rhetorical purpose or stylistic effect. In each chapter, we focus on one issue — such as coordination, parallel structures, or use of pronouns — and explore how what might seem a mechanical point can, in fact, be approached rhetorically. Thus, students can see, for instance, how and to what effect Martin Luther King Jr. uses parallel structure or how Gay Talese uses precise, active verbs.

E-Books

The Language of Composition is available in several different electronic formats to meet your students' needs:

The Language of Composition Bedford e-Book (**ISBN 978-1-4576-1833-8**) Access *The Language of Composition* from any computer via a Web browser. With a robust search engine, navigation tools, easy ways to take and share notes, and interactive exercises, Bedford e-Books support focused reading and studying. And with fast ways to rearrange chapters, add new custom pages, and embed video and audio, Bedford e-Books let teachers build just the right book for their course.

The Language of Composition Bedford e-Book to Go (**ISBN 978-1-4576-3259-4**) These downloadable, PDF-style e-books match our print books page for page, and they're ready for your tablet, computer, phone, or e-reader device. Students can take these e-books with them wherever they go.

The Language of Composition **Partner e-Books**   Students can also find PDF versions of *The Language of Composition* when they shop online at our publishing partners' sites: CourseSmart, Barnes & Noble NOOK Study, Follett CafeScribe, Chegg, and Kno.

Ancillaries

Teacher's Manual for The Language of Composition (**ISBN 978-1-4576-1834-5**) This robust teacher's manual offers suggested responses to all the questions in the book and practical approaches to teaching the full-length essays. A new Introduction to Teaching AP English Language section covers major teaching issues — from designing a curriculum to teaching writing effectively. An expanded test preparation section includes multiple-choice questions, essay prompts, and synthesis clusters to prepare students for the AP Language exam.

The Language of Composition **book companion site (bedfordstmartins.com /languageofcomp)**   This free resource includes the *Language of Composition* Media Library with links to audio, video, and texts related to the readings in *The*

Language of Composition; online reading comprehension quizzes; and access to *Re:Writing*, a free collection of Bedford/St. Martin's most popular online materials for writing, grammar, and research, including *Exercise Central*, the world's largest collection of online interactive grammar exercises.

i•claim visualizing argument   *i•claim* offers a new way to see argument. With tutorials, interactive assignments, and more than 70 multimedia arguments (including Lou Gehrig's farewell speech), *i•claim* brings argument to life.

i•cite visualizing sources   *i•cite* presents a new way to see sources. With its animated introduction to using sources, concrete tutorials, and practice exercises, *i•cite* helps students understand the hows and whys of working with sources.

To bundle *i•claim* and *i•cite* with *The Language of Composition* for only $5, use: ISBN 978-1-4576-4135-0.

Acknowledgments

We want to extend our heartfelt appreciation to the team at Bedford/St. Martin's. We've enjoyed the support, guidance, and encouragement of many talented professionals, starting with the leadership of former president Joan Feinberg, current president Denise Wydra, editor in chief Karen Henry, and director of development Erica Appel, who have been committed to this project from the start. We say a special thanks to Nancy Perry, editorial director of custom publishing, for encouraging us to explore the idea that became *The Language of Composition*. It is no exaggeration to call her role in this project visionary; *The Language of Composition* would truly not exist without her initial ideas and continuing belief in it. To our gifted editor Nathan Odell, we would like to present an academy award for his exceptional judgment, appreciation for language, energy, enthusiasm—and patience. Assigned to this project as our editor, he became our dear friend. We thank Dan McDonough, editor and marketing manager, for his creativity and faith. He brought us together at Bedford/St. Martin's and from the very start understood what we had in mind for this project. We hope the finished product lives up to his ideal. Many thanks to marketing manager Lisa Kozempel for her support, expertise, wise counsel, and enthusiasm. Also, our thanks to Emily Wunderlich, editorial assistant, a cheerful researcher and invaluable resource.

We also want to thank our many dedicated and innovative colleagues in the Advanced Placement Program at the College Board, Educational Testing Service, and classrooms across the country for sharing their knowledge of their subject matter and their passion for preparing students for success in college. We want to single out Janet Heller, formerly director of the AP Program in the Middle States Office of the College Board, for giving us incredible opportunities to teach and learn. A remarkable teacher in her own right, Janet encouraged us by example and common classroom sense to seek better ways to motivate and move all students to do their best work, work that would make them as well as us proud.

We would like to thank our reviewers, whose expertise guided us at every turn: Jennifer Barbknecht, Allison Beers, Julie Bollich, Rebecca Cartee-Haring, Allison Casper, Chad Cooley, James Dam, Dottie DePaolo, Beth Dibler, Denise Hayden, Angie Hedges, Jasara Lee Hing Hines, Robert Hornbuckle, Paula Jay, Hope Keese, Mary Kirkpatrick, Sylvia Kranish, Shaylene Krupinski, Tonita Lang, Dianne Malueg, Jenny Massey, Daniel McKenna, Linda Mirro, Lisa Moore, Sherry Neaves, Jennifer O'Hare, Beth Priem, Emily Richardson, Susan Sanchez, Shital Shah, Paul Stevenson, Rebecca Swanigan, Gwendolyn Todd, Jennifer Troy, Jason Webb, Peggy Winter, Eric Woodard, and Victoria Zavadsky.

We also want to thank our colleagues who model the high school–college partnerships that are fundamental to *The Language of Composition*: Kathleen L. Bell, John Brassil, Sandra Coker, Shirley Counsil, Robert DiYanni, Marilyn Elkins, George Gadda, Mary-Grace DeNike Gannon, Stephen Heller, David Jolliffe, Bernie Phelan, Mary-Jo Potts, Hephzibah Roskelly, Sylvia Sarrett, Ed Schmieder, and Norma Wilkerson. Their suggestions, advice, and insights have made *The Language of Composition* a better book.

We thank our families for their unflagging support and encouragement through every stage of this project. A longer list of co-authors should include our children Meredith Barnes, Christopher Shea, Kate Aufses, Michael Aufses, Alison Scanlon, Lindsay Prezzano, Maura Liguori, and Kaitlin Scanlon.

Finally, we are grateful to our students—the ones in our classrooms and the colleagues in our workshops—for teaching us well.

RENÉE H. SHEA
LAWRENCE SCANLON
ROBIN DISSIN AUFSES

Contents

5 EDUCATION 175

To what extent do our schools serve the goals of a true education?

7 THE ECONOMY 393

What is the role of the economy in our everyday lives?

office parks that encircle Washington, he solicited customers with a simple pitch: early in the morning, he would deliver some bagels and a cash basket to a company's snack room; he would return before lunch to pick up the money and the leftovers. It was an honor-system commerce scheme, and it worked.

10 LANGUAGE 699

How does the language we use reveal who we are?

when I say that. It has always bothered me that I can think of no other way to describe it other than "broken," as if it were damaged and needed to be fixed, as if it lacked a certain wholeness and soundness.

11 POPULAR CULTURE   787

To what extent does pop culture reflect our society's values?

CENTRAL ESSAY

JAMES MCBRIDE, *Hip Hop Planet*   788

To many of my generation, despite all attempts to exploit it, belittle it, numb it, classify it, and analyze it, hip hop remains an enigma, a clarion call, a cry of "I am" from the youth of the world. We'd be wise, I suppose, to start paying attention.

CLASSIC ESSAY

MARK TWAIN, *Corn-Pone Opinions*   799

Its name is Public Opinion. It is held in reverence. It settles everything. Some think it the Voice of God.

12 THE ENVIRONMENT 887

What is our responsibility to the natural environment?

Central Essay

Rachel Carson, from *Silent Spring* 888

There was a strange stillness. The birds, for example—where had they gone? Many people spoke of them, puzzled and disturbed. The feeding stations in the backyards were deserted. The few birds seen anywhere were moribund; they trembled violently and could not fly. It was a spring without voices.

Classic Essay

Ralph Waldo Emerson, from *Nature* 897

The lover of nature is he whose inward and outward senses are still truly adjusted to each other; who has retained the spirit of infancy even into the era of manhood.

Other Voices

Aldo Leopold, from *The Land Ethic* 906

It is inconceivable to me that an ethical relation to land can exist without love, respect, and admiration for land, and a high regard for its value. By value, of course I mean something far broader than mere economic value; I mean value in the philosophical sense.

Lewis Thomas, *Natural Man* 915

We still argue the details, but it is conceded almost everywhere that we are not the masters of nature that we thought ourselves; we are as dependent as the leaves or midges or fish on the rest of life. We are part of the system.

13   POLITICS   1005

What is the relationship between the citizen and the state?

1

An Introduction to Rhetoric
Using the "Available Means"

To many people, the word *rhetoric* automatically signals that trickery or deception is afoot. They assume that an advertiser is trying to manipulate a consumer, a politician wants to obscure a point, or a spin doctor is spinning. "Empty rhetoric!" is a common criticism — and at times an indictment. Yet the Greek philosopher Aristotle (384–322 B.C.E.) defined **rhetoric** as "the faculty of observing in any given case the available means of persuasion."

At its best, rhetoric is a thoughtful, reflective activity leading to effective communication, including the rational exchange of opposing viewpoints. In Aristotle's day and in ours, those who understand and can use the available means to appeal to an **audience** of one or many find themselves in a position of strength. They have the tools to resolve conflicts without confrontation, to persuade readers or listeners to support their position, or to move others to take action.

Rhetoric is not just for Roman senators in togas. You might use rhetoric to convince a friend that John Coltrane is worth listening to, explain to readers of your blog why *Night of the Living Dead* is the most influential horror movie of all time, or persuade your parents that they should buy you a car. Rhetoric is also not just about speeches. Every essay, political cartoon, photograph, and advertisement is designed to convince you of something. To simplify, we will call all of these things **texts** because they are cultural products that can be "read," meaning not just consumed and comprehended, but investigated. We need to be able to "read" between the lines, regardless of whether we're reading a political ad, a political cartoon, or a political speech. Consider documentary films: every decision — such as what lighting to use for an interview, what music to play, what to show and what to leave out — constitutes a rhetorical choice based on what the filmmaker thinks will be most persuasive.

It is part of our job as informed citizens and consumers to understand how rhetoric works so that we can be wary of manipulation or deceit, while appreciating effective and civil communication. And it is essential that each of us communicates as effectively and honestly as possible.

1

> • **ACTIVITY** •
>
> Identify an article, a speech, a video, or an advertisement that you think is manipulative or deceptive and one that is civil and effective. Use these two examples to explain what you see as the difference.

The Rhetorical Situation

Let's start out by looking at a speech that nearly everyone has read or heard: the speech that baseball player Lou Gehrig gave at an Appreciation Day held in his honor on July 4, 1939. Gehrig had recently learned that he was suffering from amyotrophic lateral sclerosis (ALS), a neurological disorder that has no cure (today it is known as Lou Gehrig's disease). Although Gehrig was a reluctant speaker, the fans' chant of "We want Lou!" brought him to the podium to deliver one of the most powerful and heartfelt speeches of all time.

Farewell Speech
Lou Gehrig

Fans, for the past two weeks you have been reading about a bad break I got. Yet today I consider myself the luckiest man on the face of the earth. I have been in ballparks for seventeen years and have never received anything but kindness and encouragement from you fans. Look at these grand men. Which of you wouldn't consider it the highlight of his career just to associate with them for even one day?

Sure, I'm lucky. Who wouldn't consider it an honor to have known Jacob Ruppert; also the builder of baseball's greatest empire, Ed Barrow; to have spent six years with that wonderful little fellow, Miller Huggins; then to have spent the next nine years with that outstanding leader, that smart student of psychology—the best manager in baseball today, Joe McCarthy? Who wouldn't feel honored to have roomed with such a grand guy as Bill Dickey?

Sure, I'm lucky. When the New York Giants, a team you would give your right arm to beat, and vice versa, sends you a gift—that's something! When everybody down to the groundskeepers and those boys in white coats remember you with trophies—that's something!

When you have a wonderful mother-in-law who takes sides with you in squabbles against her own daughter—that's something! When you have a father and mother who work all their lives so that you can have an education and build your body—it's a blessing! When you have a wife who has been a tower of strength and shown more courage than you dreamed existed—that's the finest I know!

So I close in saying that I might have been given a bad break, but I have an awful lot to live for! Thank you.

While in our time the word *rhetoric* may suggest deception, this speech reminds us that rhetoric can serve sincerity as well. No wonder one commentator wrote, "Lou Gehrig's speech almost rocked Yankee Stadium off its feet."

Occasion, Context, and Purpose

Why is this an effective speech? First of all, rhetoric is always situational. It has an **occasion**—the time and place the text was written or spoken. The occasion exists within a specific **context**—the circumstances, atmosphere, attitudes, and events surrounding the text. **Purpose** is the goal the speaker wants to achieve. In the case of Gehrig's speech, the occasion is Lou Gehrig Appreciation Day. More specifically, his moment comes at home plate between games of a doubleheader. The context is first and foremost Gehrig's recent announcement of his illness and his subsequent retirement, but as is often the case, the context goes well beyond that. Gehrig, known as the Iron Horse, held the record for consecutive games played (2,130) and was one of the greatest sluggers of all time. For such a durable and powerful athlete to fall victim to a disease that strips away strength and coordination seemed an especially cruel fate. Just a couple of weeks earlier, Gehrig was still playing ball; but by the time he gave this speech, he was so weak that his manager had to help him walk out to the mound for the ceremony.

One of Gehrig's chief purposes in delivering this speech is to thank his fans and his teammates, but he also wants to demonstrate that he remains positive: he emphasizes his past luck and present optimism and downplays his illness. He makes a single reference to the diagnosis and does so in the strong, straightforward language of an athlete: he got a "bad break." There is no blame, no self-pity, no plea for sympathy. Throughout, he maintains his focus: to thank his fans and teammates for their support and get on with watching the ballgame. Gehrig responds as a true Yankee, not just the team but the can-do Yankee spirit of America, by acknowledging his illness and accepting his fate with dignity, honor, humility, and even a touch of humor.

The Rhetorical Triangle

Another important aspect of the rhetorical situation is the relationship among the speaker, audience, and subject. One way to conceptualize the relationship among these elements is through the **rhetorical triangle**. Some refer to it as the **Aristotelian triangle** because Aristotle used a triangle to illustrate how these three elements are interrelated. How a speaker perceives the relationships among these elements will go a long way toward determining what he or she says and how he or she says it.

Let's use the rhetorical triangle (see p. 4) to analyze Gehrig's speech.

The **speaker** is the person or group who creates a text. This might be a politician who delivers a speech, a commentator who writes an article, an artist who draws a political cartoon, or even a company that commissions an advertisement.

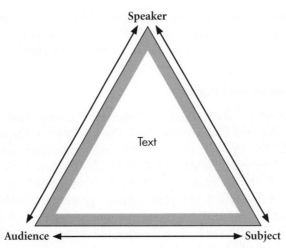

Aristotle's Rhetorical Triangle

Don't think of the speaker solely as a name, but consider a description of who the speaker is in the context of the text. The speaker of the speech we just read is not just Lou Gehrig, but baseball hero and ALS victim Lou Gehrig. Sometimes, there is a slight difference between who the speaker is in real life and the role the speaker plays when delivering the speech. This is called a **persona**. Persona comes from the Greek word for "mask"; it means the face or character that a speaker shows to his or her audience. Lou Gehrig is a famous baseball hero, but in his speech he presents himself as a common man who is modest and thankful for the opportunities he's had.

The **audience** is the listener, viewer, or reader of a text or performance, but it is important to note that there may be multiple audiences. When making rhetorical decisions, speakers ask what values their audiences hold, particularly whether the audience is hostile, friendly, or neutral and how informed it is on the topic at hand. Sure, Gehrig's audience was his teammates and the fans in the stadium that day, but it was also the teams he played against, the fans listening on the radio, and posterity—us.

The **subject** is the topic. And the subject should not be confused with the purpose, which is the goal the speaker wants to achieve. Gehrig's subject is his illness, but it is also a catalog of all the lucky breaks that preceded his diagnosis.

• ACTIVITY •

Construct and analyze a rhetorical situation for writing a review of a movie, video game, or concert. Be very specific in your analysis: What is your subject? What is your purpose? Who is your audience? What is your relationship to the audience? Remember, you need not write a full essay; just analyze the rhetorical situation.

SOAPS

In discussing the rhetorical situation surrounding a text, we've talked about some of the background that you should consider (like the occasion, context, and purpose) and relationships that are more directly related to the text (like those among the speaker, audience, and subject). One way to remember all of these things is to use the acronym **SOAPS**, which stands for Subject, Occasion, Audience, Purpose, and Speaker. It's a mnemonic device that offers a practical way to approach the concept of the rhetorical situation. Think of it as a kind of checklist that helps you organize your ideas rhetorically. Let's use SOAPS to look at the rhetorical situation in a letter written by Albert Einstein.

Widely considered the greatest scientist of the twentieth century, Einstein (1879–1955) is responsible for the theory of relativity, quantum mechanics, and other foundational scientific concepts. He won the Nobel Prize in Physics in 1921. In 1936, he wrote the following letter to a sixth-grade student, Phyllis Wright, in response to her questions: Do scientists pray? And if so, what do they pray for?

January 24, 1936

Dear Phyllis,

I have tried to respond to your question as simply as I could. Here is my answer.

Scientific research is based on the idea that everything that takes place is determined by laws of nature, and therefore this holds for the actions of people. For this reason, a research scientist will hardly be inclined to believe that events could be influenced by a prayer, i.e., by a wish addressed to a supernatural being.

However, it must be admitted that our actual knowledge of these laws is only imperfect and fragmentary, so that, actually, the belief in the existence of basic all-embracing laws in Nature also rests on a sort of faith. All the same this faith has been largely justified so far by the success of scientific research.

But, on the other hand, every one who is seriously involved in the pursuit of science becomes convinced that a spirit is manifest in the laws of the Universe—a spirit vastly superior to that of man, and one in the face of which we with our modest powers must feel humble. In this way the pursuit of science leads to a religious feeling of a special sort, which is indeed quite different from the religiosity of someone more naive.

I hope this answers your question.

Best wishes
Yours,
Albert Einstein

Subject	The explicit subject here is whether scientists pray and, if so, what they pray for. Implicitly, the subject is the nature of faith.
Occasion	The occasion is Einstein's receipt of a letter from Phyllis Wright asking questions about science and religion.
Audience	The primary audience for the letter is Phyllis herself, though the formality of his response suggests that Einstein realized that his letters would have a larger audience. (Note that he won the Nobel Prize in Physics in 1921, so by 1936 he was a world-renowned scientist.)
Purpose	Einstein's purpose is probably the most complex element here. At its most straightforward, his purpose is to respond to a sincere schoolgirl's question about science and religion. Beyond that, it seems that Einstein's purpose is to expand Phyllis's horizons a bit, to help her understand that science and religion do not necessarily represent two antagonistic ways of thinking.
Speaker	The speaker, a scientist approaching age sixty, is responding to a girl who is likely twelve, so his purpose is intertwined with that speaker–audience relationship: the wise elder in dialogue with the younger generation.

Ultimately, Einstein does not "answer" Phyllis directly at all; rather, he returns the question to her by offering different ways to think about the nature of science and religion and the way spiritual and scientific perspectives interact. Viewed in this light, Einstein's purpose can be seen as engaging a younger person — who might become a scientist — in thinking more deeply about her own question.

• ACTIVITY •

Using SOAPS, analyze the rhetorical situation in the following speech.

9/11 Speech
GEORGE W. BUSH

Good evening.

Today, our fellow citizens, our way of life, our very freedom came under attack in a series of deliberate and deadly terrorist acts.

The victims were in airplanes or in their offices — secretaries, businessmen and women, military and federal workers. Moms and dads. Friends and neighbors.

Thousands of lives were suddenly ended by evil, despicable acts of terror.

The pictures of airplanes flying into buildings, fires burning, huge structures collapsing, have filled us with disbelief, terrible sadness, and a quiet, unyielding anger.

These acts of mass murder were intended to frighten our nation into chaos and retreat. But they have failed. Our country is strong. A great people has been moved to defend a great nation.

5

Terrorist attacks can shake the foundations of our biggest buildings, but they cannot touch the foundation of America. These acts shatter steel, but they cannot dent the steel of American resolve.

America was targeted for attack because we're the brightest beacon for freedom and opportunity in the world. And no one will keep that light from shining.

Today, our nation saw evil, the very worst of human nature, and we responded with the best of America, with the daring of our rescue workers, with the caring for strangers and neighbors who came to give blood and help in any way they could.

Immediately following the first attack, I implemented our government's emergency response plans. Our military is powerful, and it's prepared. Our emergency teams are working in New York City and Washington, D.C., to help with local rescue efforts.

Our first priority is to get help to those who have been injured and to take every precaution to protect our citizens at home and around the world from further attacks. The functions of our government continue without interruption. Federal agencies in Washington which had to be evacuated today are reopening for essential personnel tonight and will be open for business tomorrow.

Our financial institutions remain strong, and the American economy will be open for business as well.

The search is under way for those who are behind these evil acts. I've directed the full resources of our intelligence and law enforcement communities to find those responsible and bring them to justice. We will make no distinction between the terrorists who committed these acts and those who harbor them.

10

Appeals to Ethos, Logos, and Pathos

Now that we understand how to assess the rhetorical situation, the next step is to use the tools of rhetoric to persuade an audience. Let's start with what Aristotle called **rhetorical appeals**. He identified three main appeals: ethos, logos, and pathos.

Ethos

Speakers appeal to **ethos** (Greek for "character") to demonstrate that they are credible and trustworthy. Think, for example, of a speech discouraging teenagers from drinking. Speakers might appeal to ethos by stressing that they are concerned parents, psychologists specializing in alcoholism or adolescent behavior, or recovering alcoholics themselves. Appeals to ethos often emphasize shared values between the speaker and the audience: when a parent speaks to other parents in the same community, they share a concern for their children's education or well-being.

Lou Gehrig brings the ethos of being a legendary athlete to his speech, yet in it he establishes a different kind of ethos — that of a regular guy and a good sport who shares the audience's love of baseball and family. And like them, he has known good luck and bad breaks.

In some instances, a speaker's reputation immediately establishes ethos. For example, the speaker may be a scholar in Russian history and economics as well as the nation's secretary of state. Or the speaker may be "the dog whisperer," a well-known animal behaviorist. In these instances, the speaker brings ethos to the text; but in other cases, a speaker establishes ethos through what he or she says in the text by sounding reasonable, acknowledging other opinions, or being thoughtful and well informed. The speaker's ethos — expertise, knowledge, experience, sincerity, common purpose with the audience, or a combination of these factors — gives the audience a reason for listening to this person on this subject.

Automatic Ethos

Let's look at an example of how a speaker's title or status automatically brings ethos to the rhetorical situation. On September 3, 1939, King George VI gave a radio address to the British people declaring that the country was at war with Germany. The very fact that he is king gives him a certain degree of automatic ethos to speak on the subject of war, yet King George also emphasizes the shared values that unite everyone.

The King's Speech (September 3, 1939)
KING GEORGE VI

> In this grave hour, perhaps the most fateful in history, I send to every household of my peoples, both at home and overseas, this message, spoken with the same depth of feeling for each one of you as if I were able to cross your threshold and speak to you myself.
>
> For the second time in the lives of most of us, we are at war. Over and over again, we have tried to find a peaceful way out of the differences between ourselves and those who are now our enemies, but it has been in vain. We have been forced into a conflict, for we are called, with our allies to meet the challenge of a principle which, if it were to prevail, would be fatal to any civilized order in the world.
>
> It is a principle which permits a state in the selfish pursuit of power to disregard its treaties and its solemn pledges, which sanctions the use of force or threat of force against the sovereignty and independence of other states. Such a principle, stripped of all disguise, is surely the mere primitive doctrine that might is right, and if this principle were established throughout the world, the freedom of our own country and of the whole British Commonwealth of nations would be in danger. But far more than this, the peoples of the world would be kept in bondage of fear, and

all hopes of settled peace and of the security of justice and liberty among nations, would be ended.

This is the ultimate issue which confronts us. For the sake of all we ourselves hold dear, and of the world order and peace, it is unthinkable that we should refuse to meet the challenge.

It is to this high purpose that I now call my people at home and my people across the seas who will make our cause their own. I ask them to stand calm and firm and united in this time of trial. The task will be hard. There may be dark days ahead, and war can no longer be confined to the battlefield, but we can only do the right as we see the right, and reverently commit our cause to God. If one and all we keep resolutely faithful to it, ready for whatever service or sacrifice it may demand, then with God's help, we shall prevail.

May He bless and keep us all.

At the outset, King George expresses his commitment to his people, his subjects, knowing that he is asking them to make their own commitment and sacrifice. As their king he is not expected to present himself as a common man, yet he establishes the ethos of a common experience. He tells them he speaks "with the same depth of feeling . . . as if I were able to cross your threshold and speak to you myself."

He uses "we" in order to speak as one of the people. He acknowledges that "we are at war" for "the second time in the lives of most of us." He also uses the inclusive first person plural possessive as he identifies "our enemies," not Britain's enemies. This personalization and emphasis on the people themselves is followed by several sentences that are much more abstract in discussion of a "principle." At the end of that discussion, King George reinforces the nation's shared values: "For the sake of all we ourselves hold dear, and of the world order and peace, it is unthinkable that we should refuse to meet the challenge."

Later on, he calls the citizenry to "this high purpose" and refers to them not as citizens or subjects but as "my people," a description that suggests a closeness rather than emphasizing the distance between a ruler and his subjects. The penultimate paragraph's references to "God" are another reminder of their shared beliefs: they worship the same god and "commit [their] cause" to him. King George brings ethos to his speech by virtue of his position, but when he assures his audience that "we shall prevail," rather than saying that England or Britain shall prevail, he is building ethos based on their common plight and common goals. They are all in this together, from king to commoner.

Building Ethos

So, what do you do if you're not a king? Writers and speakers often have to build their ethos by explaining their credentials or background to their readers, or by emphasizing shared values. You're more likely to listen to someone who is qualified to speak on a subject or who shares your interests and concerns. Following is the opening from "The Myth of the Latin Woman: I Just Met a Girl Named Maria" by Judith Ortiz Cofer. Note how she draws on her own Puerto Rican heritage as she describes her experience with prejudice as a young Latina:

from *The Myth of the Latin Woman: I Just Met a Girl Named Maria*
JUDITH ORTIZ COFER

> On a bus trip to London from Oxford University where I was earning some grad-uate credits one summer, a young man, obviously fresh from a pub, spotted me and as if struck by inspiration went down on his knees in the aisle. With both hands over his heart he broke into an Irish tenor's rendition of "Maria" from *West Side Story*. My politely amused fellow passengers gave his lovely voice the round of gentle applause it deserved. Though I was not quite as amused, I man-aged my version of an English smile: no show of teeth, no extreme contortions of the facial muscles—I was at this time of my life practicing reserve and cool. Oh, that British control, how I coveted it. But Maria had followed me to London, remind-ing me of a prime fact of my life: you can leave the Island, master the English language, and travel as far as you can, but if you are a Latina, especially one like me who so obviously belongs to Rita Moreno's gene pool, the Island travels with you.
>
> This is sometimes a very good thing—it may win you that extra minute of someone's attention. But with some people, the same things can make you an island—not so much a tropical paradise as an Alcatraz, a place nobody wants to visit. As a Puerto Rican girl growing up in the United States and wanting like most children to "belong," I resented the stereotype that my Hispanic appearance called forth from many people I met.

As Cofer develops her argument about common stereotypes of Latin women, she establishes her authority to speak on the subject of racial prejudice through her background (Puerto Rican, Latina), education (graduate student at Oxford University), and experience (firsthand encounter with ethnic bias)—and thus she gains her readers' trust.

• ACTIVITY •

Think of a situation in which you are presenting your view on the same sub-ject to two different audiences. For instance, you might be presenting your ideas on ways to stop bullying (1) to the School Board or a group of parents and (2) to a group of middle schoolers. Discuss how you would establish ethos in each situation.

Logos

Speakers appeal to **logos**, or reason, by offering clear, rational ideas. Appealing to logos (Greek for "embodied thought") means thinking logically—having a clear main idea and using specific details, examples, facts, statistics, or expert testimony to back it up. Creating a logical argument often involves defining the terms of the argument and identifying connections such as causality. It can also require considerable research. Evidence from expert sources and authorities, facts, and quantitative data can be very persuasive if selected carefully and presented accurately. Sometimes, writers and speakers add charts and graphs as a way to present such information, but often they weave this information into their argument.

Although on first reading or hearing, Lou Gehrig's speech may seem largely emotional, it is actually based on irrefutable logic. He starts with the thesis that he is "the luckiest man on the face of the earth" and supports it with two points: (1) the love and kindness he's received in his seventeen years of playing baseball, and (2) a list of great people who have been his friends, family, and teammates in that time.

Conceding and Refuting

One way to appeal to logos is to acknowledge a **counterargument**—that is, to anticipate objections or opposing views. While you might worry that raising an opposing view might poke a hole in your argument, you'll be vulnerable if you ignore ideas that run counter to your own. In acknowledging a counterargument, you agree (concede) that an opposing argument may be true or reasonable, but then you deny (refute) the validity of all or part of the argument. This combination of **concession** and **refutation** actually strengthens your own argument; it appeals to logos by demonstrating that you understand a viewpoint other than your own, you've thought through other evidence, and you stand by your view.

In longer, more complex texts, the writer may address the counterargument in greater depth, but Lou Gehrig simply concedes what some of his listeners may think—that his bad break is a cause for discouragement or despair. Gehrig refutes this by saying that he has "an awful lot to live for!" Granted, he implies his concession rather than stating it outright; but in addressing it at all, he acknowledges a contrasting way of viewing his situation—that is, a counterargument.

Let's look at an example by Alice Waters, a famous chef, food activist, and author. Writing in the *Nation*, she argues for acknowledgment of the full consequences of what she calls "our national diet":

from *Slow Food Nation*
ALICE WATERS

It's no wonder our national attention span is so short: We get hammered with the message that everything in our lives should be fast, cheap and easy—especially food.

So conditioned are we to believe that food should be almost free that even the rich, who pay a tinier fraction of their incomes for food than has ever been paid in human history, grumble at the price of an organic peach—a peach grown for flavor and picked, perfectly ripe, by a local farmer who is taking care of the land and paying his workers a fair wage. And yet, as the writer and farmer David Mas Masumoto recently pointed out, pound for pound, peaches that good still cost less than Twinkies. When we claim that eating well is an elitist preoccupation, we create a smokescreen that obscures the fundamental role our food decisions have in shaping the world. The reason that eating well in this country costs more than eating poorly is that we have a set of agricultural policies that subsidize fast food and make fresh, wholesome foods, which receive no government support, seem expensive. Organic foods seem elitist only because industrial food is artificially cheap, with its real costs being charged to the public purse, the public health, and the environment.

To develop a logical argument for better, healthier food for everyone, Waters refutes the counterargument that any food that is not "fast, cheap and easy" is "elitist." She does that by redefining terms such as "cheap," "[eating] well," "expensive," and "cost." She explains in a step-by-step fashion the "smokescreen" of price that many people use to argue that mass-produced fast food is the best alternative for all but the very wealthy. She points out that "[o]rganic foods *seem* elitist only because industrial food is *artificially* cheap" (emphasis added). Waters asks her readers to think more deeply about the relationships among availability, production, and distribution of food: she appeals to reason.

• ACTIVITY •

Following is an excerpt from an article by George Will, a columnist for the *Washington Post* and *Newsweek*, entitled "King Coal: Reigning in China." Discuss how he appeals to logos in this article on "China's ravenous appetite for coal."

---

from *King Coal: Reigning in China*
GEORGE WILL

Half of the 6 billion tons of coal burned globally each year is burned in China. A spokesman for the Sierra Club, which in recent years has helped to block construction of 139 proposed coal-fired plants in America, says, "This is undermining everything we've accomplished." America, say environmentalists, is exporting global warming.

Can something really be exported if it supposedly affects the entire planet? Never mind. America has partners in this crime against nature, if such it is. One Australian company proposes to build the Cowlitz facility; another has signed a $60 billion contract to supply Chinese power plants with Australian coal.

The *Times* says ships—all burning hydrocarbons—hauled about 690 million tons of thermal coal this year, up from 385 million in 2001. China, which imported about 150 million tons this year, was a net exporter of coal until 2009, sending abroad its low-grade coal and importing higher-grade, low-sulfur coal from, for example, the Powder River Basin of Wyoming and Montana. Because much of China's enormous coal reserves is inland, far from coastal factories, it is sometimes more economical to import American and Australian coal.

Writing in the *Atlantic* on China's appetite for coal and possible aptitude for using the old fuel in new, cleaner ways, James Fallows quotes a Chinese official saying that the country's transportation system is the only serious limit on how fast power companies increase their use of coal. One reason China is building light-rail systems is to get passenger traffic out of the way of coal trains.

Fallows reports that 15 years from now China expects that 350 million people will be living in cities that do not exist yet. This will require adding to China's electrical system a capacity almost as large as America's current capacity. The United States, China, Russia and India have 40 percent of the world's population and 60 percent of its coal.

Pathos

Pathos is an appeal to emotions, values, desires, and hopes, on the one hand, or fears and prejudices, on the other. Although an argument that appeals exclusively to the emotions is by definition weak—it's generally **propagandistic** in purpose and more **polemical** than persuasive—an effective speaker or writer understands the power of evoking an audience's emotions by using such tools as figurative language, personal anecdotes, and vivid images.

Lou Gehrig uses the informal first person (*I*) quite naturally, which reinforces the friendly sense that this is a guy who is speaking on no one's behalf but his own. He also chooses words with strong positive **connotations**: *grand, greatest, wonderful, honored, blessing.* He uses one image—*tower of strength*—that may not seem very original but strikes the right note. It is a well-known description that his audience understands—in fact, they probably have used it themselves. But, of course, the most striking appeal to pathos is the poignant contrast between Gehrig's horrible diagnosis and his public display of courage.

Let's look at a more direct example of pathos. As a vice-presidential candidate, Richard Nixon gave a speech in 1952 defending himself against allegations of inappropriate use of campaign funds. In it, he related this anecdote, which is the reason that the speech will forever be known as "the Checkers speech":

from *The Checkers Speech*
RICHARD NIXON

One other thing I probably should tell you, because if I don't they'll probably be saying this about me, too. We did get something, a gift, after the election. A man down in Texas heard Pat [his wife] on the radio mention the fact that our two youngsters

> would like to have a dog. And believe it or not, the day before we left on this campaign trip we got a message from Union Station in Baltimore, saying they had a package for us. We went down to get it. You know what it was? It was a little cocker spaniel dog in a crate that he'd sent all the way from Texas, black and white, spotted. And our little girl Tricia, the six-year-old, named it "Checkers." And you know, the kids, like all kids, love the dog, and I just want to say this, right now, that regardless of what they say about it, we're gonna keep it.

This example of pathos tugs at every possible heartstring: puppies, children, warm paternal feelings, the excitement of getting a surprise package. All of these images fill us with empathetic feelings toward Nixon: our emotions are engaged far more than our reason. Despite never truly addressing the campaign funds issue, Nixon's speech was a profound success with voters, who sent enough dog food to feed Checkers for a year! And yet, history has come to view this part of the speech as baldly manipulative.

Images and Pathos

You can often appeal to pathos by using striking imagery in your writing, so it's no surprise that images often serve the same purpose. A striking photograph, for example, may lend an emotional component that greatly strengthens an argument. Advertisers certainly make the most of photos and other visual images to entice or persuade audiences. In the accompanying example, which appeared in both the *New York Times* and the *New Yorker* magazine in 2000, the American Civil Liberties Union (ACLU) makes a dramatic assertion, an appeal to pathos through both visual images and written text, as a call to support its organization. According to its mission statement, the ACLU seeks "to defend and preserve the individual rights and liberties that the Constitution and laws of the United States guarantee everyone in this country."

The headline below the pictures reads:

> It happens every day on America's highways. Police stop drivers based on their skin color rather than for the way they are driving. For example, in Florida 80% of those stopped and searched were black and Hispanic, while they constituted only 5% of all drivers. These humiliating and illegal searches are violations of the Constitution and must be fought. Help us defend your rights. Support the ACLU.

The advertisement does not name the two men pictured, assuming the audience will recognize revered civil rights leader Martin Luther King Jr. on the left and convicted serial killer Charles Manson on the right. The headline at the top is an assertion that is bound to evoke a visceral response. The written text below the photos makes a series of logical appeals by pointing out that racial profiling accounts for the police stopping drivers on the basis of their race, and by offering statistical evidence from the state of Florida. The main appeal, however, is to pathos through the juxtaposition of a hero with a madman presented in a form reminiscent of a "wanted" poster.

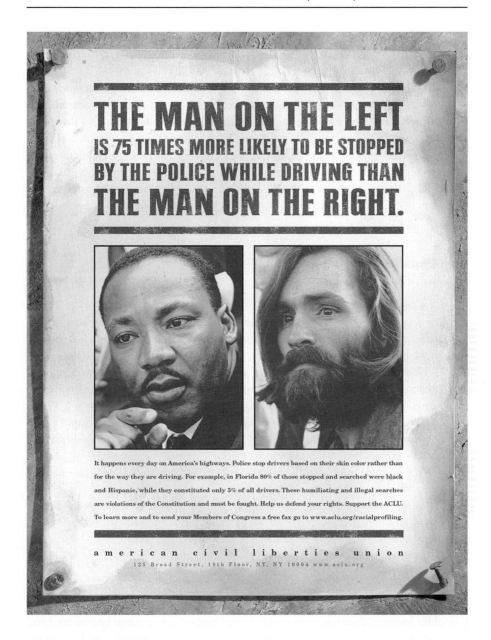

Humor and Pathos

Another way to appeal to pathos is through humor. Since we like to hear things that we already believe are true, our first reaction to anything that challenges our beliefs is often negative: we think "that's all wrong!" and get defensive or outright offended. Humor works rhetorically by wrapping a challenge to our beliefs in something that makes us feel good — a joke — and thus makes us more receptive to the new idea.

This goes not just for new ideas, but for the people who are presenting those ideas. Whether it is gentle tongue-in-cheek teasing or bitter irony, humor may help a writer to make a point without, for instance, seeming to preach to the audience or take himself or herself too seriously. Political commentator Ruth Marcus employs gentle humor in the following essay from 2010 in which she addresses the speaker of the House of Representatives and objects to the members of Congress using electronic devices during hearings and other deliberations. Even the title, a play on words, signals the humorous tone: "Crackberry Congress." Let's look at a few passages:

from *Crackberry Congress*
Ruth Marcus

Mr. Speaker, please don't.

Go ahead, if you must, and cut taxes. Slash spending. Repeal health care. I understand. Elections have consequences. But BlackBerrys and iPads and laptops on the House floor? Reconsider, before it's too late.

The current rules bar the use of a "wireless telephone or personal computer on the floor of the House." The new rules, unveiled last week, add three dangerous words. They prohibit any device "that impairs decorum."

In other words, as long as you've turned down your cellphone ringer and you're not strolling around the floor chatting with your broker or helping the kids with their homework, feel free to tap away.

If the Senate is the world's greatest deliberative body, the House is poised to be the world's greatest tweeting one.   5

A few upfront acknowledgements. First, I'm not one to throw stones. I have been known to sneak a peek, or 10, at my BlackBerry during meetings. For a time my daughter had my ringtone set to sound like a squawking chicken; when I invariably forgot to switch to vibrate, the phone would cluck during meetings. In short, I have done my share of decorum impairing.

Second, let's not get too dreamy about the House floor. John Boehner, the incoming speaker, once passed out campaign checks from tobacco companies there. One of his former colleagues once came to the chamber with a paper bag on his head to dramatize his supposed embarrassment at fellow lawmakers' overdrafts at the House bank. Worse things have happened on the House floor than a game of Angry Birds — check it out! — on the iPad.

Nonetheless, lines have to be drawn, and the House floor is not a bad place to draw them. Somehow, it has become acceptable to e-mail away in the midst of meetings. Even Emily Post has blessed what once would have been obvious rudeness, ruling that "tapping on a handheld device is okay if it's related to what's being discussed."

> The larger war may be lost, but not the battle to keep some remaining space in life free of gadgetry and its distractions. I'm not talking Walden Pond—just a few minutes of living the unplugged life. There are places—dinner table, church, school and, yes, the House floor—where multitasking is inappropriate, even disrespectful.

First of all, Marcus structures her criticism as a letter, which obviously is a fiction and sets a humorous note right away. Who, after all, would begin a letter to the Speaker of the House by saying, "please don't"? Marcus often works by teasing about "decorum," yet she makes a serious point about "connectivity" as she exaggerates her fear that "the House is poised to be the world's greatest tweeting [body]." Humor is also one of her strategies for establishing ethos in this case, as she says, "I'm not one to throw stones" and admits to checking her own BlackBerry during meetings. Overall, by taking a more lighthearted approach and not sounding like Ms. Manners, Marcus makes her point about the inappropriateness of elected officials interacting with their electronic devices while colleagues and others are debating important issues.

Marcus could have marshaled all manner of examples that illustrate the decline in civility and courtesy in modern life, but readers would likely have dismissed her as old-fashioned or shrill. By taking a humorous approach, she appeals to readers' sense of humor as well as their community values: don't we want our elected officials to forego "instantaneous communication" for more thoughtful deliberations when they are making decisions about the laws of the land?

• ACTIVITY •

General Dwight D. Eisenhower, Supreme Commander of the Allied Expeditionary Force in Europe, distributed the following Order of the Day to the military troops right before the 1944 D-Day invasion of Normandy. Discuss how General Eisenhower appeals to pathos.

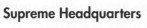

Supreme Headquarters **Allied Expeditionary Force**

Soldiers, Sailors and Airmen of the Allied Expeditionary Force!

You are about to embark upon the Great Crusade, toward which we have striven these many months. The eyes of the world are upon you. The hopes and prayers of liberty-loving people everywhere march with you. In company with our brave Allies and brothers-in-arms on other Fronts, you will bring about the destruction of the German war machine, the elimination of Nazi tyranny over the oppressed peoples of Europe, and security for ourselves in a free world.

Your task will not be an easy one. Your enemy is well trained, well equipped, and battle-hardened. He will fight savagely.

But this is the year 1944! Much has happened since the Nazi triumphs of 1940–41. The United Nations have inflicted upon the Germans great defeats, in open battle, man-to-man. Our air offensive has seriously reduced their strength in the air and their capacity to wage war on the ground. Our Home Fronts have given us an overwhelming superiority in weapons and munitions of war and placed at our disposal great reserves of trained fighting men. The tide has turned! The free men of the world are marching together to Victory!

I have full confidence in your courage, devotion to duty, and skill in battle. We will accept nothing less than full Victory!

Good Luck! And let us all beseech the blessing of Almighty God upon this great and noble undertaking.

Dwight D. Eisenhower

Combining Ethos, Logos, and Pathos

Most authors don't rely on just a single type of appeal to persuade their audience; they combine these appeals to create an effective argument. And the appeals themselves are inextricably bound together: if you lay out your argument logically, that will help to build your ethos. It is only logical to listen to an expert on a subject, so having ethos can help build a foundation for an appeal to logos. It's also possible to build your ethos based on pathos — for example, who better to speak about the pain of losing a loved one than someone who has gone through it? The best political satirists can say things that are both perfectly logical and completely hilarious, thus appealing to both logos and pathos at the same time.

Let's examine a letter that Toni Morrison, the only African American woman to win the Nobel Prize for Literature, wrote to then-senator Barack Obama endorsing him as the Democratic candidate for president in 2008. The letter was published in the *New York Times*.

Dear Senator Obama,

This letter represents a first for me—a public endorsement of a Presidential candidate. I feel driven to let you know why I am writing it. One reason is it may help gather other supporters; another is that this is one of those singular moments that nations ignore at their peril. I will not rehearse the multiple crises facing us, but of one thing I am certain: this opportunity for a national evolution (even revolution) will not come again soon, and I am convinced you are the person to capture it.

May I describe to you my thoughts?

I have admired Senator [Hillary] Clinton for years. Her knowledge always seemed to me exhaustive; her negotiation of politics expert. However I am more compelled by the quality of mind (as far as I can measure it) of a candidate. I cared little for her gender as a source of my admiration, and the little I did care was based on the fact that no liberal woman has ever ruled in America. Only conservative or "new-centrist" ones are allowed into that realm. Nor do I care very much for your race[s]. I would not support you if that was all you had to offer or because it might make me "proud."

In thinking carefully about the strengths of the candidates, I stunned myself when I came to the following conclusion: that in addition to keen intelligence, integrity, and a rare authenticity, you exhibit something that has nothing to do with age, experience, race, or gender and something I don't see in other candidates. That something is a creative imagination which coupled with brilliance equals wisdom. It is too bad if we associate it only with gray hair and old age. Or if we call searing vision naivete. Or if we believe cunning is insight. Or if we settle for finessing cures tailored for each ravaged tree in the forest while ignoring the poisonous landscape that feeds and surrounds it. Wisdom is a gift; you can't train for it, inherit it, learn it in a class, or earn it in the workplace—that access can foster the acquisition of knowledge, but not wisdom.

When, I wondered, was the last time this country was guided by such a leader?   5
Someone whose moral center was un-embargoed? Someone with courage instead of mere ambition? Someone who truly thinks of his country's citizens as "we," not "they"? Someone who understands what it will take to help America realize the virtues it fancies about itself, what it desperately needs to become in the world?

Our future is ripe, outrageously rich in its possibilities. Yet unleashing the glory of that future will require a difficult labor, and some may be so frightened of its birth they will refuse to abandon their nostalgia for the womb.

There have been a few prescient leaders in our past, but you are the man for this time.

Good luck to you and to us.

Toni Morrison

Let's take a step back. Who is Morrison's audience for this letter? Of course, she claims Senator Obama is, yet it is an open letter printed in a newspaper. Thus, we have a sense that while she does intend that he read the letter, she also understands that her public endorsement of his candidacy, and not Senator Hillary Clinton's, will have an impact on a much larger audience than Obama himself: her audience is the large national and international readership of the *Times*, readers who value the viewpoint of a Nobel Prize winner.

Given that audience, Morrison need not establish her ethos as a credible person whose opinion should carry some weight. After all, both Obama and the readers of the *New York Times*—in fact, readers in general—know her as an award-winning author, someone who has written many novels, a professor at Princeton University, and the winner of a Nobel Prize. She is not, however, a person accustomed to publicly weighing in on political campaigns, so she opens with her announcement that this endorsement is "a first" for her. She does not assume that she has the authority or position to make Senator Obama (or others) listen to her; instead, she asks, deferentially, "May I describe to you my thoughts?" As a woman in her seventies with a proven record as a respected author and thinker, she could demand that Obama listen to her, but she does not; asking a question rather than launching into her viewpoint presents herself as courteous and reasonable. The ethos she establishes is as a person who cares deeply for the future of America and is moved to speak out because she believes that the country is at a crossroads ("this is one of those singular moments that nations ignore at their peril").

Although she does not offer facts and figures nor cite expert sources, Morrison develops a logical argument. She addresses two counterarguments: (1) Senator Clinton is the better candidate, and (2) her support of Obama is driven primarily by race. In paragraph 3, she concedes and refutes both. She points out that she has "admired" Senator Clinton over the years and offers reasons; gender is not, however, among them. She effectively makes that argument also serve as evidence that she would not support Obama purely because of race, saying, "I would not support you if that was all you had to offer or because it might make me 'proud.'" In paragraph 4, Morrison provides reasons for her support of Obama. She acknowledges that he is a person of "keen intelligence, integrity, and a rare authenticity," yet those qualities are neither her only nor her chief reasons for supporting his candidacy. She claims that she sees in him "a creative imagination which coupled with brilliance equals wisdom." Once Morrison makes this point, she addresses another counterargument: that Obama is too young. She refutes that belief by claiming that wisdom is not necessarily a matter of age.

Morrison continues to develop her reasons for supporting Obama as she adds appeals to pathos. By asking a series of rhetorical questions, she calls up the shared values of the country; for instance, she asks when the country was actually guided by "[s]omeone whose moral center was un-embargoed." She chooses language likely to evoke emotions, such as her distinction between "courage instead of mere ambition." By the end of the letter, she uses images of birth ("the glory of that future will require a difficult labor, and some may be so frightened of its birth they will refuse to abandon their nostalgia for the womb") and language that pulls at our heartstrings, such as "Our future is ripe, outrageously rich."

She draws the conclusion, again appealing to logos, that given all the evidence presented in the letter Senator Obama is "the man for this time." Morrison closes with a final appeal to ethos as she emphasizes that she is an integral part of the community of the country: "Good luck to you and to us." The "us" is decidedly not just African Americans but all Americans.

• ACTIVITY •

Select one of the following rhetorical situations, and discuss how you would establish your ethos and appeal to logos and pathos.

- You are trying to persuade your skeptical parents that a "gap year"— taking a year off between high school graduation and college—will be beneficial.

- You have been asked to make a presentation to your school's principal and food service staff to propose healthier food choices in the cafeteria at a time when the overall school budget is constrained.
- You are making the case for the purchase of a specific model and make of car that will best fit your family's needs and resources.
- You are the student representative chosen to go before a group of local businesspeople to ask them to provide financial support for a proposed school trip.

Rhetorical Analysis of Visual Texts

Many visual texts are full-fledged arguments. Although they may not be written in paragraphs or have a traditional thesis, they are occasioned by specific circumstances, they have a purpose (whether it is to comment on a current event or simply to urge you to buy something), and they make a claim and support it with appeals

SOURCE: Toles © 2005 The Washington Post. Reprinted with permission of UNIVERSAL UCLICK. All rights reserved.

to authority, emotion, and reason. Consider the cartoon on page 21, which cartoonist Tom Toles drew after the death of civil-rights icon Rosa Parks in 2006. Parks was the woman who in 1955 refused to give up her seat on the bus in Montgomery, Alabama; that act came to symbolize the struggle for racial equality in the United States.

We can discuss the cartoon rhetorically, just as we've been examining texts that are exclusively verbal: The occasion is the death of Rosa Parks. The speaker is Tom Toles, a respected and award-winning political cartoonist. The audience is made up of readers of the *Washington Post* and other newspapers—that is, it's a very broad audience. The speaker can assume that his audience shares his admiration and respect for Parks and that they view her passing as the loss of a public figure as well as a private woman. Finally, the context is a memorial for a well-loved civil-rights activist, and Toles's purpose is to remember Parks as an ordinary citizen whose courage and determination brought extraordinary results. The subject is the legacy of Rosa Parks, a well-known person loved by many.

Readers' familiarity with Toles—along with his obvious respect for his subject—establishes his ethos. The image in the cartoon appeals primarily to pathos. Toles shows Rosa Parks, who was a devout Christian, as she is about to enter heaven through the pearly gates; they are attended by an angel, probably Saint Peter, who is reading a ledger. Toles depicts Parks wearing a simple coat and carrying her pocketbook, as she did while sitting on the bus so many years ago. Her features are somewhat detailed and realistic, making her stand out despite her modest posture and demeanor.

The commentary at the bottom right reads, "We've been holding it [the front row in heaven] open since 1955," a reminder that more than fifty years have elapsed since Parks resolutely sat where she pleased. The caption can be seen as an appeal to both pathos and logos. Its emotional appeal is its acknowledgment that, of course, heaven would have been waiting for this good woman; but the mention of "the front row" appeals to logic because Parks made her mark in history for refusing to sit in the back of the bus. Some readers might even interpret the caption as a criticism of how slow the country was both to integrate and to pay tribute to Parks.

• ACTIVITY •

The following advertisement is from the World Wildlife Fund (WWF), a conservation organization that "combines global reach with a foundation in science, involves action at every level from local to global, and ensures the delivery of innovative solutions that meet the needs of both people and nature."

What rhetorical strategies does the WWF use to achieve its purpose in this advertisement? Pay particular attention to the interaction of the written text with the visual elements. How does the arrangement on the page affect your response? How does the WWF appeal to ethos, logos, and pathos? How effective do you think the advertisement is in reaching its intended audience? Explain.

(See insert for color version.)

Determining Effective and Ineffective Rhetoric

Not every attempt at effective rhetoric hits its mark. A famous example of humorously ineffective rhetoric is the proposal of Mr. Collins to the high-spirited heroine Elizabeth Bennet in the novel *Pride and Prejudice* by Jane Austen. Mr. Collins, a foolish and sycophantic minister, stands to inherit the Bennet estate; thus, he assumes that any of the Bennet sisters, including Elizabeth, will be grateful for his offer of marriage. So he crafts his offer as a business proposal that is a series of reasons. Following is a slightly abridged version of Mr. Collins's proposal:

from *Pride and Prejudice*
JANE AUSTEN

My reasons for marrying are, first, that I think it a right thing for every clergyman in easy circumstances (like myself) to set the example of matrimony in his parish. Secondly, that I am convinced it will add very greatly to my happiness; and thirdly—which perhaps I ought to have mentioned earlier, that it is the particular advice and recommendation of the very noble lady whom I have the honour of calling patroness. . . . But the fact is, that being, as I am, to inherit this estate after the death of your honoured father (who, however, may live many years longer), I could not satisfy myself without resolving to chuse a wife from among his daughters, that the loss to them might be as little as possible, when the melancholy event takes place—which, however, as I have already said, may not be for several years. This has been my motive, my fair cousin, and I flatter myself it will not sink me in your esteem. And now nothing remains for me but to assure you in the most animated language of the violence of my affection. To fortune I am perfectly indifferent, and shall make no demand of that nature on your father, since I am well aware that it could not be complied with; and that one thousand pounds in the 4 per cents, which will not be yours till after your mother's decease, is all that you may ever be entitled to. On that head, therefore, I shall be uniformly silent; and you may assure yourself that no ungenerous reproach shall ever pass my lips when we are married.

Mr. Collins appeals to logos with a sequence of reasons that support his intent to marry: ministers should be married, marriage will add to his happiness, and his patroness wants him to marry. Of course, these are all advantages to himself. Ultimately, he claims that he can assure Elizabeth "in the most animated language of the violence of [his] affection," yet he offers no language at all about his emotional attachment. Finally, as if to refute the counterargument that she would not reap many benefits from the proposed alliance, he reminds her that her financial future will be grim unless she accepts his offer, and he promises to be "uniformly silent" rather than to remind her of that fact once they are married.

Where did he go wrong? Without devaluing the wry humor of Austen in her portrayal of Mr. Collins, we can conclude that at the very least he failed to understand his audience. He offers reasons for marriage that would have little appeal to Elizabeth, who does not share his businesslike and self-serving assumptions. No

Feeding Kids Meat Is

CHILD ABUSE

Fight the Fat: Go Vegan | *PeTA*

(See insert for color version.)

wonder she can hardly wait to get way from him; no wonder he responds with shocked indignation.

Unlike Mr. Collins's clearly bad attempt at rhetoric, in the real world deciding whether rhetoric hits or misses its mark is often a matter of debate. Consider the advertisement above from PETA (People for the Ethical Treatment of Animals).

It's important to note that PETA, an animal rights group, sponsors this ad. A positive reading would see the image of an overweight child about to bite into a burger as an effective attention-getter. The headline, with "meat" the only word in red, makes the bold assertion that parents who allow children to eat meat are guilty of child abuse. Since most people would not have thought of this connection, its boldness might have the shock value to make them stop and think. By choosing a particularly unappetizing burger and plump-looking kid, PETA presents an image of childhood obesity that might want to make the viewer grab the burger from the child before she gets it in her mouth! The smaller print calls for a "vegan" diet to combat obesity, asserting that replacing burgers with vegetables is a healthier alternative—a claim few people would find questionable.

But that's not the only way to interpret this ad. Claiming that allowing a child to eat a hamburger is the same as committing child abuse is a serious allegation, and it could be seen as hyperbole. If you read the large print as an unfounded exaggeration, then the ad's purpose is lost. It's unlikely that anyone would argue with the exhortation to "fight the fat," but to link consumption of any kind of meat with a heinous act of child abuse might not seem logical to every view, which could undermine the ad's effectiveness.

Let's turn to an essay, an op-ed piece that appeared in the *Washington Post* in 2011 after Japan was hit by a massive earthquake and tsunami that severely damaged nuclear reactors. Columnist Anne Applebaum uses this devastating situation to argue against further use of nuclear power. As you read the article, analyze it rhetorically and ask yourself if she is likely to achieve her purpose or if her strategies miss the mark.

If the Japanese Can't Build a Safe Reactor, Who Can?
ANNE APPLEBAUM

In the aftermath of a disaster, the strengths of any society become immediately visible. The cohesiveness, resilience, technological brilliance and extraordinary competence of the Japanese are on full display. One report from Rikuzentakata—a town of 25,000, annihilated by the tsunami that followed Friday's massive earthquake—describes volunteer firefighters working to clear rubble and search for survivors; troops and police efficiently directing traffic and supplies; survivors are not only "calm and pragmatic" but also coping "with politeness and sometimes amazingly good cheer."

Thanks to these strengths, Japan will eventually recover. But at least one Japanese nuclear power complex will not. As I write, three reactors at the Fukushima Daiichi nuclear power station appear to have lost their cooling capacity. Engineers are flooding the plant with seawater—effectively destroying it—and then letting off radioactive steam. There have been two explosions. The situation may worsen in the coming hours.

Yet Japan's nuclear power stations were designed with the same care and precision as everything else in the country. More to the point, as the only country in the world to have experienced true nuclear catastrophe, Japan had an incentive to build well, as well as the capability, laws and regulations to do so. Which leads to an unavoidable question: If the competent and technologically brilliant Japanese can't build a completely safe reactor, who can?

It can—and will—be argued that the Japanese situation is extraordinary. Few countries are as vulnerable to natural catastrophe as Japan, and the scale of this earthquake is unprecedented. But there are other kinds of extraordinary situations and unprecedented circumstances. In an attempt to counter the latest worst-possible scenarios, a Franco-German company began constructing a super-safe, "next-generation" nuclear reactor in Finland several years ago. The plant was designed to withstand the impact of an airplane—a post–Sept. 11 concern—and includes a chamber allegedly able to contain a core meltdown. But it was also meant to cost $4 billion and to be completed in 2009. Instead, after numerous setbacks, it is still unfinished—and may now cost $6 billion or more.

Ironically, the Finnish plant was meant to launch the renaissance of the nuclear   5
power industry in Europe—an industry that has, of late, enjoyed a renaissance around the world, thanks almost entirely to fears of climate change. Nuclear plants emit no carbon. As a result, nuclear plants, after a long, post-Chernobyl lull, have

became fashionable again. Some 62 nuclear reactors are under construction at the moment, a further 158 are being planned and 324 others have been proposed.

Increasingly, nuclear power is also promoted because it is safe. Which it is— except, of course, when it is not. Chances of a major disaster are tiny, one in a hundred million. But in the event of a statistically improbable major disaster, the damage could include, say, the destruction of a city or the poisoning of a country. The cost of such a potential catastrophe is partly reflected in the price of plant construction, and it partly explains the cost overruns in Finland: Nobody can risk the tiniest flaw in the concrete or the most minimal reduction in the quality of the steel.

But as we are about to learn in Japan, the true costs of nuclear power are never reflected even in the very high price of plant construction. Inevitably, the enormous costs of nuclear waste disposal fall to taxpayers, not the nuclear industry. The costs of cleanup, even in the wake of a relatively small accident, are eventually borne by government, too. Health-care costs will also be paid by society at large, one way or another. If there is true nuclear catastrophe in Japan, the entire world will pay the price.

I hope that this will never, ever happen. I feel nothing but admiration for the Japanese nuclear engineers who have been battling catastrophe for several days. If anyone can prevent a disaster, the Japanese can do it. But I also hope that a near-miss prompts people around the world to think twice about the true "price" of nuclear energy, and that it stops the nuclear renaissance dead in its tracks.

Does Applebaum miss her mark? Does she use a worst-case scenario to make her case? Do her references to September 11 and World War II make nuclear power seem alarming, or do they just make Applebaum sound alarmist? Are her fears fully justified, or is this nothing but fear mongering? Consider that she does acknowledge that Japan's situation is unusual because the country is so "vulnerable to natural catastrophe" and the earthquake that struck was unusually strong. She cites facts and figures about the efforts in Finland to build a nuclear plant that is meant to be "super-safe" and withstand every imaginable contingency. She explains that other European nations are following the Finnish lead ("158 are being planned and 324 others have been proposed") because nuclear power, which does not emit carbon dioxide, is not thought to contribute to climate change. There is quite a bit to consider, even in this relatively brief piece.

• ACTIVITY •

Following is a rhetorical analysis of the effectiveness of Applebaum's argument written by an AP student, Tamar Demby. How does she develop her position? Why do you agree or disagree with her? How might she improve her essay?

Alarmist or Alarming Rhetoric?

TAMAR DEMBY

In an age when threats to life as we know it seem to grow too enormous to face, it becomes tempting to regard any danger as an apocalypse waiting to happen. But however huge and urgent an incident appears, it is important to look at the big picture and calmly analyze the true risks of all responses. Within the context of Japan's struggle to avert a nuclear meltdown in Fukushima Prefecture, Anne Applebaum, writing for the *Washington Post*, argues against any further expansion of nuclear power. However, she undermines her own purpose by basing her argument on unsupported claims, relying on highly emotional language, and failing to establish her ethos as a credible authority on the issue.

As a journalist rather than a nuclear physicist or someone with credentials earned by education and training, she has to present a clear viewpoint supported by solid evidence. If she has a history of reporting on nuclear power issues, then she should have explained that expertise. Instead, she relies on hot-button issues such as Chernobyl to alarm her readers, who are likely an educated and well-informed audience. Even though she is writing in the midst of the crisis in Japan when no one knew what would happen to the reactors, she needs to establish a fair-minded ethos and build a more fact-based case. Unless she moves her audience to share her concern and alarm, she fails to achieve her purpose of making them see the true "cost" of nuclear power and oppose further expansion.

Applebaum's central point is spelled out in the title of her piece: "If the Japanese Can't Build a Safe Reactor, Who Can?" In order to ask and then answer this question, she must establish the supremacy of the Japanese to build a safe nuclear reactor. In her first paragraph, she highlights the strengths of the Japanese: "cohesiveness, resilience, technological brilliance and extraordinary competence" and cites examples of all these traits *except* technological brilliance — leaving the reader with no reason to agree with her assessment of Japanese technological prowess. This pattern continues in the second paragraph, as Applebaum attempts to explain that the Japanese can be expected to have built the safest possible nuclear reactors because they were "designed with the same care and precision as everything else in the country" — a statement she fails to support. Verified details seem to be reserved for viscerally effective descriptions of the situation in the Fukushima Daiichi plant. Applebaum states that the plant will not "eventually recover," as three reactors are "letting off radioactive steam . . . (and) there have been two explosions." These facts serve only to appeal to the reader's emotions, focusing on the horrifying results of the catastrophe but not addressing — or supporting — Applebaum's claims. Ultimately, Applebaum's position seems to be based more on personal alarm than analysis of facts.

• ACTIVITY •

Examine the following advertisement sponsored by the Federal Highway Administration. Analyze the rhetorical situation and appeals used in the advertisement, and determine whether you think this advertisement is effective or ineffective.

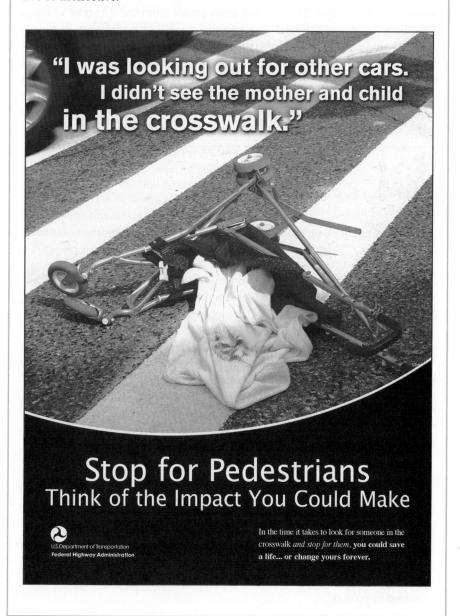

• CULMINATING ACTIVITY •

By this point, you have analyzed what we mean by the rhetorical situation, and you have learned a number of key concepts and terms. It's time to put all the ideas together to examine a series of texts on a single subject. Following are four texts related to the 1969 *Apollo 11* mission that landed the first humans on the moon. The first is a news article from the *Times* of London reporting the event; the next is a speech by William Safire that President Nixon would have given had the mission not been successful; the third is a commentary by novelist Ayn Rand; the last is a political cartoon that appeared at the time. Discuss the purpose of each text and how the interaction among speaker, audience, and subject affects the text. How does each text appeal to ethos, pathos, and logos? Finally, how effective is each text in achieving its purpose?

Man Takes First Steps on the Moon

THE *TIMES*

The following article appeared in a special 5 A.M. edition of the Times *of London.*

Neil Armstrong became the first man to take a walk on the moon's surface early today. The spectacular moment came after he had inched his way down the ladder of the fragile lunar bug Eagle while colleague Edwin Aldrin watched his movements from inside the craft. The landing, in the Sea of Tranquillity, was near perfect and the two astronauts on board Eagle reported that it had not tilted too far to prevent a take-off. The first word from man on the moon came from Aldrin: "Tranquillity base. The Eagle has landed." Of the first view of the lunar surface, he said: "There are quite a few rocks and boulders in the near area which are going to have some interesting colours in them." Armstrong said both of them were in good shape and there was no need to worry about them. They had experienced no difficulty in manoeuvring the module in the moon's gravity. There were tense moments in the mission control centre at Houston while they awaited news of the safe landing. When it was confirmed, one ground controller was heard to say: "We got a bunch of guys on the ground about to turn blue. We're breathing again." Ten minutes after landing, Aldrin radioed: "We'll get to the details of what's around here. But it looks like a collection of every variety, shape, angularity, granularity; a collection of just about every kind of rock." He added: "The colour depends on what angle you're looking at . . . rocks and boulders look as though they're going to have some interesting colours."

Armstrong says: one giant leap for mankind

From the News Team in Houston and London

It was 3.56 A.M. (British Standard Time) when Armstrong stepped off the ladder from Eagle and on to the moon's surface. The module's hatch had opened at 3.39 A.M.

"That's one small step for man but one giant leap for mankind," he said as he stepped on the lunar surface.

The two astronauts opened the hatch of their lunar module at 3.39 A.M. in preparation for Neil Armstrong's walk. They were obviously being ultra careful over the operation for there was a considerable time lapse before Armstrong moved backwards out of the hatch to start his descent down the ladder.

Aldrin had to direct Armstrong out of the hatch because he was walking backwards and could not see the ladder.

Armstrong moved on to the porch outside Eagle and prepared to switch the television cameras which showed the world his dramatic descent as he began to inch his way down the ladder.

By this time the two astronauts had spent 25 minutes of their breathing time but their oxygen packs on their backs last four hours.

When the television cameras switched on there was a spectacular shot of Armstrong as he moved down the ladder. Viewers had a clear view as they saw him stepping foot by foot down the ladder, which has nine rungs.

He reported that the lunar surface was a "very fine-grained powder."

Clutching the ladder Armstrong put his left foot on the lunar surface and reported it was like powdered charcoal and he could see his footprints on the surface. He said the L.E.M.'s engine had left a crater about a foot deep but they were "on a very level place here."

Standing directly in the shadow of the lunar module Armstrong said he could see very clearly. The light was sufficiently bright for everything to be clearly visible.

The next step was for Aldrin to lower a hand camera down to Armstrong. This was the camera which Armstrong was to use to film Aldrin when he descends from Eagle.

Armstrong then spent the next few minutes taking photographs of the area in which he was standing and then prepared to take the "contingency" sample of lunar soil.

This was one of the first steps in case the astronauts had to make an emergency take-off before they could complete the whole of their activities on the moon.

Armstrong said: "It is very pretty out here."

Using the scoop to pick up the sample Armstrong said he had pushed six to eight inches into the surface. He then reported to the mission control centre that he placed the sample lunar soil in his pocket.

The first sample was in his pocket at 4.08 A.M. He said the moon "has soft beauty all its own," like some desert of the United States. . . .

Greatest moment of time

President Nixon, watching the events on television, described it as "one of the greatest moments of our time." He told Mr. Ron Ziegler, the White House press secretary, that the last 22 seconds of the descent were the longest he had ever lived through.

Mr. Harold Wilson, in a television statement, expressed "our deep wish for a safe return at the end of what has been a most historic scientific achievement in the history of man." The Prime Minister, speaking from 10 Downing Street, said: "The first feeling of all in Britain is that this very dangerous part of the mission has been safely accomplished."

Moscow Radio announced the news solemnly as the main item in its 11.30 news broadcast. There was no immediate news of Luna 15.

At Castelgandolfo the Pope greeted news of the lunar landing by exclaiming: "Glory to God in the highest and peace on earth to men of good will!"

In an unscheduled speech from his summer residence the Pope, who followed the flight on colour television, said: "We, humble representatives of that Christ, who, coming among us from the abyss of divinity, has made to resound in the heavens this blessed voice, today we make an echo, repeating it in a celebration on the part of the whole terrestrial globe, with no more unsurpassable bounds of human existence, but openness to the expanse of endless space and a new destiny."

"Glory to God!" President Saragat of Italy said in a statement: "May this victory be a good omen for an even greater victory: the definite conquest of peace, of justice, of liberty, for all peoples of the World."

President Charles Helou of Lebanon followed the flight and landing with special dispatches from the Information Ministry. A spokesman said he would send an official message later.

In Jordan King Husain sent a congratulatory message to the astronauts and President Nixon.

In Stockholm Mr. Tage Erlander, the Swedish Prime Minister, said he planned to cable President Nixon his congratulations as soon as the astronauts returned to Earth. King Gustav Adolf was watching television at touchdown time and told friends he was "thrilled" by the Apollo performance.

In Cuba the national radio announced the moon landing 12 minutes after it was accomplished.

Sir Bernard Lovell, Director of the Jodrell Bank observatory, said: "The moment of touchdown was one of the moments of greatest drama in the history of man. The success in this part of the enterprize opens the most enormous opportunities for the future exploration of the universe."

In Event of Moon Disaster

WILLIAM SAFIRE

The following speech, revealed in 1999, was prepared by President Nixon's speechwriter, William Safire, to be used in the event of a disaster that would maroon the astronauts on the moon.

Fate has ordained that the men who went to the moon to explore in peace will stay on the moon to rest in peace.

These brave men, Neil Armstrong and Edwin Aldrin, know that there is no hope for their recovery. But they also know that there is hope for mankind in their sacrifice. These two men are laying down their lives in mankind's most noble goal: the search for truth and understanding.

They will be mourned by their families and friends; they will be mourned by their nation; they will be mourned by the people of the world; they will be mourned by a Mother Earth that dared send two of her sons into the unknown.

In their exploration, they stirred the people of the world to feel as one; in their sacrifice, they bind more tightly the brotherhood of man.

In ancient days, men looked at stars and saw their heroes in the constellations. In modern times, we do much the same, but our heroes are epic men of flesh and blood.

Others will follow, and surely find their way home. Man's search will not be denied. But these men were the first, and they will remain the foremost in our hearts. For every human being who looks up at the moon in the nights to come will know that there is some corner of another world that is forever mankind.

5

The July 16, 1969, Launch: A Symbol of Man's Greatness

AYN RAND

The following commentary by novelist Ayn Rand first appeared in the Objectivist, *a publication created by Rand and others to put forward their philosophy of objectivism, which values individualism, freedom, and reason.*

"No matter what discomforts and expenses you had to bear to come here," said a NASA guide to a group of guests, at the conclusion of a tour of the Space Center on Cape Kennedy, on July 15, 1969, "there will be seven minutes tomorrow morning that will make you feel it was worth it."

It was.

[The launch] began with a large patch of bright, yellow-orange flame shooting sideways from under the base of the rocket. It looked like a normal kind of flame and I felt an instant's shock of anxiety, as if this were a building on fire. In the next instant the flame and the rocket were hidden by such a sweep of dark red fire that the anxiety vanished: this was not part of any normal experience and could not be integrated with anything. The dark red fire parted into two gigantic wings, as if a hydrant were shooting streams of fire outward and up, toward the zenith—and between the two wings, against a pitch-black sky, the rocket rose slowly, so slowly that it seemed to hang still in the air, a pale cylinder with a blinding oval of white light at the bottom, like an upturned candle with its flame directed at the earth. Then I became aware that this was happening in total silence, because I heard the cries of birds winging frantically away from the flames. The rocket was rising faster, slanting a little, its tense white flame leaving a long, thin spiral of bluish smoke behind it. It had risen into the open blue sky, and the dark red fire had turned into enormous billows of brown smoke, when the sound reached us: it was a long, violent crack, not a rolling sound, but specifically a cracking, grinding sound, as if space were breaking apart, but it seemed irrelevant and unimportant, because it was a sound from the past and the rocket was long since speeding safely out of its reach—though it was strange to realize that only a few seconds had passed. I found myself waving to the rocket involuntarily, I heard people applauding and joined them, grasping our common motive; it was impossible to watch passively, one had to express, by some physical action, a feeling that was not triumph, but more: the feeling that that white object's unobstructed streak of motion was the only thing that mattered in the universe.

What we had seen, in naked essentials—but in reality, not in a work of art—was the concretized abstraction of man's greatness.

The fundamental significance of *Apollo 11*'s triumph is not political; it is philosophical; specifically, moral-epistemological. ⁵

The meaning of the sight lay in the fact that when those dark red wings of fire flared open, one knew that one was not looking at a normal occurrence, but at a cataclysm which, if unleashed by nature, would have wiped man out of existence—and one knew also that this cataclysm was planned, unleashed, and controlled by man, that this unimaginable power was ruled by his power and, obediently serving his purpose, was making way for a slender, rising craft. One knew that this spectacle was not the product of inanimate nature, like some aurora borealis, or of chance, or of luck, that it was unmistakably human—with "human," for once, meaning grandeur—that a purpose and a long, sustained, disciplined effort had gone to achieve this series of moments, and that man was succeeding, succeeding, succeeding! For once, if only for seven minutes, the worst among those who saw it had to feel—not "How small is man by the side of the Grand Canyon!"—but "How great is man and how safe is nature when he conquers it!"

That we had seen a demonstration of man at his best, no one could doubt—this was the cause of the event's attraction and of the stunned numbed state in which it left us. And no one could doubt that we had seen an achievement of man in his capacity as a rational being—an achievement of reason, of logic, of mathematics, of total dedication to the absolutism of reality.

Frustration is the leitmotif in the lives of most men, particularly today—the frustration of inarticulate desires, with no knowledge of the means to achieve them. In the sight and hearing of a crumbling world, *Apollo 11* enacted the story of an audacious purpose, its execution, its triumph, and the means that achieved it—the story and the demonstration of man's highest potential.

Transported

HERBLOCK

The following editorial cartoon by the famous cartoonist Herb Lock, or Herblock, appeared in the Washington Post *on July 18, 1969.*

SOURCE: A 1969 Herblock Cartoon, copyright by The Herb Block Foundation.

Glossary of Rhetorical Terms

Aristotelian triangle   See **rhetorical triangle**.

audience   The listener, viewer, or reader of a text. Most texts are likely to have multiple audiences.

> *Gehrig's audience was his teammates and fans in the stadium that day, but it was also the teams he played against, the fans listening on the radio, and posterity — us.*

concession   An acknowledgment that an opposing argument may be true or reasonable. In a strong argument, a concession is usually accompanied by a refutation challenging the validity of the opposing argument.

> *Lou Gehrig concedes what some of his listeners may think — that his bad break is a cause for discouragement or despair.*

connotation   Meanings or associations that readers have with a word beyond its dictionary definition, or denotation. Connotations are usually positive or negative, and they can greatly affect the author's tone. Consider the connotations of the words below, all of which mean "overweight."

> *That cat is* plump. *That cat is* fat. *That cat is* obese.

context   The circumstances, atmosphere, attitudes, and events surrounding a text.

> *The context for Lou Gehrig's speech is the recent announcement of his illness and his subsequent retirement, but also the poignant contrast between his potent career and his debilitating disease.*

counterargument   An opposing argument to the one a writer is putting forward. Rather than ignoring a counterargument, a strong writer will usually address it through the process of concession and refutation.

> *Some of Lou Gehrig's listeners might have argued that his bad break was a cause for discouragement or despair.*

ethos   Greek for "character." Speakers appeal to ethos to demonstrate that they are credible and trustworthy to speak on a given topic. Ethos is established by both who you are and what you say.

> *Lou Gehrig brings the ethos of being a legendary athlete to his speech, yet in it he establishes a different kind of ethos — that of a regular guy and a good sport who shares the audience's love of baseball and family. And like them, he has known good luck and bad breaks.*

logos   Greek for "embodied thought." Speakers appeal to logos, or reason, by offering clear, rational ideas and using specific details, examples, facts, statistics, or expert testimony to back them up.

> *Gehrig starts with the thesis that he is "the luckiest man on the face of the earth" and supports it with two points: (1) the love and kindness he's received in his seventeen years of playing baseball, and (2) a list of great people who have been his friends, family, and teammates.*

occasion   The time and place a speech is given or a piece is written.

> *In the case of Gehrig's speech, the occasion is Lou Gehrig Appreciation Day. More specifically, his moment comes at home plate between games of a doubleheader.*

pathos   Greek for "suffering" or "experience." Speakers appeal to pathos to emotionally motivate their audience. More specific appeals to pathos might play on the audience's values, desires, and hopes, on the one hand, or fears and prejudices, on the other.

> *The most striking appeal to pathos is the poignant contrast between Gehrig's horrible diagnosis and his public display of courage.*

persona   Greek for "mask." The face or character that a speaker shows to his or her audience.

> *Lou Gehrig is a famous baseball hero, but in his speech he presents himself as a common man who is modest and thankful for the opportunities he's had.*

polemic   Greek for "hostile." An aggressive argument that tries to establish the superiority of one opinion over all others. Polemics generally do not concede that opposing opinions have any merit.

propaganda   The spread of ideas and information to further a cause. In its negative sense, propaganda is the use of rumors, lies, disinformation, and scare tactics in order to damage or promote a cause. For more information, see *How to Detect Propaganda* on page 756.

purpose   The goal the speaker wants to achieve.

> *One of Gehrig's chief purposes in delivering his Farewell Address is to thank his fans and his teammates, but he also wants to demonstrate that he remains positive: he emphasizes his past luck and present optimism and downplays his illness.*

refutation   A denial of the validity of an opposing argument. In order to sound reasonable, refutations often follow a concession that acknowledges that an opposing argument may be true or reasonable.

> *Lou Gehrig refutes that his bad break is a cause for discouragement by saying that he has "an awful lot to live for!"*

rhetoric   As Aristotle defined the term, "the faculty of observing in any given case the available means of persuasion." In other words, it is the art of finding ways to persuade an audience.

rhetorical appeals   Rhetorical techniques used to persuade an audience by emphasizing what they find most important or compelling. The three major appeals are to ethos (character), logos (reason), and pathos (emotion).

rhetorical triangle (Aristotelian triangle)   A diagram that illustrates the interrelationship among the speaker, audience, and subject in determining a text. See p. 4.

SOAPS   A mnemonic device that stands for Subject, Occasion, Audience, Purpose, and Speaker. It is a handy way to remember the various elements that make up the rhetorical situation.

speaker   The person or group who creates a text. This might be a politician who delivers a speech, a commentator who writes an article, an artist who draws a political cartoon, or even a company that commissions an advertisement.

In his Farewell Address, the speaker is not just Lou Gehrig, but baseball hero and ALS victim Lou Gehrig, a common man who is modest and thankful for the opportunities he's had.

subject   The topic of a text. What the text is *about*.

Lou Gehrig's subject in his speech is his illness, but it is also a catalog of all the lucky breaks that preceded his diagnosis.

text   While this term generally means the written word, in the humanities it has come to mean any cultural product that can be "read"—meaning not just consumed and comprehended, but investigated. This includes fiction, nonfiction, poetry, political cartoons, fine art, photography, performances, fashion, cultural trends, and much more.

Close Reading
The Art and Craft of Analysis

Do you ever wonder how your teachers can teach the same books year after year and not be bored by them? One reason is that the works we study in school have many layers of meaning, revealing something new each time we read them. That quality is what distinguishes them from literary potato chips — works that are satisfying, even delicious, but that offer little nutritional value. A mystery, romance, gossip blog, or sports rant may absorb us completely, but usually we do not read it a second time.

How do you find the "nutritional value" in the essays, speeches, stories, and poems you study in school? Your teacher may lead you through a work, putting it in context, focusing your attention on themes and techniques, asking for a response. Or you might do these things yourself through a process called close reading. When you read closely, you develop an understanding of a text that is based first on the words themselves and then on the larger ideas those words suggest. That is, you start with the small details, and as you think about them, you discover how they affect the text's larger meaning. When you *write* a close analysis, you start with the larger meaning you've discovered and use the small details — the language itself — to support your interpretation.

Of course, as you read the speeches, essays, letters, editorials, and even blog posts in this book and in your class, you will find that many different factors dictate the stylistic choices a writer makes. Sometimes, it's the genre: a blog post will likely be less formal than, say, an acceptance speech; an editorial will be less personal than an exchange of letters between two friends. Sometimes, it's the context or rhetorical situation — considering subject matter, occasion, audience, purpose, and the persona of the speaker. Often, however, the choices writers make are related to the rhetorical strategies of the text: what words in what arrangement are most likely to create the desired effect in the audience?

Analyzing Style

As with any skill, close reading becomes easier with practice, but it's important to remember that we use it unconsciously—and instantaneously—every day as we respond to people and situations. Just as we notice body language, gestures, facial expressions, and volume in our conversations, we can understand a text better by examining its sentence structure, vocabulary, imagery, and figurative language. These elements make up the style of the written piece and help us to discover layers of meaning. Style contributes to the meaning, purpose, and effect of a text, whether it is written, oral, or visual.

A Model Analysis

Let's take a look at a very famous speech given by Queen Elizabeth I in 1588 to the English troops at Tilbury that were assembled in preparation for an attack by the Spanish Armada. Working with older pieces such as this one sometimes seems more difficult than working with texts from the twentieth or twenty-first century, yet you may find that you read the older ones more carefully and that their riches reveal themselves more quickly than you might expect. Often the biggest challenge is understanding the tone of the piece, but if you look carefully at the speaker's choices of words (also called **diction**) and how those words are arranged (called **syntax**), you will find plenty of clues.

It may help you to begin by picturing Queen Elizabeth as she might have been on that day in 1588. (Consider watching a reenactment of this speech; Helen Mirren's performance of it in the 2005 miniseries *Elizabeth I* is especially good and easy to find online.) Tradition has it that when Queen Elizabeth, known as the Virgin Queen, gave this speech, she was dressed in armor and left her bodyguards in order to walk among her subjects. Her troops were vastly outnumbered by a Spanish Armada that was the most formidable naval force in the world, and it had been preparing to invade England for three years. England, in contrast, was in a precarious financial situation that made it impossible for its troops to go on the offensive; they had to wait for the attack. The English troops were bedraggled, underpaid, and hungry.

Speech to the Troops at Tilbury
QUEEN ELIZABETH

My loving people,

We have been persuaded by some that are careful of our safety, to take heed how we commit our selves to armed multitudes, for fear of treachery; but I assure you I do not desire to live to distrust my faithful and loving people. Let tyrants fear, I have always so behaved myself that, under God, I have placed my chiefest strength and safeguard in the loyal hearts and good-will of my subjects; and therefore I am come amongst you, as you see, at this time, not for my recreation and disport, but being resolved, in the midst and heat of the battle, to live and die amongst you all; to lay down for my God, and for my kingdom, and my people, my honour and my blood, even in the dust.

I know I have the body but of a weak and feeble woman; but I have the heart and stomach of a king, and of a king of England too, and think foul scorn that Parma or Spain, or any prince of Europe, should dare to invade the borders of my realm; to which rather than any dishonour shall grow by me, I myself will take up arms, I myself will be your general, judge, and rewarder of every one of your virtues in the field.

I know already, for your forwardness you have deserved rewards and crowns; and We do assure you in the word of a prince, they shall be duly paid you. In the mean time, my lieutenant general shall be in my stead, than whom never prince commanded a more noble or worthy subject; not doubting but by your obedience to my general, by your concord in the camp, and your valour in the field, we shall shortly have a famous victory over those enemies of my God, of my kingdom, and of my people.

Using what you learned in Chapter 1, you can begin by identifying the passage's rhetorical situation. The speaker is the Queen of England, not — and this is important — the king. She is exhorting her troops to face the battle with courage and determination on the eve of a confrontation in which England is the underdog. We can analyze the passage through the rhetorical triangle, considering the interaction of subject, audience, and speaker. The subject is Queen Elizabeth's support for her troops, and the audience is those soldiers gathered around to hear her. Of course, we can assume Elizabeth knew that her words would be communicated to the larger world as well.

You can also consider the ways the queen appealed to ethos, pathos, and logos. A popular queen, walking alone but with her loyal retinue nearby, her ethos as the monarch is established; nevertheless, she begins the speech humbly by stating her confidence in her subjects. She appeals to pathos in her characterization of herself as a "weak and feeble woman," although she reassures her listeners that on the inside she is as strong as a king. Less apparent is Elizabeth's appeal to logos; we could, however, consider her promise to repay her loyal troops with "rewards and crowns" to be a logical extension of her support for them.

• ACTIVITY •

Reread the speech, and think about the rhetorical strategies and style choices that help Queen Elizabeth convey her message. Think also about the persona she creates for herself and how that helps her achieve her purpose.

You probably noticed that Elizabeth begins by speaking of herself in the first person plural. This is a convention: the "royal we," meant to show that the ruling monarch embodies the entire nation. Even though it is conventional, you can see that it helps Elizabeth create a sense of common purpose. Interestingly, she quickly moves to the singular personal pronouns, "I" and "my," appropriate in a speech she is making on the same ground (literally) as her audience. She starts off by acknowledging those who might warn her against walking among her soldiers, those who urge her to "take heed how we commit our selves to armed multitudes." She asserts her independence and fortitude here, telling the troops that she considers them her "chiefest strength" and assures them that she is not that day among them for "recreation and disport." We can imagine that Elizabeth knew the power of image and even mythmaking; there in the flesh among her soldiers, her wish to "live and die amongst you all" would inspire confidence and courage. The sentence that begins the speech creates a sense of equity between Elizabeth and her troops. The second sentence builds up to the queen's dramatic commitment to die in the dust with her subjects.

The speech switches gears a bit in the third sentence (para. 2) with the speech's most famous phrase: "I know I have the body but of a weak and feeble woman; but I have the heart and stomach of a king, and of a king of England too. . . ." Here Elizabeth reinforces her image as the Virgin Queen. She never married, most likely for political reasons, and considered herself married to England. She reminds the assembled troops that she is the daughter of a king, however, and is, therefore, connected to the long line of royalty and the divine right of kings — the idea that royal power is bestowed by God. It is worth noting that only then, when she has characterized herself as a "weak and feeble woman," does she mention the enemies: Spain, Parma (Italy), and Europe in general. These references may serve a few purposes. They appeal to the gallantry of the troops who would feel obligated as gentlemen to defend their queen; they may also be a way to suggest that an attack by Spain is a Catholic threat to English Protestantism. In either case, Elizabeth reassures her troops that she is with them every step of the way and that their "virtues in the field" will be rewarded.

The final part of the speech reinforces the earlier call for national unity and a reassurance that Elizabeth has the interests of her people at heart. She reminds the troops of the rewards they will receive and reaffirms her support for her lieutenant general, who serves "in [her] stead." The last clause invokes the rule of three — "your obedience," "your concord," "your valour" — to predict a "famous victory over those enemies of my God, of my kingdom, and of my people." Although the Armada was defeated largely by bad weather and the light English boats that were able to ride out the storms, Elizabeth's troops were certainly strengthened by her glorious words of trust and confidence.

Let's discuss the tone of Elizabeth's speech, as this is a good way to begin thinking about how to write about what you've discovered in your close reading. We often consider tone and mood together: **tone** is the speaker's attitude toward the subject as revealed by his or her choice of language, and **mood** is the feeling created by the work. As always, it's important to be able to support your description of tone and mood with evidence from the text. Elizabeth's speech at Tilbury begins with Elizabeth humbling herself to the soldiers: she drops the "royal we"; she puts her subjects before her own safety; she offers her life for her kingdom. In the second paragraph, Elizabeth makes a transition from humble (she has the body of a "weak and feeble woman") to defiant: she dares the Europeans to invade. Finally, she makes some practical concessions, promising her troops that they will be led by her most loyal lieutenant and amply rewarded for their loyalty. We could describe the tone of her speech as humble yet inspiring and defiant.

• ACTIVITY •

Read Winston Churchill's first speech to the House of Commons as Prime Minister of Britain in May 1940. Describe the tone of the speech by using two adjectives or an adjective and an adverb; then explain why you chose those words, making specific reference to the text.

Blood, Toil, Tears, and Sweat

Winston Churchill

I beg to move,

That this House welcomes the formation of a Government representing the united and inflexible resolve of the nation to prosecute the war with Germany to a victorious conclusion.

On Friday evening last I received His Majesty's commission to form a new Administration. It is the evident wish and will of Parliament and the nation that this should be conceived on the broadest possible basis and that it should include all parties, both those who supported the late Government and also the parties of the Opposition. I have completed the most important part of this task. A War Cabinet has been formed of five Members, representing, with the Opposition Liberals, the unity of the nation. The three party Leaders have agreed to serve, either in the War Cabinet or in high executive office. The three Fighting Services have been filled. It was necessary that this should be done in one single day, on account of the extreme urgency and rigour of events. A number of other positions, key positions, were filled yesterday, and I am submitting a further list to His Majesty tonight. I hope to complete the appointment of the principal Ministers during tomorrow. The appointment of the other Ministers usually takes a little longer, but I trust that, when Parliament meets again, this part of my task will be completed, and that the Administration will be complete in all respects.

I considered it in the public interest to suggest that the House should be summoned to meet today. Mr. Speaker agreed, and took the necessary steps, in accordance with the powers conferred upon him by the Resolution of the House. At the end of the proceedings today, the Adjournment of the House will be proposed until Tuesday, 21st May, with, of course, provision for earlier meeting, if need be. The business to be considered during that week will be notified to Members at the earliest opportunity. I now invite the House, by the Motion which stands in my name, to record its approval of the steps taken and to declare its confidence in the new Government.

To form an Administration of this scale and complexity is a serious undertaking in itself, but it must be remembered that we are in the preliminary stage of one of the greatest battles in history, that we are in action at many other points in Norway and in Holland, that we have to be prepared in the Mediterranean, that the air battle is continuous and that many preparations, such as have been indicated by my hon. Friend below the Gangway, have to be made here at home. In this crisis I hope I may be pardoned if I do not address the House at any length today. I hope that any of my friends and colleagues, or former colleagues, who are affected by the political reconstruction, will make allowance, all allowance, for any lack of ceremony with which it has been necessary to act. I would say to the House, as I said to those who have joined this government: "I have nothing to offer but blood, toil, tears and sweat."

We have before us an ordeal of the most grievous kind. We have before us many, many long months of struggle and of suffering. You ask, what is our policy? I can say: It is to wage war, by sea, land and air, with all our might and with all the strength that God can give us; to wage war against a monstrous tyranny, never surpassed in the dark, lamentable catalogue of human crime. That is our policy. You ask, what is our aim? I can answer in one word: It is victory, victory at all costs, victory in spite of all terror, victory, however long and hard the road may be; for without victory, there is no survival. Let that be realised; no survival for the British Empire, no survival for all that the British Empire has stood for, no survival for the urge and impulse of the ages, that mankind will move forward towards its goal. But I take up my task with buoyancy and hope. I feel sure that our cause will not be suffered to fail among men. At this time I feel entitled to claim the aid of all, and I say, "come then, let us go forward together with our united strength."

Talking with the Text

Effective close reading requires active reading, an exchange between the reader and the text that eventually reveals layers of meaning. The first step is to read and reread. That's a good start, but at some point you will have to talk back, ask questions, make comments. In other words, have a conversation with the text. Let's look at some close reading techniques that will help you talk with the text.

Asking Questions

One of the simplest ways to talk with the text is to interrogate it—ask questions. Remember that we're always trying to consider the choices writers make, so as you read, ask yourself why they chose the words or sentence patterns they did. You don't always need to know the answers to your questions; sometimes, just asking them will give you insights into a writer's choices.

Let's take a look at this excerpt from Ralph Ellison's "On Bird, Bird-Watching and Jazz," an essay in which the writer considers the legend—and style—of jazz saxophonist and composer Charlie Parker, nicknamed Yardbird. In the essay, which was published in the *Saturday Review* in 1962, Ellison refers to both Robert Reisner's *Bird: The Legend of Charlie Parker* (a collection of interviews of Parker's friends, family, and colleagues) and Roger Tory Peterson's *A Field Guide to the Birds* (the bird-watcher's bible) as he comments on jazz as art and examines the myths surrounding Parker's nickname.

from *On Bird, Bird-Watching and Jazz*
Ralph Ellison

Oddly enough, while several explanations are advanced as to how Charles Parker, Jr., became known as "Bird" ("Yardbird," in an earlier metamorphosis), none is conclusive. There is, however, overpowering internal evidence that whatever the true circumstance of his ornithological designation, it had little to do with the chicken yard. Randy roosters and operatic hens are familiars to fans of the animated cartoons, but for all the pathetic comedy of his living—and despite the crabbed and constricted character of his style—Parker was a most inventive melodist, in bird-watcher's terminology, a true songster.

This failure in the exposition of Bird's legend is intriguing, for nicknames are indicative of a change from a given to an achieved identity, whether by rise or fall, and they tell us something of the nicknamed individual's interaction with his fellows. Thus, since we suspect that more of legend is involved in his renaming than Mr. Reisner's title indicates, let us at least consult Roger Tory Peterson's *Field Guide to the Birds* for a hint as to why, during a period when most jazzmen were labeled "cats," someone hung the bird on Charlie. Let us note too that "legend" originally meant "the story of a saint," and that saints were often identified with symbolic animals.

Two species won our immediate attention, the goldfinch and the mockingbird— the goldfinch because the beatnik phrase "Bird lives," which, following Parker's death, has been chalked endlessly on Village buildings and subway walls, reminds us that during the thirteenth and fourteenth centuries a symbolic goldfinch frequently appeared in European devotional paintings. An apocryphal story has it that upon being given a clay bird for a toy, the infant Jesus brought it miraculously to life as a goldfinch. Thus the small, tawny-brown bird with a bright red patch about the base of its bill and a broad yellow band across its wings became a representative of the soul, the Passion and the Sacrifice. In more worldly late-Renaissance art, the little bird became the ambiguous symbol of death and the soul's immortality. For our own purposes, however, its song poses a major problem: it is like that of a canary— which soul or no soul, rules the goldfinch out.

> The mockingbird, *Mimus polyglottos*, is more promising. Peterson informs us that its song consists of "long successions of notes and phrases of great variety, with each phrase repeated a half dozen times before going on to the next," that mockingbirds are "excellent mimics" who "adeptly imitate a score or more species found in the neighborhood," and that they frequently sing at night—a description which not only comes close to Parker's way with a saxophone but even hints at a trait of his character. For although he *usually* sang at night, his playing was characterized by velocity, by long-continued successions of notes and phrases, by swoops, bleats, echoes, rapidly repeated bebops—I mean rebopped bebops—by mocking mimicry of other jazzmen's styles, and by interpolations of motifs from extraneous melodies, all of which added up to a dazzling display of wit, satire, burlesque and pathos. Further, he was as expert at issuing his improvisations from the dense brush as from the extreme treetops of the harmonic landscape, and there was, without doubt, as irrepressible a mockery in his personal conduct as his music.

Reread the excerpt, and see what you notice on a second reading. Jot down questions as you go, asking why Ellison might have used the language he did.

Here are some questions about Ellison's style that might come to mind, based on first and second impressions of the passage:

1. Why do the first two sentences contain qualifiers ("Oddly enough," "however")?

2. Why does Ellison suggest that his audience might be "fans of the animated cartoons"?

3. Why does Ellison think a book about bird-watching might be more edifying than a biography of Parker?

4. Why does Ellison say "hung the bird on Charlie" (para. 2) instead of "nicknamed him"?

5. What is the effect of Ellison's references to the story about the infant Jesus (para. 3)?

6. Why does Ellison provide the mockingbird's scientific name (*Mimus polyglottos*) (para. 4)?

7. How does Ellison manage to make this description of jazz sound so jazzy: "by long-continued successions of notes and phrases, by swoops, bleats, echoes, rapidly repeated bebops—I mean rebopped bebops—..." (para. 4)?

8. What is the effect of the dashes in the phrase above?

You may notice that these questions fall into the two categories we talked about in relation to Queen Elizabeth's speech: the choice of words (diction) and the way the words are arranged (syntax). When we talk about diction, we might look for interesting or powerful vocabulary, but we also consider figures of speech like **metaphors, similes, personification,** and **hyperbole.** When we consider syntax we want to notice interesting constructions like **parallelism, juxtaposition,** and **antithesis,** along with sentence types such as **compound, complex, periodic, cumulative,** and **imperative,** among others. We also might look at the **pacing** of a piece of work: Does the writer reveal details quickly or slowly? How does he or she build suspense?

Here are some questions to ask when you analyze diction:

1. What type of words draw your attention? Do they tend to be a particular part of speech, such as verbs, nouns, adjectives, or adverbs? Is the language general and abstract or specific and concrete?

2. Is the language formal, informal, colloquial, or slang?

3. Are some words nonliteral or figurative, creating **figures of speech** such as metaphors?

4. Are there words with strong connotations? Words with a particular emotional punch?

When you analyze syntax, you might ask:

1. What is the order of the parts of the sentence? Is it the usual order (subject-verb-object), or is it inverted (object-subject-verb, or any other pattern that is out of the ordinary)?

2. What are the sentences like? Are they periodic (moving toward something important at the end) or cumulative (beginning with an important idea and then adding details)?

3. Are many of the sentences simple? Complex? Compound? Are the sentences on the long side, or are they short?

4. Does the writer ask questions?

5. How does the writer connect words, phrases, and clauses?

These questions do not have simple yes or no answers. They lend themselves to discussion, but as you discuss them, be sure you can support your ideas with evidence from the text. Coming up with answers to questions like these will put you well on your way toward making an analysis of an author's style and how that style helps the author make his or her point.

• ACTIVITY •

Read the next paragraph from Ellison's essay, then generate two or three questions each about diction and syntax.

from *On Bird, Bird-Watching and Jazz*

RALPH ELLISON

Mimic thrushes, which include the catbird and brown thrasher, along with the mockingbird, are not only great virtuosi, they are the tricksters and con men of the bird world. Like Parker, who is described as a confidence man and a practical joker by several of the commentators, they take off on the songs of other birds, inflating, inverting and turning them wrong side out, and are capable of driving a prowling ("square") cat wild. Utterly irreverent and romantic, they are not beyond bugging human beings. Indeed, on summer nights in the South, when the moon hangs low, mockingbirds sing as though determined to heat every drop of romance in the sleeping adolescent's heart to fever pitch. Their song thrills and swings the entire moon-struck night to arouse one's sense of the mystery, promise and frustration of being human, alive and hot in the blood. They are as delightful to the eye as to the ear, but sometimes a similarity of voice and appearance makes for a confusion with the shrike, a species given to impaling insects and smaller songbirds on the points of thorns, and they are destroyed. They are fond of fruit, especially mulberries, and if there is a tree in your yard, there will be, along with the wonderful music, much chalky, blue-tinted evidence of their presence. Under such conditions, be careful and heed Parker's warning to his friends — who sometimes were subjected to a shrikelike treatment — "you must pay your dues to Bird."

Annotating

Another close reading technique you can use is annotation. Annotating a text requires reading with a pencil in hand. If you are not allowed to write in your book, then write on sticky notes. As you read, circle words you don't know, or write them on the sticky notes. Identify main ideas — thesis statements, topic sentences — and also words, phrases, or sentences that appeal to you, that seem important, or that you don't understand. Look for figures of speech such as metaphors, similes, and personification — as well as **imagery** and striking detail. If you don't know the technical term for something, just describe it. For example, if you come across an adjective-and-noun combination that seems contradictory, such as "meager abundance," and you don't know that the term for it is **oxymoron**, you might still note the juxtaposition of two words that have opposite meanings. Ask questions or comment on what you have read. In short, as you read, listen to the voice in your head, and write down what that voice is saying.

Let's try out this approach using a passage by Joan Didion about California's Santa Ana winds from her 1965 essay "Los Angeles Notebook." Read the passage first, and see if you can come up with some ideas about Didion's purpose. Then we will look closely at the choices she makes and the effects of those choices.

The Santa Ana Winds

Joan Didion

There is something uneasy in the Los Angeles air this afternoon, some unnatural stillness, some tension. What it means is that tonight a Santa Ana will begin to blow,
a hot wind from the northeast whining down through the Cajon and San Gorgonio
Passes, blowing up sand storms out along Route 66, drying the hills and the nerves
to flash point. For a few days now we will see smoke back in the canyons, and
hear sirens in the night. I have neither heard nor read that a Santa Ana is due, but
I know it, and almost everyone I have seen today knows it too. We know it because
we feel it. The baby frets. The maid sulks. I rekindle a waning argument with the
telephone company, then cut my losses and lie down, given over to whatever it is
in the air. To live with the Santa Ana is to accept, consciously or unconsciously, a
deeply mechanistic view of human behavior.

I recall being told, when I first moved to Los Angeles and was living on an isolated beach, that the Indians would throw themselves into the sea when the bad wind
blew. I could see why. The Pacific turned ominously glossy during a Santa Ana
period, and one woke in the night troubled not only by the peacocks screaming in
the olive trees but by the eerie absence of surf. The heat was surreal. The sky had a
yellow cast, the kind of light sometimes called "earthquake weather." My only neighbor would not come out of her house for days, and there were no lights at night,
and her husband roamed the place with a machete. One day he would tell me that
he had heard a trespasser, the next a rattlesnake.

"On nights like that," Raymond Chandler once wrote about the Santa Ana,
"every booze party ends in a fight. Meek little wives feel the edge of the carving
knife and study their husbands' necks. Anything can happen." That was the kind of
wind it was. I did not know then that there was any basis for the effect it had on all
of us, but it turns out to be another of those cases in which science bears out folk
wisdom. The Santa Ana, which is named for one of the canyons it rushes through,
is a *foehn* wind, like the *foehn* of Austria and Switzerland and the *hamsin* of Israel.
There are a number of persistent malevolent winds, perhaps the best known of which
are the *mistral* of France and the Mediterranean *sirocco*, but a *foehn* wind has
distinct characteristics: it occurs on the leeward slope of a mountain range and,
although the air begins as a cold mass, it is warmed as it comes down the mountain
and appears finally as a hot dry wind. Whenever and wherever *foehn* blows, doctors hear about headaches and nausea and allergies, about "nervousness," about
"depression." In Los Angeles some teachers do not attempt to conduct formal classes
during a Santa Ana, because the children become unmanageable. In Switzerland
the suicide rate goes up during the *foehn*, and in the courts of some Swiss cantons
the wind is considered a mitigating circumstance for crime. Surgeons are said to
watch the wind, because blood does not clot normally during a *foehn*. A few years
ago an Israeli physicist discovered that not only during such winds, but for the ten or
twelve hours which precede them, the air carries an unusually high ratio of positive

to negative ions. No one seems to know exactly why that should be; some talk about friction and others suggest solar disturbances. In any case the positive ions are there, and what an excess of positive ions does, in the simplest terms, is make people unhappy. One cannot get much more mechanistic than that.

You probably noticed that while Didion seems to be writing about a natural phenomenon — the Santa Ana winds — she is also commenting on human nature and the way nature affects human behavior. Her purpose, then, is social commentary as much as the observation of an event in nature. In addition, you may notice on a second or third reading that her tone gives you another message: the way Didion sees human nature.

Following is an annotated version of the Didion passage:

There is something uneasy in the Los Angeles air this after-noon, some unnatural stillness, some tension. What it means is that tonight a Santa Ana will begin to blow, a hot wind from the northeast whining down through the Cajon and San Gorgonio Passes, blowing up sand storms out along Route 66, drying the hills and the nerves to flash point. For a few days now we will see smoke back in the canyons, and hear sirens in the night. I have neither heard nor read that a Santa Ana is due, but I know it, and almost everyone I have seen today knows it too. We know it because we feel it. The baby frets. The maid sulks. I rekindle a waning argument with the telephone company, then cut my losses and lie down, given over to whatever it is in the air. To live with the Santa Ana is to accept, consciously or unconsciously, a deeply mechanistic view of human behavior.

I recall being told, when I first moved to Los Angeles and was living on an isolated beach, that the Indians would throw themselves into the sea when the bad wind blew. I could see why. The Pacific turned ominously glossy during a Santa Ana period, and one woke in the night troubled not only by the peacocks screaming in the olive trees but by the eerie absence of surf. The heat was surreal. The sky had a yellow cast, the kind of light sometimes called "earthquake weather." My only neighbor would not come out of her house for days, and there were no lights at night, and her husband roamed the place with a machete. One day he would tell me that he had heard a trespasser, the next a rattlesnake.

Annotations in margins:

- Long sentence
- Related words. Anxiety, foreboding
- Appeal to senses
- Short sentences
- Look up word
- Folktale?
- Echo of foreboding in opening
- Vivid images
- More anxiety words
- Personal anecdote

"On nights like that," Raymond Chandler once wrote   *Look up name*
about the Santa Ana, "every booze party ends in a fight. Meek
little wives feel the edge of the carving knife and study their
husbands' necks. Anything can happen." That was the kind of
wind it was. I did not know then that there was any basis for
the effect it had on all of us, but it turns out to be another of   *Seemingly*
those cases in which <u>science bears out folk wisdom</u>. The   *contradictory*
Santa Ana, which is named for one of the canyons it rushes   *sources of*
through, is a *foehn* wind, like the *foehn* of Austria and Switzer-   *information*
land and the *hamsin* of Israel. There are a number of <u>persistent</u>
<u>malevolent winds</u>, perhaps the best known of which are the   —*Good description*
mistral of France and the Mediterranean *sirocco*, but a *foehn*
wind has distinct characteristics: ① it occurs on the leeward
slope of a mountain range and, although the air begins as a
cold mass, it is warmed as it comes down the mountain and
appears finally as a hot dry wind. Whenever and wherever
foehn blows, ② doctors hear about headaches and nausea and
allergies, about "<u>nervousness</u>," about "<u>depression</u>." In Los Ange-   —*Why in quotes?*
les ③ some teachers do not attempt to conduct formal classes dur-
ing a Santa Ana, because the children become unmanageable.   *At least 7*
In Switzerland ④ the suicide rate goes up during the *foehn*, and   *scientific facts*
in the courts of some Swiss cantons the wind is considered ⑤ a
mitigating circumstance for crime. Surgeons are said to watch
the wind, because ⑥ blood does not clot normally during a
foehn. A few years ago an Israeli physicist discovered that not
only during such winds, but for the ten or <u>twelve hours</u> which
precede them, the air carries an unusually ⑦ high ratio of positive to negative ions. No one seems to know exactly why that
should be; some talk about friction and others suggest solar
disturbances. In any case the positive ions are there, and <u>what</u>
<u>an excess of positive ions does, in the simplest terms, is make</u>   —*Strange*
<u>people unhappy</u>. One cannot get much more mechanistic   *should be positive*
than that.

Using a Graphic Organizer

Another way to organize your thoughts about a specific text is to use a graphic
organizer. A graphic organizer lets you systematically look at short passages from a
longer text. Your teacher may divide the text for you, or you may divide it yourself;

you might use the paragraph divisions as natural breaking points, or you might consider smaller sections that seem interesting stylistically. Although a graphic organizer takes time to complete, it lets you gather a great deal of information that you can use as you prepare to write an essay.

The accompanying graphic organizer asks you to take something the writer

QUOTATION	PARAPHRASE OR SUMMARIZE
There is something uneasy in the Los Angeles air this afternoon, some unnatural stillness, some tension. What it means is that tonight a Santa Ana will begin to blow, a hot wind from the northeast whining down through the Cajon and San Gorgonio Passes, blowing up sand storms out along Route 66, drying the hills and the nerves to flash point. For a few days now we will see smoke back in the canyons, and hear sirens in the night. I have neither heard nor read that a Santa Ana is due, but I know it, and almost everyone I have seen today knows it too. We know it because we feel it. The baby frets. The maid sulks. I rekindle a waning argument with the telephone company, then cut my losses and lie down, given over to whatever it is in the air. To live with the Santa Ana is to accept, consciously or unconsciously, a deeply mechanistic view of human behavior.	The winds are creepy. They bring sand storms and cause fires. People know they're coming without being told because babies and maids act strange. The speaker picks a fight and then gives up. The Santa Ana winds make us aware that human behavior can be explained in terms of physical causes and processes.
I recall being told, when I first moved to Los Angeles and was living on an isolated beach, that the Indians would throw themselves into the sea when the bad wind blew. I could see why. The Pacific turned ominously glossy during a Santa Ana period, and one woke in the night troubled not only by the peacocks screaming in the olive trees but by the eerie absence of surf. The heat was surreal. The sky had a yellow cast, the kind of light sometimes called "earthquake weather." My only neighbor would not come out of her house for days, and there were no lights at night, and her husband roamed the place with a machete. One day he would tell me that he had heard a trespasser, the next a rattlesnake.	Didion talks about her early experiences with the winds, plus the folklore about them. She mentions things that seem weird — peacocks screeching and a very quiet ocean. She says her neighbors are strange too; one stays indoors, and the other walks around with a big knife.

has said, restate it in your own words, identify some of the devices that the writer has used, and then analyze how the writer uses those devices to make his or her point. Note that you become increasingly analytical as you move from left to right. The following graphic organizer has been filled in for you using a portion of the Joan Didion passage that we read above.

RHETORICAL STRATEGY OR STYLE ELEMENT	EFFECT OR FUNCTION
Personification: the wind whines	Giving the wind a human quality makes it even more threatening.
Cumulative sentence	She makes her point by accumulating details about what it means that the Santa Ana is beginning to blow.
Two short sentences: "The baby frets. The maid sulks."	Those simple sentences reduce human behavior to irrefutable evidence. We can't argue with what we see so clearly.
"rekindle"	Though she's talking about restarting an argument with the phone company, the word makes us think of starting a fire, like the wind does up in the hills.
Subordinate clause in the middle of that first sentence: "when I first moved to Los Angeles and was living on an isolated beach."	The clause accentuates Didion's isolation and because it's so long almost makes her experience more important than the Indians who threw themselves into the ocean.
"peacocks screaming in the olive trees"	Kind of an upside-down image. Peacocks are usually regal and elegant; these are screaming. Also olive trees are associated with peace (the olive branch). Supports the idea that the Santa Ana turns everything upside down.
Compound sentence: My only neighbor would not come out of her house for days, and there were no lights at night, and her husband roamed the place with a machete.	"And" as the coordinating conjunction makes the wife hiding and the husband with the machete equally important.
"machete"	"Machete" is associated with revolutions in banana republics, vigilantes. Suggests danger.

QUOTATION	PARAPHRASE OR SUMMARIZE
"On nights like that," Raymond Chandler once wrote about the Santa Ana, "every booze party ends in a fight. Meek little wives feel the edge of the carving knife and study their husbands' necks. Anything can happen." That was the kind of wind it was. I did not know then that there was any basis for the effect it had on all of us, but it turns out to be another of those cases in which science bears out folk wisdom.	Didion quotes a writer who describes the effects of the wind as causing women to want to kill their husbands. She says that folklore sometimes has a basis in science.
The Santa Ana, which is named for one of the canyons it rushes through, is a *foehn* wind, like the *foehn* of Austria and Switzerland and the *hamsin* of Israel. . . . A few years ago an Israeli physicist discovered that not only during such winds, but for the ten or twelve hours which precede them, the air carries an unusually high ratio of positive to negative ions.	This section gives scientific facts about the Santa Ana wind, including its generic name, *foehn*. Didion names other winds like it in other parts of the world, but says the *foehn* has its own characteristics. She names some of the effects the *foehn* has on people in various places.

Breaking the text into small sections, looking at them closely, and writing down your ideas about them helps you notice the stylistic details in Didion's writing. For example, in paragraph 1, she connects two seemingly different things in the same grammatical construction ("drying the hills and the nerves"; the technical name for this figure of speech is **zeugma**). Later in the essay she alludes to crime writer Raymond Chandler, to facts, even to some scientific data. Collecting these bits of information from the text and considering their impression on you prepares you to answer the following questions about Didion's style.

- What effect is she striving for?
- How does she create that effect?
- How does the effect serve the purpose of her writing?

From Close Reading to Analysis

No matter what technique you choose, as you interact with the text you should keep in mind that you're not only identifying techniques and strategies, but also analyzing their effect — you're moving from close reading to analysis. As you read the Didion passage, you probably got a feel for its mood. But how is that mood created? You probably noticed the anxiety-related words in the first paragraph: "uneasy," "unnatural," "tension," "flash point." There is an echo in the second paragraph: the ocean is "ominously glossy." That sense of foreboding imbues even the personal anecdote: a neighbor with a "machete," fear of a "trespasser," hints of a "rattlesnake." Didion uses the word "rekindle" to describe her effort to restart an

RHETORICAL STRATEGY OR STYLE ELEMENT	EFFECT OR FUNCTION
Allusion to Raymond Chandler	Chandler, who wrote crime fiction, was known for his hard-boiled style and cynical views. The allusion to Chandler helps create the ominous tone.
Complex sentence: "There are a number of persistent malevolent winds, perhaps the best known of which are the *mistral* of France and the Mediterranean *sirocco*, but a *foehn* wind has distinct characteristics: it occurs on the leeward slope of a mountain range and, although the air begins as a cold mass, it is warmed as it comes down the mountain and appears finally as a hot dry wind."	The details accumulate, ending in "hot dry wind," to create a picture of the "persistent malevolent winds."

ongoing argument with the phone company; it serves to remind us of the brush fires that so often threaten Southern California. Of course, if you've read other work by Joan Didion you may recognize that foreboding as a hallmark of her style. In either case, you can begin to see how Didion creates an unsettled mood through her word choice, especially in the first two paragraphs.

The passage's syntax also has a role. The second sentence in the first paragraph is long, a cumulative sentence that gathers details (and steam) as it describes the path of the Santa Ana wind and its destination in "flash point." Again, those Southern California brush fires come to mind. The sentence stands, too, in contrast to the short sentences later in the paragraph, simple declarative sentences that observe without comment the behavior that precedes the Santa Ana winds. Didion notes that she has "neither heard nor read that a Santa Ana is due"; nevertheless, the evidence is irrefutable: "The baby frets. The maid sulks."

The third paragraph is different even though it begins in the anxiety-laden mood of the first two, with its quotation from crime fiction writer Raymond Chandler. Though he is a fiction writer, Chandler is nevertheless an authority on both crime and Los Angeles. The quotation helps Didion transition to showing that sometimes "science bears out folk wisdom." What follows are at least seven examples of data—including the names and characteristics of various winds; the effects of the winds on schoolchildren, personal health, and criminals; and the changes in the atmosphere described in terms of positive and negative ions. This scientific language contrasts with the moodiness of the previous paragraphs. Notice the complex sentence that begins by noting a "number of persistent malevolent winds." Didion provides a couple of examples, foregrounding the *foehn*. The second independent clause provides the details of that wind, ending with its impact at the bottom of the mountain as a "hot dry wind."

So let's go back to those three key questions:

- What effect is Didion striving for?
- How does she create that effect?
- How does the effect serve the purpose of her writing?

For the first question, we might say that she is trying to both re-create the effect of the Santa Ana winds and explain the effect scientifically. For the second, we might say that she does this by simulating the feeling of anxiety that precedes the Santa Ana winds at the same time that she offers scientific facts and figures. The mood of foreboding, the tone of barely subdued fear and anger, and the language of violence and natural disaster are juxtaposed with the essay's pseudoscientific information. For the third question, we could agree that her purpose is to show that some human behavior is mechanistic, meaning it is less a matter of choice than a direct result of outside forces. We might go even further to say that Didion wants to scare us a bit: we sometimes can't help the way we behave. But it's not our fault. Maybe it's a full moon. Maybe a storm is brewing. Or maybe it's the Santa Ana winds.

• ACTIVITY •

Read Virginia Woolf's "The Death of the Moth," an essay in which she contemplates life and death by reflecting on the death of a small "day moth," a type of moth that is active in the daytime. Try one of the techniques you have learned for talking with the text. Then answer these questions: What effect is Woolf striving for? How does she create that effect? How does the effect serve the purpose of her writing? Try developing a thesis statement and an outline for an essay in which you analyze the way Woolf's style helps her achieve her purpose.

The Death of the Moth
VIRGINIA WOOLF

Moths that fly by day are not properly to be called moths; they do not excite that pleasant sense of dark autumn nights and ivy-blossom which the commonest yellow-underwing asleep in the shadow of the curtain never fails to rouse in us. They are hybrid creatures, neither gay like butterflies nor somber like their own species. Nevertheless the present specimen, with his narrow hay-colored wings, fringed with a tassel of the same color, seemed to be content with life. It was a pleasant morning, mid-September, mild, benignant, yet with a keener breath than that of the summer months. The plough was already scoring the field opposite the window, and where the share had been, the earth was pressed flat and gleamed with moisture. Such vigor came rolling in from the fields and the down beyond that it was difficult to keep the eyes strictly turned upon the book. The rooks too were keeping one of their annual festivities; soaring round the tree tops until it looked as if a vast net with thousands of black knots in it had been cast up into the air; which, after a few moments sank slowly down upon the trees until every twig seemed to have a knot at the end of it. Then, suddenly, the net would be thrown into the air again in a wider circle this time, with the utmost clamor and vociferation, as though to be thrown into the air and settle slowly down upon the tree tops were a tremendously exciting experience.

The same energy which inspired the rooks, the ploughmen, the horses, and even, it seemed, the lean bare-backed downs, sent the moth fluttering from side to side of his square of the windowpane. One could not help watching him. One, was, indeed, conscious of a queer feeling of pity for him. The possibilities of pleasure seemed that morning so enormous and so various that to have only a moth's part in life, and a day moth's at that, appeared a hard fate, and his zest in enjoying his meager opportunities to the full, pathetic. He flew vigorously to one corner of his compartment, and, after waiting there a second, flew across to the other. What remained for him but to fly to a third corner and then to a fourth? That was all he could do, in spite of the size of the downs, the width of the sky, the far-off smoke of houses, and the romantic voice, now and then, of a steamer out at sea. What he could do he did. Watching him, it seemed as if a fiber, very thin but pure, of the enormous energy of the world had been thrust into his frail and diminutive body. As often as he crossed the pane, I could fancy that a thread of vital light became visible. He was little or nothing but life.

Yet, because he was so small, and so simple a form of the energy that was rolling in at the open window and driving its way through so many narrow and intricate corridors in my own brain and in those of other human beings, there was something marvelous as well as pathetic about him. It was as if someone had taken a tiny bead of pure life and decking it as lightly as possible with down and feathers, had set it dancing and zigzagging to show us the true nature of life. Thus displayed one could not get over the strangeness of it. One is apt to forget all about life, seeing it humped and bossed and garnished and cumbered so that it has to move with the greatest circumspection and dignity. Again, the thought of all that life might have been had he been born in any other shape caused one to view his simple activities with a kind of pity.

After a time, tired by his dancing apparently, he settled on the window ledge in the sun, and, the queer spectacle being at an end, I forgot about him. Then, looking up, my eye was caught by him. He was trying to resume his dancing, but seemed either so stiff or so awkward that he could only flutter to the bottom of the windowpane; and when he tried to fly across it he failed. Being intent on other matters I watched these futile attempts for a time without thinking, unconsciously waiting for him to resume his flight, as one waits for a machine, that has stopped momentarily, to start again without considering the reason of its failure. After perhaps a seventh attempt he slipped from the wooden ledge and fell, fluttering his wings, on to his back on the windowsill. The helplessness of his attitude roused me. It flashed upon me that he was in difficulties; he could no longer raise himself; his legs struggled vainly. But, as I stretched out a pencil, meaning to help him to right himself, it came over me that the failure and awkwardness were the approach of death. I laid the pencil down again.

The legs agitated themselves once more. I looked as if for the enemy against which he struggled. I looked out of doors. What had happened there? Presumably it was midday, and work in the fields had stopped. Stillness and quiet had replaced the previous animation. The birds had taken themselves off to feed in the brooks. The horses stood still. Yet the power was there all the same, massed outside, indifferent, impersonal, not attending to anything in particular. Somehow it was opposed to the little hay-colored moth. It was useless to try to do anything. One could only watch the extraordinary efforts made by those tiny legs against an oncoming doom which could, had it chosen, have submerged an entire city, not merely a city, but masses of human beings; nothing, I knew, had any chance against death. Nevertheless after a pause of exhaustion the legs fluttered again. It was superb this last protest, and so frantic that he succeeded at last in righting himself. One's sympathies, of course, were all on the side of life. Also, when there was nobody to care or to know, this gigantic effort on the part of an insignificant little moth, against a power of such magnitude, to retain what no one else valued or desired to keep, moved one strangely. Again, somehow, one saw life, a pure bead. I lifted the pencil again, useless though I knew it to be. But even as I did so, the unmistakable tokens of death showed themselves. The body relaxed, and instantly grew stiff. The struggle was over. The insignificant little creature now knew death. As I looked at the dead moth, this minute wayside triumph of so great a force over so mean an antagonist filled me with wonder. Just as life had been strange a few minutes before, so death was now as strange. The moth having righted himself now lay most decently and uncomplainingly composed. O yes, he seemed to say, death is stronger than I am.

Writing a Close Analysis Essay

We're going to look now at steps you can take toward writing a close analysis essay. Good writing comes from careful reading, so the first steps will always be to read, reread, ask questions, and either annotate or create a graphic organizer for the text you will be working with. We're going to look at a 1947 letter from comedian and film star Groucho Marx. Marx performed with his brothers Zeppo, Chico, and Harpo—they were known as the Marx Brothers. The letter is a part of his correspondence with the film production company Warner Bros., which had concerns about an upcoming Marx Brothers film entitled *A Night in Casablanca*; the company worried that the title was too similar to the title of its 1942 film *Casablanca*. Read the letter carefully, and then read it again. Ask some questions, and either annotate the letter or make a graphic organizer. Pay close attention to the diction and syntax choices Marx made and how they might help him achieve his purpose.

Dear Warner Brothers,

Apparently there is more than one way of conquering a city and holding it as your own. For example, up to the time that we contemplated making a picture, I had no idea that the city of Casablanca[1] belonged exclusively to Warner Brothers. However, it was only a few days after our announcement appeared that we received a long, ominous legal document warning us not to use the name "Casablanca."

It seems that in 1471, Ferdinand Balboa Warner, your great-great-grandfather, while looking for a shortcut to the city of Burbank, had stumbled on the shores of Africa and, raising his alpenstock,[2] which he later turned in for a hundred shares of common,[3] named it Casablanca.

I just can't understand your attitude. Even if you plan on releasing your picture, I am sure that the average movie fan could learn in time to distinguish between Ingrid Bergman[4] and Harpo.[5] I don't know whether I could, but I certainly would like to try.

You claim you own Casablanca and that no one else can use that name without your permission. What about "Warner Brothers"? Do you own that too? You probably have the right to use the name Warner, but what about the name Brothers? Professionally, we were brothers long before you were. We were touring the sticks as the Marx Brothers when Vitaphone[6] was still a gleam in the inventor's eye, and even before us there had been other brothers—the Smith Brothers; the Brothers Karamazov; Dan Brouthers, an outfielder with Detroit; and "Brother, Can You Spare a Dime?" (This was originally "Brothers, Can You Spare a Dime?" but this was spreading a dime pretty thin, so they threw out one brother, gave all the money to the other one, and whittled it down to "Brother, Can You Spare a Dime?")

Now Jack, how about you? Do you maintain that yours is an original name? Well it's not. It was used long before you were born. Offhand, I can think of two Jacks—there was Jack of "Jack and the Beanstalk," and Jack the Ripper, who cut quite a figure in his day. 5

As for you, Harry, you probably sign your checks sure in the belief that you are the first Harry of all time and that all other Harrys are impostors. Offhand I can think of two Harrys that preceded you. There was Lighthorse Harry of Revolutionary fame and a Harry Appelbaum who lived on the corner of 93rd Street and Lexington Avenue. Unfortunately, Appelbaum wasn't too well-known. The last I heard of him, he was selling neckties at Weber and Heilbroner; but I'll never forget his mother, she made the best apple strudle in Yorkville.

---

[1]*Casablanca* is the title of a romantic—and perennially popular—film released by Warner Bros. in 1942 that won the Academy Award for Best Picture. It starred Humphrey Bogart in his first romantic role.—Eds.

[2]Walking stick.—Eds.

[3]Common stock in a company.—Eds.

[4]The beautiful female star of *Casablanca.*—Eds.

[5]Harpo was Groucho's brother and part of the Marx Brothers; he wore a red, curly-haired wig and did not speak, communicating instead by blowing a horn or whistling.—Eds.

[6]Vitaphone was the process developed by Warner Bros. for adding sound to film.—Eds.

Now about the Burbank studio.[7] I believe this is what you brothers call your place. Old man Burbank is gone. Perhaps you remember him. He was a great man in a garden. He was the wizard who crossed all those fruits and vegetables until he had the poor plants in such confused and jittery condition that they could never decide whether to enter the dining room on the meat platter or the dessert dish.

This is pure conjecture, of course, but who knows—perhaps Burbank's survivors aren't too happy with the fact that a plant that grinds out pictures on a quota settled in their town, appropriated Burbank's name and uses it as a front for their films. It is even possible that the Burbank family is prouder of the potato produced by the old man than they are of the fact that your studio emerged "Casablanca" or even "Gold Diggers of 1931."

This all seems to add up to a pretty bitter tirade, but I assure you it's not meant to. I love Warners. Some of my best friends are Warner Brothers. It is even possible that I am doing you an injustice and that you, yourselves, know nothing about this dog-in-the-Wanger[8] attitude. It wouldn't surprise me at all to discover that the heads of your legal department are unaware of this absurd dispute, for I am acquainted with many of them and they are fine fellows with curly black hair, double-breasted suits and a love of their fellow man that out-Saroyans Saroyan.[9]

I have a hunch that this attempt to prevent us from using the title is the brain- 10
child of some ferret-faced shyster, serving a brief apprenticeship in your legal department. I know the type well—hot out of law school, hungry for success and too ambitious to follow the natural laws of promotion. This bar sinister probably needled your attorneys, most of whom are fine fellows with curly black hair, double-breasted suits, etc., into attempting to enjoin us. Well, he won't get away with it! We'll fight him to the highest court! No pasty-faced legal adventurer is going to cause bad blood between the Warners and the Marxes. We are all brothers under the skin, and we'll remain friends till the last reel of A Night in Casablanca goes tumbling over the spool.

Sincerely,

Groucho Marx

---

[7]Movie production studios located in Burbank, California, a city close to Los Angeles where many movie production companies have their headquarters. Although there is a Luther Burbank Middle School in Burbank, the city is not named after the botanist Luther Burbank—who invented the Idaho potato—but after a dentist named David Burbank, who was originally from Maine. *Casablanca* was filmed at the Burbank studio.—Eds.

[8]A double play on words. Dog-in-the-Manger is one of Aesop's fables, about a dog that didn't eat the grain in the manger but wouldn't let the other animals eat it either. Walter Wanger was a film producer who produced the first Marx Brothers talkie.—Eds.

[9]A reference to William Saroyan, a writer and dramatist whose work was known for its optimism in the face of hardship.—Eds.

There is some doubt about whether Warner Bros. had actually objected to the title of the Marx Brothers film; but there's little doubt that this letter was primarily a publicity stunt by Groucho. In any case, it is a great example of the persuasive powers of humor. Groucho's style was instantly recognizable to fans of popular culture in the first half of the twentieth century. Now let's ask some questions to help determine the purpose of Marx's letter, what makes his style so distinctive, and how this style helps him achieve his purpose.

1. Why does Marx begin with "Apparently"?
2. Why does he say he had no idea that the city of Casablanca belonged to Warner Bros.?
3. What is the effect of Groucho's short history of Casablanca (para. 2)?
4. Would it really be difficult to distinguish between Ingrid Bergman and Harpo Marx (para. 3)?
5. Why does Marx offer so many examples of "Brothers" (para. 4)?
6. What is the effect of the parenthetical story about "Brother, Can You Spare a Dime" (para. 4)?
7. Why does Marx bring up Luther Burbank's experiments with fruits and vegetables (para. 7)?
8. Why does Marx qualify his statement that he loves Warners (para. 9) with "Some of my best friends are Warner Brothers"?
9. Why does Marx suggest that the source of Warner Bros.' concerns about his film come from an ambitious young lawyer, referring to him as a "pasty-faced legal adventurer" (para. 10)?

Developing a Thesis Statement

Answering these questions or others like them may help you to get some ideas for a thesis statement, the first step in writing a close analysis essay. You may change it as you go along, but having an idea about the argument you want to make will help you stay focused. As we mentioned, Groucho Marx uses humor to create his argument; we might even call this letter a kind of **satire** — the use of sarcasm or irony to criticize — so let's think first about Marx's purpose in writing the letter and why he might have chosen to use humor. Even if this letter was a publicity stunt, we can imagine that Marx wanted to highlight the differences between his film and the romantic adventure *Casablanca* to show Warner Bros. that it had little to fear from the Marx Brothers film *A Night in Casablanca*. It's also likely that Marx wanted to comment on the hot air that sometimes emerges from big corporations and their lawyers — especially, in this case, the enormous and powerful movie studio Warner Bros. But he chooses not to take these goals on directly.

As you think about a thesis statement, you will want to be careful that your thesis isn't too broad or just a summary:

> Groucho Marx uses humor to defend his movie.

And you will also want to make sure that it's not too narrow or just your personal opinion:

> Groucho Marx's letter to Warner Bros. is rude and disrespectful.

Most important, a close analysis essay must focus on the choices writers make to help them achieve their purpose. Here's a thesis statement that might work:

> Rather than take on Warner Bros. directly, Groucho Marx jabs and feints until the studio couldn't possibly take its own claim seriously.

A Sample Close Analysis Essay

Once you have a working thesis statement (remember, you may change it as you plan and write), think about the ways you will support it. Your essay may look closely at different style elements; it may focus on the way the writer organized the paragraphs and developed his or her argument; it may be a combination of both. It is important to cite the text, weaving quotes into your essay and explaining each example with at least two sentences of analysis or commentary. Take a look at this sample essay:

Like a boxer who weighs less than his opponent, Groucho Marx circles the great movie moguls — the Warner Bros. — baiting them, drawing them out, blinding them with his fancy footwork in his response to a letter from the studio forbidding the Marx Brothers from using the word "Casablanca" in the title of their upcoming film, *A Night in Casablanca*. Rather than take Warner Bros. on directly, Groucho Marx jabs and feints — humorously, of course — until Warner Bros. couldn't possibly take its own claim seriously.

Marx opens the letter with an intentional misunderstanding, the first way he highlights the absurdity of Warner Bros.' threat of legal action. He claims not to have understood that Warner Bros. had conquered the city of Casablanca until he received their "long, ominous legal document." It's not a big leap from there for Marx to imagine Ferdinand Balboa Warner, conveniently named after a real explorer, claiming the city of Casablanca by "raising his alpenstock." The image conjures up scenes from the lavish epics of early Hollywood, casting Warner as Moses in Cecil B. DeMille's *The Ten Commandments*. Marx extends his misunderstanding by imagining that the studio's main worry might be the trouble that the "average movie fan" will have in distinguishing Ingrid Bergman from Harpo Marx. Humbly, Marx says he "certainly would like to try." This slightly salacious offer reinforces the silliness of Warner Bros.' worries: Bergman was beautiful, blonde and dignified; Harpo Marx was a short, bewigged mute clown.

Marx creates a sense of familiarity, which serves his purpose by reminding his audience — Warner Bros. and their legal team — that they're all in the same boat, moviemakers with similar cultural knowledge, even shared heritage. Using classic Marx Brothers absurdist humor Groucho claims that he and his brothers — the Marx Brothers — have been around longer than Harry and Jack have and that they might have more right to use the word "Brothers" in their name. He piles on a list of other sets of brothers: "the Smith Brothers" (of cough drop fame), "the Brothers Karamazov" (title of a nineteenth-century Russian novel), a baseball player with the last name of "Brouthers." He even riffs a bit on the song "Brother, Can You Spare a Dime?" He gets even more personal, addressing each Warner brother by name: "Now Jack, how about you?", "As for you, Harry," and throws in some well-known examples of Harrys and Jacks, just for good measure. Unwilling to stop, Marx even questions the right of Warner Bros. to name its workplace "Burbank studio," suggesting — "pure conjecture, of course" — that Luther Burbank's survivors might not be happy to be associated with the Warner Bros.' body of work. One can imagine the effect of Marx's onslaught of examples on the movie studio's large and serious legal team, who also come under fire.

Content to let the logic of his defense rest, Marx gives Warner Bros.' legal team a break, suggesting that the letter was the brainchild of a young lawyer "hot out of law school, hungry for success and too ambitious to follow the natural laws of promotion." He claims sympathy and admiration for the heads of the legal department, "fine fellows with curly black hair, double-breasted suits and a love of their fellow man," a formulation he uses twice — the second time slightly truncated and ending in "etc." Effortlessly, Marx calls up a vision of mindless automatons, led astray by the "pasty-faced legal adventurer" who Marx calls responsible for the possible "bad blood between the Warners and the Marxes." Here he reinforces that bond between moviemaking families — "brothers under the skin" — and highlights once more the absurdity of imagining that the reputation or box office receipts of *Casablanca*, the 1942 Academy Award winner for Best Picture, will be sullied by a film made by the likes of Groucho and his brothers.

In this hilarious letter — and in the two letters that followed — Groucho Marx underscored the ridiculousness of comparing the classic *Casablanca* with the silliness of a Marx Brothers film in very much the style of his own films. Fast, clever, not especially logical, but certainly tireless, Marx wore out his bigger opponent. It took two more letters from Marx to get Warner Bros. off his back: each one outlined plots that were so far-fetched as to be nearly incomprehensible, and Warner Bros. finally gave up.

• ACTIVITY •

Read the following essay written by Christopher Morley in 1920. Annotate it or create a graphic organizer; generate some questions about its style. Develop a thesis statement, and write an essay in which you analyze the ways that the style of the essay helps Morley achieve his purpose.

On Laziness

CHRISTOPHER MORLEY

Today we rather intended to write an essay on Laziness, but were too indolent to do so.

The sort of thing we had in mind to write would have been exceedingly persuasive. We intended to discourse a little in favour of a greater appreciation of Indolence as a benign factor in human affairs.

It is our observation that every time we get into trouble it is due to not having been lazy enough. Unhappily, we were born with a certain fund of energy. We have been hustling about for a number of years now, and it doesn't seem to get us anything but tribulation. Henceforward we are going to make a determined effort to be more languid and demure. It is the bustling man who always gets put on committees, who is asked to solve the problems of other people and neglect his own.

The man who is really, thoroughly, and philosophically slothful is the only thoroughly happy man. It is the happy man who benefits the world. The conclusion is inescapable.

We remember a saying about the meek inheriting the earth. The truly meek man is the lazy man. He is too modest to believe that any ferment and hubbub of his can ameliorate the earth or assuage the perplexities of humanity.

O. Henry said once that one should be careful to distinguish laziness from dignified repose. Alas, that was a mere quibble. Laziness is always dignified, it is always reposeful. Philosophical laziness, we mean. The kind of laziness that is based upon a carefully reasoned analysis of experience. Acquired laziness. We have no respect for those who were born lazy; it is like being born a millionaire: they cannot appreciate their bliss. It is the man who has hammered his laziness out of the stubborn material of life for whom we chant praise and allelulia.

The laziest man we know—we do not like to mention his name, as the brutal world does not yet recognize sloth at its community value—is one of the greatest poets in this country; one of the keenest satirists; one of the most rectilinear thinkers. He began life in the customary hustling way. He was always too busy to enjoy himself. He became surrounded by eager people who came to him to solve their problems. "It's a queer thing," he said sadly; "no one ever comes to me asking for help in solving my problems." Finally the light broke upon him. He stopped answering letters, buying lunches for casual friends and visitors from out of town, he stopped lending money to old college pals and frittering his time away on all the useless minor matters that pester the good-natured. He sat down in a secluded cafe with his cheek against a seidel of dark beer and began to caress the universe with his intellect.

The most damning argument against the Germans is that they were not lazy enough. In the middle of Europe, a thoroughly disillusioned, indolent, and delightful old continent, the Germans were a dangerous mass of energy and bumptious

5

push. If the Germans had been as lazy, as indifferent, and as righteously laissez-fairish as their neighbours the world would have been spared a great deal.

People respect laziness. If you once get a reputation for complete, immovable, and reckless indolence the world will leave you to your own thoughts, which are generally rather interesting.

Doctor Johnson, who was one of the world's great philosophers, was lazy. Only yesterday our friend the Caliph showed us an extraordinarily interesting thing. It was a little leather-bound notebook in which Boswell jotted down memoranda of his talks with the old doctor.[10] These notes he afterward worked up into the immortal Biography. And lo and behold, what was the very first entry in this treasured little relic?

> Doctor Johnson told me in going to Ilam from Ashbourne, 22 September, 1777, that the way the plan of his Dictionary came to be addressed to Lord Chesterfield was this: He had neglected to write it by the time appointed. Dodsley suggested a desire to have it addressed to Lord C. Mr. J. laid hold of this as an excuse for delay, that it might be better done perhaps, and let Dodsley have his desire. Mr. Johnson said to his friend, Doctor Bathurst: "Now if any good comes of my addressing to Lord Chesterfield it will be ascribed to deep policy and address, when, in fact, it was only a casual excuse for laziness."

Thus we see that it was sheer laziness that led to the greatest triumph of Doctor Johnson's life, the noble and memorable letter to Chesterfield in 1775.

Mind your business is a good counsel; but mind your idleness also. It's a tragic thing to make a business of your mind. Save your mind to amuse yourself with.

The lazy man does not stand in the way of progress. When he sees progress roaring down upon him he steps nimbly out of the way. The lazy man doesn't (in the vulgar phrase) pass the buck. He lets the buck pass him. We have always secretly envied our lazy friends. Now we are going to join them. We have burned our boats or our bridges or whatever it is that one burns on the eve of a momentous decision.

Writing on this congenial topic has roused us up to quite a pitch of enthusiasm and energy.

Close Reading a Visual Text

Many of the same tools of rhetorical analysis and close reading that we have practiced on written texts are also useful for detecting how visual texts convey their

---

[10]Samuel Johnson (1709–1784) was a British scholar who wrote *A Dictionary of the English Language*. James Boswell wrote his famous biography. — Eds.

DODGE DURANGO. This is the most affordable SUV with a V-8. Dodge Durango. With nearly four tons of towing,* this baby carries around chunks of those wimpy wanna-bes in its tail pipe. For more info, call 800-4ADODGE or visit dodge.com

GRAB LIFE BY THE HORNS
DODGE

IT'S A BIG FAT JUICY CHEESEBURGER IN A LAND OF TOFU.
*Depending on model and when properly equipped.

(See insert for color version.)

messages. These tools work whether the visual texts are advertisements, photos, fine art, or political cartoons. Let's start by looking at an ad for the Dodge Durango.

The rhetorical triangle still applies: what are the relationships among the text's subject (a powerful sport utility vehicle), its audience (the potential SUV buyer), and the speaker (in this case, Dodge and the advertising agency it hired to create the ad)? The advertisement appeals to ethos in the text at the top left: it banks on associations to Dodge cars and trucks—power, dependability, toughness. Its appeals to pathos play on preconceptions about food: a cheeseburger is real food, tofu is somehow fake; cheeseburgers are what you want to eat, tofu is what you're supposed to eat; a big powerful truck is what you really want, a small fuel-efficient car is what you are supposed to have. As for logos, the Durango is affordable; it makes sense to own one. Why not enjoy life, drive an affordable SUV, and eat big juicy cheeseburgers?

When we analyze a visual text, we still look at the words, both individually and in the way they are placed on the page. Look at the text at the top left part of the ad.

> DODGE DURANGO. This is the most affordable SUV with a V-8. Dodge Durango. With nearly four tons of towing, this baby carries around chunks of those wimpy wanna-bes in its tail pipe.

Note the aggressive tone. How is that aggressiveness created? It may be the repetition of "Dodge Durango" with its hard consonant sounds; it may be the prepositional phrase announcing that the vehicle can tow four tons. It's a "baby" that carries "chunks" of its competitors in its tailpipe. The use of the colloquialism "baby" contrasts nicely with the image of the car as a predator eating the competition. The owner of a Dodge Durango will be the kind of person whose car is his or her "baby" and who is the leader of the pack, not one "of those wimpy wanna-bes." The Dodge logo—a ram's head—and slogan "grab life by the horns" appear at the top right of the ad. Both the image and the words play with the connotations of horns: strength, masculinity, and noise. The imperative sentence is a call to action that can be paraphrased as "Don't be a wimp! Enjoy life now!" Finally, the text at the bottom of the ad has yet another message. The large white letters on the dark road are boldly designed, but the message is gentle and even funny. "[B]ig fat juicy cheeseburger" acknowledges our natural desire for pleasures that are not always healthy. But who can resist when the alternative is tofu? The antecedent of *It's* is, of course, the SUV; but the pronoun suggests an understanding, an insider's wink.

We study the images in the text the same way: individually and in terms of composition, or arrangement on the page. For instance, notice that even though the Dodge logo is very aggressive, the photo is less so. In fact, the photo shows a man and a woman in the car, pulling a vintage Airstream motor home, thus suggesting not only a family atmosphere but also good taste, as Airstreams are collectibles. Perhaps it is a pitch to the rising number of women car buyers or to the use of an SUV as a less stodgy replacement for a minivan. Though the front of the Dodge Durango is outsized, a reminder of the power under the hood, the ocean and sky in the background temper the aggressiveness of the looming SUV; it looks like a beautiful day for a cool couple with great taste to be out for a ride.

So what is the advertisement's message? Or are there a few different messages? If you were to write an essay analyzing the "language" of the visual text, you might consider a thesis that argues for the ad's multiple messages. Here's one example:

> The Dodge Durango ad balances aggressiveness with humor; it appeals to men and women with its reminder that life is too short not to enjoy its guilty pleasures.

Use the following ad, or find one on your own that either appeals to you or provokes you, and analyze it as we have done with the Durango ad.

(See insert for color version.)

• CULMINATING ACTIVITY •

Look carefully at the three documents below. The first is John F. Kennedy's 1961 inaugural address. The second is an article that appeared in January 2011, first on the Web site Daily Beast and then in *Newsweek*. In "Inside Kennedy's Inauguration, 50 Years On," writer Eleanor Clift reports on what intimates of JFK remember from that cold January day. The last document is a photograph of the swearing-in ceremony.

Begin by reading the Kennedy speech and the analysis that follows. As you read the speech, take the time to generate some questions on style, annotate the speech, or create a graphic organizer, noting passages that stand out, interest you, or even confuse you. Then do the same with the Clift article: read it closely, and generate questions, annotate the article, or create a graphic organizer. Finally, study the photo, and consider the arrangement of the figures in it.

Once you have analyzed all three pieces, develop a thesis statement for an essay that compares and contrasts the styles of the three documents, focusing on how they convey the legacy of John Fitzgerald Kennedy.

Inaugural Address, January 20, 1961
JOHN F. KENNEDY

Given on a cold January afternoon in 1961, John F. Kennedy's inaugural address was hailed as a return to the tradition of political eloquence. It offers great pleasures to students of rhetoric, rewarding the close reader's efforts with details large and small that lend themselves to analysis, that inspire imitation, and that have stood the test of time.

Vice President Johnson, Mr. Speaker, Mr. Chief Justice, President Eisenhower, Vice President Nixon, President Truman, Reverend Clergy, fellow citizens:

We observe today not a victory of party but a celebration of freedom—symbolizing an end as well as a beginning—signifying renewal as well as change. For I have sworn before you and Almighty God the same solemn oath our forebears prescribed nearly a century and three-quarters ago.

The world is very different now. For man holds in his mortal hands the power to abolish all forms of human poverty and all forms of human life. And yet the same revolutionary beliefs for which our forebears fought are still at issue around the globe—the belief that the rights of man come not from the generosity of the state but from the hand of God.

We dare not forget today that we are the heirs of that first revolution. Let the word go forth from this time and place, to friend and foe alike, that the torch has been passed to a new generation of Americans—born in this century, tempered by war, disciplined by a hard and bitter peace, proud of our ancient heritage—and unwilling to witness or permit the slow undoing of those human rights to which this nation has always been committed, and to which we are committed today at home and around the world.

Let every nation know, whether it wishes us well or ill, that we shall pay any price, bear any burden, meet any hardship, support any friend, oppose any foe to assure the survival and the success of liberty.

This much we pledge—and more.   5

To those old allies whose cultural and spiritual origins we share, we pledge the loyalty of faithful friends. United there is little we cannot do in a host of co-operative ventures. Divided there is little we can do—for we dare not meet a powerful challenge at odds and split asunder.

To those new states whom we welcome to the ranks of the free, we pledge our word that one form of colonial control shall not have passed away merely to be replaced by a far more iron tyranny. We shall not always expect to find them supporting our view. But we shall always hope to find them strongly sup-porting their own freedom—and to remember that, in the past, those who foolishly sought power by riding the back of the tiger ended up inside.

To those people in the huts and villages of half the globe struggling to break the bonds of mass misery, we pledge our best efforts to help them help themselves, for whatever period is required—not because the communists may be doing it, not because we seek their votes, but because it is right. If a free society cannot help the many who are poor, it cannot save the few who are rich.

To our sister republics south of our border, we offer a special pledge—to convert our good words into good deeds—in a new alliance for progress—to assist free men and free governments in casting off the chains of poverty. But this peaceful revolution of hope cannot become the prey of hostile powers. Let all our neighbors know that we shall join with them to oppose aggression or subversion anywhere in the Americas. And let every other power know that this Hemisphere intends to remain the master of its own house.

To that world assembly of sovereign states, the United Nations, our last best   10
hope in an age where the instruments of war have far outpaced the instruments of peace, we renew our pledge of support—to prevent it from becoming merely a forum for invective—to strengthen its shield of the new and the weak—and to enlarge the area in which its writ may run.

Finally, to those nations who would make themselves our adversary, we offer not a pledge but a request: that both sides begin anew the quest for peace, before the dark powers of destruction unleashed by science engulf all humanity in planned or accidental self-destruction.

We dare not tempt them with weakness. For only when our arms are suffi-cient beyond doubt can we be certain beyond doubt that they will never be employed.

But neither can two great and powerful groups of nations take comfort from our present course—both sides overburdened by the cost of modern weapons, both rightly alarmed by the steady spread of the deadly atom, yet both racing to alter that uncertain balance of terror that stays the hand of mankind's final war.

So let us begin anew—remembering on both sides that civility is not a sign of weakness, and sincerity is always subject to proof. Let us never negotiate out of fear. But let us never fear to negotiate.

Let both sides explore what problems unite us instead of belaboring those problems which divide us.

Let both sides, for the first time, formulate serious and precise proposals for the inspection and control of arms—and bring the absolute power to destroy other nations under the absolute control of all nations.

Let both sides seek to invoke the wonders of science instead of its terrors. Together let us explore the stars, conquer the deserts, eradicate disease, tap the ocean depths and encourage the arts and commerce.

Let both sides unite to heed in all corners of the earth the command of Isaiah— to "undo the heavy burdens . . . [and] let the oppressed go free."

And if a beachhead of cooperation may push back the jungle of suspicion, let both sides join in creating a new endeavor, not a new balance of power, but a new world of law, where the strong are just and the weak secure and the peace preserved.

All this will not be finished in the first one hundred days. Nor will it be finished in the first one thousand days, nor in the life of this Administration, nor even perhaps in our lifetime on this planet. But let us begin.

In your hands, my fellow citizens, more than mine, will rest the final success or failure of our course. Since this country was founded, each generation of Americans has been summoned to give testimony to its national loyalty. The graves of young Americans who answered the call to service surround the globe.

Now the trumpet summons us again—not as a call to bear arms, though arms we need—not as a call to battle, though embattled we are—but a call to bear the burden of a long twilight struggle, year in and year out, "rejoicing in hope, patient in tribulation"—a struggle against the common enemies of man: tyranny, poverty, disease and war itself.

Can we forge against these enemies a grand and global alliance, North and South, East and West, that can assure a more fruitful life for all mankind? Will you join in that historic effort?

In the long history of the world, only a few generations have been granted the role of defending freedom in its hour of maximum danger. I do not shrink from this responsibility—I welcome it. I do not believe that any of us would exchange places with any other people or any other generation. The energy, the faith, the devotion which we bring to this endeavor will light our country and all who serve it—and the glow from that fire can truly light the world.

And so, my fellow Americans: ask not what your country can do for you— ask what you can do for your country.

My fellow citizens of the world: ask not what America will do for you, but what together we can do for the freedom of man.

Finally, whether you are citizens of America or citizens of the world, ask of us here the same high standards of strength and sacrifice which we ask of you. With a good conscience our only sure reward, with history the final judge of our deeds, let us go forth to lead the land we love, asking His blessing and His help, but knowing that here on earth God's work must truly be our own.

Let's start by looking at the rhetorical situation in Kennedy's inaugural address with SOAPS (p. 5). John F. Kennedy makes his subject not policy proposals, but the common heritage, purpose, and obligations of the American people. The occasion is the inauguration, a very cold day in January. The speech is short, only 1,343 words; its length is, perhaps, the new president's nod to the live audience standing in the cold on the Capitol grounds. The audience — those who were there on that icy morning and the millions watching on television — is vast and diverse. Kennedy was the youngest U.S. president, the first Roman Catholic president, and the winner of the election by a very small margin. His audience was, perhaps, watching more closely than usual. Knowing that, it is likely that Kennedy and his speechwriters considered their purpose to be one of unification and conciliation. As a speaker, Kennedy played up his youthful energy, giving the speech while standing coatless and hatless. The speech's strongest appeals are to pathos and ethos: Kennedy appeals to pathos, in part, by reaching his audience psychologically, asking them to consider what they can do for their country. He establishes ethos by offering America as a partner with the "citizens of the world" to champion the "freedom of man."

You may have generated questions like the ones listed below. Try your hand at answering the ones here as well as any you may have generated on your own. Don't worry if you can't answer all of them.

1. Why are so many of the words abstract? How do words like *freedom, poverty, devotion, loyalty,* and *sacrifice* set the tone of the speech?

2. Find examples of rhetorical devices such as metaphor and personification.

3. Does Kennedy use any figures of speech that might be considered clichés? Which metaphors are fresher? Is there a pattern to their use?

4. Do any words in the speech seem archaic, or old-fashioned? If so, what are they? What is their effect?

5. The speech is a succession of twenty-seven short paragraphs. Twelve paragraphs have only one sentence, eight have two, and six have three sentences. Why do you think Kennedy used these short paragraphs?

6. The speech contains two extremes of sentence length, ranging from ninety-four words (para. 3) to six words (para. 5). A high proportion of the sentences are on the short side. Why?

7. More than twenty sentences are complex sentences — that is, sentences that contain a subordinate clause. What is their effect? How are they different from the speech's simple or compound sentences?

8. The speech has many examples of antithesis in parallel grammatical structures: "To those old allies" (para. 6); "to those new states" (para. 7); "If a free society cannot help the many who are poor, it cannot save the few who are rich" (para. 8); and of course, "[A]sk not what your country can do for you — ask what you can do for your country" (para 25). What does this use of opposites suggest about the purpose of Kennedy's speech?

9. Why is the dominance of declarative sentences, which make statements, appropriate in an inaugural address?

10. Paragraph 23 consists of two rhetorical questions. How do they act as a transition to Kennedy's call for action?

11. Find examples of rhetorical schemes such as **anaphora** (the repetition of a word or phrase at the beginning of successive phrases, clauses, or lines) and **zeugma** (one verb or adjective having multiple and incongruous objects).

12. Consider the speech's many examples of parallelism: "born in this century, tempered by war, disciplined by a hard and bitter peace, proud of our ancient heritage" (para. 3); "pay any price, bear any burden, meet any hardship, support any friend, oppose any foe" (para. 4). How do they lend themselves to Kennedy's purpose?

13. Kennedy uses **hortative** sentences (language that urges or calls to action) in paragraphs 3 through 20: "Let the word," "Let both sides," and so on. Later, in paragraphs 25 and 26, he uses the imperative: "ask" and "ask not." What is the difference between the two forms, and why did he start with one and end with the other?

Look at your answers to the preceding questions. Even if you weren't able to answer them all, you may be able to see one or more patterns.

Kennedy's address is formal; the archaic diction (*asunder, foe, writ, forebears*) underscores the formality. The figures of speech make traditional yet powerful connections — *tyranny* and *iron, power* and *tiger, poverty* and *chains* — and they are a strong source of emotional persuasion. Such figures of speech as personification ("our sister republics") elevate the speech to a grand style. The image of the "beachhead of cooperation" pushing back the "jungle of suspicion" is especially vivid.

The speech's syntax reveals other meanings and adds to the development of the speech's tone. Formality is sustained by devices such as anaphora: "not as a call to bear arms, though arms we need — not as a call to battle, though embattled we are" (para. 22). The many examples of parallelism (especially antithesis) — "If a free society cannot help the many who are poor, it cannot save the few who are rich" (para. 8), juxtaposing the many and the few, the poor with the rich — are intended to unite disparate groups and also to reassure the country that despite Kennedy's narrow margin of victory he will be everyone's president.

This short address covers a lot of ground. Each of its short paragraphs reveals another one of Kennedy's principles or promises — an early version of what we now call bullet points. There are a variety of sentence types: many are very short, declarative sentences; a few are compound; and more than twenty are complex, usually beginning with the subordinate clause to allow steam to build in order to energize the sentence's main idea. The speech is a call to action, but Kennedy uses hortatory forms ("let us") more than imperatives ("ask" and "ask not"); his intention is to persuade rather than coerce. And the rhetorical questions in paragraph 23 are also reminders that the young president is building consensus rather than dictating. Finally, many sentences begin with coordinating conjunctions, such as *so, for,* and *but.* These transitional words move us smoothly from one sentence into the next and represent continuity — the passing of the torch — in the same way an inauguration helps the country make the transition to a new era.

Inside Kennedy's Inauguration, 50 Years On

ELEANOR CLIFT

This article, in which friends and family of JFK share their memories of the inauguration with reporter Eleanor Clift, originally appeared in January 2011 on the Web site Daily Beast and was then reprinted in Newsweek.

Weather forecasters had predicted light snow turning to rain on the eve of President Kennedy's inauguration, but the snow fell heavily and steadily, covering Pennsylvania Avenue with an eight-inch white blanket and forcing the Army Corps of Engineers' snow-removal force to work through the night to clear the parade route. Jan. 20, 1961, dawned sunny and cold, with gusty winds that made the 22 degrees registered at noon for the swearing-in feel like 7 degrees.

It had just begun to snow when press aide Sue Vogelsinger made her way to the Mayflower Hotel to give Harry Truman an advance copy of the inaugural speech.

She found one Secret Service agent standing guard, told him why she was there, and he said, "Sure, just knock on the door." The former president came to the door in his bedroom slippers. "Have you met Bess?" he asked, inviting the young aide in and introducing her to Mrs. Truman, who sat there knitting away.

It was a day, 50 years ago, frozen in our memories, at least those of us old enough to remember it. But the haze of history masks the random collection of personal experiences and inconveniences for those who were there.

The Mayflower was the favored gathering place for politicians and Democratic activists coming to Washington to celebrate their return to power. Journalist John Seigenthaler was having drinks at the Mayflower with two veteran New York congressmen. "What's the best inaugural you've been to?" he asked. "The one we're going to tomorrow," said Rep. Charles Buckley of New York.

5

"What about FDR?" exclaimed Seigenthaler. "What Charlie means is tomorrow night an Irish Catholic sleeps in the White House," explained Brooklyn Rep. Eugene Keogh. "We forget, looking back on it, how powerful the anti-Catholic effort was," Seigenthaler says now. "There were frozen tears of joy on the cheeks of Irish Catholics that day," says the journalist, who would go to the Justice Department as a top assistant to Robert Kennedy. "It sounds a bit cliché now to talk about the New Frontier and what it meant, and sure it was political sloganeering, but for those of us in the campaign and planning to stay on in the administration, it was a meaningful mantra—a passing of the torch and changing of the guard."

Dignitaries assembled on the inaugural platform with seating marked for the various political tribes: the Eisenhower and Nixon contingents, the Kennedy–Johnson family and friends. Philip Bobbitt, age 12, a nephew of Lyndon Johnson, sat next to Gov. Pat Brown of California (father of current governor Jerry). As Cardinal Cushing, a traditionalist with a heavy Boston accent, went on at some length with his prayer, Governor Brown leaned over to the young boy and said, "If he doesn't stop now, I'm quitting the church."

The glare from the sun made it impossible for Robert Frost to read the poem he had written for Kennedy, titled "Dedication." Bobbitt, now a law professor at Columbia University and lecturer at the University of Texas, remembers his Uncle Lyndon gallantly using his hat to try to shield the sun, but it didn't work, and Frost fell back on an earlier poem he knew well, "The Gift Outright," reciting it from memory. "We were all very excited," Bobbitt says, "but my memory is mostly about being cold."

Kathleen, the oldest of the Kennedy grandchildren, watched the swearing-in from the camera platform facing the ceremony. She was with her four younger siblings—Joe, Bobby, David, and Courtney—and to a 9-year-old, standing and cold, the whole thing felt kind of remote. "I knew I was supposed to think this was very historic, but all the adults were taller and we couldn't see well. I remember scooting up to see what I could on a small TV." She does remember how Frank Sinatra stuck his head into her bedroom to say hello: "I thought that was cool." Sinatra had recorded a Kennedy campaign song to the tune of

"High Hopes," which Kathleen sings unprompted. Another memorable moment was actress Kim Novak "tobogganing with us in the snow." Joan Kennedy had campaigned in West Virginia for her brother-in-law, going down into a coal mine with him, and sitting there that day she thought how remarkable it was that "you could be in a coal mine and two months later be inaugurated president. The contrast says a lot about democratic politics that's good." She had campaigned for Jack all over the country, but West Virginia stood out. "Jack said we had to win in West Virginia to prove that a Catholic could win because there were so few Catholics there, only 1 or 2 percent." She remembered how cold and dark and dank the mine was, and how the coal miners were so eager to meet them.

As family and friends descended on the White House, cold and hungry, Jackie Kennedy's newly appointed social secretary, Letitia Baldridge, bustled about, worrying whether there was enough heat in the corner bedrooms and whether the food passed muster with Rose Kennedy, the family matriarch. "She wanted proper little sandwiches, the kind they had at tea time, and little cream desserts—she was very thrifty, wanted to make sure we used up everything, and also that we had enough. She whispered in our ears, and when Mama Rose whispered, you jumped. . . . She was the bountiful grandmother orchestrating everybody's stomach."

10

What Ambassador Jean Kennedy Smith, the last surviving Kennedy sibling, remembers most from the inauguration is an impromptu family lunch of hot soup and sandwiches in the White House. "It was just us," she says, "my brother and sisters and their husbands, and Bobby and Teddy. We just talked about the campaign and how we won everything and that's why he was president, just jokes. And then he signed a picture for us, and it said, 'To Jean, Don't deny you did it,' and I thought how wonderful, and of course he put the same thing to Pat. He meant that we made him president. . . . He always had a terrific sense of humor. And you know he didn't seem young to us because of course he was older than all of us."

After the swearing-in, speechwriter and new special assistant to the president Richard Goodwin, hatless and coatless, walked the two miles from the Capitol to the White House. Freezing, he retreated to the White House to look for his new office, when who should he encounter walking down the hallway but "the guy I had been traveling the country with for the last year and a half—Kennedy. And he said, 'Dick, did you see the Coast Guard contingent in the parade? There was not a single black face in that delegation, and I want you to do something about it right away.'

"So I ran upstairs to my office in the West Wing and I said, 'Who's in charge of the Coast Guard?' I learned they're not under the Defense Department; they're under the Treasury Department. So I called Douglas Dillon, the new Treasury secretary. And it struck me as I went up the stairs that we'll no longer just make speeches, we actually can do something about this. I told Dillon and within a few months the Coast Guard Academy was integrated."

NBC correspondent Sander Vanocur covered the inauguration from inside the rotunda of the Capitol, watching it on TV. Print still ruled, but the networks were beginning to gain a greater foothold, and the Kennedy campaign wasn't suspicious of the press as the Nixon campaign had been, which made for a freer and easier exchange. Vanocur remembers the new president stopping by a Democratic National Committee meeting at the Mayflower, and when a reporter asked what Truman thought of the changes in the White House he'd left eight years earlier, Kennedy responded that all Truman would say about Eisenhower is "the sonofabitch moved my piano to the basement."

Sue Vogelsinger, the young press aide, ended up checking herself in to the hospital that evening, suffering from exhaustion after months on the campaign trail. She didn't get to the White House until the following day, and the next night she ran into the new president, who was walking around by himself checking out the West Wing and fretting about the state of disrepair. "This is really bad," he said, looking at the chipped floors. "You think that's bad, come see the press office," Vogelsinger told him, which he pronounced "worse than the Senate office." The press office was around the corner from the Oval Office (it still is), and the three wire machines (AP, UP and Agence France-Presse) were kept in the press secretary's private bathroom. Kennedy could hear the bells go off signaling urgent news and he'd be there. 15

Kennedy paid close attention to what journalists wrote about him. He would say, "I'd rather be Krocked than Fleesonized," a reference to liberal Democratic columnist Doris Fleeson versus the more conservative *New York Times*'s Arthur Krock. Fleeson was a Kennedy favorite, and in early May 1961, she had a medical problem and needed someone to ghostwrite her column. She was a good friend of Kennedy special assistant Fred Dutton, and he agreed to take on the task, two columns a week for three weeks. "And Fred uses this as a way to goad the president for not being liberal enough, that he's selling out on taxes," recalls Dutton's widow, Nancy. "So the president walks in with the *Washington Star* one afternoon, throws it on Dutton's desk, and says, 'Can't you control that friend of yours?'"

Fifty years after Kennedy's inauguration, the memories that linger remind us of a time when all seemed possible, when a politician could capture the imagination of a country. Those who were there knew it was special, and while Kennedy's presidency was brief, his impact endures.

Inauguration of John F. Kennedy
UNITED STATES ARMY SIGNAL CORPS

This photo, credited to the United States Army Signal Corps, shows Chief Justice Earl Warren administering the Oath of Office to John F. Kennedy during the ceremony at the Capitol on January 20, 1961. Among the notables are poet Robert Frost; former presidents Eisenhower and Truman with their wives, Mamie and Bess;

Vice President Lyndon B. Johnson and his wife, Lady Bird; as well as the new first lady, Jacqueline, seen at the lower left in her signature pillbox hat.

Glossary of Style Elements

John F. Kennedy's inaugural address is almost a textbook of style elements. The following brief glossary of terms uses examples from Kennedy's speech.

alliteration   Repetition of the same sound beginning several words or syllables in sequence.

> *[L]et us go forth to lead the land we love . . .*

allusion   Brief reference to a person, event, or place (real or fictitious) or to a work of art.

> *Let both sides unite to heed in all corners of the earth the command of Isaiah . . .*

anaphora   Repetition of a word or phrase at the beginning of successive phrases, clauses, or lines.

> *. . . not as a call to bear arms, though arms we need—not as a call to battle, though embattled we are . . .*

antimetabole   Repetition of words in reverse order.

> *[A]sk not what your country can do for you—ask what you can do for your country.*

antithesis   Opposition, or contrast, of ideas or words in a parallel construction.
[W]e shall . . . support any friend, oppose any foe . . .

archaic diction   Old-fashioned or outdated choice of words.
beliefs for which our forebears fought

asyndeton   Omission of conjunctions between coordinate phrases, clauses, or words.
[W]e shall pay any price, bear any burden, meet any hardship, support any friend, oppose any foe to assure the survival and the success of liberty.

cumulative sentence   Sentence that completes the main idea at the beginning of the sentence and then builds and adds on.
But neither can two great and powerful groups of nations take comfort from our present course—both sides overburdened by the cost of modern weapons, both rightly alarmed by the steady spread of the deadly atom, yet both racing to alter that uncertain balance of terror that stays the hand of mankind's final war.

hortative sentence   Sentence that exhorts, urges, entreats, implores, or calls to action.
Let both sides explore what problems unite us instead of belaboring those problems which divide us.

imperative sentence   Sentence used to command or enjoin.
My fellow citizens of the world: ask not what America will do for you, but what together we can do for the freedom of man.

inversion   Inverted order of words in a sentence (variation of the subject-verb-object order).
United there is little we cannot do in a host of cooperative ventures. Divided there is little we can do . . .

juxtaposition   Placement of two things closely together to emphasize similarities or differences.
[W]e are the heirs of that first revolution. Let the word go forth . . . that the torch has been passed to a new generation of Americans—born in this century . . .

metaphor   Figure of speech that compares two things without using *like* or *as.*
And if a beachhead of cooperation may push back the jungle of suspicion . . .

oxymoron   Paradoxical juxtaposition of words that seem to contradict one another.
But this peaceful revolution . . .

parallelism   Similarity of structure in a pair or series of related words, phrases, or clauses.
Let both sides explore. . . . Let both sides, for the first time, formulate serious and precise proposals. . . . Let both sides seek to invoke. . . . Let both sides unite to heed . . .

periodic sentence   Sentence whose main clause is withheld until the end.
> *To that world assembly of sovereign states, the United Nations, our last best hope in an age where the instruments of war have far outpaced the instruments of peace, we renew our pledge of support . . .*

personification   Attribution of a lifelike quality to an inanimate object or an idea.
> *with history the final judge of our deeds*

rhetorical question   Figure of speech in the form of a question posed for rhetorical effect rather than for the purpose of getting an answer.
> *Will you join in that historic effort?*

synedoche   Figure of speech that uses a part to represent the whole.
> *In your hands, my fellow citizens, more than mine, will rest the final success or failure of our course.*

zeugma   Use of two different words in a grammatically similar way that produces different, often incongruous, meanings.
> *Now the trumpet summons us again — not as a call to bear arms, though arms we need — not as a call to battle, though embattled we are — but a call to bear the burden . . .*

3

Analyzing Arguments
From Reading to Writing

Have you ever changed your mind about something? What caused you to re-examine a belief or idea? Most likely, you read or heard someone else's perspective that challenged you to think about an issue in a different way. It might have been a clear, thoughtful presentation of information, a personal story that tugged at your conscience, a startling statistic, or even a bit of humor or satire that presented a familiar issue in a new and enlightening way. It's less likely that you were bullied into reconsidering your opinion by a loud voice that belittled your ideas. By carefully and respectfully reading the viewpoints of others and considering a range of ideas on an issue, we develop a clearer understanding of our own beliefs—a necessary foundation to writing effective arguments. In this chapter, we're going to analyze elements of argument as a means of critical thinking and an essential step toward crafting your own argumentative essays.

What Is Argument?

Although we have been discussing argument in previous chapters, the focus has been primarily on rhetorical appeals and style. We'll continue examining those elements, but here we take a closer look at an argument's claim, evidence, and organization.

Let's start with some definitions. What is argument? Is it a conflict? A contest between opposing forces to prove the other side wrong? A battle with words? Or is it, rather, a process of reasoned inquiry and rational discourse seeking common ground? If it is the latter, then we engage in argument whenever we explore ideas rationally and think clearly about the world. Yet these days argument is often no more than raised voices interrupting one another, exaggerated assertions without adequate support, and scanty evidence from sources that lack credibility. We might call this "crazed rhetoric," as political commentator Tom Toles does in the following cartoon.

(See insert for color version.)

This cartoon appeared on January 16, 2011, a few days after Arizona congresswoman Gabrielle Giffords was the victim of a shooting; six people were killed and another thirteen injured. Many people saw this tragedy as stemming from vitriolic political discourse that included violent language. Toles argues that Uncle Sam, and thus the country, is in danger of being devoured by "crazed rhetoric." There may not be a "next trick" or a "taming" if the rhetorical lion continues to roar.

Is Toles's view exaggerated? Whether you answer yes or no to that question, it seems quite clear that partisanship and polarization often hold sway over dialogue and civility when people think of argument. In our discussions, however, we define **argument** as a persuasive discourse, a coherent and considered movement from a claim to a conclusion. The goal of this chapter is to avoid thinking of argument as a zero-sum game of winners and losers but, instead, to see it as a means of better understanding other people's ideas as well as your own.

In Chapter 1 we discussed concession and refutation as a way to acknowledge a counterargument, and we want to re-emphasize the usefulness of that approach.

Viewing anyone who disagrees with you as an adversary makes it very likely that the conversation will escalate into an emotional clash, and treating opposing ideas disrespectfully rarely results in mutual understanding. Twentieth-century psychologist Carl Rogers stressed the importance of replacing confrontational argument tactics with ones that promote negotiation, compromise, and cooperation. **Rogerian arguments** are based on the assumption that having a full understanding of an opposing position is essential to responding to it persuasively and refuting it in a way that is accommodating rather than alienating. Ultimately, the goal of a Rogerian argument is not to destroy your opponents or dismantle their viewpoints but rather to reach a satisfactory conclusion.

So what does a civil argument look like? Let's examine a short article that appeared in *Ode* magazine in 2009 entitled "Why Investing in Fast Food May Be a Good Thing." In this piece Amy Domini, a financial advisor and leading voice for socially responsible investing, argues the counterintuitive position that investing in the fast-food industry can be an ethically responsible choice.

Why Investing in Fast Food May Be a Good Thing
Amy Domini

My friends and colleagues know I've been an advocate of the Slow Food movement for many years. Founded in Italy 20 years ago, Slow Food celebrates harvests from small-scale family farms, prepared slowly and lovingly with regard for the health and environment of diners. Slow Food seeks to preserve crop diversity, so the unique taste of "heirloom" apples, tomatoes and other foods don't perish from the Earth. I wish everyone would choose to eat this way. The positive effects on the health of our bodies, our local economies and our planet would be incalculable. Why then do I find myself investing in fast-food companies?

The reason is social investing isn't about investing in perfect companies. (Perfect companies, it turns out, don't exist.) We seek to invest in companies that are moving in the right direction and listening to their critics. We offer a road map to bring those companies to the next level, step by step. No social standard causes us to reject restaurants, even fast-food ones, out of hand. Although we favor local, organic food, we recognize it isn't available in every community, and is often priced above the means of the average household. Many of us live more than 100 miles from a working farm.

Fast food is a way of life. In America, the average person eats it more than 150 times a year. In 2007, sales for the 400 largest U.S.-based fast-food chains totaled $277 billion, up 7 percent from 2006.

Fast food is a global phenomenon. Major chains and their local competitors open restaurants in nearly every country. For instance, in Greece, burgers and pizza are supplanting the traditional healthy Mediterranean diet of fish, olive oil and vegetables. Doctors are treating Greek children for diabetes, high cholesterol and high blood pressure—ailments rarely seen in the past.

The fast-food industry won't go away anytime soon. But in the meantime, it   5
can be changed. And because it's so enormous, even seemingly modest changes
can have a big impact. In 2006, New York City banned the use of trans-fats (a
staple of fast food) in restaurants, and in 2008, California became the first state to
do so. When McDonald's moved to non-trans-fats for making French fries, the
health benefits were widespread. Another area of concern is fast-food packaging,
which causes forest destruction and creates a lot of waste. In the U.S. alone,
1.8 million tons of packaging is generated each year. Fast-food containers make
up about 20 percent of litter, and packaging for drinks and snacks adds another
20 percent.

A North Carolina–based organization called the Dogwood Alliance has
launched an effort to make fast-food companies reduce waste and source paper
responsibly. Through a campaign called No Free Refills, the group is pressing fast-
food companies to reduce their impact on the forests of the southern U.S., the
world's largest paper-producing region. They're pushing companies to:

- Reduce the overuse of packaging.
- Maximize use of 100 percent post-consumer recycled boxboard.
- Eliminate paper packaging from the most biologically important endangered forests.
- Eliminate paper packaging from suppliers that convert natural forests into industrial pine plantations.
- Encourage packaging suppliers to source fiber from responsibly managed forests certified by the Forest Stewardship Council.
- Recycle waste in restaurants to divert paper and other material from landfills.

Will the fast-food companies adopt all these measures overnight? No. But
along with similar efforts worldwide, this movement signals that consumers and
investors are becoming more conscious of steps they can take toward a better
world—beginning with the way they eat.

While my heart will always be with Slow Food, I recognize the fast-food industry can improve and that some companies are ahead of others on that path.

Domini begins by reminding her readers of her ethos as "an advocate of the
Slow Food movement for many years." By describing some of the goals and tenets
of that movement, including the "positive effects" it can have, she establishes
common ground before she discusses her position—one that the Slow Food
advocates are not likely to embrace, at least not initially. In fact, instead of asserting her position in a strong declarative sentence, Domini asks a question that
invites her audience to hear her explanation: "Why then do I find myself investing
in fast-food companies?" She provides evidence that supports her choice to take
that action: she uses statistics to show that slow food is not available in all communities, while fast food is an expanding industry. She uses the example of Greece

to show that fast food is becoming a global phenomenon. She gives numerous examples of how fast-food companies are improving ingredients and reducing waste to illustrate how working to change fast-food practices can have a significant impact on public health and the environment. After presenting her viewpoint, Domini ends by acknowledging that her "heart will always be with Slow Food"; but that fact should not preclude her supporting those in the fast-food industry who are making socially and environmentally responsible decisions.

• ACTIVITY •

Identify at least two points in Domini's article where she might have given way to accusation or blame or where she might have dismissed the Slow Food movement as being shortsighted or elitist. Discuss how, instead, she finds common ground and promotes dialogue with her audience through civil discourse.

• ESSAY IN PROGRESS: Selecting a Topic •

What are two controversial topics that interest you? Brainstorm how you might develop an argument about each from two different viewpoints. Consider the potential for volatile or highly emotional responses to each. What could you do to encourage a civil tone and approach? Make sure to choose ideas that you could develop into a full essay. You will have an opportunity to return to them throughout the chapter.

Staking a Claim

Every argument has a **claim**—also called an assertion or proposition—that states the argument's main idea or position. A claim differs from a topic or a subject in that a claim has to be arguable. It can't just be a simple statement of fact; it has to state a position that some people might disagree with and others might agree with. Going from a simple topic to a claim means stating your informed opinion about a topic. In the essay you just read, the general topic is social investing—specifically, social investing in the fast-food industry. The arguable claim, however, is that investing in fast-food companies can be socially responsible. Notice that the topic may be a single word or a phrase, but the arguable claim has to be stated as a complete sentence.

It's important to note that neither a published author nor a student writer is likely to develop a strong claim without exploring a topic through reading about it, discussing it with others, brainstorming, taking notes, and rethinking. After looking into a topic thoroughly, then you are ready to develop a position on an issue. For example, let's use the topic of single-sex classrooms. You will notice, first of all, that a simple statement of the topic does not indicate whether you support the notion or challenge it. Let's consider several directions to take with this topic.

- Many schools have single-sex classrooms.
- Single-sex classrooms have been around for years, especially in private schools.
- Single-sex classrooms are ineffective because they do not prepare students for the realities of the workplace.

The first statement may be true, but it is easily verified and not arguable; thus, it is simply a topic and not a claim. The second statement has more detail, but it's easy to verify whether it is true or not. Since it is not arguable, it is not a claim. The third statement is a claim because it is arguable. It argues that single-sex classrooms are ineffective and that preparation for the workplace is an important way to measure the effectiveness of an education. There are those who would disagree with both statements and those who would agree with both. Thus, it presents an arguable position and is a viable claim.

• ACTIVITY •

For each of the following statements, evaluate whether it is arguable or too easily verifiable to develop into an effective argument. Try revising the ones you consider too easily verifiable to make them into arguable claims.

1. SUV owners should be required to pay an energy surcharge.
2. Charter schools are an alternative to public schools.
3. Ronald Reagan was the most charismatic president of the twentieth century.
4. Requiring students to wear uniforms improves school spirit.
5. The terms *global warming* and *climate change* describe different perspectives on this complex issue.
6. Students graduating from college today can expect to have more debt than any previous generation.
7. People who read novels are more likely to attend sports events and movies than those who do not.
8. Print newspapers will not survive another decade.
9. The competition among countries to become a site for the Olympic Games is fierce.
10. Plagiarism is a serious problem in today's schools.

Types of Claims

Typically, we speak of three types of claims: claims of fact, claims of value, and claims of policy. Each type can be used to guide entire arguments, which we would call arguments of fact, arguments of value, and arguments of policy. While it is helpful to separate the three for analysis, in practice it is not always that simple. Indeed, it is quite common for an argument to include more than one type of claim, as you will see in the following examples.

Claims of Fact

Claims of fact assert that something is true or not true. You can't argue whether Zimbabwe is in Africa or whether restaurants on Main Street serve more customers at breakfast than at lunch. These issues can be resolved and verified—in the first case by checking a map, in the second through observation or by checking sales figures. You can, however, argue that Zimbabwe has an unstable government or that restaurants on Main Street are more popular with older patrons than younger ones. Those statements are arguable: What does "unstable" mean? What does "popular" mean? Who is "older" and who is "younger"?

Arguments of fact often pivot on what exactly is "factual." Facts become arguable when they are questioned, when they raise controversy, when they challenge people's beliefs. "It's a fact that the Social Security program will go bankrupt by 2025" is a claim that could be developed in an argument of fact. Very often, so-called facts are a matter of interpretation. At other times, new "facts" call into question older ones. The claim that cell phones increase the incidence of brain tumors, for instance, requires sifting through new "facts" from medical research and scrutinizing who is carrying out the research, who is supporting it financially, and so on. Whenever you are evaluating or writing an argument of fact, it's important to approach your subject with a healthy skepticism.

In "Why Investing in Fast Food May Be a Good Thing," Domini makes two claims of fact. The argument in paragraph 3 is guided by the claim of fact that "fast food is a way of life." Is it? She supports this claim with sales statistics and information on the growth of this industry. Paragraph 4 is guided by the claim of fact that "fast food is a global phenomenon." She supports this claim with an explanation of fast-food restaurants opening "in nearly every country" and a specific example discussing the changing diet in Greece.

We commonly see arguments of fact that challenge stereotypes or social beliefs. For instance, in Chapter 8, Gender, there is an argument of fact by Matthias Mehl and his colleagues about whether women are more talkative than men (p. 557). Mehl and his colleagues recorded conversations and concluded that the differences are, in fact, very minor. Their findings call into question the stereotype that women are excessively chatty and more talkative than their male counterparts. Mehl's essay is a clear argument of fact that re-evaluates earlier "facts" and challenges a social myth.

Claims of Value

Perhaps the most common type of claim is a **claim of value**, which argues that something is good or bad, right or wrong, desirable or undesirable. Of course, just like any other claim, a claim of value must be arguable. Claims of value may be personal judgments based on taste, or they may be more objective evaluations based on external criteria. For instance, if you argue that Brad Pitt is the best leading man in Hollywood, that is simply a matter of taste. The criteria for what is "best" and what defines a "leading man" are strictly personal. Another person could argue that while Pitt might be the best-looking actor in Hollywood, Leonardo DiCaprio is more highly paid and his movies tend to make more money. That is an evaluation based on external criteria — dollars and cents.

To develop an argument from a claim of value, you must establish specific criteria or standards and then show to what extent the subject meets your criteria. Amy Domini's argument is largely one of value as she supports her claim that investing in fast-food companies can be a positive thing. The very title of Domini's essay suggests a claim of value: "Why Investing in Fast Food May Be a Good Thing." She develops her argument by explaining the impact that such investing can have on what food choices are available, and what the impact of those choices is.

Entertainment reviews — of movies, television shows, concerts, books — are good examples of arguments developed from claims of value. Take a look at this one, movie critic Roger Ebert's 1977 review of the first *Star Wars* movie. He raved. Notice how he states his four-star claim — it's a great movie! — in several ways throughout the argument and sets up his criteria at each juncture.

Star Wars
ROGER EBERT

Every once in a while I have what I think of as an out-of-the-body experience at a movie. When the ESP people use a phrase like that, they're referring to the sensation of the mind actually leaving the body and spiriting itself off to China or Peoria or a galaxy far, far away. When I use the phrase, I simply mean that my imagination has forgotten it is actually present in a movie theater and thinks it's up there on the screen. In a curious sense, the events in the movie seem real, and I seem to be a part of them.

Ebert's first criterion is whether a film transports him.

Ebert's claim of value. Stated more formally, it might read: "Star Wars is so good that it will completely draw you in."

Star Wars works like that. My list of other out-of-the-body films is a short and odd one, ranging from the artistry of *Bonnie and Clyde* or *Cries and Whispers* to the slick commercialism of *Jaws* and the brutal strength of *Taxi Driver*. On whatever level (sometimes I'm not at all sure) they engage me so immediately and powerfully that I lose my detachment, my analytical reserve. The movie's happening, and it's happening to me.

What makes the *Star Wars* experience unique, though, is that it happens on such an innocent and often funny level. It's usually violence that draws me so deeply into a movie—violence ranging from the psychological torment of a Bergman character to the mindless crunch of a shark's jaws. Maybe movies that scare us find the most direct route to our imaginations. But there's hardly any violence at all in *Star Wars* (and even then it's presented as essentially bloodless swashbuckling). Instead, there's entertainment so direct and simple that all of the complications of the modern movie seem to vaporize.

Ebert asserts that Star Wars is not just different from the other films he has cited; it is "unique."

Ebert elaborates on why it is "unique"— pointing out that its power lies in directness and simplicity rather than violence and brutality.

Star Wars is a fairy tale, a fantasy, a legend, finding its roots in some of our most popular fictions. The golden robot, lion-faced space pilot, and insecure little computer on wheels must have been suggested by the Tin Man, the Cowardly Lion, and the Scarecrow in *The Wizard of Oz*. The journey from one end of the galaxy to another is out of countless thousands of space operas. The hardware is from *Flash Gordon* out of *2001: A Space Odyssey*, the chivalry is from Robin Hood, the heroes are from Westerns, and the villains are a cross between Nazis and sorcerers. *Star Wars* taps the pulp fantasies buried in our memories, and because it's done so brilliantly, it reactivates old thrills, fears, and exhilarations we thought we'd abandoned when we read our last copy of *Amazing Stories*.

Another criterion is the effectiveness of the storytelling. Here it is literally the stuff of legends, managing somehow to be both new and nostalgic.

Ebert addresses a counterargument. He knows that many people will praise the special effects in the film. He acknowledges that they are "good"—but that is not one of his chief criteria.

The movie works so well for several reasons, and they don't all have to do with the spectacular special effects. The effects are good, yes, but great effects have been used in such movies as *Silent Running* and *Logan's Run* without setting all-time box-office records. No, I think the key to *Star Wars* is more basic than that.

5

The movie relies on the strength of pure narrative, in the most basic storytelling form known to man, the Journey. All of the best tales we remember from our childhoods had to do with heroes setting out to travel down roads filled with danger, and hoping to find treasure or heroism at the journey's end. In *Star Wars*, George Lucas takes this simple and powerful framework into outer space, and that is an inspired thing to do, because we no longer have maps on Earth that warn, "Here there be dragons." We can't fall off the edge of the map, as Columbus could, and we can't hope to find new continents of prehistoric monsters or lost tribes ruled by immortal goddesses. Not on Earth, anyway, but anything is possible in space, and Lucas goes right ahead

Ebert moves into his principal criterion: the value of the classic hero's journey that Star Wars embodies.

Another criterion: The movie is good because the characters are both familiar . . . and shows us very nearly everything. We get involved quickly, because the characters in *Star Wars* are so strongly and simply drawn and have so many small foibles and large, futile hopes for us to identify with. And then Lucas does an interesting thing. As he sends his heroes off to cross the universe and do battle with the Forces of Darth Vader, the evil Empire, and the awesome Death Star, he gives us lots of special effects, yes—ships passing into hyperspace, alien planets, an infinity of stars—but we also get a

. . . and unfamiliar. wealth of strange living creatures, and Lucas correctly guesses that they'll be more interesting for us than all the intergalactic hardware.

The most fascinating single scene, for me, was the one set in the bizarre saloon on the planet Tatooine. As that incredible collection of extraterrestrial alcoholics and bug-eyed martini drinkers lined up at the bar, and as Lucas so slyly let them exhibit characteristics that were universally human, I found myself feeling a combination of admiration and delight. *Star Wars* had placed me in the presence of really magical movie invention: Here, all mixed together, were whimsy and fantasy, simple wonderment and quietly sophisticated storytelling.

Ebert applies his criteria to one specific scene.

When Stanley Kubrick was making *2001* in the late 1960s, he threw everything he had into the special effects depicting outer space, but he finally decided not to show any aliens at all—because they were impossible to visualize, he thought. But they weren't at all, as *Star Wars* demonstrates, and the movie's delight in the possibilities of alien life forms is at least as much fun as its conflicts between the space cruisers of the Empire and the Rebels.

He reiterates his claim by emphasizing that it is not the technology of special effects but the humanity of the characters that makes the film great. And perhaps that helps to explain the movie's one weakness, which is that the final assault on the Death Star is allowed to go on too long. Maybe, having invested so much money and sweat in his special effects, Lucas couldn't bear to see them trimmed. But the magic of *Star Wars* is only dramatized by the special effects; the movie's heart is in its endearingly human (and non-human) people.

Ebert concedes that the film does have a flaw.

• ACTIVITY •

Find a review of a movie, a television show, a concert, an album or a song, or another form of popular culture. Identify the claim in the review. What criteria does the reviewer use to justify a thumbs-up or a thumbs-down?

Claims of Policy

Anytime you propose a change, you're making a **claim of policy**. It might be local: A group at your school proposes to raise money to contribute to a school in Haiti. You want your parents to let you spend more time with friends on weeknights. Or it might be a bigger issue such as a proposal for transitioning to alternative energy sources, a change in copyright laws for digital music, a shift in foreign policy, a change in legislation to allow former felons to vote.

An argument of policy generally begins with a definition of the problem (claim of fact), explains why it is a problem (claim of value), and then explains the change that needs to happen (claim of policy). Also, keep in mind that while an argument of policy usually calls for some direct action to take place, it may be a recommendation for a change in attitude or viewpoint.

Let's take a look at the opening paragraphs of an argument of policy. In this piece, published in 1999 in *Newsweek*, Anna Quindlen argues for a change in attitude toward the treatment of mental illness. Notice how she combines claims of fact and value to ground her claim of policy—that is, that attitudes toward mental illness must change so that treatment options become more available.

from *The C Word in the Hallways*
ANNA QUINDLEN

The saddest phrase I've read in a long time is this one: psychological autopsy. That's what the doctors call it when a kid kills himself and they go back over the plowed ground of his short life, and discover all the hidden markers that led to the rope, the blade, the gun.

There's a plague on all our houses, and since it doesn't announce itself with lumps or spots or protest marches, it has gone unremarked in the quiet suburbs and busy cities where it has been laying waste. [Claim of value] The number of suicides and homicides committed by teenagers, most often young men, has exploded in the last three decades, until it has become commonplace to have [Claim of fact] black-bordered photographs in yearbooks and murder suspects with acne problems. And everyone searches for reasons, and scapegoats, and solutions, most often punitive. Yet one solution continues to elude us, and that is ending the ignorance about mental health, and moving it from the margins of care and into the mainstream where it belongs. [Claim of policy] As surely as any vaccine, this would save lives.

So many have already been lost. This month Kip Kinkel was sentenced to life in prison in Oregon for the murders of his parents and a shooting rampage at his high school that killed two students. A psychiatrist who specializes in the care of adolescents testified that Kinkel, now 17, had been hearing voices since he was 12. Sam Manzie is also 17. He is serving a 70-year sentence for luring an 11-year-old boy named Eddie Werner into his New Jersey home and strangling him with the cord of an alarm clock because his Sega Genesis was out of reach. Manzie had his first psychological evaluation in the first grade.

Quindlen calls for "ending the ignorance" about mental health and its care. As she develops her argument, she supports this claim of policy by considering both personal examples and general facts about mental health in America. To arrive at this claim of policy, however, she first makes a claim of value—"There's a plague on all our houses": that is, this is a problem deserving of our attention. She then offers a claim of fact that demonstrates the scope of the problem: teenage suicide and homicide in the last decades have "exploded." Granted, all three of these claims need to be explained with appropriate evidence, and Quindlen does that in subsequent paragraphs; but at the outset, she establishes claims of value and fact that lay the foundation for the claim of policy that is the main idea of her argument.

• ACTIVITY •

Read the following argument of policy that appeared as an editorial in the *New York Times* in 2004. Annotate it to identify claims of fact, value, and policy; then describe how these interact throughout the argument.

Felons and the Right to Vote

NEW YORK TIMES EDITORIAL BOARD

About 4.7 million Americans, more than 2 percent of the adult population, are barred from voting because of a felony conviction. Denying the vote to ex-offenders is antidemocratic, and undermines the nation's commitment to rehabilitating people who have paid their debt to society. Felon disenfranchisement laws also have a sizable racial impact: 13 percent of black men have had their votes taken away, seven times the national average. But even if it were acceptable as policy, denying felons the vote has been a disaster because of the chaotic and partisan way it has been carried out.

Thirty-five states prohibit at least some people from voting after they have been released from prison. The rules about which felonies are covered and when the right to vote is restored vary widely from state to state, and often defy logic. In four states, including New York, felons on parole cannot vote, but felons on probation can. In some states, felons must formally apply for restoration of their voting rights, which state officials can grant or deny on the most arbitrary of grounds.

Florida may have changed the outcome of the 2000 presidential election when Secretary of State Katherine Harris oversaw a purge of suspected felons that removed an untold number of eligible voters from the rolls. This year, state officials are conducting a new purge that may be just as flawed. They have developed a list of 47,000 voters who may be felons, and have asked local officials to consider purging them. But the *Miami Herald* found that more than 2,100 of them may have been listed in error, because their voting rights were restored by the state's clemency process. Last week, the state acknowledged that 1,600 of those on the list should be allowed to vote.

Election officials are also far too secretive about felon voting issues, which should be a matter of public record. When Ms. Harris used inaccurate standards for purging voters, the public did not find out until it was too late. This year, the state tried to keep the 47,000 names on its list of possible felons secret, but fortunately a state court ruled this month that they should be open to scrutiny.

There is a stunning lack of information and transparency surrounding felon disenfranchisement across the country. The rules are often highly technical, and little effort is made to explain them to election officials or to the people affected. In New York, the Brennan Center for Justice at New York University Law School found that local elections offices often did not understand the law, and some demanded that felons produce documents that do not exist.

Too often, felon voting is seen as a partisan issue. In state legislatures, it is usually Democrats who try to restore voting rights, and Republicans who resist. Recently, Republicans and election officials in Missouri and South Dakota have raised questions about voter registration groups' employment of ex-felons, although they have every right to be involved in political activity. In Florida, the decision about whether a felon's right to vote will be restored lies with a panel made up of the governor and members of his cabinet. Some voting rights activists believe that Gov. Jeb Bush has moved slowly, and reinstated voting rights for few of the state's ex-felons, to help President Bush's re-election prospects.

The treatment of former felons in the electoral system cries out for reform. The cleanest and fairest approach would be simply to remove the prohibitions on felon voting. In his State of the Union address in January, President Bush announced a new national commitment to helping prisoners re-enter society. Denying them the right to vote belies this commitment.

Restoring the vote to felons is difficult, because it must be done state by state, and because ex-convicts do not have much of a political lobby. There have been legislative successes in recent years in some places, including Alabama and Nevada. But other states have been moving in the opposite direction. The best hope of reform may lie in the courts. The Atlanta-based

United States Court of Appeals for the 11th Circuit and the San Francisco-based Court of Appeals for the Ninth Circuit have ruled recently that disenfranchising felons may violate equal protection or the Voting Rights Act.

Until the whole idea of permanently depriving felons of their right to vote is wiped away, the current rules should be applied more fairly. The quality of voting roll purges must be improved. Florida should discontinue its current felon purge until it can prove that the list it is using is accurate.

Mechanisms for restoring voting rights to felons must be improved. Even in states where felons have the right to vote, they are rarely notified of this when they exit prison. Released prisoners should be given that information during the discharge process, and helped with the paperwork.

The process for felons to regain their voting rights should be streamlined. In Nevada, early reports are that the restoration of felon voting rights has had minimal effect, because the paperwork requirements are too burdensome. Ex-felons who apply to vote should have the same presumption of eligibility as other voters.

Voting rights should not be a political football. There should be bipartisan support for efforts to help ex-felons get their voting rights back, by legislators and by state and local election officials. American democracy is diminished when officeholders and political parties, for their own political gain, try to keep people from voting.

10

• ESSAY IN PROGRESS: Staking a Claim •

Choosing one of the topics you explored initially (p. 85), write three different claims that could focus an essay. Be sure each is arguable. Comment on whether your overall argument will likely include more than one type of claim.

From Claim to Thesis

To develop a claim into a thesis statement, you have to be more specific about what you intend to argue. In her essay "The C Word in the Hallways," Anna Quindlen states her main idea explicitly:

> Yet one solution continues to elude us, and that is ending the ignorance about mental health, and moving it from the margins of care and into the mainstream where it belongs. As surely as any vaccine, this would save lives.

The "policy" that Quindlen advocates changing is removing the stigma from mental illness so it can be properly treated. Her second sentence emphasizes her thesis by drawing an analogy: just as vaccines save lives by preventing disease, a shift in policy toward mental illness would save lives by preventing violence.

Sometimes in professional essays the claim may be implicit, but in the formal essays that you will write for your classes, the claim is traditionally stated explicitly as a one-sentence thesis statement that appears in the introduction of your argument. To be effective, a thesis statement must preview the essay by encapsulating in clear, unambiguous language the main point or points the writer intends to make. Let's consider several different types of thesis statements: a closed thesis, an open thesis, and a thesis that includes the counterargument.

Closed Thesis Statements

A **closed thesis** is a statement of the main idea of the argument that also previews the major points the writer intends to make. It is "closed" because it limits the number of points the writer will make. For instance, here is a closed thesis on the appeal of the Harry Potter book series:

> The three-dimensional characters, exciting plot, and complex themes of the Harry Potter series make them not only legendary children's books but enduring literary classics.

This thesis asserts that the series constitutes a "literary classic" and specifies three reasons — characters, plot, and theme — each of which would be discussed in the argument. A closed thesis often includes (or implies) the word *because*. This one might have been written as follows:

> The Harry Potter series has become legendary children's books and enduring literary classics because of its three-dimensional characters, exciting plot, and complex themes.

Indeed, that statement might be a good working thesis.

A closed thesis is a reliable way to focus a short essay, particularly one written under time constraints. Explicitly stating the points you'll make can help you organize your thoughts when you are working against the clock, and it can be a way to address specific points that are required by the prompt or argument.

Open Thesis Statements

If, however, you are writing a longer essay with five, six, or even more main points, then an open thesis is probably more effective. An **open thesis** is one that does not list all the points the writer intends to cover in an essay. If you have six or seven points in an essay, for instance, stringing them all out in the thesis will be awkward; plus, while a reader can remember two or three main points, it's confusing to keep track of a whole string of points made way back in an opening paragraph. For instance, you might argue that the Harry Potter series is far from an enduring classic because you think the main characters are either all good or all bad rather than a bit of both, the minor characters devolve into caricatures, the plot is repetitious and formulaic, the magic does not follow a logical system of rules, and so on. Imagine trying to line all those ideas up in a sentence or two having any clarity and grace at all. By making the overall point without actually stating every subpoint, an open thesis can guide an essay without being cumbersome:

> The popularity of the Harry Potter series demonstrates that simplicity trumps complexity when it comes to the taste of readers, both young and old.

Counterargument Thesis Statements

A variant of the open and closed thesis is the **counterargument thesis**, in which a summary of a counterargument, usually qualified by *although* or *but*, precedes the writer's opinion. This type of thesis has the advantage of immediately addressing the counterargument. Doing so may make an argument seem both stronger and more reasonable. It may also create a seamless transition to a more thorough concession and refutation of the counterargument later in the argument. Using the Harry Potter example again, let's look at a counterargument thesis:

> Although the Harry Potter series may have some literary merit, its popularity has less to do with storytelling than with merchandising.

This thesis concedes a counterargument that the series "may have some literary merit" before refuting that claim by saying that the storytelling itself is less popular than the movies, toys, and other merchandise that the books inspired. The thesis promises some discussion of literary merit and a critique of its storytelling (concession and refutation) but will ultimately focus on the role of the merchandising machine in making Harry Potter a household name.

Note that the thesis that considers a counterargument can also lead to a position that is a modification or qualification rather than an absolute statement of support or rejection. If, for instance, you were asked to discuss whether the success of the Harry Potter series has resulted in a reading renaissance, this thesis would let you respond not with a firm "yes" or "no," but with a qualification of "in some respects." It would allow you to ease into a critique by first recognizing its strengths before leveling your criticism that the popularity was the result of media hype rather than quality and thus will not result in a reading renaissance.

• ACTIVITY •

Develop a thesis statement that could focus an argument in response to each of the following prompts. Discuss why you think that the structure (open, closed, counterargument) you chose would be appropriate or effective.

1. Same-sex classrooms have gone in and out of favor in public education. Write an essay explaining why you would support or oppose same-sex classrooms for public schools in grades 10 through 12.

2. Write an essay supporting, challenging, or qualifying English author E. M. Forster's position in the following quotation: "I hate the idea of causes, and if I had to choose between betraying my country and betraying my friend, I hope I should have the guts to betray my country."

3. Today's world is full of conflicts and controversies. Choose a local or global issue, and write an essay that considers multiple viewpoints and proposes a solution or compromise.

4. Write an essay explaining why you agree or disagree with the following quotation: "Advertising degrades the people it appeals to; it deprives them of their will to choose."

5. Plagiarism is rampant in public high schools and colleges. In fact, some people argue that the definition of *plagiarism* has changed with the proliferation of the Internet. Write an essay explaining what you believe the appropriate response of a teacher should be to a student who turns in a plagiarized essay or exam.

• **ESSAY IN PROGRESS: Developing a Thesis** •

Now that you understand the different types of claims and how to develop them into thesis statements, you can begin drafting an argument. Select one of the claims you worked with in the activity on page 95. Draft two different thesis statements that might guide an essay on the subject. Which one do you think is more promising for a full argumentative essay? Why?

Presenting Evidence

Once a writer has established a claim and developed a thesis statement, the next step is to support it with effective evidence. What evidence to present, how much is necessary, and how to present it are all rhetorical choices guided by an understanding of the audience. A person speaking to a group of scientists will more likely need facts and figures to persuade her audience, while one writing an essay for a local newspaper might want to use an anecdote to grab the audience's attention. Amy Domini, knowing that her audience—the generally affluent and liberal readers of *Ode* magazine—will include many who are hostile to fast food, presents evidence regarding the positive changes that fast-food companies are making, as well as numerical evidence showing that fast food is a growing phenomenon

that could have either a positive or a negative impact on health and the environment. Keep audience in mind throughout this discussion of evidence, particularly in terms of whether your audience would be persuaded more by formal or
informal sources.

Relevant, Accurate, and Sufficient Evidence

Regardless of the type of evidence a writer chooses to use, it should always be
relevant, accurate, and sufficient. Relevant evidence is evidence that specifically
applies to the argument being made. To argue that a particular car is superior
from a dependability standpoint, bringing in evidence about its maintenance
record would be relevant, but talking about its hand-tooled leather seats would
not. Generally, good writers do not leave the relevance of a piece of evidence to
the reader's imagination; they explicitly spell out what the relationship is between
an example and the argument at hand.

Presenting accurate information means taking care to quote sources correctly without misrepresenting what the sources are saying or taking the information out of context. One way to ensure that you have accurate evidence is to
get it from a credible source. Think carefully about the bias any source might
have. Is it partisan or backed financially by a company or industry group? Even
statistical data can be inaccurate if it is from a source that has gathered the data
in a way that fits its own agenda. Accuracy can also be a matter of the audience's
perception. You should choose sources that they will find credible. If you want
accurate dependability information about a car, some reliable sources might be a
reputable mechanic, a magazine reviewer who has compared the car's performance to other similar cars, or simply someone who has owned the car for a long
time.

Finally, you should include a sufficient amount of evidence to support your
thesis. If you based your entire argument about the car's dependability on an
interview with a single mechanic, that would not be persuasive. A mechanic only
sees the cars that break down, so perhaps his viewpoint is overly negative.

Logical Fallacies

Before we turn to specific types of evidence, let's consider **logical fallacies**: potential vulnerabilities or weaknesses in an argument. Practically speaking, the logical
breakdown in most weak arguments occurs in the use of evidence, since evidence
is what we use to prove arguments. So a more practical definition of a fallacy
might be a failure to make a logical connection between the claim and the evidence used to support that claim. Fallacies may be accidental, but they can also be
used deliberately to manipulate or deceive.

Regardless of whether they are intentional or unintentional, logical fallacies
work against the clear, civil discourse that should be at the heart of argument. By

checking for logical fallacies in a published argument that you're analyzing, you can identify weak points; by checking for fallacies in your own writing, you can revise to strengthen your argument. It's more important that you notice these fallacies and be able to describe what you see than it is to be able to label them by their technical name. The concepts are more important than the terms.

Fallacies of Relevance

One characteristic of evidence we have just discussed is relevance. Fallacies that result from using evidence that's irrelevant to the claim fall under the general heading of red herrings. (The term derives from the dried fish that trainers used to distract dogs when teaching them to hunt foxes.) A **red herring** occurs when a speaker skips to a new and irrelevant topic in order to avoid the topic of discussion. If Politician X says, "We can debate these regulations until the cows come home, but what the American people want to know is, when are we going to end this partisan bickering?" she has effectively avoided providing evidence on the benefits or detriments of the regulations by trying to change the subject to that of partisanship.

One common type of red herring is an ***ad hominem* fallacy**. *Ad hominem* is Latin for "to the man"; the phrase refers to the diversionary tactic of switching the argument from the issue at hand to the character of the other speaker. If you argue that a park in your community should not be renovated because the person supporting it was arrested during a domestic dispute, then you are guilty of *ad hominem*—arguing against the person rather than addressing the issue. This fallacy is frequently misunderstood to mean that *any* instance of questioning someone's character is *ad hominem*. Not so. It is absolutely valid to call a person's character into question if it is *relevant* to the topic at hand. For example, if a court case hinges on the testimony of a single witness and that person happens to be a con artist, then his character is absolutely relevant in deciding whether he is a credible witness.

Analogy is the most vulnerable type of evidence because it is always susceptible to the charge that two things are not comparable, resulting in a **faulty analogy**. However, some analogies are more vulnerable than others, particularly those that focus on irrelevant or inconsequential similarities between two things. Whenever analogy is used, it's important to gauge whether the dissimilarities outweigh the similarities. Advertisements sometimes draw faulty analogies to appeal to pathos; for example, an ad for a very expensive watch might picture a well-known athlete or a ballet dancer and draw an analogy between the precision and artistry of (1) the person and (2) the mechanism. When writers use analogy to add drama to a claim, it's important to question whether the similarities really fit and illuminate the point or simply add emotional appeal. For instance, to argue that "we put animals who are in irreversible pain out of their misery, so we should do the same for people" asks the reader to ignore significant and profound differences between animals and people. The analogy may at first glance appeal to emotions, but it is logically irrelevant.

Fallacies of Accuracy

Using evidence that is either intentionally or unintentionally inaccurate will result in a fallacy. The most common example of inaccurate evidence resulting in a fallacy is one called the straw man. A **straw man fallacy** occurs when a speaker chooses a deliberately poor or oversimplified example in order to ridicule and refute an opponent's viewpoint. For example, consider the following scenario. Politician X proposes that we put astronauts on Mars in the next four years. Politician Y ridicules this proposal by saying that his opponent is looking for "little green men in outer space." Politician Y is committing a straw man fallacy by inaccurately representing Politician X's proposal, which is about space exploration and scientific experimentation, not "little green men."

Another fallacy that results from using inaccurate evidence is the **either/or fallacy**, also called a **false dilemma**. In this fallacy, the speaker presents two extreme options as the only possible choices. For instance:

> Either we agree to higher taxes, or our grandchildren will be mired
> in debt.

This statement offers only two ways to view the issue, and both are extreme and inaccurate.

Fallacies of Insufficiency

Perhaps the most common of fallacies occurs when evidence is insufficient. We call this a **hasty generalization**, meaning that there is not enough evidence to support a particular conclusion. For instance: "Smoking isn't bad for you; my great aunt smoked a pack a day and lived to be 90." It could be that the story of the speaker's aunt is true, but this single anecdote does not provide enough evidence to discredit the results of years of medical research.

Another fallacy resulting from insufficient evidence is circular reasoning. **Circular reasoning** involves repeating the claim as a way to provide evidence, resulting in no evidence at all. For instance, a student who asserts, "You can't give me a C; I'm an A student" is guilty of circular reasoning; that is, the "evidence" that she should get an A is that she is an A student. The so-called evidence is insufficient because it is a mere repetition of the claim. You can frequently spot circular reasoning in advertising. For instance: "Buy this shampoo because it's the best shampoo!" or "Shop at this store because it's a shopper's paradise."

We will discuss other common logical fallacies as we examine specific types of evidence.

First-Hand Evidence

First-hand evidence is something you *know*, whether it's from personal experience, anecdotes you've heard from others, observations, or your general knowledge of events.

Personal Experience

The most common type of first-hand evidence is personal experience. Bringing in personal experience adds a human element and can be an effective way to appeal to pathos. For example, when writing about whether you do or do not support single-sex classrooms, you might describe your experience as a student, or you might use your observations about your school or classmates to inform your argument. Personal experience is a great way to make an abstract issue more human, and it is an especially effective technique in the introduction and conclusion of an argument. Personal experience can interest readers and draw them in, but they'll need more than just your perspective to be persuaded.

Personal experience works best if the writer can speak as an insider. For instance, you can speak knowledgeably about the issue of single-sex classrooms because you have inside knowledge about classrooms and how they work. In the following essay about the environmentalist movement, Jennifer Oladipo argues that minorities need to become more involved: "The terms *environmentalist* and *minority* conjure two distinct images in most people's minds — a false dichotomy that seriously threatens any chance of pulling the planet out of its current ecological tailspin." As a member of a minority group herself, she uses her personal experience as both an entrance into the essay and a source of evidence.

Why Can't Environmentalism Be Colorblind?
JENNIFER OLADIPO

> In nearly two years of volunteering and working at an urban nature preserve, I have never seen another face like mine come through our doors. At least, I've not seen another black woman come for a morning hike or native-wildlife program. The few I do encounter are teachers and chaperones with school groups, or aides assisting people with disabilities. When I commute by bus to the preserve, located in the middle of Louisville, Kentucky, I disembark with blacks and other minorities. Yet none of them ever seems to make it to the trails.
>
> I might have assumed they simply weren't interested, but then I saw that none of the center's newsletters were mailed to predominantly minority areas of town, nor did any press releases go to popular minority radio stations or newspapers. Not ever, as far as I could tell. Although the nature center seeks a stronger community presence and feels the same budget pinch as other small nonprofits, it has missed large swaths of the community with its message.

The terms *environmentalist* and *minority* conjure two distinct images in most people's minds—a false dichotomy that seriously threatens any chance of pulling the planet out of its current ecological tailspin. Some people think this country is on the precipice of a societal shift that will make environmental stewardship an integral part of our collective moral code. But that is not going to happen as long as we as a nation continue to think and act as if "green" automatically means "white."

Assumptions about who is amenable to conservation values cost the environmental movement numbers and dollars. Religion, capitalism, and even militarism learned ages ago to reach actively across the racial spectrum. In terms of winning over minorities, they have left environmentalism in the dust. Not until I joined an environmental-journalism organization was my mailbox flooded with information about serious environmental issues—even though I have been volunteering in organic gardens, hiking, and camping for years. I had received solicitations for credit cards and political parties, fast-food coupons, and a few Books of Mormon— but I had to seek out environmental groups.

Minorities make up one-third of the population, and we are growing as an   5 economic and financial force as our numbers increase. We are a key to maintaining the energy that environmentalism has gained as a result of intense mainstream attention. That momentum will peter out without more people to act on the present sense of urgency. Imagine the power of 100 million Asians, African Americans, Latinos, and Native Americans invested in sustainable living, joining green organizations, voting for politicians and laws that protect the environment.

Nobody benefits from the perception that enjoying and caring for the environment is an exclusively white lifestyle. The truth is that brown, yellow, red, and black people like to go backpacking, too. Those of us with the means are buying organic, local, and hybrid. If environmentalism continues to appear mostly white and well-off, it will continue to be mostly white and well-off, even as racial and economic demographics change. The environmental movement will continue to overlook the nuances, found in diversity of experience, that reveal multiple facets of environmental problems—and their solutions.

Sooner or later, even global warming will be pushed off magazine covers, television screens, and the congressional floor. Before that time, we need to have in place something even more impressive: a racially diverse, numerically astounding mass of environmentalists ready to pick up the ball and run with it.

Oladipo writes most of her essay around her personal experience working in a Kentucky nature preserve, explaining why she chose the work and pointing out the lack of "another face like mine" in that setting. She also describes her experience working for an "environmental-journalism organization" and spending time outdoors. Although she primarily draws on her own experiences in her essay, she also uses some statistics and a reasonable tone to make a persuasive case.

....

FALLACY ALERT: Hasty Generalization

As we described previously (p. 100), a hasty generalization is a fallacy in which there is not enough evidence to support a particular conclusion. When using personal experience as evidence, it is important to remember that while it might provide some ethos to speak on a topic and it may be an effective way to appeal to pathos, personal experience is rarely universal proof.

EXAMPLE: Pulling wisdom teeth is just another unnecessary and painful medical procedure. I still have all of mine, and they haven't given me any problems.

....

Anecdotes

First-hand evidence also includes anecdotes about other people that you've either observed or been told about. Like personal experience, anecdotes can be a useful way to appeal to pathos.

In the following excerpt from an op-ed piece, Fabiola Santiago argues against the policy that children born in the United States to immigrants, including those who are undocumented, must be treated as nonresidents when it comes to receiving state services. To make the case about the specific unfairness of imposing out-of-state tuition on Florida residents who fall into this category, Santiago uses an anecdote as part of her evidence.

In College, These American Citizens Are Not Created Equal

FABIOLA SANTIAGO

> "I lift my lamp beside the golden door!" — Lady Liberty

> On Saturday, the day after its 125th anniversary celebration, the Statue of Liberty will close its doors for a year-long, $27 million renovation of the monument's interior. One could only hope that the nation's soul will undergo some transformation as well. Emma Lazarus, the descendant of Sephardic Jews expelled from Spain who wrote in 1883 "The New Colossus," the moving sonnet at the base of the statue in New York harbor, would shed mournful tears at the lack of compassion for immigrants these days. She would weep at the ease with which words of disdain are spoken by some who lead and aspire to lead, and at the underhanded way in which ill-willed actions are taken against immigrants and their children. Lady Liberty's "golden door" is not only jammed, slammed shut, or slightly ajar depending on where you come from, but we've fallen so low on the scale of our founding values that in the United States of America of today not all U.S. citizens are created equal. There are states like Florida, Alabama, and Arizona where politicians and bureaucrats use the system to discriminate, to create classes of

Americans, to disenfranchise some of the most deserving among us. The latest low blow was unveiled by a class-action lawsuit and a bill filed in the Florida Legislature last week. Under rules established by the state's Department of Education and the university system's Board of Governors, students like Wendy Ruiz—born and raised in Miami—have to pay out-of-state tuition at rates that are more than three times what other Florida resident students pay for their education. Ruiz has lived in the state all her life. She has a Florida birth certificate, a Florida driver's license, and is registered to vote in Florida. But while other Miami Dade College students pay about $1,266 per term in tuition, she must pay $4,524 because the state considers her a dependent of nonresidents. Here's an institution that is supposed to defend education punishing a young American for the sins of her parents, who are undocumented immigrants. But we should all aspire to have neighbors like the Ruizes, who raised a daughter like Wendy, willing to work three part-time jobs to pay her tuition while maintaining a 3.7 grade-point average. "I know that I will be successful because I have never wanted something so bad in my life like I want this," Ruiz said of her education. Who knows what more Wendy Ruiz might accomplish, what more she could become if she were able to pay all of her attention to her education without the unfair financial burden of paying extravagantly unfair fees.

Santiago could have provided facts and figures about the legislative policy in question. Instead, she focuses on one person, Wendy Ruiz. Santiago points out that Ruiz "has lived in the state all her life. She has a Florida birth certificate, a Florida driver's license, and is registered to vote in Florida." Santiago then explains the difference in tuition for residents vs. nonresidents, noting that Wendy is a model citizen "willing to work three part-time jobs to pay her tuition." She even quotes Wendy's comments about the premium she places on education. In this example, Santiago is not writing about herself, but she is telling an anecdote about another person that gives a human face to the argument. She appeals to pathos by describing the situation of Wendy Ruiz, being careful to point out that her situation typifies that of others who would suffer from a proposed policy.

Current Events

Current events are another type of evidence that is accessed first-hand through observation. Staying abreast of what is happening locally, nationally, and globally ensures a store of information that can be used as evidence in arguments. Remember that current events can be interpreted in many ways, so seek out multiple perspectives and be on the lookout for bias. Here is an example from an essay by the political analyst Fareed Zakaria about the plight of the American education system. He wrote the article around the time of the death of Steve Jobs, the founder of Apple, when details of Jobs's life were in the national news. In "When

Will We Learn?" Zakaria argues for the improvement of our public education system, citing Jobs and his partner, Steve Wozniak, as evidence of the impact of a strong high school education.

> For the past month, we have all marveled at the life of Steve Jobs, the adopted son of working-class parents, who dropped out of college and became one of the great technologists and businessmen of our time. How did he do it? He was, of course, an extraordinary individual, and that explains much of his success, but his environment might also have played a role. Part of the environment was education. And it is worth noting that Jobs got a great secondary education. The school he attended, Homestead High in Cupertino, Calif., was a first-rate public school that gave him a grounding in both the liberal arts and technology. It did the same for Steve Wozniak, the more technically oriented co-founder of Apple Computer, whom Jobs met at that same school.
>
> In 1972, the year Jobs graduated, California's public schools were the envy of the world. They were generally rated the finest in the country, well funded and well run, with excellent teachers. These schools were engines of social mobility that took people like Jobs and Wozniak and gave them an educational grounding that helped them rise.

Second-Hand Evidence

Second-hand evidence is evidence that is accessed through research, reading, and investigation. It includes factual and historical information, expert opinion, and quantitative data. Anytime you cite what someone else knows, not what you know, you are using second-hand evidence. While citing second-hand evidence may occasionally appeal to pathos and certainly may establish a writer's ethos, the central appeal is to logos — reason and logic.

Historical Information

A common type of second-hand evidence is historical information — verifiable facts that a writer knows from research. This kind of evidence can provide background and context to current debates; it also can help establish the writer's ethos because it shows that he or she has taken the time and effort to research the matter and become informed. One possible pitfall is that historical events are complicated. You'll want to keep your description of the events brief, but be sure not to misrepresent the events. In the following paragraph from *Hate Speech: The History of an American Controversy* (1994), author Samuel Walker provides historical information to establish the "intolerance" of the 1920s era.

> The 1920s are remembered as a decade of intolerance. Bigotry was as much a symbol of the period as Prohibition, flappers, the stock market boom, and Calvin Coolidge. It was the only time when the Ku Klux Klan paraded en masse through

> the nation's capital. In 1921 Congress restricted immigration for the first time in American history, drastically reducing the influx of Catholics and Jews from southern and eastern Europe, and the nation's leading universities adopted admission quotas to restrict the number of Jewish students. The Sacco and Vanzetti case, in which two Italian American anarchists were executed for robbery and murder in a highly questionable prosecution, has always been one of the symbols of the anti-immigrant tenor of the period.

To support the claim that the 1920s was a period characterized by bigotry, Walker cites a series of historical examples: the KKK, immigration laws, restriction targeting certain ethnicities, and a high-profile court case.

Historical information is often used to develop a point of comparison or contrast to a more contemporary situation. In the following paragraph from Charles Krauthammer's op-ed "The 9/11 'Overreaction'? Nonsense," the political commentator does exactly that by comparing the War on Terror to previous military campaigns in U.S. history.

> True, in both [the Iraq and Afghanistan] wars there was much trial, error and tragic loss. In Afghanistan, too much emphasis on nation-building. In Iraq, the bloody middle years before we found our general and our strategy. But cannot the same be said of, for example, the Civil War, the terrible years before Lincoln found his general? Or the Pacific campaign of World War II, with its myriad miscalculations, its often questionable island-hopping, that cost infinitely more American lives?

Notice that Krauthammer's historical evidence is brief but detailed enough to both show his grasp of the history and explicitly lay out his comparison. Simply saying, "These wars are no different from the Civil War or World War II" would have been far too vague and thus ineffective.

FALLACY ALERT: *Post Hoc Ergo Propter Hoc*

The name of the ***post hoc ergo propter hoc*** fallacy is Latin for "after which therefore because of which." What that means is that it is incorrect to always claim that something is a cause just because it happened earlier. In other words, correlation does not imply causation.

EXAMPLE: We elected Johnson as president and look where it got us: hurricanes, floods, stock market crashes.

That's a simple example, but in reality causality is very tricky to prove because few things have only one cause. When using historical evidence, you should be especially aware of this fallacy. Check your facts. Consider the complexity of the situation. Proceed with caution.

Expert Opinion

Most everyone is an expert on something! And how often do we bolster our viewpoint by pointing out that so-and-so agrees with us? Expert opinion is a more formal variation on that common practice. An expert is someone who has published research on a topic or whose job or experience gives him or her specialized knowledge. Sometimes, you might cite the viewpoint of an individual who is an "expert" in a local matter but who is not widely recognized. If, for instance, you are writing about school policy, you might cite the opinion of a teacher or student government officer. The important point is to make certain that your expert is seen as credible by your audience so that his or her opinion will add weight to your argument.

Following is an excerpt from "Just a Little Princess" by Peggy Orenstein in which she critiques what she calls "the princess culture" that Disney promotes. In this paragraph, she is commenting on the phenomenon of "Supergirl." Note the use of an expert—and how that expert is identified—as evidence.

> The princess as superhero is not irrelevant. Some scholars I spoke with say that given its post-9/11 timing, princess mania is a response to a newly dangerous world. "Historically, princess worship has emerged during periods of uncertainty and profound social change," observes Miriam Forman-Brunell, a historian at the University of Missouri–Kansas City. Francis Hodgson Burnett's original *Little Princess* was published at a time of rapid urbanization, immigration and poverty; Shirley Temple's film version was a hit during the Great Depression. "The original folk tales themselves," Forman-Brunell says, "spring from medieval and early modern European culture that faced all kinds of economic and demographic and social upheaval—famine, war, disease, terror of wolves. Girls play savior during times of economic crisis and instability." That's a heavy burden for little shoulders. Perhaps that's why the magic wand has become an essential part of the princess get-up. In the original stories—even the Disney versions of them—it's not the girl herself who's magic: it's the fairy godmother. Now if Forman-Brunell is right, we adults have become the cursed creatures whom girls have the thaumaturgic [miraculous] power to transform.

Orenstein is careful to present credentials (in this case, a university professor) and to either quote or paraphrase the relevant information as evidence. She quotes Forman-Brunell and then comments on this expert's viewpoint. Orenstein may have held the same opinion about fairy godmothers and their impact on girls' views of themselves, but the findings of a researcher add credibility to the argument.

. . . .

FALLACY ALERT: Appeal to False Authority

Appeal to false authority occurs when someone who has no expertise to speak on an issue is cited as an authority. A TV star, for instance, is not a medical expert, even though pharmaceutical advertisements often use celebrity endorsements. When choosing whom to cite as an expert, be sure to verify the person's background and qualifications.

Quantitative Evidence

Quantitative evidence includes things that can be represented in numbers: statistics, surveys, polls, census information. This type of evidence can be persuasive in its appeal to logos. Amy Domini cites numerical evidence in her essay to support her contention that "[f]ast food is a way of life. In America, the average person eats it more than 150 times a year. In 2007, sales for the 400 largest U.S.-based fast-food chains totaled $277 billion, up 7 percent from 2006" (see p. 83).

Quantitative evidence need not be all percentages and dollar figures, however. In the article on American education, Fareed Zakaria compares the education situation of the United States with that of other countries by citing quantitative information without a lot of numbers and figures.

> U.S. schoolchildren spend less time in school than their peers abroad. They have shorter school days and a shorter school year. Children in South Korea will spend almost two years more in school than Americans by the end of high school. Is it really so strange that they score higher on tests?
>
> If South Korea teaches the importance of hard work, Finland teaches another lesson. Finnish students score near the very top on international tests, yet they do not follow the Asian model of study, study and more study. Instead they start school a year later than in most countries, emphasize creative work and shun tests for most of the year. But Finland has great teachers, who are paid well and treated with the same professional respect that is accorded to doctors and lawyers. They are found and developed through an extremely competitive and rigorous process. All teachers are required to have master's degrees, and only 1 in 10 applicants is accepted to the country's teacher-training programs.

Zakaria includes quantitative data—two more years of school for Korean students than their American counterparts, a highly competitive process for teacher-training programs that accept only one of every ten applicants—as part of his overall discussion. He could have cited dollar amounts as evidence of how well paid teachers are in Finland, but in the context of this column he makes the point and moves on; perhaps if he were writing for a more scholarly or skeptical audience, he would have thought it necessary to provide even more information.

FALLACY ALERT: Bandwagon Appeal

Bandwagon appeal (or *ad populum* **fallacy**) occurs when evidence boils down to "everybody's doing it, so it must be a good thing to do." Sometimes, statistics can be used to prove that "everybody's doing it" and thus give a bandwagon appeal the appearance of cold, hard fact.

EXAMPLE: You should vote to elect Rachel Johnson — she has a strong lead in the polls!

Polling higher does not necessarily make Senator Johnson the "best" candidate, only the most popular.

• ACTIVITY •

Identify the logical fallacy in each of the following examples.

1. What's the problem? All my friends have a curfew of midnight!
2. A person who is honest will not steal, so my client, an honest person, clearly is not guilty of theft.
3. Her economic plan is impressive, but remember: this is a woman who spent six weeks in the Betty Ford Center getting treatment for alcoholism.
4. Since Mayor Perry has been in office, our city has had a balanced budget; if he were governor, the state budget would finally be balanced.
5. If we outlaw guns, only outlaws will have guns.
6. Smoking is dangerous because it is harmful to your health.
7. He was last year's MVP, and he drives a Volvo. That must be a great car.
8. A national study of grades 6–8 showed that test scores went down last year and absenteeism was high; this generation is going to the dogs.

• ACTIVITY •

Annotate the essay below by identifying the different types of first- and second-hand evidence presented to develop the argument. Analyze how each type of evidence appeals to ethos, logos, pathos, or a combination of those.

Terror's Purse Strings
DANA THOMAS

Luxury fashion designers are busily putting final touches on the handbags they will present during the spring-summer 2008 women's wear shows, which begin next week in New York City's Bryant Park. To understand the importance of the handbag in fashion today consider this: According to consumer surveys conducted by Coach, the average American woman was buying two new handbags a year in 2000; by 2004, it was more than four. And the average luxury bag retails for 10 to 12 times its production cost.

"There is a kind of an obsession with bags," the designer Miuccia Prada told me. "It's so easy to make money."

Counterfeiters agree. As soon as a handbag hits big, counterfeiters around the globe churn out fake versions by the thousands. And they have no trouble selling them. Shoppers descend on Canal Street in New York, Santee Alley in Los Angeles and flea markets and purse parties around the country to pick up knockoffs for one-tenth the legitimate bag's retail cost, then pass them off as real.

"Judges, prosecutors, defense attorneys shop here," a private investigator told me as we toured the counterfeit section of Santee Alley. "Affluent people from Newport Beach." According to a study by the British law firm Davenport Lyons, two-thirds of British consumers are "proud to tell their family and friends" that they bought fake luxury fashion items.

At least 11 percent of the world's clothing is fake, according to 2000 figures from the Global Anti-Counterfeiting Group in Paris. Fashion is easy to copy: counterfeiters buy the real items, take them apart, scan the pieces to make patterns and produce almost-perfect fakes.

Most people think that buying an imitation handbag or wallet is harmless, a victimless crime. But the counterfeiting rackets are run by crime syndicates that also deal in narcotics, weapons, child prostitution, human trafficking and terrorism. Ronald K. Noble, the secretary general of Interpol, told the House of Representatives Committee on International Relations that profits from the sale of counterfeit goods have gone to groups associated with Hezbollah, the Shiite terrorist group, paramilitary organizations in Northern Ireland and FARC, the Revolutionary Armed Forces of Colombia.

Sales of counterfeit T-shirts may have helped finance the 1993 World Trade Center bombing, according to the International AntiCounterfeiting Coalition. "Profits from counterfeiting are one of the three main sources of income supporting international terrorism," said Magnus Ranstorp, a terrorism expert at the University of St. Andrews, in Scotland.

Most fakes today are produced in China, a good many of them by children. Children are sometimes sold or sent off by their families to work in clandestine factories that produce counterfeit luxury goods. Many in the West consider this an urban myth. But I have seen it myself.

On a warm winter afternoon in Guangzhou, I accompanied Chinese police officers on a factory raid in a decrepit tenement. Inside, we found two dozen children, ages 8 to 13, gluing and sewing together fake luxury-brand handbags. The police confiscated everything, arrested the owner and sent the children out. Some punched their timecards, hoping to still get paid. (The average Chinese factory worker earns about $120 a month; the counterfeit factory worker earns half that or less.) As we made our way back to the police vans, the children threw bottles and cans at us. They were now jobless and, because the factory owner housed them, homeless. It was *Oliver Twist* in the 21st century.

What can we do to stop this? Much like the war on drugs, the effort to protect luxury brands must go after the source: the counterfeit manufacturers. The company that took me on the Chinese raid is one of the only luxury-goods makers that works directly with Chinese authorities to shut down factories, and it has one of the lowest rates of counterfeiting.

Luxury brands also need to teach consumers that the traffic in fake goods has many victims. But most companies refuse to speak publicly about counterfeiting — some won't even authenticate questionable items for concerned customers — believing, like Victorians, that acknowledging despicable actions tarnishes their sterling reputations.

So it comes down to us. If we stop knowingly buying fakes, the supply chain will dry up and counterfeiters will go out of business. The crime syndicates will have far less money to finance their illicit activities and their terrorist plots. And the children? They can go home.

10

• ESSAY IN PROGRESS: Using Evidence •

Choose one of the thesis statements you developed on page 97, and develop three paragraphs of support, using a different type of evidence in each. You will probably have to do some research if you want to use historical information, expert testimony, or quantitative data.

Shaping Argument

The shape — that is, the organization or arrangement — of an argument reflects a host of factors, including audience and purpose, but it usually follows one of several patterns. We'll discuss classical oration, induction and deduction, and the Toulmin model as four common ways to structure an argument. Keep in mind that writers often modify these structures as needed. The essential point to remember is that the organization should fit the ideas, rather than forcing ideas to fit into a prescribed organizational pattern.

The Classical Oration

Classical rhetoricians outlined a five-part structure for an oratory, or speech, that writers still use today, although perhaps not always consciously:

- The **introduction** (***exordium***) introduces the reader to the subject under discussion. In Latin, *exordium* means "beginning a web," which is an apt description for an introduction. Whether it is a single paragraph or several, the introduction draws the readers into the text by piquing their interest, challenging them, or otherwise getting their attention. Often the introduction is where the writer establishes ethos.

- The **narration** (*narratio*) provides factual information and background material on the subject at hand, thus beginning the developmental paragraphs, or establishes why the subject is a problem that needs addressing. The level of detail a writer uses in this section depends largely on the audience's knowledge of the subject. Although classical rhetoric describes narration as appealing to logos, in actuality it often appeals to pathos because the writer attempts to evoke an emotional response about the importance of the issue being discussed.

- The **confirmation** (*confirmatio*), usually the major part of the text, includes the development or the proof needed to make the writer's case—the nuts and bolts of the essay, containing the most specific and concrete detail in the text. The confirmation generally makes the strongest appeal to logos.

- The **refutation** (*refutatio*), which addresses the counterargument, is in many ways a bridge between the writer's proof and conclusion. Although classical rhetoricians recommended placing this section at the end of the text as a way to anticipate objections to the proof given in the confirmation section, this is not a hard-and-fast rule. If opposing views are well known or valued by the audience, a writer will address them before presenting his or her own argument. The counterargument's appeal is largely to logos.

- The **conclusion** (*peroratio*)—whether it is one paragraph or several—brings the essay to a satisfying close. Here the writer usually appeals to pathos and reminds the reader of the ethos established earlier. Rather than simply repeating what has gone before, the conclusion brings all the writer's ideas together and answers the question, so what? Writers should remember the classical rhetoricians' advice that the last words and ideas of a text are those the audience is most likely to remember.

An example of the classical model at work is the piece below written in 2006 by Sandra Day O'Connor, a former Supreme Court justice, and Roy Romer, then superintendent of the Los Angeles Unified School District.

Not by Math Alone
SANDRA DAY O'CONNOR AND ROY ROMER

> Fierce global competition prompted President Bush to use the State of the Union address to call for better math and science education, where there's evidence that many schools are falling short. | Introduction

We should be equally troubled by another shortcoming in American schools: Most young people today simply do not have an adequate understanding of how our government and political system work, and they are thus not well prepared to participate as citizens.

This country has long exemplified democratic practice to the rest of the world. With the attention we are paying to advancing democracy abroad, we ought not neglect it at home.

Two-thirds of 12th-graders scored below "proficient" on the last national civics assessment in 1998, and only 9 percent could list two ways a democracy benefits from citizen participation. Yes, young people remain highly patriotic, and many volunteer in their communities. But most are largely disconnected from current events and issues.

A healthy democracy depends on the participation of citizens, and that participation is learned behavior; it doesn't just happen. As the 2003 report "The Civic Mission of Schools" noted: "Individuals do not automatically become free and responsible citizens, but must be educated for citizenship." That means civic learning—educating students for democracy—needs to be on par with other academic subjects.

Narration 5

This is not a new idea. Our first public schools saw education for citizenship as a core part of their mission. Eighty years ago, John Dewey said, "Democracy needs to be reborn in every generation and education is its midwife."

But in recent years, civic learning has been pushed aside. Until the 1960s, three courses in civics and government were common in American high schools, and two of them ("civics" and "problems of democracy") explored the role of citizens and encouraged students to discuss current issues. Today those courses are very rare.

What remains is a course on "American government" that usually spends little time on how people can—and why they should—participate. The effect of reduced civic learning on civic life is not theoretical. Research shows that the better people understand our history and system of government, the more likely they are to vote and participate in the civic life.

Confirmation

We need more and better classes to impart the knowledge of government, history, law and current events that students need to understand and participate in a democratic republic. And we also know that much effective civic learning takes place beyond the classroom—in extracurricular activity, service work that is connected to class work, and other ways students experience civic life.

Preserving our democracy should be reason enough to promote civic learning. But there are other benefits. Understanding society and how we relate to each other fosters the attitudes essential for success in college, work and communities; it enhances student learning in other subjects.

Economic and technological competitiveness is essential, and America's economy and technology have flourished because of the rule of law and the "assets" of a free and open society. Democracy has been good for business and for economic well-being. By the same token, failing to hone the civic tools of democracy will have economic consequences.

Bill Gates—a top business and technology leader—argues strongly that schools have to prepare students not only for college and career but for citizenship as well.

None of this is to diminish the importance of improving math and science education. This latest push, as well as the earlier emphasis on literacy, deserves support. It should also be the occasion for a broader commitment, and that means restoring education for democracy to its central place in school. *Refutation*

We need more students proficient in math, science and engineering. We also need them to be prepared for their role as citizens. Only then can self-government work. Only then will we not only be more competitive but also remain the beacon of liberty in a tumultuous world. *Conclusion*

Sandra Day O'Connor retired as an associate justice of the Supreme Court. Roy Romer, a former governor of Colorado, is superintendent of the Los Angeles Unified School District. They are co-chairs of the national advisory council of the Campaign for the Civic Mission of Schools.

Sandra Day O'Connor and Roy Romer follow the classical model very closely. The opening two paragraphs are an introduction to the main idea the authors develop. In fact, the last sentence of paragraph 2 is their two-part claim, or thesis: "Most young people today simply do not have an adequate understanding of how our government and political system work, and they are thus not well prepared to participate as citizens." O'Connor's position as a former Supreme Court justice establishes her ethos as a reasonable person, an advocate for justice, and a concerned citizen. Romer's biographical note at the end of the article suggests similar qualities. The authors use the pronoun "we" in the article to refer not only to themselves but to all of "us" who are concerned about American society. The opening phrase, "Fierce global competition," connotes a sense of urgency, and the warning that we are not adequately preparing our young people to participate as citizens is sure to evoke an emotional response of concern, even alarm.

In paragraphs 3 to 6—the narration—the authors provide background information, including facts that add urgency to their point. They cite statistics, quote from research reports, even call on the well-known educator John Dewey. They also include a definition of "civic learning," a key term in their argument. Their facts-and-figures appeal is largely to logos, though the language of "a healthy democracy" certainly engages the emotions.

Paragraphs 7 to 12 present the bulk of the argument—the confirmation—by offering reasons and examples to support the case that young people lack the knowledge necessary to be informed citizens. The authors link civic learning to other subjects as well as to economic development. They quote Bill Gates, chairman of Microsoft, who has spoken about the economic importance of a well-informed citizenry.

In paragraph 13, O'Connor and Romer briefly address a major objection—the refutation—that we need to worry more about math and science education than about civic learning. While they concede the importance of math, science, and literacy, they point out that it is possible to increase civic education without undermining the gains made in those other fields.

The final paragraph—the conclusion—emphasizes the importance of a democracy to a well-versed citizenry, a point that stresses the shared values of the authors with their audience. The appeal to pathos is primarily through the vivid language, particularly the final sentence with its emotionally charged description "beacon of liberty," a view of their nation that most Americans hold dear.

Induction and Deduction

Induction and deduction are ways of reasoning, but they are often effective ways to structure an entire argument as well.

Induction

Induction (from the Latin *inducere*, "to lead into") means arranging an argument so that it leads from particulars to universals, using specific cases to draw a conclusion. For instance:

> Regular exercise promotes weight loss.
>
> Exercise lowers stress levels.
>
> Exercise improves mood and outlook.
>
> GENERALIZATION: Exercise contributes to better health.

We use induction in our everyday lives. For example, if your family and friends have owned several cars made by Subaru that have held up well, then you are likely to conclude inductively that Subaru makes good cars. Yet induction is also used in more technical situations. Even the scientific method is founded on inductive reasoning. Scientists use experiments to determine the effects in certain cases, and from there they might infer a universal scientific principle. For instance, if bases neutralize acids in every experiment conducted, then it can reasonably be inferred that all bases neutralize acids. The process of induction involves collecting evidence and then drawing an inference based on that evidence in order to reach a conclusion.

When you write a full essay developed entirely by reasons, one after another supporting the main point, then your entire argument is inductive. For instance, suppose you are asked to take a position on whether the American Dream is alive and well today. As you examine the issue, you might think of examples from your own community that demonstrate that the Dream is not a reality for the average citizen; you might study current events and think about the way societal expectations have changed; you might use examples from fiction you have read, such as the novel *Tortilla Curtain* by T. Corraghessan Boyle or movies such as *Boyz N the Hood*, where economic pressures limit the characters' horizons. All of this evidence together supports the inference that the American Dream no longer exists for the average person. To write that argument, you would support your claim with a series of reasons explained through concrete examples: you would argue inductively.

Arguments developed inductively can never be said to be true or false, right or wrong. Instead, they can be considered strong or weak, so it's important to consider possible vulnerabilities—in particular, the exception to the rule. Let's consider an example from politics. An argument written in favor of a certain political candidate might be organized inductively around reasons that she is the best qualified person for the job because of her views on military spending, financial aid for college students, and states' rights. However, the argument is vulnerable to an objection that her views on, for instance, the death penalty or environmental issues weaken her qualifications. Essentially, an argument structured inductively cannot lead to certainty, only probability.

Let's look at an excerpt from *Outliers* by Malcolm Gladwell for an example of how an argument can be structured largely by induction. Gladwell uses various types of evidence here to support his conclusion that "[w]hen it comes to math . . . Asians have a built-in advantage."

from *Outliers*
MALCOLM GLADWELL

Take a look at the following list of numbers: 4, 8, 5, 3, 9, 7, 6. Read them out loud. Now look away and spend twenty seconds memorizing that sequence before saying them out loud again.

If you speak English, you have about a 50 percent chance of remembering that sequence perfectly. If you're Chinese, though, you're almost certain to get it right every time. Why is that? Because as human beings we store digits in a memory loop that runs for about two seconds. We most easily memorize whatever we can say or read within that two-second span. And Chinese speakers get that list of numbers—4, 8, 5, 3, 9, 7, 6—right almost every time because, unlike English, their language allows them to fit all those seven numbers into two seconds.

That example comes from Stanislas Dehaene's book *The Number Sense*. As Dehaene explains:

> Chinese number words are remarkably brief. Most of them can be uttered in less than one-quarter of a second (for instance, 4 is "si" and 7 "qi"). Their English equivalents—"four," "seven,"—are longer: pronouncing them takes about one-third of a second. The memory gap between English and Chinese apparently is entirely due to this difference in length. In languages as diverse as Welsh, Arabic, Chinese, English and Hebrew, there is a reproducible correlation between the time required to pronounce numbers in a given language and the memory span of its speakers. In this domain, the prize for efficacy goes to the Cantonese dialect of Chinese, whose brevity grants residents of Hong Kong a rocketing memory span of about 10 digits.

It turns out that there is also a big difference in how number-naming systems in Western and Asian languages are constructed. In English, we say fourteen, sixteen, seventeen, eighteen, and nineteen, so one might expect that we would also say oneteen, twoteen, threeteen, and fiveteen. But we don't. We use a different form: eleven, twelve, thirteen, and fifteen. Similarly, we have forty and sixty, which sound like the words they are related to (four and six). But we also say fifty and thirty and twenty, which sort of sound like five and three and two, but not really. And, for that matter, for numbers above twenty, we put the "decade" first and the unit number second (twenty-one, twenty-two), whereas for the teens, we do it the other way around (fourteen, seventeen, eighteen). The number system in English is highly irregular. Not so in China, Japan, and Korea. They have a logical counting system. Eleven is ten-one. Twelve is ten-two. Twenty-four is two-tens-four and so on.

That difference means that Asian children learn to count much faster than   5
American children. Four-year-old Chinese children can count, on average, to forty. American children at that age can count only to fifteen, and most don't reach forty until they're five. By the age of five, in other words, American children are already a *year* behind their Asian counterparts in the most fundamental of math skills.

The regularity of their number system also means that Asian children can perform basic functions, such as addition, far more easily. Ask an English-speaking seven-year-old to add thirty-seven plus twenty-two in her head, and she has to convert the words to numbers (37 + 22). Only then can she do the math: 2 plus 7 is 9 and 30 and 20 is 50, which makes 59. Ask an Asian child to add three-tens-seven and two-tens-two, and then the necessary equation is right there, embedded in the sentence. No number translation is necessary: It's five-tens-nine.

"The Asian system is transparent," says Karen Fuson, a Northwestern University psychologist who has closely studied Asian-Western differences. "I think that it makes the whole attitude toward math different. Instead of being a rote learning thing, there's a pattern I can figure out. There is an expectation that I can do this. There is an expectation that it's sensible. For fractions, we say three-fifths. The Chinese is literally 'out of five parts, take three.' That's telling you conceptually what a fraction is. It's differentiating the denominator and the numerator."

The much-storied disenchantment with mathematics among Western children starts in the third and fourth grades, and Fuson argues that perhaps a part of that disenchantment is due to the fact that math doesn't seem to make sense; its linguistic structure is clumsy; its basic rules seem arbitrary and complicated.

Asian children, by contrast, don't feel nearly the same bafflement. They can hold more numbers in their heads and do calculations faster, and the way fractions are expressed in their languages corresponds exactly to the way a fraction actually is—and maybe that makes them a little more likely to enjoy math, and maybe because they enjoy math a little more, they try a little harder and take more math classes and are more willing to do their homework, and on and on, in a kind of virtuous circle.

When it comes to math, in other words, Asians have a built-in advantage.   10

In each paragraph, Gladwell provides reasons backed by evidence. He begins in the opening two paragraphs by drawing in the reader with an anecdotal example that (he assumes) will demonstrate his point: if you speak English, you won't do as well as if you speak Chinese. In paragraph 3, he provides additional support by citing an expert who has written a book entitled *The Number Sense.* In the next two paragraphs, he discusses differences in the systems of Western and Asian languages that explain why Asian children learn certain basic skills that put them ahead of their Western counterparts at an early age. In paragraphs 6 and 7, he raises another issue—attitude toward problem solving—and provides evidence from an expert to explain the superiority of Asian students. By this point, Gladwell has provided enough specific information—from facts, experts, examples—to support an inference that is a generalization. In this case, he concludes that "[w]hen it comes to math . . . Asians have a built-in advantage." Gladwell's reasoning and the structure of his argument are inductive.

Deduction

When you argue using **deduction**, you reach a conclusion by starting with a general principle or universal truth (a major premise) and applying it to a specific case (a minor premise). Deductive reasoning is often structured as a **syllogism**, a logical structure that uses the major premise and minor premise to reach a necessary conclusion. Let's use the same example about exercise that we used to demonstrate induction, but now we'll develop a syllogism to argue deductively:

MAJOR PREMISE: Exercise contributes to better health.

MINOR PREMISE: Yoga is a type of exercise.

CONCLUSION: Yoga contributes to better health.

The strength of deductive logic is that if the first two premises are true, then the conclusion is logically valid. Keep in mind, though, that if either premise is false (or questionable in any way), then the conclusion is subject to challenge. Consider the following:

MAJOR PREMISE: Celebrities are role models for young people.

MINOR PREMISE: Lindsey Lohan is a celebrity.

CONCLUSION: Lindsey Lohan is a role model for young people.

As you can see in this example, the conclusion is logically valid—but is it true? You can challenge the conclusion by challenging the veracity of the major premise—that is, whether all celebrities are role models for young people.

Deduction is a good way to combat stereotypes that are based on faulty premises. Consider this one:

MAJOR PREMISE: Women are poor drivers.

MINOR PREMISE: Ellen is a woman.

CONCLUSION: Ellen is a poor driver.

Breaking this stereotype down into a syllogism clearly shows the faulty logic. Perhaps some women, just as some men, are poor drivers, but to say that women in general drive poorly is to stereotype by making a hasty generalization. Breaking an idea down into component parts like this helps expose the basic thinking, which then can yield a more nuanced argument. This example might be qualified, for instance, by saying that *some* women are poor drivers; thus, Ellen *might* be a poor driver.

• ESSAY IN PROGRESS: Shaping an Argument •

Write an outline that shows how you could structure the argument you are crafting either inductively or deductively. If you are using induction, cite at least four specifics that lead to your generalization (claim). If using deduction, break the overall reasoning of the essay into a syllogism with both a major and a minor premise and a conclusion.

Combining Induction and Deduction

While some essays are either completely inductive or completely deductive, it's more common for an essay to combine these methods depending on the situation. Induction — a series of examples — may be used to verify a major premise, then that premise can become the foundation for deductive reasoning. The Declaration of Independence is an example of deductive and inductive logic at work. Thomas Jefferson and the framers drafted this document to prove that the colonies were justified in their rebellion against King George III.

The Declaration of Independence

THOMAS JEFFERSON

In CONGRESS, July 4, 1776
The unanimous Declaration of the thirteen united States of America

When in the Course of human events it becomes necessary for one people to dissolve the political bands which have connected them with another and to assume among the powers of the earth, the separate and equal station to which the Laws of Nature and of Nature's God entitle them, a decent respect to the opinions of mankind requires that they should declare the causes which impel them to the separation.

We hold these truths to be self-evident, that all men are created equal, that they are endowed by their Creator with certain unalienable Rights, that among these are Life, Liberty and the pursuit of Happiness. — That to secure these rights, Governments are instituted among Men, deriving their just powers from the consent of the governed, — That whenever any Form of Government becomes destructive of these ends, it is the Right of the People to alter or to abolish it, and to institute new Government, laying its foundation on such principles and organizing its powers in such form, as to them shall seem most likely to effect their Safety and Happiness. Prudence, indeed, will dictate that Governments long established should not be changed for light and transient causes; and accordingly all experience hath shewn that mankind are more disposed to suffer, while evils are sufferable than to right themselves by abolishing the forms to which they are accustomed. But when a long train of abuses and usurpations, pursuing invariably the same Object evinces a design to reduce them under absolute Despotism, it is their right, it is their duty, to throw off such Government, and to provide new Guards for their future security. — Such has been the patient sufferance of these Colonies; and such is now the necessity which constrains them to alter their former Systems of Government. The history of the present King of Great Britain is a history of repeated injuries and usurpations, all having in direct object the establishment of an absolute Tyranny over these States. To prove this, let Facts be submitted to a candid world.

He has refused his Assent to Laws, the most wholesome and necessary for the public good.

He has forbidden his Governors to pass Laws of immediate and pressing importance, unless suspended in their operation till his Assent should be obtained; and when so suspended, he has utterly neglected to attend to them.

He has refused to pass other Laws for the accommodation of large districts of 5 people, unless those people would relinquish the right of Representation in the Legislature, a right inestimable to them and formidable to tyrants only.

He has called together legislative bodies at places unusual, uncomfortable, and distant from the depository of their Public Records, for the sole purpose of fatiguing them into compliance with his measures.

He has dissolved Representative Houses repeatedly, for opposing with manly firmness his invasions on the rights of the people.

He has refused for a long time, after such dissolutions, to cause others to be elected, whereby the Legislative Powers, incapable of Annihilation, have returned to the People at large for their exercise; the State remaining in the mean time exposed to all the dangers of invasion from without, and convulsions within.

He has endeavoured to prevent the population of these States; for that purpose obstructing the Laws for Naturalization of Foreigners; refusing to pass others to encourage their migrations hither, and raising the conditions of new Appropriations of Lands.

He has obstructed the Administration of Justice by refusing his Assent to Laws 10 for establishing Judiciary Powers.

He has made Judges dependent on his Will alone for the tenure of their offices, and the amount and payment of their salaries.

He has erected a multitude of New Offices, and sent hither swarms of Officers to harass our people and eat out their substance.

He has kept among us, in times of peace, Standing Armies without the Consent of our legislatures.

He has affected to render the Military independent of and superior to the Civil Power.

He has combined with others to subject us to a jurisdiction foreign to our con- 15 stitution, and unacknowledged by our laws; giving his Assent to their Acts of pretended Legislation:

For quartering large bodies of armed troops among us:

For protecting them, by a mock Trial from punishment for any Murders which they should commit on the Inhabitants of these States:

For cutting off our Trade with all parts of the world:

For imposing Taxes on us without our Consent:

For depriving us in many cases, of the benefit of Trial by Jury: 20

For transporting us beyond Seas to be tried for pretended offences:

For abolishing the free System of English Laws in a neighbouring Province, establishing therein an Arbitrary government, and enlarging its Boundaries so as to render it at once an example and fit instrument for introducing the same absolute rule into these Colonies:

For taking away our Charters, abolishing our most valuable Laws and altering fundamentally the Forms of our Governments:

For suspending our own Legislatures, and declaring themselves invested with power to legislate for us in all cases whatsoever.

He has abdicated Government here, by declaring us out of his Protection and waging War against us. 25

He has plundered our seas, ravaged our coasts, burnt our towns, and destroyed the lives of our people.

He is at this time transporting large Armies of foreign Mercenaries to compleat the works of death, desolation, and tyranny, already begun with circumstances of Cruelty & Perfidy scarcely paralleled in the most barbarous ages, and totally unworthy the Head of a civilized nation.

He has constrained our fellow Citizens taken Captive on the high Seas to bear Arms against their Country, to become the executioners of their friends and Brethren, or to fall themselves by their Hands.

He has excited domestic insurrections amongst us, and has endeavoured to bring on the inhabitants of our frontiers, the merciless Indian Savages whose known rule of warfare, is an undistinguished destruction of all ages, sexes and conditions.

In every stage of these Oppressions We have Petitioned for Redress in the most humble terms: Our repeated Petitions have been answered only by repeated injury. A Prince, whose character is thus marked by every act which may define a Tyrant, is unfit to be the ruler of a free people. 30

Nor have We been wanting in attentions to our British brethren. We have warned them from time to time of attempts by their legislature to extend an unwarrantable jurisdiction over us. We have reminded them of the circumstances of our emigration and settlement here. We have appealed to their native justice and magnanimity, and we have conjured them by the ties of our common kindred to disavow these usurpations, which would inevitably interrupt our connections and correspondence. They too have been deaf to the voice of justice and of consanguinity. We must, therefore, acquiesce in the necessity, which denounces our Separation, and hold them, as we hold the rest of mankind, Enemies in War, in Peace Friends.

We, therefore, the Representatives of the united States of America, in General Congress, Assembled, appealing to the Supreme Judge of the world for the rectitude of our intentions, do, in the Name, and by Authority of the good People of these Colonies, solemnly publish and declare, That these united Colonies are, and of Right ought to be Free and Independent States, that they are Absolved from all Allegiance to the British Crown, and that all political connection between them and the State of Great Britain, is and ought to be totally dissolved; and that as Free and Independent States, they have full Power to levy War, conclude Peace, contract Alliances, establish Commerce, and to do all other Acts and Things which Independent States may of right do. —And for the support of this Declaration, with a firm reliance on the protection of Divine Providence, we mutually pledge to each other our Lives, our Fortunes, and our sacred Honor.

The argument of the entire document can be distilled into this syllogism:

MAJOR PREMISE: Citizens have a right to rebel against a despot.

MINOR PREMISE: King George III is a despot.

CONCLUSION: Citizens have a right to rebel against King George III.

However, most of the text is inductive evidence—or "facts . . . submitted to a candid world," as Jefferson called them. The document lists one example ("fact") after another of the king's behavior that support the generalization that he is a despot. For instance, "He has made Judges dependent on his Will alone," "He has affected to render the Military independent of and superior to the Civil Power," "He has plundered our seas," and "He has excited domestic insurrections amongst us." The evidence is overwhelming: the king is a despot; the colonists have every right to declare their independence.

• ACTIVITY •

Modeled on the Declaration of Independence, the Declaration of Sentiments by Elizabeth Cady Stanton was presented on July 19, 1848, at the Seneca Falls Convention. Analyze the use of induction and deduction to support the claim and develop the argument.

The Declaration of Sentiments
ELIZABETH CADY STANTON

When, in the course of human events, it becomes necessary for one portion of the family of man to assume among the people of the earth a position different from that which they have hitherto occupied, but one to which the laws of nature and of nature's God entitle them, a decent respect to the opinions of mankind requires that they should declare the causes that impel them to such a course.

We hold these truths to be self-evident: that all men and women are created equal; that they are endowed by their Creator with certain inalienable rights; that among these are life, liberty, and the pursuit of happiness; that to secure these rights governments are instituted, deriving their just powers from the consent of the governed. Whenever any form of Government becomes destructive of these ends, it is the right of those who suffer from it to refuse allegiance to it, and to insist upon the institution of a new government, laying its foundation on such principles, and organizing its powers in such form as to them shall seem most likely to effect their safety and happiness. Prudence, indeed, will dictate that governments long established should not be changed for light and transient causes; and accordingly, all experience hath shown that mankind are more disposed to suffer, while evils are sufferable, than to right themselves by abolishing the forms to which they are accustomed. But when a long train of abuses and usurpations, pursuing invariably the same object, evinces a design to reduce them under absolute despotism, it is their duty to throw off such government, and to provide new guards for their future security. Such has been the patient sufferance of the women under this government, and such is now the necessity which constrains them to demand the equal station to which they are entitled.

The history of mankind is a history of repeated injuries and usurpations on the part of man toward woman, having in direct object the establishment of an absolute tyranny over her. To prove this, let facts be submitted to a candid world.

He has never permitted her to exercise her inalienable right to the elective franchise.

He has compelled her to submit to laws, in the formation of which she had no voice. 5

He has withheld from her rights which are given to the most ignorant and degraded men—both natives and foreigners.

Having deprived her of this first right of a citizen, the elective franchise, thereby leaving her without representation in the halls of legislation, he has oppressed her on all sides.

He has made her, if married, in the eye of the law, civilly dead.

He has taken from her all right in property, even to the wages she earns.

He has made her, morally, an irresponsible being, as she can commit many crimes with impunity, provided they be done in the presence of her husband. In the covenant of marriage, she is compelled to promise obedience to her husband, he becoming, to all intents and purposes, her master—the law giving him power to deprive her of her liberty, and to administer chastisement. 10

He has so framed the laws of divorce, as to what shall be the proper causes of divorce; in case of separation, to whom the guardianship of the children shall be given; as to be wholly regardless of the happiness of women—the law, in all cases, going upon the false supposition of the supremacy of man, and giving all power into his hands.

After depriving her of all rights as a married woman, if single and the owner of property, he has taxed her to support a government which recognizes her only when her property can be made profitable to it.

He has monopolized nearly all the profitable employments, and from those she is permitted to follow, she receives but a scanty remuneration.

He closes against her all the avenues to wealth and distinction, which he considers most honorable to himself. As a teacher of theology, medicine, or law, she is not known.

He has denied her the facilities for obtaining a thorough education—all colleges being closed against her.

15

He allows her in Church as well as State, but a subordinate position, claiming Apostolic authority for her exclusion from the ministry, and, with some exceptions, from any public participation in the affairs of the Church.

He has created a false public sentiment, by giving to the world a different code of morals for men and women, by which moral delinquencies which exclude women from society, are not only tolerated but deemed of little account in man.

He has usurped the prerogative of Jehovah himself, claiming it as his right to assign for her a sphere of action, when that belongs to her conscience and her God.

He has endeavored, in every way that he could to destroy her confidence in her own powers, to lessen her self-respect, and to make her willing to lead a dependent and abject life.

Now, in view of this entire disfranchisement of one-half the people of this country, their social and religious degradation,—in view of the unjust laws above mentioned, and because women do feel themselves aggrieved, oppressed, and fraudulently deprived of their most sacred rights, we insist that they have immediate admission to all the rights and privileges which belong to them as citizens of these United States.

20

In entering upon the great work before us, we anticipate no small amount of misconception, misrepresentation, and ridicule; but we shall use every instrumentality within our power to effect our object. We shall employ agents, circulate tracts, petition the State and national Legislatures, and endeavor to enlist the pulpit and the press in our behalf. We hope this Convention will be followed by a series of Conventions, embracing every part of the country.

Using the Toulmin Model

A useful way of both analyzing and structuring an argument is through the **Toulmin model**, an approach to argument created by British philosopher Stephen Toulmin in his book *The Uses of Argument* (1958). The Toulmin model is an effective tool in uncovering the assumptions that underlie arguments. Although at first this method—particularly its terminology—may seem complicated, it is actually very practical because it helps with analysis, structuring, qualifying a thesis, and understanding abstract arguments. Once mastered, it can be a very powerful tool.

The Toulmin model has six elements: claim, support (evidence), warrant (the assumption), backing, qualifier, and reservation. We have already discussed claims, which are arguable assertions. Toulmin defined a claim as "a conclusion whose merits we are seeking to establish." You have also already learned about support or evidence. A **warrant** expresses the **assumption** necessarily shared by the speaker and the audience. Similar to the minor premise of a syllogism, the assumption links the claim to the evidence; in other words, if the speaker and audience do not share the same assumption regarding the claim, all the evidence in the world won't be enough to sway them. **Backing** consists of further assurances or data without which the assumption lacks authority. The **qualifier**, when used (for example, *usually, probably, maybe, in most cases, most likely*), tempers the claim a bit, making it less absolute. The **reservation** explains the terms and conditions necessitated by the qualifier. In many cases, the argument will contain a **rebuttal** that gives voice to objections.

The following diagram illustrates the Toulmin model at work:

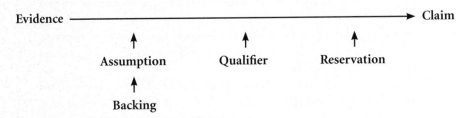

A Toulmin analysis will follow this form:

> Because (evidence as support), therefore (claim), since (assumption), on account of (backing), unless (reservation).

If there is a qualifier (such as *usually* or *maybe*), it will precede the claim. Here is a simple illustration:

> Because it is raining, therefore I should take my umbrella, since it will keep me dry.

You will immediately recognize the tacit assumption (that an umbrella will keep you dry) given explicit expression in the warrant. The backing would be "on account of the fact that the material is waterproof," and the reservation might be "unless there is a hole in it." In this case, the backing and reservation are so obvious that they don't need to be stated. The diagram below illustrates this argument—a simple one indeed, but one that demonstrates the process:

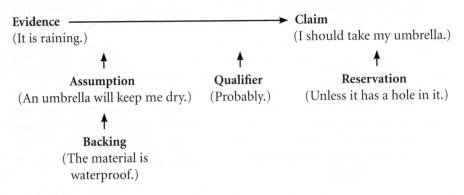

Fully expressed, this Toulmin argument would read:

> Because it is raining, therefore I should probably take my umbrella, since it will keep me dry on account of its waterproof material, unless, of course, there is a hole in it.

Analyzing Assumptions

You will note how the Toulmin model gives expression to the usually unspoken but necessary assumption. The Toulmin model shows us that assumptions are the link between a claim and the evidence used to support it. And, really, we should say "assumptions" here, because arguments of any complexity are always based on multiple assumptions. If your audience shares those assumptions, it is more likely to agree with the claim, finding the argument to be sound; if your audience does not, then the assumption becomes yet another claim requiring evidence. And if you were asked to analyze an argument in order to determine whether you support or challenge its claim, finding vulnerabilities in the assumptions would be the place to begin.

Let's take a look at how assumptions can become arguable claims by revisiting a piece that you read earlier in this chapter, Amy Domini's article "Why Investing in Fast Food May Be a Good Thing." We will see that by using the Toulmin method you could paraphrase her argument as follows:

> Because the fast food industry continues to grow and is not going away, therefore even those of us who support Slow Food should invest in it, since investing has the power to persuade businesses to change.

The last part expresses one of the assumptions the audience must agree on in order for Domini's argument to be persuasive. Does investing have the power to persuade business to change?

Two examples from the education article by Fareed Zakaria will further illustrate the method. Paraphrased according to Toulmin, one of Zakaria's arguments would run as follows:

> Because Chinese and South Korean children spend almost two years more in school than do Americans, therefore they outperform Americans on tests, since increased instructional time is responsible for increased test scores.

Do you agree with the assumption that increased instructional time is responsible for increased test scores? Alternatively, revealing another assumption, one might say:

> Because foreign students spend more time in school and achieve higher test scores, therefore they receive a better education, since quality of education and learning is indicated by test scores, on account of their accuracy in assessing learning.

Again, the assumption here might very well be debatable. Is learning indicated by test scores?

Sometimes, in the development of an argument, claims are presented implicitly early in the piece and more explicitly later. For an example, let's return to "The C Word in the Hallways" by Anna Quindlen. In the article, she makes several claims and supports them with credible evidence. Still, if you are to agree with her position, it is necessary to agree with the assumptions on which her arguments rest. Using the Toulmin model can help you to discover what they are, especially when the claim is implicit, as in the following:

> So many have already been lost. This month Kip Kinkel was sentenced to life in prison in Oregon for the murders of his parents and a shooting rampage at his high school that killed two students. A psychiatrist who specializes in the care of adolescents testified that Kinkel, now 17, had been hearing voices since he was 12. Sam Manzie is also 17. He is serving a 70-year sentence for luring an 11-year-old boy named Eddie Werner into his New Jersey home and strangling him with the cord of an alarm clock because his Sega Genesis was out of reach. Manzie had his first psychological evaluation in the first grade.

Using the Toulmin model, Quindlen's implicit argument here might be paraphrased as follows:

> Because Kinkel's and Manzie's mental illnesses were known for several years before they committed murder, therefore mental health care could have saved lives, since psychological intervention would have prevented them from committing these heinous acts.

As you finish the article, you come to realize that the entire argument rests on that assumption. Indeed, would psychological intervention have had that result? It certainly provokes discussion, which means that it is perhaps a point of vulnerability in Quindlen's argument.

• ACTIVITY •

For each of the following statements, identify the assumption that would link the claim to its support. Use the following format to discover the assumption: "Because (support), therefore (claim), since (assumption), on account of (backing), unless (reservation)." Decide whether each of the statements would require a qualifier.

1. Grades should be abolished because they add stress to the learning experience.

2. Until you buy me a diamond, I won't know that you love me!

3. Everyone should read novels because they make us more understanding of human foibles and frailties.

4. If we want to decrease gang violence, we should legalize drugs.
5. Don't get married if you believe that familiarity breeds contempt.
6. WiFi should be available to everyone without cost since the Internet has become a vital part of our lives.
7. You must obey her because she is your mother.
8. Because improving the educational system in this country is essential to competing with the other industrialized nations, we need to equip all classrooms with the latest computer technology.

From Reading to Writing

The Toulmin model can help you not only analyze the arguments that you read but also to bring logic and order to those that you write. Of course, the Toulmin language shouldn't be used directly in your essays because it often sounds stiff and lacks the nuance of more natural writing. But if you eliminate some of the artificial constructions and awkward phrasings—*because, therefore, since*—it can help you create a strong thesis statement, or at least think through the logic of your argument fully so that you can compose one that is strong and persuasive.

Let's walk through the process of refining an argument topic using the Toulmin model. We'll begin by responding to an argument about the increased visual nature of our print media, including textbooks:

> One reason education in this country is so bad is that the textbooks are crammed full of fluff like charts and graphs and pictures.

Let's restate this argument using the Toulmin model and look at its component parts.

> Because textbook authors are filling their books with charts, graphs, and pictures, therefore the quality of education is declining in this country, since less written information equals less learning.

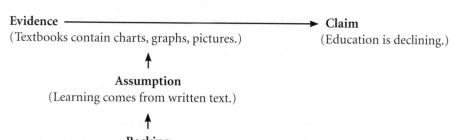

Evidence ⟶ **Claim**
(Textbooks contain charts, graphs, pictures.) (Education is declining.)

↑

Assumption
(Learning comes from written text.)

↑

Backing
(Traditionally, students have been learning from written text.)

Studying the argument this way, we find that the original argument has a vulnerability in that it assumes students only learn from printed text and not from visual material.

We can also use Toulmin to craft a response, using a simple template such as this: "Because_____, therefore_____, since_____, on account of_____, unless_____." Just because it's a template doesn't mean it has to tie your hands intellectually. You can put forth any viewpoint you like. Here is one response, just as an example:

> Because charts, graphs, and pictures provide information, therefore they do not hinder the education system, since that information is a supplement to written text.

In this case, we did not include a qualifier or a reservation.

Evidence **Claim**
(Charts, graphs, pictures provide information.)   (Visuals do not hinder education.)

Assumption
(Visual information supplements written text.)

Backing
(Students learn from a variety of media.)

You would then use that statement to develop your position and to write the thesis for your essay. The following example presents the claim but doesn't argue with the data: it acknowledges its validity, as far as it goes (this creates a reasonable tone and appeals to ethos and logos), and then zeros in on the assumption with a pair of rhetorical questions:

> Much of the argument is indisputable; however, some of it can be interpreted in different ways. Take, for instance, the criticism of textbooks for using too many visuals, particularly of a map replacing a topographical description. Is the map really a bad thing? Are any of the charts and graphs bad things?

The essay would then go on to argue the value of visuals not as replacements for but as supplements to written texts, developing a qualified and reasoned argument.

• ACTIVITY •

Complete each of the following templates, using an argument from this chapter (e.g., "Crazed Rhetoric" by Tom Toles, "Why Investing in Fast Food

May Be a Good Thing" by Amy Domini, or "*Star Wars*" by Roger Ebert). Use at least two different texts.

1. In his/her argument _____ concludes _____ and supports the conclusion with such evidence as _____ and _____. To link this conclusion with the evidence, he/she makes the assumption that _____.

2. Although what _____ says about _____ may be true in some cases, his/her position fails to take _____ into account. A closer look at _____ reveals _____.

3. While the position advanced by X may seem reasonable, it assumes _____. If that were so, then _____. It might be more reasonable to consider _____.

4. One way to look at X would be to say _____; but if that were the case, then _____. Of course, another view might be _____. Yet another way to consider X might be _____.

5. Position X would be sound only if we chose to ignore _____. When we consider _____, then _____. In addition, _____.

6. Wouldn't it be wonderful if we could all agree about _____? The trouble is, _____. X says _____ and Y says _____. How can we come to a compromise that recognizes _____?

Analyzing Visual Texts as Arguments

In this section, we'll focus on how to analyze visual texts that present arguments. A visual argument can be an advertisement, a political cartoon, a photograph, a bumper sticker, a T-shirt, a hat, a Web page, or even a piece of fine art. Yet the tools to analyze argument — identifying the claims, analyzing the way evidence is used, thinking critically about the artist's assumptions, examining how the piece is structured, considering appeals to ethos, pathos, and logos — are fairly similar for both visual and written arguments.

Although the tools that artists use to make their arguments are primarily visual strategies such as the placement of figures and objects and the use of color, the process of analysis is the same as with any text: look carefully, take note of every detail, make connections about your observations, and draw conclusions. Again, as with any written text, it's important to know what occasioned the visual image and, if possible, who the artist intended as his or her audience.

Following is a checklist to use with any visual text:

- Where did the visual first appear? Who is the audience? Who is the speaker or artist? Does this person have political or organizational affiliations that are important to understanding the text?
- What do you notice first? Where is your eye drawn? What is your overall first impression?
- What topic does the visual address or raise? Does the visual make a claim about that topic?
- Does the text tell or suggest a narrative or story? If so, what is the point?
- What emotions does the visual text evoke? How do color or light and shadow contribute to evoking emotions?
- Are the figures realistic, caricatures, distorted? What is the effect?
- Are any of the images visual allusions that would evoke emotions or memories in viewers?
- What cultural values are viewers likely to bring to the images?
- What claim does the visual make about the issue(s) it addresses?

Let's use this checklist to analyze a four-frame cartoon entitled *Rat Race* that appeared on the United Kingdom Web site polyp.org.uk.

- **Where did the visual first appear? Who is the audience? Who is the speaker? Does this person have political or organizational affiliations that are important to understanding the text?** This cartoon first appeared in *Ethical Consumer* magazine, a publication whose mission is to provide information to consumers about products and brands that are socially and environmentally responsible. The magazine has an obvious bias against buying products for the sake of status rather than necessity, and against companies or organizations motivated primarily by profit. The readers of *Ethical Consumer* are likely to be practical or even frugal, to frown upon materialism, and to be skeptical of big business.

- **What do you notice first? Where is your eye drawn? What is your overall first impression?** Although there's quite a bit going on in these frames, your eye is probably drawn most immediately to the written text that is in bold: WORK HARDER / EARN MORE MONEY / BUY MORE THINGS / KEEP GOING. Since the written text appears in the same place within each frame, it also might be seen as a way to structure the piece.

- **What topic does the visual address or raise? Does the visual make a claim about that topic?** With rats racing all over the place within frames and from frame to frame, clearly the topic is the rat race—an allusion to the well-known expression. Even at this early stage of analysis, the artist's claim that the rat race is a never-ending cycle of working to earn money to buy material possessions becomes pretty clear.

(See insert for color version.)
SOURCE: www.polyp.org.uk.

- **Does the text tell or suggest a narrative or story? If so, what is the point?** The frames constitute a story, a narrative: the key "characters" are rats that seem to be caught in a maze; the idea of a trap is emphasized by the rats' bodies appearing in pieces, fragmented, with only one example of a whole body being in the picture. The sign at the top ("Happiness is just around the corner!") is repeated in each frame, a slogan that seems to cheer the rats on and keep them on task.

- **What emotions does the visual text evoke? How do color or light and shadow contribute to evoking emotions?** You might feel a range of emotions being evoked. First of all, it's hard not to see something comic about the bug-eyed rats with human expressions who are frantically running either from or toward something, though it's not clear which. Red usually evokes an alarm button in viewers. The background is a little more subtle, but the closer you look, the world beyond the "maze" goes from lighter to darker shades, suggesting a workday, the morning-until-night routine. That background does not have any trees or natural shapes but, rather, industrial-looking smokestacks and buildings.

- **Are the figures realistic, caricatures, distorted? What is the effect?** The rats themselves are caricatures, distortions with huge heads and eyes. They never interact with one another but are depicted as looking at the signs or maybe watching one another; there's no contact between or among them.

- **Are any of the images visual allusions that would evoke emotions or memories in viewers?** We've already noted the overarching allusion to "the rat race," a common expression people use to refer to a situation that involves ceaseless activity with little meaning. In addition, the signs on the walls of each frame remind us of advertisements that entice us to buy things or acquire luxuries. They're promises of a better physical appearance or lifestyle.

- **What cultural values are viewers likely to bring to the images?** Viewers are likely to be familiar with the cultural values implicit in such advertising ploys, though maybe more subtle ones, to grab their attention and make them want to spend money. The artist leads us clearly to the irony of committing to the draining rat race in order to "spoil yourself" and "escape from it all."

- **What claim does the visual make about the issue(s) it addresses?** Let's take stock of what we have observed thus far and connect some of those observations. We have exaggerated images of rats in a maze working to make money to buy things that require them to continue working to make money to pay for those things and the next things that promise happiness. The red color and the exaggerated characteristics of the mice signal a fevered urgency that the cartoon's overall message mocks. The rats live crowded, frantic lives driven by the pursuit of material goods and fueled by ads, slogans, and other external stimuli. It's true that we are making an inferential leap, but given all these specifics, we can fairly conclude that the artist's claim is one of value: "the rat race just isn't worth it!" Or, to state it more formally, "the constant striving to make money in order to spend money can never bring satisfaction, only more striving."

If we think about this analysis in the terms of argument we have used throughout this chapter, each of the four frames might be thought of as a paragraph. In each one the artist refutes a counterargument: happiness is just around the corner if you work harder, if you earn more money, if you buy more things, if you keep going. These slogans become assertions that the drawings refute as the rats become increasingly frantic within the confines of the boxes and as day turns to night. The argument seems to be organized inductively because as each slogan (assertion) is refuted by the images of the rats who are anything but happy as they face yet another "corner," the viewer draws the conclusion that the rat race is thankless, useless, and never a route to happiness.

Photographs are another type of visual text that can make powerful arguments. How often do we look at the photograph on the front page of a newspaper or news site before we read the lead story? The photo in that case may greatly impact how we read the written text by shaping our attitude toward the piece, or even by leading us to form conclusions before reading so much as a single word.

In fact, photographic images carry additional power because they seem "real," authentic, images of truth frozen in time. No political cartoon has ever claimed to be "reality." But it is important to understand that while photographs may be more "real" than a drawing, they nevertheless are artificial. The photographer must decide how to light a scene, what to focus on, when to take the picture, what to put inside the frame and outside of it, and how to compose the shot in order to convey the desired meaning. Unfortunately, combining the power of the photographic image has at times resulted in the irresistible temptation to pose or construct an image to make a point. But even if the image is not doctored, a photograph is constructed to tell a story, evoke emotions, and make a strong argument.

Let's examine an iconic photograph called *The Steerage*, taken in 1907 by photographer Alfred Stieglitz (see p. 136). We might start with a definition of *steerage*, which is the cheapest accommodation on a passenger ship — originally the compartments containing the steering apparatus. Stieglitz did not take the photograph for a particular publication because by this point he was already a highly regarded artist who championed the relatively new medium of photography as an art form. The context is the early twentieth century, when immigration to the United States was at a high point. The photograph depicts the wealthier classes aboard ship on the deck above the poorer classes, who are housed in the steerage. Notice how your eye is immediately drawn to the empty gangway that separates the two groups. This point of focus raises the issue of separation, even segregation.

This time, instead of going through the checklist step-by-step as we did with *Rat Race*, let's just think about how the style of this photo might be seen as evidence used to make its claim. In what ways might that gangway be symbolic? Why would Stieglitz choose the moment when it is empty? What story is this photograph telling? Note the similarities and differences between the two groups depicted. Stieglitz juxtaposes them. Some differences, such as dress, are stark; yet what similarities do you see? How does Stieglitz want his audience — his viewers — to experience the people in this scene? Why do you suppose we see the group in the top more straight on, face-to-face, while the people in the lower level in many instances have their backs to us? Think about the time period, and ask yourself what cultural values the viewers — those who frequent art galleries and are familiar with artists of the day — bring to this image. Granted, the technology did not make color photos an option, but notice the many shades of light and dark, the shadows, the highlighted areas: What mood does this moment frozen in time suggest? How does the evocation of mood add to the pathos of the scene? What claim — or claims — is Stieglitz making through this visual image?

Alfred Stieglitz, *The Steerage.* SOURCE: Digital image © The Museum of Modern Art / licensed by SCALA / Art Resource, NY.

• ACTIVITY •

The Heroes of 2001 stamp depicts a photograph taken at Ground Zero after the September 11 terrorist attacks on the Twin Towers in New York City. Analyze the photograph's argument, and explain why it is or is not an effective choice for a stamp for the U.S. Postal Service.

(See insert for color version.)

• ESSAY IN PROGRESS: Using Visual Evidence •

Find a visual text—a political cartoon, advertisement, photograph, or the like—that supports or enhances the argument you have been developing. Write a paragraph or two explaining how the visual text makes its own argument.

• CULMINATING ACTIVITY •

The political cartoon and article that follow make similar claims about the Nobel Peace Prize awarded to President Barack Obama in 2009, but in very different ways. The Tom Toles cartoon appeared in the *Washington Post*; the article appeared in the London *Times*. Discuss the way each argument is developed and the likely impact of each on its audience.

Comment: Absurd Decision on Obama Makes a Mockery of the Nobel Peace Prize

MICHAEL BINYON

The award of this year's Nobel Peace Prize to President Obama will be met with widespread incredulity, consternation in many capitals and probably deep embarrassment by the President himself.

Rarely has an award had such an obvious political and partisan intent. It was clearly seen by the Norwegian Nobel Committee as a way of expressing European gratitude for an end to the Bush Administration, approval for the election of America's first black president and hope that Washington will honour its promise to re-engage with the world.

Instead, the prize risks looking preposterous in its claims, patronising in its intentions and demeaning in its attempt to build up a man who has barely begun his period in office, let alone achieved any tangible outcome for peace.

The pretext for the prize was Mr. Obama's decision to "strengthen international diplomacy and co-operation between peoples." Many people will point out that, while the President has indeed promised to "reset" relations with Russia and offer a fresh start to relations with the Muslim world, there is little so far to show for his fine words.

East–West relations are little better than they were six months ago, and any change is probably due largely to the global economic downturn; and America's vaunted determination to re-engage with the Muslim world has failed to make any concrete progress towards ending the conflict between the Israelis and the Palestinians. 5

There is a further irony in offering a peace prize to a president whose principal preoccupation at the moment is when and how to expand the war in Afghanistan.

The spectacle of Mr. Obama mounting the podium in Oslo to accept a prize that once went to Nelson Mandela, Aung San Suu Kyi and Mother Theresa would be all the more absurd if it follows a White House decision to send up to 40,000 more U.S. troops to Afghanistan. However just such a war may be deemed in Western eyes, Muslims would not be the only group to complain that peace is hardly compatible with an escalation in hostilities.

The Nobel Committee has made controversial awards before. Some have appeared to reward hope rather than achievement: the 1976 prize for the two peace campaigners in Northern Ireland, Betty Williams and Mairead Corrigan, was clearly intended to send a signal to the two battling communities in Ulster. But the political influence of the two winners turned out, sadly, to be negligible.

In the Middle East, the award to Menachem Begin of Israel and Anwar Sadat of Egypt in 1978 also looks, in retrospect, as naive as the later award to Yassir Arafat, Shimon Peres and Yitzhak Rabin—although it could be argued that both the Camp David and Oslo accords, while not bringing peace, were at least attempts to break the deadlock.

Mr. Obama's prize is more likely, however, to be compared with the most contentious prize of all: the 1973 prize to Henry Kissinger and Le Duc Tho for their negotiations to end the Vietnam War. Dr. Kissinger was branded a warmonger for his support for the bombing campaign in Cambodia; and the Vietnamese negotiator was subsequently seen as a liar whose government never intended to honour a peace deal but was waiting for the moment to attack South Vietnam. 10

Mr. Obama becomes the third sitting U.S. President to receive the prize. The committee said today that he had "captured the world's attention." It is certainly true that his energy and aspirations have dazzled many of his supporters. Sadly, it seems they have so bedazzled the Norwegians that they can no longer separate hopes from achievement. The achievements of all previous winners have been diminished.

> • **ESSAY IN PROGRESS: First Draft** •
>
> Write a full argument that includes at least three different types of evidence and a visual text. You have been developing this essay throughout the chapter: use the texts and drafts you've developed thus far, as you like, but do not hesitate to rethink and revise. Suggested length: 500–700 words.

Glossary of Argument Terms and Fallacies

ad hominem   Latin for "to the man," this fallacy refers to the specific diversionary tactic of switching the argument from the issue at hand to the character of the other speaker. If you argue that a park in your community should not be renovated because the person supporting it was arrested during a domestic dispute, then you are guilty of *ad hominem*.

ad populum (**bandwagon appeal**)   This fallacy occurs when evidence boils down to "everybody's doing it, so it must be a good thing to do."
You should vote to elect Rachel Johnson — she has a strong lead in the polls!
Polling higher does not necessarily make Senator Johnson the "best" candidate, only the most popular.

appeal to false authority   This fallacy occurs when someone who has no expertise to speak on an issue is cited as an authority. A TV star, for instance, is not a medical expert, even though pharmaceutical advertisements often use celebrity endorsements.

argument   A process of reasoned inquiry; a persuasive discourse resulting in a coherent and considered movement from a claim to a conclusion.

assumption   See **warrant**.

backing   In the Toulmin model, backing consists of further assurances or data without which the assumption lacks authority. For an example, see **Toulmin model**.

bandwagon appeal   See *ad populum*.

begging the question   A fallacy in which a claim is based on evidence or support that is in doubt. It "begs" a question whether the support itself is sound.
Giving students easy access to a wealth of facts and resources online allows them to develop critical thinking skills.

circular reasoning   A fallacy in which the writer repeats the claim as a way to provide evidence.
You can't give me a C; I'm an A student!

claim   Also called an assertion or a proposition, a claim states the argument's main idea or position. A claim differs from a topic or subject in that a claim has to be arguable.

claim of fact   A claim of fact asserts that something is true or not true.

> *The number of suicides and homicides committed by teenagers, most often young men, has exploded in the last three decades . . .*
>
> —ANNA QUINDLEN

claim of policy   A claim of policy proposes a change.

> *Yet one solution continues to elude us, and that is ending the ignorance about mental health, and moving it from the margins of care and into the mainstream where it belongs.*
>
> —ANNA QUINDLEN

claim of value   A claim of value argues that something is good or bad, right or wrong.

> *There's a plague on all our houses, and since it doesn't announce itself with lumps or spots or protest marches, it has gone unremarked in the quiet suburbs and busy cities where it has been laying waste.*
>
> —ANNA QUINDLEN

classical oration, the   Five-part argument structure used by classical rhetoricians. The five parts are:

introduction (*exordium*)   Introduces the reader to the subject under discussion.

narration (*narratio*)   Provides factual information and background material on the subject at hand or establishes why the subject is a problem that needs addressing.

confirmation (*confirmatio*)   Usually the major part of the text, the confirmation includes the proof needed to make the writer's case.

refutation (*refutatio*)   Addresses the counterargument. It is a bridge between the writer's proof and conclusion.

conclusion (*peroratio*)   Brings the essay to a satisfying close.

closed thesis   A closed thesis is a statement of the main idea of the argument that also previews the major points the writer intends to make.

> *The three-dimensional characters, exciting plot, and complex themes of the Harry Potter series make them not only legendary children's books but also enduring literary classics.*

deduction   Deduction is a logical process whereby one reaches a conclusion by starting with a general principle or universal truth (a major premise) and applying it to a specific case (a minor premise). The process of deduction is usually demonstrated in the form of a syllogism:

MAJOR PREMISE: Exercise contributes to better health.

MINOR PREMISE: Yoga is a type of exercise.

CONCLUSION: Yoga contributes to better health.

either/or (false dilemma)   A fallacy in which the speaker presents two extreme options as the only possible choices.

Either we agree to higher taxes, or our grandchildren will be mired in debt.

fallacy   See **logical fallacy**.

faulty analogy   A fallacy that occurs when an analogy compares two things that are not comparable. For instance, to argue that because we put animals who are in irreversible pain out of their misery, we should do the same for people, asks the reader to ignore significant and profound differences between animals and people.

first-hand evidence   Evidence based on something the writer *knows*, whether it's from personal experience, observations, or general knowledge of events.

hasty generalization   A fallacy in which a faulty conclusion is reached because of inadequate evidence.

Smoking isn't bad for you; my great aunt smoked a pack a day and lived to be 90.

induction — From the Latin *inducere*, "to lead into"; a logical process whereby the writer reasons from particulars to universals, using specific cases in order to draw a conclusion, which is also called a generalization.

> Regular exercise promotes weight loss.
>
> Exercise lowers stress levels.
>
> Exercise improves mood and outlook.
>
> GENERALIZATION: Exercise contributes to better health.

logical fallacy   Logical fallacies are potential vulnerabilities or weaknesses in an argument. They often arise from a failure to make a logical connection between the claim and the evidence used to support it.

open thesis   An open thesis is one that does not list all the points the writer intends to cover in an essay.

The popularity of the Harry Potter series demonstrates that simplicity trumps complexity when it comes to the taste of readers, both young and old.

post hoc ergo propter hoc   This fallacy is Latin for "after which therefore because of which," meaning that it is incorrect to always claim that something is a cause just because it happened earlier. One may loosely summarize this fallacy by saying that correlation does not imply causation.

We elected Johnson as president and look where it got us: hurricanes, floods, stock market crashes.

qualifier   In the Toulmin model, the qualifier uses words like *usually, probably, maybe, in most cases,* and *most likely* to temper the claim, making it less absolute. For an example, see **Toulmin model**.

quantitative evidence   Quantitative evidence includes things that can be measured, cited, counted, or otherwise represented in numbers — for instance, statistics, surveys, polls, census information.

rebuttal In the Toulmin model, a rebuttal gives voice to possible objections. For an example, see **Toulmin model**.

reservation In the Toulmin model, a reservation explains the terms and conditions necessitated by the qualifier. For an example, see **Toulmin model**.

Rogerian arguments Developed by psychiatrist Carl Rogers, Rogerian arguments are based on the assumption that having a full understanding of an opposing position is essential to responding to it persuasively and refuting it in a way that is accommodating rather than alienating.

second-hand evidence Evidence that is accessed through research, reading, and investigation. It includes factual and historical information, expert opinion, and quantitative data.

straw man A fallacy that occurs when a speaker chooses a deliberately poor or oversimplified example in order to ridicule and refute an idea.

> *Politician X proposes that we put astronauts on Mars in the next four years. Politician Y ridicules this proposal by saying that his opponent is looking for "little green men in outer space."*

syllogism A logical structure that uses the major premise and minor premise to reach a necessary conclusion.

> MAJOR PREMISE: Exercise contributes to better health.
>
> MINOR PREMISE: Yoga is a type of exercise.
>
> CONCLUSION: Yoga contributes to better health.

Toulmin model An approach to analyzing and constructing arguments created by British philosopher Stephen Toulmin in his book *The Uses of Argument* (1958). The Toulmin model can be stated as a template:

> Because (evidence as support), therefore (claim), since (warrant or assumption), on account of (backing), unless (reservation).
>
> *Because it is raining, therefore I should probably take my umbrella, since it will keep me dry on account of its waterproof material, unless, of course, there is a hole in it.*

warrant In the Toulmin model, the warrant expresses the assumption necessarily shared by the speaker and the audience.

4

Synthesizing Sources
Entering the Conversation

We all draw on the ideas of others as we develop our own positions, regardless of the topic. Whether you are explaining your opinion about an issue specific to your community (such as whether to allow skateboarding in public parks), or you are developing a position on a national or global issue (such as whether to change immigration policies), you should know as much as possible about the topic. Rather than make a quick response that reflects an opinion based only on what you already know, you must research and read sources — what others have written. Then you can develop your own *informed* opinion, a measured response that considers multiple perspectives and possibilities. We call this process **synthesis**, which involves considering various viewpoints in order to create a new and more informed viewpoint.

Think of it this way: You show up at a party. There are a dozen different conversations going on. You approach one group of people who are having a heated debate. You'll need to listen for a while to understand what the specific topic is, what has already been said, who is taking what side, and what they're not saying. Then, by either expanding on what others are saying, challenging what others are saying, or filling in a gap in their understanding, you will begin to enter this conversation and make your own contribution. And that's what synthesis is all about: entering the conversation that society is having about a topic. You enter the conversation by carefully reading and understanding the perspectives and ideas surrounding an issue, examining your own ideas on the matter, and then synthesizing these views into a more informed position than the one you began with.

When you're learning about a subject, look for reliable sources. Be aware of the **bias** that a source brings to the topic. Consider the speaker: What does he or she believe in? How might the speaker's position provide personal gain? Don't look for a pro-and-con debate that represents only polarized views; look for a range of viewpoints. This might sound like a lot to keep in mind, but don't worry, you work with sources all the time. When you decide to buy a new cell phone, you gather information by exploring different sources. You might consult *Consumer Reports* and other technology magazines. You'd compare prices and technical specs. You'd ask your friends for their opinions and experiences, and you might go to a computer store and talk with the experts. You might read reviews online or use forums as a quick source for many opinions. But you might not talk to your grandfather, who may be new to cell phones himself, nor would you get all of your information from a salesperson, who likely works on commission. The final result of your inquiry is a purchase, not an essay, but you just synthesized a range of sources in order to make the argument to yourself that the phone you chose is the best fit for you.

• ACTIVITY •

Write a brief paragraph about a time that you used multiple sources to help make a decision. You can choose something as simple as a decision about which movie to see or which shoes to purchase or as serious as which colleges to apply to. Discuss how each source contributed to your decision and how you decided which ones were more or less influential. You may consult written sources as well as more informal ones such as conversations.

Using Sources to Inform an Argument

As we discussed in Chapter 3, many different types of evidence can serve to support an argument. But it is important to remember that your sources should enhance, not replace, your argument. You may worry that the ideas of others are so persuasive that you have nothing new to say. Or you may think that the more sources you cite, the more impressed your reader (especially your teacher) will be. But as you develop your skills in writing synthesis essays, you will find that the sources inform your own ideas and demonstrate your understanding of opposing views. What *you* have to say is the main event; *your* position is central.

In the following example, Laura Hillenbrand, author of *Seabiscuit*, a Pulitzer Prize–winning book about a champion racehorse who beat the odds, maintains her own voice throughout even when she uses the work of experts to help make a point. (She identifies them in a section at the end of the book.) But whether she is quoting directly or paraphrasing, she never gets lost in the sources or allows them to overwhelm her ideas.

from *Seabiscuit*
LAURA HILLENBRAND

To pilot a racehorse is to ride a half-ton catapult. It is without question one of the most formidable feats in sport. The extraordinary athleticism of the jockey is unparalleled: A study of the elements of athleticism conducted by Los Angeles exercise physiologists and physicians found that of all major sports competitors, jockeys may be, pound for pound, the best overall athletes. They have to be. To begin with, there are the demands on balance, coordination, and reflex. A horse's body is a constantly shifting topography, with a bobbing head and neck and roiling muscle over the shoulders, back, and rump. On a running horse, a jockey does not sit in the saddle, he crouches over it, leaning all of his weight on his toes, which rest on the thin metal bases of stirrups dangling about a foot from the horse's topline. When a horse is in full stride, the only parts of the jockey that are in continuous contact with the animal are the insides of the feet and ankles—everything else is balanced in midair. In other words, jockeys squat on the pitching backs of their mounts, a task much like perching on the grille of a car while it speeds down a twisting, potholed freeway in traffic. The stance is, in the words of University of North Carolina researchers, "a situation of dynamic imbalance and ballistic opportunity." The center of balance is so narrow that if jockeys shift only slightly rearward, they will flip right off the back. If they tip more than a few inches forward, a fall is almost inevitable. A thoroughbred's neck, while broad from top to bottom, is surprisingly narrow in width, like the body of a fish. Pitching up and down as the horse runs, it offers little for the jockey to grab to avoid plunging to the ground and under the horse's hooves.

Jockey (video), Tel-Air Productions, 1980.

A. E. Waller et al., "Jockey Injuries in the United States," *Journal of the American Medical Association*, 2000; vol. 283, no. 10.

Rather than citing her sources within the text, Hillenbrand includes the information about the sources she cites at the end of her book. The first item is a video-tape about the study by Los Angeles exercise physiologists and physicians; the second is an article in a medical journal. Both acknowledge that she turned to authorities—sources—to deepen and supplement her own knowledge about the mechanics and physics of how a racehorse and a jockey move as one entity.

• ACTIVITY •

In the following passage from *A Level Playing Field: African American Athletes and the Republic of Sports*, Gerald L. Early discusses the complex character of Jackie Robinson, the first black athlete to play in major league baseball. What is the purpose of the sources Early chooses to include? How do they enhance or detract from his own voice? What is the purpose of each of the notes documenting the sources?

---

from *A Level Playing Field*
GERALD L. EARLY

But 1949 was also Robinson's year of liberation. According to Branch Rickey, known as the Mahatma by sportswriters, the Dodgers executive who signed Robinson and who pushed for integration: "For three years [that was the agreement] this boy was to turn the other cheek. He did, day after day, until he had no other to turn. They were both beat off. There were slight slip-ups on occasion in that first year in Montreal."[1]

Robinson had agreed to ignore all slights, insults, and abuses that he endured on the playing field during his first three years as a professional ballplayer in the white leagues. This generated, naturally, a certain public sympathy, as Robinson did, indeed, endure much abuse, and he did not have a natural or an easy camaraderie with most of his white teammates. He became almost a perfect Gandhi-like figure of sacrifice and forbearance, and he created the paradigm for how integration was to proceed in the United States in the 1950s and early 1960s—the Noble Negro who, through his nobility, a mystical product of his American heritage of suffering but enduring devotion to the foundational principles of American life, legitimates white institutions as he integrates them. As the *New York Times* put it in 1950, "The going wasn't easy. Jackie Robinson met open or covert hostility with the spirit of a gallant gentleman. He kept his temper, he kept his poise and he played good baseball. Now he has won his battle. No fan threatens to riot, no player threatens to go on strike when Jackie Robinson, or any one of several Negroes, takes the field."[2] This is the Robinson that is always remembered when his career is reexamined today. He is almost always sentimentalized.

But it must be remembered that Robinson played major league baseball with the Dodgers for ten years, only two of which were under this agreement. (The agreement also included the year in Montreal.) So for most of his career as a big league ballplayer, Robinson did not act in any sort of self-sacrificing non-violent way. He was a tough, almost chip-on-the-shoulder player, a particularly aggressive athlete who usually took umbrage at the least slight or unfairness he felt on the field. He understood that high-performance sports were about intimidation, and he was not about to be intimidated.[3]

---

1. Branch Rickey, with Robert Riger, *The American Diamond: A Documentary of the Game of Baseball* (New York: Simon & Schuster, 1965), p. 46.
2. "Jackie Robinson's New Honor," *New York Times*, December 8, 1950.
3. "In 1950, and the years to come, Jack battled with umpires over matters not simply of judgment but of ethics, in his growing belief that the umpires, all white, were abusing their power in order to put him in his place." See Rampersad, *Jackie Robinson*, p. 229; see also Jackie Robinson, "Now I Know Why They Boo Me!" *Look*, January 25, 1955, pp. 22–28.

Using Sources to Appeal to an Audience

If you were writing an in-class essay, would you take the time to put together a bibliography? Of course not. But you would prepare a bibliography for a formal research paper because that writing has a different purpose and the audience has different expectations. A writer must analyze the rhetorical situation in order to determine what is appropriate, even when it comes to sources and documentation. (See the rhetorical triangle, p. 4.)

Now let's consider a topic and examine how sources were used and identified for three different audiences. The following excerpts are from three pieces about indirect speech by the linguist and cognitive scientist Steven Pinker.

The first example is from an article in *Time* magazine written for a general audience of readers interested primarily in understanding the basics of Pinker's ideas. (The rest of this article appears on pp. 745–8.)

from *Words Don't Mean What They Mean*

Why don't people just say what they mean? The reason is that conversational partners are not modems downloading information into each other's brains. People are very, very touchy about their relationships. Whenever you speak to someone, you are presuming the two of you have a certain degree of familiarity—which your words might alter. So every sentence has to do two things at once: convey a message and continue to negotiate that relationship.

The clearest example is ordinary politeness. When you are at a dinner party and want the salt, you don't blurt out, "Gimme the salt." Rather, you use what linguists call a whimperative, as in "Do you think you could pass the salt?" or "If you could pass the salt, that would be awesome."

Taken literally, these sentences are inane. The second is an overstatement, and the answer to the first is obvious. Fortunately, the hearer assumes that the speaker is rational and listens between the lines. Yes, your point is to request the salt, but you're doing it in such a way that first takes care to establish what linguists call "felicity conditions," or the prerequisites to making a sensible request. The underlying rationale is that the hearer not be given a command but simply be asked or advised about one of the necessary conditions for passing the salt. Your goal is to have your need satisfied without treating the listener as a flunky who can be bossed around at will.

Note that there are no formal sources cited. The technical terms that are introduced—*whimperative* and *felicity conditions*—are more playful than technical, and Pinker makes no attempt to cite the academic origin of these terms or the other ideas in this article. He does not go into the research that led to these conclusions. His goal in this brief article for the general reader is to inform and keep moving.

The audience for Pinker's book *The Stuff of Thought: Language as a Window into Human Nature* is interested in exploring his subject more deeply, and his use and citation of sources becomes correspondingly more extensive and formal.

from *The Stuff of Thought*

The double message conveyed with an implicature is nowhere put to greater use than in the commonest kind of indirect speech of all, politeness. Politeness in linguistics does not refer to social etiquette, like eating your peas without using your knife, but to the countless adjustments that speakers make to avoid the equally countless ways that their listeners might be put off. People are very, very touchy, and speakers go to great lengths not to step on their toes. In their magisterial work *Politeness: Some Universals in Language Use*, the anthropologists Penelope Brown and Stephen Levinson . . . extended Grice's theory by showing how people all over the world use politeness to lubricate their social interactions.[1]

Politeness Theory begins with Erving Goffman's observation that when people interact they constantly worry about maintaining a nebulous yet vital commodity called "face" (from the idiom "to save face").[2] Goffman defined face as a positive social value that a person claims for himself. Brown and Levinson divide it into positive face, the desire to be approved (specifically, that other people want for you what you want for yourself), and negative face, the desire to be unimpeded or autonomous. The terminology, though clumsy, points to a fundamental duality in social life, which has been discovered in many guises and goes by many names: solidarity and status, connection and autonomy, communion and agency, intimacy and power, communal sharing and authority ranking.[3]

---

1. Brown & Levinson, 1987b. See also Brown, 1987; Brown & Gilman, 1972; Fraser, 1990; Green, 1996; Holtgraves, 2002.
2. Goffman, 1967.
3. Fiske, 1992; Fiske, 2004; Haslam, 2004; Holtgraves, 2002.

While this is not a scientific study, it is also not a brief and breezy article in a magazine with a very wide readership. The audience of a book of this sort has some interest in this topic—they have chosen to read a whole book on linguistics and cognition—and because of that, Pinker feels comfortable not just summarizing the latest thinking in the field, but introducing terminology common to research in linguistics and tracing the origins of concepts back to their academic origins. He also formally (and fully) cites his sources using extensive endnotes that appear at the back of the book.

Finally, take a look at this selection from a scholarly article by Pinker in the academic journal *Intercultural Pragmatics*.

from *The Evolutionary Social Psychology of Off-Record Indirect Speech Acts*

The double message conveyed with an implicature is nowhere put to greater use than in the commonest kind of indirect speech, politeness. In their seminal work *Politeness: Some Universals in Language Use*, Brown and Levinson (1987b) extended Grice's theory by showing how people in many (perhaps all) cultures use politeness to lubricate their social interactions.

Politeness Theory begins with Goffman's (1967) observation that when people interact they constantly worry about maintaining a commodity called "face" (from the idiom "to save face"). Goffman defined face as a positive social value that a person claims for himself. Brown and Levinson divide it into positive face, the desire to be approved (specifically, that other people want for you what you want for yourself), and negative face, the desire to be unimpeded or autonomous. The terminology points to a fundamental duality in social life which goes by many names: solidarity and status, connection and autonomy, communion and agency, intimacy and power, communal sharing and authority ranking (Fiske 1992, 2004; Haslam 2004; Holtgraves 2002). Later we will see how these wants come from two of the three major social relations in human life.

Brown and Levinson argue that Grice's Cooperative Principle applies to the maintenance of face as well as to the communication of data. Conversationalists work together, each trying to maintain his own face and the face of his partner. The challenge is that most kinds of speech pose at least some threat to the face of the hearer. The mere act of initiating a conversation imposes a demand on the hearer's time and attention. Issuing an imperative challenges her status and autonomy. Making a request puts her in the position where she might have to refuse, earning her a reputation as stingy or selfish. Telling something to someone implies that she was ignorant of the fact in the first place. And then there are criticisms, boasts, interruptions, outbursts, the telling of bad news, and the broaching of divisive topics, all of which can injure the hearer's face directly.

At the same time, people have to get on with the business of life, and in doing so they have to convey requests and news and complaints. The solution is to make amends with politeness: the speaker sugarcoats his utterances with niceties that reaffirm his concern for the hearer or that acknowledge her autonomy. Brown and Levinson call the stratagems positive and negative politeness, though better terms are sympathy and deference.

References

Brown, Penelope, and Stephen C. Levinson. 1987a. Introduction to the reissue: A review of recent work. In *Politeness: Some universals in language use.* New York: Cambridge University Press.

—. 1987b. *Politeness: Some universals in language usage.* New York: Cambridge University Press.

Fiske, Alan P. 1992. The four elementary forms of sociality: Framework for a unified theory of social relations. *Psychological Review,* 99: 689–723.

—. 2004. Four modes of constituting relationships: Consubstantial assimilation; space, magnitude, time, and force; Concrete procedures; Abstract symbolism. In N. Haslam (ed.), *Relational models theory: A contemporary overview.* Mahwah: Erlbaum Associates.

Goffman, Erving. 1959. *The presentation of self in everyday life.* New York: Doubleday.

—. 1967. On face-work: An analysis of ritual elements in social interaction. In *Interaction ritual: Essays on face-to-face behavior.* New York: Random House.

Grice, Herbert P. 1975. Logic and conversation. In P. Cole & J. L. Morgan (eds.), *Syntax & Semantics* Vol. 3: Speech acts. New York: Academic Press.

Haslam, Nick. (ed.). 2004. *Relational models theory: A contemporary overview.* Mahwah: Erlbaum Associates.

Holtgraves, Tom M. 2002. *Language as social action.* Mahwah: Erlbaum Associates.

Notice that for this academic audience of researchers and scholars who bring a good deal of prior knowledge to the text, Pinker chooses other scholarly works as his sources and documents them thoroughly in a style that gives those sources more emphasis. Rather than just putting the citations at the back of the book, he embeds the source names throughout for direct reference and then includes a detailed Works Cited list at the end of the article. Many readers, likely familiar with these sources, will find Pinker's text more authoritative because he has included them.

As you can see, the type of evidence and the way it is documented depends on audience and situation. But what does all of this have to do with the writing you will be doing? The texts we have examined in this chapter were written by journalists, professors, and scholars; the sources they use and the ways they document them are appropriate for their audiences. In school, you have probably written essays for which you were required to use outside sources, sources that were assigned to you, or sources that were part of your classroom readings. Keep in mind that your goal in a synthesis essay is the same as that of professional writers: to use sources to support and illustrate your own ideas and to establish your credibility as a reasonable and informed writer. Whether your teacher wants you to make informal in-text citations or use formal in-text parenthetical documentation and an end-of-paper Works Cited list, as prescribed by the Modern Language Association (MLA), you must document sources to give credit where credit is due.

• ACTIVITY •

To set themselves apart, columnists for print and online publications establish a viewpoint and style. The types of sources they use and the way they use them are part of that style. Using three columns by one writer, analyze the columnist's audience by examining the types of sources he or she uses. You might consider a political commentator, a sportswriter, a movie or music reviewer, or a columnist in a local publication.

Conversation
Mandatory Community Service

In this section, we will walk you through the process of writing a synthesis essay: understanding the task, analyzing a series of readings, and writing an argument using them.

Here is your prompt:

> Using the following documents on community service requirements in high schools, write an essay explaining whether you believe that high schools in general — or your specific school or district — should make community service mandatory. Incorporate references to or quotations from a minimum of three of these sources in your essay.

Before reading the texts, think about how the sources will help you complete the assignment. As we've discussed, sources can illustrate or support your own ideas. If you think that community service requirements are worthwhile, then you can look to your sources to help you make that point. But it's important not to reject texts that disagree with your position or are not directly relevant to it. In fact, you might use a text that presents an opinion in opposition to yours as a counterargument, and then concede and refute it. Most important, keep an open mind while you read the sources so your thesis shows that you understand the complexity of the subject of community service.

Sources

1. **Neil Howe and William Strauss,** from *Millennials Rising*
2. **The Dalton School,** *Community Service Mission Statement*
3. *Detroit News, Volunteering Opens Teen's Eyes to Nursing*
4. **Dennis Chaptman,** *Study: "Resume Padding" Prevalent in College-Bound Students Who Volunteer*
5. **Arthur Stukas, Mark Snyder, and E. Gil Clary,** from *The Effects of "Mandatory Volunteerism" on Intentions to Volunteer*
6. **Mark Hugo Lopez,** from *Youth Attitudes toward Civic Education and Community Service Requirements*

1. from *Millennials Rising*

NEIL HOWE AND WILLIAM STRAUSS

The following excerpt from a 2000 book by two social historians tries to define the characteristics of Americans who are coming of age in a new millennium.

The definition of "community service" has morphed from one generation to the next, dating back to World War II. For the Silent Generation [the generation that came of age in the 1940s], community deed-doing was channeled by the Selective Service law, which pushed young males toward socially acceptable deferments such as teaching, science, or even marriage. For leading-edge Boomers, the term "community service" often meant cleaning hospital bedpans to avoid Vietnam — or for the more radically minded, spurring oppressed neighborhoods to vent their grievances against the "establishment." When the draft ended, in 1973, first-wave Boomers had eliminated mandatory civic duty for their later cohorts and the generation to follow. Growing up in the era of the Volunteer Army, Gen Xers developed their own ethic of volunteerism, de-emphasizing great crusades in favor of simple acts of charity to help needy people. For teenagers, "community service" came to mean punishment for drunk drivers and Breakfast Club miscreants.

By the Millennial era [people born between 1982 and 2002], the notion of volunteering gave way to a more compulsory "service learning," which is now often required for graduation from middle or high school. Bolstered by Acts of Congress in 1990 and 1993, which created the Learn and Serve America program, the integration of community service with academic study has spread to schools everywhere. From 1984 to 1999, the share of high schools offering any kind of community service program grew from 17 to 83 percent, and the share with "service learning" grew from 9 to 46 percent. Two-thirds of all public schools at all grade levels now have students engaged in community work, often . . . as part of the curriculum.

A new Millennial service ethic is emerging, built around notions of collegial (rather than individual) action, support for (rather than resistance against) civic institutions, and the tangible doing of good deeds. Surveys show that five of every six Millennials believe their generation has the greatest duty to improve the environment — and that, far more than older people, Millennials would impose extra civic duties on themselves, including taxes to achieve results.

2. *Community Service Mission Statement*

The Dalton School

The following mission statement is from a small private school in Manhattan.

Community Service is something that needs to be done. Community Service situates our moral center; it teaches us through experience — about the relationship between empathy and responsibility, about what it takes to be part of a community, in essence, about being human. Inherent in the notion of Community Service are the feelings of optimism and empowerment: we are optimistic that the world can change for the better and when empowered to effect that change, we as individuals can make a difference. There are no more important lessons that we can learn and teach.

For Survival

We are members of many communities: family, school, neighborhood, city, country, religion, and ethnic group. It is from these communities that we gain our sustenance. We must each play a role in contributing to our communities so that these communities can continue to survive and prosper. Benevolent action is essential to the survival and prosperity of any community. We must engage in Community Service because it needs to be done and because we need our communities to survive.

For a Moral Center

Community Service is vital to the healthy community. A community that takes without giving back, that is indifferent to the needs of its fellow members, that is only concerned with individual measures of success, is a weak, unsound community. The strength of a community can be found in its moral center; the ability to articulate and act upon a defined moral center will fortify a community. The moral center of a community, that place where we can find the values of empathy, compassion, and caring, is the basis for civic responsibility and the success of that community.

For Personal Enrichment

Doing Community Service is empowering. When an individual goes out in the world and interacts with other people in the spirit of bettering, that individual makes a contribution and will feel a sense of accomplishment.

We are reminded all too often of the cynicism, indifference, and isolation that exists in our society. Community Service, the taking of physical action, reminds us of our connection and ability to connect. It is important to study the great actions of others, but participating in Community Service enables the individual to learn for himself and to teach herself.

For the Institutional Community

Our school is a place of learning; we need to integrate the ideals of Community Service into our academic curriculum. Because Community Service embodies experiential learning, locating a moral center, community health, because it is about empowerment and making the world a better place, because these issues are at the core of being, we need to do it. The desire to act comes from a pride, caring, and respect for a community. Community Service must be harnessed to foster a sense of community in a school, a neighborhood, and beyond.

3. *Volunteering Opens Teen's Eyes to Nursing*

The following human interest story appeared in the *Detroit News* in 2008.

If you asked 13-year-olds to make a list of their favorite after-school activities, visiting with the elderly probably wouldn't be a top choice. But it would be for John Prueter, son of Keith and Barbara Prueter of Essexville, who says he'd spend time with older generations every day if he could.

"All the older people are nice people," he said. "They like to see young people come visit in these homes." Prueter, a seventh-grader at Cramer Junior High School, spends much of his after-school time at the Alterra Sterling House, an assisted-living home in Hampton Township.

Prueter got into volunteering with the elderly almost two years ago when his great-grandmother, Mable Post, suffered a stroke. Always close to her, Prueter visited her regularly when she was in the hospital. After 100 days, she was transferred to Alterra, where she still lives. Now, instead of coming just to visit a relative, he comes to volunteer and visit with everyone. He is the youngest of Alterra's regular volunteers and one of the most frequent visitors.

Prueter spends his time there helping with activities such as cooking and gardening, playing games with residents and just chatting with them. He speaks to the residents on a level that makes them feel good, said Pam O'Laughlin, executive director for Alterra's Bay City campus. "He has a unique ability to communicate with these folks," she said. "He's not timid. They look forward to him coming." Prueter sometimes takes the residents small gifts, such as cake on a birthday, and often calls them when he cannot come in.

He's willing to help Alterra's staff with any activities, O'Laughlin said. For example, he helped residents make cheesecakes for Easter. He helps with gardening and crafts, and calls the bingo games each Sunday. He also helps with mail delivery, assists nurses and helps residents get ready for special trips or concerts.

Virginia Ball, an 85-year-old resident, says Prueter visits with her regularly when he stops in. He runs and answers her phone when he hears it ringing down the hall and helps out with other tasks. "He'll offer to fold laundry," she said. But if there is nothing to do to help, Prueter will just sit in her room and chat. "He seems to enjoy talking to older people," Ball said.

His service at Alterra earned him an outstanding youth volunteer award from Veterans of Foreign Wars Post 6950. Prueter wants to be in the marching band when he moves up to Garber High School. But he says he doesn't plan on letting practice get in the way of his visits to Alterra. Even after high school, Prueter hopes to continue working with the elderly by studying nursing. He says he became interested in the field because of his volunteer work.

His dream job, he says, is working where he volunteers now.

4. *Study: "Resume Padding" Prevalent in College-Bound Students Who Volunteer*

DENNIS CHAPTMAN

The following article appeared in 2006 in the *University of Wisconsin–Madison News*, a newsletter published by the university's communication office.

Although the rates of volunteerism among high schoolers appear to be healthy, a study by a UW–Madison researcher suggests that "resume-padding"—not simple altruism—may be the driving force.

Lewis Friedland, a professor of journalism and mass communication, says his research in Madison-area high schools "calls into question some of the vibrancy apparent in the high rate of youth volunteerism."

"The near universality of this college resume padding really surprised me," Friedland says.

The high schoolers Friedland, along with sociology doctoral candidate Shauna Morimoto and other students, interviewed held an overwhelming belief that volunteering would be a key to college admission.

"Resume padding is a symptom of the extraordinary pressure put on young people to achieve a college education, and the very explicit understanding that a college education is a means to a decent life in the middle class," the study found. 5

Many young people said that their motive in becoming involved was to make a stronger case to please college admissions officers—regardless of whether they were applying to an Ivy League school, a state university or a technical college.

But Friedland notes that, despite the widespread beliefs of college-bound students, service criteria usually only come into play in truly selective schools, those with an admissions rate of 50 percent or less.

Friedland says that civic activities are part of the expectation of high-achievers in high school, while others recognize their more precarious position. They see that college is within reach, but only if they perform enough of the "right" activities outside of the classroom.

"Young people have a lot of different motivations, some altruistic, some genuinely religious, some genuinely civic. But they rarely appeared in a pure form," Friedland says. . . .

One implication of the study, which has yet to be proven, is that when civic 10 engagement and volunteerism are used to achieve a short-term goal, the long-term effect of that activity may decline, Friedland says.

"We are faced with a generation of young people coming up in a different world," he says. "Their attachments are more fleeting and there is a lack of attachment that seems to pervade."

5. from *The Effects of "Mandatory Volunteerism" on Intentions to Volunteer*

ARTHUR STUKAS, MARK SNYDER, AND E. GIL CLARY

The following is from an article that appeared in 1999 in the professional journal *Psychological Science*.

Two studies suggest that community service requirements can have negative effects on students' intentions to volunteer freely in the future but only when students feel that they aren't ready to volunteer or that the requirement is too controlling. Students who are ready to volunteer should be less influenced by requirements to serve.

Students who were not "ready" to volunteer were less affected by the free choice condition — that is, researchers were able to persuade them to volunteer while making sure that they still felt that it was their free choice and they were more likely to want to volunteer in the future than "not ready" students who had been required. Students were just as likely to want to continue volunteering after being required as after having a free choice to volunteer. To avoid the negative effects of mandatory volunteer programs on students' motivation, institutions should design these programs to contain an element of free choice and to offer programs that allow students to choose the type of volunteer activity they will engage in or allow them to combine personal interests and skills with their service requirements. Researchers found that students who initially did not want to volunteer found that they actually enjoyed helping others if requirements were applied gently and with their input and involvement in the process.

6. from *Youth Attitudes toward Civic Education and Community Service Requirements*

MARK HUGO LOPEZ

The following graphs are from an academic study conducted in 2002 by the the Center for Information and Research on Civic Learning and Engagement.

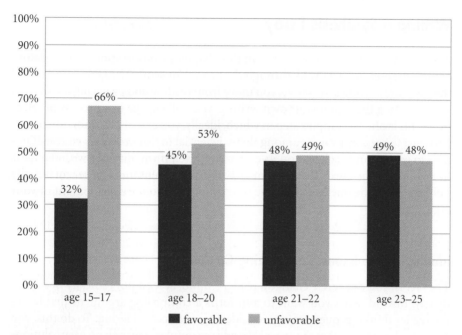

Graph 1 Attitudes toward Requiring Community Service for a High School Diploma, by Age. SOURCE: CIRCLE/Council for Excellence in Government Youth Survey, 2002.

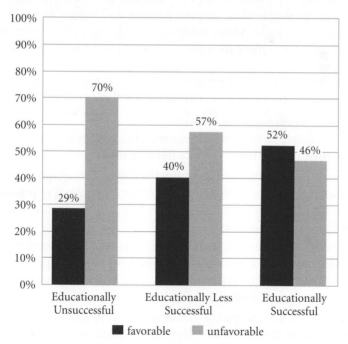

Graph 2 Attitudes toward Requiring Community Service for a High School Diploma, by Level of Educational Success. SOURCE: CIRCLE/Council for Excellence in Government Youth Survey, 2002.

Writing a Synthesis Essay

Now that you have read the sources in this chapter's Conversation on mandatory community service, let's walk through the process of synthesizing the sources and then writing a synthesis essay. As you move from reading and analyzing the sources to integrating them into your own writing, you will engage in a process of selection. This is often a complex step in which, ideally, you explore the individual texts and start to see connections among them. Essential to this process is your willingness to understand each text on its own terms, even if you disagree with the ideas or position; in fact, texts that present viewpoints different from those you initially hold are often the ones that become most important to the development of your argument.

Identifying the Issues: Recognizing Complexity

The fact is, you can rarely change a reader's mind, at least not radically or immediately. Instead, what you want to aim for is a compelling argument that leaves the reader thinking, questioning, considering, and reconsidering. To do this, you have to acknowledge that the issue at hand is a complex one with no easy solutions and a variety of valid perspectives on the matter. You want to present a reasonable idea in a voice that is logical, sincere, and informed. To write a qualified argument, you must anticipate objections to your position and recognize and respect the complexities of your topic. A reasonable voice recognizes that there are more than two sides to an issue — more than pro–con, which is the written equivalent of a shouting match.

Careful reading has already revealed some of the complexities surrounding the issue of mandatory community service in schools. Let's explore a few.

- Source 1, the excerpt from *Millennials Rising*, describes what community service has meant for various generations, ranging from Selective Service in the early twentieth century to service learning today.

- Source 2, the mission statement from the Dalton School, offers an argument for community service based on morality and a sense of responsibility to a community. However, the statement is from a small private school. Might this limit its wider application?

- Source 3, "Volunteering Opens Teen's Eyes to Nursing," is quite positive and possibly persuasive if you are writing in support of community service. However, it focuses on the experience of a seventh-grader, which might not be relevant to high schools.

- Source 4, on resume padding, is a good counterexample to Source 3. It reports on the cynical attitude of students who perform community service specifically to bolster their college applications. Would nationwide mandatory community service eliminate this issue? Would it make it more difficult for truly altruistic students to distinguish themselves?

- Source 5, on mandatory volunteerism, reports that requiring community service may discourage future involvement, making it less likely that volunteering will become a lifelong habit. Does this finding ring true for you?

- Source 6, the graphs from Mark Hugo Lopez's study, raise further questions about required community service. Graph 1 shows that support for requiring such service is weakest among those currently in school and is evenly split among those over the age of twenty-one. Does this finding suggest that community service is "good medicine" for high school students, who will eventually appreciate the experience? Graph 2 shows that young people with greater levels of education ("Educationally Successful," signifying completion of a BA or some college work, as opposed to only a high school education) are more likely to support a community service requirement in high schools.

Formulating Your Position

Before you formulate your position, it might be helpful to take stock of the issues. In analyzing the texts on community service, the following issues emerge:

- Does requiring community service devalue it?
- Does requiring it discourage future participation?
- Does the positive experience that most volunteers have offset their initial reluctance to participate?
- How does the structure of the community service program affect its perceived value? Is it part of academic study? Are there choices?
- How would making community service mandatory affect the fact that many students volunteer for selfish reasons, namely, padding their resumes for college?
- What values about community and education underlie a service requirement?
- Does requiring volunteer work go beyond the jurisdiction of schools? If it's not done during school hours, are the requirements violating students' rights? After all, mandatory community service is a punishment for minor criminals.
- What influence does socioeconomic status play in such a requirement? For example, if students need to earn money in their free time, can required community service programs be designed to accommodate them?
- How does a school system determine how many hours of service to require?

These questions—and others you might have—illustrate the complexity of the issue and ensure that you do not develop an argument that is one-sided or polarized between yes and no. Instead, you are now prepared to write a documented essay that reflects the complexities surrounding the topic.

With these questions and issues in mind, you can begin to formulate a thesis, or claim, that captures your position on the topic. Consider the following working thesis statements:

- Community service can be extremely valuable in the development of both character and academics, but the negative effects of forcing students to participate by making it a graduation requirement more than offset the benefits.

- Though students may not recognize the value of community service until later in life, high schools should require community service to instill a sense of civic responsibility and encourage a lifelong habit of helping others.

- High schools should encourage students to participate in community service and reward those who do so without making participation mandatory for graduation.

- Required community service programs are beneficial to both the individuals who participate and the communities being served, as long as students have some choice in the type of service they engage in.

Although you might want to tailor one of these working thesis statements to use in your essay, each one suggests a clear focus while acknowledging the complexities of the issue.

• ACTIVITY •

Of the thesis statements above, select one you *disagree with*. Then, using the readings in the Conversation on mandatory community service, find three pieces of evidence supporting that thesis.

Framing Quotations

When writing with sources, it's important not to simply summarize or paraphrase the sources. You need to use the sources to strengthen your own argument. One easy way to make sure the sources are working for you is to include a sentence or two of explanation or commentary with each quote. You might use a lead-in sentence, so your readers know what to look for, as is demonstrated below:

> Even without a service learning requirement, today's youth have shown that they are enthusiastic about serving the community. Howe and Strauss indicate that five out of six Millennials "believe their generation has the greatest duty to improve the environment" and would accept additional "civic duties" to bring about needed change.

Alternatively, you might follow a quote with a sentence or two of commentary to remind readers of your point and how the quote reinforces it, as you see here:

The Dalton School, a small private high school, phrases it hopefully in the mission statement, which speaks of "empowering" students and "situating our moral center." It continues on to argue (rather ominously) that "we must engage in community service because . . . we need our communities to survive." The strong goals stated in this argument are certainly attractive, but their loftiness seems far removed from what a student might practically aim to achieve. In this regard, the Dalton School's teaching goals are admirable but impractical because they seem to forget the individual student.

And, of course, be careful not to represent ideas or words as your own if they are not: give credit where it is due!

Integrating Quotations

When using multiple sources in your writing, it becomes even more important to incorporate the quotations in a way that is both clear and interesting. You want the transition from your own voice to others' words and ideas to be smooth and natural sounding. The most effective way to accomplish this is to integrate the quotations into your own sentences. This may be a bit challenging, but the benefit is seamless prose. When you integrate quotations in this way, the reader can follow your ideas and see the sources in the context of your argument. Be sure that the result is a grammatically correct and syntactically fluent sentence, like this one:

> Howe and Strauss indicate that five out of six Millennials "believe their generation has the greatest duty to improve the environment" and would accept additional "civic duties" to bring about needed change.

• ACTIVITY •

Below you will find a paragraph written using the mission statement from the Dalton School as a source. Read the paragraph, and then revise it in order to make more effective use of the source.

Proponents of mandatory service learning programs often argue that whether a student chooses for himself or not, the spirit of service is important for students to learn and for schools to teach. The Dalton School, a small private high school, opens its mission statement by asserting, "Community Service is something that needs to be done." The argument is that this experience "teaches us through experience—about the relationship between empathy and responsibility, about what it takes to be part of a community, in essence, about being human." The strong goals of the Dalton School's program are attractive because they emphasize the importance of having each individual "play a role in contributing to our communities so that these communities can continue to survive and prosper." The contribution this experience makes to academic growth is not the only emphasis, though it is important: "Our school is a place of learning; we

> need to integrate the ideals of Community Service into our academic curriculum." The heart of the Dalton School's program is, however, what they term the "moral center" that "will fortify a community." This is more than merely service; it is "that place where we can find the values of empathy, compassion, and caring" and "is the basis for civic responsibility and the success of that community."

Citing Sources

Since you will be quoting from several works, you have to keep track of your sources for your reader. In timed situations, you'll probably include only the source number or the author's name in parentheses after the quote or paraphrase, like this:

> Modern Americans will recognize the term "service learning," a phrase made familiar by the two-thirds of public schools that have integrated community service into the educational curriculum (Howe and Strauss).

You need to cite paraphrases as well, not just direct quotes. Anytime you are using someone else's ideas, you must give them credit.

Another, more elegant, option is to mention the author and title of the work in the sentence introducing or including the quote:

> Howe and Strauss indicate that five out of six Millennials "believe their generation has the greatest duty to improve the environment" and would accept additional "civic duties" to bring about needed change.

If you are writing a more formal research paper, you will likely need to follow MLA documentation procedures, including a Works Cited page. Ask your teacher if you are unclear about what is required for an assignment. Guidelines for MLA documentation appear in the back of this book.

As you go through the readings and other texts in the following chapters, you will join conversations on a range of topics, reflecting on and integrating the ideas of others from different times and places into your own thinking and writing. Each chapter includes a Conversation in which you will practice this skill with a series of texts (including visuals) related to the chapter's theme. You should also be aware of the conversations going on around you all the time. How do people call on sources to reinforce their positions? And how do people enter an ongoing conversation and move it forward?

A Sample Synthesis Essay

Following is a brief synthesis essay about community service that incorporates the sources we have discussed. Note how the viewpoint expressed in the thesis statement remains central, with sources supplementing and supporting that view.

Americans today will recognize the term "service learning," a phrase made familiar by the two-thirds of public schools that have integrated community service into the educational curriculum (Howe and Strauss). However, according to Neil Howe and William Strauss's book *Millennials Rising*, the term only came into our vocabulary with the newest, or "Millennial," generation of Americans. In the past, people simply "volunteered." Creating a new policy to enforce an age-old practice seems superfluous, and studies show that it actually discourages high school students from performing public service. Because mandating public service is unnecessary and can have a negative effect on students' attitudes, schools should encourage students to participate in community service without making it mandatory for graduation.

Discussion of the evolution of the terms — from "service learning" to "volunteering" — leads up to the thesis.

Thesis statement indicates the main argument about making public service mandatory.

Even without a service learning requirement, today's youth have shown that they are enthusiastic about serving the community. Howe and Strauss indicate that five out of six Millennials "believe their generation has the greatest duty to improve the environment" and would accept additional "civic duties" to bring about needed change. Indeed, students are investing themselves in service activities for reasons other than to fulfill a school requirement.

Topic Sentence #1 focuses on the author's first point and makes an assertion that will be supported by sources.

Quotation from one source supports the point made in the topic sentence.

A *Detroit News* article introduces us to thirteen-year-old John Prueter, for example, who began volunteering at an assisted-living home when his great-grandmother became a resident there. Prueter had "always [been] close to" his great-grandmother, and this genuine, personal investment in his work, the article tells us, was what made the experience meaningful for him. Prueter's example demonstrates that the most beneficial service experiences — for the individual and the community — are those that students can and do choose for themselves.

A second source brings up another dimension to the assertion in Topic Sentence #1.

It has also been shown that making public service compulsory can extinguish the natural spirit of volunteerism. According to two studies published in the journal *Psychological Science*, harsh requirements mandating community service "can have negative effects on students' intentions to volunteer freely in the future." The same studies also found that students were more likely to volunteer in the future if they began volunteering out of "free choice." Furthermore, the sense that service learning is "required" not only to graduate high school but to get into a good college has driven many students to volunteer out of self-interest rather than altruism. "Many young people said that their motive in becoming involved was to make a stronger case to please college admissions officers,"

Topic Sentence #2 raises a second point — that is, the negative consequences of "making public service compulsory."

The writer provides several sentences of discussion of the source being cited.

reported an article in the *University of Wisconsin–Madison News*. High schools should not support this distorted mind-set by explicitly requiring public service; rather, they should allow authentic enthusiasm and encourage service projects of the students' own choosing.

Second source supporting the topic sentence. The writer integrates quotations into her own sentences.

Topic Sentence #3 raises a counterargument.

Proponents of mandatory service learning programs may argue that whether a student chooses it for himself or not, the spirit of service is important to learn and to teach. The Dalton School, a small private high school, phrases it hopefully in the mission statement, which speaks of "empowering" students and "situating our moral center." It continues on to argue (rather ominously) that "we must engage in community service because . . . we need our communities to survive." The strong goals stated in this argument are certainly attractive, but their loftiness seems far removed from

The opening clause is a concession to the counterargument.

The last two sentences refute the counterargument.

what a student might practically aim to achieve. In this regard, the Dalton School's teaching goals are admirable but impractical because they seem to forget the individual student. And as Prueter's case demonstrates, individual interest and personal investment are essential for service experiences to truly last.

On both sides of the debate, we should agree that the ultimate goal of "service learning" is precisely that — teaching an experience that will last. Even the Dalton School admits to the reality of school as a stop along the way to what happens when

The conclusion opens with common ground.

The writer returns to two of her sources to emphasize the importance of choice in community service activities.

"an individual goes out in the world." The issue thus concerns not just how to get students started volunteering, but how to maintain that desire to serve. At thirteen, John Prueter already knows that "his dream job . . . is working where he volunteers now." His story, along with the data supporting "free choice" in service projects, proves that the surest way to have students volunteer in the future is to allow them experiences that are personally valuable. Those experiences will come not from any heavy-handed school requirement, but from support and, most important, the freedom of choice.

The concluding paragraph answers the "so what?" question. The writer goes beyond simple repetition of the thesis. Note that the writer returns to the terminology — "service learning" — from the opening paragraph.

Culminating Conversation

The Dumbest Generation?

Students today live and learn in a world with vastly more complex technology than that of previous generations. Many people see this new technology as a way to expand and distribute knowledge. They call it the information age. Others lament the constant distractions that accompany this onslaught of information. But, of course, there is a long tradition of critics bemoaning the harmful effects of technological change on younger generations. In his best-selling book *The Dumbest Generation*, social critic and professor Mark Bauerlein claims that — as his book's title suggests — those under age thirty constitute the "dumbest" generation in modern history. In his explanation of why he wrote the book, Bauerlein says, "I've noticed in the last ten years that students are no less intelligent, no less ambitious, but there are two big differences: Reading habits have slipped, along with general knowledge. You can quote me on this: You guys don't know anything."

Carefully read the following eight sources, including the introductory information for each source. Then synthesize information from at least three of the sources, and incorporate it into a coherent, well-developed essay that evaluates the claim that those under age thirty are "the dumbest generation."

Make sure that your own argument is central; use the sources to illustrate and support your reasoning. Avoid merely summarizing the sources. Indicate clearly which sources you are drawing from, whether through direct quotation, paraphrase, or summary. You may cite the sources as Source 1, Source 2, and so on, or by putting the author's name in parentheses.

Sources

1. **Mark Bauerlein,** *The Dumbest Generation*
2. **Sharon Begley,** *The Dumbest Generation? Don't Be Dumb*
3. **Mizuko Ito et al.,** *Living and Learning with New Media: Summary of Findings from the Digital Youth Project*
4. **Nicholas Carr,** *Is Google Making Us Stupid?*
5. **R. Smith Simpson,** *Are We Getting Our Share of the Best?*
6. **Steven Johnson,** *Your Brain on Video Games*
7. **Clive Thompson,** *The New Literacy*
8. **Roz Chast,** *Shelved* (cartoon)

1. *The Dumbest Generation*

MARK BAUERLEIN

The following is excerpted from a 2008 book about the effects of digital media on young people by Mark Bauerlein, an English professor and researcher at Emory University.

This is the paradox of the Dumbest Generation. For the young American, life has never been so yielding, goods so plentiful, schooling so accessible, diversion so easy, and liberties so copious. The material gains are clear, and each year the traits of worldliness and autonomy seem to trickle down into ever-younger age groups. But it's a shallow advent. As the survey research shows, knowledge and skills haven't kept pace, and the intellectual habits that complement them are slipping. The advantages of twenty-first century teen life keep expanding, the eighties and nineties economy and the digital revolution providing miraculously quick and effortless contact with information, wares, amusements, and friends. The mind should profit alongside the youthful ego, the thirst for knowledge satisfied as much as the craving for fun and status. But the enlightenment hasn't happened. Young Americans have much more access and education than their parents did, but in the 2007 Pew survey on "What Americans Know: 1989–2007," 56 percent of 18- to 29-year-olds possessed low knowledge levels, while only 22 percent of 50- to 64-year-olds did. In other words, the advantages don't show up in intellectual outcomes. The mental equipment of the young falls short of their media, money, e-gadgets, and career plans. The 18-year-old may have a Visa card, cell phone, MySpace page, part-time job, PlayStation 2, and an admissions letter from State U., but ask this wired and on-the-go high school senior a few intellectual questions and the façade of in-the-know-ness crumbles.

2. *The Dumbest Generation? Don't Be Dumb*

Sharon Begley

The following is excerpted from an article by science columnist Sharon Begley that appeared in *Newsweek* in May 2010.

A more fundamental problem is what Bauerlein has in mind by "dumbest." If it means "holding the least knowledge," then he has a case. Gen Y cares less about knowing information than knowing where to find information. . . . And it is a travesty that employers are spending $1.3 billion a year to teach basic writing skills, as a 2003 survey of managers found. But if dumb means lacking such fundamental cognitive capacities as the ability to think critically and logically, to analyze an argument, to learn and remember, to see analogies, to distinguish fact from opinion . . . well, here Bauerlein is on shakier ground.

First, IQ scores in every country that measures them, including the United States, have been rising since the 1930s. Since the tests measure not knowledge but pure thinking capacity—what cognitive scientists call fluid intelligence, in that it can be applied to problems in any domain—then Gen Y's ignorance of facts (or of facts that older people think are important) reflects not dumbness but choice. And who's to say they are dumb because fewer of them than of their grandparents' generation care who wrote the oratorio "Messiah" (which 35 percent of college seniors knew in 2002, compared with 56 percent in 1955)? Similarly, we suspect that the decline in the percentage of college freshmen who say it's important to keep up with political affairs, from 60 percent in 1966 to 36 percent in 2005, reflects at least in part the fact that in 1966 politics determined whether you were going to get drafted and shipped to Vietnam. The apathy of 2005 is more a reflection of the world outside Gen-Yers' heads than inside, and one that we bet has changed tack with the historic candidacy of Barack Obama. Alienation is not dumbness.

Bauerlein is not the first scholar to pin the blame for a younger generation's intellectual shortcomings on new technology (television, anyone?), in this case indicting "the digital age." But there is no empirical evidence that being immersed in instant messaging, texting, iPods, videogames and all things online impairs thinking ability. "The jury is still out on whether these technologies are positive or negative" for cognition, says Ken Kosik of the University of California, Santa Barbara, codirector of the Neuroscience Research Institute there. "But they're definitely changing how people's brains process information." In fact, basic principles of neuroscience offer reasons to be optimistic. "We are gradually changing from a nation of callused hands to a nation of agile brains," says cognitive scientist Marcel Just of Carnegie Mellon University. "Insofar as new information technology exercises our minds and provides more information, it has to be improving thinking ability."

3. *Living and Learning with New Media: Summary of Findings from the Digital Youth Project*

Mizuko Ito et al.

The following is excerpted from a 2008 study of the effects of digital media on young people.

In both friendship-driven and interest-driven online activity, youth create and navigate new forms of expression and rules for social behavior. In the process, young people acquire various forms of technical and media literacy by exploring new interests, tinkering, and "messing around" with new forms of media. They may start with a Google search or "lurk" in chat rooms to learn more about their burgeoning interest. Through trial and error, youth add new media skills to their repertoire, such as how to create a video or customize games or their MySpace page. Teens then share their creations and receive feedback from others online. By its immediacy and breadth of information, the digital world lowers barriers to self-directed learning.

Others "geek out" and dive into a topic or talent. Contrary to popular images, geeking out is highly social and engaged, although usually not driven primarily by local friendships. Youth turn instead to specialized knowledge groups of both teens and adults from around the country or world, with the goal of improving their craft and gaining reputation among expert peers. What makes these groups unique is that while adults participate, they are not automatically the resident experts by virtue of their age. Geeking out in many respects erases the traditional markers of status and authority.

New media allow for a degree of freedom and autonomy for youth that is less apparent in a classroom setting. Youth respect one another's authority online, and they are often more motivated to learn from peers than from adults. Their efforts are also largely self-directed, and the outcome emerges through exploration, in contrast to classroom learning that is oriented toward set, predefined goals.

4. *Is Google Making Us Stupid?*

Nicholas Carr

The following is from an article in the summer 2008 issue of the *Atlantic*, a national magazine.

Over the past few years I've had an uncomfortable sense that someone, or something, has been tinkering with my brain, remapping the neural circuitry, reprogramming the memory. My mind isn't going—so far as I can tell—but it's changing. I'm not thinking the way I used to think. I can feel it most strongly when I'm reading. Immersing myself in a book or a lengthy article used to be easy. My mind would get caught up in the narrative or the turns of the argument, and I'd spend hours strolling through long stretches of prose. That's rarely the case anymore. Now my concentration often starts to drift after two or three pages. I get fidgety, lose the thread, begin looking for something else to do. I feel as if I'm always dragging my wayward brain back to the text. The deep reading that used to come naturally has become a struggle.

I think I know what's going on. For more than a decade now, I've been spending a lot of time online, searching and surfing and sometimes adding to the great databases of the Internet. The Web has been a godsend to me as a writer. Research that once required days in the stacks or periodical rooms of libraries can now be done in minutes. A few Google searches, some quick clicks on hyperlinks, and I've got the telltale fact or pithy quote I was after. Even when I'm not working, I'm as likely as not to be foraging in the Web's info-thickets reading and writing e-mails, scanning headlines and blog posts, watching videos and listening to podcasts, or just tripping from link to link to link. (Unlike footnotes, to which they're sometimes likened, hyperlinks don't merely point to related works; they propel you toward them.)

For me, as for others, the Net is becoming a universal medium, the conduit for most of the information that flows through my eyes and ears and into my mind. The advantages of having immediate access to such an incredibly rich store of information are many, and they've been widely described and duly applauded. "The perfect recall of silicon memory," *Wired*'s Clive Thompson has written, "can be an enormous boon to thinking." But that boon comes at a price. As the media theorist Marshall McLuhan pointed out in the 1960s, media are not just passive channels of information. They supply the stuff of thought, but they also shape the process of thought. And what the Net seems to be doing is chipping away my capacity for concentration and contemplation. My mind now expects to take in information the way the Net distributes it: in a swiftly moving stream of particles. Once I was a scuba diver in the sea of words. Now I zip along the surface like a guy on a Jet Ski.

5. *Are We Getting Our Share of the Best?*

R. Smith Simpson

The following is excerpted from a 1962 article in the U.S. government's *Foreign Service Journal.*

My initial surprise was to find among the candidates an abysmal ignorance of so elementary a subject as the geography of the United States. Few could even place accurately the principal rivers: one with so descriptive a name as the Ohio was not infrequently identified as being "somewhere west of the Mississippi." Few could name the principal seaports, and, of course, any requirement demanding such detailed familiarity with this country as identifying the states comprising the "wheat belt" or the "corn belt" was completely beyond the average candidate's depth.

As to elementary economics and social data, most could only guess at the population, labor force, and gross national product of their country. Many did not know what constituted "gross national product." They had no clear idea as to the principal products of their country, nor as to its exports and imports. They could name a few of each, but had no notion of their relative importance and had given no thought to the role of imports in the American economy.

As with elementary geographic and economic aspects of the United States, so with historical, sociological, and cultural. Americans abroad are asked a great many questions about their country. How did the United States acquire the Panama Canal? What is its status now? Who started our war with Spain (or Mexico) and what came out of it? When did our labor movement start and where does it stand now? How does a Jimmy Hoffa get control of a powerful union? What were some of the reform movements in American history? What became of them?

A good half of our candidates could answer such questions with only the thinnest recital of facts; many could not discuss them at all. Some could not recall ever having heard of the Populist movement; few knew its connection with Woodrow Wilson's "New Freedom." Asked if he knew anything about the Progressive movement, one candidate replied, "Oh, yes, that was LaFollette's movement." To the question, "Where did LaFollette come from?" he could only reply vaguely, "Somewhere out West."

6. *Your Brain on Video Games*

STEVEN JOHNSON

The following is excerpted from an article in the July 2005 issue of *Discover,* a popular science magazine.

To understand why games might be good for the mind, begin by shedding the cliché that they are about improving hand-eye coordination and firing virtual weapons. The majority of video games on the best-seller list contain no more bloodshed than a game of Risk. The most popular games are not simply difficult in the sense of challenging manual dexterity; they challenge *mental* dexterity as well. The best-selling game of all time, *The Sims,* involves almost no hand-eye coordination or quick reflexes. One manages a household of characters, each endowed with distinct drives and personality traits, each cycling through an endless series of short-term needs (companionship, say, or food), each enmeshed in a network of relationships with other characters. Playing the game is a nonstop balancing act: sending one character off to work, cleaning the kitchen with another, searching through the classifieds for work with another. Even a violent game like *Grand Theft Auto* involves networks of characters that the player must navigate and master, picking up clues and detecting patterns. The text walk-through for *Grand Theft Auto III*—a document that describes all the variables involved in playing the game through to the finish—is 53,000 words long, the length of a short novel. But despite the complexity of these environments, most gamers eschew reading manuals or walk-throughs altogether, preferring to feel their way through the game space. . . .

Among all popular media today, video games are unique in their reliance on the regime of competence principle. Movies or television shows don't start out with simple dialogue or narrative structures and steadily build in complexity depending on the aptitude of individual viewers. Books don't pause midchapter to confirm that their readers' vocabularies have progressed enough to move on to more complicated words. By contrast, the training structure of video games dates back to the very origins of the medium; even Pong got more challenging as a player's skills improved. Moreover, only a fraction of today's games involve explicit violence, and sexual content is a rarity. But the regime of competence is everywhere.

7. *The New Literacy*

CLIVE THOMPSON

The following is excerpted from the August 2009 issue of *Wired*, a popular technology magazine.

As the school year begins, be ready to hear pundits fretting once again about how kids today can't write—and technology is to blame. Facebook encourages narcissistic blabbering, video and PowerPoint have replaced carefully crafted essays, and texting has dehydrated language into "bleak, bald, sad shorthand" (as University College of London English professor John Sutherland has moaned). An age of illiteracy is at hand, right?

Andrea Lunsford isn't so sure. Lunsford is a professor of writing and rhetoric at Stanford University, where she has organized a mammoth project called the Stanford Study of Writing to scrutinize college students' prose. From 2001 to 2006, she collected 14,672 student writing samples—everything from in-class assignments, formal essays, and journal entries to emails, blog posts, and chat sessions. Her conclusions are stirring.

"I think we're in the midst of a literacy revolution the likes of which we haven't seen since Greek civilization," she says. For Lunsford, technology isn't killing our ability to write. It's reviving it—and pushing our literacy in bold new directions.

The first thing she found is that young people today write far more than any generation before them. That's because so much socializing takes place online, and it almost always involves text. Of all the writing that the Stanford students did, a stunning 38 percent of it took place out of the classroom—life writing, as Lunsford calls it. Those Twitter updates and lists of 25 things about yourself add up.

It's almost hard to remember how big a paradigm shift this is. Before the Internet came along, most Americans never wrote anything, ever, that wasn't a school assignment. Unless they got a job that required producing text (like in law, advertising, or media), they'd leave school and virtually never construct a paragraph again.

But is this explosion of prose good, on a technical level? Yes. Lunsford's team found that the students were remarkably adept at what rhetoricians call *kairos*—assessing their audience and adapting their tone and technique to best get their point across. The modern world of online writing, particularly in chat and on discussion threads, is conversational and public, which makes it closer to the Greek tradition of argument than the asynchronous letter and essay writing of 50 years ago.

8. *Shelved*

Roz Chast

The following cartoon appeared on the cover of the *New Yorker* in October 2010.

(See insert for color version.)

Education

*To what extent do our schools serve the goals
of a true education?*

Education is a concept as difficult to define as it is essential to our identity. What makes a person educated? Is a skilled artisan with no formal schooling educated? Is a wise grandmother with eighty years of life experience but only a third-grade education educated? Is Bill Gates, who dropped out of Harvard as a junior to found Microsoft, more or less educated than his classmates who stayed in school? When we are seeking education, are we looking for knowledge, wisdom, skills, or all three?

Describing the purpose of education raises even more questions. Is it to prepare citizens to participate in a democracy? Is it to teach practical skills for the workforce? Or is it to make us more knowledgeable about ourselves and our culture — to know, in the words of the British poet Matthew Arnold, "the best that is known and thought in the world"?

Even Arnold's focus begs several questions: What is "best"? How do we balance what the American educator John Dewey called "mechanical efficiency" with a deep understanding of "democratic ideals"? Should schools impart values as well as knowledge? Do mainstream ideas take precedence over the concerns of individual groups?

Such philosophical questions are often lost in the practical realities of schooling. Advocates of accountability are prescribing more standardized testing, while critics are sounding alarms about the negative effects. We are far from agreement about the best way to teach and learn, tasks made even more challenging by the demands of the international marketplace. What information and skills do students need to compete in a global economy?

The selections in this chapter explore many of these issues. They ask how choices of required reading affect students and whether the humdrum routine of drill contributes to an education. The writers give us an insider's view of what it means to feel excluded from mainstream education by attitude, textbooks, economics, or choice. They discuss how schools in the United States compare with those in other countries. And they ask whether the American high school is obsolete. Together, they lead us to reflect on what education means and whether — and how — our schools embody that vision.

I Know Why the Caged Bird Cannot Read

How American High School Students
Learn to Loathe Literature

FRANCINE PROSE

 Francine Prose, who was born in the late 1940s, is a reporter, essayist, critic, and editor. She has also written more than twenty books, including poetry, fiction, and children's literature. Her novel *Blue Angel* (2000) was a finalist for the National Book Award, and her nonfiction works *The Lives of the Muses: Nine Women and the Artists They Inspired* (2002) and *Reading Like a Writer: A Guide for People Who Love Books and Those Who Want to Write Them* (2006) were both national best sellers. She has received numerous grants and awards, including Guggenheim and Fulbright fellowships. She is most recently the author of the satiric novel *My New American Life* (2011). Prose is currently a book reviewer for a number of magazines and periodicals, including the *New York Times Book Review* and *O*. The following essay, published in *Harper's* in September 1999, is a critique of the quality of required reading in American high schools.

Books discussed in this essay include:
I Know Why the Caged Bird Sings by Maya Angelou. Bantam Books, 1983.
To Kill a Mockingbird by Harper Lee. Warner Books, 1988.
Teaching Values through Teaching Literature by Margaret Dodson.
    Eric/Edinfo Press, 1993.
Teaching the Novel by Becky Alano. Eric/Edinfo Press, 1989.
Teaching Literature by Women Authors by Carolyn Smith McGowen.
    Eric/Edinfo Press, 1993.

Like most parents who have, against all odds, preserved a lively and still evolving passion for good books, I find myself, each September, increasingly appalled by the dismal lists of texts that my sons are doomed to waste a school year reading. What I get as compensation is a measure of insight into why our society has come to admire Montel Williams and Ricki Lake so much more than Dante and Homer. Given the dreariness with which literature is taught in many American classrooms, it seems miraculous that any sentient teenager would view reading as a source of pleasure. Traditionally, the love of reading has been born and nurtured in high school English class — the last time many students will find themselves in a roomful of people who have all read the same text and are, in theory, prepared to discuss it. High school — even more than college — is where literary tastes and allegiances are formed: what we read in adolescence is imprinted on our brains as the dreary notions of childhood crystallize into hard data.

The intense loyalty adults harbor for books first encountered in youth is one probable reason for the otherwise baffling longevity of vintage mediocre novels, books that teachers may themselves have read in adolescence; it is also the most plausible explanation for the peculiar [1998] Modern Library list of the "100 Best Novels of the 20th Century," a roster dominated by robust survivors from the tenth-grade syllabus. *Darkness at Noon, Lord of the Flies, Brave New World*, and *The Studs Lonigan Trilogy* all speak, in various ways, to the vestigial teenage psyches of men of a certain age. The parallel list drawn up by students (younger, more of them female) in the Radcliffe Publishing Course reflects the equally romantic and tacky tastes (*Gone with the Wind, The Fountainhead*) of a later generation of adolescent girls.

Given the fact that these early encounters with literature leave such indelible impressions, it would seem doubly important to make sure that high school students are actually reading literature. Yet every opportunity to instill adolescents with a lifelong affinity for narrative, for the ways in which the vision of an artist can percolate through an idiosyncratic use of language, and for the supple gymnastics of a mind that exercises the mind of the reader is being squandered on regimens of trash and semi-trash, taught for reasons that have nothing to do with how well a book is written. In fact, less and less attention is being paid to what has been written, let alone how; it's become a rarity for a teacher to suggest that a book might be a work of art composed of words and sentences, or that the choice of these words and sentences can inform and delight us. We hear that more books are being bought and sold than ever before, yet no one, as far as I know, is arguing that we are producing and becoming a nation of avid readers of serious literature.

Much has been made of the lemminglike fervor with which our universities have rushed to sacrifice complexity for diversity; for decades now, critics have decried our plummeting scholastic standards and mourned the death of cultural literacy without having done one appreciable thing to raise the educational bar or revive our moribund culture. Meanwhile, scant notice has been paid, except by exasperated parents, to the missed opportunities and misinformation that form the true curriculum of so many high school English classes.

My own two sons, now twenty-one and seventeen, have read (in public and private schools) Shakespeare, Hawthorne, and Melville. But they've also slogged repeatedly through the manipulative melodramas of Alice Walker and Maya Angelou, through sentimental, middlebrow favorites (*To Kill a Mockingbird* and *A Separate Peace*), the weaker novels of John Steinbeck, the fantasies of Ray Bradbury. My older son spent the first several weeks of sophomore English discussing the class's summer assignment, *Ordinary People*, a weeper and former bestseller by Judith Guest about a "dysfunctional" family recovering from a teenage son's suicide attempt.

Neither has heard a teacher suggest that he read Kafka, though one might suppose that teenagers might enjoy the transformative science-fiction aspects of

The Metamorphosis, a story about a young man so alienated from *his* "dysfunctional" family that he turns—embarrassingly for them—into a giant beetle. No instructor has ever asked my sons to read Alice Munro, who writes so lucidly and beautifully about the hypersensitivity that makes adolescence a hell.

In the hope of finding out that my children and my friends' children were exceptionally unfortunate, I recently collected eighty or so reading lists from high schools throughout the country. Because of how overworked teachers are, how hard to reach during the school day, as well as the odd, paranoid defensiveness that pervades so many schools, obtaining these documents seemed to require more time and dogged perseverance than obtaining one's FBI surveillance files—and what I came away with may not be a scientifically accurate survey. Such surveys have been done by the National Council of Teachers of English (published in the 1993 NCTE research report, *Literature in the Secondary Schools*), with results that both underline and fail to reflect what I found.

What emerges from these photocopied pages distributed in public, private, and Catholic schools as well as in military academies, in Manhattan and Denver, in rural Oregon and urban Missouri, is a numbing sameness, unaffected by geography, region, or community size. Nearly every list contains at least one of Shakespeare's plays. Indeed, in the NCTE report, Shakespeare (followed closely by John Steinbeck) tops the rosters of "Ten Most Frequently Required Authors of Book-Length Works, Grades 9–12."

Yet in other genres—fiction and memoir—the news is far more upsetting. On the lists sampled, Harper Lee's *To Kill a Mockingbird* and Maya Angelou's *I Know Why the Caged Bird Sings* are among the titles that appear most often, a grisly fact that in itself should inspire us to examine the works that dominate our children's literary education.

First published in 1970, *I Know Why the Caged Bird Sings* is what we have since 10
learned to recognize as a "survivor" memoir, a first-person narrative of victimization and recovery. Angelou transports us to her childhood in segregated Arkansas, where she was raised by her grandmother and was mostly content, despite the unpleasantness of her white neighbors, until, after a move to St. Louis, eight-year-old Maya was raped by her mother's boyfriend.

One can see why this memoir might appeal to the lazy or uninspired teacher, who can conduct the class as if the students were the studio audience for Angelou's guest appearance on *Oprah*. The author's frequently vented distrust of white society might rouse even the most sluggish or understandably disaffected ninth-graders to join a discussion of racism; her victory over poverty and abuse can be used to address what one fan, in a customer book review on Amazon.com, celebrated as "transcending that pain, drawing from it deeper levels of meaning about being truly human and truly alive." Many chapters end with sententious epigrams virtually begging to serve as texts for sophomoric rumination on such questions as: What does Angelou mean when she writes, "If growing up is painful for the Southern Black girl, being aware of her displacement is rust on the razor that threatens the throat"?

But much more terrifying than the prospect of Angelou's pieties being dissected for their deeper meaning is the notion of her language being used as a model of "poetic" prose style. Many of the terrible mysteries that confront teachers of college freshman composition can be solved simply by looking at Angelou's writing. Who told students to combine a dozen mixed metaphors in one paragraph? Consider a typical passage from Angelou's opaque prose: "Weekdays revolved on a sameness wheel. They turned into themselves so steadily and inevitably that each seemed to be the original of yesterday's rough draft. Saturdays, however, always broke the mold and dared to be different." Where do students learn to write stale, inaccurate similes? "The man's dead words fell like bricks around the auditorium and too many settled in my belly." Who seriously believes that murky, turgid, convoluted language of this sort constitutes good writing? "Youth and social approval allied themselves with me and we trammeled memories of slights and insults. The wind of our swift passage remodeled my features. Lost tears were pounded to mud and then to dust. Years of withdrawal were brushed aside and left behind, as hanging ropes of parasitic moss."

To hold up this book as a paradigm of memoir, of thought—of literature—is akin to inviting doctors convicted of malpractice to instruct our medical students. If we want to use Angelou's work to educate our kids, let's invite them to parse her language, sentence by sentence; ask them precisely what it means and ask why one would bother obscuring ideas that could be expressed so much more simply and felicitously.

Narrated affably enough by a nine-year-old girl named Scout, *To Kill a Mockingbird* is the perennially beloved and treacly account of growing up in a small Southern town during the Depression. Its hero is Scout's father, the saintly Atticus Finch, a lawyer who represents everything we cherish about justice and democracy and the American Way, and who defends a black man falsely accused of rape by a poor white woman. The novel has a shadow hero, too, the descriptively named Boo Radley, a gooney recluse who becomes the occasion for yet another lesson in tolerance and compassion.

Such summary reduces the book, but not by all that much. To read the novel is, for most, an exercise in wish-fulfillment and self-congratulation, a chance to consider thorny issues of race and prejudice from a safe distance and with the comfortable certainty that the reader would *never* harbor the racist attitudes espoused by the lowlifes in the novel. We (the readers) are Scout, her childhood is our childhood, and Atticus Finch is our brave, infinitely patient American Daddy. And that creepy big guy living alone in the scary house turns out to have been watching over us with protective benevolent attention.

Maya Angelou and Harper Lee are not the only authors on the lists. The other most popular books are *The Great Gatsby*, *The Scarlet Letter*, *The Adventures of Huckleberry Finn*, and *The Catcher in the Rye*. John Steinbeck (*The Pearl, Of Mice and Men, The Red Pony, The Grapes of Wrath*) and Toni Morrison (*Song of Solomon, Sula, The Bluest Eye, Beloved*) are the writers — after Shakespeare — represented by the largest number of titles. Also widely studied are the novels of more dubious literary merit: John Knowles's *A Separate Peace*, William Golding's *Lord of the Flies*, Elie Wiesel's *Night*, and Ray Bradbury's *Fahrenheit 451, Dandelion Wine, The October Country*, and *Something Wicked This Way Comes*. Trailing behind these favorites, Orwell (*Nineteen Eighty-Four* and *Animal Farm*) is still being read, as are the Brontës (*Wuthering Heights* and *Jane Eyre*).

How astonishing then that students exposed to such a wide array of masterpieces and competent middlebrow entertainments are not mobbing their libraries and bookstores, demanding heady diets of serious or semi-serious fiction! And how puzzling that I should so often find myself teaching bright, eager college undergraduate and graduate students, would-be writers handicapped not merely by how little literature they have read but by their utter inability to read it; many are nearly incapable of doing the close line-by-line reading necessary to disclose the most basic information in a story by Henry James or a seemingly more straightforward one by Katherine Mansfield or Paul Bowles.

The explanation, it turns out, lies in how these books, even the best of them, are being presented in the classroom. My dogged search for reading lists flushed out, in addition to the lists themselves, course descriptions, teaching guides, and anecdotes that reveal how English literature is being taught to high school students. Only rarely do teachers propose that writing might be worth reading closely. Instead, students are informed that literature is principally a vehicle for the soporific moral blather they suffer daily from their parents. The present vogue for teaching "values" through literature uses the novel as a springboard for the sort of discussion formerly conducted in civics or ethics classes — areas of study that, in theory, have been phased out of the curriculum but that, in fact, have been retained and cleverly substituted for what we used to call English. English — and everything about it that is inventive, imaginative, or pleasurable — is beside the point in classrooms, as is everything that constitutes style and that distinguishes writers, one from another, as precisely as fingerprints or DNA mapping.

The question is no longer what the writer has written but rather who the writer is — specifically, what ethnic group or gender identity an author represents. A motion passed by the San Francisco Board of Education in March 1998 mandates that "works of literature read in class in grades nine to eleven by each high school student must include works by writers of color which reflect the diversity of culture, race, and class of the students of the San Francisco Unified School District. . . . The writers who are known to be lesbian, gay, bisexual or transgender, shall be appropriately identified in the curriculum." Meanwhile, aesthetic beauty — felicitous or accurate language, images, rhythm, wit, the satisfaction of recognizing something in fiction that seems fresh and true — is simply too frivolous, suspect, and elitist even to mention.

Thus the fragile *To Kill a Mockingbird* is freighted with tons of sociopolitical ballast. A "Collaborative Program Planning Record of Learning Experience," which   20

I obtained from the Internet, outlines the "overall goal" of teaching the book ("To understand problems relating to discrimination and prejudice that exist in our present-day society. To understand and apply these principles to our own lives") and suggests topics for student discussion: "What type of people make up your community? Is there any group of people . . . a person (NO NAMES PLEASE) or type of person in your community that you feel uncomfortable around?"

A description of "The Family in Literature," an elective offered by the Princeton Day School—a course including works by Sophocles and Eugene O'Neill— begins: "Bruce Springsteen once tried to make us believe that 'No one can break the ties that bind / You can't for say-yay-yay-yay-yay-yay-yake the ties that bind.' He has since divorced his wife and married his back-up singer. So what are these ties and just how strong are they, after all?" With its chilling echoes of New Age psychobabble, Margaret Dodson's *Teaching Values through Teaching Literature*, a sourcebook for high school English teachers, informs us that the point of Steinbeck's *Of Mice and Men* is "to show how progress has been made in the treatment of the mentally disadvantaged, and that more and better roles in society are being devised for them [and to] establish that mentally retarded people are human beings with the same needs and feelings that everyone else experiences."

An eighth-grader studying Elie Wiesel's overwrought *Night* in a class taught by a passionate gay-rights advocate came home with the following notes: "Many Jews killed during the Holocaust, but many *many* homosexuals murdered by Nazis. Pink triangle—Silence equals death."

It's cheering that so many lists include *The Adventures of Huckleberry Finn*— but not when we discover that this moving, funny novel is being taught not as a work of art but as a piece of damning evidence against that bigot, Mark Twain. A friend's daughter's English teacher informed a group of parents that the only reason to study *Huckleberry Finn* was to decide whether it was a racist text. Instructors consulting *Teaching Values through Teaching Literature* will have resolved this debate long before they walk into the classroom to supervise "a close reading of *Huckleberry Finn* that will reveal the various ways in which Twain undercuts Jim's humanity: in the minstrel routines with Huck as the 'straight man'; in generalities about Blacks as unreliable, primitive and slow-witted. . . ."

Luckily for the teacher and students required to confront this fictional equivalent of a minstrel show, Mark Twain can be rehabilitated—that is to say, revised. In classes that sound like test screenings used to position unreleased Hollywood films, focus groups in which viewers are invited to choose among variant endings, students are polled for possible alternatives to Huck's and Tom Sawyer's actions— should Tom have carried out his plan to "free" Jim?—and asked to speculate on what the fictional characters might have or should have done to become better people and atone for the sins of their creators.

In the most unintentionally hilarious of these lesson plans, a chapter entitled 25 "*Ethan Frome*: An Avoidable Tragedy," Dodson warns teachers to expect resistance to their efforts to reform Wharton's characters and thus improve her novel's outcome: "Students intensely dislike the mere suggestion that Ethan should have honored his commitment to Zeena and encouraged Mattie to date Dennie Eady, yet this would surely have demonstrated greater love than the suicide attempt."

Thus another puzzle confronting college and even graduate school instructors— Why do students so despise dead writers?—is partly explained by the adversarial stance that these sourcebooks adopt toward authors of classic texts. Teachers are counseled "to help students rise above Emerson's style of stating an idea bluntly, announcing reservations, and sometimes even negating the original idea" and to present "a method of contrasting the drab, utilitarian prose of *Nineteen Eighty-four* with a lyric poem 'To a Darkling Thrush,' by Thomas Hardy." Why not mention that such works have been read for years—for a reason!—and urge students to figure out what that reason is? Doesn't it seem less *valuable* to read Emily Dickinson's work as the brain-damaged mumblings of a demented agoraphobic than to approach the subject of Dickinson, as Richard Sewell suggests in his biography of her, on our knees? No one's suggesting that canonical writers should be immune to criticism. Dickens's anti-Semitism, Tolstoy's overly romantic ideas about the peasantry, Kipling's racism, are all problematic, and merit discussion. But to treat the geniuses of the past as naughty children, amenable to reeducation by the children of the present, evokes the educational theory of the Chinese Revolution.

No wonder students are rarely asked to consider what was actually written by these hopeless racists and sociopaths. Instead, they're told to write around the books, or, better yet, write their own books. Becky Alano's depressing *Teaching the Novel* advises readers of Sylvia Plath's *The Bell Jar* to construct a therapeutic evaluation of its suicidal heroine ("Do you think she is ready to go home? What is your prognosis for her future?") and lists documents to be written as supplements to *Macbeth* (a script of the TV evening news announcing the murders; a psychiatrist's report on Lady Macbeth, or her suicide note to her husband; Macbeth's entry in *Who's Who*, or his obituary).

How should prospective readers of Anne Frank's *The Diary of a Young Girl* prepare? Carolyn Smith McGowen's *Teaching Literature by Women Authors* suggests: "Give each student a paper grocery bag. Explain that to avoid being sent to a concentration camp, many people went into hiding. Often they could take with them only what they could carry. . . . Ask your students to choose the items they would take into hiding. These items must fit into the grocery bag." A class attempting to interpret an Emily Dickinson poem can be divided into three groups, each group interpreting the poem based on one of Freud's levels of consciousness; thus the little ids, egos, and superegos can respond to the Dickinson poem according to the category of awareness to which their group has been assigned.

Those who might have supposed that one purpose of fiction was to deploy the powers of language to connect us, directly and intimately, with the hearts and souls of others, will be disappointed to learn that the whole point is to make us examine ourselves. According to Alano, *The Catcher in the Rye* will doubtless suggest an incident "in which you felt yourself to be an 'outsider' like Holden. Why did you feel outside? What finally changed your situation?" Stephen Crane's *The Red*

Badge of Courage should make us compare our anxieties ("Describe an event that you anticipated with fear. . . . Was the actual event worth the dread?") with those of its Civil War hero. And what does *The Great Gatsby* lead us to consider? "Did you ever pursue a goal with single-minded devotion? . . . Would you have gained your end in any other way?" Are we to believe that the average eleventh-grader has had an experience comparable to that of Jay Gatsby—or F. Scott Fitzgerald? And is it any wonder that teenagers should complete these exercises with little but contempt for the writer who so pointlessly complicated and obfuscated a personal true story that sixteen-year-olds could have told so much more interestingly themselves?

I remember when it dawned on me that I might, someday, grow old. I was in the eleventh grade. Our marvelous and unusual English teacher had assigned us to read *King Lear*—that is, to read every line of *King Lear*. (As I recall, we were asked to circle every word or metaphor having to do with eyes and vision, a tedious process we grumbled about but that succeeded in focusing our attention.) Although I knew I would never ever resemble the decrepit adults around me, Shakespeare's genius, his poetry, his profound, encyclopedic understanding of personality, managed to persuade me that I could *be* that mythical king—an imaginative identification very different from whatever result I might have obtained by persuading myself that my own experience was the *same* as Lear's. I recall the hallucinatory sense of having left my warm bedroom, of finding myself—old, enraged, alone, despised—on that heath, in that dangerous storm. And I remember realizing, after the storm subsided, that language, that mere words on the page, had raised that howling tempest.

Lear is still the Shakespeare play I like best. I reread it periodically, increasingly moved now that age is no longer a theoretical possibility, and now that its portrayal of Lear's behavior so often seems like reportage. A friend whose elderly boss is ruining his company with irrational tests of fealty and refusals to cede power needs only six words to describe the situation at work: *King Lear*, Act One, Scene One.

Another high school favorite was the King James Version of the Book of Revelation. I don't think I'd ever heard of Armageddon, nor did I believe that when the seals of a book were opened horses would fly out. What delighted me was the language, the cadences and the rhythms, and the power of the images: the four horsemen, the beast, the woman clothed with the sun.

But rather than exposing students to works of literature that expand their capacities and vocabularies, sharpen their comprehension, and deepen the level at which they think and feel, we either offer them "easy" (Steinbeck, Knowles, Angelou, Lee) books that "anyone" can understand, or we serve up the tougher works predigested. We no longer believe that books were written one word at a time, and deserve to be read that way. We've forgotten the difference between a student who has never read a nineteenth-century novel and an idiot incapable of reading one. When my son was assigned *Wuthering Heights* in tenth-grade English, the complex sentences, archaisms, multiple narrators, and interwoven stories seemed, at first, like a foreign language. But soon enough, he caught on and reported being moved almost to tears by the cruelty of Heathcliff's treatment of Isabella.

In fact, it's not difficult to find fiction that combines clear, beautiful, accessible, idiosyncratic language with a narrative that conveys a complex worldview. But to use such literature might require teachers and school boards to make fresh choices, selections uncontaminated by trends, clichés, and received ideas. If educators continue to assume that teenagers are interested exclusively in books about teenagers, there *is* engaging, truthful fiction about childhood and adolescence, written in ways that remind us why someone might like to read. There is, for example, Charles Baxter's precise and evocative "Gryphon." And there are the carefully chosen details, the complex sentences, and the down-to-earth diction in Stuart Dybek's great Chicago story, "Hot Ice."

If English class is the only forum in which students can talk about racism and ethnic identity, why not teach Hilton Als's *The Women*, Flannery O'Connor's "Everything That Rises Must Converge," or any of the stories in James Alan McPherson's *Hue and Cry*, all of which eloquently and directly address the subtle, powerful ways in which race affects every tiny decision and gesture? Why not introduce our kids to the clarity and power of James Baldwin's great story "Sonny's Blues"? 35

My suspicion is that the reason such texts are not used as often as *I Know Why the Caged Bird Sings* is precisely the reason why they *should* be taught—that is, because they're complicated. Baldwin, Als, and McPherson reject obvious "lessons" and familiar arcs of abuse, self-realization, and recovery; they actively refute simplistic prescriptions about how to live.

Great novels can help us master the all-too-rare skill of tolerating—of being able to hold in mind—ambiguity and contradiction. Jay Gatsby has a shady past, but he's also sympathetic. Huck Finn is a liar, but we come to love him. A friend's student once wrote that Alice Munro's characters weren't people he'd choose to hang out with but that reading her work always made him feel "a little less petty and judgmental." Such benefits are denied to the young reader exposed only to books with banal, simple-minded moral equations as well as to the student encouraged to come up with reductive, wrong-headed readings of multilayered texts.

The narrator of *Caged Bird* is good, her rapist is bad; Scout and Atticus Finch are good, their bigoted neighbors are bad. But the characters in James Alan McPherson's "Gold Coast" are a good deal more lifelike. The cantankerous, bigoted, elderly white janitor and the young African American student, his temporary assistant, who puts up with the janitor's bullshit and is simultaneously cheered and saddened by the knowledge that he's headed for greater success than the janitor will ever achieve, both embody mixtures of admirable and more dubious qualities. In other words, they're more like humans. It's hard to imagine the lesson plans telling students exactly how to feel about these two complex plausible characters.

No one's suggesting that every existing syllabus be shredded; many books on the current lists are great works of art. But why not *tell* the students that, instead of suggesting that Mark Twain be posthumously reprimanded? Why not point out how convincingly he captured the workings of Huck's mind, the inner voice of a kid trying desperately to sew a crazy quilt of self together from the ragged scraps around him? Why not celebrate the accuracy and vigor with which he translated the rhythms of American speech into written language?

In simplifying what a book is allowed to tell us — Twain's novel is wholly about racism and not at all about what it's like to *be* Huck Finn — teachers pretend to spark discussion but actually prevent it. They claim to relate the world of the book to the world of experience, but by concentrating on the student's own history they narrow the world of experience down to the personal and deny students *other* sorts of experience — the experience of what's in the book, for starters. One reason we read writers from other times or cultures is to confront alternatives — of feeling and sensibility, of history and psyche, of information and ideas. To experience the heartbreaking matter-of-factness with which Anne Frank described her situation seems more useful than packing a paper bag with Game Boys, cigarettes, and CDs so that we can go into hiding and avoid being sent to the camps.

The pleasure of surrender to the world of a book is only one of the pleasures that this new way of reading — and teaching — denies. In blurring the line between reality and fiction (What happened to you that was exactly like what happened to Hester Prynne?), it reduces our respect for imagination, beauty, art, thought, and for the way that the human spirit expresses itself in words.

Writers have no choice but to believe that literature will survive, that it's worth some effort to preserve the most beautiful, meaningful lyrics or narratives, the record of who we were, and are. And if we want our children to begin an extended love affair with reading and with what great writing can do, we *want* them to get an early start — or any start, at all. Teaching students to value literary masterpieces is our best hope of awakening them to the infinite capacities and complexities of human experience, of helping them acknowledge and accept complexity and ambiguity, and of making them love and respect the language that allows us to smuggle out, and send one another, our urgent, eloquent dispatches from the prison of the self.

That may be what writers — and readers — desire. But if it's not occurring, perhaps that's because our culture wants it less urgently than we do. Education, after all, is a process intended to produce a product. So we have to ask ourselves: What sort of product is being produced by the current system? How does it change when certain factors are added to, or removed from, our literature curriculum? And is it really in the best interests of our consumer economy to create

40

a well-educated, smart, highly literate society of fervent readers? Doesn't our epidemic dumbing-down have undeniable advantages for those institutions (the media, the advertising industry, the government) whose interests are better served by a population not trained to read too closely or ask too many questions?

On the most obvious level, it's worth noting that books are among the few remaining forms of entertainment not sustained by, and meant to further, the interests of advertising. Television, newspapers, and magazines are busily instilling us with new desires and previously unsuspected needs, while books sell only themselves. Moreover, the time we spend reading is time spent away from media that have a greater chance of alchemically transmuting attention into money.

But of course what's happening is more complex and subtle than that, more closely connected to how we conceive of the relation between intellect and spirit. The new-model English-class graduate — the one who has been force-fed the gross oversimplifications proffered by these lesson plans and teaching manuals — values empathy and imagination less than the ability to make quick and irreversible judgments, to entertain and maintain simplistic immovable opinions about guilt and innocence, about the possibilities and limitations of human nature. Less comfortable with the gray areas than with sharply delineated black and white, he or she can work in groups and operate by consensus, and has a resultant, residual distrust for the eccentric, the idiosyncratic, the annoyingly . . . individual. 45

What I've described is a salable product, tailored to the needs of the economic and political moment. What results from these educational methods is a mode of thinking (or, more accurately, of *not* thinking) that equips our kids for the future: Future McDonald's employees. Future corporate board members. Future special prosecutors. Future makers of 100-best-books lists who fondly recall what they first read in high school — and who may not have read anything since. And so the roster of literary masterpieces we pass along to future generations will continue its downward shift, and those lightweight, mediocre high school favorites will continue to rise, unburdened by gravity, to the top of the list.

Questions for Discussion

1. Francine Prose states, "Traditionally, the love of reading has been born and nurtured in high school English class" (para. 1). Do you think this is generally the case? Describe your experience on this subject.

2. What does Prose mean when she writes, "[B]y concentrating on the student's own history they [teachers] narrow the world of experience down to the personal and deny students *other* sorts of experience — the experience of what's in the book, for starters" (para. 40)? Do you agree with Prose's statement? Why or why not?

3. What is Prose implying in the following statement about what she calls the "new-model English-class graduate": "But of course what's happening is more complex and subtle than that [seeing books as unconnected to advertising], more

closely connected to how we conceive of the relation between intellect and spirit" (para. 45)?

4. Whom does Prose blame for this state of affairs? Does assigning blame affect the cogency of her argument?

5. This essay was written in 1999. Do you think Prose would or could make the same argument today? Why or why not?

Questions on Rhetoric and Style

1. Discuss three appeals to ethos in this essay. What different roles, or personae, does Prose use to establish her ethos?

2. Prose's opening paragraph includes such words as *appalled, dismal,* and *dreariness*— all with negative connotations. Why does she start out with such strong language? Does she risk putting off readers who do not share her views? Why or why not? What other examples of strongly emotional language do you find in the essay?

3. Prose makes several key assumptions about the role and impact of reading literary works in high school. What are they?

4. What appeals does she make to logos?

5. Prose cites many different novels and plays. Does she assume her audience is familiar with some of them? All of them? Explain why it matters whether the audience knows the works.

6. According to Prose, "To hold up [*I Know Why the Caged Bird Sings*] as a paradigm of memoir, of thought—of literature—is akin to inviting doctors convicted of malpractice to instruct our medical students" (para. 13). Do you agree with this analogy? Explain your answer. What other examples of figurative language can you find in this essay?

7. Toward the end of the essay (paras. 35, 39, and 43), Prose uses a series of rhetorical questions. What is her purpose in piling one rhetorical question on top of another?

8. Would Prose have strengthened her argument by including interviews with a few high school students or teachers? Why or why not?

9. According to Prose, why are American high school students learning to loathe literature? Try to find at least four or five reasons.

10. Does she propose a solution or recommendations to change this situation? If she does not offer a solution, is her argument weakened? Explain your answer.

Suggestions for Writing

1. Prose is highly critical of the quality of both *I Know Why the Caged Bird Sings* and *To Kill a Mockingbird*. If you have read either, write an evaluation of her criticism of the book. Pay particular attention to the quotations she selects; is she setting up a straw man—that is, an argument that can be easily refuted?

2. Prose is skeptical of the practice of using literary works to teach values. Write an essay in which you support or challenge her position. Be specific in your references to novels, plays, or poems.

3. Prose writes, "Great novels can help us master the all-too-rare skill of tolerating— of being able to hold in mind—ambiguity and contradiction" (para. 37). Select a novel you know well, and explain the "ambiguity and contradiction" at its heart.
4. Collect the required reading lists from several schools (or classes) in different geographical regions, and compare and contrast them. Are there differences in quality as well as quantity? Are any of the books Prose discusses included on them? Do the books appeal to boys as well as girls? Is there opportunity for choice? Write an essay analyzing these lists from Prose's point of view.

from *Education*

RALPH WALDO EMERSON

 Ralph Waldo Emerson (1803–1882), perhaps best known for his essay "Self-Reliance" (1841), was one of America's most influential thinkers and writers. After graduating from Harvard Divinity School, he followed nine generations of his family into the ministry but practiced for only a few years. In 1836, he and other like-minded intellectuals, including Henry David Thoreau, founded the Transcendental Club, and that same year he published his influential essay "Nature" (1836). Known as a great orator, Emerson made his living as a popular lecturer on a wide range of topics. From 1821 to 1826, he taught in city and country schools and later served on a number of school boards, including the Concord School Committee and the Board of Overseers of Harvard College. Emerson's essay "Education," from which the following excerpt is taken, was put together posthumously from his writings published in the *American Scholar* and from his commencement addresses.

I believe that our own experience instructs us that the secret of Education lies in respecting the pupil. It is not for you to choose what he shall know, what he shall do. It is chosen and foreordained, and he only holds the key to his own secret. By your tampering and thwarting and too much governing he may be hindered from his end and kept out of his own. Respect the child. Wait and see the new product of Nature. Nature loves analogies, but not repetitions. Respect the child. Be not too much his parent. Trespass not on his solitude.

But I hear the outcry which replies to this suggestion — Would you verily throw up the reins of public and private discipline; would you leave the young child to the mad career of his own passions and whimsies, and call this anarchy a respect for the child's nature? I answer — Respect the child, respect him to the end, but also respect yourself. Be the companion of his thought, the friend of his friendship, the lover of his virtue — but no kinsman of his sin. Let him find you so true to yourself that you are the irreconcilable hater of his vice and the imperturbable slighter of his trifling.

The two points in a boy's training are, to keep his *naturel* and train off all but that — to keep his *naturel*, but stop off his uproar, fooling, and horseplay — keep his nature and arm it with knowledge in the very direction to which it points. Here are the two capital facts, Genius and Drill. This first is the inspiration in the well-born healthy child, the new perception he has of nature. Somewhat he sees in forms or hears in music or apprehends in mathematics, or believes practicable in mechanics or possible in political society, which no one else sees or hears or believes. This is the perpetual romance of new life, the invasion of God into the old dead world, when he sends into quiet houses a young soul with a thought which is not met, looking for something which is not there, but which ought to be there: the thought is dim but it is sure, and he casts about restless for means and masters to verify it; he makes wild attempts to explain himself and invoke the aid and consent of the by-standers. Baffled for want of language and methods to convey his meaning, not yet clear to himself, he conceives that thought not in this house or town, yet in some other house or town is the wise master who can put him in possession of the rules and instruments to execute his will. Happy this child with a bias, with a thought which entrances him, leads him, now into deserts now into cities, the fool of an idea. Let him follow it in good and in evil report, in good or bad company; it will justify itself; it will lead him at last into the illustrious society of the lovers of truth.

In London, in a private company, I became acquainted with a gentleman, Sir Charles Fellowes, who, being at Xanthos, in the Aegean Sea, had seen a Turk point with his staff to some carved work on the corner of a stone almost buried in the soil. Fellowes scraped away the dirt, was struck with the beauty of the sculptured ornaments, and, looking about him, observed more blocks and fragments like this. He returned to the spot, procured laborers and uncovered many blocks. He went back to England, bought a Greek grammar and learned the language; he read history and studied ancient art to explain his stones; he interested Gibson the sculptor; he invoked the assistance of the English Government; he called in the succor of Sir Humphry Davy to analyze the pigments; of experts in coins, of scholars and connoisseurs; and at last in his third visit brought home to England such statues and marble reliefs and such careful plans that he was able to reconstruct, in the British Museum where it now stands, the perfect model of the Ionic trophy-monument, fifty years older than the Parthenon of Athens, and which had been destroyed by earthquakes, then by iconoclast Christians, then by savage Turks. But mark that in the task he had achieved an excellent education, and become associated with distinguished scholars whom he had interested in his pursuit; in short, had formed a college for himself; the enthusiast had found the master, the masters, whom he sought. Always genius seeks genius, desires nothing so much as to be a pupil and to find those who can lend it aid to perfect itself.

Nor are the two elements, enthusiasm and drill, incompatible. Accuracy is 5 essential to beauty. The very definition of the intellect is Aristotle's: "that by which we know terms or boundaries." Give a boy accurate perceptions. Teach him the difference between the similar and the same. Make him call things by their right names. Pardon in him no blunder. Then he will give you solid satisfaction as long as he lives. It is better to teach the child arithmetic and Latin grammar than rhetoric or moral philosophy, because they require exactitude of performance; it is made certain that the lesson is mastered, and that power of performance is worth more than the knowledge. He can learn anything which is important to him now that the power to learn is secured: as mechanics say, when one has learned the use of tools, it is easy to work at a new craft.

Letter by letter, syllable by syllable, the child learns to read, and in good time can convey to all the domestic circle the sense of Shakespeare. By many steps each just as short, the stammering boy and the hesitating collegian, in the school debates, in college clubs, in mock court, comes at last to full, secure, triumphant unfolding of his thought in the popular assembly, with a fullness of power that makes all the steps forgotten.

But this function of opening and feeding the human mind is not to be fulfilled by any mechanical or military method; is not to be trusted to any skill less large than Nature itself. You must not neglect the form, but you must secure the essentials. It is curious how perverse and intermeddling we are, and what vast pains and cost we incur to do wrong. Whilst we all know in our own experience and apply natural methods in our own business — in education our common sense fails us, and we are continually trying costly machinery against nature, in patent schools and academies and in great colleges and universities.

The natural method forever confutes our experiments, and we must still come back to it. The whole theory of the school is on the nurse's or mother's knee. The child is as hot to learn as the mother is to impart. There is mutual delight. The joy of our childhood in hearing beautiful stories from some skillful aunt who loves to tell them, must be repeated in youth. The boy wishes to learn to skate, to coast, to catch a fish in the brook, to hit a mark with a snowball or a stone; and a boy a little older is just as well pleased to teach him these sciences. Not less delightful is the mutual pleasure of teaching and learning the secret of algebra, or of chemistry, or of good reading and good recitation of poetry or of prose, or of chosen facts in history or in biography.

Nature provided for the communication of thought by planting with it in the receiving mind a fury to impart it. 'Tis so in every art, in every science. One burns to tell the new fact, the other burns to hear it. See how far a young doctor will ride or walk to witness a new surgical operation. I have seen a carriage-maker's shop emptied of all its workmen into the street, to scrutinize a new pattern from New York. So in literature, the young man who has taste for poetry, for fine images, for noble thoughts, is insatiable for this nourishment, and forgets all the world for the more learned friend — who finds equal joy in dealing out his treasures.

Happy the natural college thus self-instituted around every natural teacher; the young men of Athens around Socrates; of Alexander around Plotinus; of Paris around Abelard; of Germany around Fichte, or Niebuhr, or Goethe: in short the natural sphere of every leading mind. But the moment this is organized, difficulties begin. The college was to be the nurse and home of genius; but, though every young man is born with some determination in his nature, and is a potential genius; is at last to be one; it is, in the most, obstructed and delayed, and, whatever they may hereafter be, their senses are now opened in advance of their minds. They are more sensual than intellectual. Appetite and indolence they have, but no enthusiasm. These come in numbers to the college: few geniuses: and the teaching comes to be arranged for these many, and not for those few. Hence the instruction seems to require skillful tutors, of accurate and systematic mind, rather than ardent and inventive masters. Besides, the youth of genius are eccentric, won't drill, are irritable, uncertain, explosive, solitary, not men of the world, not good for every-day association. You have to work for large classes instead of individuals; you must lower your flag and reef your sails to wait for the dull sailors; you grow departmental, routinary, military almost with your discipline and college police. But what doth such a school to form a great and heroic character? What abiding Hope can it inspire? What Reformer will it nurse? What poet will it breed to sing to the human race? What discoverer of Nature's laws will it prompt to enrich us by disclosing in the mind the statute which all matter must obey? What fiery soul will it send out to warm a nation with his charity? What tranquil mind will it have fortified to walk with meekness in private and obscure duties, to wait and to suffer? Is it not manifest that our academic institutions should have a wider scope; that they should not be timid and keep the ruts of the last generation, but that wise men thinking for themselves and heartily seeking the good of mankind, and counting the cost of innovation, should dare to arouse the young to a just and heroic life; that the moral nature should be addressed in the school-room, and children should be treated as the high-born candidates of truth and virtue?

So to regard the young child, the young man, requires, no doubt, rare patience: a patience that nothing but faith in the remedial forces of the soul can give. You see his sensualism; you see his want of those tastes and perceptions which make the power and safety of your character. Very likely. But he has something else. If he has his own vice, he has its correlative virtue. Every mind should be allowed to make its own statement in action, and its balance will appear. In these judgments one needs that foresight which was attributed to an eminent reformer, of whom it was said "his patience could see in the bud of the aloe the blossom at the end of a hundred years." Alas for the cripple Practice when it seeks to come up with the bird Theory, which flies before it. Try your design on the best school. The scholars are of all ages and temperaments and capacities. It is difficult to class them, some are too young, some are slow, some perverse. Each requires so much consideration, that the morning hope of the teacher, of a day of love and progress, is often closed at evening by despair. Each single case, the more it is considered, shows more to be done; and the strict conditions of the hours, on one side, and the number of tasks, on the other. Whatever becomes of our method, the conditions stand fast—six hours, and thirty, fifty, or a hundred and fifty pupils. Something must be done, and done speedily, and in this distress the wisest are tempted to adopt violent means, to proclaim martial law, corporal punishment, mechanical arrangement, bribes, spies, wrath, main strength and ignorance, in lieu of that wise genial providential influence they had hoped, and yet hope at some future day to adopt. Of course the devotion to details reacts injuriously on the teacher. He cannot indulge his genius, he cannot delight in personal relations with young friends, when his eye is always on the clock, and twenty classes are to be dealt with before the day is done. Besides, how can he please himself with genius, and foster modest virtue? A sure proportion of rogue and dunce finds its way into every school and requires a cruel share of time, and the gentle teacher, who wished to be a Providence to youth, is grown a martinet,[1] sore with suspicions; knows as much vice as the judge of a police court, and his love of learning is lost in the routine of grammars and books of elements.

A rule is so easy that it does not need a man to apply it; an automaton, a machine, can be made to keep a school so. It facilitates labor and thought so much that there is always the temptation in large schools to omit the endless task of meeting the wants of each single mind, and to govern by steam. But it is at frightful cost. Our modes of Education aim to expedite, to save labor; to do for masses what cannot be done for masses, what must be done reverently, one by one: say rather, the whole world is needed for the tuition of each pupil. The advantages of this system of emulation and display are so prompt and obvious, it is such a time-saver, it is so energetic on slow and on bad natures, and is of so easy application, needing no sage or poet, but any tutor or schoolmaster in his first term can apply it — that it is not strange that this calomel[2] of culture should be a popular medicine. On the other hand, total abstinence from this drug, and the adoption of simple discipline and the following of nature involves at once immense claims on the time, the thoughts, on the Life of the teacher. It requires time, use, insight, event, all the great lessons and assistances of God; and only to think of using it implies character and profoundness; to enter on this course of discipline is to be good and great. It is precisely analogous to the difference between the use of corporal punishment and the methods of love. It is so easy to bestow on a bad boy a blow, overpower him, and get obedience without words, that in this world of hurry and distraction, who can wait for the returns of reason and the conquest of self; in the uncertainty too whether that will ever come? And yet the familiar observation of the universal compensations might suggest the fear that so summary a stop of a bad humor was more jeopardous than its continuance.

Now the correction of this quack practice is to import into Education the wisdom of life. Leave this military hurry and adopt the pace of Nature. Her secret is patience. Do you know how the naturalist learns all the secrets of the forest, of plants, of birds, of beasts, of reptiles, of fishes, of the rivers and the sea? When he goes into the woods the birds fly before him and he finds none; when he goes to the river bank, the fish and the reptile swim away and leave him alone. His secret is patience; he sits down, and sits still; he is a statue; he is a log. These creatures have no value for their time, and he must put as low a rate on his. By dint of obstinate sitting still, reptile, fish, bird and beast, which all wish to return to their haunts, begin to return. He sits still; if they approach, he remains passive as the stone he sits upon. They lose their fear. They have curiosity too about him. By and by the curiosity masters the fear, and they come swimming, creeping and flying towards him; and as he is still immovable, they not only resume their haunts and

---

[1]A strict disciplinarian. Originally a type of whip. — Eds.
[2]A mercury compound once used as a laxative, purgative, or disinfectant. — Eds.

their ordinary labors and manners, show themselves to him in their work-day trim, but also volunteer some degree of advances towards fellowship and good understanding with a biped who behaves so civilly and well. Can you not baffle the impatience and passion of the child by your tranquility? Can you not wait for him, as Nature and Providence do? Can you not keep for his mind and ways, for his secret, the same curiosity you give to the squirrel, snake, rabbit, and the sheldrake[3] and the deer? He has a secret; wonderful methods in him; he is—every child—a new style of man; give him time and opportunity. Talk of Columbus and Newton! I tell you the child just born in yonder hovel is the beginning of a revolution as great as theirs. But you must have the believing and prophetic eye. Have the self-command you wish to inspire. Your teaching and discipline must have the reserve and taciturnity of Nature. Teach them to hold their tongues by holding your own. Say little; do not snarl; do not chide; but govern by the eye. See what they need, and that the right thing is done.

I confess myself utterly at a loss in suggesting particular reforms in our ways of teaching. No discretion that can be lodged with a school-committee, with the overseers or visitors of an academy, of a college, can at all avail to reach these difficulties and perplexities, but they solve themselves when we leave institutions and address individuals. The will, the male power, organizes, imposes its own thought and wish on others, and makes that military eye which controls boys as it controls men; admirable in its results, a fortune to him who has it, and only dangerous when it leads the workman to overvalue and overuse it and precludes him from finer means. Sympathy, the female force—which they must use who have not the first—deficient in instant control and the breaking down of resistance, is more subtle and lasting and creative. I advise teachers to cherish mother-wit. I assume that you will keep the grammar, reading, writing and arithmetic in order; 'tis easy and of course you will. But smuggle in a little contraband wit, fancy, imagination, thought. If you have a taste which you have suppressed because it is not shared by those about you, tell them that. Set this law up, whatever becomes of the rules of the school: they must not whisper, much less talk; but if one of the young people says a wise thing, greet it, and let all the children clap their hands. They shall have no book but school-books in the room; but if one has brought in a Plutarch or Shakespeare or Don Quixote or Goldsmith or any other good book, and understands what he reads, put him at once at the head of the class. Nobody shall be disorderly, or leave his desk without permission, but if a boy runs from his bench, or a girl, because the fire falls, or to check some injury that a little dastard is indicting behind his desk on some helpless sufferer, take away the medal from the head of the class and give it on the instant to the brave rescuer. If a child happens to show that he knows any fact about astronomy, or plants, or birds, or rocks, or history, that interests him and you, hush all the

---

[3]A type of duck.—Eds.

classes and encourage him to tell it so that all may hear. Then you have made your school-room like the world. Of course you will insist on modesty in the children, and respect to their teachers, but if the boy stops you in your speech, cries out that you are wrong and sets you right, hug him!

To whatsoever upright mind, to whatsoever beating heart I speak, to you it is committed to educate men. By simple living, by an illimitable soul, you inspire, you correct, you instruct, you raise, you embellish all. By your own act you teach the beholder how to do the practicable. According to the depth from which you draw your life, such is the depth not only of your strenuous effort, but of your manners and presence. The beautiful nature of the world has here blended your happiness with your power. Work straight on in absolute duty, and you lend an arm and an encouragement to all the youth of the universe. Consent yourself to be an organ of your highest thought, and lo! suddenly you put all men in your debt, and are the fountain of an energy that goes pulsing on with waves of benefit to the borders of society, to the circumference of things.

Questions for Discussion

1. In this essay, Ralph Waldo Emerson describes his view of an ideal education. What are its defining characteristics?
2. In what ways is Emerson's advice appropriate to a child's first teacher—his or her parents?
3. Why does Emerson believe "[i]t is better to teach the child arithmetic and Latin grammar than rhetoric or moral philosophy" (para. 5)?
4. In what ways does this essay point out the education system's effect on teachers as well as students?
5. What exactly is the "natural method" to which Emerson refers (para. 8)?
6. Why does Emerson criticize schools as bureaucratic institutions (para. 10)?
7. Emerson refers to educating "a boy" and "a man" and uses masculine pronouns when referring to students. As a reader, does this gender bias affect how receptive you are to Emerson's ideas? Are his ideas equally applicable to women? If you do not think so, then how would they need to be changed to be applicable to both men and women, boys and girls?
8. Describe the adult that Emerson imagines would emerge from an education based on the principles he supports.

Questions on Rhetoric and Style

1. What does Emerson mean when he says, "Nature loves analogies, but not repetitions" (para. 1)?
2. Why is the relationship between "Genius and Drill," as Emerson explains it, paradoxical (para. 3)?

3. Paragraph 4 is taken up almost entirely by an extended example. What is Emerson's purpose in developing this long explanation?

4. Identify at least three examples of figurative language that Emerson uses to advance his argument, and explain their effect. In responding, consider the following line from paragraph 11: "Alas for the cripple Practice when it seeks to come up with the bird Theory, which flies before it."

5. Identify examples of the following rhetorical strategies in paragraph 13, and explain their effect: rhetorical questions, sentence variety and pacing, analogy, allusion, and imperative sentences.

6. Examine Emerson's appeals to pathos through highly emotional and evocative diction.

7. Rephrase the following sentence in contemporary language: "And yet the familiar observation of the universal compensations might suggest the fear that so summary a stop of a bad humor was more jeopardous than its continuance" (para. 12).

8. Explain why you do or do not interpret the opening line of paragraph 14 as ironic: "I confess myself utterly at a loss in suggesting particular reforms in our ways of teaching."

9. Why does Emerson believe that the "will, the male power" (para. 14) will be of less benefit to the child than "[s]ympathy, the female force"?

10. What is Emerson's purpose in shifting among the pronouns *I*, *we*, and *you*?

11. How would you describe Emerson's tone in this essay?

Suggestions for Writing

1. In paragraph 12, Emerson makes the following assertion about education in his time: "Our modes of Education aim to expedite, to save labor; to do for masses what cannot be done for masses, what must be done reverently, one by one: say rather, the whole world is needed for the tuition of each pupil." What does he mean? (You might have to look up the meaning of *tuition* in this context.) Do you think that public education today still resembles Emerson's description? Explain.

2. If you were responsible for the education of a child, which of Emerson's assertions about education would you choose as your guiding principle? Write an essay explaining why you would choose that principle over another of Emerson's beliefs.

3. Explain why you agree or disagree with Emerson's assertion that "every young man [and woman] is born with some determination in his [or her] nature, and is a potential genius" (para. 10).

4. Write a response to Emerson in the voice of Francine Prose, explaining why you agree or disagree with the issues he raises and the positions he takes.

5. Evaluate your own schooling according to the criteria presented in paragraph 10.

A Talk to Teachers

James Baldwin

James Baldwin (1924–1987) was one of the most influential figures in American literature during the latter half of the twentieth century. His novels include *Go Tell It on the Mountain* (1953), *Giovanni's Room* (1956), *If Beale Street Could Talk* (1974), and *Just Above My Head* (1979). A sharp social critic of race relations and sexual identity, Baldwin wrote numerous essays that were collected in *Notes of a Native Son* (1955), *The Fire Next Time* (1963), and *The Devil Finds Work* (1976). He also wrote poetry and plays. By the late 1940s, Baldwin had moved to Europe. He lived in France and Turkey for most of the rest of his life, but he returned at times to the United States to lecture and participate in the civil rights movement. He delivered the following speech to a group of New York City schoolteachers in 1963, the height of the movement for equality for African Americans.

Let's begin by saying that we are living through a very dangerous time. Everyone in this room is in one way or another aware of that. We are in a revolutionary situation, no matter how unpopular that word has become in this country. The society in which we live is desperately menaced, not by [Nikita] Khrushchev,[1] but from within. So any citizen of this country who figures himself as responsible — and particularly those of you who deal with the minds and hearts of young people — must be prepared to "go for broke." Or to put it another way, you must understand that in the attempt to correct so many generations of bad faith and cruelty, when it is operating not only in the classroom but in society, you will meet the most fantastic, the most brutal, and the most determined resistance. There is no point in pretending that this won't happen.

Since I am talking to schoolteachers and I am not a teacher myself, and in some ways am fairly easily intimidated, I beg you to let me leave that and go back to what I think to be the entire purpose of education in the first place. It would seem to me that when a child is born, if I'm the child's parent, it is my obligation and my high duty to civilize that child. Man is a social animal. He cannot exist without a society. A society, in turn, depends on certain things which everyone within that society takes for granted. Now, the crucial paradox which confronts us here is that the whole process of education occurs within a social framework and is designed to perpetuate the aims of society. Thus, for example, the boys and girls who were born during the era of the Third Reich, when educated to the purposes of the Third Reich, became barbarians. The paradox of education is precisely this — that as one begins to become conscious one begins to examine the society in which he is being educated. The purpose of education, finally, is to create in a

---

[1] Premier of the Soviet Union, 1958–1964. — Eds.

person the ability to look at the world for himself, to make his own decisions, to say to himself this is black or this is white, to decide for himself whether there is a God in heaven or not. To ask questions of the universe, and then learn to live with those questions, is the way he achieves his own identity. But no society is really anxious to have that kind of person around. What societies really, ideally, want is a citizenry which will simply obey the rules of society. If a society succeeds in this, that society is about to perish. The obligation of anyone who thinks of himself as responsible is to examine society and try to change it and to fight it—at no matter what risk. This is the only hope society has. This is the only way societies change.

Now, if what I have tried to sketch has any validity, it becomes thoroughly clear, at least to me, that any Negro who is born in this country and undergoes the American educational system runs the risk of becoming schizophrenic. On the one hand he is born in the shadow of the stars and stripes and he is assured it represents a nation which has never lost a war. He pledges allegiance to that flag which guarantees "liberty and justice for all." He is part of a country in which any-one can become president, and so forth. But on the other hand he is also assured by his country and his countrymen that he has never contributed anything to civilization—that his past is nothing more than a record of humiliations gladly endured. He is assumed by the republic that he, his father, his mother, and his ancestors were happy, shiftless, watermelon-eating darkies who loved Mr. Charlie and Miss Ann,[2] that the value he has as a black man is proven by one thing only—his devotion to white people. If you think I am exaggerating, examine the myths which proliferate in this country about Negroes.

All this enters the child's consciousness much sooner than we as adults would like to think it does. As adults, we are easily fooled because we are so anxious to be fooled. But children are very different. Children, not yet aware that it is dangerous to look too deeply at anything, look at everything, look at each other, and draw their own conclusions. They don't have the vocabulary to express what they see, and we, their elders, know how to intimidate them very easily and very soon. But a black child, looking at the world around him, though he cannot know quite what to make of it, is aware that there is a reason why his mother works so hard, why his father is always on edge. He is aware that there is some reason why, if he sits down in the front of the bus, his father or mother slaps him and drags him to the back of the bus. He is aware that there is some terrible weight on his parents' shoulders which menaces him. And it isn't long—in fact it begins when he is in school—before he discovers the shape of his oppression.

Let us say that the child is seven years old and I am his father, and I decide to   5
take him to the zoo, or to Madison Square Garden, or to the U.N. Building, or to any of the tremendous monuments we find all over New York. We get into a bus and we go from where I live on 131st Street and Seventh Avenue downtown through

---

[2]Figurative characters invented by African slaves to represent male and female slave masters, respectively.—Eds.

the park and we get into New York City, which is not Harlem. Now, where the boy lives — even if it is a housing project — is in an undesirable neighborhood. If he lives in one of those housing projects of which everyone in New York is so proud, he has at the front door, if not closer, the pimps, the whores, the junkies — in a word, the danger of life in the ghetto. And the child knows this, though he doesn't know why.

I still remember my first sight of New York. It was really another city when I was born — where I was born. We looked down over the Park Avenue streetcar tracks. It was Park Avenue, but I didn't know what Park Avenue meant *downtown*. The Park Avenue I grew up on, which is still standing, is dark and dirty. No one would dream of opening a Tiffany's on that Park Avenue, and when you go downtown you discover that you are literally in the white world. It is rich — or at least it looks rich. It is clean — because they collect garbage downtown. There are doormen. People walk about as though they owned where they are — and indeed they do. And it's a great shock. It's very hard to relate yourself to this. You don't know what it means. You know — you know instinctively — that none of this is for you. You know this before you are told. And who is it for and who is paying for it? And why isn't it for you?

Later on when you become a grocery boy or messenger and you try to enter one of those buildings a man says, "Go to the back door." Still later, if you happen by some odd chance to have a friend in one of those buildings, the man says, "Where's your package?" Now this by no means is the core of the matter. What I'm trying to get at is that by this time the Negro child has had, effectively, almost all the doors of opportunity slammed in his face, and there are very few things he can do about it. He can more or less accept it with an absolutely inarticulate and dangerous rage inside — all the more dangerous because it is never expressed. It is precisely those silent people whom white people see every day of their lives — I mean your porter and your maid, who never say anything more than "Yes, Sir" and "No, Ma'am." They will tell you it's raining if that is what you want to hear, and they will tell you the sun is shining if *that* is what you want to hear. They really hate you — really hate you because in their eyes (and they're right) you stand between them and life. I want to come back to that in a moment. It is the most sinister of the facts, I think, which we now face.

There is something else the Negro child can do, too. Every street boy — and I was a street boy, so I know — looking at the society which has produced him, looking at the standards of that society which are not honored by anybody, looking at your churches and the government and the politicians, understands that this structure is operated for someone else's benefit — not for his. And there's no reason in it for him. If he is really cunning, really ruthless, really strong — and many of us are — he becomes a kind of criminal. He becomes a kind of criminal because that's the only way he can live. Harlem and every ghetto in this city — every ghetto in this country — is full of people who live outside the law. They wouldn't dream of calling a policeman. They wouldn't, for a moment, listen to any of those professions of which we are so proud on the Fourth of July. They have turned away from this country forever and totally. They live by their wits and really long to see the day when the entire structure comes down.

The point of all this is that black men were brought here as a source of cheap labor. They were indispensable to the economy. In order to justify the fact that men were treated as though they were animals, the white republic had to brainwash itself into believing that they were, indeed, animals and *deserved* to be treated like animals. Therefore it is almost impossible for any Negro child to discover anything about his actual history. The reason is that this "animal," once he suspects his own worth, once he starts believing that he is a man, has begun to attack the entire power structure. This is why America has spent such a long time keeping the Negro in his place. What I am trying to suggest to you is that it was not an accident, it was not an act of God, it was not done by well-meaning people muddling into something which they didn't understand. It was a deliberate policy hammered into place in order to make money from black flesh. And now, in 1963, because we have never faced this fact, we are in intolerable trouble.

The Reconstruction, as I read the evidence, was a bargain between the North   10 and South to this effect: "We've liberated them from the land—and delivered them to the bosses." When we left Mississippi to come North we did not come to freedom. We came to the bottom of the labor market, and we are still there. Even the Depression of the 1930s failed to make a dent in Negroes' relationship to white workers in the labor unions. Even today, so brainwashed is this republic that people seriously ask in what they suppose to be good faith, "What does the Negro want?" I've heard a great many asinine questions in my life, but that is perhaps the most asinine and perhaps the most insulting. But the point here is that people who ask that question, thinking that they ask it in good faith, are really the victims of this conspiracy to make Negroes believe they are less than human.

In order for me to live, I decided very early that some mistake had been made somewhere. I was not a "nigger" even though you called me one. But if I was a "nigger" in your eyes, there was something about *you*—there was something *you* needed. I had to realize when I was very young that I was none of those things I was told I was. I was not, for example, happy. I never touched a watermelon for all kinds of reasons that had been invented by white people, and I knew enough about life by this time to understand that whatever you invent, whatever you project, is you! So where we are now is that a whole country of people believe I'm a "nigger," and I *don't*, and the battle's on! Because if I am not what I've been told I am, then it means that *you're* not what you thought *you* were *either*! And that is the crisis.

It is not really a "Negro revolution" that is upsetting the country. What is upsetting the country is a sense of its own identity. If, for example, one managed to change the curriculum in all the schools so that Negroes learned more about themselves and their real contributions to this culture, you would be liberating not only Negroes, you'd be liberating white people who know nothing about their own history. And the reason is that if you are compelled to lie about one aspect of anybody's history, you must lie about it all. If you have to lie about my real role here, if you have to pretend that I hoed all that cotton just because I loved you, then you have done something to yourself. You are mad.

Now let's go back a minute. I talked earlier about those silent people — the porter and the maid — who, as I said, don't look up at the sky if you ask them if it is raining, but look into your face. My ancestors and I were very well trained. We understood very early that this was not a Christian nation. It didn't matter what you said or how often you went to church. My father and my mother and my grandfather and my grandmother knew that Christians didn't act this way. It was as simple as that. And if that was so there was no point in dealing with white people in terms of their own moral professions, for they were not going to honor them. What one did was to turn away, smiling all the time, and tell white people what they wanted to hear. But people always accuse you of reckless talk when you say this.

All this means that there are in this country tremendous reservoirs of bitterness which have never been able to find an outlet, but may find an outlet soon. It means that well-meaning white liberals place themselves in great danger when they try to deal with Negroes as though they were missionaries. It means, in brief, that a great price is demanded to liberate all those silent people so that they can breathe for the first time and *tell* you what they think of you. And a price is demanded to liberate all those white children — some of them near forty — who have never grown up, and who never will grow up, because they have no sense of their identity.

What passes for identity in America is a series of myths about one's heroic ancestors. It's astounding to me, for example, that so many people really appear to believe that the country was founded by a band of heroes who wanted to be free. That happens not to be true. What happened was that some people left Europe because they couldn't stay there any longer and had to go someplace else to make it. That's all. They were hungry, they were poor, they were convicts. Those who were making it in England, for example, did not get on the *Mayflower*. That's how the country was settled. Not by Gary Cooper. Yet we have a whole race of people, a whole republic, who believe the myths to the point where even today they select political representatives, as far as I can tell, by how closely they resemble Gary Cooper. Now this is dangerously infantile, and it shows in every level of national life. When I was living in Europe, for example, one of the worst revelations to me was the way Americans walked around Europe buying this and buying that and insulting everybody — not even out of malice, just because they didn't know any better. Well, that is the way they have always treated me. They weren't cruel, they just didn't know you were alive. They didn't know you had any feelings.

What I am trying to suggest here is that in the doing of all this for 100 years or more, it is the American white man who has long since lost his grip on reality. In some peculiar way, having created this myth about Negroes, and the myth about his own history, he created myths about the world so that, for example, he was astounded that some people could prefer [Fidel] Castro, astounded that there are people in the world who don't go into hiding when they hear the word "Communism," astounded that Communism is one of the realities of the twentieth century which we will not overcome by pretending that it does not exist. The political level in this country now, on the part of people who should know better, is abysmal.

The Bible says somewhere that where there is no vision the people perish. I don't think anyone can doubt that in this country today we are menaced — intolerably menaced — by a lack of vision.

It is inconceivable that a sovereign people should continue, as we do so abjectly, to say, "I can't do anything about it. It's the government." The government is the creation of the people. It is responsible to the people. And the people are responsible for it. No American has the right to allow the present government to say, when Negro children are being bombed and hosed and shot and beaten all over the Deep South, that there is nothing we can do about it. There must have been a day in this country's life when the bombing of the children in Sunday School would have created a public uproar and endangered the life of a Governor [George] Wallace. It happened here and there was no public uproar.

I began by saying that one of the paradoxes of education was that precisely at the point when you begin to develop a conscience, you must find yourself at war with your society. It is your responsibility to change society if you think of yourself as an educated person. And on the basis of the evidence — the moral and political evidence — one is compelled to say that this is a backward society. Now if I were a teacher in this school, or any Negro school, and I was dealing with Negro children, who were in my care only a few hours of every day and would then return to their homes and to the streets, children who have an apprehension of their future which with every hour grows grimmer and darker, I would try to teach them — I would try to make them know — that those streets, those houses, those dangers, those agonies by which they are surrounded, are criminal. I would try to make each child know that these things are the result of a criminal conspiracy to destroy him. I would teach him that if he intends to get to be a man, he must at once decide that he is stronger than this conspiracy and that he must never make his peace with it. And that one of his weapons for refusing to make his peace with it and for destroying it depends on what he decides he is worth. I would teach him that there are currently very few standards in this country which are worth a man's respect. That it is up to him to begin to change these standards for the sake of the life and the health of the country. I would suggest to him that the popular culture — as represented, for example, on television and in comic books and in movies — is based on fantasies created by very ill people, and he must be aware that these are fantasies that have nothing to do with reality. I would teach him that the press he reads is not as free as it says it is — and that he can do something about that, too. I would try to make him know that just as American history is longer, larger, more various, more beautiful, and more terrible than anything anyone has ever said about it, so is the world larger, more daring, more beautiful and more terrible, but principally larger—and that it belongs to him. I would teach him that he doesn't have to be bound by the expediencies of any given administration, any given policy, any given morality; that he has the right and the necessity to examine everything. I would try to show him that one has not learned anything about Castro when one says, "He is a Communist." This is a way of his learning something about Castro, something about Cuba, something, in time, about the world. I would suggest to him that he is living, at the moment, in an enormous province. America is not the world and if America is going to become a nation, she must find a way—and this child must help her to find a way to use the tremendous potential and tremendous energy which this child represents. If this country does not find a way to use that energy, it will be destroyed by that energy.

Exploring the Text

1. What relationship does James Baldwin establish with his audience in the opening two paragraphs? How does he establish his ethos?
2. What is the "crucial paradox which confronts us here" (para. 2)?
3. Identify four appeals to pathos in paragraphs 3–5.
4. What is the effect of Baldwin's emphasizing his personal experience when he begins paragraph 6 with "I still remember my first sight of New York"?
5. Analyze Baldwin's use of pronouns in paragraphs 8 and 9. What is his purpose in alternating between first, second, and third person?
6. How would you describe Baldwin's perspective on history? What is the effect of using historical events to support his argument?
7. Why, in paragraph 11, does Baldwin use the term *nigger*? What effect would have been lost—or gained—had he used a less provocative term?
8. What does Baldwin mean when he writes, "What passes for identity in America is a series of myths about one's heroic ancestors" (para. 15)?
9. What is the effect of the short two-sentence paragraph 17?
10. Identify examples of parallelism and repetition in the final, long paragraph. Discuss how Baldwin uses these strategies to achieve his purpose.
11. Where in this speech does Baldwin appeal to logos?
12. How would you describe Baldwin's overall tone? Cite specific passages to support your description.

School

KYOKO MORI

Kyoko Mori, who was born in Kobe, Japan, in 1957, earned both an MA and a PhD from the University of Wisconsin. She was a Briggs-Copeland lecturer at Harvard University for several years; she joined the creative writing faculty at George Mason University in Virginia in 2005. She is the author of three nonfiction books, several novels, and numerous essays, many of which have appeared in the annual *Best American Essays*. In her memoir, *Polite Lies: On Being a Woman Caught between Cultures* (1999), she reflects on the differences between Japan and America. The following selection is a chapter from that book focusing on differences in education.

During our senior year at college, some of my classmates said they could hardly wait to graduate, to join "the real world." They couldn't concentrate on classes, knowing that they would soon be out of school forever. I didn't feel the same way at all. School seemed as "real" to me as "the outside world"—only more interesting.

I still don't trust the distinction often made between school and "the real world," which implies that there is something insubstantial or artificial about school. The business meetings I attended in Milwaukee as an interpreter confirmed my suspicion that arcane and "academic" discussions don't happen only at colleges. The directors of two small companies, one Japanese and the other American, once had a twenty-minute debate about whether the plastic cover of a particular camera lens should be "pumpkin yellow" or "the yellow of raincoats." What each man meant by these terms was unclear to the other and had to be redefined many times over. This is the conversation I recall now when I attend academic conferences and cannot understand what is being said about a book I have read more than once.

School and "the real world" both have their absurd moments, but school is where people go when they are not satisfied with their "real world" lives and want a change. Many Americans in their thirties and forties go back to college to get trained for a different line of work or to pursue a lifelong interest they couldn't afford to study earlier. Until they are in need of such second chances, most Americans take colleges for granted because they are always there—almost any adult can get into some college at any age.

Being able to go back to school is a particularly American opportunity. My Japanese friends will never be able to do the same. In Japan, school does not give anyone a second chance. Many of my Japanese friends are married women with money who already have college degrees. But none of them can go back to college to earn a second degree in art, education, or social work, as their American counterparts may do.

Recently, a few Japanese colleges have started accepting applications from adults who have been out of school for years, but these colleges are exceptions. The only   5 way most people can get into a college in Japan is to take and pass the entrance examination for that particular college immediately after graduating from high school. The number of exams a student can sit for in a given year is limited since many schools give their exams on the same day.

A student who does not get into any college will have to wait a year, attending a cram school. There is a word for a student in this situation—*ronin* (floating person). In feudal times, the word referred to samurai whose clan had been dissolved. Feudal *ronin* had to roam around until they could find a new master to serve. To be a modern *ronin* is scarcely better: while their friends move on to colleges or jobs, *ronin* must float around for a year without any allegiance. In Japan, anyone who doesn't belong to the right group at the right time feels like a failure. If a *ronin* can't get into a college after a year at a cram school, he or she usually gives up and settles for a low-paying job rather than spending another year floating around.

In the States, young people who don't feel ready for college can work for a few years and then apply when they feel more motivated or mature. Young Japanese people don't have the same chance. For older adults to go back to school to have a second chance—at a job or an artistic career or personal fulfillment—is practically impossible.

The very accessibility of schools in America adds to the perception that they are not real or substantial enough. Many Americans who criticize their own school system for being "too easy" idealize the Japanese school system because they are drawn to its rough image. The details Americans cite as the merits of the Japanese system actually reflect their ideal of the mythical "real world" where people must work hard—long hours, the emphasis on discipline and basic skills, the tough competition among peers. These people admire the Japanese school system because they see it as a samurai version of their own fantasies about the American work ethic.

My education at a traditional Japanese grade school was nothing so glorious. Day-to-day life at a Japanese public school was harsh but also boring. Until I transferred to a private school in seventh grade, I didn't learn anything that I couldn't have learned at home by reading and memorizing the same books with my mother's help.

Recently when I was in Japan, I was asked why I did not write my novels in Japanese, why I did not at least translate my own work. The question surprised me at first. The people who asked knew that for twelve years I have lived in a small Wisconsin town where I have few opportunities to speak Japanese. No one can write novels in a language she has not spoken every day for more than a decade. But there is another reason I could not possibly have written my novels or poems in Japanese: I was never taught to write in what was my native language. My public education in Japan prepared me to make the correct letters to spell out the correct sounds, but that is not the same as teaching me how to write.

When I started the first grade at six, I had not been taught to read at home—at least not in a formal way. Because my mother read to me all the time, I had memorized my favorite books and could read along with her. Sometimes, when my mother and I were standing on the street corner waiting for a taxi, I noticed that I could read the license plates of the cars passing by. I would read the plates and she would nod and smile because I was right, but no big fuss was made about my being able to read. Most of the other kids starting school with me were the same way: we sort of knew how to read because of our mothers, but we hadn't been formally trained.

In first grade, we were taught the fifty phonetic signs that make up the Japanese alphabet, a dozen simple pictorial characters, and the basic numbers. By the end of the year, everyone in our class could read our textbooks and write simple messages to our family and friends in our sprawling, uneven handwriting. People who admire the Japanese education system are partially right. Japanese schools *are* very good at teaching skills like basic writing—which can only be learned through memorization and repeated practice.

Once we learned the alphabet and some pictorial characters, my classmates and I wrote compositions about our families, our vacations, our friends. Occasionally, our teachers had us write stories and poems as well. In summer, we were given notebooks in which we had to keep "picture diaries": on the upper, blank, half we drew pictures, and on the lower, lined, half we wrote sentences about what we did every day. These assignments gave us a lot of practice at writing.

When we got to the upper grades, though, our assignments changed. We no longer wrote stories or poems; our compositions weren't about our personal experiences or feelings. Almost every writing assignment was a book report or a summary of our reading. We had to follow a very strict formula, organizing our thoughts under predetermined headings like "plot," "characters," "setting," "themes," "what we learned from the book." If we didn't follow the format, we got poor grades.

The grades didn't always make sense. Luckily, I did well most of the time, but I wasn't sure what I did right aside from adhering to the format. The only suggestions I got were circled corrections where I had used the wrong pictorial characters or general remarks about my bad penmanship. 15

A few of my friends didn't do so well, but they were never given suggestions for improvement. They would simply get low grades and comments like "Your writing needs improvement," "You didn't really follow the directions for the assignment," or "I can see you tried some but you still have a long way to go." Often, our teachers openly scolded pupils. In front of the whole class, my friends were told to "pay better attention" and to "try harder." It didn't matter that most of them were serious and well-behaved students, not lazy and inattentive troublemakers; they were already trying hard, trying to pay attention.

No matter what the subject, our teachers never gave us very clear advice about how to do better. When I couldn't understand long division or fractions and decimals in math, I felt bad at first. On the timed tests we had every day, I could finish only half the problems before the teacher's stopwatch beeped, telling us to put down our pencils. The results were put up on the wall, and my name was always near the bottom. I was told to "try harder," but none of my teachers spent extra time with me to go over what I was doing wrong. Since I wasn't given a real chance to improve, I decided after a while that I didn't really care how I did.

Over and over again, our Japanese education offered this sort of harsh judgment combined with vague exhortation. In every subject, kids who didn't do well were made to feel ashamed and yet given no chance to improve. The humiliation was especially obvious in physical education classes. At our grade school we were expected to learn to swim in the same way we were expected to learn to write: by sheer repetition and "trying harder." We were left to swim around on our own, but the pool hours weren't just for fun. Each of us had to wear a cloth swim-cap with the symbol that indicated our skill level. Students who couldn't swim at all were singled out by the big red circle sewn on top of their caps. "Red mark, red mark, you'll sink like a big hammer," some of the other kids taunted, and the teachers did nothing to stop them. I was glad that I already knew how to swim by the time I started school.

For those of us who could swim, there were monthly tests to determine how far we could go without stopping. For every five or ten meters we could swim, our mothers sewed red or black lines on the side of our caps. Those who could swim fifty meters in the crawl, sidestroke, or breaststroke got the best marks on their caps: five all-black lines. In fifth grade, when I passed the test for fifty meters, my teachers praised me for having "tried so hard," even though I was able to do so well only because my mother had taught me to swim in the river near her parents' home. Unlike my teachers, my mother enjoyed giving specific instructions. She drew diagrams on paper to show me what my arms and legs should be doing for crawl and sidestroke. Then she made me lie down on the sand on the river bank to practice the arm and leg movements. Once I was in the water, she stood on the bank shouting out instructions like "Stretch your arms all the way," "Turn your head sideways." When my form was wrong, she showed me by imitating me— exaggerating my awkward movements and making me laugh. "I don't look like *that*," I protested, but I knew exactly what I needed to improve.

I did not learn how to write in Japanese because even at the private school I 20 attended after seventh grade, Japanese language classes were taught by older men who had studied classical Japanese literature or Chinese poetry at the national universities before the war. They were the most conservative and traditional of all our teachers. In their classes, we read the works of famous authors and wrote essays to answer questions like: "What is the theme?" "When does the main character realize the importance of morality?" "What important Buddhist philosophy is expressed in this passage?" All the writing we did for our extracurricular activities—for skits or school newspapers and magazines—was supervised by younger teachers who did not teach Japanese.

During those same years, we learned how to write in English. Our English teachers were young Japanese women who had studied in the States or England,

and American women from small Midwestern towns who had just graduated from college. In their classes, we wrote essays about our families, friends, hobbies, future dreams—personal subjects we had not written about at school since third grade. We were given plenty of instruction about the specifics of writing: word choice, description, style. Our essays came back with comments both about our writing and about the thoughts we had expressed. I looked forward to writing essays and reading my teachers' comments. By the time I was a high school senior, I wanted to be a writer, and English was the only language I could write in.

To study writing, I had to go to an American college. Creative writing was not—and still is not—offered at Japanese colleges, in English or in Japanese. I don't know how Japanese writers learn to write, since most of them, as children, must have had the same kind of education I had. There are no schools or writers' conferences where a person can study creative writing as an adult. I have never heard of people getting together to form a writing group or workshop.

Writing is not something that comes naturally to the chosen few. Most American writers of my generation didn't just learn to write on their own. Without the classes we took in creative writing and modern literature, we wouldn't have known what to read, how to read it, how to pay attention to form and content. We needed to be shown how to write good dialogue, smooth transitions, pared-down but vivid character descriptions. These things didn't come naturally. It would have taken us thirty years to learn, on our own, the same skills we learned in eight years of college and graduate school. My friends at graduate school came from average Midwestern homes; they were not children of famous writers. School gave us a chance we would never have had otherwise. In America, we are proof that the romantic notion of the natural writer is a myth. In Japan, where no formal training is offered in writing, the myth may be a sad reality that prevents many people from becoming writers.

My stepmother used the traditional method of harsh judgment even though she was not a teacher. When Michiko came to live with my family, I was twelve and already knew how to cook and bake simple foods like omelettes and chocolate chip cookies and how to clean up the kitchen. But my attempts to help Michiko always ended in disaster. She complained endlessly about how I had not been taught to do things the "proper way." Everything I did, from drying the dishes to sweeping the floor, was wrong. "I can't believe that you don't know how to do this," she would scold in her shrill voice, and yet she never showed me exactly what the "proper way" was. When I asked, "What do you mean? What am I doing wrong?" she would scream, "If I have to tell you, then it's no good. I can't show you something you should already know." I was supposed to watch her silently and learn on my own through observation, but she made me too nervous to concentrate. I had no idea what I was supposed to be looking for. If I gave up and asked, "Do you mean the way I am holding the broom or are you saying that I should start over there instead of here?" she would stomp out of the kitchen without a word.

I know that Michiko's silent and judgmental manner was a manifestation of her meanspiritedness, but she didn't invent the method. The tradition of not giving specific instruction comes from Zen. In traditional Zen philosophy, satori or enlightenment is considered to be beyond human description. Since no one can describe satori or ways to attain it, the teacher-monk asks his disciples a series of koans—questions meant to puzzle and disturb rather than to provide answers. The whole purpose of the koan is to break down the disciples' reliance on their own intellect by humiliating them. At its worst, the teaching technique amounts to intellectual or spiritual hazing. The disciples are supposed to hit bottom and suffer terrible despair before they can open their eyes to satori and experience beauty and peace that is beyond logic or description.

To my American friends who took up Zen in college, this style of teaching seemed liberating because of its apparent emphasis on a larger and unexplainable truth instead of minute and trivial details. After years of American education, my friends were tired of specific instruction. All the rules they had to learn about writing good paragraphs or improving their tennis swings struck them as fussy and superficial. Zen taught them that everything they had learned in their Western education was an illusion that needed to be shattered. The very destructiveness and uncertainty of enlightenment sounded uplifting.

But in the Zen-style teaching actually practiced in Japan, students are not liberated from minute details. The details are everything. A beginning calligraphy student writes the same letters over and over, trying to make her brush strokes look exactly like her master's. If she puts one dot five millimeters too far to the right, her work is considered flawed. The master does not point out her mistake. "No, not right yet," he grunts. "Do it over." Until the student can see for herself that her dot is in the wrong place, she will have to keep copying the same letters— she has not reached "enlightenment."

In America, students are often drilled on the details of grammar or form and yet are forgiven for the minor mistakes they make in their writing. Their teacher might say, "You have a couple of awkward sentences and punctuation mistakes here, but your paper is excellent overall. Your ideas are good and you write with a wonderful voice." Hearing comments like these, my friends concluded that their teachers were being inconsistent. If the minor details weren't important in the end, why did the teachers spend so much time on them?

The paradox about the two styles of teaching is that neither emphasizes what it considers to be truly important. In calligraphy and other traditional arts derived from Zen, following the correct form is everything—there is no possibility that you can make a few minor mistakes and still "get" the spirit or the essence of the "truth"—and yet instruction consists of vague exhortation about "following the right balance" and "working hard." In America, where teachers actually value the overall spirit of the work, they spend most of their time talking about details.

This paradox reflects a common ground all teachers share. No matter what and how we teach, we believe that what we value the most is beyond our meager ability to describe. We are struck dumb with admiration at the things we value, so we try to teach the secondary things that we think are easier to talk about. Like most American writing teachers, I value the overall spirit or genuine voice in my students' work and yet nag them about the smaller details of technique like trimming their lines or writing better dialogue. Mine is a Western approach—the same method of instruction is apparent even in the Bible, which gives God a name that cannot be spoken, while offering book after book detailing the laws about how to build a temple or what foods should not be eaten together.

My Japanese teachers, who thought that detail was everything, must have felt that precision was so important that it could not be described: only the truly enlightened can be in perfect harmony with the correct form. In the meantime, they must have reasoned, they could at least talk about the value of hard work, something everyone can easily understand. The contradiction we share points to the difficulty of teaching anything: trying to pass on knowledge that seems so clear to ourselves to people who don't have that knowledge. When my stepmother complained, "How can I teach you something you should already know?" she was expressing in its meanest form the universal frustration of teachers.

In spite of our shared frustration, though, I have a hard time forgiving some of my former teachers in Japan because they never seemed humbled by the near impossibility of their task. Many of my teachers felt entitled to be both strict and arbitrary—strict about their own authority and the rules of the system and yet so arbitrary and lax about helping us.

In Japan, whether you are in school or at your private karate, judo, or *ikebana*[1] lesson, you can never question the authority of the teacher, whom you address simply as "sensei," literally, "one whose life comes first." Unless there are multiple teachers who need to be distinguished from one another, you do not even use their family names, much less first names (which you most likely do not know). The teacher is like the biblical God, whom you cannot name.

Students are not expected to question the competence of their teachers or the usefulness of their assignments, any more than Zen disciples can rebel against their master and his koans. Japanese students who study at American universities are amazed that at the end of the semester most universities ask their students to evaluate their teachers. Even though students in Japan complain to each other about their teachers, they would never think of writing an evaluation or filing official grievances.

In the teaching of many traditional Japanese art forms, the teacher's author-   35
ity is backed up by a complete hierarchy called *ie* that controls instruction. Even the choice of this word, since it means both "house" and "family origin," reflects high expectations of allegiance. What is described in English as a "school" (such

---

[1]Japanese art of flower arrangement.—Eds.

as a school of writing or painting) is actually a "family" in Japanese. Each *ie* is structured like a family hierarchy: at the top is the head teacher, called *iemoto* (source of the house), and under him are various assistant teachers who, in turn, take their own assistants. All these teachers are licensed by the *ie*. A beginner in *ikebana* or Japanese dance will study with a minor assistant teacher for a few years and then move on to a more advanced teacher. There are various levels of competence awarded along the way, but every advancement must be approved by the *ie*.

The system makes it impossible for a student to challenge any teacher's decision, since the teacher can invoke the authority of the whole clanlike hierarchy. Teachers can make any arbitrary decision so long as it can be backed up by the *ie*. When my cousin Kazumi studied *ikebana*, she was disillusioned by the unfair judgments her teachers made every year about who should be allowed to advance to the next level of competence. There were no tests or lists of tasks and qualities that determined the advancements. Who advanced and who didn't seemed entirely up to the teachers' whims. People who were related to any of the teachers rose through the ranks much faster than those who weren't.

Whether or not they won an advancement to the next level, all the students were required to attend the annual certificate ceremony in their best kimonos. The year of the Kobe earthquake Kazumi received a letter from her *ie* advising students to rent a good kimono to attend the annual ceremony if theirs had been destroyed in the earthquake.

"I had been disillusioned with *ikebana* for some time anyway," Kazumi told me, "but the letter was the last straw. I couldn't believe that the teachers thought this was a time for people to be worrying about their kimonos. Even though the letter said that we didn't necessarily have to have a nice kimono if our family had suffered such a great damage that we had no money, the tone was very condescending—and it was obvious that they were really saying that we should rent one no matter what the cost. They didn't write and say, 'We are so sorry about the earthquake. We would be so happy if you could still come to the annual ceremony in spite of the damage many of you must have suffered, and of course, you can wear whatever you would like.'"

She switched to Dutch-style flower arrangement even though it, too, has a nationwide association that oversees its teaching and licensing. Like *ikebana*, Dutch flower arrangement has different levels of teachers and different levels of competence, but Kazumi sees a big difference between the two. To advance from one to the next in the Dutch style, people take tests in which each person is given a bucket of flowers to make into a table arrangement, a small bouquet, and a corsage; a group of judges scores the results. Everybody has the same amount of time, the same number of arrangements to complete, similar flowers in the bucket, and the same group of judges. Evaluation isn't arbitrary the way it was for *ikebana*. In the lessons she took—mostly from Dutch teachers—plenty of specific instruction was given about colors, textures, shapes, and the flowers themselves. Her teachers looked at her work and gave her suggestions—something none of her *ikebana* teachers ever did.

Until I talked to Kazumi, I was hoping that even though my Japanese friends   40 could not go back to school in their thirties and forties, they might be able to take private lessons or receive training through volunteer work in order to pursue some of their interests. Even in small towns like Green Bay, many people my age can learn new skills, pursue their hobbies, or work for causes they believe in without enrolling in school.

My Japanese friends do not have similar chances to learn something new or feel useful. There are very few volunteer organizations in Japan for nature conservation, crisis intervention, helping children, or working with families who are poor or homeless. The few soup kitchens one might find in big Japanese cities are operated by international organizations like the Salvation Army. People who work at them are mostly foreigners. A nice Japanese housewife is not expected to do volunteer work for strangers. "If she has time to help people she doesn't even know," her relatives would grumble, "why doesn't she do more to help her own kids study? Why doesn't she run for an office in the P.T.A. at their school?" Most middle-class Japanese people seem to think that poor people deserve to be poor— it's their own fault or the fault of their families and relatives. Nobody should expect help from total strangers. As for conserving nature, that is the job of biologists. My friends have a hard time justifying their passion for gardening to their husbands and in-laws. If they were to spend their afternoons taking care of injured wildlife or clearing marshes of trash instead of cleaning their houses and preparing special meals for their children, their families would probably disown them.

Nice housewives like my friends can take private lessons only if they can be justified as genteel means of cultivating fine, feminine tastes—like *ikebana*, tea, koto and samisen[2] music—but these are the traditional Japanese arts with the strict *ie* structure. Joining the *ie* would involve my friends in another burdensome system of duties and obligations, something they already experience in every facet of their lives.

In so many ways, Japan is a place of no second chances. Many of my friends are in very unhappy marriages. They write to me about the shouting and shoving matches they have with their husbands, about the night they tried to run away, only to have the husband chase them down the street, catch them, and drag them home. Unable to run away, my friends lock themselves up in the guest room or sleep in their daughters' rooms to avoid sleeping with their husbands. For most American women, leaving a bad marriage like theirs would be nothing but happiness. My friends stay because divorce still carries a big stigma in Japan. If they leave their

---

[2]Traditional Japanese instruments. A koto has thirteen strings of fixed tonality and is plucked, like a harp. A samisen has three strings on a fingerboard and is picked, like a banjo.—Eds.

husbands, they may never be able to see their children again. Certainly, they will not be able to marry again and try another chance at marriage. Nobody marries a divorced middle-aged woman in Japan.

Life in Japan is like an unending stint at a school where you have to keep taking tests — giving your answers under pressure without help or guidance, knowing that you will get no second chance if you make a mistake. Japanese people have to make many of the big decisions of their lives — whom to marry, what company to join — without detailed information, since it is rude to ask direct questions even at *omiai* meetings[3] and job interviews. They have no choice but to trust authority and do their best, just as they were supposed to do in school. If their job or marriage turns out to be a disappointment, they will be given the same vague exhortations they heard from their teachers: keep trying, work hard, pay attention.

There is nothing intrinsically wrong with trying harder. Sometimes when I 45 see my former students in Green Bay seeming to flounder — waiting on tables or working clerical jobs they hate, the whole time talking about their big plans to "go back to school" soon — I think maybe a little Japanese perseverance might not hurt them. I know that for them or for anyone else, going back to school does not guarantee a job or happiness. Within school, too, when my students complain that everything we read in a modern American literature class is depressing or that I simply do not "like" their work (when every poem they wrote in the class is a love poem in couplets), I long for a little Japanese respect for authority. Some of my students would be better off if they trusted me a little rather than questioning my decisions at every turn. Still, I would rather have students who question too much than those who assume that I know best and don't owe them any explanations. No one should have power that is unjustified and unjustifiable, regardless of how convenient or efficient it may seem for the smooth running of the classroom, the educational system, or the country.

The problem with the Japanese system, ultimately, is that individual freedom — to question the teacher, to disagree — is sacrificed for the supposed convenience and protection of the whole group. The system works well for people who feel no desire to rebel. The Japanese *ie* system my cousin complained about does ensure that anyone who perseveres in a given art form will have some recognition; periodically, every student is asked to take part in public exhibitions or concerts. Most Japanese students have public-performance opportunities many of my American friends — artists and musicians — don't.

But for me — as well as for my cousin — the price is too high. The security comes with too many obligations. The *ie* system asks that you trust your teachers who have not earned or deserved your trust. What you are required to have is blind faith in the *ie*: like the church or the mosque, the *ie* is an institution that is designed to inspire total obedience to its rules. In Japan, if you reject your chance to enjoy

---

[3]Meetings in which two singles and their families meet to determine whether they would be a suitable match for marriage. — Eds.

the security that comes from joining the right group such as an *ie*, an elite school, a good company, or a respectable family, you will have to leave the country or live in it as an outcast. Life in Japan resembles the harshest interpretation of a religious faith: the Koran or the sword, either you are with Christ or against him, either you join the sheltering umbrella of Japanese security or you have nothing. In school and elsewhere, people are rewarded for obeying the rules diligently, never for taking a chance and being different, or for asking good questions.

But words like *security* and *uncertainty* are misleading. Because Dutch-style flower arrangement is not as popular as *ikebana* and the association does not provide the same kind of protection that a traditional *ie* gives its teachers, my cousin is struggling to get enough students for the classes she offers. She has quit her clerical job, which she did not like, and committed herself to the life of a flower-arrangement teacher. She isn't going to get a second chance at being a clerk or going back to *ikebana*. My cousin's life is uncertain and insecure. But daily, as she arranges her own flowers and watches her students cutting and arranging theirs, she is certain of other things. She knows when she is making a good arrangement and when she is not. In Dutch-style arrangements, my cousin has learned what colors and shapes look pleasing; she has a firm sense of what she considers beautiful. She also knows that she will tell her students exactly what she thinks about their work rather than keeping her criticism to herself or being vague. Kazumi feels a certainty about truth, beauty, honesty. That is the only certainty worth choosing.

Exploring the Text

1. According to Kyoko Mori, what are the major differences between the Japanese and American educational systems? Summarize them.
2. Why does she place the phrase "the real world" in quotation marks (para. 1)?
3. What is the effect of Mori's introducing Japanese terms, especially *ronin* (para. 6), at the beginning of the essay?
4. Does Mori's reliance on personal experience limit or enhance her analysis? Explain.
5. What does Mori mean by the "romantic notion of the natural writer" (para. 23)? To what extent do you believe that writing skill is a matter of "natural" talent?
6. What is the "paradox" that Mori refers to in paragraph 30?
7. What is Mori's purpose in including her cousin Kazumi's experience (paras. 36–39)?
8. Describe the arrangement of this essay. At the most general level, it is organized as a comparison/contrast, but it is made up of eight sections that are separated by space within the text. Would you say that this structure is governed more by logos or pathos?
9. Apart from the fact that her book is written in English, how do you know that Western readers are her audience?

10. How would you describe Mori's attitude toward Japan in this essay? Is she sympathetic? Harsh? Ambivalent? Cite specific passages to support your response.
11. How does your own experience in school compare with Mori's as she describes it in paragraphs 15–19?

Superman and Me

SHERMAN ALEXIE

Sherman J. Alexie Jr. (b. 1966), a member of the Spokane and the Coeur d'Alene tribes, grew up on the Spokane Reservation in Washington state. A graduate of Washington State University, he has published more than twenty books, most notably *The Lone Ranger and Tonto Fistfight in Heaven* (1993), *The Absolutely True Diary of a Part-Time Indian* (2007), and *War Dances* (2009), which won the PEN/Faulkner Award for best American fiction. One of the stories in the *Lone Ranger* collection was the basis for the movie *Smoke Signals* (1999), for which Alexie wrote the screenplay. An activist for Native American rights and culture, Alexie wrote the following essay describing the impact of reading on his life. It was originally published in the *Los Angeles Times* in 1998 for a series called "The Joy of Reading and Writing."

I learned to read with a Superman comic book. Simple enough, I suppose. I cannot recall which particular Superman comic book I read, nor can I remember which villain he fought in that issue. I cannot remember the plot, nor the means by which I obtained the comic book. What I can remember is this: I was 3 years old, a Spokane Indian boy living with his family on the Spokane Indian Reservation in eastern Washington state. We were poor by most standards, but one of my parents usually managed to find some minimum-wage job or another, which made us middle-class by reservation standards. I had a brother and three sisters. We lived on a combination of irregular paychecks, hope, fear and government surplus food.

My father, who is one of the few Indians who went to Catholic school on purpose, was an avid reader of westerns, spy thrillers, murder mysteries, gangster epics, basketball player biographies and anything else he could find. He bought his books by the pound at Dutch's Pawn Shop, Goodwill, Salvation Army and Value Village. When he had extra money, he bought new novels at supermarkets, convenience stores and hospital gift shops. Our house was filled with books. They were stacked in crazy piles in the bathroom, bedrooms and living room. In a fit of unemployment-inspired creative energy, my father built a set of bookshelves and soon filled them with a random assortment of books about the Kennedy assassination, Watergate, the Vietnam War and the entire 23-book series of the Apache westerns. My father loved books, and since I loved my father with an aching devotion, I decided to love books as well.

I can remember picking up my father's books before I could read. The words themselves were mostly foreign, but I still remember the exact moment when I first understood, with a sudden clarity, the purpose of a paragraph. I didn't have the vocabulary to say "paragraph," but I realized that a paragraph was a fence that held words. The words inside a paragraph worked together for a common purpose. They had some specific reason for being inside the same fence. This knowledge delighted me. I began to think of everything in terms of paragraphs. Our reservation was a small paragraph within the United States. My family's house was a paragraph, distinct from the other paragraphs of the LeBrets to the north, the Fords to our south and the Tribal School to the west. Inside our house, each family member existed as a separate paragraph but still had genetics and common experiences to link us. Now, using this logic, I can see my changed family as an essay of seven paragraphs: mother, father, older brother, the deceased sister, my younger twin sisters and our adopted little brother.

At the same time I was seeing the world in paragraphs, I also picked up that Superman comic book. Each panel, complete with picture, dialogue and narrative, was a three-dimensional paragraph. In one panel, Superman breaks through a door. His suit is red, blue and yellow. The brown door shatters into many pieces. I look at the narrative above the picture. I cannot read the words, but I assume it tells me that "Superman is breaking down the door." Aloud, I pretend to read the words and say, "Superman is breaking down the door." Words, dialogue, also float out of Superman's mouth. Because he is breaking down the door, I assume he says, "I am breaking down the door." Once again, I pretend to read the words and say aloud, "I am breaking down the door." In this way, I learned to read.

This might be an interesting story all by itself. A little Indian boy teaches himself to read at an early age and advances quickly. He reads *Grapes of Wrath* in kindergarten when other children are struggling through *Dick and Jane*. If he'd been anything but an Indian boy living on the reservation, he might have been called a prodigy. But he is an Indian boy living on the reservation and is simply an oddity. He grows into a man who often speaks of his childhood in the third-person, as if it will somehow dull the pain and make him sound more modest about his talents.

5

A smart Indian is a dangerous person, widely feared and ridiculed by Indians and non-Indians alike. I fought with my classmates on a daily basis. They wanted me to stay quiet when the non-Indian teacher asked for answers, for volunteers, for help. We were Indian children who were expected to be stupid. Most lived up to those expectations inside the classroom but subverted them on the outside. They struggled with basic reading in school but could remember how to sing a few dozen powwow songs. They were monosyllabic in front of their non-Indian teachers but could tell complicated stories and jokes at the dinner table. They submissively ducked their heads when confronted by a non-Indian adult but would slug it out with the Indian bully who was 10 years older. As

Indian children, we were expected to fail in the non-Indian world. Those who failed were ceremonially accepted by other Indians and appropriately pitied by non-Indians.

I refused to fail. I was smart. I was arrogant. I was lucky. I read books late into the night, until I could barely keep my eyes open. I read books at recess, then during lunch and in the few minutes left after I had finished my classroom assignments. I read books in the car when my family traveled to powwows or basketball games. In shopping malls, I ran to the bookstores and read bits and pieces of as many books as I could. I read the books my father brought home from the pawnshops and secondhand. I read the books I borrowed from the library. I read the backs of cereal boxes. I read the newspaper. I read the bulletins posted on the walls of the school, the clinic, the tribal offices, the post office. I read junk mail. I read auto-repair manuals. I read magazines. I read anything that had words and paragraphs. I read with equal parts joy and desperation. I loved those books, but I also knew that love had only one purpose. I was trying to save my life.

Despite all the books I read, I am still surprised I became a writer. I was going to be a pediatrician. These days, I write novels, short stories, and poems. I visit schools and teach creative writing to Indian kids. In all my years in the reservation school system, I was never taught how to write poetry, short stories or novels. I was certainly never taught that Indians wrote poetry, short stories and novels. Writing was something beyond Indians. I cannot recall a single time that a guest teacher visited the reservation. There must have been visiting teachers. Who were they? Where are they now? Do they exist? I visit the schools as often as possible. The Indian kids crowd the classroom. Many are writing their own poems, short stories and novels. They have read my books. They have read many other books. They look at me with bright eyes and arrogant wonder. They are trying to save their lives. Then there are the sullen and already defeated Indian kids who sit in the back rows and ignore me with theatrical precision. The pages of their notebooks are empty. They carry neither pencil nor pen. They stare out the window. They refuse and resist. "Books," I say to them. "Books," I say. I throw my weight against their locked doors. The door holds. I am smart. I am arrogant. I am lucky. I am trying to save our lives.

Exploring the Text

1. What figure of speech is the following: "We lived on a combination of irregular paychecks, hope, fear and government surplus food" (para. 1)? What is its effect?
2. In what ways does the description of Sherman Alexie's father play against stereotypes of Native Americans?
3. What is the effect of Alexie's analogy of a paragraph to a fence (para. 3)?
4. What does Alexie mean when he describes "an Indian boy" who "grows into a man who often speaks of his childhood in the third-person" (para. 5)?

5. In paragraph 7, Alexie deliberately uses a number of short, simple sentences. What effect do you think he is trying to achieve?

6. This eight-paragraph essay is divided into two distinct sections. Why? How would you describe its arrangement? How does it suit Alexie's overall purpose?

7. Discuss Alexie's use of parallel structure and repetition in the last two paragraphs. Pay particular attention to the final sentence in each.

8. Who is the audience for this essay? Cite specific passages to support your response.

9. What is your first memory of books and reading? Do you associate it with a specific person or setting? How has your early experience affected your attitude toward books and reading?

10. Alexie writes that he read to save his life, and many others have written that books opened up worlds and possibilities that gave them a new life. Do you believe that reading and books can still have that power? Explain.

11. Will you read books — plain old two-dimensional print texts with pictures — to your children? During these times of Kindles and e-books and iPads and other electronic means of presenting what traditionally existed on paper, do you think that books per se will be important to the next generation? Explain the reasons for your view.

Me Talk Pretty One Day

David Sedaris

One of America's premier humorists, David Sedaris (b. 1956) is a playwright, essayist, and frequent contributor to National Public Radio. Five of his essay collections have been best sellers, including *Naked* (1997), *Holidays on Ice* (1997), *Me Talk Pretty One Day* (2000), *Dress Your Family in Corduroy and Denim* (2004), and *When You Are Engulfed in Flames* (2008). His most recent book is *Squirrel Seeks Chipmunk: A Modest Bestiary* (2010), a collection of humorous short stories. Sedaris has been nominated for three Grammy Awards for Best Spoken Word and Best Comedy Album. Much of his satiric humor is autobiographical and self-effacing as he points out the foolishness and foibles of the human condition.

At the age of forty-one, I am returning to school and have to think of myself as what my French textbook calls "a true debutant." After paying my tuition, I was issued a student ID, which allows me a discounted entry fee at movie theaters, puppet shows, and Festyland, a far-flung amusement park that advertises with billboards picturing a cartoon stegosaurus sitting in a canoe and eating what appears to be a ham sandwich.

I've moved to Paris with the hopes of learning the language. My school is an easy ten-minute walk from my apartment, and on the first day of class I arrived early, watching as the returning students greeted one another in the school lobby. Vacations were recounted, and questions were raised concerning mutual friends with names like Kang and Vlatnya. Regardless of their nationalities, everyone spoke in what sounded to me like excellent French. Some accents were better than others, but the students exhibited an ease and confidence I found intimidating. As an added discomfort, they were all young, attractive, and well dressed, causing me to feel not unlike Pa Kettle[1] trapped backstage after a fashion show.

The first day of class was nerve-racking because I knew I'd be expected to perform. That's the way they do it here — it's everybody into the language pool, sink or swim. The teacher marched in, deeply tanned from a recent vacation, and proceeded to rattle off a series of administrative announcements. I've spent quite a few summers in Normandy, and I took a monthlong French class before leaving New York. I'm not completely in the dark, yet I understood only half of what this woman was saying.

"If you have not *meimslsxp* or *lgpdmurct* by this time, then you should not be in this room. Has everyone *apzkiubjxow*? Everyone? Good, we shall begin." She spread out her lesson plan and sighed, saying, "All right, then, who knows the alphabet?"

It was startling because (a) I hadn't been asked that question in a while and (b) I realized, while laughing, that I myself did *not* know the alphabet. They're the same letters, but in France they're pronounced differently. I know the shape of the alphabet but had no idea what it actually sounded like.

"Ahh." The teacher went to the board and sketched the letter *a*. "Do we have anyone in the room whose first name commences with an *ahh*?"

Two Polish Annas raised their hands, and the teacher instructed them to present themselves by stating their names, nationalities, occupations, and a brief list of things they liked and disliked in this world. The first Anna hailed from an industrial town outside of Warsaw and had front teeth the size of tombstones. She worked as a seamstress, enjoyed quiet times with friends, and hated the mosquito.

"Oh, really," the teacher said. "How very interesting. I thought that everyone loved the mosquito, but here, in front of all the world, you claim to detest him. How is it that we've been blessed with someone as unique and original as you? Tell us, please?"

The seamstress did not understand what was being said but knew that this was an occasion for shame. Her rabbity mouth huffed for breath, and she stared down at her lap as though the appropriate comeback were stitched somewhere alongside the zipper of her slacks.

The second Anna learned from the first and claimed to love sunshine and detest lies. It sounded like a translation of one of those Playmate of the Month data sheets, the answers always written in the same loopy handwriting: "Turn-ons:

---

[1]Ma and Pa Kettle were comic film characters from the 1940s to 1950s. They were caricatures of unsophisticated country folk. — Eds.

Mom's famous five-alarm chili! Turnoffs: insecurity and guys who come on too strong!!!!"

The two Polish Annas surely had clear notions of what they loved and hated, but like the rest of us, they were limited in terms of vocabulary, and this made them appear less than sophisticated. The teacher forged on, and we learned that Carlos, the Argentine bandonion player, loved wine, music, and, in his words, "making sex with the womens of the world." Next came a beautiful young Yugoslav who identified herself as an optimist, saying that she loved everything that life had to offer.

The teacher licked her lips, revealing a hint of the saucebox we would later come to know. She crouched low for her attack, placed her hands on the young woman's desk, and leaned close, saying, "Oh yeah? And do you love your little war?"

While the optimist struggled to defend herself, I scrambled to think of an answer to what had obviously become a trick question. How often is one asked what he loves in this world? More to the point, how often is one asked and then publicly ridiculed for his answer? I recalled my mother, flushed with wine, pounding the tabletop late one night, saying, "Love? I love a good steak cooked rare. I love my cat, and I love . . ." My sisters and I leaned forward, waiting to hear our names. "Tums," our mother said. "I love Tums."

The teacher killed some time accusing the Yugoslavian girl of masterminding a program of genocide, and I jotted frantic notes in the margins of my pad. While I can honestly say that I love leafing through medical textbooks devoted to severe dermatological conditions, the hobby is beyond the reach of my French vocabulary, and acting it out would only have invited controversy.

When called upon, I delivered an effortless list of things that I detest: blood sausage, intestinal pâtés, brain pudding. I'd learned these words the hard way. Having given it some thought, I then declared my love for IBM typewriters, the French word for *bruise*, and my electric floor waxer. It was a short list, but still I managed to mispronounce *IBM* and assign the wrong gender to both the floor waxer and the typewriter. The teacher's reaction led me to believe that these mistakes were capital crimes in the country of France.

"Were you always this *palicmkrexis*?" she asked. "Even a *fiuscrzsa ticiwelmun* knows that a typewriter is feminine."

I absorbed as much of her abuse as I could understand, thinking — but not saying — that I find it ridiculous to assign a gender to an inanimate object incapable of disrobing and making an occasional fool of itself. Why refer to Lady Crack Pipe or Good Sir Dishrag when these things could never live up to all that their sex implied?

The teacher proceeded to belittle everyone from German Eva, who hated laziness, to Japanese Yukari, who loved paintbrushes and soap. Italian, Thai, Dutch, Korean, and Chinese — we all left class foolishly believing that the worst was over. She'd shaken us up a little, but surely that was just an act designed to weed out the deadweight. We didn't know it then, but the coming months would teach us what is was like to spend time in the presence of a wild animal, something completely unpredictable. Her temperament was not based on a series of good and bad days, but, rather, good and bad moments. We soon learned to dodge chalk and protect our heads and stomachs whenever she approached us with a question. She hadn't yet punched anyone, but it seemed wise to protect ourselves against the inevitable.

Though we were forbidden to speak anything but French, the teacher would occasionally use us to practice any of her five fluent languages.

"I hate you," she said to me one afternoon. Her English was flawless. "I really, really hate you." Call me sensitive, but I couldn't help but take it personally. 20

After being singled out as a lazy *kfdtinvfm*, I took to spending four hours a night on my homework, putting in even more time whenever we were assigned an essay. I suppose I could have gotten by with less, but I was determined to create some sort of identity for myself: David the hard worker, David the cut-up. We'd have one of those "complete this sentence" exercises, and I'd fool with the thing for hours, invariably settling on something like "A quick run around the lake? I'd love to! Just give me a moment while I strap on my wooden leg." The teacher, through word and action, conveyed the message that if this was my idea of an identity, she wanted nothing to do with it.

My fear and discomfort crept beyond the borders of the classroom and accompanied me out onto the wide boulevards. Stopping for coffee, asking directions, depositing money in my bank account: these things were out of the question, as they involved having to speak. Before beginning school, there'd been no shutting me up, but now I was convinced that everything I said was wrong. When the phone rang, I ignored it. If someone asked me a question, I pretended to be deaf. I knew my fear was getting the best of me when I started wondering why they don't sell cuts of meat in vending machines.

My only comfort was the knowledge that I was not alone. Huddled in the hallways and making the most of our pathetic French, my fellow students and I engaged in the sort of conversation commonly overheard in refugee camps.

"Sometime me cry alone at night."

"That be common for I, also, but be more strong, you. Much work and some- 25 day you talk pretty. People start love you soon. Maybe tomorrow, okay."

Unlike the French class I had taken in New York, here there was no sense of competition. When the teacher poked a shy Korean in the eyelid with a freshly sharpened pencil, we took no comfort in the fact that, unlike Hyeyoon Cho, we all knew the irregular past tense of the verb *to defeat*. In all fairness, the teacher hadn't meant to stab the girl, but neither did she spend much time apologizing, saying only, "Well, you should have been *vkkdyo* more *kdeynfulh*."

Over time it became impossible to believe that any of us would ever improve. Fall arrived and it rained every day, meaning we would now be scolded for the water dripping from our coats and umbrellas. It was mid-October when the teacher singled me out, saying, "Every day spent with you is like having a cesarean section." And it struck me that, for the first time since arriving in France, I could understand every word that someone was saying.

Understanding doesn't mean that you can suddenly speak the language. Far from it. It's a small step, nothing more, yet its rewards are intoxicating and deceptive. The teacher continued her diatribe and I settled back, bathing in the subtle beauty of each new curse and insult.

"You exhaust me with your foolishness and reward my efforts with nothing but pain, do you understand me?"

The world opened up, and it was with great joy that I responded, "I know the 30 thing that you speak exact now. Talk me more, you, plus, please, plus."

Exploring the Text

1. How does David Sedaris establish a humorous tone in the first two paragraphs? What details contribute to this tone?
2. How does Sedaris manage to make us laugh at the other students without seeming to mock or make fun of them? What effect does he achieve by including actual dialogue?
3. How does Sedaris characterize the teacher? Is she intentionally cruel, an effective teacher, an overly strict disciplinarian? Is she portrayed as a stereotype? Refer to specific details and passages from the essay to explain your response.
4. What does Sedaris mean when he writes that "understanding" another language is "a small step, nothing more, yet its rewards are intoxicating and deceptive" (para. 28)?
5. Sedaris uses both understatement and hyperbole in this essay. Identify two examples of each, and explain the effect.
6. Like most humorists, Sedaris makes a serious point through laughter and comedy. What is his point in this essay? Try stating it in one or two sentences.
7. Sedaris describes what for most of us would be a very unusual class — that is, a class in a foreign country with students from all over the world. Yet, for this essay to be funny, it must resonate with us to some extent. What aspect of the experience of being a student does Sedaris count on as common ground between himself and his readers?
8. In *Laughter: An Essay on the Meaning of the Comic*, philosopher Henri Bergson writes, "Several have defined man as 'an animal which laughs.' They might equally as well have defined him as an animal which is laughed at; for if any other animal, or some lifeless object, produces the same effect, it is always because of some resemblance to man, or the stamp he gives it or the use he puts it to." Does "Me Talk Pretty One Day" more effectively present people as creatures who laugh or are laughed at?

Best in Class

Margaret Talbot

A senior fellow at the New America Foundation, a nonpartisan think tank, Margaret Talbot (b. 1961) writes about the cultural politics of the United States in the twenty-first century. She has been an editor at *Lingua Franca* and the *New Republic,* and currently she is a staff writer for the *New Yorker.* In the following selection, which appeared in 2005 in the *New Yorker,* Talbot examines the impact of naming a single valedictorian, multiple valedictorians, or none at all.

Daniel Kennedy remembers when he still thought that valedictorians were a good thing. Kennedy, a wiry fifty-nine-year-old who has a stern buzz cut, was in 1997 the principal of Sarasota High School, in Sarasota, Florida. Toward the end of the school year, it became apparent that several seniors were deadlocked in the race to become valedictorian. At first, Kennedy saw no particular reason to worry. "My innocent thought was What possible problem could those great kids cause?" he recalled last month, during a drive around Sarasota. "And I went blindly on with my day."

The school had a system in place to break ties. "If the G.P.A.s were the same, the award was supposed to go to the kid with the most credits," Kennedy explained. It turned out that one of the top students, Denny Davies, had learned of this rule, and had quietly arranged to take extra courses during his senior year, including an independent study in algebra. "The independent study was probably a breeze, and he ended up with the most credits," Kennedy said.

Davies was named valedictorian. His chief rivals for the honor were furious — in particular, a girl named Kylie Barker, who told me recently that she had wanted to be valedictorian "pretty much forever."

Kennedy recalled, "Soon, the kids were doing everything they could to battle it out." As we drove past sugary-white beaches, high-rise hotels, and prosperous strip malls, he told me that the ensuing controversy "effectively divided the school and the community." Kennedy took the position that Davies had followed the school's own policy, which he had been resourceful enough to figure out, and whether he should have been allowed to load on an easy extra class was beside the point. He'd done it, and he hadn't broken any rules. Davies's guidance counsellor, Paul Storm, agreed. In an interview with the Sarasota *Herald-Tribune* at the time, he said of Davies, "He's very clever. He said, 'I want to be valedictorian. I've figured out I need to do this and that. Can you help me?' Denny had a good strategy, and this strategy was available to anyone who was a competitor."

Barker's supporters argued that what Davies had done was a sneaky way of 5 gaming the system. "It never crossed my mind to approach it as a *strategy,*" Barker, who is . . . pursuing a Ph.D. in chemistry at Northwestern University, said. "I just thought it was something you worked really hard for." Kimberly Belcher, who was ranked third that year, and who is now studying for a doctorate in theology at Notre Dame University, told me, "Among our friends, who were sort of the Academic Olympics and National Honor Society types, it was a big deal. Most of the people I knew thought that it was unfair of Denny to use what we thought of as a loophole to take a class that was too easy for him, and to do it secretly. We felt betrayed. I'm not angry anymore, but, boy, I was angry then." Davies, who is now a captain in the Air Force, and is stationed in Germany, said that he didn't care to comment about the dispute, except to say that he was a "firm believer in the idea that people benefit from healthy competition."

During the final weeks of the school year, Kennedy was meeting with both sets of riled parents, and students were buttonholing him in the hallway. "I'm telling you, it was hostile!" he said. Some teachers considered boycotting graduation; students talked about booing Davies when he walked out onstage. Kylie Barker's mom, Cheryl, said that she recalls getting a call in the middle of the day from Kylie's chemistry teacher, Jim Harshman, who asked her to pick up Kylie from school, saying, "She's in a pressure cooker here, and she's about to burst."

Kennedy tried to broker a compromise. Davies had suggested that he and Barker be named co-valedictorians, and Kennedy embraced the idea. But the Barkers weren't excited about it. "The principal was trying to make everybody happy, and when you do that there's always somebody who isn't," Cheryl Barker said. "I guess it was me."

Kennedy remembers finally "convincing everybody to agree reluctantly — and I do mean *extremely* reluctantly — to have co-valedictorians." He went on, "I have been in education basically my whole life, and I've been to a lot of graduations in my time. But I dreaded this one. Sarasota High is a big school — three thousand kids — and there were probably seven thousand people in the audience. At that time, it felt like half of the students in the room hated one of those two valedictorians and half hated the other. The tension was so thick that I was sitting up there in my cap and gown sweating buckets the whole time." In the end, both students got through their speeches — Kylie's was about integrity — without incident. But Kennedy, a likeable traditionalist who has been married to his childhood sweetheart for thirty-seven years, concluded that it was time to get rid of valedictorians at Sarasota High.

Kennedy convened a committee to consider various alternatives, and it was decided that from then on all students in the top ten per cent of the class — which at Sarasota means about seventy-five people — would march in first during graduation and have an asterisk printed next to their names on the program. "Students and parents got to see more kids recognized," Kennedy said. "It made everybody feel better."

Sarasota is a competitive school district — while visiting the area, I saw a car 10 with a bumper sticker that read, "My Child Was Student of the Month at Tuttle Elementary" — but most of the local high schools have followed Kennedy's lead.

Riverview High School has also eliminated valedictorians and salutatorians; Booker High School ended the tradition last year. Four years ago, North Port High opened near Sarasota. George Kennedy, its principal, recalled thinking that it "would be easier to just start out without valedictorians, so we wouldn't be taking something away later on." He added, "There's an awful lot of clawing and scratching to get to the top. You have families at some schools coming in freshman year saying, 'How can my kid get to No. 1?' And the pressure that puts on teachers is inexcusable. 'Valedictorian' is an antiquated title, and I think it has more negative connotations and effects than positive ones."

When Kennedy left Sarasota High to form a charter school, the Sarasota Military Academy, in 2001, he did not even consider having a valedictorian. Kennedy has an amiable way about him, but he's not kidding when he says, "My advice to other principals is, Whatever you do, do *not* name a valedictorian. Any principal who does is facing peril."

At one time, it was obvious who the best students in a school were. But now the contenders for the valedictorian title, especially at large, top-performing suburban high schools, are numerous and determined. Many schools offer Advanced Placement courses—and sometimes honors and International Baccalaureate classes—extra weight when a student's G.P.A. is calculated, so that an A earns 5.0 points, versus 4.0 in a regular class. Students who fill their schedules with A.P. classes, as the ambitious ones tend to do, can end up with G.P.A.s well above 4.0.

Jim Conrey is the director of public information at Adlai Stevenson High School, in Lincolnshire, Illinois—a public school with forty-five hundred students that is well funded enough to have such a thing as a director of public information. Students at the top of their class, Conrey said, are often separated by one thousandth of a decimal point. A few years ago, a school committee issued a report saying that "parents routinely phone the principal's office to express their concern over the competitive nature of our numerical ranking practice. Minuscule differences between the ranks of two students can often be perceived as major differences. Is a student ranked No. 1 in a given class really the 'best' student in that class?" As of this year, Stevenson High will no longer have a valedictorian and a salutatorian. Instead, students can apply to speak at graduation, and a faculty panel will select two winners. "If you go to a really good school, you could be ranked a hundred and thirty-fourth in your class and still be a really good student," Conrey said.

Between 1990 and 2000, the over-all mean G.P.A. of high-school students increased from 2.68 to 2.94, which is attributable in part to grade inflation and in part to the fact that students are working harder. Last year, more than a million students took at least one A.P. course. During the nineteen-nineties, the percentage of students taking A.P. or International Baccalaureate classes in math more than doubled, from 4.4 per cent of graduating seniors to 9.5 per cent. My own high school, North Hollywood High, in Los Angeles, had three or four A.P. classes when I graduated, in 1979 (a time when we were told that our most illustrious alumnus was Bert Convy, the game-show host; Susan Sontag had gone there, too, but nobody mentioned her). Now it has twenty-two.

Some schools, responding to the critique that competition has got too bruising, have decided that naming a single valedictorian is part of the reason that today's students have become so anxious. (Many small private schools came to this conclusion long ago, and never adopted the valedictorian tradition.) An organization called Stressed Out Students, which is headed by Denise Clark Pope, a Stanford education professor, has a list of about twenty-five schools, mostly in the Bay Area and Silicon Valley, that have pledged to try to make students and their parents less driven. Pope told me that "it would be healthier to eliminate valedictorians or change the rules, so that, for example, anyone who wants to can put their hat in the ring, and then there can be a vote for the best graduation speaker. Then you get a person who really wants to give a speech. It's not an academic contest."

A number of schools now call everyone who gets a 4.0 or higher a valedictorian. At Cleveland High School, in the San Fernando Valley, there will be thirty-two valedictorians this year. At Mission San Jose, in Northern California, there will be twenty-three. "We have such an outstanding student body that it was just hard to get that definitive," Stuart Kew, the principal of Mission San Jose, said. "Occasionally, we get the criticism that it's so watered down it doesn't mean anything. But the students don't feel that way." On graduation day, each of the school's many valedictorians will speak at a ceremony, where, one hopes, the chairs will be comfortable.

The single-valedictorian tradition is also being endangered by lawsuits. In 2003, Brian Delekta, who narrowly missed having the highest G.P.A. in his class, sued his school district, near Port Huron, Michigan, asking that he be credited with an A-plus, instead of an A, for a work-study class that he took at his mother's law firm. (In addition, Delekta asked for a restraining order on the publication of class rankings.) In another case that year, Blair Hornstine, a senior at Moorestown High School, in New Jersey, and the daughter of a New Jersey superior-court judge, sued the local board of education to be named the school's sole valedictorian; she also asked for two hundred thousand dollars in compensatory damages and more than two million dollars in punitive damages. Hornstine had an unspecified illness that caused "substantial fatigue," and, with the consent of the school district, she had taken many of her classes at home, with private tutors. Her transcript showed twenty-three A-pluses, nine A's, and a single A-minus; two-thirds of her classes were A.P. courses. Her weighted G.P.A. was 4.6894, which reportedly put her .055 points ahead of her closest competitor, Kenneth Mirkin.

The school board, however, decided that Hornstine's home instruction had given her an unfair advantage and that she should share the valedictorian title with Mirkin. Judge Freda Wolfson sided with Hornstine. The defendants, she wrote, "should revel in the success" of their accommodation to a student's disability "and the academic star it has produced," instead of seeking "to diminish the honor that she has rightly earned." In her ruling, Judge Wolfson nevertheless made a larger point about the insidious effects of naming a top student. "The fierceness of the competition in Moorestown High School is evidenced by the widespread involvement of parents in this dispute, which may have been fueled by the school's emphasis on grade-based distinctions," she wrote. "While the school's Handbook states that it seeks to minimize competition by no longer reporting class rank . . . elsewhere it heightens the levels of competition by naming a valedictorian." The case inspired a mocking Web site, the Blair Hornstine Project, and a flood of vitriolic Internet commentary; Hornstine was so excoriated by critics in her home town that she did not even attend graduation. The Moorestown Board of Education acknowledged no wrongdoing but eventually agreed to an out-of-court settlement, under which Hornstine was reportedly paid sixty thousand dollars. (Harvard, which had admitted her to the Class of 2007, rescinded the offer not long after a local paper for which Hornstine had written a column revealed that she had plagiarized material.)

I recently spoke to some students who had been involved in legal actions over the naming of a valedictorian, and they seemed to share a common attitude toward the experience. On the one hand, they shrugged off the importance of the honor—they had gone on to colleges where valedictorians were so plentiful that to have claimed bragging rights would have been seriously uncool. On the other hand, they could easily recall their high-school state of mind, and feel indignant all over again, utterly convinced that they had done the right thing. In 2003, Sarah Bird, a senior at Plano West Senior High School, in Plano, Texas, requested a hearing before the local school board. Another student, Jennifer Wu, had been named sole valedictorian, although her G.P.A. was virtually identical to Bird's. Bird had played on the school's basketball team. The sport was treated like a physical-education course by the school, and for several semesters she had been given unweighted A's. This had put her at a disadvantage, Bird felt. The hearing, at which Bird's lawyer asked that the two students be named co-valedictorians, involved some very close parsing. Brent William Bailey, Bird's lawyer, told me, "Going in, the other girl had a G.P.A. of 4.46885 and Sarah had 4.46731 — so that was a difference of .00154. Then the calculations were redone and Sarah came out with a G.P.A. of 4.47647." The school board granted Bird's request. "I was prepared to go ahead with a lawsuit if it hadn't gone our way," Bailey recalled. Wu, who expressed unhappiness over the decision to the *Dallas Morning News*, then requested a hearing of her own, to question the way the process was handled. Wu is now a sophomore at Harvard, where she is a premed student. We spoke just before finals, and she clearly had other things on her mind. "Nobody in college cares about your having been valedictorian," she said. "My roommate had no idea I was valedictorian. It doesn't come up, and I don't think about it." Still, when I asked Wu why she had complained to the school board, she said, "I wanted to make sure the school knew how traumatic something like this can be—thinking you're competing under one set of rules, and having an expectation because of that, and then finding out you're competing under another."

*   *   *

Stephanie Klotz's academic ambitions made her stand out at Valley View High, in   20
Germantown, Ohio, from which she graduated in 2001. "We weren't from here
originally," Klotz told me. "My dad had been in the military, and we'd lived in
Pennsylvania, Idaho, Texas, and upstate New York. I knew there was a big world
out there, and I was going to go out and conquer it. I wasn't going to get married
right out of high school and be a housewife with twenty kids." Klotz paused, but not
for long. "I mean, Germantown is a place with only three stoplights. I come from
a very educated family, and expectations are set at a higher level than they are in
a small farming town." Then, too, Klotz said, she was always kind of a "nerd—a
science nerd, a nature nerd." She continued, "My dad went deer hunting when I
was three years old, and they were cutting up the deer next door, because my mom
wouldn't let it in the house, and I was, like, 'Daddy, can I play with the head?'" As
a young girl, she loved accompanying her father, an anesthetist, to the hospital,
where she was allowed to observe surgeries. At Valley View, where football is very
popular—T-shirts bear the slogan "Valley View Football Is Life. Nothing Else
Matters"—Klotz was often unhappy. She doesn't like football, and was captain of
the dance team, which, she said, "got me made fun of—that and being smart. I'd
say, 'I want to see *you* do a kick line for an hour!'" She also worked with the town's
rescue squad ("I was so service-oriented; I did hundreds and hundreds of hours of
service work"), loved science, and hated English and history. She was often "bored
to tears" in classes that she found insufficiently challenging, but she got straight A's
anyway, as well as tens of thousands of dollars in college-scholarship money.

Several weeks before the school year ended, the principal of Valley View told
Klotz that she and four other students would share the valedictorian title. Klotz
thought the decision was odd—as she recalled, one of the girls had got a B—but
she let it go. "Notices were sent out, relatives notified," her father, Randy Klotz,
said. Three of the students had G.P.A.s above 4.0 because they'd taken at least one
A.P. course, whereas Stephanie, whose G.P.A. was 4.0, had not. (Instead of taking
A.P. history in her junior year, Stephanie, who hoped to become a doctor, had
decided to take another chemistry course.) Three weeks before graduation, Stephanie
was told that the school was reversing its decision: she and Megan Keener, another
girl with a 4.0 G.P.A., wouldn't be valedictorians after all. (Keener, too, lacked A.P.
credits, though she had been taking classes at local colleges.) Two students with
G.P.A.s above 4.0 would be named co-valedictorians, and a third would be salutatorian. "I would be nothing," Klotz recalled.

When Klotz told her parents, they complained first to the principal, then several times to the school board. Finally, the family hired a lawyer and sued the school
district, the superintendent, and the principal of Valley View. A judge in the Common Plea Court of Montgomery County, Ohio, sided with the Klotzes, and, days
before graduation, issued an order reinstating Klotz and Keener as valedictorians.

"At first, I was, like, I'm seventeen, I can't be dealing with this before I graduate from high school," Klotz told me. "I'm not strong enough. And then I thought,

I need to fight for the people who are coming after me, who really aren't strong enough to fight." Graduation day, she recalled, "was kind of a comedy event, really. I was sitting there, bored, twirling my tassels." Klotz said that she wasn't allowed to speak, because the decision to reinstate her title was made just before graduation day. One of the valedictorians who did speak, she recalled, "read that Dr. Seuss book 'Oh, the Places You'll Go!' to the audience. I mean, she read practically the entire book." Klotz remembers being given "so many academic awards and plaques, it was ridiculous. Every time I sat down, I had to get up again to get an award. I had so many plaques I literally couldn't carry them off the stage, and I'm, like, 'Oh, yeah, right, I'm not valedictorian?'"

Klotz graduated magna cum laude from the University of Dayton in May, and will start medical school at the University of Cincinnati in August. At college, Klotz realized that she was "a little fish in a big sea with a lot of valedictorians." But she's glad that she sued: she learned that she could be a fighter when she needed to be, and she showed Germantown that she couldn't be "walked all over." Klotz, who is engaged to be married to a social worker, is working as a waitress until school starts. To her fiancé's chagrin, she's been watching a lot of "trauma-and-E.R. shows" at home. (He lacks her strong stomach.) "There's so much focus on all the terrible things youths in our society do — murdering each other, using drugs — that I think it's good to focus on the positive things, as opposed to people who are dropping out and are failures," she said. "There are all these special programs to keep kids in school, give them a special experience, make them feel special. So much of classroom experience is focused on these kids who are *lacking*. There's nothing to reward the kids who are self-motivated and are working hard."

The first public high school in the United States, Boston's English Classical School, was founded in 1821. Within a few decades, the practice of designating a valedictorian had become an established tradition in American high schools. There was little public financing of secondary schools and a good deal of hostility to them, at least until the eighteen-eighties. High schools were so widely criticized as palaces of privilege, teaching Latin to the children of the rich, that Horace Mann, the education reformer, tried for a while to come up with a new name for "high school," reasoning that perhaps the phrase implied "superior and exclusive," William J. Reese notes in his 1995 history *The Origins of the American High School*. (In fact, many high-school students in the nineteenth century were middle-class girls training to support themselves as teachers.) By 1900, roughly ten per cent of American adolescents were enrolled in high school, and public funding remained relatively small.

The graduation ceremony, and in particular the valedictory, served an important purpose for proponents of publicly funded secondary education. A clever graduate declaiming loftily was something to show off to the local taxpayers, and, besides, graduation ceremonies were popular entertainments in an age that lacked television and radio and honored elocution and oratory. "By the late eighteen-fifties, approximately four thousand spectators attended the graduation exercises at Philadelphia's Central High School — and twice that number was turned away," Reese writes. "Eight to ten thousand citizens arrived for the event in Cleveland in the eighteen-seventies." In smaller towns, five hundred or more people might show up to see five or six graduates.

The valedictorian prize also celebrated people who weren't often publicly recognized: studious girls. In the nineteenth century, young women largely outperformed young men in American high schools. They generally won more prizes, graduated at higher rates, and displayed lovelier penmanship. At graduation, girls would read while sitting or standing on a low step, since it wasn't considered proper for them to speak from a platform. Still, the opportunity to appear before an audience of hundreds or thousands, to be singled out for one's academic achievements, must have been heady at a time when modesty and self-effacement were the constant counsel for young women.

In 1981, two professors, Terry Denny and Karen Arnold, began following the lives of eighty-one high-school valedictorians — forty-six women and thirty-five men from Illinois. (Their sample is, admittedly, narrow.) According to Arnold's 1995 book *Lives of Promise: What Becomes of High School Valedictorians*, these students continued to distinguish themselves academically in college; a little less than sixty per cent pursued graduate studies. By their early thirties, most were "working in high-level, prestigious, secure professions" — they were lawyers, accountants, professors, doctors, engineers. Arnold totted up fifteen Ph.D.s, six law degrees, three medical degrees, and twenty-two master's degrees in her group. The valedictorians got divorced at a lower rate than did the population at large, were less likely to use alcohol and drugs, and tended to be active in their communities. At the same time, Arnold, who stays in touch with her cohort, has found that few of the valedictorians seem destined for intellectual eminence or for creative work outside of familiar career paths. Dedicated to the well-rounded ideal — to be a valedictorian, after all, you must excel in classes that don't interest you or are poorly taught — the valedictorians had "used their strong work ethic to pursue multiple academic and extracurricular interests. None was obsessed with a single talent area to which he or she subordinated school and social involvement." This marks a difference, Arnold said, from what we know about many eminent achievers, who tend to evince an early passion for a particular field. For these people, Arnold writes, a "powerful early interest evolves into lifelong, intensive, even obsessive involvement in the talent area." She goes on, "Exceptional adult achievers often recall formal schooling as a disliked distraction." Valedictorians, by contrast, conformed to the expectations of school and carefully chose careers that were likely to be socially and financially secure: "As a rule, valedictorians relegated their early interests to hobbies, second majors, or regretted dead ends. The serious athletes among the valedictorians never pursued sports occupations. Most of the high school musicians hung up their instruments during college."

Becoming a valedictorian at a top high school is a grueling trajectory — involving perhaps a dozen A.P. classes and hours of study each night. Sometimes students cave in to the pressure. In 2002, Audrey Lin, one of Mission San Jose's many vale-dictorians, admitted that she had cheated to get to the top in high school, and gave back her valedictorian plaque. Lin, who is now a student at Berkeley, made her confession in conjunction with the release of a study by the Josephson Institute of Ethics, in which three-quarters of the high-school students surveyed acknowl-edged having cheated on a test the previous year; ten years earlier, the number had been sixty-one per cent.

In some ways, it seems that the valedictorian is a status designed for a simpler   30
time, when few people aspired to college. It isn't entirely suited to a brutally com-petitive age in which the dividing line between those who go to college and those who don't may be the most significant fissure in American society, and in which the children (and parents) of the upper middle classes have been convinced that going to an exceedingly selective college is the only way to insure wealth and happiness.

Still, perhaps something is lost if schools eliminate valedictorians. Like spell-ing bees, the contest for valedictorian offers a pleasing image of a purer meritoc-racy, in which learning and performing by the rules leave one hard-working person standing. It seems sad to abolish the tradition — and faintly ridiculous to honor too large a group. (If we're trying to be more sensitive, doesn't it make ordinary students feel *worse* when they can't be one of several dozen valedictori-ans?) Maybe the answer is to stick to one valedictorian but to make the rules of the contest clear, and to be sure everyone knows them. Maybe the honor should go to the student who is not necessarily the smartest but the most adept at run-ning a peculiarly American kind of academic marathon, one that requires prodi-gious energy, tactical savvy, and a Tracy Flick–like determination. (Remember the Reese Witherspoon character from *Election*?)

"Over the past ten years, a lot of school districts have been abolishing the valedictorian, and I'm against that," Karen Arnold told me. "On the day we allow anybody who's always wanted to be a quarterback to play on the high-school foot-ball team, *then* we can get rid of valedictorians. If we rank anything, we ought to rank what we say is most central to school, which is to say, academic learning."

A few weeks ago, I met Cheryl Barker, the mother of Kylie, the girl at Sarasota High School who, as it turned out, was one of the last two valedictorians at the school. Her daughter went to Furman University, in South Carolina, then to Northwest-ern. Cheryl Barker was a waitress when Kylie was in high school, and she is now the manager of a family-style restaurant in Sarasota. Her husband owns a print shop, and they have two younger children, a daughter who is graduating from Florida State this year and plans to go to law school, and a son who just graduated in the top ten per cent from Sarasota High.

Cheryl Barker still marvels at how hard Kylie worked, how determined she was, how she never missed a day of school, how she'd go to the library all the time to use the computer because they didn't have one at home. Barker thinks that it was a mistake for the high school to stop naming a valedictorian and a salutatorian. "Those kids all know who the No. 1 and 2 are, anyway," she told me over coffee. "Everyone's so afraid of getting sued or losing their jobs these days that they try too hard to candy-coat things." But, she added, "there are some kids who what they're good at is studying. That's what they do. They deserve something special to strive for. They do."

· ·

Exploring the Text

1. Margaret Talbot spends a good deal of time at the outset of the essay describing the situation at Sarasota High School and then returns to it at the end; however, her primary subject is neither that school nor its students. What is her rhetorical strategy in examining this one school in such depth?

2. In paragraph 14, Talbot refers to her own experience in high school. What is the effect of this personal element?

3. In this essay, Talbot surveys a range of perspectives on the issue of valedictorians. Identify at least four of them.

4. Why does Talbot rely so heavily on interviews with students? Why would this approach appeal to her audience?

5. Beginning with paragraph 25, Talbot presents some historical background on the American high school. How would the effect of this information have differed if she had opened the article with it?

6. To what extent do you think that the analogy Karen Arnold draws in paragraph 32 is valid? She says, "On the day we allow anybody who's always wanted to be a quarterback to play on the high-school football team, *then* we can get rid of valedictorians."

7. Does this essay rely more heavily on logos or pathos? Cite specific examples to illustrate your response.

8. Where do Talbot's sympathies lie? Does she believe that naming a single valedictorian is right or wrong? Identify passages that support your response.

This Is Water

Some Thoughts, Delivered on a Significant Occasion, about Living a Compassionate Life

DAVID FOSTER WALLACE

David Foster Wallace (1962–2008) was an American novelist and essayist and a professor at Pomona College in Claremont, California. His first novel, *Infinite Jest* (1996), was named by *Time* magazine as one of the 100 Greatest Novels from 1923 to 2006. Raised mainly in central Illinois by an English professor mother and a philosophy professor father, he graduated with a BA from Amherst College and an MFA in creative writing from the University of Arizona. He published two short-story collections, *Brief Interviews with Hideous Men* (1999) and *Oblivion* (2004); his unfinished novel, *The Pale King*, was published in 2011. He received numerous literary awards and fellowships, including the Lannan Award for Fiction and the Whiting Award, and in 1997 he received a MacArthur Foundation "genius" grant. One of the brightest literary stars of his generation, Wallace, who suffered from depression most of his life, committed suicide in 2008. Following is the 2005 commencement address that Wallace delivered at Kenyon College in Gambier, Ohio; it was published in book form under the title *This Is Water*.

There are these two young fish swimming along, and they happen to meet an older fish swimming the other way, who nods at them and says, "Morning, boys, how's the water?" And the two young fish swim on for a bit, and then eventually one of them looks over at the other and goes, "What the hell is water?"

If at this moment, you're worried that I plan to present myself here as the wise old fish explaining what water is to you younger fish, please don't be. I am not the wise old fish. The immediate point of the fish story is that the most obvious, ubiquitous, important realities are often the ones that are the hardest to see and talk about. Stated as an English sentence, of course, this is just a banal platitude—but the fact is that, in the day-to-day trenches of adult existence, banal platitudes can have life-or-death importance. That may sound like hyperbole, or abstract nonsense.

A huge percentage of the stuff that I tend to be automatically certain of is, it turns out, totally wrong and deluded. Here's one example of the utter wrongness of something I tend to be automatically sure of: Everything in my own immediate experience supports my deep belief that I am the absolute center of the universe, the realest, most vivid and important person in existence. We rarely talk about this sort of natural, basic self-centeredness, because it's so socially repulsive, but it's pretty much the same for all of us, deep down. It is our default-setting, hard-wired into our boards at birth. Think about it: There is no experience you've had that you were not at the absolute center of. The world as you experience it is right there in front of you, or behind you, to the left or right of you, on your TV, or your monitor, or whatever. Other people's thoughts and feelings have to be communicated to you somehow, but your own are so immediate, urgent, *real*—you get the idea. But please don't worry that I'm getting ready to preach to you about compassion or other-directedness or the so-called "virtues." This is not a matter of virtue—it's a matter of my choosing to do the work of somehow altering or getting free of my natural, hard-wired default-setting, which is to be deeply and literally self-centered, and to see and interpret everything through this lens of self.

People who can adjust their natural default-setting this way are often described as being "well adjusted," which I suggest to you is not an accidental term.

Given the triumphal academic setting here, an obvious question is how much of this work of adjusting our default-setting involves actual knowledge or intellect. This question gets tricky. Probably the most dangerous thing about college education, at least in my own case, is that it enables my tendency to over-intellectualize stuff, to get lost in abstract arguments inside my head instead of simply paying attention to what's going on right in front of me. Paying attention to what's going on inside me. As I'm sure you guys know by now, it is extremely difficult to stay alert and attentive instead of getting hypnotized by the constant monologue inside your own head. Twenty years after my own graduation, I have come gradually to understand that the liberal-arts cliché about "teaching you how to think" is actually shorthand for a much deeper, more serious idea: "Learning how to think" really means learning how to exercise some control over how and what you think. It means being conscious and aware enough to choose what you pay attention to and to choose how you construct meaning from experience. Because if you cannot exercise this kind of choice in adult life, you will be totally hosed. Think of the old cliché about "the mind being an excellent servant but a terrible master." This, like many clichés, so lame and unexciting on the surface, actually expresses a great and terrible truth. It is not the least bit coincidental that adults who commit suicide with firearms almost always shoot themselves in the head. And the truth is that most of these suicides are actually dead long before they pull the trigger. And I submit that this is what the real, no-bull value of your liberal-arts education is supposed to be about: How to keep from going through your comfortable, prosperous, respectable adult life dead, unconscious, a slave to your head and to your natural default-setting of being uniquely, completely, imperially alone, day in and day out.

That may sound like hyperbole, or abstract nonsense. So let's get concrete. The plain fact is that you graduating seniors do not yet have any clue what "day in, day out" really means. There happen to be whole large parts of adult American life that nobody talks about in commencement speeches. One such part involves boredom, routine, and petty frustration. The parents and older folks here will know all too well what I'm talking about.

By way of example, let's say it's an average day, and you get up in the morning, go to your challenging job, and you work hard for nine or ten hours, and at the end of the day you're tired, and you're stressed out, and all you want is to go home and have a good supper and maybe unwind for a couple of hours and then hit the rack early because you have to get up the next day and do it all again. But then you remember there's no food at home — you haven't had time to shop this week, because of your challenging job — and so now after work you have to get in your car and drive to the supermarket. It's the end of the workday, and the traffic's very bad, so getting to the store takes way longer than it should, and when you finally get there the supermarket is very crowded, because of course it's the

time of day when all the other people with jobs also try to squeeze in some grocery shopping, and the store's hideously, fluorescently lit, and infused with soul-
killing Muzak or corporate pop, and it's pretty much the last place you want to be,
but you can't just get in and quickly out: You have to wander all over the huge, over-
lit store's crowded aisles to find the stuff you want, and you have to maneuver your
junky cart through all these other tired, hurried people with carts, and of course
there are also the glacially slow old people and the spacey people and the ADHD
kids who all block the aisle and you have to grit your teeth and try to be polite as
you ask them to let you by, and eventually, finally, you get all your supper supplies,
except now it turns out there aren't enough checkout lanes open even though it's
the end-of-the-day-rush, so the checkout line is incredibly long, which is stupid
and infuriating, but you can't take your fury out on the frantic lady working the
register.

Anyway, you finally get to the checkout line's front, and pay for your food,
and wait to get your check or card authenticated by a machine, and then get told
to "Have a nice day" in a voice that is the absolute voice of *death*, and then you
have to take your creepy flimsy plastic bags of groceries in your cart through the
crowded, bumpy, littery parking lot, and try to load the bags in your car in such a
way that everything doesn't fall out of the bags and roll around in the trunk on
the way home, and then you have to drive all the way home through slow, heavy,
SUV-intensive rush-hour traffic, et cetera, et cetera.

The point is that petty, frustrating crap like this is exactly where the work of
choosing comes in. Because the traffic jams and crowded aisles and long checkout
lines give me time to think, and if I don't make a conscious decision about how to
think and what to pay attention to, I'm going to be pissed and miserable every time
I have to food-shop, because my natural default-setting is the certainty that situations like this are really all about *me*, about my hungriness and my fatigue and my
desire to just get home, and it's going to seem, for all the world, like everybody else
is just *in my way*, and who are all these people in my way? And look at how repulsive most of them are and how stupid and cow-like and dead-eyed and nonhuman
they seem here in the checkout line, or at how annoying and rude it is that people
are talking loudly on cell phones in the middle of the line, and look at how deeply
unfair this is: I've worked really hard all day and I'm starved and tired and I can't
even get home to eat and unwind because of all these stupid g-d- *people.*

Or, of course, if I'm in a more socially conscious form of my default-setting,   10
I can spend time in the end-of-the-day traffic jam being angry and disgusted at
all the huge, stupid, lane-blocking SUV's and Hummers and V-12 pickup trucks
burning their wasteful, selfish, forty-gallon tanks of gas, and I can dwell on the
fact that the patriotic or religious bumper stickers always seem to be on the biggest, most disgustingly selfish vehicles driven by the ugliest, most inconsiderate and
aggressive drivers, who are usually talking on cell phones as they cut people off in
order to get just twenty stupid feet ahead in a traffic jam, and I can think about
how our children's children will despise us for wasting all the future's fuel and

probably screwing up the climate, and how spoiled and stupid and disgusting we all are, and how it all just *sucks*, and so on and so forth. . . .

Look, if I choose to think this way, fine, lots of us do — except that thinking this way tends to be so easy and automatic it doesn't *have* to be a choice. Thinking this way is my natural default-setting. It's the automatic, unconscious way that I experience the boring, frustrating, crowded parts of adult life when I'm operating on the automatic, unconscious belief that I am the center of the world and that my immediate needs and feelings are what should determine the world's priorities. The thing is that there are obviously different ways to think about these kinds of situations. In this traffic, all these vehicles stuck and idling in my way: It's not impossible that some of these people in SUV's have been in horrible auto accidents in the past and now find driving so traumatic that their therapist has all but ordered them to get a huge, heavy SUV so they can feel safe enough to drive; or that the Hummer that just cut me off is maybe being driven by a father whose little child is hurt or sick in the seat next to him, and he's trying to rush to the hospital, and he's in a way bigger, more legitimate hurry than I am — it is actually *I* who am in *his* way. Or I can choose to force myself to consider the likelihood that everyone else in the supermarket's checkout line is just as bored and frustrated as I am, and that some of these people probably have much harder, more tedious or painful lives than I do, overall.

Again, please don't think that I'm giving you moral advice, or that I'm saying you're "supposed to" think this way, or that anyone expects you to just automatically do it, because it's hard, it takes will and mental effort, and if you're like me, some days you won't be able to do it, or you just flat-out won't want to. But most days, if you're aware enough to give yourself a choice, you can choose to look differently at this fat, dead-eyed, over-made lady who just screamed at her little child in the checkout line — maybe she's not usually like this; maybe she's been up three straight nights holding the hand of her husband who's dying of bone cancer, or maybe this very lady is the low-wage clerk at the Motor Vehicles Dept. who just yesterday helped your spouse resolve a nightmarish red-tape problem through some small act of bureaucratic kindness. Of course, none of this is likely, but it's also not impossible — it just depends on what you want to consider. If you're automatically sure that you know what reality is and who and what is really important — if you want to operate on your default-setting — then you, like me, will not consider possibilities that aren't pointless and annoying. But if you've really learned how to think, how to pay attention, then you will know you have other options. It will actually be within your power to experience a crowded, loud, slow, consumer-hell-type situation as not only meaningful but sacred, on fire with the same force that lit the stars — compassion, love, the sub-surface unity of all things. Not that that mystical stuff's necessarily true: The only thing that's capital-T True is that you get to *decide* how you're going to try to see it. You get to consciously decide what has meaning and what doesn't. You get to decide what to worship. . . .

Because here's something else that's true. In the day-to-day trenches of adult life, there is actually no such thing as atheism. There is no such thing as not worshipping. Everybody worships. The only choice we get is *what* to worship. And an outstanding reason for choosing some sort of God or spiritual-type thing to worship—be it J.C. or Allah, be it Yahweh or the Wiccan mother-goddess or the Four Noble Truths or some infrangible set of ethical principles—is that pretty much anything else you worship will eat you alive. If you worship money and things—if they are where you tap real meaning in life—then you will never have enough. Never feel you have enough. It's the truth. Worship your own body and beauty and sexual allure and you will always feel ugly, and when time and age start showing, you will die a million deaths before they finally plant you. On one level, we all know this stuff already—it's been codified as myths, proverbs, clichés, bromides, epigrams, parables: the skeleton of every great story. The trick is keeping the truth up-front in daily consciousness. Worship power—you will feel weak and afraid, and you will need ever more power over others to keep the fear at bay. Worship your intellect, being seen as smart—you will end up feeling stupid, a fraud, always on the verge of being found out. And so on.

Look, the insidious thing about these forms of worship is not that they're evil or sinful; it is that they are *unconscious*. They are default-settings. They're the kind of worship you just gradually slip into, day after day, getting more and more selective about what you see and how you measure value without ever being fully aware that that's what you're doing. And the world will not discourage you from operating on your default-settings, because the world of men and money and power hums along quite nicely on the fuel of fear and contempt and frustration and craving and the worship of self. Our own present culture has harnessed these forces in ways that have yielded extraordinary wealth and comfort and personal freedom. The freedom to be lords of our own tiny skull-sized kingdoms, alone at the center of all creation. This kind of freedom has much to recommend it. But of course there are all different kinds of freedom, and the kind that is most precious you will not hear much talked about in the great outside world of winning and achieving and displaying. The really important kind of freedom involves attention, and awareness, and discipline, and effort, and being able truly to care about other people and to sacrifice for them, over and over, in myriad petty little unsexy ways, every day. That is real freedom. The alternative is unconsciousness, the default-setting, the "rat race"—the constant gnawing sense of having had and lost some infinite thing.

I know that this stuff probably doesn't sound fun and breezy or grandly inspirational. What it is, so far as I can see, is the truth with a whole lot of rhetorical bullshit pared away. Obviously, you can think of it whatever you wish. But please don't dismiss it as some finger-wagging Dr. Laura sermon. None of this is about morality, or religion, or dogma, or big fancy questions of life after death. The capital-T Truth is about life *before* death. It is about making it to 30, or maybe 50, without wanting to shoot yourself in the head. It is about simple awareness—awareness of what

15

is so real and essential, so hidden in plain sight all around us, that we have to keep reminding ourselves, over and over: "This is water, this is water."

It is unimaginably hard to do this, to stay conscious and alive, day in and day out.

. . . .

Exploring the Text

1. What is the purpose of the anecdote with which David Foster Wallace opens the speech? What is the effect of his returning to the line "This is water" again near the end of the speech and repeating it there?

2. What does Wallace mean when he refers to the "natural, hard-wired default-setting" of himself and others (para. 3)? To what extent do you think that most of us are "deeply and literally self-centered"?

3. Wallace points out that the phrase "being 'well-adjusted' . . . is not an accidental term" (para. 4); in the next sentence he refers to "this work of adjusting our default-setting" (para. 5). Reflect on the word *adjust*, its denotations and connotations. Why does Wallace emphasize the deliberate choice of this word?

4. What does Wallace mean in the following sentences: "'Learning how to think' really means learning how to exercise some control over how and what you think. It means being conscious and aware enough to choose what you pay attention to and to choose how you construct meaning from experience" (para. 5)? What view of "thinking" does he seem to be arguing against?

5. What effect does Wallace achieve by using the hypothetical narrative of "an average day" in paragraphs 7–11?

6. Examine the syntax in one or two paragraphs of this piece. In paragraph 7, for instance, how does the form of the sentence beginning "It's the end of the workday" reinforce its content?

7. Throughout the speech, Wallace emphasizes that he is not offering "banal platitude[s]" (para. 2) or "moral advice" (para. 12). Why? What is he concerned about avoiding? Explain whether you think he is successful.

8. Wallace contends that once we have "really learned how to think, how to pay attention," then "[i]t will actually be within your power to experience a crowded, loud, slow, consumer-hell-type situation as not only meaningful but sacred, on fire with the same force that lit the stars—compassion, love, the sub-surface unity of all things" (para. 12). What is the causal link between attention and experience that he is asserting?

9. In paragraphs 13 and 14, Wallace discusses the concept of worship, claiming, "There is no such thing as not worshipping." Do you agree? Do you think that he risked offending members of his audience in his use of *worship* to mean something other than traditional religions? Why or why not?

10. How does he make the transition from the concept and forms of worship to his definition of "real freedom" (para. 14)? What is the connection?

11. In paragraph 14, Wallace asserts, "That is real freedom." How does he define "real freedom" in this speech? To what extent — and why — do you agree with him?

12. Throughout this speech, Wallace shifts between sophisticated, formal diction and colloquial language. Find examples of the latter, and discuss how appropriate and effective you think they are within the context of this speech.

13. Throughout this speech, Wallace builds a tension between two ways of being/living in the world. What are they? How does he explain and illustrate each to build his argument for the superiority of one over the other?

14. According to one researcher, a commencement speech has four major characteristics: it acknowledges the graduates, creates an identification between the graduates and the speaker, presents the world and its challenges, and instills hope. To what extent does this speech embody these characteristics? Cite specific passages to support and illustrate your response.

15. If someone asked you what this speech is about, how would you answer in under ten words? Explain your response.

Eleven

Sandra Cisneros

One of the first Latina writers to achieve commercial success, Sandra Cisneros (b. 1954) is a novelist, short-story writer, and poet, best known for *The House on Mango Street* (1983), a collection of connected stories and sketches. Recipient of many awards, including a MacArthur Foundation "genius" grant, Cisneros has published the short-story collection *Woman Hollering Creek* (1991), the poetry collections *My Wicked Wicked Ways* (1987) and *Loose Woman* (1994), and the novel *Caramelo* (2002). The *New York Times Book Review* says Cisneros "embraces . . . the endless variety of Mexican and American culture — songs and stories, jokes and legends, furniture and food." The story "Eleven" explores the nature of power in the classroom.

What they don't understand about birthdays and what they never tell you is that when you're eleven, you're also ten, and nine, and eight, and seven, and six, and five, and four, and three, and two, and one. And when you wake up on your eleventh birthday you expect to feel eleven, but you don't. You open your eyes and everything's just like yesterday, only it's today. And you don't feel eleven at all. You feel like you're still ten. And you are — underneath the year that makes you eleven.

Like some days you might say something stupid, and that's the part of you that's still ten. Or maybe some days you might need to sit on your mama's lap because you're scared, and that's the part of you that's five. And maybe one day when you're all grown up maybe you will need to cry like if you're three, and that's okay. That's what I tell Mama when she's sad and needs to cry. Maybe she's feeling three.

Because the way you grow old is kind of like an onion or like the rings inside a tree trunk or like my little wooden dolls that fit one inside the other, each year inside the next one. That's how being eleven years old is.

You don't feel eleven. Not right away. It takes a few days, weeks even, sometimes even months before you say Eleven when they ask you. And you don't feel smart eleven, not until you're almost twelve. That's the way it is.

Only today I wish I didn't have only eleven years rattling inside me like pennies in a tin Band-Aid box. Today I wish I was one hundred and two instead of eleven because if I was one hundred and two I'd have known what to say when Mrs. Price put the red sweater on my desk. I would've known how to tell her it wasn't mine instead of just sitting there with that look on my face and nothing coming out of my mouth.

"Whose is this?" Mrs. Price says, and she holds the red sweater up in the air for all the class to see. "Whose? It's been sitting in the coatroom for a month."

"Not mine," says everybody. "Not me."

"It has to belong to somebody," Mrs. Price keeps saying, but nobody can remember. It's an ugly sweater with red plastic buttons and a collar and sleeves all stretched out like you could use it for a jump rope. It's maybe a thousand years old and even if it belonged to me I wouldn't say so.

Maybe because I'm skinny, maybe because she doesn't like me, that stupid Sylvia Saldívar says, "I think it belongs to Rachel." An ugly sweater like that, all raggedy and old, but Mrs. Price believes her. Mrs. Price takes the sweater and puts it right on my desk, but when I open my mouth nothing comes out.

"That's not, I don't, you're not . . . Not mine," I finally say in a little voice that was maybe me when I was four.

"Of course it's yours," Mrs. Price says. "I remember you wearing it once." Because she's older and the teacher, she's right and I'm not.

Not mine, not mine, not mine, but Mrs. Price is already turning to page thirty-two, and math problem number four. I don't know why but all of a sudden I'm feeling sick inside, like the part of me that's three wants to come out of my eyes, only I squeeze them shut tight and bite down on my teeth real hard and try to remember today I am eleven, eleven. Mama is making a cake for me tonight, and when Papa comes home everybody will sing Happy birthday, happy birthday to you.

But when the sick feeling goes away and I open my eyes, the red sweater's still sitting there like a big red mountain. I move the red sweater to the corner of my desk with my ruler. I move my pencil and books and eraser as far from it as possible. I even move my chair a little to the right. Not mine, not mine, not mine.

In my head I'm thinking how long till lunchtime, how long till I can take the red sweater and throw it over the schoolyard fence, or leave it hanging on a parking meter, or bunch it up into a little ball and toss it in the alley. Except when math period ends Mrs. Price says loud and in front of everybody, "Now, Rachel, that's enough," because she sees I've shoved the red sweater to the tippy-tip corner of my desk and it's hanging all over the edge like a waterfall, but I don't care.

"Rachel," Mrs. Price says. She says it like she's getting mad. "You put that sweater on right now and no more nonsense." 15

"But it's not —"

"Now!" Mrs. Price says.

This is when I wish I wasn't eleven, because all the years inside of me — ten, nine, eight, seven, six, five, four, three, two, and one — are pushing at the back of my eyes when I put one arm through one sleeve of the sweater that smells like cottage cheese, and then the other arm through the other and stand there with my arms apart like if the sweater hurts me and it does, all itchy and full of germs that aren't even mine.

That's when everything I've been holding in since this morning, since when Mrs. Price put the sweater on my desk, finally lets go, and all of a sudden I'm crying in front of everybody. I wish I was invisible but I'm not. I'm eleven and it's my birthday today and I'm crying like I'm three in front of everybody. I put my head down on the desk and bury my face in my stupid clown-sweater arms. My face all hot and spit coming out of my mouth because I can't stop the little animal noises from coming out of me, until there aren't any more tears left in my eyes, and it's just my body shaking like when you have the hiccups, and my whole head hurts like when you drink milk too fast.

But the worst part is right before the bell rings for lunch. That stupid Phyllis 20 Lopez, who is even dumber than Sylvia Saldívar, says she remembers the red sweater is hers! I take it off right away and give it to her, only Mrs. Price pretends like everything's okay.

Today I'm eleven. There's a cake Mama's making for tonight, and when Papa comes home from work we'll eat it. There'll be candles and presents and everybody will sing Happy birthday, happy birthday to you, Rachel, only it's too late.

I'm eleven today. I'm eleven, ten, nine, eight, seven, six, five, four, three, two, and one, but I wish I was one hundred and two. I wish I was anything but eleven, because I want today to be far away already, far away like a runaway balloon, like a tiny *o* in the sky, so tiny-tiny you have to close your eyes to see it.

Exploring the Text

1. Why do you think Sandra Cisneros chose to tell "Eleven" from the viewpoint of the young girl rather than of an omniscient narrator? What effect does this have?
2. What is the source of Mrs. Price's authority? Is it solely "[b]ecause she's older and the teacher" (para. 11)?

3. In what ways does Cisneros's juxtaposition of home life and school life make for an effective rhetorical strategy?
4. Discuss the figurative language in this story, especially the similes. What purposes do they serve?
5. How is this a story about having a voice in society, about who gets to talk and who gets heard?

The Spirit of Education

NORMAN ROCKWELL

Norman Rockwell (1894–1978) was a popular American painter and illustrator best known for his depictions of everyday life and positive American values. His first cover for the *Saturday Evening Post* appeared in 1916, and over three hundred fol-

(See insert for color version.)

lowed during the next forty-seven years. In the early 1960s, he began working for *Look* magazine, where he turned to more political concerns such as civil rights and space exploration. In 1977, Rockwell received the nation's highest civilian honor, the Presidential Medal. On the facing page is a Rockwell painting, *The Spirit of Education*, that was featured on the cover of the *Saturday Evening Post* in 1934.

Exploring the Text

1. Examine the props carefully. What are the "tools" of education, according to Norman Rockwell's image?
2. On the basis of this depiction alone, who is excluded from Rockwell's ideal vision of education?
3. What assumptions about education does Rockwell make in this illustration?
4. In 1934, the United States was in the midst of the Great Depression. How does this painting encourage an optimistic outlook on the future?

What I Learned

A Sentimental Education from Nursery School through Twelfth Grade

Roz Chast

Roz Chast (b. 1954) grew up in Brooklyn, the child of two schoolteachers, and received a BFA from the Rhode Island School of Design, where she studied graphic design and painting. After she graduated, as she says on her Web site, she "reverted to type and began drawing cartoons once again." More than a thousand of her cartoons have been published in the *New Yorker* magazine since 1978. A collection of twenty-five years of her work was published in *Theories of Everything* (2006). She collaborated with comedian and novelist Steve Martin on the children's book *The Alphabet from A to Y with a Bonus Letter Z!* (2007); she has also written the children's book *Too Busy Marco* (2010) and a collection of cartoons entitled *What I Hate: From A–Z* (2011). She has won numerous awards and received an Honorary Doctorate of Fine Arts from Pratt Institute and the Art Institute of Boston. Chast is known for her wry commentaries on the experiences of ordinary life such as going to school, which the following cartoon depicts. She has written of her own experience: "I doodled all the time in school—that is what kept me from going completely out of my head."

WHAT I LEARNED:

(See insert for color version.)

A Sentimental Education

...and boys played Cars and Trucks.

VROOM, VROOM!

BAM BAM BAM BAM!

RMMMMM, RMMM, RMMM

ACME

I liked the Art Corner.

Ooh! Is that a horsie?

No.

I learned that it was very unlikely that I'd become an Olympic anything.

GET THE BALL!
GET THE BALL!
GET THE BALL!
GET THE BALL!
GET THE BALL!
GET THE BALL!
GET THE BALL!

Up through sixth grade, I learned lots of stuff: addition; spelling; all about explorers; how to do a chain stitch; subtraction; how to read and write; multiplication; fractions; how banks worked (a little); how to play punchball (theoretically); division; where crops came from; about planets; what was meant by "Current Events"; about George Washington and Johnny Appleseed; that a heart wasn't shaped like a heart at all; and lots, lots more.

E-I R-E-C-E-I-V-E

DAILY TIMES

OUR FRIEND, WHEAT

OUR FRIEND, CORN

371 86

MID-BROOKLYN BANK FOR SAVINGS

PENSEY PINKY

16 40687

THE STORY OF COLUMBUS
LEIF ERIKSSON
MAGELLAN'S TALE
WHO WAS VASCO da GAMA?

La, la, la.

APPLE SEEDS

AaBb Ff

And, of course, I was learning more about being good.

• Do homework.
• Be neat.
• Be organized.
• Be quiet.
• Pay attention.
• BE GOOD!!

It wasn't until junior high that I really started to wonder about the whole setup.

Class, today we're going to memorize all the prepositions.

Oh, my GOD...

Why did we have to learn this? Who said?

...so the sine of a 36° angle is 0.5877853.

What is the Elgin-Marcy Treaty of 1854?

Can anyone tell me the atomic weight of...

FROM NURSERY SCHOOL THROUGH TWELFTH GRADE

After that, I went to a large public high school where we were sorted into three piles based on our probable futures.

ACADEMIC

COMMERCIAL

ACME CO. May I help you?

GENERAL

This was called "tracking"— a process that had probably begun back in kindergarten.

I got pretty good at half-listening. I tried to pay full attention, but sometimes it was impossible.

Maybe I would have been just as bored at an "alternative" school.

Today we're going to make goat cheese!

Then we're going to practice our yoga!

Who knows?

Anyway, one day during math I had an epiphany:

I don't care about any of this.

I had wanted to "BE GOOD," but there were limits.

But what if you want to be a trigonometrist?

Trust me, I won't.

R.-Chast

Exploring the Text

1. Identify one part of this cartoon, a single frame or several, that you find to be an especially effective synergy of written and visual text. Why do you think the section you chose works so well?

2. On the second page, the middle frame is a large one with a whole list of what Roz Chast learned "Up through sixth grade." Is she suggesting that all these things are foolish or worthless? Explain your response.

3. The three-page cartoon presents a narrative, a story. Discuss the extent to which Chast uses the techniques of a fiction writer, such as plot, character, and setting.

4. Chast subtitles her cartoon "A Sentimental Education . . . ," which is a reference to a French novel of that title written by Gustave Flaubert in 1869. The American writer Henry James described *A Sentimental Education* as far inferior to Flaubert's earlier and more successful novel *Madame Bovary*; in fact, he characterized the 1869 work as "elaborately and massively dreary." Why do you think Chast uses this reference to Flaubert's novel? Or do you think that she is not specifically alluding to Flaubert but, rather, to more generalized "sentimental" notions of education? Consider her audience as you respond to these questions.

5. What, ultimately, is Chast's critique? What is the relationship she sees among learning, K–12 school, and education?

Conversation
The American High School

Each of the following texts presents a viewpoint on the American high school.

Sources

1. **Horace Mann,** from *Report of the Massachusetts Board of Education*
2. **Todd Gitlin,** *The Liberal Arts in an Age of Info-Glut*
3. **Leon Botstein,** *Let Teenagers Try Adulthood*
4. **Edward Koren,** *Two Scoreboards* (cartoon)
5. **Diane Ravitch,** *Stop the Madness*
6. **Eric A. Hanushek et al.,** from *U.S. Math Performance in Global Perspective* (tables)
7. **David Barboza,** from *Shanghai Schools' Approach Pushes Students to Top of Tests*

After you have read, studied, and synthesized these pieces, enter the conversation with one of the suggested topics on pp. 266–7.

1. from *Report of the Massachusetts Board of Education*

HORACE MANN

The following selection is taken from an official 1848 policy document by Horace Mann (1796–1859), who is known as the father of American public education.

Intellectual Education as a Means of Removing Poverty, and Securing Abundance

. . . According to the European theory, men are divided into classes,—some to toil and earn, others to seize and enjoy. According to the Massachusetts theory, all are to have an equal chance for earning, and equal security in the enjoyment of what they earn. The latter tends to equality of condition; the former, to the grossest inequalities. . . .

But is it not true that Massachusetts, in some respects, instead of adhering more and more closely to her own theory, is becoming emulous of the baneful examples of Europe? The distance between the two extremes of society is lengthening, instead of being abridged. With every generation, fortunes increase on the one hand, and some new privation is added to poverty on the other. We are verging towards those extremes of opulence and of penury, each of which unhumanizes the human mind. A perpetual struggle for the bare necessaries of life, without the ability to obtain them, makes men wolfish. Avarice, on the other hand, sees, in all the victims of misery around it, not objects for pity and succor, but only crude materials to be worked up into more money.

I suppose it to be the universal sentiment of all those who mingle any ingredient of benevolence with their notions on political economy, that vast and overshadowing private fortunes are among the greatest dangers to which the happiness of the people in a republic can be subjected. Such fortunes would create a feudalism of a new kind, but one more oppressive and unrelenting than that of the middle ages. The feudal lords in England and on the Continent never held their retainers in a more abject condition of servitude than the great majority of foreign manufacturers and capitalists hold their operatives and laborers at the present day. The means employed are different; but the similarity in results is striking. What force did then, money does now. The villein[1] of the middle ages had no spot of earth on which he could live, unless one were granted to him by his lord. The operative or laborer of the present day has no employment, and therefore no bread, unless the capitalist will accept his services. The vassal had no shelter but such as his master provided for him. Not one in five thousand of English operatives or farm-laborers is able to build or own even a hovel; and therefore they must accept such shelter as capital offers them. The baron prescribed his own terms to his retainers: those terms were peremptory, and the serf must submit or perish. The British manufacturer or farmer prescribes the rate of wages he will give to his work-people; he reduces these wages under whatever pretext he pleases; and they, too, have no alternative but submission or starvation. In some respects, indeed, the condition of the modern dependent is more forlorn than that of the corresponding serf class in former times. Some attributes of the patriarchal relation did spring up between the lord and his lieges to soften the harsh relations subsisting between them. Hence came some oversight of the condition of children, some relief in sickness, some protection and support in the decrepitude of age. But only in instances comparatively few have kindly offices smoothed the rugged relation between British capital and British labor. The children of the work-people are abandoned to their fate; and notwithstanding the privations they suffer, and the dangers they threaten, no power in the realm has yet been able to secure them an education; and when the adult laborer is prostrated by sickness, or eventually worn out by toil and age, the poorhouse, which has all along been his destination, becomes his destiny. . . .

Now, surely nothing but universal education can counterwork this tendency to the domination of capital and servility of labor. If one class possesses all the wealth and the education, while the residue of society is ignorant and poor, it

---

[1]In a feudal society, a serf who has the right to own property. — Eds.

matters not by what name the relation between them may be called: the latter, in fact and in truth, will be the servile dependants and subjects of the former. But, if education be equally diffused, it will draw property after it by the strongest of all attractions, for such a thing never did happen, and never can happen, as that an intelligent and practical body of men should be permanently poor. Property and labor in different classes are essentially antagonistic; but property and labor in the same class are essentially fraternal. The people of Massachusetts have, in some degree, appreciated the truth, that the unexampled prosperity of the State—its comfort, its competence, its general intelligence and virtue—is attributable to the education, more or less perfect, which all its people have received: but are they sensible of a fact equally important; namely, that it is to this same education that two-thirds of the people are indebted for not being today the vassals of as severe a tyranny, in the form of capital, as the lower classes of Europe are bound to in the form of brute force?

Education, then, beyond all other devices of human origin, is the great equal- 5
izer of the conditions of men,—the balance-wheel of the social machinery. I do not here mean that it so elevates the moral nature as to make men disdain and abhor the oppression of their fellow-men. This idea pertains to another of its attributes. But I mean that it gives each man the independence and the means by which he can resist the selfishness of other men. It does better than to disarm the poor of their hostility towards the rich: it prevents being poor. Agrarianism is the revenge of poverty against wealth. The wanton destruction of the property of others—the burning of hay-ricks and corn-ricks, the demolition of machinery because it supersedes hand-labor, the sprinkling of vitriol on rich dresses—is only agrarianism run mad. Education prevents both the revenge and the madness. On the other hand, a fellow-feeling for one's class or caste is the common instinct of hearts not wholly sunk in selfish regards for person or for family. The spread of education, by enlarging the cultivated class or caste, will open a wider area over which the social feelings will expand; and, if this education should be universal and complete, it would do more than all things else to obliterate factitious distinctions in society. . . .

For the creation of wealth, then,—for the existence of a wealthy people and a wealthy nation,—intelligence is the grand condition. The number of improvers will increase as the intellectual constituency, if I may call it, increases. In former times, and in most parts of the world even at the present day, not one man in a million has ever had such a development of mind as made it possible for him to become a contributor to art or science. Let this development precede, and contribu- tions, numberless, and of inestimable value, will be sure to follow. That political economy, therefore, which busies itself about capital and labor, supply and demand, interest and rents, favorable and unfavorable balances of trade, but leaves out of account the element of a widespread mental development, is nought but stupendous folly. The greatest of all the arts in political economy is to change a consumer into a producer; and the next greatest is to increase the producer's producing power,—an end to be directly attained by increasing his intelligence. For mere delving, an ignorant man is but little better than a swine, whom he so much resembles in his appetites, and surpasses in his powers of mischief.

Questions

1. Why does Horace Mann begin with a description of the "feudal lords in England and on the Continent" (para. 3)?
2. What does Mann mean by the following statement: "Property and labor in different classes are essentially antagonistic; but property and labor in the same class are essentially fraternal" (para. 4)?
3. When Mann uses the term *intelligence*, does he mean innate ability or developed skill?
4. Describe Mann's style in this excerpt. In what ways is it appropriate for his audience?
5. Identify one claim Mann makes and explain whether you believe it remains true today.

2. *The Liberal Arts in an Age of Info-Glut*

Todd Gitlin

In the following selection, which ran in the *Chronicle of Higher Education* in 1998, author and university professor Todd Gitlin argues that studying the liberal arts is even more important now in this age of mass media.

The glut of images is, in many respects, unprecedented, and so is the challenge it poses for education and the arts. On average, Americans watch television, or are in its presence, for more than four hours a day — half the waking hours that are not taken up with work (and sometimes even then). For the sake of argument, let us suppose that, during those hours of watching television, the representative American tunes in to six fictional programs. Those might include half-hour comedies, hour-long dramas, and two-hour movies. (Actually, thanks to remote-control devices, many viewers see more than one program at a time. More than two-thirds of cable subscribers surf channels, and the younger they are, the more they surf.)

For simplicity's sake, assume 16 minutes of commercials per hour on commercial channels — say, 40 distinct commercials per hour. That gives us roughly 160 more short units of mass-mediated message per day. For viewers who watch news shows, throw in, as a conservative estimate, 30 separate news items every day. Add trailers for upcoming shows and trivia quizzes. Add sporting events. Add videocassettes. Add billboards along the highway, on street corners, on buses. Add newspaper and magazine stories and advertisements, video and computer games, books — especially lightweight fiction. Add the photo-studded displays of wiggling, potentially meaningful units of information and disinformation that flood into millions of households and offices through the Internet. Read me! Notice me! Click on me! All told, we are exposed to thousands of mass-produced stories a month, not counting thousands more freestanding images and labels that flash into the corners of our consciousness.

Note, too, that this imagescape has a sound track—the vast quantities of performed music and other auditory stimuli, including songs, sound effects, tapes, compact disks, voice-mail filler—all the currents and ejaculations of organized sound that have become the background of our lives.

Now, it is true that no one but impressionable psychotics could be held in thrall for long by most of the minuscule dramas and depictions we find in popular culture. We experience most of the messages minimally, as sensations of the moment. But some part of the imagescape is nearly always clamoring for attention. Caught in the cross hairs of what the comedy writer Larry Gelbart has called "weapons of mass distraction," how shall we know, deeply, who we are? How shall we find still points in a turning world? How shall we learn to govern ourselves?

What does it mean, this information for which we are to be grateful and   5
upgrade our facilities? When a neo-Nazi creates a World Wide Web site that maintains that Auschwitz was not a death camp, he is, technically, adding as much "information" to the gross informational product as when someone posts an analysis of global warming. Garbage in, garbage sloshing around. When people "chat" about the weather in Phoenix or Paris, they are circulating information, but this does not mean they are either deepening their sensibilities or improving their democratic capacity to govern themselves. Long before Hollywood or computers, the French observer Alexis de Tocqueville wrote of America: "What is generally sought in the productions of mind is easy pleasure and information without labor." Toward that very end, the genius of our consumer-oriented marketplace has been to produce the Walkman, the remote-control device, and the computer mouse.

When information piles up higgledy-piggledy—when information becomes the noise of our culture—the need to teach the lessons of the liberal arts is urgent. Students need "chaff detectors." They need some orientation to philosophy, history, language, literature, music, and arts that have lasted more than 15 minutes. In a high-velocity culture, the liberal arts have to say, "Take your time." They have to tell students, "Trends are fine, but you need to learn about what endures."

Faculty members in the liberal arts need to say: "We don't want to add to your information glut, we want to offer some ground from which to perceive the rest of what you will see. Amid the weightless fluff of a culture of obsolescence, here is Jane Austen on psychological complication, Balzac on the pecuniary squeeze. Here is Dostoyevsky wrestling with God, Melville with nothingness, Douglass with slavery. Here is Rembrandt's religious inwardness, Mozart's exuberance, Beethoven's longing. In a culture of chaff, here is wheat."

The point is not simply to help us find our deepest individual beings. It is also to help new generations discover that they are not that different from the common run of humanity. Common concerns about life and death, right and wrong, beauty and ugliness persist throughout the vicissitudes of individual life, throughout our American restlessness, global instabilities, the multiple livelihoods that we must shape in an age of retraining, downsizing, and resizing. We badly need continuities to counteract vertigo as we shift identities, careen through careers and cultural changes.

Finally, we need to cultivate the liberal arts in a democratic spirit—not necessarily for the sake of piety before the past (though that spirit is hardly ruled out), but to pry us out of parochialism. In preparation for citizenship, the liberal arts tell us that human beings have faced troubles before; they tell us how people have managed, well and badly. Access to a common, full-blooded humanities curriculum will help our students cross social boundaries in their imaginations. Studying a common core of learning will help orient them to common tasks as citizens; it will challenge or bolster—make them think through—their views and, in any case, help them understand why not everyone in the world (or in their classroom) agrees with them.

Regardless of one's views of the curricular conflicts of our time, surely no one   10
who is intellectually serious can help but notice how students of all stripes arrive at college with shallow and scattered educations, ill-prepared to learn. They are greeted by budget pressures and shortsighted overseers. A strong liberal-arts curriculum could teach them about their history, their social condition, themselves. Today's common curriculum would not be that of 1950—anymore than 1950's was that of 1900. What overlap it would have with the past would generate cultural ballast. Surely the academic left and right (and center) might find some common ground in the quest to offer a higher education that is democratically useful, citizenly, and smart.

Questions

1. Why does Todd Gitlin explain in detail the television-watching habits of most Americans? How does this information lay the foundation for his argument?
2. How does the style of paragraph 2, which begins "For simplicity's sake," reflect its content? Pay special attention to the sentence structure.
3. What effect does Gitlin's use of such emotional terms and references as "impressionable psychotics" (para. 3) and "neo-Nazi" (para. 4) have on his audience?
4. What is his purpose in quoting nineteenth-century critic Alexis de Tocqueville (para. 5)?
5. Gitlin offers several reasons for the importance of the liberal arts. What are they? Why does he present them in the order that he does?
6. This selection is from a longer article about the need for a common core curriculum in colleges. To what extent do you think that its argument is relevant to high schools as well?

3. *Let Teenagers Try Adulthood*

LEON BOTSTEIN

The following opinion piece, published in the *New York Times* in 1999, was written by Leon Botstein, president of Bard College and author of *Jefferson's Children: Education and the Promise of American Culture* (1997).

The national outpouring after the Littleton [Columbine High School] shootings has forced us to confront something we have suspected for a long time: the American high school is obsolete and should be abolished. In the . . . month [after the shootings] high school students present and past [came] forward with stories about cliques and the artificial intensity of a world defined by insiders and outsiders, in which the insiders hold sway because of superficial definitions of good looks and attractiveness, popularity and sports prowess.

The team sports of high school dominate more than student culture. A community's loyalty to the high school system is often based on the extent to which varsity teams succeed. High school administrators and faculty members are often former coaches, and the coaches themselves are placed in a separate, untouchable category. The result is that the culture of the inside elite is not contested by the adults in the school. Individuality and dissent are discouraged.

But the rules of high school turn out not to be the rules of life. Often the high school outsider becomes the more successful and admired adult. The definitions of masculinity and femininity go through sufficient transformation to make the game of popularity in high school an embarrassment. No other group of adults young or old is confined to an age-segregated environment, much like a gang in which individuals of the same age group define each other's world. In no workplace, not even in colleges or universities, is there such a narrow segmentation by chronology.

Given the poor quality of recruitment and training for high school teachers, it is no wonder that the curriculum and the enterprise of learning hold so little sway over young people. When puberty meets education and learning in modern America, the victory of puberty masquerading as popular culture and the tyranny of peer groups based on ludicrous values meet little resistance.

By the time those who graduate from high school go on to college and realize [5] what really is at stake in becoming an adult, too many opportunities have been lost and too much time has been wasted. Most thoughtful young people suffer the high school environment in silence and in their junior and senior years mark time waiting for college to begin. The Littleton killers, above and beyond the psychological demons that drove them to violence, felt trapped in the artificiality of the high school world and believed it to be real. They engineered their moment of undivided attention and importance in the absence of any confidence that life after high school could have a different meaning.

Adults should face the fact that they don't like adolescents and that they have used high school to isolate the pubescent and hormonally active adolescent away from both the picture-book idealized innocence of childhood and the more accountable world of adulthood. But the primary reason high school doesn't work anymore, if it ever did, is that young people mature substantially earlier in the late 20th century than they did when the high school was invented. For example, the age of first menstruation has dropped at least two years since the beginning of this century, and not surprisingly, the onset of sexual activity has dropped in proportion. An institution intended for children in transition now holds young adults back well beyond the developmental point for which high school was originally designed.

Furthermore, whatever constraints to the presumption of adulthood among young people may have existed decades ago have now fallen away. Information and images, as well as the real and virtual freedom of movement we associate with adulthood, are now accessible to every 15- and 16-year-old.

Secondary education must be rethought. Elementary school should begin at age 4 or 5 and end with the sixth grade. We should entirely abandon the concept of the middle school and junior high school. Beginning with the seventh grade, there should be four years of secondary education that we may call high school. Young people should graduate at 16 rather than 18.

They could then enter the real world, the world of work or national service, in which they would take a place of responsibility alongside older adults in mixed company. They could stay at home and attend junior college, or they could go away to college. For all the faults of college, at least the adults who dominate the world of colleges, the faculty, were selected precisely because they were exceptional and different, not because they were popular. Despite the often cavalier attitude toward teaching in college, at least physicists know their physics, mathematicians know and love their mathematics, and music is taught by musicians, not by graduates of education schools, where the disciplines are subordinated to the study of classroom management.

For those 16-year-olds who do not want to do any of the above, we might con-   10
struct new kinds of institutions, each dedicated to one activity, from science to dance, to which adolescents could devote their energies while working together with professionals in those fields.

At 16, young Americans are prepared to be taken seriously and to develop the motivations and interests that will serve them well in adult life. They need to enter a world where they are not in a lunchroom with only their peers, estranged from other age groups and cut off from the game of life as it is really played. There is nothing utopian about this idea; it is immensely practical and efficient, and its implementation is long overdue. We need to face biological and cultural facts and not prolong the life of a flawed institution that is out of date.

Questions

1. In the first paragraph, Leon Botstein states, "[T]he American high school is obsolete and should be abolished." Why? What specific reasons does he provide?
2. What does Botstein mean by "the rules of high school turn out not to be the rules of life" (para. 3)?

3. What is Botstein's proposed solution?
4. Where does Botstein address a counterargument? Does he refute (or concede) in sufficient detail to be persuasive?
5. Which parts of Botstein's reasoning do you find to be the strongest? The weakest? Explain.

4. *Two Scoreboards*

EDWARD KOREN

Edward Koren is best known for his work in the *New Yorker*, where he has published more than nine hundred cartoons, including the following one from 2002, which comments on the relationship between athletics and academics.

Questions

1. Consider the words and the images separately. What is the relationship between them? Do the images support the words or vice versa?
2. What point does the cartoon make about the relationship between sports and academics? Do you agree with Edward Koren's thesis?
3. What does the American flag add to the cartoon's impact?

5. *Stop the Madness*

DIANE RAVITCH

Diane Ravitch (b. 1938) is a former Assistant Secretary of Education and currently a research professor of education at New York University. The following excerpt from her book *The Death and Life of the Great American School System: How Testing and Choice Are Undermining Education* (2010) appeared on the Web site of the National Education Association, the largest professional association and union of educators in America.

On "No Child Left Behind"

I was initially supportive of NCLB. Who could object to ensuring that children mastered the basic skills of reading and mathematics? Who could object to an annual test of those skills? Certainly not I.

My support for NCLB remained strong until November 30, 2006. That was the day I went to a conference at the American Enterprise Institute, a well-respected conservative think tank in Washington, D.C. The conference examined whether the major remedies prescribed by NCLB—especially choice and after-school tutoring—were effective. Was the "NCLB toolkit" working? The various presentations that day demonstrated that state education departments were drowning in new bureaucratic requirements, procedures, and routines, and that none of the prescribed remedies was making a difference.

I started to doubt the entire approach to school reform that NCLB represented. I started to see the danger of the culture of testing that was spreading through every school in every community, town, city and state.

The most toxic flaw in NCLB was its legislative command that all students in every school must be proficient in reading and mathematics by 2014, including students with special needs, students whose native language is not English, students who are homeless and lacking in any societal advantage, and students who have every societal advantage but are not interested in their schoolwork. All will be proficient by 2014. And if they are not, then their schools and teachers will suffer the consequences.

The 2014 goal is a timetable for the demolition of public education in the United States. The goal of 100 percent proficiency has placed thousands of public schools at risk of being privatized, turned into charters, or closed. And indeed, scores of schools in New York City, Chicago, Washington, D.C., and other districts were closed because they were unable to meet the unreasonable demands of NCLB. Superintendents in those districts boasted of how many schools they had closed, as if it were a badge of honor rather than an admission of defeat.

As the clock ticks toward 2014, ever larger numbers of public schools will be forced to close or become charter schools, relinquish control to state authorities, become privately managed, or undergo some other major restructuring. Yet, to date, there is no substantial body of evidence that demonstrates that low-performing schools can be turned around by any of the remedies prescribed in the law. Furthermore, [NCLB's] simpleminded and singular focus on test scores distorts and degrades the meaning and practice of education.

One of the unintended consequences of NCLB was the shrinkage of time available to teach anything other than reading and math. Other subjects, including history, science, the arts, geography, even recess, were curtailed in many schools. Reading and mathematics were the only subjects that counted in calculating a school's adequate yearly progress, and even in these subjects, instruction gave way to intensive test preparation. Test scores became an obsession. Many school districts invested heavily in test-preparation materials and activities. Test-taking skills and strategies took precedence over knowledge. Teachers used the tests from previous years to prepare their students, and many of the questions appeared in precisely the same format every year; sometimes the exact same questions reappeared on the state tests. In urban schools, where there are many low-performing students, drill and practice became a significant part of the daily routine.

NCLB assumed that shaming schools that were unable to lift test scores every year — and the people who work in them — would lead to higher scores. It assumed that low scores are caused by lazy teachers and lazy principals. Perhaps most naively, it assumed that higher test scores on standardized tests of basic skills are synonymous with good education. Its assumptions were wrong.

On Her Favorite Teacher

My favorite teacher was Mrs. Ruby Ratliff. More than fifty years ago, she was my homeroom teacher at San Jacinto High School in Houston, and I was lucky enough to get into her English class as a senior.

Mrs. Ratliff was gruff and demanding. She did not tolerate foolishness or 10 disruptions. She had a great reputation among students. When it came time each semester to sign up for classes, there was always a long line outside her door. What I remember most about her was what she taught us. We studied the greatest writers of the English language, not their long writings like novels (no time for that), but their poems and essays. I still recall a class discussion of Shelley's "Ozymandias," and the close attention that thirty usually rowdy adolescents paid to a poem about a time and place we could barely imagine. Now, many years later, in times of stress or sadness, I still turn to poems that I first read in Mrs. Ratliff's class.

She had a red pen and she used it freely. Still, she was always sure to make a comment that encouraged us to do a better job. Clearly she had multiple goals for her students, beyond teaching literature and grammar. She was also teaching about character and personal responsibility. These are not the sorts of things that appear on any standardized test.

At our graduation, she made a gift of a line or two of poetry to each of the students in her homeroom. I got these two: "To strive, to seek, to find, and not to yield," the last line of Tennyson's "Ulysses," which we had read in class, and "among them, but not of them," from Byron's "Childe Harold's Pilgrimage," which we had not read in class. As she did in class, Mrs. Ratliff used the moment to show us how literature connected to our own lives, without condescending into shallow "relevance." I think these were the best graduation presents I got, because they are the only ones I remember a half century later.

I think of Mrs. Ratliff when I hear the latest proposals to improve the teaching force. I believe Mrs. Ratliff was a great teacher, but I don't think she would have been considered "great" if she had been judged by the kind of hard data that is used now. How would the experts have measured what we learned? We never took a multiple-choice test. We wrote essays and took written tests in which we had to explain our answers, not check a box or fill in a bubble. If she had been evaluated by the grades she gave, she would have been in deep trouble, because she did not award many A grades. An observer might have concluded that she was a very ineffective teacher.

Would any school today recognize her ability to inspire her students to love literature? Would she get a bonus for expecting her students to use good grammar, accurate spelling, and good syntax? Would she win extra dollars for insisting that her students write long essays and for grading them promptly? I don't think so. And let's face it: She would be stifled not only by the data mania of her supervisors, but by the jargon, the indifference to classical literature, and the hostility to her manner of teaching that now prevail in our schools. . . .

On How to Improve Our Schools

What, then, can we do to improve schools and education? Plenty.   15

We must first of all have a vision of what good education is. We should have goals that are worth striving for. Everyone involved in educating children should ask themselves why we educate. What is a well-educated person? What knowledge is of most worth? What do we hope for when we send our children to school? What do we want them to learn and accomplish by the time they graduate from school?

Certainly we want them to be able to read and write and be numerate. But that is not enough. We want to prepare them for a useful life. We want them to be able to think for themselves when they are out in the world on their own. We want them to have good character and to make sound decisions about their life, their work, and their health. We want them to face life's joys and travails with courage and humor. We hope that they will be kind and compassionate in their dealings with others. We want them to have a sense of justice and fairness. We want them to understand our nation and our world and the challenges we face. We want them to be active, responsible citizens, prepared to think issues through carefully, to listen to differing views, and to reach decisions rationally. We want them to learn science and mathematics so they understand the problems of modern life and participate in finding solutions. We want them to enjoy the rich artistic and cultural heritage of our society and other societies.

If these are our goals, the current narrow, utilitarian focus of our national testing regime is not sufficient to reach any of them. Indeed, to the extent that we make the testing regime our master, we may see our true goals recede farther and farther into the distance. By our current methods, we may be training (not educating) a generation of children who are repelled by learning, thinking that it means only drudgery, worksheets, test preparation, and test-taking.

Our nation's commitment to provide universal, free public education has been a crucial element in the successful assimilation of millions of immigrants and in the ability of generations of Americans to improve their lives. As we seek to reform our schools, we must take care to do no harm. In fact, we must take care to make our public schools once again the pride of our nation. To the extent that we strengthen them, we strengthen our democracy.

Questions

1. What effect does Diane Ravitch achieve by opening with an explanation of how and why she changed her mind on the No Child Left Behind (NCLB) legislation?
2. What does she mean by "toxic flaw" (para. 4)? What other criticisms does she level at NCLB?
3. Ravitch ends the first section of her article by enumerating why NCLB's "assumptions were wrong" (para. 8). How does that analysis connect with the following section, where she describes her "favorite teacher"?
4. What are the traits of Mrs. Ratliff that make Ravitch remember her so many years later?
5. What point is Ravitch making when she asserts, "An observer might have concluded that [Mrs. Ratliff] was a very ineffective teacher" (para. 13)?
6. In paragraph 17, Ravitch lists what most of us want our education to include, but her list would be difficult to quantify and measure. Why do you believe these qualities should or should not be goals of public education?
7. What is the difference between "training" and "educating" that Ravitch implies in paragraph 18?

6. from *U.S. Math Performance in Global Perspective*

Eric A. Hanushek et al.

The following two charts appeared in a study by professors from Stanford University, Harvard University, and Munich University. This study compares student math performance internationally based on results from the 2009 Program for International Student Assessment (PISA) exam.

Class of 2009: Percentage of students at advanced level in math in U.S. states and countries participating in PISA 2006.

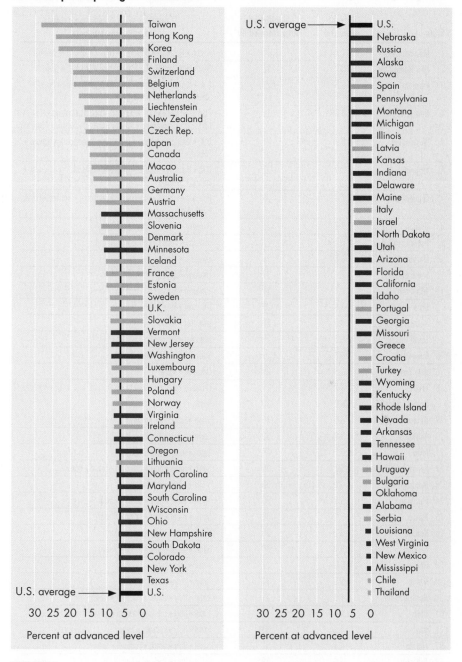

FIGURE 1

NOTE: Excludes participating countries below 1 percent: Romania, Brazil, Argentina, Azerbaijan, Mexico, Montenegro, Qatar, Tunisia, Colombia, Indonesia, Jordan, and Kyrgyzstan.

Percentages of all students at the advanced level per state and countries with similar and higher percentages at the advanced level in overall student population.

State	Percent advanced	Significantly outperformed by*	Countries with similar percentages of advanced students**
1. Massachusetts	11.4%	14	Austria • Germany • Denmark • France • Iceland • Slovenia
2. New Hampshire	10.8	16	Denmark • Estonia • France • Iceland • Slovenia • Sweden
3. Vermont	8.8	22	U.K. • Hungary • Ireland • Luxembourg • Norway • Poland • Slovakia
4. New Jersey	8.7	18	Estonia • France • U.K. • Hungary • Ireland • Iceland • Lithuania • Luxembourg • Norway • Poland • Slovakia • Sweden
4. Washington	8.7	21	U.K. • Hungary • Ireland • Lithuania • Luxembourg • Norway • Poland • Slovakia • Sweden
6. Virginia	7.9	22	U.K. • Hungary • Ireland • Lithuania • Luxembourg • Norway • Poland • Slovakia
7. Connecticut	7.8	23	Hungary • Ireland • Lithuania • Luxembourg • Norway • Poland • Slovakia
8. Oregon	7.3	25	Hungary • Ireland • Lithuania • Poland
9. North Carolina	7.1	27	Slovakia • Ireland • Lithuania • Poland
10. Maryland	6.8	29	Lithuania • Russia
11. South Carolina	6.7	29	Lithuania • Russia
11. Wisconsin	6.7	29	Lithuania • Russia
13. Ohio	6.6	29	Lithuania • Russia
14. New Hampshire	6.5	29	Lithuania • Russia
14. South Dakota	6.5	29	Lithuania • Russia
16. Colorado	6.3	29	Spain • Lithuania • Russia
16. New York	6.3	29	Lithuania • Russia
18. Texas	6.2	29	Lithuania • Russia
United States	6.0	30	Russia
19. Nebraska	6.0	29	Spain • Lithuania • Russia
20. Alaska	5.8	30	Spain • Latvia • Russia
21. Iowa	5.7	30	Spain • Latvia • Russia
21. Pennsylvania	5.7	30	Spain • Israel • Italy • Lithuania • Latvia • Russia
23. Montana	5.6	30	Spain • Latvia • Russia
24. Michigan	5.5	30	Spain • Israel • Italy • Latvia • Russia
25. Illinois	5.4	30	Spain • Israel • Italy • Latvia • Russia
26. Kansas	5.2	30	Spain • Israel • Italy • Latvia • Russia
27. Indiana	5.1	30	Spain • Israel • Italy • Latvia • Russia
28. Delaware	5.0	32	Israel • Italy • Latvia
28. Maine	5.0	32	Israel • Italy • Latvia
30. North Dakota	4.8	32	Israel • Italy • Latvia • Portugal • Turkey
31. Utah	4.7	32	Israel • Italy • Latvia • Portugal • Turkey
32. Arizona	4.6	33	Israel • Italy • Portugal • Turkey
32. Florida	4.6	32	Israel • Italy • Latvia • Portugal • Turkey
34. California	4.5	33	Israel • Italy • Portugal • Turkey
34. Idaho	4.5	33	Israel • Italy • Portugal • Turkey

State	Percent advanced	Significantly outperformed by*	Countries with similar percentages of advanced students**
36. Georgia	4.3	34	Greece • Israel • Portugal • Turkey
37. Missouri	4.1	35	Greece • Portugal • Turkey
38. Wyoming	3.5	37	Croatia • Turkey
39. Kentucky	3.4	37	Croatia • Turkey
40. Rhode Island	3.3	37	Croatia • Turkey
41. Nevada	3.1	38	Turkey
42. Arkansas	3.0	38	Bulgaria • Turkey
43. Tennessee	2.9	38	Bulgaria • Turkey
44. Hawaii	2.5	38	Bulgaria • Turkey • Uruguay
45. Oklahoma	2.4	38	Bulgaria • Serbia • Turkey • Uruguay
46. Alabama	2.3	38	Bulgaria • Serbia • Turkey • Uruguay
47. Louisiana	1.7	42	Bulgaria
48. West Virginia	1.4	42	Bulgaria
48. New Mexico	1.4	42	Bulgaria
50. Mississippi	1.3	42	Turkey

FIGURE 2

*Number of countries whose percent advanced was statistically significantly higher
**Countries where the percentage of students at the advanced level did not differ significantly from state. If no country had similar percentage, the country with the percentage just higher than that of state is listed.

Questions

1. According to Figure 1, how many states have higher advanced-level math achievement than the overall United States?
2. Based on the top-ten ranked countries, what conclusions can you draw? Now look at the top-twenty ranked countries and states; how does your observation change?
3. According to Figure 2, do most states rank closer to developing or to developed countries in advanced math skills?
4. Based on information from Figure 2, what hypotheses can you develop about the competitiveness of U.S. students in the global market? Develop at least two hypotheses.
5. What questions might you ask about the data that is used as the basis for these two charts? What specific information would you need either to challenge or to draw conclusions from these charts?

7. from *Shanghai Schools' Approach Pushes Students to Top of Tests*

David Barboza

The following excerpt from a 2010 *New York Times* article compares the approach to instruction in Shanghai with that in the United States.

SHANGHAI—In Li Zhen's ninth-grade mathematics class here last week, the morning drill was geometry. Students at the middle school affiliated with Jing'An Teachers' College were asked to explain the relative size of geometric shapes by using Euclid's theorem of parallelograms.

"Who in this class can tell me how to demonstrate two lines are parallel without using a proportional segment?" Ms. Li called out to about 40 students seated in a cramped classroom.

One by one, a series of students at this medium-size public school raised their hands. When Ms. Li called on them, they each stood politely by their desks and usually answered correctly. They returned to their seats only when she told them to sit down.

Educators say this disciplined approach helps explain the announcement this month that 5,100 15-year-olds in Shanghai outperformed students from about 65 countries on an international standardized test that measured math, science and reading competency.

American students came in between 15th and 31st place in the three catego- 5
ries. France and Britain also fared poorly.

Experts said comparing scores from countries and cities of different sizes is complicated. They also said that the Shanghai scores were not representative of China, since this fast-growing city of 20 million is relatively affluent. Still, they were impressed by the high scores from students in Shanghai.

The results were seen as another sign of China's growing competitiveness. The United States rankings are a "wake-up call," said Arne Duncan, the secretary of education.

Although it was the first time China had taken part in the test, which was administered by the Organization for Economic Cooperation and Development, based in Paris, the results bolstered this country's reputation for producing students with strong math and science skills.

Many educators were also surprised by the city's strong reading scores, which measured students' proficiency in their native Chinese.

The Shanghai students performed well, experts say, for the same reason students 10
from other parts of Asia—including South Korea, Singapore and Hong Kong—do: Their education systems are steeped in discipline, rote learning and obsessive test preparation.

Public school students in Shanghai often remain at school until 4 P.M., watch very little television and are restricted by Chinese law from working before the age of 16.

"Very rarely do children in other countries receive academic training as intensive as our children do," said Sun Baohong, an authority on education at the Shanghai Academy of Social Sciences. "So if the test is on math and science, there's no doubt Chinese students will win the competition."

But many educators say China's strength in education is also a weakness. The nation's education system is too test-oriented, schools here stifle creativity and parental pressures often deprive children of the joys of childhood, they say.

"These are two sides of the same coin: Chinese schools are very good at pre-paring their students for standardized tests," Jiang Xueqin, a deputy principal at Peking University High School in Beijing, wrote in an opinion article published in the *Wall Street Journal* shortly after the test results were announced. "For that reason, they fail to prepare them for higher education and the knowledge economy."

In an interview, Mr. Jiang said Chinese schools emphasized testing too much, and produced students who lacked curiosity and the ability to think critically or independently.

"It creates very narrow-minded students," he said. "But what China needs now is entrepreneurs and innovators."

This is a common complaint in China. Educators say an emphasis on stan-dardized tests is partly to blame for the shortage of innovative start-ups in China. And executives at global companies operating here say they have difficulty find-ing middle managers who can think creatively and solve problems.

In many ways, the system is a reflection of China's Confucianist past. Children are expected to honor and respect their parents and teachers.

"Discipline is rarely a problem," said Ding Yi, vice principal at the middle school affiliated with Jing'An Teachers' College. "The biggest challenge is a student who chronically fails to do his homework."

While the quality of schools varies greatly in China (rural schools often lack sufficient money, and dropout rates can be high), schools in major cities typically produce students with strong math and science skills.

Shanghai is believed to have the nation's best school system, and many stu-dents here gain admission to America's most selective colleges and universities.

In Shanghai, teachers are required to have a teaching certificate and to undergo a minimum of 240 hours of training; higher-level teachers can be required to have up to 540 hours of training. There is a system of incentives and merit pay, just like the systems in some parts of the United States.

"Within a teacher's salary package, 70 percent is basic salary," said Xiong Bingqi, a professor of education at Shanghai Jiaotong University. "The other 30 percent is called performance salary."

Still, teacher salaries are modest, about $750 a month before bonuses and allowances—far less than what accountants, lawyers or other professionals earn.

Questions

1. What does the description of class at the start of the article (paras. 1–3) establish about public school in Shanghai?
2. According to this article, what are the strengths and weaknesses of China's approach to education?
3. In what ways do Chinese families and society in general support the "discipline, rote learning and obsessive test preparation" (para. 10) emphasized in schools?
4. Why is this approach "a reflection of China's Confucianist past" (para. 18)?

5. What characteristics and skills are prized in a global marketplace, according to this article?

Making Connections

1. How would Todd Gitlin respond to the report on the schools in Shanghai? Would he be likely to recommend de-emphasizing math and science?

2. Which author in this Conversation do you think Diane Ravitch would have the most in common with? Why?

3. Based on his beliefs about the interconnection of democracy and education, do you think that Horace Mann would approve or disapprove of standardized testing as we know it today? Explain your response. To what extent does standardized testing contribute to "the balance-wheel of the social machinery" (para. 5), as Mann describes education?

4. In what ways does the low-ranking achievement in math of American students challenge Leon Botstein's position? In what ways does it support his position?

Entering the Conversation

As you respond to the following prompts, support your argument with references to at least three of the sources in this conversation on the American high school. For help using sources, see Chapter 4.

1. Write an essay explaining whether you agree with Leon Botstein's critique of the American high school (p. 254).

2. Using the texts in this conversation on the American high school, as well as your own insights into high school, identify two serious problems with the educational system, and propose recommendations for addressing them. Cite at least two sources from the conversation in your response.

3. John Dewey, the father of experiential education, described the interaction of education and democracy as follows:

> Democratic society is peculiarly dependent for its maintenance upon the use in forming a course of study of criteria which are broadly human. Democracy cannot flourish where the chief influences in selecting subject matter of instruction are utilitarian ends narrowly conceived for the masses, and, for the higher education of the few, the traditions of a specialized cultivated class. The notion that the "essentials" of elementary education are the three R's mechanically treated, is based upon ignorance of the essentials needed for realization of democratic ideals. . . . A curriculum which acknowledges the social responsibilities of education must present situations

where problems are relevant to the problems of living together, and where observation and information are calculated to develop social insight and interest.

—*Democracy and Education*, 1916

Write an essay explaining the extent to which you believe that high schools today are preparing citizens to achieve Dewey's vision. Draw on your experience and observation, and cite at least three of the readings from the conversation to develop your argument.

4. Suppose you had the freedom to design a high school that you want to attend. What would be the prevailing philosophy of the school? What would be three or four key characteristics of the school that implement this philosophy? Draw on at least three of the sources from the Conversation in your discussion.

Student Writing

Argument: Using Personal Experiences as Evidence

The following essay is one AP student's response to the following prompt.

James Baldwin delivered "A Talk to Teachers" to a group of educators in New York City in 1963 — over forty years ago. Do the problems and prejudices he discussed still exist, or are they history?

As you read, consider how the student explains and supports his viewpoint.

A Talk to High School Teachers

Tyler Wilchek

In James Baldwin's "A Talk to Teachers," he writes a social criticism of public schools and describes how the problems are reflected in the larger society. Forty-two years later, some of the problems Baldwin mentions still exist in public schools. If I were to give a talk to teachers today, I would be sure to talk about segregation in different parts of a typical school such as class level, athletics, and social situations. Regular, honors, and Advanced Placement classes definitely have trends linking race to the difficulty of the class. Also, sports are often dominated by particular races, so teams end up with predominantly one race. Last, social situations during lunch prove race is still a factor.

In my school a link can be made between the race of students and the level of classes enrolled in. Often in AP and honors classes, the students are predominantly white. In regular classes, the students are predominantly African American and Hispanic. This trend reflects the experiences Baldwin discusses in his essay. Used to the more "undesirable" part of the city that he grew up in, he knows that downtown Park Avenue is not really meant for him. Baldwin writes, "You know — you know instinctively — that none of this is for you. You know this before you are told." He points out that he feels unwelcome and shunned from this part of Park Avenue. I feel as if this is how African American students feel today towards advanced-level classes. The low enrollment of African American students in upper-level classes can perhaps be explained by the premise that Baldwin brings up. Minority students believe that they cannot be accepted in the society of advanced-level classes. Although expectations can sometime define how much a person can push himself, if students believe that they are not meant for honors classes, they will not attempt to try them. African American students often do not have people raising their expectations. Therefore, when they look at honors courses, their perception is already denying any chance for success. They assume, rightly or wrongly, that these classes are not for them.

Another problem in high schools today is segregation in athletics. As an active member of two varsity sports at my high school for three years, I have noticed the "white sports" and the "black sports." Participating in two almost exclusively white sports (swimming and lacrosse) has shown me that sports teams are just as segregated as classes. In the sports that I play, involvement and encouragement from parents is essential for success. Swimming requires parents to volunteer at meets and pay for membership to pools, while lacrosse is just not as popular a sport as basketball or football. It is much harder for black people to succeed in swimming and lacrosse because of the lack of opportunities. Baldwin agrees that black children are not given a fair opportunity to succeed in life. Baldwin states that "the Negro child has had, effectively, almost all the doors of opportunity slammed in his face, and there are very few things he can do about it." African American children do not have these doors of opportunity in sports such as swimming and lacrosse. Many black students do not have the thousand dollars a year to swim or hundreds of dollars to purchase lacrosse equipment. These doors of opportunity are just not available for minority students in high school. At my school, basketball and football are dominated by African American students because the equipment is more readily available and there are more opportunities to play.

Last, public high schools are segregated in social situations, such as where students choose to eat lunch in the cafeteria. Each and every student has his own group of friends, his own place to sit, his home sweet home, during every lunch period. There are very distinct areas for each group of students. But usually these students are linked by more than common interests; they are also linked by race. The most distinct areas in my school are probably the Asian math-and-science magnet section, the Gothic (white) students near the trophy cases, the African American students near the lunch line, and the Hispanic students in the hallway. Students today feel a sense of security when they are with people of their own race, and so they choose to isolate themselves with people of their own race.

Segregation is the core problem that exists in public high schools today. Although Baldwin wrote his essay many years ago, the issue of race still plays a large part in public education. The lack of African American enrollment in advanced classes, segregation in sports teams, and racial isolation in the cafeteria illustrate that this is still very much a problem today. Although there have been improvements over the past forty years, segregation is still a concern for public schools.

Questions

1. How has Tyler drawn connections to James Baldwin's essay? Examine places where he refers specifically to Baldwin's essay. Should Tyler have added more explicit references, perhaps even quotations? Explain.
2. Assuming that the third sentence ("If I were to give a talk to teachers today . . .") is Tyler's thesis, would you recommend eliminating the following three sentences? If so, why? If not, what do you think they add to the introductory paragraph?
3. Are the specific details in this essay one of its strengths or weaknesses? Explain.
4. Try rewriting a paragraph of this essay in the third person. Do you think Tyler's decision to write in the first person is more effective, or would the distance achieved by the third person have given his position greater weight?
5. Tyler opens his final paragraph with the statement, "Segregation is the core problem that exists in public high schools today." How well do you think he has prepared for and supported this conclusion?

Grammar as Rhetoric and Style

Appositives

An appositive is a noun or noun phrase that tells you more about a nearby noun or pronoun. In each sentence below, the appositive is bracketed. The arrow shows the noun or pronoun that the appositive describes.

It turned out that one of the top students, Denny Davies, had learned of this rule.

—Margaret Talbot

Kennedy, a wiry fifty-nine-year-old who has a stern buzz cut, was in 1997 the principal of Sarasota High School.

—Margaret Talbot

In 1981, two professors . . . began following the lives of eighty-one high-school valedictorians—forty-six women and thirty-five men from Illinois.

—Margaret Talbot

Japanese people have to make many of the big decisions of their lives—whom to marry, what company to join—without detailed information.

—Kyoko Mori

We were given plenty of instruction about the specifics of writing: word choice, description, style.

—Kyoko Mori

When my cousin Kazumi studied *ikebana*, she was disillusioned by the unfair judgments her teachers made every year.

—Kyoko Mori

Punctuation and Appositives

The last example given does not use punctuation to set off the appositive from the rest of the sentence, but the others do. Here's why: If the appositive is not essential to the meaning of the sentence but is more of an aside or parenthetical remark, then the writer uses punctuation to set off the appositive. If the appositive *is* essential to the meaning of the sentence, then the writer does *not* set off the appositive with punctuation marks. Include what is essential; exclude what is not. In the second example given, the description of the principal is a minor detail, so Margaret Talbot sets off the appositive with commas. In the final sentence, Kyoko Mori thought it essential that she personalize the anecdote by telling the reader *which* cousin she is describing, so she does not punctuate the appositive.

Choosing Punctuation

If your appositive needs punctuation, you can set off the appositive in one of three ways. First, you can use one or two commas.

> The principal of Sarasota High School in 1997 was Daniel Kennedy, a wiry fifty-nine-year-old who has a stern buzz cut.

> Kennedy, a wiry fifty-nine-year-old who has a stern buzz cut, was in 1997 the principal of Sarasota High School.

> —Margaret Talbot

Second, you can use one or two dashes.

> In 1981, two professors . . . began following the lives of eighty-one high-school valedictorians—forty-six women and thirty-five men from Illinois.

> —Margaret Talbot

Japanese people have to make many of the big decisions of their lives—whom to marry, what company to join—without detailed information.

—Kyoko Mori

Third, you can use a colon.

We were given plenty of instruction about the specifics of writing: word choice, description, style.

—Kyoko Mori

Dashes emphasize the appositive more than commas do. Furthermore, if an appositive contains its own internal commas, then one dash, two dashes, or a colon makes it easier to read the complete sentence.

Position of Appositive: Before or after the Noun?

All the examples so far in this lesson have shown an appositive coming *after* the noun or pronoun it details. Although that is the most common use of an appositive, it can come before the noun or pronoun as well.

A wiry fifty-nine-year-old who has a stern buzz cut, Daniel Kennedy was the principal of Sarasota High School in 1997.

Whether you put the appositive before or after the noun it details is a stylistic choice. If in doubt, read the sentence aloud with several surrounding sentences to determine which placement sounds better.

Rhetorical and Stylistic Strategy

An appositive serves two rhetorical and stylistic functions:

- First, an appositive can *clarify* a term by providing a proper noun or a synonym for the term, by defining or explaining the term, or by getting more specific.

PROPER NOUN   Its hero is Scout's father, the saintly Atticus Finch.

—Francine Prose

SYNONYM   . . . an automaton, a machine, can be made to keep a school so.

—Ralph Waldo Emerson

LONGER DEFINITION   First published in 1970, *I Know Why the Caged Bird Sings* is what we have since learned to recognize as a "survivor" memoir, a first-person narrative of victimization and recovery.

— FRANCINE PROSE

EXPLANATION   [O]ne might suppose that teenagers might enjoy the transformative science-fiction aspects of *The Metamorphosis*, a story about a young man so alienated from *his* "dysfunctional" family that he turns . . . into a giant beetle.

— FRANCINE PROSE

SPECIFICITY   Yet in other genres — fiction and memoir — the news is far more upsetting.

— FRANCINE PROSE

• Second, an appositive can *smooth* choppy writing. Note how stilted each of the following items is compared with the preceding versions.

Its hero is Scout's father. His name is Atticus Finch. He is saintly.

An automaton is a machine. An automaton can be made to keep a school so.

I Know Why the Caged Bird Sings was first published in 1970. It is what we have since learned to recognize as a "survivor" memoir. A "survivor" memoir is a first-person narrative. The narrative deals with victimization and recovery.

[O]ne might suppose that teenagers might enjoy the transformative science-fiction aspects of *The Metamorphosis*. *The Metamorphosis* is a story about a young man.

Yet in other genres the news is far more upsetting. Other genres are fiction and memoir.

• **EXERCISE 1** •

Identify the appositive in each of the following sentences and the word or phrase it details.

1. My father, a truly exceptional man, worked at an ordinary job and was unknown outside the small town where he lived.

2. His rage passes description — the sort of rage that is only seen when rich folk that have more than they can enjoy suddenly lose something that they have long had but have never before used or wanted.
   — J. R. R. Tolkien, *The Hobbit*

3. [W. E. B.] DuBois saw the grandeur and degradation in a single unifying thought — slavery was the West's tragic flaw; yet it was tragic precisely because of the greatness of the civilization that encompassed it.
— Dinesh D'Souza, "Equality and the Classics"

4. The eruptions in the early part of our century — the time of world wars and emergent modernity — were premonitions of a sort.
— Sven Birkerts, *The Gutenberg Elegies*

5. Evidently I need this starting point — the world as it appeared before people bent it to their myriad plans — from which to begin dreaming up my own myriad, imaginary hominid agendas.
— Barbara Kingsolver, "Knowing Our Place"

6. The war America waged in Vietnam, the first to be witnessed day after day by television cameras, introduced the home front to new tele-intimacy with death and destruction.
— Susan Sontag, *Regarding the Pain of Others*

7. The restaurant's signature dish, a tantalizing fish taco, is also one of the least expensive entrees on the menu.

• EXERCISE 2 •

Provide the correct punctuation for each of the following sentences by using a dash, comma, or colon to separate the appositive from the rest of the sentence. Or, if a sentence does not need punctuation around the appositive, for that sentence write "NP" for "no punctuation." Be ready to explain why your choice of punctuation is the most effective in each case.

1. Several West African countries Nigeria, Ghana, Benin, Cameroon, and Togo were at some time in their history under colonial rule.

2. The mayoral candidate's rally opened to throngs of people an unusually large turnout for a cold, rainy day.

3. The British parliamentary system has two branches the House of Lords and the House of Commons.

4. The fifth canon of rhetoric style includes a writer's choices of diction and syntax.

5. One of our most popular poets Billy Collins is also one of our most gifted.

6. The surgeons reconstructed his hand the most damaged part of his body.

7. The rewards of hard work both physical and mental are often intangible.

8. Nadine Gordimer a white South African author won the Nobel Prize for Literature in 1991 when the country was still under the rule of apartheid.

9. Don't you think that businesses should close on July 4 the birthday of our country?

• EXERCISE 3 •

Combine each of the following pairs of sentences into one more fluent and coherent sentence by using an appositive. Be sure to punctuate correctly.

1. The *Times* is a world-renowned newspaper. It is delivered to my house every day.

2. Dolores Cunningham is the first mayor in our town's history to increase jobs during her four-year term. She is an advocate of the supply-side theory of economics.

3. A major health problem for teenagers is bulimia. Bulimia is a potentially life-threatening eating disorder.

4. My car is in the parking lot. It's an old blue station wagon with a dent in the fender.

5. That call was from Bridget. She's the top student in my calculus class.

6. The Edwardsville Tigers are the only baseball team ever to lose a series that it had led three games to none. They will be forever remembered for this colossal choke.

7. Warren G. Harding defeated James Cox in the 1920 presidential election by 26 percentage points. This was the biggest landslide victory in the history of U.S. presidential elections.

8. The service opened to the choir's rendition of Handel's "Hallelujah Chorus." That performance was a smashing success.

• EXERCISE 4 •

Identify the appositives in the following sentences from "I Know Why the Caged Bird Can't Read," and explain their effect. Note that all are direct quotations.

1. Traditionally, the love of reading has been born and nurtured in high school English class—the last time many students will find themselves in a roomful of people who have all read the same text and are, in theory, prepared to discuss it.

2. The intense loyalty adults harbor for books first encountered in youth is one probable reason for the otherwise baffling longevity of vintage

mediocre novels, books that teachers may themselves have read in adolescence. . . .

3. My older son spent the first several weeks of sophomore English discussing the class's summer assignment, *Ordinary People*, a weeper and former bestseller by Judith Guest about a "dysfunctional" family recovering from a teenage son's suicide attempt.

4. Yet in other genres—fiction and memoir—the news is far more upsetting.

5. First published in 1970, *I Know Why the Caged Bird Sings* is what we have since learned to recognize as a "survivor" memoir, a first-person narrative of victimization and recovery.

6. Its hero is Scout's father, the saintly Atticus Finch, a lawyer who represents everything we cherish about justice and democracy and the American Way.

7. The novel has a shadow hero, too, the descriptively named Boo Radley, a gooney recluse who becomes the occasion for yet another lesson in tolerance and compassion.

8. To read the novel is, for most, an exercise in wish-fulfillment and self-congratulation, a chance to consider thorny issues of race and prejudice from a safe distance and with the comfortable certainty that the reader would *never* harbor the racist attitudes espoused by the lowlifes in the novel.

9. The question is no longer what the writer has written but rather who the writer is—specifically, what ethnic group or gender identity an author represents.

10. Meanwhile, aesthetic beauty—felicitous or accurate language, images, rhythm, wit, the satisfaction of recognizing something in fiction that seems fresh and true—is simply too frivolous, suspect, and elitist even to mention.

• EXERCISE 5 •

Each of the following sentences includes one or more appositives. Identify the appositives, explain their effect, and then write a sentence of your own using that sentence as a model.

1. And on the basis of the evidence—the moral and political evidence—one is compelled to say that this is a backward society.

—James Baldwin, A Talk to Teachers

2. So to regard the young child, the young man, requires, no doubt, rare patience: a patience that nothing but faith in the medial forces of the soul can give. —Ralph Waldo Emerson, *Education*

3. In their classes, we wrote essays about our families, friends, hobbies, future dreams—personal subjects we had not written about at school since third grade. —Kyoko Mori, *School*

4. I am also other selves: a late starter, a casualty of the culture wars of the 1960s, an alienated adolescent sopping up pop culture and dreaming of escape, an American kid growing up in the 1950s, playing touch football and watching *I Love Lucy*.
   —Sven Birkerts, *The Gutenberg Elegies*

5. Mr. Somervell—a most delightful man, to whom my debt is great—was charged with the duty of teaching the stupidest boys the most regarded thing—namely, to write mere English.
   —Winston Churchill, *A Roving Commission: My Early Life*

Suggestions for Writing

Education

Now that you have examined a number of readings and other texts that focus on education, explore this topic yourself by synthesizing your own ideas and the readings. You might want to do more research or use readings from other classes as you write.

1. Many see standardized testing as the answer to improving public education in the United States. Thus, students face district- and state-mandated tests as well as national ones. What do you think? Write an essay discussing whether standardized testing is an effective way to improve instruction and performance. Be sure to research the topic, and broaden the scope of your essay beyond your own experience.

2. Homeschooling has become a popular alternative to public or private school for an increasing number of students in the United States. Research this trend by consulting print and electronic resources and, if possible, by interviewing someone involved with homeschooling. Would Ralph Waldo Emerson (p. 189) or Horace Mann (p. 248) support or oppose this method of education? Write an essay exploring both the benefits and the liabilities of homeschooling.

3. Many people believe that children should be required to attend at least one year of school prior to kindergarten. Write an essay explaining why tax dol-

lars should or should not be used to pay for mandatory, government-funded preschool. You might want to do some research to develop and support your position.

4. Write your own "Talk to Teachers," addressing either the teachers in your school or teachers in general. To start this assignment, replace the name *Khrushchev* with the word *terrorism* in the opening paragraph of James Baldwin's "A Talk to Teachers" (p. 197). How does this substitution set the stage for your more contemporary view?

5. Write a roundtable discussion among three or four of the authors in this chapter as they discuss *one* of the following quotations:

   • The only real education comes from what goes counter to you.

   —ANDRÉ GIDE

   • I have never let my schooling interfere with my education.

   —MARK TWAIN

   • Education is not filling a bucket but lighting a fire.

   —WILLIAM BUTLER YEATS

   • Rewards and punishments are the lowest form of education.

   —CHUANG-TZU

6. According to Francine Prose, "Education, after all, is a process intended to produce a product." Examine your school or another part of an educational system (for example, your school district, a Montessori class, a private religion-affiliated school). Describe specific parts of the educational process, and the "product" they strive to produce. Think of this as a cause-and-effect essay, with the process as the cause and the product as the effect.

7. Write a comparison/contrast of the high school classroom as you've experienced it in the United States with the high school experience in another country. If you've attended school in another country, you can use your own experience; if you know someone who has, you might interview that person; or you can research the topic in print and electronic sources. Consider how the classroom, including the relationship of teacher and student, reflects the values of the larger society.

8. Congratulations class of 2035! What will high school be like for the next generation? Write an essay explaining what changes you anticipate for high schools in the not-too-distant future. Will the high school be pretty much the same as yours? Will students interact with teachers solely online? Or will future students face a backlash to a more traditional model? What books will students be reading? Will they be reading at all? Can you imagine yourself as one of the teachers?

9. Create your own version of Roz Chast's "What I Learned," presenting your thoughts on education as a cartoon with a narrative line. Feel free to develop your own illustration style, rather than emulating hers.

10. Write your own humorous account of a learning experience, either in a traditional classroom or in a different context. Use some of David Sedaris's rhetorical strategies, such as dialogue, a self-deprecating persona, or hyperbolic descriptions.

11. Suppose you are delivering the commencement address at your high school. Consider David Foster Wallace's speech and the characteristics of commencement addresses in general, and write one that is tailored to your school and community. Keep in mind that, unlike Wallace at Kenyon College, you are writing as an insider speaking to fellow classmates.

6

Community

*What is the relationship of the individual
to the community?*

How can an individual maintain integrity and pursue personal dreams while contributing to the overall society? This is the central question facing every community. In the United States, we pride ourselves on rugged individualism and the pioneering spirit; at the same time, we believe in collective values. In other parts of the world, people perceive the balance of the individual and the community differently, but the history and literature of most societies depict the struggle of the individual to live life in good faith or conscience while being part of a community.

In the twenty-first century, the speed of our lives and an increasingly global perspective are redefining what a community is. The word *community* itself is changing, coming to mean a group of like-minded people sharing common interests, when in the past it referred to a group of people of various skills and interests cooperating with one another in order to survive. Geography and uniformity, once the main criteria of a community, now bow to technology and diversity, which today underlie the definition of ethnic communities, the intelligence community, or online communities, for example. Consider the notion of the "gated community." Is the phrase an expression of a different kind of community, one defined not by inclusion but rather by exclusion?

We find—and forge—communities based on geography, ethnicity, race, religion, marital status, occupation, class, economic status, gender, political affiliation, shared interest, or even language. Are those features more important than values, principles, and ideals? Or do we belong to various communities based on distinct criteria? How can we belong to several communities simultaneously?

The readings in this chapter explore the balance of individual concerns and community values, and they examine how different types of communities arise, some intentionally, some coincidentally. As you discuss these ideas, consider how people form communities, how individuals gain membership, how the community contributes to an individual's identity, and how outsiders perceive the community. Such discussions will help you formulate questions about the meaning of community in your own life.

Letter from Birmingham Jail

MARTIN LUTHER KING JR.

 Martin Luther King Jr. (1929–1968) was one of the most influential leaders of the civil rights movement of the 1950s and 1960s. Dr. King was born in Atlanta, Georgia, and grew up in the Ebenezer Baptist Church, where his father and grandfather were ministers. He earned a BA at Morehouse College, a divinity degree at Crozer Theological Seminary, and a PhD in theology at Boston University, all by the age of 26. In 1957, he founded the Southern Christian Leadership Conference and later led numerous protests against segregation by practicing the Gandhian doctrine of nonviolent resistance. In 1963, while King was in Birmingham, Alabama, eight clergymen published a letter in the *Post-Herald* criticizing his presence and his strategies. From the cell where he was jailed for demonstrating, King responded by writing what has come to be known as "Letter from Birmingham Jail."

The following is the public statement directed to Martin Luther King Jr. by eight Alabama clergymen that occasioned King's letter.

We the undersigned clergymen are among those who, in January, issued "an appeal for law and order and common sense," in dealing with racial problems in Alabama. We expressed understanding that honest convictions in racial matters could properly be pursued in the courts, but urged that decisions of those courts should in the meantime be peacefully obeyed.

Since that time there has been some evidence of increased forbearance and a willingness to face facts. Responsible citizens have undertaken to work on various problems which cause racial friction and unrest. In Birmingham, recent public events have given indication that we all have opportunity for a new constructive and realistic approach to racial problems.

However, we are now confronted by a series of demonstrations by some of our Negro citizens, directed and led in part by outsiders. We recognize the natural impatience of people who feel that their hopes are slow in being realized. But we are convinced that these demonstrations are unwise and untimely.

We agree rather with certain local Negro leadership which has called for honest and open negotiation of racial issues in our area. And we believe this kind of facing of issues can best be accomplished by citizens of our own metropolitan area, white and Negro, meeting with their knowledge and experience of the local situation. All of us need to face that responsibility and find proper channels for its accomplishment.

Just as we formerly pointed out that "hatred and violence have no sanction in our religious and political traditions," we also point out that such actions as incite to hatred and violence, however technically peaceful those actions may be, have not contributed to the resolution of our local problems. We do not believe that these days of new hope are days when extreme measures are justified in Birmingham.

We commend the community as a whole, and the local news media and law enforcement officials in particular, on the calm manner in which these demonstrations have been handled. We urge the public to continue to show restraint should the demonstrations continue, and the law enforcement officials to remain calm and continue to protect our city from violence.

We further strongly urge our own Negro community to withdraw support from these demonstrations, and to unite locally in working peacefully for a better Birmingham. When rights are consistently denied, a cause should be pressed in the courts and in negotiations among local leaders, and not in the streets. We appeal to both our white and Negro citizenry to observe the principles of law and order and common sense.

BISHOP C. C. J. CARPENTER, D.D., LL.D., Episcopalian Bishop of Alabama

BISHOP JOSEPH A. DURICK, D.D., Auxiliary Bishop, Roman Catholic Diocese of Mobile, Birmingham

RABBI MILTON L. GRAFMAN, Temple Emanu-El, Birmingham, Alabama

BISHOP PAUL HARDIN, Methodist Bishop of the Alabama–West Florida Conference

BISHOP NOLAN B. HARMON, Bishop of the North Alabama Conference of the Methodist Church

REV. GEORGE M. MURRAY, D.D., LL.D., Bishop Coadjutor, Episcopal Diocese of Alabama

REV. EDWARD V. RAMAGE, Moderator, Synod of the Alabama Presbyterian Church in the United States

REV. EARL STALLINGS, Pastor, First Baptist Church, Birmingham, Alabama

April 12, 1963

My Dear Fellow Clergymen:

While confined here in the Birmingham city jail, I came across your recent statement calling my present activities "unwise and untimely." Seldom do I pause to answer criticism of my work and ideas. If I sought to answer all the criticisms that cross my desk, my secretaries would have little time for anything other than such correspondence in the course of the day, and I would have no time for constructive work. But since I feel that you are men of genuine good will and that your criticisms are sincerely set forth, I want to try to answer your statement in what I hope will be patient and reasonable terms.

I think I should indicate why I am here in Birmingham, since you have been influenced by the view which argues against "outsiders coming in." I have the honor of serving as president of the Southern Christian Leadership Conference, an organization operating in every southern state, with headquarters in Atlanta, Georgia. We have some eighty-five affiliated organizations across the South, and one of them is the Alabama Christian Movement for Human Rights. Frequently we share staff, educational, and financial resources with our affiliates. Several months ago the affiliate here in Birmingham asked us to be on call to engage in a nonviolent direct-action program if such were deemed necessary. We readily consented, and when the hour came we lived up to our promise. So I, along with several members of my staff, am here because I was invited here. I am here because I have organizational ties here.

But more basically, I am in Birmingham because injustice is here. Just as the prophets of the eighth century B.C. left their villages and carried their "thus saith the Lord" far beyond the boundaries of their home towns, and just as the Apostle Paul left his village of Tarsus and carried the gospel of Jesus Christ to the far corners of the Greco-Roman world, so am I compelled to carry the gospel of freedom beyond my own home town. Like Paul, I must constantly respond to the Macedonian call for aid.

Moreover, I am cognizant of the interrelatedness of all communities and states. I cannot sit idly by in Atlanta and not be concerned about what happens in Birmingham. Injustice anywhere is a threat to justice everywhere. We are caught in an inescapable network of mutuality, tied in a single garment of destiny. Whatever affects one directly, affects all indirectly. Never again can we afford to live with the narrow, provincial "outside agitator" idea. Anyone who lives inside the United States can never be considered an outsider anywhere within its bounds.

You deplore the demonstrations taking place in Birmingham. But your statement, I am sorry to say, fails to express a similar concern for the conditions that brought about the demonstrations. I am sure that none of you would want to rest content with the superficial kind of social analysis that deals merely with effects and does not grapple with underlying causes. It is unfortunate that demonstrations are taking place in Birmingham, but it is even more unfortunate that the city's white power structure left the Negro community with no alternative.

In any nonviolent campaign there are four basic steps: collection of the facts to determine whether injustices exist; negotiation; self-purification; and direct action. We have gone through all these steps in Birmingham. There can be no gainsaying the fact that racial injustice engulfs this community. Birmingham is

5

probably the most thoroughly segregated city in the United States. Its ugly record of brutality is widely known. Negroes have experienced grossly unjust treatment in the courts. There have been more unsolved bombings of Negro homes and churches in Birmingham than in any other city in the nation. These are the hard, brutal facts of the case. On the basis of these conditions, Negro leaders sought to negotiate with the city fathers. But the latter consistently refused to engage in good-faith negotiation.

Then, last September, came the opportunity to talk with leaders of Birmingham's economic community. In the course of the negotiations, certain promises were made by the merchants — for example, to remove the stores' humiliating racial signs. On the basis of these promises, the Reverend Fred Shuttlesworth and the leaders of the Alabama Christian Movement for Human Rights agreed to a moratorium on all demonstrations. As the weeks and months went by, we realized that we were the victims of a broken promise. A few signs, briefly removed, returned; the others remained.

As in so many past experiences, our hopes had been blasted, and the shadow of deep disappointment settled upon us. We had no alternative except to prepare for direct action, whereby we would present our very bodies as a means of laying our case before the conscience of the local and the national community. Mindful of the difficulties involved, we decided to undertake a process of self-purification. We began a series of workshops on nonviolence, and we repeatedly asked ourselves: "Are you able to accept blows without retaliating?" "Are you able to endure the ordeal of jail?" We decided to schedule our direct-action program for the Easter season, realizing that except for Christmas, this is the main shopping period of the year. Knowing that a strong economic withdrawal program would be the by-product of direct action, we felt that this would be the best time to bring pressure to bear on the merchants for the needed change.

Then it occurred to us that Birmingham's mayoral election was coming up in March, and we speedily decided to postpone action until after election day. When we discovered that the Commissioner of Public Safety, Eugene "Bull" Connor, had piled up enough votes to be in the runoff, we decided again to postpone action until the day after the runoff so that the demonstrations could not be used to cloud the issues. Like many others, we wanted to see Mr. Connor defeated, and to this end we endured postponement after postponement. Having aided in this community need, we felt that our direct-action program could be delayed no longer.

You may well ask, "Why direct action? Why sit-ins, marches, and so forth? Isn't negotiation a better path?" You are quite right in calling for negotiation. Indeed, this is the very purpose of direct action. Nonviolent direct action seeks to create such a crisis and foster such a tension that a community which has constantly refused to negotiate is forced to confront the issue. It seeks so to dramatize the issue that it can no longer be ignored. My citing the creation of tension as part of the work of the nonviolent-resister may sound rather shocking. But I must confess that I am not afraid of the word "tension." I have earnestly opposed violent tension, but there is a type of constructive, nonviolent tension which is necessary for growth. Just as Socrates felt that it was necessary to create a tension in the mind so that individuals could rise from the bondage of myths and half-truths to the unfettered realm of creative analysis and objective appraisal, so must we see the need for nonviolent gadflies to create the kind of tension in society that will help men rise from the dark depths of prejudice and racism to the majestic heights of understanding and brotherhood.

The purpose of our direct-action program is to create a situation so crisis-packed that it will inevitably open the door to negotiation. I therefore concur with you in your call for negotiation. Too long has our beloved Southland been bogged down in a tragic effort to live in monologue rather than dialogue.

One of the basic points in your statement is that the action that I and my associates have taken in Birmingham is untimely. Some have asked: "Why didn't you give the new city administration time to act?" The only answer that I can give to this query is that the new Birmingham administration must be prodded about as much as the outgoing one, before it will act. We are sadly mistaken if we feel that the election of Albert Boutwell as mayor will bring the millennium to Birmingham. While Mr. Boutwell is a much more gentle person than Mr. Connor, they are both segregationists, dedicated to maintenance of the status quo. I have hoped that Mr. Boutwell will be reasonable enough to see the futility of massive resistance to desegregation. But he will not see this without pressure from devotees of civil rights. My friends, I must say to you that we have not made a single gain in civil rights without determined legal and nonviolent pressure. Lamentably, it is an historical fact that privileged groups seldom give up their privileges voluntarily. Individuals may see the moral light and voluntarily give up their unjust posture, but, as Reinhold Niebuhr[1] has reminded us, groups tend to be more immoral than individuals.

We know through painful experience that freedom is never voluntarily given by the oppressor; it must be demanded by the oppressed. Frankly, I have yet to engage in a direct-action campaign that was "well timed" in the view of those who have not suffered unduly from the disease of segregation. For years now I have heard the word "Wait!" It rings in the ear of every Negro with piercing familiarity. This "Wait" has almost always meant "Never." We must come to see, with one of our distinguished jurists, that "justice too long delayed is justice denied."

We have waited for more than 340 years for our constitutional and God-given rights. The nations of Asia and Africa are moving with jet-like speed toward gaining political independence, but we still creep at horse-and-buggy pace toward gaining a cup of coffee at a lunch counter. Perhaps it is easy for those who have never felt the stinging darts of segregation to say, "Wait." But when you have seen

---

[1] Niebuhr (1892–1971) was a U.S. clergyman and a Protestant theologian.—Eds.

vicious mobs lynch your mothers and fathers at will and drown your sisters and brothers at whim; when you have seen hate-filled policemen curse, kick, and even kill your black brothers and sisters; when you see the vast majority of your twenty million Negro brothers smothering in an airtight cage of poverty in the midst of an affluent society; when you suddenly find your tongue twisted and your speech stammering as you seek to explain to your six-year-old daughter why she can't go to the public amusement park that has just been advertised on television, and see tears welling up in her eyes when she is told that Funtown is closed to colored children, and see ominous clouds of inferiority beginning to form in her little mental sky, and see her beginning to distort her personality by developing an unconscious bitterness toward white people; when you have to concoct an answer for a five-year-old son who is asking, "Daddy, why do white people treat colored people so mean?"; when you take a cross-country drive and find it necessary to sleep night after night in the uncomfortable corners of your automobile because no motel will accept you; when you are humiliated day in and day out by nagging signs reading "white" and "colored"; when your first name becomes "nigger," your middle name becomes "boy" (however old you are) and your last name becomes "John," and your wife and mother are never given the respected title "Mrs."; when you are harried by day and haunted by night by the fact that you are a Negro, living constantly at tiptoe stance, never quite knowing what to expect next, and are plagued with inner fears and outer resentments; when you are forever fighting a degenerating sense of "nobodiness"—then you will understand why we find it difficult to wait. There comes a time when the cup of endurance runs over, and men are no longer willing to be plunged into the abyss of despair. I hope, sirs, you can understand our legitimate and unavoidable impatience.

You express a great deal of anxiety over our willingness to break laws. This is 15 certainly a legitimate concern. Since we so diligently urge people to obey the Supreme Court's decision of 1954 outlawing segregation in the public schools, at first glance it may seem rather paradoxical for us consciously to break laws. One may well ask: "How can you advocate breaking some laws and obeying others?" The answer lies in the fact that there are two types of laws: just and unjust. I would be the first to advocate obeying just laws. One has not only a legal but a moral responsibility to obey just laws. Conversely, one has a moral responsibility to disobey unjust laws. I would agree with St. Augustine that "an unjust law is no law at all."

Now, what is the difference between the two? How does one determine whether a law is just or unjust? A just law is a man-made code that squares with the moral law or the law of God. An unjust law is a code that is out of harmony with the moral law. To put it in the terms of St. Thomas Aquinas: An unjust law is a human law that is not rooted in eternal law and natural law. Any law that uplifts human personality is just. Any law that degrades human personality is unjust. All segregation statutes are unjust because segregation distorts the soul and damages the personality. It gives the segregator a false sense of superiority and the segregated a false sense of inferiority. Segregation, to use the terminology of the Jewish philosopher Martin Buber, substitutes an "I-it" relationship for an "I-thou" relationship and ends up relegating persons to the status of things. Hence segregation is not only politically, economically, and sociologically unsound, it is morally wrong and sinful. Paul Tillich[2] has said that sin is separation. Is not segregation an existential expression of man's tragic separation, his awful estrangement, his terrible sinfulness? Thus it is that I can urge men to obey the 1954 decision of the Supreme Court, for it is morally right; and I can urge them to disobey segregation ordinances, for they are morally wrong.

Let us consider a more concrete example of just and unjust laws. An unjust law is a code that a numerical or power majority group compels a minority group to obey but does not make binding on itself. This is *difference* made legal. By the same token, a just law is a code that a majority compels a minority to follow and that it is willing to follow itself. This is *sameness* made legal.

Let me give another explanation. A law is unjust if it is inflicted on a minority that, as a result of being denied the right to vote, had no part in enacting or devising the law. Who can say that the legislature of Alabama which set up that state's segregation laws was democratically elected? Throughout Alabama all sorts of devious methods are used to prevent Negroes from becoming registered voters, and there are some counties in which, even though Negroes constitute a majority of the population, not a single Negro is registered. Can any law enacted under such circumstances be considered democratically structured?

Sometimes a law is just on its face and unjust in its application. For instance, I have been arrested on a charge of parading without a permit. Now, there is nothing wrong in having an ordinance which requires a permit for a parade. But such an ordinance becomes unjust when it is used to maintain segregation and to deny citizens the First-Amendment privilege of peaceful assembly and protest.

I hope you are able to see the distinction I am trying to point out. In no sense do I advocate evading or defying the law, as would the rabid segregationist. That would lead to anarchy. One who breaks an unjust law must do so openly, lovingly, and with a willingness to accept the penalty. I submit that an individual who breaks a law that conscience tells him is unjust, and who willingly accepts the penalty of imprisonment in order to arouse the conscience of the community over its injustice, is in reality expressing the highest respect for law.

Of course, there is nothing new about this kind of civil disobedience. It was evidenced sublimely in the refusal of Shadrach, Meshach, and Abednego to obey the laws of Nebuchadnezzar, on the ground that a higher moral law was at stake. It was practiced superbly by the early Christians, who were willing to face hungry lions and the excruciating pain of chopping blocks rather than submit to certain unjust laws of the Roman Empire. To a degree, academic freedom is a reality

20

---

[2]Tillich (1886–1965) was a German American philosopher and a Christian theologian. — Eds.

today because Socrates practiced civil disobedience. In our own nation, the Boston Tea Party represented a massive act of civil disobedience.

We should never forget that everything Adolf Hitler did in Germany was "legal" and everything the Hungarian freedom fighters did in Hungary was "illegal." It was "illegal" to aid and comfort a Jew in Hitler's Germany. Even so, I am sure that, had I lived in Germany at the time, I would have aided and comforted my Jewish brothers. If today I lived in a Communist country where certain principles dear to the Christian faith are suppressed, I would openly advocate disobeying that country's antireligious laws.

I must make two honest confessions to you, my Christian and Jewish brothers. First, I must confess that over the past few years I have been gravely disappointed with the white moderate. I have almost reached the regrettable conclusion that the Negro's great stumbling block in his stride toward freedom is not the White Citizen's Counciler or the Ku Klux Klanner, but the white moderate, who is more devoted to "order" than to justice; who prefers a negative peace which is the absence of tension to a positive peace which is the presence of justice; who constantly says, "I agree with you in the goal you seek, but I cannot agree with your methods of direct action"; who paternalistically believes he can set the timetable for another man's freedom; who lives by a mythical concept of time and who constantly advises the Negro to wait for a "more convenient season." Shallow understanding from people of good will is more frustrating than absolute misunderstanding from people of ill will. Lukewarm acceptance is much more bewildering than outright rejection.

I had hoped that the white moderate would understand that law and order exist for the purpose of establishing justice and that when they fail in this purpose they become the dangerously structured dams that block the flow of social progress. I had hoped that the white moderate would understand that the present tension in the South is a necessary phase of the transition from an obnoxious negative peace, in which the Negro passively accepted his unjust plight, to a substantive and positive peace, in which all men will respect the dignity and worth of human personality. Actually, we who engage in nonviolent direct action are not the creators of tension. We merely bring to the surface the hidden tension that is already alive. We bring it out in the open, where it can be seen and dealt with. Like a boil that can never be cured so long as it is covered up but must be opened with all its ugliness to the natural medicines of air and light, injustice must be exposed, with all the tension its exposure creates, to the light of human conscience and the air of national opinion, before it can be cured.

In your statement you assert that our actions, even though peaceful, must be ²⁵ condemned because they precipitate violence. But is this a logical assertion? Isn't this like condemning a robbed man because his possession of money precipitated the evil act of robbery? Isn't this like condemning Socrates because his unswerving commitment to truth and his philosophical inquiries precipitated the act by the misguided populace in which they made him drink hemlock? Isn't this like condemning Jesus because his unique God-consciousness and never-ceasing devotion to God's will precipitated the evil act of crucifixion? We must come to see that, as the federal courts have consistently affirmed, it is wrong to urge an individual to cease his efforts to gain his basic constitutional rights because the quest may precipitate violence. Society must protect the robbed and punish the robber.

I had also hoped that the white moderate would reject the myth concerning time in relation to the struggle for freedom. I have just received a letter from a white brother in Texas. He writes: "All Christians know that the colored people will receive equal rights eventually, but it is possible that you are in too great a religious hurry. It has taken Christianity almost two thousand years to accomplish what it has. The teachings of Christ take time to come to earth." Such an attitude stems from a tragic misconception of time, from the strangely irrational notion that there is something in the very flow of time that will inevitably cure all ills. Actually, time itself is neutral; it can be used either destructively or constructively. More and more I feel that the people of ill will have used time much more effectively than have the people of good will. We will have to repent in this generation not merely for the hateful words and actions of the bad people, but for the appalling silence of the good people. Human progress never rolls in on wheels of inevitability; it comes through the tireless efforts of men willing to be co-workers with God, and without this hard work, time itself becomes an ally of the forces of social stagnation. We must use time creatively, in the knowledge that the time is always ripe to do right. Now is the time to make real the promise of democracy and transform our pending national elegy into a creative psalm of brotherhood. Now is the time to lift our national policy from the quicksand of racial injustice to the solid rock of human dignity.

You speak of our activity in Birmingham as extreme. At first I was rather disappointed that fellow clergymen would see my nonviolent efforts as those of an extremist. I began thinking about the fact that I stand in the middle of two opposing forces in the Negro community. One is a force of complacency, made up in part of Negroes who, as a result of long years of oppression, are so drained of self-respect and a sense of "somebodiness" that they have adjusted to segregation; and in part of a few middle-class Negroes who, because of a degree of academic and economic security and because in some ways they profit by segregation, have become insensitive to the problems of the masses. The other force is one of bitterness and hatred, and it comes perilously close to advocating violence. It is expressed in the various black nationalist groups that are springing up across the nation, the largest and best-known being Elijah Muhammad's Muslim movement. Nourished by the Negro's frustration over the continued existence of racial discrimination, this movement is made up of people who have lost faith in America, who have absolutely repudiated Christianity, and who have concluded that the white man is an incorrigible "devil."

I have tried to stand between these two forces, saying that we need emulate neither the "do-nothingism" of the complacent nor the hatred and despair of the black nationalist. For there is the more excellent way of love and nonviolent protest. I am grateful to God that, through the influence of the Negro church, the way of nonviolence became an integral part of our struggle.

If this philosophy had not emerged, by now many streets of the South would, I am convinced, be flowing with blood. And I am further convinced that if our white brothers dismiss as "rabble-rousers" and "outside agitators" those of us who employ nonviolent direct action, and if they refuse to support our nonviolent efforts, millions of Negroes will, out of frustration and despair, seek solace and security in black-nationalist ideologies—a development that would inevitably lead to a frightening racial nightmare.

Oppressed people cannot remain oppressed forever. The yearning for freedom eventually manifests itself, and that is what has happened to the American Negro. Something within has reminded him of his birthright of freedom, and something without has reminded him that it can be gained. Consciously or unconsciously, he has been caught up by the *Zeitgeist*,[3] and with his black brothers of Africa and his brown and yellow brothers of Asia, South America, and the Caribbean, the United States Negro is moving with a sense of great urgency toward the promised land of racial justice. If one recognizes this vital urge that has engulfed the Negro community, one should readily understand why public demonstrations are taking place. The Negro has many pent-up resentments and latent frustrations, and he must release them. So let him march; let him make prayer pilgrimages to the city hall; let him go on freedom rides—and try to understand why he must do so. If his repressed emotions are not released in nonviolent ways, they will seek expression through violence; this is not a threat but a fact of history. So I have not said to my people, "Get rid of your discontent." Rather, I have tried to say that this normal and healthy discontent can be channeled into the creative outlet of nonviolent direct action. And now this approach is being termed extremist.

But though I was initially disappointed at being categorized as an extremist, as I continued to think about the matter I gradually gained a measure of satisfaction from the label. Was not Jesus an extremist for love: "Love your enemies, bless them that curse you, do good to them that hate you, and pray for them which despitefully use you, and persecute you." Was not Amos an extremist for justice: "Let justice roll down like waters and righteousness like an ever-flowing stream." Was not Paul an extremist for the Christian gospel: "I bear in my body the marks of the Lord Jesus." Was not Martin Luther an extremist: "Here I stand; I cannot do otherwise, so help me God." And John Bunyan: "I will stay in jail to the end of my days before I make a butchery of my conscience." And Abraham Lincoln: "This nation cannot survive half slave and half free." And Thomas Jefferson: "We hold these truths to be self-evident, that all men are created equal. . . ." So the question is not whether we will be extremists, but what kind of extremists we will be. Will

30

---

[3]German, "spirit of the time."—Eds.

we be extremists for hate or for love? Will we be extremists for the preservation of injustice or for the extension of justice? In that dramatic scene on Calvary's hill three men were crucified. We must never forget that all three were crucified for the same crime—the crime of extremism. Two were extremists for immorality, and thus fell below their environment. The other, Jesus Christ, was an extremist for love, truth, and goodness, and thereby rose above his environment. Perhaps the South, the nation, and the world are in dire need of creative extremists.

I had hoped that the white moderate would see this need. Perhaps I was too optimistic; perhaps I expected too much. I suppose I should have realized that few members of the oppressor race can understand the deep groans and passionate yearnings of the oppressed race, and still fewer have the vision to see that injustice must be rooted out by strong, persistent, and determined action. I am thankful, however, that some of our white brothers in the South have grasped the meaning of this social revolution and committed themselves to it. They are still all too few in quantity, but they are big in quality. Some—such as Ralph McGill, Lillian Smith, Harry Golden, James McBride Dabbs, Ann Braden, and Sarah Patton Boyle—have written about our struggle in eloquent and prophetic terms. Others have marched with us down nameless streets of the South. They have languished in filthy, roach-infested jails, suffering the abuse and brutality of policemen who view them as "dirty nigger-lovers." Unlike so many of their moderate brothers and sisters, they have recognized the urgency of the moment and sensed the need for powerful "action" antidotes to combat the disease of segregation.

Let me take note of my other major disappointment. I have been so greatly disappointed with the white church and its leadership. Of course, there are some notable exceptions. I am not unmindful of the fact that each of you has taken some significant stands on this issue. I commend you, Reverend [Earl] Stallings, for your Christian stand on this past Sunday, in welcoming Negroes to your worship service on a nonsegregated basis. I commend the Catholic leaders of this state for integrating Spring Hill College several years ago.

But despite these notable exceptions, I must honestly reiterate that I have been disappointed with the church. I do not say this as one of those negative critics who can always find something wrong with the church. I say this as a minister of the gospel, who loves the church; who was nurtured in its bosom; who has been sustained by its spiritual blessings and who will remain true to it as long as the cord of life shall lengthen.

When I was suddenly catapulted into the leadership of the bus protest in Montgomery, Alabama, a few years ago, I felt we would be supported by the white church. I felt that the white ministers, priests, and rabbis of the South would be among our strongest allies. Instead, some have been outright opponents, refusing to understand the freedom movement and misrepresenting its leaders; all too many others have been more cautious than courageous and have remained silent behind the anesthetizing security of stained-glass windows.

35

In spite of my shattered dreams, I came to Birmingham with the hope that the white religious leadership of this community would see the justice of our cause and, with deep moral concern, would serve as the channel through which our just grievances could reach the power structure. I had hoped that each of you would understand. But again I have been disappointed.

I have heard numerous southern religious leaders admonish their worshipers to comply with a desegregation decision because it is the law, but I have longed to hear white ministers declare: "Follow this decree because integration is morally right and because the Negro is your brother." In the midst of blatant injustices inflicted upon the Negro, I have watched white church men stand on the sideline and mouth pious irrelevancies and sanctimonious trivialities. In the midst of a mighty struggle to rid our nation of racial and economic injustice, I have heard many ministers say: "Those are social issues, with which the gospel has no real concern." And I have watched many churches commit themselves to a completely otherworldly religion which makes a strange, un-Biblical distinction between body and soul, between the sacred and the secular.

I have traveled the length and breadth of Alabama, Mississippi, and all the other southern states. On sweltering summer days and crisp autumn mornings I have looked at the South's beautiful churches with their lofty spires point-ing heavenward. I have beheld the impressive outlines of her massive religious-education buildings. Over and over I have found myself asking: "What kind of people worship here? Who is their God? Where were their voices when the lips of Governor [Ross] Barnett dripped with words of interposition and nullification? Where were they when Governor [George] Wallace gave a clarion call for defiance and hatred? Where were their voices of support when bruised and weary Negro men and women decided to rise from the dark dungeons of complacency to the bright hills of creative protest?"

Yes, these questions are still in my mind. In deep disappointment I have wept over the laxity of the church. But be assured that my tears have been tears of love. There can be no deep disappointment where there is not deep love. Yes, I love the church. How could I do otherwise? I am in the rather unique position of being the son, the grandson, and the great-grandson of preachers. Yes, I see the church as the body of Christ. But, oh! How we have blemished and scarred that body through social neglect and through fear of being nonconformists.

There was a time when the church was very powerful—in the time when the early Christians rejoiced at being deemed worthy to suffer for what they believed. In those days the church was not merely a thermometer that recorded the ideas and principles of popular opinion; it was a thermostat that transformed the mores of society. Whenever the early Christians entered a town, the people in power became disturbed and immediately sought to convict the Christians for being "disturbers of the peace" and "outside agitators." But the Christians pressed on, in the conviction that they were "a colony of heaven," called to obey God rather than man. Small in number, they were big in commitment. They were too

40

God-intoxicated to be "astronomically intimidated." By their effort and example they brought an end to such ancient evils as infanticide and gladiatorial contests.

Things are different now. So often the contemporary church is a weak, ineffectual voice with an uncertain sound. So often it is an archdefender of the status quo. Far from being disturbed by the presence of the church, the power structure of the average community is consoled by the church's silent—and often even vocal—sanction of things as they are.

But the judgment of God is upon the church as never before. If today's church does not recapture the sacrificial spirit of the early church, it will lose its authenticity, forfeit the loyalty of millions, and be dismissed as an irrelevant social club with no meaning for the twentieth century. Every day I meet young people whose disappointment with the church has turned into outright disgust.

Perhaps I have once again been too optimistic. Is organized religion too inextricably bound to the status quo to save our nation and the world? Perhaps I must turn my faith to the inner spiritual church, the church within the church, as the true *ekklesia* and the hope of the world. But again I am thankful to God that some noble souls from the ranks of organized religion have broken loose from the paralyzing chains of conformity and joined us as active partners in the struggle for freedom. They have left their secure congregations and walked the streets of Albany, Georgia, with us. They have gone down the highways of the South on tortuous rides for freedom. Yes, they have gone to jail with us. Some have been dismissed from their churches, have lost the support of their bishops and fellow ministers. But they have acted in the faith that right defeated is stronger than evil triumphant. Their witness has been the spiritual salt that has preserved the true meaning of the gospel in these troubled times. They have carved a tunnel of hope through the dark mountain of disappointment.

I hope the church as a whole will meet the challenge of this decisive hour. But even if the church does not come to the aid of justice, I have no despair about the future. I have no fear about the outcome of our struggle in Birmingham, even if our motives are at present misunderstood. We will reach the goal of freedom in Birmingham and all over the nation, because the goal of America is freedom. Abused and scorned though we may be, our destiny is tied up with America's destiny. Before the pilgrims landed at Plymouth, we were here. Before the pen of Jefferson etched the majestic words of the Declaration of Independence across the pages of history, we were here. For more than two centuries our forebears labored in this country without wages: they made cotton king; they built the homes of their masters while suffering gross injustice and shameful humiliation—and yet out of a bottomless vitality they continued to thrive and develop. If the inexpressible cruelties of slavery could not stop us, the opposition we now face will surely fail. We will win our freedom because the sacred heritage of our nation and the eternal will of God are embodied in our echoing demands.

Before closing I feel impelled to mention one other point in your statement 45 that has troubled me profoundly. You warmly commended the Birmingham police force for keeping "order" and "preventing violence." I doubt that you would have so warmly commended the police force if you had seen its dogs sinking their teeth into unarmed, nonviolent Negroes. I doubt that you would so quickly commend the policemen if you were to observe their ugly and inhumane treatment of Negroes here in the city jail; if you were to watch them push and curse old Negro women and young Negro girls; if you were to see them slap and kick old Negro men and young boys; if you were to observe them, as they did on two occasions, refuse to give us food because we wanted to sing our grace together. I cannot join you in your praise of the Birmingham police department.

It is true that the police have exercised a degree of discipline in handling the demonstrators. In this sense they have conducted themselves rather "nonviolently" in public. But for what purpose? To preserve the evil system of segregation. Over the past few years I have consistently preached that nonviolence demands that the means we use must be as pure as the ends we seek. I have tried to make clear that it is wrong to use immoral means to attain moral ends. But now I must affirm that it is just as wrong, or perhaps even more so, to use moral means to preserve immoral ends. Perhaps Mr. Connor and his policemen have been rather nonviolent in public, as was Chief Pritchett in Albany, Georgia, but they have used the moral means of nonviolence to maintain the immoral end of racial injustice. As T. S. Eliot has said, "The last temptation is the greatest treason: To do the right deed for the wrong reason."

I wish you had commended the Negro sit-inners and demonstrators of Birmingham for their sublime courage, their willingness to suffer, and their amazing discipline in the midst of great provocation. One day the South will recognize its real heroes. They will be the James Merediths, with the noble sense of purpose that enables them to face jeering and hostile mobs, and with the agonizing loneliness that characterizes the life of the pioneer. They will be old, oppressed, battered Negro women, symbolized in a seventy-two-year-old woman in Montgomery, Alabama, who rose up with a sense of dignity and with her people decided not to ride segregated buses, and who responded with ungrammatical profundity to one who inquired about her weariness: "My feets is tired, but my soul is at rest." They will be the young high school and college students, the young ministers of the gospel and a host of their elders, courageously and nonviolently sitting in at lunch counters and willingly going to jail for conscience' sake. One day the South will know that when these disinherited children of God sat down at lunch counters, they were in reality standing up for what is best in the American dream and for the most sacred values in our Judaeo-Christian heritage, thereby bringing our nation back to those great wells of democracy which were dug deep by the founding fathers in their formulation of the Constitution and the Declaration of Independence.

Never before have I written so long a letter. I'm afraid it is much too long to take your precious time. I can assure you that it would have been much shorter if I had been writing from a comfortable desk, but what else can one do when he is alone in a narrow jail cell, other than write long letters, think long thoughts, and pray long prayers?

If I have said anything in this letter that overstates the truth and indicates an unreasonable impatience, I beg you to forgive me. If I have said anything that understates the truth and indicates my having a patience that allows me to settle for anything less than brotherhood, I beg God to forgive me.

I hope this letter finds you strong in the faith. I also hope that circumstances   50
will soon make it possible for me to meet each of you, not as an integrationist or a civil-rights leader but as a fellow clergyman and a Christian brother. Let us all hope that the dark clouds of racial prejudice will soon pass away and the deep fog of misunderstanding will be lifted from our fear-drenched communities, and in some not too distant tomorrow the radiant stars of love and brotherhood will shine over our great nation with all their scintillating beauty.

Yours for the cause of Peace and Brotherhood,
Martin Luther King Jr.

. . . .

Questions for Discussion

1. Martin Luther King writes as a member of several communities, some overlapping, some in conflict. What are they? Focusing on two or three, explain how he defines himself within each.
2. What is the meaning of *ekklesia* (para. 43)? What does King mean when he invokes "the true *ekklesia*"?
3. How does King balance the twin appeals to religion and patriotism throughout "Letter from Birmingham Jail"? Do you think he puts more emphasis on religion or patriotism? Why do you think he makes that choice?
4. In the later 1960s, Alice Walker wrote an essay titled "The Civil Rights Movement: What Good Was It?" How would you answer her question today? What good do you believe has resulted from the civil rights movement?

Questions on Rhetoric and Style

1. What is King's tone in the opening paragraph? How might you make an argument for its being ironic?
2. Why does King arrange paragraphs 2–4 in the order that he does? How would reversing the order change the impact?
3. How do King's allusions to biblical figures and events appeal to both ethos and pathos?
4. Why does King go into such detail to explain the basic principles and process of the nonviolent protest movement?
5. In sentence 2 of paragraph 14, what is the effect of juxtaposing the rate of change in Asian and African cultures with the rate of change in American culture?

6. In the long sentence in paragraph 14 (beginning with "But when you have seen"), why does King arrange the "when" clauses in the order that he does? Try repositioning them, and then discuss the difference in effect.
7. What rhetorical strategies are used in paragraph 25? Identify at least four.
8. What are the chief rhetorical strategies used in paragraph 31? Identify at least five.
9. Why does King wait until paragraph 45 to address the alleged commendable behavior of the Birmingham police in "preventing violence"?
10. Trace one of the following patterns of figurative language throughout King's letter: darkness and light, high and low, sickness and health.
11. King uses repetition of single words or phrases, of sentence structures, and of sounds. Focusing on a passage of one or more paragraphs, discuss the effect of this use of repetition.
12. Considering the final three paragraphs as King's conclusion, discuss whether you believe it is rhetorically effective.

Suggestions for Writing

1. Write an essay analyzing the style of this letter, paying close attention to how the stylistic devices and resources of language contribute to achieving King's purpose.
2. King spends nearly half of his letter addressing counterarguments before he launches into his main argument to the clergymen. Write an essay analyzing this argument. What are his major claims, his assumptions, the types of evidence he uses?
3. Compare and contrast the rhetorical strategies King employs in "Letter from Birmingham Jail" with those he uses in another piece, such as the "I Have a Dream" speech or the introduction to *Why We Can't Wait* (which appeared on the 1989 AP Language exam). Why are certain strategies more appropriate for a speech than for an essay or a letter?
4. Select a quotation from King's letter, and explain (1) why you find it compelling or (2) on what grounds you would challenge it. Cite evidence from your own experience or reading to support your position. Possible quotations to focus on include:
   a. "Injustice anywhere is a threat to justice everywhere." (para. 4)
   b. ". . . freedom is never voluntarily given by the oppressor; it must be demanded by the oppressed." (para. 13)
   c. "Shallow understanding from people of good will is more frustrating than absolute misunderstanding from people of ill will." (para. 23)
5. Describe a time when your participation in, or loyalty to, two different communities conflicted. Explain the nature of the conflict and how you resolved it.

Where I Lived, and What I Lived For

HENRY DAVID THOREAU

Henry David Thoreau (1817–1862) was a philosopher, poet, essayist, and naturalist as well as an outspoken social critic. He was born in Concord, Massachusetts, and was educated at Harvard. He worked in a variety of professions, from land surveyor to teacher to pencil maker. Strongly influenced by his neighbor and friend Ralph Waldo Emerson, Thoreau considered himself a fierce patriot who honored his country and its ideals, if not always its government. He spoke out against the war against Mexico, and slavery—specifically the Fugitive Slave Act—and defended the abolitionist John Brown. He is best known for *Walden, or Life in the Woods*, published in 1854, which is his account of living in a cabin on Walden Pond for two years. This selection is from the second chapter of *Walden*.

I went to the woods because I wished to live deliberately, to front only the essential facts of life, and see if I could not learn what it had to teach, and not, when I came to die, discover that I had not lived. I did not wish to live what was not life, living is so dear; nor did I wish to practice resignation, unless it was quite necessary. I wanted to live deep and suck out all the marrow of life, to live so sturdily and Spartan-like as to put to rout all that was not life, to cut a broad swath and shave close, to drive life into a corner, and reduce it to its lowest terms, and, if it proved to be mean, why then to get the whole and genuine meanness of it, and publish its meanness to the world; or if it were sublime, to know it by experience, and be able to give a true account of it in my next excursion. For most men, it appears to me, are in a strange uncertainty about it, whether it is of the devil or of God, and have *somewhat hastily* concluded that it is the chief end of man here to "glorify God and enjoy him forever."[1]

Still we live meanly, like ants; though the fable tells us that we were long ago changed into men; like pygmies we fight with cranes;[2] it is error upon error, and clout upon clout, and our best virtue has for its occasion a superfluous and evi-

---

[1] The first question and answer in the Westminster Catechism, a statement of religious doctrine that came out of the Protestant Reformation, is "Q: What is the chief end of man? A: To glorify God and enjoy him forever."—Eds.

[2] Allusions to the Greek fable of the Myrmidons (ant-people), and to Book III of the *Iliad*, respectively. The *Iliad* draws a parallel between the Trojan War and the mythological war between the cranes and the pygmies.—Eds.

table wretchedness. Our life is frittered away by detail. An honest man has hardly need to count more than his ten fingers, or in extreme cases he may add his ten toes, and lump the rest. Simplicity, simplicity, simplicity! I say, let your affairs be as two or three, and not a hundred or a thousand; instead of a million count half a dozen, and keep your accounts on your thumb-nail. In the midst of this chopping sea of civilized life, such are the clouds and storms and quicksands and thousand-and-one items to be allowed for, that a man has to live, if he would not founder and go to the bottom and not make his port at all, by dead reckoning, and he must be a great calculator indeed who succeeds. Simplify, simplify. Instead of three meals a day, if it be necessary eat but one; instead of a hundred dishes, five; and reduce other things in proportion. Our life is like a German Confederacy, made up of petty states, with its boundary forever fluctuating, so that even a German cannot tell you how it is bounded at any moment. The nation itself, with all its so-called internal improvements, which, by the way are all external and superficial, is just such an unwieldy and overgrown establishment, cluttered with furniture and tripped up by its own traps, ruined by luxury and heedless expense, by want of calculation and a worthy aim, as the million households in the land; and the only cure for it, as for them, is in a rigid economy, a stern and more than Spartan simplicity of life and elevation of purpose. It lives too fast. Men think that it is essential that the *Nation* have commerce, and export ice, and talk through a telegraph, and ride thirty miles an hour, without a doubt, whether *they* do or not; but whether we should live like baboons or like men, is a little uncertain. If we do not get out sleepers,[3] and forge rails, and devote days and nights to the work, but go to tinkering upon our *lives* to improve *them*, who will build railroads? And if railroads are not built, how shall we get to heaven in season? But if we stay at home and mind our business, who will want railroads? We do not ride on the railroad; it rides upon us. Did you ever think what those sleepers are that underlie the railroad? Each one is a man, an Irishman, or a Yankee man. The rails are laid on them, and they are covered with sand, and the cars run smoothly over them. They are sound sleepers, I assure you. And every few years a new lot is laid down and run over, so that, if some have the pleasure of riding on a rail, others have the misfortune to be ridden upon. And when they run over a man that is walking in his sleep, a supernumerary sleeper in the wrong position, and wake him up, they suddenly stop the cars, and make a hue and cry about it, as if this were an exception. I am glad to know that it takes a gang of men for every five miles to keep the sleepers down and level in their beds as it is, for this is a sign that they may sometimes get up again.

Why should we live with such hurry and waste of life? We are determined to be starved before we are hungry. Men say that a stitch in time saves nine, and so they take a thousand stitches today to save nine tomorrow. As for *work*, we haven't

---

[3]Here, *sleepers* means "railroad ties." — Eds.

any of any consequence. We have the Saint Vitus' dance,[4] and cannot possibly keep our heads still. If I should only give a few pulls at the parish bell-rope, as for a fire, that is, without setting the bell, there is hardly a man on his farm in the outskirts of Concord, notwithstanding that press of engagements which was his excuse so many times this morning, nor a boy, nor a woman, I might almost say, but would foresake all and follow that sound, not mainly to save property from the flames, but, if we will confess the truth, much more to see it burn, since burn it must, and we, be it known, did not set it on fire—or to see it put out, and have a hand in it, if that is done as handsomely; yes, even if it were the parish church itself. Hardly a man takes a half-hour's nap after dinner, but when he wakes he holds up his head and asks, "What's the news?" as if the rest of mankind had stood his sentinels. Some give directions to be waked every half-hour, doubtless for no other purpose; and then, to pay for it, they tell what they have dreamed. After a night's sleep the news is as indispensable as the breakfast. "Pray tell me anything new that has happened to a man anywhere on this globe"—and he reads it over his coffee and rolls, that a man has had his eyes gouged out this morning on the Wachito River; never dreaming the while that he lives in the dark unfathomed mammoth cave of this world, and has but the rudiment of an eye himself.

For my part, I could easily do without the post-office. I think that there are very few important communications made through it. To speak critically, I never received more than one or two letters in my life—I wrote this some years ago—that were worth the postage. The penny-post is, commonly, an institution through which you seriously offer a man that penny for his thoughts which is so often safely offered in jest. And I am sure that I never read any memorable news in a newspaper. If we read of one man robbed, or murdered, or killed by accident, or one house burned, or one vessel wrecked or one steamboat blown up, or one cow run over on the Western Railroad, or one mad dog killed, or one lot of grasshoppers in the winter—we never need read of another. One is enough. If you are acquainted with the principle, what do you care for a myriad instances and applications? To a philosopher all *news*, as it is called, is gossip, and they who edit and read it are old women over their tea. Yet not a few are greedy after this gossip. There was such a rush, as I hear, the other day at one of the offices to learn the foreign news by the last arrival, that several large squares of plate glass belonging to the establishment were broken by the pressure—news which I seriously think a ready wit might write a twelvemonth, or twelve years, beforehand with sufficient accuracy. As for Spain, for instance, if you know how to throw in Don Carlos and the Infanta, and Don Pedro and Seville and Granada, from time to time in the right propor-tions—they may have changed the names a little since I saw the papers—and serve up a bullfight when other entertainments fail, it will be true to the letter, and give us as good an idea of the exact state or ruin of things in Spain as the most

---

[4]A disease that causes the victim to twitch uncontrollably. St. Vitus is the patron saint of dancers.—Eds.

succinct and lucid reports under this head in the newspapers; and as for England, almost the last significant scrap of news from that quarter was the revolution of 1649; and if you have learned the history of her crops for an average year, you never need attend to that thing again, unless your speculations are of a merely pecuniary character. If one may judge who rarely looks into the newspapers, nothing new does ever happen in foreign parts, a French revolution not excepted.

What news! how much more important to know what that is which was never old! "Kieou-pe-yu (great dignitary of the state of Wei) sent a man to Khoung-tseu to know his news. Khoung-tseu caused the messenger to be seated near him, and questioned him in these terms: What is your master doing? The messenger answered with respect: My master desires to diminish the number of his faults, but he cannot come to the end of them. The messenger being gone, the philosopher remarked: What a worthy messenger! What a worthy messenger!" The preacher, instead of vexing the ears of drowsy farmers on their day of rest at the end of the week — for Sunday is the fit conclusion of an ill-spent week, and not the fresh and brave beginning of a new one — with this one other draggle-tail of a sermon, should shout with thundering voice, "Pause! Avast! Why so seeming fast, but deadly slow?"

Shams and delusions are esteemed for soundless truths, while reality is fabulous. If men would steadily observe realities only, and not allow themselves to be deluded, life, to compare it with such things as we know, would be like a fairy tale and the Arabian Nights' Entertainments. If we respected only what is inevitable and has a right to be, music and poetry would resound along the streets. When we are unhurried and wise, we perceive that only great and worthy things have any permanent and absolute existence, that petty fears and petty pleasures are but the shadow of the reality. This is always exhilarating and sublime. By closing the eyes and slumbering, and consenting to be deceived by shows, men establish and confirm their daily life of routine and habit everywhere, which still is built on purely illusory foundations. Children, who play life, discern its true law and relations more clearly than men, who fail to live it worthily, but who think that they are wiser by experience, that is, by failure. I have read in a Hindoo book, that "there was a king's son, who, being expelled in infancy from his native city, was brought up by a forester, and, growing up to maturity in that state, imagined himself to belong to the barbarous race with which he lived. One of his father's ministers having discovered him, revealed to him what he was, and the misconception of his character was removed, and he knew himself to be a prince. So soul," continues the Hindoo philosopher, "from the circumstances in which it is placed, mistakes its own character, until the truth is revealed to it by some holy teacher and then it knows itself to be *Brahme*."[5] I perceive that we inhabitants of New England live this mean life that we do because our vision does not penetrate the surface of things. We think that that *is* which *appears* to be. If a man should walk through

---

[5]One of the three main Hindu gods, now spelled *Brahma*. — Eds.

this town and see only the reality, where, think you, would the "Milldam"[6] go to? If he should give us an account of the realities he beheld there, we should not recognize the place in his description. Look at the meetinghouse, or a courthouse, or a jail, or a shop, or a dwelling-house, and say what that thing really is before a true gaze, and they would all go to pieces in your account of them. Men esteem truth remote, in the outskirts of the system behind the farthest star, before Adam and after the last man. In eternity there is indeed something true and sublime. But all these times and places and occasions are now and here. God himself culminates in the present moment, and will never be more divine in the lapse of all the ages. And we are enabled to apprehend at all what is sublime and noble only by the perpetual instilling and drenching of the reality that surrounds us. The universe constantly and obediently answers to our conceptions; whether we travel fast or slow, the track is laid for us. Let us spend our lives in conceiving then. The poet or the artist never yet had so fair and noble a design but some of his posterity at least could accomplish it.

Let us spend one day as deliberately as Nature, and not be thrown off the track by every nutshell and mosquito's wing that falls on the rails. Let us rise early and fast, or breakfast, gently and without perturbation; let company come and let company go, let the bells ring and the children cry—determined to make a day of it. Why should we knock under and go with the stream? Let us not be upset and overwhelmed in that terrible rapid and whirlpool called a dinner, situated in the meridian shallows. Weather this danger and you are safe, for the rest of the way is downhill. With unrelaxed nerves, with morning vigor, sail by it, looking another way, tied to the mast like Ulysses. If the engine whistles, let it whistle till it is hoarse for its pains. If the bell rings, why should we run? We will consider what kind of music they are like. Let us settle ourselves and work and wedge our feet downward through the mud and slush of opinion, and prejudice, and tradition, and delusion, and appearance, that alluvion[7] which covers the globe, through Paris and London, through New York and Boston and Concord, through Church and State, through poetry and philosophy and religion, till we come to a hard bottom and rocks in place, which we can call *reality*, and say, This is, and no mistake; and then begin, having a *point d'appui*,[8] below freshet and frost and fire, a place where you might found a wall or a state, or set a lamppost safely, or perhaps a gauge, not a Nilometer, but a Realometer, that future ages might know how deep a freshet of shams and appearances had gathered from time to time. If you stand right fronting and face to face to a fact, you will see the sun glimmer on both its surfaces, as if it were a cimeter,[9] and feel its sweet edge dividing you

---

[6]Concord's business center.—Eds.
[7]The flow of water against a shore.—Eds.
[8]French, "foundation."—Eds.
[9]Also known as a *scimeter* or *scimitar*, a curved bladed sword traditionally used in the Middle East.—Eds.

through the heart and marrow, and so you will happily conclude your mortal career. Be it life or death, we crave only reality. If we are really dying, let us hear the rattle in our throats and feel cold in the extremities; if we are alive, let us go about our business.

Time is but the stream I go afishing in. I drink at it; but while I drink I see the sandy bottom and detect how shallow it is. Its thin current slides away but eternity remains. I would drink deeper; fish in the sky, whose bottom is pebbly with stars. I cannot count one. I know not the first letter of the alphabet. I have always been regretting that I was not as wise as the day I was born. The intellect is a cleaver; it discerns and rifts its way into the secret of things. I do not wish to be any more busy with my hands than is necessary. My head is hands and feet. I feel all my best faculties concentrated in it. My instinct tells me that my head is an organ for burrowing, as some creatures use their snout and fore paws, and with it I would mine and burrow my way through these hills. I think that the richest vein is somewhere hereabouts, so by the divining-rod and thin rising vapors, I judge; and here I will begin to mine.

. . . .

Questions for Discussion

1. What is Henry David Thoreau calling for early in paragraph 2 when he writes, "Simplicity, simplicity, simplicity!"?
2. Thoreau writes, "We do not ride on the railroad; it rides upon us" (para. 2). Consider an electronic device (such as a laptop computer, a smartphone, a tablet, or an MP3 player). What would Thoreau say about it? Has this device helped to simplify our lives, or has it had a negative impact on them?
3. What does Thoreau mean when he says, "As for *work*, we haven't any of any consequence" (para. 3)? What is his definition of *work*?
4. How do you interpret this assertion: "Shams and delusions are esteemed for soundless truths, while reality is fabulous" (para. 6)? Use that as a topic sentence, and develop it with examples from your own experience.
5. Do you think Thoreau's advice and sentiments in this essay are meant as recommendations for living one's entire life or as suggestions for periodically reflecting on life's true meaning? Is he suggesting isolation as a lifestyle?
6. In today's terms, how would you characterize Thoreau's politics? Is he very conservative or very progressive? Is he somewhere in between?

Questions on Rhetoric and Style

1. In the first paragraph, how does Thoreau use antitheses to describe his purpose in going to live in the woods?

2. Paragraph 2 opens with a simile and continues its lengthy development with more similes and an extended metaphor. Identify these and explain their effect.

3. Throughout the text, Thoreau uses repetition, particularly parallel structure. Identify three or four examples and analyze their effect. Try to find ones that illustrate different effects.

4. Thoreau opens paragraph 3 with a rhetorical question. How effectively does the rest of the paragraph answer it — or does he intend to "answer" the question?

5. What does Thoreau mean by the phrase "starved before we are hungry" in the second sentence of paragraph 3? What other examples of paradox do you find in this excerpt from *Walden*?

6. Compare the probable rhetorical effect of paragraph 4 at the time it was written with its effect today.

7. What is the purpose of the parable in paragraph 5? In telling this story, what assumptions does Thoreau make about his audience?

8. In paragraph 6, Thoreau sets forth a series of "if . . . then" statements to support his opening sentence. Explain the deductive logic in at least one of these statements, specifying the major and minor premises and conclusion. Note that the assumption may be unexpressed.

9. What is the meaning of the allusion to Ulysses in paragraph 7?

10. In what ways do the ideas Thoreau presents in paragraph 6 become the foundation for the beliefs he expresses in paragraph 7? For instance, how do the ideas explained in paragraph 6 lead to his exhortation, "If the engine whistles, let it whistle till it is hoarse for its pains"?

11. Sometimes, even the slightest stylistic feature can work effectively as a rhetorical strategy. What is the effect of the alliterative phrase "freshet and frost and fire" in paragraph 7?

12. In the concluding paragraph, Thoreau develops two metaphors regarding time and the intellect. What are they? What is their effect?

Suggestions for Writing

1. In paragraph 5, Thoreau writes, "What news! how much more important to know what that is which was never old!" Write an essay in which you evaluate Thoreau's own writing according to this thought. Consider how this essay appeals to two audiences: Thoreau's contemporaries and today's readers.

2. In this essay, Thoreau extols the virtues of individualism and self-sufficiency. Discuss how living according to these virtues can jeopardize the community; consider specific circumstances when such jeopardy might occur.

3. Write a response to Thoreau, telling him how modern technology has influenced how we communicate. Acknowledge how he did or did not anticipate our modern condition.

4. Using the reflective style of Thoreau, write your own philosophical essay entitled "Where I Live, and What I Live For" (note present tense).

Aria

A Memoir of a Bilingual Childhood

RICHARD RODRIGUEZ

> Richard Rodriguez is a literary scholar, memoirist, essayist, journalist, and televi-
> sion commentator known for his controversial positions—especially his stands
> against bilingual education and affirmative action. Born in 1944 in San Francisco
> to Mexican immigrants, he grew up in Sacramento, California. Rodriguez received
> a BA from Stanford University and an MA from Columbia University, and he stud-
> ied for his doctorate at the University of California at Berkeley. He is best known
> for his autobiography, *Hunger of Memory: The Education of Richard Rodriguez*
> (1982). He is also the author of *Days of Obligation: An Argument with My Mexi-
> can Father* (1992), which was a finalist for the Pulitzer Prize, and *Brown: The
> Last Discovery of America* (2002). The following selection from a chapter in *Hun-
> ger of Memory* (originally an essay for *The American Scholar*), contrasts the pub-
> lic world of Rodriguez's Catholic grammar school with the private world of his
> family.

1

I remember to start with that day in Sacramento—a California now nearly thirty
years past—when I first entered a classroom, able to understand some fifty stray
English words.

The third of four children, I had been preceded to a neighborhood Roman
Catholic school by an older brother and sister. But neither of them had revealed
very much about their classroom experiences. Each afternoon they returned, as
they left in the morning, always together, speaking in Spanish as they climbed the
five steps of the porch. And their mysterious books, wrapped in shopping-bag
paper, remained on the table next to the door, closed firmly behind them.

An accident of geography sent me to a school where all my classmates were
white, many the children of doctors and lawyers and business executives. All my
classmates certainly must have been uneasy on that first day of school—as most
children are uneasy—to find themselves apart from their families in the first
institution of their lives. But I was astonished.

The nun said, in a friendly but oddly impersonal voice, "Boys and girls, this
is Richard Rodriguez." (I heard her sound out: *Rich-heard Road-ree-guess.*) It
was the first time I had heard anyone name me in English. "Richard," the nun
repeated more slowly, writing my name down in her black leather book. Quickly
I turned to see my mother's face dissolve in a watery blur behind the pebbled
glass door.

*   *   *

Many years later there is something called bilingual education—a scheme pro-   5
posed in the late 1960s by Hispanic-American social activists, later endorsed by a
congressional vote. It is a program that seeks to permit non-English-speaking
children, many from lower-class homes, to use their family language as the language of school. (Such is the goal its supporters announce.) I hear them and
am forced to say no: It is not possible for a child—any child—ever to use his
family's language in school. Not to understand this is to misunderstand the public uses of schooling and to trivialize the nature of intimate life—a family's
"language."

Memory teaches me what I know of these matters; the boy reminds the adult.
I was a bilingual child, a certain kind—socially disadvantaged—the son of
working-class parents, both Mexican immigrants.

In the early years of my boyhood, my parents coped very well in America. My
father had steady work. My mother managed at home. They were nobody's victims. Optimism and ambition led them to a house (our home) many blocks from
the Mexican south side of town. We lived among *gringos* and only a block from
the biggest, whitest houses. It never occurred to my parents that they couldn't live
wherever they chose. Nor was the Sacramento of the fifties bent on teaching them
a contrary lesson. My mother and father were more annoyed than intimidated by
those two or three neighbors who tried initially to make us unwelcome. ("Keep
your brats away from my sidewalk!") But despite all they achieved, perhaps
because they had so much to achieve, any deep feeling of ease, the confidence of
"belonging" in public was withheld from them both. They regarded the people at
work, the faces in crowds, as very distant from us. They were the others, *los gringos*. That term was interchangeable in their speech with another, even more telling, *los americanos*.

I grew up in a house where the only regular guests were my relations. For
one day, enormous families of relatives would visit and there would be so many
people that the noise and the bodies would spill out to the backyard and front
porch. Then, for weeks no one came by. (It was usually a salesman who rang the
door bell.) Our house stood apart. A gaudy yellow in a row of white bungalows.
We were the people with the noisy dog. The people who raised pigeons and chickens. We were the foreigners on the block. A few neighbors smiled and waved. We
waved back. But no one in the family knew the names of the old couple who lived
next door; until I was seven years old, I did not know the names of the kids who
lived across the street.

In public, my father and mother spoke a hesitant, accented, not always grammatical English. And they would have to strain—their bodies tense—to catch
the sense of what was rapidly said by *los gringos*. At home they spoke Spanish. The
language of their Mexican past sounded in counterpoint to the English of public
society. The words would come quickly, with ease. Conveyed through those
sounds was the pleasing, soothing, consoling reminder of being at home.

During those years when I was first conscious of hearing, my mother and father addressed me only in Spanish; in Spanish I learned to reply. By contrast, English (*inglés*), rarely heard in the house, was the language I came to associate with *gringos*. I learned my first words of English overhearing my parents speak to strangers. At five years of age, I knew just enough English for my mother to trust me on errands to stores one block away. No more.

I was a listening child, careful to hear the very different sounds of Spanish and English. Wide-eyed with hearing, I'd listen to sounds more than words. First, there were English (*gringo*) sounds. So many words were still unknown that when the butcher or the lady at the drugstore said something to me, exotic polysyllabic sounds would bloom in the midst of their sentences. Often, the speech of people in public seemed to me very loud, booming with confidence. The man behind the counter would literally ask, "What can I do for you?" But by being so firm and so clear, the sound of his voice said that he was a *gringo*; he belonged in public society.

I would also hear then the high nasal notes of middle-class American speech. The air stirred with sound. Sometimes, even now, when I have been traveling abroad for several weeks, I will hear what I heard as a boy. In hotel lobbies or airports, in Turkey or Brazil, some Americans will pass, and suddenly I will hear it again — the high sound of American voices. For a few seconds I will hear it with pleasure, for it is now the sound of *my* society — a reminder of home. But inevitably — already on the flight headed for home — the sound fades with repetition. I will be unable to hear it anymore.

When I was a boy, things were different. The accent of *los gringos* was never pleasing nor was it hard to hear. Crowds at Safeway or at bus stops would be noisy with sound. And I would be forced to edge away from the chirping chatter above me.

I was unable to hear my own sounds, but I knew very well that I spoke English poorly. My words could not stretch far enough to form complete thoughts. And the words I did speak I didn't know well enough to make into distinct sounds. (Listeners would usually lower their heads, better to hear what I was trying to say.) But it was one thing for *me* to speak English with difficulty. It was more troubling for me to hear my parents speak in public: their high-whining vowels and guttural consonants; their sentences that got stuck with "eh" and "ah" sounds; the confused syntax; the hesitant rhythm of sounds so different from the way *gringos* spoke. I'd notice, moreover, that my parents' voices were softer than those of *gringos* we'd meet.

I am tempted now to say that none of this mattered. In adulthood I am embarrassed by childhood fears. And, in a way, it didn't matter very much that my parents could not speak English with ease. Their linguistic difficulties had no serious consequences. My mother and father made themselves understood at the county hospital clinic and at government offices. And yet, in another way, it mattered very much — it was unsettling to hear my parents struggle with English.

Hearing them, I'd grow nervous, my clutching trust in their protection and power weakened.

There were many times like the night at a brightly lit gasoline station (a blaring white memory) when I stood uneasily, hearing my father. He was talking to a teenaged attendant. I do not recall what they were saying, but I cannot forget the sounds my father made as he spoke. At one point his words slid together to form one word — sounds as confused as the threads of blue and green oil in the puddle next to my shoes. His voice rushed through what he had left to say. And, toward the end, reached falsetto notes, appealing to his listener's understanding. I looked away to the lights of passing automobiles. I tried not to hear anymore. But I heard only too well the calm, easy tones in the attendant's reply. Shortly afterward, walking toward home with my father, I shivered when he put his hand on my shoulder. The very first chance that I got, I evaded his grasp and ran on ahead into the dark, skipping with feigned boyish exuberance.

But then there was Spanish. *Español*: my family's language. *Español*: the language that seemed to me a private language. I'd hear strangers on the radio and in the Mexican Catholic church across town speaking in Spanish, but I couldn't really believe that Spanish was a public language, like English. Spanish speakers, rather, seemed related to me, for I sensed that we shared — through our language — the experience of feeling apart from *los gringos*. It was thus a ghetto Spanish that I heard and I spoke. Like those whose lives are bound by a barrio, I was reminded by Spanish of my separateness from *los otros, los gringos* in power. But more intensely than for most barrio children — because I did not live in a barrio — Spanish seemed to me the language of home. (Most days it was only at home that I'd hear it.) It became the language of joyful return.

A family member would say something to me and I would feel myself specially recognized. My parents would say something to me and I would feel embraced by the sounds of their words. Those sounds said: *I am speaking with ease in Spanish. I am addressing you in words I never use with* los gringos, *I recognize you as someone special, close, like no one outside. You belong with us. In the family.*

(*Ricardo.*)

At the age of five, six, well past the time when most other children no longer easily notice the difference between sounds uttered at home and words spoken in public, I had a different experience. I lived in a world magically compounded of sounds. I remained a child longer than most; I lingered too long, poised at the edge of language — often frightened by the sounds of *los gringos*, delighted by the sounds of Spanish at home. I shared with my family a language that was startlingly different from that used in the great city around us.

For me there were none of the gradations between public and private society so normal to a maturing child. Outside the house was public society; inside the house was private. Just opening or closing the screen door behind me was an important experience. I'd rarely leave home all alone or without reluctance.

20

Walking down the sidewalk, under the canopy of tall trees, I'd warily notice the—suddenly—silent neighborhood kids who stood warily watching me. Nervously, I'd arrive at the grocery store to hear there the sounds of the *gringo*— foreign to me—reminding me that in this world so big, I was a foreigner. But then I'd return. Walking back toward our house, climbing the steps from the sidewalk, when the front door was open in summer, I'd hear voices beyond the screen door talking in Spanish. For a second or two, I'd stay, linger there, listening. Smiling, I'd hear my mother call out, saying in Spanish (words): "Is that you, Richard?" All the while her sounds would assure me: *You are home now; come closer; inside. With us.*

"*Sí*," I'd reply.

Once more inside the house I would resume (assume) my place in the family. The sounds would dim, grow harder to hear. Once more at home, I would grow less aware of that fact. It required, however, no more than the blurt of the doorbell to alert me to listen to sounds all over again. The house would turn instantly still while my mother went to the door. I'd hear her hard English sounds. I'd wait to hear her voice return to soft-sounding Spanish, which assured me, as surely as did the clicking tongue of the lock on the door, that the stranger was gone.

Plainly, it is not healthy to hear such sounds so often. It is not healthy to distinguish public words from private sounds so easily. I remained cloistered by sounds, timid and shy in public, too dependent on voices at home. And yet it needs to be emphasized: I was an extremely happy child at home. I remember many nights when my father would come back from work, and I'd hear him call out to my mother in Spanish, sounding relieved. In Spanish, he'd sound light and free notes he never could manage in English. Some nights I'd jump up just at hearing his voice. With *mis hermanos* I would come running into the room where he was with my mother. Our laughing (so deep was the pleasure!) became screaming. Like others who know the pain of public alienation, we transformed the knowledge of our public separateness and made it consoling—the reminder of intimacy. Excited, we joined our voices in a celebration of sounds. *We are speaking now the way we never speak out in public. We are alone—together*, voices sounded, surrounded to tell me. Some nights, no one seemed willing to loosen the hold sounds had on us. At dinner, we invented new words. (Ours sounded Spanish, but made sense only to us.) We pieced together new words by taking, say, an English verb and giving it Spanish endings. My mother's instructions at bedtime would be lacquered with mock-urgent tones. Or a word like sí would become, in several notes, able to convey added measures of feeling. Tongues explored the edges of words, especially the fat vowels. And we happily sounded that military drum roll, the twirling roar of the Spanish *r*. Family language: my family's sounds. The voices of my parents and sisters and brother. Their voices insisting: *You belong here. We are family members. Related. Special to one another. Listen!* Voices singing and sighing, rising, straining, then surging, teeming with pleasure that burst syllables into fragments of laughter. At times it seemed there was steady quiet only when, from another room, the rustling whispers of my parents faded and I moved closer to sleep.

2

Supporters of bilingual education today imply that students like me miss a great deal by not being taught in their family's language. What they seem not to recognize is that, as a socially disadvantaged child, I considered Spanish to be a private language. What I needed to learn in school was that I had the right—and the obligation—to speak the public language of *los gringos*. The odd truth is that my first-grade classmates could have become bilingual, in the conventional sense of that word, more easily than I. Had they been taught (as upper-middle-class children are often taught early) a second language like Spanish or French, they could have regarded it simply as that: another public language. In my case such bilingualism could not have been so quickly achieved. What I did not believe was that I could speak a single public language.

Without question, it would have pleased me to hear my teachers address me in Spanish when I entered the classroom. I would have felt much less afraid. I would have trusted them and responded with ease. But I would have delayed— for how long postponed?—having to learn the language of public society. I would have evaded—and for how long could I have afforded to delay?—learning the great lesson of school, that I had a public identity.

Fortunately, my teachers were unsentimental about their responsibility. What they understood was that I needed to speak a public language. So their voices would search me out, asking me questions. Each time I'd hear them, I'd look up in surprise to see a nun's face frowning at me. I'd mumble, not really meaning to answer. The nun would persist, "Richard, stand up. Don't look at the floor. Speak up. Speak to the entire class, not just to me!" But I couldn't believe that the English language was mine to use. (In part, I did not want to believe it.) I continued to mumble. I resisted the teacher's demands. (Did I somehow suspect that once I learned public language my pleasing family life would be changed?) Silent, waiting for the bell to sound, I remained dazed, diffident, afraid.

Because I wrongly imagined that English was intrinsically a public language and Spanish an intrinsically private one, I easily noted the difference between classroom language and the language of home. At school, words were directed to a general audience of listeners. ("Boys and girls.") Words were meaningfully ordered. And the point was not self-expression alone but to make oneself understood by many others. The teacher quizzed: "Boys and girls, why do we use that word in this sentence? Could we think of a better word to use there? Would the sentence change its meaning if the words were differently arranged? And wasn't there a better way of saying much the same thing?" (I couldn't say. I wouldn't try to say.)

Three months. Five. Half a year passed. Unsmiling, ever watchful, my teachers noted my silence. They began to connect my behavior with the difficult progress my older sister and brother were making. Until one Saturday morning three nuns arrived at the house to talk to our parents. Stiffly, they sat on the blue living room sofa. From the doorway of another room, spying the visitors, I noted the incongruity—the clash of two worlds, the faces and voices of school intruding upon the familiar setting of home. I overheard one voice gently wondering, "Do your children speak only Spanish at home, Mrs. Rodriguez?" While another voice added, "That Richard especially seems so timid and shy."

That Rich-heard!

30

With great tact the visitors continued, "Is it possible for you and your husband to encourage your children to practice their English when they are home?" Of course, my parents complied. What would they not do for their children's well-being? And how could they have questioned the Church's authority which those women represented? In an instant, they agreed to give up the language (the sounds) that had revealed and accentuated our family's closeness. The moment after the visitors left, the change was observed. "*Ahora*, speak to us *en inglés*," my father and mother united to tell us.

At first, it seemed a kind of game. After dinner each night, the family gathered to practice "our" English. (It was still then *inglés*, a language foreign to us, so we felt drawn as strangers to it.) Laughing, we would try to define words we could not pronounce. We played with strange English sounds, often over-anglicizing our pronunciations. And we filled the smiling gaps of our sentences with familiar Spanish sounds. But that was cheating, somebody shouted. Everyone laughed. In school, meanwhile, like my brother and sister, I was required to attend a daily tutoring session. I needed a full year of special attention. I also needed my teachers to keep my attention from straying in class by calling out, *Rich-heard*—their English voices slowly prying loose my ties to my other name, its three notes, *Ri-car-do*. Most of all I needed to hear my mother and father speak to me in a moment of seriousness in broken—suddenly heartbreaking—English. The scene was inevitable: One Saturday morning I entered the kitchen where my parents were talking in Spanish. I did not realize that they were talking in Spanish however until, at the moment they saw me, I heard their voices change to speak English. Those *gringo* sounds they uttered startled me. Pushed me away. In that moment of trivial misunderstanding and profound insight, I felt my throat twisted by unsounded grief. I turned quickly and left the room. But I had no place to escape to with Spanish. (The spell was broken.) My brother and sisters were speaking English in another part of the house.

Again and again in the days following, increasingly angry, I was obliged to hear my mother and father: "Speak to us *en inglés*." (*Speak.*) Only then did I determine to learn classroom English. Weeks after, it happened: One day in school I raised my hand to volunteer an answer. I spoke out in a loud voice. And I did not think it remarkable when the entire class understood. That day, I moved very far from the disadvantaged child I had been only days earlier. The belief, the calming assurance that I belonged in public, had at last taken hold.

Shortly after, I stopped hearing the high and loud sounds of *los gringos*. A more and more confident speaker of English, I didn't trouble to listen to *how* strangers sounded, speaking to me. And there simply were too many English-speaking people in my day for me to hear American accents anymore. Conversations quickened. Listening to persons who sounded eccentrically pitched voices, I usually noted their sounds for an initial few seconds before I concentrated on *what* they were saying. Conversations became content-full. Transparent. Hearing someone's *tone* of voice — angry or questioning or sarcastic or happy or sad — I didn't distinguish it from the words it expressed. Sound and word were thus tightly wedded. At the end of a day, I was often bemused, always relieved, to realize how "silent," though crowded with words, my day in public had been. (This public silence measured and quickened the change in my life.)

At last, seven years old, I came to believe what had been technically true since my birth: I was an American citizen. 35

But the special feeling of closeness at home was diminished by then. Gone was the desperate, urgent, intense feeling of being at home; rare was the experience of feeling myself individualized by family intimates. We remained a loving family, but one greatly changed. No longer so close; no longer bound tight by the pleasing and troubling knowledge of our public separateness. Neither my older brother nor sister rushed home after school anymore. Nor did I. When I arrived home there would often be neighborhood kids in the house. Or the house would be empty of sounds.

Following the dramatic Americanization of their children, even my parents grew more publicly confident. Especially my mother. She learned the names of all the people on our block. And she decided we needed to have a telephone installed in the house. My father continued to use the word *gringo*. But it was no longer charged with the old bitterness or distrust. (Stripped of any emotional content, the word simply became a name for those Americans not of Hispanic descent.) Hearing him, sometimes, I wasn't sure if he was pronouncing the Spanish word *gringo* or saying gringo in English.

Matching the silence I started hearing in public was a new quiet at home. The family's quiet was partly due to the fact that, as we children learned more and more English, we shared fewer and fewer words with our parents. Sentences needed to be spoken slowly when a child addressed his mother or father. (Often the parent wouldn't understand.) The child would need to repeat himself. (Still the parent misunderstood.) The young voice, frustrated, would end up saying, "Never mind" — the subject was closed. Dinners would be noisy with the clinking of knives and forks against dishes. My mother would smile softly between her remarks; my father at the other end of the table would chew and chew at his food, while he stared over the heads of his children.

My *mother!* My *father!* After English became my primary language, I no longer knew what words to use in addressing my parents. The old Spanish words (those tender accents of sound) I had used earlier — *mamá* and *papá* — I couldn't use anymore. They would have been too painful reminders of how much had changed in my life. On the other hand, the words I heard neighborhood kids call their parents seemed equally unsatisfactory. *Mother* and *Father; Ma, Papa, Pa, Dad, Pop* (how I hated the all-American sound of that last word especially) — all these terms I felt were unsuitable, not really terms of address for *my* parents. As a result, I never used them at home. Whenever I'd speak to my parents, I would try to get their attention with eye contact alone. In public conversations, I'd refer to "my parents" or "my mother and father."

My mother and father, for their part, responded differently, as their children   40 spoke to them less. She grew restless, seemed troubled and anxious at the scarcity of words exchanged in the house. It was she who would question me about my day when I came home from school. She smiled at small talk. She pried at the edges of my sentences to get me to say something more. (What?) She'd join conversations she overheard, but her intrusions often stopped her children's talking. By contrast, my father seemed reconciled to the new quiet. Though his English improved somewhat, he retired into silence. At dinner he spoke very little. One night his children and even his wife helplessly giggled at his garbled English pronunciation of the Catholic Grace before Meals. Thereafter he made his wife recite the prayer at the start of each meal, even on formal occasions, when there were guests in the house. Hers became the public voice of the family. On official business, it was she, not my father, one would usually hear on the phone or in stores, talking to strangers. His children grew so accustomed to his silence that, years later, they would speak routinely of his shyness. (My mother would often try to explain: Both his parents died when he was eight. He was raised by an uncle who treated him like little more than a menial servant. He was never encouraged to speak. He grew up alone. A man of few words.) But my father was not shy, I realized, when I'd watch him speaking Spanish with relatives. Using Spanish, he was quickly effusive. Especially when talking with other men, his voice would spark, flicker, flare alive with sounds. In Spanish, he expressed ideas and feelings he rarely revealed in English. With firm Spanish sounds, he conveyed confidence and authority English would never allow him.

The silence at home, however, was finally more than a literal silence. Fewer words passed between parent and child, but more profound was the silence that resulted from my inattention to sounds. At about the time I no longer bothered to listen with care to the sounds of English in public, I grew careless about listening to the sounds family members made when they spoke. Most of the time I heard someone speaking at home and didn't distinguish his sounds from the words people uttered in public. I didn't even pay much attention to my parents' accented and ungrammatical speech. At least not at home. Only when I was with them in public would I grow alert to their accents. Though, even then, their sounds caused me less and less concern. For I was increasingly confident of my own public identity.

I would have been happier about my public success had I not sometimes recalled what it had been like earlier, when my family had conveyed its intimacy through a set of conveniently private sounds. Sometimes in public, hearing a stranger, I'd hark back to my past. A Mexican farmworker approached me downtown to ask directions to somewhere. "*¿Hijito...?*" he said. And his voice summoned deep longing. Another time, standing beside my mother in the visiting room of a Carmelite convent, before the dense screen which rendered the nuns shadowy figures, I heard several Spanish-speaking nuns — their busy, singsong overlapping voices — assure us that yes, yes, we were remembered, all our family was remembered in their prayers. (Their voices echoed faraway family sounds.) Another day, a dark-faced old woman — her hand light on my shoulder — steadied herself against me as she boarded a bus. She murmured something I couldn't quite comprehend. Her Spanish voice came near, like the face of a never-before-seen relative in the instant before I was kissed. Her voice, like so many of the Spanish voices I'd hear in public, recalled the golden age of my youth. Hearing Spanish then, I continued to be a careful, if sad, listener to sounds. Hearing a Spanish-speaking family walking behind me, I turned to look. I smiled for an instant, before my glance found the Hispanic-looking faces of strangers in the crowd going by.

Today I hear bilingual educators say that children lose a degree of "individuality" by becoming assimilated into public society. (Bilingual schooling was popularized in the seventies, that decade when middle-class ethnics began to resist the process of assimilation — the American melting pot.) But the bilingualists simplistically scorn the value and necessity of assimilation. They do not seem to realize that there are *two* ways a person is individualized. So they do not realize that while one suffers a diminished sense of *private* individuality by becoming assimilated into public society, such assimilation makes possible the achievement of *public* individuality.

The bilingualists insist that a student should be reminded of his difference from others in mass society, his heritage. But they equate mere separateness with individuality. The fact is that only in private — with intimates — is separateness from the crowd a prerequisite for individuality. (An intimate draws me apart, tells me that I am unique, unlike all others.) In public, by contrast, full individuality is achieved, paradoxically, by those who are able to consider themselves members of the crowd. Thus it happened for me: Only when I was able to think of myself as an American, no longer an alien in *gringo* society, could I seek the rights and opportunities necessary for full public individuality. The social and political advantages I enjoy as a man result from the day that I came to believe that my name, indeed, is *Rich-heard Road-ree-guess*. It is true that my public society today is often impersonal. (My public society is usually mass society.) Yet despite the anonymity of the crowd and despite the fact that the individuality I achieve in public is often tenuous — because it depends on my being one in a crowd — I celebrate the day I acquired my new name. Those middle-class ethnics who scorn assimilation seem to me filled with decadent self-pity, obsessed by the burden of public life. Dangerously, they romanticize public separateness and they trivialize the dilemma of the socially disadvantaged.

My awkward childhood does not prove the necessity of bilingual education. 45
My story discloses instead an essential myth of childhood—inevitable pain. If I
rehearse here the changes in my private life after my Americanization, it is finally
to emphasize the public gain. The loss implies the gain: The house I returned to
each afternoon was quiet. Intimate sounds no longer rushed to the door to greet
me. There were other noises inside. The telephone rang. Neighborhood kids ran
past the door of the bedroom where I was reading my schoolbooks—covered
with shopping-bag paper. Once I learned public language, it would never again be
easy for me to hear intimate family voices. More and more of my day was spent
hearing words. But that may only be a way of saying that the day I raised my hand
in class and spoke loudly to an entire roomful of faces, my childhood started to end.

Exploring the Text

1. According to Richard Rodriguez, how can language define community—both
   negatively and positively?
2. What does Rodriguez mean in the following statement? "It is not possible for a
   child—any child—ever to use his family's language in school. Not to understand this is to misunderstand the public uses of schooling and to trivialize the
   nature of intimate life—a family's 'language'" (para. 5). Write an essay defending, challenging, or modifying Rodriguez's assertion. Support your argument
   with evidence from your experience, observation, or reading.
3. What is an aria? Why do you think Rodriguez chose it for his title? Is it an appropriate title? Is it effective?
4. Explain how Rodriguez establishes his ethos in the opening four paragraphs.
5. What does Rodriguez mean when he says, "[I]n a way, it didn't matter very much
   that my parents could not speak English with ease. . . . And yet, in another way, it
   mattered very much" (para. 15)?
6. Rodriguez admits, "Matching the silence I started hearing in public was a new
   quiet at home" (para. 38). Later he says, "The silence at home, however, was
   finally more than a literal silence" (para. 41). Does he convince you that this
   change in family relationships is worthwhile in terms of his "dramatic Americanization" (para. 37)?
7. What does Rodriguez mean in the following statement: "[W]hile one suffers a
   diminished sense of *private* individuality by becoming assimilated into public
   society, such assimilation makes possible the achievement of *public* individuality"
   (para. 43)?
8. In several sections, Rodriguez makes his point by narrative (such as the moment
   in school when he first hears his name). How does narrative contribute to the
   effectiveness of Rodriguez's argument?
9. What major counterarguments does Rodriguez address? (He does not address
   them all at once; identify specific passages.)

10. Rodriguez develops his argument largely through his own experience and opinions, but without quantitative data from research or the views of experts. How convincing is he? Do you think more formal evidence would have strengthened his argument? Explain.

11. In this essay, Richard Rodriguez describes a clash of two communities—his private family community and his public community of both the school and middle-class America as a whole. How do these competing communities impact the development of his personal identity?

12. In a 1994 interview, Rodriguez made the following comment about multiculturalism: "Multiculturalism, as it is expressed in the platitudes of the American campus, is not multiculturalism. It is an idea about culture that has a specific genesis, a specific history, and a specific politics. What people mean by multiculturalism is different hues of themselves. They don't mean Islamic fundamentalists or skinheads. They mean other brown and black students who share opinions like theirs. It isn't diversity. It's a pretense to diversity." Do you agree with Rodriguez?

The Family That Stretches (Together)

Ellen Goodman

Pulitzer Prize–winning journalist Ellen Goodman (b. 1941) was a syndicated columnist from 1976 until her retirement in 2010. She received her BA from Radcliffe College and later was a fellow at the Nieman Foundation for Journalism at Harvard. She began her career as a researcher for *Newsweek* and was later a reporter for the *Detroit Free Press* and the *Boston Globe*. She published her first book, *Turning Points*, in 1979 and then collections of her columns, including *Making Sense* (1989), *Value Judgments* (1993), and *Paper Trail: Common Sense in Uncommon Times* (2004). She is co-author of *I Know Just What You Mean: The Power of Friendship in Women's Lives* (2000). In 1994, Goodman was the first Lorry I. Lokey Visiting Professor of Professional Journalism at Stanford University. The following essay originally appeared in the *Boston Globe* in 1983.

The girl is spending the summer with her extended family. She doesn't put it this way. But as we talk on the beach, the ten-year-old lists the people who are sharing the same house this month with the careful attention of a genealogist.

First of all there is her father—visitation rights awarded him the month of August. Second of all there is her father's second wife and two children by her first marriage. All that seems perfectly clear. A stepmother and two stepbrothers.

Then there are the others, she slowly explains. There is her stepmother's sister for example. The girl isn't entirely sure whether this makes the woman a stepaunt, or whether her baby is a stepcousin. Beyond that, the real puzzle is whether her stepaunt's husband's children by his first marriage have any sort of official relationship to her at all. It does, we both agree, seem a bit fuzzy.

Nevertheless, she concludes, with a certainty that can only be mustered by the sort of a ten-year-old who keeps track of her own Frequent Flier coupons, "We are in the same family." With that she closes the subject and focuses instead on her peanut butter and jelly.

I am left to my thoughts. My companion, in her own unselfconscious way, is   5 a fine researcher. She grasps the wide new family configurations that are neglected by census data takers and social scientists.

After all, those of us who grew up in traditional settings remember families which extended into elaborate circles of aunts, uncles, and cousins. There were sides to this family, names and titles to be memorized. But they fit together in a biological pattern.

Now, as my young friend can attest, we have fewer children and more divorces. We know that as many as 50 percent of recent marriages may end. About 75 percent of divorced women and 83 percent of divorced men then remarry. Of those remarriages, 59 percent include a child from a former marriage.

So, our families often extend along lines that are determined by decrees, rather than genes. If the nucleus is broken, there are still links forged in different directions.

The son of a friend was asked to produce a family tree for his sixth-grade class. But he was dissatisfied with his oak. There was no room on it for his step-grandfather, though the man had married his widowed grandmother years ago.

More to the point, the boy had to create an offshoot for his new baby half-   10 brother that seemed too distant. He couldn't find a proper place for the uncle — the ex-uncle to be precise — whom he visited last summer with his cousin.

A family tree just doesn't work, he complained. He would have preferred to draw family bushes.

The reality is that divorce has created kinship ties that rival the most complex tribe. These are not always easy relationships. The children and even the adults whose family lives have been disrupted by divorce and remarriage learn that people they love do not necessarily love each other. This extended family does not gather for reunions and Thanksgivings.

But when it works, it can provide a support system of sorts. I have seen the nieces, nephews — even the dogs — of one marriage welcomed as guests into another. There are all sorts of relationships that survive the marital ones, though there are no names for these kinfolk, no nomenclature for this extending family.

Not long ago, when living together first became a common pattern, people couldn't figure out what to call each other. It was impossible to introduce the man you lived with as a "spouse equivalent." It was harder to refer to the woman your son lived with as his lover, mistress, housemate.

It's equally difficult to describe the peculiar membership of this new lineage.   15 Does your first husband's mother become a mother-out-law? Is the woman no longer married to your uncle an ex-aunt? We have nieces and nephews left dangling like participles from other lives and stepfamilies entirely off the family tree.

Our reality is more flexible and our relationships more supportive than our language. But for the moment, my ten-year-old researcher is right. However accidentally, however uneasily, "We are in the same family."

. . . .

Exploring the Text

1. Ellen Goodman begins her column by establishing that she is taking a walk on the beach, where she meets a ten-year-old who prompts her to reflect on the nature of family. What are the benefits and liabilities of Goodman making herself a character in her own column?

2. Do you agree that the ten-year-old, "in her own unselfconscious way, is a fine researcher" (para. 5)? Why or why not? What effect does Goodman achieve by letting the girl provide the subject and viewpoint rather than raising it on her own?

3. Examine Goodman's use of evidence. What actual facts and figures does she call on in her essay? Would having more, along with expert testimony from academic researchers, psychologists, and the like, have strengthened her viewpoint? Explain.

4. Overall, what is Goodman's attitude toward a society where the norm has become families that "are determined by decrees, rather than genes" (para. 8)? Cite specific passages to support your response.

5. What does Goodman mean by this statement: "Our reality is more flexible and our relationships more supportive than our language" (para. 16)? What are some examples outside of family connections that might illustrate this point?

6. How would you describe the tone of this essay? Is Goodman tolerant, critical, optimistic, skeptical, reflective—or a combination of these or other descriptors?

7. Goodman wrote this essay in 1983. To what extent do you think that it remains true today?

8. Elsewhere, Goodman has written that she is interested in exploring the importance "for all of us to make links between our personal lives and public issues." In what ways does this essay encourage us to make those links?

Walking the Path between Worlds

Lori Arviso Alvord

The first Navajo woman surgeon, Lori Arviso Alvord (b. 1958) is currently the associate dean of student and minority affairs and assistant professor of surgery at Dartmouth Medical School. She received her BA from Dartmouth College and her

MD from Stanford University. At the start of her career, she served as a general surgeon in the Indian Health Service in her native New Mexico. She has been honored with numerous awards, including the Governor's Award for Outstanding Women from the State of New Mexico (1992) and the Outstanding Women in Medicine Award from the University of Missouri–Kansas City School of Medicine (2001). Her autobiography, *The Scalpel and the Silver Bear* (1999), describes her efforts to combine Navajo healing practices with Western medicine. The following passage from that book focuses on her journey from the reservation to Dartmouth.

Today Navajo children are still standing on the playgrounds where I stood, facing the critical decision I would face after I graduated from high school: to leave the rez, or to stay and cleave to traditional ways. To let the desert live inside them, or to try to wash it away. They too hear the voice of the wind and the desert, smell the strong smells of our people, and feel the ways we came from. "*Decide*," the world whispers to them, "*you must choose.*"

I chose to leave and get an education, following the path of the books I loved so much. But leaving Dinetah was a frightening prospect. Navajo people believe we are safe within the four sacred mountains that bound the Navajo reservation — Mount Taylor, San Francisco Peak, Blanca Peak, and the La Plata Range. In our creation stories it is the place of our origins, of our emergence to the surface of the earth from other worlds below, the place where Changing Woman and First Man, Coyote, the Twins, and the monsters in our legends roamed. These mountains are central to everything in our lives. To leave this place is to invite imbalance, to break our precious link with the tribe, to leave the Walk of Beauty, and to court danger. It was a dangerous step, that into the unknown, unguarded world.

In our song called the Mountain Chant, each of the sacred mountains is honored. The words describe each mountain and its special qualities.

> The mountain to the east is Sisna'jin
> It is standing out.
> The strong White Bead is standing out
> A living mountain is standing out . . .
> The mountain to the south is Tsoodził   5
> It is standing out.
> The strong turquoise is standing out
> A living mountain is standing out . . .
> The mountain to the west is Dook'o'oosłííd.
> It is standing out.   10
> The strong white shell is standing out.
> A living mountain is standing out . . .
> The mountain to the north is Dibé Ntsaa.
> It is standing out.

> The strong jet is standing out.   15
> A living mountain is standing out . . .[1]

If I left, I would leave the enclosed and sacred world within the strong mountains, standing out.

I made good grades in high school, but I had received a very marginal education. I had a few good teachers, but teachers were difficult to recruit to our schools and they often didn't stay long. Funding was often inadequate. I spent many hours in classrooms where, I now see, very little was being taught. Nevertheless my parents always assumed, quite optimistically, that all their children would go to college. I don't remember any lectures from my father on the importance of higher education—just the quiet assurance that he and my mother and Grandmother all believed in us.

My college plans were modest; I assumed I would attend a nearby state   5
school. But then I happened to meet another Navajo student who was attending Princeton. I had heard of Princeton but had no idea where it was. I asked him how many Indians were there. He replied, "Five." I couldn't even imagine a place with only five Indians, since our town was 98 percent Indian. Then he mentioned Dartmouth, which had about fifty Indians on campus, and I felt a little better. *Ivy League* was a term I had heard, but I had no concept of its meaning. No one from my high school had ever attended an Ivy League college.

At my request, my high school counselor gave me the applications for all the Ivy League schools, but I only completed Dartmouth's because I knew there were fifty Indians there.

I waited anxiously, and one day the letter came. I was accepted, early decision. I was only sixteen years old. As I was only half Navajo in blood, I wondered if this meant it would be only half as dangerous to me to leave Dinetah, the place between the sacred mountains. Half of me belonged in Dinetah, but the other half of me belonged in that other world too, I figured. Still, in my heart I was all Navajo, and I instinctively felt afraid of the move. I had seen those who went away and came back: the Vietnam veterans, broken and lost, who aimlessly wandered the streets of Gallup, the others who came back but had forgotten Navajo ways.

My memories of my arrival in Hanover, New Hampshire, are mostly of the color green. Green cloaked the hillsides, crawled up the ivied walls, and was reflected in the river where the Dartmouth crew students sculled. For a girl who had never been far from Crownpoint, New Mexico, the green felt incredibly juicy, lush, beautiful, and threatening. Crownpoint had had vast acreage of sky and sand, but aside from the pastel scrub brush, mesquite, and chamiso, practically the only growing things there were the tiny stunted pines called piñon trees. Yet it is beautiful; you can see the edges and contours of red earth stretching all the way

---

[1] Aileen O'Bryan, *Navajo Indian Myths* (New York: Dover, 1994).

to the box-shaped faraway cliffs and the horizon. No horizon was in sight in Hanover, only trees. I felt claustrophobic.

If the physical contrasts were striking, the cultural ones were even more so. Although I felt lucky to be there, I was in complete culture shock. I thought people talked too much, laughed too loud, asked too many personal questions, and had no respect for privacy. They seemed overly competitive and put a higher value on material wealth than I was used to. Navajos placed much more emphasis on a person's relations to family, clan, tribe, and the other inhabitants of the earth, both human and nonhuman, than on possessions. Everyone at home followed unwritten codes for behavior. We were taught to be humble and not to draw attention to ourselves, to favor cooperation over competition (so as not to make ourselves "look better" at another's expense or hurt someone's feelings), to value silence over words, to respect our elders, and to reserve our opinions until they were asked for.

Understanding the culture of Dartmouth was like taking a course in itself. I 10 didn't know the meaning of fraternities or the class system (divided into the haves and the have-nots) which were so important there at first. Had the parents of my fellow students taught them survival skills through camping, tracking, and hunting? Did I have any interest in making four-story-high sculptures out of ice for Winter Carnival? Did they respect their elders, their parents? Did I know which fork to use at a formal dinner? What sort of ceremonies did their "tribes" practice? While they pondered such burning questions as the opening day of ski season, I was struggling just to stay warm during the frozen New Hampshire winter and not slip on the ice!

Indian reservations and pueblos could almost be seen as tiny Third World countries, lacking as they did electricity, indoor plumbing, and paved roads. When the Native American students arrived at Dartmouth, one of the first things we were told was that we could attend high tea at Sanborn Hall at four o'clock daily. I walked around the campus in awe, like a peasant visiting the castle of a great king.

The very stately, beautiful, and affluent campus could be intimidating and alienating. The college's unofficial mascot was the "Dartmouth Indian," a tomahawk-wielding red man whose presence was everywhere on the campus, in spite of the Native community's protests. He was like those TV Indians we had watched when we were little and thought so alien. Imagine young Native students seeing white students wearing loincloths and paint on their faces, jumping around with toy tomahawks. Like the rest of the Native community, I was shocked by this caricature.

I remember, distinctly, feeling alienated while walking around Dartmouth's campus that first year. By my sophomore year I understood what it meant to be invisible. People looked right through me—I moved around the campus as unseen as the air. Outside of my freshman roommate, Anne, I never made a close non-Indian friend. I wonder if other students of color felt the same way.

I was very homesick, wishing I didn't have to miss so many familiar events: the Navajo tribal fairs, the Zuni Shalako, the Laguna feast days, the Santa Fe Indian market, the Gallup ceremonial. Everyone at home was having a great time eating wonderful food—roasted corn from the Shiprock market, posole, red chile stew, venison jerky—and I was stuck in a library far away. I missed watching the Apache Devil Dancers and the Pueblo Buffalo Dancers. I missed the sight of Navajo traditional clothing, emblazoned with silver and turquoise, and the pink-and-purple-splashed sunsets of New Mexico. I missed that smell—that smell we had tried to wash away at our laundromat so long ago—the smell of wildness, the desert, and the Navajo world.

Sometimes I wondered: If I'd had a *kinaaldá* ceremony, could I have been   15 stronger, more independent, better able to face this loneliness and alienation, less unassured. The *kinaaldá* is part of the Blessing Way set of ceremonies performed for girls when they reach puberty. Blessing Way tells the story of Changing Woman (a central Navajo deity), and the *kinaaldá* celebrates her coming into womanhood. The family and community gather around her, she is sung to, and her female relatives massage her from head to toe, giving her the power and strength of womanhood. A large corn cake is baked underground in a corn husk–lined pit, and the girl sprinkles cornmeal over the top. Each day for four days, she runs for a mile toward the new sun, toward her new life. It gives a young woman strength and power, confidence and security, as she goes through menses for the first time. She takes that strength and those "good thoughts" with her into the world. I could have used that assurance. Because my family was less traditional, my sisters and I did not have *kinaaldá* ceremonies, although we attended those of our cousins. Nevertheless, since the Navajo culture is matriarchal, I think I was better prepared as a woman in a "man's world" than many white women I met.

A few things at Dartmouth, however, were comforting and did make me feel at home. For one thing, dogs roamed the campus freely. They didn't belong to anybody in particular but to everybody and were fed and cared for by the entire campus. Muttlike, wily, always after something to eat, they reminded me naturally of rez dogs. And everywhere I looked playful squirrels ran around, reminding me of the prairie dogs who run around their prairie dog cities on the mesas and sit up on their hind legs to watch the cars drive by.

Academically, due to my strong reading background, I held my own in classes like literature and social sciences, but I was totally unprepared for the physical and life sciences. After receiving the only D of my entire life in calculus, I retreated from the sciences altogether. The high school at Crownpoint had not prepared me adequately to compete with the Ivy Leaguers. Furthermore, I had an additional problem. As I mentioned earlier, Navajos are taught from the youngest age never to draw attention to ourselves. So Navajo children do not raise their hands in class. At a school like Dartmouth, the lack of participation was seen as a sign not of humility but lack of interest and a disengaged attitude. My Navajo humility was combined with a deep feeling of academic inferiority; it was hard to compete with students who had taken calculus and read Chaucer in high school. I sat in the back and tried not to reveal my ignorance.

This sense of being torn between worlds was reflected even in my studies: I chose a double major, psychology and sociology, modified with Native American studies. I received honors in my freshman seminar as well as in two Native American studies courses that stressed writing. As a result, I found myself thinking of teaching Native American studies as a career, and perhaps also becoming a writer.

In fact, I loved Dartmouth's Native American program. It had the tough job of recruiting students like us, who were very high risk. We frequently had had only marginal high school preparation; many were reluctant to come to school so far from home; and like skittish wild horses, some would turn tail and run home at the least provocation. We found great comfort in one another, for although we came from many different tribes, our experiences at Dartmouth were similar: We all felt disconnected from the mainstream student body. For the women, it was even worse. At the time I arrived on the scene, Dartmouth had only recently changed from an all-male to a coed student body, and many of the men resented the presence of women on campus. Referred to as cohogs instead of coeds, women were shunned for dates; instead girls were bused in from nearby women's colleges on weekends. Social life was dominated by the fraternities, and, if we went to their parties at all, we were often ignored.

For all these reasons, the few Native American students at Dartmouth   20
coalesced into a solid community who did almost everything together. Our group was made up of Paiutes, Sioux, Cherokees, Chippewas, Navajos, Pueblos, and many other tribes. We were friends, lovers, rivals, enemies. I have been a part of many other groups since then, but nothing compared in intensity to the experience of being a member of that Native American student group.

Though we often felt as though we didn't belong at Dartmouth, the ironic truth is that we did belong, or rather, we were entitled to be there. Eleazar Wheelock, the Connecticut minister who founded Dartmouth College in 1769, did so with funds that came from King George II, who wished to establish a place to "educate the savages." The college flourished, but for literally hundreds of years its original founding purpose was not honored. "Educating savages" was not on the real agenda; it had simply been a way to get land and money. Before the 1960s fewer than twenty Native students graduated from Dartmouth. Then in the 1970s the Native American studies program was developed by college president John Kemeny and writer Michael Dorris, and Dartmouth began to take its mission in earnest.

We Indian students all knew why we were there. Without the vision of Kemeny and Dorris, we would never have had an opportunity to set foot on the grounds of such an institution, let alone actually enroll. We were there because of the generous scholarships the college had given us, and the money from our tribes.

Some years later, reflecting back on my college experiences, I realized something else. The outside, non-Indian world is tribeless, full of wandering singular souls, seeking connection through societies, clubs, and other groups. White people know what it is to be a family, but to be a tribe is something of an altogether different sort. It provides a feeling of inclusion in something larger, of having a set place in the universe where one always belongs. It provides connectedness and a blueprint for how to live.

At Dartmouth the fraternities and sororities seemed to be attempts to claim or create tribes. Their wild and crazy parties that often involved drugs and sex seemed to me to be unconscious re-creations of rituals and initiation ceremonies. But the fraternities emphasized exclusion as much as inclusion, and their rituals involved alcohol and hazing initiations. Although they developed from a natural urge for community, they lacked much that a real tribe has.

I began to honor and cherish my tribal membership, and in the years that followed I came to understand that such membership is central to mental health, to spiritual health, to physical health. A tribe is a community of people connected by blood or heart, by geography and tradition, who help one another and share a belief system. Community and tribe not only reduce the alienation people feel but in doing so stave off illness. In a sense they are a form of preventive medicine. Most Americans have lost their tribal identities, although at one time, most likely, everyone belonged to a tribe. One way to remedy this is to find and establish groups of people who can nurture and support one another. The Native American students at Dartmouth had become such a group. 25

Our new "tribe" had its ceremonies. Each year, in a primitive outdoor amphitheater called the Bema where concerts and plays were sometimes put on, we held a campus powwow. Feathered fancy dancers and women in "jingle dresses" or in beaded and brightly colored fabric would spin and step to the drums of Plains Indians or to songs from an invited singer from a pueblo. The women would whirl, their shawls swirling and twisting into corkscrew shapes around them. They'd dance to two big hide-stretched drums, encircled by the men, who struck the drums rhythmically and sang. Their voices wove and resonated, rose and fell above the steady heartbeat of the drums. This ceremony was a chance for the Native and non-Native communities to come together as one. I felt then, briefly, that I belonged.

In the evening after the powwow the singing and drumming would continue at a party called a "49"—but here the ancient rhythms were mixed with modern English lyrics. The songs we sang could be romantic, funny, or political; they could be about reservation life and pickup trucks or the Bureau of Indian Affairs. They always sounded the same though, with a blend of voices rising around a drumbeat, and a melody that pulled out our memories of childhood songs.

Dartmouth was good for me. Singing with the other students melted some of my historical grief and anger into a larger powerful force, a force I would take with me into the world. I gained a new kind of family and tribe, with new songs that held us together. Once again, songs had the power to heal.

Exploring the Text

1. What different views of community did Lori Arviso Alvord experience as she moved from her home in New Mexico to college at Dartmouth?
2. What is Alvord's primary method of organization in this essay?
3. What is the effect of including the Mountain Chant?
4. What impact does the physical landscape in Hanover have on Alvord? Why does she describe the landscape of both Hanover and New Mexico in such detail?
5. Which details of life on the reservation does Alvord recall in paragraph 15? Cite specific ones, and explain their importance. Why is the *kinaałdá* ceremony especially significant?
6. Describe Alvord's tone in the two paragraphs on the history of Dartmouth and its Native American studies program (paras. 21–22). Cite specific language and examples to support your response.
7. What is the distinction Alvord makes between a family and a tribe? To what extent do you agree with her?
8. Ultimately, what is Alvord's attitude toward Dartmouth? Cite specific paragraphs to support your response.
9. What does Alvord mean in the concluding paragraph by "my historical grief and anger"?

Health and Happiness

ROBERT D. PUTNAM

Robert D. Putnam (b. 1941) is the Peter and Isabel Malkin Professor of Public Policy at Harvard University, former dean of the John F. Kennedy School of Government, and founder of the Saguaro Seminar, a program dedicated to fostering civic engagement in America. He received his undergraduate degree from Swarthmore College, won a Fulbright Fellowship to Balliol College at Oxford University, and received both his MA and PhD from Yale University. He was the 2006 recipient of the Skytte Prize, the most prestigious international award for scholarly achievement in political science. Among the ten books Putnam has authored or co-authored, three are considered his most influential: *Bowling Alone: The Collapse and Revival of American Community* (1995), *Better Together: Restoring the American Community* (2003), and *American Grace* (2010), a study of religion and public life. *Bowling Alone* argues that civic, social, associational, and political connections—what is called "social capital"—have decreased dramatically during the latter half of the twentieth century. Following is a chapter analyzing the impact of social connectedness on physical and psychological health. Based on extensive research, this enormously popular book introduced a wide audience to Putnam's groundbreaking ideas.

Of all the domains in which I have traced the consequences of social capital, in none is the importance of social connectedness so well established as in the case of health and well-being. Scientific studies of the effects of social cohesion on physical and mental health can be traced to the seminal work of the nineteenth-century sociologist Émile Durkheim, *Suicide*. Self-destruction is not merely a personal tragedy, he found, but a sociologically predictable consequence of the degree to which one is integrated into society—rarer among married people, rarer in more tightly knit religious communities, rarer in times of national unity, and more frequent when rapid social change disrupts the social fabric. Social connectedness matters to our lives in the most profound way.

In recent decades public health researchers have extended this initial insight to virtually all aspects of health, physical as well as psychological. Dozens of painstaking studies from Alameda (California) to Tecumseh (Michigan) have established beyond reasonable doubt that social connectedness is one of the most powerful determinants of our well-being. The more integrated we are with our community, the less likely we are to experience colds, heart attacks, strokes, cancer, depression, and premature death of all sorts. Such protective effects have been confirmed for close family ties, for friendship networks, for participation in social events, and even for simple affiliation with religious and other civic associations. In other words, both *machers** and *schmoozers* enjoy these remarkable health benefits.

After reviewing dozens of scientific studies, sociologist James House and his colleagues have concluded that the *positive* contributions to health made by social integration and social support rival in strength the *detrimental* contributions of well-established biomedical risk factors like cigarette smoking, obesity, elevated blood pressure, and physical inactivity. Statistically speaking, the evidence for the health consequences of social connectedness is as strong today as was the evidence for the health consequences of smoking at the time of the first surgeon general's report on smoking. If the trends in social disconnection are as pervasive as I argued in section II, then "bowling alone" represents one of the nation's most serious public health challenges.[1]

Although researchers aren't entirely sure why social cohesion matters for health, they have a number of plausible theories. First, social networks furnish tangible assistance, such as money, convalescent care, and transportation, which reduces psychic and physical stress and provides a safety net. If you go to church regularly, and then you slip in the bathtub and miss a Sunday, someone is more likely to notice. Social networks also may reinforce healthy norms—socially isolated people are more likely to smoke, drink, overeat, and engage in other health-damaging behaviors. And socially cohesive communities are best able to organize politically to ensure first-rate medical services.[2]

Finally, and most intriguingly, social capital might actually serve as a physiological triggering mechanism, stimulating people's immune systems to fight dis-

5

---

*Yiddish: ambitious person, big shot, schemer.—Eds.

ease and buffer stress. Research now under way suggests that social isolation has measurable biochemical effects on the body. Animals who have been isolated develop more extensive atherosclerosis (hardening of the arteries) than less isolated animals, and among both animals and humans loneliness appears to decrease the immune response and increase blood pressure. Lisa Berkman, one of the leading researchers in the field, has speculated that social isolation is "a chronically stressful condition to which the organism respond[s] by aging faster."[3]

Some studies have documented the strong correlation between connectedness and health at the community level. Others have zeroed in on individuals, both in natural settings and in experimental conditions. These studies are for the most part careful to account for confounding factors—the panoply of other physiological, economic, institutional, behavioral, and demographic forces that might also affect an individual's health. In many cases these studies are longitudinal: they check on people over many years to get a better understanding of what lifestyle changes might have caused people's health to improve or decline. Thus researchers have been able to show that social isolation *precedes* illness to rule out the possibility that the isolation was caused by illness. Over the last twenty years more than a dozen large studies of this sort in the United States, Scandinavia, and Japan have shown that *people who are socially disconnected are between two and five times more likely to die from all causes, compared with matched individuals who have close ties with family, friends, and the community.*[4]

A recent study by researchers at the Harvard School of Public Health provides an excellent overview of the link between social capital and physical health across the United States.[5] Using survey data from nearly 170,000 individuals in all fifty states, these researchers found, as expected, that people who are African American, lack health insurance, are overweight, smoke, have a low income, or lack a college education are at greater risk for illness than are more socio-economically advantaged individuals. But these researchers also found an astonishingly strong relationship between poor health and low social capital. States whose residents were most likely to report fair or poor health were the same states in which residents were most likely to distrust others.[6] Moving from a state with a wealth of social capital to a state with very little social capital (low trust, low voluntary group membership) increased one's chances of poor to middling health by roughly 40–70 percent. When the researchers accounted for individual residents' risk factors, the relationship between social capital and individual health remained. Indeed, the researchers concluded that if one wanted to improve one's health, moving to a high-social-capital state would do almost as much good as quitting smoking. These authors' conclusion is complemented by our own analysis. We found a strong positive relationship between a comprehensive index of public health and the Social Capital Index, along with a strong negative correlation between the Social Capital Index and all-cause mortality rates.[7] (See table 1 for the measure of public health and health care and figure 1 for the correlations of public health and mortality with social capital.)

TABLE 1: WHICH STATE HAS THE BEST HEALTH AND HEALTH CARE?

MORGAN-QUITNO HEALTHIEST STATE RANKINGS (1993–1998):

1. Births of low birth weight as a percent of all births (–)
2. Births to teenage mothers as a percent of live births (–)
3. Percent of mothers receiving late or no prenatal care (–)
4. Death rate (–)
5. Infant mortality rate (–)
6. Estimated age adjusted death rate by cancer (–)
7. Death rate by suicide (–)
8. Percent of population not covered by health insurance (–)
9. Change in percent of population uninsured (–)
10. Health care expenditures as a percent of gross state product (–)
11. Per capita personal health expenditures (–)
12. Estimate rate of new cancer cases (–)
13. AIDS rate (–)
14. Sexually transmitted disease rate (–)
15. Percent of population lacking access to primary care (–)
16. Percent of adults who are binge drinkers (–)
17. Percent of adults who smoke (–)
18. Percent of adults overweight (–)
19. Days in past month when physical health was "not good" (–)
20. Community hospitals per 1,000 square miles (+)
21. Beds in community hospitals per 100,000 population (+)
22. Percent of children aged 19–35 months fully immunized (+)
23. Safety belt usage rate (+)

The state-level findings are suggestive, but far more definitive evidence of the benefits of community cohesion is provided by a wealth of studies that examine individual health as a function of individual social-capital resources. Nowhere is the connection better illustrated than in Roseto, Pennsylvania.[8] This small Italian American community has been the subject of nearly forty years of in-depth study, beginning in the 1950s when medical researchers noticed a happy but puzzling phenomenon. Compared with residents of neighboring towns, Rosetans just didn't die of heart attacks. Their (age-adjusted) heart attack rate was less than half that of their neighbors; over a seven-year period not a single Roseto resident under forty-seven had died of a heart attack. The researchers looked for the usual explanations: diet, exercise, weight, smoking, genetic predisposition, and so forth. But none of these explanations held the answer—indeed, Rosetans were actually more likely to have some of these risk factors than were people in neighboring towns. The researchers then began to explore Roseto's social dynamics. The town had been founded in the nineteenth century by people from the same southern Italian village. Through local leadership these immigrants had created a mutual aid society, churches, sports clubs, a labor union, a newspaper, Scout troops, and a park and athletic field. The residents had also developed a tight-knit community where conspicuous displays of wealth were scorned and family values and good behaviors reinforced. Rosetans learned to draw on one another for financial,

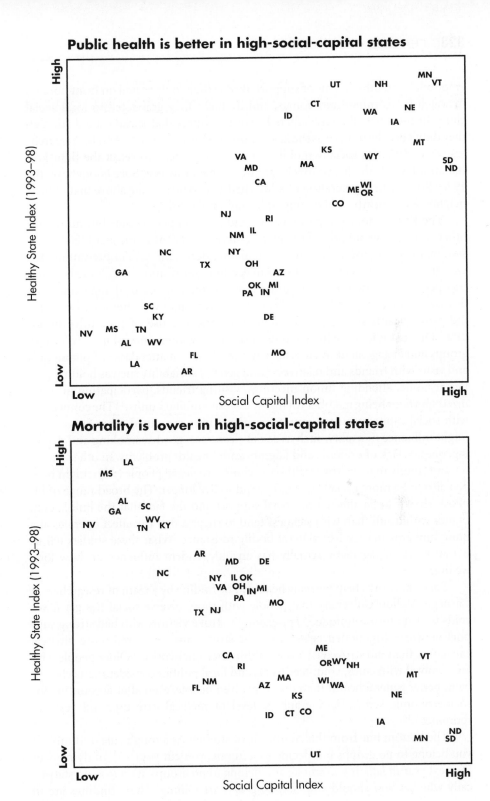

FIGURE 1: Health Is Better in High-Social-Capital States

emotional, and other forms of support. By day they congregated on front porches to watch the comings and goings, and by night they gravitated to local social clubs. In the 1960s the researchers began to suspect that social capital (though they didn't use the term) was the key to Rosetans' healthy hearts. And the researchers worried that as socially mobile young people began to reject the tight-knit Italian folkways, the heart attack rate would begin to rise. Sure enough, by the 1980s Roseto's new generation of adults had a heart attack rate above that of their neighbors in a nearby and demographically similar town.

The Roseto story is a particularly vivid and compelling one, but numerous other studies have supported the medical researchers' intuition that social cohesion matters, not just in preventing premature death, but also in preventing disease and speeding recovery. For example, a long-term study in California found that people with the fewest social ties have the highest risk of dying from heart disease, circulatory problems, and cancer (in women), even after accounting for individual health status, socioeconomic factors, and use of preventive health care.[9] Other studies have linked lower death rates with membership in voluntary groups and engagement in cultural activities;[10] church attendance;[11] phone calls and visits with friends and relatives;[12] and general sociability such as holding parties at home, attending union meetings, visiting friends, participating in organized sports, or being members of highly cohesive military units.[13] The connection with social capital persisted even when the studies examined other factors that might influence mortality, such as social class, race, gender, smoking and drinking, obesity, lack of exercise, and (significantly) health problems. In other words, it is not simply that healthy, health-conscious, privileged people (who might happen also to be more socially engaged) tend to live longer. The broad range of illnesses shown to be affected by social support and the fact that the link is even tighter with death than with sickness tend to suggest that the effect operates at a quite fundamental level of general bodily resistance. What these studies tell us is that social engagement actually has an independent influence on how long we live.

Social networks help you stay healthy. The finding by a team of researchers at Carnegie Mellon University that people with more diverse social ties get fewer colds is by no means unique.[14] For example, stroke victims who had strong support networks functioned better after the stroke, and recovered more physical capacities, than did stroke victims with thin social networks.[15] Older people who are involved with clubs, volunteer work, and local politics consider themselves to be in better general health than do uninvolved people, even after accounting for socioeconomic status, demographics, level of medical care use, and years in retirement.[16]

The bottom line from this multitude of studies: As a rough rule of thumb, if you belong to no groups but decide to join one, you cut your risk of dying over the next year *in half.* If you smoke and belong to no groups, it's a toss-up statistically whether you should stop smoking or start joining. These findings are in

10

some ways heartening: it's easier to join a group than to lose weight, exercise regularly, or quit smoking.

But the findings are sobering, too. As we saw in section II, there has been a general decline in social participation over the past twenty-five years. Figure 2 shows that this same period witnessed a significant decline in self-reported health, despite tremendous gains in medical diagnosis and treatment. Of course, by many objective measures, including life expectancy, Americans are healthier than ever before, but these self-reports indicate that we are feeling worse.[17] These self-reports are in turn closely linked to social connectedness, in the sense that it is precisely less connected Americans who are feeling worse. These facts alone do not *prove* that we are suffering physically from our growing disconnectedness, but taken in conjunction with the more systematic evidence of the health effects of social capital, this evidence is another link in the argument that the erosion of social capital has measurable ill effects.

We observed in chapter 14 the remarkable coincidence that during the same years that social connectedness has been declining, depression and even suicide have been increasing. We also noted that this coincidence has deep generational roots, in the sense that the generations most disconnected socially also suffer

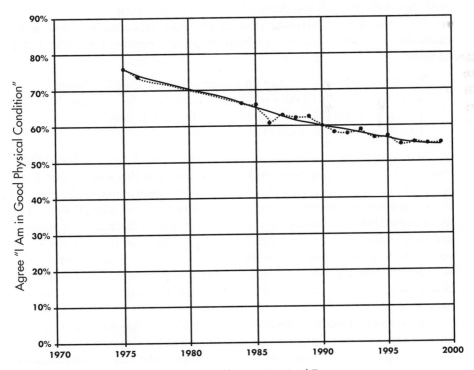

FIGURE 2: Americans Don't Feel As Healthy As We Used To

most from what some public health experts call "Agent Blue." In any given year 10 percent of Americans now suffer from major depression, and depression imposes the fourth largest total burden of any disease on Americans overall. Much research has shown that social connections inhibit depression. Low levels of social support directly predict depression, even controlling for other risk factors, and high levels of social support lessen the severity of symptoms and speed recovery. Social support buffers us from the stresses of daily life. Face-to-face ties seem to be more therapeutic than ties that are geographically distant. In short, even within the single domain of depression, we pay a very high price for our slackening social connectedness.[18]

Countless studies document the link between society and psyche: people who have close friends and confidants, friendly neighbors, and supportive co-workers are less likely to experience sadness, loneliness, low self-esteem, and problems with eating and sleeping. Married people are consistently happier than people who are unattached, all else being equal. These findings will hardly surprise most Americans, for in study after study people themselves report that good relationships with family members, friends, or romantic partners—far more than money or fame—are prerequisites for their happiness.[19] The single most common finding from a half century's research on the correlates of life satisfaction, not only in the United States but around the world, is that happiness is best predicted by the breadth and depth of one's social connections.[20]

We can see how social capital ranks as a producer of warm, fuzzy feelings by examining a number of questions from the DDB Needham Life Style survey archives:

"I wish I could leave my present life and do something entirely different."
"I am very satisfied with the way things are going in my life these days."
"If I had my life to live over, I would sure do things differently."
"I am much happier now than I ever was before."

Responses to these items are strongly intercorrelated, so I combined them into a single index of happiness with life. Happiness in this sense is correlated with material well-being. Generally speaking, as one rises up the income hierarchy, life contentment increases. So money can buy happiness after all. But not as much as marriage. Controlling for education, age, gender, marital status, income, and civic engagement, the marginal "effect" of marriage on life contentment is equivalent to moving roughly seventy percentiles up the income hierarchy— say, from the fifteenth percentile to the eighty-fifty percentile.[21] In round numbers, getting married is the "happiness equivalent" of quadrupling your annual income.[22]

What about education and contentment? Education has important indirect links to happiness through increased earning power, but controlling for income (as well as age, gender, and the rest), what is the marginal correlation of education itself with life satisfaction? In round numbers the answer is that four additional years of education—attending college, for example—is the "happiness equivalent" of roughly doubling your annual income.

Having assessed in rough-and-ready terms the correlations of financial capital (income), human capital (education), and one form of social capital (marriage) with life contentment, we can now ask equivalent questions about the correlations between happiness and various forms of social interaction. Let us ask about regular club members (those who attend monthly), regular volunteers (those who do so monthly), people who entertain regularly at home (say, monthly), and regular (say, biweekly) churchgoers. The differences are astonishingly large. Regular club attendance, volunteering, entertaining, or church attendance is the happiness equivalent of getting a college degree or more than doubling your income. Civic connections rival marriage and affluence as predictors of life happiness.[23]

If monthly club meetings are good, are daily club meetings thirty times better? The answer is no. Figure 3 shows what economists might call the "declining marginal productivity" of social interaction with respect to happiness. The biggest happiness returns to volunteering, clubgoing, and entertaining at home appear to come between "never" and "once a month." There is very little gain in happiness after about one club meeting (or party or volunteer effort) every three weeks. After fortnightly encounters, the marginal correlation of additional social interaction with happiness is actually negative—another finding that is consistent with common experience! Churchgoing, on the other hand, is somewhat different, in that at least up through weekly attendance, the more the merrier.

This analysis is, of course, phrased intentionally in round numbers, for the underlying calculations are rough and ready. Moreover the direction of causation

20

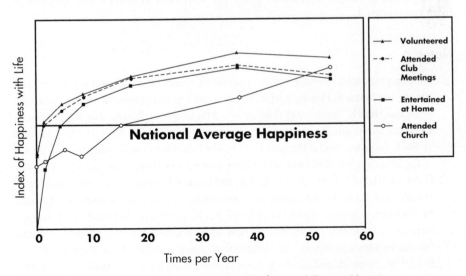

FIGURE 3: Social Connectedness (at Least in Moderation) Fosters Happiness

remains ambiguous. Perhaps happy people are more likely than unhappy people to get married, win raises at work, continue in school, attend church, join clubs, host parties, and so on. My present purpose is merely to illustrate that social connections have profound links with psychological well-being. The Beatles got it right: we all "get by with a little help from our friends."

In the decades since the Fab Four topped the charts, life satisfaction among adult Americans has declined steadily. Roughly half the decline in contentment is associated with financial worries, and half is associated with declines in social capital: lower marriage rates and decreasing connectedness to friends and community. Not all segments of the population are equally gloomy. Survey data show that the slump has been greatest among young and middle-aged adults (twenty to fifty-five). People over fifty-five—our familiar friends from the long civic generation—are actually *happier* than were people their age a generation ago.[24]

Some of the generational discrepancy is due to money worries: despite rising prosperity, young and middle-aged people feel less secure financially. But some of the disparity is also due to social connectedness. Young and middle-aged adults today are simply less likely to have friends over, attend church, or go to club meetings than were earlier generations. Psychologist Martin Seligman argues that more of us are feeling down because modern society encourages a belief in personal control and autonomy more than a commitment to duty and common enterprise. This transformation heightens our expectations about what we can achieve through choice and grit and leaves us unprepared to deal with life's inevitable failures. Where once we could fall back on social capital—families, churches, friends—these no longer are strong enough to cushion our fall.[25] In our personal lives as well as in our collective life, the evidence of this chapter suggests, we are paying a significant price for a quarter century's disengagement from one another.

Notes

1. For comprehensive overviews of the massive literature on health and social connectedness, see James S. House, Karl R. Landis, and Debra Umberson, "Social Relationships and Health," *Science* 241 (1988): 540–545; Lisa F. Berkman, "The Role of Social Relations in Health Promotion," *Psychosomatic Medicine* 57 (1995): 245–254; and Teresa E. Seeman, "Social Ties and Health: The Benefits of Social Integration," *Annual of Epidemiology* 6 (1996): 442–451. Other useful recent overviews include Benjamin C. Amick III, Sol Levine, Alvin R. Tarlov, and Diana Chapman Walsh, eds., *Society and Health* (New York: Oxford University Press, 1995), esp. Donald L. Patrick and Thomas M. Wickizer, "Community and Health," 46–92; Richard G. Wilkinson, *Unhealthy Societies: From Inequality to Well-Being* (New York: Routledge, 1996); Linda K. George, "Social Factors and Illness," in *Handbook of Aging and the Social Sciences*, 4th ed., Robert H. Binstock and Linda K. George, eds. (New York: Academic Press, 1996), 229–252; Frank W. Young and Nina Glasgow, "Voluntary Social Participation and

Health," *Research on Aging* 20 (1998): 339–362; Sherman A. James, Amy J. Schulz, and Juliana van Olphen, "Social Capital, Poverty, and Community Health: An Exploration of Linkages," in *Using Social Capital,* Saegert, Thompson, and Warren, eds.

2. B. H. Kaplan, J. C. Cassel, and S. Gore, "Social Support and Health," *Medical Care* (supp.) 15, no. 5 (1977): 47–58; L. F. Berkman, "The Relationship of Social Networks and Social Support to Morbidity and Mortality," in S. Cohen and S. L. Syme, eds., *Social Support and Health* (Orlando, Fla.: Academic Press, 1985), 241–262; J. S. House, D. Umberson, and K. R. Landis, "Structures and Processes of Social Support," *Annual Review of Sociology* 14 (1988): 293–318; Ichiro Kawachi, Bruce P. Kennedy, and Roberta Glass, "Social Capital and Self-Rated Health: A Contextual Analysis," *American Journal of Public Health* 89 (1999): 1187–1193.

3. Lisa Berkman, "The Changing and Heterogeneous Nature of Aging and Longevity: A Social and Biomedical Perspective," *Annual Review of Gerontology and Geriatrics* 8 (1988): 37–68; Lisa Berkman and Thomas Glass, "Social Integration, Social Networks, Social Support, and Health," in *Social Epidemiology*, Lisa F. Berkman and Ichiro Kawachi, eds. (New York, Oxford University Press, 2000), 137–174; T. E. Seeman, L. F. Berkman, and D. Blazer, et al., "Social Ties and Support and Neuroendocrine Function: The MacArthur Studies of Successful Aging," *Annals of Behavioral Medicine* 16 (1994): 95–106; Sheldon Cohen, "Health Psychology: Psychological Factors and Physical Disease from the Perspective of Human Psychoneuroimmunology," *Annual Review of Psychology* 47 (1996): 113–142.

4. Berkman and Glass, "Social Integration, Social Networks, Social Support, and Health."

5. Kawachi et al., "Social Capital and Self-Rated Health."

6. The Pearson's *r* coefficient between the fraction reporting they were in fair or poor health and the (demographically weighted) state mistrust ranking (low, medium, high) was 0.71; the *r* coefficient between fraction of population in fair/poor health and the (demographically weighted) state "helpfulness" ranking (low, medium, high) was -0.66.

7. The Pearson's *r* coefficient between the Social Capital Index and the Morgan-Quitno health index (1991–98) across the fifty states equals 0.78, which is strong by conventional social science standards; the comparable correlation between the Social Capital Index and the age-adjusted all-cause mortality rate is -.81. Thanks to Ichiro Kawachi for providing this measure of death rates.

8. Thanks to Kimberly Lochner for bringing the history of Roseto to my attention and for introducing me to the literature on the health effects of social connectedness. The key studies of Roseto are J. G. Bruhn and S. Wolf, *The Roseto Story: An Anatomy of Health* (Norman, Okla.: University of Oklahoma Press, 1979); S. Wolf and J. G. Bruhn, *The Power of Clan: The Influence of Human Relationships on Heart Disease* (New Brunswick, N.J.: Transaction Publishers, 1993); B. Egolf, J. Lasker, S. Wolf, and L. Potvin, "The Roseto Effect: A Fifty-Year Comparison of Mortality Rates," *American Journal of Epidemiology* 125, no. 6 (1992): 1089–1092.

9. L. F. Berkman and S. L. Syme, "Social Networks, Host Resistance and Mortality: A Nine Year Follow-up of Alameda County Residents," *American Journal of Epidemiology* 109 (1979): 186–204.

10. J. House, C. Robbins, and H. Metzner, "The Association of Social Relationships and Activities with Mortality: Prospective Evidence from the Tecumseh Community Health Study," *American Journal of Epidemiology* 116, no. 1 (1982): 123–140. This finding held for men only.

11. House, Robbins, and Metzner (1982); this finding held for women only. T. E. Seeman, G. A. Kaplan, L. Knudsen, R. Cohen, and J. Guralnik, "Social Network Ties and Mortality among the Elderly in the Alameda County Study," *American Journal of Epidemiology* 126, no. 4 (1987): 714–723; this study found that social isolation predicted mortality only in people over sixty.

12. D. Blazer, "Social Support and Mortality in an Elderly Community Population," *American Journal of Epidemiology* 115, no. 5 (1982): 684–694; K. Orth-Gomer and J. V. Johnson, "Social Network Interaction and Mortality," *Journal of Chronic Diseases* 40, no. 10 (1987): 949–957.

13. L. Welin, G. Tibblin, K. Svardsudd, B. Tibblin, S. Ander-Peciva, B. Larsson, and L. Wilhelmsen, "Prospective Study of Social Influences on Mortality," The *Lancet*, April 20, 1985, 915–918; Frederick J. Manning and Terrence D. Fullerton, "Health and Well-Being in Highly Cohesive Units of the U.S. Army," *Journal of Applied Social Psychology* 18 (1988): 503–519.

14. Sheldon Cohen et al., "Social Ties and Susceptibility to the Common Cold," *Journal of the American Medical Association* 277 (June 25, 1997): 1940–1944.

15. A. Colantonio, S. V. Kasl, A. M. Ostfeld, and L. Berkman, "Psychosocial Predictors of Stroke Outcomes in an Elderly Population," *Journal of Gerontology* 48, no. 5 (1993): S261–S268.

16. Young and Glasgow, "Voluntary Social Participation and Health."

17. Angus Deaton and C. H. Paxson, "Aging and Inequality in Income and Health," *American Economic Review* 88 (1998): 252, report "there has been no improvement, and possibly some deterioration, in health status across cohorts born after 1945, and there were larger improvements across those born before 1945."

18. R. C. Kessler et al., "Lifetime and 12-Month Prevalence of DSM-III-R Psychiatric Disorders in the United States," *Archives of General Psychiatry* 51 (1994): 8–19; C. J. Murray and A. D. Lopez, "Evidence-Based Health Policy—Lessons from the Global Burden of Disease Study," *Science* 274 (1996): 740–743; L. I. Pearlin et al., "The Stress Process"; G. A. Kaplan et al., "Psychosocial Predictors of Depression"; A. G. Billings and R. H. Moos, "Life Stressors and Social Resources Affect Posttreatment Outcomes among Depressed Patients," *Journal of Abnormal Psychiatry* 94 (1985): 140–153; C. D. Sherbourne, R. D. Hays, and K. B. Wells, "Personal and Psychosocial Risk Factors for Physical and Mental Health Outcomes and Course of Depression among Depressed Patients," *Journal of Consulting and Clinical Psychology* 63 (1995): 345–355; T. E. Seeman and L. F. Berkman, "Structural Characteristics of Social Networks and Their Relationship with Social Support in the Elderly: Who Provides Support," *Social Science and Medicine* 26 (1988): 737–749. I am indebted to Julie Donahue for her fine work on this topic.

19. L. I. Pearlin, M. A. Lieberman, E. G. Menaghan, and J. T. Mullan, "The Stress Process," *Journal of Health and Social Behavior* 22, no. 4 (1981): 337–356; A. Billings and R. Moos,

"Social Support and Functioning among Community and Clinical Groups: A Panel Model," *Journal of Behavioral Medicine* 5, no. 3 (1982): 295–311; G. A. Kaplan, R. E. Roberts, T. C. Camacho, and J. C. Coyne, "Psychosocial Predictors of Depression," *American Journal of Epidemiology* 125, no. 2 (1987), 206–220; P. Cohen, E. L. Struening, G. L. Muhlin, L. E. Genevie, S. R. Kaplan, and H. B. Peck, "Community Stressors, Mediating Conditions and Well-being in Urban Neighborhoods," *Journal of Community Psychology* 10 (1982): 377–391; David G. Myers, "Close Relationships and Quality of Life," in D. Kahneman, E. Diener, and N. Schwartz, eds., *Well-being: The Foundation of Hedonic Psychology* (New York: Russell Sage Foundation, 1999).

20. Michael Argyle, *The Psychology of Happiness* (London: Methuen, 1987); Ed Diener, "Subjective Well-being," *Psychological Bulletin* 95 (1984): 542–575; Ed Deiner, "Assessing Subjective Well-being," *Social Indicators Research*, 31 (1994): 103–175; David G. Myers and Ed Deiner, "Who Is Happy?" *Psychological Science* 6 (1995): 10–19; Ruut Veenhoven, "Developments in Satisfaction-Research," *Social Indicators Research*, 37 (1996): 1–46; and works cited there.

21. In these data and in most studies the effect of marriage on life happiness is essentially identical among men and women, contrary to some reports that marriage has a more positive effect on happiness among men.

22. Income in successive Life Style surveys is measured in terms of income brackets, defined in dollars of annual income. To enhance comparability over time, we have translated each of these brackets in each annual survey into its mean percentile ranking in that year's income distribution. The effect of income measured in percentiles on contentment is not linear, but that is offset by the fact that the translation of income in dollars to income percentiles is also not linear. Thus the "happiness equivalent" of any particular change in income is accurate in its order of magnitude, but not in detail.

23. The results here are based on multiple regression analyses on the DDB Needham Life Style sample, including age, gender, education, income, marital status, as well as our various measures of civic engagement. The results are essentially identical for men and women, except that the effects of education and of social connections on happiness are slightly greater among women. Income, education, and social connections all have a greater effect among single people than among married people. For example, the effects of club meetings on the happiness of single people is twice as great as on the happiness of married people. In other words, absent marriage, itself a powerful booster of life contentment, other factors become more important. Conversely, even among the poor, uneducated, and socially isolated, marriage provides a fundamental buffer for contentment.

24. Author's analysis of DDB Needham Life Style and Harris poll data.

25. Martin E. P. Seligman, "Boomer Blues," *Psychology Today*, October 1988, 50–55.

Exploring the Text

1. Robert D. Putnam opens with consideration of suicide. Why does he use suicide, perhaps the most profound expression of isolation, as a way to introduce an analysis of social connectedness?

2. What is the purpose of Note 1 from the perspective of both the audience and the author?

3. What theories does Putnam review to explain the positive effects of social connectedness and the negative effects of its absence?

4. What evidence do the Notes present to support Putnam's claim that Lisa Berkman is "one of the leading researchers in the field" (para. 5)?

5. What evidence does Putnam provide in his discussion of the "astonishingly strong relationship between poor health and low social capital" (para. 7)?

6. Putnam discusses at length a classic study of the Italian American community in Roseto, Pennsylvania (para. 8). What have researchers learned from this example?

7. In this chapter, Putnam uses several graphs and charts. Discuss how they function in presenting his arguments — that is, do they add information that is not in the written text, do they confirm it, do they expand on it? Consider each individually.

8. What is the causal relationship between marriage and happiness? Between education and happiness? Between money and happiness? Which, according to Putnam, is strongest? What evidence does he provide?

9. Does Putnam's allusion to the musical group the Beatles and his quotation from one of their famous songs (para. 20) strike you as out of place or a welcome lighter note? Is it effective or ineffective in the context of this essay?

10. Select three sequential paragraphs at random for analysis. Look at the syntax, diction, and point of view. What rhetorical strategies does Putnam use to make technical and specialized research accessible to a more general audience?

11. After looking over all of Putnam's notes for this chapter, classify them into three or four different purposes. Specifically, how do these notes complement the written and visual text in the chapter without interrupting the flow of the analysis?

12. Discuss why you agree or disagree with the position of psychologist Martin Seligman, as described by Putnam: "more of us are feeling down because modern society encourages a belief in personal control and autonomy more than a commitment to duty and common enterprise" (para. 22).

13. If you were asked to develop a series of suggestions to the area where you live for a "healthier environment" based on Putnam's research, what would you recommend?

14. Identify one or two of the ways people establish social connectedness — for example, by belonging to an organized religion, volunteering, participating in associations, spending time with friends. What role(s) do you think social media might play in increasing social capital?

Home at Last

Dinaw Mengestu

Dinaw Mengestu, born in Addis Ababa, Ethiopia, in 1978, immigrated to the United States in 1980. He received a BA from Georgetown University and an MFA from Columbia University. His first novel, *The Beautiful Things That Heaven Bears* (2007), was named a *New York Times* Notable Book. He published his second novel, *How to Read the Air*, in 2010, the year he was also named one of the *New Yorker*'s "20 under 40" Writers to Watch. Mengestu was the Lannan Visiting Writer at Georgetown University in 2007. After having spent a number of years in New York, he currently lives with his wife and son in Paris. The following essay was included in *Brooklyn Was Mine* (2008), a collection of essays about living in Brooklyn, New York.

At twenty-one I moved to Brooklyn hoping that it would be the last move I would ever make — that it would, with the gradual accumulation of time, memory, and possessions, become that place I instinctively reverted back to when asked, "So, where are you from?" I was born in Ethiopia like my parents and their parents before them, but it would be a lie to say I was *from* Ethiopia, having left the country when I was only two years old following a military coup and civil war, losing in the process the language and any direct memory of the family and culture I had been born into. I simply am Ethiopian, without the necessary "from" that serves as the final assurance of our identity and origin.

Since leaving Addis Ababa in 1980, I've lived in Peoria, Illinois; in a suburb of Chicago; and then finally, before moving to Brooklyn, in Washington, D.C., the de facto capital of the Ethiopian immigrant. Others, I know, have moved much more often and across much greater distances. I've only known a few people, however, that have grown up with the oddly permanent feeling of having lost and abandoned a home that you never, in fact, really knew, a feeling that has nothing to do with apartments, houses, or miles, but rather the sense that no matter how far you travel, or how long you stay still, there is no place that you can always return to, no place where you fully belong. My parents, for all that they had given up by leaving Ethiopia, at least had the certainty that they had come from some place. They knew the country's language and culture, had met outside of coffee shops along Addis's main boulevard in the early days of their relationship, and as a result, regardless of how mangled by violence Ethiopia later became, it was irrevocably and ultimately theirs. Growing up, one of my father's favorite sayings was, "Remember, you are Ethiopian," even though, of course, there was nothing for me to remember apart from the bits of nostalgia and culture my parents had imparted. What remained had less to do with the idea that I was from Ethiopia and more to do with the fact that I was not from America.

I can't say when exactly I first became aware of that feeling—that I was always going to and never from—but surely I must have felt it during those first years in Peoria, with my parents, sister, and me always sitting on the edge of whatever context we were now supposed to be a part of, whether it was the all-white Southern Baptist Church we went to every weekend, or the nearly all-white Catholic schools my sister and I attended first in Peoria and then again in Chicago at my parents' insistence. By that point my father, haunted by the death of his brother during the revolution and the ensuing loss of the country he had always assumed he would live and die in, had taken to long evening walks that he eventually let me accompany him on. Back then he had a habit of sometimes whispering his brother's name as he walked ("Shibrew," he would mutter) or whistling the tunes of Amharic songs that I had never known. He always walked with both hands firmly clasped behind his back, as if his grief, transformed into something real and physical, could be grasped and secured in the palms of his hands. That was where I first learned what it meant to lose and be alone. The lesson would be reinforced over the years whenever I caught sight of my mother sitting by herself on a Sunday afternoon, staring silently out of our living room's picture window, recalling, perhaps, her father who had died after she left, or her mother, four sisters, and one brother in Ethiopia—or else recalling nothing at all because there was no one to visit her, no one to call or see. We had been stripped bare here in America, our lives confined to small towns and urban suburbs. We had sacrificed precisely those things that can never be compensated for or repaid—parents, siblings, culture, a memory to a place that dates back more than half a generation. It's easy to see now how even as a family we were isolated from one another—my parents tied and lost to their past; my sister and I irrevocably assimilated. For years we were strangers even among ourselves.

By the time I arrived in Brooklyn I had little interest in where I actually landed. I had just graduated college and had had enough of the fights and arguments about not being "black" enough, as well as the earlier fights in high school hallways and street corners that were fought for simply being black. Now it was enough, I wanted to believe, to simply be, to say I was in Brooklyn and Brooklyn was home. It wasn't until after I had signed the lease on my apartment that I even learned the name of the neighborhood I had moved into: Kensington, a distinctly regal name at a price that I could afford; it was perfect, in other words, for an eager and poor writer with inflated ambitions and no sense of where he belonged.

After less than a month of living in Kensington I had covered almost all of the 5 neighborhood's streets, deliberately committing their layouts and routines to memory in a first attempt at assimilation. There was an obvious and deliberate echo to my walks, a self-conscious reenactment of my father's routine that I adopted to stave off some of my own emptiness. It wasn't just that I didn't have any deep personal relationships here, it was that I had chosen this city as the place to redefine, to ground, to secure my place in the world. If I could bind myself to Kensington physically, if I could memorize and mentally reproduce in accurate detail the various shades of the houses on a particular block, then I could stake my own claim to it, and in doing so, no one could tell me who I was or that I didn't belong.

On my early-morning walks to the F train I passed in succession a Latin American restaurant and grocery store, a Chinese fish market, a Halal butcher shop, followed by a series of Pakistani and Bangladeshi takeout restaurants. This cluster of restaurants on the corner of Church and McDonald, I later learned, sold five-dollar plates of lamb and chicken biryani in portions large enough to hold me over for a day, and in more financially desperate times, two days. Similarly, I learned that the butcher and fish shop delivery trucks arrived on most days just as I was making my way to the train. If I had time, I found it hard not to stand and stare at the refrigerated trucks with their calf and sheep carcasses dangling from hooks, or at the tanks of newly arrived bass and catfish flapping around in a shallow pool of water just deep enough to keep them alive.

It didn't take long for me to develop a fierce loyalty to Kensington, to think of the neighborhood and my place in it as emblematic of a grander immigrant narrative. In response to that loyalty, I promised to host a "Kensington night" for the handful of new friends that I eventually made in the city, an evening that would have been comprised of five-dollar lamb biryani followed by two-dollar Budweisers at Denny's, the neighborhood's only full-fledged bar—a defunct Irish pub complete with terribly dim lighting and wooden booths. I never hosted a Kensington night, however, no doubt in part because I had established my own private relationship to the neighborhood, one that could never be shared with others in a single evening of cheap South Asian food and beer. I knew the hours of the call of the muezzin that rang from the mosque a block away from my apartment. I heard it in my bedroom every morning, afternoon, and evening, and if I was writing when it called out, I learned that it was better to simply stop and admire it. My landlord's father, an old gray-haired Chinese immigrant who spoke no English, gradually smiled at me as I came and went, just as I learned to say hello, as politely as possible, in Mandarin every time I saw him. The men behind the counters of the Bangladeshi takeout places now knew me by sight. A few, on occasion, slipped an extra dollop of vegetables or rice into my to-go container, perhaps because they worried that I wasn't eating enough. One in particular, who was roughly my age, spoke little English, and smiled wholeheartedly whenever I came in, gave me presweetened tea and free bread, a gesture that I took to be an acknowledgment that, at least for him, I had earned my own, albeit marginal, place here.

And so instead of sitting with friends in a brightly lit fluorescent restaurant with cafeteria-style service, I found myself night after night quietly walking around the neighborhood in between sporadic fits of writing. Kensington was no more beautiful by night than by day, and perhaps this very absence of grandeur allowed me to feel more at ease wandering its streets at night. The haphazard gathering of immigrants in Kensington had turned it into a place that even some-one like me, haunted and conscious of race and identity at every turn, could slip and blend into.

Inevitably on my way home I returned to the corner of Church and McDon-ald with its glut of identical restaurants. On warm nights, I had found it was the perfect spot to stand and admire not only what Kensington had become with the most recent wave of migration, but what any close-knit community—whether its people came here one hundred years ago from Europe or a decade ago from Africa, Asia, or the Caribbean—has provided throughout Brooklyn's history: a second home. There, on that corner, made up of five competing South Asian res-taurants of roughly equal quality, dozens of Pakistani and Bangladeshi men gath-ered one night after another to drink chai out of paper cups. The men stood there talking for hours, huddled in factions built in part, I imagine, around restaurant loyalties. Some nights I sat in one of the restaurants and watched from a corner table with a book in hand as an artificial prop. A few of the men always stared, curious no doubt as to what I was doing there. Even though I lived in Kensington, when it came to evening gatherings like this, I was the foreigner and tourist. On other nights I ordered my own cup of tea and stood a few feet away on the edge of the sidewalk, near the subway entrance or at the bus stop, and silently stared. I had seen communal scenes like this before, especially while living in Washington, D.C., where there always seemed to be a cluster of Ethiopians, my age or older, gathered together outside coffee shops and bars all over the city, talking in Amharic with an ease and fluency that I admired and envied. They told jokes that didn't require explanation and debated arguments that were decades in the making. All of this was coupled with the familiarity and comfort of speaking in our native tongue. At any given moment, they could have told you without hesitancy where they were from. And so I had watched, hardly understanding a word, hoping somehow that the simple act of association and observation was enough to draw me into the fold.

Here, then, was a similar scene, this one played out on a Brooklyn corner with a culture and history different from the one I had been born into, but familiar to me nonetheless. The men on that corner in Kensington, just like the people I had known throughout my life, were immigrants in the most complete sense of the word—their loyalties still firmly attached to the countries they had left one, five, or twenty years earlier. If there was one thing I admired most about them, it was that they had succeeded, at least partly, in re-creating in Brooklyn some of what they had lost when they left their countries of origin. Unlike the solitary and private walks my father and I took, each of us buried deep in thoughts that had nowhere to go, this nightly gathering of Pakistani and Bangladeshi men was a makeshift reenactment of home. Farther down the road from where they stood were the few remaining remnants of the neighborhood's older Jewish community—one synagogue, a kosher deli—proof, if one was ever needed, that Brooklyn is always reinventing itself, that there is room here for us all.

While the men stood outside on the corner, their numbers gradually increasing until they spilled out into the street as they talked loudly among themselves, I once again played my own familiar role of quiet, jealous observer and secret admirer. I have no idea what those men talked about, if they discussed politics, sex, or petty complaints about work. It never mattered anyway. The substance of the conversation belonged to them, and I couldn't have cared less. What I had wanted and found in them, what I admired and adored about Kensington, was the assertion that we can rebuild and remake ourselves and our communities over and over again, in no small part because there have always been corners in Brooklyn to do so on. I stood on that corner night after night for the most obvious of reasons—to be reminded of a way of life that persists regardless of context; to feel, however foolishly, that I too was attached to something.

Exploring the Text

1. Dinaw Mengestu opens the essay with a paragraph of commentary before he provides a more chronological account of his early life. What is the effect on you as a reader? What do you know about the narrator from this paragraph? How do you interpret the final sentence?

2. How does the form of the following sentence, taken from paragraph 2, reinforce its meaning?

   I've only known a few people, however, that have grown up with the oddly permanent feeling of having lost and abandoned a home that you never, in fact, really knew, a feeling that has nothing to do with apartments, houses, or miles, but rather the sense that no matter how far you travel, or how long you stay still, there is no place that you can always return to, no place where you fully belong.

3. One of the themes that Mengestu develops in this essay is isolation. What are the different ways that isolation manifests itself in different people and settings in the communities he describes?

4. What does Mengestu do to make his "first attempt at assimilation" (para. 5)? How does his new, chosen identity as a "poor writer with inflated ambitions" (para. 4) contribute to this attempt?

5. What does he mean when he writes that he begins to think of himself as "emblematic of a grander immigrant narrative" (para. 7)?

6. What are the qualities about Kensington, Brooklyn, that appeal to Mengestu and draw him in? In what ways does he interact with his neighborhood?

7. In what ways has Brooklyn served as "a second home" (para. 9) to different groups over the years, as explained in this essay?

8. Mengestu describes himself in various ways: for example, "haunted and conscious of race and identity at every turn" (para. 8), "foreigner and tourist" (para. 9), "quiet, jealous observer" (para. 11). Who is he by the end of the essay—one of

these, a combination of them, or something else entirely? Consider what he means by the qualifying phrase "however foolishly" in the final line of the essay.

9. Discuss the role of walking, taking walks, or being a walker in this essay. What different ways of walking and motivations for it does Mengestu describe? In what ways does walking take on metaphoric meaning?

10. According to this essay, how does Mengestu define "community"? What does the concept mean to him? Is it the same as "home"?

Facebook Friendonomics

Scott Brown

Scott Brown (b. 1976) became *New York* magazine's theater critic in the fall of 2010. After graduating from Harvard, he was a senior writer for *Entertainment Weekly* and a columnist for *Wired* magazine, where the following essay appeared in 2008. He is the co-author (with Anthony King) of the off-Broadway comedy *Gutenberg! The Musical!*

Hey, want to be my friend? It's more than possible; it's probable. Hell, we may already be friends—I haven't checked my email in a few minutes. And once we are, we will be, as they say, 4-eva. A perusal of my Facebook Friend roster reveals that I, a medium-social individual of only middling lifetime popularity, have never lost a friend. They're all there: elementary school friends, high school friends, college friends, work friends, friends of friends, friends of ex-girlfriends—the constellation of familiar faces crowds my Friendbox like medals on Mussolini's chest. I'm Friend-rich—at least onscreen. I've never lost touch with anyone, it seems. What I've lost is the right to lose touch. This says less about my innate lovability, I think, than about the current inflated state of Friendonomics.

Think of it as the Long Tail of Friendship—in the age of queue-able social priorities, Twitter-able status updates, and amaranthine cloud memory, keeping friends requires almost no effort at all. We have achieved Infinite Friendspace, which means we need never drift from old pals nor feel the poignant tug of passive friend-loss. It also means that even the flimsiest of attachments—the chance convention buddy, the cube-mate from the '90s, the bar-napkin hookup—will be preserved, in perpetuity, under the flattering, flattening banner of "Friend." (Sure, you can rank and categorize them to your heart's content, but who'd be callous enough to actually categorize a hookup under "Hookup"?)

It has been argued that this Infinite Friendspace is an unalloyed good. But while this plays nicely into our sentimental ideal of lifelong friendship, it's having at least three catastrophic effects. First, it encourages hoarding. We squirrel away Friends the way our grandparents used to save nickels—obsessively, desperately, as if we'll run out of them some day. (Of course, they lived through the Depression. And we lived through—what, exactly? Middle school? *90210*? The Electric Slide?) Humans are natural pack rats, and given the chance we'll stockpile anything of nominal value. Friends are the currency of the socially networked world; therefore, it follows that more equals better. But the more Friends you have, the less they're worth—and, more to the point, the less human they are. People become mere collectibles, like Garbage Pail Kids. And call me a buzz kill, but I don't want to be anyone's Potty Scotty.

Second, Friending has subsumed the ol' Rolodex. Granted, it's often convenient to have all of your contacts under one roof. But the great thing about the Rolodex was that it never talked back, it didn't throw virtual octopi or make you take movie quizzes, and it never, ever poked you. The Rolodex just sat there. It was all business.

Third, and most grave, we've lost our right to lose touch. "A friend may well   5
be reckoned the masterpiece of Nature," Emerson wrote, not bothering to add, "and like most things natural, friendship is biodegradable." We scrawl "Friends Forever" in yearbooks, but we quietly realize, with relief, that some bonds are meant to be shed, like snakeskin or a Showtime subscription. It's nature's way of allowing you to change, adapt, evolve, or devolve as you wish—and freeing you from the exhaustion of multifront friend maintenance. Fine, you can "Remove Friend," but what kind of monster actually does that? Deletion is scary—and, we're told, unnecessary in the Petabyte Age. That's what made good old-fashioned losing touch so wonderful—friendships, like long-forgotten photos and mixtapes, would distort and slowly whistle into oblivion, quite naturally, nothing personal. It was sweet and sad and, though you'd rarely admit it, necessary.

And maybe that's the answer: A Facebook app we'll call the Fade Utility. Untended Friends would gradually display a sepia cast on the picture, a blurring of the neglected profile—perhaps a coffee stain might appear on it or an unrelated phone number or grocery list. The individual's status updates might fade and get smaller. The user may then choose to notice and reach out to the person in some meaningful way—no pokes! Or they might pretend not to notice. Without making a choice, they could simply let that person go. Would that really be so awful?

I realize that I may lose a few Friends by saying this. I invite them to remove me. Though I think they'll find it harder than they imagine. I've never lost a Friend, you see, and I'm starting to worry I never will.

Exploring the Text

1. The title "Facebook Friendonomics" is a play on *Freakonomics*, the title of a best-selling book by Stephen J. Dubner and Steven D. Levitt that looks at the economics of everyday phenomena (see p. 342). Knowing this allusion, explain whether you think this is a good title for Scott Brown's article.

2. What is Brown's main point? Is he arguing against Facebook and social networks in general? What are the major points of his argument? Do you find one particularly strong or weak? Explain.

3. Where does Brown address the counterargument? Do you think that he fleshes it out sufficiently or glosses over it?

4. Brown proposes one solution to the problem he defines: "A Facebook app we'll call the Fade Utility" (para. 6). Is he serious? Does his facetious or sarcastic tone undermine his argument?

5. How does Brown use humor to make his point? Analyze two specific examples. How would you characterize the humor? Is it gentle ribbing, stinging sarcasm, or bitter irony?

6. Explain why Brown's use of humor is appropriate to his subject and his audience, the readers of *Wired* magazine. Cite specific words and phrases to support your analysis.

7. Explain why you agree or disagree with the following assertion that Brown makes: "Friends are the currency of the socially networked world; therefore, it follows that more equals better. But the more Friends you have, the less they're worth — and, more to the point, the less human they are. People become mere collectibles . . ." (para. 3).

Small Change

Why the Revolution Will Not Be Tweeted

MALCOLM GLADWELL

Author of four best-selling books, Malcolm Gladwell (b. 1963) grew up in Ontario, Canada, the son of an English university professor father and a Jamaican therapist mother. He has been a staff writer with the *New Yorker* magazine since 1996, and in 2005 he was named one of *Time* magazine's 100 Most Influential People. His books include *The Tipping Point: How Little Things Make a Big Difference* (2000), *Blink: The Power of Thinking without Thinking* (2005), and *Outliers: The Story of Success* (2008). Gladwell's *What the Dog Saw* (2009) is a compilation of articles published in the *New Yorker*. His writing often explores the implications of research in the social sciences and psychology. The following article, which appeared in the *New Yorker* in 2010, compares the intricate network of activists who brought about the civil rights movement with the social media networks that have sprung up on the Internet.

At four-thirty in the afternoon on Monday, February 1, 1960, four college students sat down at the lunch counter at the Woolworth's in downtown Greensboro, North Carolina. They were freshmen at North Carolina A. & T., a black college a mile or so away.

"I'd like a cup of coffee, please," one of the four, Ezell Blair, said to the waitress. "We don't serve Negroes here," she replied.

The Woolworth's lunch counter was a long L-shaped bar that could seat sixty-six people, with a standup snack bar at one end. The seats were for whites. The snack bar was for blacks. Another employee, a black woman who worked at the steam table, approached the students and tried to warn them away. "You're acting stupid, ignorant!" she said. They didn't move. Around five-thirty, the front doors to the store were locked. The four still didn't move. Finally, they left by a side door. Outside, a small crowd had gathered, including a photographer from the Greensboro *Record*. "I'll be back tomorrow with A. & T. College," one of the students said.

By next morning, the protest had grown to twenty-seven men and four women, most from the same dormitory as the original four. The men were dressed in suits and ties. The students had brought their schoolwork, and studied as they sat at the counter. On Wednesday, students from Greensboro's "Negro" secondary school, Dudley High, joined in, and the number of protesters swelled to eighty. By Thursday, the protesters numbered three hundred, including three white women, from the Greensboro campus of the University of North Carolina. By Saturday, the sit-in had reached six hundred. People spilled out onto the street. White teenagers waved Confederate flags. Someone threw a firecracker. At noon, the A. & T. football team arrived. "Here comes the wrecking crew," one of the white students shouted.

By the following Monday, sit-ins had spread to Winston-Salem, twenty-five miles away, and Durham, fifty miles away. The day after that, students at Fayetteville State Teachers College and at Johnson C. Smith College, in Charlotte, joined in, followed on Wednesday by students at St. Augustine's College and Shaw University, in Raleigh. On Thursday and Friday, the protest crossed state lines, surfacing in Hampton and Portsmouth, Virginia, in Rock Hill, South Carolina, and in Chattanooga, Tennessee. By the end of the month, there were sit-ins throughout the South, as far west as Texas. "I asked every student I met what the first day of the sitdowns had been like on his campus," the political theorist Michael Walzer wrote in *Dissent*. "The answer was always the same: 'It was like a fever. Everyone wanted to go.'" Some seventy thousand students eventually took part. Thousands were arrested and untold thousands more radicalized. These events in the early sixties became a civil-rights war that engulfed the South for the rest of the decade — and it happened without e-mail, texting, Facebook, or Twitter.

The world, we are told, is in the midst of a revolution. The new tools of social media have reinvented social activism. With Facebook and Twitter and the like, the traditional relationship between political authority and popular will has been upended, making it easier for the powerless to collaborate, coördinate, and give voice to their concerns. When ten thousand protesters took to the streets in Moldova in the spring of 2009 to protest against their country's Communist government, the action was dubbed the Twitter Revolution, because of the means by which the demonstrators had been brought together. A few months after that, when student protests rocked Tehran, the State Department took the unusual step of asking Twitter to suspend scheduled maintenance of its Web site, because the Administration didn't want such a critical organizing tool out of service at the height of the demonstrations. "Without Twitter the people of Iran would not have felt empowered and confident to stand up for freedom and democracy," Mark Pfeifle, a former national-security adviser, later wrote, calling for Twitter to be nominated for the Nobel Peace Prize. Where activists were once defined by their causes, they are now defined by their tools. Facebook warriors go online to push for change. "You are the best hope for us all," James K. Glassman, a former senior State Department official, told a crowd of cyber activists at a recent conference sponsored by Facebook, A. T. & T., Howcast, MTV, and Google. Sites like Facebook, Glassman said, "give the U.S. a significant competitive advantage over terrorists. Some time ago, I said that Al Qaeda was 'eating our lunch on the Internet.' That is no longer the case. Al Qaeda is stuck in Web 1.0. The Internet is now about interactivity and conversation."

These are strong, and puzzling, claims. Why does it matter who is eating whose lunch on the Internet? Are people who log on to their Facebook page really the best hope for us all? As for Moldova's so-called Twitter Revolution, Evgeny Morozov, a scholar at Stanford who has been the most persistent of digital evangelism's critics, points out that Twitter has scant internal significance in Moldova, a country where very few Twitter accounts exist. Nor does it seem to have been a revolution, not least because the protests—as Anne Applebaum suggested in the *Washington Post*—may well have been a bit of stagecraft cooked up by the government. (In a country paranoid about Romanian revanchism, the protesters flew a Romanian flag over the Parliament building.) In the Iranian case, meanwhile, the people tweeting about the demonstrations were almost all in the West. "It is time to get Twitter's role in the events in Iran right," Golnaz Esfandiari wrote, this past summer, in *Foreign Policy*. "Simply put: There was no Twitter Revolution inside Iran." The cadre of prominent bloggers, like Andrew Sullivan, who championed the role of social media in Iran, Esfandiari continued, misunderstood the situation. "Western journalists who couldn't reach—or didn't bother reaching?—people on the ground in Iran simply scrolled through the English-language tweets post with tag #iranelection," she wrote. "Through it all, no one seemed to wonder why people trying to coordinate protests in Iran would be writing in any language other than Farsi."

Some of this grandiosity is to be expected. Innovators tend to be solipsists. They often want to cram every stray fact and experience into their new model. As the historian Robert Darnton has written, "The marvels of communication technology in the present have produced a false consciousness about the past—even a sense that communication has no history, or had nothing of importance to consider before the days of television and the Internet." But there is something else at work here, in the outsized enthusiasm for social media. Fifty years after one of the most extraordinary episodes of social upheaval in American history, we seem to have forgotten what activism is.

■■
■■

Greensboro in the early nineteen-sixties was the kind of place where racial insub- ordination was routinely met with violence. The four students who first sat down at the lunch counter were terrified. "I suppose if anyone had come up behind me and yelled 'Boo,' I think I would have fallen off my seat," one of them said later. On the first day, the store manager notified the police chief, who immediately sent two officers to the store. On the third day, a gang of white toughs showed up at the lunch counter and stood ostentatiously behind the protesters, ominously muttering epithets such as "burr-head nigger." A local Ku Klux Klan leader made an appearance. On Saturday, as tensions grew, someone called in a bomb threat, and the entire store had to be evacuated.

The dangers were even clearer in the Mississippi Freedom Summer Project of 1964, another of the sentinel campaigns of the civil-rights movement. The Student Nonviolent Coordinating Committee recruited hundreds of Northern, largely white unpaid volunteers to run Freedom Schools, register black voters, and raise civil-rights awareness in the Deep South. "No one should go *anywhere* alone, but certainly not in an automobile and certainly not at night," they were instructed. Within days of arriving in Mississippi, three volunteers—Michael Schwerner, James Chaney, and Andrew Goodman—were kidnapped and killed, and, during the rest of the summer, thirty-seven black churches were set on fire and dozens of safe houses were bombed; volunteers were beaten, shot at, arrested, and trailed by pickup trucks full of armed men. A quarter of those in the program dropped out. Activism that challenges the status quo—that attacks deeply rooted problems—is not for the faint of heart.

What makes people capable of this kind of activism? The Stanford sociologist Doug McAdam compared the Freedom Summer dropouts with the participants who stayed, and discovered that the key difference wasn't, as might be expected, ideological fervor. "*All* of the applicants—participants and withdrawals alike—emerge as highly committed, articulate supporters of the goals and values of the summer program," he concluded. What mattered more was an applicant's degree of personal connection to the civil-rights movement. All the volunteers were required to provide a list of personal contacts—the people they wanted kept apprised of their activities—and participants were far more likely than dropouts to have close friends who were also going to Mississippi. High-risk activism, McAdam concluded, is a "strong-tie" phenomenon.

This pattern shows up again and again. One study of the Red Brigades, the Italian terrorist group of the nineteen-seventies, found that seventy per cent of recruits had at least one good friend already in the organization. The same is true of the men who joined the mujahideen in Afghanistan. Even revolutionary

10

actions that look spontaneous, like the demonstrations in East Germany that led to the fall of the Berlin Wall, are, at core, strong-tie phenomena. The opposition movement in East Germany consisted of several hundred groups, each with roughly a dozen members. Each group was in limited contact with the others: at the time, only thirteen per cent of East Germans even had a phone. All they knew was that on Monday nights, outside St. Nicholas Church in downtown Leipzig, people gathered to voice their anger at the state. And the primary determinant of who showed up was "critical friends"—the more friends you had who were critical of the regime, the more likely you were to join the protest.

So one crucial fact about the four freshmen at the Greensboro lunch counter—David Richmond, Franklin McCain, Ezell Blair, and Joseph McNeil—was their relationship with one another. McNeil was a roommate of Blair's in A. & T.'s Scott Hall dormitory. Richmond roomed with McCain one floor up, and Blair, Richmond, and McCain had all gone to Dudley High School. The four would smuggle beer into the dorm and talk late into the night in Blair and McNeil's room. They would all have remembered the murder of Emmett Till in 1955, the Montgomery bus boycott that same year, and the showdown in Little Rock in 1957. It was McNeil who brought up the idea of a sit-in at Woolworth's. They'd discussed it for nearly a month. Then McNeil came into the dorm room and asked the others if they were ready. There was a pause, and McCain said, in a way that works only with people who talk late into the night with one another, "Are you guys chicken or not?" Ezell Blair worked up the courage the next day to ask for a cup of coffee because he was flanked by his roommate and two good friends from high school.

The kind of activism associated with social media isn't like this at all. The platforms of social media are built around weak ties. Twitter is a way of following (or being followed by) people you may never have met. Facebook is a tool for efficiently managing your acquaintances, for keeping up with the people you would not otherwise be able to stay in touch with. That's why you can have a thousand "friends" on Facebook, as you never could in real life.

This is in many ways a wonderful thing. There is strength in weak ties, as the sociologist Mark Granovetter has observed. Our acquaintances—not our friends—are our greatest source of new ideas and information. The Internet lets us exploit the power of these kinds of distant connections with marvelous efficiency. It's terrific at the diffusion of innovation, interdisciplinary collaboration, seamlessly matching up buyers and sellers, and the logistical functions of the dating world. But weak ties seldom lead to high-risk activism.

In a new book called *The Dragonfly Effect: Quick, Effective, and Powerful Ways to Use Social Media to Drive Social Change*, the business consultant Andy Smith and the Stanford Business School professor Jennifer Aaker tell the story of Sameer Bhatia, a young Silicon Valley entrepreneur who came down with acute myelogenous leukemia. It's a perfect illustration of social media's strengths. Bhatia needed a bone-marrow transplant, but he could not find a match among his relatives and friends. The odds were best with a donor of his ethnicity, and there were few South Asians in the national bone-marrow database. So Bhatia's business partner sent out an e-mail explaining Bhatia's plight to more than four hundred of their acquaintances, who forwarded the e-mail to their personal contacts; Facebook pages and YouTube videos were devoted to the Help Sameer campaign. Eventually, nearly twenty-five thousand new people were registered in the bone-marrow database, and Bhatia found a match.

But how did the campaign get so many people to sign up? By not asking too much of them. That's the only way you can get someone you don't really know to do something on your behalf. You can get thousands of people to sign up for a donor registry, because doing so is pretty easy. You have to send in a cheek swab and — in the highly unlikely event that your bone marrow is a good match for someone in need — spend a few hours at the hospital. Donating bone marrow isn't a trivial matter. But it doesn't involve financial or personal risk; it doesn't mean spending a summer being chased by armed men in pickup trucks. It doesn't require that you confront socially entrenched norms and practices. In fact, it's the kind of commitment that will bring only social acknowledgment and praise.

The evangelists of social media don't understand this distinction; they seem to believe that a Facebook friend is the same as a real friend and that signing up for a donor registry in Silicon Valley today is activism in the same sense as sitting at a segregated lunch counter in Greensboro in 1960. "Social networks are particularly effective at increasing motivation," Aaker and Smith write. But that's not true. Social networks are effective at increasing *participation* — by lessening the level of motivation that participation requires. The Facebook page of the Save Darfur Coalition has 1,282,339 members, who have donated an average of nine cents apiece. The next biggest Darfur charity on Facebook has 22,073 members, who have donated an average of thirty-five cents. Help Save Darfur has 2,797 members, who have given, on average, fifteen cents. A spokesperson for the Save Darfur Coalition told *Newsweek*, "We wouldn't necessarily gauge someone's value to the advocacy movement based on what they've given. This is a powerful mechanism to engage this critical population. They inform their community, attend events, volunteer. It's not something you can measure by looking at a ledger." In other words, Facebook activism succeeds not by motivating people to make a real sacrifice but by motivating them to do the things that people do when they are not motivated enough to make a real sacrifice. We are a long way from the lunch counters of Greensboro.

⁂

The students who joined the sit-ins across the South during the winter of 1960 described the movement as a "fever." But the civil-rights movement was more like a military campaign than like a contagion. In the late nineteen-fifties, there had   20 been sixteen sit-ins in various cities throughout the South, fifteen of which were formally organized by civil-rights organizations like the N.A.A.C.P. and CORE. Possible locations for activism were scouted. Plans were drawn up. Movement activists held training sessions and retreats for would-be protesters. The Greensboro Four were a product of this groundwork: all were members of the N.A.A.C.P. Youth Council. They had close ties with the head of the local N.A.A.C.P. chapter. They had been briefed on the earlier wave of sit-ins in Durham, and had been part of a series of movement meetings in activist churches. When the sit-in movement spread from Greensboro throughout the South, it did not spread indiscriminately. It spread to those cities which had preexisting "movement centers"—a core of dedicated and trained activists ready to turn the "fever" into action.

The civil-rights movement was high-risk activism. It was also, crucially, strategic activism: a challenge to the establishment mounted with precision and discipline. The N.A.A.C.P. was a centralized organization, run from New York according to highly formalized operating procedures. At the Southern Christian Leadership Conference, Martin Luther King, Jr., was the unquestioned authority. At the center of the movement was the black church, which had, as Aldon D. Morris points out in his superb 1984 study, *The Origins of the Civil Rights Movement*, a carefully demarcated division of labor, with various standing committees and disciplined groups. "Each group was task-oriented and coordinated its activities through authority structures," Morris writes. "Individuals were held accountable for their assigned duties, and important conflicts were resolved by the minister, who usually exercised ultimate authority over the congregation."

This is the second crucial distinction between traditional activism and its online variant: social media are not about this kind of hierarchical organization. Facebook and the like are tools for building *networks*, which are the opposite, in structure and character, of hierarchies. Unlike hierarchies, with their rules and procedures, networks aren't controlled by a single central authority. Decisions are made through consensus, and the ties that bind people to the group are loose.

This structure makes networks enormously resilient and adaptable in low-risk situations. Wikipedia is a perfect example. It doesn't have an editor, sitting in New York, who directs and corrects each entry. The effort of putting together each entry is self-organized. If every entry in Wikipedia were to be erased tomorrow, the content would swiftly be restored, because that's what happens when a network of thousands spontaneously devote their time to a task.

There are many things, though, that networks don't do well. Car companies sensibly use a network to organize their hundreds of suppliers, but not to design their cars. No one believes that the articulation of a coherent design philosophy is best handled by a sprawling, leaderless organizational system. Because networks don't have a centralized leadership structure and clear lines of authority, they have real difficulty reaching consensus and setting goals. They can't think strategically; they are chronically prone to conflict and error. How do you make difficult choices about tactics or strategy or philosophical direction when everyone has an equal say?

The Palestine Liberation Organization originated as a network, and the 25 international-relations scholars Mette Eilstrup-Sangiovanni and Calvert Jones argue in a recent essay in *International Security* that this is why it ran into such trouble as it grew: "Structural features typical of networks—the absence of central authority, the unchecked autonomy of rival groups, and the inability to arbitrate quarrels through formal mechanisms—made the P.L.O. excessively vulnerable to outside manipulation and internal strife."

In Germany in the nineteen-seventies, they go on, "the far more unified and successful left-wing terrorists tended to organize hierarchically, with professional management and clear divisions of labor. They were concentrated geographically in universities, where they could establish central leadership, trust, and camaraderie through regular, face-to-face meetings." They seldom betrayed their comrades in arms during police interrogations. Their counterparts on the right were organized as decentralized networks, and had no such discipline. These groups were regularly infiltrated, and members, once arrested, easily gave up their comrades. Similarly, Al Qaeda was most dangerous when it was a unified hierarchy. Now that it has dissipated into a network, it has proved far less effective.

The drawbacks of networks scarcely matter if the network isn't interested in systemic change—if it just wants to frighten or humiliate or make a splash—or if it doesn't need to think strategically. But if you're taking on a powerful and organized establishment you have to be a hierarchy. The Montgomery bus boycott required the participation of tens of thousands of people who depended on public transit to get to and from work each day. It lasted a *year*. In order to persuade those people to stay true to the cause, the boycott's organizers tasked each local black church with maintaining morale, and put together a free alternative private carpool service, with forty-eight dispatchers and forty-two pickup stations. Even the White Citizens Council, King later said, conceded that the carpool system moved with "military precision." By the time King came to Birmingham, for the climactic showdown with Police Commissioner Eugene (Bull) Connor, he had a budget of a million dollars, and a hundred full-time staff members on the ground, divided into operational units. The operation itself was divided into steadily escalating phases, mapped out in advance. Support was maintained through consecutive mass meetings rotating from church to church around the city.

Boycotts and sit-ins and nonviolent confrontations—which were the weapons of choice for the civil-rights movement—are high-risk strategies. They leave little room for conflict and error. The moment even one protester deviates from the script and responds to provocation, the moral legitimacy of the entire protest is compromised. Enthusiasts for social media would no doubt have us believe that King's task in Birmingham would have been made infinitely easier had he been able to communicate with his followers through Facebook, and contented himself with tweets from a Birmingham jail. But networks are messy: think of the ceaseless pattern of correction and revision, amendment and debate, that characterizes Wikipedia. If Martin Luther King, Jr., had tried to do a wiki-boycott in

Montgomery, he would have been steamrollered by the white power structure. And of what use would a digital communication tool be in a town where ninety-eight per cent of the black community could be reached every Sunday morning at church? The things that King needed in Birmingham—discipline and strategy—were things that online social media cannot provide.

The bible of the social-media movement is Clay Shirky's *Here Comes Everybody*. Shirky, who teaches at New York University, sets out to demonstrate the organizing power of the Internet, and he begins with the story of Evan, who worked on Wall Street, and his friend Ivanna, after she left her smart phone, an expensive Sidekick, on the back seat of a New York City taxicab. The telephone company transferred the data on Ivanna's lost phone to a new phone, whereupon she and Evan discovered that the Sidekick was now in the hands of a teen-ager from Queens, who was using it to take photographs of herself and her friends.

When Evan e-mailed the teen-ager, Sasha, asking for the phone back, she   30 replied that his "white ass" didn't deserve to have it back. Miffed, he set up a Web page with her picture and a description of what had happened. He forwarded the link to his friends, and they forwarded it to their friends. Someone found the MySpace page of Sasha's boyfriend, and a link to it found its way onto the site. Someone found her address online and took a video of her home while driving by; Evan posted the video on the site. The story was picked up by the news filter Digg. Evan was now up to ten e-mails a minute. He created a bulletin board for his readers to share their stories, but it crashed under the weight of responses. Evan and Ivanna went to the police, but the police filed the report under "lost," rather than "stolen," which essentially closed the case. "By this point millions of readers were watching," Shirky writes, "and dozens of mainstream news outlets had covered the story." Bowing to the pressure, the N.Y.P.D. reclassified the item as "stolen." Sasha was arrested, and Evan got his friend's Sidekick back.

Shirky's argument is that this is the kind of thing that could never have happened in the pre-Internet age—and he's right. Evan could never have tracked down Sasha. The story of the Sidekick would never have been publicized. An army of people could never have been assembled to wage this fight. The police wouldn't have bowed to the pressure of a lone person who had misplaced something as trivial as a cell phone. The story, to Shirky, illustrates "the ease and speed with which a group can be mobilized for the right kind of cause" in the Internet age.

Shirky considers this model of activism an upgrade. But it is simply a form of organizing which favors the weak-tie connections that give us access to information over the strong-tie connections that help us persevere in the face of danger. It shifts our energies from organizations that promote strategic and disciplined activity and toward those which promote resilience and adaptability. It makes it easier for activists to express themselves, and harder for that expression to have any impact. The instruments of social media are well suited to making the existing social order more efficient. They are not a natural enemy of the status quo. If you are of the opinion that all the world needs is a little buffing around the edges, this should not trouble you. But if you think that there are still lunch counters out there that need integrating, it ought to give you pause.

Shirky ends his story of the Sidekick by asking, portentously, "What happens next?"—no doubt imagining future waves of digital protesters. But he has already answered the question. What happens next is more of the same. A networked, weak-tie world is good at things like helping Wall Streeters get phones back from teen-age girls. *Viva la revolución.*

Exploring the Text

1. Most of Malcolm Gladwell's readers are familiar with the lunch counter event at Woolworth's in Greensboro, North Carolina, that catalyzed the civil rights movement. Why, then, does he begin by retelling it and providing such detail in the opening section? How does this serve as a foundation for the argument he develops? Consider both what he tells and *how* he tells it.

2. What does he mean when he writes, "Where activists were once defined by their causes, they are now defined by their tools" (para. 7)? Do you agree or disagree with this idea? Explain why.

3. What is the key point Gladwell makes in the paragraph beginning, "Some of this grandiosity is to be expected" (para. 9)? How does he connect his statement "Innovators tend to be solipsists" with the assertion that ends the paragraph, that "we seem to have forgotten what activism is"?

4. How does Gladwell define "high-risk activism" (paras. 11–12)? Why does he believe that activism based on today's social media cannot qualify as "high risk"? Consider the contrast between "weak ties" and "strong ties" as part of your definition.

5. What is the purpose of the example of Sameer Bhatia, who found a bone marrow donor through social networking (para. 17)? Do you find it persuasive, or is it too exceptional?

6. What is the distinction between increasing motivation and increasing participation that Gladwell makes (para. 19)? Why is this distinction important to his argument?

7. Throughout this essay, Gladwell relies heavily on expert testimony. He cites scholars and researchers as well as business analysts and State Department officials and security advisors. Choose two examples, and discuss how Gladwell uses one to support his argument and the other to examine a counterargument.

8. In order to make his argument against the belief that the "new tools of social media have reinvented social activism" (para. 7), Gladwell must delineate precisely the central qualities of social activism. What are they? Refer to specific passages in the text to support your analysis.

9. Gladwell does not entirely discount the power of social media. What benefits or positive impacts does he grant to social media? Do you find his term "digital

evangelism" (para. 8) a critical description, a particularly apt one, or simply a colorful one? Why?

10. Gladwell uses many examples from fairly recent history, such as the fall of the Berlin Wall and protests in Moldova and Tehran, yet he repeatedly returns to the civil rights movement of the 1960s. Why? Does doing so strengthen his argument by adding coherence and depth, or weaken it by over-relying on a single example? Explain your viewpoint.

11. Compare the opening example at the lunch counter with that of the closing one about Evan and Ivanna in terms of such rhetorical strategies as narrative pacing, sensory detail, setting, dialogue, and point of view. Are they more similar or different? In what ways?

12. At key junctures in the essay, Gladwell makes sharp personal comments. In fact, his ending "*Viva la revolución*" could be read as downright sarcastic. What others do you notice? Do these editorial comments add vitality and voice to the essay, or do they undercut the argument with a mocking tone? Explain your response.

13. Choose one of the following assertions that Gladwell makes, and challenge it by referring to an example of social activism in the United States or abroad during the past five years:
   • "Our acquaintances—not our friends—are our greatest source of new ideas and information" (para. 16).
   • Networks "can't think strategically; they are chronically prone to conflict and error" (para. 24).
   • "The things that King needed in Birmingham—discipline and strategy—were things that online social media cannot provide" (para. 28).
   • "The instruments of social media are well suited to making the existing social order more efficient. They are not a natural enemy of the status quo" (para. 32).

Child of the Americas

Aurora Levins Morales

Daughter of a Puerto Rican mother and a Jewish father, Aurora Levins Morales (b. 1954) lived in Puerto Rico until she was thirteen, when her family moved to Chicago. She received her undergraduate degree from Franconia University in New Hampshire and her MA and PhD from the Union Institute in Ohio. She co-authored with her mother *Getting Home Alive* (1986), a collection of short stories, essays, and poetry. In 1999, she published *Medicine Stories: History, Culture, and the Politics of Integrity*, followed by *Remedios: Stories of Earth and Iron from the History of Puertorriqueñas* in 2001. An activist and writer, Morales currently divides her time between the San Francisco Bay Area and Minneapolis. In the poem that follows, she celebrates her mixed heritage.

I am a child of the Americas,
a light-skinned mestiza of the Caribbean,
a child of many diaspora, born into this continent at a crossroads.

I am a U.S. Puerto Rican Jew,
a product of the ghettos of New York I have never known.   5
An immigrant and the daughter and granddaughter of immigrants.
I speak English with passion: it's the tongue of my consciousness,
a flashing knife blade of crystal, my tool, my craft.

I am Caribeña, island grown. Spanish is in my flesh,
ripples from my tongue, lodges in my hips: 10
the language of garlic and mangoes,
the singing in my poetry, the flying gestures of my hands.
I am of Latinoamerica, rooted in the history of my continent:
I speak from that body.

I am not africa. Africa is in me, but I cannot return.   15
I am not taína. Taíno is in me, but there is no way back.
I am not european. Europe lives in me, but I have no home there.

I am new. History made me. My first language was spanglish.
I was born at the crossroads
and I am whole.   20

Exploring the Text

1. How does the speaker describe herself? What characteristics does she emphasize?
2. Why does Aurora Levins Morales introduce those characteristics in the order that she does? That is, why does she choose not to open with her Jewish or African heritage, for instance?
3. What examples of parallel structure do you find? What is their effect?
4. How do you interpret the line "Europe lives in me, but I have no home there" (l. 17)?
5. What is the tone of the poem? Is the speaker defiant, hopeful, angry, confused, ambivalent, proud? Cite specific words and phrases to support your response.
6. Which of the following descriptions of the United States do you think the speaker would prefer: melting pot, salad bowl, mosaic? Why? To which community or communities would the speaker say she belongs?
7. What is the argument that Morales makes? Try explaining it in terms of induction and deduction.

Freedom from Want

Norman Rockwell

Norman Rockwell (1894 –1978) was a popular American painter and illustrator best known for his depictions of everyday life and positive American values. His first cover for the *Saturday Evening Post* appeared in 1916, and over three hundred followed during the next forty-seven years. In the early 1960s, he began working for *Look* magazine, where he turned to more political concerns such as civil rights and space exploration. In 1977, Rockwell received the nation's highest civilian honor, the Presidential Medal. The 1943 painting shown on the following page appeared in the *Saturday Evening Post* as part of Rockwell's Four Freedoms series. These illustrations depict the "four essential human freedoms" delineated in President Franklin Delano Roosevelt's Message to Congress on January 6, 1941: freedom of speech and expression, freedom of every person to worship God in his own way, freedom from want, and freedom from fear. The Thanksgiving scene shows Rockwell's interpretation of freedom from want, which, in Roosevelt's words, "means economic understandings which will secure to every nation a healthy peacetime life for its inhabitants—everywhere in the world." This painting appeared in the magazine with the headline, "Ours . . . to fight for."

Exploring the Text

1. What is the perspective of the viewer? Where are the participants in the painting looking? As a viewer, do you feel you are an observer or a participant in the community depicted in the painting? Why?

2. How does the painting embody the descriptors Roosevelt used—"healthy" and "peacetime"?

3. In the 1940s, who would likely have felt included in the world shown in this painting? Who might have felt excluded? How does the composition of the image contribute to your thinking on this issue?

4. Was Rockwell successful in depicting Roosevelt's vision of "economic understandings which will secure to every nation a healthy peacetime life for its inhabitants— everywhere in the world"? Explain.

Freedom from Want (1943, oil on canvas, 45.75" x 35.5"). (See insert for color version.)

The Last Thanksgiving

Roz Chast

Roz Chast (b. 1954) grew up in Brooklyn, the child of two schoolteachers, and received a BFA from the Rhode Island School of Design, where she studied graphic design and painting. After she graduated, as she says on her Web site, she "reverted to type and began drawing cartoons once again." More than a thousand of her cartoons have been published in the *New Yorker* magazine since 1978. A collection of twenty-five years of her work was published in *Theories of Everything* (2006). She collaborated with comedian and novelist Steve Martin on the children's book *The Alphabet from A to Y with a Bonus Letter Z!* (2007); she has also written the children's book *Too Busy Marco* (2010) and a collection of cartoons entitled *What I Hate: From A – Z* (2011). She has won numerous awards and received an Honorary Doctorate of Fine Arts from Pratt Institute and the Art Institute of Boston. This cartoon appeared as the cover of the *New Yorker* in 2010.

Exploring the Text

1. Thanksgiving is a holiday that inspires both delight and dread: many see it as their favorite since it has no religious affiliation but is simply a celebration of bounty and fellowship; others recall or anticipate gatherings that abound with conflict and misunderstanding. On the surface, it seems that Roz Chast focuses on only one of these views, but in fact a case can be made that she captures both. What specifics can you cite to make that case?
2. Clearly, Chast's imaginary dinner guests are quite different from those in Rockwell's painting. Yet in what ways does Chast's depiction of Thanksgiving reflect the same American values that Rockwell's does?
3. What do you think is Chast's purpose in this cartoon? Is it simply to amuse? To ridicule? To provoke reflection? Explain.
4. What is Chast's argument in this cartoon? Is Chast making a point about Thanksgiving in general or the nature of community in the twenty-first century in particular? Or both? Cite specific details in the cartoon to support your response.

The Black Experience Is Everywhere

Nissan Motor Company

The following advertisement from the Nissan Motor Company appeared in *Vibe* magazine in March 2007.

(See insert for color version.)

Exploring the Text

1. This ad claims that "the black experience is everywhere." Do you think that that is true, or is that a fiction concocted for this ad? Do you think that the scene in this ad is believable? Consider the meaning of the barbershop in African American culture. Explain.

2. The ultimate purpose of any advertisement is to sell more products, but modern advertising often is more sly than that. Imagine that you are the creator of this ad, but it has not yet been approved by your boss. Write up a brief explanation of the rationale behind this ad and its benefit to the company. Be sure to answer the question: how will this sell more cars?

3. Do you find this advertisement flattering, offensive, inspiring, exploitive, or simply provocative? Why? Notice that the company motto is "SHIFT_respect." How does that affect your reading?

4. Using the Toulmin method described in Chapter 3, examine the argument put forth in this ad.

5. What does this ad have to say about the meaning of community in the twenty-first century?

Conversation
The Individual's Responsibility to the Community

Each of the following texts presents a view of the individual's responsibility to the community.

Sources

1. **Andrew Carnegie,** from *The Gospel of Wealth*
2. **Bertrand Russell,** *The Happy Life*
3. **Garrett Hardin,** from *Lifeboat Ethics*
4. **Peter Singer,** from *The Singer Solution to World Poverty*
5. **Zapiro (Jonathan Shapiro),** *World Economic Forum* (cartoon)
6. *Christian Science Monitor* **Editorial Board,** *Warren Buffett, Bill Gates, and the Billionaire Challenge*
7. *Der Spiegel* **Online,** *Negative Reaction to Charity Campaign*

After using the questions to discuss individual selections, synthesize the pieces through one of the suggested assignments on page 379.

1. from *The Gospel of Wealth*

ANDREW CARNEGIE

Following is a selection from *The Gospel of Wealth*, an extended essay written by American industrialist Andrew Carnegie in 1889. It outlines his belief that the rich have a responsibility to use their wealth to create a better society.

Those who would administer wisely must, indeed, be wise, for one of the serious obstacles to the improvement of our race is indiscriminate charity. It were better for mankind that the millions of the rich were thrown into the sea than so spent as to encourage the slothful, the drunken, the unworthy. Of every thousand dollars spent in so-called charity to-day, it is probable that $950 is unwisely spent; so spent, indeed, as to produce the very evils which it proposes to mitigate or cure. A well-known writer of philosophic books admitted the other day that he had given a quarter of a dollar to a man who approached him as he was coming to visit the house of his friend. He knew nothing of the habits of this beggar; knew not the use that would be made of this money, although he had every reason to suspect that it would be spent improperly. This man professed to be a disciple of Herbert Spencer;[1] yet the quarter-dollar given that night will probably work more injury than all the money which its thoughtless donor will ever be able to give in true charity will do good. He only gratified his own feelings, saved himself from annoyance,—and this was probably one of the most selfish and very worst actions of his life, for in all respects he is most worthy.

In bestowing charity, the main consideration should be to help those who will help themselves; to provide part of the means by which those who desire to improve may do so; to give those who desire to rise the aids by which they may rise; to assist, but rarely or never to do all. Neither the individual nor the race is improved by alms-giving. Those worthy of assistance, except in rare cases, seldom require assistance. The really valuable men of the race never do, except in cases of accident or sudden change. Every one has, of course, cases of individuals brought to his own knowledge where temporary assistance can do genuine good, and these he will not overlook. But the amount which can be wisely given by the individual for individuals is necessarily limited by his lack of knowledge of the circumstances connected with each. He is the only true reformer who is as careful and as anxious not to aid the unworthy as he is to aid the worthy, and, perhaps, even more so, for in alms-giving more injury is probably done by rewarding vice than by relieving virtue.

The rich man is thus almost restricted to following the examples of Peter Cooper, Enoch Pratt of Baltimore, Mr. Pratt of Brooklyn, Senator Stanford, and others, who know that the best means of benefiting the community is to place within its reach the ladders upon which the aspiring can rise—parks, and means of recreation, by which men are helped in body and mind; works of art, certain to give pleasure and improve the public taste; and public institutions of various kinds, which will improve the general condition of the people;—in this manner returning their surplus wealth to the mass of their fellows in the forms best calculated to do them lasting good.

Thus is the problem of Rich and Poor to be solved. The laws of accumulation will be left free; the laws of distribution free. Individualism will continue, but the millionaire will be but a trustee for the poor; intrusted for a season with a great part of the increased wealth of the community, but administering it for the community far better than it could or would have done for itself. The best minds will thus have reached a stage in the development of the race in which it is clearly seen that there is no mode of disposing of surplus wealth creditable to thoughtful and

---

[1]British philosopher and scientist Herbert Spencer (1820–1903) was an early proponent of evolution and coined the term "survival of the fittest." He is notorious for the concept of social Darwinism, which tried to apply the notion of "survival of the fittest" to human civilization. The logical conclusion was that the poor were less "fit" for survival, so helping them was counterproductive for society as a whole. Social Darwinism was also used to justify racism, eugenics, and Nazism.—Eds.

earnest men into whose hands it flows save by using it year by year for the general good. This day already dawns. Men may die without incurring the pity of their fellows, still sharers in great business enterprises from which their capital cannot be or has not been withdrawn, and is left chiefly at death for public uses, yet the man who dies leaving behind him millions of available wealth, which was his to administer during life, will pass away "unwept, unhonored, and unsung," no matter to what uses he leaves the dross which he cannot take with him. Of such as these public verdict will then be: "The man who dies thus rich dies disgraced."

Such, in my opinion, is the true Gospel concerning Wealth, obedience to which is destined some day to solve the problem of the Rich and the Poor, and to bring "Peace on earth, among men Good-Will." 5

Questions

1. If Andrew Carnegie believes that "in alms-giving more injury is probably done by rewarding vice than by relieving virtue" (para. 2), then what is his recommendation for "the best means of benefiting the community" (para. 3)? Do you agree or disagree with his analysis?

2. Carnegie claims that the best way to improve the situation of the poor "is to place within its reach the ladders upon which the aspiring can rise." The "ladders" he mentions are "parks, and means of recreation, by which men are helped in body and mind" (para. 3). Do you think that this is an effective plan? Explain. What assumption(s) about the relationship between rich and poor does this viewpoint suggest?

3. When Carnegie claims that "the millionaire will be but a trustee for the poor" (para. 4), what assumption about the relationship between the rich and the poor is he making?

4. What overall responsibility does wealth confer, according to Carnegie's assertion that "the man who dies leaving behind him millions of available wealth, which was his to administer during life, will pass away 'unwept, unhonored, and unsung,' no matter to what uses he leaves the dross which he cannot take with him" (para. 4)?

5. What attitude toward money and wealth is suggested by Carnegie's title, "The Gospel of Wealth"? To what extent do you think that his philosophy is consistent with the spirit of the title?

2. *The Happy Life*

Bertrand Russell

In the following selection from his book *The Conquest of Happiness* (1930), British philosopher Bertrand Russell reflects on the meaning of happiness.

The happy life is to an extraordinary extent the same as the good life. Professional moralists have made too much of self-denial, and in so doing have put the emphasis in the wrong place. Conscious self-denial leaves a man self-absorbed and vividly aware of what he has sacrificed; in consequence it fails often of its immediate object and almost always of its ultimate purpose. What is needed is not self-denial, but that kind of direction of interest outward which will lead spontaneously and naturally to the same acts that a person absorbed in the pursuit of his own virtue could only perform by means of conscious self-denial. I have written in this book [*The Conquest of Happiness*] as a hedonist, that is to say, as one who regards happiness as the good, but the acts to be recommended from the point of view of the hedonist are on the whole the same as those to be recommended by the sane moralist. The moralist, however, is too apt, though this is not, of course, universally true, to stress the act rather than the state of mind. The effects of an act upon the agent will be widely different according to his state of mind at the moment. If you see a child drowning and save it as the result of a direct impulse to bring help, you will emerge none the worse morally. If, on the other hand, you say to yourself, "It is the part of virtue to succor the helpless, and I wish to be a virtuous man, therefore I must save this child," you will be an even worse man afterwards than you were before. What applies in this extreme case, applies in many other instances that are less obvious.

There is another difference, somewhat more subtle, between the attitude towards life that I have been recommending and that which is recommended by the traditional moralists. The traditional moralist, for example, will say that love should be unselfish. In a certain sense he is right, that is to say, it should not be selfish beyond a point, but it should undoubtedly be of such a nature that one's own happiness is bound up in its success. If a man were to invite a lady to marry him on the ground that he ardently desired her happiness and at the same time considered that she would afford ideal opportunities of self-abnegation, I think it may be doubted whether she would be altogether pleased. Undoubtedly we should desire the happiness of those whom we love, but not as an alternative to our own. In fact, the whole antithesis between self and the rest of the world, which is implied in the doctrine of self-denial, disappears as soon as we have any genuine interest in persons or things outside ourselves. Through such interests a man comes to feel himself part of the stream of life, not a hard separate entity like a billiard ball, which can have no relation with other such entities except that of collision. All unhappiness depends upon some kind of disintegration or lack of integration; there is disintegration within the self through lack of coordination between the conscious and the unconscious mind; there is lack of integration between the self and society, where the two are not knit together by the force of objective interests and affections. The happy man is the man who does not suffer from either of these failures of unity, whose personality is neither divided against itself nor pitted against the world. Such a man feels himself a citizen of the universe; enjoying freely the spectacle that it offers and the joys that it affords, untroubled by the thought of death because he feels himself not really separate from those who will come after him. It is in such profound instinctive union with the stream of life that the greatest joy is to be found.

Questions

1. In the opening paragraph, Bertrand Russell says, "The happy life is to an extraordinary extent the same as the good life." What does he mean? Is this statement paradoxical?
2. According to Russell, what would the traditional moralist say about the belief that "love should be unselfish" (para. 2)?
3. What does Russell mean by his claim that "the whole antithesis between self and the rest of the world . . . disappears as soon as we have any genuine interest in persons or things outside ourselves" (para. 2)?
4. In the second paragraph, how does Russell construct his argument?
5. Do you find Russell's simile of the billiard ball effective or ineffective? Explain why.
6. What does Russell mean by "a citizen of the universe" (para. 2)?

3. from *Lifeboat Ethics*

GARRETT HARDIN

In the following selection from his 1974 *Psychology Today* article, human ecologist Garrett Hardin presents a classic argument on the implications of population growth.

Environmentalists use the metaphor of the earth as a "spaceship" in trying to persuade countries, industries, and people to stop wasting and polluting our natural resources. Since we all share life on this planet, they argue, no single person or institution has the right to destroy, waste, or use more than a fair share of its resources.

But does everyone on earth have an equal right to an equal share of its resources? The spaceship metaphor can be dangerous when used by misguided idealists to justify suicidal policies for sharing our resources through uncontrolled immigration and foreign aid. In their enthusiastic but unrealistic generosity, they confuse the ethics of a spaceship with those of a lifeboat.

A true spaceship would have to be under the control of a captain, since no ship could possibly survive if its course were determined by committee. Spaceship Earth certainly has no captain; the United Nations is merely a toothless tiger, with little power to enforce any policy upon its bickering members.

If we divide the world crudely into rich nations and poor nations, two thirds of them are desperately poor, and only one third comparatively rich, with the United States the wealthiest of all. Metaphorically each rich nation can be seen as a lifeboat full of comparatively rich people. In the ocean outside each lifeboat swim the poor of the world, who would like to get in, or at least to share some of the wealth. What should the lifeboat passengers do?

First, we must recognize the limited capacity of any lifeboat. For example, a 5 nation's land has a limited capacity to support a population and as the current [1974] energy crisis has shown us, in some ways we have already exceeded the carrying capacity of our land.

Adrift in a Moral Sea

So here we sit, say 50 people in our lifeboat. To be generous, let us assume it has room for 10 more, making a total capacity of 60. Suppose the 50 of us in the lifeboat see 100 others swimming in the water outside, begging for admission to our boat or for handouts. We have several options: we may be tempted to try to live by the Christian ideal of being "our brother's keeper," or by the Marxist ideal of "to each according to his needs." Since the needs of all in the water are the same, and since they can all be seen as "our brothers," we could take them all into our boat, making a total of 150 in a boat designed for 60. The boat swamps, everyone drowns. Complete justice, complete catastrophe.

Since the boat has an unused excess capacity of 10 more passengers, we could admit just 10 more to it. But which 10 do we let in? How do we choose? Do we pick the best 10, "first come, first served"? And what do we say to the 90 we exclude? If we do let an extra 10 into our lifeboat, we will have lost our "safety factor," an engineering principle of critical importance. For example, if we don't leave room for excess capacity as a safety factor in our country's agriculture, a new plant disease or a bad change in the weather could have disastrous consequences.

Suppose we decide to preserve our small safety factor and admit no more to the lifeboat. Our survival is then possible although we shall have to be constantly on guard against boarding parties.

While this last solution clearly offers the only means of our survival, it is morally abhorrent to many people. Some say they feel guilty about their good luck. My reply is simple: "Get out and yield your place to others." This may solve the problem of the guilt-ridden person's conscience, but it does not change the ethics of the lifeboat. The needy person to whom the guilt-ridden person yields his place will not himself feel guilty about his good luck. If he did, he would not climb aboard. The net result of conscience-stricken people giving up their unjustly held seats is the elimination of that sort of conscience from the lifeboat.

This is the basic metaphor within which we must work out our solutions. Let us 10 now enrich the image, step by step, with substantive additions from the real world, a world that must solve real and pressing problems of overpopulation and hunger.

The harsh ethics of the lifeboat become even harsher when we consider the reproductive differences between the rich nations and the poor nations. The people inside the lifeboats are doubling in numbers every 87 years; those swimming around outside are doubling, on the average, every 35 years, more than twice as fast as the rich. And since the world's resources are dwindling, the difference in prosperity between the rich and the poor can only increase.

As of 1973, the U.S. had a population of 210 million people, who were increasing by 0.8 percent per year. Outside our lifeboat, let us imagine another 210 million people (say the combined populations of Colombia, Ecuador, Venezuela, Morocco, Pakistan, Thailand and the Philippines) who are increasing at a rate of 3.3 percent per year. Put differently, the doubling time for this aggregate population is 21 years, compared to 87 years for the U.S.

The harsh ethics of the lifeboat become harsher when we consider the reproductive differences between rich and poor.

Multiplying the Rich and the Poor

Now suppose the U.S. agreed to pool its resources with those seven countries, with everyone receiving an equal share. Initially the ratio of Americans to non-Americans in this model would be one-to-one. But consider what the ratio would be after 87 years, by which time the Americans would have doubled to a population of 420 million. By then, doubling every 21 years, the other group would have swollen to 354 billion. Each American would have to share the available resources with more than eight people.

But, one could argue, this discussion assumes that current population trends will continue, and they may not. Quite so. Most likely the rate of population increase will decline much faster in the U.S. than it will in the other countries, and there does not seem to be much we can do about it. In sharing with "each according to his needs," we must recognize that needs are determined by population size, which is determined by the rate of reproduction, which at present is regarded as a sovereign right of every nation, poor or not. This being so, the philanthropic load created by the sharing ethic of the spaceship can only increase. 15

The Tragedy of the Commons

The fundamental error of spaceship ethics, and the sharing it requires, is that it leads to what I call "the tragedy of the commons." Under a system of private property, the men who own property recognize their responsibility to care for it, for if they don't they will eventually suffer. A farmer, for instance, will allow no more cattle in a pasture than its carrying capacity justifies. If he overloads it, erosion sets in, weeds take over, and he loses the use of the pasture.

If a pasture becomes a commons open to all, the right of each to use it may not be matched by a corresponding responsibility to protect it. Asking everyone to use it with discretion will hardly do, for the considerate herdsman who refrains from overloading the commons suffers more than a selfish one who says his needs are greater. If everyone would restrain himself, all would be well; but it takes only one less than everyone to ruin a system of voluntary restraint. In a crowded world of less than perfect human beings, mutual ruin is inevitable if there are no controls. This is the tragedy of the commons.

One of the major tasks of education today should be the creation of such an acute awareness of the dangers of the commons that people will recognize its many varieties. For example, the air and water have become polluted because they are treated as commons. Further growth in the population or per-capita conversion of natural resources into pollutants will only make the problem worse. The same holds true for the fish of the oceans. Fishing fleets have nearly disappeared in many parts of the world, technological improvements in the art of fishing are hastening the day of complete ruin. Only the replacement of the system of the commons with a responsible system of control will save the land, air, water and oceanic fisheries.

Pure Justice vs. Reality

Clearly, the concept of pure justice produces an infinite regression to absurdity. Centuries ago, wise men invented statutes of limitations to justify the rejection of such pure justice, in the interest of preventing continual disorder. The law zealously defends property rights, but only relatively recent property rights. Drawing a line after an arbitrary time has elapsed may be unjust, but the alternatives are worse.

We are all the descendants of thieves, and the world's resources are inequitably distributed. But we must begin the journey to tomorrow from the point where we are today. We cannot remake the past. We cannot safely divide the wealth equitably among all peoples so long as people reproduce at different rates. To do so would guarantee that our grandchildren and everyone else's grandchildren would have only a ruined world to inhabit.

To be generous with one's own possessions is quite different from being generous with those of posterity. We should call this point to the attention of those who from a commendable love of justice and equality, would institute a system of the commons, either in the form of a world food bank, or of unrestricted immigration. We must convince them if we wish to save at least some parts of the world from environmental ruin.

Without a true world government to control reproduction and the use of available resources, the sharing ethic of the spaceship is impossible. For the foreseeable future, our survival demands that we govern our actions by the ethics of a lifeboat, harsh though they may be. Posterity will be satisfied with nothing less.

Questions

1. What are the implications of the two central metaphors—the spaceship and the lifeboat—that Garrett Hardin uses for his argument? Is contrasting these two an effective rhetorical strategy? Discuss your answer.

2. Hardin uses population growth statistics to make projections to support his argument. Have these projections proven true? (You will need to do some research.)
3. What does Hardin mean by "the tragedy of the commons" (para. 16)?
4. Hardin relies mainly on the logic of his arguments, but he also uses strong connotative language. How do expressions such as "toothless tiger" (para. 3) and "conscience-stricken people" (para. 9) affect the reader?
5. What does Hardin mean by "pure justice" (para. 19)? Do you agree with his use of the phrase? Why or why not?
6. Hardin's essay was published in *Psychology Today* in 1974. To what extent do you think his basic argument can apply to today's world?

4. from *The Singer Solution to World Poverty*

Peter Singer

In the following selection first published in the *New York Times Magazine* in 1999, bioethicist Peter Singer argues for the individual's responsibility to the world community.

In the Brazilian film *Central Station*, Dora is a retired schoolteacher who makes ends meet by sitting at the station writing letters for illiterate people. Suddenly she has an opportunity to pocket $1,000. All she has to do is persuade a homeless 9-year-old boy to follow her to an address she has been given. (She is told he will be adopted by wealthy foreigners.) She delivers the boy, gets the money, spends some of it on a television set and settles down to enjoy her new acquisition. Her neighbor spoils the fun, however, by telling her that the boy was too old to be adopted—he will be killed and his organs sold for transplantation. Perhaps Dora knew this all along, but after her neighbor's plain speaking, she spends a troubled night. In the morning Dora resolves to take the boy back.

Suppose Dora had told her neighbor that it is a tough world, other people have nice new TV's too, and if selling the kid is the only way she can get one, well, he was only a street kid. She would then have become, in the eyes of the audience, a monster. She redeems herself only by being prepared to bear considerable risks to save the boy.

At the end of the movie, in cinemas in the affluent nations of the world, people who would have been quick to condemn Dora if she had not rescued the boy go home to places far more comfortable than her apartment. In fact, the average family in the United States spends almost one-third of its income on things that are no more necessary to them than Dora's new TV was to her. Going out to nice restaurants, buying new clothes because the old ones are no longer stylish, vacationing at beach resorts—so much of our income is spent on things not essential to the preservation of our lives and health. Donated to one of a number of charitable agencies, that money could mean the difference between life and death for children in need.

All of which raises a question: In the end, what is the ethical distinction between a Brazilian who sells a homeless child to organ peddlers and an American who already has a TV and upgrades to a better one—knowing that the money could be donated to an organization that would use it to save the lives of kids in need?

Of course, there are several differences between the two situations that could support different moral judgments about them. For one thing, to be able to consign a child to death when he is standing right in front of you takes a chilling kind of heartlessness; it is much easier to ignore an appeal for money to help children you will never meet. Yet for a utilitarian philosopher like myself—that is, one who judges whether acts are right or wrong by their consequences—if the upshot of the American's failure to donate the money is that one more kid dies on the streets of a Brazilian city, then it is, in some sense, just as bad as selling the kid to the organ peddlers. But one doesn't need to embrace my utilitarian ethic to see that, at the very least, there is a troubling incongruity in being so quick to condemn Dora for taking the child to the organ peddlers while, at the same time, not regarding the American consumer's behavior as raising a serious moral issue.

In his 1996 book, *Living High and Letting Die*, the New York University philosopher Peter Unger presented an ingenious series of imaginary examples designed to probe our intuitions about whether it is wrong to live well without giving substantial amounts of money to help people who are hungry, malnourished or dying from easily treatable illnesses like diarrhea. Here's my paraphrase of one of these examples:

Bob is close to retirement. He has invested most of his savings in a very rare and valuable old car, a Bugatti, which he has not been able to insure. The Bugatti is his pride and joy. In addition to the pleasure he gets from driving and caring for his car, Bob knows that its rising market value means that he will always be able to sell it and live comfortably after retirement. One day when Bob is out for a drive, he parks the Bugatti near the end of a railway siding and goes for a walk up the track. As he does so, he sees that a runaway train, with no one aboard, is running down the railway track. Looking farther down the track, he sees the small figure of a child very likely to be killed by the runaway train. He can't stop the train and the child is too far away to warn of the danger, but he can throw a switch that will divert the train down the siding where his Bugatti is parked. Then nobody will be killed—but the train will destroy his Bugatti. Thinking of his joy in owning the car and the financial security it represents, Bob decides not to throw the switch. The child is killed. For many years to come, Bob enjoys owning his Bugatti and the financial security it represents.

Bob's conduct, most of us will immediately respond, was gravely wrong. Unger agrees. But then he reminds us that we, too, have opportunities to save the lives of children. We can give to organizations like UNICEF or Oxfam America. How much would we have to give one of these organizations to have a high probability of saving the life of a child threatened by easily preventable diseases? (I do not believe that children are more worth saving than adults, but since no one can argue that children have brought their poverty on themselves, focusing on them simplifies the issues.) Unger called up some experts and used the information they provided to offer some plausible estimates that include the cost of raising money, administrative expenses and the cost of delivering aid where it is most needed. By his calculation, $200 in donations would help a sickly 2-year-old transform into a healthy 6-year-old—offering safe passage through childhood's most dangerous years. To show how practical philosophical argument can be, Unger even tells his readers that they can easily donate funds by using their credit card and calling one of these toll-free numbers: (800) 367-5437 for Unicef; (800) 693-2687 for Oxfam America.

Now you, too, have the information you need to save a child's life. How should you judge yourself if you don't do it? Think again about Bob and his Bugatti. Unlike Dora, Bob did not have to look into the eyes of the child he was sacrificing for his own material comfort. The child was a complete stranger to him and too far away to relate to in an intimate, personal way. Unlike Dora, too, he did not mislead the child or initiate the chain of events imperiling him. In all these respects, Bob's situation resembles that of people able but unwilling to donate to overseas aid and differs from Dora's situation.

If you still think that it was very wrong of Bob not to throw the switch that would have diverted the train and saved the child's life, then it is hard to see how you could deny that it is also very wrong not to send money to one of the organizations listed above. Unless, that is, there is some morally important difference between the two situations that I have overlooked. 10

Is it the practical uncertainties about whether aid will really reach the people who need it? Nobody who knows the world of overseas aid can doubt that such uncertainties exist. But Unger's figure of $200 to save a child's life was reached after he had made conservative assumptions about the proportion of the money donated that will actually reach its target.

One genuine difference between Bob and those who can afford to donate to overseas aid organizations but don't is that only Bob can save the child on the tracks, whereas there are hundreds of millions of people who can give $200 to overseas aid organizations. The problem is that most of them aren't doing it. Does this mean that it is all right for you not to do it?

Suppose that there were more owners of priceless vintage cars—Carol, Dave, Emma, Fred and so on, down to Ziggy—all in exactly the same situation as Bob, with their own siding and their own switch, all sacrificing the child in order to preserve their own cherished car. Would that make it all right for Bob to do the same? To answer this question affirmatively is to endorse follow-the-crowd ethics—the kind of ethics that led many Germans to look away when the Nazi atrocities were being committed. We do not excuse them because others were behaving no better.

We seem to lack a sound basis for drawing a clear moral line between Bob's situation and that of any reader of this article with $200 to spare who does not donate it to an overseas aid agency. These readers seem to be acting at least as badly as Bob was acting when he chose to let the runaway train hurtle toward the unsuspecting child. In the light of this conclusion, I trust that many readers will reach for the phone and donate that $200. Perhaps you should do it before reading further.

Now that you have distinguished yourself morally from people who put their vintage cars ahead of a child's life, how about treating yourself and your partner to dinner at your favorite restaurant? But wait. The money you will spend at the restaurant could also help save the lives of children overseas! True, you weren't planning to blow $200 tonight, but if you were to give up dining out just for one month, you would easily save that amount. And what is one month's dining out, compared to a child's life? There's the rub. Since there are a lot of desperately needy children in the world, there will always be another child whose life you could save for another $200. Are you therefore obliged to keep giving until you have nothing left? At what point can you stop?

Hypothetical examples can easily become farcical. Consider Bob. How far past losing the Bugatti should he go? Imagine that Bob had got his foot stuck in the track of the siding, and if he diverted the train, then before it rammed the car it would also amputate his big toe. Should he still throw the switch? What if it would amputate his foot? His entire leg?

As absurd as the Bugatti scenario gets when pushed to extremes, the point it raises is a serious one: only when the sacrifices become very significant indeed would most people be prepared to say that Bob does nothing wrong when he decides not to throw the switch. Of course, most people could be wrong; we can't decide moral issues by taking opinion polls. But consider for yourself the level of sacrifice that you would demand of Bob, and then think about how much money you would have to give away in order to make a sacrifice that is roughly equal to that. It's almost certainly much, much more than $200. For most middle-class Americans, it could easily be more like $200,000.

Isn't it counterproductive to ask people to do so much? Don't we run the risk that many will shrug their shoulders and say that morality, so conceived, is fine for saints but not for them? I accept that we are unlikely to see, in the near or even medium-term future, a world in which it is normal for wealthy Americans to give the bulk of their wealth to strangers. When it comes to praising or blaming people for what they do, we tend to use a standard that is relative to some conception of normal behavior. Comfortably off Americans who give, say, 10 percent of their income to overseas aid organizations are so far ahead of most of their equally comfortable fellow citizens that I wouldn't go out of my way to chastise them for not doing more. Nevertheless, they should be doing much more, and they are in no position to criticize Bob for failing to make the much greater sacrifice of his Bugatti.

At this point various objections may crop up. Someone may say: "If every citizen living in the affluent nations contributed his or her share I wouldn't have to make such a drastic sacrifice, because long before such levels were reached, the resources would have been there to save the lives of all those children dying from lack of food or medical care. So why should I give more than my fair share?" Another, related, objection is that the Government ought to increase its overseas aid allocations, since that would spread the burden more equitably across all taxpayers.

Yet the question of how much we ought to give is a matter to be decided in the real world—and that, sadly, is a world in which we know that most people do not, and in the immediate future will not, give substantial amounts to overseas aid agencies. We know, too, that at least in the next year, the United States Government is not going to meet even the very modest United Nations–recommended target of 0.7 percent of gross national product; at the moment it lags far below that, at 0.09 percent, not even half of Japan's 0.22 percent or a tenth of Denmark's 0.97 percent. Thus, we know that the money we can give beyond that theoretical "fair share" is still going to save lives that would otherwise be lost. While the idea that no one need do more than his or her fair share is a powerful one, should it prevail if we know that others are not doing their fair share and that children will die preventable deaths unless we do more than our fair share? That would be taking fairness too far. 20

Thus, this ground for limiting how much we ought to give also fails. In the world as it is now, I can see no escape from the conclusion that each one of us with wealth surplus to his or her essential needs should be giving most of it to help people suffering from poverty so dire as to be life-threatening. That's right: I'm saying that you shouldn't buy that new car, take that cruise, redecorate the house or get that pricey new suit. After all, a $1,000 suit could save five children's lives.

So how does my philosophy break down in dollars and cents? An American household with an income of $50,000 spends around $30,000 annually on necessities, according to the Conference Board, a nonprofit economic research organization. Therefore, for a household bringing in $50,000 a year, donations to help the world's poor should be as close as possible to $20,000. The $30,000 required for necessities holds for higher incomes as well. So a household making $100,000 could cut a yearly check for $70,000. Again, the formula is simple: whatever money you're spending on luxuries, not necessities, should be given away.

Now, evolutionary psychologists tell us that human nature just isn't sufficiently altruistic to make it plausible that many people will sacrifice so much for strangers. On the facts of human nature, they might be right, but they would be wrong to draw a moral conclusion from those facts. If it is the case that we ought to do things that, predictably, most of us won't do, then let's face that fact head-on. Then, if we value the life of a child more than going to fancy restaurants, the next time we dine out we will know that we could have done something better with our money. If that makes living a morally decent life extremely arduous, well, then that is the way things are. If we don't do it, then we should at least know that we are failing to live a morally decent life — not because it is good to wallow in guilt but because knowing where we should be going is the first step toward heading in that direction.

When Bob first grasped the dilemma that faced him as he stood by that railway switch, he must have thought how extraordinarily unlucky he was to be placed in a situation in which he must choose between the life of an innocent child and the sacrifice of most of his savings. But he was not unlucky at all. We are all in that situation.

Questions

1. Peter Singer opens his essay by describing a situation from a movie, yet it could be argued that seeing movies is, in fact, a luxury that one advocating his position should forgo. To what extent does this interpretation undermine Singer's argument?
2. The example of Bob and his Bugatti is hypothetical. Is this a rhetorical strategy that strengthens or weakens Singer's argument? Explain your response.
3. Note the places where Singer addresses the counterargument. Where does he concede, and where does he refute?
4. When does Singer use the pronoun *we*? When does he use *you*? How does this shift reflect and contribute to appeals to ethos and pathos?
5. This selection appeared in the *New York Times Magazine* (1999). What does that fact tell you about the audience to whom Singer is appealing? To what extent do you think he is effective in reaching them?

5. *World Economic Forum*

Zapiro

The following cartoon by South African cartoonist Zapiro (Jonathan Shapiro) takes as its context the World Economic Forum, a meeting of international leaders from business, industry, government, and academia who meet annually in Davos, Switzerland, to explore solutions to a wide range of global economic issues.

Questions

1. How are the participants—both the two entering the room and those already inside—depicted? Consider appearance and activity.
2. What does the setting illustrated resemble? Does it seem to be, for instance, a lecture hall?
3. What is a one-sentence summary of the argument that the cartoonist is making?

6. *Warren Buffett, Bill Gates, and the Billionaire Challenge*

CHRISTIAN SCIENCE MONITOR EDITORIAL BOARD

This 2010 article from the *Christian Science Monitor* describes the proposal of two superwealthy philanthropists to their billionaire counterparts.

America's superwealthy are being hit up hard for their money on two fronts this year—for charity and for higher taxes. At the least, these new appeals may serve as a reminder for everyone in how best to give back to society.

One front is a gentle arm-twisting campaign by Warren Buffett and Bill Gates to persuade fellow billionaires to commit half of their wealth to good causes. In just a few short weeks, the two men have won over 38 of those listed on the Forbes 400 list of wealthiest Americans to make that pledge.

About half of those asked have so far said yes, often saying they see their giving as an investment in society. Their names range from New York Mayor Michael Bloomberg to eBay founder Pierre Omidyar. In all, they have a combined net worth of more than $200 billion.

But money for charity isn't the main point. As Mr. Buffett, head of Berkshire Hathaway investments, said: "At its core, the Giving Pledge is about asking wealthy families to have important conversations about their wealth and how it will be used."

Such family and peer pressure certainly has its uses if they encourage generosity. The Buffett-Gates campaign in particular may also help create useful publicity for a broad political discussion about government tax rates. In coming weeks, Congress will decide whether to eliminate the Bush-era tax cuts for families earning more than $250,000 — the other proposal to wrest money for the public good away from the rich.

High-profile philanthropy by this large number of super-rich is indeed a rare display of heartfelt concern about others. It sets an example for those of more modest means to make more donations. "By giving, we inspire others to give of themselves, whether their money or their time," says New York's mayor, who earned his wealth publishing financial news.

The Giving Pledge campaign may also help dampen the harsh rhetoric of class warfare in the coming fight over the Bush tax cuts.

The willingness of both rich and poor to pay taxes — "the price of civilization," as Justice Learned Hand called them — is critical to a functioning government. But the debate on Capitol Hill mostly centers on data and arguments from economists about the effects of tax rates on private investments and the budget deficit, or the tax burdens on each income group. Economics is not really a science, however, so it's hard for either side to win those debates.

Rather, the setting of tax rates is a democratic exercise, even though for many Americans the paying of taxes seems coercive — like an IRS agent citing jail time if you don't pay up. That's why each elected official must give voice to their constituents' willingness to be taxed, just as Buffett and Mr. Gates have quietly drawn out the rich to say how much they would give to charity.

Sen. Barbara Boxer (D) of California is one lawmaker who says the rich are ready to pony up more in taxes. "Those people who are making that kind of money, they've told me that they feel fine contributing to this country," she says. Such statements are far better than the usual practice of demonizing the wealthy.

But then Jon Kyl (R) of Arizona makes an opposing point by highlighting a wealthy small-business man, Craig Fritsche, the owner of Tart Lumber in Virginia. "Do we need to raise taxes on people who create the jobs in our country?" asks Mr. Kyl.

Congress sets the priorities for both government spending and taxes. Lawmakers must reflect the will of voters to contribute to the wider community, but also persuade them to be taxed more—or on different types of income—when that is needed.

It is the type of task that Gates and Buffett have learned well as they continue to hold private dinners with more billionaires to ask them to make the Giving Pledge. "We hope to come back in six months and surprise you more," Buffett said, "or at least surprise ourselves."

Questions

1. What is the "Giving Pledge" proposed by Bill Gates and Warren Buffett to the Forbes 400 wealthiest Americans?
2. Why do Gates and Buffett assert that "money for charity isn't the main point" (para. 4) of their proposal?
3. Why do they believe that their approach is better than imposing higher taxes on those earning the highest incomes?

7. *Negative Reaction to Charity Campaign*

DER SPIEGEL ONLINE

The following article appeared in *Der Spiegel* Online, the English-language version of a German news source. The interview is with Peter Krämer, a multi-millionaire shipping magnate who criticizes the Giving Pledge.

Germany's super-rich have rejected an invitation by Bill Gates and Warren Buffett to join their "Giving Pledge" to give away most of their fortune. The pledge has been criticized in Germany, with millionaires saying donations shouldn't replace duties that would be better carried out by the state.

Last week, Microsoft founder Bill Gates attempted to convince billionaires around the world to agree to give away half their money to charity. But in Germany, the "Giving Pledge," backed by 40 of the world's wealthiest people, including Gates and Warren Buffett, has met with skepticism, SPIEGEL has learned.

"For most people that is too ostentatious," said the asset manager of one of the billionaires contacted by Gates, adding that many of the people contacted had already transferred larger proportions of their assets than the Americans to charitable foundations.

Dietmar Hopp, the co-founder of the SAP business software company, has transferred some €2.9 billion to a foundation. Klaus Tschira, another founder of SAP, has handed more than half of his wealth to a foundation.

Peter Krämer, a Hamburg-based shipping magnate and multimillionaire, has emerged as one of the strongest critics of the "Giving Pledge." Krämer, who donated millions of euros in 2005 to "Schools for Africa," a program operated by UNICEF, explained his opposition to the Gates initiative in a SPIEGEL interview.

5

SPIEGEL: Forty superwealthy Americans have just announced that they would donate half of their assets, at the very latest after their deaths. As a person who often likes to say that rich people should be asked to contribute more to society, what were your first thoughts?

KRÄMER: I find the U.S. initiative highly problematic. You can write donations off in your taxes to a large degree in the USA. So the rich make a choice: Would I rather donate or pay taxes? The donors are taking the place of the state. That's unacceptable.

SPIEGEL: But doesn't the money that is donated serve the common good?

KRÄMER: It is all just a bad transfer of power from the state to billionaires. So it's not the state that determines what is good for the people, but rather the rich want to decide. That's a development that I find really bad. What legitimacy do these people have to decide where massive sums of money will flow?

SPIEGEL: It is their money at the end of the day.   10

KRÄMER: In this case, 40 superwealthy people want to decide what their money will be used for. That runs counter to the democratically legitimate state. In the end the billionaires are indulging in hobbies that might be in the common good, but are very personal.

SPIEGEL: Do the donations also have to do with the fact that the idea of state and society is such a different one in the United States?

KRÄMER: Yes, one cannot forget that the U.S. has a desolate social system and that alone is reason enough that donations are already a part of everyday life there. But it would have been a greater deed on the part of Mr. Gates or Mr. Buffett if they had given the money to small communities in the U.S. so that they can fulfill public duties.

SPIEGEL: Should wealthy Germans also give up some of their money?

KRÄMER: No, not in this form. It would make more sense, for example, to   15
work with and donate to established organizations.

Questions

1. What is the primary reason Peter Krämer finds the premise of the Giving Pledge "problematic" (para. 7)?
2. Do you agree or disagree with Krämer that "it would have been a greater deed on the part of Mr. Gates or Mr. Buffett if they had given the money to small communities in the U.S. so that they can fulfill public duties" (para. 13)?

Making Connections

1. What is the most basic difference between Peter Singer's and Garrett Hardin's worldviews?

2. In what ways are the philosophies of Singer and Andrew Carnegie similar?

3. In what ways might Hardin object to Zapiro's argument in the cartoon on the World Economic Forum?

4. Is the viewpoint of Peter Krämer, the German multimillionaire, more similar to that of Carnegie or Hardin? Explain.

5. How does Bertrand Russell's concept of self-denial in the following quotation reflect the assumptions that underlie Bill Gates's and Warren Buffett's Giving Pledge: "the whole antithesis between self and the rest of the world, which is implied in the doctrine of self-denial, disappears as soon as we have any genuine interest in persons or things outside ourselves"? (See Russell, para. 2.)

Entering the Conversation

As you respond to the following prompts, support your argument with references to at least three of the seven sources in this Conversation on the Individual's Responsibility to the Community. For help using sources, see Chapter 4.

1. How can "the good life" be lived well? Explain your position, first by defining the term and then by presenting your own view within the context of the sources.

2. Write an essay explaining which of the seven perspectives represented in these readings you find most compelling. Make sure you explain why you have come to this conclusion.

3. Suppose that a proposal is made to vary college tuition according to the student's (or parents') annual income. Essentially, tuition payment would be determined according to criteria similar to that used to levy income tax, so that those who earn the most will pay the most. Write an essay explaining why you would support or oppose this proposal.

4. Pose a question on a controversial issue, such as "Should the United States intervene in a conflict in another region?" or "Should individual citizens of affluent countries contribute a portion of their income to fight AIDS in Africa?" Then write a roundtable discussion that includes any five participants: Andrew Carnegie, Bertrand Russell, Peter Singer, Garrett Hardin, Bill Gates, and Warren Buffett. You might do this assignment as a group, with different members role-playing the authors.

Student Writing

Synthesis: Incorporating Sources into a Revision

Following are two versions of an essay. The first is a draft that student Martin Copeland wrote in response to this prompt:

> Explain why you believe that fraternities, sororities, or both do or do not build community or provide a positive community environment for their members.

The second essay is Martin's revision after he researched the topic of fraternities and sororities further. Using the questions following each version of the essay, discuss specific ways in which the second is an improvement over the first, and suggest ways for further improvement. (Note: Both the draft and the revision were written outside class without time constraints.)

Draft

From the outside, it is very difficult to tell exactly what fraternities and sororities do or don't do for their members. What an outsider can do, however, is give an honest opinion of his or her perception of fraternities and sororities, which I feel, is very valuable to the organizations. It can allow members to understand how their organizations are perceived, what are the misconceptions, and why they may or may not be attracting new members.

Having established my outside perspective, I believe that the general idea and philosophy of fraternities and sororities is to provide a positive community environment for their members, and that in their purest form, fraternities and sororities can do just that. Unfortunately, most fraternities and sororities are not in their "purest form," and have been corrupted by wayward members so that now, they do not provide a positive community environment for their members.

It is important to understand the language of "positive community environment." Were the question only concerned with providing a community environment for their members, my answer would have been an enthusiastic "yes." Fraternities and sororities are perhaps the closest groups on college campuses. On many campuses, they live, study, and party together. The "rush" process alone is enough to bring several wannabe members together as one cohesive unit. Often, within fraternities and sororities, students make lifetime friends and professional contacts; they build a support system away from home that for many students is the ship that keeps them afloat in the vast ocean that is college.

The problem, however, lies in the fact that the question included the word "positive." For all of the great things fraternities and sororities do for their members, much of it, though pleasurable, does not seem positive. We have all heard stories of fraternities and sororities placing their pledges in compromising and even dangerous situations all for the sake of brotherhood or sisterhood. Such stories are more frequent than these organizations would have the general public believe. The process that pledges have to endure to make it to the positive community environment can often humiliate them, bringing them down to the point that they feel that walking away from such a group would make the person less than the others. Admittedly, that brings into question the self-esteem of the pledge, but it also makes me question why an overwhelming number of students with self-esteem issues are drawn to fraternities and sororities. Instead of being uplifting societies focused on the growth and maturity of its members, the community environment can often become a crutch, which is anything but positive.

In essence, my argument is not that fraternities and sororities are bad, because without more specific definition of the terms analyzed, of course bad examples will run rampant. My argument, however, is that as a whole, it seems that fraternities and sororities have departed from their true purposes; they have lost touch with the principles and values upon which they were founded. Finding those principles again and rebuilding their lost legacies would be an amazing step toward becoming truly positive community environments, and it would take work from all such groups in order to fix the way outsiders perceive the groups as a whole.

Questions

1. The student has written in the first person, using both *I* and *we*. Is that decision appropriate or inappropriate for this assignment and topic? Why?
2. The thesis statement is "closed," with specification of the essay's major points clearly identified. As a reader, do you find this type of thesis helpful or limiting?
3. What effect does the figurative language ("the ship that keeps them afloat," para. 3) have on you as a reader?
4. What attempts does Martin make to develop a balanced tone and perspective?

Revision

After writing the draft, Martin did some reading and research on the topic. The following revision shows his expanded view and use of sources.

Fraternities and Sororities

Martin Copeland

From the outside, it is very difficult to tell exactly what fraternities and sororities do or don't do for their members. What an outsider can do, however, is give an honest opinion of his or her perception to members to help them understand how their organizations are perceived, what the misconceptions are, and why they may have difficulty attracting new members. The general idea and philosophy of fraternities and sororities is to provide a positive community environment for their members, and in their purest form, they can do just that. Unfortunately, most fraternities and sororities are not in their "purest form" and have been corrupted by what might be a minority of highly visible members.

It is important to understand the language of "positive community environment." Were the question concerned only with sororities and fraternities providing a community environment for their members, my answer would have been an enthusiastic yes. Fraternities and sororities are perhaps the closest groups on college campuses. On many campuses, they live, study, and party together. The "rush" process alone is enough to bring several wannabe members together as one cohesive unit. Often, within fraternities and sororities, students make lifetime friends and professional contacts. In his explanation of why he is proud to be part of a fraternity, Douglas Luetjen points out that "all but eight U.S. presidents since 1856 have been regular or honorary members of a college fraternity. And . . . 85% of the Fortune 500 executives are fraternity members."

Furthermore, in a sorority or a fraternity, students can build a support system away from home that for many is the ship that keeps them afloat in the vast ocean that is college. Anne Remington begins her article for *Parent Times*, an online magazine from the University of Iowa, with a story about a freshman who felt that no one remembered her birthday until her Alpha Chi Omega sisters began singing to her: "And in that instance, she knew she had found a new 'home.'" Remington continues to describe Greek-letter organizations that appeal to specific minorities and that provide a "sense of belonging" for many students who are away from home for the first time.

The problem, however, lies in the fact that the question included the word "positive." For all of the great things fraternities and sororities do for their members, much of it, though pleasurable, does not always seem positive. We have all heard stories of fraternities and sororities placing their pledges in compromising and even dangerous situations all for the sake of brotherhood or sisterhood. Such stories are more frequent than these organizations would have the general public believe. The process that pledges have to endure to make it to the positive community environment can often humiliate them, bringing them down to the point that they feel that walking away from such a group would make them less than the others.

A major problem with fraternities and sororities is drinking and the negative behaviors that accompany it. According to a study at the University of Washington, 85% of those living in Greek houses drank at least one to two times per week, 37% three to four times (Baer et al.). Another national study reported that sorority members are nearly twice as likely to become binge drinkers than their nonsorority counterparts, and 75% of fraternity members were self-described binge drinkers (Wechsler). This study also reported higher incidences of missed classes and unprotected sex among fraternity and sorority members.

In essence, my argument is not that fraternities and sororities are necessarily a negative community environment, but they do promote negative and potentially dangerous behaviors. As a whole, it seems that too many fraternities and sororities have become "organized saloons" (Cross) and departed from the principles and values upon which they were founded: "scholarship, relationships, leadership, and service" (Remington). Finding those principles again and rebuilding their lost legacies will be a step toward becoming truly positive community environments, though it will take the work of many individuals to change the way outsiders perceive fraternities and sororities.

Works Cited

Baer, J.S., D. R. Kivlahan, and G.A. Marlatt. "High-Risk Drinking across the Transition from High School to College." *Alcoholism: Clinical and Experimental Research* 19.1 (1995): 54–61.

Cross, Charles R. "Why I'm Proud I'm Not a Greek." *Columns: University of Washington Alumni Magazine* September 2001: XX. Web. 6 Mar. 2004. <http://www.washington.edu/alumni/columns/sept01/greekdebate1.html>.

Luetjen, Douglas A. "Why I'm Proud I'm a Greek." *Columns: University of Washington Alumni Magazine* September 2001: XX. Web. 6 Mar. 2004. <http://www.washington.edu/alumni/columns/sept01/greekdebate1.html>.

Remington, Anne. "It's All Greek to Me." *Parent Times Online* Winter 2004–2005: n. pag. U of Iowa. Web. 15 Mar. 2004. <http://www.uiowa.edu/~ptimes/issues04-05/winter04-05/greek.html>.

Wechsler, Henry. Binge Drinking on American College Campuses: A New Look at an Old Problem. *Harvard School of Public Health* (1995). Web. 20 Mar. 2004. <http://www.hsph.harvard.edu/cas/Documents/monograph_2000/cas_mono_2000.pdf>.

Questions

1. Cite three changes Martin has made, and discuss their effect.
2. The revised essay is written primarily in the third person. Is this point of view more effective? Why or why not?
3. Do the sources Martin has chosen help to balance his argument, or do they favor one viewpoint?
4. Do the sources give Martin's voice more authority? If so, explain how. If you do not think so, explain why not. Did he cite his sources properly? How does that affect his authority?
5. Is the revision more effective as an argument? Explain your answer, with specific references to the initial draft and the revision.
6. Find and read one or more of the sources. Are the quotations and references effective? Would you have made other choices? Why or why not?

Grammar as Rhetoric and Style

Parallel Structures

Sentences or parts of a sentence are parallel when structures within them take the same form. Parallelism is important at the level of the word, the phrase, and the clause.

Words

> Why should we live with such hurry and waste of life?
>
> — HENRY DAVID THOREAU

In this sentence, the words hurry and waste, both nouns, follow the preposition with; hurry and waste are parallel.

> In eternity there is indeed something true and sublime.
>
> — HENRY DAVID THOREAU

In this sentence, the words true and sublime, both adjectives, modify the pronoun something; true and sublime are parallel.

Phrases

> Men esteem truth remote, in the outskirts of the system behind the farthest star, before Adam and after the last man.
>
> — HENRY DAVID THOREAU

To modify the adjective remote in this first sentence, Thoreau uses parallel prepositional phrases: in the outskirts, before the farthest star, before Adam, and after the last man.

> More difficult because there is no zeitgeist to read, no template to follow, no mask to wear.
>
> — ANNA QUINDLEN

And in the preceding sentence, Anna Quindlen uses three parallel nouns each preceded by no and each followed by an infinitive: no zeitgeist to read, no template to follow, and no mask to wear.

Clauses

"Where I Lived, and What I Lived For"
— Title of an essay by Henry David Thoreau

The title of Thoreau's essay consists of two parallel dependent, or subordinate, clauses; one begins with where, and the other begins with what.

[W]e perceive that only great and worthy things have any permanent and absolute existence, that petty fears and petty pleasures are but the shadow of the reality.
— Henry David Thoreau

The preceding example contains two parallel dependent clauses, each beginning with that and functioning as an object of the verb perceive.

If we are really dying, let us hear the rattle in our throats and feel cold in the extremities; if we are alive, let us go about our business.
— Henry David Thoreau

This example begins with a dependent clause (If . . . dying) followed by an independent, or main, clause (let . . . extremities); then, after the semicolon, Thoreau presents another dependent-independent construction, parallel to the first.

Lack of Parallelism

To fully appreciate the power of the parallelism created by Thoreau and Quindlen in the preceding examples, consider what happens when supposedly equal elements of a sentence do not follow the same grammatical or syntactical form — that is, when they are not parallel with each other.

Why should we live with such hurry and to waste life?

This version of Thoreau's sentence tries to modify the verb should live by coordinating a prepositional phrase, with such hurry, with an infinitive phrase, to waste life. The two phrases are not parallel with each other, and as a result, the sentence lacks balance and force.

Parallelism can be tricky when the elements — words, phrases, or clauses — are separated by modifiers or other syntactical elements. The following sentence may not at first glance seem to lack parallelism:

It [the process of friendships fading] was sweet and sad and, though you'd rarely admit it, a necessity.

When you analyze carefully, you notice that sweet and sad are adjectives, and necessity is a noun. Notice that in the actual sentence that Scott Brown wrote in "Friendonomics," he makes all three words parallel adjectives:

> It was sweet and sad, and though you'd rarely admit it, necessary.
>
> — SCOTT BROWN

The fact that all three are adjectives underscores the unity in the qualities Brown argues is the natural ebb and flow of friendships fading: it's sweet and sad and also necessary.

Parallelism is often at its most effective at the level of the clause, but, again, it may be difficult to keep track. Let's use an example from Malcolm Gladwell. Here it is without parallel structure:

> In other words, Facebook activism succeeds not by motivating people to make a real sacrifice but when people are motivated to do things even though they are not motivated enough to make a real sacrifice.

That sentence makes sense — once you've untangled all the motivations! — but the emphasis Gladwell intends is on the not: people are *not* motivated by x *but* by y. In the sentence that actually appears in his essay, he repeats the phrase by motivating and thus uses parallel structure to emphasize the contrast:

> In other words, Facebook activism succeeds not by motivating people to make a real sacrifice but by motivating them to do the things that people do when they are not motivated enough to make a real sacrifice.
>
> — MALCOLM GLADWELL

Rhetorical and Stylistic Strategy

Looking first at the parallel sentences at the beginning of this lesson and then at the rewrites that lack parallelism, you can see that writers use parallelism on the level of the word, phrase, or clause as a rhetorical and stylistic device to emphasize ideas, to contrast ideas, or to connect ideas.

Following are the names, definitions, and examples of specific types of parallelism:

anaphora: Repetition of a word or phrase at the beginning of successive phrases, clauses, or lines.

> *But when you have seen vicious mobs lynch your mothers and fathers at will and drown your sisters and brothers at whim; when you have seen hate-filled policemen curse, kick, and even kill your black brothers and sisters; . . . when you are forever*

fighting a degenerating sense of "nobodiness"—then you will understand why we find it difficult to wait.

— MARTIN LUTHER KING JR.

In this example, form follows function. Just as King is saying that African Americans have had to endure unjust treatment as they waited for full civil rights, this series of parallel clauses makes the reader wait—and wait—for the main point in the independent clause.

antimetabole: Repetition of words in reverse order.

We do not ride on the railroad; it rides upon us.

— HENRY DAVID THOREAU

Ask not what your country can do for you; ask what you can do for your country.

— JOHN F. KENNEDY

The example above from President Kennedy is, perhaps, his most famous quote. Part of what makes this quote so "quotable" is that the repetition inherent in antimetabole makes it dramatic and easy to remember. Because the pattern of the two clauses is so similar, the listener only needs to remember one pattern. Because that sentence pattern is repeated, it gives the listener two chances to understand the entire sentence and places extra emphasis on the second part. It is almost as if Kennedy is repeating a point for emphasis. Keep an eye out for antimetabole in modern political soundbites.

antithesis: Opposition, or contrast, of ideas or words in a parallel construction.

[F]reedom is never voluntarily given by the oppressor; it must be demanded by the oppressed.

— MARTIN LUTHER KING JR.

One has not only a legal but a moral responsibility to obey just laws. Conversely, one has a moral responsibility to disobey unjust laws.

— MARTIN LUTHER KING JR.

That's one small step for man, one giant leap for mankind.

— NEIL ARMSTRONG

In all three of these examples, the parallel structure creates a clear comparison between two things in order to emphasize the difference between them. *Given by the oppressor* is contrasted in meaning and in placement with *demanded by the oppressed*. Notice also how the parallel prepositional phrases *by the oppressor* and *by the oppressed* call attention to the tension between oppressor and oppressed.

zeugma: Use of two different words in a grammatically similar way that produces different, often incongruous, meanings.

Someone sent me a T-shirt not long ago that read "Well-Behaved Women Don't Make History." They don't make good lawyers, either, or doctors or businesswomen.

— ANNA QUINDLEN

You are free to execute your laws and your citizens as you see fit.

— STAR TREK: THE NEXT GENERATION

In this example, the zeugma is created when the verb *make* takes many different nouns as its direct object: *history*, but also, *lawyers, doctors,* and *businesswomen.* While all of these words are nouns, they do not have the same meanings — *history* is not an occupation, while all the other nouns are. There is a consistency in the pattern, but an inconsistency in the meaning of the words. Quindlen exploits the ironic inconsistency of the zeugma to draw a connection between two things that her audience might not otherwise think of as connected: activists who fought for women's rights, and women today who are trying to build their careers.

• EXERCISE 1 •

Identify the parallel structure in words, phrases, or clauses in each of the following sentences.

1. "A penny saved is a penny earned." (Benjamin Franklin)
2. Was this act the work of a genius or a lunatic?
3. This situation is a problem not only for the students but also for the teachers.
4. Heather learned to work fast, ask few questions, and generally keep a low profile.
5. After you finish your homework and before you check your email, please do your chores.

• EXERCISE 2 •

Correct the faulty parallelism in the following sentences.

1. My new exercise program and going on a strict diet will help me lose the weight I gained over the holidays.
2. As part of his accounting business, Rick has private clients, does some pro bono work, and corporations.
3. Try not to focus on the mistakes that you've made; what you've learned from them should be your focus instead.
4. A new job is likely to cause a person anxiety and working extra hours to make a good impression.
5. A competent physician will assess a patient's physical symptoms, and mental attitude will also be considered.

• EXERCISE 3 •

Identify the parallel structures in the following sentences from Martin Luther King Jr.'s "Letter from Birmingham Jail," and explain their effect.

1. So I, along with several members of my staff, am here because I was invited here. I am here because I have organizational ties here. (para. 2)

2. We are caught in an inescapable network of mutuality, tied in a single garment of destiny. (para. 4)

3. Whatever affects one directly, affects all indirectly. (para. 4)

4. In any nonviolent campaign there are four basic steps: collection of the facts to determine whether injustices exist; negotiation; self-purification; and direct action. (para. 6)

5. An unjust law is a code that a numerical or power majority group compels a minority group to obey but does not make binding on itself. This is *difference* made legal. By the same token, a just law is a code that a majority compels a minority to follow and that it is willing to follow itself. This is *sameness* made legal. (para. 17)

6. Was not Jesus an extremist for love: "Love your enemies, bless them that curse you, do good to them that hate you, and pray for them which despitefully use you, and persecute you." Was not Amos an extremist for justice: "Let justice roll down like waters and righteousness like an ever-flowing stream." Was not Paul an extremist for the Christian gospel: "I bear in my body the marks of the Lord Jesus." Was not Martin Luther an extremist: "Here I stand; I cannot do otherwise, so help me God." And John Bunyan: "I will stay in jail to the end of my days before I make a butchery of my conscience." And Abraham Lincoln: "This nation cannot survive half slave and half free." And Thomas Jefferson: "We hold these truths to be self-evident, that all men are created equal. . . ." (para. 31)

7. If I have said anything in this letter that overstates the truth and indicates an unreasonable impatience, I beg you to forgive me. If I have said anything that understates the truth and indicates my having a patience that allows me to settle for anything less than brotherhood, I beg God to forgive me. (para. 49)

• EXERCISE 4 •

The following paragraph is from Toni Morrison's Nobel Lecture, delivered in 1993 when she won the Nobel Prize for Literature. Find examples of parallel structure; identify whether the construction is a word, clause, or phrase; and explain its effect.

The systematic looting of language can be recognized by the tendency of its users to forgo its nuanced, complex, mid-wifery properties for menace and subjugation. Oppressive language does more than represent violence; it is violence; does more than represent the limits of knowledge; it limits knowledge. Whether it is obscuring state language or the faux-language of mindless media; whether it is the proud but calcified language of the academy or the commodity driven language of science; whether it is the malign language of law-without-ethics, or language designed for the estrangement of minorities, hiding its racist plunder in its literary cheek—it must be rejected, altered and exposed. It is the language that drinks blood, laps vulnerabilities, tucks its fascist boots under crinolines of respectability and patriotism as it moves relentlessly toward the bottom line and the bottomed-out mind. Sexist language, racist language, theistic language—all are typical of the policing languages of mastery, and cannot, do not permit new knowledge or encourage the mutual exchange of ideas.

• EXERCISE 5 •

Each of the following sentences is an example of parallelism. Identify the type of parallelism, explain its effect, and then model a sentence of your own on the example.

1. To spend too much time in studies is sloth; to use them too much for ornament is affectation; to make judgment wholly by their rules is the humour of a scholar. — FRANCIS BACON

2. Alas, art is long, and life is short. — BENJAMIN FRANKLIN

3. Flowers are as common here . . . as people are in London.

— OSCAR WILDE

4. Where justice is denied, where poverty is enforced, where ignorance prevails, and where any one class is made to feel that society is in an organized conspiracy to oppress, rob, and degrade them, neither persons nor property will be safe. — FREDERICK DOUGLASS

5. He carried a strobe light and the responsibility for the lives of his men.

— TIM O'BRIEN

Suggestions for Writing

Community

Now that you have examined a number of texts that focus on community, explore this topic yourself by synthesizing your own ideas and the readings. You might want to do more research or use readings from other classes as you write.

1. Cell phones, e-mail, social networking sites, blogs, and other electronic communication have made our world smaller and increased the pace at which we live life. Have these inventions also given us a new sense of community or opened up communities that would otherwise be closed to us? Have they lowered or expanded our standards of what *community* means?

2. Write about the discussion that might ensue among several of the writers you have studied in this chapter if they were to focus on the following question: What are the characteristics of a productive and successful community at the start of the twenty-first century?

3. Creating a community of like-minded people is the principle behind the development of many charter schools. Select a charter school in your area, and examine it as an intentional community, defined as "a group of people who have chosen to live together with a common purpose, working cooperatively to create a lifestyle that reflects their shared core values."

4. Was the Ku Klux Klan in the nineteenth and twentieth centuries a community? Many would argue yes, that it fit most definitions of *community*. It was, however, one of many so-called communities that might be seen as counterproductive. Choose another controversial community (such as the punk community, a country club, or a secret society), examine its structure and purpose, and argue for or against its value to its members and to the larger community.

5. Many colleges and universities are developing what they call living-learning communities, in which students choose to live together as a group centered around a theme, which could be anything from Chinese culture to women in science. Some critics believe such groupings are limiting because the students are not exposed to different viewpoints and interests. Others object because they believe segregation based on race, ethnicity, or religion does not contribute to the mission of higher education. What do you think of living-learning communities? Will you choose to live in one when you go to college? Why or why not?

6. Examine a community that is organized around shared values but not geographic proximity. What holds that community together? What do members gain from it? Why does it continue?

7. Following is a description of a coffeehouse called Java from the novel *Queen of Dreams* by Chitra Banerjee Divakaruni.

> Java demands nothing from them [customers] except their money. It allows them to remain unknown. . . . And yet they have community, too, as much of it as they want: the comfortable company of a roomful of nameless-faceless folks just like themselves, happy to be alone, to gaze into middle distance, to notice no one.

Discuss this concept of community, explain how it can function for some, and describe examples of it that you have seen.

8. Write an essay about making the transition from one community to another and how that change affects your sense of self. The transition might be from one country to another or simply from one neighborhood or group of friends to another. Include descriptions of the communities as well as your own emotional responses. You might also include photographs as part of the essay.

9. The author Kurt Vonnegut Jr. wrote, "What should young people do with their lives today? Many things, obviously. But the most daring thing is to create stable communities in which the terrible disease of loneliness can be cured." Write a speech that you would deliver to a group of your peers (identify which group) that uses Vonnegut's idea as your main point and recommends ways to "create stable communities."

The Economy

What is the role of the economy in our everyday lives?

Hardly a day goes by without people hearing something about the economy—good or bad. Just what is this grand presence that inserts itself into our lives? Generally, "the economy" refers to the production, trade, and consumption of goods and services. And economics is the study of that process. It is generally broken into macroeconomics and microeconomics: the former refers to the economy at large, and the latter refers to the economic considerations and transactions that we make in our everyday lives.

For most of us, our experience of the economy begins first with consumption of goods, and then with work. We perform labor in order to purchase goods, especially those that are necessary to life. And yet it's not so simple. How do we choose what work to do? What counts as important work? Should work do more than pay the bills—should it satisfy the soul? And what exactly do we mean by "necessary for life"?

Our national mythology—the American Dream—is based on the belief that hard work will not go unrewarded. Yet recently that dream seems increasingly difficult to realize. We consume more and more but produce less and less. For the first time in history, we are participating in a truly global economy. Ultimately, what will be the outcome of such extreme shifts?

The authors and artists whose work you find in this chapter offer different perspectives on the meaning of economics in our lives. In the central work, Barbara Ehrenreich tells of her experience trying to make a living earning minimum wage; and in our classic essay, Jonathan Swift poses a novel solution to the woes of the destitute in eighteenth-century Ireland. Eric Schlosser (p. 431) asks whether we can enjoy the fruits of labor without exploiting the laborers, and Matthew B. Crawford (p. 449) looks at the nature of work itself, discussing what he calls "knowledge work" and "manual work." Other authors in this chapter consider the plight of the poor and the future of the American Dream. Finally, we enter a conversation about materialism in American culture. Do we insist on consuming more than we need—more, in fact, than is good for us and for the world? Or is our consumption of goods and services a realization of the American Dream?

from *Serving in Florida*

Barbara Ehrenreich

Best-selling author Barbara Ehrenreich (b. 1941) started out as a scientist. But after receiving her PhD in biology from Rockefeller University, she pursued a career in the academic world only briefly before starting to write for magazines such as *Time* and the *Progressive*. A social critic with a decidedly liberal bent, her sardonic sensibility often animates her writing. Some of her recent books include *Nickel and Dimed: On (Not) Getting By in America* (2001), *Bait and Switch: The (Futile) Pursuit of the American Dream* (2005), and *Bright-Sided: How the Relentless Pursuit of Positive Thinking Has Undermined America* (2009). To research her most famous book, *Nickel and Dimed*, a study of the working poor in the United States, Ehrenreich worked undercover as a server, maid, and salesclerk; and she tried to live on the wages she received. The following excerpt from "Serving in Florida," a chapter in *Nickel and Dimed*, describes Ehrenreich's experience working in a restaurant named Jerry's.

Picture a fat person's hell, and I don't mean a place with no food. Instead there is everything you might eat if eating had no bodily consequences — the cheese fries, the chicken-fried steaks, the fudge-laden desserts — only here every bite must be paid for, one way or another, in human discomfort. The kitchen is a cavern, a stomach leading to the lower intestine that is the garbage and dishwashing area, from which issue bizarre smells combining the edible and the offal: creamy carrion, pizza barf, and that unique and enigmatic Jerry's scent, citrus fart. The floor is slick with spills, forcing us to walk through the kitchen with tiny steps, like Susan McDougal[1] in leg irons. Sinks everywhere are clogged with scraps of lettuce, decomposing lemon wedges, water-logged toast crusts. Put your hand down on any counter and you risk being stuck to it by the film of ancient syrup spills, and this is unfortunate because hands are utensils here, used for scooping up lettuce onto the salad plates, lifting out pie slices, and even moving hash browns from one plate to another. The regulation poster in the single unisex rest room admonishes us to wash our hands thoroughly, and even offers instructions for doing so, but there is always some vital substance missing — soap, paper towels, toilet paper — and I never found all three at once. You learn to stuff your pockets

---

[1]Susan McDougal was imprisoned in 1996 for contempt of court, fraud, and conspiracy in connection with the failed Whitewater land deal involving President Bill Clinton and First Lady Hillary Rodham Clinton. The Clintons were never charged with any wrongdoing. — Eds.

with napkins before going in there, and too bad about the customers, who must eat, although they don't realize it, almost literally out of our hands.

The break room summarizes the whole situation: there is none, because there are no breaks at Jerry's. For six to eight hours in a row, you never sit except to pee. Actually, there are three folding chairs at a table immediately adjacent to the bathroom, but hardly anyone ever sits in this, the very rectum of the gastroarchitectural system. Rather, the function of the peri-toilet area is to house the ashtrays in which servers and dishwashers leave their cigarettes burning at all times, like votive candles, so they don't have to waste time lighting up again when they dash back here for a puff. Almost everyone smokes as if their pulmonary well-being depended on it — the multinational mélange of cooks; the dishwashers, who are all Czechs here; the servers, who are American natives — creating an atmosphere in which oxygen is only an occasional pollutant. My first morning at Jerry's, when the hypoglycemic shakes set in, I complain to one of my fellow servers that I don't understand how she can go so long without food. "Well, I don't understand how *you* can go so long without a cigarette," she responds in a tone of reproach. Because work is what you do for others; smoking is what you do for yourself. I don't know why the antismoking crusaders have never grasped the element of defiant self-nurturance that makes the habit so endearing to its victims — as if, in the American workplace, the only thing people have to call their own is the tumors they are nourishing and the spare moments they devote to feeding them.

Now, the Industrial Revolution is not an easy transition, especially, in my experience, when you have to zip through it in just a couple of days. I have gone from craft work straight into the factory, from the air-conditioned morgue of the Hearthside directly into the flames. Customers arrive in human waves, sometimes disgorged fifty at a time from their tour buses, peckish and whiny. Instead of two "girls" on the floor at once, there can be as many as six of us running around in our brilliant pink-and-orange Hawaiian shirts. Conversations, either with customers or with fellow employees, seldom last more than twenty seconds at a time. On my first day, in fact, I am hurt by my sister servers' coldness. My mentor for the day is a supremely competent, emotionally uninflected twenty-three-year-old, and the others, who gossip a little among themselves about the real reason someone is out sick today and the size of the bail bond someone else has had to pay, ignore me completely. On my second day, I find out why. "Well, it's good to see *you* again," one of them says in greeting. "Hardly anyone comes back after the first day." I feel powerfully vindicated — a survivor — but it would take a long time, probably months, before I could hope to be accepted into this sorority.

I start out with the beautiful, heroic idea of handling the two jobs at once, and for two days I almost do it: working the breakfast/lunch shift at Jerry's from 8:00 till 2:00, arriving at the Hearthside a few minutes late, at 2:10, and attempting to hold out until 10:00. In the few minutes I have between jobs, I pick up a spicy chicken sandwich at the Wendy's drive-through window, gobble it down in the car, and change from khaki slacks to black, from Hawaiian to rust-colored polo. There is a problem, though. When, during the 3:00–4:00 dead time, I finally sit down to wrap silver, my flesh seems to bond to the seat: I try to refuel with a purloined cup of clam chowder, as I've seen Gail and Joan do dozens of times, but Stu catches me and hisses "No *eating*!" although there's not a customer around to be offended by the sight of food making contact with a server's lips. So I tell Gail I'm going to quit, and she hugs me and says she might just follow me to Jerry's herself.

But the chances of this are minuscule. She has left the flophouse and her annoying roommate and is back to living in her truck. But, guess what, she reports to me excitedly later that evening, Phillip has given her permission to park overnight in the hotel parking lot, as long as she keeps out of sight, and the parking lot should be totally safe since it's patrolled by a hotel security guard! With the Hearthside offering benefits like that, how could anyone think of leaving? This must be Phillip's theory, anyway. He accepts my resignation with a shrug, his main concern being that I return my two polo shirts and aprons.

Gail would have triumphed at Jerry's, I'm sure, but for me it's a crash course in exhaustion management. Years ago, the kindly fry cook who trained me to waitress at a Los Angeles truck stop used to say: Never make an unnecessary trip; if you don't have to walk fast, walk slow; if you don't have to walk, stand. But at Jerry's the effort of distinguishing necessary from unnecessary and urgent from whenever would itself be too much of an energy drain. The only thing to do is to treat each shift as a one-time-only emergency: you've got fifty starving people out there, lying scattered on the battlefield, so get out there and feed them! Forget that you will have to do this again tomorrow, forget that you will have to be alert enough to dodge the drunks on the drive home tonight — just burn, burn, burn! Ideally, at some point you enter what servers call a "rhythm" and psychologists term a "flow state," where signals pass from the sense organs directly to the muscles, bypassing the cerebral cortex, and a Zen-like emptiness sets in. I'm on a 2:00–10:00 P.M. shift now, and a male server from the morning shift tells me about the time he "pulled a triple" — three shifts in a row, all the way around the clock — and then got off and had a drink and met this girl, and maybe he shouldn't tell me this, but they had sex right then and there and it was like *beautiful*.

But there's another capacity of the neuromuscular system, which is pain. I start tossing back drugstore-brand ibuprofens as if they were vitamin C, four before each shift, because an old mouse-related repetitive-stress injury in my upper back has come back to full-spasm strength, thanks to the tray carrying. In my ordinary life, this level of disability might justify a day of ice packs and stretching. Here I comfort myself with the Aleve commercial where the cute blue-collar guy asks: If you quit after working four hours, what would your boss say? And the not-so-cute blue-collar guy, who's lugging a metal beam on his back, answers: He'd fire me, that's what. But fortunately, the commercial tells us, we workers can exert the same kind of authority over our painkillers that our bosses exert over us. If Tylenol doesn't want to work for more than four hours, you just fire its ass and switch to Aleve.

True, I take occasional breaks from this life, going home now and then to catch up on e-mail and for conjugal visits (though I am careful to "pay" for everything I eat here, at $5 for a dinner, which I put in a jar), seeing *The Truman Show* with friends and letting them buy my ticket. And I still have those what-am-I-doing-here moments at work, when I get so homesick for the printed word that I obsessively reread the six-page menu. But as the days go by, my old life is beginning to look exceedingly strange. The e-mails and phone messages addressed to my former self come from a distant race of people with exotic concerns and far too much time on their hands. The neighborly market I used to cruise for produce now looks forbiddingly like a Manhattan yuppie emporium. And when I sit down one morning in my real home to pay bills from my past life, I am dazzled by the two- and three-figure sums owed to outfits like Club Body Tech and Amazon.com.

Management at Jerry's is generally calmer and more "professional" than at the Hearthside, with two exceptions. One is Joy, a plump, blowsy woman in her early thirties who once kindly devoted several minutes of her time to instructing me in the correct one-handed method of tray carrying but whose moods change disconcertingly from shift to shift and even within one. The other is B.J., aka B.J. the Bitch, whose contribution is to stand by the kitchen counter and yell, "Nita, your order's up, move it!" or "Barbara, didn't you see you've got another table out there? Come *on*, girl!" Among other things, she is hated for having replaced the whipped cream squirt cans with big plastic whipped-cream-filled baggies that have to be squeezed with both hands—because, reportedly, she saw or thought she saw employees trying to inhale the propellant gas from the squirt cans, in the hope that it might be nitrous oxide. On my third night, she pulls me aside abruptly and brings her face so close that it looks like she's planning to butt me with her forehead. But instead of saying, "You're fired," she says, "You're doing fine." The only trouble is I'm spending time chatting with customers: "That's how they're getting you." Furthermore I am letting them "run me," which means harassment by sequential demands: you bring the catsup and they decide they want extra Thousand Island; you bring that and they announce they now need a side of fries, and so on into distraction. Finally she tells me not to take her wrong. She tries to say things in a nice way, but "you get into a mode, you know, because everything has to move so fast."[2]

I mumble thanks for the advice, feeling like I've just been stripped naked by the crazed enforcer of some ancient sumptuary law: No chatting for *you*, girl. No

10

---

[2]In *Workers in a Lean World: Unions in the International Economy* (Verso, 1997), Kim Moody cites studies finding an increase in stress-related workplace injuries and illness between the mid-1980s and the early 1990s. He argues that rising stress levels reflect a new system of "management by stress" in which workers in a variety of industries are being squeezed to extract maximum productivity, to the detriment of their health.

fancy service ethic allowed for the serfs. Chatting with customers is for the good-looking young college-educated servers in the downtown carpaccio and ceviche joints, the kids who can make $70–$100 a night. What had I been thinking? My job is to move orders from tables to kitchen and then trays from kitchen to tables. Customers are in fact the major obstacle to the smooth transformation of information into food and food into money — they are, in short, the enemy. And the painful thing is that I'm beginning to see it this way myself. There are the traditional asshole types — frat boys who down multiple Buds and then make a fuss because the steaks are so emaciated and the fries so sparse — as well as the variously impaired — due to age, diabetes, or literacy issues — who require patient nutritional counseling. The worst, for some reason, are the Visible Christians — like the ten-person table, all jolly and sanctified after Sunday night service, who run me mercilessly and then leave me $1 on a $92 bill. Or the guy with the crucifixion T-shirt (SOMEONE TO LOOK UP TO) who complains that his baked potato is too hard and his iced tea too icy (I cheerfully fix both) and leaves no tip at all. As a general rule, people wearing crosses or wwjd? ("What Would Jesus Do?") buttons look at us disapprovingly no matter what we do, as if they were confusing waitressing with Mary Magdalene's original profession.

I make friends, over time, with the other "girls" who work my shift: Nita, the tattooed twenty-something who taunts us by going around saying brightly, "Have we started making money yet?" Ellen, whose teenage son cooks on the graveyard shift and who once managed a restaurant in Massachusetts but won't try out for management here because she prefers being a "common worker" and not "ordering people around." Easygoing fiftyish Lucy, with the raucous laugh, who limps toward the end of the shift because of something that has gone wrong with her leg, the exact nature of which cannot be determined without health insurance. We talk about the usual girl things — men, children, and the sinister allure of Jerry's chocolate peanut-butter cream pie — though no one, I notice, ever brings up anything potentially expensive, like shopping or movies. As at the Hearthside, the only recreation ever referred to is partying, which requires little more than some beer, a joint, and a few close friends. Still, no one is homeless, or cops to it anyway, thanks usually to a working husband or boyfriend. All in all, we form a reliable mutual-support group: if one of us is feeling sick or overwhelmed, another one will "bev" a table or even carry trays for her. If one of us is off sneaking a cigarette or a pee, the others will do their best to conceal her absence from the enforcers of corporate rationality.[3]

---

[3]Until April 1998, there was no federally mandated right to bathroom breaks. According to Marc Linder and Ingrid Nygaard, authors of *Void Where Prohibited: Rest Breaks and the Right to Urinate on Company Time* (Cornell University Press, 1997), "The right to rest and void at work is not high on the list of social or political causes supported by professional or executive employees, who enjoy personal workplace liberties that millions of factory workers can only dream about. . . .

But my saving human connection—my oxytocin [hormone] receptor, as it were—is George, the nineteen-year-old Czech dishwasher who has been in this country exactly one week. We get talking when he asks me, tortuously, how much cigarettes cost at Jerry's. I do my best to explain that they cost over a dollar more here than at a regular store and suggest that he just take one from the half-filled packs that are always lying around on the break table. But that would be unthinkable. Except for the one tiny earring signaling his allegiance to some vaguely alternative point of view, George is a perfect straight arrow—crew-cut, hardworking, and hungry for eye contact. "Czech Republic," I ask, "or Slovakia?" and he seems delighted that I know the difference. "Vaclav Havel," I try, "Velvet Revolution, Frank Zappa?" "Yes, yes, 1989," he says, and I realize that for him this is already history.

My project is to teach George English. "How are you today, George?" I say at the start of each shift. "I am good, and how are you today, Barbara?" I learn that he is not paid by Jerry's but by the "agent" who shipped him over—$5 an hour, with the agent getting the dollar or so difference between that and what Jerry's pays dishwashers. I learn also that he shares an apartment with a crowd of other Czech "dishers," as he calls them, and that he cannot sleep until one of them goes off for his shift, leaving a vacant bed. We are having one of our ESL sessions late one afternoon when B.J. catches us at it and orders "Joseph" to take up the rubber mats on the floor near the dishwashing sinks and mop underneath. "I thought your name was George," I say loud enough for B.J. to hear as she strides off back to the counter. Is she embarrassed? Maybe a little, because she greets me back at the counter with "George, Joseph—there are so many of them!" I say nothing, neither nodding nor smiling, and for this I am punished later, when I think I am ready to go and she announces that I need to roll fifty more sets of silverware, and isn't it time I mixed up a fresh four-gallon batch of blue-cheese dressing? May you grow old in this place, B.J., is the curse I beam out at her when I am finally permitted to leave. May the syrup spills glue your feet to the floor.

I make the decision to move closer to Key West. First, because of the drive. Second and third, also because of the drive: gas is eating up $4–$5 a day, and although Jerry's is as high-volume as you can get, the tips average only 10 percent, and not just for a newbie like me. Between the base pay of $2.15 an hour and the obligation to share tips with the busboys and dishwashers, we're averaging only about $7.50 an hour. Then there is the $30 I had to spend on the regulation tan slacks worn by Jerry's servers—a setback it could take weeks to absorb. (I had combed the town's two downscale department stores hoping for something cheaper

---

While we were dismayed to discover that workers lacked an acknowledged right to void at work, [the workers] were amazed by outsiders' naïve belief that their employers would permit them to perform this basic bodily function when necessary. . . . A factory worker, not allowed a break for six-hour stretches, voided into pads worn inside her uniform; and a kindergarten teacher in a school without aides had to take all twenty children with her to the bathroom and line them up outside the stall door while she voided."

but decided in the end that these marked-down Dockers, originally $49, were more likely to survive a daily washing.) Of my fellow servers, everyone who lacks a working husband or boyfriend seems to have a second job: Nita does something at a computer eight hours a day; another welds. Without the forty-five-minute commute, I can picture myself working two jobs and still having the time to shower between them.

So I take the $500 deposit I have coming from my landlord, the $400 I have   15 earned toward the next month's rent, plus the $200 reserved for emergencies, and use the $1,100 to pay the rent and deposit on trailer number 46 in the Overseas Trailer Park, a mile from the cluster of budget hotels that constitute Key West's version of an industrial park. Number 46 is about eight feet in width and shaped like a barbell inside, with a narrow region—because of the sink and the stove— separating the bedroom from what might optimistically be called the "living" area, with its two-person table and half-sized couch. The bathroom is so small my knees rub against the shower stall when I sit on the toilet, and you can't just leap out of the bed, you have to climb down to the foot of it in order to find a patch of floor space to stand on. Outside, I am within a few yards of a liquor store, a bar that advertises "free beer tomorrow," a convenience store, and a Burger King—but no supermarket or, alas, laundromat. By reputation, the Overseas park is a nest of crime and crack, and I am hoping at least for some vibrant multicultural street life. But desolation rules night and day, except for a thin stream of pedestrians heading for their jobs at the Sheraton or the 7-Eleven. There are not exactly people here but what amounts to canned labor, being preserved between shifts from the heat.

In line with my reduced living conditions, a new form of ugliness arises at Jerry's. First we are confronted—via an announcement on the computers through which we input orders—with the new rule that the hotel bar, the Driftwood, is henceforth off-limits to restaurant employees. The culprit, I learn through the grapevine, is the ultraefficient twenty-three-year-old who trained me—another trailer home dweller and a mother of three. Something had set her off one morning, so she slipped out for a nip and returned to the floor impaired. The restriction mostly hurts Ellen, whose habit it is to free her hair from its rubber band and drop by the Driftwood for a couple of Zins before heading home at the end of her shift, but all of us feel the chill. Then the next day, when I go for straws, I find the dry-storage room locked. It's never been locked before; we go in and out of it all day—for napkins, jelly containers, Styrofoam cups for takeout. Vic, the portly assistant manager who opens it for me, explains that he caught one of the dishwashers attempting to steal something and, unfortunately, the miscreant will be with us until a replacement can be found—hence the locked door. I neglect to ask what he had been trying to steal but Vic tells me who he is—the kid with the buzz cut and the earring, you know, he's back there right now.

I wish I could say I rushed back and confronted George to get his side of the story. I wish I could say I stood up to Vic and insisted that George be given a translator and allowed to defend himself or announced that I'd find a lawyer who'd handle the case pro bono. At the very least I should have testified as to the kid's honesty. The mystery to me is that there's not much worth stealing in the dry-storage room, at least not in any fenceable quantity: "Is Gyorgi here, and am having 200—maybe 250—catsup packets. What do you say?" My guess is that he had taken—if he had taken anything at all—some Saltines or a can of cherry pie mix and that the motive for taking it was hunger.

So why didn't I intervene? Certainly not because I was held back by the kind of moral paralysis that can mask as journalistic objectivity. On the contrary, something new—something loathsome and servile—had infected me, along with the kitchen odors that I could still sniff on my bra when I finally undressed at night. In real life I am moderately brave, but plenty of brave people shed their courage in POW camps, and maybe something similar goes on in the infinitely more congenial milieu of the low-wage American workplace. Maybe, in a month or two more at Jerry's, I might have regained my crusading spirit. Then again, in a month or two I might have turned into a different person altogether—say, the kind of person who would have turned George in.

Questions for Discussion

1. Does Barbara Ehrenreich seem to be exaggerating the workplace as she describes it in this selection? If you have worked in a restaurant, does her description of the environment match your experience?

2. What is Ehrenreich's attitude toward her coworkers? Does she appreciate them? Is she condescending? How do you react to her observations?

3. Early in the selection, as Ehrenreich pays bills left over from her "real life," she reflects, "[My] old life is beginning to look exceedingly strange" (para. 8). At the end, she asks, "So why didn't I intervene [with George]?" (para. 18). Does the experience of "serving in Florida" change Ehrenreich? Cite specific passages to support your response.

4. According to Ehrenreich, who is to blame for the situation of those who work at low-paying jobs in restaurants? Are there heroes and villains, or does the workplace itself change the people who are part of it?

5. Overall, what is your attitude toward Ehrenreich and her method of research? Does choosing to live as one of the working poor for a short time—as a kind of visitor or tourist—give her an accurate picture of their lives? Explain whether you find her presentation of them respectful, convincing, sympathetic, patronizing, superficial, or some combination of these. Cite specific passages.

6. Ehrenreich's essay delivers strong implications about the U.S. economy. What is the relationship between the macroeconomy and the microeconomy in the essay? Which is more prominent? Identify places where she addresses each. What implications does her essay make about each?

Questions on Rhetoric and Style

1. Ehrenreich opens the selection with "Picture a fat person's hell ..." (para. 1). What is the intended effect? Does she want to shock or disgust the reader? Is she being humorous?

2. Ehrenreich describes the kitchen in terms of bodily organs and functions. What response is she trying to evoke? Is she successful? (See paras. 1 and 2.)

3. Ehrenreich provides fairly extensive commentary in footnotes. What is the effect of this strategy? In the footnotes, is her tone different from the one used in the body of the piece? Explain.

4. Ehrenreich uses lively, emotionally charged language throughout. Identify one passage and analyze the diction, especially the connotations of the words. Suggestions: the paragraph beginning "Now, the Industrial Revolution is not an easy transition ..." (para. 3) or "I make friends, over time, with the other 'girls' who work my shift ..." (para. 11).

5. Ehrenreich occasionally uses crude expressions. Are they appropriate? What is her intended effect in shifting to diction that is not only informal but, some would say, crass?

6. In this selection Ehrenreich is both outsider and insider; that is, she is the writer observing the environment in which she is playing a role. How does she make this narrative stance work? Does she shift abruptly between describing what is going on and commenting about it, or does she move smoothly between the two? Discuss by citing specific passages.

7. Discuss specific instances of humor in this selection. Is it primarily ironic humor? Aggressively sarcastic? Affectionately amusing? Cite specific passages in your response.

8. What elements of fiction does Ehrenreich employ? Consider such elements as figurative language, dialogue, narrative commentary, and description of people and settings.

9. In this selection, Ehrenreich does not state a thesis or indicate directly what her purpose is; instead, she works by inference and implication. What is her purpose? State it directly in a sentence that begins, "In this selection, Ehrenreich ..."

10. At times, Ehrenreich seems to raise tangential issues. When she describes her coworker smoking, for instance, she writes: "Because work is what you do for others; smoking is what you do for yourself. I don't know why the antismoking crusaders have never grasped the element of defiant self-nurturance that makes the habit so endearing to its victims — as if, in the American workplace, the only thing people have to call their own is the tumors they are nourishing and the spare moments they devote to feeding them" (para. 2). What is the effect of this commentary? What is its relevance to Ehrenreich's overall purpose?

11. How does Ehrenreich establish her ethos in this selection? What part does her relationship with George play in her appeal to ethos?

12. Who is Ehrenreich's audience? Base your answer on the tone you detect in specific passages.

Suggestions for Writing

1. Using Ehrenreich as a model, describe a negative work experience (for example, you may have found a boss to be arrogant or you may have encountered prejudice or bias). You can narrate—and comment—but also use dialogue, as Ehrenreich does, to make the situation come alive for your readers.

2. In "Evaluation," the final chapter of *Nickel and Dimed*, Ehrenreich observes:

   > Some odd optical property of our highly polarized and unequal society makes the poor almost invisible to their economic superiors. The poor can see the affluent easily enough—on television, for example, or on the covers of magazines. But the affluent rarely see the poor or, if they do catch sight of them in some public space, rarely know what they're seeing, since—thanks to consignment stores and, yes, Wal-Mart—the poor are usually able to disguise themselves as members of the more comfortable classes.

   Write an essay supporting or challenging Ehrenreich's analysis.

3. *Nickel and Dimed* takes place from 1998 to 2000. Write an essay explaining whether the author's experience would be the same or different in today's economy.

4. Write an editorial for a newspaper on a topic related to the issues Ehrenreich raises—for example, a minimum wage, health care, working conditions.

5. How much is the minimum wage? Develop a budget for living for one month as a single person earning the minimum wage (plus tips if applicable) in your geographical area. What kind of living accommodations could you afford? How much money would you have available for food? What would your transportation costs be?

A Modest Proposal

Jonathan Swift

Perhaps best known for *Gulliver's Travels* (1726), which has mistakenly come to be thought of as a children's novel, Jonathan Swift (1667–1745) was born in Ireland to English parents. He was educated at Trinity College, was ordained a minister, and was appointed dean of Saint Patrick's Cathedral in Dublin in 1713. For years he addressed the political problems of his day by publishing pamphlets on contemporary social issues, some of them anonymously. For one, it is believed that a reward of 300 pounds was offered to anyone who would "discover" the authorship. Among these pamphlets is the well-known essay "A Modest Proposal for Preventing the Children of Poor People in Ireland from Being a Burden to Their Parents or Country, and for Making Them Beneficial to the Publick," widely known as "A Modest Proposal." As a model of elegant prose and cogent argument, it has gained deserved fame. After reading it, you will understand what *Swiftian* means and why Swift is regarded as one of the world's premier satirists.

It is a melancholy object to those who walk through this great town or travel in the country, when they see the streets, the roads, and cabin doors, crowded with beggars of the female sex, followed by three, four, or six children, all in rags and importuning every passenger for an alms. These mothers instead of being able to work for their honest livelihood, are forced to employ all their time in strolling to beg sustenance for their helpless infants: who as they grow up either turn thieves for want of work, or leave their dear native country to fight for the pretender[1] in Spain, or sell themselves to the Barbadoes.

I think it is agreed by all parties that this prodigious number of children in the arms, or on the backs, or at the heels of their mothers, and frequently of their fathers, is in the present deplorable state of the kingdom a very great additional grievance; and, therefore, whoever could find out a fair, cheap, and easy method of making these children sound, useful members of the commonwealth, would deserve so well of the public as to have his statue set up for a preserver of the nation.

But my intention is very far from being confined to provide only for the children of professed beggars; it is of a much greater extent, and shall take in the whole number of infants at a certain age who are born of parents in effect as little able to support them as those who demand our charity in the streets.

---

[1] James Francis Edward, son of deposed Catholic King James II. His claim to the throne was not considered legitimate; thus, he was a pretender to the throne. — Eds.

As to my own part, having turned my thoughts for many years upon this important subject, and maturely weighed the several schemes of our projectors, I have always found them grossly mistaken in their computation. It is true, a child just dropped from its dam may be supported by her milk for a solar year, with little other nourishment; at most not above the value of 2s., which the mother may certainly get, or the value in scraps, by her lawful occupation of begging; and it is exactly at one year old that I propose to provide for them in such a manner as instead of being a charge upon their parents or the parish, or wanting food and raiment for the rest of their lives, they shall on the contrary contribute to the feeding, and partly to the clothing, of many thousands.

There is likewise another great advantage in my scheme, that it will prevent those voluntary abortions, and that horrid practice of women murdering their bastard children, alas! too frequent among us! sacrificing the poor innocent babes I doubt more to avoid the expense than the shame, which would move tears and pity in the most savage and inhuman breast.

The number of souls in this kingdom being usually reckoned one million and a half, of these I calculate there may be about 200,000 couple whose wives are breeders; from which number I subtract 30,000 couple who are able to maintain their own children (although I apprehend there cannot be so many, under the present distress of the kingdom); but this being granted, there will remain 170,000 breeders. I again subtract 50,000 for those women who miscarry, or whose children die by accident or disease within the year. There only remain 120,000 children of poor parents annually born. The question therefore is, how this number shall be reared and provided for? which, as I have already said, under the present situation of affairs, is utterly impossible by all the methods hitherto proposed. For we can neither employ them in handicraft of agriculture; we neither build houses (I mean in the country) nor cultivate land; they can very seldom pick up a livelihood by stealing, till they arrive at six years old, except where they are of towardly parts, although I confess they learn the rudiments much earlier; during which time they can, however, be properly looked upon only as probationers; as I have been informed by a principal gentleman in the county of Cavan, who protested to me that he never knew above one or two instances under the age of six, even in a part of the kingdom so renowned for the quickest proficiency in that art.

I am assured by our merchants, that a boy or a girl before twelve years old is no salable commodity; and even when they come to this age they will not yield above 3£ or 3£ 2s. 6d.[2] at most on the exchange; which cannot turn to account either to the parents or kingdom, the charge of nutriment and rags having been at least four times that value.

I shall now therefore humbly propose my own thoughts, which I hope will not be liable to the least objection.

---

[2] 3 pounds, 2 shillings, 6 pence (denominations of English money). — Eds.

I have been assured by a very knowing American of my acquaintance in London, that a young healthy child well nursed is at a year old a most delicious, nourishing, and wholesome food, whether stewed, roasted, baked, or broiled; and I make no doubt that it will equally serve in a fricassee or a ragout.

I do therefore humbly offer it to public consideration that of the 120,000 children already computed, 20,000 may be reserved for breed, whereof only one-fourth part to be males; which is more than we allow to sheep, black cattle, or swine; and my reason is, that these children are seldom the fruits of marriage, a circumstance not much regarded by our savages; therefore one male will be sufficient to serve four females. That the remaining 100,000 may, at a year old, be offered in sale to the persons of quality and fortune through the kingdom; always advising the mother to let them suck plentifully in the last month, so as to render them plump and fat for a good table. A child will make two dishes at an entertainment for friends; and when the family dines alone, the fore and hind quarter will make a reasonable dish, and seasoned with a little pepper or salt will be very good boiled on the fourth day, especially in winter. 10

I have reckoned upon a medium that a child just born will weigh 12 pounds, and in a solar year, if tolerably nursed, will increase to 28 pounds.

I grant this food will be somewhat dear, and therefore very proper for landlords, who, as they have already devoured most of the parents, seem to have the best title to the children.

Infants' flesh will be in season throughout the year, but more plentiful in March, and a little before and after: for we are told by a grave author, an eminent French physician, that fish being a prolific diet, there are more children born in Roman Catholic countries about nine months after Lent than at any other season; therefore, reckoning a year after Lent, the markets will be more glutted than usual, because the number of popish infants is at least three to one in this kingdom: and therefore it will have one other collateral advantage, by lessening the number of papists among us.

I have already computed the charge of nursing a beggar's child (in which list I reckon all cottagers, laborers, and four-fifths of the farmers) to be about 2s. per annum, rags included; and I believe no gentleman would repine to give 10s. for the carcass of a good fat child, which, as I have said, will make four dishes of excellent nutritive meat, when he has only some particular friend or his own family to dine with him. Thus the squire will learn to be a good landlord, and grow popular among the tenants; the mother will have 8s. net profit, and be fit for work till she produces another child.

Those who are more thrifty (as I must confess the times require) may flay the carcass; the skin of which artificially dressed will make admirable gloves for ladies, and summer boots for fine gentlemen. 15

As to our city of Dublin, shambles may be appointed for this purpose in the most convenient parts of it, and butchers we may be assured will not be wanting: although I rather recommend buying the children alive, and dressing them hot from the knife as we do roasting pigs.

A very worthy person, a true lover of his country, and whose virtues I highly esteem, was lately pleased in discoursing on this matter to offer a refinement upon my scheme. He said that many gentlemen of this kingdom, having of late destroyed their deer, he conceived that the want of venison might be well supplied by the bodies of young lads and maidens, not exceeding fourteen years of age nor under twelve; so great a number of both sexes in every country being now ready to starve for want of work and service; and these to be disposed of by their parents, if alive, or otherwise by their nearest relations. But with due deference to so excellent a friend and so deserving a patriot, I cannot be altogether in his sentiments; for as to the males, my American acquaintance assured me from frequent experience that their flesh was generally tough and lean, like that of our schoolboys by continual exercise, and their taste disagreeable; and to fatten them would not answer the charge. Then as to the females, it would, I think, with humble submission be a loss to the public, because they soon would become breeders themselves: and besides, it is not improbable that some scrupulous people might be apt to censure such a practice (although indeed very unjustly), as a little bordering upon cruelty; which, I confess, has always been with me the strongest objection against any project, how well soever intended.

But in order to justify my friend, he confessed that this expedient was put into his head by the famous Psalmanazar, a native of the island Formosa,[3] who came from thence to London about twenty years ago: and in conversation told my friend, that in his country when any young person happened to be put to death, the executioner sold the carcass to persons of quality as a prime dainty; and that in his time the body of a plump girl of fifteen, who was crucified for an attempt to poison the emperor, was sold to his imperial majesty's prime minister of state, and other great mandarins of the court, in joints from the gibbet, at 400 crowns. Neither indeed can I deny, that if the same use were made of several plump young girls in this town, who without one single groat to their fortunes cannot stir abroad without a chair, and appear at the playhouse and assemblies in foreign fineries which they never will pay for, the kingdom would not be the worse.

Some persons of a desponding spirit are in great concern about the vast number of poor people, who are aged, diseased, or maimed, and I have been desired to employ my thoughts what course may be taken to ease the nation of so grievous an encumbrance. But I am not in the least pain upon that matter, because it is very well known that they are every day dying and rotting by cold and famine, and filth and vermin, as fast as can be reasonably expected. And as to the young laborers, they are now in as hopeful condition: They cannot get work, and consequently pine away for want of nourishment, to a degree that if at any time they are accidentally hired to common labor, they have not strength to perform it; and thus the country and themselves are happily delivered from the evils to come.

---

[3]Taiwan. Psalmanazar was later found to be a fraud. His book on Formosa and its culture described cannibalistic religious rituals. — Eds.

I have too long digressed, and therefore shall return to my subject. I think the $\quad$ 20
advantages by the proposal which I have made are obvious and many, as well as
of the highest importance.

For first, as I have already observed, it would greatly lessen the number of
papists, with whom we are yearly overrun, being the principal breeders of the
nation as well as our most dangerous enemies; and who stay at home on purpose
to deliver the kingdom to the Pretender, hoping to take their advantage by the
absence of so many good Protestants, who have chosen rather to leave their country
than stay at home and pay tithes against their conscience to an Episcopal curate.

Secondly, The poor tenants will have something valuable of their own, which
by law may be made liable to distress and help to pay their landlord's rent, their
corn and cattle being already seized, and money a thing unknown.

Thirdly, Whereas the maintenance of 100,000 children from two years old and
upward, cannot be computed at less than 10s. a-piece per annum, the nation's stock
will be thereby increased £50,000 per annum, beside the profit of a new dish introduced to the tables of all gentlemen of fortune in the kingdom who have any refinement in taste. And the money will circulate among ourselves, the goods being
entirely of our own growth and manufacture.

Fourthly, The constant breeders beside the gain of 8s. sterling per annum by
the sale of their children, will be rid of the charge of maintaining them after the
first year.

Fifthly, This food would likewise bring great custom to taverns where the vint- $\quad$ 25
ners will certainly be so prudent as to procure the best receipts for dressing it to
perfection, and consequently have their houses frequented by all the fine gentlemen, who justly value themselves upon their knowledge in good eating; and a
skilful cook who understands how to oblige his guests, will contrive to make it as
expensive as they please.

Sixthly, This would be a great inducement to marriage, which all wise nations
have either encouraged by rewards or enforced by laws and penalties. It would
increase the care and tenderness of mothers toward their children, when they were
sure of a settlement for life to the poor babes, provided in some sort by the public,
to their annual profit instead of expense. We should see an honest emulation among
the married women, which of them would bring the fattest child to the market.
Men would become as fond of their wives during the time of their pregnancy as
they are now of their mares in foal, their cows in calf, their sows when they are
ready to farrow; nor offer to beat or kick them (as is too frequent a practice) for
fear of a miscarriage.

Many other advantages might be enumerated. For instance, the addition of
some thousand carcasses in our exportation of barreled beef, the propagation of
swine's flesh, and improvement in the art of making good bacon, so much wanted
among us by the great destruction of pigs, too frequent at our table; which are no
way comparable in taste or magnificence to a well-grown, fat, yearling child, which
roasted whole will make a considerable figure at a lord mayor's feast or any other
public entertainment. But this and many others I omit, being studious of brevity.

Supposing that 1,000 families in this city would be constant customers for infants' flesh, besides others who might have it at merry-meetings, particularly at weddings and christenings, I compute that Dublin would take off annually about 20,000 carcasses; and the rest of the kingdom (where probably they will be sold somewhat cheaper) the remaining 80,000.

I can think of no one objection that will possibly be raised against this proposal unless it should be urged that the number of people will be thereby much lessened in the kingdom. This I freely own, and it was indeed one principal design in offering it to the world. I desire the reader will observe, that I calculate my remedy for this one individual kingdom of Ireland and for no other that ever was, is, or I think ever can be upon earth. Therefore let no man talk to me of other expedients: of taxing our absentees at 5s. a pound: of using neither clothes nor household furniture except what is of our own growth and manufacture: of utterly rejecting the materials and instruments that promote foreign luxury: of curing the expensiveness of pride, vanity, idleness, and gaming in our women: of introducing a vein of parsimony, prudence, and temperance: of learning to love our country, in the want of which we differ even from Laplanders and the inhabitants of Topinamboo[4]: of quitting our animosities and factions; nor acting any longer like the Jews, who were murdering one another at the very moment their city was taken: of being a little cautious not to sell our country and conscience for nothing: of teaching landlords to have at least one degree of mercy toward their tenants: lastly, of putting a spirit of honesty, industry, and skill into our shopkeepers; who, if a resolution could now be taken to buy only our native goods, would immediately unite to cheat and exact upon us in the price, the measure, and the goodness, nor could ever yet be brought to make one fair proposal of just dealing, though often and earnestly invited to it.

Therefore I repeat, let no man talk to me of these and the like expedients, till he has at least some glimpse of hope that there will be ever some hearty and sincere attempt to put them in practice.

But as to myself, having been wearied out for many years with offering vain, idle, visionary thoughts, and at length utterly despairing of success, I fortunately fell upon this proposal; which, as it is wholly new, so it has something solid and real, of no expense and little trouble, full in our own power, and whereby we can incur no danger in disobliging England. For this kind of commodity will not bear exportation, the flesh being of too tender a consistence to admit a long continuance in salt, although perhaps I could name a country which would be glad to eat up our whole nation without it.

After all, I am not so violently bent upon my own opinion as to reject any offer proposed by wise men, which shall be found equally innocent, cheap, easy, and effectual. But before something of that kind shall be advanced in contradiction to my scheme, and offering a better, I desire the author or authors will be

30

---

[4]"Laplanders" refers to Norwegians, and "Topinamboo" is a region in Brazil.—Eds.

pleased maturely to consider two points. First, as things now stand, how they will be able to find food and raiment for 100,000 useless mouths and backs. And secondly, there being a round million of creatures in human figure throughout this kingdom, whose subsistence put into a common stock would leave them in debt 2,000,000£, sterling, adding those who are beggars by profession to the bulk of farmers, cottagers, and laborers, with the wives and children who are beggars in effect; I desire those politicians who dislike my overture, and may perhaps be so bold as to attempt an answer, that they will first ask the parents of these mortals, whether they would not at this day think it a great happiness to have been sold for food at a year old in the manner I prescribe, and thereby have avoided such a perpetual scene of misfortunes as they have since gone through by the oppression of landlords, the impossibility of paying rent without money or trade, the want of common sustenance, with neither house nor clothes to cover them from the inclemencies of the weather, and the most inevitable prospect of entailing the like or greater miseries upon their breed for ever.

I profess, in the sincerity of my heart, that I have not the least personal interest in endeavoring to promote this necessary work, having no other motive than the public good of my country, by advancing our trade, providing for infants, relieving the poor, and giving some pleasure to the rich. I have no children by which I can propose to get a single penny; the youngest being nine years old, and my wife past childbearing.

Questions for Discussion

1. What were the social conditions in Ireland that occasioned the writing of Jonathan Swift's essay? Does the essay indicate what Swift considers to be the causes of these conditions? Does the government—the state—have a responsibility for the condition of its poor? Does Swift target anybody in particular with his satire? How can you tell?
2. Would a modern audience be more or less offended by Swift's proposal? Explain your reasoning.
3. Of the six advantages Swift enumerates (paras. 21–26), which one might be considered the most sardonic? Explain.
4. Explain how Swift uses the essay to satirize both his subject and the vehicle he employs—that is, a political proposal itself.
5. What is Swift's overall purpose? Why did he choose such a provocative approach?
6. The modern reader may notice the misogyny in Swift's essay. Does it affect your opinion of the essay? Does it make Swift's criticism of society less powerful?
7. Several eighteenth-century writers made allusions to "A Modest Proposal" in the titles of their satiric essays. For example, Philip Skelton made his irony obvious by calling an essay "Some Proposals for the Revival of Christianity." Why do you think Swift's title was considered such a useful satiric tool?

8. By publishing such an outrageous text, what might Swift have hoped to bring about among the people of Ireland?

Questions on Rhetoric and Style

1. How does Swift want the reader to view his speaker? That is, how would Swift want his reader to describe the persona he adopts?
2. At what point in the essay did you recognize that Swift's proposal is meant to be satiric? Do you think a modern audience would get the joke faster than Swift's contemporaries did?
3. Note Swift's diction in the first seven paragraphs. How does it show quantification and dehumanization? Explain the purpose of Swift's specific word choices.
4. At the beginning of the essay, Swift explains the anticipated results before revealing the actual proposal. Explain the rhetorical purpose of such a strategy.
5. In paragraph 9, why doesn't Swift end the sentence after the word *food*? Explain the purpose and effect of the modifiers included there.
6. Identify examples of appeals to values such as thrift and patriotism. Explain the rhetorical strategy behind each example.
7. Consider the additional proposal that Swift mentions in paragraph 17. Explain the rhetorical strategy at work in that paragraph.
8. Which targets does Swift ironically identify in paragraphs 21 and 22? Note the rhetorical progression of paragraphs 21–26. By using such a method, what is Swift satirizing?
9. What are the assumptions behind each of Swift's claims in paragraphs 21–26? Explain them.
10. Read carefully paragraphs 29–31. What are the "expedients" that Swift discusses there? How does irony serve his rhetorical purpose in this section?
11. To what do the "vain, idle, visionary thoughts" (para. 31) refer? What is Swift's tone here?
12. How does the final paragraph of the essay contribute to Swift's rhetorical purpose?

Suggestions for Writing

1. "A Modest Proposal" is remarkably consistent in its ironic voice throughout. There are, however, some places where Swift's own voice intrudes. Write an essay showing how these breaks in tone reveal Swift's own attitude toward his subject.
2. Read carefully paragraphs 20–26. Then write an essay explaining how Swift uses resources of language to develop his positions. Consider diction, voice, pacing, and other rhetorical features to support your position.
3. Write an essay explaining the influence of Swift on a contemporary example of satire. One example, by political commentator Christopher Buckley about mad cow disease, was published in the *New Yorker* (April 15, 1996) and titled "A Moodest Proposal." Another example might be the satiric news program *The Colbert Report*.

4. Write a response to Swift in the voice of an economist sympathetic to Swift's views, or in the voice of someone who takes the proposal seriously, challenging Swift's argument.
5. Write your own "modest proposal" about an economic condition in today's society. Be sure to specify who your audience is — whether you intend your piece to be published in a national magazine, your local newspaper, or your school newspaper.

from *The Roots of Honor*

John Ruskin

John Ruskin (1819–1900) was born in London, the only child of a wine importer. He was educated at home and studied at King's College, London, and at Oxford. A precocious young man, he started writing articles at age fifteen and became a highly influential art critic, publishing his first great work, *Modern Painters*, in five volumes between 1843 and 1860. He later turned to social and political concerns, writing such works as the three-volume *The Stones of Venice* (1851–1853), *Unto This Last* (1860), and *Sesame and Lilies* (1865). *Unto This Last* addresses social reform and economics; it includes "The Roots of Honor," excerpted here. Ruskin held an Oxford professorship from 1870 to 1880, when he resigned for health reasons. He had bouts of madness until 1883, when he was reelected to his professorship. Astoundingly prolific, Ruskin wrote over 250 works on art, ornithology, politics, history, economics, geology, literature, mythology, and what we would now call environmental science. He also wrote a fantasy novel, *The King of the Golden River* (1841), and worked on his autobiography, *Praeterita*, from 1885 to 1889. Ruskin's thought on art and political economy has been highly influential. *Unto This Last* had a profound influence on Mahatma Gandhi, and Ruskin continues to influence such contemporary writers as Wendell Berry, whose work is included in this chapter (p. 484).

Now there can be no question but that the tact, foresight, decision, and other mental powers required for the successful management of a large mercantile concern, if not such as could be compared with those of a great lawyer, general, or divine, would at least match the general conditions of mind required in the subordinate officers of a ship, or of a regiment, or in the curate of a country parish. If, therefore, all the efficient members of the so-called liberal professions are still, somehow, in public estimate of honor, preferred before the head of a commercial firm, the reason must lie deeper than in the measurement of their several powers of mind.

And the essential reason for such preference will be found to lie in the fact that the merchant is presumed to act always selfishly. His work may be very necessary to the community; but the motive of it is understood to be wholly personal. The merchant's first object in all his dealings must be (the public believe) to get as much for himself, and leave as little to his neighbor (or customer) as possible. Enforcing this upon him, by political statute, as the necessary principle of his action; recommending it to him on all occasions, and themselves reciprocally adopting it; proclaiming vociferously, for law of the universe, that a buyer's function is to cheapen, and a seller's to cheat—the public, nevertheless, involuntarily condemn the man of commerce for his compliance with their own statement, and stamp him forever as belonging to an inferior grade of human personality.

This they will find, eventually, they must give up doing. They must not cease to condemn selfishness; but they will have to discover a kind of commerce which is not exclusively selfish. Or, rather, they will have to discover that there never was, or can be, any other kind of commerce; that this which they have called commerce was not commerce at all, but cozening; and that a true merchant differs as much from a merchant according to laws of modern political economy, as the hero of the "Excursion" from Autolycus.[1] They will find that commerce is an occupation which gentlemen will every day see more need to engage in, rather than in the businesses of talking to men or slaying them; that, in true commerce, as in true preaching, or true fighting, it is necessary to admit the idea of occasional voluntary loss; that sixpences have to be lost, as well as lives, under a sense of duty; that the market may have its martyrdoms as well as the pulpit; and trade its heroisms, as well as war.

May have—in the final issue, must have—and only has not had yet, because men of heroic temper have always been misguided in their youth into other fields, not recognizing what is in our days, perhaps, the most important of all fields; so that, while many a zealous person loses his life in trying to teach the form of a gospel, very few will lose a hundred pounds in showing the practice of one.

The fact is, that people never have had clearly explained to them the true functions of a merchant with respect to other people. I should like the reader to be very clear about this.

Five great intellectual professions, relating to daily necessities of life, have hitherto existed—three exist necessarily in every civilized nation:

The Soldier's profession is to *defend* it.
The Pastor's, to *teach* it.
The Physician's, to *keep it in health*.
The Lawyer's, to *enforce justice* in it.
The Merchant's, to *provide* for it.

And the duty of all these men is, on due occasion, to *die* for it.

"On due occasion," namely:

The Soldier, rather than leave his post in battle.
The Physician, rather than leave his post in plague.
The Pastor, rather than teach Falsehood.
The Lawyer, rather than countenance Injustice.
The Merchant—What is *his* "due occasion" of death?

It is the main question for the merchant, as for all of us. For, truly, the man who does not know when to die, does not know how to live.

---

[1] By the "Excursion," Ruskin is playfully referring to the *Odyssey* and its hero, Odysseus. In contrast, Odysseus's grandfather, Autolycus, was a child of Hermes, and thus a thief. It was said he could never be caught. —Eds.

Observe, the merchant's function (or manufacturer's, for in the broad sense in which it is here used the word must be understood to include both) is to provide for the nation. It is no more his function to get profit for himself out of that provision than it is a clergyman's function to get his stipend. The stipend is a due and necessary adjunct, but not the object, of his life, if he be a true clergyman, any more than his fee (or *honorarium*) is the object of life to a true physician. Neither is his fee the object of life to a true merchant. All three, if true men, have a work to be done irrespective of fee — to be done even at any cost, or for quite the contrary of fee; the pastor's function being to teach, the physician's to heal, and the merchant's, as I have said, to provide. That is to say, he has to understand to their very root the qualities of the things he deals in, and the means of obtaining or producing it; and he has to apply all his sagacity and energy to the producing or obtaining it in perfect state, and distributing it at the cheapest possible price where it is most needed.

And because the production or obtaining of any commodity involves necessarily the agency of many lives and hands, the merchant becomes in the course of his business the master and governor of large masses of men in a more direct, though less confessed way, than a military officer or pastor; so that on him falls, in great part, the responsibility for the kind of life they lead; and it becomes his duty, not only to be always considering how to produce what he sells in the purest and cheapest forms, but how to make the various employments involved in the production, or transference of it, most beneficial to the men employed.

And as into these two functions, requiring for their right exercise the highest intelligence, as well as patience, kindness, and tact, the merchant is bound to put all his energy, so for their just discharge he is bound, as soldier or physician is bound, to give up, if need be, his Life, in such way as it may be demanded of him. Two main points he has in his Providing function to maintain: first, his engagements (faithfulness to engagements being the real root of all possibilities in commerce); and secondly, the perfectness and purity of the thing provided; so that, rather than fail in any engagement, or consent to any deterioration, adulteration, or unjust and exorbitant price of that which he provides, he is bound to meet fearlessly any form of distress, poverty, or labor, which may, through maintenance of these points, come upon him.

Again: in his office as governor of the men employed by him, the merchant or manufacturer is invested with a distinctly paternal authority and responsibility. In most cases, a youth entering a commercial establishment is withdrawn altogether from home influence; his master must become his father, else he has, for practical and constant help, no father at hand: in all cases the master's authority, together with the general tone and atmosphere of his business, and the character of the men with whom the youth is compelled in the course of it to associate, have more immediate and pressing weight than the home influence, and will usually neutralize it either for good or evil; so that the only means which the master has of doing justice to the men employed by him is to ask himself sternly whether he is dealing with such subordinate as he would with his own son, if compelled by circumstances to take such a position.

Supposing the captain of a frigate saw it right, or were by any chance obliged, to place his own son in the position of a common sailor; as he would then treat his son, he is bound always to treat every one of the men under him. So, also, supposing the master of a manufactory saw it right, or were by any chance obliged, to place his own son in the position of an ordinary workman; as he would then treat his son, he is bound always to treat every one of his men. This is the only effective, true, or practicable RULE which can be given on this point of political economy.

And as the captain of a ship is bound to be the last man to leave his ship in case of wreck, and to share his last crust with the sailors in case of famine, so the manufacturer, in any commercial crisis or distress, is bound to take the suffering of it with his men, and even to take more of it for himself than he allows his men to feel; as a father would in a famine, shipwreck, or battle, sacrifice himself for his son.

All which sounds very strange: the only real strangeness in the matter being, nevertheless, that it should so sound. For all this is true, and that not partially nor theoretically, but everlastingly and practically: all other doctrine than this respecting matters political being false in premises, absurd in deduction, and impossible in practice, consistently with any progressive state of national life; all the life which we now possess as a nation showing itself in the resolute denial and scorn, by a few strong minds and faithful hearts, of the economic principles taught to our multitudes, which principles, so far as accepted, lead straight to national destruction. Respecting the modes and forms of destruction to which they lead, and, on the other hand, respecting the farther practical working of true polity, I hope to reason further in a following paper.

15

Exploring the Text

1. What is the "preference" John Ruskin refers to at the beginning of the second paragraph? According to Ruskin, who is responsible for it? The merchant himself? The public? Explain.
2. How does Ruskin characterize commerce in paragraphs 3 and 4? What has changed since 1862? What has not?
3. How reasonable are Ruskin's statements about the five great professions (para. 6)? Do you agree that the merchant's profession is not, as many would say, to make money, but to provide for the country?
4. Ruskin writes, "For, truly, the man who does not know when to die, does not know how to live" (para. 8). What does Ruskin mean to suggest with this epigrammatic statement? How might it apply to your life?
5. Explain the nature of the comparison Ruskin makes between the merchant and the clergyman (para. 9).

6. In paragraph 9, Ruskin writes of the pastor, the physician, and the merchant, "All three, if true men. . . ." What are the purpose and effect of the qualifier "if true men"?
7. What, according to Ruskin, is the duty of the merchant as described in paragraphs 10 and 11?
8. What is the nature of the analogy developed in paragraphs 12–14? Do you find it reasonable and persuasive? Explain.
9. Ruskin concludes, "All which sounds very strange: the only real strangeness in the matter being, nevertheless, that it should so sound" (para. 15). Does it "sound strange" to you? Do you agree that the *sounding strange* is the only strange thing about it? Why does he conclude this way?

The Atlanta Exposition Address

Booker T. Washington

Born a slave in West Virginia, Booker T. Washington (1856–1915) was an influential educator and the founder of Tuskegee Normal and Industrial Institute in Alabama. After emancipation, he worked in salt mines and coal mines and then literally walked two hundred miles to attend the Hampton Institute in Virginia, which was then an industrial school for African Americans and Native Americans. There, he paid his tuition and board by working as a janitor. Graduating with honors in 1875, Washington taught at the Hampton Institute until 1881. Stressing the importance of learning a trade and developing self-confidence, Washington's pragmatism appealed to African Americans living in the post-Reconstruction South. He was criticized by the NAACP and other organizations for promoting accommodation rather than resistance to Southern white supremacy. He worked behind the scenes, however, to sponsor civil rights suits and advocate on behalf of Historically Black Colleges and Universities. Washington delivered the following speech in 1895 before the Cotton States and International Exposition in Atlanta to promote the economic ascendancy of the South.

MR. PRESIDENT AND GENTLEMEN OF THE BOARD OF DIRECTORS AND CITIZENS.

One-third of the population of the South is of the Negro race. No enterprise seeking the material, civil, or moral welfare of this section can disregard this element of our population and reach the highest success. I but convey to you, Mr. President and Directors, the sentiment of the masses of my race when I say that in no way have the value and manhood of the American Negro been more fittingly and generously recognized than by the managers of this magnificent Exposition at every stage of its progress. It is a recognition that will do more to cement the friendship of the two races than any occurrence since the dawn of our freedom.

Not only this, but the opportunity here afforded will awaken among us a new era of industrial progress. Ignorant and inexperienced, it is not strange that in the first years of our new life we began at the top instead of at the bottom; that a seat in Congress or the state legislature was more sought than real estate or industrial skill; that the political convention of stump speaking had more attractions than starting a dairy farm or truck garden.

A ship lost at sea for many days suddenly sighted a friendly vessel. From the mast of the unfortunate vessel was seen a signal, "Water, water; we die of thirst!" The answer from the friendly vessel at once came back, "Cast down your bucket where you are." A second time the signal, "Water, water; send us water!" ran up from the distressed vessel, and was answered, "Cast down your bucket where you are." And a third and fourth signal for water was answered, "Cast down your bucket where you are." The captain of the distressed vessel, at last heeding the injunction, cast down his bucket, and it came up full of fresh, sparkling water from the mouth of the Amazon River. To those of my race who depend on bettering their condition in a foreign land or who underestimate the importance of cultivating friendly relations with the Southern white man, who is their next-door neighbour, I would say: "Cast down your bucket where you are"—cast it down in making friends in every manly way of the people of all races by whom we are surrounded.

Cast it down in agriculture, mechanics, in commerce, in domestic service, and in the professions. And in this connection it is well to bear in mind that whatever other sins the South may be called to bear, when it comes to business pure and simple, it is in the South that the Negro is given a man's chance in the commercial world, and in nothing is this Exposition more eloquent than in emphasizing this chance. Our greatest danger is that in the great leap from slavery to freedom we may overlook the fact that the masses of us are to live by the productions of our hands, and fail to keep in mind that we shall prosper in proportion as we learn to dignify and glorify common labour and put brains and skill into the common occupations of life; shall prosper in proportion as we learn to draw the line between the superficial and the substantial, the ornamental gewgaws of life and the useful. No race can prosper till it learns that there is as much dignity in tilling a field as in writing a poem. It is at the bottom of life we must begin, and not at the top. Nor should we permit our grievances to overshadow our opportunities.

To those of the white race who look to the incoming of those of foreign birth and strange tongue and habits for the prosperity of the South, were I permitted I would repeat what I say to my own race, "Cast down your bucket where you are." Cast it down among the eight millions of Negroes whose habits you know, whose fidelity and love you have tested in days when to have proved treacherous meant the ruin of your firesides. Cast down your bucket among these people who have, without strikes and labour wars, tilled your fields, cleared your forests, builded your railroads and cities, and brought forth treasures from the bowels of the earth, and helped make possible this magnificent representation of the progress of the South. Casting down your bucket among my people, helping and encouraging them as you are doing on these grounds, and to education of head, hand, and heart, you

5

will find that they will buy your surplus land, make blossom the waste places in your fields, and run your factories. While doing this, you can be sure in the future, as in the past, that you and your families will be surrounded by the most patient, faithful, law-abiding, and unresentful people that the world has seen. As we have proved our loyalty to you in the past, in nursing your children, watching by the sickbed of your mothers and fathers, and often following them with tear-dimmed eyes to their graves, so in the future, in our humble way, we shall stand by you with a devotion that no foreigner can approach, ready to lay down our lives, if need be, in defence of yours, interlacing our industrial, commercial, civil, and religious life with yours in a way that shall make the interests of both races one. In all things that are purely social we can be as separate as the fingers, yet one as the hand in all things essential to mutual progress.

There is no defence or security for any of us except in the highest intelligence and development of all. If anywhere there are efforts tending to curtail the fullest growth of the Negro, let these efforts be turned into stimulating, encouraging, and making him the most useful and intelligent citizen. Effort or means so invested will pay a thousand per cent interest. These efforts will be twice blessed—"blessing him that gives and him that takes."

There is no escape through law of man or God from the inevitable:—

The laws of changeless justice bind
   Oppressor with oppressed;
And close as sin and suffering joined
   We march to fate abreast.

Nearly sixteen millions of hands will aid you in pulling the load upward, or they will pull against you the load downward. We shall constitute one-third and more of the ignorance and crime of the South, or one-third its intelligence and progress; we shall contribute one-third to the business and industrial prosperity of the South, or we shall prove a veritable body of death, stagnating, depressing, retarding every effort to advance the body politic.

Gentlemen of the Exposition, as we present to you our humble effort at an exhibition of our progress, you must not expect overmuch. Starting thirty years ago with ownership here and there in a few quilts and pumpkins and chickens (gathered from miscellaneous sources), remember the path that has led from these to the inventions and production of agricultural implements, buggies, steam-engines, newspapers, books, statuary, carving, paintings, the management of drug-stores and banks, has not been trodden without contact with thorns and thistles. While we take pride in what we exhibit as a result of our independent efforts, we do not for a moment forget that our part in this exhibition would fall far short of your expectations but for the constant help that has come to our educational life, not only from the Southern states, but especially from Northern philanthropists, who have made their gifts a constant stream of blessing and encouragement.

The wisest among my race understand that the agitation of questions of   10
social equality is the extremest folly, and that progress in the enjoyment of all the

privileges that will come to us must be the result of severe and constant struggle rather than of artificial forcing. No race that has anything to contribute to the markets of the world is long in any degree ostracized. It is important and right that all privileges of the law be ours, but it is vastly more important that we be prepared for the exercises of these privileges. The opportunity to earn a dollar in a factory just now is worth infinitely more than the opportunity to spend a dollar in an opera-house.

In conclusion, may I repeat that nothing in thirty years has given us more hope and encouragement, and drawn us so near to you of the white race, as this opportunity offered by the Exposition; and here bending, as it were, over the altar that represents the results of the struggles of your race and mine, both starting practically empty-handed three decades ago, I pledge that in your effort to work out the great and intricate problem which God has laid at the doors of the South, you shall have at all times the patient, sympathetic help of my race; only let this be constantly in mind, that, while from representations in these buildings of the product of field, of forest, of mine, of factory, letters, and art, much good will come, yet far above and beyond material benefits will be that higher good, that, let us pray God, will come, in a blotting out of sectional differences and racial animosities and suspicions, in a determination to administer absolute justice, in a willing obedience among all classes to the mandates of law. This, then, coupled with our material prosperity, will bring into our beloved South a new heaven and new earth.

Exploring the Text

1. What are Booker T. Washington's goals as articulated in this speech? What does he believe is the best way to achieve them?

2. What appeals to ethos does Washington make in the opening paragraphs? What additional appeals to ethos does he make as the speech proceeds?

3. What is the point of the story Washington tells in paragraph 3 about a "ship lost at sea"? What is the rhetorical effect?

4. This speech has come to be known by the sentence "Cast down your bucket where you are" (para. 3). What does Washington mean by this exhortation?

5. In what types of work does Washington want African Americans to engage? Are such jobs as readily available now as they were at the time of his speech? To what extent do his ideas apply in our current economy?

6. How do you interpret Washington's concluding statement in paragraph 5: "In all things that are purely social we can be as separate as the fingers, yet one as the hand in all things essential to mutual progress"?

7. Why is the Shakespeare quotation in paragraph 6 ("'blessing him that gives and him that takes'") appropriate to the point Washington is making?

8. Discuss two possible—and contrasting—interpretations of Washington's assertion: "The opportunity to earn a dollar in a factory just now is worth infinitely

more than the opportunity to spend a dollar in an opera-house" (para. 10). In today's age of globalization and outsourcing, when many of our factory jobs have gone to foreign workers, does this statement still apply? Rewrite the sentence, replacing "factory" with a contemporary place of employment. Does the new sentence effectively update the idea? Why or why not?

9. Where in this speech does Washington implicitly argue against racial stereotypes and advocate American values of rugged individualism and a strong work ethic? How have racial stereotypes changed since then? Is our work ethic as strong now as it once was?

10. Discuss the importance of the occasion and audience of this speech. How do these factors influence its form and content?

11. In the introduction to Washington's autobiography, *Up from Slavery*, Henry Louis Gates Jr. and Nellie McKay make the following observation: "To some, Washington's autobiography seems to paper over centuries of accumulated white responsibility for the evils of slavery, and instead of demanding the reform of white American institutions, it calls for African American conformity to the dominant myth of individualism in the United States. To other readers, however, Washington's message in *Up from Slavery* puts its priorities exactly where they had to be—on the necessity of self-help within the African American community" (*Norton Anthology of African American Literature*). Which view is closer to yours? Cite specific passages to support your position.

On Dumpster Diving

Lars Eighner

Lars Eighner was born in Corpus Christi, Texas, in 1948 and grew up primarily in Houston. As a child, he studied creative writing at the Corpus Christi Fine Arts Colony, and after graduating from Lamar High School, he attended the University of Texas at Austin. After losing his job at the state asylum in Austin, Eighner became homeless for three years. "On Dumpster Diving," an account of being homeless with his dog, Lizbeth, was published as "My Daily Dives in the Dumpster" in *Harper's* magazine in 1991 and was revised to become part of Eighner's 1993 memoir, *Travels with Lizbeth: Three Years on the Road and on the Streets*. Eighner's work has appeared in the *Threepenny Review*, *Harper's*, the *Washington Post*, the *Utne Reader*, and the *New York Times Book Review*.

Long before I began Dumpster diving I was impressed with Dumpsters, enough so that I wrote the Merriam-Webster research service to discover what I could about the word "Dumpster." I learned from them that "Dumpster" is a proprietary word belonging to the Dempster Dumpster company.

Since then I have dutifully capitalized the word although it was lowercased in almost all of the citations Merriam-Webster photocopied for me. Dempster's word is too apt. I have never heard these things called anything but Dumpsters. I do not know anyone who knows the generic name for these objects. From time to time, however, I hear a wino or hobo give some corrupted credit to the original and call them Dipsy Dumpsters.

I began Dumpster diving about a year before I became homeless.

I prefer the term "scavenging" and use the word "scrounging" when I mean to be obscure. I have heard people, evidently meaning to be polite, using the word "foraging," but I prefer to reserve that word for gathering nuts and berries and such which I do also according to the season and the opportunity. "Dumpster diving" seems to me to be a little too cute and, in my case, inaccurate because I lack the athletic ability to lower myself into the Dumpsters as the true divers do, much to their increased profit.

I like the frankness of the word "scavenging," which I can hardly think of with-   5
out picturing a big black snail on an aquarium wall. I live from the refuse of others. I am a scavenger. I think it a sound and honorable niche, although if I could I would naturally prefer to live the comfortable consumer life, perhaps — and only perhaps — as a slightly less wasteful consumer owing to what I have learned as a scavenger.

While my dog Lizbeth and I were still living in the house on Avenue B in Austin, as my savings ran out, I put almost all my sporadic income into rent. The necessities of daily life I began to extract from Dumpsters. Yes, we ate from Dumpsters. Except for jeans, all my clothes came from Dumpsters. Boom boxes, candles, bedding, toilet paper, medicine, books, a typewriter, a virgin male love doll, change sometimes amounting to many dollars: I acquired many things from the Dumpsters.

I have learned much as a scavenger. I mean to put some of what I have learned down here, beginning with the practical art of Dumpster diving and proceeding to the abstract.

What is safe to eat?

After all, the finding of objects is becoming something of an urban art. Even respectable employed people will sometimes find something tempting sticking out of a Dumpster or standing beside one. Quite a number of people, not all of them of the bohemian type, are willing to brag that they found this or that piece in the trash. But eating from Dumpsters is the thing that separates the dilettanti from the professionals.

Eating safely from the Dumpsters involves three principles: using the senses   10
and common sense to evaluate the condition of the found materials, knowing the Dumpsters of a given area and checking them regularly, and seeking always to answer the question "Why was this discarded?"

Perhaps everyone who has a kitchen and a regular supply of groceries has, at one time or another, made a sandwich and eaten half of it before discovering mold on the bread or got a mouthful of milk before realizing the milk had turned. Nothing of the sort is likely to happen to a Dumpster diver because he is constantly reminded that most food is discarded for a reason. Yet a lot of perfectly good food can be found in Dumpsters.

Canned goods, for example, turn up fairly often in the Dumpsters I frequent. All except the most phobic people would be willing to eat from a can even if it came from a Dumpster. Canned goods are among the safest of foods to be found in Dumpsters, but are not utterly foolproof.

Although very rare with modern canning methods, botulism is a possibility. Most other forms of food poisoning seldom do lasting harm to a healthy person. But botulism is almost certainly fatal and often the first symptom is death. Except for carbonated beverages, all canned goods should contain a slight vacuum and suck air when first punctured. Bulging, rusty, dented cans and cans that spew when punctured should be avoided, especially when the contents are not very acidic or syrupy.

Heat can break down the botulin, but this requires much more cooking than most people do to canned goods. To the extent that botulism occurs at all, of course, it can occur in cans on pantry shelves as well as in cans from Dumpsters. Need I say that home-canned goods found in Dumpsters are simply too risky to be recommended.

From time to time one of my companions, aware of the source of my provisions, will ask, "Do you think these crackers are really safe to eat?" For some reason it is most often the crackers they ask about.

This question always makes me angry. Of course I would not offer my companion anything I had doubts about. But more than that I wonder why he cannot evaluate the condition of the crackers for himself. I have no special knowledge and I have been wrong before. Since he knows where the food comes from, it seems to me he ought to assume some of the responsibility for deciding what he will put in his mouth.

For myself I have few qualms about dry foods such as crackers, cookies, cereal, chips, and pasta if they are free of visible contaminates and still dry and crisp. Most often such things are found in the original packaging, which is not so much a positive sign as it is the absence of a negative one.

Raw fruits and vegetables with intact skins seem perfectly safe to me, excluding of course the obviously rotten. Many are discarded for minor imperfections which can be pared away. Leafy vegetables, grapes, cauliflower, broccoli, and similar things may be contaminated by liquids and may be impractical to wash.

Candy, especially hard candy, is usually safe if it has not drawn ants. Chocolate is often discarded only because it has become discolored as the cocoa butter de-emulsified. Candying after all is one method of food preservation because pathogens do not like very sugary substances.

All of these foods might be found in any Dumpster and can be evaluated with some confidence largely on the basis of appearance. Beyond these are foods which cannot be correctly evaluated without additional information.

I began scavenging by pulling pizzas out of the Dumpster behind a pizza delivery shop. In general prepared food requires caution, but in this case I knew when the shop closed and went to the Dumpster as soon as the last of the help left.

Such shops often get prank orders, called "bogus." Because help seldom stays long at these places pizzas are often made with the wrong topping, refused on delivery for being cold, or baked incorrectly. The products to be discarded are boxed up because inventory is kept by counting boxes: A boxed pizza can be written off; an unboxed pizza does not exist.

I never placed a bogus order to increase the supply of pizzas and I believe no one else was scavenging in this Dumpster. But the people in the shop became suspicious and began to retain their garbage in the shop overnight.

While it lasted I had a steady supply of fresh, sometimes warm pizza. Because I knew the Dumpster I knew the source of the pizza, and because I visited the Dumpster regularly I knew what was fresh and what was yesterday's.

The area I frequent is inhabited by many affluent college students. I am not here by chance; the Dumpsters in this area are very rich. Students throw out many good things, including food. In particular they tend to throw everything out when they move at the end of a semester, before and after breaks, and around midterm when many of them despair of college. So I find it advantageous to keep an eye on the academic calendar. 25

The students throw food away around the breaks because they do not know whether it has spoiled or will spoil before they return. A typical discard is a half jar of peanut butter. In fact nonorganic peanut butter does not require refrigeration and is unlikely to spoil in any reasonable time. The student does not know that, and since it is Daddy's money, the student decides not to take a chance.

Opened containers require caution and some attention to the question "Why was this discarded?" But in the case of discards from student apartments, the answer may be that the item was discarded through carelessness, ignorance, or wastefulness. This can sometimes be deduced when the item is found with many others, including some that are obviously perfectly good.

Some students, and others, approach defrosting a freezer by chucking out the whole lot. Not only do the circumstances of such a find tell the story, but also the mass of frozen goods stays cold for a long time and items may be found still frozen or freshly thawed.

Yogurt, cheese, and sour cream are items that are often thrown out while they are still good. Occasionally I find a cheese with a spot of mold, which of course I just pare off, and because it is obviously why such a cheese was discarded, I treat it with less suspicion than an apparently perfect cheese found in similar circumstances. Yogurt is often discarded, still sealed, only because the expiration date on the carton had passed. This is one of my favorite finds because yogurt will keep several days, even in warm weather.

Students throw out canned goods and staples at the end of semesters and when they give up college at midterm. Drugs, pornography, spirits, and the like are often discarded when parents are expected—Dad's day, for example. And 30 spirits also turn up after big party weekends, presumably discarded by the newly reformed. Wine and spirits, of course, keep perfectly well even once opened.

My test for carbonated soft drinks is whether they still fizz vigorously. Many juices or other beverages are too acid or too syrupy to cause much concern provided they are not visibly contaminated. Liquids, however, require some care.

One hot day I found a large jug of Pat O'Brien's Hurricane mix. The jug had been opened, but it was still ice cold. I drank three large glasses before it became apparent to me that someone had added the rum to the mix, and not a little rum. I never tasted the rum and by the time I began to feel the effects I had already ingested a very large quantity of the beverage. Some divers would have considered this a boon, but being suddenly and thoroughly intoxicated in a public place in the early afternoon is not my idea of a good time.

I have heard of people maliciously contaminating discarded food and even handouts, but mostly I have heard of this from people with vivid imaginations who have had no experience with the Dumpsters themselves. Just before the pizza shop stopped discarding its garbage at night, jalapeños began showing up on most of the discarded pizzas. If indeed this was meant to discourage me it was a wasted effort because I am a native Texan.

For myself, I avoid game, poultry, pork, and egg-based foods whether I find them raw or cooked. I seldom have the means to cook what I find, but when I do I avail myself of plentiful supplies of beef which is often in very good condition. I suppose fish becomes disagreeable before it becomes dangerous. The dog is happy to have any such thing that is past its prime and, in fact, does not recognize fish as food until it is quite strong.

Home leftovers, as opposed to surpluses from restaurants, are very often bad. 35 Evidently, especially among students, there is a common type of personality that carefully wraps up even the smallest leftover and shoves it into the back of the refrigerator for six months or so before discarding it. Characteristic of this type are the reused jars and margarine tubs which house the remains.

I avoid ethnic foods I am unfamiliar with. If I do not know what it is supposed to look like when it is good, I cannot be certain I will be able to tell if it is bad.

No matter how careful I am I still get dysentery at least once a month, oftener in warm weather. I do not want to paint too romantic a picture. Dumpster diving has serious drawbacks as a way of life.

I learned to scavenge gradually, on my own. Since then I have initiated several companions into the trade. I have learned that there is a predictable series of stages a person goes through in learning to scavenge.

At first the new scavenger is filled with disgust and self-loathing. He is ashamed of being seen and may lurk around, trying to duck behind things, or he may try to dive at night.

(In fact, most people instinctively look away from a scavenger. By skulking 40 around, the novice calls attention to himself and arouses suspicion. Diving at night is ineffective and needlessly messy.)

Every grain of rice seems to be a maggot. Everything seems to stink. He can wipe the egg yolk off the found can, but he cannot erase the stigma of eating garbage out of his mind.

That stage passes with experience. The scavenger finds a pair of running shoes that fit and look and smell brand new. He finds a pocket calculator in perfect working order. He finds pristine ice cream, still frozen, more than he can eat or keep. He begins to understand: People do throw away perfectly good stuff, a lot of perfectly good stuff.

At this stage, Dumpster shyness begins to dissipate. The diver, after all, has the last laugh. He is finding all manner of good things which are his for the taking. Those who disparage his profession are the fools, not he.

He may begin to hang onto some perfectly good things for which he has neither a use nor a market. Then he begins to take note of the things which are not perfectly good but are nearly so. He mates a Walkman with broken earphones and one that is missing a battery cover. He picks up things which he can repair.

At this stage he may become lost and never recover. Dumpsters are full of things of some potential value to someone and also of things which never have much intrinsic value but are interesting. All the Dumpster divers I have known come to the point of trying to acquire everything they touch. Why not take it, they reason, since it is all free. 45

This is, of course, hopeless. Most divers come to realize that they must restrict themselves to items of relatively immediate utility. But in some cases the diver simply cannot control himself. I have met several of these pack-rat types. Their ideas of the values of various pieces of junk verge on the psychotic. Every bit of glass may be a diamond, they think, and all that glistens, gold.

I tend to gain weight when I am scavenging. Partly this is because I always find far more pizza and doughnuts than water-packed tuna, nonfat yogurt, and fresh vegetables. Also I have not developed much faith in the reliability of Dumpsters as a food source, although it has been proven to me many times. I tend to eat as if I have no idea where my next meal is coming from. But mostly I just hate to see food go to waste and so I eat much more than I should. Something like this drives the obsession to collect junk.

As for collecting objects, I usually restrict myself to collecting one kind of small object at a time, such as pocket calculators, sunglasses, or campaign buttons. To live on the street I must anticipate my needs to a certain extent: I must pick up and save warm bedding I find in August because it will not be found in Dumpsters in November. But even if I had a home with extensive storage space I could not save everything that might be valuable in some contingency.

I have proprietary feelings about my Dumpsters. As I have suggested, it is no accident that I scavenge from Dumpsters where good finds are common. But my limited experience with Dumpsters in other areas suggests to me that it is the population of competitors rather than the affluence of the dumpers that most affects the feasibility of survival by scavenging. The large number of competitors is what puts me off the idea of trying to scavenge in places like Los Angeles.

Curiously, I do not mind my direct competition, other scavengers, so much   50
as I hate the can scroungers.

People scrounge cans because they have to have a little cash. I have tried scrounging cans with an able-bodied companion. Afoot a can scrounger simply cannot make more than a few dollars a day. One can extract the necessities of life from the Dumpsters directly with far less effort than would be required to accumulate the equivalent value in cans.

Can scroungers, then, are people who *must* have small amounts of cash. These are drug addicts and winos, mostly the latter because the amounts of cash are so small.

Spirits and drugs do, like all other commodities, turn up in Dumpsters and the scavenger will from time to time have a half bottle of a rather good wine with his dinner. But the wino cannot survive on these occasional finds; he must have his daily dose to stave off the DTs. All the cans he can carry will buy about three bottles of Wild Irish Rose.

I do not begrudge them the cans, but can scroungers tend to tear up the Dumpsters, mixing the contents and littering the area. They become so specialized that they can see only cans. They earn my contempt by passing up change, canned goods, and readily hockable items.

There are precious few courtesies among scavengers. But it is a common   55
practice to set aside surplus items: pairs of shoes, clothing, canned goods, and such. A true scavenger hates to see good stuff go to waste and what he cannot use he leaves in good condition in plain sight.

Can scroungers lay waste to everything in their path and will stir one of a pair of good shoes to the bottom of the Dumpster, to be lost or ruined in the muck. Can scroungers will even go through individual garbage cans, something I have never seen a scavenger do.

Individual garbage cans are set out on the public easement only on garbage days. On other days going through them requires trespassing close to a dwelling. Going through individual garbage cans without scattering litter is almost impossible. Litter is likely to reduce the public's tolerance of scavenging. Individual garbage cans are simply not as productive as Dumpsters; people in houses and duplexes do not move as often and for some reason do not tend to discard as much useful material. Moreover, the time required to go through one garbage can that serves one household is not much less than the time required to go through a Dumpster that contains the refuse of twenty apartments.

But my strongest reservation about going through individual garbage cans is that this seems to me a very personal kind of invasion to which I would object if I were a householder. Although many things in Dumpsters are obviously meant never to come to light, a Dumpster is somehow less personal.

I avoid trying to draw conclusions about the people who dump in the Dumpsters I frequent. I think it would be unethical to do so, although I know many people will find the idea of scavenger ethics too funny for words.

Dumpsters contain bank statements, bills, correspondence, and other docu-   60
ments, just as anyone might expect. But there are also less obvious sources of

information. Pill bottles, for example. The labels on pill bottles contain the name of the patient, the name of the doctor, and the name of the drug. AIDS drugs and antipsychotic medicines, to name but two groups, are specific and seldom prescribed for any other disorders. The plastic compacts for birth control pills usually have complete label information.

Despite all of this sensitive information, I have had only one apartment resident object to my going through the Dumpster. In that case it turned out the resident was a university athlete who was taking bets and who was afraid I would turn up his wager slips.

Occasionally a find tells a story. I once found a small paper bag containing some unused condoms, several partial tubes of flavored sexual lubricant, a partially used compact of birth control pills, and the torn pieces of a picture of a young man. Clearly she was through with him and planning to give up sex altogether.

Dumpster things are often sad—abandoned teddy bears, shredded wedding books, despaired-of sales kits. I find many pets lying in state in Dumpsters. Although I hope to get off the streets so that Lizbeth can have a long and comfortable old age, I know this hope is not very realistic. So I suppose when her time comes she too will go into a Dumpster. I will have no better place for her. And after all, for most of her life her livelihood has come from the Dumpster. When she finds something I think is safe that has been spilled from the Dumpster I let her have it. She already knows the route around the best Dumpsters. I like to think that if she survives me she will have a chance of evading the dog catcher and of finding her sustenance on the route.

Silly vanities also come to rest in the Dumpsters. I am a rather accomplished needleworker. I get a lot of materials from the Dumpsters. Evidently sorority girls, hoping to impress someone, perhaps themselves, with their mastery of a womanly art, buy a lot of embroider-by-number kits, work a few stitches horribly, and eventually discard the whole mess. I pull out their stitches, turn the canvas over, and work an original design. Do not think I refrain from chuckling as I make original gifts from these kits.

I find diaries and journals. I have often thought of compiling a book of literary found objects. And perhaps I will one day. But what I find is hopelessly commonplace and bad without being, even unconsciously, camp. College students also discard their papers. I am horrified to discover the kind of paper which now merits an A in an undergraduate course. I am grateful, however, for the number of good books and magazines the students throw out.

In the area I know best I have never discovered vermin in the Dumpsters, but there are two kinds of kitty surprise. One is alley cats which I meet as they leap, claws first, out of Dumpsters. This is especially thrilling when I have Lizbeth in tow. The other kind of kitty surprise is a plastic garbage bag filled with some ponderous, amorphous mass. This always proves to be used cat litter.

City bees harvest doughnut glaze and this makes the Dumpster at the doughnut shop more interesting. My faith in the instinctive wisdom of animals is always

65

shaken whenever I see Lizbeth attempt to catch a bee in her mouth, which she does whenever bees are present. Evidently some birds find Dumpsters profitable, for birdie surprise is almost as common as kitty surprise of the first kind. In hunting season all kinds of small game turn up in Dumpsters, some of it sadly, not entirely dead. Curiously, summer and winter, maggots are uncommon.

The worst of the living and near-living hazards of the Dumpsters are the fire ants. The food that they claim is not much of a loss, but they are vicious and aggressive. It is very easy to brush against some surface of the Dumpster and pick up half a dozen or more fire ants, usually in some sensitive area such as the under-arm. One advantage of bringing Lizbeth along as I make Dumpster rounds is that, for obvious reasons, she is very alert to ground-based fire ants. When Lizbeth recognizes the signs of fire ant infestation around our feet she does the Dance of the Zillion Fire Ants. I have learned not to ignore this warning from Lizbeth, whether I perceive the tiny ants or not, but to remove ourselves at Lizbeth's first pas de bourrée.[1] All the more so because the ants are the worst in the months I wear flip-flops, if I have them.

(Perhaps someone will misunderstand the above. Lizbeth does the Dance of the Zillion Fire Ants when she recognizes more fire ants than she cares to eat, not when she is being bitten. Since I have learned to react promptly, she does not get bitten at all. It is the isolated patrol of fire ants that falls in Lizbeth's range that deserves pity. Lizbeth finds them quite tasty.)

By far the best way to go through a Dumpster is to lower yourself into it. 70 Most of the good stuff tends to settle at the bottom because it is usually weightier than the rubbish. My more athletic companions have often demonstrated to me that they can extract much good material from a Dumpster I have already been over.

To those psychologically or physically unprepared to enter a Dumpster, I rec-ommend a stout stick, preferably with some barb or hook at one end. The hook can be used to grab plastic garbage bags. When I find canned goods or other objects loose at the bottom of a Dumpster I usually can roll them into a small bag that I can then hoist up. Much Dumpster diving is a matter of experience for which nothing will do except practice.

Dumpster diving is outdoor work, often surprisingly pleasant. It is not entirely predictable; things of interest turn up every day and some days there are finds of great value. I am always very pleased when I can turn up exactly the thing I most wanted to find. Yet in spite of the element of chance, scavenging more than most other pursuits tends to yield returns in some proportion to the effort and intel-ligence brought to bear. It is very sweet to turn up a few dollars in change from a Dumpster that has just been gone over by a wino.

The land is now covered with cities. The cities are full of Dumpsters. I think of scavenging as a modern form of self-reliance. In any event, after ten years of

---

[1]A transitional ballet step. — Eds.

government service, where everything is geared to the lowest common denominator, I find work that rewards initiative and effort refreshing. Certainly I would be happy to have a sinecure again, but I am not heartbroken not to have one anymore.

I find from the experience of scavenging two rather deep lessons. The first is to take what I can use and let the rest go by. I have come to think that there is no value in the abstract. A thing I cannot use or make useful, perhaps by trading, has no value however fine or rare it may be. I mean useful in a broad sense — so, for example, some art I would think useful and valuable, but other art might be otherwise for me.

I was shocked to realize that some things are not worth acquiring, but now I think it is so. Some material things are white elephants that eat up the possessor's substance. 75

The second lesson is of the transience of material being. This has not quite converted me to a dualist, but it has made some headway in that direction. I do not suppose that ideas are immortal, but certainly mental things are longer-lived than other material things.

Once I was the sort of person who invests material objects with sentimental value. Now I no longer have those things, but I have the sentiments yet.

Many times in my travels I have lost everything but the clothes I was wearing and Lizbeth. The things I find in Dumpsters, the love letters and ragdolls of so many lives, remind me of this lesson. Now I hardly pick up a thing without envisioning the time I will cast it away. This I think is a healthy state of mind. Almost everything I have now has already been cast out at least once, proving that what I own is valueless to someone.

Anyway, I find my desire to grab for the gaudy bauble has been largely sated. I think this is an attitude I share with the very wealthy — we both know there is plenty more where what we have came from. Between us are the rat-race millions who have confounded their selves with the objects they grasp and who nightly scavenge the cable channels looking for they know not what.

I am sorry for them. 80

. . . .

Exploring the Text

1. What is the effect of Lars Eighner's attention to language in the first five paragraphs? Does this opening appeal more to ethos, logos, or pathos? Explain.

2. In paragraph 7, Eighner identifies the rhetorical direction he plans to follow. What is the effect of such information?

3. Note the technical and clinical nature of much of the first part (paras. 1–37) of the essay. In paragraph 19, for example, Eighner writes of de-emulsification and the behavior of pathogens. What is the effect of such scientific language and information?

4. The wealth of goods that Eighner is able to salvage from Dumpsters would suggest that our society is wasteful—at least on the micro level. What might be the effect of such wasteful habits on the macroeconomy?

5. Identify and explain two examples of irony in the section about students (paras. 25–30). What does this section suggest about their relationship to the economy at large?

6. Paragraph 37 concludes, "I do not want to paint too romantic a picture. Dumpster diving has serious drawbacks as a way of life." What is the effect of these sentences? What is their rhetorical purpose?

7. Note the careful distinction Eighner makes between the "true scavenger" and the "can scrounger" (paras. 50–56). What purpose does it serve?

8. Eighner addresses homelessness in America. How successfully does he debunk the stereotype of homeless people as indolent and uneducated?

9. Explain the irony in paragraph 73 where Eighner writes, "I think of scavenging as a modern form of self-reliance."

10. Explain the irony in the closing passage (paras. 78–80). In the sentence "This I think is a healthy state of mind," what does *this* refer to? Do you agree with Eighner's claim? Explain.

11. How would you characterize Eighner's attitudes toward wealth and materialism as revealed especially in paragraphs 74–80? What implications do they have regarding the economy at large?

12. Eighner is obviously an intelligent man who writes well. What does it suggest about our economy that such a person as he could become homeless and resort to Dumpster diving? Does our society have an obligation to help those in similar situations? Explain.

from *In the Strawberry Fields*

Eric Schlosser

Born in 1959 and raised in New York and Los Angeles, Eric Schlosser graduated from Princeton University with a degree in American history and studied British history at Oxford University. In addition to working as a correspondent for the *Atlantic*, he has published articles in such periodicals as the *New Yorker*, the *Nation*, *Rolling Stone*, and *Vanity Fair*. His 2001 book about the food industry, *Fast Food Nation: The Dark Side of the American Meal*, became a best seller and was adapted into a film in 2006. Schlosser also participated in the making of the 2009 documentary film *Food Inc*. His second best seller, *Reefer Madness: Sex, Drugs, and Cheap Labor in the American Black Market* (2003), grew out of his articles on the enforcement of marijuana laws and illegal immigration in California. It includes "In the Strawberry Fields," an earlier version of which appeared in the *Atlantic Monthly* in 1995.

La Fruta del Diablo

It was mid-April when I visited Watsonville, and heavy rains had recently flooded hundreds of acres. Bright blue plastic barrels from a Smuckers plant were scattered across local strawberry fields and embedded in the mud. Many fields that hadn't been flooded still had been damaged by the rains. I met with strawberry workers at an old labor camp — a small slum set amid rolling hills and strawberry fields not far from town. For most of the year this bleak collection of gray wooden barracks housed about 350 residents, mainly strawberry workers and their families. But at the peak of the harvest hundreds more crammed into its forty apartments. In the mid-1990s there'd been a major outbreak of tuberculosis at the camp, fueled by its crowded living quarters and poor building design. The bedrooms occupied a central corridor of the barracks; none had a window. The tenants paid $500 a month for their two-bedroom apartments and felt lucky to have a roof over their heads. As I walked around the camp, there were children everywhere, running and playing in the courtyards, oblivious of the squalor.

The sky was overcast, more bad weather was coming, and a year's income for these workers would be determined in the next few months. Half a dozen strawberry pickers, leaning against parked cars, told me that at this point in the season they usually worked in the fields eight or ten hours a day. Only one of them was employed at the moment. Every morning the others visited the strawberry farm on a nearby hillside, inquired about work, and were turned away. The foreman, who had hired them for years, said to try again next week.

Harvest work in the strawberry fields, like most seasonal farmwork in California, is considered "at will." There is no contract, no seniority, no obligation beyond the day-to-day. A grower hires and fires workers as necessary, without need for explanation. It makes no difference whether the migrant has been an employee for six days or for six years. The terms of employment are laid down on a daily basis. If a grower wants slow and careful work, wages are paid by the hour. If a grower wants berries quickly removed from the field, the wages are piece-rate, providing an incentive to move fast. A migrant often does not know how long the workday will last or what the wage rate will be until he or she arrives at the field that morning. There might be two weeks of ten-hour days followed by a week of no work at all, depending upon the weather and the market.

This system did not arise because growers are innately mean and heartless. Harvests are unpredictable from beginning to end. Many growers try to guarantee their workers a certain amount of income each week. Among other things, it makes good business sense to have reliable and capable workers returning each year. And yet there is no denying where the power lies.

The strawberry has long been known to migrants as *la fruta del diablo* — the fruit of the devil. Picking strawberries is some of the lowest-paid, most difficult, and therefore least desirable farmwork in California. Strawberries are fragile and bruise easily. They must be picked with great care, especially the berries that will

5

be sold fresh at the market. Market berries are twisted, not pulled, off the stem to preserve a green cap on top. Workers must select only berries of the proper size, firmness, shape, and color. They must arrange the berries neatly in baskets to catch the shopper's eye. Learning how to pick strawberries correctly can take weeks. The worker is often responsible not only for gathering and packing the fruit but also for tending the plants. The drip irrigation system has to be continually checked. Shoots and runners have to be removed. Rotting berries have to be tossed away, or they will spoil the rest. When a piece-rate wage is being paid, workers must perform these tasks and pick berries as fast as they can. There is a strong undercurrent of anxiety in a field being harvested at piece-rate. Workers move down the furrows pushing small wheelbarrows; they pause, bend over, brush away leaves to their left and right, pick berries, place them in boxes, check the plants, and move on, all in one fluid motion. Once their boxes are filled, they rush to have them tallied at the end of the field, rush back, and begin the process again.

Strawberry plants are four or five inches high and grow from beds eight to twelve inches high. You must bend at the waist to pick the fruit, which explains why the job is so difficult. Bending over that way for an hour can cause a stiff back; doing so for ten to twelve hours a day, weeks at a time, can cause excruciating pain and lifelong disabilities. Most strawberry pickers suffer back pain. As would be expected, the older you get, the more your back hurts. Farmworkers, like athletes, also decline in speed as they age. The fastest strawberry pickers tend to be in their late teens and early twenties. Most migrants quit picking strawberries in their mid-thirties, although some highly skilled women do work longer. Age discrimination is commonplace in the fields — it is purely a question of efficiency.

The hourly wages vary considerably, depending on the grower, the type of strawberry being picked, the time of year, and often, the skill of the worker. Wages are higher in Watsonville and the Salinas than in Southern California, because of the greater distance from Mexico. Growers producing top-quality berries for the fresh market may pay as much as $8 or $10 an hour. At the height of the season, when berries are plentiful and growers pay a piece-rate of $1.25 a box, the fastest workers can earn more than $150 a day. But wages at that level only last for a month or so, and even during that period most workers can't attain them. When a crew of thirty picks at a piece-rate, three or four will earn $10 an hour, five or six will earn at or below the state minimum wage, $6.75 an hour, and the rest will earn somewhere in between.

The availability of work, not the pay scale, is of greatest concern to migrants. Despite the hardships that accompany the job, there is an oversupply of people hoping to pick strawberries. The fear of unemployment haunts all farmworkers in California today. Each harvest brings a new struggle to line up enough jobs for a decent income. The average migrant spends half the year working and a few months looking for work.

Another constant worry is finding a place to sleep. Santa Cruz and Monterey counties have some of the highest housing costs in the country. Long popular with tourists and wealthy retirees, the area has also attracted commuters from Silicon Valley. The residents of Watsonville and Salinas are determined to preserve the local farm economy, despite enormous pressure from developers. Agricultural land that currently sells for $40,000 an acre could be sold for many times that amount if it were rezoned; there are strawberry fields overlooking the Pacific Ocean. The determination to preserve agricultural land has not, however, extended to providing shelter for agricultural workers. Since 1980 the acreage around Watsonville and Salinas devoted to strawberries has more than doubled and the tonnage of strawberries produced there has nearly quadrupled. But the huge influx of migrant workers required to pick these berries has been forced to compete for a supply of low-income housing that's been inadequate for decades.

The few remaining labor camps for single men are grim places. I toured one   10
that was a group of whitewashed buildings surrounded by chain-link fences and barbed wire. Desolate except for a rosebush in front of the manager's office, it looked like a holding pen or an old minimum-security prison. A nearby camp was reputed to be one of the best of its kind. Inside the barracks, the walls were freshly painted and the concrete floor was clean. A typical room was roughly twelve feet by ten feet, unheated, and occupied by four men. Sheets of plywood separated the steel cots. For $80 a week, a price far too high for most migrants, you got a bed and two meals a day. I've seen nicer horse barns.

Nevertheless, the labor camps are often preferable to the alternatives. When migrants stay in residential neighborhoods, they must pool their resources. In Watsonville three to four families will share a small house, seven or eight people to a room. Migrants routinely pay $100 to $200 a month to sleep in a garage with anywhere from four to ten other people. A survey of garages in Soledad found 1,500 inhabitants—a number roughly equal to one-eighth of the town's official population. At the peak of the harvest the housing shortage becomes acute. Migrants at the labor camps sometimes pay to sleep in parked cars. The newest migrant workers, who lack family in the area and haven't yet learned the ropes, often sleep outdoors in the wooded sections of Prunedale, trespassing, moving to a different hiding place each night. On hillsides above the Salinas Valley, hundreds of strawberry pickers have been found living in caves.

Locked into Dependence

The immigration history of Guadalupe, California, can be read in the names and faces adorning headstones at its small cemetery. The Swiss and Italian and Portuguese surnames belong to families who settled in the Santa Maria Valley around the turn of the last century, growing beans and sugar beets, running cattle, and raising dairy herds. The Chinese, Japanese, and Filipino names belong to the first wave of farmworkers, some of whom managed to acquire land of their own. Spanish surnames greatly outnumber the rest, marking the recent graves along with plastic flowers and the images of saints. There is a sepulchral custom in Guadalupe, practiced for generations: most of the headstones bear sepia-tinted photographs of the deceased. Walking through the graveyard, one sees at a glance the slightly different ethnic traits and the subtle variations in skin color—long the basis of economic status and rivalry. Now all these faces stare in the same direction from the same place, arranged like crops in long, straight rows.

For most of the twentieth century, the Santa Maria Valley had a diverse farm economy. Although migrants were a large seasonal presence, the area lacked the huge industrial farms that dominated the landscape elsewhere in California. The acreage around Guadalupe was devoted primarily to field crops and irrigated pasture. The cattle ranches and dairy farms were owned and managed by local families. Fruits and vegetables, though an important source of revenue, occupied a small portion of the agricultural land.

Then, from the early 1970s to the late 1980s, the Santa Maria Valley was transformed. As field crops and dairy products became less profitable, farmers either switched to high-value crops or quit farming. Much of the land was bought by outside corporations, such as Mobil and the Bank of America. Irrigated pastures became strawberry fields (dotted with oil wells) on leased land. The number of migrant workers soared. In 1960 Guadalupe's population was 18 percent Latino; today it is about 85 percent Latino. The middle classes fled to the nearby city of Santa Maria, leaving behind a rural underclass.

Juan Vicente Palerm has spent the last two decades studying the social and economic changes in the Santa Maria Valley. The director of the University of California's Institute for Mexico and the United States, Palerm is an anthropologist by training. His early fieldwork traced the lives of Spanish guest workers in northern Europe—migrants imported by treaty to labor in the factories and fields. He is an imposing figure, with the graying beard of a patriarch, and has a remarkable grasp not only of labor market dynamics, but also of how every crop in the valley is planted, tended, marketed, and sold. I spent a day with Palerm and one of his graduate students, Manolo Gonzalez (who picked strawberries for a year as part of his research), driving the side streets of Guadalupe, touring the fields, and discussing how the growers of California and the peasants of rural Mexico created an agricultural system that has locked them into mutual dependence.

By relying on poor migrants from Mexico, California growers established a wage structure that discouraged American citizens from seeking farmwork. The wages offered at harvest were too low to sustain a family in the United States, but they were up to ten times as high as any wages Mexican peasants could earn in their native villages. A system evolved in which the cheap labor of Mexican migrants subsidized California agriculture, while remittances from that farmwork preserved rural communities in Mexico that otherwise might have collapsed. For decades the men of Mexican villages have traveled north to the fields of California, leaving behind women, children, and the elderly to look after their small farms. Migrant work in California has long absorbed Mexican surplus labor, while Mexico has in effect paid for the education, health care, and retirement of California's farmworkers.

Whenever migrants decided to settle in California, however, they disrupted the smooth workings of this system, by imposing higher costs on the state — especially if they married and raised children. That is why the Immigration and Naturalization Service (INS) used to round up and deport illegal immigrants in California immediately after the harvest. Nevertheless, millions of Mexican farmworkers have settled in the United States over the years, most of them becoming American citizens. Although agricultural employment has long been a means of entering U.S. society, low wages and poor working conditions have made it an occupation that most immigrants and their children hope to escape. Farm labor is more physically demanding and less financially rewarding than almost any other kind of work. A migrant who finds a job in a factory can triple his or her income. As a result, the whole system now depends upon a steady supply of illegal immigrants to keep farm wages low and to replace migrants who have either retired to Mexico or found better jobs in California.

Juan Vicente Palerm believes that today there are not only more migrants shuttling back and forth from Mexico but also more Mexican farmworkers settling permanently in California. Throughout the state towns like Guadalupe, Calexico, Cutler, and McFarland are becoming enclaves of rural poverty. In the Santa Maria Valley the increased production of fruits and vegetables, higher yields per acre, and an extended growing season have created thousands of full- and part-time jobs for farmworkers. Broccoli fields now occupy more than 20,000 acres, requiring a large supply of resident workers for a staggered harvest that lasts most of the year. Celery and cauliflower production has also increased the number of full-time jobs. Perhaps 40 percent of the farm labor in the valley is currently performed by workers who live there. Many farmworkers now own houses. But the strawberry fields have drawn thousands of poor migrants to the area. Only 12 percent of the work force at a strawberry farm can claim year-round employment. And cultivating the fruit is so labor-intensive — twenty-five times as labor-intensive as cultivating broccoli — that strawberry production now employs more farmworkers than the production of all the vegetables grown in the valley combined. Most strawberry pickers hope to find jobs in the neighboring vegetable fields, where the wages are better and the work is less arduous. Turnover rates are extremely high in the strawberry work force. But there is no impending shortage of potential migrants. The rural population of Mexico has tripled since the 1940s. "In terms of absolute numbers," Palerm says, "there are far more Mexican peasants today than ever before."

Twenty-five years ago academic texts declared that California agriculture — with its large-scale irrigation, sophisticated farming practices, corporate structure, and low-wage, imported labor — was unique. That is no longer true. Southern Spain is fast becoming the "California of Europe," borrowing many of the same techniques to grow the same high-value crops and relying on illegal immigrants from North Africa. Southern Italy and Mediterranean France are adopting the system as well. Mexico, Guatemala, and Chile, with the aid of foreign investors, are recreating California's industrialized agriculture in Latin America, producing some crops that now compete with those grown in the United States. Improvements in transportation systems and cooling technology have created an international market for commodities that until recent years were rarely exported. Juan Vicente Palerm believes that the cultivation of fruits and vegetables for processing will increasingly shift from California to Mexico, where labor costs are much lower. Mexico will produce the frozen vegetables for TV dinners, while California grows artichokes, broccoli, strawberries, and asparagus for the fresh market. The harvest of these specialty crops, however, cannot easily be mechanized: their high value is closely linked to their unblemished appearance. The prosperity of California agriculture increasingly depends on uninterrupted access to Mexico's peasantry.

Most of the strawberry workers in the Santa Maria Valley are Mixtec Indians— [20] some of the poorest and most exploited people in the Western Hemisphere. Soil erosion and declining crop yields in the mountains of western Oaxaca have forced the Mixtecs to become migrant workers. According to Michael Kearney, a professor of anthropology at the University of California at Riverside, their choice is simple: "Migrate or starve." Mixtecs now dominate the lowest-paid jobs in California agriculture. In Tijuana you often see wives and children of Mixtec farmworkers, small and dark and beautiful, dressed in the bright colors of their native villages, selling Chiclets to tourists on the street.

Until the 1970s almost all the Mexican farmworkers in California were mestizos with strong links to communities already in the state. The new migrants present social workers with unusual challenges. In addition to the ninety-two dialects of Mixtec, there are at least half a dozen other pre-Columbian languages spoken by the indigenous peoples of Oaxaca. Perhaps one-fifth of the Mixtec farmworkers in California speak little English or Spanish. Throughout their migratory route Mixtecs are the victims of robbery and discrimination. In central Mexico they must run a gauntlet of officials demanding bribes. In Tijuana they are preyed upon by smugglers, rapists, and thieves. In the Imperial Desert, east of San Diego, they risk their lives crossing the border. Two or three migrants now die there from exposure every week.

In Guadalupe many of the settled farmworkers resent the new arrivals from Oaxaca. Illegal immigrants often crossed picket lines during the 1980s, helping to drive the UFW from the valley. Adjusted for inflation, the hourly wages have declined, and there is widespread underemployment. Labor contractors now actively recruit illegals, who work for less money and raise fewer objections than legal residents. At harvest time Guadalupe's population of roughly 5,700 swells by as much as one-third, placing greater demands on local services. Palerm's researchers once discovered twenty-two people living in a two-bedroom apartment.

Despite the hardships of the long journey, Mixtecs hoping to sustain their native villages have a strong incentive to find work in California. Wages in Oaxaca are about two or three dollars a day. Wages in the strawberry fields of Baja California are about five dollars a day. A Mixtec farmworker in the Santa Maria Valley, making ten dollars an hour at the peak of the strawberry harvest, can earn more in one day than he or she could earn back home in a month. . . .

Bowing Down to the Market

One morning in San Diego County, I met a strawberry grower named Doug. We sat and talked in a trailer on the edge of his field. Doug's father and his grandfather had both been sent to an internment camp for Japanese Americans during World War II. Upon their release, the grandfather bought a used truck. At first he worked for other farmers, then he leased some land. He spoke no English and so Doug's father, still a teenager, assumed an important role in the business. The two grew vegetables with success and eventually shifted to strawberries, shipping and processing the fruit as well. On the land where their original farm once stood, there are now condominiums, a park, and a school. Doug grows strawberries a few miles inland. His fields are surrounded by chain-link fences topped with barbed wire. An enormous real estate development, with hundreds of Spanish-style condo units, is creeping up the hills toward his farm. Many of the farmers nearby have already sold their land. Doug has spent most of his life in strawberry fields, learning every aspect of the business first-hand, but now isn't sure he wants his children to do the same.

"Farming's not a glamorous business," Doug said. "Farmers don't have a high status in this community. In fact, we're resented by most people." With all the hassles today from the state and from his neighbors, he sometimes asks himself, "Hey, why do this?" Selling the land would make him instantly rich. Instead, he worries about water costs, about theft, about the strawberries from New Zealand he saw in the market the other day. Rain had wiped out a quarter of his early-season berries, just when the market price was at its peak. Doug cannot understand the hostility toward growers in California. After all, agriculture preserves open land. He thinks Americans don't appreciate how lucky they are to have cheap food. He doesn't understand why anyone would impede strawberry production by limiting his access to migrants. "My workers are helping themselves," he said. "I've picked strawberries, and let me tell you, there is no harder work. I respect these people. They work damn hard. And my jobs are open to anyone who wants to apply." Every so often college kids visit the ranch, convinced that picking strawberries would be a nice way to earn some extra money. Doug laughed. "They don't last an hour out here." 25

We stepped from the trailer into bright sunshine. Workers moved down the furrows under close supervision. Doug takes great pride in being a third-generation grower. He is smart, well educated, meticulous, and it showed in his field. But I wondered if Doug and his workers would still be there in a few years.

Doug picked a berry and handed it to me, a large Chandler that was brilliantly red. I took a bite. The strawberry was warm and sweet and fragrant, with a slightly bitter aftertaste from the soil.

That evening I inadvertently met some of Doug's workers. Ricardo Soto, a young lawyer at CRLA, had brought me to the edge of an avocado orchard to visit a hidden encampment of migrant workers. Perhaps one-third of the farmworkers in northern San Diego County—about 7,000 people—are now homeless. An additional 9,000 of their family members are homeless, too. Many are living outdoors. The shortage of low-income housing became acute in the early 1980s, and large shantytowns began to appear, some containing hundreds of crude shacks. As suburbs encroached on agricultural land in northern San Diego County, wealthy commuters and strawberry pickers became neighbors. At one large shantytown I visited, women were doing their laundry in a stream not far from a walled compound with tennis courts, a pool, and a sign promising country club living. The suburbanites do not like living beside Mexican farmworkers. Instead of providing low-income housing, local authorities have declared states of emergency, passed laws to forbid curbside hiring, and bulldozed many of the large encampments. San Diego growers appalled by the living conditions of their migrants have tried to build farmworker housing near the fields—only to encounter fierce resistance from neighboring home-owners. Although the shantytowns lower nearby property values, permanent farmworker housing might reduce property values even more. "When people find out you want to build housing for your migrants," one grower told me, "they just go ballistic."

The new encampments are smaller and built to avoid detection. At the end of a driveway, near a chain-link fence, I met a young Mixtec who lived in such an encampment. His name was Francisco, and he was eighteen years old. He looked deeply exhausted. He had just picked strawberries for twelve hours at Doug's farm. I asked what he thought of Doug as a boss. "Not bad," he said politely.

The previous year Francisco had picked strawberries from April until July. 30 He had saved $800 during that period and had wired all of it to his mother and father in the village of San Sebastian Tecomaxtlahuaca. This was Francisco's second season in the fields, but he had not seen much of San Diego County. He was too afraid of getting caught. His days were spent at the farm, his nights at the encampment. He picked strawberries six days a week, sometimes seven, for ten or twelve hours a day. "When there's work," Francisco said, "you have to work." Each morning he woke up around four-thirty and walked for half an hour to reach Doug's field.

At dusk, thirteen tired men in dirty clothes approached us. They were all from Francisco's village. They worked together at Doug's farm and stayed at the same encampment. They knew one another's families back home and looked after one another here. The oldest was forty-three and the youngest looked about fifteen. All the men were illegals. All were sick with coughs, but none dared to see a doctor. As the sun dropped behind the hills, clouds of mosquitoes descended, and yet the migrants seemed too tired to notice. They lay on their backs, on their sides, resting on the hard ground as though it were a sofa.

Francisco offered to show me their encampment. We squeezed through a hole in the chain-link fence and through gaps in rusting barbed wire, and climbed a winding path enclosed by tall bushes. It felt like a medieval maze. As we neared the camp, I noticed beer cans and food wrappers littering the ground. We came upon the first shack—short and low, more like a tent, just silver trash bags draped over a wooden frame. A little farther up the path stood three more shacks in a small clearing. They were built of plywood and camouflaged. Branches and leaves had been piled on their roofs. The land-owner did not know the migrants lived here, and the encampment would be difficult to find. These migrants were hiding out, like criminals or Viet Cong. Garbage was everywhere. Francisco pointed to his shack, which was about five feet high, five feet wide, and seven feet long. He shared it with two other men. He had a good blanket. But when it rained at night the roof leaked, and the men would go to work soaking wet the next day and dry off in the sun. Francisco had never lived this way before coming to San Diego. At home he always slept in a bed.

Beyond the sheds, bushes crowded the path again, and then it reached another clearing, where two battered lawn chairs had been placed at the edge of the hill. There was a wonderful view of strawberry fields, new houses, and the lights of the freeway in the distance.

Driving back to my motel that night, I thought about the people of Orange County, one of the richest counties in the nation—big on family values, yet bankrupt from financial speculation, unwilling to raise taxes to pay for their own children's education, unwilling to pay off their debts, whining about the injustice of it, and blaming all their problems on illegal immigrants. And I thought about Francisco, their bogeyman, their scapegoat, working ten hours a day at one of the hardest jobs imaginable, and sleeping on the ground every night, for months, so that he could save money and send it home to his parents.

We have been told for years to bow down before "the market." We have placed our faith in the laws of supply and demand. What has been forgotten, or ignored, is that the market rewards only efficiency. Every other human value gets in its way. The market will drive wages down like water, until they reach the lowest possible level. Today that level is being set not in Washington or New York or Sacramento but in the fields of Baja California and the mountain villages of Oaxaca. That level is about five dollars a day. No deity that men have ever worshipped is more ruthless and more hollow than the free market unchecked; there is no reason why shantytowns should not appear on the outskirts of every American city. All those who now consider themselves devotees of the market should take a good look at what is happening in California. Left to its own devices, the free market always seeks a work force that is hungry, desperate, and cheap—a work force that is anything but free.

35

Notes (by paragraph)

8 *spends half the year working:* According to the latest NAWS survey, the average farmworker spent 47 percent of his or her time in the United States doing farmwork, 19 percent residing but not working, and 8 percent in nonfarm work. See "NAWS, 1997–98," p. 24.

9   *Since 1980, the acreage around Watsonville and Salinas:* In 1980 there were 4,270 acres of strawberries in the area that produced about 96,000 tons of strawberries. In 2000 there were 11,570 acres that produced about 365,000 tons of strawberries. See "California Strawberry Acreage and Yield by Major Areas, 1972 through 1994," California Strawberry Commission, and the Agricultural Commission crop reports for Monterey County and Santa Cruz County, 2000.

11   *A survey of garages in Soledad:* Meuter interview.
hundreds of strawberry pickers have been found living in caves: A decade ago, a large encampment was found near a strawberry farm in Prunedale. Smaller encampments are discovered from time to time in the area. See Roya Camp, "Shanty Camp Draws Aid; Field Workers Found Living in Makeshift Caves," *Salinas Californian,* August 28, 1991; Everett Messick and Susan Ferris, "Authorities to Move Laborers Out of Caves; Seeks Housing for 200 Migrants in Castroville, Salinas Areas," *Monterey Herald,* August 29, 1991; "Back Wages Sought for Farmworkers," *Watsonville Register-Pajaronian,* September 3, 1991.

14   *Guadalupe's population was 18 percent Latino:* Cited in Juan Vicente Palerm, "Farm Labor Needs and Farmworkers in California, 1970 to 1989," *California Agricultural Studies, 91–92,* Labor Market Information Division, State Employment Development Department, April 1991, p. 21.
today it is about 85 percent Latino: According to the U.S. Census Bureau, Guadalupe's population was 84.5 percent Latino in 2000. The actual proportion was most likely higher, given the perennial undercount of Latinos by the census.

16   *up to ten times as high as any wages Mexican peasants could earn:* See Juan Vicente Palerm with Jose Ignacio Urquiola, "A Binational System of Agricultural Production: The Case of the Mexican Bajio and California," in Daniel G. Aldrich, Jr., and Lorenzo Meyer, eds., *Mexico and the United States: Neighbors in Crisis* (San Bernardino, Calif.: Borgo Press, 1993), p. 327.
preserved rural communities in Mexico that otherwise might have collapsed: According to Michael Kearney, a professor of anthropology at the University of California, Northridge, some villages in Oaxaca now derive 80 percent of their annual income from remittances sent home by migrant workers in California. Interview with Michael Kearney. See also "Binational System," pp. 311, 346; Michael Kearney, "Mixtec Ethnicity: Social Identity, Political Consciousness, and Political Activism," *Latin American Research Review* 25 (2): 74–77.

18   *Juan Vicente Palerm believes:* Palerm interview.
Perhaps 40 percent of the farm labor: Cited in Palerm, "Immigrant and Migrant Farmworkers in the Santa Maria Valley, California," Center for Survey Methods Research, Bureau of the Census, 1994, p. 11.
twenty-five times as labor-intensive as cultivating broccoli: Broccoli production requires 80 man-hours per acre; strawberry production requires about 2,000 man-hours per acre. See "Immigrant and Migrant," pp. 4, 6.
The rural population of Mexico: Palerm interview.

20   *"Migrate or starve":* Kearney interview.

21 *Perhaps one-fifth of the Mixtec farmworkers:* Interview with Agimiro Morales, Coalition of Indian Communities of Oaxaca.

Two or three migrants now die there from exposure: One hundred and three migrants were found dead in California's Imperial Desert during 2001. Cited in Kenny Klein, "Search Ended for Immigrants Missing in Imperial Desert," *Desert Sun* (Palm Springs), August 15, 2002. The official death toll no doubt understates the number of migrant deaths; many bodies lie undiscovered in remote areas of the desert. For a good account of why INS policies have made crossing the border so treacherous, see Wayne A. Cornelius, "Death at the Border: Efficacy and Unintended Consequences of U.S. Immigration Control Policy," *Population and Development Review*, December 1, 2001.

23 *Wages in Oaxaca:* Morales interview.

Wages in the strawberry fields of Baja California: Kearney interview.

28 *Perhaps one-third of the farmworkers in northern San Diego County:* Cited in Dan Weisman, "Farmworkers Often Homeless: Estimated 7,000 in North Country Lack Housing," *North Country Times*, March 21, 2000.

Exploring the Text

1. Note Eric Schlosser's title, "In the Strawberry Fields." Compare the imagery evoked by the Beatles song "Strawberry Fields" and the ceremonial place in New York's Central Park with Schlosser's description in paragraphs 1 and 2.
2. How does Schlosser use the resources of language to characterize the work of the strawberry pickers in paragraph 6?
3. What are some of the particular hardships facing the strawberry pickers? Which one does Schlosser say is the worst?
4. Explain the rhetorical shift that Schlosser makes from "La Fruta del Diablo" to "Locked into Dependence."
5. According to Schlosser, how has economics changed the land and the population?
6. Schlosser concludes paragraphs 16 and 17 with claims. Analyze his arguments according to the Toulmin model as explained in Chapter 3.
7. What aspects of strawberry production differ significantly from the production of broccoli, celery, or cauliflower (para. 18)? How does this affect the lives of the workers?
8. Explain the nature of the economic imperative that concludes the section "Locked into Dependence" (para. 23).
9. How do you feel about the conditions described in the selection? Does reading it influence your attitude toward eating strawberries? Toward migrant workers? Explain.
10. Why does Schlosser conclude with narration and personal experience?
11. How would you characterize Schlosser's tone in the concluding paragraphs (34–35)? Do you agree with his conclusions? Why or why not?
12. Select an example of a general statement, such as the one that concludes the first section: "On hillsides above the Salinas Valley, hundreds of strawberry pickers

have been found living in caves." Then read the endnote that corresponds to the sentence. Explain the relationship between the endnote and the text. What is the rhetorical function of the endnote? Overall, what effect do the endnotes have on ethos and logos? Explain.

What the Bagel Man Saw

STEPHEN J. DUBNER AND STEVEN D. LEVITT

Stephen J. Dubner (b. 1963) and Steven D. Levitt (b. 1967) are the authors of the best sellers *Freakonomics* (2005) and *SuperFreakonomics* (2009). Dubner lives in New York City. In addition to *Freakonomics* and *SuperFreakonomics*, he is the author of *Turbulent Souls (Choosing My Religion)* (1998), *Confessions of a Hero-Worshiper* (2003), and a children's book, *The Boy with Two Belly Buttons* (2007). He has written for publications including the *New York Times Magazine*, the *New Yorker*, and *Time*. In addition, his journalism has been anthologized in *The Best American Sportswriting* and *The Best American Crime Writing*. He has taught English at Columbia University, where he earned an MFA and played in a rock band. Steven Levitt is a professor of economics at the University of Chicago, where he directs the Becker Center on Chicago Price Theory. In 2004, he was awarded the John Bates Clark Medal, which recognizes the most influential economist in America under the age of forty. More recently, he was named one of *Time* magazine's "100 People Who Shape Our World." Levitt received his BA from Harvard University in 1989, and his PhD from MIT in 1994, and he has taught at Chicago since 1997. "What the Bagel Man Saw" first appeared in the *New York Times Magazine* in 2004.

Once upon a time, Paul F. dreamed big dreams. While studying agricultural economics at Cornell, he wanted to end world hunger. Instead, after doctoral work at M.I.T., he wound up taking a job with a research institute in Washington, analyzing the weapons expenditures of the United States Navy. This was in 1962. After four years came more of the same: analyst jobs with the Bureau of the Budget, the Institute for Defense Analyses, the President's Commission on Federal Statistics. Still, he dreamed. He had "potent research ideas," as he recalls them now, which the Environmental Protection Agency failed to appreciate. He developed a statistical means of predicting cancer clusters, but because he was an economist and not a doctor, he couldn't make headway with the National Cancer Institute. He still loved the art of economics — the data-gathering, the statistical manipulation, the problem-solving — but it had led him to a high-level dead end. He was well paid and unfulfilled. "I'd go to the office Christmas party, and people would introduce me to their wives or husbands as the guy who brings in the bagels," he says. "'Oh! You're the guy who brings in the bagels!' Nobody ever said, 'This is the guy in charge of the public research group.'"

The bagels had begun as a casual gesture: a boss treating his employees whenever they won a new research contract. Then he made it a habit. Every Friday, he would bring half a dozen bagels, a serrated knife, some cream cheese. When employees from neighboring floors heard about the bagels, they wanted some, too. Eventually he was bringing in 15 dozen bagels a week. He set out a cash basket to recoup his costs. His collection rate was about 95 percent; he attributed the underpayment to oversight.

In 1984, when his research institute fell under new management, he took a look at his career and grimaced. "I was sick of every aspect of the whole thing," he says. "I was discouraged. I was tired of chasing contracts. So I said to management: 'I'm getting out of this. I'm going to sell bagels.'"

His economist friends thought he had lost his mind. They made oblique remarks (and some not so oblique) about "a terrible waste of talent." But his wife supported his decision. They had retired their mortgage; the last of their three children was finishing college. Driving around the office parks that encircle Washington, he solicited customers with a simple pitch: early in the morning, he would deliver some bagels and a cash basket to a company's snack room; he would return before lunch to pick up the money and the leftovers. It was an honor-system commerce scheme, and it worked. Within a few years, he was delivering 700 dozen bagels a week to 140 companies and earning as much as he had ever made as a research analyst. He had thrown off the shackles of cubicle life and made himself happy.

He had also—quite without meaning to—designed a beautiful economic 5
experiment. By measuring the money collected against the bagels taken, he could tell, down to the penny, just how honest his customers were. Did they steal from him? If so, what were the characteristics of a company that stole versus a company that did not? Under what circumstances did people tend to steal more, or less?

As it happens, his accidental study provides a window onto a subject that has long stymied academics: white-collar crime. (Yes, shorting the bagel man is white-collar crime, writ however small.) Despite all the attention paid to companies like Enron, academics know very little about the practicalities of white-collar crime. The reason? There aren't enough data.

A key fact of white-collar crime is that we hear about only the very slim fraction of people who are caught. Most embezzlers lead quiet and theoretically happy lives; employees who steal company property are rarely detected. With street crime, meanwhile, that is not the case. A mugging or a burglary or a murder is usually counted whether or not the criminal is caught. A street crime has a victim, who typically reports the crime to the police, which generates data, which in turn generate thousands of academic papers by criminologists, sociologists and economists. But white-collar crime presents no obvious victim. Whom, exactly, did the masters of Enron steal from? And how can you measure something if you don't know to whom it happened, or with what frequency, or in what magnitude?

Paul F.'s bagel business was different. It did present a victim. The victim was Paul F.

It is 3:32 A.M., and Paul F. is barreling down a dark Maryland road when he jams on the brakes and swears. "I forgot my hearing aids," he mutters. He throws the gearshift into reverse and proceeds to drive backward nearly as fast as he had been driving forward.

He is 72, and his business is still thriving. (Thus his request to mask his full name and his customers' identities: he is wary of potential competitors poaching his clients.) His daughter, son-in-law and one other employee now make most of the deliveries. Today is Friday, which is the only day Paul F. still drives. Semi-retirement has left him more time to indulge his economist self and tally his data. He now knows, for instance, that in the past eight years he has delivered 1,375,103 bagels, of which 1,255,483 were eaten. (He has also delivered 648,341 doughnuts, of which 608,438 were eaten.) 10

He knows a good deal about the payment rate, too. When he first went into business, he expected 95 percent payment, based on the experience at his own office. But just as crime tends to be low on a street where a police car is parked, the 95 percent rate was artificially high: Paul F.'s presence had deterred theft. Not only that, but those bagel eaters knew the provider and had feelings (presumably good ones) about him. A broad swath of psychological and economic research has argued that people will pay different amounts for the same item depending on who is providing it. The economist Richard Thaler, in his 1985 "Beer on the Beach" study, showed that a thirsty sunbather would pay $2.65 for a beer delivered from a resort but only $1.50 for the same beer if it came from a shabby grocery store.

In the real world, Paul F. learned to settle for less than 95 percent. Now he considers companies "honest" if the payment is 90 percent or more. "Averages between 80 percent and 90 percent are annoying but tolerable," he says. "Below 80 percent, we really have to grit our teeth to continue."

In recent years, he has seen two remarkable trends in overall payment rates. The first was a long, slow decline that began in 1992. "All my friends say: 'Aha! Clinton!'" Paul F. says. "Although I must say that most of my friends are conservative and inclined to see such things where others might not." The second trend revealed in Paul F.'s data was even starker. Entering the summer of 2001, the over-all payment rate had slipped to about 87 percent. Immediately after Sept. 11, the rate spiked a full 2 percent and hasn't slipped much since. (If a 2 percent gain in payment doesn't sound like much, think of it this way: the nonpayment rate fell from 13 percent to 11 percent, which amounts to a 15 percent decline in theft.) Because many of Paul F.'s customers are affiliated with national security, there may be a patriotic element to this 9/11 effect. Or it may represent a more general surge in empathy. Whatever the reason, Paul F. was grateful for the boost. He expends a great deal of energy hectoring his low-paying customers, often in the form of a typewritten note. "The cost of bagels has gone up dramatically since the beginning of the year," reads one. "Unfortunately, the number of bagels and dough-nuts that disappear without being paid for has also gone up. Don't let that con-tinue. I don't imagine that you would teach your children to cheat, so why do it yourselves?"

He is impatient and cantankerous but in sum agreeable. Dressed in jeans and sneakers, with busy eyes and a wavy fringe of gray hair, he awoke this Friday at 3 A.M. Working out of his garage, he first loaded 50 cardboard trays of doughnuts—a local bakery delivered them overnight—into the back of his van. He drives an unmarked white Ford E-150 rigged with a bagel-warming compartment. (The van was never stopped during the D.C. sniper attacks, but Paul F.'s tendency to park at the curb caused problems in the near aftermath of 9/11. One customer left a note saying: "Please park in a parking space. You are freaking a lot of people out.")

After the doughnuts, Paul F. loaded two dozen money boxes, which he made 15
himself out of plywood. A money slot is cut into the top. When he started out, he left behind an open basket for the cash, but too often the money vanished. Then he tried a coffee can with a slot in its plastic lid, which also proved too tempting. The wooden box has worked well. Each year he drops off about 7,000 boxes and loses, on average, just one to theft. This is an intriguing statistic: the same people who routinely steal more than 10 percent of his bagels almost never stoop to stealing his money box—a tribute to the nuanced social calculus of theft. From Paul F.'s perspective, an office worker who eats a bagel without paying is committing a crime; the office worker apparently doesn't think so. This distinction probably has less to do with the admittedly small amount of money involved than with the context of the "crime." (The same office worker who fails to pay for his bagel might also help himself to a long slurp of soda while he's filling a glass in a self-serve restaurant, but it is extremely unlikely that he will leave the restaurant without paying.)

After retrieving his hearing aids, he heads for the bagel shop that provides him with roughly 50 dozen bagels, in six flavors, every day. He drives nearly 80 m.p.h. along empty highways and discusses what he has learned about honesty. He is leery of disparaging individual companies or even most industries, for fear it will hurt his business. But he will say that the telecom companies have robbed him blind, and another bagel-delivery man found that law firms aren't worth the trouble. He also says he believes that employees further up the corporate ladder cheat more than those down below. He reached this conclusion in part after delivering for years to one company spread out over three floors—an executive floor on top and two lower floors with sales, service and administrative employees. Maybe, he says, the executives stole bagels out of a sense of entitlement. (Or maybe cheating is how they got to be executives.) His biggest surprise? "I had idly assumed that in places where security clearance was required for an individual to have a job, the employees would be more honest than elsewhere. That hasn't turned out to be true."

Since he started delivering bagels, Paul F. has kept rigorous data—which, when run through a computer and measured against external factors ranging from the local weather to the unemployment rate, can tell some interesting stories. Other conclusions, meanwhile, are purely intuitive, based on Paul F.'s 20-year exposure to bagel behavior.

He has identified two great overriding predictors of a company's honesty: morale and size. Paul F. has noted a strong correlation between high payment rates and an office where people seem to like their boss and their work. (This is one of his intuitive conclusions.) He also gleans a higher payment rate from smaller offices. (This one is firmly supported by the data.) An office with a few dozen employees generally outpays by 3 percent to 5 percent an office with a few hundred employees. This may seem counterintuitive: in a bigger office, a bigger crowd is bound to convene around the bagel table—providing more witnesses to make sure you drop your money in the box. (Paul F. currently charges $1 for a bagel and 50 cents for a doughnut.) But in the big-office/small-office comparison, bagel crime seems to mirror street crime. There is far less crime per capita in rural areas than in cities, in large part because a rural criminal is more likely to be known (and therefore caught). Also, a rural community tends to exert greater social incentives against crime, the main one being shame.

The bagel data also show a correlation between payment rate and the local rate of unemployment. Intuition might have argued that these two factors would be negatively correlated—that is, when unemployment is low (and the economy is good), people would tend to be freer with their cash. "But I found that as the unemployment rate goes down, dishonesty goes up," Paul F. says. "My guess is that a low rate of unemployment means that companies are having to hire a lower class of employee." The data also show that the payment rate does not change when he raises bagel prices, though volume may temporarily fall.

If the payment tendencies that Paul F. has noted so far might be called macro trends, it is the micro trends—those reflecting personal mood—that are perhaps most compelling. Weather, for instance, has a major effect on the payment rate. Unseasonably pleasant weather inspires people to pay a significantly higher rate. Unseasonably cold weather, meanwhile, makes people cheat prolifically; so does heavy rain and wind. But worst are the holidays. The week of Christmas produces a 2 percent drop in payment rates—again, a 15 percent increase in theft, an effect on the same order, in reverse, as 9/11. Thanksgiving is nearly as bad; the week of Valentine's Day is also lousy, as is the week straddling April 15. There are, however, a few good holidays: July 4, Labor Day and Columbus Day. The difference in the two sets of holidays? The low-cheating holidays represent little more than an extra day off from work. The high-cheating holidays are freighted with miscellaneous anxieties and the high expectations of loved ones. 20

As considerable as these oscillations may be, the fact is that a poorly paying office rarely turns into a well-paying office, or vice versa. This has led Paul F. to believe in a sobering sort of equilibrium: honest people are honest, and cheaters will cheat regardless of the circumstance. "One time when I was cleaning up leftovers," he recalls, "a man came and took a doughnut while I was standing there, and started to walk away without putting any money in the box. I never challenge people about paying, but in that place, despite notes and appeals to management, the payment rate had been abysmal, and I was fed up. I said to the guy, 'Are you going to pay for that?' And he said, 'Oh, I left my wallet in my car,' and started to put the doughnut back. Now I knew, and he knew that I knew, that he hadn't left his wallet in the car, but he was too cheap to pay 50 cents for a doughnut and too brazen to say, 'Oh, I'm sorry, I just wasn't thinking,' which is what anyone with half a conscience would say."

Once the van is loaded up with fresh bagels, sorted by the dozen into white paper bags that Paul F. had earlier labeled with customers' names, he begins his rounds. It is 5:02 A.M. The first stop is an office building in northern Virginia. His routine is nearly always the same. He grabs one of the magnetic ID cards dangling from his rearview mirror, hangs it from his neck, jumps around to the side of the van, loads up a cardboard box with bagels, doughnuts and a cash box and practically sprints inside. In the snack room, he dumps the bagels from their bag, folds back the top of the doughnut tray, plunks his money box on the table and hustles out. Then back into the van, which he drives maniacally even from one office-park cul-de-sac to the next. (When a woman in a Lexus tarries at the entrance to one parking lot, he calls her terrible names.) Another office building, another ID card, another delivery. You can tell the defense contractors by the art on the walls: achingly sensual black-and-white photographs of missiles and armored personnel carriers. Some of the break rooms have vending machines whose offerings — "Spicy Chicken Biscuit" and "Chopped Beefsteak Sandwich" — look so vile that the simple appeal of a warm, fresh bagel becomes all the more apparent.

By 9 A.M., he has made all his deliveries. At 11, he will start picking up leftovers and the money boxes. Until then, it is time for his weekly Friday morning breakfast with a dozen of his old economist friends. They meet in the ground-floor cafeteria of the office building where one of them now works. They swap gossip, tax tips, Ziploc bags of pipe tobacco.

These are some of the same friends who 20 years ago told Paul F. that his bagel business would never work. People cannot be trusted, they said. Their conversation this morning continues along those lines. One man cites a story he heard about a toll-collector strike in England. During the strike, drivers were asked simply to put their money into a box. As it turned out, the government collected more toll money during the strike — which suggests that the drivers were at least fairly honest, but also that the toll collectors had been skimming like mad. Another economist at the table is now a tax preparer. He ticks off a long list of common tax evasions his clients try to use — lying about the cost basis of stocks is perhaps the favorite — and reminds the others that the United States tax code is, like Paul F.'s bagel business, largely built on an honor system.

Amid all the talk of cheating, lying and scamming, Paul F. takes the floor to   25
declare his faith in humankind. "You guys know the story about the Rings of Gyges, right?" he says.

A man named Gyges, he explains, came upon a cave and, inside it, a skeleton wearing a ring. When Gyges put on the ring, he found that it made him invisible. Now he was faced with a choice: would he use his invisibility for good or evil? The story comes from Plato's *Republic*. It was told by a student named Glaucon, in challenge to a Socratic teaching about honesty and justice. "Socrates was arguing against the idea that people will be dishonest if given the chance," Paul F. says. "His point was that people are good, even without enforcement."

But Paul F. doesn't tell his friends how Glaucon's story ends. Gyges actually did woeful things once he got the ring—seduced the queen, murdered the king and so on. The story posed a moral question: could any man resist the temptation of evil if he knew his acts could not be witnessed? Glaucon seemed to think the answer was no. But Paul F. sides with Socrates—for he knows that the answer, at least 89 percent of the time, is yes.

Exploring the Text

1. What rhetorical effect does the "fairy tale" opening "Once upon a time . . ." have?
2. What is the major implication developed in the first paragraph?
3. As Stephen Dubner and Steven Levitt develop their essay, they use a great deal of quantification. Note three particular examples. How does their use of numbers affect their argument?
4. What is the nature of the appeals in Paul F.'s typewritten notes (para. 13)?
5. What do the writers mean by the phrase "the nuanced social calculus of theft" (para. 15)?
6. Find and explain an example of humor. How does the humor affect the argument developed by the authors?
7. Of the two predictors presented in paragraph 18, which do you think is the more compelling? Also, which deterrent do you think would be stronger—the fear of being caught or the shame associated with the crime?
8. According to the authors, what is the difference between macro and micro trends as they apply to payment for bagels? Do you find the authors' position compelling? Why or why not?
9. Do you agree with the way that Dubner and Levitt characterize "honest people" and "cheaters"? Explain.
10. Identify the point where the essay moves toward conclusion. Explain the appeal the writers use there. What is its effect on the reader?
11. How does the story of Gyges (paras. 26–27) contribute to the piece as a whole? Do you find it to be an effective conclusion?
12. In summary, what, exactly, was it that "the bagel man saw"? How does that relate to the economy as a whole?

The Case for Working with Your Hands

MATTHEW B. CRAWFORD

A philosopher, writer, and mechanic, Matthew B. Crawford grew up in the San Francisco Bay area with a theoretical physicist for a father and worked his way through high school and college as an electrician. He earned a degree in physics at the University of California at Santa Barbara and a PhD in political philosophy at the

University of Chicago, where he was a fellow at the Committee on Social Thought. Crawford has done research on ocean surface temperature at the Scripps Institute of Oceanography in La Jolla, California. He has also done emission control research, taught high school Latin, and worked on a white-collar assembly line, where his job was to write summaries of scientific journal articles that he did not understand. Currently a fellow at the Institute for Advanced Studies in Culture at the University of Virginia, he owns and operates Shockoe Moto, an independent motorcycle repair shop in Richmond, Virginia. "The Case for Working with Your Hands" originally appeared in the *New York Times Magazine* in 2009. That year also saw the publication of Crawford's best seller, *Shop Class as Soulcraft: An Inquiry into the Value of Work*, and in 2010 he published *The Case for Working with Your Hands: Or Why Office Work Is Bad for Us and Fixing Things Feels Good.*

The television show *Deadliest Catch* depicts commercial crab fishermen in the Bering Sea. Another, *Dirty Jobs*, shows all kinds of grueling work; one episode featured a guy who inseminates turkeys for a living. The weird fascination of these shows must lie partly in the fact that such confrontations with material reality have become exotically unfamiliar. Many of us do work that feels more surreal than real. Working in an office, you often find it difficult to see any tangible result from your efforts. What exactly have you accomplished at the end of any given day? Where the chain of cause and effect is opaque and responsibility diffuse, the experience of individual agency can be elusive. *Dilbert, The Office* and similar portrayals of cubicle life attest to the dark absurdism with which many Americans have come to view their white-collar jobs.

Is there a more "real" alternative (short of inseminating turkeys)?

High-school shop-class programs were widely dismantled in the 1990s as educators prepared students to become "knowledge workers." The imperative of the last 20 years to round up every warm body and send it to college, then to the cubicle, was tied to a vision of the future in which we somehow take leave of material reality and glide about in a pure information economy. This has not come to pass. To begin with, such work often feels more enervating than gliding. More fundamentally, now as ever, somebody has to actually do things: fix our cars, unclog our toilets, build our houses.

When we praise people who do work that is straightforwardly useful, the praise often betrays an assumption that they had no other options. We idealize them as the salt of the earth and emphasize the sacrifice for others their work may entail. Such sacrifice does indeed occur—the hazards faced by a lineman restoring power during a storm come to mind. But what if such work answers as well to a basic human need of the one who does it? I take this to be the suggestion of Marge Piercy's poem "To Be of Use," which concludes with the lines "The pitcher longs for water to carry/and a person for work that is real." Beneath our gratitude for the lineman may rest envy.

This seems to be a moment when the useful arts have an especially compel-ling economic rationale. A car mechanics' trade association reports that repair 5 shops have seen their business jump significantly in the current recession: people aren't buying new cars; they are fixing the ones they have. The current downturn is likely to pass eventually. But there are also systemic changes in the economy, arising from information technology, that have the surprising effect of making the manual trades—plumbing, electrical work, car repair—more attractive as careers. The Princeton economist Alan Blinder argues that the crucial distinction in the emerging labor market is not between those with more or less education, but between those whose services can be delivered over a wire and those who must do their work in person or on site. The latter will find their livelihoods more secure against outsourcing to distant countries. As Blinder puts it, "You can't hammer a nail over the Internet." Nor can the Indians fix your car. Because they are in India.

If the goal is to earn a living, then, maybe it isn't really true that 18-year-olds need to be imparted with a sense of panic about getting into college (though they certainly need to learn). Some people are hustled off to college, then to the cubicle, against their own inclinations and natural bents, when they would rather be learning to build things or fix things. One shop teacher suggested to me that "in schools, we create artificial learning environments for our children that they know to be contrived and undeserving of their full attention and engagement. Without the opportunity to learn through the hands, the world remains abstract and distant, and the passions for learning will not be engaged."

A gifted young person who chooses to become a mechanic rather than to accumulate academic credentials is viewed as eccentric, if not self-destructive. There is a pervasive anxiety among parents that there is only one track to success for their children. It runs through a series of gates controlled by prestigious institutions. Further, there is wide use of drugs to medicate boys, especially, against their natural tendency toward action, the better to "keep things on track." I taught briefly in a public high school and would have loved to have set up a Ritalin fogger in my classroom. It is a rare person, male or female, who is naturally inclined to sit still for 17 years in school, and then indefinitely at work.

The trades suffer from low prestige, and I believe this is based on a simple mistake. Because the work is dirty, many people assume it is also stupid. This is not my experience. I have a small business as a motorcycle mechanic in Richmond, Va., which I started in 2002. I work on Japanese and European motorcycles, mostly older bikes with some "vintage" cachet that makes people willing to spend money on them. I have found the satisfactions of the work to be very much bound up with the intellectual challenges it presents. And yet my decision to go into this line of work is a choice that seems to perplex many people.

After finishing a Ph.D. in political philosophy at the University of Chicago in 2000, I managed to stay on with a one-year postdoctoral fellowship at the university's Committee on Social Thought. The academic job market was utterly bleak. In a state of professional panic, I retreated to a makeshift workshop I set up in the basement of a Hyde Park apartment building, where I spent the winter tearing down an old Honda motorcycle and rebuilding it. The physicality of it, and the clear specificity of what the project required of me, was a balm. Stumped by a starter motor that seemed to check out in every way but wouldn't work, I started asking around at Honda dealerships. Nobody had an answer; finally one service manager told me to call Fred Cousins of Triple O Service. "If anyone can help you, Fred can."

I called Fred, and he invited me to come to his independent motorcycle-repair shop, tucked discreetly into an unmarked warehouse on Goose Island. He told me to put the motor on a certain bench that was free of clutter. He checked the electrical resistance through the windings, as I had done, to confirm there was no short circuit or broken wire. He spun the shaft that ran through the center of the motor, as I had. No problem: it spun freely. Then he hooked it up to a battery. It moved ever so slightly but wouldn't spin. He grasped the shaft, delicately, with three fingers, and tried to wiggle it side to side. "Too much free play," he said. He suggested that the problem was with the bushing (a thick-walled sleeve of metal) that captured the end of the shaft in the end of the cylindrical motor housing. It was worn, so it wasn't locating the shaft precisely enough. The shaft was free to move too much side to side (perhaps a couple of hundredths of an inch), causing the outer circumference of the rotor to bind on the inner circumference of the motor housing when a current was applied. Fred scrounged around for a Honda motor. He found one with the same bushing, then used a "blind hole bearing puller" to extract it, as well as the one in my motor. Then he gently tapped the new, or rather newer, one into place. The motor worked! Then Fred gave me an impromptu dissertation on the peculiar metallurgy of these Honda starter-motor bushings of the mid-'70s. Here was a scholar.

Over the next six months I spent a lot of time at Fred's shop, learning, and put in only occasional appearances at the university. This was something of a regression: I worked on cars throughout high school and college, and one of my early jobs was at a Porsche repair shop. Now I was rediscovering the intensely absorbing nature of the work, and it got me thinking about possible livelihoods.

As it happened, in the spring I landed a job as executive director of a policy organization in Washington. This felt like a coup. But certain perversities became apparent as I settled into the job. It sometimes required me to reason backward, from desired conclusion to suitable premise. The organization had taken certain positions, and there were some facts it was more fond of than others. As its figure-head, I was making arguments I didn't fully buy myself. Further, my boss seemed intent on retraining me according to a certain cognitive style — that of the corporate world, from which he had recently come. This style demanded that I project an image of rationality but not indulge too much in actual reasoning. As I sat in my K Street office, Fred's life as an independent tradesman gave me an image that I kept coming back to: someone who really knows what he is doing, losing himself in work that is genuinely useful and has a certain integrity to it. He also seemed to be having a lot of fun.

Seeing a motorcycle about to leave my shop under its own power, several days after arriving in the back of a pickup truck, I don't feel tired even though I've been standing on a concrete floor all day. Peering into the portal of his helmet, I think

I can make out the edges of a grin on the face of a guy who hasn't ridden his bike in a while. I give him a wave. With one of his hands on the throttle and the other on the clutch, I know he can't wave back. But I can hear his salute in the exuberant "bwaaAAAAP!" of a crisp throttle, gratuitously revved. That sound pleases me, as I know it does him. It's a ventriloquist conversation in one mechanical voice, and the gist of it is "Yeah!"

After five months at the think tank, I'd saved enough money to buy some tools I needed, and I quit and went into business fixing bikes. My shop rate is $40 per hour. Other shops have rates as high as $70 per hour, but I tend to work pretty slowly. Further, only about half the time I spend in the shop ends up being billable (I have no employees; every little chore falls to me), so it usually works out closer to $20 per hour — a modest but decent wage. The business goes up and down; when it is down I have supplemented it with writing. The work is sometimes frustrating, but it is never irrational.

And it frequently requires complex thinking. In fixing motorcycles you come   15 up with several imagined trains of cause and effect for manifest symptoms, and you judge their likelihood before tearing anything down. This imagining relies on a mental library that you develop. An internal combustion engine can work in any number of ways, and different manufacturers have tried different approaches. Each has its own proclivities for failure. You also develop a library of sounds and smells and feels. For example, the backfire of a too-lean fuel mixture is subtly different from an ignition backfire.

As in any learned profession, you just have to know a lot. If the motorcycle is 30 years old, from an obscure maker that went out of business 20 years ago, its tendencies are known mostly through lore. It would probably be impossible to do such work in isolation, without access to a collective historical memory; you have to be embedded in a community of mechanic-antiquarians. These relationships are maintained by telephone, in a network of reciprocal favors that spans the country. My most reliable source, Fred, has such an encyclopedic knowledge of obscure European motorcycles that all I have been able to offer him in exchange is deliveries of obscure European beer.

There is always a risk of introducing new complications when working on old motorcycles, and this enters the diagnostic logic. Measured in likelihood of screw-ups, the cost is not identical for all avenues of inquiry when deciding which hypothesis to pursue. Imagine you're trying to figure out why a bike won't start. The fasteners holding the engine covers on 1970s-era Hondas are Phillips head, and they are almost always rounded out and corroded. Do you really want to check the condition of the starter clutch if each of eight screws will need to be drilled out and extracted, risking damage to the engine case? Such impediments have to be taken into account. The attractiveness of any hypothesis is determined in part by physical circumstances that have no logical connection to the diagnostic problem at hand. The mechanic's proper response to the situation cannot be anticipated by a set of rules or algorithms.

There probably aren't many jobs that can be reduced to rule-following and still be done well. But in many jobs there is an attempt to do just this, and the perversity of it may go unnoticed by those who design the work process. Mechanics face something like this problem in the factory service manuals that we use. These manuals tell you to be systematic in eliminating variables, presenting an idealized image of diagnostic work. But they never take into account the risks of working on old machines. So you put the manual away and consider the facts before you. You do this because ultimately you are responsible to the motorcycle and its owner, not to some procedure.

Some diagnostic situations contain a lot of variables. Any given symptom may have several possible causes, and further, these causes may interact with one another and therefore be difficult to isolate. In deciding how to proceed, there often comes a point where you have to step back and get a larger gestalt. Have a cigarette and walk around the lift. The gap between theory and practice stretches out in front of you, and this is where it gets interesting. What you need now is the kind of judgment that arises only from experience; hunches rather than rules. For me, at least, there is more real thinking going on in the bike shop than there was in the think tank.

Put differently, mechanical work has required me to cultivate different intellectual habits. Further, habits of mind have an ethical dimension that we don't often think about. Good diagnosis requires attentiveness to the machine, almost a conversation with it, rather than assertiveness, as in the position papers produced on K Street. Cognitive psychologists speak of "metacognition," which is the activity of stepping back and thinking about your own thinking. It is what you do when you stop for a moment in your pursuit of a solution, and wonder whether your understanding of the problem is adequate. The slap of worn-out pistons hitting their cylinders can sound a lot like loose valve tappets, so to be a good mechanic you have to be constantly open to the possibility that you may be mistaken. This is a virtue that is at once cognitive and moral. It seems to develop because the mechanic, if he is the sort who goes on to become good at it, internalizes the healthy functioning of the motorcycle as an object of passionate concern. How else can you explain the elation he gets when he identifies the root cause of some problem? [20]

This active concern for the motorcycle is reinforced by the social aspects of the job. As is the case with many independent mechanics, my business is based entirely on word of mouth. I sometimes barter services with machinists and metal fabricators. This has a very different feel than transactions with money; it situates me in a community. The result is that I really don't want to mess up anybody's motorcycle or charge more than a fair price. You often hear people complain about mechanics and other tradespeople whom they take to be dishonest or incompetent. I am sure this is sometimes justified. But it is also true that the mechanic deals with a large element of chance.

I once accidentally dropped a feeler gauge down into the crankcase of a Kawasaki Ninja that was practically brand new, while performing its first scheduled valve adjustment. I escaped a complete tear-down of the motor only through an operation that involved the use of a stethoscope, another pair of trusted hands and the sort of concentration we associate with a bomb squad. When finally I laid my fingers on that feeler gauge, I felt as if I had cheated death. I don't remember ever feeling so alive as in the hours that followed.

Often as not, however, such crises do not end in redemption. Moments of elation are counterbalanced with failures, and these, too, are vivid, taking place right before your eyes. With stakes that are often high and immediate, the manual trades elicit heedful absorption in work. They are punctuated by moments of pleasure that take place against a darker backdrop: a keen awareness of catastrophe as an always-present possibility. The core experience is one of individual responsibility, supported by face-to-face interactions between tradesman and customer.

Contrast the experience of being a middle manager. This is a stock figure of ridicule, but the sociologist Robert Jackall spent years inhabiting the world of corporate managers, conducting interviews, and he poignantly describes the "moral maze" they feel trapped in. Like the mechanic, the manager faces the possibility of disaster at any time. But in his case these disasters feel arbitrary; they are typically a result of corporate restructurings, not of physics. A manager has to make many decisions for which he is accountable. Unlike an entrepreneur with his own business, however, his decisions can be reversed at any time by someone higher up the food chain (and there is always someone higher up the food chain). It's important for your career that these reversals not look like defeats, and more generally you have to spend a lot of time managing what others think of you. Survival depends on a crucial insight: you can't back down from an argument that you initially made in straightforward language, with moral conviction, without seeming to lose your integrity. So managers learn the art of provisional thinking and feeling, expressed in corporate doublespeak, and cultivate a lack of commitment to their own actions. Nothing is set in concrete the way it is when you are, for example, pouring concrete.

Those who work on the lower rungs of the information-age office hierarchy 25 face their own kinds of unreality, as I learned some time ago. After earning a master's degree in the early 1990s, I had a hard time finding work but eventually landed a job in the Bay Area writing brief summaries of academic journal articles, which were then sold on CD-ROMs to subscribing libraries. When I got the phone call offering me the job, I was excited. I felt I had grabbed hold of the passing world — miraculously, through the mere filament of a classified ad — and reeled myself into its current. My new bosses immediately took up residence in my imagination, where I often surprised them with my hidden depths. As I was shown to my cubicle, I felt a real sense of being honored. It seemed more than spacious enough. It was my desk, where I would think my thoughts — my unique contribution to a common enterprise, in a real company with hundreds of employees. The regularity of the cubicles made me feel I had found a place in the order of things. I was to be a knowledge worker.

But the feel of the job changed on my first day. The company had gotten its start by providing libraries with a subject index of popular magazines like *Sports Illustrated*. Through a series of mergers and acquisitions, it now found itself offering not just indexes but also abstracts (that is, summaries), and of a very different kind of material: scholarly works in the physical and biological sciences, humanities, social sciences and law. Some of this stuff was simply incomprehensible to anyone but an expert in the particular field covered by the journal. I was reading articles in Classical Philology where practically every other word was in Greek. Some of the scientific journals were no less mysterious. Yet the categorical difference between, say, *Sports Illustrated* and *Nature Genetics* seemed not to have impressed itself on the company's decision makers. In some of the titles I was assigned, articles began with an abstract written by the author. But even in such cases I was to write my own. The reason offered was that unless I did so, there would be no "value added" by our product. It was hard to believe I was going to add anything other than error and confusion to such material. But then, I hadn't yet been trained.

My job was structured on the supposition that in writing an abstract of an article there is a method that merely needs to be applied, and that this can be done without understanding the text. I was actually told this by the trainer, Monica, as she stood before a whiteboard, diagramming an abstract. Monica seemed a perfectly sensible person and gave no outward sign of suffering delusions. She didn't insist too much on what she was telling us, and it became clear she was in a position similar to that of a veteran Soviet bureaucrat who must work on two levels at once: reality and official ideology. The official ideology was a bit like the factory service manuals I mentioned before, the ones that offer procedures that mechanics often have to ignore in order to do their jobs.

My starting quota, after finishing a week of training, was 15 articles per day. By my 11th month at the company, my quota was up to 28 articles per day (this was the normal, scheduled increase). I was always sleepy while at work, and I think this exhaustion was because I felt trapped in a contradiction: the fast pace demanded complete focus on the task, yet the pace also made any real concentration impossible. I had to actively suppress my own ability to think, because the more you think, the more the inadequacies in your understanding of an author's argument come into focus. This can only slow you down. To not do justice to an author who had poured himself into the subject at hand felt like violence against what was best in myself.

The quota demanded, then, not just dumbing down but also a bit of moral re-education, the opposite of the kind that occurs in the heedful absorption of mechanical work. I had to suppress my sense of responsibility to the article itself, and to others—to the author, to begin with, as well as to the hapless users of the database, who might naïvely suppose that my abstract reflected the author's work. Such detachment was made easy by the fact there was no immediate consequence for me; I could write any nonsense whatever.

Now, it is probably true that every job entails some kind of mutilation. I used to work as an electrician and had my own business doing it for a while. As an electrician you breathe a lot of unknown dust in crawl spaces, your knees get bruised, your neck gets strained from looking up at the ceiling while installing lights or ceiling fans and you get shocked regularly, sometimes while on a ladder. Your hands are sliced up from twisting wires together, handling junction boxes made out of stamped sheet metal and cutting metal conduit with a hacksaw. But none of this damage touches the best part of yourself.

You might wonder: Wasn't there any quality control? My supervisor would periodically read a few of my abstracts, and I was sometimes corrected and told not to begin an abstract with a dependent clause. But I was never confronted with an abstract I had written and told that it did not adequately reflect the article. The quality standards were the generic ones of grammar, which could be applied without my supervisor having to read the article at hand. Rather, my supervisor and I both were held to a metric that was conjured by someone remote from the work process—an absentee decision maker armed with a (putatively) profit-maximizing calculus, one that took no account of the intrinsic nature of the job. I wonder whether the resulting perversity really made for maximum profits in the long term. Corporate managers are not, after all, the owners of the businesses they run.

At lunch I had a standing arrangement with two other abstracters. One was from my group, a laconic, disheveled man named Mike whom I liked instantly. He did about as well on his quota as I did on mine, but it didn't seem to bother him too much. The other guy was from beyond the partition, a meticulously groomed Liberian named Henry who said he had worked for the C.I.A. He had to flee Liberia very suddenly one day and soon found himself resettled near the office parks of Foster City, Calif. Henry wasn't going to sweat the quota. Come 12:30, the three of us would hike to the food court in the mall. This movement was always thrilling. It involved traversing several "campuses," with ponds frequented by oddly real seagulls, then lunch itself, which I always savored. (Marx writes that under conditions of estranged labor, man "no longer feels himself to be freely active in any but his animal functions.") Over his burrito, Mike would recount the outrageous things he had written in his abstracts. I could see my own future in such moments of sabotage—the compensating pleasures of a cubicle drone. Always funny and gentle, Mike confided one day that he was doing quite a bit of heroin. On the job. This actually made some sense.

How was it that I, once a proudly self-employed electrician, had ended up among these walking wounded, a "knowledge worker" at a salary of $23,000? I had a master's degree, and it needed to be used. The escalating demand for academic credentials in the job market gives the impression of an ever-more-knowledgeable society, whose members perform cognitive feats their unschooled parents could scarcely conceive of. On paper, my abstracting job, multiplied a millionfold, is precisely what puts the futurologist in a rapture: we are getting to be so smart! Yet my M.A. obscures a more real stupidification of the work I secured with that credential, and a wage to match. When I first got the degree, I felt as if I had been inducted to a certain order of society. But despite the beautiful ties I wore, it turned out to be a more proletarian existence than I had known as an electrician. In that job I had made quite a bit more money. I also felt free and active, rather than confined and stultified.

A good job requires a field of action where you can put your best capacities to work and see an effect in the world. Academic credentials do not guarantee this.

Nor can big business or big government—those idols of the right and the left—reliably secure such work for us. Everyone is rightly concerned about economic growth on the one hand or unemployment and wages on the other, but the character of work doesn't figure much in political debate. Labor unions address important concerns like workplace safety and family leave, and management looks for greater efficiency, but on the nature of the job itself, the dominant political and economic paradigms are mute. Yet work forms us, and deforms us, with broad public consequences.

The visceral experience of failure seems to have been edited out of the career trajectories of gifted students. It stands to reason, then, that those who end up making big decisions that affect all of us don't seem to have much sense of their own fallibility, and of how badly things can go wrong even with the best of intentions (like when I dropped that feeler gauge down into the Ninja). In the boardrooms of Wall Street and the corridors of Pennsylvania Avenue, I don't think you'll see a yellow sign that says "Think Safety!" as you do on job sites and in many repair shops, no doubt because those who sit on the swivel chairs tend to live remote from the consequences of the decisions they make. Why not encourage gifted students to learn a trade, if only in the summers, so that their fingers will be crushed once or twice before they go on to run the country?

There is good reason to suppose that responsibility has to be installed in the foundation of your mental equipment—at the level of perception and habit. There is an ethic of paying attention that develops in the trades through hard experience. It inflects your perception of the world and your habitual responses to it. This is due to the immediate feedback you get from material objects and to the fact that the work is typically situated in face-to-face interactions between tradesman and customer.

An economy that is more entrepreneurial, less managerial, would be less subject to the kind of distortions that occur when corporate managers' compensation is tied to the short-term profit of distant shareholders. For most entrepreneurs, profit is at once a more capacious and a more concrete thing than this. It is a calculation in which the intrinsic satisfactions of work count—not least, the exercise of your own powers of reason.

Ultimately it is enlightened self-interest, then, not a harangue about humility or public-spiritedness, that will compel us to take a fresh look at the trades. The good life comes in a variety of forms. This variety has become difficult to see; our field of aspiration has narrowed into certain channels. But the current perplexity in the economy seems to be softening our gaze. Our peripheral vision is perhaps recovering, allowing us to consider the full range of lives worth choosing. For anyone who feels ill suited by disposition to spend his days sitting in an office, the question of what a good job looks like is now wide open.

. . . .

Exploring the Text

1. What does Matthew B. Crawford mean by "such confrontations with material reality"? Do you agree that "[m]any of us do work that feels more surreal than real" (para. 1)?

2. In paragraph 4, Crawford quotes the last two lines of Marge Piercy's poem, "To Be of Use." How effective is his use of the poem?

3. What is the nature of economist Alan Blinder's "crucial distinction" (para. 5)? What implications does it have for the world of work?

4. Do you agree with Crawford's characterization of schooling and learning (paras. 6–7)? Does it fit with your own experience and observation? To what extent? If it doesn't, explain why.

5. How does Crawford build his ethos in paragraph 7?

6. Note the particular detail with which Crawford characterizes Fred (para. 10). Do you agree with Crawford's conclusion about Fred: "Here was a scholar"? Why or why not?

7. What is ironic about Crawford's job at the policy organization in Washington (para. 12)? How does that irony contribute to Crawford's characterization of work?

8. Crawford writes, "The attractiveness of any hypothesis is determined in part by physical circumstances that have no logical connection to the diagnostic problem at hand" (para. 17). Two paragraphs later he writes, "For me, at least, there is more real thinking going on in the bike shop than there was in the think tank." How does this humorous remark relate to the meaning of the first statement?

9. What is the virtue that, according to Crawford, is "at once cognitive and moral" (para. 20)? Do you agree with his claim?

10. Think of an experience you have had that in some way resembles the one Crawford describes in paragraph 22. Were your feelings similar to Crawford's? How effectively does the writer appeal to the experience of his audience?

11. Paragraph 24 concludes with a claim about managers. Explain how Crawford develops his argument, using the Toulmin model described and demonstrated in Chapter 3.

12. What did Crawford learn from his job as a writer of abstracts (paras. 25–32)? How does that experience support the claims he makes earlier in the essay?

13. Paragraph 30 concludes, "But none of this damage touches the best part of yourself." What, as implied by Crawford, is "the best part of yourself"? Do you agree?

14. How effective is the rhetorical question that concludes paragraph 36?

15. Crawford concludes that the economy will be improved by "enlightened self-interest" (para. 39). Do you agree with his assessment?

16. In an interview about his book *Shop Class as Soulcraft: An Inquiry into the Value of Work*, Crawford has said,

There's knowledge work and there's manual work, and the idea that these are two very different things seemed very bogus to me. I needed to make the case for how much thinking goes on in the trades. And that this can be a life worth choosing—if you're someone who likes to use your brain at work. And once you get into that, it becomes a very interesting question of psychology: how using your hands and using your mind are connected. Another thing that prompted the book is the year that I spent teaching high school Latin, which I was barely qualified to do. There's some simile here to be made with fools rushing in. At any rate, the kids were being told that they had to take this course to get their SAT scores up—because everyone has to get into college. The class was something of a disaster: Half of them were jacked up on Ritalin just trying to stay awake. I felt like if I had been able to take some of these kids aside and say, "Hey, let's build a deck," or, "Let's overhaul an engine," they would have perked right up.

How effectively does this essay serve as a response to the situation Crawford describes in the interview?

How to Restore the American Dream

FAREED ZAKARIA

Fareed Zakaria was born in 1964 in Mumbai (then Bombay), where he attended the Cathedral and John Connon School before moving to the United States. He earned a BA from Yale University and a PhD in political science from Harvard University. *Esquire* magazine has called him "one of the 21 most important people of the 21st Century," and *Foreign Policy* named him one of the top 100 global thinkers. After spending ten years overseeing all of *Newsweek's* editions abroad, Zakaria became *Time* magazine's Editor at Large in 2010. His cover stories and columns on economics and politics have received many awards, including a 2010 National Magazine Award, and reach more than twenty-five million readers weekly. Before joining *Newsweek* in 2000, he spent eight years as managing editor of *Foreign Affairs*, a post he took on at only twenty-eight years of age. Prior to joining *Foreign Affairs*, Zakaria managed a major research project on American foreign policy at Harvard University, where he taught international relations and political philosophy. He is the author of *From Wealth to Power: The Unusual Origins of America's World Role* (1998), which has been translated into several languages, and *The Future of Freedom* (2003), a *New York Times* best seller. "How to Restore the American Dream" appeared in *Time* magazine on October 21, 2010.

The American dream for me, growing up in India in the 1970s, looked something like the opening credits of *Dallas*. The blockbuster TV series began with a kaleidoscope of big, brassy, sexy images—tracts of open land, shiny skyscrapers, fancy cars, cowboy businessmen and the very dreamy Victoria

Principal. We watched bootlegged copies of the show, passed around on old Betamax cassettes. America (certainly the CBS soap-opera version of America) seemed dazzling and larger than life, especially set against the stagnant backdrop of India in the 1970s. Everyone I knew was fascinated by the U.S., whether they admitted it or not. Politicians who denounced the country by day would go home in the evenings and plot to send their kids to college in "the States."

Of course, the 1970s were actually tough times in America—stagflation,[1] malaise, the aftermath of Vietnam and Watergate—but they were brutal in the rest of the world. Hyperinflation racked most third-world countries; coups and martial law were familiar occurrences, even affecting staunchly democratic India, where emergency rule was enforced from 1975 to 1977. Set against this atmosphere of despair, the U.S. looked like a shining city on a hill.

A few years later, when I got to America on a college scholarship, I realized that the real American Dream was somewhat different from *Dallas*. I visited college friends in their hometowns and was struck by the spacious suburban houses and the gleaming appliances—even when their parents had simple, modest jobs. The modern American Dream, for me, was this general prosperity and well-being for the average person. European civilization had produced the great cathedrals of the world. America had the two-car garage. And this middle-class contentment created a country of optimists. Compared with the fatalism and socialist lethargy that was pervasive in India in those days, Americans had a sunny attitude toward life that was utterly refreshing.

But when I travel from America to India these days, as I did recently, it's as if the world has been turned upside down. Indians are brimming with hope and faith in the future. After centuries of stagnation, their economy is on the move, fueling animal spirits and ambition. The whole country feels as if it has been unlocked. Meanwhile, in the U.S., the mood is sour. Americans are glum, dispirited and angry. The middle class, in particular, feels under assault. In a *Newsweek* poll in September, 63% of Americans said they did not think they would be able to maintain their current standard of living. Perhaps most troubling, Americans are strikingly fatalistic about their prospects. The can-do country is convinced that it can't.

Americans have good reasons to worry. We have just gone through the worst recession since the Great Depression. The light at the end of the tunnel is dim at best. Sixteen months into the recovery, the unemployment rate is higher than it was in the depths of all but one of the postwar recessions. And as government spending is being pared back, the economy is showing new signs of weakness. 5

Some experts say that in every recession Americans get gloomy and then recover with the economy. This slump is worse than most; so is the mood. Once demand returns, they say, jobs will come back and, with them, optimism. But Americans are far more apprehensive than usual, and their worries seem to go

---

[1]Stagnant economic growth combined with a high rate of inflation.—Eds.

beyond the short-term debate over stimulus vs. deficit reduction. They fear that we are in the midst of not a cyclical downturn but a structural shift, one that poses huge new challenges to the average American job, pressures the average American wage and endangers the average American Dream. The middle class, many Americans have come to believe, is being hollowed out. I think they are right.

Going Global

For a picture of the global economy, look at America's great corporations, which are thriving. IBM, Coca-Cola, PepsiCo, Google, Microsoft, Apple, Intel and Caterpillar are all doing well. And they share a strategy that is becoming standard for success. First, technology has produced massive efficiencies over the past decade. Jack Welch explained the process succinctly on CNBC last September. "Technology has changed the game in jobs," he said. "We had technology bumping around for years in the '80s and '90s, and [we were] trying to make it work. And now it's working. . . . You couple the habits [of efficiency] from a deep recession [with] an exponential increase in technology, and you're not going to see jobs for a long, long time." Welch gave as an example a company owned by the private-equity firm with which he is affiliated. In 2007 the business had 26,000 employees and generated $12 billion in revenue. It will return to those revenue numbers by 2013 but with only 14,000 employees. "Companies have learned to do more with less," Welch said.

Next, companies have truly gone global. The companies on the S&P 500 generate 46% of their profits outside the U.S., and for many of the biggest American names, the proportion is much higher. You might think of Coca-Cola as the quintessentially American company. In fact it is a vast global enterprise, operating in 206 countries. "We have a factory in Ramallah that employs 2,000 people. We have a factory in Afghanistan. We have factories everywhere," explains Muhtar Kent, the CEO of Coke. Nearly 80% of Coca-Cola's revenue comes from outside the U.S., and an even greater percentage of its employees are in foreign countries. "We are a global company that happens to be headquartered in Atlanta," says Kent.

America's great corporations access global markets, easy credit, new technologies and high-quality labor at a low price. Many have had to cut jobs at home, where demand is weak, and have added them in the emerging markets that are booming. They are not "outsourcing" jobs. That word makes little sense anymore. They simply invest in growth areas and cut back in places where the economy is weak. None of them will ever give up on the American market — it is too large, too profitable and too central to their businesses — but the marginal dollar is more likely to be invested abroad than in the U.S.

While businesses have a way to navigate this new world of technological change and globalization, the ordinary American worker does not. Capital and technology are mobile; labor isn't. American workers are located in America. And this is a country with one of the highest wages in the world, because it is one of 10 the richest countries in the world. That makes it more difficult for the American middle-class worker to benefit from technology and global growth in the same way that companies do.

At this point, economists will protest. Historically, free trade has been beneficial to rich and poor. By forcing you out of industries in which you are inefficient, trade makes you strengthen those industries in which you are world-class. That's right in theory, and it has been right in practice. As countries have traded with one another over the past two centuries, they have prospered, and average living standards in those countries (primarily in the Western world) have soared. Those places that kept themselves protected (mostly communist and third-world nations) found that they had crappy industries, shoddy goods, massive corruption and slow growth.

And yet something feels different this time. Technology and globalization are working together at warp speed, creating a powerful new reality. Many more goods and services can now be produced anywhere on the globe. China and India have added literally hundreds of millions of new workers to the global labor pool, producing the same goods and services as Western workers at a fraction of the price. Far from being basket-case economies and banana republics, many developing economies are now stable and well managed, and companies can do business in them with ease. At some point, all these differences add up to mean that global competition is having quite a new impact on life in the U.S.

Two weeks ago, for example, I sat in a Nano, the revolutionary car being produced by Tata Motors in India. It's a nice, comfortable midgetmobile, much like Mercedes-Benz's Smart car, except that rather than costing $22,000, it costs about $2,400. Tata plans to bring it to the U.S. in two to three years. Properly equipped with air bags and other safety features, it will retail at $7,000. Leave aside the car itself, whose price will surely put a downward pressure on U.S. carmakers. Just think about car parts. Every part in the Nano is made to global standards but manufactured in India at about a tenth of what it would cost in America. When Ford orders its next set of car parts, will they be made in Michigan or Mumbai?

This is not a hypothetical. Steven Rattner, who helped restructure the automobile industry, tells the story of getting a new General Motors plant online in Michigan by bringing management and unions together. "The unions agreed to allow 40% of the new plant to operate at $14-an-hour wages," he says, "which is half of GM's normal wages. The management agreed to invest in this new plant. But here's the problem: workers at GM's Mexican operations make $7 an hour, and today they are as productive as American workers. And think of this: $14 an hour translates into about $35,000 a year. That's below the median family income. The whole experience left me frightened about the fate of the American worker."

Alan Blinder is also worried. A distinguished economist and Princeton professor, Blinder is a former vice chairman of the board of governors of the Federal Reserve. In a now famous essay in *Foreign Affairs*, he argues that while we recognize the pressures placed on manufacturing jobs by international competition, technology ensures that service jobs are now similarly exposed. Since the service sector

15

is a much larger part of the economy, Blinder estimates that 28 million to 42 million jobs will be "susceptible" to being shipped offshore—jobs such as customer-service representative and stock analyst, which we tend to think of as local. Blinder understands the benefits of free trade but worries that the new wave of offshoring is so big and fast that Western societies will have difficulty adjusting. The crucial distinction for the future, he argues, might be not between highly educated and less educated workers but between those jobs that can be done abroad and those—such as nurse or pilot—that cannot.

You can divide the American workforce in many ways, but any way you slice it, you see the same trend. People who get paid a decent wage for skilled but routine work in manufacturing or services are getting squeezed by a pincer movement of technology and globalization. David Autor, an MIT economist, has done an important study on what he calls "the polarization of job opportunities" in America. Autor finds that job growth divides neatly into three categories. On one side are managerial, professional and technical occupations, held by highly educated workers who are comfortable in the global economy. Jobs have been plentiful in this segment for the past three decades. On the other end are service occupations, those that involve "helping, caring for or assisting others," such as security guard, cook and waiter. Most of these workers have no college education and get hourly wages that are on the low end of the scale. Jobs in this segment too have been growing robustly.

In between are the skilled manual workers and those in white collar operations like sales and office management. These jobs represent the beating heart of the middle class. Those in them make a decent living, usually above the median family income ($49,777), and they mostly did fine in the two decades before 2000. But since then, employment growth has lagged the economy in general. And in the Great Recession, it has been these middle-class folks who have been hammered. Why? Autor is cautious and tentative, but it would seem that technology, followed by global competition, has played the largest role in making less valuable the routine tasks that once epitomized middle-class work.

Recapturing the Dream

So what is the solution? It's easier to identify the wrong answer than the right one. It would be pointless and damaging to try to go down a protectionist route, though polls show a stunning drop of support for free trade, even among college-educated professionals, its usual cheerleaders. But technology is a much larger driver of the hollowing out than trade. You cannot shut down this new world. How would you stop people from sending one another e-mails, which is what a lot of offshoring comes down to these days? Nor can you help a modern economy by shielding industries from world-class competitors, which just encourages greater inefficiency. I grew up in an economy made up of those kinds of industries, all tightly protected from "foreign exploitation and domination." It added up to stagnation and backwardness.

There are solutions, but they are hard and involve painful changes — in companies, government programs and personal lifestyles. For more than a generation, Americans have been unwilling to make these adjustments. Instead, we found an easier way to goose the economy: expand consumption. During the early 1950s, personal consumer expenditures made up 60% to 65% of the U.S.'s GDP.[2] But starting in the early 1980s, facing slower growth, we increased our personal spending substantially, giving rise to new economic activity in the country. Consumption grew to 70% of GDP by 2001 and has stayed there ever since. Unfortunately, this rise in consumption was not triggered by a rise in income. Wages have been largely stagnant. It was facilitated, rather, by an increase in credit, so that now the average American family has no fewer than 13 credit cards. Household debt rose from $680 billion in 1974 to $14 trillion in 2008. This pattern repeated itself in government, except on a much larger scale. People everywhere — from California to New Jersey — wanted less taxes but more government. Local, state and federal governments obliged, taking on massive debts. A generation's worth of economic growth has been generated by an unsustainable expansion of borrowing.

That is why the current economic debate between another stimulus and deficit reduction is frustrating. Right now, there is a strong case for government stimulus, since no one else is doing much spending. But then what? What happens after another year of federal spending? Consumers still might be cautious; do we really want them to spend like they did in the old days? Is the strategy simply to reinflate the housing bubble? In recent years, the left and the right in America have conspired in feeding consumption spending. The left expands government, much of which means more consumption (pensions, health care). The right focuses obsessively on tax cuts, which have a similar effect. The political system, pandering to today's constituents, encourages both tendencies. But when will we invest for our children's economy?

What We Need to Do Now

Ultimately American jobs are created from the bottom up by companies, not from the top down by government fiat. But there are measures we can take that will encourage the process. Here are the key ones:

Shift from consumption to investment.   Fundamentally, America needs to move from consumption to investment. Everyone agrees that the best way to create good jobs in the U.S. is to create new industries and companies and to innovate within old ones. This means large investments in research, technology and development. As a society, this needs to become our strongest focus.

Despite substantial increases and important new projects under the Obama Administration, the federal government is still not spending as much on R&D as a

---

[2]Gross Domestic Product — The value of the goods produced and services rendered in a single year. — Eds.

percentage of GDP as it did in the 1950s. I would argue that it should be spending twice that level, which would be 6% of GDP. In the 1950s, the U.S. had a huge manufacturing base that could absorb millions of semiskilled workers. Today, manufacturing is a small part of the economy and faces intense global competition. The only good jobs that will stay in the U.S. are jobs related to knowledge and innovation. Additionally, in the 1950s, America was the only research lab in town, accounting for the vast majority of global scientific spending. Today, countries around the world are entering the arena. Two weeks ago, South Korea—a country of just 50 million people!—announced plans to invest $35 billion in renewable-energy projects. We should pay for this with a 5% national sales tax—call it an American innovation tax—which would be partly offset by a small reduction in income taxes. This would have the twin benefits of tamping down consumption and yielding some additional funds. All the proceeds from the tax should be focused on future generations, because we need to invest massively in growth.

The often overlooked aspect of investment is investment in people. America has been able to create the future in large measure because it has tapped into the energies and work of immigrants. It has managed to invest in human capital by taking smart, motivated people from around the globe, educating them in the planet's best higher-education system and then unleashing them in a dynamic economy. In this crucial realm, the U.S. is now disinvesting. After training the world's best and brightest—often at public expense—we don't find ways to make sure they stay here by giving them a green card but rather insist that they leave and take their knowledge to another country, where they will invent, inspire, and build and pay taxes. Every year, we send tens of thousands of the smartest Indians and Chinese back home, which is a great investment—in the future of those countries.

Training and education.   "Most jobs that will have good prospects in the future   25 will be complicated," says Louis Gerstner, the former CEO of American Express and IBM. "They will involve being able to juggle data, symbols, computer programs in some way or the other, no matter what the task. To do this, workers will need to be educated and often retrained." We need more and better education at every level, especially job retraining. So far, most retraining efforts in the U.S. have not worked very well. But they have worked in countries that have been able to retain a manufacturing base, like Germany and parts of Northern Europe. There, some of the most successful programs are apprenticeships—which cover only 0.3% of the total U.S. workforce.

There are advantages to the U.S. system. We don't stream people too early in their lives, and we allow for more creative thinking. But the path to good jobs for the future is surely to expand apprenticeship programs substantially so industry can find the workers it needs. This would require a major initiative, a training triangle in which the government funds, the education system teaches and industry hires—though to have an effect, the program would have to be on the scale of the GI Bill.

Fiscal sanity.   To pay for such initiatives, the government needs to get its house in order. The single most important aspect of this is getting health care costs under control, followed by other entitlement programs, especially pensions at the state level. Government today spends vast sums of money on current consumption — health care and pensions being a massive chunk of it — which leaves little money for anything else. We need a radical rebalancing of American government so it can free up resources to fund future growth.

Benchmark, benchmark, benchmark.   There is now global competition for growth, which means the U.S. has to constantly ask itself what other countries are doing well and how it might adapt — looking, for example, at what other countries are doing with their corporate tax rates or their health care systems and asking why and where we fall short. Americans have long resisted such an approach, but if someone else is doing tax policy, tort litigation, health care or anything else better, we have to ask why.

There are things the U.S. does well. Most new jobs in America are created by start-ups and small companies, so the ease of doing business is crucial — and there's good news there. The World Bank has a ranking of countries measured by the "ease of doing business," and the U.S. is No. 4. That's very good, but there's a catch. Those rankings are divided into several categories. In most, like "starting a business," the U.S. does well. But in one category it's only 61st in the world, and that is "paying taxes."

The American tax code is a monstrosity, cumbersome and inefficient. It is 16,000 pages long and riddled with exemptions and loopholes, specific favors to special interests. As such, it represents the deep, institutionalized corruption at the heart of the American political process, in which it is now considered routine to buy a member of Congress's support for a particular, narrow provision that will be advantageous for your business. 30

The Work Ahead

My proposals are inherently difficult because they ask the left and right to come together, cut some spending, pare down entitlements, open up immigration for knowledge workers, rationalize the tax code — and then make large investments in education and training, research and technology, innovation and infrastructure. But the fact that it is a solution that crosses political borders should make it more palatable, not less. And time is crucial. The U.S. has considerable advantages, but every day other countries try to find ways to attract growth within their borders. People often note that America's political system is broken. Perhaps the truth is more awkward: America needs radical change, and it has an 18th century system determined to check and balance the absolute power of a monarchy. It is designed for gridlock at a moment when quick and large-scale action is our only hope.

When I left India, the marginal tax rate was 97.5%, corporate taxation was punitive, and business was stifled or went underground. Were I to move from New York City to Mumbai today, my personal tax rate would drop, as would every other rate, from corporate to capital-gains taxes. (The long-term capital-tax rate in India is zero.) Singapore now ranks as the No. 1 country for ease of doing business, with a top tax rate of 20%. I know permanent residents working in the U.S. who are thinking of giving up their green cards to move to Singapore. To an Indian of my generation, this would have been unthinkable. The green card was a passport to the American Dream. But for young Indians, there are many new dreams out there, and new passports.

But there are reasons for optimism. The U.S. faces huge challenges, but it also has enormous advantages. "I've always been bullish on America," says Coke's Kent. "It's the largest, richest market in the world. Look at the demographics alone. North America is the only part of the industrialized world that will be growing in people. It now has a higher birthrate than Mexico, for the first time in history." Or listen to Alcoa's German-born Klaus Kleinfeld, previously the head of Siemens: "I know the things that America has that are unique. The openness, the diversity, the dynamism—you don't have it anywhere else. If you keep all these things, build on them, I still believe in the American Dream."

The term *American Dream* was coined during the Great Depression. The historian James Truslow Adams published *The Epic of America* in 1931, in an atmosphere of even greater despair than today's. He wanted to call his book *The American Dream*, but his publishers objected. No one will pay $3.50 for a book about a "dream," they said. Still, Adams used the phrase so often that it entered the lexicon. The American Dream, he said, was of "a better, richer and happier life for all our citizens of every rank, which is the greatest contribution we have made to the thought and welfare of the world. That dream or hope has been present from the start. Ever since we became an independent nation, each generation has seen an uprising of ordinary Americans to save the American Dream from the forces which appear to be overwhelming it."

Today, those forces really do look overwhelming. But challenges like them have been beaten back before—and can be again.   35

. . . .

Exploring the Text

1. How does Fareed Zakaria's characterization of the American Dream compare with your own?

2. What is the rhetorical shift that Zakaria uses between paragraphs 3 and 4? How does it prepare the reader for what he says about "the experts" in paragraph 6?

3. What are the consequences of technology that Zakaria discusses at the beginning of the second section, "Going Global"? Research the Luddites, who rebelled against mechanization in the textile industry in nineteenth-century England. To what extent are we now facing a problem similar to the one that they faced?

4. Zakaria makes the claim that "none of them [corporations] will ever give up on the American market" (para. 9). Analyze his argument according to the Toulmin model that you learned about in Chapter 3.
5. What is the crucial distinction that Zakaria makes in paragraph 15? Compare and contrast this distinction with the one that Matthew B. Crawford makes in "The Case for Working with Your Hands" (p. 449).
6. How does Zakaria describe the relationship between consumerism and credit? What does he suggest the consequences will be?
7. As he concludes the second section of the essay, how does Zakaria appeal to logos and pathos? Which is the stronger appeal?
8. How does Zakaria compare the advantages and disadvantages of economic approaches in the United States as opposed to Europe and Asia (paras. 21–30)? What is the approach that Americans have resisted? Why has that been the case?
9. What is the nature of the complaint Zakaria makes in paragraph 31? Does his strong characterization help or hinder his case? Explain.
10. Zakaria begins many of his paragraphs with short, simple sentences, and then he develops them with varied syntax. Identify three paragraphs in which this is the case. How does such a style contribute to his essay as a whole?
11. What do you find most surprising in Zakaria's essay? Most compelling?
12. Zakaria ends on an optimistic note. Do you share his optimism? Why or why not?

To Be of Use

Marge Piercy

Born in Detroit, Michigan, in 1936, Marge Piercy is a poet, novelist, and social activist. She was the first member of her family to go to college. After attending the University of Michigan on a scholarship, she went on to earn a master's degree from Northwestern University. Her first volume of poems, *Breaking Camp*, was published in 1968. She has published over a dozen books of poetry, including *Colors Passing through Us* (2003), *The Art of Blessing the Day: Poems with a Jewish Theme* (1999), *What Are Big Girls Made Of?* (1997), *Available Light* (1988), *The Moon Is Always Female* (1980), and *To Be of Use* (1973). She is also the author of more than a dozen novels, in which she explores science fiction, feminism, history, and social issues. Among these works are *Three Women* (1999), *Storm Tide* (written with her husband, Ira Wood in 1998), *Woman on the Edge of Time* (1976), and the best-selling *Gone to Soldiers* (1988), an epic story of World War II. Piercy lives on Cape Cod in Massachusetts.

The people I love the best
jump into work head first
without dallying in the shallows
and swim off with sure strokes almost out of sight.

They seem to become natives of that element,   5
the black sleek heads of seals
bouncing like half-submerged balls.

I love people who harness themselves, an ox to a heavy cart,
who pull like water buffalo, with massive patience,
who strain in the mud and the muck to move things forward,   10
who do what has to be done, again and again.

I want to be with people who submerge
in the task, who go into the fields to harvest
and work in a row and pass the bags along,
who are not parlor generals and field deserters   15
but move in a common rhythm
when the food must come in or the fire be put out.

The work of the world is common as mud.
Botched, it smears the hands, crumbles to dust.
But the thing worth doing well done   20
has a shape that satisfies, clean and evident.
Greek amphoras for wine or oil,
Hopi vases that held corn, are put in museums
but you know they were made to be used.
The pitcher cries for water to carry   25
and a person for work that is real.

Exploring the Text

1. What is the effect of the extended metaphor that Marge Piercy develops in the first seven lines of the poem? What is the effect of the shift to a new metaphor for the following four lines?
2. After the word "submerge" (l. 12), the poem shifts from figurative to literal language through line 17. How does this shift express Piercy's attitude?
3. What are "parlor generals" and "field deserters" (l. 15)? What function do they serve in the poem?
4. What does Piercy suggest through the juxtaposed phrases "the food must come in" and "the fire be put out" (l. 17)?
5. How would you describe the speaker's attitude toward the amphoras and vases that we see in museums?
6. In "The Case for Working with Your Hands" (p. 449), Matthew B. Crawford refers to Piercy's poem, specifically its two concluding lines. How does the poem inform Crawford's position regarding work? Find another section of the poem that would likely appeal to Crawford. Explain your selection.

The Great GAPsby Society

JEFF PARKER

Jeff Parker (b. 1959) is an editorial cartoonist for *Florida Today*. A member of the National Cartoonists Society and the Association of American Editorial Cartoonists, he was nominated in 1997 and 1998 for the NCS Reuben Award for editorial cartooning. His cartoons have been included in many editions of Pelican Books' *Best Editorial Cartoons of the Year*.

Exploring the Text

1. The title of this cartoon alludes to the novel *The Great Gatsby* by F. Scott Fitzgerald. Why is the allusion appropriate? If you haven't read the novel to which the title alludes, does the cartoon still make sense?
2. Try summarizing the point, or message, of the cartoon. How does the verbal summary change the impact of the visual?
3. What does the audience have to know in order to get the full impact of the cartoon? Will readers who have jobs at the "quickee mart" or places such as McDonald's feel insulted or mocked? Explain.

4. What is the purpose of the expression "old sport"? How does it contribute to the characterization of the man in the suit?
5. How do you think Barbara Ehrenreich, whose "from *Serving in Florida*" appears on page 394, would respond to this cartoon? Would the cartoon effectively illustrate her work? Which other readings from this chapter would the cartoon enhance?

This Modern World

A "Handy" Guide to the Housing Market

TOM TOMORROW

Tom Tomorrow is the pen name of political cartoonist Dan Perkins, creator of the weekly feature "This Modern World," which appears in approximately eighty newspapers across the United States and on the Web site Salon.com. His work has appeared in publications including the *New York Times*, the *New Yorker*, *Spin*, *Mother Jones*, *Esquire*, the *Economist*, the *Nation*, *U.S. News and World Report*, and the *American Prospect*. In 2009, he created the cover art for the Pearl Jam album *Backspacer*. He is also the author of a book for children, *The Very Silly Mayor* (2009). He received the first place Robert F. Kennedy Award for Excellence in Journalism in 1998 and in 2003. The cartoon on the facing page features The Invisible Hand, a character based on the notion that an invisible hand guides the marketplace so that the pursuit of profit ultimately ensures the greater good. The phrase "invisible hand" derives from the following passage from Adam Smith's highly influential book *The Wealth of Nations* (1776):

> But it is only for the sake of profit that any man employs a capital in the support of industry; and he will always, therefore, endeavour to employ it in the support of that industry of which the produce is likely to be of the greatest value, or to exchange for the greatest quantity either of money or of other goods. . . .
>
> As every individual, therefore, endeavours as much as he can both to employ his capital in the support of domestic industry, and so to direct that industry that its produce may be of the greatest value; every individual necessarily labours to render the annual revenue of the society as great as he can. He generally, indeed, neither intends to promote the public interest, nor knows how much he is promoting it. By preferring the support of domestic to that of foreign industry, he intends only his own security; and by directing that industry in such a manner as its produce may be of the greatest value, he intends only his own gain, and he is in this, as in many other cases, led by an invisible hand to promote an end which was no part of his intention. Nor is it always the worse for the society that it was no part of it. By pursuing his own interest he frequently promotes that of the society more effectually than when he really intends to promote it. I have never known much good done by those who affected to trade for the public good. It is an affectation, indeed, not very common among merchants, and very few words need be employed in dissuading them from it.

(See insert for color version.)

Exploring the Text

1. The main character of the cartoon is modeled on economist Adam Smith's "invisible hand." How well does the hand in the cartoon express what Smith says in the quotation on the facing page?

2. How would you characterize the tone of The Invisible Hand—that is, the main speaker in the cartoon? How does his diction contribute to that tone?

3. What is Tom Tomorrow's attitude toward The Invisible Hand? Is he critical? Is he supportive? How can you tell?

4. What is the rhetorical function of the statement following "ER" in frame 5?

5. Why is the secondary character a young boy? What is his rhetorical function?

6. What is ironic about the "solution" posed in frames 7 and 8? What does Tomorrow suggest about the contemporary relationship between government and business?

7. What does the cartoon suggest about the free market economy?

8. Compare this cartoon with Jonathan Swift's essay (p. 404). Are they rhetorically similar? Thematically similar? Explain.

Materialism in American Culture

Each of the following texts presents a viewpoint on materialism in American culture:

Sources

1. **Henry David Thoreau,** from *Economy*
2. **John Kenneth Galbraith,** from *The Dependence Effect*
3. **Phyllis Rose,** *Shopping and Other Spiritual Adventures in America Today*
4. **Wendell Berry,** *Waste*
5. **Juliet Schor,** *The New Consumerism*
6. **Joan Smith,** *Shop-happy*
7. **Virginia Postrel,** *In Praise of Chain Stores*
8. **Scott DeCarlo,** Forbes *Price Index of Luxury Goods Keeps Pace with Inflation* (table)

After you have read, studied, and synthesized these pieces, enter the conversation by responding to one of the prompts on page 500–01.

1. from *Economy*

HENRY DAVID THOREAU

In the following excerpt from "Economy," the first chapter of his classic book *Walden* (1854), Henry David Thoreau discusses the necessities of life.

Let us consider for a moment what most of the trouble and anxiety which I have referred to is about, and how much it is necessary that we be troubled, or, at least, careful. It would be some advantage to live a primitive and frontier life, though in the midst of an outward civilization, if only to learn what are the gross necessaries of life and what methods have been taken to obtain them; or even to look over the old day-books of the merchants, to see what it was that men most commonly bought at the stores, what they stored, that is, what are the grossest groceries. For the improvements of ages have had but little influence on the essential laws of man's existence; as our skeletons, probably, are not to be distinguished from those of our ancestors.

By the words, *necessary of life*, I mean whatever, of all that man obtains by his own exertions, has been from the first, or from long use has become, so important to human life that few, if any, whether from savageness, or poverty, or philosophy, ever attempt to do without it. To many creatures there is in this sense but one necessary of life, Food. To the bison of the prairie it is a few inches of palatable grass, with water to drink; unless he seeks the Shelter of the forest or the mountain's shadow.

474

None of the brute creation requires more than Food and Shelter. The necessaries of life for man in this climate may, accurately enough, be distributed under the several heads of Food, Shelter, Clothing, and Fuel; for not till we have secured these are we prepared to entertain the true problems of life with freedom and a prospect of success. Man has invented, not only houses, but clothes and cooked food; and possibly from the accidental discovery of the warmth of fire, and the consequent use of it, at first a luxury, arose the present necessity to sit by it. We observe cats and dogs acquiring the same second nature. By proper Shelter and Clothing we legitimately retain our own internal heat; but with an excess of these, or of Fuel, that is, with an external heat greater than our own internal, may not cookery properly be said to begin? Darwin, the naturalist, says of the inhabitants of Tierra del Fuego,[1] that while his own party, who were well clothed and sitting close to a fire, were far from too warm, these naked savages, who were farther off, were observed, to his great surprise, "to be streaming with perspiration at undergoing such a roasting." So, we are told, the New Hollander[2] goes naked with impunity, while the European shivers in his clothes. Is it impossible to combine the hardiness of these savages with the intellectualness of the civilized man? According to Liebig,[3] man's body is a stove, and food the fuel which keeps up the internal combustion in the lungs. In cold weather we eat more, in warm less. The animal heat is the result of a slow combustion, and disease and death take place when this is too rapid; or for want of fuel, or from some defect in the draught, the fire goes out. Of course the vital heat is not to be confounded with fire; but so much for analogy. It appears, therefore, from the above list, that the expression, *animal life*, is nearly synonymous with the expression, *animal heat*; for while Food may be regarded as the Fuel which keeps up the fire within us, — and Fuel serves only to prepare that Food or to increase the warmth of our bodies by addition from without, — Shelter and Clothing also serve only to retain the *heat* thus generated and absorbed.

The grand necessity, then, for our bodies, is to keep warm, to keep the vital heat in us. What pains we accordingly take, not only with our Food, and Clothing, and Shelter, but with our beds, which are our nightclothes, robbing the nests and breasts of birds to prepare this shelter within a shelter, as the mole has its bed of grass and leaves at the end of its burrow! The poor man is wont to complain that this is a cold world; and to cold, no less physical than social, we refer directly a great part of our ails. The summer, in some climates, makes possible to man a sort of Elysian[4] life. Fuel, except to cook his Food, is then unnecessary; the sun is his fire, and many of the fruits are sufficiently cooked by its rays; while Food generally is more various, and more easily obtained, and Clothing and Shelter are wholly or

---

[1]The southernmost tip of South America. — Eds.
[2]Native Australian. — Eds.
[3]Justus von Liebig (1803–1873), German chemist and author of *Animal Chemistry* (1842). — Eds.
[4]In Greek mythology, a paradise in the afterlife. — Eds.

half unnecessary. At the present day, and in this country, as I find by my own experience, a few implements, a knife, an axe, a spade, a wheelbarrow, &c., and for the studious, lamplight, stationery, and access to a few books, rank next to necessaries, and can all be obtained at a trifling cost. Yet some, not wise, go to the other side of the globe, to barbarous and unhealthy regions, and devote themselves to trade for ten or twenty years, in order that they may live,—that is, keep comfortably warm,—and die in New England at last. The luxuriously rich are not simply kept comfortably warm, but unnaturally hot; as I implied before, they are cooked, of course *à la mode*.

Most of the luxuries, and many of the so called comforts of life, are not only not indispensable, but positive hinderances to the elevation of mankind. With respect to luxuries and comforts, the wisest have ever lived a more simple and meagre life than the poor. The ancient philosophers, Chinese, Hindoo, Persian, and Greek, were a class than which none has been poorer in outward riches, none so rich in inward. We know not much about them. It is remarkable that *we* know so much of them as we do. The same is true of the more modern reformers and benefactors of their race. None can be an impartial or wise observer of human life but from the vantage ground of what *we* should call voluntary poverty. Of a life of luxury the fruit is luxury, whether in agriculture, or commerce, or literature, or art. There are nowadays professors of philosophy, but not philosophers. Yet it is admirable to profess because it was once admirable to live. To be a philosopher is not merely to have subtle thoughts, nor even to found a school, but so to love wisdom as to live according to its dictates, a life of simplicity, independence, magnanimity, and trust. It is to solve some of the problems of life, not only theoretically, but practically. The success of great scholars and thinkers is commonly a courtier-like success, not kingly, not manly. They make shift to live merely by conformity, practically as their fathers did, and are in no sense the progenitors of a nobler race of men. But why do men degenerate ever? What makes families run out? What is the nature of the luxury which enervates and destroys nations? Are we sure that there is none of it in our own lives? The philosopher is in advance of his age even in the outward form of his life. He is not fed, sheltered, clothed, warmed, like his contemporaries. How can a man be a philosopher and not maintain his vital heat by better methods than other men?

When a man is warmed by the several modes which I have described, what does he want next? Surely not more warmth of the same kind, as more and richer food, larger and more splendid houses, finer and more abundant clothing, more numerous incessant and hotter fires, and the like. When he has obtained those things which are necessary to life, there is another alternative than to obtain the superfluities; and that is, to adventure on life now, his vacation from humbler toil having commenced. The soil, it appears, is suited to the seed, for it has sent its radicle[5] downward, and it may now send its shoot upward also with confidence.

5

---

[5]The first shoot that emerges from a seed during germination.—Eds.

Why has man rooted himself thus firmly in the earth, but that he may rise in the same proportion into the heavens above? — for the nobler plants are valued for the fruit they bear at last in the air and light, far from the ground, and are not treated like the humbler esculents,[6] which, though they may be biennials, are cultivated only till they have perfected their root, and often cut down at top for this purpose, so that most would not know them in their flowering season.

I do not mean to prescribe rules to strong and valiant natures, who will mind their own affairs whether in heaven or hell, and perchance build more magnificently and spend more lavishly than the richest, without ever impoverishing themselves, not knowing how they live, — if, indeed, there are any such, as has been dreamed; nor to those who find their encouragement and inspiration in precisely the present condition of things, and cherish it with the fondness and enthusiasm of lovers, — and, to some extent, I reckon myself in this number; I do not speak to those who are well employed, in whatever circumstances, and they know whether they are well employed or not; — but mainly to the mass of men who are discontented, and idly complaining of the hardness of their lot or of the times, when they might improve them. There are some who complain most energetically and inconsolably of any, because they are, as they say, doing their duty. I also have in my mind that seemingly wealthy, but most terribly impoverished class of all, who have dross,[7] but know not how to use it, or get rid of it, and thus have forged their own golden or silver fetters.

Questions

1. Thoreau makes much use of analogy and metaphor, saying, in fact, at one point, "So much for analogy" (para. 2). Select three examples of analogy and/or metaphor from this selection, and explain how they contribute to Thoreau's argument.

2. Being extremely economical in his assessment even for his own time, Thoreau denotes what he calls "grand necessity" and what he considers near necessities (para. 3). And he writes, "Most of the luxuries, and many of the so called comforts of life, are not only not indispensable, but positive hinderances to the elevation of mankind" (para. 4). Do you agree with this statement? What would you add to his list today? Which things that Thoreau would consider luxuries do we now deem as necessities?

3. Thoreau writes, "There are nowadays professors of philosophy, but not philosophers. Yet it is admirable to profess because it was once admirable to live" (para. 4). What does he mean? To what extent does he speak to our time as well as his own?

4. How would you describe Thoreau's tone in the first two sentences of paragraph 5? How is his attitude relevant to our current economy?

5. Who is Thoreau's intended audience? How does he characterize that audience in paragraph 6? Is such an audience living today?

---

[6]Edible things. — Eds.
[7]Waste matter. — Eds.

2. from *The Dependence Effect*

JOHN KENNETH GALBRAITH

In the following chapter from the Fortieth Anniversary Edition of his 1958 book, *The Affluent Society*, John Kenneth Galbraith discusses the nature of consumerism in America.

The notion that wants do not become less urgent the more amply the individual is supplied is broadly repugnant to common sense. It is something to be believed only by those who wish to believe. Yet the conventional wisdom must be tackled on its own terrain. Intertemporal comparisons of an individual's state of mind do rest on technically vulnerable ground. Who can say for sure that the deprivation which afflicts him with hunger is more painful than the deprivation which afflicts him with envy of his neighbor's new car? In the time that has passed since he was poor, his soul may have become subject to a new and deeper searing. And where a society is concerned, comparisons between marginal satisfactions when it is poor and those when it is affluent will involve not only the same individual at different times but different individuals at different times. The scholar who wishes to believe that with increasing affluence there is no reduction in the urgency of desires and goods is not without points for the debate. However plausible the case against him, it cannot be proven. In the defense of the conventional wisdom, this amounts almost to invulnerability.

However, there is a flaw in the case. If the individual's wants are to be urgent, they must be original with himself. They cannot be urgent if they must be contrived for him. And above all, they must not be contrived by the process of production by which they are satisfied. For this means that the whole case for the urgency of production, based on the urgency of wants, falls to the ground. One cannot defend production as satisfying wants if that production creates the wants.

Were it so that a man on arising each morning was assailed by demons which instilled in him a passion sometimes for silk shirts, sometimes for kitchenware, sometimes for chamber pots, and sometimes for orange squash, there would be every reason to applaud the effort to find the goods, however odd, that quenched this flame. But should it be that his passion was the result of his first having cultivated the demons, and should it also be that his effort to allay it stirred the demons to ever greater and greater effort, there would be question as to how rational was his solution. Unless restrained by conventional attitudes, he might wonder if the solution lay with more goods or fewer demons.

So it is that if production creates the wants it seeks to satisfy, or if the wants emerge *pari passu*[1] with the production, then the urgency of the wants can no longer be used to defend the urgency of the production. Production only fills a void that it has itself created.

---

[1]Latin, "on equal footing."—Eds.

II

The point is so central that it must be pressed. Consumer wants can have bizarre, 5
frivolous or even immoral origins, and an admirable case can still be made for a
society that seeks to satisfy them. But the case cannot stand if it is the process of
satisfying wants that creates the wants. For then the individual who urges the
importance of production to satisfy these wants is precisely in the position of the
onlooker who applauds the efforts of the squirrel to keep abreast of the wheel that
is propelled by his own efforts.

That wants are, in fact, the fruit of production will now be denied by few serious scholars. And a considerable number of economists, though not always in full
knowledge of the implications, have conceded the point. In the observation cited
at the end of the preceding chapter, Keynes noted that needs of "the second class,"
i.e., those that are the result of efforts to keep abreast or ahead of one's fellow
being, "may indeed be insatiable; for the higher the general level, the higher still
are they.[2] And emulation has always played a considerable role in the views of
other economists of want creation. One man's consumption becomes his neighbor's wish. This already means that the process by which wants are satisfied is also
the process by which wants are created. The more wants that are satisfied, the
more new ones are born. . . .

III

The even more direct link between production and wants is provided by the institutions of modern advertising and salesmanship. These cannot be reconciled with
the notion of independently determined desires, for their central function is to
create desires — to bring into being wants that previously did not exist.[3] This is
accomplished by the producer of the goods or at his behest. A broad empirical
relationship exists between what is spent on production of consumer goods and
what is spent in synthesizing the desires for that production. A new consumer product must be introduced with a suitable advertising campaign to arouse an interest
in it. The path for an expansion of output must be paved by a suitable expansion
in the advertising budget. Outlays for the manufacturing of a product are not more
important in the strategy of modern business enterprise than outlays for the

---

[2]J. M. Keynes, *Essays in Persuasion*, "Economic Possibilities for Our Grandchildren" (London:
Macmillan, 1931), p. 365.

[3]Advertising is not a simple phenomenon. It is also important in competitive strategy and want
creation is, ordinarily, a complementary result of efforts to shift the demand curve of the individual firm at the expense of others or (less importantly, I think) to change its shape by increasing
the degree of product differentiation. Some of the failure of economists to identify advertising
with want creation may be attributed to the undue attention that its use in purely competitive
strategy has attracted. It should be noted, however, that the competitive manipulation of consumer
desire is only possible, at least on any appreciable scale, when such need is not strongly felt.

manufacturing of demand for the product. None of this is novel. All would be regarded as elementary by the most retarded student in the nation's most primitive school of business administration. The cost of this want formation is formidable. In 1987, total advertising expenditure—though, as noted, not all of it may be assigned to the synthesis of wants—amounted to approximately one hundred and ten billion dollars. The increase in previous years was by an estimated six billion dollars a year. Obviously, such outlays must be integrated with the theory of consumer demand. They are too big to be ignored.

But such integration means recognizing that wants are dependent on production. It accords to the producer the function both of making the goods and of making the desires for them. It recognizes that production, not only passively through emulation, but actively through advertising and related activities, creates the wants it seeks to satisfy.

The businessman and the lay reader will be puzzled over the emphasis which I give to a seemingly obvious point. The point is indeed obvious. But it is one which, to a singular degree, economists have resisted. They have sensed, as the layman does not, the damage to established ideas which lurks in these relationships. As a result, incredibly, they have closed their eyes (and ears) to the most obtrusive of all economic phenomena, namely, modern want creation.

This is not to say that the evidence affirming the dependence of wants on advertising has been entirely ignored. It is one reason why advertising has so long been regarded with such uneasiness by economists. Here is something which cannot be accommodated easily to existing theory. More pervious scholars have speculated on the urgency of desires which are so obviously the fruit of such expensively contrived campaigns for popular attention. Is a new breakfast cereal or detergent so much wanted if so much must be spent to compel in the consumer the sense of want? But there has been little tendency to go on to examine the implications of this for the theory of consumer demand and even less for the importance of production and productive efficiency. These have remained sacrosanct. More often, the uneasiness has been manifested in a general disapproval of advertising and advertising men, leading to the occasional suggestion that they shouldn't exist. Such suggestions have usually been ill received in the advertising business.

And so the notion of independently determined wants still survives. In the face of all the forces of modern salesmanship, it still rules, almost undefiled, in the textbooks. And it still remains the economist's mission—and on few matters is the pedagogy so firm—to seek unquestionably the means for filling these wants. This being so, production remains of prime urgency. We have here, perhaps, the ultimate triumph of the conventional wisdom in its resistance to the evidence of the eyes. To equal it, one must imagine a humanitarian who was long ago persuaded of the grievous shortage of hospital facilities in the town. He continues to importune the passersby for money for more beds and refuses to notice that the town doctor is deftly knocking over pedestrians with his car to keep up the occupancy.

And in unraveling the complex, we should always be careful not to overlook the obvious. The fact that wants can be synthesized by advertising, catalyzed by salesmanship, and shaped by the discreet manipulations of the persuaders shows that they are not very urgent. A man who is hungry need never be told of his need for food. If he is inspired by his appetite, he is immune to the influence of Messrs. Batten, Barton, Durstine & Osborn. The latter are effective only with those who are so far removed from physical want that they do not already know what they want. In this state alone, men are open to persuasion.

IV

The general conclusion of these pages is of such importance for this essay that it had perhaps best be put with some formality. As a society becomes increasingly affluent, wants are increasingly created by the process by which they are satisfied. This may operate passively. Increases in consumption, the counterpart of increases in production, act by suggestion or emulation to create wants. Expectation rises with attainment. Or producers may proceed actively to create wants through advertising and salesmanship. Wants thus come to depend on output. In technical terms, it can no longer be assumed that welfare is greater at an all-round higher level of production than at a lower one. It may be the same. The higher level of production has, merely, a higher level of want creation necessitating a higher level of want satisfaction. There will be frequent occasion to refer to the way wants depend on the process by which they are satisfied. It will be convenient to call it the Dependence Effect.

Questions

1. Why is the proposition that Galbraith explains at the beginning of the essay "repugnant to common sense"? Why is it true nonetheless?
2. What is the presumed answer to the rhetorical question that Galbraith poses in paragraph 1? How would you answer?
3. Galbraith writes, "Production only fills a void that it has itself created" (para. 4). What might be the consequences of such a paradox as he describes? Where in the essay does Galbraith return to this same paradox? Explain.
4. In paragraph 12, Galbraith writes, "In this state alone men are open to persuasion." What is the state to which he refers?
5. In his final paragraph, Galbraith describes what he calls the "Dependence Effect." Paraphrase what he means by that phrase. What implications does it have for your idea of the American Dream?
6. Galbraith wrote this essay over fifty years ago. To what extent do you think his ideas still apply to our economy today?

3. *Shopping and Other Spiritual Adventures in America Today*

PHYLLIS ROSE

In the following selection, which originally appeared in the *New York Times* in 1984, Phyllis Rose discusses the role that shopping plays in our lives.

Last year a new Waldbaum's Food Mart opened in the shopping mall on Route 66. It belongs to the new generation of superduper-markets open twenty-four hours that have computerized checkout. I went to see the place as soon as it opened and I was impressed. There was trail mix in Lucite bins. There was freshly made pasta. There were coffee beans, four kinds of tahini, ten kinds of herb teas, raw shrimp in shells and cooked shelled shrimp, fresh-squeezed orange juice. Every sophistication known to the big city, even goat's cheese covered with ash, was now available in Middletown, Conn. People raced from the warehouse aisle to the bagel bin to the coffee beans to the fresh fish market, exclaiming at all the new things. Many of us felt elevated, graced, complimented by the presence of this food palace in our town.

This is the wonderful egalitarianism of American business. Was it Andy Warhol who said that the nice thing about Coke is, no can is any better or worse than any other? Some people may find it dull to cross the country and find the same chain stores with the same merchandise from coast to coast, but it means that my town is as good as yours, my shopping mall as important as yours, equally filled with wonders.

Imagine what people ate during the winter as little as seventy-five years ago. They ate food that was local, long-lasting, and dull, like acorn squash, turnips, and cabbage. Walk into an American supermarket in February and the world lies before you: grapes, melons, artichokes, fennel, lettuce, peppers, pistachios, dates, even strawberries, to say nothing of ice cream. Have you ever considered what a triumph of civilization it is to be able to buy a pound of chicken livers? If you lived on a farm and had to kill a chicken when you wanted to eat one, you wouldn't ever accumulate a pound of chicken livers.

Another wonder of Middletown is Caldor, the discount department store. Here is man's plenty: tennis racquets, panty hose, luggage, glassware, records, toothpaste. Timex watches, Cadbury's chocolate, corn poppers, hair dryers, warm-up suits, car wax, light bulbs, television sets. All good quality at low prices with exchanges cheerfully made on defective goods. There are worse rules to live by. I feel good about America whenever I walk into this store, which is almost every mid-winter Sunday afternoon, when life elsewhere has closed down. I go to Caldor the way English people go to pubs: out of sociability. To get away from my house. To widen my horizons. For culture's sake. Caldor provides me too with a welcome sense of seasonal change. When the first outdoor grills and lawn furniture appear there, it's as exciting a sign of spring as the first crocus or robin.

Someone told me about a Soviet émigré who practices English by declaiming, 5
at random, sentences that catch his fancy. One of his favorites is, "Fifty percent off
all items today only." Refugees from Communist countries appreciate our supermarkets and discount department stores for the wonders they are. An Eastern European scientist visiting Middletown wept when she first saw the meat counter at
Waldbaum's. On the other hand, before her year in America was up, her pleasure
turned sour. She wanted everything she saw. Her approach to consumer goods
was insufficiently abstract, too materialistic. We Americans are beyond a simple,
possessive materialism. We're used to abundance and the possibility of possessing
things. The things, and the possibility of possessing them, will still be there next
week, next year. So today we can walk the aisles calmly.

It is a misunderstanding of the American retail store to think we go there
necessarily to buy. Some of us shop. There's a difference. Shopping has many purposes, the least interesting of which is to acquire new articles. We shop to cheer
ourselves up. We shop to practice decision-making. We shop to be useful and
productive members of our class and society. We shop to remind ourselves how
much is available to us. We shop to remind ourselves how much is to be striven
for. We shop to assert our superiority to the material objects that spread themselves before us.

Shopping's function as a form of therapy is widely appreciated. You don't
really need, let's say, another sweater. You need the feeling of power that comes
with buying or not buying it. You need the feeling that someone wants something
you have — even if it's just your money. To get the benefit of shopping, you needn't
actually purchase the sweater, any more than you have to marry every man you
flirt with. In fact, window-shopping, like flirting, can be more rewarding, the same
high without the distressing commitment, the material encumbrance. The purest
form of shopping is provided by garage sales. A connoisseur goes out with no goal
in mind, open to whatever may come his or her way, secure that it will cost very
little. Minimum expense, maximum experience. Perfect shopping.

I try to think of the opposite, a kind of shopping in which the object is all-
important, the pleasure of shopping at a minimum. For example, the purchase of
blue jeans. I buy new blue jeans as seldom as possible because the experience is so
humiliating. For every pair that looks good on me, fifteen look grotesque. But
even shopping for blue jeans at Bob's Surplus on Main Street — no frills, bare-
bones shopping — is an event in the life of the spirit. Once again I have to come
to terms with the fact that I will never look good in Levi's. Much as I want to be
mainstream, I never will be.

In fact, I'm doubly an oddball, neither Misses nor Junior, but Misses Petite. I
look in the mirror, I acknowledge the disparity between myself and the ideal, I
resign myself to making the best of it: I will buy the Lee's Misses Petite. Shopping
is a time of reflection, assessment, spiritual self-discipline.

It is appropriate, I think, that Bob's Surplus has a communal dressing room. 10
I used to shop only in places where I could count on a private dressing room with

a mirror inside. My impulse then was to hide my weaknesses. Now I believe in sharing them. There are other women in the dressing room at Bob's Surplus trying on blue jeans who look as bad as I do. We take comfort from one another. Sometimes a woman will ask me which of two items looks better. I always give a definite answer. It's the least I can do. I figure we are all in this together, and I emerge from the dressing room not only with a new pair of jeans but with a renewed sense of belonging to a human community.

When a Solzhenitsyn[1] rants about American materialism, I have to look at my digital Timex and check what year this is. Materialism? Like conformism, a hot moral issue of the fifties, but not now. How to spread the goods, maybe. Whether the goods are the Good, no. Solzhenitsyn, like the visiting scientist who wept at the beauty of Waldbaum's meat counter but came to covet everything she saw, takes American materialism too materialistically. He doesn't see its spiritual side. Caldor, Waldbaum's, Bob's Surplus — these, perhaps, are our cathedrals.

Questions

1. Read once again the title of the essay. What assumption underlies the title? If, as Rose says, Caldor, Waldbaum's, and Bob's Surplus were the "cathedrals" (para. 11) of her time — the 1980s — what are our "cathedrals" now? Consider the impact of online shopping. How has that phenomenon changed the economic landscape that Rose describes?

2. How does Rose go about undermining our conventional attitudes concerning materialism? Does she consider Americans to be too materialistic? Explain.

3. How does Rose characterize buying and shopping in paragraphs 6 and 7? Do you agree with her?

4. How does Rose's use of analogy and self-characterization appeal to her audience? How does it contribute to her argument?

5. Writing in 1984, Rose saw materialism and conformism as issues from the 1950s, already dated thirty years in the past; now, another thirty years later, to what extent does Rose speak to the economic issues of our time?

4. *Waste*

WENDELL BERRY

In the following essay from his 1990 collection, *What Are People For?*, Wendell Berry discusses the waste that we produce as a result of production and consumption.

---

[1]Russian author Aleksandr Solzhenitsyn (1918–2008) gave a famous commencement address at Harvard University in 1978, in which he warned of the moral and spiritual dangers of having a national ethos based primarily on material gain.—Eds.

As a country person, I often feel that I am on the bottom end of the waste problem. I live on the Kentucky River about ten miles from its entrance into the Ohio. The Kentucky, in many ways a lovely river, receives an abundance of pollution from the eastern Kentucky coal mines and the central Kentucky cities. When the river rises, it carries a continuous raft of cans, bottles, plastic jugs, chunks of styrofoam, and other imperishable trash. After the floods subside, I, like many other farmers, must pick up the trash before I can use my bottomland fields. I have seen the Ohio, whose name (*Oyo* in Iroquois) means "beautiful river," so choked with this manufactured filth that an ant could crawl dry-footed from Kentucky to Indiana. The air of both river valleys is seriously polluted. Our roadsides and roadside fields lie under a constant precipitation of cans, bottles, the plastic-ware of fast food joints, soiled plastic diapers, and sometimes whole bags of garbage. In our county we now have a "sanitary landfill" which daily receives, in addition to our local production, fifty to sixty large truckloads of garbage from Pennsylvania, New Jersey, and New York.

Moreover, a close inspection of our countryside would reveal, strewn over it from one end to the other, thousands of derelict and worthless automobiles, house trailers, refrigerators, stoves, freezers, washing machines, and dryers; as well as thousands of unregulated dumps in hollows and sink holes, on streambanks and roadsides, filled not only with "disposable" containers but also with broken toasters, television sets, toys of all kinds, furniture, lamps, stereos, radios, scales, coffee makers, mixers, blenders, corn poppers, hair dryers, and microwave ovens. Much of our waste problem is to be accounted for by the intentional flimsiness and unrepairability of the labor-savers and gadgets that we have become addicted to.

Of course, my sometime impression that I live on the receiving end of this problem is false, for country people contribute their full share. The truth is that we Americans, all of us, have become a kind of human trash, living our lives in the midst of a ubiquitous damned mess of which we are at once the victims and the perpetrators. We are all unwilling victims, perhaps; and some of us even are unwilling perpetrators, but we must count ourselves among the guilty nonetheless. In my household we produce much of our own food and try to do without as many frivolous "necessities" as possible—and yet, like everyone else, we must shop, and when we shop we must bring home a load of plastic, aluminum, and glass containers designed to be thrown away, and "appliances" designed to wear out quickly and be thrown away.

I confess that I am angry at the manufacturers who make these things. There are days when I would be delighted if certain corporation executives could somehow be obliged to eat their products. I know of no good reason why these containers and all other forms of manufactured "waste"—solid, liquid, toxic, or whatever—should not be outlawed. There is no sense and no sanity in objecting to the desecration of the flag while tolerating and justifying and encouraging as a daily business the desecration of the country for which it stands.

But our waste problem is not the fault only of producers. It is the fault of an economy that is wasteful from top to bottom—a symbiosis of an unlimited greed at the top and a lazy, passive, and self-indulgent consumptiveness at the bottom— 5 and all of us are involved in it. If we wish to correct this economy, we must be careful to understand and to demonstrate how much waste of human life is involved in our waste of the material goods of Creation. For example, much of the litter that now defaces our country is fairly directly caused by the massive secession or exclusion of most of our people from active participation in the food economy. We have made a social ideal of minimal involvement in the growing and cooking of food. This is one of the dearest "liberations" of our affluence. Nevertheless, the more dependent we become on the *industries* of eating and drinking, the more waste we are going to produce. The mess that surrounds us, then, must be understood not just as a problem in itself but as a symptom of a greater and graver problem: the centralization of our economy, the gathering of the productive property and power into fewer and fewer hands, and the consequent destruction, everywhere, of the local economies of household, neighborhood, and community.

This is the source of our unemployment problem, and I am not talking just about the unemployment of eligible members of the "labor force." I mean also the unemployment of children and old people, who, in viable household and local economies, would have work to do by which they would be useful to themselves and to others. The ecological damage of centralization and waste is thus inextricably involved with human damage. For we have, as a result, not only a desecrated, ugly, and dangerous country in which to live until we are in some manner poisoned by it, and a constant and now generally accepted problem of unemployed or unemployable workers, but also classrooms full of children who lack the experience and discipline of fundamental human tasks, and various institutions full of still capable old people who are useless and lonely.

I think that we must learn to see the trash on our streets and roadsides, in our rivers, and in our woods and fields, not as the side effects of "more jobs" as its manufacturers invariably insist that it is, but as evidence of good work *not* done by people able to do it.

Questions

1. What is the rhetorical effect of the long lists in the sentence that makes up most of paragraph 2?
2. What is ironic about the "unwilling" addiction that Berry talks about in paragraphs 2–4? How does the repetition of "must" contribute to this irony?
3. Berry writes, "There is no sense and no sanity in objecting to the desecration of the flag while tolerating and justifying and encouraging as a daily business the desecration of the country for which it stands (para. 4)." What allusion does the statement make? What is the major assumption that underlies its claim? Do you agree with Berry's position? Why or why not?
4. Rather than say "consumerism," Berry refers to our "consumptiveness," which he describes as "lazy, passive, and self-indulgent" (para. 5). What is the rhetorical effect of such diction?

5. According to Berry, what is the damage—both ecological and psychological—caused by centralization and waste? Do you agree with his concluding assessment of modern America? Why or why not?

5. *The New Consumerism*

Juliet Schor

In the following selection from her 1999 essay in the *Boston Review,* "The New Politics of Consumption," Juliet Schor discusses consumer culture in the United States.

A new politics of consumption should begin with daily life, and recent developments in the sphere of consumption. I describe these developments as "the new consumerism," by which I mean an upscaling of lifestyle norms; the pervasiveness of conspicuous, status goods and of competition for acquiring them; and the growing disconnect between consumer desires and incomes.

Social comparison and its dynamic manifestation—the need to "keep up"—have long been part of American culture. My term is "competitive consumption," the idea that spending is in large part driven by a comparative or competitive process in which individuals try to keep up with the norms of the social group with which they identify—a "reference group." Although the term is new, the idea is not. Thorstein Veblen, James Duesenberry, Fred Hirsch, and Robert Frank have all written about the importance of relative position as a dominant spending motive. What's new is the redefinition of reference groups: today's comparisons are less likely to take place between or among households of similar means. Instead, the lifestyles of the upper middle class and the rich have become a more salient point of reference for people throughout the income distribution. Luxury, rather than mere comfort, is a widespread aspiration.

One reason for this shift to "upscale emulation" is the decline of the neighborhood as a focus of comparison. Economically speaking, neighborhoods are relatively homogeneous groupings. In the 1950s and '60s, when Americans were keeping up with the Joneses down the street, they typically compared themselves to other households of similar incomes. Because of this focus on neighbors, the gap between aspirations and means tended to be moderate.

But as married women entered the workforce in larger numbers—particularly in white collar jobs—they were exposed to a more economically diverse group of people, and became more likely to gaze upward. Neighborhood contacts correspondingly declined, and the workplace became a more prominent point of reference. Moreover, as people spent less time with neighbors and friends, and more time on the family-room couch, television became more important as a source of consumer cues and information. Because television shows are so heavily skewed to the "lifestyle of the rich and upper middle class," they inflate the viewer's perceptions of what others have, and by extension what is worth acquiring—what one must have in order to avoid being "out of it."

Trends in inequality also helped to create the new consumerism. Since the 1970s, the distribution of income and wealth have shifted decisively in the direction of the top 20 percent. The share of after-tax family income going to the top 20 percent rose from 41.4 percent in 1979 to 46.8 percent in 1996. The share of wealth controlled by the top 20 percent rose from 81.3 percent in 1983 to 84.3 percent in 1997. This windfall resulted in a surge in conspicuous spending at the top. Remember the 1980s—the decade of greed and excess? Beginning with the super-rich, whose gains have been disproportionately higher, and trickling down to the merely affluent, visible status spending was the order of the day. Slowed down temporarily by the recession during the early 1990s, conspicuous luxury consumption has intensified during the current boom. Trophy homes, diamonds of a carat or more, granite countertops, and sport utility vehicles are the primary consumer symbols of the late 1990s. Television, as well as films, magazines, and newspapers, ensures that the remaining 80 percent of the nation is aware of the status purchasing that has swept the upper echelons.

In the meantime, upscale emulation had become well established. Researchers Susan Fournier and Michael Guiry found that 35 percent of their sample aspired to reach the top 6 percent of the income distribution, and another 49 percent aspired to the next 12 percent. Only 15 percent reported that they would be satisfied with "living a comfortable life"—that is, being middle class. But 85 percent of the population cannot earn the six-figure incomes necessary to support upper-middle-class lifestyles. The result is a growing aspirational gap: with desires persistently outrunning incomes, many consumers find themselves frustrated. One survey of U.S. households found that the level of income needed to fulfill one's dreams doubled between 1986 and 1994, and is currently more than twice the median household income.

The rapid escalation of desire and need, relative to income, also may help to explain the precipitous decline in the savings rate—from roughly 8 percent in 1980, to 4 percent in the early 1990s, to the current level of zero. (The stock market boom may also be inducing households not to save; but financial assets are still highly concentrated, with half of all households at net worths of $10,000 or less, including the value of their homes.) About two-thirds of American households do not save in a typical year. Credit card debt has skyrocketed, with unpaid balances now averaging about $7,000 and the typical household paying $1,000 each year in interest and penalties. These are not just low-income households. Bankruptcy rates continue to set new records, rising from 200,000 a year in 1980 to 1.4 million in 1998.

*   *   *

The new consumerism, with its growing aspirational gap, has begun to jeopardize the quality of American life. Within the middle class—and even the upper middle class—many families experience an almost threatening pressure to keep up, both for themselves and their children. They are deeply concerned about the rigors of the global economy, and the need to have their children attend "good" schools. This means living in a community with relatively high housing costs. For some households this also means providing their children with advantages purchased on the private market (computers, lessons, extra-curriculars, private schooling). Keeping two adults in the labor market—as so many families do, to earn the incomes to stay middle class—is expensive, not only because of the second car, child-care costs, and career wardrobe. It also creates the need for time-saving, but costly, commodities and services, such as take-out food and dry cleaning, as well as stress-relieving experiences. Finally, the financial tightrope that so many households walk—high expenses, low savings—is a constant source of stress and worry. While precise estimates are difficult to come by, one can argue that somewhere between a quarter and half of all households live paycheck-to-paycheck.

These problems are magnified for low-income households. Their sources of income have become increasingly erratic and inadequate, on account of employment instability, the proliferation of part-time jobs, and restrictions on welfare payments. Yet most low-income households remain firmly integrated within consumerism. They are targets for credit card companies, who find them an easy mark. They watch more television, and are more exposed to its desire-creating properties. Low-income children are more likely to be exposed to commercials at school, as well as home. The growing prominence of the values of the market, materialism, and economic success make financial failure more consequential and painful.

These are the effects at the household level. The new consumerism has also 10 set in motion another dynamic: it siphons off resources that could be used for alternatives to private consumption. We use our income in four basic ways: private consumption, public consumption, private savings, and leisure. When consumption standards can be met easily out of current income, there is greater willingness to support public goods, save privately, and cut back on time spent at work (in other words, to "buy leisure"). Conversely, when lifestyle norms are upscaled more rapidly than income, private consumption "crowds out" alternative uses of income. That is arguably what happened in the 1980s and 1990s: resources shifting into private consumption, and away from free time, the public sector, and saving. Hours of work have risen dramatically, saving rates have plummeted, public funds for education, recreation, and the arts have fallen in the wake of a grass-roots tax revolt. The timing suggests a strong coincidence between these developments and the intensification of competitive consumption—though I would have to do more systematic research before arguing causality. Indeed, this scenario makes good sense of an otherwise surprising finding: that indicators of "social health" or "genuine progress" (i.e., basic quality-of-life measures) began to diverge from Gross Domestic Product in the mid-1970s, after moving in tandem for decades. Can it be that consuming and prospering are no longer compatible states?

Questions

1. Of the three developments of the "new consumerism" that Schor explains, which is the most subjective?
2. Do you agree with Schor that "luxury, rather than mere comfort, is a widespread aspiration" (para. 2)? Identify the three reasons she offers to explain this paradigm shift. Which, in your view, is the most important? Why?
3. Provide three examples of statistical information that Schor uses. What effect does such data have on the cogency of her argument?
4. What is the nature of the "disconnect" that Schor discusses in paragraphs 6 and 7?
5. How accurate is Schor's characterization of modern American family life? Has it changed since she wrote this article in 1999? Do her descriptions still apply? Explain.
6. In paragraph 10, Schor makes several claims without offering specific evidence. How persuasive are her arguments? Why does she not offer substantive data to support her assertions?
7. Analyze the argument Schor develops in the final paragraph. How effectively does her evidence support her claims? How does she appeal to ethos? How persuasive is her argument?

6. *Shop-happy*

Joan Smith

In the following selection from the May 11, 2000, edition of *Salon*, Joan Smith responds to the ideas of Juliet Schor.

The other night, my 3-year-old nephew and I received an unexpected economics lesson in the form of a picture book called "Rainbow Fish." The plot is deceptively simple: Rainbow Fish is an underwater denizen distinguished by a set of unusually attractive silver scales. A small, blue fish asks R.F. to give him one of his scales and R.F. refuses. Shunned, as a result, by all of the other fish, R.F. consults a wise old octopus, who encourages him to reconsider. Give your scales away, the octopus advises. You won't be as pretty, but the other fish will like you and you'll be happy. So he does and he is. The end.

My nephew understood immediately that the book was about sharing, but he is also at the age of the perpetual "why?" and trying to answer his whys about R.F.'s epiphany, I felt queasy. It's important that children learn to share, but this clumsy little book's more prominent message is that people will like you if you give them your possessions, particularly the possessions they envy. The unwitting moral of "Rainbow Fish" is that you *can* buy love.

Anyone who reads to children knows that such ill-conceived homilies abound, but what's interesting about these sloppily reasoned kids books is what they tell us about our own atavistic beliefs. It seems to me that "Rainbow Fish" unwittingly exposes the confusion inherent in one of our most deep-seated convictions—that materialism, the love and acquisition of things, is intrinsically evil.

In her interesting new book, "Do Americans Shop Too Much?" Harvard economist Juliet Schor laments what she calls the "new consumerism," a frenzy for "high-status" goods she attributes to the increased concentration of wealth at the top of the economic ladder: "Trophy homes, diamonds of a carat or more, granite countertops, and sport utility vehicles are the primary consumer symbols of the late 1990s." This rampant consumption is unfortunate, she argues, not only because it squanders environmental resources but because it forces people on the lower rungs of the income ladder to try to keep up.

Schor believes that we consume competitively, with an eye on the consumption   5
habits of the proverbial Joneses—except that the Joneses, who used to live down the street and were probably our socioeconomic peers, are no longer our frames of reference. Now, because of television, more sophisticated marketing techniques and the fact that most women are working in jobs, our new frame of reference, she argues, is *Lifestyles of the Rich and Famous*.

This, Schor says, explains one of the more disturbing trends of the past 30 years: that while our buying power has doubled, we are increasingly dissatisfied. Her solution? To limit consumption by taxing luxury goods. This, she believes, would take the pressure off those of us struggling so hard to keep up with all the new stock-market and dot-com millionaires.

But the urge to buy is so much more complicated than Schor—perhaps limited by the brevity of her essay, perhaps by an academic discipline whose theories have often proved irrelevant in the real world—even begins to suggest. Status is clearly not the main reason most people buy things. Just because I see the Joneses' SUV and think, "I, too, would love to own an SUV," doesn't mean that I am competing with them. It could simply be that I think owning an SUV seems like a pretty good idea.

Personally, I can't stand SUVs because they guzzle gas, block my view and represent a transportation menace. But I don't have children; both of my sisters, who own Chevy Suburbans, do. One borrowed a Suburban for a vacation with her husband, his mother and the couple's three small daughters and became addicted to all of that wonderful space. The other has a weakness for labor-saving devices and imagined easily carting her two sons and all of their friends to Little League games *and* having plenty of room in the back to stash their equipment.

Wanting to acquire the things that we see and like is as natural as breathing. Babies want to touch things, taste them, bash them against the wall. We appease them with shining objects, distract them with new toys. When one child sees another child playing with a toy, he or she wants it not because of envy of the other child's relative social position but because it looks like fun. When we see other people having sex, eating an ice-cream cone, setting a table with pretty dishes or using a clever new tool and want to do the same, it's not necessarily because we're jockeying for position. It could be that we, too, just want to have fun.

Of course, we do sometimes buy things with status in mind—a nice suit for   10
a job interview, a cool pair of shoes in junior high, a certain kind of car or house because we imagine it contributing to our allure. But the mundane truth is that things, especially new things, just *please* us. Examining something, taking it home, rearranging our homes to accommodate it—it's all part of what social psychologists describe as the human need to affect (and be affected by) our surroundings. Even the urge to create is connected to the urge to acquire.

If, as Schor notes, "the level of income needed to fulfill one's dreams doubled between 1986 and 1994," it's because there are so many more interesting and relatively affordable things to dream about. Some of them didn't even exist in 1986, and others—personal computers and cars, for instance—are so much cheaper now. The most compelling reason to buy these new things is not the status they afford but their promise to make life easier and/or more fun. Parents are using pagers and cellphones to keep in touch with their teenagers. Teenagers are using them to keep in constant contact with their friends.

And if SUVs are mainly status symbols, why has there never been the same sudden widespread interest in acquiring Mercedeses? SUVs are more the equivalent of the 1950s station wagon, an updated version of a car with enough space to accommodate a family. With gas almost obscenely cheap and car companies building light trucks that are both comfortable and easy to drive, the popularity of SUVs seems in retrospect almost inevitable.

And if we are breaking records in running up credit card debt and declaring bankruptcy, isn't it less because we are trying to keep up with rich people than because credit has never been so widely available or collective economic optimism so high? One of the most profound cultural gaps in contemporary America is between my generation—people in their 40s and 50s—and our parents, whose formative experience was the Great Depression. A growing number of us have never experienced widespread poverty and unemployment without the security of a government safety net. If this were the fable of the grasshopper and the ant, we would be grasshoppers who had never experienced winter.

Schor calls for controlling consumption—thus protecting us from the "new" emphasis on "luxury, expensiveness, exclusivity, rarity, uniqueness, and distinction"—by taxing "high-end versions" of products. "Why not stand for consumption that is democratic, egalitarian, and available to all?" It's ironic that Ralph Nader is the author of an enthusiastic foreword to Schor's essay when the consumer movement he launched some 30 years ago is, along with the counterculture of the 1960s, at least in part responsible for our hunger for high-quality goods.

Paul Hawken, co-founder of upscale garden tool company Smith & Hawken,   15
predicted in his 1983 book, "The Next Economy," both the growing gap between rich and poor and an increased demand (among the new rich) for quality. Should

we penalize people for buying fine art when reproductions are so much cheaper? For buying hardcover books instead of mass-market paperbacks? For paying more for whole wheat when they could be surviving on Wonder Bread?

Of the nine responses by an assortment of scholars that follow Schor's essay, the most compelling are (unexpectedly) from an assistant professor of advertising at the University of Illinois, Douglas Holt, and an associate professor of marketing at the University of Wisconsin, Craig J. Thompson. Holt argues that it's almost impossible to control consumption anyway, given today's market in which companies compete to appropriate every new idea the instant it becomes popular. "The market would find the nonstatus values that Schor's agenda encourages and turn them into salable goods," writes Holt, citing businesses that have already exploited symbols of the counterculture, from Benetton to the Nature Company to Ben & Jerry's.

And in his essay, "A New Puritanism?" Thompson maintains that any "moral critique of consumerism is steeped in a phobia of feminization and an infatuation with puritanical asceticism. It effects a rejection of the sensual and emotive aspects of human experience and an extreme suspicion of 'unproductive' pleasures." He suggests that if sex sells at least in part because it is a forbidden pleasure, we might become less compulsive shoppers if we allowed ourselves to truly savor the shopping experience.

Yet the real weakness of Schor's approach is her assumption that happiness is a function of relative affluence and the pressure to consume. In Schor's world, Rainbow Fish can indeed buy happiness—for everyone—by giving up whatever he has that might provoke envy. (Never mind that people envy all sorts of things they *can't* buy—good looks and good health, talent, confidence, charisma.) While it's clear that unfettered consumption is a threat to the planet, and it's well established that, despite our unprecedented affluence, Americans are increasingly unhappy, a far more satisfying analysis of this crisis is David G. Myers' "The American Paradox: Spiritual Hunger in an Age of Plenty."

A professor of psychology at Hope College in Holland, Mich., Myers helped pioneer the study of happiness (as opposed to the discipline's traditional focus on psychopathology), and he has spent most of his career deconstructing the components of psychological well-being. One of the most interesting things researchers like Myers have discovered is that the old saw is true: Money does not buy happiness. Subjective well-being has no relation to income once people can afford the basic necessities of life.

Myers argues that the true source of our new dissatisfaction is embedded in American culture—and in the same free market that has made us wealthy. Both encourage a radical individualism that lies "at the heart of the American dream." On the one hand, he says, people who live in democratic countries that guarantee basic individual freedoms tend to be happier than people who don't. "Yet for today's radical individualism, we pay a price: a social recession that imperils children [Myers reports that the teen suicide rate has tripled over the past 30 years], 20 corrodes civility, and diminishes happiness. When individualism is taken to an extreme, individuals becomes its ironic casualties."

In Myers' view, the problem is cultural, not economic, and therefore requires a constellation of social and political corrections. We have allowed the free market, which has benefited us in many ways, to determine values—and the free market values only one thing: money. "Pretend some devil wanted to design a program to corrode families," he writes. "They might begin by lowering the job prospects and earning power of young men. To accomplish this they might encourage corporate CEO's to act like yesteryear's robber barons and redirect rewards to themselves. Justifying their actions with talk of freedom, they might also deregulate television, legalize gambling, structure taxes to penalize marriage, and shrink the value of the minimum wage (which was created to be a 'family living wage' that protected families and children)." Sound familiar?

Not that Myers wants to abolish the free market. "Capitalism, as Winston Churchill might have put it, is the worst economic system, except for all the others," he writes. But citing studies showing that people who believe in God and/or participate in community activities tend to be happier than people who don't, Myers sees the solution in an emerging communitarian movement that transcends the culture wars: "one that affirms liberals' indictment of the demoralizing effects of poverty and conservatives' indictment of toxic media models." People who feel connected to others—through their churches and other community activities—are more likely to take responsibility for one another and for the culture as a whole, he argues.

We have a long tradition of changing the way we do things even without market incentives, Myers points out. We do it when enough people come to believe that we are being hurt in ways that can't be calculated on a balance sheet. Thus, we've abolished slavery, regulated polluters and outlawed child labor and sexual harassment. Already, we've begun to encourage the auto industry to redesign SUVs to make them less dangerous to other vehicles, and we are moving to hold them to the same fuel efficiency standards that apply to cars.

Myers is an optimist, perhaps, but he sees people coming together "on the common ground of concern for our children and their future"—more of them going to church, more (both liberal and conservative) speaking the same language when they talk about the family and about moral values. In Myers' world, Rainbow Fish would find happiness not by renouncing his material good fortune but by recognizing that (no matter his momentary status) he is inescapably responsible for and connected to all the other fish in the sea.

Questions

1. What are the purpose and effect of the opening paragraphs about *Rainbow Fish*? How effective are they?

2. In paragraph 7, Smith writes, "But the urge to buy is so much more complicated than Schor . . . even begins to suggest." Identify three counterarguments that Smith

develops. How effectively does she use them to support her claim about Schor? Explain with specific references to both articles.

3. Smith refers to Ralph Nader and Paul Hawken (paras. 14–15). What is the purpose for each reference? Which one more effectively supports her argument?

4. How does Smith respond to Schor's idea of a new luxury tax? Explain.

5. What do you consider Smith's most compelling claim? Do you agree with her? Explain.

7. *In Praise of Chain Stores*

Virginia Postrel

In the following essay from the December 2006 issue of the *Atlantic*, Virginia Postrel discusses the advantages of chain stores.

Every well-traveled cosmopolite knows that America is mind-numbingly monotonous — "the most boring country to tour, because everywhere looks like everywhere else," as the columnist Thomas Friedman once told Charlie Rose. Boston has the same stores as Denver, which has the same stores as Charlotte or Seattle or Chicago. We live in a "Stepford world," says Rachel Dresbeck, the author of *Insiders' Guide to Portland, Oregon*. Even Boston's historic Faneuil Hall, she complains, is "dominated by the Gap, Anthropologie, Starbucks, and all the other usual suspects. Why go anywhere? Every place looks the same." This complaint is more than the old worry, dating back to the 1920s, that the big guys are putting Mom and Pop out of business. Today's critics focus less on what isn't there — Mom and Pop — than on what is. Faneuil Hall actually has plenty of locally owned businesses, from the Geoclassics store selling minerals and jewelry, to Pizzeria Regina ("since 1926"). But you do find the same chains everywhere.

The suburbs are the worst. Take Chandler, Arizona, just south of Phoenix. At Chandler Fashion Center, the area's big shopping mall, you'll find P. F. Chang's, California Pizza Kitchen, Chipotle Mexican Grill, and the Cheesecake Factory. Drive along Chandler's straight, flat boulevards, and you'll see Bed Bath & Beyond and Linens-n-Things; Barnes & Noble and Borders; PetSmart and Petco; Circuit City and Best Buy; Lowe's and Home Depot; CVS and Walgreens. Chandler has the Apple Store and Pottery Barn, the Gap and Ann Taylor, Banana Republic and DSW, and, of course, Target and Wal-Mart, Starbucks and McDonald's. For people allergic to brands, Chandler must be hell — even without the 110-degree days.

One of the fastest-growing cities in the country, Chandler is definitely the kind of place urbanists have in mind as they intone, "When every place looks the same, there is no such thing as place anymore." Like so many towns in America, it has lost much of its historic character as a farming community. The annual Ostrich Festival still honors one traditional product, but these days Chandler raises more subdivisions and strip malls than ostrich plumes or cotton, another former staple. Yet it still refutes the common assertion that national chains are a blight on the landscape, that they've turned American towns into an indistinguishable "geography of nowhere."

The first thing you notice in Chandler is that, as a broad empirical claim, the cliché that "everywhere looks like everywhere else" is obvious nonsense. Chandler's land and air and foliage are peculiar to the desert Southwest. The people dress differently. Even the cookie-cutter housing developments, with their xeriscaping[1] and washed-out desert palette, remind you where you are. Forget New England clapboard, Carolina columns, or yellow Texas brick. In the intense sun of Chandler, the red-tile roofs common in California turn a pale, pale pink.

Stores don't give places their character. Terrain and weather and culture do.   5
Familiar retailers may take some of the discovery out of travel — to the consternation of journalists looking for obvious local color — but by holding some of the commercial background constant, chains make it easier to discern the real differences that define a place: the way, for instance, that people in Chandler come out to enjoy the summer twilight, when the sky glows purple and the dry air cools.

Besides, the idea that America was once filled with wildly varied business establishments is largely a myth. Big cities could, and still can, support more retail niches than small towns. And in a less competitive national market, there was certainly more variation in business efficiency — in prices, service, and merchandise quality. But the range of retailing *ideas* in any given town was rarely that great. One deli or diner or lunch counter or cafeteria was pretty much like every other one. A hardware store was a hardware store, a pharmacy a pharmacy. Before it became a ubiquitous part of urban life, Starbucks was, in most American cities, a radically new idea.

Chains do more than bargain down prices from suppliers or divide fixed costs across a lot of units. They rapidly spread economic discovery — the scarce and costly knowledge of what retail concepts and operational innovations actually work. That knowledge can be gained only through the expensive and time-consuming process of trial and error. Expecting each town to independently invent every new business is a prescription for real monotony, at least for the locals. Chains make a large range of choices available in more places. They increase local variety, even as they reduce the differences from place to place. People who mostly stay put get to have experiences once available only to frequent travelers, and this loss of exclusivity is one reason why frequent travelers are the ones who complain. When Borders was a unique Ann Arbor institution, people in places like Chandler — or, for that matter, Philadelphia and Los Angeles — didn't have much in the way of bookstores. Back in 1986, when California Pizza Kitchen was an innovative local restaurant about to open its second location, food writers at the L.A. *Daily News* declared it "the kind of place every neighborhood should have." So what's wrong if the country has 158 neighborhood CPKs instead of one or two?

---

[1]Landscaping designed to minimize water consumption. — Eds.

The process of multiplication is particularly important for fast-growing towns like Chandler, where rollouts of established stores allow retail variety to expand as fast as the growing population can support new businesses. I heard the same refrain in Chandler that I've heard in similar boomburgs elsewhere, and for similar reasons. "It's got all the advantages of a small town, in terms of being friendly, but it's got all the things of a big town," says Scott Stephens, who moved from Manhattan Beach, California, in 1998 to work for Motorola. Chains let people in a city of 250,000 enjoy retail amenities once available only in a huge metropolitan center. At the same time, familiar establishments make it easier for people to make a home in a new place. When Nissan recently moved its headquarters from Southern California to Tennessee, an unusually high percentage of its Los Angeles–area employees accepted the transfer. "The fact that Starbucks are everywhere helps make moving a lot easier these days," a rueful Greg Whitney, vice president of business development for the Los Angeles County Economic Development Corporation, told the *Los Angeles Times* reporter John O'Dell. Orth Hedrick, a Nissan product manager, decided he could stay with the job he loved when he turned off the interstate near Nashville and realized, "You could really be Anywhere, U.S.A. There's a great big regional shopping mall, and most of the stores and restaurants are the same ones we see in California. Yet a few miles away you're in downtown, and there's lots of local color, too."

Contrary to the rhetoric of bored cosmopolites, most cities don't exist primarily to please tourists. The children toddling through the Chandler mall hugging their soft Build-A-Bear animals are no less delighted because kids can also build a bear in Memphis or St. Louis. For them, this isn't tourism; it's life — the experiences that create the memories from which the meaning of a place arises over time. Among Chandler's most charming sights are the business-casual dads joining their wives and kids for lunch in the mall food court. The food isn't the point, let alone whether it's from Subway or Dairy Queen. The restaurants merely provide the props and setting for the family time. When those kids grow up, they'll remember the food court as happily as an older generation recalls the diners and motels of Route 66 — not because of the businesses' innate appeal but because of the memories they evoke.

The contempt for chains represents a brand-obsessed view of place, as if 10 store names were all that mattered to a city's character. For many critics, the name on the store really *is* all that matters. The planning consultant Robert Gibbs works with cities that want to revive their downtowns, and he also helps developers find space for retailers. To his frustration, he finds that many cities actually turn away national chains, preferring a moribund downtown that seems authentically local. But, he says, the same local activists who oppose chains "want specialty retail that sells exactly what the chains sell — the same price, the same fit, the same qualities, the same sizes, the same brands, even." You can show people pictures of a Pottery Barn with nothing but the name changed, he says, and they'll love the store. So downtown stores stay empty, or sell low-value tourist items like candles and kites, while the chains open on the edge of town. In the name of urbanism, officials and activists in cities like Ann Arbor and Fort Collins, Colorado, are driving business to the suburbs. "If people like shopping at the Banana Republic or the Gap, if that's your market — or Payless Shoes — why not?" says an exasperated Gibbs. "Why not sell the goods and services people want?"

Questions

1. Do you agree with the characterization of America with which Postrel begins her essay? Why or why not?
2. According to Postrel in paragraph 7, what are the main things that chain stores do? Do her claims square with your own observations and experience? Explain.
3. What are the economic effects of chains, according to Postrel?
4. Postrel quotes Orth Hedrick, a Nissan product manager: "You could really be Anywhere, U.S.A. There's a great big regional shopping mall, and most of the stores and restaurants are the same ones we see in California. Yet a few miles away you're in downtown, and there's lots of local color, too" (para. 8). What is Hedrick's tone? Rewrite the third sentence to give the speaker an entirely different tone and attitude toward chains.
5. What does Postrel imply about people who are against chain stores?

8. Forbes *Price Index of Luxury Goods Keeps Pace with Inflation*

Scott DeCarlo

The following chart is excerpted from one posted on the *Forbes* magazine Web site on September 23, 2010. *Forbes* is a business bi-weekly that is famous for its lists, such as "The Forbes 400," which identifies the richest Americans.

ITEM	2010 PRICE	CHANGE FROM 2009
Coat/Natural Russian sable, Maximilian at Bloomingdale's	$200,000	14%
Silk Dress/Bill Blass Ltd., classic	$1,900	−21%
Loafers/Gucci	$495	0%
Shirts/1 dozen cotton, bespoke, Turnbull & Asser, London	$4,200	0%
Shoes/Men's black calf wing tip, custom-made, John Lobb, London	$4,187	−11%
School/Preparatory, Groton, 1-year tuition, room, board	$48,895	4%
University/Harvard, 1-year tuition, room, board, insurance	$50,723	4%

Opera/Two tickets, six performances Metropolitan Opera, Saturday night, parterre box	$4,265	−3%
Caviar/Imperial Special Reserve Stellatus, 1 kilo, Petrossian, Los Angeles, CA & N.Y., N.Y.	$19,600	NA
Champagne/Dom Perignon vintage 2000, case, Sherry-Lehmann, N.Y.	$1,799	0%
Dinner at La Tour d'Argent*/Paris, estimated per person (including wine and tip)	$426	−15%
Flowers in season/Arrangements for 6 rooms, changed weekly, Christatos & Koster, N.Y., per month	$8,175	0%
Hotel/1-bedroom suite, Four Seasons, N.Y.	$4,650	0%
Face-lift/American Academy of Facial Plastic & Reconstructive Surgery	$17,000	0%
Lawyer/Established N.Y. firm, Schlesinger, Gannon & Lazetera LLP, average hourly fee for estate planning by partner	$875	3%
Perfume/1 oz. Joy, by Jean Patou	$450	13%
Motor yacht/Hatteras 80 MY (with 1,550hp Caterpillar C-32 engines)	$5,281,600	0%
Shotguns*/Pair of James Purdey & Sons (12 gauge Side-by-Side), Griffin & Howe, Bernardsville, NJ & Greenwich, CT	$185,954	−1%
Swimming pool/Olympic (50 meters), Mission Pools, Escondido, CA	$1,476,000	−5%
Tennis court/Clay, Putnam, Tennis and Recreation, Harwinton, CT	$55,000	0%
Automobile/Rolls-Royce Phantom	$380,000	0%
Magazine/*Forbes*, 1-year subscription	$60	0%
Duffel Bag/Louis Vuitton, Keepall Bandouliere, 55 centimeters	$1,225	0%
Watch/Patek Philippe classic men's in gold (Calatrava), alligator strap	$17,400	NA
Purse/Hermes, Kelly Bag, calfskin, rigid, 28 centimeters	$7,300	NA

*Currency exchange as of Aug. 31, 2010.

Questions

1. Which item on the list is the most surprising to you? Which is the least? Why?
2. Which items on the list are within the grasp of the majority of consumers? Which are completely out of range? What do you consider luxuries in your own life? How do they compare with those on the list?
3. In his *Philosophical Dictionary* (1764), the French author Voltaire wrote, "People have declaimed against luxury for two thousand years, in verse and in prose, and people have always delighted in it." Do more people declaim or delight in luxury? Which do you find yourself doing more? How does this chart affect your view of luxury? Of wealth? Of consumerism and materialism? Of the economy? Refer to Voltaire's epigrammatic statement in your response.

4. Do you think people should pay more in taxes — pay what we call a "luxury tax" — on purchases of items such as those on this list? Why or why not?

Making Connections

1. In her essay "In Praise of Chain Stores," Virginia Postrel quotes consultant Robert Gibbs: "'If people like shopping at the Banana Republic or the Gap, if that's your market — or Payless Shoes — why not?' says an exasperated Gibbs. 'Why not sell the goods and services people want?'" (para. 10). How would Wendell Berry reply to Gibbs's question? Juliet Schor? John Kenneth Galbraith? Henry David Thoreau? Joan Smith? Provide a brief response of a sentence or two for each.

2. How might Thoreau, Berry, Galbraith, Schor, Smith, Phyllis Rose, or Postrel respond to the *Forbes* Price Index of Luxury Goods? Write a one- to two-sentence response from each.

3. Why are the words "necessities" and "liberations" in quotation marks in "Waste" by Berry? How would Thoreau regard Berry's use of "necessities"? How would Rose regard his use of "liberations"? Explain.

4. Compare Schor's concluding rhetorical question with Galbraith's main idea. How would he answer her question?

5. Thoreau describes luxuries and "comforts" as "hinderances to the elevation of mankind" (para. 4). Rose sees the "spiritual side of shopping" and views it as a "time of reflection, assessment, spiritual self-discipline" (para. 9). Imagine a brief dialogue between the two writers. What would each say?

6. How would Rose respond to Smith's argument?

7. Smith remarks, "The most compelling reason to buy these new things is not the status they afford but their promise to make life easier and/or more fun" (para. 11). Which of the writers in this Conversation would agree? Which would disagree? Why? Do you agree?

8. Compare what Postrel says in paragraph 9 with the main ideas in the piece by Rose (p. 482).

Entering the Conversation

As you respond to the following prompts, support your argument with references to at least three sources in this Conversation on materialism in American culture. For help using sources, see Chapter 4.

1. Write an essay identifying the major issues discussed in the selections and taking a position on what you view as the most important idea. Which of the selections most nearly share a perspective on the topic? Which ones most obviously present opposing positions?

2. Paraphrase the basic argument advanced by John Kenneth Galbraith (p. 478). Then, in an essay in which you refer to three of the other selections in the Conversation, carefully support, refute, or qualify his position.

3. Are Americans overly materialistic? Or is such a claim too simplistic? Which of the writers in the Conversation would agree with either position? What is *your* position? Write an essay that answers that question, using as sources at least three of the selections in the Conversation.

4. You have read Smith's response to Schor. Now write an answer from Schor to Smith. Quote at least two other voices from the chapter in your response.

5. In "Economy," Thoreau writes, "Most of the luxuries, and many of the so called comforts of life, are not only not indispensable, but positive hinderances to the elevation of mankind" (para. 4). He also poses two questions that address both microeconomics and macroeconomics: "What is the nature of the luxury which enervates and destroys nations?" and "Are we sure there is none of it in our own lives?" (para. 4). Write an essay in which you take a position on his first statement and also answer the questions that he poses. Refer to other selections in the chapter as well as to your own observations and experience as you develop your essay.

Student Writing

Rhetorical Analysis:
Analyzing a Prose Passage

The following prompt calls for a close analysis of a passage from Lars Eighner's essay, "On Dumpster Diving," on page 421 of this chapter.

> Paragraphs 1 through 7 serve as an introduction to Lars Eighner's "Dumpster Diving." Read the passage carefully and write an essay explaining how Eighner uses rhetorical strategies to introduce his subject to his reader.

Here is the first draft of an essay from student Jonathan Ellis in response to the prompt. Read the draft carefully, thinking about ways that it could be improved through revision. Consider rhetoric and style as well as content. Then respond to the questions that follow.

Draft

Lars Eighner's essay "Dumpster Diving" serves as a driving force for Eighner's extensive memoir, *Travels with Lizbeth* (1993). The larger piece chronicles a three-year period of Eighner's life during which he was homeless. "Dumpster Diving" details a core aspect of his homelessness, explaining the means by which Eighner obtained his food, clothing, and other necessities. The first seven paragraphs of the essay underscore not only the carelessness of the consumer but also the mindfulness of those who depend on the consumer's refuse to survive. Throughout the introduction of "Dumpster Diving," Eighner conveys a message to the reader that individuals should make much more utility of their possessions and stop taking them for granted. This message is then reiterated in the rest of the passage as Eighner "put[s] . . . what I have learned down here [in the essay], beginning with the practical art of Dumpster diving and proceeding to the abstract."

Eighner begins the passage by mentioning the origins of the term "Dumpster." Eighner enlightens the reader on the roots of the word as a trademark of the Dempster Dumpster company (para. 1). This is a rather unusual way to begin the piece because a word such as "Dumpster" is rarely deemed interesting enough to research or explore. However, this insight given to the reader emphasizes the lack of knowledge that people really have about Dumpsters. Often, people view "Dumpster" as a quite negative term because of its association with waste items. The fact that "Dumpster" is merely a proprietary word of a company that specializes in garbage disposal seldom crosses the mind. Instead, "Dumpster" is treated with ill repute — the same ill repute that consumers treat their personal items with when they discard them into Dumpsters. Eighner gives "Dumpster" a more favorable portrayal, even "dutifully capitaliz[ing] the word although it was lowercased in almost all of the citations Merriam-Webster photocopied for me" (para. 2). Through this "dutiful capitalization" he divulges a more accurate meaning of Dumpsters as seen through the eyes of the "wino[s]" and "hobo[s]" (para. 2) who rely on them for sustenance and supplies; for the homeless view a Dumpster in the same way that those with housing view a refrigerator — as primary food storage.

Eighner is also very particular with the phrase "Dumpster diving." Despite the attractive alliteration, Eighner states that this depiction of the process by which he amasses his essentials "seems to me to be a little too cute and, in my case, inaccurate because I lack the athletic ability to lower myself into the Dumpsters as the true divers do, much to their increased profit" (para. 4). Rather than "diving," Eighner broaches some more fitting terms within the fourth paragraph, such as "scavenging," "scrounging," and "foraging." These terms commensurately capture the reality of the activity rather than giving a euphemism such as "diving." Dumpster diving is not an athlete leaping into a Dumpster with style or grace. Dumpster diving is the way of life for those who have no place to live and no other means of obtaining provisions. Eighner is not coy in his description, later delivering a fairly sordid illustration followed by a one-two punch of concise parallel statements: "I like the frankness of the word 'scavenging,' which I can hardly think of without picturing a big black snail on an aquarium wall. I live from the refuse of others. I am a scavenger" (para. 5). The author reveals to the reader the cold, hard truth of Dumpster diving by being direct and guileless — no smoke and mirrors.

The fact that Eighner takes pride in his "scavenger" status accentuates value in what would otherwise be an unenviable position. Eighner writes, "I think it a sound and honorable niche, although if I could I would naturally prefer to live the comfortable consumer life, perhaps — and only perhaps — as a slightly less wasteful consumer owing to what I have learned as a scavenger" (para. 5). As a scavenger, he is much thriftier with what he has than the "consumer." He has come to appreciate his belongings more than the lavish consumer, who is unaware of how it feels to be homeless, and has no apparent reason to be mindful with his property. Eighner stresses how wasteful the consumer truly is when he provides a laundry list of necessities that he acquired from Dumpsters — a list that includes a few luxury items as well: "Except for jeans, all my clothes came from Dumpsters. Boom boxes, candles, bedding, toilet paper, medicine, books, a typewriter, a virgin male love doll, change sometimes amounting to many dollars: I acquired many things from the Dumpsters" (para. 6). Such indulgences, Eighner reveals, as boom boxes, a typewriter, and even money are discarded for the "scavengers" to dig out of the Dumpsters. By stating that he extracted the "necessities of daily life" from Dumpsters and then proceeding to list items that are not essential and yet are thrown away encapsulates the improvident nature of the larger culture. Eighner's powerful paradox imparts the lessons he learned without a roof over his head to the readers with a roof over theirs.

Lars Eighner and his dog, Lizbeth, suffered a great deal on the streets, relying on the litter of others. While they were destitute of a home, however, they were not destitute of frugality. The opening seven paragraphs detail the misconceived gentler notions on Dumpster diving and provide a striking critique of society for the reader to mull over as he or she reads the rest of the essay. "On Dumpster Diving" is a life lesson to the extravagant users, misusers, and abusers of objects. The narrator Eighner had his home, his savings, and ultimately his lifestyle stripped away from him. The same can happen to anyone, especially to the person who takes his or her own life for granted. However, it is better to read about Eighner's experiences and alter one's ways than to undergo Eighner's experiences.

Questions

1. What are the chief strengths of the draft?
2. What do you see as its deficiencies?
3. How can the essay be revised for improvement?

Revision

Now read Jonathan's revision, and answer the questions that follow.

Rhetorical Analysis of "Dumpster Diving"

Jonathan Ellis

Lars Eighner's essay "On Dumpster Diving" details a core aspect of the three-year period when the author and his canine companion were homeless. The text explains the means by which Eighner obtained his food, clothing, and other necessities. The first seven paragraphs of the essay underscore not only the carelessness of the consumer but also the mindfulness of those who depend on the consumer's refuse to survive. In addition, these paragraphs uncover the truth and allay the misconceptions that people have about the disgusting activity of Dumpster diving. Throughout the introduction of "On Dumpster Diving," Eighner conveys a message to the reader that individuals should make much more utility of their possessions and stop taking them for granted. He communicates this primarily with his attitude toward the audience, his high-class diction, and his personal storytelling. With these rhetorical strategies, Eighner makes the topic of Dumpster diving interesting rather than nauseating.

From the very onset of the passage, Lars Eighner utilizes a jocular voice with the reader. He begins the passage by mentioning the origins of the term "Dumpster," enlightening the reader on the roots of the word as a trademark of the Dempster Dumpster company (para. 1). Eighner then goes on to note how he "dutifully capitalized the word although it was lowercased in almost all of the citations Merriam-Webster photocopied for me" (para. 2). On one level, this excerpt is quite comical considering that Eighner is both deeply researching the name of a waste receptacle and paying special attention to capitalizing the term in his writing. On a second level, however, this sentence has a very grave connotation. The effect of this sentence is to glorify dumpsters, which are in fact the sources of property for the homeless. Through his "dutiful capitalization" he divulges a more accurate meaning of Dumpsters as seen through the eyes of the "wino[s]" and "hobo[s]" that rely on them for sustenance and supplies. His hybrid tone allows the reader to enjoy Eighner's passage without worry over the squalor of Dumpster diving, the matter Eighner is addressing. The humor gives readers an opportunity to audibly chortle along with the essay and thus sustain interest in the piece; the gravity of his tone shows a different side of dumpster diving — not as something degrading, but as a way of life. This double-edged sword that is Eighner's tone is evident throughout the rest of the introduction and the rest of the entire piece.

Eighner is also very particular with his diction, as well as the phrase "Dumpster diving." The expression itself "seems to me [Eighner] to be a little too cute and, in my case, inaccurate because I lack the athletic ability to lower myself into the Dumpsters as the true divers do, much to their increased profit" (para. 4). A very funny line indeed this is; in addition to sounding droll, however, Eighner sounds deadly serious in his mention of dumpster diving as not merely a recreational art form, but a lifestyle and necessary skill for the homeless to have in order to survive. Eighner broaches some more "fitting" terms for this activity within the fourth paragraph, such as "scavenging," "scrounging," and "foraging" — and even these are used in partial jest. Nevertheless,

Eighner's humor is not to be confused with coyness on the subject. The narrator later delivers a fairly sordid illustration bolstered by the use of anaphora: "I like the frankness of the word 'scavenging,' which I can hardly think of without picturing a big black snail on an aquarium wall. I live from the refuse of others. I am a scavenger" (para. 5). The author reveals to the reader the cold, hard truth of Dumpster diving by being direct and guileless — no smoke and mirrors. In doing this he continues to change the attitude of his audience about Dumpster diving for the better, showing his readers a more practical and less repugnant side of the story. Surely after reading Eighner's piece, the reader will no longer simply look at a Dumpster and retch; for he or she will know the true value of the Dumpster and the importance of Dumpster diving as told by the author.

The fact that Eighner takes pride in his "scavenger" status accentuates worth in what would otherwise be an unenviable position. Eighner writes, "I think it a sound and honorable niche, although if I could I would naturally prefer to live the comfortable consumer life, perhaps — and only perhaps — as a slightly less wasteful consumer owing to what I have learned as a scavenger" (para. 5). The "perhaps — and only perhaps" double qualifier is important. Without the "and only perhaps" portion of this sentence, Eighner risks estranging the reader early in his essay. The last thing he desires to do is sound preachy and condescending, and the extra qualifier prevents him from doing so. As a man who already knows how it feels to be without a home, Eighner has already established great ethos in his essay; he does not want to lose it here. Rather than sounding overbearing, Eighner comes across as humble and cordial to his audience, allowing his audience to feel comfortable with Eighner as a narrator.

However, regardless of how amiable Eighner tries to be with his readers, the fact is this: as a scavenger, he is much thriftier with what he has than the "consumer." He has come to appreciate his belongings more than the lavish consumer, who is unaware of how it feels to be homeless and has no apparent reason to be mindful with his property. Eighner stresses how wasteful the consumer truly is when he provides a laundry list of necessities that he acquired from Dumpsters — a list that includes a few luxury items as well: "Except for jeans, all my clothes came from Dumpsters. Boom boxes, candles, bedding, toilet paper, medicine, books, a typewriter, a virgin male love doll, change sometimes amounting to many dollars: I acquired many things from the Dumpsters" (para. 6). Such indulgences, Eighner reveals, as boom boxes, a typewriter, and even money are discarded for the "scavengers" to dig out of the Dumpsters. Eighner's powerful paradox — stating that he extracted the "necessities of life" from Dumpsters and then proceeding to list items that are not essential and yet are thrown away — imparts the lessons he learned without a roof over his head to the readers with a roof over theirs. Through this rhetorical strategy he encapsulates the profligate nature of the larger culture. Eighner hopes that, by giving such an astounding exposition, those spendthrifts who might be reading his essay will go forth and be less prodigal with their personal belongings.

Lars Eighner and his dog, Lizbeth, suffered a great deal on the streets, relying on the litter of others. While they were destitute of a home, however, they were not destitute of frugality. The opening seven paragraphs detail the misconceived gentler notions on Dumpster diving and provide a striking critique of society for the reader to mull over as he or she reads the rest of the essay. "On Dumpster Diving" is a life lesson to the extravagant users, misusers, and abusers of objects. The narrator Eighner had his home, his savings, and ultimately his lifestyle stripped away from him. The same can happen to anyone, especially to the person who takes his or her own life for granted. However, it is better to read about Eighner's experiences and alter one's ways than to undergo Eighner's experiences.

Questions

1. What are three minor changes in the revision?
2. What are three major changes in the revision?
3. Write a brief essay that discusses the changes made in this final draft in terms of content, rhetoric, and style and then evaluates the success of the revision.

Grammar as Rhetoric and Style
Short Simple Sentences and Fragments

Short Simple Sentences

A simple sentence, strictly defined, has a subject and verb: it consists of one independent clause. A simple sentence may have a compound subject, a compound verb, a modifier, and an object or a complement, but it still is one independent clause.

The following examples of simple sentences appear in Barbara Ehrenreich's "Serving in Florida."

> There is a problem, though.
> But the chances of this are minuscule.
> This must be Phillip's theory, anyway.
> Finally she tells me not to take her wrong.
> What had I been thinking?

Sometimes simple sentences can be rather long:

> The e-mails and phone messages addressed to my former self come from a distant race of people with exotic concerns and far too much time on their hands.

This example from Ehrenreich consists of twenty-eight words.

Sentence Fragments

A sentence fragment is an incomplete sentence, often the result of careless writing; an effective fragment, however, is an incomplete sentence that readers understand to be complete. Some fragments are missing a subject, a verb, or both; other fragments have a subject and verb but are dependent clauses. Consider the fragment in blue from Dubner and Levitt's "What the Bagel Man Saw."

> Despite all the attention paid to companies like Enron, academics know very little about the practicalities of white-collar crime. The reason? There aren't enough data.

This fragment, which asks a question, has neither a subject nor a verb. If we added a subject and verb to make it a complete sentence, it might read like this:

> Despite all the attention paid to companies like Enron, academics know very little about the practicalities of white-collar crime. And what is the reason for this? There aren't enough data.

Posing a question is a common use for fragments, but they can also be used to express doubt, surprise, shock, or perhaps outrage, as in this example from Fareed Zakaria:

> And in the Great Recession, it has been these middle-class folks who have been hammered. Why?

This one-word fragment, another question, has neither a subject nor a verb. If we added a subject and verb to make it a complete sentence, it might read like this:

> And in the Great Recession, it has been these middle-class folks who have been hammered. Why is this the case?

In the following example, Phyllis Rose poses a rhetorical question with a fragment:

> When a Solzhenitsyn rants about American materialism, I have to look at my digital Timex and check what year this is. Materialism?

Lest you think that fragments are more common to contemporary than classic writing, consider this example from Thoreau:

> When a man is warmed by the several modes which I have described, what does he want next? Surely not more warmth of the same kind, as more and richer food, larger and more splendid houses, finer and more abundant clothing, more numerous incessant and hotter fires, and the like.

Here the fragment is used not to ask, but to answer a rhetorical question. The missing subject, *he*, and verb, *would [not] want*, are understood. The fragment creates a sense of impatience that conveys Thoreau's tone of exasperation.

The following example from John Ruskin shows how fragments can provide both economy of expression and emphasis:

> And the duty of all these men is, on due occasion, to *die* for it.
> "On due occasion," namely:
>
> The Soldier, rather than leave his post in battle.
> The Physician, rather than leave his post in plague.
> The Pastor, rather than teach Falsehood.
> The lawyer, rather than countenance Injustice.

The antecedent of "it" is "every civilized nation." Rewritten as a complete sentence, the first fragment would read: "The due occasion for the soldier would be to die for his civilized nation rather than leave his post in battle." And so on for the others. (You will doubtless notice that "And so on for the others" is a fragment that we hope you will agree is deliberately and effectively used.)

Fragments also suggest the rhythm and patterns of natural speech. Read the following sentences from "The Case for Working with Your Hands," by Matthew B. Crawford, in which Crawford relates Fred's attempt to fix a starter motor.

> He spun the shaft that ran through the center of the motor, as I had. No problem: it spun freely. Then he hooked it up to a battery. It moved ever so slightly but wouldn't spin. He grasped the shaft, delicately, with three fingers, and tried to wiggle it side to side. "Too much free play," he said.

The first fragment delivers the natural mental response to the activity; the second one, quoted, delivers Fred's natural expression. "'There is too much free play,' he said," simply would not ring true.

Using Short Sentences Rhetorically

A series of simple sentences can become monotonous, but one or two short simple sentences can be rhetorically effective in a number of situations:

- after several long sentences
- as a summary of what the writer has just said
- as a transition between sentences or paragraphs

Essentially, one or two short simple sentences create emphasis by contrast. As a writer, when you juxtapose one or two short simple sentences with several longer ones, you call attention to the short simple ones. Consider this example from Dubner and Levitt:

A key fact of white-collar crime is that we hear about only the very slim fraction of people who are caught. Most embezzlers lead quiet and theoretically happy lives; employees who steal company property are rarely detected. With street crime, meanwhile, that is not the case. A mugging or a burglary or a murder is usually counted whether or not the criminal is caught. A street crime has a victim, who typically reports the crime to the police, which generates data, which in turn generate thousands of academic papers by criminologists, sociologists and economists. But white-collar crime presents no obvious victim. Whom, exactly, did the masters of Enron steal from? And how can you measure something if you don't know to whom it happened, or with what frequency, or in what magnitude?

Paul F.'s bagel business was different. It did present a victim. The victim was Paul F.

Notice how the short simple sentences of the second paragraph (each structured simply as subject + adjective, subject + direct object, and subject + complement) stand out after the longer sentences of the previous paragraph. Their similar structure adds even more emphasis.

In some instances, writers choose to use sentence fragments, especially short ones. Although most of the time you will avoid fragments, occasionally you might use one for effect. What's important is that you use the fragment as you would use a short simple sentence—*deliberately*, for a special reason:

- to make a transition
- to signal a conclusion
- to economize expression
- to emphasize an important point

A word of caution, however. Use both short simple sentences and fragments sparingly. Used intentionally and infrequently, both can be effective. Overused, they lose their punch or become more of a gimmick than a valuable technique. Also, consider whether your audience will interpret a fragment as a grammatical error. If you are confident that your audience will recognize your deliberate use of a fragment, then use it. But if you think your instructor or reader will assume you made a mistake, then it's better to write a complete sentence. Again, if you use fragments infrequently, then your audience is more likely to know you're deliberately choosing what is technically an incomplete sentence.

• EXERCISE 1 •

Identify the simple sentences in the following selection from "In the Strawberry Fields" by Eric Schlosser.

The few remaining labor camps for single men are grim places. I toured one that was a group of whitewashed buildings surrounded by chain-link fences and barbed wire. Desolate except for a rosebush in front of the manager's office, it looked like a holding pen or an old minimum-security prison. A nearby camp was reputed to be one of the best of its kind. Inside the barracks, the walls were freshly painted and the concrete floor was clean. A typical room was roughly twelve feet by ten feet, unheated, and occupied by four men. Sheets of plywood separated the steel cots. For $80 a week, a price far too high for most migrants, you got a bed and two meals a day. I've seen nicer horse barns.

Nevertheless, the labor camps are often preferable to the alternatives. When migrants stay in residential neighborhoods, they must pool their resources. In Watsonville three to four families will share a small house, seven or eight people to a room. Migrants routinely pay $100 to $200 a month to sleep in a garage with anywhere from four to ten other people. A survey of garages in Soledad found 1,500 inhabitants—a number roughly equal to one-eighth of the town's official population. At the peak of the harvest the housing shortage becomes acute. Migrants at the labor camps sometimes pay to sleep in parked cars. The newest migrant workers, who lack family in the area and haven't yet learned the ropes, often sleep outdoors in the wooded sections of Prunedale, trespassing, moving to a different hiding place each night. On hillsides above the Salinas Valley, hundreds of strawberry pickers have been found living in caves.

· EXERCISE 2 ·

Revise the selection in Exercise 1 by turning it into a series of short simple sentences. Then revise it again to eliminate the simple sentences entirely by turning every sentence into a compound, complex, or compound-complex sentence. How do your revisions change the effect? Read the original excerpt; then read your revisions aloud, and listen to the difference.

· EXERCISE 3 ·

Identify the short simple sentences and fragments in the following passage from "Shopping and Other Spiritual Adventures in America Today" by Phyllis Rose. Discuss their effect.

Someone told me about a Soviet émigré who practices English by declaiming, at random, sentences that catch his fancy. One of his favorites is, "Fifty percent off all items today only." Refugees from Communist countries appreciate our supermarkets and discount department stores for the wonders they are. An Eastern European scientist visiting Middletown wept when she first saw the meat counter at Waldbaum's. On the other hand, before her year in America was up, her pleasure turned sour. She wanted everything she saw. Her approach to consumer goods was insufficiently abstract, too materialistic. We Americans are beyond a simple, possessive materialism. We're used to abundance and the possibility of possessing things. The things, and the possibility of possessing them, will still be there next week, next year. So today we can walk the aisles calmly.

It is a misunderstanding of the American retail store to think we go there necessarily to buy. Some of us shop. There's a difference. Shopping has many purposes, the least interesting of which is to acquire new articles. We shop to cheer ourselves up. We shop to practice decision-making. We shop to be useful and productive members of our class and society. We shop to remind ourselves how much is available to us. We shop to remind ourselves how much is to be striven for. We shop to assert our superiority to the material objects that spread themselves before us.

Shopping's function as a form of therapy is widely appreciated. You don't really need, let's say, another sweater. You need the feeling of power that comes with buying or not buying it. You need the feeling that someone wants something you have — even if it's just your money. To get the benefit of shopping, you needn't actually purchase the sweater, any more than you have to marry every man you flirt with. In fact, window-shopping, like flirting, can be more rewarding, the same high without the distressing commitment, the material encumbrance. The purest form of shopping is provided by garage sales. A connoisseur goes out with no goal in mind, open to whatever may come his or her way, secure that it will cost very little. Minimum expense, maximum experience. Perfect shopping.

• EXERCISE 4 •

Find six examples of short simple sentences or fragments in the selections presented in this chapter. Explain their effect in the context of the paragraphs in which you find them.

Suggestions for Writing

The Economy

Now that you have examined a number of texts focusing on economics, explore one dimension of this topic by synthesizing your own ideas and those in the readings. You might want to do more research or use readings from other classes as you prepare for the following assignments.

1. In *The Souls of Black Folk* (1903), African American intellectual W. E. B. DuBois took Booker T. Washington to task. Acknowledging that Washington "stands as the one recognized spokesman of his ten million fellows and one of the most notable figures in a nation of seventy million," DuBois criticizes him for promoting "a gospel of Work and Money to such an extent as apparently almost completely to overshadow the higher aims of life." Read Chapter 3 of DuBois's *The Souls of Black Folk* called "Of Mr. Booker T. Washington and Others," and then explain whether you agree with Washington or DuBois. You might also want to read Dudley Randall's poem "Booker T. and W.E.B.," which captures and comments on the debate between Washington and DuBois. The selections by DuBois and Randall can both be found at bedfordstmartins.com/languageofcomp.

2. How has the economy been portrayed in popular culture, either in the past or today? You might consider films such as *Wall Street: Money Never Sleeps* (2010), *Inside Job* (2010), and *Margin Call* (2011), periodicals such as the *Onion*, or television programs such as *The Colbert Report*. Select one genre, such as movies, comedy shows, or cartoons. Do they extol the virtues of labor? Do they ennoble work? Do they satirize economics and economists? Explain using examples.

3. In *City of God*, St. Augustine tells the story of a pirate captured by Alexander the Great. "The Emperor asked him, 'How dare you molest the seas?' The pirate replied, 'How dare you molest the whole world? Because I do it with a small boat, I am called a pirate and a thief. You, with a great fleet, molest the world and are called an emperor.'" St. Augustine "approved of the pirate's response." In our time, there are many who bemoan the greed with which our financial system is riddled, while observing at the same time the punishments meted out to the poor for minor offenses. Consider the implications of the pirate's response and St. Augustine's thought. Write an essay in which you evaluate the application of the story to our nation's current economic situation, using the works presented in this chapter for support.

4. In "The Singer Solution to World Poverty" (p. 369), first published in the *New York Times Magazine* in 1999, philosopher and bioethicist Peter Singer writes,

"So how does my philosophy break down in dollars and cents? An American household with an income of $50,000 spends around $30,000 annually on necessities, according to the Conference Board, a nonprofit economic research organization. Therefore, for a household bringing in $50,000 a year, donations to help the world's poor should be as close as possible to $20,000. The $30,000 required for necessities holds for higher incomes as well. So a household making $100,000 a year could cut a yearly check for $70,000. Again, the formula is simple: whatever money you're spending on luxuries, not necessities, should be given away" (para. 22). What effect would Singer's solution have on the economy? Write a response to Singer in which you refer to the "*Forbes Price Index of Luxury Goods*" (p. 498) and at least two other selections from this chapter.

5. Write a response to Barbara Ehrenreich, Eric Schlosser, or Fareed Zakaria in the voice of a financially successful or powerful contemporary person, such as Donald Trump or Bill Gates. Indicate areas of common ground as well as disagreement.

6. John Ruskin, whom you have read in this chapter, wrote about duty and responsibility as those values relate to business. To what extent do his views relate to our contemporary economy? Focus on both the microeconomic and macroeconomic implications.

7. In "The Arts of Selling," one of the essays in *Brave New World Revisited* (1958), Aldous Huxley, author of the dystopian novel *Brave New World*, wrote about advertising. Read the following paragraph from that work, and compare Huxley's ideas with those presented in John Kenneth Galbraith's contemporaneous piece, "The Dependence Effect." Write an essay in which you compare the two and evaluate which one comments more cogently and eloquently on our nation's economy. Refer to at least two other selections in this chapter for support.

> Effective rational propaganda becomes possible only when there is a clear understanding, on the part of all concerned, of the nature of symbols and of their relations to the things and events symbolized. Irrational propaganda depends for its effectiveness on the general failure to understand the nature of symbols. Simpleminded people tend to equate the symbol with what it stands for, to attribute to things and events some of the qualities expressed by the words in terms of which the propagandist has chosen, for his own purposes, to talk about them. Consider a simple example. Most cosmetics are made of lanolin, which is a mixture of purified wool fat and water beaten up into an emulsion. This emulsion has many valuable properties: it penetrates the skin, it does not become rancid, it is mildly antiseptic and so forth. But the commercial propagandists do not speak about the genuine virtues of the emulsion. They give it some picturesquely voluptuous name, talk ecstatically and misleadingly about feminine beauty and show pictures of gorgeous blondes nourishing their tissues with skin food. "The cosmetic

manufacturers," one of their number has written, "are not selling lanolin, they are selling hope." For this hope, this fraudulent implication of a promise that they will be transfigured, women will pay ten or twenty times the value of the emulsion which the propagandists have so skillfully related, by means of misleading symbols, to a deep-seated and almost universal feminine wish — the wish to be more attractive to members of the opposite sex. The principles underlying this kind of propaganda are extremely simple. Find some common desire, some widespread unconscious fear or anxiety; think out some way to relate this wish or fear to the product you have to sell; then build a bridge of verbal or pictorial symbols over which your customer can pass from fact to compensatory dream, and from the dream to the illusion that your product, when purchased, will make the dream come true. "We no longer buy oranges, we buy vitality. We do not buy just an auto, we buy prestige." And so with all the rest. In toothpaste, for example, we buy, not a mere cleanser and antiseptic, but release from the fear of being sexually repulsive. In vodka and whisky we are not buying a protoplasmic poison which, in small doses, may depress the nervous system in a psychologically valuable way; we are buying friendliness and good fellowship, the warmth of Dingley Dell and the brilliance of the Mermaid Tavern. With our laxatives we buy the health of a Greek god, the radiance of one of Diana's nymphs. With the monthly best seller we acquire culture, the envy of our less literate neighbors and the respect of the sophisticated. In every case the motivation analyst has found some deep-seated wish or fear, whose energy can be used to move the customer to part with cash and so, indirectly, to turn the wheels of industry. Stored in the minds and bodies of countless individuals, this potential energy is released by, and transmitted along, a line of symbols carefully laid out so as to bypass rationality and obscure the real issue.

8. Write an argument defending or challenging the large salaries paid to athletes, movie stars, or corporate executives. Develop a logical argument with clearly drawn reasons — or write your response as a satire.

9. In the following excerpts, Adam Smith and Henry David Thoreau consider price and cost as features of economy. Write an essay in which you compare the two and evaluate which speaks more accurately and eloquently to our time. In your essay, refer to at least three of the selections presented in this chapter as support.

> The real price of everything, what everything is really worth to the man who has acquired it, and who wants to dispose of it or exchange for something else, is the toil and trouble which it can save for himself, and which it can impose on other people.
>
> —ADAM SMITH, *The Wealth of Nations*, 1776

> If it is asserted that civilization is a real advance on the condition of man, — and I think that it is, though only the wise improve their advantages, — it must

be shown that it has produced better dwellings without making them more costly; and the cost of a thing is the amount of what I will call life which is required to be exchanged for it, immediately or in the long run.

— HENRY DAVID THOREAU, *Walden*, 1854

10. Which of the following quotations most accurately captures your attitude toward work and the economy? Write an essay about why the quotation speaks to you. In your essay, refer to the selections presented in this chapter.

- Never work just for money or for power. They won't save your soul or help you sleep at night.

— MARIAN WRIGHT EDELMAN

- Work for something because it is good, not just because it stands a chance to succeed.

— VACLAV HAVEL

- There is no way of keeping profits up but by keeping wages down.

— DAVID RICARDO

- Every man is rich or poor according to the degree to which he can afford the necessaries, conveniences, and amusements of human life.

— ADAM SMITH

- It is easier for a camel to pass through the eye of a needle, than for a rich man to enter into the kingdom of God.

— MATTHEW 19:24

- Capital is dead labor that, vampire-like, lives only by sucking living labor, and lives the more, the more labor it sucks.

— KARL MARX

- I am opposed to millionaires, but it would be dangerous to offer me the position.

— MARK TWAIN

- I'd like to live as a poor man with lots of money.

— PABLO PICASSO

Gender

What is the impact of the gender roles that society creates and enforces?

"Why can't a woman be more like a man?" asks the exasperated Henry Higgins in *My Fair Lady* when he fails to understand his indomitable pupil, Eliza Doolittle. Why, indeed! The question of gender differences and roles has baffled and angered us, delighted and confused us.

What is the distinction between sex and gender? The former refers to biological identity; the latter has come to mean behavior that is learned. Some "socially constructed" gender roles result from beliefs about the proper way to behave. When do gender roles become stereotypes of what it means to be a woman or a man? These ideas vary according to culture and time. A look at men in the eighteenth century wearing wigs of curls tells us that what is considered appropriate in one context is wholly inappropriate in another.

What other forces define gender roles? How does ethnicity contribute to the expectations of what is masculine or feminine behavior? How does setting—a small town, an athletic field, a formal dinner—affect a group's expectations?

Such issues take on even greater importance in the context of bias. When do socially constructed roles hinder individual expression or choice? Why are certain professions dominated by men and others by women? How do beliefs about sex or gender affect public policy, including education?

These are the questions taken up in this chapter, starting with an exploration into what "scientific evidence" has been marshaled to "prove" the intellectual superiority of men over women. Other selections focus on the social pressure to behave "like a man" and the communication differences between men and women. The serious economic and even medical consequences of beliefs about gender are also considered.

The fictional Professor Higgins was, in fact, asking a rhetorical question, but the authors presented in this chapter answer his question in specific and provocative ways that are bound to challenge—and deepen—our thinking about gender roles.

Women's Brains

STEPHEN JAY GOULD

Paleontologist and evolutionary biologist Stephen Jay Gould (1941–2002) was a professor of geology and zoology at Harvard University from 1967 until his death. His major scientific work was the theory of punctuated equilibrium, a theory of evolutionary biology that builds on the work of Charles Darwin by suggesting that evolution occurs sporadically, rather than gradually over a long period of time. Gould is the author of numerous scientific texts, including *The Mismeasure of Man* (1981); *Wonderful Life: The Burgess Shale and the Nature of History* (1989); his magnum opus, *The Structure of Evolutionary Theory* (2002); and *The Hedgehog, the Fox, and the Magister's Pox: Mending the Gap between Science and the Humanities* (2003). Gould also wrote for a more general audience in his column in *Natural History*, where the following essay originally appeared in 1980.

In the Prelude to *Middlemarch*, George Eliot lamented the unfulfilled lives of talented women:

> Some have felt that these blundering lives are due to the inconvenient indefiniteness with which the Supreme Power has fashioned the natures of women: if there were one level of feminine incompetence as strict as the ability to count three and no more, the social lot of women might be treated with scientific certitude.

Eliot goes on to discount the idea of innate limitation, but while she wrote in 1872, the leaders of European anthropometry were trying to measure "with scientific certitude" the inferiority of women. Anthropometry, or measurement of the human body, is not so fashionable a field these days, but it dominated the human sciences for much of the nineteenth century and remained popular until intelligence testing replaced skull measurement as a favored device for making invidious comparisons among races, classes, and sexes. Craniometry, or measurement of the skull, commanded the most attention and respect. Its unquestioned leader, Paul Broca (1824–80), professor of clinical surgery at the Faculty of Medicine in Paris, gathered a school of disciples and imitators around himself. Their work, so meticulous and apparently irrefutable, exerted great influence and won high esteem as a jewel of nineteenth-century science.

Broca's work seemed particularly invulnerable to refutation. Had he not measured with the most scrupulous care and accuracy? (Indeed, he had. I have the greatest respect for Broca's meticulous procedure. His numbers are sound. But science is an inferential exercise, not a catalog of facts. Numbers, by themselves, specify nothing. All depends upon what you do with them.) Broca depicted himself as an apostle of objectivity, a man who bowed before facts and cast aside superstition and sentimentality. He declared that "there is no faith, however respectable, no interest, however legitimate, which must not accommodate itself to the progress of human knowledge and bend before truth." Women, like it or not, had smaller brains than men and, therefore, could not equal them in intelligence. This fact, Broca argued, may reinforce a common prejudice in male society, but it is also a scientific truth. L. Manouvrier, a black sheep in Broca's fold, rejected the inferiority of women and wrote with feeling about the burden imposed upon them by Broca's numbers:

> Women displayed their talents and their diplomas. They also invoked philosophical authorities. But they were opposed by *numbers* unknown to Condorcet or to John Stuart Mill. These numbers fell upon poor women like a sledge hammer, and they were accompanied by commentaries and sarcasms more ferocious than the most misogynist imprecations of certain church fathers. The theologians had asked if women had a soul. Several centuries later, some scientists were ready to refuse them a human intelligence.

Broca's argument rested upon two sets of data: the larger brains of men in modern societies, and a supposed increase in male superiority through time. His most extensive data came from autopsies performed personally in four Parisian hospitals. For 292 male brains, he calculated an average weight of 1,325 grams; 140 female brains averaged 1,144 grams for a difference of 181 grams, or 14 percent of the male weight. Broca understood, of course, that part of this difference could be attributed to the greater height of males. Yet he made no attempt to measure the effect of size alone and actually stated that it cannot account for the entire difference because we know, a priori, that women are not as intelligent as men (a premise that the data were supposed to test, not rest upon):

> We might ask if the small size of the female brain depends exclusively upon the small size of her body. Tiedemann has proposed this explanation. But we must not forget that women are, on the average, a little less intelligent than men, a difference which we should not exaggerate but which is, nonetheless, real. We are therefore permitted to suppose that the relatively small size of the female brain depends in part upon her physical inferiority and in part upon her intellectual inferiority.

In 1873, the year after Eliot published *Middlemarch*, Broca measured the cranial capacities of prehistoric skulls from L'Homme Mort cave. Here he found a difference of only 99.5 cubic centimeters between males and females, while modern populations range from 129.5 to 220.7. Topinard, Broca's chief disciple, explained the increasing discrepancy through time as a result of differing evolutionary pressures upon dominant men and passive women:

> The man who fights for two or more in the struggle for existence, who has all the responsibility and the cares of tomorrow, who is constantly active in combating the environment and human rivals, needs more brain than the woman whom he must protect and

5

nourish, the sedentary woman, lacking any interior occupations, whose role is to raise children, love, and be passive.

In 1879, Gustave Le Bon, chief misogynist of Broca's school, used these data to publish what must be the most vicious attack upon women in modern scientific literature (no one can top Aristotle). I do not claim his views were representative of Broca's school, but they were published in France's most respected anthropological journal. Le Bon concluded:

> In the most intelligent races, as among the Parisians, there are a large number of women whose brains are closer in size to those of gorillas than to the most developed male brains. This inferiority is so obvious that no one can contest it for a moment; only its degree is worth discussion. All psychologists who have studied the intelligence of women, as well as poets and novelists, recognize today that they represent the most inferior forms of human evolution and that they are closer to children and savages than to an adult, civilized man. They excel in fickleness, inconstancy, absence of thought and logic, and incapacity to reason. Without doubt there exist some distinguished women, very superior to the average man, but they are as exceptional as the birth of any monstrosity, as, for example, of a gorilla with two heads; consequently, we may neglect them entirely.

Nor did Le Bon shrink from the social implications of his views. He was horrified by the proposal of some American reformers to grant women higher education on the same basis as men:

> A desire to give them the same education, and, as a consequence, to propose the same goals for them, is a dangerous chimera. . . . The day when, misunderstanding the inferior occupations which nature has given her, women leave the home and take part in our battles; on this day a social revolution will begin, and everything that maintains the sacred ties of the family will disappear.

Sound familiar?[1]

I have reexamined Broca's data, the basis for all this derivative pronouncement, and I find his numbers sound but his interpretation ill-founded, to say the least. The data supporting his claim for increased difference through time can be easily dismissed. Broca based his contention on the samples from L'Homme Mort alone—only seven male and six female skulls in all. Never have so little data yielded such far-ranging conclusions.

In 1888, Topinard published Broca's more extensive data on the Parisian hospitals. Since Broca recorded height and age as well as brain size, we may use modern statistics to remove their effect. Brain weight decreases with age, and Broca's women were, on average, considerably older than his men. Brain weight increases

---

[1]When I wrote this essay, I assumed that Le Bon was a marginal, if colorful, figure. I have since learned that he was a leading scientist, one of the founders of social psychology, and best known for a seminal study on crowd behavior, still cited today (*La psychologie des foules*, 1895), and for his work on unconscious motivation.

with height, and his average man was almost half a foot taller than his average woman. I used multiple regression, a technique that allowed me to assess simultaneously the influence of height and age upon brain size. In an analysis of the data for women, I found that, at average male height and age, a woman's brain would weigh 1,212 grams. Correction for height and age reduces Broca's measured difference of 181 grams by more than a third, to 113 grams.

I don't know what to make of this remaining difference because I cannot assess other factors known to influence brain size in a major way. Cause of death has an important effect: degenerative disease often entails a substantial diminution of brain size. (This effect is separate from the decrease attributed to age alone.) Eugene Schreider, also working with Broca's data, found that men killed in accidents had brains weighing, on average, 60 grams more than men dying of infectious diseases. The best modern data I can find (from American hospitals) records a full 100-gram difference between death by degenerative arteriosclerosis and by violence or accident. Since so many of Broca's subjects were very elderly women, we may assume that lengthy degenerative disease was more common among them than among the men.

More importantly, modern students of brain size still have not agreed on a proper measure for eliminating the powerful effect of body size. Height is partly adequate, but men and women of the same height do not share the same body build. Weight is even worse than height, because most of its variation reflects nutrition rather than intrinsic size—fat versus skinny exerts little influence upon the brain. Manouvrier took up this subject in the 1880s and argued that muscular mass and force should be used. He tried to measure this elusive property in various ways and found a marked difference in favor of men, even in men and women of the same height. When he corrected for what he called "sexual mass," women actually came out slightly ahead in brain size.

Thus, the corrected 113-gram difference is surely too large; the true figure is probably close to zero and may as well favor women as men. And 113 grams, by the way, is exactly the average difference between a 5 foot 4 inch and a 6 foot 4 inch male in Broca's data. We would not (especially us short folks) want to ascribe greater intelligence to tall men. In short, who knows what to do with Broca's data? They certainly don't permit any confident claim that men have bigger brains than women.

To appreciate the social role of Broca and his school, we must recognize that his statements about the brains of women do not reflect an isolated prejudice toward a single disadvantaged group. They must be weighed in the context of a general theory that supported contemporary social distinctions as biologically ordained. Women, blacks, and poor people suffered the same disparagement, but women bore the brunt of Broca's argument because he had easier access to data on women's brains. Women were singularly denigrated but they also stood as surrogates for other disenfranchised groups. As one of Broca's disciples wrote in 1881: "Men of the black races have a brain scarcely heavier than that of white women." This juxtaposition extended into many other realms of anthropological argument, particularly to claims that, anatomically and emotionally, both women and blacks were like white children—and that white children, by the theory of recapitulation, represented an ancestral (primitive) adult stage of human evolution. I do not regard as empty rhetoric the claim that women's battles are for all of us.

Maria Montessori did not confine her activities to educational reform for young children. She lectured on anthropology for several years at the University of Rome, and wrote an influential book entitled *Pedagogical Anthropology* (English edition, 1913). Montessori was no egalitarian. She supported most of Broca's work and the theory of innate criminality proposed by her compatriot Cesare Lombroso. She measured the circumference of children's heads in her schools and inferred that the best prospects had bigger brains. But she had no use for Broca's conclusions about women. She discussed Manouvrier's work at length and made much of his tentative claim that women, after proper correction of the data, had slightly larger brains than men. Women, she concluded, were intellectually superior, but men had prevailed heretofore by dint of physical force. Since technology has abolished force as an instrument of power, the era of women may soon be upon us: "In such an epoch there will really be superior human beings, there will really be men strong in morality and in sentiment. Perhaps in this way the reign of women is approaching, when the enigma of her anthropological superiority will be deciphered. Woman was always the custodian of human sentiment, morality and honor."

This represents one possible antidote to "scientific" claims for the constitutional inferiority of certain groups. One may affirm the validity of biological distinctions but argue that the data have been misinterpreted by prejudiced men with a stake in the outcome, and that disadvantaged groups are truly superior. In recent years, Elaine Morgan has followed this strategy in her *Descent of Woman*, a speculative reconstruction of human prehistory from the woman's point of view—and as farcical as more famous tall tales by and for men. 15

I prefer another strategy. Montessori and Morgan followed Broca's philosophy to reach a more congenial conclusion. I would rather label the whole enterprise of setting a biological value upon groups for what it is: irrelevant and highly injurious. George Eliot well appreciated the special tragedy that biological labeling imposed upon members of disadvantaged groups. She expressed it for people like herself—women of extraordinary talent. I would apply it more widely—not only to those whose dreams are flouted but also to those who never realize that they may dream—but I cannot match her prose. In conclusion, then, the rest of Eliot's prelude to *Middlemarch*:

> The limits of variation are really much wider than anyone would imagine from the sameness of women's coiffure and the favorite love stories in prose and verse. Here and there a cygnet is reared uneasily among the ducklings in the brown pond, and never finds the living stream in fellowship with its own oary-footed kind. Here and there is born a Saint Theresa, foundress of nothing, whose loving heartbeats and sobs after an unattained goodness tremble off and are dispersed among hindrances instead of centering in some long-recognizable deed.

Questions for Discussion

1. Stephen Jay Gould's argument focuses on research about women's brain size, but — more important — what does he say about the nature of scientific inquiry — that is, about how scientists think?

2. What does Gould mean when he says, "Women were singularly denigrated but they also stood as surrogates for other disenfranchised groups" (para. 13)?

3. Why does Gould say, "I do not regard as empty rhetoric the claim that women's battles are for all of us" (para. 13)? Is he being patronizing? Does such a personal comment undermine his scientific credibility? Explain.

4. Gould's essay was published in 1980, and it centers on research conducted a century before that. What case can you make that Gould's true subject was not women but assumptions about the abilities of certain groups?

5. Would individuals accustomed to scientific texts have an easier time reading this essay? Why or why not? How do your own experience and prior knowledge of a topic affect your reading process?

Questions on Rhetoric and Style

1. What purposes do the quotations in this essay from George Eliot's novel *Middlemarch* serve? Why does Gould, when introducing the quotation from Broca in paragraph 5, refer to Eliot? Why are quotations from Eliot, whose real name was Mary Anne Evans, especially appropriate for Gould's essay?

2. In paragraph 3, Gould states, "I have the greatest respect for Broca's meticulous procedure. His numbers are sound." Despite this praise, Gould goes on to refute Broca's findings. What vulnerability does Gould find in Broca's conclusions? Does Gould's praise of Broca strengthen or weaken his own argument? Explain.

3. Gould builds two parallel arguments: one on scientific method, another on speculative conclusions. In which passages does he question the scientific method(s) rather than the findings themselves? How does Gould weave these sources together in order to make his own point?

4. How does each of the individuals Gould cites — Paul Broca, L. Manouvrier, Gustave Le Bon, and Maria Montessori — contribute to the development of his argument? Does each make a separate point, or do they reinforce one another? Could Gould have eliminated any of them without damaging his argument? Explain your reasoning.

5. At the end of paragraph 7, Gould adds a footnote reassessing an earlier point. Does this admission add or detract from his credibility?

6. Paragraphs 9 through 12 work as a unit to develop a single point that is integral to the overall essay. What is this point? How do paragraphs 9–12 develop the point?

7. In paragraph 13, Gould shows how Broca and his colleagues extended their conclusions to other groups. What is Gould's purpose in developing this point as elaborately as he does?

8. Why is questioning Maria Montessori's research and conclusions an effective strategy? What criticism might Gould be guarding against in doing so?

9. In the final two paragraphs, how does Gould bring together both of his arguments—that is, his argument against the actual scientific research and his argument about the conclusions drawn from that research?

10. This essay has a strong appeal to logos, as would be expected of a scientific argument. How does Gould also appeal to pathos? How does that appeal add to the persuasiveness of his argument?

11. Most of the time Gould writes in the third person, but he uses first person occasionally. Explain why you think those shifts strengthen or weaken the essay.

12. How would you characterize the audience for whom Gould is writing? Do you think fellow scientists are among them? Explain why or why not.

Suggestions for Writing

1. In paragraph 3, Gould asserts that "[n]umbers, by themselves, specify nothing. All depends upon what you do with them." Support, challenge, or qualify Gould's assertion by referring to statistics used in science, politics, economics, sports, or another applicable field.

2. Find an essay written for a specialized audience (for example, an essay about technology in a scientific journal or a computer magazine). Rewrite it for a more general audience.

3. In paragraph 13, Gould refers to "a general theory that supported contemporary social distinctions as biologically ordained" in the late nineteenth century. In the twenty-first century, many continue to argue for nature over nurture—that is, for biology rather than socialization—as the causal agent for skills and talents of specific groups of people. Write an essay explaining whether you believe heredity or environment is the principal determinant of human characteristics. You may use yourself as an example and may cite Gould's essay, but you should also do research in other sources to explore how the nature-nurture debate has fared in particular historical contexts.

4. Write an essay using scientific data to develop an argument that has ethical or social implications. For example, use statistical data to make (a) a case about the impact of global warming or (b) a proposal to address what is being called the obesity epidemic in the United States. Frame the essay with a quotation (as Gould does), a description, or an anecdote.

5. Consider another myth or stereotype about women based on biology that has prevailed at some point in history—perhaps one that continues to have some credibility, such as women are more emotional, more intuitive, better at child care, or worse at math and science. Write an argument challenging the myth by using scientific evidence.

Professions for Women

Virginia Woolf

 A prolific novelist, critic, and essayist, Virginia Woolf was born in London in 1882. Her novels, particularly *Mrs. Dalloway* (1925) and *To the Lighthouse* (1927), are renowned for their penetrating psychological insight. Her novels are known for their use of interior monologue, or stream of consciousness. Woolf is also noted for her nonfiction, especially for such works as *The Common Reader* (1925), *A Room of One's Own* (1929), and *Three Guineas* (1938). Having struggled with mental illness for much of her life, she drowned herself in 1941. "Professions for Women," delivered as a talk in 1931 to the Women's Service League, was included in *Death of a Moth and Other Essays* (1942).

When your secretary invited me to come here, she told me that your Society is concerned with the employment of women and she suggested that I might tell you something about my own professional experiences. It is true I am a woman; it is true I am employed; but what professional experiences have I had? It is difficult to say. My profession is literature; and in that profession there are fewer experiences for women than in any other, with the exception of the stage — fewer, I mean, that are peculiar to women. For the road was cut many years ago — by Fanny Burney, by Aphra Behn, by Harriet Martineau, by Jane Austen, by George Eliot — many famous women, and many more unknown and forgotten, have been before me, making the path smooth, and regulating my steps. Thus, when I came to write, there were very few material obstacles in my way. Writing was a reputable and harmless occupation. The family peace was not broken by the scratching of a pen. No demand was made upon the family purse. For ten and sixpence one can buy paper enough to write all the plays of Shakespeare — if one has a mind that way. Pianos and models, Paris, Vienna and Berlin, masters and mistresses, are not needed by a writer. The cheapness of writing paper is, of course, the reason why women have succeeded as writers before they have succeeded in the other professions.

But to tell you my story — it is a simple one. You have only got to figure to yourselves a girl in a bedroom with a pen in her hand. She had only to move that pen from left to right — from ten o'clock to one. Then it occurred to her to do what is simple and cheap enough after all — to slip a few of those pages into an envelope, fix a penny stamp in the corner, and drop the envelope into the red box at the corner. It was thus that I became a journalist; and my effort was rewarded on the first day of the following month — a very glorious day it was for me — by a letter from an editor containing a cheque for one pound ten shillings and sixpence. But to show you how little I deserve to be called a professional woman, how little I know of the struggles and difficulties of such lives, I have to admit that instead of spending that sum upon bread and butter, rent, shoes and stockings, or butcher's bills, I went out and bought a cat—a beautiful cat, a Persian cat, which very soon involved me in bitter disputes with my neighbours.

What could be easier than to write articles and to buy Persian cats with the profits? But wait a moment. Articles have to be about something. Mine, I seem to remember, was about a novel by a famous man. And while I was writing this review, I discovered that if I were going to review books I should need to do battle with a certain phantom. And the phantom was a woman, and when I came to know her better I called her after the heroine of a famous poem, The Angel in the House.[1] It was she who used to come between me and my paper when I was writing reviews. It was she who bothered me and wasted my time and so tormented me that at last I killed her. You who come of a younger and happier generation may not have heard of her—you may not know what I mean by the Angel in the House. I will describe her as shortly as I can. She was intensely sympathetic. She was immensely charming. She was utterly unselfish. She excelled in the difficult arts of family life. She sacrificed herself daily. If there was chicken, she took the leg; if there was a draught she sat in it—in short she was so constituted that she never had a mind or a wish of her own, but preferred to sympathize always with the minds and wishes of others. Above all—I need not say it—she was pure. Her purity was supposed to be her chief beauty—her blushes, her great grace. In those days—the last of Queen Victoria—every house had its Angel. And when I came to write I encountered her with the very first words. The shadow of her wings fell on my page; I heard the rustling of her skirts in the room. Directly, that is to say, I took my pen in my hand to review that novel by a famous man, she slipped behind me and whispered: "My dear, you are a young woman. You are writing about a book that has been written by a man. Be sympathetic; be tender; flatter; deceive; use all the arts and wiles of our sex. Never let anybody guess that you have a mind of your own. Above all, be pure." And she made as if to guide my pen. I now record the one act for which I take some credit to myself, though the credit rightly belongs to some excellent ancestors of mine who left me a certain sum of money—shall we say five hundred pounds a year?—so that it was not necessary for me to depend solely on charm for my living. I turned upon her and caught her by the throat. I did my best to kill her. My excuse, if I were to be had up in a court of law, would be that I acted in self-defence. Had I not killed her she would have killed me. She would have plucked the heart out of my writing. For, as I found, directly I put pen to paper, you cannot review even a novel without having a mind of your own, without expressing what you think to be the truth about human relations, morality, sex. And all these questions, according to the Angel of the House, cannot be dealt

---

[1] "The Angel in the House" is a nineteenth-century poem about a self-sacrificing heroine; for many, she represented the ideal Victorian woman.—Eds.

with freely and openly by women; they must charm, they must conciliate, they must — to put it bluntly — tell lies if they are to succeed. Thus, whenever I felt the shadow of her wing or the radiance of her halo upon my page, I took up the inkpot and flung it at her. She died hard. Her fictitious nature was of great assistance to her. It is far harder to kill a phantom than a reality. She was always creeping back when I thought I had despatched her. Though I flatter myself that I killed her in the end, the struggle was severe; it took much time that had better have been spent upon learning Greek grammar; or in roaming the world in search of adventures. But it was a real experience; it was an experience that was found to befall all women writers at that time. Killing the Angel in the House was part of the occupation of a woman writer.

But to continue my story. The Angel was dead; what then remained? You may say that what remained was a simple and common object — a young woman in a bedroom with an inkpot. In other words, now that she had rid herself of falsehood, that young woman had only to be herself. Ah, but what is "herself"? I mean, what is a woman? I assure you, I do not know. I do not believe that you know. I do not believe that anybody can know until she has expressed herself in all the arts and professions open to human skill. That indeed is one of the reasons why I have come here — out of respect for you, who are in process of showing us by your experiments what a woman is, who are in process of providing us, by your failures and successes, with that extremely important piece of information.

But to continue the story of my professional experiences. I made one pound ten and six by my first review; and I bought a Persian cat with the proceeds. Then I grew ambitious. A Persian cat is all very well, I said; but a Persian cat is not enough. I must have a motor car. And it was thus that I became a novelist — for it is a very strange thing that people will give you a motor car if you will tell them a story. It is a still stranger thing that there is nothing so delightful in the world as telling stories. It is far pleasanter than writing reviews of famous novels. And yet, if I am to obey your secretary and tell you my professional experiences as a novelist, I must tell you about a very strange experience that befell me as a novelist. And to understand it you must try first to imagine a novelist's state of mind. I hope I am not giving away professional secrets if I say that a novelist's chief desire is to be as unconscious as possible. He has to induce in himself a state of perpetual lethargy. He wants life to proceed with the utmost quiet and regularity. He wants to see the same faces, to read the same books, to do the same things day after day, month after month, while he is writing, so that nothing may break the illusion in which he is living — so that nothing may disturb or disquiet the mysterious nosings about, feelings round, darts, dashes and sudden discoveries of that very shy and illusive spirit, the imagination. I suspect that this state is the same both for men and women. Be that as it may, I want you to imagine me writing a novel in a state of trance. I want you to figure to yourselves a girl sitting with a pen in her hand, which for minutes, and indeed for hours, she never dips into the inkpot. The image that comes to my mind when I think of this girl is the image of a fisherman lying sunk in dreams on the verge of a deep lake with a rod held out over the water. She was letting her imagination sweep unchecked round every rock and cranny of the world that lies submerged in the depths of our unconscious being. Now came the experience, the experience that I believe to be far commoner with women writers than with men. The line raced through the girl's fingers. Her imagination had rushed away. It had sought the pools, the depths, the dark places where the largest fish slumber. And then there was a smash. There was an explosion. There was foam and confusion. The imagination had dashed itself against something hard. The girl was roused from her dream. She was indeed in a state of the most acute and difficult distress. To speak without figure she had thought of something, something about the body, about the passions which it was unfitting for her as a woman to say. Men, her reason told her, would be shocked. The consciousness of what men will say of a woman who speaks the truth about her passions had roused her from her artist's state of unconsciousness. She could write no more. The trance was over. Her imagination could work no longer. This I believe to be a very common experience with women writers—they are impeded by the extreme conventionality of the other sex. For though men sensibly allow themselves great freedom in these respects, I doubt that they realize or can control the extreme severity with which they condemn such freedom in women.

These then were two very genuine experiences of my own. These were two of the adventures of my professional life. The first—killing the Angel in the House—I think I solved. She died. But the second, telling the truth about my own experiences as a body, I do not think I solved. I doubt that any woman has solved it yet. The obstacles against her are still immensely powerful—and yet they are very difficult to define. Outwardly, what is simpler than to write books? Outwardly, what obstacles are there for a woman rather than for a man? Inwardly, I think, the case is very different; she has still many ghosts to fight, many prejudices to overcome. Indeed it will be a long time still, I think, before a woman can sit down to write a book without finding a phantom to be slain, a rock to be dashed against. And if this is so in literature, the freest of all professions for women, how is it in the new professions which you are now for the first time entering?

Those are the questions that I should like, had I time, to ask you. And indeed, if I have laid stress upon these professional experiences of mine, it is because I believe that they are, though in different forms, yours also. Even when the path is nominally open—when there is nothing to prevent a woman from being a doctor, a lawyer, a civil servant—there are many phantoms and obstacles, as I believe, looming in her way. To discuss and define them is I think of great value and importance; for thus only can the labour be shared, the difficulties be solved. But besides this, it is necessary also to discuss the ends and the aims for which we are fighting, for which we are doing battle with these formidable obstacles. Those aims cannot be taken for granted; they must be perpetually questioned and examined. The whole position, as I see it—here in this hall surrounded by women practising for the first time in history I know not how many different professions—is one of extraordinary interest and importance. You have won rooms of your own in the house hitherto exclusively owned by men. You are able, though not without great labour and effort, to pay the rent. You are earning your five hundred pounds a year. But this freedom is only a beginning; the room is your own, but it is still bare. It has to be furnished; it has to be decorated; it has to be shared. How are you going to furnish it, how are you going to decorate it? With whom are you going to share it, and upon what terms? These, I think, are questions of the utmost importance and interest. For the first time in history you are able to ask them; for the first time you are able to decide for yourselves what the answers should be. Willingly would I stay and discuss those questions and answers—but not tonight. My time is up; and I must cease.

Questions for Discussion

1. According to Virginia Woolf, what are the two main obstacles to women's professional identity? Are these still the two main obstacles, or does the contemporary woman face different hurdles? Explain.

2. Research the origin of "The Angel in the House" (para. 3). Why is this an appropriate or effective frame of reference for Woolf?

3. What do you think Woolf means in paragraph 5 when she asserts that "a novelist's chief desire is to be as unconscious as possible"? Do you agree that someone who writes fiction should be "unconscious"? Why do you think a novelist would want to be "unconscious" or would benefit from being "unconscious"?

4. In paragraphs 5 and 6, Woolf explores the consequences of being unable to tell "the truth" about her own "experiences as a body." What does she mean? Why does she believe that surmounting this obstacle is more difficult—perhaps impossible at the time she was writing—than "killing the Angel in the House"?

5. In her final paragraph, Woolf apologizes to a certain extent for dwelling on her own experience, and then points out that her "professional experiences . . . are, though in different forms," also the experiences of her audience. What exactly is she asking of her audience here?

6. In an online essay, Barbara Wahl Ledingham makes the following assertion about the relevance of Woolf's essay to women in the twenty-first century:

> We must claim and have knowledge of our feminists, our artists, our mothers, our leaders, and our organizers, women like Susan B. Anthony . . . or Margaret Sanger. . . . All of these women acted despite persecution. Their sacrifice is responsible for many of the rights we take for granted today, but the biggest challenge is confronting our own Angel in the House, our own inner phantom, the one that keeps us from . . . defining and owning our own lives.
>
> With a kind of uncanny prescience, Woolf's words follow us seventy years later, haunting us with their veracity and timelessness. They are a gauge by which to measure not only our exterior accomplishments but also our inner state, and they serve as a warning not to lose consciousness or become apathetic about either realm.

After summarizing what Ledingham is saying, explain why you agree or disagree with her analysis.

Questions on Rhetoric and Style

1. How does Woolf present herself in the opening paragraph? What relationship is she establishing with her audience?
2. Identify an example in the opening paragraph of each of the following, and explain its effect: understatement, parallel structure, rhetorical question, irony, and metonymy.
3. What is the effect of the personal anecdote in paragraph 2? Does the anecdote appeal mainly to logos or pathos? Why is it especially effective for Woolf's audience?
4. What does Woolf mean in the following description of the Angel in the House: "The shadow of her wings fell on my page; I heard the rustling of her skirts in the room" (para. 3)?
5. Discuss the effect of the short, simple sentences that Woolf uses in paragraph 3. How do they contribute to her tone as she describes the Angel in the House?
6. In paragraph 3, Woolf tells how she did her "best to kill [the Angel in the House]." Examine the words and images she uses to describe this act. Do you believe the violence of her descriptions to be appropriate? Explain why or why not.
7. How does the shift in person in paragraph 4 serve Woolf's purpose? In what ways is this a transitional paragraph?
8. What is the effect in paragraph 5 of Woolf's referring to a novelist as *he*? Should Woolf have used *she* as though she were referring to herself? Why or why not?
9. Summarize the extended analogy Woolf develops in paragraph 5 to describe "a girl sitting with a pen in her hand." Explain its effect.
10. Would you characterize the language at the end of paragraph 5, where Woolf writes about "the body," to be delicate and genteel or euphemistic? Explain, keeping in mind the historical context of the work.
11. By the time of this speech, Woolf's extended essay *A Room of One's Own* was well known as a feminist manifesto: Woolf claimed that every woman requires a separate income and a room of her own if she is to become an independent, productive woman. How does Woolf embellish this metaphor of a room of one's own in paragraph 7? What is the effect?
12. What is Woolf's overall tone in this speech? Because the tone evolves and shifts throughout the text, determining the overall tone is complex. Identify passages where Woolf displays various tones, sometimes in order to assume a specific persona, and then develop a description of the overall tone. You will probably need to use two words (possibly joined with *but* or *yet*) or a phrase rather than a single word. Does Woolf display anger, bitterness, resignation, aggression, apology, combativeness? Or does she show a combination of these emotions or others?

Suggestions for Writing

1. Write an essay analyzing the rhetorical strategies Woolf uses in this speech to reach her specific audience. Pay attention to the way she uses the tools of the novelist, such as characterization, scene setting, highly textured and specific descriptive detail, and figurative language.

2. Imagine that you have been invited to deliver a speech entitled "Professions for Women" to an audience of your peers, male and female. Cite Woolf to support your speech's thesis, or propose a counterargument to Woolf's position. Also, be sure to describe the audience and occasion of your speech.

3. If you have read any of Virginia Woolf's fiction (either her short stories or the novels *Mrs. Dalloway* or *To the Lighthouse*, for example), discuss how this essay informs them.

4. In *A Room of One's Own*, Woolf asks, what if Shakespeare had had a sister? She calls her Judith and considers whether circumstances would have encouraged or allowed Judith to write great plays. Write an essay comparing and contrasting the ideas and style of that essay with those in "Professions for Women."

5. In the final paragraph of her speech, Woolf says, "Even when the path is nominally open — when there is nothing to prevent a woman from being a doctor, a lawyer, a civil servant — there are many phantoms and obstacles, as I believe, looming in her way." Write an essay in which you defend, challenge, or modify that statement with regard to women today in the United States *or* to women in another country where gender equality might be more problematic. Pay particular attention to what you see as the "phantoms and obstacles."

The Speech of Miss Polly Baker

BENJAMIN FRANKLIN

> Benjamin Franklin (1706–1790) was a scholar, diplomat, author, scientist, business-man, and inventor. One of the Founding Fathers, he helped draft the Declaration of Independence, and he was a delegate to the Constitutional Convention. In 1741, he began publishing *Poor Richard's Almanac*, a very popular and influential maga-zine that established his reputation (under a pseudonym) as a satirist and secured his fortune. He made important contributions to science, especially in the understanding of electricity. He was ambassador to France from 1776 to 1785 and governor of Pennsylvania from 1785 to 1788. Toward the end of his life, he became a prominent abolitionist. The following essay initially appeared in 1747 in a London paper. Sub-sequently, American publications picked it up. For several decades, the story was accepted as having been written by a woman named Polly Baker, but eventually Franklin admitted that he had written it to criticize a legal system that penalized mothers but not fathers for having children out of wedlock. Although there has been some controversy, most scholars accept Franklin as the author, including the editors of *The Papers of Benjamin Franklin* published by the American Philosophical Society and Yale University.

The Speech of Miss Polly Baker, before a Court of Judicature, at Connecti-cut near Boston in New-England; where she was prosecuted the Fifth Time, for having a Bastard Child: Which influenced the Court to dispense with her Punishment, and induced one of her Judges to marry her the next Day.

May it please the Honourable Bench to indulge me in a few Words: I am a poor unhappy Woman, who have no Money to fee Lawyers to plead for me, being hard put to it to get a tolerable Living. I shall not trouble your Honours with long Speeches; for I have not the Presumption to expect, that you may, by any Means, be prevailed on to deviate in your Sentence from the Law, in my Favour. All I humbly hope is, That your Honours would charitably move the Governor's Good-ness on my Behalf, that my Fine may be remitted. This is the Fifth Time, Gentle-men, that I have been dragged before your Court on the same Account; twice I have paid heavy Fines, and twice have been brought to Publick Punishment, for want of Money to pay those Fines. This may have been agreeable to the Laws, and I don't dispute it; but since Laws are sometimes unreasonable in themselves, and therefore repealed, and others bear too hard on the Subject in particular Circum-stances; and therefore there is left a Power somewhat to dispense with the Execu-tion of them; I take the Liberty to say, That I think this Law, by which I am punished, is both unreasonable in itself, and particularly severe with regard to me, who have always lived an inoffensive Life in the Neighbourhood where I was born, and defy my Enemies (if I have any) to say I ever wronged Man, Woman, or Child.

Abstracted from the Law, I cannot conceive (may it please your Honours) what the Nature of my Offence is. I have brought Five fine Children into the World, at the Risque of my Life; I have maintained them well by my own Industry, without burthening the Township, and would have done it better, if it had not been for the heavy Charges and Fines I have paid. Can it be a Crime (in the Nature of Things I mean) to add to the Number of the King's Subjects, in a new Country that really wants People? I own it, I should think it a Praise-worthy, rather than a punishable Action. I have debauched no other Woman's Husband, nor enticed any Youth; these Things I never was charged with, nor has any one the least Cause of Complaint against me, unless, perhaps, the Minister, or Justice, because I have had Children without being married, by which they have missed a Wedding Fee. But, can ever this be a Fault of mine?

I appeal to your Honours. You are pleased to allow I don't want Sense; but I must be stupified to the last Degree, not to prefer the Honourable State of Wedlock, to the Condition I have lived in. I always was, and still am willing to enter into it; and doubt not my behaving well in it, having all the Industry, Frugality, Fertility, and Skill in Economy, appertaining to a good Wife's Character. I defy any Person to say, I ever refused an Offer of that Sort: On the contrary, I readily consented to the only Proposal of Marriage that ever was made me, which was when I was a Virgin; but too easily confiding in the Person's Sincerity that made it, I unhappily lost my own Honour, by trusting to his; for he got me with Child, and then forsook me: That very Person you all know; he is now become a Magistrate of this Country; and I had Hopes he would have appeared this Day on the Bench, and have endeavoured to moderate the Court in my Favour; then I should have scorned to have mentioned it; but I must now complain of it, as unjust and unequal, That my Betrayer and Undoer, the first Cause of all my faults and Miscarriages (if they must be deemed such) should be advanced to Honour and Power in the Government, that punishes my Misfortunes with Stripes and Infamy.

I should be told, 'tis like, That were there no Act of Assembly in the Case, the Precepts of Religion are violated by my Transgressions. If mine, then, is a religious Offence, leave it to religious Punishments. You have already excluded me from the Comforts of your Church-Communion. Is not that sufficient? You believe I have offended Heaven, and must suffer eternal Fire: Will not that be sufficient? What Need is there, then, of your additional Fines and Whipping?   5

I own, I do not think as you do; for, if I thought what you call a Sin, was really such, I could not presumptuously commit it. But, how can it be believed, that Heaven is angry at my having Children, when to the little done by me towards it, God has been pleased to add his Divine Skill and admirable Workmanship in the Formation of their Bodies, and crowned it, by furnishing them with rational and immortal Souls. Forgive me, Gentlemen, if I talk a little extravagantly on these

Matters; I am no Divine, but if you, Gentlemen, must be making Laws, do not turn natural and useful Actions into Crimes, by your Prohibitions. But take into your wise Consideration, the great and growing Number of Batchelors in the Country, many of whom from the mean Fear of the Expences of a Family, have never sincerely and honourably courted a Woman in their Lives; and by their Manner of Living, leave unproduced (which is little better than Murder) Hundreds of their Posterity to the Thousandth Generation. Is not this a greater Offence against the Publick Good, than mine? Compel them, then, by Law, either to Marriage, or to pay double the Fine of Fornication every Year.

What must poor young Women do, whom Custom have forbid to solicit the Men, and Who cannot force themselves upon Husbands, when the Laws take no Care to provide them any; and yet severely punish them if they do their Duty without them; the Duty of the first and great Command of Nature, and of Nature's God, *Encrease and Multiply*. A Duty, from the steady Performance of which, nothing has been able to deter me; but for its Sake, I have hazarded the Loss of the Publick Esteem, and have frequently endured Publick Disgrace and Punishment; and therefore ought, in my humble Opinion, instead of a Whipping, to have a Statue erected to my Memory.

Exploring the Text

1. How does Benjamin Franklin develop Polly Baker into a sympathetic character? What ethos does the character establish at the outset?
2. What is the basic argument that Polly makes? Try explaining it through a syllogism, a series of syllogisms, or the Toulmin model (see Chapter 3).
3. What evidence does Polly present in her defense?
4. How does Polly anticipate counterarguments? What examples of concession and refutation do you find?
5. What is the effect of the rhetorical questions Polly asks? Refer to specific examples in your response.
6. How does Polly tailor her argument (or does she?) to the particular audience of the magistrates?
7. Outline the logic of Polly's argument that she should, in fact, be rewarded instead of punished. Go a step further, and show how she turns the law's logic on itself to argue that the bachelors in the community are the ones guilty of "a greater Offence against the Publick Good" (para. 6).
8. What instances of a double standard does Polly point out? Pay close attention to the examples of men's behavior being seen in an entirely different light than women's in the same situation.
9. How do the diction and syntax establish Polly as a humble, obedient woman?
10. If you did not know that Polly was a fictional character created by an author whose intent is to criticize a practice or system, what clues might you notice that suggest

something is below the surface? Consider elements of satire such as hyperbole, understatement, connotative language, double entendres, and puns.

11. What does Franklin achieve by writing in the voice of a woman and creating this fictional scenario rather than simply writing a straightforward criticism of a system that he believes treats women unfairly?

12. Compare and contrast the rhetorical strategies used by Franklin with those of Jonathan Swift in his satire "A Modest Proposal" (p. 404).

Letters

JOHN AND ABIGAIL ADAMS

John Adams (1735–1826), one of America's Founding Fathers, was the second president of the United States. His wife, Abigail Smith Adams (1744–1818), was also dedicated to the cause of independence and wrote frequently to him on the conditions of wartime Boston, which was held by the British for most of the war. The city was liberated by George Washington's army just before these letters were written. In the following two letters, Abigail writes to her husband in Philadelphia, where he is serving in the Continental Congress, and John responds as both husband and politician. Abigail presses her husband to "remember the ladies" as he and his colleagues are discussing freedom from tyranny. Given the time period, her exhortation did not refer to women's suffrage but rather to laws regarding such matters as inheritance and spousal abuse. You can view these letters at bedfordstmartins.com/languageofcomp.

From Abigail to John

Braintree, March 31, 1776
I wish you would ever write me a Letter half as long as I write you; and tell me if you may where your Fleet are gone? What sort of Defence Virginia can make against our common Enemy? Whether it is so situated as to make an able Defence? Are not the Gentery Lords and the common people vassals, are they not like the uncivilized Natives Brittain represents us to be? I hope their Riffel Men who have shewen themselves very savage and even Blood thirsty; are not a specimen of the Generality of the people.

I . . . am willing to allow the Colony great merrit for having produced a Washington but they have been shamefully duped by a Dunmore.[1]

I have sometimes been ready to think that the passion for Liberty cannot be Eaquelly Strong in the Breasts of those who have been accustomed to deprive their

---

[1]The Fourth Earl of Dunmore (John Murray) was the British colonial governor of Virginia from 1771 to 1776. He opposed independence for the colonies and was forced to return to England. — Eds.

fellow Creatures of theirs. Of this I am certain that it is not founded upon that generous and christian principal of doing to others as we would that others should do unto us.

Do not you want to see Boston; I am fearfull of the small pox, or I should have been in before this time. I got Mr. Crane to go to our House and see what state it was in. I find it has been occupied by one of the Doctors of a Regiment, very dirty, but no other damage has been done to it. The few things which were left in it are all gone. Cranch has the key which he never deliverd up. I have wrote to him for it and am determined to get it cleand as soon as possible and shut it up. I look upon it a new acquisition of property, a property which one month ago I did not value at a single Shilling, and could with pleasure have seen it in flames.

The Town in General is left in a better state than we expected, more oweing to a percipitate flight than any Regard to the inhabitants, tho some individuals discoverd a sense of honour and justice and have left the rent of the Houses in which they were, for the owners and the furniture unhurt, or if damaged sufficent to make it good.

Others have committed abominable Ravages. The Mansion House of your President is safe and the furniture unhurt whilst both the House and Furniture of the Solisiter General have fallen a prey to their own merciless party. Surely the very Fiends feel a Reverential awe for Virtue and patriotism, whilst they Detest the paricide[2] and traitor.

I feel very differently at the approach of spring to what I did a month ago. We knew not then whether we could plant or sow with safety, whether when we had toild we could reap the fruits of our own industery, whether we could rest in our own Cottages, or whether we should not be driven from the sea coasts to seek shelter in the wilderness, but now we feel as if we might sit under our own vine and eat the good of the land.

I feel a gaieti de Coar[3] to which before I was a stranger. I think the Sun looks brighter, the Birds sing more melodiously, and Nature puts on a more chearfull countanance. We feel a temporary peace, and the poor fugitives are returning to their deserted habitations.

Tho we felicitate ourselves, we sympathize with those who are trembling least the Lot of Boston should be theirs. But they cannot be in similar circumstances unless pusilanimity and cowardise should take possession of them. They have time and warning given them to see the Evil and shun it. — I long to hear that you have declared an independency — and by the way in the new Code of Laws which I suppose it will be necessary for you to make I desire you would Remember the Ladies, and be more generous and favourable to them than your ancestors. Do not put such unlimited power into the hand of the Husbands. Remember all Men would be tyrants if they could. If perticuliar care and attention is not paid to the Ladies we

---

[2]A son who murdered his father, also known as a *patricide*. — Eds.
[3]French (correctly spelled gaieté de coeur), happiness of heart. — Eds.

are determined to foment a Rebelion, and will not hold ourselves bound by any Laws in which we have no voice, or Representation.

That your Sex are Naturally Tyrannical is a Truth so thoroughly established as to admit of no dispute, but such of you as wish to be happy willingly give up the harsh title of Master for the more tender and endearing one of Friend. Why then, not put it out of the power of the vicious and the Lawless to use us with cruelty and indignity with impunity. Men of Sense in all Ages abhor those customs which treat us only as the vassals of your Sex. Regard us then as Beings placed by providence under your protection and in immitation of the Supreem Being make use of that power only for our happiness.

From John to Abigail

April 14, 1776

You justly complain of my short Letters, but the critical State of Things and the Multiplicity of Avocations must plead my Excuse. You ask where the Fleet is. The inclosed Papers will inform you. You ask what Sort of Defence Virginia can make. I believe they will make an able Defence. Their Militia and minute Men have been some time employed in training them selves and they have Nine Battallions of regulars as they call them, maintained among them, under good Officers, at the Continental Expence. They have set up a Number of Manufactories of Fire Arms, which are busily employed. They are tolerably supplied with Powder, and are successfull and assiduous, in making Salt Petre. Their neighbouring Sister or rather Daughter Colony of North Carolina, which is a warlike Colony, and has several Battallions at the Continental Expence, as well as a pretty good Militia, are ready to assist them, and they are in very good Spirits, and seem determined to make a brave Resistance. — The Gentry are very rich, and the common People very poor.

This Inequality of Property, gives an Aristocratical Turn to all their Proceedings, and occasions a strong Aversion in their Patricians, to Common Sense. But the Spirit of these Barons, is coming down, and it must submit.

It is very true, as you observe they have been duped by Dunmore. But this is a Common Case. All the Colonies are duped, more or less, at one Time and another. A more egregious Bubble was never blown up, than the Story of Commissioners coming to treat with the Congress. Yet it has gained Credit like a Charm, not only without but against the clearest Evidence. I never shall forget the Delusion, which seized our best and most sagacious Friends the dear Inhabitants of Boston, the Winter before last. Credulity and the Want of Foresight, are Imperfections in the human Character, that no Politician can sufficiently guard against.

You have given me some Pleasure, by your Account of a certain House in Queen Street. I had burned it, long ago, in Imagination. It rises now to my View like a Phoenix. — What shall I say of the Solicitor General? I pity his pretty Children, I pity his Father, and his sisters. I wish I could be clear that it is no moral Evil to pity him and his Lady. Upon Repentance they will certainly have a large Share in the

Compassions of many. But . . . let Us take Warning and give it to our Children. Whenever Vanity, and Gaiety, a Love of Pomp and Dress, Furniture, Equipage, Buildings, great Company, expensive Diversions, and elegant Entertainments get the better of the Principles and Judgments of Men or Women there is no knowing where they will stop, nor into what Evils, natural, moral, or political, they will lead us.

Your Description of your own Gaiety de Coeur, charms me. Thanks be to God   15
you have just Cause to rejoice—and may the bright Prospect be obscured by no Cloud.

As to Declarations of Independency, be patient. Read our Privateering Laws, and our Commercial Laws. What signifies a Word.

As to your extraordinary Code of Laws, I cannot but laugh. We have been told that our Struggle has loosened the bands of Government every where. That Children and Apprentices were disobedient—that schools and Colledges were grown turbulent—that Indians slighted their Guardians and Negroes grew insolent to their Masters.

But your Letter was the first Intimation that another Tribe more numerous and powerfull than all the rest were grown discontented.—This is rather too coarse a Compliment but you are so saucy, I wont blot it out.

Depend upon it, We know better than to repeal our Masculine systems. Altho they are in full Force, you know they are little more than Theory. We dare not exert our Power in its full Latitude. We are obliged to go fair, and softly, and in Practice you know We are the subjects. We have only the Name of Masters, and rather than give up this, which would compleatly subject Us to the Despotism of the Peticoat, I hope General Washington, and all our brave Heroes would fight. I am sure every good Politician would plot, as long as he would against Despotism, Empire, Monarchy, Aristocracy, Oligarchy, or Ochlocracy.[4]—A fine Story indeed. I begin to think the Ministry as deep as they are wicked. After stirring up Tories, Landjobbers, Trimmers, Bigots, Canadians, Indians, Negroes, Hanoverians, Hessians, Russians, Irish Roman Catholicks, Scotch Renegadoes, at last they have stimulated the[e] to demand new Priviledges and threaten to rebell.

. . . .

Exploring the Text

1. What ethos does Abigail Adams establish in the opening paragraph? How do the questions contribute to the persona she presents?
2. Abigail describes Boston in considerable detail. What is the general impression she tries to convey? Why do you think she chose the details she did?
3. When Abigail exhorts John Adams to "remember the Ladies," she also points out that "all Men would be tyrants if they could" (para. 9) and that "your Sex are Naturally Tyrannical" (para. 10). How does she make such statements without sounding accusatory or alienating her husband? Explain.

---

[4]Mob rule.—Eds.

4. When John tells Abigail that he "cannot but laugh" (para. 17) at her suggestions for laws, is he dismissing her? Is he disrespectful to her? Explain.
5. Is the last paragraph of John's letter written tongue-in-cheek, or is he serious? What does he mean by "the Despotism of the Peticoat" (para. 19)? How do you interpret this ending?
6. Describe the overall tone of each of these letters. Based on the tone and the information in the letters, describe the relationship between John and Abigail Adams. What evidence of intimacy do you find in each letter?
7. Imagine that Abigail and John Adams had access to e-mail, and rewrite these two letters as e-mail correspondence.

I Want a Wife

JUDY BRADY

Judy Brady was born in San Francisco in 1937 and earned a BFA in painting from the University of Iowa in 1962. She has been active in political and environmental movements as an editor and author. She edited *Women and Cancer* (1990) and *One in Three: Women with Cancer Confront an Epidemic* (1991). Brady's work has also appeared in periodicals such as *Greenpeace* magazine and the *Women's Review of Books*. Since appearing in the premiere issue of *Ms.* magazine in 1971, "I Want a Wife" has become a classic piece of feminist writing and humor. It was reprinted as "I [Still] Want a Wife" in *Ms.* in 1990.

I belong to that classification of people known as wives. I am A Wife. And, not altogether incidentally, I am a mother.

Not too long ago a male friend of mine appeared on the scene fresh from a recent divorce. He had one child, who is, of course, with his ex-wife. He is looking for another wife. As I thought about him while I was ironing one evening, it suddenly occurred to me that I, too, would like to have a wife. Why do I want a wife?

I would like to go back to school so that I can become economically independent, support myself, and, if need be, support those dependent upon me. I want a wife who will work and send me to school. And while I am going to school I want a wife to take care of my children. I want a wife to keep track of the children's doctor and dentist appointments. And to keep track of mine, too. I want a wife to make sure my children eat properly and are kept clean. I want a wife who will wash the children's clothes and keep them mended. I want a wife who is a good nurturant attendant to my children, who arranges for their schooling, makes sure that they have an adequate social life with their peers, takes them to the park, the zoo, etc. I want a wife who takes care of the children when they are sick, a wife who arranges to be around when the children need special care, because, of course, I cannot miss classes at school. My wife must arrange to lose time at work and not lose the job. It may mean a small cut in my wife's income from time to time, but I guess I can tolerate that. Needless to say, my wife will arrange and pay for the care of the children while my wife is working.

I want a wife who will take care of my physical needs. I want a wife who will keep my house clean. A wife who will pick up after my children, a wife who will pick up after me. I want a wife who will keep my clothes clean, ironed, mended, replaced when need be, and who will see to it that my personal things are kept in their proper place so that I can find what I need the minute I need it. I want a wife who cooks the meals, a wife who is a good cook. I want a wife who will plan the menus, do the necessary grocery shopping, prepare the meals, serve them pleasantly, and then do the cleaning up while I do my studying. I want a wife who will care for me when I am sick and sympathize with my pain and loss of time from school. I want a wife to go along when our family takes a vacation so that someone can continue to care for me and my children when I need a rest and change of scene.

I want a wife who will not bother me with rambling complaints about a wife's duties. But I want a wife who will listen to me when I feel the need to explain a rather difficult point I have come across in my course of studies. And I want a wife who will type my papers for me when I have written them. 5

I want a wife who will take care of the details of my social life. When my wife and I are invited out by my friends, I want a wife who will take care of the babysitting arrangements. When I meet people at school that I like and want to entertain, I want a wife who will have the house clean, will prepare a special meal, serve it to me and my friends, and not interrupt when I talk about things that interest me and my friends. I want a wife who will have arranged that the children are fed and ready for bed before my guests arrive so that the children do not bother us. I want a wife who takes care of the needs of my guests so that they feel comfortable, who makes sure that they have an ashtray, that they are passed the hors d'oeuvres, that they are offered a second helping of the food, that their wine glasses are replenished when necessary, that their coffee is served to them as they like it. And I want a wife who knows that sometimes I need a night out by myself.

I want a wife who is sensitive to my sexual needs, a wife who makes love passionately and eagerly when I feel like it, a wife who makes sure that I am satisfied. And, of course, I want a wife who will not demand sexual attention when I am not in the mood for it. I want a wife who assumes the complete responsibility for birth control, because I do not want more children. I want a wife who will remain sexually faithful to me so that I do not have to clutter up my intellectual life with jealousies. And I want a wife who understands that my sexual needs may entail more than just strict adherence to monogamy. I must, after all, be able to relate to people as fully as possible.

If, by chance, I find another person more suitable as a wife than the wife I already have, I want the liberty to replace my present wife with another one. Naturally, I will expect a fresh new life; my wife will take the children and be solely responsible for them so that I am left free.

When I am through with school and have a job, I want my wife to quit working and remain at home so that my wife can more fully and completely take care of a wife's duties.

My God, who *wouldn't* want a wife?   10

. . . .

Exploring the Text

1. How does the opening paragraph set the tone for the entire essay? Note details such as the form and progression of sentences, the use of capitalization, and the qualifying phrases.
2. What is the effect of Judy Brady repeating the sentence (or clause) "I want a wife" again and again? What is the effect of Brady's use of pronouns in referring to herself and "her" wife?
3. What is the overall structure of her argument? Consider breaking this essay into a straightforward syllogism or analyzing it using the Toulmin model presented in Chapter 3.
4. How would you describe the progression of the paragraphs? Does Brady go from most to least or from least to most, or does she follow another organizational principle? Why is her choice effective?
5. What elements of satire does Brady use? How does she, for instance, use hyperbole? Understatement? Humor? Irony? Others?
6. Although Brady never uses the term *sexism* (or *feminism*), what gender inequities does she catalog in this essay?
7. Even though this essay was published in 1971, when the feminist movement was a strong political force, it has remained popular for decades. Why? Some of the details seem dated, such as the references to a typewriter and ashtrays. Do you think that the situation Brady describes is still relevant? Or is the essay mainly a historical document that is a reminder of times past?
8. How might you apply the same rhetorical strategies that Brady uses in this essay to another one entitled "I Want a Husband"?

Just Walk on By

A Black Man Ponders His Power to Alter Public Space

BRENT STAPLES

An author and editorial writer for the *New York Times*, Brent Staples (b. 1951) grew up in Pennsylvania in a family of nine children. He received his BA from Widener University and his PhD in psychology from the University of Chicago. His memoir, *Parallel Time: Growing Up in Black and White* (1994), won the Anisfield-Wolf Book

Award, which recognizes books that contribute to a deeper appreciation of cultural diversity. The following essay originally appeared in *Ms.* magazine in 1986.

My first victim was a woman—white, well dressed, probably in her early twenties. I came upon her late one evening on a deserted street in Hyde Park, a relatively affluent neighborhood in an otherwise mean, impoverished section of Chicago. As I swung onto the avenue behind her, there seemed to be a discreet, uninflammatory distance between us. Not so. She cast back a worried glance. To her, the youngish black man—a broad six feet two inches with a beard and billowing hair, both hands shoved into the pockets of a bulky military jacket—seemed menacingly close. After a few more quick glimpses, she picked up her pace and was soon running in earnest. Within seconds she disappeared into a cross street.

That was more than a decade ago. I was twenty-two years old, a graduate student newly arrived at the University of Chicago. It was in the echo of that terrified woman's footfalls that I first began to know the unwieldy inheritance I'd come into—the ability to alter public space in ugly ways. It was clear that she thought herself the quarry of a mugger, a rapist, or worse. Suffering a bout of insomnia, however, I was stalking sleep, not defenseless wayfarers. As a softy who is scarcely able to take a knife to a raw chicken—let alone hold it to a person's throat—I was surprised, embarrassed, and dismayed all at once. Her flight made me feel like an accomplice in tyranny. It also made it clear that I was indistinguishable from the muggers who occasionally seeped into the area from the surrounding ghetto. That first encounter, and those that followed, signified that a vast, unnerving gulf lay between nighttime pedestrians—particularly women—and me. And I soon gathered that being perceived as dangerous is a hazard in itself. I only needed to turn a corner into a dicey situation, or crowd some frightened, armed person in a foyer somewhere, or make an errant move after being pulled over by a policeman. Where fear and weapons meet—and they often do in urban America—there is always the possibility of death.

In that first year, my first away from my hometown, I was to become thoroughly familiar with the language of fear. At dark, shadowy intersections in Chicago, I could cross in front of a car stopped at a traffic light and elicit the *thunk, thunk, thunk, thunk* of the driver—black, white, male, or female—hammering down the door locks. On less traveled streets after dark, I grew accustomed to but never comfortable with people who crossed to the other side of the street rather than pass me. Then there were the standard unpleasantries with police, doormen, bouncers, cabdrivers, and others whose business is to screen out troublesome individuals *before* there is any nastiness.

I moved to New York nearly two years ago and I have remained an avid night walker. In central Manhattan, the near-constant crowd cover minimizes tense one-on-one street encounters. Elsewhere—visiting friends in Soho, where sidewalks are narrow and tightly spaced buildings shut out the sky—things can get very taut indeed.

Black men have a firm place in New York mugging literature. Norman Podhoretz 5
in his famed (or infamous) 1963 essay, "My Negro Problem—And Ours," recalls
growing up in terror of black males; they "were tougher than we were, more ruthless," he writes—and as an adult on the Upper West Side of Manhattan, he continues, he cannot constrain his nervousness when he meets black men on certain
streets. Similarly, a decade later, the essayist and novelist Edward Hoagland extols
a New York where once "Negro bitterness bore down mainly on other Negroes."
Where some see mere panhandlers, Hoagland sees "a mugger who is clearly screwing up his nerve to do more than just *ask* for money." But Hoagland has "the New
Yorker's quick-hunch posture for broken-field maneuvering," and the bad guy
swerves away.

I often witness that "hunch posture," from women after dark on the warren-
like streets of Brooklyn where I live. They seem to set their faces on neutral and, with
their purse straps strung across their chests bandolier style, they forge ahead as
though bracing themselves against being tackled. I understand, of course, that the
danger they perceive is not a hallucination. Women are particularly vulnerable to
street violence, and young black males are drastically overrepresented among the
perpetrators of that violence. Yet these truths are no solace against the kind of
alienation that comes of being ever the suspect, against being set apart, a fearsome
entity with whom pedestrians avoid making eye contact.

It is not altogether clear to me how I reached the ripe old age of twenty-two
without being conscious of the lethality nighttime pedestrians attributed to me.
Perhaps it was because in Chester, Pennsylvania, the small, angry industrial town
where I came of age in the 1960s, I was scarcely noticeable against a backdrop of
gang warfare, street knifings, and murders. I grew up one of the good boys, had
perhaps a half-dozen fistfights. In retrospect, my shyness of combat has clear
sources.

Many things go into the making of a young thug. One of those things is the
consummation of the male romance with the power to intimidate. An infant discovers that random flailings send the baby bottle flying out of the crib and crashing to the floor. Delighted, the joyful babe repeats those motions again and again,
seeking to duplicate the feat. Just so, I recall the points at which some of my boyhood friends were finally seduced by the perception of themselves as tough guys.
When a mark cowered and surrendered his money without resistance, myth and
reality merged—and paid off. It is, after all, only manly to embrace the power to
frighten and intimidate. We, as men, are not supposed to give an inch of our lane
on the highway; we are to seize the fighter's edge in work and in play and even in
love; we are to be valiant in the face of hostile forces.

Unfortunately, poor and powerless young men seem to take all this nonsense
literally. As a boy, I saw countless tough guys locked away; I have since buried several, too. They were babies, really—a teenage cousin, a brother of twenty-two, a
childhood friend in his midtwenties—all gone down in episodes of bravado played
out in the streets. I came to doubt the virtues of intimidation early on. I chose, perhaps even unconsciously, to remain a shadow—timid, but a survivor.

The fearsomeness mistakenly attributed to me in public places often has a per-   10
ilous flavor. The most frightening of these confusions occurred in the late 1970s
and early 1980s when I worked as a journalist in Chicago. One day, rushing into the
office of a magazine I was writing for with a deadline story in hand, I was mistaken for a burglar. The office manager called security and, with an ad hoc posse,
pursued me through the labyrinthine halls, nearly to my editor's door. I had no
way of proving who I was. I could only move briskly toward the company of someone who knew me.

Another time I was on assignment for a local paper and killing time before an
interview. I entered a jewelry store on the city's affluent Near North Side. The
proprietor excused herself and returned with an enormous red Doberman pin-
scher straining at the end of a leash. She stood, the dog extended toward me,
silent to my questions, her eyes bulging nearly out of her head. I took a cursory
look around, nodded, and bade her good night. Relatively speaking, however, I
never fared as badly as another black male journalist. He went to nearby Wauke-
gan, Illinois, a couple of summers ago to work on a story about a murderer who
was born there. Mistaking the reporter for the killer, police hauled him from his
car at gunpoint and but for his press credentials would probably have tried to
book him. Such episodes are not uncommon. Black men trade tales like this all
the time.

In "My Negro Problem—And Ours," Podhoretz writes that the hatred he
feels for blacks makes itself known to him through a variety of avenues—one
being his discomfort with that "special brand of paranoid touchiness" to which
he says blacks are prone. No doubt he is speaking here of black men. In time, I
learned to smother the rage I felt at so often being taken for a criminal. Not to do
so would surely have led to madness—via that special "paranoid touchiness" that
so annoyed Podhoretz at the time he wrote the essay.

I began to take precautions to make myself less threatening. I move about
with care, particularly late in the evening. I give a wide berth to nervous people on
subway platforms during the wee hours, particularly when I have exchanged business clothes for jeans. If I happen to be entering a building behind some people
who appear skittish, I may walk by, letting them clear the lobby before I return, so
as not to seem to be following them. I have been calm and extremely congenial on
those rare occasions when I've been pulled over by the police.

And on late-evening constitutionals along streets less traveled by, I employ
what has proved to be an excellent tension-reducing measure: I whistle melodies
from Beethoven and Vivaldi and the more popular classical composers. Even
steely New Yorkers hunching toward nighttime destinations seem to relax, and
occasionally they even join in the tune. Virtually everybody seems to sense that a
mugger wouldn't be warbling bright, sunny selections from Vivaldi's *Four Seasons*.
It is my equivalent of the cowbell that hikers wear when they know they are in
bear country.

Exploring the Text

1. What is the impact of the opening sentence, "My first victim was a woman . . ."? How is Brent Staples using the term "victim"? How does the meaning of the sentence and the term change as you read and reread the essay?

2. In what ways does the description at the beginning resemble a scene from a novel? What mood does Staples set with the details and specific words he chooses? Pay close attention to modifiers and verbs.

3. Staples opens paragraph 2 with the short, simple sentence "That was more than a decade ago," an objective statement that indicates the passage of time. Does this sentence jolt you as a reader? Disappoint you? Explain why you think it is or is not an effective follow-up to the opening paragraph.

4. What examples does Staples provide to illustrate "the language of fear" (para. 3)?

5. In what ways does Staples acknowledge that the "victim's" response is not unwarranted? What explanations does he provide for her behavior? To what extent does he blame her? Does he want us as readers to blame or be more sympathetic toward her?

6. What is his purpose in quoting Norman Podhoretz and Edward Hoagland? Are they providing support for his viewpoint, a contrasting viewpoint, expert testimony, or something else?

7. Is Staples being ironic when he writes, "I began to take precautions to make myself less threatening" (para. 13)? Cite specific parts of the text to support your viewpoint.

8. Is the final paragraph intended to be flippant? Humorous? Explain whether you find it an effective conclusion to the essay.

9. How would you describe the overall tone of this essay? You might consider a phrase rather than a single word to capture the complexity of this piece. Support your reading with specific references to Staples's language.

10. In 1994, Staples incorporated this essay into his memoir, *Parallel Time*, but he revised it substantially. Below, you will find the first two paragraphs from that revised version. Compare those paragraphs with the originals. Why do you think Staples made the changes he did? In your opinion, did they improve the essay?

> At night, I walked to the lakefront whenever the weather permitted. I was headed home from the lake when I took my first victim. It was late fall, and the wind was cutting. I was wearing my navy pea jacket, the collar turned up, my hands snug in the pockets. Dead leaves scuttled in shoals along the streets. I turned out of Blackstone Avenue and headed west on 57th Street, and there she was, a few yards ahead of me, dressed in business clothes and carrying a briefcase. She looked back at me once, then again, and picked up her pace. She looked back again and started to run. I stopped where I was and looked up at the surrounding windows. What did this look like to people peeking out through their blinds? I was out walking. But what if someone had thought they'd seen something they hadn't and called the police. I

held back the urge to run. Instead, I walked south to The Midway, plunged into its darkness, and remained on The Midway until I reached the foot of my street.

I'd been a fool. I'd been walking the streets grinning good evening at people who were frightened to death of me. I did violence to them by just being. How had I missed this? I kept walking at night, but from then on I paid attention.

11. Staples first wrote this essay in 1986. Do you think the essay is dated? Explain why you do or do not feel that many people in today's society continue to perceive young African American males as threatening.

The Myth of the Latin Woman
I Just Met a Girl Named María

Judith Ortiz Cofer

Poet, novelist, and essayist Judith Ortiz Cofer was born in Puerto Rico in 1952 and grew up in New Jersey. She is currently the Regents' and Franklin Professor of English and Creative Writing at the University of Georgia. Among her many publications are the young adult novel *If I Could Fly* (2011), the novel *The Meaning of Consuelo* (2004), her memoirs *Silent Dancing: A Partial Remembrance of a Puerto Rican Childhood* (1990) and *Woman in Front of the Sun: Becoming a Writer* (2000), and her collection of prose and poetry, *The Latin Deli* (1993). She has won many awards, including the Anisfield-Wolf Award in Race Relations and the Americas Award for Children's and Young Adult Literature; she was nominated for the Pulitzer Prize in 1989. In the following selection, originally published in *Glamour* in 1992, Cofer examines the impact of stereotyping.

On a bus trip to London from Oxford University where I was earning some graduate credits one summer, a young man, obviously fresh from a pub, spotted me and as if struck by inspiration went down on his knees in the aisle. With both hands over his heart he broke into an Irish tenor's rendition of "María" from *West Side Story*.[1] My politely amused fellow passengers gave his lovely voice the round of gentle applause it deserved. Though I was not quite as amused, I managed my version of an English smile: no show of teeth, no extreme contortions of the facial muscles — I was at this time of my life practicing reserve and cool. Oh, that British control, how I coveted it. But María had followed me to

---

[1] *West Side Story* was a Broadway musical (1957) and then a feature film (1961). Based on *Romeo and Juliet*, the story deals with the conflicts between two New York City gangs — a Puerto Rican gang and a white ethnic gang. The Puerto Rican actress Rita Moreno, mentioned later in this paragraph, had a major role in the movie. — Eds.

London, reminding me of a prime fact of my life; you can leave the Island, master the English language, and travel as far as you can, but if you are a Latina, especially one like me who so obviously belongs to Rita Moreno's gene pool, the Island travels with you.

This is sometimes a very good thing—it may win you that extra minute of someone's attention. But with some people, the same things can make *you* an island—not so much a tropical paradise as an Alcatraz, a place nobody wants to visit. As a Puerto Rican girl growing up in the United States and wanting like most children to "belong," I resented the stereotype that my Hispanic appearance called forth from many people I met.

Our family lived in a large urban center in New Jersey during the sixties, where life was designed as a microcosm of my parents' casas on the island. We spoke in Spanish, we ate Puerto Rican food bought at the bodega, and we practiced strict Catholicism complete with Saturday confession and Sunday mass at a church where our parents were accommodated into a one-hour Spanish mass slot, performed by a Chinese priest trained as a missionary for Latin America.

As a girl I was kept under strict surveillance, since virtue and modesty were, by cultural equation, the same as family honor. As a teenager I was instructed on how to behave as a proper señorita. But it was a conflicting message girls got, since the Puerto Rican mothers also encouraged their daughters to look and act like women and to dress in clothes our Anglo friends and their mothers found too "mature" for our age. It was, and is, cultural, yet I often felt humiliated when I appeared at an American friend's party wearing a dress more suitable to a semiformal than to a playroom birthday celebration. At Puerto Rican festivities, neither the music nor the colors we wore could be too loud. I still experience a vague sense of letdown when I'm invited to a "party" and it turns out to be a marathon conversation in hushed tones rather than a fiesta with salsa, laughter, and dancing—the kind of celebration I remember from my childhood.

I remember Career Day in our high school, when teachers told us to come dressed as if for a job interview. It quickly became obvious that to the barrio girls, "dressing up" sometimes meant wearing ornate jewelry and clothing that would be more appropriate (by mainstream standards) for the company Christmas party than as daily office attire. That morning I had agonized in front of my closet, trying to figure out what a "career girl" would wear because, essentially, except for Marlo Thomas on TV, I had no models on which to base my decision. I knew how to dress for school: at the Catholic school I attended we all wore uniforms; I knew how to dress for Sunday mass, and I knew what dresses to wear for parties at my relatives' homes. Though I do not recall the precise details of my Career Day outfit, it must have been a composite of the above choices. But I remember a comment my friend (an Italian-American) made in later years that coalesced my impressions of that day. She said that at the business school she was attending the Puerto Rican girls always stood out for wearing "everything at once." She meant, of course, too much jewelry, too many accessories. On that day at school, we were simply

5

made the negative models by the nuns who were themselves not credible fashion experts to any of us. But it was painfully obvious to me that to the others, in their tailored skirts and silk blouses, we must have seemed "hopeless" and "vulgar." Though I now know that most adolescents feel out of step much of the time, I also know that for the Puerto Rican girls of my generation that sense was intensified. The way our teachers and classmates looked at us that day in school was just a taste of the culture clash that awaited us in the real world, where prospective employers and men on the street would often misinterpret our tight skirts and jingling bracelets as a come-on.

Mixed cultural signals have perpetuated certain stereotypes—for example, that of the Hispanic woman as the "Hot Tamale" or sexual firebrand. It is a one-dimensional view that the media have found easy to promote. In their special vocabulary, advertisers have designated "sizzling" and "smoldering" as the adjectives of choice for describing not only the foods but also the women of Latin America. From conversations in my house I recall hearing about the harassment that Puerto Rican women endured in factories where the "boss men" talked to them as if sexual innuendo was all they understood and, worse, often gave them the choice of submitting to advances or being fired.

It is custom, however, not chromosomes, that leads us to choose scarlet over pale pink. As young girls, we were influenced in our decisions about clothes and colors by the women—older sisters and mothers who had grown up on a tropical island where the natural environment was a riot of primary colors, where showing your skin was one way to keep cool as well as to look sexy. Most important of all, on the island, women perhaps felt freer to dress and move more provocatively, since, in most cases, they were protected by the traditions, mores, and laws of a Spanish/Catholic system of morality and machismo whose main rule was: *You may look at my sister, but if you touch her I will kill you.* The extended family and church structure could provide a young woman with a circle of safety in her small pueblo on the island; if a man "wronged" a girl, everyone would close in to save her family honor.

This is what I have gleaned from my discussions as an adult with older Puerto Rican women. They have told me about dressing in their best party clothes on Saturday nights and going to the town's plaza to promenade with their girlfriends in front of the boys they liked. The males were thus given an opportunity to admire the women and to express their admiration in the form of *piropos*: erotically charged street poems they composed on the spot. I have been subjected to a few piropos while visiting the Island, and they can be outrageous, although custom dictates that they must never cross into obscenity. This ritual, as I understand it, also entails a show of studied indifference on the woman's part; if she is "decent," she must not acknowledge the man's impassioned words. So I do understand how things can be lost in translation. When a Puerto Rican girl dressed in her idea of what is attractive meets a man from the mainstream culture who has been trained to react to certain types of clothing as a sexual signal, a clash is likely to take place. The line

I first heard based on this aspect of the myth happened when the boy who took me to my first formal dance leaned over to plant a sloppy overeager kiss painfully on my mouth, and when I didn't respond with sufficient passion said in a resentful tone: "I thought you Latin girls were supposed to mature early"—my first instance of being thought of as a fruit or vegetable—I was supposed to *ripen*, not just grow into womanhood like other girls.

It is surprising to some of my professional friends that some people, including those who should know better, still put others "in their place." Though rarer, these incidents are still commonplace in my life. It happened to me most recently during a stay at a very classy metropolitan hotel favored by young professional couples for their weddings. Late one evening after the theater, as I walked toward my room with my new colleague (a woman with whom I was coordinating an arts program), a middle-aged man in a tuxedo, a young girl in satin and lace on his arm, stepped directly into our path. With his champagne glass extended toward me, he exclaimed, "Evita!"

Our way blocked, my companion and I listened as the man half-recited, half-bellowed "Don't Cry for Me, Argentina." When he finished, the young girl said: "How about a round of applause for my daddy?" We complied, hoping this would bring the silly spectacle to a close. I was becoming aware that our little group was attracting the attention of the other guests. "Daddy" must have perceived this too, and he once more barred the way as we tried to walk past him. He began to shout-sing a ditty to the tune of "La Bamba"—except the lyrics were about a girl named María whose exploits all rhymed with her name and gonorrhea. The girl kept saying "Oh, Daddy" and looking at me with pleading eyes. She wanted me to laugh along with the others. My companion and I stood silently waiting for the man to end his offensive song. When he finished, I looked not at him but at his daughter. I advised her calmly never to ask her father what he had done in the army. Then I walked between them and to my room. My friend complimented me on my cool handling of the situation. I confessed to her that I really had wanted to push the jerk into the swimming pool. I knew that this same man—probably a corporate executive, well educated, even worldly by most standards—would not have been likely to regale a white woman with a dirty song in public. He would perhaps have checked his impulse by assuming that she could be somebody's wife or mother, or at least *somebody* who might take offense. But to him, I was just an Evita or a María: merely a character in his cartoon-populated universe.

Because of my education and my proficiency with the English language, I have acquired many mechanisms for dealing with the anger I experience. This was not true for my parents, nor is it true for the many Latin women working at menial jobs who must put up with stereotypes about our ethnic group such as: "They make good domestics." This is another facet of the myth of the Latin woman in the United States. Its origin is simple to deduce. Work as domestics, waitressing, and factory jobs are all that's available to women with little English and few skills. The myth of the Hispanic menial has been sustained by the same media phenomenon that made "Mammy" from *Gone with the Wind* America's idea of the black woman for generations: María, the housemaid or counter girl, is now indelibly etched into the national psyche. The big and the little screens have presented us with the picture of the funny Hispanic maid, mispronouncing words and cooking up a spicy storm in a shiny California kitchen.

This media-engendered image of the Latina in the United States has been documented by feminist Hispanic scholars, who claim that such portrayals are partially responsible for the denial of opportunities for upward mobility among Latinas in the professions. I have a Chicana friend working on a Ph.D. in philosophy at a major university. She says her doctor still shakes his head in puzzled amazement at all the "big words" she uses. Since I do not wear my diplomas around my neck for all to see, I too have on occasion been sent to that "kitchen," where some think I obviously belong.

One such incident that has stayed with me, though I recognize it as a minor offense, happened on the day of my first public poetry reading. It took place in Miami in a boat-restaurant where we were having lunch before the event. I was nervous and excited as I walked in with my notebook in my hand. An older woman motioned me to her table. Thinking (foolish me) that she wanted me to autograph a copy of my brand-new slender volume of verse, I went over. She ordered a cup of coffee from me, assuming that I was the waitress. Easy enough to mistake my poems for menus, I suppose. I know that it wasn't an intentional act of cruelty, yet of all the good things that happened that day, I remember that scene most clearly, because it reminded me of what I had to overcome before anyone would take me seriously. In retrospect I understand that my anger gave my reading fire, that I have almost always taken doubts in my abilities as a challenge — and that the result is, most times, a feeling of satisfaction at having won a convert when I see the cold, appraising eyes warm to my words, the body language change, the smile that indicates that I have opened some avenue for communication. That day I read to that woman and her lowered eyes told me that she was embarrassed at her little faux pas, and when I willed her to look up at me, it was my victory, and she graciously allowed me to punish her with my full attention. We shook hands at the end of the reading, and I never saw her again. She has probably forgotten the whole thing but maybe not.

Yet I am one of the lucky ones. My parents made it possible for me to acquire a stronger footing in the mainstream culture by giving me the chance at an education. And books and art have saved me from the harsher forms of ethnic and racial prejudice that many of my Hispanic *compañeras* have had to endure. I travel a lot around the United States, reading from my books of poetry and my novel, and the reception I most often receive is one of positive interest by people who want to know more about my culture. There are, however, thousands of Latinas without the privilege of an education or the entrée into society that I have. For them life is a struggle against the misconceptions perpetuated by the myth of the Latina as whore, domestic, or criminal. We cannot change this by legislating the way people look at us. The transformation, as I see it, has to occur at a much more individual level. My personal goal in my public life is to try to replace the old pervasive stereotypes and myths about Latinas with a much more interesting set of realities. Every time I give a reading, I hope the stories I tell, the dreams and fears I examine in my work, can achieve some universal truth which will get my audience past the particulars of my skin color, my accent, or my clothes.

I once wrote a poem in which I called us Latinas "God's brown daughters." 15
This poem is really a prayer of sorts, offered upward, but also, through the human-to-human channel of art, outward. It is a prayer for communication, and for respect. In it, Latin women pray "in Spanish to an Anglo God / With a Jewish heritage," and they are "fervently hoping / that if not omnipotent / at least He be bilingual."

Exploring the Text

1. What is the effect of Judith Ortiz Cofer's opening paragraph? Does her anger draw you in or distance you?
2. Note the times when Cofer explains rather than denies the basis for stereotyping. For instance, rather than deny that Latinas prefer vivid colors, she explains that this preference reflects the bright landscape of their homelands. Does this strategy work, or do you think Cofer is playing to the stereotype?
3. Note the sections of the essay that refer to personal experience. Does Cofer's use of personal experience weaken her argument or make it more effective? Explain. Would the essay be more effective with less—or more—personal experience? Explain your view.
4. What do Cofer's experiences on the bus, in the hotel, and at the poetry reading have in common? Could she have omitted any of them from her essay? Do you find her behavior toward the man in the "very classy metropolitan hotel" (para. 9) unnecessarily cruel? Explain.
5. How does Cofer broaden the argument from her personal experience to larger concerns, including other stereotypes (or stereotypes of other communities)?
6. Cofer ends by quoting one of her own poems. Is this effective? Why or why not?
7. Who do you think is Cofer's audience for this essay? Does it include the woman at the poetry reading who asks Cofer for a cup of coffee?
8. According to Cofer, "Mixed cultural signals have perpetuated certain stereotypes—for example, that of the Hispanic woman as the 'Hot Tamale' or sexual firebrand. It is a one-dimensional view that the media have found easy to promote. In their special vocabulary, advertisers have designated 'sizzling' and 'smoldering' as the adjectives of choice for describing not only the foods but also the women of Latin America" (para. 6). Does this assertion—that the media promotes stereotypes—apply today? In answering, consider Cofer's example of Latin American women, or choose another group, such as African Americans, older people, or people from the Middle East.

There Is No Unmarked Woman

Deborah Tannen

A linguist by training, Deborah Tannen (b. 1945) is the best-selling author of more than fifteen books, including *You Just Don't Understand: Women and Men in Conversation* (1990), in which she argues that "communication between men and women can be like cross-cultural communication, prey to a clash of conversational styles." Her most recent book is *You Were Always Mom's Favorite!: Sisters in Conversation throughout Their Lives* (2009). Winner of numerous fellowships and awards, Dr. Tannen is a professor of linguistics at Georgetown University. The following essay is part of a longer piece Tannen wrote for the *New York Times*, "Wears Jump Suit. Sensible Shoes. Uses Husband's Last Name." She contrasts the impact that appearance, especially clothing, has on perceptions of men and women.

Some years ago I was at a small working conference of four women and eight men. Instead of concentrating on the discussion I found myself looking at the three other women at the table, thinking how each had a different style and how each style was coherent.

One woman had dark brown hair in a classic style, a cross between Cleopatra and Plain Jane. The severity of her straight hair was softened by wavy bangs and ends that turned under. Because she was beautiful, the effect was more Cleopatra than plain.

The second woman was older, full of dignity and composure. Her hair was cut in a fashionable style that left her with only one eye, thanks to a side part that let a curtain of hair fall across half her face. As she looked down to read her prepared paper, the hair robbed her of bifocal vision and created a barrier between her and the listeners.

The third woman's hair was wild, a frosted blond avalanche falling over and beyond her shoulders. When she spoke she frequently tossed her head, calling attention to her hair and away from her lecture.

Then there was makeup. The first woman wore facial cover that made her skin smooth and pale, a black line under each eye and mascara that darkened already dark lashes. The second wore only a light gloss on her lips and a hint of shadow on her eyes. The third had blue bands under her eyes, dark blue shadow, mascara, bright red lipstick, and rouge; her fingernails flashed red.

I considered the clothes each woman had worn during the three days of the conference: In the first case, man-tailored suits in primary colors with solid-color blouses. In the second, casual but stylish black T-shirts, a floppy collarless jacket and baggy slacks or a skirt in neutral colors. The third wore a sexy jumpsuit; tight sleeveless jersey and tight yellow slacks; a dress with gaping armholes and an indulged tendency to fall off one shoulder.

Shoes? No. 1 wore string sandals with medium heels; No. 2, sensible, comfortable walking shoes; No. 3, pumps with spike heels. You can fill in the jewelry, scarves, shawls, sweaters—or lack of them.

As I amused myself finding coherence in these styles, I suddenly wondered why I was scrutinizing only the women. I scanned the eight men at the table. And then I knew why I wasn't studying them. The men's styles were unmarked.

The term "marked" is a staple of linguistic theory. It refers to the way language alters the base meaning of a word by adding a linguistic particle that has no meaning on its own. The unmarked form of a word carries the meaning that goes without saying—what you think of when you're not thinking anything special.

The unmarked tense of verbs in English is the present—for example, *visit*. To indicate past, you mark the verb by adding *ed* to yield *visited*. For future, you add a word: *will visit*. Nouns are presumed to be singular until marked for plural, typically by adding *s* or *es*, so *visit* becomes *visits* and *dish* becomes *dishes*.

The unmarked forms of most English words also convey "male." Being male is the unmarked case. Endings like *ess* and *ette* mark words as "female." Unfortunately, they also tend to mark them for frivolousness. Would you feel safe entrusting your life to a doctorette? Alfre Woodard, who was an Oscar nominee for best supporting actress, says she identifies herself as an actor because "actresses worry about eyelashes and cellulite, and women who are actors worry about the characters we are playing." Gender markers pick up extra meanings that reflect common associations with the female gender: not quite serious, often sexual.

Each of the women at the conference had to make decisions about hair, clothing, makeup, and accessories, and each decision carried meaning. Every style available to us was marked. The men in our group had made decisions, too, but the range from which they chose was incomparably narrower. Men can choose styles that are marked, but they don't have to, and in this group none did. Unlike the women, they had the option of being unmarked.

Take the men's hair styles. There was no marine crew cut or oily longish hair falling into eyes, no asymmetrical, two-tiered construction to swirl over a bald top. One man was unabashedly bald; the others had hair of standard length, parted on one side, in natural shades of brown or gray or graying. Their hair obstructed no views, left little to toss or push back or run fingers through and, consequently, needed and attracted no attention. A few men had beards. In a business setting, beards might be marked. In this academic gathering, they weren't.

There could have been a cowboy shirt with string tie or a three-piece suit or a necklaced hippie in jeans. But there wasn't. All eight men wore brown or blue slacks and nondescript shirts of light colors. No man wore sandals or boots; their shoes were dark, closed, comfortable, and flat. In short, unmarked.

Although no man wore makeup, you couldn't say the men didn't wear makeup in the sense that you could say a woman didn't wear makeup. For men, no makeup is unmarked.

I asked myself what style we women could have adopted that would have been unmarked, like the men's. The answer was none. There is no unmarked woman.

There is no woman's hairstyle that can be called standard, that says nothing about her. The range of women's hairstyles is staggering, but a woman whose hair has no particular style is perceived as not caring about how she looks, which can disqualify her from many positions, and will subtly diminish her as a person in the eyes of some.

Women must choose between attractive shoes and comfortable shoes. When our group made an unexpected trek, the woman who wore flat, laced shoes arrived first. Last to arrive was the woman in spike heels, shoes in hand and a handful of men around her.

If a woman's clothing is tight or revealing (in other words, sexy), it sends a message — an intended one of wanting to be attractive, but also a possibly unintended one of availability. If her clothes are not sexy, that too sends a message, lent meaning by the knowledge that they could have been. There are thousands of cosmetic products from which women can choose and myriad ways of applying them. Yet no makeup at all is anything but unmarked. Some men see it as a hostile refusal to please them.

Women can't even fill out a form without telling stories about themselves. 20 Most forms give four titles to choose from. "Mr." carries no meaning other than that the respondent is male. But a woman who checks "Mrs." or "Miss" communicates not only whether she has been married but also whether she has conservative tastes in forms of address — and probably other conservative values as well. Checking "Ms." declines to let on about marriage (checking "Mr." declines nothing since nothing was asked), but it also marks her as either liberated or rebellious, depending on the observer's attitudes and assumptions.

I sometimes try to duck these variously marked choices by giving my title as "Dr." — and in so doing risk marking myself as either uppity (hence sarcastic responses like "Excuse *me*!") or an overachiever (hence reactions of congratulatory surprise like "Good for you!").

All married women's surnames are marked. If a woman takes her husband's name, she announces to the world that she is married and has traditional values. To some it will indicate that she is less herself, more identified by her husband's identity. If she does not take her husband's name, this too is marked, seen as worthy of comment: She has *done* something; she has "kept her own name." A man is never said to have "kept his own name" because it never occurs to anyone that he might have given it up. For him using his own name is unmarked.

A married woman who wants to have her cake and eat it too may use her surname plus his, with or without a hyphen. But this too announces her marital status and often results in a tongue-tying string. In a list (Harvey O'Donovan, Jonathan Feldman, Stephanie Woodbury McGillicutty), the woman's multiple name stands out. It is marked.

I have never been inclined toward biological explanations of gender differences in language, but I was intrigued to see Ralph Fasold bring biological phenomena to bear on the question of linguistic marking in his book *The Sociolinguistics of Language*. Fasold stresses that language and culture are particularly unfair in treating women as the marked case because biologically it is the male that is marked. While two X chromosomes make a female, two Y chromosomes make nothing. Like the linguistic markers *s*, *es*, or *ess*, the Y chromosome doesn't "mean" anything unless it is attached to a root form—an X chromosome.

Developing this idea elsewhere Fasold points out that girls are born with fully female bodies, while boys are born with modified female bodies. He invites men who doubt this to lift up their shirts and contemplate why they have nipples.

In his book, Fasold notes "a wide range of facts which demonstrates that female is the unmarked sex." For example, he observes that there are a few species that produce only females, like the whiptail lizard. Thanks to parthenogenesis,[1] they have no trouble having as many daughters as they like. There are no species, however, that produce only males. This is no surprise, since any such species would become extinct in its first generation.

Fasold is also intrigued by species that produce individuals not involved in reproduction, like honeybees and leaf-cutter ants. Reproduction is handled by the queen and a relatively few males; the workers are sterile females. "Since they do not reproduce," Fasold said, "there is no reason for them to be one sex or the other, so they default, so to speak, to female."

Fasold ends his discussion of these matters by pointing out that if language reflected biology, grammar books would direct us to use "she" to include males and females and "he" only for specifically male referents. But they don't. They tell us that "he" means "he or she," and that "she" is used only if the referent is specifically female. This use of "he" as the sex-indefinite pronoun is an innovation introduced into English by grammarians in the eighteenth and nineteenth centuries, according to Peter Mühlhäusler and Rom Harré in *Pronouns and People*. From at least about 1500, the correct sex-indefinite pronoun was "they," as it still is in casual spoken English. In other words, the female was declared by grammarians to be the marked case.

Writing this article may mark me not as a writer, not as a linguist, not as an analyst of human behavior, but as a feminist—which will have positive or negative, but in any case powerful, connotations for readers. Yet I doubt that anyone reading Ralph Fasold's book would put that label on him.

I discovered the markedness inherent in the very topic of gender after writing a book on differences in conversational style based on geographical region, ethnicity, class, age, and gender. When I was interviewed, the vast majority of journalists wanted to talk about the differences between women and men. While I thought I was simply

---

[1] Asexual reproduction in females that does not require fertilization by males.—Eds.

describing what I observed—something I had learned to do as a researcher—merely mentioning women and men marked me as a feminist for some.

When I wrote a book devoted to gender differences in ways of speaking, I sent the manuscript to five male colleagues, asking them to alert me to any interpretation, phrasing, or wording that might seem unfairly negative toward men. Even so, when the book came out, I encountered responses like that of the television talk show host who, after interviewing me, turned to the audience and asked if they thought I was male-bashing.

Leaping upon a poor fellow who affably nodded in agreement, she made him stand and asked, "Did what she say accurately describe you?" "Oh, yes," he answered. "That's me exactly." "And what she said about women—does that sound like your wife?" "Oh yes," he responded. "That's her exactly." "Then why do you think she's male-bashing?" He answered, with disarming honesty, "Because she's a woman and she's saying things about men."

To say anything about women and men without marking oneself as either feminist or anti-feminist, male-basher or apologist for men seems as impossible for a woman as trying to get dressed in the morning without inviting interpretations of her character.

Sitting at the conference table musing on these matters, I felt sad to think that we women didn't have the freedom to be unmarked that the men sitting next to us had. Some days you just want to get dressed and go about your business. But if you're a woman, you can't, because there is no unmarked woman.

Exploring the Text

1. What is the effect of opening the essay with elaborate descriptions of the women's appearance?
2. Do Deborah Tannen's references to her personal experiences strengthen or weaken the argument about marked versus unmarked people? Explain.
3. What is the effect of Tannen's turning to "biological explanations of gender differences in language" (para. 24)? Does this discussion support or challenge her thesis about marked women?
4. In paragraph 32, what is the impact of Tannen's presenting the television anecdote as a conversation rather than a straight narrative?
5. Identify examples of subjective description, technical explanation, personal opinion, and argumentative conclusions in the essay. How effective is Tannen in embedding a technical analysis into a social commentary? Discuss.
6. Tannen uses the framing, or envelope, technique—opening and closing an essay with the same reference, quotation, or anecdote. What effect does this have?
7. Tannen wrote this essay in 1993. Is it outdated, or is it even more relevant today? Consider her thesis in light of other cultures or ethnicities or time periods. In a country where women's choices in dress are restricted by social mores, for example, is Tannen's claim applicable?

8. In the last paragraph, Tannen argues that women should have the "freedom to be unmarked." What does she mean by this? Do you think an unmarked woman is possible in our culture today?

Are Women Really More Talkative Than Men?

Matthias R. Mehl et al.

> The principal researcher, Matthias R. Mehl, is an assistant professor of psychology at the University of Arizona. He earned an MA in psychology from Friedrich-Alexander University in Germany and a PhD in social and personality psychology from the University of Texas at Austin. In 2008, the Society for Personality and Social Psychology named him one of the ten most cited assistant professors in the field. He describes his research interests as "naturalistic person-environment interactions . . . how psychological responses to upheaval change over time, and how social interactions facilitate coping." Others on the research team for this article were Simine Vazire, Nairan Ramirez-Esparza, Richard Slatcher, and James Pennebaker. This article appeared in *Science* magazine in 2007.

Sex differences in conversational behavior have long been a topic of public and scientific interest (*1, 2*). The stereotype of female talkativeness is deeply engrained in Western folklore and often considered a scientific fact. In the first printing of her book, neuropsychiatrist Brizendine reported, "A woman uses about 20,000 words per day while a man uses about 7,000" (*3*). These numbers have since circulated throughout television, radio, and print media (e.g., CBS, CNN, National Public Radio, *Newsweek*, the *New York Times*, and the *Washington Post*). Indeed, the 20,000-versus-7000 word estimates appear to have achieved the status of a cultural myth in that comparable differences have been cited in the media for the past 15 years (*4*).

In reality, no study has systematically recorded the natural conversations of large groups of people for extended periods of time. Consequently, there have not been the necessary data for reliably estimating differences in daily word usage among women and men (*5*). Extrapolating from a reanalysis of tape-recorded daily conversations from 153 participants from the British National Corpus (*6*), Liberman recently estimated that women speak 8805 words and men 6073 words per day. However, he acknowledged that these estimates may be problematic because no information was available regarding when participants decided to turn off their manual tape recorders (*4*).

Over the past 8 years, we have developed a method for recording natural language using the electronically activated recorder (EAR) (*7*). The EAR is a digital voice recorder that unobtrusively tracks people's real-world moment-to-moment interactions. It operates by periodically recording snippets of ambient sounds, including conversations, while participants go about their daily lives. Because of the covert digital recording, it is impossible for participants to control or even to sense when the EAR is on or off. For the purpose of this study, the EAR can be used to track naturally spoken words and to estimate how many words women and men use over the course of a day.

In the default paradigm, participants wear the EAR for several days during their waking hours. The device is programmed to record for 30 s every 12.5 min. All captured words spoken by the participant are transcribed. The number of spoken words per day can then be estimated by extrapolating from a simple word count, the number of sampled sound files, and the recording time per sound file.

We addressed the question about sex differences in daily word use with data from six samples based on 396 participants (210 women and 186 men) that were conducted between 1998 and 2004. Five of the samples were composed of university students in the United States, and the sixth, university students in Mexico. Table 1 provides background information on the samples along with estimates for the number of words that female and male participants spoke per day (8). 5

The data suggest that women spoke on average 16,215 (SD = 7301) words and men 15,669 (SD = 8633) words over an assumed period of, on average, 17 waking hours. Expressed in a common effect-size metric (Cohen's $d = 0.07$), this sex difference in daily word use (546 words) is equal to only 7% of the standardized variability among women and men. Further, the difference does not meet conventional thresholds for statistical significance ($P = 0.248$, one-sided test). Thus, the data fail to reveal a reliable sex difference in daily word use. Women and men both use on average about 16,000 words per day, with very large individual differences around this mean.

A potential limitation of our analysis is that all participants were university students. The resulting homogeneity in the samples with regard to sociodemographic characteristics may have affected our estimates of daily word usage. However, none of the samples provided support for the idea that women have substantially larger lexical budgets than men. Further, to the extent that sex differences in daily word use are assumed to be biologically based, evolved adaptations (3), they should be detectable among university students as much as in more diverse samples. We therefore conclude, on the basis of available empirical evidence, that the widespread and highly publicized stereotype about female talkativeness is unfounded.

References and Notes

1. R. Lakoff, *Language and Woman's Place* (Harper, New York, 1975).
2. L. Litosseliti, *Gender and Language: Theory and Practice* (Arnold, London, 2006).
3. L. Brizendine, *The Female Brain* (Morgan Road, New York, 2006).

TABLE 1

Estimated number of words spoken per day for female and male study participants across six samples. $N = 396$. Year refers to the year when the data collection started; duration refers to the approximate number of days participants wore the EAR; the weighted average weighs the respective sample group mean by the sample size of the group.

SAMPLE	YEAR	LOCATION	DURATION	AGE RANGE (YEARS)	SAMPLE SIZE (N) WOMEN	SAMPLE SIZE (N) MEN	ESTIMATED AVERAGE NUMBER (SD) OF WORDS SPOKEN PER DAY WOMEN	ESTIMATED AVERAGE NUMBER (SD) OF WORDS SPOKEN PER DAY MEN
1	2004	USA	7 days	18–29	56	56	18,443 (7460)	16,576 (7871)
2	2003	USA	4 days	17–23	42	37	14,297 (6441)	14,060 (9065)
3	2003	Mexico	4 days	17–25	31	20	14,704 (6215)	15,022 (7864)
4	2001	USA	2 days	17–22	47	49	16,177 (7520)	16,569 (9108)
5	2001	USA	10 days	18–26	7	4	15,761 (8985)	24,051 (10,211)
6	1998	USA	4 days	17–23	27	20	16,496 (7914)	12,867 (8343)
						Weighted average	16,215 (7301)	15,669 (8633)

4. M. Liberman, *Sex-Linked Lexical Budgets*, http://itre.cis.upenn.edu/~myl/languagelog/archives/003420.html (first accessed 12 December 2006).

5. D. James, J. Drakich, in *Gender and Conversational Interaction*, D. Tannen, Ed. (Oxford Univ. Press, New York, 1993), pp. 281–313.

6. P. Rayson, G. Leech, M. Hodges, *Int. J. Corpus Linguist*, **2**, 133 (1997).

7. M. R. Mehl, J. W. Pennebaker, M. Crow, J. Dabbs, J. Price, *Behav. Res. Methods Instrum Comput*, **33**, 517 (2001).

8. Details on methods and analysis are available on *Science* Online.

9. This research was supported by a grant from the National Institute of Mental Health (MH 52391). We thank V. Dominguez, J. Greenberg, S. Holleran, C. Mehl, M. Peterson, and T. Schmader for their valuable feedback.

Exploring the Text

1. What is the stereotype that Matthias Mehl and his research team sought to debunk? Is discussing this stereotype an effective way to open the article? Explain your answer.

2. How does Mehl establish that his research will not merely duplicate previous studies? What is original about the work he and his colleagues have been doing?

3. What is meant by "the default paradigm" (para. 4)?

4. What information do you gain from Table 1 that is not in the written text? Explain why you believe that this is or is not an effective way to convey additional information.

5. Mehl and his colleagues are careful to explain their hypothesis, methodology, and findings, including some limitations of their study. What other questions do you think they have left unanswered or unexamined? What questions might guide further research?

6. Judging from the References and Notes, how would you characterize the type of research Mehl and his colleagues conducted?

7. This article reports a scientific study and its findings. In what ways is it the same as a conventional essay of explanation or argument? In what ways does it differ? Cite specific passages to support your response.

8. In an interview on National Public Radio, Mehl made the following statement about the importance of debunking the stereotype of the "female chatterbox" and the "silent male": "It puts men into the gender box, that in order to be a good male, we'd better not talk—[that] silence is golden. The stereotype puts unfortunate constraints on men and women—the idea that you can only happily be a woman if you're talkative and you can only be happy as a man if you're reticent. The study relieves those gender constraints." Do you agree or disagree with Mehl's interpretation of the study's impact? Why?

9. Mehl's research has proved to be of interest to a wider, nonspecialist audience. What rhetorical strategies does he employ in this article to make it accessible to readers who are not professional psychologists or linguists without diluting the research itself? Examine one of the reports on his work, and discuss how the analysis of his

research is reported—specifically, how the reporting differs from Mehl's own article. See, for instance, "Stereotypes of Quiet Men, Chatty Women Not Sound Science" from the *Washington Post*; "Study: Women Don't Talk More Than Men" from ABC News; and "Men 'No Less Chatty than Women'" from BBC News.

Barbie Doll

MARGE PIERCY

American poet, novelist, and activist Marge Piercy (b. 1936) grew up in Michigan in a working-class family during the Depression. She graduated from Northwestern University with an MA and went on to write more than thirty books, including novels and volumes of poetry. She is known for her highly personal free verse and her themes of feminism and social protest. "Barbie Doll," from her 1973 collection *To Be of Use*, comments on the popular icon—and children's toy—of the same name.

This girlchild was born as usual
and presented dolls that did pee-pee
and miniature GE stoves and irons
and wee lipsticks the color of cherry candy.
Then in the magic of puberty, a classmate said: 5
You have a great big nose and fat legs.

She was healthy, tested intelligent,
possessed strong arms and back,
abundant sexual drive and manual dexterity.
She went to and fro apologizing.   10
Everyone saw a fat nose on thick legs.

She was advised to play coy,
exhorted to come on hearty,
exercise, diet, smile and wheedle.
Her good nature wore out   15
like a fan belt.
So she cut off her nose and her legs
and offered them up.

In the casket displayed on satin she lay
with the undertaker's cosmetics painted on,   20
a turned-up putty nose,
dressed in a pink and white nightie.

Doesn't she look pretty? everyone said.
Consummation at last.
To every woman a happy ending.   25

. . . .

Exploring the Text

1. Identify several stereotypes that Marge Piercy draws on in this poem. Why is *girlchild* — one word — an appropriate term?
2. What images and colors does Piercy use to depict the girlchild?
3. Who is the speaker in the poem?
4. How does the way the girl is encouraged to behave run counter to her natural inclinations?
5. How does the speaker entwine other commentaries into the poem? Why? Are these voices in the mind of the girlchild real or imagined?
6. What is the speaker's tone in this poem? What specific lines and images lead you to your understanding of tone?

Chancellor Séguier at the Entry of Louis XIV into Paris in 1660

CHARLES LE BRUN

and

The Chancellor Séguier on Horseback

KEHINDE WILEY

Charles Le Brun (1619–1690) was responsible for the production of paintings, sculpture, and decorative objects commissioned by the French government during the reign of Louis XIV. The monarch had extravagant tastes and favored artists whose work reflected the opulence of the period. Although known as a fine portrait painter, Le Brun preferred a narrative style, believing that a painting told a story through symbols, costumes, and gestures — as in the one shown here depicting Pierre Séguier, Duke of Villemor, the Lord Chief Justice of France. He and his entourage are shown entering Paris in August 1660 to celebrate the marriage of Louis XIV and his wife, Maria Theresa, daughter of the king of Spain. Those shown would be counselors, treasurers, secretaries, court ushers, and the like who took part in the procession.

Kehinde Wiley was born in 1977 in Los Angeles, lives in New York City, and maintains studios in several cities worldwide, including Beijing and Dakar. He holds a BFA from the San Francisco Art Institute and an MFA from Yale. Wiley is a photorealist painter whose work is inspired by traditional portraitists, such as Sir Joshua Reynolds, Thomas Gainsborough, Titian, and Jean-Auguste-Dominique Ingres. His paintings are in the permanent collections of the Columbus Museum of Art, the Studio Museum in Harlem, the Walker Art Center, the Miami Art Museum, and the Detroit Institute of Arts, among others. To create paintings such as this one, Wiley often seeks out average African American men and asks them to select a painting from one of the old masters such as Titian or Ingres. Then they strike a pose from one of those paintings. In an interview with *Art in America*, Wiley said of his work, "Black masculinity has been codified in a fixed way. I'm not trying to provide a direct corrective, but . . . there is a certain desire in my work to tie the urban street and the way it's been depicted with elements that are not necessarily coded as masculine."

Chancellor Séguier at the Entry of Louis XIV into Paris in 1660 (c. 1661, oil on canvas, 295 x 357 cm.) (See insert for color version.)

The Chancellor Séguier on Horseback (2005, oil on canvas, 108" x 144") (See insert for color version.)

Exploring the Texts

1. The men in Charles Le Brun's painting are dressed in the height of fashion for their day. How would you characterize it? Note differences between the eminence on horseback and the others. What specific elements of dress seem to define the male image? Note the hair, hats, and shoes.
2. The entourage pictured in Le Brun's painting was intended as a sign to the cheering Parisians that a new epoch of peace and glory had dawned. What elements of this painting attest to affluence and power?
3. What symbols of African American culture or hip-hop culture does Kehinde Wiley include in his painting?
4. Wiley applies the visual vocabulary and conventions of glorification, wealth, and prestige to his subject matter. In this painting, what is the fashion code? How does the appearance of these men define the image of today's young, urban African American male?
5. What is the effect of Wiley's melding of late Renaissance prototypes and hip-hop street style? Is Wiley being critical of one or the other — or both? Is he celebrating or criticizing (or both) what one reviewer called "the hyper-masculine posturing of hip-hop culture"?

6. In a review of one of Wiley's shows, an art critic asks, "Do his big, flashy pictures of young African-American men recast as the kings, dandies, prophets, and saints of European portraiture subvert the timeworn ruses of Western art and its hierarchies of race, class and sex?" Based on these two paintings, how would you answer that question? To expand your response, you might look at other paintings by Wiley on his Web site, www.kehindewiley.com.

Defining Masculinity

The following six texts comment directly or indirectly on definitions and images of masculinity in today's society:

Sources
1. **Leonard McCombe,** *Marlboro Man* (photo)
2. **Paul Theroux,** *Being a Man*
3. **Gretel Ehrlich,** *About Men*
4. **Rebecca Walker,** *Putting Down the Gun*
5. **Mark Bauerlein and Sandra Stotsky,** *Why Johnny Won't Read*
6. **David Brooks,** *Mind over Muscle*

After you have read, studied, and synthesized these pieces, enter the conversation by responding to one of the prompts on page 580.

1. *Marlboro Man*

Leonard McCombe

This iconic photograph, taken by Leonard McCombe, was used by the Philip Morris Company to transform Marlboro cigarettes from the feminine appeal of being "Mild as May" to a more rugged image that appealed to men. When this campaign began in 1955, sales were at $5 billion; by 1957, they had jumped to $20 billion despite growing health concerns over cigarettes. McCombe took this photo of Clarence Hailey Young, a ranch foreman in Texas, in 1949.

Questions

1. How does the composition of the photograph contribute to its effect? Why is the focus exclusively on the face rather than a longer shot that would include the entire body?
2. What is the effect of the subject's gaze not meeting the eyes of the viewer?
3. *Life* magazine assigned McCombe to do a story that dispelled the glamorous image of cowboys seen in Hollywood movies of the period and, instead, documented the hardworking life of ranchers. What stereotypes about cowboys or the West does the photo exploit — or combat?
4. Why do you think that this photo caught the eye of legendary advertising executive Leo Burnett as a good choice for his campaign to transform the image of Marlboro cigarettes?

2. *Being a Man*

PAUL THEROUX

In the following essay, part of the collection *Sunrise with Seamonsters* (1985), novelist and travel writer Paul Theroux examines society's views of masculinity.

There is a pathetic sentence in the chapter "Fetishism" in Dr. Norman Cameron's book *Personality Development and Psychopathology*. It goes, "Fetishists are nearly always men; and their commonest fetish is a woman's shoe." I cannot read that sentence without thinking that it is just one more awful thing about being a man — and perhaps it is an important thing to know about us.

I have always disliked being a man. The whole idea of manhood in America is pitiful, in my opinion. This version of masculinity is a little like having to wear an ill-fitting coat for one's entire life (by contrast, I imagine femininity to be an oppressive sense of nakedness). Even the expression "Be a man!" strikes me as insulting and abusive. It means: Be stupid, be unfeeling, obedient, soldierly and stop thinking. Man means "manly"—how can one think about men without considering the terrible ambition of manliness? And yet it is part of every man's life. It is a hideous and crippling lie; it not only insists on difference and connives at superiority, it is also by its very nature destructive—emotionally damaging and socially harmful.

The youth who is subverted, as most are, into believing in the masculine ideal is effectively separated from women and he spends the rest of his life finding women a riddle and a nuisance. Of course, there is a female version of this male affliction. It begins with mothers encouraging little girls to say (to other adults) "Do you like my new dress?" In a sense, little girls are traditionally urged to please adults with a kind of coquettishness, while boys are enjoined to behave like monkeys towards each other. The nine-year-old coquette proceeds to become womanish in a subtle power game in which she learns to be sexually indispensable, socially decorative and always alert to a man's sense of inadequacy.

Femininity—being lady-like—implies needing a man as witness and seducer; but masculinity celebrates the exclusive company of men. That is why it is so grotesque; and that is also why there is no manliness without inadequacy—because it denies men the natural friendship of women.

It is very hard to imagine any concept of manliness that does not belittle women,   5 and it begins very early. At an age when I wanted to meet girls—let's say the treacherous years of thirteen to sixteen—I was told to take up a sport, get more fresh air, join the Boy Scouts, and I was urged not to read so much. It was the 1950s and if you asked too many questions about sex you were sent to camp—boy's camp, of course: the nightmare. Nothing is more unnatural or prison-like than a boy's camp, but if it were not for them we would have no Elks' Lodges, no pool rooms, no boxing matches, no Marines.

And perhaps no sports as we know them. Everyone is aware of how few in number are the athletes who behave like gentlemen. Just as high school basketball teaches you how to be a poor loser, the manly attitude towards sports seems to be little more than a recipe for creating bad marriages, social misfits, moral degenerates, sadists, latent rapists and just plain louts. I regard high school sports as a drug far worse than marijuana, and it is the reason that the average tennis champion, say, is a pathetic oaf.

Any objective study would find the quest for manliness essentially right-wing, puritanical, cowardly, neurotic and fueled largely by a fear of women. It is also certainly philistine. There is no book-hater like a Little League coach. But indeed all the creative arts are obnoxious to the manly ideal, because at their best the arts are pursued by uncompetitive and essentially solitary people. It makes it very hard for a creative youngster, for any boy who expresses the desire to be alone seems to be saying that there is something wrong with him.

It ought to be clear by now that I have something of an objection to the way we turn boys into men. It does not surprise me that when the President of the United

States [George W. Bush] has his customary weekend off he dresses like a cowboy—it is both a measure of his insecurity and his willingness to please. In many ways, American culture does little more for a man than prepare him for modeling clothes in the L. L. Bean catalogue. I take this as a personal insult because for many years I found it impossible to admit to myself that I wanted to be a writer. It was my guilty secret, because being a writer was incompatible with being a man.

There are people who might deny this, but that is because the American writer, typically, has been so at pains to prove his manliness that we have come to see literariness and manliness as mingled qualities. But first there was a fear that writing was not a manly profession—indeed, not a profession at all. (The paradox in American letters is that it has always been easier for a woman to write and for a man to be published.) Growing up, I had thought of sports as wasteful and humiliating, and the idea of manliness was a bore. My wanting to become a writer was not a flight from that oppressive role-playing, but I quickly saw that it was at odds with it. Everything in stereotyped manliness goes against the life of the mind. The Hemingway personality is too tedious to go into here, and in any case his exertions are well-known, but certainly it was not until this aberrant behavior was examined by feminists in the 1960s that any male writer dared question the pugnacity in Hemingway's fiction. All the bullfighting and arm wrestling and elephant shooting diminished Hemingway as a writer, but it is consistent with a prevailing attitude in American writing: one cannot be a male writer without first proving that one is a man.

It is normal in America for a man to be dismissive or even somewhat apologetic about being a writer. Various factors make it easier. There is a heartiness about journalism that makes it acceptable—journalism is the manliest form of American writing and, therefore, the profession the most independent-minded women seek (yes, it is an illusion, but that is my point). Fiction-writing is equated with a kind of dispirited failure and is only manly when it produces wealth—money is masculinity. So is drinking. Being a drunkard is another assertion, if misplaced, of manliness. The American male writer is traditionally proud of his heavy drinking. But we are also a very literal-minded people. A man proves his manhood in America in old-fashioned ways. He kills lions, like Hemingway; or he hunts ducks, like Nathanael West; or he makes pronouncements like, "A man should carry enough knife to defend himself with," as James Jones once said to a *Life* interviewer. Or he says he can drink you under the table. But even tiny drunken William Faulkner loved to mount a horse and go fox hunting, and Jack Kerouac roistered up and down Manhattan in a lumberjack shirt (and spent every night of *The Subterraneans*[1] with his mother in Queens). And we are familiar with the lengths to which Norman Mailer[2] is prepared, in his endearing way, to prove that he is just as much a monster as the next man.

10

---

[1]A 1960 film based on Jack Kerouac's novel about the lifestyle of 1950s Beats.—Eds.
[2]An American journalist and novelist.—Eds.

When the novelist John Irving was revealed as a wrestler, people took him to be a very serious writer; and even a bubble reputation like Erich (*Love Story*) Segal's was enhanced by the news that he ran the marathon in a respectable time. How surprised we would be if Joyce Carol Oates were revealed as a sumo wrestler or Joan Didion active in pumping iron. "Lives in New York City with her three children" is the typical woman writer's biographical note, for just as the male writer must prove he has achieved a sort of muscular manhood, the woman writer—or rather her publicists—must prove her motherhood.

There would be no point in saying any of this if it were not generally accepted that to be a man is somehow—even now in feminist-influenced America—a privilege. It is on the contrary an unmerciful and punishing burden. Being a man is bad enough; being manly is appalling (in this sense, women's lib has done much more for men than for women). It is the sinister silliness of men's fashions, and a clubby attitude in the arts. It is the subversion of good students. It is the so-called "Dress Code" of the Ritz-Carlton Hotel in Boston, and it is the institutionalized cheating in college sports. It is the most primitive insecurity.

And this is also why men often object to feminism but are afraid to explain why: of course women have a justified grievance, but most men believe—and with reason—that their lives are just as bad.

Questions

1. Much of this essay consists of negative descriptions of what it means to Paul Theroux to be masculine or a man. Why does he offer such strong images and assertions?

2. Do you agree or disagree with Theroux when he writes, "It is very hard to imagine any concept of manliness that does not belittle women, and it begins very early" (para. 5)? Explain.

3. How does Theroux prepare his readers for the turn the essay takes in paragraph 12 when he says, "There would be no point in saying any of this if it were not generally accepted that to be a man is somehow—even now in feminist-influenced America—a privilege"? What does this statement reveal about Theroux's overall purpose in this piece?

4. Theroux's essay was written in 1983. Which of his points are outdated? Which ones do you think remain true today?

3. *About Men*

Gretel Ehrlich

In the following essay from *The Solace of Open Spaces* (1984), author and documentary filmmaker Gretel Ehrlich compares the popular view of the cowboy with her own experiences.

When I'm in New York but feeling lonely for Wyoming I look for the Marlboro ads in the subway. What I'm aching to see is horseflesh, the glint of a spur, a line of distant mountains, brimming creeks, and a reminder of the ranchers and cowboys I've ridden with for the last eight years. But the men I see in those posters with their stern, humorless looks remind me of no one I know here. In our hellbent earnestness to romanticize the cowboy we've ironically disesteemed his true character. If he's "strong and silent" it's because there's probably no one to talk to. If he "rides away into the sunset" it's because he's been on horseback since four in the morning moving cattle and he's trying, fifteen hours later, to get home to his family. If he's "a rugged individualist" he's also part of a team: ranch work is teamwork and even the glorified open-range cowboys of the 1880s rode up and down the Chisholm Trail in the company of twenty or thirty other riders. Instead of the macho, trigger-happy man our culture has perversely wanted him to be, the cowboy is more apt to be convivial, quirky, and softhearted. To be "tough" on a ranch has nothing to do with conquests and displays of power. More often than not, circumstances—like the colt he's riding or an unexpected blizzard—are overpowering him. It's not toughness but "toughing it out" that counts. In other words, this macho, cultural artifact the cowboy has become is simply a man who possesses resilience, patience, and an instinct for survival. "Cowboys are just like a pile of rocks—everything happens to them. They get climbed on, kicked, rained and snowed on, scuffed up by wind. Their job is 'just to take it,'" one old-timer told me.

A cowboy is someone who loves his work. Since the hours are long—ten to fifteen hours a day—and the pay is $30 he has to. What's required of him is an odd mixture of physical vigor and maternalism. His part of the beef-raising industry is to birth and nurture calves and take care of their mothers. For the most part his work is done on horseback and in a lifetime he sees and comes to know more animals than people. The iconic myth surrounding him is built on American notions of heroism: the index of a man's value as measured in physical courage. Such ideas have perverted manliness into a self-absorbed race for cheap thrills. In a rancher's world, courage has less to do with facing danger than with acting spontaneously—usually on behalf of an animal or another rider. If a cow is stuck in a boghole he throws a loop around her neck, takes his dally (a half hitch around the saddle horn), and pulls her out with horsepower. If a calf is born sick, he may take her home, warm her in front of the kitchen fire, and massage her legs until dawn. One friend, whose favorite horse was trying to swim a lake with hobbles on, dove under water and cut her legs loose with a knife, then swam her to shore, his arm around her neck lifeguard-style, and saved her from drowning. Because these incidents are usually linked to someone or something outside himself, the westerner's courage is selfless, a form of compassion.

The physical punishment that goes with cowboying is greatly underplayed. Once fear is dispensed with, the threshold of pain rises to meet the demands of the job. When Jane Fonda asked Robert Redford (in the film *Electric Horseman*) if he was sick as he struggled to his feet one morning, he replied, "No, just bent." For once the movies had it right. The cowboys I was sitting with laughed in agreement. Cowboys are rarely complainers; they show their stoicism by laughing at themselves.

If a rancher or cowboy has been thought of as a "man's man" — laconic, hard-drinking, inscrutable — there's almost no place in which the balancing act between male and female, manliness and femininity, can be more natural. If he's gruff, handsome, and physically fit on the outside, he's androgynous at the core. Ranchers are midwives, hunters, nurturers, providers, and conservationists all at once. What we've interpreted as toughness — weathered skin, calloused hands, a squint in the eye and a growl in the voice — only masks the tenderness inside. "Now don't go telling me these lambs are cute," one rancher warned me the first day I walked into the football-field-sized lambing sheds. The next thing I knew he was holding a black lamb. "Ain't this little rat good-lookin'?"

So many of the men who came to the West were southerners — men looking   5
for work and a new life after the Civil War — that chivalrousness and strict codes of honor were soon thought of as western traits. There were very few women in Wyoming during territorial days, so when they did arrive (some as mail-order brides from places like Philadelphia) there was a stand-offishness between the sexes and a formality that persists now. Ranchers still tip their hats and say, "Howdy, ma'am" instead of shaking hands with me.

Even young cowboys are often evasive with women. It's not that they're Jekyll and Hyde creatures — gentle with animals and rough on women — but rather, that they don't know how to bring their tenderness into the house and lack the vocabulary to express the complexity of what they feel. Dancing wildly all night becomes a metaphor for the explosive emotions pent up inside, and when these are, on occasion, released, they're so battery-charged and potent that one caress of the face or one "I love you" will peal for a long while.

The geographical vastness and the social isolation here make emotional evolution seem impossible. Those contradictions of the heart between respectability, logic, and convention on the one hand, and impulse, passion, and intuition on the other, played out wordlessly against the paradisical beauty of the West, give cowboys a wide-eyed but drawn look. Their lips pucker up, not with kisses but with immutability. They may want to break out, staying up all night with a lover just to talk, but they don't know how and can't imagine what the consequences will be. Those rare occasions when they do bare themselves result in confusion. "I feel as if I'd sprained my heart," one friend told me a month after such a meeting.

My friend Ted Hoagland wrote, "No one is as fragile as a woman but no one is as fragile as a man." For all the women here who use "fragileness" to avoid work or as a sexual ploy, there are men who try to hide theirs, all the while clinging to an adolescent dependency on women to cook their meals, wash their clothes, and keep the ranch house warm in winter. But there is true vulnerability in evidence here. Because these men work with animals, not machines or numbers, because they live outside in landscapes of torrential beauty, because they are confined to a place and a routine embellished with awesome variables, because calves die in the arms that pulled others into life, because they go to the mountains as if on a pilgrimage to find out what makes a herd of elk tick, their strength is also a softness, their toughness, a rare delicacy.

Questions

1. Gretel Ehrlich opens with a reference to the Marlboro Man (pp. 566–7), a lone and rugged-looking cowboy who represented Marlboro in its cigarette advertising for many years. With this reference and her description of the Wyoming landscape, what effect does she achieve in the first three sentences of her essay?
2. In the first paragraph, Ehrlich claims that by romanticizing the cowboy, we have "disesteemed his true character" (para. 1). How does she define that "true character"?
3. What does Ehrlich mean when she calls the cowboy "an odd mixture of physical vigor and maternalism" (para. 2)?
4. In paragraphs 5 and 6, Ehrlich analyzes the cowboy's relationship with women. How has the cowboy's history defined the way he interacts with women?
5. How does the paradoxical statement by Ted Hoagland that "[n]o one is as fragile as a woman but no one is as fragile as a man" (para. 8) distill the points Ehrlich makes throughout the essay?

4. *Putting Down the Gun*

Rebecca Walker

In the following excerpt from her introduction to the essay collection *What Makes a Man: 22 Writers Imagine the Future* (2004), Rebecca Walker, journalist, activist, and author of the memoir *Black White Jewish*, looks at the pressures boys experience to conform to certain societal expectations.

The idea for this book was born one night after a grueling conversation with my then eleven-year-old son. He had come home from his progressive middle school unnaturally quiet and withdrawn, shrugging off my questions of concern with uncharacteristic irritability. Where was the sunny, chatty boy I dropped off that morning? What had befallen him in the perilous halls of middle school? I backed off but kept a close eye on him, watching for clues.

After a big bowl of his favorite pasta, he sat on a sofa in my study and read his science textbook as I wrote at my desk. We both enjoyed this simple yet profound togetherness, the two of us focused on our own projects yet palpably connected. As we worked under the soft glow of paper lanterns, with the heat on high and our little dog snoring at his feet, my son began to relax. I could feel a shift as he began to remember, deep in his body, that he was home, that he was safe, that he didn't have to brace to protect himself from the expectations of the outside world.

An hour or so passed like this before he announced that he had a question. He had morphed back into the child I knew, and was lying down with a colorful blanket over his legs, using one hand to scratch behind the dog's ears. "I've been thinking that maybe I should play sports at school."

"Sports?" I replied with surprise, swiveling around and leaning back in my chair. "Any sport in mind, or just sports in general?"

A nonchalant shrug. "Maybe softball, I like softball."   5

I cocked my head to one side. "What brought this on?"

"I don't know," he said. "Maybe girls will like me if I play sports."

Excuse me?

My boy is intuitive, smart, and creative beyond belief. At the time he loved animals, Japanese anime, the rap group Dead Prez, and everything having to do with snowboarding. He liked to help both of his grandmothers in the garden. He liked to read science fiction. He liked to climb into bed with me and lay his head on my chest. He liked to build vast and intricate cities with his Legos, and was beginning what I thought would be a lifelong love affair with chess.

Maybe girls would like him if he played sports?   10

Call me extreme, but I felt like my brilliant eleven-year-old daughter had come home and said, "Maybe boys will like me if I stop talking in class." Or my gregarious African-American son had told me, "Maybe the kids will like me if I act white."

I tried to stay calm as he illuminated the harsh realities of his sixth grade social scene. In a nutshell, the girls liked the jocks the best, and sometimes deigned to give the time of day to the other team, the computer nerds. Since he wasn't allowed to play violent computer games — we forbade them in our house — he was having trouble securing his place with the latter, hence his desire to assume the identity of the former. When I asked about making friends based on common interests rather than superficial categories, he got flustered. "You don't understand," he said huffily. "Boys talk about sports, like their matches and who scored what and stuff, or they talk about new versions of computer games or tricks they learned to get to higher levels." Tears welled up in his eyes. "I don't have anything to talk about."

He was right; until that moment I had had no idea, but suddenly the truth of being a sixth-grade boy in America crystallized before me. My beautiful boy and every other mother's beautiful boy had what essentially boiled down to two options: fight actually in sport, or fight virtually on the computer. Athlete, gladiator, secret agent, Tomb Raider. The truth of his existence, his many likes and dislikes, none of them having to do with winning or killing of any kind, had no social currency. My son could compete and score, perform and win, or be an outcast or worse, invisible, his unique gifts unnoticed and unharvested, the world around him that much more impoverished.

That night I went to sleep with several things on my mind: the conversation I planned to have with the head of my son's school about the need for a comprehensive, curricular interrogation of the contours of masculinity; the way girls find themselves drawn to more "traditional" displays of masculinity because they are more unsure than ever about how to experience their own femininity; and the many hours and endless creativity I would have to devote to ensuring that my son's true self would not be entirely snuffed out by the cultural imperative.

And then there was the final and most chilling thought of all: 15

A bat, a "joy stick." What's next, a gun?

It occurred to me that my son was being primed for war, was being prepared to pick up a gun. The first steps were clear: Tell him that who he is authentically is not enough; tell him that he will not be loved unless he abandons his own desires and picks up a tool of competition; tell him that to really be of value he must stand ready to compete, dominate, and, if necessary, kill, if not actually then virtually, financially, athletically.

If one's life purpose is obscured by the pressure to conform to a generic type and other traces of self are ostracized into shadow, then just how difficult is it to pick up a gun, metaphoric or literal, as a means of self-definition, as a way of securing what feels like personal power?

Questions

1. Rebecca Walker focuses on her own son as she develops her thesis. Is doing so an effective strategy to reach her audience? Explain whether the addition of quantitative evidence would have strengthened or weakened the introduction. As you develop your response, take into account what you believe Walker's purpose is.

2. Do you think the pressure Walker's son was experiencing was simply standard peer pressure, or do you agree with her that the pressure was tied to gender roles? Explain.

3. Do you agree with this statement: "My beautiful boy and every other mother's beautiful boy had what essentially boiled down to two options: fight actually in sport, or fight virtually on the computer" (para. 13)?

4. What does Walker mean by "the cultural imperative" (para. 14)?

5. Trace the causal links that Walker makes in order to move from the pressure her son feels to participate in competitive sports to her worry that he "was being primed for war" (para. 17). Do you find any faulty linkages in her logic? If so, identify and explain.

5. *Why Johnny Won't Read*

MARK BAUERLEIN AND SANDRA STOTSKY

In the following 2005 *Washington Post* column, Mark Bauerlein and Sandra Stotsky, researchers involved in the National Endowment for the Arts and the National Assessment of Educational Progress, examine the reading habits and preferences of boys.

When the National Endowment for the Arts last summer [2004] released "Reading at Risk: A Survey of Literary Reading in America," journalists and commentators were quick to seize on the findings as a troubling index of the state of literary culture. The survey showed a serious decline in both literary reading and book reading in general by adults of all ages, races, incomes, education levels and regions.

But in all the discussion, one of the more worrisome trends went largely unnoticed. From 1992 to 2002, the gender gap in reading by young adults widened considerably. In overall book reading, young women slipped from 63 percent to 59 percent, while young men plummeted from 55 percent to 43 percent.

Placed in historical perspective, these findings fit with a gap that has existed in the United States since the spread of mass publishing in the mid-19th century. But for the gap to have grown so much in so short a time suggests that what was formerly a moderate difference is fast becoming a decided marker of gender identity: Girls read; boys don't.

The significance of the gender gap is echoed in two other recent studies. In September the Bureau of Labor Statistics issued the "American Time Use Survey," a report on how Americans spend their hours, including work, school, sleep and leisure. The survey found that in their leisure time young men and women both read only eight minutes per day. But the equality is misleading, because young men enjoy a full 56 minutes more leisure than young women—approximately six hours for men and five for women.

The other report, "Trends in Educational Equity of Girls and Women: 2004," is from the Education Department. Between 1992 and 2002, among high school seniors, girls lost two points in reading scores and boys six points, leaving a 16-point differential in their averages on tests given by the National Assessment of Educational Progress. In the fall semester of kindergarten in 1998, on a different test, girls outperformed boys by 0.9 points. By the spring semester, the difference had nearly doubled, to 1.6 points.

Although one might expect the schools to be trying hard to make reading appealing to boys, the K–12 literature curriculum may in fact be contributing to the problem. It has long been known that there are strong differences between boys and girls in their literary preferences. According to reading interest surveys, both boys and girls are unlikely to choose books based on an "issues" approach, and children are not interested in reading about ways to reform society—or themselves. But boys prefer adventure tales, war, sports and historical nonfiction, while girls prefer stories about personal relationships and fantasy. Moreover, when given choices, boys do not choose stories that feature girls, while girls frequently select stories that appeal to boys.

Unfortunately, the textbooks and literature assigned in the elementary grades do not reflect the dispositions of male students. Few strong and active male role models can be found as lead characters. Gone are the inspiring biographies of the most important American presidents, inventors, scientists and entrepreneurs. No military valor, no high adventure. On the other hand, stories about adventurous and brave women abound. Publishers seem to be more interested in avoiding "masculine" perspectives or "stereotypes" than in getting boys to like what they are assigned to read.

At the middle school level, the kind of quality literature that might appeal to boys has been replaced by Young Adult Literature, that is, easy-to-read, short novels about teenagers and problems such as drug addiction, teenage pregnancy, alcoholism, domestic violence, divorced parents and bullying. Older literary fare has also been replaced by something called "culturally relevant" literature — texts that appeal to students' ethnic group identification on the assumption that sharing the leading character's ethnicity will motivate them to read.

There is no evidence whatsoever that either of these types of reading fare has turned boys into lifelong readers or learners. On the contrary, the evidence is accumulating that by the time they go on to high school, boys have lost their interest in reading about the fictional lives, thoughts and feelings of mature individuals in works written in high-quality prose, and they are no longer motivated by an exciting plot to persist in the struggle they will have with the vocabulary that goes with it.

Last year the National Assessment Governing Board approved a special study of gender differences in reading as part of its research agenda over the next five years. The study will examine how differences in theme, the leading character's gender, and genre, among other factors, bear upon the relative reading performance of boys and girls. With its focus on the content of reading rather than process, this study will, one hopes, give us some ideas on what needs to be done to get boys reading again.

10

Questions

1. What types of evidence dominate in this essay? Is the purpose of the essay to inform or to persuade?
2. Do you agree with Mark Bauerlein and Sandra Stotsky's analysis of the literary preferences of girls and boys? Explain.
3. Taking the opening two paragraphs as the authors' introduction, how do they capture their readers' interest?

6. *Mind over Muscle*

DAVID BROOKS

The following is a 2005 editorial by columnist David Brooks that appeared in the *New York Times*.

Once upon a time, it was a man's world. Men possessed most of the tools one needed for power and success: muscles, connections, control of the crucial social institutions.

But then along came the information age to change all that. In the information age, education is the gateway to success. And that means this is turning into a woman's world, because women are better students than men.

From the first days of school, girls outperform boys. The gap is sometimes small, but over time slight advantages accumulate into big ones. In surveys, kindergarten teachers report that girls are more attentive than boys and more persistent at tasks. Through elementary school, girls are less likely to be asked to repeat a grade. They are much less likely to be diagnosed with a learning disability.

In high school, girls get higher grades in every subject, usually by about a quarter of a point, and have a higher median class rank. They are more likely to take advanced placement courses and the hardest math courses, and are more likely to be straight-A students. They have much higher reading and writing scores on national assessment tests. Boys still enjoy an advantage on math and science tests, but that gap is smaller and closing.

Girls are much more likely to be involved in the school paper or yearbook, to be elected to student government and to be members of academic clubs. They set higher goals for their post-high-school career. (This data is all from the Department of Education.) 5

The differences become monumental in college. Women are more likely to enroll in college and they are more likely to have better applications, so now there are hundreds of schools where the female-male ratio is 60 to 40. About 80 percent of the majors in public administration, psychology and education are female. And here's the most important piece of data: Until 1985 or so, male college graduates outnumbered female college graduates. But in the mid-80's, women drew even, and ever since they have been pulling away at a phenomenal rate.

This year [2005], 133 women will graduate from college for every 100 men. By decade's end, according to Department of Education projections, there will be 142 female graduates for every 100 male graduates. Among African-Americans, there are 200 female grads for every 100 male grads.

The social consequences are bound to be profound. The upside is that by sheer force of numbers, women will be holding more and more leadership jobs. On the negative side, they will have a harder and harder time finding marriageable men with comparable education levels. One thing is for sure: in 30 years the notion that we live in an oppressive patriarchy that discriminates against women will be regarded as a quaint anachronism.

There are debates about why women have thrived and men have faltered. Some say men are imprisoned by their anti-intellectual machismo. Others say the educational system has been overly feminized. Boys are asked to sit quietly for hours at a stretch under conditions where they find it harder to thrive.

But Thomas G. Mortensen of the Pell Institute observes that these same 10 trends—thriving women, faltering men—are observable across the world. In most countries, and in nearly all developed countries, women are graduating from high school and college at much higher rates than men. Mortensen writes, "We conclude that the issue is far less driven by a nation's culture than it is by basic differences between males and females in the modern world."

In other words, if we want to help boys keep up with girls, we have to have an honest discussion about innate differences between the sexes. We have to figure out why poor girls who move to middle-class schools do better, but poor boys who make the same move often do worse. We have to absorb the obvious lesson of every airport bookstore, which is that men and women like to read totally different sorts of books, and see if we can apply this fact when designing curriculums. If boys like to read about war and combat, why can't there be books about combat on the curriculum?

Would elementary school boys do better if they spent more time outside the classroom and less time chained to a desk? Or would they thrive more in a rigorous, competitive environment?

For 30 years, attention has focused on feminine equality. During that time honest discussion of innate differences has been stifled (ask Larry Summers[1]). It's time to look at the other half.

Questions

1. What is David Brooks's main point in this essay? Why doesn't he state it directly at the outset?
2. What is the effect of using the standard fairy-tale opening, "Once upon a time . . ."?
3. Do you agree with Brooks's cause-effect analysis that in the information age, "this is turning into a woman's world" (para. 2)? Why or why not?
4. Do you agree with Brooks that in the near future "women will be holding more and more leadership jobs" and "will have a harder and harder time finding marriageable men with comparable education levels" (para. 8)? Why or why not?
5. What type of evidence does Brooks cite in order to give his position weight?

Making Connections

1. In what ways does the study reported by Mark Bauerlein and Sandra Stotsky support or challenge the more personal commentary of Paul Theroux?

2. Would Rebecca Walker likely agree or disagree with David Brooks's claim that we need "to have an honest discussion about innate differences between the sexes" (para. 11)? Why or why not?

3. How does Gretel Ehrlich's essay reflect or conflict with the image of the Marlboro Man?

4. On the face of it, Walker and Theroux seem at odds; yet despite their quite different perspectives, they share a number of concerns. What are the most obvious differences? What are the more subtle commonalities?

---

[1]Lawrence Summers was president of Harvard University when he claimed that differences in ability were one reason why women were underrepresented in scientific fields. Summers eventually resigned his post. — Eds.

5. How might Ehrlich respond to Theroux's contention that being a man in America is "an unmerciful and punishing burden" (para. 12)? How would Brooks?

Entering the Conversation

As you respond to each of the following prompts, support your argument with references to at least three of the sources in this Conversation on Defining Masculinity. For help using sources, see Chapter 4.

1. Suppose you are part of a community group deciding whether to experiment with single-sex classrooms in grades 9–12 in an effort to raise the achievement level and character development of boys. Based on the readings in this Conversation and your own knowledge and experience, discuss the three or four major issues that you believe should be taken into consideration.

2. Using the readings presented here and your own knowledge and research, write an argument defining what you see as the central issue facing boys and young men in our society. Recommend at least one way to address the issue.

3. Rebecca Walker edited the anthology *What Makes a Man*. Write an essay answering that question. Cite authors in this Conversation on Defining Masculinity who support your point of view, or explain why you disagree with authors in the Conversation.

4. Choose one or two assertions that authors in this Conversation section make that you believe are questionable, perhaps even stereotypes. Write an essay illustrating how popular culture and the media promote or reinforce such beliefs. For example, David Brooks writes, "[W]omen are better students than men" (para. 2); Rebecca Walker speculates that boys' choices "boiled down to two options: fight actually in sport, or fight virtually on the computer" (para. 13).

Student Writing

Argument: Supporting an Assertion

In the following prompt, the writer is asked to take a side in the debate over single-sex education.

> In "Fee-Paying Parents Lose Faith in Single Sex Education," an article filed on telegraph .co.uk, the online version of an English newspaper, John Clare covers the debate about single-sex schools, citing examples of formerly single-sex private schools that have

become, or are planning to become, coeducational. Read the excerpt from the article below, and then choose one side of the argument to defend in an essay.

The head teachers of co-educational schools say that girls' parents are increasingly rejecting the arguments of those such as Brenda Despontin, this year's president of the Girls' Student Association (GSA), who maintains that "girls' brains are wired differently; it follows that adolescents need to be taught differently."

Girls, insists Dr. Despontin, the head of Haberdashers', Monmouth, are "short-changed" in co-ed classrooms. "Boys dominate teacher time, organising themselves quickly to the task, often with a degree of ruthlessness, while girls sharing a classroom with boys hold back, through shyness or a desire to cooperate," she says.

"Oh, no they don't," chorus co-educational school heads. "They learn how to succeed in a co-ed world." Boys' parents, they add, recognise and welcome the "civilising" influence of the opposite sex.

Brian Tannenbaum, an eleventh-grade student, argues for coeducation in his response. Read his essay, and consider its strengths and weaknesses. Then answer the questions about how Brian develops his argument.

Coeducational Schools

Brian Tannenbaum

"In a world that taught them how to think, she showed them how to live." This is the tagline from *Mona Lisa Smile*, a movie set in 1953 when freethinking art-history teacher Katherine Watson came to teach at Wellesley College, arguably at that time the best women's college in the nation, and one of the top colleges in the world. From the beginning of the movie, it is evident that the Wellesley women are both intelligent and competitive. As Ms. Watson discovers in her very first class, every single student had read the art-history textbook before being given any assignments. Would these women have read the textbook if they were at Yale, Harvard, or Princeton? Is it imaginable that these brilliant thinkers would take a secondary position to their male counterparts at coeducational universities? Why should women be separated from men in learning environments? Single-sex schools are both discriminatory and do not prepare their students for the real adult world where both males and females live mutually.

Segregation existed throughout the South until the 1950s, when *Brown v. Board of Education* argued that segregation of black children in the public schools was unconstitutional because it violated the Fourteenth Amendment. Is being denied admission to a school because of race any different from being denied because of sex? It seems unconstitutional that a college, such as Wellesley, has a right to deny a potential student because the applicant is a male. A person is born with both a sex and a race, and since denying someone of the black race is unconstitutional, denying someone of the male sex must be also. How would the world react if a university only admitted white students?

Advocates of single-sex education argue that males distract females and vice versa in coeducational schools. If only one sex is taught in a school, they believe, there will be no distractions and the students can focus on their studies. Although this position may seem logical, there is one major flaw. The workforce is composed of both males and females. If men and women are not able to interact as adolescents, how can they possibly interact as adults? Boys and girls must be exposed to each other so they can learn how to coexist and cooperate. Our world is based on the fundamental relationship between a man and a female. This relationship must be formed from the beginning so our world can continue to function. If the sexes are considered a distraction to each other in elementary and secondary schools, imagine the disturbance if they are first introduced to each other in the working world.

Dr. Brenda Despontin believes that "girls' brains are wired differently" and "boys dominate teacher time" in coeducational schools. Dr. Despontin sets the male brain as the standard norm and, therefore, declares the female brain to be a deviation. Ironically, this female scholar is reverting to ancient times when women were considered inferior to men. I happen to know, firsthand, that female students are outspoken in the classroom and realize they must assert their beliefs in front of males to ensure that they will not be considered the inferior sex. Young girls must be around young boys to develop the social and emotional skills that will prepare them for the coeducational world. And on the other end of the spectrum, young boys must be around young girls to guarantee healthy relationships between males and females.

The second part of the *Mona Lisa Smile* tagline says that Ms. Watson taught the Wellesley women another way of living, helping them become more than what my mother declares herself to be — a domestic engineer. Males and females must interact at a young age to ensure proper relationships between the sexes. Perhaps what is most wrong with single-sex schools is the loss of diversity. Should anyone go to school with people who are just the same as they are?

Questions

1. What is most appealing or effective about this essay? As you respond, reflect on how your own view (that is, whether you agree or disagree with Brian) affects what you find most appealing or effective.
2. Are Brian's outside sources — a film, a Supreme Court case — helpful in making his argument? Explain why or why not.
3. If you were making suggestions for revision, would you recommend adding more external sources? If so, what kind would you suggest?

4. Brian draws an analogy between segregation by race and sex. Explain whether you think this strategy strengthens or weakens his argument.
5. Does referring to his mother as "a domestic engineer" strengthen or weaken Brian's argument?
6. What is the effect of the rhetorical questions in the essay's first and last paragraphs?

Grammar as Rhetoric and Style
Pronouns

As you well know, a pronoun takes the place of a noun (called the *antecedent*). Unlike a noun, however, a pronoun defines the viewpoint in your writing. Are you talking about yourself (first person), are you talking directly to the audience (second person), or are you referring to a person who is neither the speaker nor the audience (third person)? This section considers two points of pronoun usage that affect viewpoint: (1) consistency of pronouns in a sentence or passage, and (2) sexist pronouns.

Consistency: Viewpoint and Number

Pronouns must agree with one another and with their antecedents in number and in viewpoint (person). The following table summarizes which personal pronouns are singular and which are plural, as well as which are first person, second person, and third person:

VIEWPOINT	NUMBER	
	SINGULAR	PLURAL
First person	*I, me, my, mine*	*we, us, our, ours*
Second person	*you, your, yours*	*you, your, yours*
Third person	*he, him, his*	*they, them, their, theirs*
	she, her, hers	
	it, its	
	one, one's	

If you use pronouns to refer to an antecedent more than once in a sentence or paragraph, it's important that they be consistent in person and number. Consider the following sentence:

> If, by chance, *you* find another person more suitable as a wife than the wife *I* already have, *I* want the liberty to replace *my* present wife with another one.

This sentence shifts viewpoint from second person to first-person singular, and as a result it is confusing to the reader.

When corrected, the sentence maintains a consistent first-person singular viewpoint:

> If, by chance, *I* find another person more suitable as a wife than the wife *I* already have, *I* want the liberty to replace *my* present wife with another one.

> — Judy Brady

Consistency is also important when using *indefinite pronouns.* (An indefinite pronoun is one that does not have a specific antecedent.) Consider the singular indefinite pronoun *one* as it is used here:

> *One* cannot think well, love well, sleep well, if *one* has not dined well.

> — Virginia Woolf

This sentence begins with the singular indefinite pronoun *one* and sticks with *one.* The sentence would be much less effective if it said:

> *One* cannot think well, love well, sleep well, if *you* have not dined well.

Note, though, that Virginia Woolf could have opted to use the second person:

> *You* cannot think well, love well, sleep well, if *you* have not dined well.

Woolf's use of the third person adds a formality to the tone — through the more distanced *one* — while the second-person *you* sounds more conversational.

Sexist Pronoun Usage

When a third-person singular pronoun (*he, she, it*) could refer to either a male or a female, writers have several options: they can combine the male and female pronouns, using *or*; they can use the plural form of the pronoun, being careful to adjust the rest of the sentence accordingly; or they can alternate the gender of the pronouns.

Consider the following sentences from Virginia Woolf's "Professions for Women."

> I hope I am not giving away professional secrets if I say that a *novelist's* chief desire is to be as unconscious as possible. *He* has to induce in *himself* a state of perpetual lethargy.

The pronouns *he* and *himself* in the second sentence refer to the antecedent *novelist* in the first sentence. In using *he* and *himself,* Woolf was not only following standard grammatical practice of the 1930s but also underscoring the reality that during her lifetime most published novelists were indeed male. But the world and the English language have changed, and using the generic *he, his, him, himself* to refer to any individual is not as acceptable today as it was when Woolf wrote. How would writers today handle a discussion of an unidentified novelist? One possibility would be to use the term *his/her* or *his or her*:

> I hope I am not giving away professional secrets if I say that a *novelist*'s chief desire is to be as unconscious as possible. *He or she* has to induce in *himself or herself* a state of perpetual lethargy.

If writers need to make only one or two references to an unspecified antecedent, perhaps they can get away with *he or she* and *himself or herself*, though even the two references in this sentence are awkward. But if there are many references to the antecedent, as in the Woolf passage that follows, the *or* construction becomes monotonous or downright annoying:

> I hope I am not giving away professional secrets if I say that a *novelist*'s chief desire is to be as unconscious as possible. *He or she* has to induce in *himself or herself* a state of perpetual lethargy. *He or she* wants life to proceed with the utmost quiet and regularity. *He or she* wants to see the same faces, to read the same books, to do the same things day after day, month after month, while *he or she* is writing, so that nothing may break the illusion in which *he or she* is living.

The most straightforward revision would be to change the unspecified singular noun to an unspecified plural noun:

> I hope I am not giving away professional secrets if I say that the chief desire of *novelists* is to be as unconscious as possible. *They* have to induce in *themselves* a state of perpetual lethargy. *They* want life to proceed with the utmost quiet and regularity. *They* want to see the same faces, to read the same books, to do the same things day after day, month after month, while *they* are writing, so that nothing may break the illusion in which *they* are living.

Another possibility for large sections of an essay is to shift between male and female pronouns, using *he* or *him* or *his* for a while, then shifting to *she* or *her* or *hers*, and shifting yet again. Generally, writers seem to like this approach more than readers, who can lose track of what they are reading about, especially if the shift in gender happens too frequently.

Rhetorical and Stylistic Strategy

Although maintaining a consistent viewpoint is a matter of grammatical accuracy, selecting which viewpoint to use is a rhetorical decision. If the writing is formal, then the third person is generally the most appropriate choice. For example, most teachers expect a research paper to be written in the third person. If the essay is more informal and draws on the writer's personal experience, then the first person (singular or plural) works well. The second person — *you* — is generally reserved for informal writing, such as a newspaper column, where the writer is addressing readers as though they are in conversation, or for speeches, where the writer is directly addressing an audience.

In the second part of this section, we focused on sexist pronouns. Why do we recommend that you eliminate pronouns that some people think of as sexist? After all, there is nothing grammatically wrong with Virginia Woolf's use of a male pronoun to refer to an indefinite singular noun such as *novelist*. But language choice sometimes involves more than grammatical correctness. Throughout this book, you are reading about how to appeal to audiences and how to make audiences find you credible. One way to impress readers is to be sensitive to their likes and dislikes—in this case, to their own attitudes toward sexist language. Many of your readers will appreciate any steps you take in your writing to establish common ground with them. In pronoun usage, meet your readers' expectations that an indefinite singular noun might just as easily refer to a woman as to a man.

Remember, grammatical correctness and a writer's purpose go hand in hand.

• EXERCISE 1 •

Correct all errors in the following sentences that result from sexist pronouns or inconsistencies in pronoun person or number.

1. Popular culture once provided us with a common vocabulary, but now you have a hard time keeping up with the jargon.

2. For a runner to keep up his pace, one must pay attention to nutrition.

3. If one measures her country's commitment to education by dollars allocated, you can see that it's not our top priority.

4. Baseball fans pay so much attention to percentages that you almost always have a sense of the improbability or likelihood of an event actually occurring.

5. Most of the time a teacher tries to tailor writing assignments to interest his students.

6. Everyone is wondering who the next Democratic presidential candidate will be and if he will be a charismatic leader.

7. A doctor should treat his patients respectfully by listening to them no matter how busy they are.

8. We hoped to get a free pass to the movie, but the mall was so crowded that you didn't have a chance.

9. You should try to stop arguments before they start; otherwise, one might become involved in a conflict that gets more complicated than we thought possible.

10. When one is as strong a student as Chong is, you're not surprised that he passed the bar on his first try.

• EXERCISE 2 •

The following paragraph is taken from the essay "I Want a Wife" by Judy Brady (p. 539). Discuss the effect of the pronouns *I* and *my*. How many times does Brady use them? How does this repetition help to achieve her purpose?

I would like to go back to school so that I can become economically independent, support myself, and, if need be, support those dependent upon me. I want a wife who will work and send me to school. And while I am going to school I want a wife to take care of my children. I want a wife to keep track of the children's doctor and dentist appointments. And to keep track of mine, too. I want a wife to make sure my children eat properly and are kept clean. I want a wife who will wash the children's clothes and keep them mended. I want a wife who is a good nurturant attendant to my children, who arranges for their schooling, makes sure that they have an adequate social life with their peers, takes them to the park, the zoo, etc. I want a wife who takes care of the children when they are sick, a wife who arranges to be around when the children need special care, because, of course, I cannot miss classes at school. My wife must arrange to lose time at work and not lose the job. It may mean a small cut in my wife's income from time to time, but I guess I can tolerate that. Needless to say, my wife will arrange and pay for the care of the children while my wife is working.

• EXERCISE 3 •

The following excerpt is from "Professions for Women" by Virginia Woolf (p. 525). It includes both the first and third person. Rewrite it entirely in the first person—for example, with *I* and *we women*. Then discuss the effect of your changes. Consider the excerpt in the context of the entire essay.

These then were two very genuine experiences of my own. These were two of the adventures of my professional life. The first—killing the Angel in the House—I think I solved. She died. But the second, telling the truth about my own experiences as a body, I do not think I solved. I doubt that any woman has solved it yet. The obstacles against her are still immensely powerful—and yet they are very difficult to define. Outwardly, what is simpler than to write books? Outwardly, what obstacles are there for a woman rather than for a man? Inwardly, I think, the case is very different;

she has still many ghosts to fight, many prejudices to overcome. Indeed
it will be a long time still, I think, before a woman can sit down to write
a book without finding a phantom to be slain, a rock to be dashed
against. And if this is so in literature, the freest of all professions for
women, how is it in the new professions which you are now for the first
time entering?

• EXERCISE 4 •

Think of an example of gender stereotyping that drives you crazy. Perhaps
it's a television or movie character, an incident from the news, or a pop culture personality who seems to play to stereotypical expectations of male or
female behavior. Write two paragraphs explaining your outrage. In one, use
the first person, singular or plural, so that your identity is front and center;
then rewrite it in third person so that your gender is not a part of the voice.
Discuss the different effects of the two.

Suggestions for Writing
Gender

Now that you have examined a number of readings and other texts that focus on
gender, including gender stereotypes and their consequences, explore one dimension of this topic by synthesizing your own ideas and the readings. You might want
to do more research or use readings from other classes as you prepare for the following projects.

1. From popular magazines and newspapers, collect ads that reflect stereotypes
   about the roles of men and women, as well as ads that show men and women
   in a more progressive light. You might work in groups to collect and analyze the
   ads. Make lists of both kinds of ads. Determine which kinds of products show
   men and women in stereotyped roles and which show men and women breaking gender stereotypes. Which stereotypes are more common in these ads —
   stereotypes about women or about men? Then, working individually, write a
   report that discusses what the ads show about American values, beliefs, and
   attitudes toward gender roles.

2. Write a personal narrative in which you describe a role that your family or
   friends expected of you but that you either refused to play or struggled against.
   Explain the origin and nature of the expectation, as well as your reasons for not

wanting to fulfill it. Include a discussion of the reactions you have gotten as you challenged the role or expectation.

3. To explore the idea that gender roles are socially constructed rather than biologically determined, do some research into other cultures and times. Report on a role that our society believes is gender-specific (for example, the nurturing mother, the protective male) but that another culture or people from another period viewed quite differently.

4. The Internet is arguably gender-neutral. When you do not know other users' background, physical traits, style of dress, and so on, you have to judge them only by their words. Some observers believe that the anonymity of the Internet allows people to move outside of expected gender roles. Does the Internet affect you that way? Are you more willing to be confrontational online, for example? Are you funnier? Does your online voice resemble who you are in person? Write an essay exploring how gender does or does not influence your online communication style.

5. Write a roundtable conversation that you might have with three authors in this chapter about *one* of the following quotations:

   - The curse of too many women has been that they have this privilege of refuge in the home. —PEARL BUCK
   - There are two kinds of spiritual law, two kinds of conscience, one in man and another, altogether different, in women. They do not understand each other. —HENRIK IBSEN
   - The discovery is, of course, that "man" and "woman" are fictions, caricatures, cultural constructs. As models they are reductive, totalitarian, inappropriate to human becoming. As roles they are static, demeaning to the female, dead-ended for males and females both. —ANDREA DWORKIN
   - You see a lot of smart guys with dumb women but you hardly ever see a smart woman with a dumb guy. —ERICA JONG

6. Examine a popular movie in terms of gender roles, and write about it. In what ways do the characters reflect conventional roles, and in what ways do they step out of those roles?

7. Write a "myth-buster" essay. Take a stereotype based on gender (such as "women are bad drivers" or "men are more prone to violent behavior than women"), and debunk it by conducting research. Use quantitative information as well as anecdotal or personal experience as evidence. Consider how this myth originated and who benefits from perpetuating it.

8. In his book *Men Are from Mars, Women Are from Venus*, John Gray writes, "A man's sense of self is defined through his ability to achieve results. . . . A woman's sense of self is defined through her feelings and the quality of

her relationships." Write an essay supporting, challenging, or modifying these statements. Use examples from your own experience and selections from this chapter.

9. Several of the authors in this Conversation on Defining Masculinity raise questions about the reading required in school. Working in groups, develop a list of books the girls like, and one the boys like; then try to reach a consensus on at least two or three selections that both groups find interesting. Write an essay analyzing the process and explaining the results. As part of your inquiry, you might visit www.guysread.com.

10. In "Mind over Muscle," David Brooks asserts: "One thing is for sure: in 30 years the notion that we live in an oppressive patriarchy that discriminates against women will be regarded as a quaint anachronism." Write an essay explaining why you agree or disagree with Brooks's prediction.

Sports

How do the values of sports affect the way we see ourselves?

Love them or hate them, sports are a central part of our modern world. Athletes are cultural icons; sports dominate television, radio, even film. Once the purview of men and boys, the subject of sports — opinions on its ethics, its future, its place in society — is now open to everyone. And in some ways, the line separating the professional from the spectator has blurred. Weekend athletes train like professionals; even couch potatoes participate in fantasy leagues.

We speak the language of sports. We are asked to play to win, play by the rules, play fair, be team players, be good sports. We're taught to be good losers; we're reminded that the best defense is a good offense — and the other way around. We're told that life is a game of chance, but that we can sometimes level the playing field. These exhortations are as at home in a grade school kickball game as they are in politics and business. Why are we so comfortable with this shorthand?

The questions raised by sports are out of proportion to the tiny number of people who play professional sports and are front and center in the news-earning salaries that top those of movie stars. At their best, sports pros are hailed as role models; at their worst, as scourges on society. Is our attraction to professional athletes healthy? Do we learn from their grit, from their strength and commitment to training, or do they encourage unhealthy narcissism and dangerous habits?

The selections in this chapter explore many of the questions raised by our interest in sports and the effect of that interest on everyday life. The readings look at the star power of our professional athletes and the thrill of tapping into our own potential for athletic achievement. They ask questions about ethics; they make us think about whether our passion for both following and participating in sports is a way for us to, at least temporarily, avoid the demands of real life. Finally, they ask whether the language of the playing field and the model of the professional athlete enliven communication and help us become better people.

The Silent Season of a Hero

Gay Talese

 Gay Talese (b. 1932) began life on the small island of Ocean City, New Jersey. As the son of a southern Italian immigrant growing up Catholic in a Protestant town, Talese identified himself as an outsider. He is known for writing the "unnoticed story," reporting the angle ignored by others or the news that others thought was not newsworthy. Recognized for his elegant style, Talese is considered one of the founders of *New Journalism*, a term coined in the 1960s to describe the work of writers like Talese, Tom Wolfe, and Hunter S. Thompson. New Journalism is characterized by the use of elements of fiction to get at the story behind the story. New Journalists set scenes, include dialogue, and accept their own presence as part of the drama of the story. The following selection appeared in *Esquire* in 1966.

"I would like to take the great DiMaggio fishing," the old man said. "They say his father was a fisherman. Maybe he was as poor as we are and would understand."
— ERNEST HEMINGWAY, *The Old Man and the Sea*

It was not quite spring, the silent season before the search for salmon, and the old fishermen of San Francisco were either painting their boats or repairing their nets along the pier or sitting in the sun talking quietly among themselves, watching the tourists come and go, and smiling, now, as a pretty girl paused to take their picture. She was about 25, healthy and blue-eyed and wearing a turtleneck sweater, and she had long, flowing blonde hair that she brushed back a few times before clicking her camera. The fishermen, looking at her, made admiring comments, but she did not understand because they spoke a Sicilian dialect; nor did she understand the tall gray-haired man in a dark suit who stood watching her from behind a big bay window on the second floor of DiMaggio's Restaurant that overlooks the pier.

He watched until she left, lost in the crowd of newly arrived tourists that had just come down the hill by cable car. Then he sat down again at the table in the restaurant, finishing his tea and lighting another cigarette, his fifth in the last half hour. It was 11:30 in the morning. None of the other tables was occupied, and the only sounds came from the bar, where a liquor salesman was laughing at something the headwaiter had said. But then the salesman, his briefcase under his arm, headed for the door, stopping briefly to peek into the dining room and call out, "See you later, Joe." Joe DiMaggio turned and waved at the salesman. Then the room was quiet again.

At 51, DiMaggio was a most distinguished-looking man, aging as gracefully as he had played on the ball field, impeccable in his tailoring, his nails manicured, his 6-foot-2 body seeming as lean and capable as when he posed for the portrait that hangs in the restaurant and shows him in Yankee Stadium, swinging from the heels at a pitch thrown 20 years ago. His gray hair was thinning at the crown, but just barely, and his face was lined in the right places, and his expression, once as sad and haunted as a matador's, was more in repose these days, though, as now, tension had returned and he chain-smoked and occasionally paced the floor and looked out the window at the people below. In the crowd was a man he did not wish to see.

The man had met DiMaggio in New York. This week he had come to San Francisco and had telephoned several times, but none of the calls had been returned because DiMaggio suspected that the man, who had said he was doing research on some vague sociological project, really wanted to delve into DiMaggio's private life and that of DiMaggio's former wife, Marilyn Monroe. DiMaggio would never tolerate this. The memory of her death is still very painful to him, and yet, because he keeps it to himself, some people are not sensitive to it. One night in a supper club, a woman who had been drinking approached his table, and when he did not ask her to join him, she snapped:

"All right, I guess I'm *not* Marilyn Monroe." 5

He ignored her remark, but when she repeated it, he replied, barely controlling his anger, "No—I wish you were, but you're not."

The tone of his voice softened her, and she asked, "Am I saying something wrong?"

"You already have," he said. "Now will you please leave me alone?"

His friends on the wharf, understanding him as they do, are very careful when discussing him with strangers, knowing that should they inadvertently betray a confidence, he will not denounce them but rather will never speak to them again; this comes from a sense of propriety not inconsistent in the man who also, after Marilyn Monroe's death, directed that fresh flowers be placed on her grave "forever."

Some of the older fishermen who have known DiMaggio all his life remem- 10
ber him as a small boy who helped clean his father's boat, and as a young man who sneaked away and used a broken oar as a bat on the sandlots nearby. His father, a small mustachioed man known as Zio Pepe, would become infuriated and call him *lagnuso*, lazy, *meschino*, good-for-nothing, but in 1936 Zio Pepe was among those who cheered when Joe DiMaggio returned to San Francisco after his first season with the New York Yankees and was carried along the wharf on the shoulders of the fishermen.

The fishermen also remember how, after his retirement in 1951, DiMaggio brought his second wife, Marilyn, to live near the wharf, and sometimes they would be seen early in the morning fishing off DiMaggio's boat, the *Yankee Clipper*, now docked quietly in the marina, and in the evening they would be sitting and talking on the pier. They had arguments, too, the fishermen knew, and one night Marilyn was seen running hysterically, crying, as she ran, along the road away from the pier, with Joe following. But the fishermen pretended they did not see this; it was none of their affair. They knew that Joe wanted her to stay in San Francisco and avoid the sharks in Hollywood, but she was confused and torn then — "She was a child," they said — and even today DiMaggio loathes Los Angeles and many of the people in it. He no longer speaks to his onetime friend, Frank Sinatra, who had befriended Marilyn in her final years, and he also is cool to Dean Martin and Peter Lawford and Lawford's former wife, Pat, who once gave a party at which she introduced Marilyn Monroe to Robert Kennedy, and the two of them danced often that night, Joe heard, and he did not take it well. He was possessive of her that year, his close friends say, because Marilyn and he had planned to remarry; but before they could she was dead, and DiMaggio banned the Lawfords and Sinatra and many Hollywood people from her funeral. When Marilyn Monroe's attorney complained that DiMaggio was keeping her friends away, DiMaggio answered coldly, "If it weren't for those friends persuading her to stay in Hollywood, she would still be alive."

Joe DiMaggio now spends most of the year in San Francisco, and each day tourists, noticing the name on the restaurant, ask the men on the wharf if they ever see him. Oh, yes, the men say, they see him nearly every day; they have not seen him yet this morning, they add, but he should be arriving shortly. So the tourists continue to walk along the piers past the crab vendors, under the circling sea gulls, past the fish-'n'-chip stands, sometimes stopping to watch a large vessel steaming toward the Golden Gate Bridge, which, to their dismay, is painted red. Then they visit the Wax Museum, where there is a life-size figure of DiMaggio in uniform, and walk across the street and spend a quarter to peer through the silver telescopes focused on the island of Alcatraz, which is no longer a federal prison. Then they return to ask the men if DiMaggio has been seen. Not yet, the men say, although they notice his blue Impala parked in the lot next to the restaurant. Sometimes tourists will walk into the restaurant and have lunch and will see him sitting calmly in a corner signing autographs and being extremely gracious with everyone. At other times, as on this particular morning when the man from New York chose to visit, DiMaggio was tense and suspicious.

When the man entered the restaurant from the side steps leading to the dining room, he saw DiMaggio standing near the window, talking with an elderly maître d' named Charles Friscia. Not wanting to walk in and risk intrusion, the man asked one of DiMaggio's nephews to inform Joe of his presence. When DiMaggio got the message, he quickly turned and left Friscia and disappeared through an exit leading down to the kitchen.

Astonished and confused, the visitor stood in the hall. A moment later Friscia appeared and the man asked, "Did Joe leave?"

"Joe who?" Friscia replied.   15

"Joe DiMaggio!"

"Haven't seen him," Friscia said.

"You haven't *seen* him! He was standing right next to you a second ago!"

"It wasn't me," Friscia said.

"You were standing next to him. I saw you. In the dining room."   20

"You must be mistaken," Friscia said, softly, seriously. "It wasn't me."

"You *must* be kidding," the man said angrily, turning and leaving the restaurant. Before he could get to his car, however, DiMaggio's nephew came running after him and said, "Joe wants to see you."

He returned, expecting to see DiMaggio waiting for him. Instead he was handed a telephone. The voice was powerful and deep and so tense that the quick sentences ran together.

"You are invading my rights. I did not ask you to come. I assume you have a lawyer. You must have a lawyer, get your lawyer!"

"I came as a friend," the man interrupted.   25

"That's beside the point," DiMaggio said. "I have my privacy. I do not want it violated. You'd better get a lawyer. . . ." Then, pausing, DiMaggio asked, "Is my nephew there?"

He was not.

"Then wait where you are."

A moment later DiMaggio appeared, tall and red-faced, erect and beautifully dressed in his dark suit and white shirt with the gray silk tie and the gleaming silver cuff links. He moved with his big steps toward the man and handed him an airmail envelope unopened that the man had written from New York.

"Here," DiMaggio said. "This is yours."   30

Then DiMaggio sat down at a small table. He said nothing, just lit a cigarette and waited, legs crossed, his head held high and back so as to reveal the intricate construction of his nose, a fine sharp tip above the big nostrils and tiny bones built out from the bridge, a great nose.

"Look," DiMaggio said, more calmly, "I do not interfere with other people's lives. And I do not expect them to interfere with mine. There are things about my life, personal things, that I refuse to talk about. And even if you asked my brothers, they would be unable to tell you about them because they do not know. There are things about me, so many things, that they simply do not know. . . ."

"I don't want to cause trouble," the man said. "I think you're a great man, and . . ."

"I'm not great," DiMaggio cut in. "I'm not great," he repeated softly. "I'm just a man trying to get along."

Then DiMaggio, as if realizing that he was intruding upon his own privacy,   35
abruptly stood up. He looked at his watch.

"I'm late," he said, very formal again. "I'm 10 minutes late. You're making me late."

The man left the restaurant. He crossed the street and wandered over to the pier, briefly watching the fishermen hauling their nets and talking in the sun, seemingly very calm and contented. Then, after he turned and was headed back toward the parking lot, a blue Impala stopped in front of him and Joe DiMaggio leaned out the window and asked, "Do you have a car?" His voice was very gentle.

"Yes," the man said.

"Oh," DiMaggio said. "I would have given you a ride."

Joe DiMaggio was not born in San Francisco but in Martinez, a small fishing   40
village 25 miles northeast of the Golden Gate. Zio Pepe had settled there after leaving Isola delle Femmine, an islet off Palermo where the DiMaggios had been fishermen for generations. But in 1915, hearing of the luckier waters off San Francisco's wharf, Zio Pepe left Martinez, packing his boat with furniture and family, including Joe, who was one year old.

San Francisco was placid and picturesque when the DiMaggios arrived, but there was a competitive undercurrent and struggle for power along the pier. At dawn the boats would sail out to where the bay meets the ocean and the sea is rough, and later the men would race back with their hauls, hoping to beat their fellow fishermen to shore and sell it while they could. Twenty or 30 boats would sometimes be trying to gain the channel shoreward at the same time, and a fisherman had to know every rock in the water, and later know every bargaining trick along the shore, because the dealers and restaurateurs would play one fisherman off against the other, keeping the prices down. Later the fishermen became wiser and organized, predetermining the maximum amount each fisherman would catch, but there were always some men who, like the fish, never learned, and so heads would sometimes be broken, nets slashed, gasoline poured onto their fish, flowers of warning placed outside their doors.

But these days were ending when Zio Pepe arrived, and he expected his five sons to succeed him as fishermen, and the first two, Tom and Michael, did; but a third, Vincent, wanted to sing. He sang with such magnificent power as a young man that he came to the attention of the great banker, A. P. Giannini, and there were plans to send him to Italy for tutoring and the opera. But there was hesitation around the DiMaggio household and Vince never went; instead, he played ball with the San Francisco Seals and sports writers misspelled his name.

It was DeMaggio until Joe, at Vince's recommendation, joined the team and became a sensation, being followed later by the youngest brother, Dominic, who was also outstanding. All three later played in the big leagues, and some writers like to say that Joe was the best hitter, Dom the best fielder, Vince the best singer, and Casey Stengel once said: "Vince is the only player I ever saw who could strike out three times in one game and not be embarrassed. He'd walk into the clubhouse whistling. Everybody would be feeling sorry for him, but Vince always thought he was doing good."

After he retired from baseball Vince became a bartender, then a milkman, now a carpenter. He lives 40 miles north of San Francisco in a house he partly built, has been happily married for 34 years, has four grandchildren, has in the closet one of Joe's tailor-made suits that he has never had altered to fit, and when people ask him if he envies Joe he always says, "No, maybe Joe would like to have what I have." The brother Vincent most admired was Michael, "a big earthy man, a dreamer, a fisherman who wanted things but didn't want to take from Joe, or to work in the restaurant. He wanted a bigger boat, but wanted to earn it on his own. He never got it." In 1953, at the age of 44, Michael fell from his boat and drowned.

Since Zio Pepe's death at 77 in 1949, Tom at 62, the oldest brother—two of   45
his four sisters are older—has become nominal head of the family and manages the restaurant that was opened in 1937 as Joe DiMaggio's Grotto. Later Joe sold out his share, and now Tom is the co-owner with Dominic. Of all the brothers, Dominic, who was known as the "Little Professor" when he played with the Boston Red Sox, is the most successful in business. He lives in a fashionable Boston suburb with his wife and three children and is president of a firm that manufactures fiber cushion materials and grossed more than $3,500,000 last year.

Joe DiMaggio lives with his widowed sister, Marie, in a tan stone house on a quiet residential street not far from Fisherman's Wharf. He bought the house almost 30 years ago for his parents, and after their deaths he lived there with Marilyn Monroe. Now it is cared for by Marie, a slim and handsome dark-eyed woman who has an apartment on the second floor, Joe on the third. There are some baseball trophies and plaques in the small room off DiMaggio's bedroom, and on his dresser are photographs of Marilyn Monroe, and in the living room downstairs is a small painting of her that DiMaggio likes very much; it reveals only her face and shoulders and she is wearing a wide-brimmed sun hat, and there is a soft, sweet smile on her lips, an innocent curiosity about her that is the way he saw her and the way he wanted her to be seen by others—a simple girl, "a warm, big-hearted girl," he once described her, "that everybody took advantage of."

The publicity photographs emphasizing her sex appeal often offend him, and a memorable moment for Billy Wilder, who directed her in *The Seven-Year Itch*, occurred when he spotted DiMaggio in a large crowd of people gathered on Lexington Avenue in New York to watch a scene in which Marilyn, standing over a subway grating to cool herself, had her skirts blown high by a sudden wind blow. "What the hell is going on here?" DiMaggio was overheard to have said in the crowd, and Wilder recalled, "I shall never forget the look of death on Joe's face."

He was then 39, she was 27. They had been married in January of that year, 1954, despite disharmony in temperament and time; he was tired of publicity, she was thriving on it; he was intolerant of tardiness, she was always late. During their honeymoon in Tokyo an American general had introduced himself and asked if, as a patriotic gesture, she would visit the troops in Korea. She looked at Joe. "It's your honeymoon," he said, shrugging, "go ahead if you want to."

She appeared on 10 occasions before 100,000 servicemen, and when she returned, she said, "It was so wonderful, Joe. You never heard such cheering."

"Yes, I have," he said.   50

Across from her portrait in the living room, on a coffee table in front of a sofa, is a sterling-silver humidor that was presented to him by his Yankee teammates at a time when he was the most talked-about man in America, and when Les Brown's band had recorded a hit that was heard day and night on the radio.

> From Coast to Coast, that's all you hear
>   Of Joe the One-Man Show.
> He's glorified the horsehide sphere,
>   Jolting Joe DiMaggio . . .
> Joe . . . Joe . . . DiMaggio . . .
>   we want you on our side . . .

The year was 1941, and it began for DiMaggio in the middle of May after the Yankees had lost four games in a row, seven of their last nine, and were in fourth place, five and a half games behind the leading Cleveland Indians. On May 15, DiMaggio hit only a first-inning single in a game that New York lost to Chicago 13–1; he was barely hitting .300, and had greatly disappointed the crowds that had seen him finish with a .352 average the year before and .381 in 1939.

He got a hit in the next game, and the next, and the next. On May 24, with the Yankees losing 6–5 to Boston, DiMaggio came up with runners on second and third and singled them home, winning the game, extending his streak to 10 games. But it went largely unnoticed. Even DiMaggio was not conscious of it until it had reached 29 games in mid-June. Then the newspapers began to dramatize it, the public became aroused, they sent him good-luck charms of every description, and DiMaggio kept hitting, and radio announcers would interrupt programs to announce the news, and then the song again: "Joe . . . Joe . . . DiMaggio . . . we want you on our side . . ."

Sometimes DiMaggio would be hitless his first three times up, the tension would build, it would appear that the game would end without his getting another chance — but he always would, and then he would hit the ball against the left-field wall, or through the pitcher's legs, or between two leaping infielders. In the forty-first game, the first of a doubleheader in Washington, DiMaggio tied an American League record that George Sisler had set in 1922. But before the second game began, a spectator sneaked onto the field and into the Yankees' dugout and stole DiMaggio's favorite bat. In the second game, using another of his bats, DiMaggio lined out twice and flied out. But in the seventh inning, borrowing one of his old bats that a teammate was using, he singled and broke Sisler's record, and he was only three games away from surpassing the major-league record of 44 set in 1897 by Willie Keeler while playing for Baltimore when it was a National League franchise.

An appeal for the missing bat was made through the newspapers. A man from Newark admitted the crime and returned it with regrets. And on July 2 at Yankee Stadium, DiMaggio hit a home run into the left-field stands. The record was broken.

He also got hits on the next 11 games, but on July 17 in Cleveland, at a night game attended by 67,468, he failed against two pitchers, Al Smith and Jim

55

Bagby, Jr., although Cleveland's hero was really its third baseman, Ken Keltner, who in the first inning lunged to his right to make a spectacular backhanded stop of a drive and, from the foul line behind third base, threw DiMaggio out. DiMaggio received a walk in the fourth inning. But in the seventh he again hit a hard shot at Keltner, who again stopped it and threw him out. DiMaggio hit sharply toward the shortstop in the eighth inning, the ball taking a bad hop, but Lou Boudreau speared it off his shoulder and threw to the second baseman to start a double play and DiMaggio's streak was stopped at 56 games. But the New York Yankees were on their way to winning the pennant by 17 games, and the World Series too, and so in August, in a hotel suite in Washington, the players threw a surprise party for DiMaggio and toasted him with champagne and presented him with his Tiffany silver humidor that is now in San Francisco in his living room. . . .

Marie was in the kitchen making toast and tea when DiMaggio came down for breakfast; his gray hair was uncombed but, since he wears it short, it was not untidy. He said good morning to Marie, sat down, and yawned. He lit a cigarette. He wore a blue wool bathrobe over his pajamas. It was 8:00 A.M. He had many things to do today and he seemed cheerful. He had a conference with the president of Continental Television, Inc., a large retail chain in California of which he is a partner and vice-president; later he had a golf date, and then a big banquet to attend, and, if that did not go on too long and if he were not too tired afterward, he might have a date.

Picking up the morning paper, not rushing to the sports page, DiMaggio read the front-page news, the people problems of 1966; Kwame Nkrumah was overthrown in Ghana, students were burning their draft cards (DiMaggio shook his head), the flu epidemic was spreading through the whole state of California. Then he flipped inside through the gossip columns, thankful they did not have him in there today — they had printed an item about his dating "an electrifying airline hostess" not long ago, and they also spotted him at dinner with Dori Lane, "the frantic frugger" in Whisky à Go Go's glass cage — and then he turned to the sports page and read a story about how the injured Mickey Mantle may never regain his form.

It happened all so quickly, the passing of Mantle, or so it seemed; he had succeeded DiMaggio, who had succeeded Ruth, but now there was no great young power hitter coming up, and the Yankee management, almost desperate, had talked Mantle out of retirement, and on September 18, 1965, they gave him a "day" in New York during which he received several thousand dollars' worth of gifts — an automobile, two quarter horses, free vacation trips to Rome, Nassau, Puerto Rico — and DiMaggio had flown to New York to make the introduction before 50,000: it had been a dramatic day, an almost holy day for the believers who had jammed the grandstands early to witness the canonization of a new stadium saint. Cardinal [Francis] Spellman was on the committee, President

[Lyndon] Johnson sent a telegram, the day was officially proclaimed by the Mayor of New York, an orchestra assembled in the center field in front of the trinity of monuments to Ruth, [Lou] Gehrig, [Miller] Huggins; and high in the grandstands, billowing in the breeze of early autumn, were white banners that read: "Don't Quit, Mick," "We Love the Mick."

The banner had been held by hundreds of young boys whose dreams had been fulfilled so often by Mantle, but also seated in the grandstands were older men, paunchy and balding, in whose middle-aged minds DiMaggio was still vivid and invincible, and some of them remembered how one month before, during a pregame exhibition at Old-Timers' Day in Yankee Stadium, DiMaggio had hit a pitch into the left-field seats, and suddenly thousands of people had jumped wildly to their feet, joyously screaming — the great DiMaggio had returned, they were young again, it was yesterday.

But on this sunny September day at the stadium, the feast day of Mickey Mantle, DiMaggio was not wearing No. 5 on his back or a black cap to cover his graying hair; he was wearing a black suit and white shirt and blue tie, and he stood in one corner of the Yankees' dugout waiting to be introduced by Red Barber, who was standing near home plate behind a silver microphone. In the outfield Guy Lombardo's Royal Canadians were playing soothing, soft music; and moving slowly back and forth over the sprawling green grass between the left-field bullpen and the infield were two carts driven by grounds keepers and containing dozens and dozens of large gifts for Mantle — a 6-foot, 100-pound Hebrew National salami, a Winchester rifle, a mink coat for Mrs. Mantle, a set of Wilson golf clubs, a year's supply of Chunky Candy. DiMaggio smoked a cigarette, but cupped it in his hands as if not wanting to be caught in the act by teen-aged boys near enough to peek down into the dugout. Then, edging forward a step, DiMaggio poked his head out and looked up. He could see nothing above except the packed, towering green grandstands that seemed a mile high and moving, and he could see no clouds or blue sky, only a sky of faces. Then the announcer called out his name — *"Joe DiMaggio!"* — and suddenly there was a blast of cheering that grew louder and louder, echoing and reechoing within the big steel canyon, and DiMaggio stomped out his cigarette and climbed up the dugout steps and onto the soft green grass, the noise resounding in his ears, he could almost feel the breeze, the breath of 50,000 lungs upon him, 100,000 eyes watching his every move, and for the briefest instant as he walked he closed his eyes.

Then in his path he saw Mickey Mantle's mother, a smiling woman wearing an orchid, and he gently reached out for her elbow, holding it as he led her toward the microphone next to the other dignitaries lined up on the infield. Then he stood, very erect and without expression as the cheers softened and the stadium settled down.

Mantle was still in the dugout, in uniform, standing with one leg on the top step, and lined on both sides of him were the other Yankees who, when the ceremony was over, would play the Detroit Tigers. Then into the dugout, smiling,

60

came Senator Robert Kennedy, accompanied by two tall curly-haired assistants with blue eyes, Fordham freckles. Jim Farley was the first on the field to notice the Senator, and Farley muttered, loud enough for others to hear, "Who the hell invited *him*?"

Toots Shor and some of the other committeemen standing near Farley looked into the dugout, and so did DiMaggio, his glance seeming cold, but he remained silent. Kennedy walked up and down within the dugout, shaking hands with the Yankees, but he did not walk onto the field.

"Senator," said Yankees' manager Johnny Keane, "why don't you sit down?"   65 Kennedy quickly shook his head, smiled. He remained standing, and then one Yankee came over and asked about getting relatives out of Cuba, and Kennedy called over one of his aides to take down the details in a notebook.

On the infield the ceremony went on, Mantle's gifts continued to pile up — a Mobilette motorbike, a Sooner Schooner wagon barbecue, a year's supply of Chock Full O' Nuts coffee, a year's supply of Topps Chewing Gum — and the Yankee players watched, and Maris seemed glum.

"Hey, Rog," yelled a man with a tape recorder, Murray Olderman, "I want to do a 30-second tape with you."

Maris swore angrily, shook his head.

"Why don't you ask Richardson? He's a better talker than me."

"Yes, but the fact that it comes from you . . ."   70

Maris swore again. But finally he went over and said in an interview that Mantle was the finest player of his era, a great competitor, a great hitter.

Fifteen minutes later, standing behind the microphone at home plate, Di-Maggio was telling the crowd, "I'm proud to introduce the man who succeeded me in center field in 1951," and from every corner of the stadium, the cheering, whistling, clapping came down. Mantle stepped forward. He stood with his wife and children, posed for the photographers kneeling in front. Then he thanked the crowd in a short speech, and, turning, shook hands with the dignitaries standing nearby. Among them now was Senator Kennedy, who had been spotted in the dugout five minutes before by Red Barber, and been called out and introduced. Kennedy posed with Mantle for a photographer, then shook hands with the Mantle children, and with Toots Shor and James Farley and others. DiMaggio saw him coming down the line and at the last second he backed away, casually, hardly anybody noticing it, and Kennedy seemed not to notice it either, just swept past, shaking more hands. . . .

Finishing his tea, putting aside the newspaper, DiMaggio went upstairs to dress, soon he was waving good-bye to Marie and driving toward his business appointment in downtown San Francisco with his partners in the retail television business. DiMaggio, while not a millionaire, has invested wisely and has always had, since his retirement from baseball, executive positions with big companies that have paid him well. He also was among the organizers of the Fisherman's National Bank of San Francisco last year, and, though it never came about, he demonstrated an acuteness that impressed those businessmen who had thought of him only in terms of baseball. He has had offers to manage big-league baseball teams but always has rejected them, saying, "I have enough trouble taking care of my own problems without taking on the responsibilities of 25 ball players."

So his only contact with baseball these days, excluding public appearances, is his unsalaried job as a batting coach each spring in Florida with the New York Yankees, a trip he would make once again on the following Sunday, three days away, if he could accomplish what for him is always the dreaded responsibility of packing, a task made no easier by the fact that he lately had fallen into the habit of keeping his clothes in two places—some hang in his closet at home, some hang in the back room of a saloon called Reno's.

Reno's is a dimly lit bar in the center of San Francisco. A portrait of DiMaggio 75 swinging a bat hangs on the wall, in addition to portraits of other star athletes, and the clientele consists mainly of the sporting crowd and newspapermen, people who know DiMaggio quite well and around whom he speaks freely on a number of subjects and relaxes as he can in few other places. The owner of the bar is Reno Barsocchini, a broad-shouldered and handsome man of 51 with graying wavy hair who began as a fiddler in Dago Mary's tavern 35 years ago. He later became a bartender there and elsewhere, including DiMaggio's Restaurant, and now he is probably DiMaggio's closest friend. He was the best man at the DiMaggio-Monroe wedding in 1954, and when they separated nine months later in Los Angeles, Reno rushed down to help DiMaggio with the packing and drove him back to San Francisco. Reno will never forget the day.

Hundreds of people were gathered around the Beverly Hills home that DiMaggio and Marilyn had rented, and photographers were perched in the trees watching the windows, and others stood on the lawn and behind the rose bushes waiting to snap pictures of anybody who walked out of the house. The newspapers that day played all the puns—"Joe Fanned on Jealousy"; "Marilyn and Joe—Out at Home"—and the Hollywood columnists, to whom DiMaggio was never an idol, never a gracious host, recounted instances of incompatibility, and Oscar Levant said it all proved that no man could be a success in two national pastimes. When Reno Barsocchini arrived, he had to push his way through the mob, then bang on the door for several minutes before being admitted. Marilyn Monroe was upstairs in bed. Joe DiMaggio was downstairs with his suitcases, tense and pale, his eyes bloodshot.

Reno took the suitcase and golf clubs out to DiMaggio's car, and then DiMaggio came out of the house, the reporters moving toward him, the lights flashing.

"Where are you going?" they yelled.

"I'm driving to San Francisco," he said, walking quickly.

"Is that going to be your home?" 80

"That is my home and always has been."

"Are you coming back?"

DiMaggio turned for a moment, looking up at the house.

"No," he said, "I'll never be back."

Reno Barsocchini, except for a brief falling-out over something he will not   85
discuss, has been DiMaggio's trusted companion ever since, joining him whenever he can on the golf course or on the town, otherwise waiting for him in the
bar with other middle-aged men. They may wait for hours sometimes, waiting
and knowing that when he arrives he may wish to be alone; but it does not seem
to matter, they are endlessly awed by him, moved by the mystique, he is a kind of
male Garbo. They know that he can be warm and loyal if they are sensitive to
his wishes, but they must never be late for an appointment to meet him. One
man, unable to find a parking place, arrived a half hour late once, and DiMaggio
did not talk to him again for three months. They know, too, when dining at
night with DiMaggio, that he generally prefers male companions and occasionally one or two young women, but never wives; wives gossip, wives complain,
wives are trouble, and men wishing to remain close to DiMaggio must keep their
wives at home.

When DiMaggio strolls into Reno's bar, the men wave and call out his name
and Reno Barsocchini smiles and announces, "Here's the Clipper!"—the "Yankee
Clipper" being a nickname from his baseball days.

"Hey Clipper, Clipper," Reno had said two nights before, "where you been,
Clipper? . . . Clipper, how 'bout a belt?"

DiMaggio refused the offer of a drink, ordering instead a pot of tea, which he
prefers to all other beverages except before a date, when he will switch to vodka.

"Hey, Joe," a sports writer asked, a man researching a magazine piece on golf,
"why is it that a golfer, when he starts getting older, loses his putting touch first?
Like [Sam] Snead and [Ben] Hogan, they can still hit a ball well off the tee, but on
the greens they lose the strokes."

"It's the pressure of age," DiMaggio said, turning around on his barstool.   90
"With age you get jittery. It's true of golfers, it's true of any man when he gets into
his 50s. He doesn't take chances like he used to. The younger golfer, on the greens,
he'll stroke his putts better. The older man, he becomes hesitant. A little uncertain. Shaky. When it comes to taking chances, the younger man, even when driving a car, will take chances that the older man won't."

"Speaking of chances," another man said, one of the group that had gathered
around DiMaggio, "did you see that guy on crutches in here last night?"

"Yeah, had his leg in a cast," a third said. "Skiing."

"I would never ski," DiMaggio said. "Men who ski must be doing it to impress
a broad. You see these men, some of them 40, 50, getting onto skis. And later you
see them all bandaged up, broken legs."

"But skiing's a very sexy sport, Joe. All the clothes, the tight pants, the fire-
places in the ski lodge, the bear rug—Christ nobody goes to ski. They just go out
there to get it cold so they can warm it up."

"Maybe you're right," DiMaggio said. "I might be persuaded."   95

"Want a belt, Clipper?" Reno asked.

DiMaggio thought for a second, then said, "All right—first belt tonight."

Now it was noon, a warm sunny day. DiMaggio's business meeting with the television retailers had gone well; he had made a strong appeal to George Shahood, president of Continental Television, Inc., which has eight retail outlets in Northern California, to put prices on color television sets and increase the sales volume, and Shahood had conceded it was worth a try. Then DiMaggio called Reno's bar to see if there were any messages, and now he was in Lefty O'Doul's car being driven along Fisherman's Wharf toward the Golden Gate Bridge en route to a golf course 30 miles upstate. Lefty O'Doul was one of the great hitters in the National League in the early thirties, and later he managed the San Francisco Seals when DiMaggio was the shining star. Though O'Doul is now 69, 18 years older than DiMaggio, he nevertheless possesses great energy and spirit, is a hard-drinking, boisterous man with a big belly and roving eye; and when DiMaggio, as they drove along the highway toward the golf club, noticed a lovely blonde at the wheel of a car nearby and exclaimed, "Look at *that* tomato!" O'Doul's head suddenly spun around, he took his eyes off the road, and yelled, "Where, *where?*" O'Doul's golf game is less than what it was—he used to have a two-handicap—but he still shoots in the 80s, as does DiMaggio.

DiMaggio's drives range between 250 and 280 yards when he doesn't sky them, and his putting is good, but he is distracted by a bad back that both pains him and hinders the fullness of his swing. On the first hole, waiting to tee off, DiMaggio sat back watching a foursome of college boys ahead swinging with such freedom. "Oh," he said with a sigh, "to have *their* backs."

DiMaggio and O'Doul were accompanied around the golf course by Ernie 100
Nevers, the former football star, and two brothers who are in the hotel and movie-distribution business. They moved quickly up and down the green hills in electric golf carts, and DiMaggio's game was exceptionally good for the first nine holes. But then he seemed distracted, perhaps tired, perhaps even reacting to a conversation of a few minutes before. One of the movie men was praising the film *Boeing, Boeing*, starring Tony Curtis and Jerry Lewis, and the man asked DiMaggio if he had seen it.

"No," DiMaggio said. Then he added, swiftly, "I haven't seen a film in eight years."

DiMaggio hooked a few shots, was in the woods. He took a No. 9 iron and tried to chip out. But O'Doul interrupted DiMaggio's concentration to remind him to keep the face of the club closed. DiMaggio hit the ball. It caromed off the side of his club, went skipping like a rabbit through the high grass down toward a pond. DiMaggio rarely displays any emotion on a golf course, but now, without saying a word, he took his No. 9 iron and flung it into the air. The club landed in a tree and stayed up there.

"Well," O'Doul said casually, "there goes *that* set of clubs."

DiMaggio walked to the tree. Fortunately the club had slipped to the lower branch, and DiMaggio could stretch up on the cart and get it back.

From p. 23

Protecting the Future of Nature

Ten million people in sub-Saharan Africa make a living fishing. In the past three decades the number of fish in their waters has declined by 50 percent. Around the world, oceans and the life they support are at risk. WWF is at work in more than 40 countries, developing responsible fishing practices and collaborating with governments and coastal communities on managing their fisheries while safeguarding livelihoods. We can protect marine populations from overfishing and still ensure a catch big enough to feed fishermen, their families and you.

Be Part of Our Work   worldwildlife.org

From p. 25

Feeding Kids Meat Is

CHILD ABUSE

Fight the Fat: Go Vegan   *PeTA*

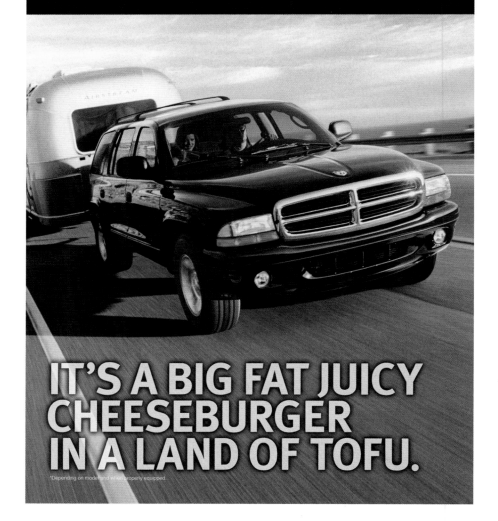

From p. 68

From p. 82

From p. 133

www.polyp.org.uk

From p. 137

From p. 174

Norman Rockwell, *The Spirit of Education* (1934, oil on canvas, 32" x 24").

WHAT I LEARNED:

My earliest school-related memory is of being brought to nursery school in a small van along with a bunch of other kids...

and an aide came over and told me to stop talking to myself.

If you talk to yourself, people will think you're CRAZY!

I learned other stuff that year: that most kids were nice...

Do you want to play?

O.K.

that some were not so nice...

Do you want to play?

No.

...and some were to be avoided.

I'm gonna punch you inna tit!

What's a tit?

I learned many gum facts...

If you swallow your gum, your guts get all stuck together and you die. It happened to my sister's friend's neighbor.

I learned that a girl's name could be Muffin.

I learned how to make an ashtray out of clay.

Well, look at that!

But mostly I was learning about being good...

• Do what Teacher says.
• Listen to Teacher.
• Do not annoy Teacher.
• Pay attention to Teacher.
• BE GOOD!

After that, I went to a grade school in my neighborhood.

P.S. 217

I learned that girls played House...

Do you want to Iron or Take Care of the Baby?

A Sentimental Education

...and boys played Cars and Trucks.

VROOM, VROOM!

BAM BAM BAM BAM!

RMMMM! RMMM! RMMM!

ACME

I liked the Art Corner.

Ooh! Is that a horsie?

No.

I learned that it was very unlikely that I'd become an Olympic anything.

GET THE BALL!
GET THE BALL!
GET THE BALL!
GET THE BALL!
GET THE BALL!
GET THE BALL!
GET THE BALL!

Up through sixth grade, I learned lots of stuff: addition; spelling; all about explorers; how to do a chain stitch; subtraction; how to read and write; multiplication; fractions; how banks worked (a little); how to play punchball (theoretically); division; where crops came from; about planets; what was meant by "Current Events"; about George Washington and Johnny Appleseed; that a heart wasn't shaped like a heart at all; and lots, lots more.

E-I
R-E-C-I-E-V-E

PENSEY! PINKY!

DAILY TIMES

OUR FRIEND WHEAT

OUR FRIEND CORN

MID-BROOKLYN BANK FOR SAVINGS

La, la, la.

371 × 86

16 / 40687

THE STORY OF COLUMBUS
LEIF ERIKSSON
MAGELLAN'S TALE
WHO WAS VASCO DA GAMA?

APPLE SEEDS

Aa Bb   Ff

And, of course, I was learning more about being good.

- Do homework.
- Be neat.
- Be organized.
- Be quiet.
- Pay attention.
- **BE GOOD!!**

It wasn't until junior high that I really started to wonder about the whole setup.

Class, today we're going to memorize all the prepositions.

Oh, my GOD...

Why did we have to learn this? Who said?

...so the sine of a 36° angle is 0.5877853.

What is the Elgin-Marcy Treaty of 1854?

Can anyone tell me the atomic weight of...

FROM NURSERY SCHOOL THROUGH TWELFTH GRADE

After that, I went to a large public high school where we were sorted into three piles based on our probable futures.

ACADEMIC

COMMERCIAL

GENERAL

This was called "tracking" — a process that had probably begun back in kindergarten.

I got pretty good at half-listening. I tried to pay full attention, but sometimes it was impossible.

Maybe I would have been just as bored at an "alternative" school.

Who knows?

Anyway, one day during math I had an epiphany:

I had wanted to "BE GOOD," but there were limits.

From p. 357

Norman Rockwell, *Freedom from Want* (1943, oil on canvas, 45.75" x 35.5").

From p. 359

From p. 473

THIS MODERN WORLD

by TOM TOMORROW

THIS WEEK: A "HANDY" GUIDE TO THE HOUSING MARKET--FEATURING THE **INVISIBLE HAND OF THE FREE MARKET!**

IF YOU'RE INVISIBLE, HOW COME I CAN **SEE** YOU?

IT'S THE MAGIC OF THE MARKET, SON! NOW--LET'S GET **STARTED!**

BACK IN THE **OLDEN** DAYS, BANKERS USED TO INSIST ON ALL SORTS OF "DOCUMENTATION" BEFORE THEY'D GIVE SOMEONE A HOUSING LOAN--EVEN IF THAT PERSON **REALLY** WANTED A LOAN!

BUT THEN **I** INTERVENED-- INTRODUCING THOSE BANKERS TO MY FRIENDS ON **WALL STREET,** WHO STARTED **BUYING** MORTGAGE LOANS FROM BANKS AND SELLING THEM TO **INVESTORS!**

THINGS BEGAN TO LOOSEN UP WHEN LENDERS NO LONGER HAD TO WORRY ABOUT PETTY DETAILS LIKE BEING **REPAID!** AND EVENTUALLY THE **SUBPRIME** MARKET TOOK OFF--AND **THEN** WHAT A PARTY WE HAD!

RATES WERE LOW, MONEY WAS PLENTIFUL, AND HOUSING PRICES **SKYROCKETED**--ER--I MEAN TO SAY, ROSE TO THEIR **PROPER VALUATION,** AS DETERMINED BY THE INHERENT **RATIONALITY** OF THE **FREE MARKET!**

HEH, HEH.

YEAH, THINGS WERE GOING **GREAT**--UNTIL MILLIONS OF BORROWERS INEXPLICABLY BEGAN TO **DEFAULT** ON THEIR LOANS! NO ONE COULD HAVE SEEN **THAT** COMING!

BUT WASN'T IT **INEVITABLE** THAT--

AHEM! ABSOLUTELY **NO ONE!** BUT NOT TO WORRY! AS ALWAYS, THE INVISIBLE HAND OF THE FREE MARKET HAS THE **SOLUTION!**

WHICH IS...?

A MASSIVE **GOVERNMENT BAILOUT!** PROBLEM **SOLVED!** ON TO THE **NEXT** OPPORTUNITY!

I GOTTA SAY, YOU DON'T SEEM VERY RATIONAL TO **ME.**

TELL IT TO THE **HAND,** KID.

TOM TOMORROW©2007... www.thismodernworld.com

Charles Le Brun, *Chancellor Séguier at the Entry of Louis XIV into Paris in 1660* (c. 1661, oil on canvas, 295 x 357 cm.).

From p. 564

Kehinde Wiley, *The Chancellor Séguier on Horseback* (2005, oil on canvas, 108" x 144").

From p. 670

From p. 767

From p. 826

From p. 873

From p. 954

From pp. 956–57

LET'S GO FURTHER ON ONE LITRE OF FUEL.

We must learn to use energy more efficiently. For over 25 years, the
Shell Eco-marathon has supported teams worldwide who explore
ways to maximise fuel economy. The current record holder is capable
of travelling 3,771 km on the equivalent of one litre of fuel. This spirit
epitomises our relationship with car manufacturers, finding ways
to make cars more efficient. And is typical of our ambition
to help build a better energy future. www.shell.com/letsgo

LET'S GO.

United States: The Caven family of California
Food expenditure for one week: $159.18
Favorite foods: Beef stew, berry yogurt sundae, clam chowder, ice cream

Kuwait: The Al Haggan family of Kuwait City
Food expenditure for one week: 63.63 dinar or $221.45
Family recipe: Chicken biryani with basmati rice

From p. 960

Bhutan: The Namgay family of Shingkhey Village
Food expenditure for one week: 224.93 ngultrum or $5.03
Family recipe: Mushroom, cheese, pork

Ecuador: The Ayme family of Tingo
Food expenditure for one week: $31.55
Family recipe: Potato soup with cabbage

Chad: The Aboubakar family of Breidjing Camp
Food expenditure for one week: 685 CFA francs or $1.23
Favorite foods: Soup with fresh sheep meat

Germany: The Melander family of Bargteheide
Food expenditure for one week: 375.39 euros or $500.07
Favorite foods: Fried potatoes with onions, bacon and herring, fried noodles with eggs and cheese, pizza, vanilla pudding

From pp. 1116–17

Christiansted

Christiansted National Historic Site
St. Croix, Virgin Islands

National Park Service
U.S. Department of the Interior

"Every time I get advice," DiMaggio muttered to himself, shaking his head   105
slowly and walking toward the pond, "I shank it."

Later, showered and dressed, DiMaggio and the others drove to a banquet
about 10 miles from the golf course. Somebody had said it was going to be an
elegant dinner, but when they arrived they could see it was more like a county
fair; farmers were gathered outside a big barnlike building, a candidate for sheriff
was distributing leaflets at the front door, and a chorus of homely ladies was
inside singing "You Are My Sunshine."

"How did we get sucked into this?" DiMaggio asked, talking out of the side of
his mouth, as they approached the building.

"O'Doul," one of the men said. "It's his fault. Damned O'Doul can't turn
anything down."

"Go to hell," O'Doul said.

Soon DiMaggio and O'Doul and Ernie Nevers were surrounded by the   110
crowd, and the woman who had been leading the chorus came rushing over and
said, "Oh, Mr. DiMaggio, it certainly is a pleasure having you."

"It's a pleasure being here, ma'am," he said, forcing a smile.

"It's too bad you didn't arrive a moment sooner. You'd have heard our
singing."

"Oh, I heard it," he said, "and I enjoyed it very much."

"Good, good," she said. "And how are your brothers, Dom and Vic?"

"Fine. Dom lives near Boston. Vince is in Pittsburgh."   115

"Why, *hello* there, Joe," interrupted a man with wine on his breath, patting
DiMaggio on the back, feeling his arm. "Who's gonna take it this year, Joe?"

"Well, I have no idea," DiMaggio said.

"What about the Giants?"

"Your guess is as good as mine."

"Well, you can't count the Dodgers out," the man said.   120

"You sure can't," DiMaggio said.

"Not with all that pitching."

"Pitching is certainly important," DiMaggio said.

Everywhere he goes the question seems the same, as if he has some special
vision into the future of new heroes, and everywhere he goes, too, older men grab
his hand and feel his arm and predict that he could still go out there and hit one,
and the smile on DiMaggio's face is genuine. He tries hard to remain as he
was—he diets, he takes steambaths, he is careful; and flabby men in the locker
rooms of golf clubs sometimes steal peeks at him when he steps out of the shower,
observing the tight muscles across his chest, the flat stomach, the long sinewy
legs. He has a young man's body, very pale and little hair; his face is dark and
lined, however, parched by the sun of several seasons. Still he is always an impressive figure at banquets such as this—an "immortal" sports writers called him,
and that is how they have written about him and others like him, rarely suggesting that such heroes might ever be prone to the ills of mortal men, carousing,

drinking, scheming; to suggest this would destroy the myth, would disillusion small boys, would infuriate rich men who own ball clubs and to whom baseball is a business dedicated to profit and in pursuit of which they trade mediocre players' flesh as casually as boys trade players' pictures on bubble-gum cards. And so the baseball hero must always act the part, must preserve the myth, and none does it better than DiMaggio, none is more patient when drunken old men grab an arm and ask, "Who's gonna take it this year, Joe?"

Two hours later, dinner and the speeches over, DiMaggio was slumped in O'Doul's car headed back to San Francisco. He edged himself up, however, when O'Doul pulled into a gas station in which a pretty red-haired girl sat on a stool, legs crossed, filing her fingernails. She was about 22, wore a tight black skirt and tighter white blouse. 125

"Look at *that*," DiMaggio said.

"Yeah," O'Doul said.

O'Doul turned away when a young man approached, opened the gas tank, began wiping the windshield. The young man wore a greasy white uniform on the front of which was printed the name "Burt." DiMaggio kept looking at the girl, but she was not distracted from her fingernails. Then he looked at Burt, who did not recognize him. When the tank was full, O'Doul paid and drove off. Burt returned to his girl; DiMaggio slumped down in the front seat and did not open his eyes again until they arrived in San Francisco.

"Let's go see Reno," DiMaggio said.

"No, I gotta go see my old lady," O'Doul said. So he dropped DiMaggio off in front of the bar, and a moment later Reno's voice was announcing in the smoky room, "Hey, here's the Clipper!" The men waved and offered to buy him a drink. DiMaggio ordered a vodka and sat for an hour at the bar talking to a half-dozen men around him. Then a blonde girl who had been with friends at the other end of the bar came over, and somebody introduced her to DiMaggio. He bought her a drink, offered her a cigarette. Then he struck a match and held it. His hand was unsteady. 130

"Is that me that's shaking?" he asked.

"It must be," said the blonde. "I'm calm."

Two nights later, having collected his clothes out of Reno's back room, DiMaggio boarded a jet; he slept crossways on three seats, then came down the steps as the sun began to rise in Miami. He claimed his luggage and golf clubs, put them into the trunk of a waiting automobile, and less than an hour later he was being driven into Fort Lauderdale, past palm-lined streets, toward the Yankee Clipper Hotel.

"All my life it seems I've been on the road traveling," he said, squinting through the windshield into the sun. "I never get a sense of being in any one place."

Arriving at the Yankee Clipper Hotel, DiMaggio checked into the largest suite. People rushed through the lobby to shake hands with him, to ask for his 135 autograph, to say, "Joe, you look great." And early the next morning, and for the next 30 mornings, DiMaggio arrived punctually at the baseball park and wore his uniform with the famous No. 5, and the tourists seated in the sunny grandstands clapped when he first appeared on the field each time, and then they watched with nostalgia as he picked up a bat and played "pepper" with the younger Yankees, some of whom were not even born when, 25 years ago this summer, he hit in 56 straight games and became the most celebrated man in America.

But the younger spectators in the Fort Lauderdale park, and the sports writers, too, were more interested in Mantle and Maris, and nearly every day there were news dispatches reporting how Mantle and Maris felt, what they did, what they said, even though they said and did very little except walk around the field frowning when photographers asked for another picture and when sports writers asked how they felt.

After seven days of this, the big day arrived—Mantle and Maris would swing a bat—and a dozen sports writers were gathered around the big batting cage that was situated beyond the left-field fence; it was completely enclosed in wire, meaning that no baseball could travel more than 30 or 40 feet before being trapped in rope; still Mantle and Maris would be swinging, and this, in spring, makes news.

Mantle stepped in first. He wore black gloves to help prevent blisters. He hit right-handed against the pitching of a coach named Vern Benson, and soon Mantle was swinging hard, smashing line drives against the nets, going *ahhh ahhh* as he followed through with his mouth open.

Then Mantle, not wanting to overdo it on his first day, dropped his bat in the dirt and walked out of the batting cage. Roger Maris stepped in. He picked up Mantle's bat.

"This damn thing must be 38 ounces," Maris said. He threw the bat down   140
into the dirt, left the cage, and walked toward the dugout on the other side of the field to get a lighter bat.

DiMaggio stood among the sports writers behind the cage, then turned when Vern Benson, inside the cage, yelled, "Joe, wanna hit some?"

"No chance," DiMaggio said.

"Com'on Joe," Benson said.

The reporters waited silently. Then DiMaggio walked slowly into the cage and picked up Mantle's bat. He took his position at the plate but obviously it was not the classic DiMaggio stance; he was holding the bat about two inches from the knob, his feet were not so far apart, and when DiMaggio took a cut at Benson's first pitch, fouling it, there was none of that ferocious follow-through, the blurred bat did not come whipping all the way around, the No. 5 was not stretched full across his broad back.

DiMaggio fouled Benson's second pitch, then he connected solidly with the   145
third, the fourth, the fifth. He was just meeting the ball easily, however, not smashing it, and Benson called out, "I didn't know you were a choke hitter, Joe."

"I am now," DiMaggio said, getting ready for another pitch.

He hit three more squarely enough, and then he swung again and there was a hollow sound.

"Ohhh," DiMaggio yelled, dropping his bat, his fingers stung. "I was waiting for that one." He left the batting cage, rubbing his hands together. The reporters watched him. Nobody said anything. Then DiMaggio said to one of them, not in anger or in sadness, but merely as a simply stated fact, "There was a time when you couldn't get me out of there."

Questions for Discussion

1. How does Gay Talese create a picture of Joe DiMaggio at loose ends that nevertheless suggests his heroism?
2. What does Talese tell us about the position of sports in American popular culture?
3. Talese describes DiMaggio as "a kind of male Garbo," referring to the legendary, reclusive film star Greta Garbo (para. 85). The comparison suggests that DiMaggio's detachment was a masculine ideal. Does this ideal still resonate? How does it square with the image of today's superstar athletes? Does our media-crazy era demand more engagement from our heroes? Are we still capable of being "moved by the mystique" (para. 85)?
4. Talese has said that his work is a highly personal response to the world as an Italian American outsider. What evidence do you find that it is an outsider's voice? How does the authorial voice of an outsider add nuance to the profile of Joe DiMaggio?
5. Why is spring the silent season? Consider the title from the perspective of fishing and baseball.

Questions on Rhetoric and Style

1. What is the effect of juxtaposing details of Joe DiMaggio's legendary baseball prowess with details of his everyday life in San Francisco as a retired athlete?
2. Why does "The Silent Season of a Hero" open with a quotation from Hemingway's *The Old Man and the Sea*? Cite specific passages from Talese's essay to support your answer.
3. The "tall gray-haired man in a dark suit" in the first paragraph is obviously Joe DiMaggio, but Talese waits until the end of paragraph 2 to name him. What is the effect of delaying identification of the essay's subject?
4. Characterize the narrator. Does he step forward at any time? Who is the "man from New York" (para. 12)? Who is asked by the narrator to comment on DiMaggio?
5. Although DiMaggio was a baseball player, the essay sometimes sounds as if it's about a fisherman. Trace both the language of baseball and the language of fishing. Which is predominant?
6. Talese suggests — but doesn't come out and say — that Joe DiMaggio and Marilyn Monroe were competitive about their celebrity. How does Talese use Monroe's

mythical status to develop his portrait of DiMaggio? Is he sympathetic to her? Does his profile of DiMaggio deepen our understanding of Monroe, or does she remain as tantalizingly out of reach as she seems to have been to DiMaggio? Explain your responses.

7. Several parts of the essay—especially paragraphs 3 and 41—evoke Hemingway. How do the images and language of those allusions create another level of meaning? How do they add to the portrait of DiMaggio?

8. What is the overall tone of the essay? How does Talese achieve his tone? How does the tone add a layer of meaning?

9. Talese notes that sportswriters have called DiMaggio an "immortal" (para. 124). How does the essay both support and debunk that myth?

10. Explain the assumptions Talese makes about his audience based on his portrait of DiMaggio as an aging hero.

Suggestions for Writing

1. Write an essay in which you analyze the strategies that Talese uses in paragraphs 116–124 to add complexity and nuance to his portrayal of Joe DiMaggio.

2. In this profile of the Yankee player, Talese doesn't hide the fact that DiMaggio smokes, drinks alcohol, and is dismissive of women. Write an essay in which you examine the responsibility of sportswriters. Should they airbrush their subjects to ensure that they meet their obligations as role models? Or should sportswriters give us the unvarnished truth?

3. Examine the parts of the selection that are about Marilyn Monroe, especially the anecdote about her performing for the troops in Korea (paras. 48–50). Write an essay about how, in the absence of details about why her marriage to DiMaggio failed, the language suggests that perhaps the marriage could not accommodate two egos as strong as DiMaggio's and Monroe's. Read other accounts of the marriage to see if they support or contradict Talese's, and refer to them in your essay.

4. Read "Sinatra Has a Cold," Talese's profile of Frank Sinatra. Compare and contrast it with "The Silent Season of a Hero." How is the author's voice similar or different? Compare the treatment of DiMaggio and Sinatra as embodiments of a masculine ideal.

5. Paragraphs 53–56 recount DiMaggio's 1941 hitting streak, which ended at a record-breaking fifty-six games. During this streak, the New York Yankees went from fourth place in the American League to victory in the World Series. The missing bat—returned by a rueful fan—seems to have been the magic charm. Compare this account with other tales of heroes who depend on the power of a sword, a shield, or some other special piece of equipment.

The Four Horsemen

GRANTLAND RICE

 Known as the Dean of American Sports Writers, Grantland Rice (1880–1954) was born in Murfreesboro, Tennessee. He attended Vanderbilt University, where he majored in Latin and Greek, and worked at newspapers in Nashville, Atlanta, New York, and Washington, D.C. In addition to writing about sports, Rice published books of light verse. One of his most frequently quoted poetic couplets is "For when the One Great Scorer comes to mark against your name, / He writes—not that you won or lost—but how you played the Game." Rice's style was easy to recognize; he elevated the sporting events he reported on beyond mere games. He made heroes out of the athletes he admired, including Jack Dempsey, Babe Ruth, Babe Didrikson Zaharias, and the horse Seabiscuit. In this famous 1924 piece from the *New York Herald Tribune*, Rice reports on the football game between Notre Dame and Army, which was played at the Polo Grounds in New York City.

Outlined against a blue-gray October sky, the Four Horsemen rode again. In dramatic lore they are known as Famine, Pestilence, Destruction and Death. These are only aliases. Their real names are Stuhldreher, Miller, Crowley and Layden. They formed the crest of the South Bend cyclone before which another fighting Army football team was swept over the precipice at the Polo Grounds yesterday afternoon as 55,000 spectators peered down on the bewildering panorama spread on the green plain below.

A cyclone can't be snared. It may be surrounded, but somewhere it breaks through to keep on going. When the cyclone starts from South Bend, where the candle lights still gleam through the Indiana sycamores, those in the way must take to storm cellars at top speed.

Yesterday the cyclone struck again as Notre Dame beat the Army, 13 to 7, with a set of backfield stars that ripped and crashed through a strong Army defense with more speed and power than the warring cadets could meet.

Notre Dame won its ninth game in twelve Army starts through the driving power of one of the greatest backfields that ever churned up the turf of any gridiron in any football age. Brilliant backfields may come and go, but in Stuhldreher, Miller, Crowley and Layden, covered by a fast and charging line, Notre Dame can take its place in front of the field.

Coach McEwan sent one of his finest teams into action, an aggressive organization that fought to the last play around the first rim of darkness, but when Rockne rushed his Four Horsemen to the track they rode down everything in sight. It was in vain that 1,400 gray-clad cadets pleaded for the Army line to hold. 5

610

The Army line was giving all it had, but when a tank tears in with the speed of a motorcycle, what chance had flesh and blood to hold? The Army had its share of stars as Garbisch, Farwick, Wilson, Wood, Ellinger and many others, but they were up against four whirlwind backs who picked up at top speed from the first step as they swept through scant openings to slip on by the secondary defense. The Army had great backs in Wilson and Wood, but the Army had no such quartet, who seemed to carry the mixed blood of the tiger and the antelope.

Rockne's light and tottering line was just about as tottering as the Rock of Gibraltar. It was something more than a match for the Army's great set of forwards, who had earned their fame before. Yet it was not until the second period that the first big thrill of the afternoon set the great crowd into a cheering whirl and brought about the wild flutter of flags that are thrown to the wind in exciting moments. At the game's start Rockne sent in almost entirely a second-string cast. The Army got the jump and began to play most of the football. It was the Army attack that made three first downs before Notre Dame had caught its stride. The South Bend cyclone opened like a zephyr.

And then, in the wake of a sudden cheer, out rushed Stuhldreher, Miller, Crowley and Layden, the four star backs who helped to beat Army a year ago. Things were to be a trifle different now. After a short opening flurry in the second period, Wood, of the Army, kicked out of bounds on Notre Dame's 20 yard line. There was no sign of a tornado starting. But it happened to be at just this spot that Stuhldreher decided to put on his attack and began the long and dusty hike.

On the first play the fleet Crowley peeled off 15 yards and the cloud from the west was now beginning to show signs of lightning and thunder. The fleet, powerful Layden got 6 yards more and then Don Miller added 10. A forward pass from Stuhldreher to Crowley added 12 yards, and a moment later Don Miller ran 20 yards around Army's right wing. He was on his way to glory when Wilson, hurtling across the right of way, nailed him on the 10 yard line and threw him out of bounds. Crowley, Miller and Layden—Miller, Layden and Crowley—one or another, ripping and crashing through, as the Army defense threw everything it had in the way to stop this wild charge that had now come 70 yards. Crowley and Layden added 5 yards more and then, on a split play, Layden went 10 yards across the line as if he had just been fired from the black mouth of a howitzer.

In that second period Notre Dame made eight first downs to the Army's none, which shows the unwavering power of the Western attack that hammered relentlessly and remorselessly without easing up for a second's breath. The Western line was going its full share, led by the crippled Walsh with a broken hand.

But there always was Miller or Crowley or Layden, directed through the right spot by the cool and crafty judgment of Stuhldreher, who picked his plays with the finest possible generalship. The South Bend cyclone had now roared 85 yards to a touchdown through one of the strongest defensive teams in the game. The

10

cyclone had struck with too much speed and power to be stopped. It was the preponderance of Western speed that swept the Army back.

The next period was much like the second. The trouble began when the alert Layden intercepted an Army pass on the 48 yard line. Stuhldreher was ready for another march.

Once again the cheering cadets began to call for a rallying stand. They are never overwhelmed by any shadow of defeat as long as there is a minute of fighting left. But silence fell over the cadet sector for just a second as Crowley ran around the Army's right wing for 15 yards, where Wilson hauled him down on the 33 yard line. Walsh, the Western captain, was hurt in the play but soon resumed. Miller got 7 and Layden got 8 and then, with the ball on the Army's 20 yard line, the cadet defense rallied and threw Miller in his tracks. But the halt was only for the moment. On the next play Crowley swung out and around the Army's left wing, cut in and then crashed over the line for Notre Dame's second touchdown.

On two other occasions the Notre Dame attack almost scored. Yeomans saved one touchdown by intercepting a pass on his 5 yard line as he ran back 35 yards before he was nailed by two tacklers. It was a great play in the nick of time. On the next drive Miller and Layden in two hurricane dashes took the ball 42 yards to the Army's 14 yard line, where the still game Army defense stopped four plunges on the 9 yard line and took the ball.

Up to this point the Army had been outplayed by a crushing margin. Notre Dame had put underway four long marches and two of these had yielded touchdowns. Even the stout and experienced Army line was meeting more than it could hold. Notre Dame's brilliant backs had been provided with the finest possible interference, usually led by Stuhldreher, who cut down tackler after tackler by diving at some rival's flying knees. Against this, each Army attack had been smothered almost before it got underway. Even the great Wilson, the star from Penn State, one of the great backfield runners of his day and time, rarely had a chance to make any headway through a massed wall of tacklers who were blocking every open route.

The sudden change came late in the third quarter, when Wilson, raging like a wild man, suddenly shot through a tackle opening to run 34 yards before he was finally collared and thrown with a jolt. A few minutes later Wood, one of the best of all punters, kicked out of bounds on Notre Dame's 5 yard line. Here was the chance. Layden was forced to kick from behind his own goal. The punt soared up the field as Yeomans called for a free catch on the 35 yard line. As he caught the ball he was nailed and spilled by a Western tackler, and the penalty gave the Army 15 yards, with the ball on Notre Dame's 20 yard line.

At this point Harding was rushed to quarter in place of Yeomans, who had been one of the leading Army stars. On the first three plays the Army reached the 12 yard line, but it was now fourth down, with two yards to go. Harding's next play was the feature of the game.

15

As the ball was passed, he faked a play to Wood, diving through the line, held the oval for just a half breath, then, tucking the same under his arm, swung out around Notre Dame's right end. The brilliant fake worked to perfection. The entire Notre Dame defense had charged forward in a surging mass to check the line attack and Harding, with open territory, sailed on for a touchdown. He traveled those last 12 yards after the manner of food shot from guns. He was over the line before the Westerners knew what had taken place. It was a fine bit of strategy, brilliantly carried over by every member of the cast.

The cadet sector had a chance to rip open the chilly atmosphere at last, and most of the 55,000 present joined in the tribute to football art. But that was Army's last chance to score. From that point on, it was seesaw, up and down, back and forth, with the rivals fighting bitterly for every inch of ground. It was harder now to make a foot than it had been to make 10 yards. Even the all-star South Bend cast could no longer continue to romp for any set distances, as Army tacklers, inspired by the touchdown, charged harder and faster than they had charged before.

The Army brought a fine football team into action, but it was beaten by a faster and smoother team. Rockne's supposedly light, green line was about as heavy as Army's, and every whit as aggressive. What is even more important, it was faster on its feet, faster in getting around.

It was Western speed and perfect interference that once more brought the Army doom. The Army line couldn't get through fast enough to break up the attacking plays; and once started, the bewildering speed and power of the Western backs slashed along for 8, 10, and 15 yards on play after play. And always in front of these offensive drivers could be found the whirling form of Stuhldreher, taking the first man out of the play as cleanly as though he had used a hand grenade at close range. This Notre Dame interference was a marvelous thing to look upon.

It formed quickly and came along in unbroken order, always at terrific speed, carried by backs who were as hard to drag down as African buffaloes. On receiving the kick-off, Notre Dame's interference formed something after the manner of the ancient flying wedge, and they drove back up the field with the runner covered from 25 and 30 yards at almost every chance. And when a back such as Harry Wilson finds few chances to get started, you can figure upon the defensive strength that is barricading the road. Wilson is one of the hardest backs in the game to suppress, but he found few chances yesterday to show his broken-field ability. You can't run through a broken field unless you get there.

One strong feature of the Army play was its headlong battle against heavy odds. Even when Notre Dame had scored two touchdowns and was well on its way to a third, the Army fought on with fine spirit until the touchdown chance came at last. And when the chance came, Coach McEwan had the play ready for the final march across the line. The Army has a better team than it had last year. So has Notre Dame. We doubt that any team in the country could have beaten

Rockne's array yesterday afternoon, East or West. It was a great football team brilliantly directed, a team of speed, power and team play. The Army has no cause to gloom over its showing. It played first-class football against more speed than it could match.

Those who have tackled a cyclone can understand.

. . . .

Questions for Discussion

1. In the time when Grantland Rice wrote, the only people reading his recap who had actually seen the game were those in attendance, unlike today when fans can watch a game on television, listen to it on the radio, stream it on the Internet, or follow it on their phones. How do you think this difference in the sports fan's experience has affected sportswriting? How did Rice make the game come alive for his readers?

2. Can you discern a bias? Does Rice seem to favor one team over the other? If so, how can you tell? If not, how does he maintain his neutrality?

3. While most readers consider "The Four Horsemen" an example of great sportswriting, it has also been roundly criticized. What faults can you find in Rice's writing?

4. Rice has been compared to epic poets such as Homer for the way he created myths out of the events and athletes he reported on. What do you think Rice would have thought of today's sports media with their close scrutiny of athletes, both on the field and off?

5. Rice's lead (the first paragraph of a news article) gave the four Notre Dame football stars — none of whom weighed more than 162 pounds or stood taller than six feet — the name the Four Horsemen, but it was a clever student publicity man (who later became the sports editor of the *Chicago Tribune*) who posed the four players on horses and created the legend. Analyze the photo on the facing page, and consider how it compares to the instant and ever-changing images of players and games we see today.

Questions on Rhetoric and Style

1. How does Rice's lead set the stage for the story?

2. What assumptions does Rice make about his readership? How can you tell?

3. Characterize the tone of "The Four Horsemen." Is the tone consistent throughout, or does it change over the course of the piece?

4. Rice was known for his poetic style. Certainly metaphors are a hallmark of that style. Identify at least four metaphors, and describe their effects.

5. Remembering that few of his readers would have seen the game he is describing, consider how Rice re-creates the event for his readers. Look carefully at his descriptions of the scene and the fans, as well as his description of the game.

6. Rice calls Notre Dame (from South Bend, Indiana) "West" or "Westerners" repeatedly (paras. 8–10, 12, 15, 17, 20, 22). He calls the Army team (from West Point, New York) "East" only once (para. 22). Why might he have characterized Notre Dame as the western team (even though Indiana is in the Midwest)? Why do you think he only calls Army "East" once?

7. With few exceptions, Rice identifies the players — even the "Four Horsemen" — by last name only. What is the effect of that decision?

8. In the New Testament of the Bible, the Four Horsemen of the Apocalypse are summoned forth when Jesus opens a scroll that is closed with seven seals. As he opens the first four seals, four riders come forth, representing Conquest, War, Famine, and Death — the apocalyptic vision of the Last Judgment. Rice surely was alluding to the Bible but may have also been referring to a popular silent film of 1921, called *The Four Horsemen of the Apocalypse*, starring matinee idol Rudolph Valentino. How do these allusions help Rice re-create the thrilling game?

9. Rice's extravagant style may feel overblown to us now, but he comes from a storytelling tradition that characterized sportswriting in the early twentieth century. According to David Maraniss, Pulitzer Prize–winning biographer of Vince Lombardi, sportswriters like Rice "served as the nation's tribe of storytellers, popular artists invested with enormous powers to reinforce cultural mores and shape the public imagination." In what ways does "The Four Horsemen" reinforce cultural

mores and shape the public's imagination? What rhetorical strategies does Rice use to make his story so influential?

Suggestions for Writing

1. Rewrite "The Four Horsemen" using only eight hundred words, the typical word count of sports columns today.

2. The nineteenth-century American poet Walt Whitman called baseball the "hurrah game!" and wrote this about it: "Well — it's our game: that's the chief fact in connection with it: America's game: has the snap, go, fling, of the American atmosphere — belongs as much to our institutions, fits into them as significantly, as our constitutions, laws: is just as important in the sum total of our historic life." Write an essay in which you show how Whitman may have influenced Grantland Rice's style and outlook in "The Four Horsemen."

3. Simon Maxwell Apter, writing in *Lapham's Quarterly* (2010), says, "It's a minor-league mind that chooses to make sport of sports. Not that there aren't major-league authors who do so, among them George Orwell ('Serious sport is war minus the shooting') and H.L. Mencken ('It is impossible to imagine Goethe or Beethoven being good at billiards or golf')." Write an essay in which you support, challenge, or qualify Apter's, Orwell's, or Mencken's assertion.

4. In his memoir, *An Accidental Sportswriter* (2011), Robert Lipsyte says the following about Grantland Rice:

   > [T]he writer who likens a ballplayer to Hercules or Grendel's mother is displaying the ultimate contempt — the ballplayer no longer exists as a person or a performer, but as an object, a piece of matter to be used, in this case, for the furtherance of the sportswriter's career by pandering to the emotional titillation of the reader/fan. Rice populated the press boxes with lesser talents who insisted, like the old master, that they were just sunny fellows who loved kids' games and the jolly apes who played them.

   Write an essay in which you agree or disagree with Lipsyte's assessment of Rice's style and portrayal of athletes.

The Proper Place for Sports

Theodore Roosevelt

Theodore Roosevelt (1858–1919) was only forty-two when he became the twenty-sixth president of the United States following William McKinley's assassination in 1901. During his first term he spearheaded the construction of the Panama Canal, and during his second he won the Nobel Peace Prize—the first American to do so—for his mediation in the Russo-Japanese War of 1904–1905. Prior to holding office, he commanded the famed Rough Riders, an all-volunteer cavalry that led the charge on San Juan Hill in the Spanish-American War, for which he was awarded the Congressional Medal of Honor. Roosevelt led what he called the "strenuous life," which included being a cowboy in the Wild West, going on safari in Africa, and exploring the Amazon basin. His letters to his children, originally published in 1919, capture Roosevelt's view that "for unflagging interest and enjoyment, a household of children, if things go reasonably well, certainly makes all other forms of success and achievement lose their importance by comparison." In the following 1903 letter to his son Ted, Roosevelt puts participation in sports in perspective.

White House, Oct. 4, 1903.

Dear Ted:

In spite of the "Hurry! Hurry!" on the outside of your envelope, I did not like to act until I had consulted Mother and thought the matter over; and to be frank with you, old fellow, I am by no means sure that I am doing right now. If it were not that I feel you will be so bitterly disappointed, I would strongly advocate your acquiescing in the decision to leave you off the second squad this year. I am proud of your pluck, and I greatly admire football—though it was not a game I was ever able to play myself, my qualities resembling Kermit's rather than yours. But the very things that make it a good game make it a rough game, and there is always the chance of your being laid up. Now, I should not in the least object to your being laid up for a season if you were striving for something worth while, to get on the Groton school team, for instance, or on your class team when you entered Harvard—for of course I don't think you will have the weight to entitle you to try for the 'varsity. But I am by no means sure that it *is* worth your while to run the risk of being laid up for the sake of playing in the second squad when you are a fourth former, instead of when you are a fifth former. I do not know that the risk is balanced by the reward. However, I have told the Rector that as you feel so strongly about it, I think that the chance of your damaging yourself in body is outweighed by the possibility of bitterness of spirit if you could not play. Understand me, I should think mighty little of you if you permitted chagrin to make you bitter on some point where it was evidently right for you to suffer the chagrin. But in this case I am uncertain, and I shall give you the benefit of the doubt.

617

If, however, the coaches at any time come to the conclusion that you ought not to be in the second squad, why you must come off without grumbling.

I am delighted to have you play football. I believe in rough, manly sports. But I do not believe in them if they degenerate into the sole end of any one's existence. I don't want you to sacrifice standing well in your studies to any over-athleticism; and I need not tell you that character counts for a great deal more than either intellect or body in winning success in life. Athletic proficiency is a mighty good servant, and like so many other good servants, a mighty bad master. Did you ever read Pliny's letter to Trajan, in which he speaks of [it] being advisable to keep the Greeks absorbed in athletics, because it distracted their minds from all serious pursuits, including soldiering, and prevented their ever being dangerous to the Romans? I have not a doubt that the British officers in the Boer War had their efficiency partly reduced because they had sacrificed their legitimate duties to an inordinate and ridiculous love of sports. A man must develop his physical prowess up to a certain point; but after he has reached that point there are other things that count more. In my regiment nine-tenths of the men were better horsemen than I was, and probably two-thirds of them better shots than I was, while on the average they were certainly hardier and more enduring. Yet after I had had them a very short while they all knew, and I knew too, that nobody else could command them as I could. I am glad you should play football; I am glad that you should box; I am glad that you should ride and shoot and walk and row as well as you do. I should be very sorry if you did not do these things. But don't ever get into the frame of mind which regards these things as constituting the end to which all your energies must be devoted, or even the major portion of your energies.

Yes, I am going to speak at Groton on prize day. I felt that while I was President, and while you and Kermit were at Groton I wanted to come up there and see you, and the Rector wished me to speak, and so I am very glad to accept.

By the way, I am working hard to get Renown accustomed to automobiles. He is such a handful now when he meets them that I seriously mind encountering them when Mother is along. Of course I do not care if I am alone, or with another man, but I am uneasy all the time when I am out with Mother. Yesterday I tried Bleistein over the hurdles at Chevy Chase. The first one was new, high and stiff, and the old rascal never rose six inches, going slap through it. I took him at it again and he went over all right.

I am very busy now, facing the usual endless worry and discouragement, and trying to keep steadily in mind that I must not only be as resolute as Abraham Lincoln in seeking to achieve decent ends, but as patient, as uncomplaining, and as even-tempered in dealing, not only with knaves, but with the well-meaning foolish people, educated and uneducated, who by their unwisdom give the knaves their chance.

5

Exploring the Text

1. Theodore Roosevelt is credited with having said, "In short, in life, as in a football game, the principle to follow is: Hit the line hard; don't foul and don't shirk, but hit the line hard!" In what ways does the letter to Ted offer similar advice? How is the advice tempered for his young son? Does the letter contradict the "hit the line hard" quotation in any way? Explain your response.

2. Roosevelt argues against sports if they "degenerate into the sole end of any one's existence" (para. 2). What examples does he give to support his argument? Are they effective? Do they withstand the test of time? Can you apply his argument to participation in sports today? If so, how?

3. What assumptions about his son underlie Roosevelt's argument?

4. Characterize the letter's tone. Do some parts seem more presidential than fatherly? Identify and explain.

5. How does the first paragraph of the letter balance appeals to logos and pathos?

6. Analyze the following two sentences, considering the effects of Roosevelt's diction. In which ways does the language support or undermine his argument?

> Understand me, I should think mighty little of you if you permitted chagrin to make you bitter on some point where it was evidently right for you to suffer the chagrin. (para. 1)

> I don't want you to sacrifice standing well in your studies to any over-athleticism; and I need not tell you that character counts for a great deal more than either intellect or body in winning success in life. (para. 2)

7. Roosevelt begins the letter by saying he did not hurry his response because he wanted to confer with Ted's mother. He doesn't mention her again until paragraph 4. What is the effect of this rhetorical decision?

8. How does Roosevelt achieve his measured response to what was obviously a sense of urgency in the letter to which he is responding? Look particularly at the ways he uses the word *if*.

9. Think about this letter in light of the current generation of parents, considered by many to be overly involved in their children's lives. Could one accuse Roosevelt of being an early-twentieth-century soccer dad?

An Innocent at Rinkside

William Faulkner

William Faulkner (1897–1962) grew up in Oxford, Mississippi. Except for some time in the Canadian and then the British Royal Air Force during World War I, a bookstore in New York City, and a newspaper in New Orleans, Faulkner seldom left Oxford. His fiction—including *The Sound and the Fury* (1929), *Light in August* (1932), *Absalom, Absalom!* (1936), and *Intruder in the Dust* (1962), among others—takes place in the imaginary Yoknapatawpha County and features a revolving cast of recurring characters. Faulkner won the Nobel Prize in Literature in 1949. The piece presented here, offering Faulkner's impressions of his first National Hockey League game, appeared in *Sports Illustrated* in 1955.

The vacant ice looked tired, though it shouldn't have. They told him it had been put down only a few minutes ago following a basketball game, and after the hockey match it would be taken up again to make room for something else. But it looked not expectant but resigned, like the mirror simulating ice in the Christmas store window, not before the miniature fir trees and reindeer and cosy lamplit cottage were arranged upon it, but after they had been dismantled and cleared away.

Then it was filled with motion, speed. To the innocent, who had never seen it before, it seemed discorded and inconsequent, bizarre and paradoxical like the frantic darting of the weightless bugs which run on the surface of stagnant pools. Then it would break, coalesce through a kind of kaleidoscopic whirl like a child's toy, into a pattern, a design almost beautiful, as if an inspired choreographer had drilled a willing and patient and hard-working troupe of dancers—a pattern, a design which was trying to tell him something, say something to him urgent and important and true in that second before, already bulging with the motion and the speed, it began to disintegrate and dissolve.

Then he learned to find the puck and follow it. Then the individual players would emerge. They would not emerge like the sweating barehanded behemoths from the troglodyte mass of football, but instead as fluid and fast and effortless as rapier thrusts or lightning—Richard with something of the passionate glittering fatal alien quality of snakes, Geoffrion like an agile ruthless precocious boy who maybe couldn't do anything else but then he didn't need to; and others—the veteran Laprade, still with the know-how and the grace. But he had time too now, or rather time had him, and what remained was no longer expendable that recklessly, heedlessly, successfully; not enough of it left now to buy fresh passion and fresh triumph with.

Like the Rapier

Excitement: men in rapid, hard, close physical conflict, not just with bare hands, but armed with the knife blades of skates and the hard, fast, deft sticks which could break bones when used right. He had noticed how many women were among the spectators, and for just a moment he thought that perhaps this was why—that here actual male blood could flow, not from the crude impact of a heavier fist but from the rapid and delicate stroke of weapons, which, like the European rapier or the frontier pistol, reduced mere size and brawn to its proper perspective to the passion and the will. But only for a moment because he, the innocent, didn't like that idea either. It was the excitement of speed and grace, with the puck for catalyst, to give it reason, meaning.

He watched it—the figure-darted glare of ice, the concentric tiers rising in   5
sections stipulated by the hand-lettered names of the individual fanclub idols, vanishing upward into the pall of tobacco smoke trapped by the roof—the roof which stopped and trapped all that intent and tense watching, and concentrated it downward upon the glare of ice frantic and frenetic with motion; until the byproduct of the speed and the motion—their violence—had no chance to exhaust itself upward into space and so leave on the ice only the swift glittering changing pattern. And he thought how perhaps something is happening to sport in America (assuming that by definition sport is something you do yourself, in solitude or not, because it is fun), and that something is the roof we are putting over it and them. Skating, basketball, tennis, track meets and even steeplechasing have moved indoors; football and baseball function beneath covers of arc lights and in time will be rain- and coldproofed too. There still remain the proper working of a fly over trout water or the taking of a rise of birds in front of a dog or the right placing of a bullet in a deer or even a bigger animal which will hurt you if you don't. But not for long: in time that will be indoors too beneath lights and the trapped pall of spectator tobacco, the concentric sections bearing the name and device of the lion or the fish as well as that of the Richard or Geoffrion of the scoped rifle or four-ounce rod.

The Same Little Boys

But (to repeat) not for long, because the innocent did not quite believe that either. We—Americans—like to watch; we like the adrenalic discharge of vicarious excitement or triumph or success. But we like to do also: the discharge of the personal excitement of the triumph and the fear to be had from actually setting the horse at the stone wall or pointing the overcanvased sloop or finding by actual test if you can line up two sights and one buffalo in time. There must have been little boys in that throng too, frantic with the slow excruciating passage of time, panting for the hour when they would be Richard or Geoffrion or Laprade—the same little Negro boys whom the innocent has seen shadow-boxing in front of a photograph of Joe Louis in his own Mississippi town, the same little Norwegian boys he watched staring up the snowless slope of the Holmenkollen jump one July day in the hills above Oslo.

Exploring the Text

1. How does William Faulkner bring to life a game that many people have only seen on television?
2. Find examples of figurative language — similes and metaphors in particular. What is the effect of these literary devices, which are more common in fiction and poetry than in sportswriting?
3. Faulkner refers to himself as "the innocent" and in the third person. Why do you think he has avoided the first person? Do you think this is an effective technique? Explain your response.
4. What statement does Faulkner make about the future of sports? To what extent have his predictions come true?
5. What do you think Faulkner's sports biases are? How can you tell?

The Cruelest Sport

JOYCE CAROL OATES

> Joyce Carol Oates was born in Lockport, New York, in 1938. With a typewriter she received at age fourteen, Oates wrote "novel after novel" in high school and college in order to train herself to be a writer. Oates, who received a bachelor's degree from Syracuse University and a master's in English from the University of Wisconsin, is currently the Roger S. Berlind Distinguished Professor of the Humanities at Princeton. She is the youngest author to receive the National Book Award — for her novel *Them* (1969). Novelist, playwright, poet, and journalist, Oates is highly prolific, having published more than thirty novels, including *Black Water* (1992), *We Were the Mulvaneys* (1996), and *The Falls* (2004). Her work often addresses the violence and suspense lurking beneath ordinary life. This essay was originally published in the *New York Review of Books* in February 1992.

And if the body does not do fully as much as the soul?
And if the body were not the soul, what is the soul?
> — WALT WHITMAN, "I Sing the Body Electric"

A boxer's victory is gained in blood.

> — Greek inscription

Professional boxing is the only major American sport whose primary, and often murderous, energies are not coyly deflected by such artifacts as balls and pucks. Though highly ritualized, and as rigidly bound by rules, traditions, and taboos as any religious ceremony, it survives as the most primitive and terrifying of contests: two men, near-naked, fight each other in a brightly lit, elevated space roped in like an animal pen (though the ropes were originally to keep rowdy spectators out); two men climb into the ring from which only one, symbolically, will climb out. (Draws do occur in boxing, but are rare, and unpopular.)

Boxing is a stylized mimicry of a fight to the death, yet its mimesis is an uncertain convention, for boxers do sometimes die in the ring, or as a consequence of a bout; their lives are sometimes, perhaps always, shortened by the stress and punishment of their careers (in training camps no less than in official fights). Certainly, as in the melancholy case of Muhammad Ali, the most acclaimed and beloved heavyweight in boxing history, the quality of the boxer's post-retirement life is frequently diminished. For the great majority of boxers, past and present, life in the ring is nasty, brutish, and short — and not even that remunerative.

Yet, for inhabitants of the boxing world, the ideal conclusion of a fight is a knockout, and not a decision; and this, ideally, not the kind in which a man is counted "out" on his feet, still less a TKO ("technical knockout" — from injuries), but a knockout in the least ambiguous sense — one man collapsed and unconscious, the other leaping about the ring with his gloves raised in victory, the very embodiment of adolescent masculine fantasy. Like a tragedy in which no one dies, the fight lacking a classic knockout seems unresolved, unfulfilled: the strength, courage, ingenuity, and desperation of neither boxer have been adequately measured. Catharsis is but partial, the Aristotelian principle of an action complete in itself has been thwarted. (Recall the fury of young Muhammad Ali at the too-readily-defeated Sonny Liston in their second, notorious title fight, of 1965: instead of going to a neutral corner, Ali stood over his fallen opponent with his fist cocked, screaming, "Get up and fight, sucker!")

This is because boxing's mimesis is not that of a mere game, but a powerful analogue of human struggle in the rawest of life-and-death terms. When the analogue is not evoked, as, in most fights, it is not, the action is likely to be unengaging, or dull; "boxing" is the art, but "fighting" is the passion. The delirium of the crowd at one of those matches called "great" must be experienced firsthand to be believed (Frazier–Ali I, 1971, Hagler–Hearns, 1986, for instance); identification with the fighters is so intense, it is as if barriers between egos dissolve, and one is in the presence of a Dionysian rite of cruelty, sacrifice, and redemption. "The nearest thing to death," Ali described it, after his third title match with Joe Frazier, in 1975, which he won when the fight was stopped after the fourteenth round. Or: "This is some way to make a living, isn't it?" as the superlightweight Saoul Mamby said, badly battered after a title fight with the champion Billy Costello, in 1984.

A romance of (expendable) maleness — in which The Fight is honored, and even great champions come, and go. 5

⸭

For these reasons, among others, boxing has long been America's most popularly despised sport: a "so-called" sport, even a "meta-" or an "anti-" sport: a "vicious exploitation of maleness"[1] as prostitution and pornography may be said to be a vicious exploitation of femaleness. It is not, contrary to common supposition, the most dangerous sport (the American Medical Association, arguing for boxing's abolition, acknowledges that it is statistically less dangerous than speedway racing, thoroughbred racing, downhill skiing, professional football, et al.), but it is the most spectacularly and pointedly cruel sport, its intention being to stun one's opponent's brain; to affect the orgasmic communal "knockout" that is the culminating point of the rising action of the ideal fight. The humanitarian argues that boxing's very intentions are obscene, which sets it apart, theoretically at least, from purer (i.e., Caucasian) establishment sports bracketed above.

Boxing is only possible if there is an endless supply of young men hungry to leave their impoverished ghetto neighborhoods, more than willing to substitute the putative dangers of the ring for the more evident, possibly daily, dangers of the street; yet it is rarely advanced as a means of eradicating boxing that poverty itself be abolished; that it is the social conditions feeding boxing that are obscene. The pious hypocrisy of Caucasian moralists vis-à-vis the sport that has become almost exclusively the province of black and ethnic minorities has its analogue in a classic statement of President Bush's of some months ago, that he is worried about the amount of "filth" flooding America by way of televised hearings and trials: not that the Clarence Thomas–Anita Hill hearing and the William Kennedy Smith rape trial revealed "filth" at the core of certain male–female relations in our society, but that public airings of such, the very hearings and trials, are the problem. Ban the spectacle, and the obscenity will cease to exist.

Black boxers from the time of Jack Johnson (the first and most flamboyant of the world's black heavyweight champions, 1908–1915) through Joe Louis, Sugar Ray Robinson, Muhammad Ali, Larry Holmes, Sugar Ray Leonard, and Mike Tyson have been acutely conscious of themselves as racially *other* from the majority of their audiences, whom they must please in one way or another, as black villains, or honorary whites. (After his pulverizing defeat of the "good, humble Negro" Floyd Patterson, in a heavyweight title match in 1962, Sonny Liston gloated in his role as black villain; when he lost so ingloriously to Muhammad Ali, a brash new-style black who drew upon Jack Johnson, Sugar Ray Robinson, and even the campy professional wrestler Gorgeous George for his own public persona, Liston lost his mystique, and his career soon ended.)

To see race as a predominant factor in American boxing is inevitable, but the moral issues, as always in this paradoxical sport, are ambiguous. Is there a moral distinction between the spectacle of black slaves in the Old South being forced by their white owners to fight, for purposes of gambling, and the spectacle of contemporary blacks fighting for multimillion-dollar paydays, for TV coverage from Las Vegas and Atlantic City? When, in 1980, in one of the most cynically promoted boxing matches in history, the aging and ailing Muhammad Ali fought the young heavyweight champion Larry Holmes, in an "execution" of a fight that was stopped after ten rounds, did it alleviate the pain, or the shame, that Ali was guaranteed $8 million for the fight? (Of which, with characteristic finesse, promoter Don King cheated him of nearly $1 million.) Ask the boxers.

Boxing today is very different from the boxing of the past, which allowed a 10 man to be struck repeatedly while trying to get to his feet (Dempsey–Willard, 1919), or to be knocked down seven times in three wholly one-sided rounds (Patterson–Johansson I, 1959), or so savagely and senselessly struck in the head with countless unanswered blows that he died in a coma ten days later (Griffith–Paret, 1962); the more immediate danger, for any boxer fighting a Don King opponent, is that the fight will be stopped prematurely, by a zealous referee protective of King's investment.

As boxing is "reformed," it becomes less satisfying on a deep, unconscious level, more nearly resembling amateur boxing; yet, as boxing remains primitive, brutal, bloody, and dangerous, it seems ever more anachronistic, if not in fact obscene, in a society with pretensions of humanitarianism. Its exemplary figure is that of the warrior, of some mythopoeic time before weapons were invented; the triumph of physical genius, in a technologically advanced world in which the physical counts for very little, set beside intellectual skills. Even in the gritty world of the underclass, who, today, would choose to fight with mere *fists*? Guns abound, death to one's opponents at a safe distance is possible even for children. Mike Tyson's boast, after his defeat of the twelve-to-one underdog Carl Williams in a heavyweight title defense of 1989, "I want to fight, fight, fight and destruct the world," strikes a poignantly hollow note, even if we knew nothing of subsequent disastrous events in Tyson's life and career.[2]

Consider the boxing trainer's time-honored adage: *They all go if you hit them right.*

These themes are implicit in Thomas Hauser's *Muhammad Ali: His Life and Times* and *The Black Lights: Inside the World of Professional Boxing*, but it is only in the latter work that theoretical, historical, and psychological issues are considered — Hauser sees boxing as "the red light district of professional sports," in which individuals of exceptional talent, courage, and integrity nonetheless prevail. His Ali is the heftier and more ambitious of the two, befitting its prodigious subject — the most famous athlete of all time, until recent years the most highly paid athlete of all time. An authorized biography, it would appear to be definitive, and is certainly exhaustive; Hauser spent thousands of hours with his subject, as well as approximately two hundred other people, and was given access to Ali's medical records. The text arranges these testimonies into a chronological history in which (is this New Age biography?) the author's voice alternates with, but rarely comments upon, still less criticizes, what these others have said. Compassionate, intelligent, fair-minded, *Muhammad Ali: His Life and Times* might have benefited from further editing and paraphrase. Specific subjects (an imminent fight, financial deals, Ali's marital problems, Ali's health problems, the Nation of Islam, et al.) become lost in a welter of words; frequently, it is difficult to locate dates, even for important fights. And no ring record of Ali in the appendix!—a baffling omission, as if Ali's performance as an athlete were not the primary reason for the book.

As it happens, Hauser's succinct commentary on the Ali phenomenon and his shrewd analysis of the boxing world, including Don King's role in it, in his earlier book, *The Black Lights*, can provide, for the reader of the biography, a kind of companion gloss; the books are helpfully read in tandem. It is a remark of Ali's, in 1967, that gives *The Black Lights* its ominous title:

> They say when you get hit and hurt bad you see black lights—the black lights of unconsciousness. But I don't know nothing about that. I've had twenty-eight fights and twenty-eight wins. I ain't never been stopped.

Muhammad Ali, born Cassius Marcellus Clay in Louisville, Kentucky, on January 17, 1942, grandson of a slave, began boxing at the age of twelve, and, by eighteen, had fought 108 amateur bouts. How is it possible that the young man who, in his twenties, would astonish the world not just with the brilliance of his boxing but the sharpness of his wit seems to have been a dull-average student in high school who graduated 376th out of a class of 391? In 1966, his score on a mental aptitude test was an Army IQ of 78, well below military qualification. In 1975, Ali confessed to a reporter that he "can't read too good" and had not read ten pages of all the material written about him. I remember the television interview in which, asked what else he might have done with his life, Ali paused, for several seconds, clearly not knowing how to reply. All he'd ever known, he said finally, was boxing.

Mental aptitude tests cannot measure genius except in certain narrow ranges, and the genius of the body, the play of lightning-swift reflexes coupled with unwavering precision and confidence, eludes comprehension. All great boxers possess this genius, which scrupulous training hones, but can never create. "Styles make fights," as Ali's great trainer Angelo Dundee says, and "style" was young Ali's trademark. Yet even after early wins over such veterans as Archie Moore and Henry Cooper, the idiosyncrasies of Ali's style aroused skepticism in boxing experts. After winning the Olympic gold medal in 1960, Ali was described by A. J. Leibling as "skittering . . . like a pebble over water." Everyone could see that this brash young boxer held his hands too low; he leaned away from punches instead of properly slipping them; his jab was light and flicking; he seemed to be perpetually on the brink of disaster. As a seven-to-one underdog in his first title fight with Sonny Liston, the twenty-two-year-old challenger astounded the experts with his performance, which was like none other they had ever seen in the heavyweight division; he so out-boxed and demoralized Liston that Liston "quit on his stool" after the sixth round. A new era in boxing had begun, like a new music.

> Ali rode the crest of a new wave of athletes—competitors who were both big and fast. . . . Ali had a combination of size and speed that had never been seen in a fighter

15

before, along with incredible will and courage. He also brought a new style to boxing. Jack Dempsey changed fisticuffs from a kind of constipated science where fighters fought in a tense defensive style to a wild sensual assault. Ali revolutionized boxing the way black basketball players have changed basketball today. He changed what happened in the ring, and elevated it to a level that was previously unknown.

—LARRY MERCHANT, quoted in *Muhammad Ali*

In the context of contemporary boxing—the sport is in one of its periodic slumps—there is nothing more instructive and rejuvenating than to see again these old, early fights of Ali's, when, as his happy boast had it, he floated like a butterfly and stung like a bee and threw punches faster than opponents could see—like the "mystery" right to the temple of Liston that felled him, in the first minute of the first round of their rematch. These early fights, the most brilliant being against Cleveland Williams, in 1966, predate by a decade the long, grueling, punishing fights of Ali's later career, whose accumulative effects hurt Ali irrevocably, resulting in what doctors call, carefully, his "Parkinsonianism"—to distinguish it from Parkinson's disease. There is a true visceral shock in observing a heavyweight with the grace, agility, swiftness of hands and feet, defensive skills, and ring cunning of a middleweight Ray Robinson, or a featherweight Willie Pep—like all great athletes, Ali has to be seen to be believed.

In a secular, yet pseudo-religious and sentimental nation like the United States, it is quite natural that sports stars emerge as "heroes"—"legends"—"icons." Who else? George Santayana described religion as "another world to live in" and no world is so set off from the disorganization and disenchantment of the quotidian than the world, or worlds, of sports. Hauser describes, in considerable detail, the transformation of the birth of Ali out of the unexpectedly stubborn and idealistic will of young Cassius Clay: how, immediately following his first victory over Liston, he declared himself a convert to the Nation of Islam (more popularly known as the Black Muslims) and "no longer a Christian." He repudiated his "slave name" of Cassius Marcellus Clay to become Muhammad Ali (a name which, incidentally, *The New York Times*, among other censorious white publications, would not honor through the 1960s). Ali became, virtually overnight, a spokesman for black America as no other athlete, certainly not the purposefully reticent Joe Louis, had ever done—"I don't have to be what you want me to be," he told white America. "I'm free to be me." Two years later, refusing to be inducted into the army to fight in Vietnam, Ali, beleaguered by reporters, uttered one of the memorable incendiary remarks of that era: "Man, I ain't got no quarrel with them Vietcong."

How ingloriously white America responded to Ali: the government retaliated by overruling a judge who had granted Ali the status of conscientious objector, fined Ali $10,000, and sentenced him to five years in prison; he was stripped of his heavyweight title and deprived of his license to box. Eventually, the U.S. Supreme

Court would overturn the conviction, and, as the tide of opinion shifted in the country, in the early 1970s as the Vietnam War wound down Ali returned triumphantly to boxing again, and regained the heavyweight title not once but twice. Years of exile during which he'd endured the angry self-righteousness of the conservative white press seemed, wonderfully, not to have embittered him. He had become a hero. He had entered myth.

Yet the elegiac title of Angelo Dundee's chapter in Dave Anderson's *In the Corner*[3] — "We Never Saw Muhammad Ali at His Best" — defines the nature of Ali's sacrifice for his principles, and the loss to boxing. When, after the three-and-a-half-year layoff, Ali returned to the ring, he was of course no longer the seemingly invincible boxer he'd been; he'd lost his legs, thus his primary line of defense. Like the maturing writer who learns to replace the incandescent head-on energies of youth with what is called technique, Ali would have to descend into his physical being and experience for the first time the punishment ("the nearest thing to death") that is the lot of the great boxer willing to put himself to the test. As Ali's personal physician at that time, Ferdie Pacheco, said, 20

> [Ali] discovered something which was both very good and very bad. Very bad in that it led to the physical damage he suffered later in his career; very good in that it eventually got him back the championship. He discovered that he could take a punch.

The secret of Ali's mature success, and the secret of his tragedy: *he could take a punch.*

For the remainder of his twenty-year career, Muhammad Ali took punches, many of the kind that, delivered to a nonboxer, would kill him or her outright — from Joe Frazier in their three exhausting marathon bouts, from George Foreman, from Ken Norton, Leon Spinks, Larry Holmes. Where in his feckless youth Ali was a dazzling figure combining, say, the brashness of Hotspur and the insouciance of Lear's Fool, he became in these dark, brooding, increasingly willed fights the closest analogue boxing contains to Lear himself; or, rather, since there is no great fight without two great boxers, the title matches Ali–Frazier I (which Frazier won by a decision) and Ali–Frazier III (which Ali won, just barely, when Frazier virtually collapsed after the fourteenth round) are boxing's analogues to *King Lear* — ordeals of unfathomable human courage and resilience raised to the level of classic tragedy. These somber and terrifying boxing matches make us weep for their very futility; we seem to be in the presence of human experience too profound to be named — beyond the strategies and diminishments of language. The mystic's dark night of the soul, transmogrified as a brutal meditation of the body.

And Ali–Foreman, Zaire, 1974: the occasion of the infamous "rope-a-dope" defense, by which the thirty-two-year-old Ali exhausted his twenty-six-year-old opponent by the inspired method of, simply, and horribly, allowing him to punch himself out on Ali's body and arms. This is a fight of such a magical quality that even to watch it closely is not to see how it was done, its fairy-tale reversal in the eighth round executed. (One of Norman Mailer's most impassioned books, *The Fight*, is about this fight; watching a tape of Ali on the ropes enticing, and infuriating, and frustrating, and finally exhausting his opponent by an offense in the guise of a defense, I pondered what sly lessons of masochism Mailer absorbed from being at ringside that day, what deep-imprinted resolve to outwear all adversaries.)

These hard-won victories began irreversible loss: progressive deterioration of Ali's kidneys, hands, reflexes, stamina. By the time of that most depressing of modern-day matches, Ali–Holmes, 1980, when Ali was thirty-eight years old, Ferdie Pacheco had long departed the Ali camp, dismissed for having advised Ali to retire; those who supported Ali's decision to fight, like the bout's promoter, Don King, had questionable motives. Judging from Hauser's information, it is a wonder that Ali survived this fight at all: the fight was, in Sylvester Stallone's words, "like watching an autopsy on a man who's still alive." (In *The Black Lights*, Hauser describes the bedlam that followed this vicious fight at Caesar's Palace, Las Vegas, where gamblers plunged in an orgy of gambling, as in a frenzy of feeding, or copulation: "Ali and Holmes had done their job.") Incredibly, Ali was allowed to fight once more, with Trevor Berbick, in December 1981, before retiring permanently.

Hauser's portrait of Ali is compassionate and unjudging: Is the man to be blamed for having been addicted to his body's own adrenaline, or are others to be blamed for indulging him—and exploiting him? The brash rap-style egoism of young Cassius Clay underwent a considerable transformation during Ali's long public career, yet strikes us, perhaps, as altered only in tone: "Boxing was just to introduce me to the world," Ali has told his biographer. Mystically involved in the Nation of Islam, Ali sincerely believes himself an international emissary for peace, love, and understanding (he who once wreaked such violence upon his opponents!); and who is to presume to feel sorry for one who will not feel sorry for himself?

The Black Lights: Inside the World of Professional Boxing describes a small, self-contained arc—a few years in the career of a boxer named Billy Costello, at one time a superlightweight titleholder from Kingston, New York. Like *Muhammad Ali*, it is a sympathetic study of its primary subject, Costello, his manager Mike Jones, and their families and associates; yet, in the interstices of a compelling narrative taking us through the preparation for a successful title defense of 1984, it illuminates aspects of the boxing world generally unknown to outsiders—the routine and discipline of the boxer in training; the complex role of the fight manager; the exhausting contractual negotiations; the state of this "red-light district"—

> Professional boxing is no longer worthy of civilized society. It's run by self-serving crooks, who are called promoters. . . . Except for the fighters, you're talking about human scum. . . . Professional boxing is utterly immoral. It's not capable of reformation. I now favor the abolition of professional boxing. You'll never clean it up. Mud can never be clean.
>
> —HOWARD COSELL, quoted in *The Black Lights*

Like others sympathetic with boxers, who are in fact poorly paid, nonunionized workers with no benefits in a monopolistic business without antitrust control, Hauser argues strongly for a national association to regulate the sport; a federal advisory panel to protect boxers from exploitation. His portrait of Billy Costello allows us to see why a young man will so eagerly risk injuries in the ring, which is perceived as a lifeline, and not a place of exploitation; why he will devote himself to the rigors of training in a sport in which, literally, one's entire career can end within a few seconds.

Black Lights ends dramatically, with Costello retaining his title against a thirty-seven-year-old opponent, Saoul Mamby, and with his hope of moving up in weight and making more money. Since its publication in 1986, the book has become a boxing classic; it is wonderfully readable, and, unlike *Ali*, judiciously proportioned. Yet to end the book with this victory is surely misleading, and even, to this reader, perplexing. The "black lights of unconsciousness" would be experienced by Billy Costello shortly, in a bout with a dazzlingly arrogant and idiosyncratic Ali-inspired young boxer named, at that time, "Lightning" Lonnie Smith, who would KO Costello in one of those nightmares all boxers have, before a hometown audience in Kingston. Following that devastating loss, Costello would fight the aging Alexis Arguello, one of the great lightweights of contemporary times, who would beat him savagely and end his career. To end with a tentative victory and not supply at least a coda to take us to the collapse of Billy Costello's career deprives *Black Lights* of the significance it might have had—for boxing is about failure far more than it is about success. In the words of the battered Saoul Mamby, "I'll miss it. I love boxing. Everything passed too soon."

Notes

1. See Gerald Early's brilliantly corrosive essays on boxing in *Tuxedo Junction: Essays on American Culture* (Ecco, 1989).
2. See Montieth Illingworth, *Mike Tyson: Money, Myth and Betrayal* (Birch Lane, 1991), p. 330.
3. See both Dave Anderson, *In the Corner: Great Boxing Trainers Talk about Their Art* (Morrow, 1991), and Ronald K. Fried, *Corner Men: Great Boxing Trainers* (Four Walls, Eight Windows, 1991). Irresistibly readable and informative books of interviews: Angelo

Dundee, Eddie Futch, Ray Arcel, Charley Goldman, Lou Duva, Emanuel Steward, Kevin Rooney, et al.

. . . .

Exploring the Text

1. What does Joyce Carol Oates think about boxing?
2. What do the two epigraphs—one from Walt Whitman and the other a Greek inscription—suggest about how Oates will approach the subject of boxing?
3. Oates alludes to Thomas Hobbes, a seventeenth-century philosopher, who described the life of man as "nasty, brutish, and short," to characterize the life of a boxer (para. 2), adding "and not even that remunerative." What is the effect of this allusion? What other literary allusions does Oates make? How do they help her develop her ideas about boxing?
4. What rhetorical strategies does Oates use in paragraph 6 to respond to the counterargument that boxing is "America's most popularly despised sport"?
5. In paragraph 9, Oates states that American boxing is about race, but that the moral issues are ambiguous, posing a rhetorical question about whether there is a moral distinction between "the spectacle of black slaves in the Old South being forced by their white owners to fight . . . and the spectacle of contemporary blacks fighting for multimillion-dollar paydays. . . ." Do you think there is a moral distinction? Does Oates answer the question? If so, how does her answer differ from yours?
6. Explain why Oates finds the sport of boxing paradoxical. Give examples to support your answer.
7. Oates cites African American writer Gerald Early (para. 6), who compared boxing's exploitation of maleness to prostitution and pornography's exploitation of femaleness. Do you agree? Explain why or why not.
8. Look carefully at paragraph 21, in which Oates creates a parallel between Muhammad Ali's later fights with Joe Frazier and Shakespeare's dark tragedy, *King Lear*. What is the effect of this comparison? How does the allusion help you understand the complexity of the sport of boxing and Oates's feelings about it?

A Spectator's Notebook

KRIS VERVAECKE

A native of Nebraska, Kris Vervaecke is a graduate of the Iowa Writers' Workshop. She has published essays and stories in literary magazines and in books such as *Of Mothers and Sons: Women Writers Talk about Having Sons and Raising Men* (2001), *The Healing Circle: Authors Writing of Recovery* (1998), and *Writers on Sports* (1998), where this essay appeared.

When I was a girl, I played brutish softball on hot summer days in a cow pasture with the other girls in the neighborhood, a neighborhood which was actually a scattering of a few houses outside the city limits of Omaha. These were homes inhabited almost solely by females: There was the widow Edgerton and her daughter, the Hellerman twin girls, the Kosinsky girl, two Martin girls, and three Vervaecke girls, of which I was the oldest. The Hellerman, Kosinsky, Martin, and Vervaecke fathers were gone all day and most evenings, some not returning even at night, except for Mr. Hellerman, who created a kind of father emergency for the rest of us by rolling into their driveway Monday through Friday evenings at 5:30 sharp. (Nancy Kosinsky's father did sometimes drink at home instead of out, which created another sort of father emergency, because he'd dress up in his Shriner's outfit and ride roughshod over everyone's lawns in his little Shriner's jeep, shearing through my mother's canna bed, sending up humiliations of red petals.) We envied the Hellerman girls, but the other mothers said that Mr. Hellerman was a very *nice* man, but not a *man's* man— a distinction I found confusing, along with the implication that a *real* woman would want a *man's* man.

No mother or father or brother ever came down to the pasture to coach or referee our games, so we girls were left to our own devices. Mary Hellerman and I were always the captains of opposing teams; no one challenged this arrangement because it was understood that the whole point of the game was to build tension between Mary and me until we had no choice but to lay down our bats and balls and injure each other.

The pretense for our fights was an alleged infraction of the rules, which were crudely drawn, like the diamond, in the rising dust. Mary would accuse me, or I'd accuse her, and our shouts ("You cheater! You fat, ugly liar!") would bring us close enough to smell each other. The Herefords would lift their heads in mild interest; the other girls would draw near. Then we'd sharpen our taunts until one of us landed the first slap. I still remember the satisfaction of smacking Mary's bony, sunburned arm. And the coarseness of her long brown hair, coated with sweat and dust, sticking to my fingers as I pulled it. She was several inches taller than I, which allowed me to punch her stomach. Her mother never seemed to make her cut her fingernails, so Mary left long furrows down my arms. Blood! What a thrill and relief it was to see it bubbling up through our sultry sleep of resignation and resentment.

Later some boys moved into the neighborhood, and most of the girls retreated inside to talk about them on the telephone. I played baseball and football with the boys: They were stuck halfway out of nowhere, too, and so they needed me and sometimes even weeny-armed Mary, to play. These games were also primitive, tackle-and-roll-in-the-cow-dirt affairs. Then, one January afternoon during my eighth-grade year, running laps around the gymnasium for seventh-period coed gym class, I broke out in a sweat. Perspiration spread under the sleeves of my prison blue uniform like twin maps of Texas, and, quite abruptly, it mattered to me that my corporeality was revealing itself so grossly in the presence of boys. In panic and humiliation, I plastered my arms to my sides, slowed down to a trot, and became a girl.

It would be years before it dawned on me that a game might be more than a   5
prelude to a fight, more than a release from preadolescent boredom. Through the eyes of my daughter and sons, who play in school and community league sports, I began to see a game as a sustaining drama dreamed up by the will and the scarcely imaginable possibilities of the body. And although I see that *the game* claims vital parts of their imaginations, I can never experience it in the same way.

Driving home from work, I catch part of a radio quiz show:

> GAME SHOW HOST: Question number one. Who won the 1991 Super Bowl?
> *BUZZ!*
> MALE CONTESTANT: The New York Giants!
> HOST: Sorry. I'm afraid that's not the right answer.
> MALE CONTESTANT: But it is! The Giants beat the Buffalo Bills, 20–19, in Tampa Stadium!
> HOST: Sorry! Who won the 1991 Super Bowl?
> *BUZZ!*
> FEMALE CONTESTANT: I don't know, and I don't care!
> HOST (ALSO FEMALE): Yes!!! That's correct!!! [*BELLS RING AND WHISTLES SOUND.*] Yeah!!! Congratulations!!!

I'd be a whiz on that show. Although I grew up in the Nebraska vortex of Big Red football and *should* be capable of being swept up by my nation's preoccupation, even as a kid, I was too *embarrassed.* I hated it when everybody was supposed to dress in red, gather around the television set, and feel excited. Or maybe it is closer to the truth to say that I was embarrassed to find that it was over watching a football game that the passions of others were aroused, while *I,* who was usually the one to go around *feeling* things, could not manufacture even a fleeting rivalrous impulse toward the state of Oklahoma, a wind-worn, sun-dulled place much like the place I lived.

Years later, after living on the West Coast, I returned to Nebraska, showing up one autumn Saturday to do some research at the university library. In my characteristically oblivious way, I had failed to find out whether there was a home game, and so it took two hours to make my way through the traffic in Lincoln, and, finally parked, through the throngs of hoarse, red-polyester-suited people to the library door.

Where I found the door locked and library closed, because it was a Big Red Saturday.

Fortunately for me and my prejudices, my kids — Ben, Emily, and Andrew — were never interested in playing football. Basketball's their game, and sometimes soccer, or tennis. They run track and practice martial arts. When Ben went through a Dan Quayle phase when he was fifteen—deciding that when he was grown he would abandon the income bracket to which his mother belongs and possibly even vote Republican—he took up golf, practiced every day for an entire summer, and won the city championship for his age division. For a few moments, he was a kind of celebrity, at least to some sweet old men we ran into at the grocery store. I was proud of him, but he was already discarding the polo shirts he'd begun wearing and letting his golf clubs gather dust. He started paying more attention to politics and environmental policy and thinking about what he wanted to do with his life. I suspected it was closely listening to Republicans that soured him on golf, but I can't say for sure, because I wanted only to listen and observe, not pry. Sports has been one of the ways he's defined and differentiated himself, stretched far beyond and past his mother, surprising her with the slam dunk.

For me, the experience of raising children has no equivalent in terror and love. For   10 long stretches of years as a single parent, I've watched as *the game* dreamed up my sons and daughter, giving them things I could not, letting them shed, for the game's duration, grief, rage, loneliness, or boredom, and allowing them to take on skill and cunning, filling them with inspiration and determination, sometimes awe.

December 1987. At ten years old, a stubby little blond boy, Ben sits in rapt attention during any game, understanding it intuitively, committing himself wholly. At a Kansas Jayhawks basketball game, I take him down to the court so he can watch his team jog into the locker room. We are so close to their immense, shining bodies that, as Milt Newton trots past (he'd scored eighteen points and accomplished several steals), Ben is able to scoop up, into his cupped palm, a few drops of Newton's sweat. For a moment, Ben holds his breath, staring down at his glistening palm. Then he straightens and begins carefully applying the sweat to his own skin, up and down his arms, patting it into his very pores.

August 1992. Over speed bumps so pronounced you need a forty-thousand-dollar vehicle to get to the other side with your teeth intact, I wind up the narrow road to the country club, to which we don't belong, to pick up Ben after his eighteen holes. He is nowhere to be seen. It's 105 degrees, and so I get out of the car, with my book, and settle myself under the stingy shade of an ornamental tree next to the parking lot.

"Mom!" I hear Ben say. "What are you doing?"

"Well, I'm just waiting for you," I say, bewildered.

"Get up! Get up!" he says.   15

After we're settled in the car, I ask what's wrong.

He struggles, not wanting to hurt my feelings. Wiping sweat from his forehead, he then passes his hand over his eyes.

"Sitting in the grass?" he finally reproaches, a bit incredulous. I don't get it. "Mom, my God, you looked like a hippie!"

August 1995. Everything has been loaded into the car: clothes, photos of the family members and the dogs; Ben's iguana ("Jay") is resting securely among the rocks in his aquarium, wedged, in the backseat, between the lifting equipment and the reference books I insist he take. We've hugged and cried and said everything there is to say about his going off to college. He does not want me to drive to the university with him, not this time; we've already done this for parent orientation and his enrollment in the honors program. He says he'll look like a baby if his mom helps him move into the dorm.

"One more thing before I leave," he says. "Mom, will you watch this with me?"   20

He slides Michael Jordan's *Air Time* into the VCR, and, sitting together on the couch, we endure the strains of the background music massacred by the worn-out sound track on our VCR. As we watch Jordan's volitant performance, his pure, vibrant grace and athleticism, the way, under pressure, his quotient of joy increases—he fakes, spins, and drives through, dunking over the head of somebody who's at least seven feet tall—Ben says, "I get chills, Mom, I really do."

Unsophisticated? My son, whose father died, as Jordan's did a few years ago, a senseless, violent death: What spiritual toll does that exact on a child? What does he understand the body to mean, knowing his father's body was robbed of life?

I remember his martial arts phase, which followed the Republican golf phase, all the demonstrations I attended of Filipino, Korean, and Chinese stylized fighting: Ben whirling nunchuks, throwing and catching knives, breaking the requisite boards and bricks. At home, when his sister or brother or the dog came up behind him, he'd leap up and chop the air, spinning off an instantaneous dramatization of his charged, secure masculinity. Then he'd get down on the floor to reassure the startled dog. "It's okay, baby," he'd croon. "Benny would never hurt you."

He doesn't need a role model, exactly, isn't interested in the personal or moral failures of athletes, isn't drawn to their celebrity. Instead he needs the example of pure jubilation in the body, the triumph of spirit, strength, determination, and talent.

I teach at a small liberal arts college thirty miles from where I live, a Division III   25
school with an active athletic program. While the college cannot offer athletic scholarships, many of the students are there primarily to play sports, and it is their athletic not scholastic achievement that inspires the college to find sufficient financial aid for them to attend. These are mostly white kids from farms, or towns such as Beebeetown, Mechanicsville, Altoona, Correctionville, or What Cheer, Iowa. (I listen closely as my students tell me the names of their towns, hoping for an ironic inflection, but I'm always disappointed.) Some of the students are fairly bright, but, because they were stars of their high school classes—football, wrestling, basketball, track, or golf—they haven't read any books.

I don't mean that they haven't read many books, or that they haven't read the great books. I mean that, except for comic books, they haven't read even one book, that is, you know, sitting down, opening a book, and reading it, beginning sentence to the next, sentence by sentence, paragraph by paragraph, all the way to the end. They've simply been passed from one class to the next without doing the work.

"Do we really have to read the whole thing?" they ask me plaintively, as we begin the first book on the syllabus.

Because my children and I live in a university community that insists on higher educational standards than most (although, believe me, these standards are nothing to boast about), by the time my children were in fifth grade they could read and write better than most of my college freshmen. Because my children attend a public school where, although there are drugs and skirmishes and occasionally weapons, there is a reasonable expectation of safety and order and the opportunity to be educated, they will be able to compete with their academic achievements, not a reverse layup or three-point shot. They are fortunate because games are play for them. On the other hand, because my children are not particularly gifted athletes, they've not had the playing time or attention from coaches that their more talented or parent-coached peers have had. All three of them need those things, not because they will bring glory to their schools, but because we all need joy in our physicality. When I travel to a school in Altoona or someplace like it to attend one of my daughter's basketball games, at first I'm distracted by my awareness that this town is one of countless others where we're failing to sufficiently educate some, if not many, of the children. Then I pick a spot in the bleachers several rows behind where her team will sit and wait for my daughter to come jogging in.

As Emily bounces onto the floor in her green-and-gold uniform, her eyes scan the crowd to meet mine. She's always happy before a game, and now, a few minutes before the whistle, she's luminous with excitement. The girls warm up, shoot, huddle, then go to the bench. Emily's one of the shorter girls, but she moves fast. I take inordinate pride in the fact that it wouldn't occur to her to go out for cheerleading. Sometimes when I pick her up after practice, ready with food she can stuff into her mouth, she cannot contain her exuberance: "Mom, I swear to God! We worked so hard, it was the most fun I've had in my entire life!" Sometimes, watching them practice, I think back to our cow-pasture softball and wish, well, that Mary and I had learned to play the game.

The girls are on the sidelines, waiting for the game to begin. I look at Emily's golden brown head among all the other bright heads with their French and corn-row braids (the girls braid each others' hair as they ride the bus to the game). The whistle blows, the ball's in play; the air is filled with shouts and squeaking shoes and the bouncing of the ball. Each time there is a substitution of players I watch my daughter's slender back lift with hope then go slack with disappointment. Unlike most of the other parents, I do not give a damn whether West High's teams win State or anything else; I want all the kids to have their playing time. The game wears on; West High is once again kicking butt. Not until the last minute or two of the game, when her team has maintained a twenty-point lead over the second half, do Emily and several other girls get to play.

She maintains her composure until we get in the car, then crumples in humiliation. Once we're on the highway, forty miles to home, freezing rain coats our windows, but I can't see well enough to find a safe place to pull off. I drive with trepidation over the slippery road, through the foggy darkness, while Emily cries so hard it sounds as though she will break apart. "Mommy, I'm such a failure!" she weeps. At first my attempts to comfort her only increase her misery, so I shut up. I'm left to listen and worry about the road and think my resentful thoughts. I remember all the years in elementary school when she was "benched" in the classroom—left to do bulletin boards for the teacher—because she'd already mastered what was being taught. I think about the studies that suggest that girls who compete in athletics are far less likely to drink or take drugs or become pregnant.

To make myself feel better, I remember her thirteenth birthday, when she was the high scorer on her team with nineteen points. I can still see her dribbling the ball down the court, passing, rebounding, shooting, so far from any self-consciousness about her body it was as though the game had dreamed her up, supplying her with a body that moved as though sure of itself and its momentary grace.

One of Ben's names for his younger brother, Andrew, is "Trancer." Years ago, when Andrew played outfield in Little League, he often faced *away* from the batter in deep contemplation, and it was only with difficulty that his coach or I would pull his attention away from his thoughts and redirect it toward the real danger he might be smacked in the back of the skull by the ball.

"Andrew, get your head in the game!" the coach would holler, but Andrew never actually did. It worked out better when he went out for track. Long-distance running gave him plenty of time to think. Until recently, I thought the last thing he'd ever want to be was a jock.

July 1996. A Saturday morning, the window open while I work at home, bringing in the breeze fragrant with freshly cut grass and the steady *thump thump thump* of the basketball on the driveway. Andrew, who has just turned fourteen, bounces a ball in order to think. Two hours might pass in bouncing and shooting hoops before he appears in the office, as if from a dream, to tell me what's on his mind.

He wanders in wearing a wrinkled T-shirt and shorts, barefoot, his dark hair mussed. I'm surprised again by how graceful and muscular he is, how tall—five-foot-ten last time I measured him—but it seems possible that he's grown another inch since I fed him breakfast.

He plops down on a chair next to mine. Up close there's a little acne and a few whiskers, new this year, and the chickenpox scar on his cheek from when he was three.

"Hi, Mom." Here's something familiar: It's obvious he hasn't gotten around to brushing his teeth. He's lost in thought. "I love you, Mom," he says absently.

"I love you," I say, patting his rather huge and hairy knee, adding, "You look like a derelict."

He registers this and looks pleased.   40

Then he wakes up, turns toward me, says in a voice heavy with portent, "Tomorrow."

"Tomorrow," I say cheerfully, because this is my role: to refute the objections he'll make because he's scared to go to the two-week writing scholarship workshop that begins the next day.

"It's going to suck! They'll treat us like babies, probably make us go to bed at ten o'clock!"

This will be the first time he's been away from home for two weeks, one of the few times he's ever been away, even to stay with family. Three summers ago, when he stayed at my mother's, he got so homesick he went on a hunger strike so that he could come home. Since that time, he's grown a foot, his voice has dropped an octave, and his shin bones are as thick as the beef bones we buy for the puppy to chew.

"Oh, I doubt it," I say. "They chose you based on your manuscripts and test   45
scores, so they know you're not babies."

"Yeah," he says. "But I bet everybody will already know each other except for me."

"They come from all over the state, so I don't know how they'd already know each other."

"Yeah, well, I don't care," he says, sounding satisfied. "They're probably all a bunch of nerds, anyway."

"Probably."

"What do you think?" he asks, pushing up the sleeve of his T-shirt, revealing   50
what I can genuinely describe to him as an amazingly well-developed biceps.

"Wow," I say, trying to take in the irony — or anti-irony — that all that grunting and weight lifting in the basement had been in preparation for a smart kids' workshop.

The next day I drive him to the university where the workshop will be held; after the three-hour orientation, I am to return to drive him to the dorm. At the appointed time, I pull into the parking lot. There is a cluster of girls at the shelter, surreptitiously watching the boys playing basketball. I scan the crowd of boys as they jump and shoot, and four times I think spot my son, but from this distance and with the sun in my eyes, I can't discern Andrew from the others. As I step out of the car to go look for him, he opens the passenger door.

"Mom!" he says. "Get in the car!"

His face is flushed, jaw set. Someone might see me, confirming the rumor he has a mother.

"How was it?" I ask, backing out.   55

"It sucks," he says. "We're on such a short leash. WE HAVE TO GO TO BED AT TEN O'CLOCK! And the boys are like all into role-playing games, though some of them are pretending to be intellectuals. It sucks so bad you wouldn't believe it. The books they go around recommending to each other are like science-fiction stuff they think is great literature."

"That's too bad," I say.

"It might be okay, though," he says. "Some of the kids are pretty cool."

"That's good," I say, noticing the lovely cumulus between us and the enormous sky.

"One kid asked me what kind of game system I have, and I said, 'Game system?' And he said, 'You know like Sega or Super Nintendo,' and I said, 'Game system? I don't play game systems.'"

"You really shut him off," I say.

"Well, I didn't really shut him off," he says, hedging.

Trailing him down the hall of the dorm where he'll live for the next two weeks, I watch as he nods to the other boys. As he unlocks the door to his room, he whispers, "Nobody I couldn't take if I had to," and grins before giving me the briefest and most furtive of hugs good-bye.

Over the next two weeks, he phones only once, and, in a breezy tone, tells me he's having, definitely, the best time of his life. My friend who lives across the street from the dorm and has promised to spy on my child, reports that every evening Andrew's out shooting hoops with the R.A. and a couple of the other scholarship guys.

In the remarks at the closing ceremony, Andrew's muscles emerge as a kind of theme, and, in the final ritual of parting, each kid autographs my son's manly biceps.

When I mention to Ben that I'm writing an essay about sports, he looks stricken. "I don't think that's a good idea, Mom," he says, honesty overriding tact. "I mean it's not something you can read about and understand in that way. You have to have a feel for it, an intuition. You have to *love* it."

"I'm not pretending to love it," I say a bit defensively.

Is there anything about sports I love?

Closing my eyes, I remember swinging my bat and solidly hitting the ball, the shudder of the connection a physical exultation traveling down my arm. I remember tossing the bat aside, and, as though suddenly released into the wild, racing through the shimmering heat, toeing each dried cow pie base and sliding into home.

I remember running hard, free of ambivalence, of pity. I remember the powdery dirt and the minty smell of the weeds and the unreasonable beauty of the sky.

"Mom," someone is calling. "*Mom!*"

I open my eyes.

"You're as bad as Andrew," Emily informs me. "Why are you just sitting here?"

"I was remembering when I was a kid, playing softball."

"Oh, my gosh," she says, mildly exasperated, "playing in the dirt with your friends doesn't count, Mom. I thought you were going to write about when I was the high scorer on my basketball team with nineteen points. On my thirteenth birthday, remember?" 75

"When did I say I was going to write about that?"

"You didn't, but I told you you should. It was so awesome. We were playing Southeast, the gym was packed, and everybody from Northwest was yelling my name. I kept throwing the ball up there, and it kept going in. My team was pounding the floor, yelling 'Em-i-ly!' Then I did a layup, and it won the game. Don't you remember?"

"Of course, I remember."

"Well, all right then," she says, satisfied. "*That's* the story to tell."

Exploring the Text

1. Kris Vervaecke describes as "brutish" the softball she played as a young girl in Nebraska (para. 1). What satisfactions did she derive from the game? How did the game define her and her nemesis, Mary Hellerman?

2. Vervaecke describes her neighborhood as "inhabited almost solely by females" (para. 1). How does that fact connect to the game she and her friends play? How might it connect to the end of Vervaecke's sports career, when she "became a girl" (para. 4)?

3. How does paragraph 5 provide a transition to Vervaecke's role as the mother of athletes?

4. How and why does Vervaecke characterize herself as an uninterested spectator (paras. 6–8)? What rhetorical strategies does she use? Are they effective? Explain your response.

5. At the beginning of the second section (para. 10), Vervaecke says that sports has given her children what she, as a single mother, could not: "letting them shed, for the game's duration, grief, rage, loneliness, or boredom, and allowing them to take on skill and cunning, filling them with inspiration and determination, sometimes awe" (para. 10). How does each of the anecdotes that follow illustrate some part of that statement?

6. Why does Vervaecke begin the third section (para. 25), which is about a game in which her daughter Emily barely plays, by noting that the athletes who attend the college where she teaches have never read a book?

7. What is the connection between Andrew's enjoyment of the writing workshop and his highly developed biceps (paras. 35–65)?

8. In what ways does the last section of the essay connect playing sports, watching sports, and motherhood—the main threads of the piece? Why does the essay end with Emily's exasperation at her mother's memory of playing softball?

Barbaro, The Heart in the Winner's Circle

JANE SMILEY

Jane Smiley was born in 1949 in Los Angeles and grew up in a suburb of St. Louis. She went to Vassar College and received her MA and PhD from the University of Iowa. She taught creative writing at Iowa State University for fifteen years. Her novel *A Thousand Acres* (1991) won the Pulitzer Prize for Fiction. Her other works include the novels *The Greenlanders* (1988), *Ordinary Love and Good Will* (1989), *Moo* (1995), *Horse Heaven* (2000), and *Private Lives* (2010); nonfiction works such as *Thirteen Ways of Looking at the Novel* (2005); and articles including "Say It Ain't So, Huck: Second Thoughts on Mark Twain's Masterpiece" (*Harper's*, 1996). The piece that follows was the *Washington Post*'s obituary for Barbaro, the racehorse who died in 2007. He won the Kentucky Derby in 2006 but broke two legs a few weeks later in the Preakness Stakes, which resulted in his death.

Nine years ago, I had a thoroughbred mare who came down with colic in the night, and was too far gone to save by the time she was found at 6 A.M. After she was euthanized, I remember staring at her body, which was stretched out in the grass, running my hands over her. Her coat was shining. Her haunch was rounded and firm. Her feet and legs were perfect. Only that one thing had been wrong, that twist in her gut, but it was enough, and it killed her. So it is with all horses.

They are engineered so close to the margins of what is physically possible that when one thing fails, it can cause the failure of the whole animal.

So it was with Barbaro, who was euthanized yesterday. When we saw his pictures over the last months, his ears were up, he was attentive and beautiful and interested. He looked pretty good, except for those casts.

His vets warned us all along that the odds were against him, but we didn't really believe them. They had hope, too. How could a horse who appeared so full of life break his leg and be so suddenly close to death? His head was fine. His back was fine. His lungs and heart and chest were fine. In fact, after a while, his broken leg was fairly fine. It was another leg that was so worrisome, since the weight of his body constantly bearing down on the delicate structures inside his foot eventually damaged and destroyed them.

A horse's hoof is wondrous structure — the outside horn is lined with delicate membranes and blood vessels that feed and support the bones of the foot. The bones of the foot are analogous to a person's fingertips, since a horse's knee is analogous to a person's wrist. The racehorse carries a thousand pounds at 35 to 40 miles per hour using a few slender bones supported by an apparatus of ligaments and tendons that have no analogues in human anatomy. Every part of the system depends on every other part. What happened to Barbaro was that the engineering couldn't take it. When it was right, as in the Kentucky Derby, it was perfectly right, and when it became wrong, it became irredeemably wrong.

Some observers have been angered by the outpouring of sympathy toward Barbaro, but there is something extra large about the death of a horse.

And the death of a thoroughbred seems to me to be even more shocking, because thoroughbreds have been bred to press on and prevail where other breeds of horse throw in the towel. When we saw Barbaro in last May's Kentucky Derby fly away from the field so gracefully and effortlessly, he was doing something thoroughbreds have been bred to do for 300 years—to sense the encroaching fatigue of three-quarters of a mile at top speed and want only to run faster, to push ahead and take the lead.

We say that thoroughbreds have "blood," meaning the DNA of desert Arab horses, and "heart," meaning fortitude, desire and competitive spirit.

It was heart that we saw in Barbaro, not only on Derby Day, but also on Preakness Day, when he stood injured in the middle of the track, touching his toe to the ground and snatching it up again, somehow impatient, somehow not truly aware of the pain, somehow still ready to get going.

I watched the Preakness with some lifelong racing people. When Barbaro was   10
injured, we turned the TV off. All of us had seen it before; everyone who loves racing has seen it all too many times. It is the paradox of racing. His dynamic beauty and his exceptional heart were gifts Barbaro inherited from his racing forebears, who had the luck and toughness to run and win and prove themselves worthy of reproducing.

And then, during his medical saga, he showed that he was intelligent, too. According to a friend of mine who talked to trainer Michael Matz in the summer, Barbaro knew when he needed some pain relief—he would stand by the sling and shake it until they put him in it, and when he was tired of it, he would shake himself so that it rattled, signaling he was ready to be taken out. And then he would go to his stall and lie down.

Did he want to survive? It seemed as though he did.

In a great racehorse, the heart and mind do the running, and the body tries to hold up.

Yes, to those who don't care about horses, terrible things are happening all over the world these days, and they demand from many people an unprecedented level of endurance, but we horse lovers say: This, too? That this beautiful and innocent animal should also die?

When I think of Barbaro, I like to think also of some of the tough ones—John   15
Henry, Seabiscuit, a horse I bred a mare to once named Loyal Pal. Among the three of them, they ran hundreds of times. They managed to avoid the bad steps and the bad luck, to go to the races as if a race were a trot in the park, coming back afterward to a bucket of grain and a long nap. Sometimes, thousands of fans thrilled to their exploits. Sometimes, the only ones watching were the owner, the trainer and a few punters. Like Barbaro, they did it because they were born and

bred to do it, because a thoroughbred loves to run, and because they didn't know what it meant not to keep on trying.

. . . .

Exploring the Text

1. How is Jane Smiley's piece both similar to and different from an obituary?
2. How does Smiley establish ethos?
3. Why do you think Smiley uses the personal pronoun in paragraph 4?
4. Why do you think Smiley provides anatomical information about horses in paragraph 5? What is the effect of that information?
5. What do you think Smiley means by "the paradox of racing" (para. 10)?
6. What purpose do the rhetorical questions in paragraphs 12 and 14 serve?
7. To whom does Smiley seem to be responding in paragraph 14? What issue might she be commenting on when she says "to those who don't care about horses"?
8. Is Smiley convincing when she says she knows what a horse is thinking: "a thoroughbred loves to run" (para. 15)? Explain your answer.

Offensive Play

How Different Are Dogfighting and Football?

MALCOLM GLADWELL

Malcolm Gladwell was born in England in 1963. He was raised in rural Ontario, Canada, and graduated from the University of Toronto, Trinity College. From 1986 to 1996 he worked at the *Washington Post*, where he covered business and science and was the newspaper's New York City bureau chief. Since 1996 he has been a staff writer with the *New Yorker* magazine. Gladwell's books include *The Tipping Point: How Little Things Make a Big Difference* (2000), *Blink: The Power of Thinking without Thinking* (2005), and *Outliers: The Story of Success* (2008). The piece presented here appeared in the *New Yorker* in 2009, at about the time that football player Michael Vick was released from prison, where he served a 23-month term for felony charges connected to illegal dogfighting.

One evening in August, Kyle Turley was at a bar in Nashville with his wife and some friends. It was one of the countless little places in the city that play live music. He'd ordered a beer, but was just sipping it, because he was driving home. He had eaten an hour and a half earlier. Suddenly, he felt a sensation of heat. He was light-headed, and began to sweat. He had been having episodes like that with increasing frequency during the past year—headaches, nausea. One month, he had vertigo every day, bouts in which he felt as if he were stuck to a wall. But this was worse. He asked his wife if he could sit on her stool for a moment. The warmup band was still playing, and he remembers saying, "I'm just going to take a nap right here until the next band comes on." Then he was lying on the floor, and someone was standing over him. "The guy was freaking out," Turley recalled. "He was saying, 'Damn, man, I couldn't find a pulse,' and my wife said, 'No, no. You were breathing.' I'm, like, 'What? What?'"

They picked him up. "We went out in the parking lot, and I just lost it," Turley went on. "I started puking everywhere. I couldn't stop. I got in the car, still puking. My wife, she was really scared, because I had never passed out like that before, and I started becoming really paranoid. I went into a panic. We get to the emergency room. I started to lose control. My limbs were shaking, and I couldn't speak. I was conscious, but I couldn't speak the words I wanted to say."

Turley is six feet five. He is thirty-four years old, with a square jaw and blue eyes. For nine years, before he retired, in 2007, he was an offensive lineman in the National Football League. He knew all the stories about former football players. Mike Webster, the longtime Pittsburgh Steeler and one of the greatest players in N.F.L. history, ended his life a recluse, sleeping on the floor of the Pittsburgh Amtrak station. Another former Pittsburgh Steeler, Terry Long, drifted into chaos and killed himself four years ago by drinking antifreeze. Andre Waters, a former defensive back for the Philadelphia Eagles, sank into depression and pleaded with his girlfriend—"I need help, somebody help me"—before shooting himself in the head. There were men with aching knees and backs and hands, from all those years of playing football. But their real problem was with their heads, the one part of their body that got hit over and over again.

"Lately, I've tried to break it down," Turley said. "I remember, every season, multiple occasions where I'd hit someone so hard that my eyes went cross-eyed, and they wouldn't come uncrossed for a full series of plays. You are just out there, trying to hit the guy in the middle, because there are three of them. You don't remember much. There are the cases where you hit a guy and you'd get into a collision where everything goes *off*. You're dazed. And there are the others where you are involved in a big, long drive. You start on your own five-yard line, and drive all the way down the field—fifteen, eighteen plays in a row sometimes. Every play: collision, collision, collision. By the time you get to the other end of the field, you're seeing spots. You feel like you are going to black out. Literally, these white explosions— *boom, boom, boom* —lights getting dimmer and brighter, dimmer and brighter.

"Then, there was the time when I got knocked unconscious. That was in St. Louis, in 2003. My wife said that I was out a minute or two on the field. But I was *gone* for about four hours after that. It was the last play of the third quarter. We were playing the Packers. I got hit in the back of the head. I saw it on film a little while afterward. I was running downfield, made a block on a guy. We fell to the ground. A guy was chasing the play, a little guy, a defensive back, and he jumped over me as I was coming up, and he kneed me right in the back of the head. *Boom!* 5

"They sat me down on the bench. I remember Marshall Faulk coming up and joking with me, because he knew that I was messed up. That's what happens in the N.F.L: 'Oooh. You got effed up. Oooh.' The trainer came up to me and said, 'Kyle, let's take you to the locker room.' I remember looking up at a clock, and there was only a minute and a half left in the game — and I had no idea that much time had elapsed. I showered and took all my gear off. I was sitting at my locker. I don't remember anything. When I came back, after being hospitalized, the guys were joking with me because Georgia Frontiere" — then the team's owner — "came in the locker room, and they said I was butt-ass naked and I gave her a big hug. They were dying laughing, and I was, like, 'Are you serious? I did that?'

"They cleared me for practice that Thursday. I probably shouldn't have. I don't know what damage I did from that, because my head was really hurting. But when you're coming off an injury you're frustrated. I wanted to play the next game. I was just so mad that this happened to me that I'm overdoing it. I was just going after guys in practice. I was really trying to use my head more, because I was so frustrated, and the coaches on the sidelines are, like, 'Yeah. We're going to win this game. He's going to lead the team.' That's football. You're told either that you're hurt or that you're injured. There is no middle ground. If you are hurt, you can play. If you are injured, you can't, and the line is whether you can walk and if you can put on a helmet and pads."

Turley said that he loved playing football so much that he would do it all again. Then he began talking about what he had gone through in the past year. The thing that scared him most about that night at the bar was that it felt exactly like the time he was knocked unconscious. "It was identical," he said. "It was my worst episode ever."

※

In August of 2007, one of the highest-paid players in professional football, the quarterback Michael Vick, pleaded guilty to involvement in a dogfighting ring. The police raided one of his properties, a farm outside Richmond, Virginia, and found the bodies of dead dogs buried on the premises, along with evidence that some of the animals there had been tortured and electrocuted. Vick was suspended from football. He was sentenced to twenty-three months in prison. The dogs on his farm were seized by the court, and the most damaged were sent to an animal sanctuary in Utah for rehabilitation. When Vick applied for reinstatement to the National Football League, this summer, he was asked to undergo psychiatric testing. He then met with the commissioner of the league, Roger Goodell, for four and a half hours, so that Goodell could be sure that he was genuinely remorseful.

"I probably considered every alternative that I could think of," Goodell told   10
reporters, when he finally allowed Vick back into the league. "I reached out to an awful lot of people to get their views — not only on what was right for the young man but also what was right for our society and the N.F.L."

Goodell's job entails dealing with players who have used drugs, driven drunk and killed people, fired handguns in night clubs, and consorted with thugs and accused murderers. But he clearly felt what many Americans felt as well—that dogfighting was a moral offense of a different order.

Here is a description of a dogfight given by the sociologists Rhonda Evans and Craig Forsyth in "The Social Milieu of Dogmen and Dogfights," an article they published some years ago in the journal *Deviant Behavior*. The fight took place in Louisiana between a local dog, Black, owned by a man named L.G., and Snow, whose owner, Rick, had come from Arizona:

> The handlers release their dogs and Snow and Black lunge at one another. Snow rears up and overpowers Black, but Black manages to come back with a quick locking of the jaws on Snow's neck. The crowd is cheering wildly and yelling out bets. Once a dog gets a lock on the other, they will hold on with all their might. The dogs flail back and forth and all the while Black maintains her hold.

In a dogfight, whenever one of the dogs "turns"—makes a submissive gesture with its head—the two animals are separated and taken back to their corners. Each dog, in alternation, then "scratches"—is released to charge at its opponent. After that first break, it is Snow's turn to scratch. She races toward Black:

> Snow goes straight for the throat and grabs hold with her razor-sharp teeth. Almost immediately, blood flows from Black's throat. Despite a serious injury to the throat, Black manages to continue fighting back. They are relentless, each battling the other and neither willing to accept defeat. This fighting continues for an hour. [Finally, the referee] gives the third and final pit call. It is Black's turn to scratch and she is severely wounded. Black manages to crawl across the pit to meet her opponent. Snow attacks Black and she is too weak to fight back. L.G. realizes that this is it for Black and calls the fight. Snow is declared the winner.

Afterward, Snow's owner collects his winnings; L.G. carries Black from the ring. "Her back legs are broken and blood is gushing from her throat," Evans and Forsyth write. "A shot rings out barely heard over the noise in the barn. Black's body is wrapped up and carried by her owner to his vehicle."

It's the shot ringing out that seals the case against dogfighting. L.G. willingly submitted his dog to a contest that culminated in her suffering and destruction. And why? For the entertainment of an audience and the chance of a payday. In the nineteenth century, dogfighting was widely accepted by the American public. But we no longer find that kind of transaction morally acceptable in a sport. "I was not aware of dogfighting and the terrible things that happen around dogfighting," Goodell said, explaining why he responded so sternly in the Vick case. One wonders whether, had he spent as much time talking to Kyle Turley as he did to Michael Vick, he'd start to have similar doubts about his own sport.

In 2003, a seventy-two-year-old patient at the Veterans Hospital in Bedford, 15
Massachusetts, died, fifteen years after receiving a diagnosis of dementia. Patients
in the hospital's dementia ward are routinely autopsied, as part of the V.A.'s
research efforts, so the man's brain was removed and "fixed" in a formaldehyde
solution. A laboratory technician placed a large slab of the man's cerebral tissue
on a microtome—essentially, a sophisticated meat slicer—and, working along
the coronal plane, cut off dozens of fifty-micron shavings, less than a hairbreadth
thick. The shavings were then immunostained—bathed in a special reagent that
would mark the presence of abnormal proteins with a bright, telltale red or brown
stain on the surface of the tissue. Afterward, each slice was smoothed out and
placed on a slide.

The stained tissue of Alzheimer's patients typically shows the two trademarks
of the disease—distinctive patterns of the proteins beta-amyloid and tau. Beta-
amyloid is thought to lay the groundwork for dementia. Tau marks the critical
second stage of the disease: it's the protein that steadily builds up in brain cells,
shutting them down and ultimately killing them. An immunostain of an Alzheimer's patient looks, under the microscope, as if the tissue had been hit with a
shotgun blast: the red and brown marks, corresponding to amyloid and tau, dot
the entire surface. But this patient's brain was different. There was damage only
to specific surface regions of his brain, and the stains for amyloid came back
negative. "This was all tau," Ann McKee, who runs the hospital's neuropathology
laboratory, said. "There was not even a whiff of amyloid. And it was the most
extraordinary damage. It was one of those cases that really took you aback." The
patient may have been in an Alzheimer's facility, and may have looked and acted
as if he had Alzheimer's. But McKee realized that he had a different condition,
called chronic traumatic encephalopathy (C.T.E.), which is a progressive neurological disorder found in people who have suffered some kind of brain trauma.
C.T.E. has many of the same manifestations as Alzheimer's: it begins with behavioral and personality changes, followed by disinhibition and irritability, before
moving on to dementia. And C.T.E. appears later in life as well, because it takes a
long time for the initial trauma to give rise to nerve-cell breakdown and death.
But C.T.E. isn't the result of an endogenous disease. It's the result of injury.
The patient, it turned out, had been a boxer in his youth. He had suffered from
dementia for fifteen years because, decades earlier, he'd been hit too many times
in the head.

McKee's laboratory does the neuropathology work for both the giant Framingham heart study, which has been running since 1948, and Boston University's New England Centenarian Study, which analyzes the brains of people who
are unusually long-lived. "I'm looking at brains constantly," McKee said. "Then I
ran across another one. I saw it and said, 'Wow, it looks just like the last case.' This
time, there was no known history of boxing. But then I called the family, and
heard that the guy had been a boxer in his twenties." You can't see tau except in an
autopsy, and you can't see it in an autopsy unless you do a very particular kind of

screen. So now that McKee had seen two cases, in short order, she began to wonder: how many people who we assume have Alzheimer's—a condition of mysterious origin—are actually victims of preventable brain trauma?

McKee linked up with an activist named Chris Nowinski, a former college football player and professional wrestler who runs a group called the Sports Legacy Institute, in Boston. In his football and wrestling careers, Nowinski suffered six concussions (that he can remember), the last of which had such severe side effects that he has become a full-time crusader against brain injuries in sports. Nowinski told McKee that he would help her track down more brains of ex-athletes. Whenever he read an obituary of someone who had played in a contact sport, he'd call up the family and try to persuade them to send the player's brain to Bedford. Usually, they said no. Sometimes they said yes. The first brain McKee received was from a man in his mid-forties who had played as a linebacker in the N.F.L. for ten years. He accidentally shot himself while cleaning a gun. He had at least three concussions in college, and eight in the pros. In the years before his death, he'd had memory lapses, and had become more volatile. McKee immunostained samples of his brain tissue, and saw big splotches of tau all over the frontal and temporal lobes. If he hadn't had the accident, he would almost certainly have ended up in a dementia ward.

Nowinski found her another ex-football player. McKee saw the same thing. She has now examined the brains of sixteen ex-athletes, most of them ex-football players. Some had long careers and some played only in college. Some died of dementia. Some died of unrelated causes. Some were old. Some were young. Most were linemen or linebackers, although there was one wide receiver. In one case, a man who had been a linebacker for sixteen years, you could see, without the aid of magnification, that there was trouble: there was a shiny tan layer of scar tissue, right on the surface of the frontal lobe, where the brain had repeatedly slammed into the skull. It was the kind of scar you'd get only if you used your head as a battering ram. You could also see that some of the openings in the brain were larger than you'd expect, as if the surrounding tissue had died and shrunk away. In other cases, everything seemed entirely normal until you looked under the microscope and saw the brown ribbons of tau. But all sixteen of the ex-athlete brains that McKee had examined—those of the two boxers, plus the ones that Nowinski had found for her—had something in common: every one had abnormal tau.

The other major researcher looking at athletes and C.T.E. is the neuropathologist Bennet Omalu. He diagnosed the first known case of C.T.E. in an ex-N.F.L. player back in September of 2002, when he autopsied the former Pittsburgh Steelers center Mike Webster. He also found C.T.E. in the former Philadelphia Eagles defensive back Andre Waters, and in the former Steelers linemen Terry Long and Justin Strzelczyk, the latter of whom was killed when he drove the wrong way down a freeway and crashed his car, at ninety miles per hour, into a tank truck. Omalu has only once failed to find C.T.E. in a professional football

20

player, and that was a twenty-four-year-old running back who had played in the N.F.L. for only two years.

"There is something wrong with this group as a cohort," Omalu says. "They forget things. They have slurred speech. I have had an N.F.L. player come up to me at a funeral and tell me he can't find his way home. I have wives who call me and say, 'My husband was a very good man. Now he drinks all the time. I don't know why his behavior changed.' I have wives call me and say, 'My husband was a nice guy. Now he's getting abusive.' I had someone call me and say, 'My husband went back to law school after football and became a lawyer. Now he can't do his job. People are suing him.'"

McKee and Omalu are trying to make sense of the cases they've seen so far. At least some of the players are thought to have used steroids, which has led to the suggestion that brain injury might in some way be enhanced by drug use. Many of the players also share a genetic risk factor for neurodegenerative diseases, so perhaps deposits of tau are the result of brain trauma coupled with the weakened ability of the brain to repair itself. McKee says that she will need to see at least fifty cases before she can draw any firm conclusions. In the meantime, late last month the University of Michigan's Institute for Social Research released the findings of an N.F.L.-funded phone survey of just over a thousand randomly selected retired N.F.L. players—all of whom had played in the league for at least three seasons. Self-reported studies are notoriously unreliable instruments, but, even so, the results were alarming. Of those players who were older than fifty, 6.1 per cent reported that they had received a diagnosis of "dementia, Alzheimer's disease, or other memory-related disease." That's five times higher than the national average for that age group. For players between the ages of thirty and forty-nine, the reported rate was nineteen times the national average. (The N.F.L. has distributed five million dollars to former players with dementia.)

"A long time ago, someone suggested that the [C.T.E. rate] in boxers was twenty per cent," McKee told me. "I think it's probably higher than that among boxers, and I also suspect that it's going to end up being higher than that among football players as well. Why? Because every brain I've seen has this. To get this number in a sample this small is really unusual, and the findings are so far out of the norm. I only can say that because I have looked at thousands of brains for a long time. This isn't something that you just see. I did the same exact thing for all the individuals from the Framingham heart study. We study them until they die. I run these exact same proteins, make these same slides—and we never see this."

McKee's laboratory occupies a warren of rooms, in what looks like an old officers' quarters on the V.A. campus. In one of the rooms, there is an enormous refrigerator, filled with brains packed away in hundreds of plastic containers. Nearby is a tray with small piles of brain slices. They look just like the ginger shavings that come with an order of sushi. Now McKee went to the room next to her office, sat down behind a microscope, and inserted one of the immunostained slides under the lens.

"This is Tom McHale," she said. "He started out playing for Cornell. Then he   25
went to Tampa Bay. He was the man who died of substance abuse at the age of
forty-five. I only got fragments of the brain. But it's just showing huge accumula-
tions of tau for a forty-five-year-old — ridiculously abnormal."

She placed another slide under the microscope. "This individual was forty-nine
years old. A football player. Cognitively intact. He never had any rage behavior.
He had the distinctive abnormalities. Look at the hypothalamus." It was dark with
tau. She put another slide in. "This guy was in his mid-sixties," she said. "He died
of an unrelated medical condition. His name is Walter Hilgenberg. Look at the
hippocampus. It's wall-to-wall tangles. Even in a bad case of Alzheimer's, you
don't see that." The brown pigment of the tau stain ran around the edge of the
tissue sample in a thick, dark band. "It's like a big river."

McKee got up and walked across the corridor, back to her office. "There's one
last thing," she said. She pulled out a large photographic blowup of a brain-tissue
sample. "This is a kid. I'm not allowed to talk about how he died. He was a good
student. This is his brain. He's eighteen years old. He played football. He'd been
playing football for a couple of years." She pointed to a series of dark spots on the
image, where the stain had marked the presence of something abnormal. "He's
got all this tau. This is frontal and this is insular. Very close to insular. Those same
vulnerable regions." This was a teen-ager, and already his brain showed the kind
of decay that is usually associated with old age. "This is completely inappropriate," she said. "You don't see tau like this in an eighteen-year-old. You don't see tau
like this in a *fifty*-year-old."

McKee is a longtime football fan. She is from Wisconsin. She had two statu-
ettes of Brett Favre, the former Green Bay Packers quarterback, on her bookshelf.
On the wall was a picture of a robust young man. It was McKee's son — nineteen
years old, six feet three. If he had a chance to join the N.F.L., I asked her, what
would she advise him? "I'd say, 'Don't. Not if you want to have a life after football.'"

At the core of the C.T.E. research is a critical question: is the kind of injury being
uncovered by McKee and Omalu incidental to the game of football or inherent in
it? Part of what makes dogfighting so repulsive is the understanding that violence
and injury cannot be removed from the sport. It's a feature of the sport that dogs
almost always get hurt. Something like stock-car racing, by contrast, is dangerous,
but not unavoidably so.

In 2000 and 2001, four drivers in NASCAR's élite Sprint Cup Series were   30
killed in crashes, including the legendary Dale Earnhardt. In response, NASCAR
mandated stronger seats, better seat belts and harnesses, and ignition kill switches,
and completed the installation of expensive new barriers on the walls of its
racetracks, which can absorb the force of a crash much better than concrete.
The result is that, in the past eight years, no one has died in NASCAR's three
national racing series. Stock-car fans are sometimes caricatured as bloodthirsty,

eagerly awaiting the next spectacular crash. But there is little blood these days in NASCAR crashes. Last year, at Texas Motor Speedway, Michael McDowell hit an oil slick, slammed head first into the wall at a hundred and eighty miles per hour, flipped over and over, leaving much of his car in pieces on the track, and, when the vehicle finally came to a stop, crawled out of the wreckage and walked away. He raced again the next day. So what is football? Is it dogfighting or is it stock-car racing?

Football faced a version of this question a hundred years ago, after a series of ugly incidents. In 1905, President Theodore Roosevelt called an emergency summit at the White House, alarmed, as the historian John Sayle Watterson writes, "that the brutality of the prize ring had invaded college football and might end up destroying it." Columbia University dropped the sport entirely. A professor at the University of Chicago called it a "boy-killing, man-mutilating, money-making, education-prostituting, gladiatorial sport." In December of 1905, the presidents of twelve prominent colleges met in New York and came within one vote of abolishing the game. But the main objection at the time was to a style of play — densely and dangerously packed offensive strategies — that, it turns out, could be largely corrected with rule changes, like the legalization of the forward pass and the doubling of the first-down distance from five yards to ten. Today, when we consider subtler and more insidious forms of injury, it's far from clear whether the problem is the style of play or the play itself.

Take the experience of a young defensive lineman for the University of North Carolina football team, who suffered two concussions during the 2004 season. His case is one of a number studied by Kevin Guskiewicz, who runs the university's Sports Concussion Research Program. For the past five seasons, Guskiewicz and his team have tracked every one of the football team's practices and games using a system called HITS, in which six sensors are placed inside the helmet of every player on the field, measuring the force and location of every blow he receives to the head. Using the HITS data, Guskiewicz was able to reconstruct precisely what happened each time the player was injured.

"The first concussion was during preseason. The team was doing two-a-days," he said, referring to the habit of practicing in both the morning and the evening in the preseason. "It was August 9th, 9:55 A.M. He has an 80-g hit to the front of his head. About ten minutes later, he has a 98-g acceleration to the front of his head." To put those numbers in perspective, Guskiewicz explained, if you drove your car into a wall at twenty-five miles per hour and you weren't wearing your seat belt, the force of your head hitting the windshield would be around 100 gs: in effect, the player had two car accidents that morning. He survived both without incident. "In the evening session, he experiences this 64-g hit to the same spot, the front of the head. Still not reporting anything. And then this happens." On his laptop, Guskiewicz ran the video from the practice session. It was a simple drill: the lineman squaring off against an offensive player who wore the number 76. The other player ran toward the lineman and brushed past him, while delivering a glancing blow to the defender's helmet. "Seventy-six does a little quick elbow. It's 63 gs, the lowest of the four, but he sustains a concussion."

"The second injury was nine weeks later," Guskiewicz continued. "He's now recovered from the initial injury. It's a game out in Utah. In warmups, he takes a 76-g blow to the front of his head. Then, on the very first play of the game, on kickoff, he gets popped in the earhole. It's a 102-g impact. He's part of the wedge." He pointed to the screen, where the player was blocking on a kickoff: "Right here." The player stumbled toward the sideline. "His symptoms were significantly worse than the first injury." Two days later, during an evaluation in Guskiewicz's clinic, he had to have a towel put over his head because he couldn't stand the light. He also had difficulty staying awake. He was sidelined for sixteen days.

When we think about football, we worry about the dangers posed by the heat and the fury of competition. Yet the HITS data suggest that practice—the routine part of the sport—can be as dangerous as the games themselves. We also tend to focus on the dramatic helmet-to-helmet hits that signal an aggressive and reckless style of play. Those kinds of hits can be policed. But what sidelined the U.N.C. player, the first time around, was an accidental and seemingly innocuous elbow, and none of the blows he suffered that day would have been flagged by a referee as illegal. Most important, though, is what Guskiewicz found when he reviewed all the data for the lineman on that first day in training camp. He didn't just suffer those four big blows. He was hit in the head *thirty-one times* that day. What seems to have caused his concussion, in other words, was his cumulative exposure. And why was the second concussion—in the game at Utah—so much more serious than the first? It's not because that hit to the side of the head was especially dramatic; it was that it came after the 76-g blow in warmup, which, in turn, followed the concussion in August, which was itself the consequence of the thirty prior hits that day, and the hits the day before that, and the day before that, and on and on, perhaps back to his high-school playing days. 35

This is a crucial point. Much of the attention in the football world, in the past few years, has been on concussions—on diagnosing, managing, and preventing them—and on figuring out how many concussions a player can have before he should call it quits. But a football player's real issue isn't simply with repetitive concussive trauma. It is, as the concussion specialist Robert Cantu argues, with repetitive *subconcussive* trauma. It's not just the handful of big hits that matter. It's lots of little hits, too.

That's why, Cantu says, so many of the ex-players who have been given a diagnosis of C.T.E. were linemen: line play lends itself to lots of little hits. The HITS data suggest that, in an average football season, a lineman could get struck in the head a thousand times, which means that a ten-year N.F.L. veteran, when you bring in his college and high-school playing days, could well have been hit in the head eighteen thousand times: that's thousands of jarring blows that shake the brain from front to back and side to side, stretching and weakening and tearing the connections among nerve cells, and making the brain increasingly vulnerable to long-term damage. People with C.T.E., Cantu says, "aren't necessarily people with a high, recognized concussion history. But they are individuals who collided heads on every play—repetitively doing this, year after year, under levels that were tolerable for them to continue to play."

But if C.T.E. is really about lots of little hits, what can be done about it? Turley says that it's impossible for an offensive lineman to do his job without "using his head." The position calls for the player to begin in a crouch and then collide with the opposing lineman when the ball is snapped. Helmet-to-helmet contact is inevitable. Nowinski, who played football for Harvard, says that "proper" tackling technique is supposed to involve a player driving into his opponent with his shoulder. "The problem," he says, "is that, if you're a defender and you're trying to tackle someone and you decide to pick a side, you're giving the other guy a way to go—and people will start running around you." Would better helmets help? Perhaps. And there have been better models introduced that absorb more of the shock from a hit. But, Nowinski says, the better helmets have become—and the more invulnerable they have made the player seem—the more athletes have been inclined to play recklessly.

"People love technological solutions," Nowinski went on. "When I give speeches, the first question is always: 'What about these new helmets I hear about?' What most people don't realize is that we are decades, if not forever, from having a helmet that would fix the problem. I mean, you have two men running into each other at full speed and you think a little bit of plastic and padding could absorb that 150 gs of force?"

At one point, while he was discussing his research, Guskiewicz showed a videotape from a 1997 college football game between Arizona and Oregon. In one sequence, a player from Oregon viciously tackles an Arizona player, bringing his head up onto the opposing player's chin and sending his helmet flying with the force of the blow. To look at it, you'd think that the Arizona player would be knocked unconscious. Instead, he bounces back up. "This guy does not sustain a concussion," Guskiewicz said. "He has a lip laceration. Lower lip, that's it. Now, same game, twenty minutes later." He showed a clip of an Arizona defensive back making a dramatic tackle. He jumps up, and, as he does so, a teammate of his chest-bumps him in celebration. The defensive back falls and hits his head on the ground. "That's a Grade 2 concussion," Guskiewicz said. "It's the fall to the ground, combined with the bounce off the turf."

The force of the first hit was infinitely greater than the second. But the difference is that the first player saw that he was about to be hit and tensed his neck, which limited the sharp back-and-forth jolt of the head that sends the brain crashing against the sides of the skull. In essence, he was being hit not in the head but in the head, neck, and torso—an area with an effective mass three times greater. In the second case, the player didn't see the hit coming. His head took the full force of the blow all by itself. That's why he suffered a concussion. But how do you insure, in a game like football, that a player is never taken by surprise?

40

Guskiewicz and his colleagues have come up with what they believe is a much better method of understanding concussion. They have done a full cognitive workup of the players on the U.N.C. team, so that they can track whatever effect might arise from the hits each player accumulates during his four years. U.N.C.'s new coach, Butch Davis, has sharply cut back on full-contact practices, reducing the toll on the players' heads. Guskiewicz says his data show that a disproportionate number of serious head impacts happen on kickoffs, so he wonders whether it might make sense, in theory, anyway, to dispense with them altogether. But, like everyone else who's worried about football, he still has no idea what the inherent risks of the game are. What if you did everything you could, and banned kickoffs and full-contact practices and used the most state-of-the-art techniques for diagnosing and treating concussion, and behaved as responsibly as NASCAR has in the past several years—and players were still getting too many dangerous little hits to the head?

After the tape session, Guskiewicz and one of his colleagues, Jason Mihalik, went outside to watch the U.N.C. football team practice, a short walk down the hill from their office. Only when you see football at close range is it possible to understand the dimensions of the brain-injury problem. The players were huge—much larger than you imagine them being. They moved at astonishing speeds for people of that size, and, long before you saw them, you heard them: the sound of one two-hundred-and-fifty-pound man colliding with another echoed around the practice facility. Mihalik and Guskiewicz walked over to a small building, just off to the side of the field. On the floor was a laptop inside a black storage crate. Next to the computer was an antenna that received the signals from the sensors inside the players' helmets. Mihalik crouched down and began paging through the data. In one column, the HITS software listed the top hits of the practice up to that point, and every few moments the screen would refresh, reflecting the plays that had just been run on the field. Forty-five minutes into practice, the top eight head blows on the field measured 82 gs, 79 gs, 75 gs, 79 gs, 67 gs, 60 gs, 57 gs, and 53 gs. One player, a running back, had received both the 79 gs and the 60 gs, as well as another hit, measuring 27.9 gs. This wasn't a full-contact practice. It was "shells." The players wore only helmets and shoulder pads, and still there were mini car crashes happening all over the field.

The most damaged, scarred, and belligerent of Michael Vick's dogs—the hardest cases—were sent to the Best Friends Animal Sanctuary, on a thirty-seven-hundred-acre spread in the canyons of southern Utah. They were housed in a specially modified octagon, a one-story, climate-controlled cottage, ringed by individual dog runs. The dogs were given a final walk at 11 P.M. and woken up at 7 A.M., to introduce them to a routine. They were hand-fed. In the early months, the staff took turns sleeping in the octagon—sometimes in the middle, sometimes in a cot in one of the runs—so that someone would be with the dogs twenty-four hours a day. Twenty-two of Vick's pit bulls came to Best Friends in January of 2008, and all but five of them are still there.

Ray lunged at his handlers when he first came to Best Friends. He can't be with other dogs. Ellen lies on the ground and wants her stomach scratched, and when the caregivers slept in the octagon she licked them all night long. Her face is lopsided, as if it had been damaged from fighting. She can't be with other dogs, either. Georgia has a broken tail, and her legs and snout are covered with scars. She has no teeth. At some point, in her early life, they had been surgically removed. The court-ordered evaluation of the Vick dogs labelled Meryl, a medium-sized brown-and-white pit-bull mix, "human aggressive," meaning that she is never allowed to be taken out of the Best Friends facility. "She had a hard time meeting people — she would preëmpt anyone coming by charging and snapping at them," Ann Allums, one of the Best Friends dog trainers, said, as she walked around Meryl's octagon, on a recent fall day.

She opened the gate to Meryl's dog run and crouched down on the ground next to her. She hugged the dog, and began playfully wrestling with her, as Meryl's tail thumped happily. "She really doesn't mind new people," Allums said. "She's very happy and loving. I feel totally comfortable with her. I can grab and kiss her." She gave Meryl another hug. "I am building a relationship," she said. "She needed to see that when people were around bad things would not happen."

What happens at Best Friends represents, by any measure, an extravagant gesture. These are dogs that will never live a normal life. But the kind of crime embodied by dogfighting is so morally repellent that it demands an extravagant gesture in response. In a fighting dog, the quality that is prized above all others is the willingness to persevere, even in the face of injury and pain. A dog that will not do that is labelled a "cur," and abandoned. A dog that keeps charging at its opponent is said to possess "gameness," and game dogs are revered.

In one way or another, plenty of organizations select for gameness. The Marine Corps does so, and so does medicine, when it puts young doctors through the exhausting rigors of residency. But those who select for gameness have a responsibility not to abuse that trust: if you have men in your charge who would jump off a cliff for you, you cannot march them to the edge of the cliff — and dogfighting fails this test. Gameness, Carl Semencic argues, in *The World of Fighting Dogs* (1984), is no more than a dog's "desire to please an owner at any expense to itself." The owners, Semencic goes on,

> understand this desire to please on the part of the dog and capitalize on it. At any organized pit fight in which two dogs are really going at each other wholeheartedly, one can observe the owner of each dog changing his position at pit-side in order to be in sight of his dog at all times. The owner knows that seeing his master rooting him on will make a dog work all the harder to please its master.

This is why Michael Vick's dogs weren't euthanized. The betrayal of loyalty requires an act of social reparation.

Professional football players, too, are selected for gameness. When Kyle Turley   50
was knocked unconscious, in that game against the Packers, he returned to practice four days later because, he said, "I didn't want to miss a game." Once, in the
years when he was still playing, he woke up and fell into a wall as he got out of
bed. "I start puking all over," he recalled. "So I said to my wife, 'Take me to practice.' I didn't want to miss practice." The same season that he was knocked unconscious, he began to have pain in his hips. He received three cortisone shots, and
kept playing. At the end of the season, he discovered that he had a herniated disk.
He underwent surgery, and four months later was back at training camp. "They
put me in full-contact practice from day one," he said. "After the first day, I knew
I wasn't right. They told me, 'You've had the surgery. You're fine. You should just
fight through it.' It's like you're programmed. You've got to go without question — *I'm a warrior. I can block that out of my mind.* I go out, two days later. Full
contact. Two-a-days. My back locks up again. I had re-herniated the same disk
that got operated on four months ago, and bulged the disk above it." As one of
Turley's old coaches once said, "He plays the game as it should be played, all out,"
which is to say that he put the game above his own well-being.

Turley says he was once in the training room after a game with a young linebacker who had suffered a vicious hit on a kickoff return. "We were in the cold
tub, which is, like, forty-five degrees, and he starts passing out. In the cold tub. I
don't know anyone who has ever passed out in the cold tub. That's supposed to
wake you up. And I'm, like, slapping his face. 'Richie! Wake up!' He said, 'What,
what? I'm cool.' I said, 'You've got a concussion. You have to go to the hospital.' He
said, 'You know, man, I'm fine.'" He wasn't fine, though. That moment in the cold
tub represented a betrayal of trust. He had taken the hit on behalf of his team. He
was then left to pass out in the cold tub, and to deal — ten and twenty years down
the road — with the consequences. No amount of money or assurances about risk
freely assumed can change the fact that, in this moment, an essential bond had
been broken. What football must confront, in the end, is not just the problem of
injuries or scientific findings. It is the fact that there is something profoundly
awry in the relationship between the players and the game.

"Let's assume that Dr. Omalu and the others are right," Ira Casson, who co-
chairs an N.F.L. committee on brain injury, said. "What should we be doing differently? We asked Dr. McKee this when she came down. And she was honest, and
said, 'I don't know how to answer that.' No one has any suggestions — assuming
that you aren't saying no more football, because, let's be honest, that's not going
to happen." Casson began to talk about the research on the connection between
C.T.E. and boxing. It had been known for eighty years. Boxers ran a twenty-
percent risk of dementia. Yet boxers continue to box. Why? Because people still go
to boxing matches.

"We certainly know from boxers that the incidence of C.T.E. is related to the
length of your career," he went on. "So if you want to apply that to football — and
I'm not saying it does apply — then you'd have to let people play six years and

then stop. If it comes to that, maybe we'll have to think about that. On the other hand, nobody's willing to do this in boxing. Why would a boxer at the height of his career, six or seven years in, stop fighting, just when he's making million-dollar paydays?" He shrugged. "It's a violent game. I suppose if you want to you could play touch football or flag football. For me, as a Jewish kid from Long Island, I'd be just as happy if we did that. But I don't know if the fans would be happy with that. So what else do you do?"

Casson is right. There is nothing else to be done, not so long as fans stand and cheer. We are in love with football players, with their courage and grit, and nothing else — neither considerations of science nor those of morality — can compete with the destructive power of that love.

In "Dogmen and Dogfights," Evans and Forsyth write: 55

> When one views a staged dog fight between pit bulls for the first time, the most macabre aspect of the event is that the only sounds you hear from these dogs are those of crunching bones and cartilage. The dogs rip and tear at each other; their blood, urine and saliva splatter the sides of the pit and clothes of the handlers. . . . The emotions of the dogs are conspicuous, but not so striking, even to themselves, are the passions of the owners of the dogs. Whether they hug a winner or in the rare case, destroy a dying loser, whether they walk away from the carcass or lay crying over it, their fondness for these fighters is manifest.

Exploring the Text

1. The subtitle of Malcolm Gladwell's article asks, "How different are dogfighting and football?" Does he explicitly answer the question? What does he think? What do you think?
2. What elements of fiction does Gladwell use to create his story?
3. Why do you think Gladwell introduces Kyle Turley so early in his piece? What are your impressions of Turley? How does Gladwell's characterization of him help Gladwell develop his argument?
4. The article shifts gears in paragraph 9, moving from football to dogfighting. What strategies does Gladwell use to introduce the subject of dogfighting and Michael Vick? How does he establish his credibility on the subject?
5. Paragraphs 16–29 are about research into chronic traumatic encephalopathy (C.T.E.), a condition that has symptoms similar to Alzheimer's but is the result of head trauma. How does Gladwell make this scientific study accessible to the lay reader? How does he bring the statistics of the disease to life?
6. Why does Gladwell provide some personal background for neuropathologist Ann McKee in paragraph 28?
7. Having read "Offensive Play," what do you think is the answer to the question Gladwell poses in paragraph 29: "is the kind of injury being uncovered by McKee and Omalu incidental to the game of football or inherent in it?" How is that

question connected to the questions he asks in the next paragraph: "So what is football? Is it dogfighting or is it stock-car racing?"

8. Gladwell describes early efforts to reform football in paragraph 31. The visual text on page 668 is a cartoon from that era. How are Gladwell's arguments similar to and different from the argument made by the cartoon?

9. Paragraph 49 comprises only two sentences. In what ways are those two sentences central to Gladwell's argument? How are the ideas in that paragraph illustrated in paragraph 51?

10. How does Gladwell appeal to logos in the conclusion of "Offensive Play"?

Why I Love My Job

RICK REILLY

Born in Boulder, Colorado, in 1958, Richard Paul "Rick" Reilly was a longtime columnist for *Sports Illustrated*, but in 2007 he joined ESPN as a back-page columnist for *ESPN The Magazine* and as a regular columnist for ESPN.com. He has also published a number of books, including the autobiographical *Who's Your Caddy?* (2003) and a golf novel, *Missing Links* (1996), and its sequel, *Shanks for Nothing* (2007). Reilly is known for his humorous—and sometimes scathing—writing. This column appeared in the December 14, 2009, edition of *ESPN The Magazine*, the 100-years-in-review issue.

When I was a college sophomore and just starting to write for the Boulder sports section, my journalism professor edged me aside, looked me in the eye and said, "You're better than sports."

Lurching into my fifth decade in this business, I still think she's wrong. I will never be better than sports. This is why:

Sports is real. It can't be faked. If you're Henry Fonda's son and you want to act, you get to act. If you're Chelsea Clinton and want to govern, you get to govern. But just because you're Nolan Ryan's son doesn't mean you get to pitch in the Show. Money, family, looks mean diddly in sports. If Tom Brady suddenly can't throw the 30-yard out, he's benched, dimple or no dimple.

Sports is Oprah for guys. I knew a Boston dad and son who hadn't spoken in five years. Some disagreement that just grew too big to see around. But when the Red Sox won it all in 2004, the son came home. They hugged and cried and laughed, and if you think it was about baseball, you don't know men.

Sports fans can be buried in a coffin that is painted in their favorite team's colors and logo. Anybody buried in a Chicago Symphony Orchestra coffin lately?

Sports has mercy. The big and strong take care of the small and weak. In an Illinois prep football game this year, a Downers Grove South kick returner broke

5

into the open at the 40 and was gone. Except, when he got to the 1-yard line, he stopped and went out of bounds. He and his teammates wanted to get an autistic teammate the only touchdown of his life. He got it on the second play. Ever see that on Wall Street?

Sports is woven deeper into American life than you know. You may change religion or politics, but not teams. "I was raised a Packers fan and taught my kids the same," writes a mom in Milwaukee. "Everyone comes to my house for games. My oldest son is battling addiction, and he comes too. We shout and curse and eat green and gold food. Whatever the joy or drama in our lives, we live and die with the Packers together."

Sports has no gray areas. It's black or white, win or lose, hero or goat. Nobody has to form a committee to figure it out. Not true in dance or art. Who was better, head to head, Matisse or Monet? If it were sports, we'd know. (Matisse, 13–8.)

Sports is unscripted. President Obama just went to China, a trip choreographed from touchdown to takeoff. He knew exactly where he'd sit and eat and what he'd say. Knew it before he left. And yet, in the PGA Championship this year, a nobody named Y. E. Yang came from behind to beat the god named Tiger Woods. No wonder Obama doesn't watch *Headline News*. He watches *SportsCenter*.

College football teams fill 100,000-seat stadiums. Seen the history department do that?   10

Sports has honor. In a Texas girls high school volleyball playoff this season, one of the East Texas Christian Academy girls suffered a head injury and was taken away on a stretcher. The East Texas girls were too upset to continue and forfeited. But their opponents—Summit Christian—refused. They insisted on rescheduling. They said they couldn't win that way. And yet last year in Alaska, Senator Ted Stevens (R) ran for reelection despite seven felony convictions.

Sports has the best words, and every CEO steals them. It's a slam dunk. It's a grand slam. It's a complete whiff. And yet, in 32 years, I have never heard an athlete say, "That was just a total filibuster out there!"

If sportswriters are so trivial, why did Frank Sinatra want to be one? Hell, the first Heisman winner, Jay Berwanger, turned his nose up at being the NFL's No. 1 draft pick in 1936 to write for the *Chicago Daily News*. Berwanger said, "It paid better."

Sports has a heart the size of a knuckleball mitt. A man in Oahu named Chris Pablo once found a golf ball stamped with the words BEAT LEUKEMIA. Weird, since he'd just learned he had leukemia. Pablo decided he hadn't found the ball, the ball had found him. His story got out and, next thing you know, hundreds of people volunteered for bone marrow donation. Now there are purposely lost balls on courses all over the country that say BEAT LEUKEMIA. Golfers find them and feel obligated to help. Sometimes they don't just save $3—they save a life. Lastly—and most important—sports is the place where beer tastes best.

So here's to you, professor. I'm glad to know I'm not better than sports. But   15
you did show me I'm better than one thing: advice from professors.

Exploring the Text

1. How would you describe the tone of "Why I Love My Job"?
2. Why do you think Rick Reilly says he is "Lurching into [his] fifth decade" (para. 2)? What is the effect of the word "lurching"?
3. Describe the structure of "Why I Love My Job." Do you think it is effective? Why?
4. In what ways does Reilly appeal to pathos?
5. There is a common thread in the examples Reilly uses to develop his argument. Describe that thread, and analyze at least three of the examples.
6. Reilly begins his piece with a comment from his journalism professor and ends with his response to the professor. What is the effect of this framing device?
7. In May 2011, Rick Reilly was the graduation speaker at his alma mater, the School of Journalism and Mass Communication at the University of Colorado. He urged the graduates to "get out there and say things that people have never said before." Does he follow his own advice here? Do you find his ideas original, or have you heard them before? Explain your view.

The Great Game

CAROLINE ALEXANDER

> Born in 1956, Caroline Alexander graduated from Florida State University, where she received a Rhodes Scholarship to study at Oxford University. She subsequently came back to FSU to tutor football players in reading and writing and wrote *Battle's End* (1995) about her experience and the lives of the players she worked with. She has written for the *New Yorker*, *Granta*, and *National Geographic*. Her books include *The Endurance: Shackleton's Legendary Antarctic Expedition* (1996) and *The War That Killed Achilles: The True Story of Homer's Iliad and the Trojan War* (2009). The essay presented here appeared in *Lapham's Quarterly* in 2010.

In 1977 I spent what was to be the first of three summers at Fort Sam Houston in San Antonio, Texas, working out in blurring near-hundred-degree heat at the U.S. Modern Pentathlon Training Center, opened that year for the first time to women. Modern pentathlon is a composite competition, devised in 1912 by Baron Pierre de Coubertin, the founder of the modern Olympics, to mirror the prestigious pentathlon centerpiece of the ancient games. The eccentric selection of modern events, however — show jumping, épée fencing, pistol shooting, swimming, and cross-country running — was predicated on the belief, already anachronistic in 1912, that these were the skills a good soldier should possess. In my day, the majority of American male pentathletes, as well as a sprinkling of the inaugural group of women, held rank. The indelible military cast of some memories of this time now seem surreal, such as practicing cavalry drills on the parade field, or shooting, dueling style, at the range. "How you score is between God and your conscience," our marine-sergeant coach would say. America's most conspicuous modern pentathlete was the twenty-six-year-old West Point graduate George Patton, who came in fifth at the event's premiere in 1912, having performed poorly in the shooting.

The equation of sport with war, or more dangerously, war with sport, is universal and enduring, but occasionally lurches into particularly sharp focus. As is made clear in *The War Lovers: Roosevelt, Lodge, Hearst, and the Rush to Empire, 1898*, Evan Thomas' new book about the easily avoidable steps that led to the Spanish American war, personal fixations on exercise and competitive strife morphed with appalling ease into national policy.

"In the last two decades of the nineteenth century, the young men of the upper and middle classes took to sweaty gyms, lifting weights and tossing medicine balls," Thomas writes. Although manifested in very different ways, this susceptibility to sports mania was shared by three of the key figures directing America's rush to war with Spain. Henry Cabot Lodge, the influential senator from Massachusetts, had been "a frail boy and, though he tried, never very adept at games," reading books of tales of derring-do as a substitute for action. For William Randolph Hearst, the publisher of the war-mongering *New York Morning Journal*, sports could be counted on to sell papers: one of the first big stories he had commissioned when taking over the *Journal* had been the annual Princeton–Yale football game. When the battleship *Maine* was blown up in Havana harbor by what was trumpeted as enemy action but was probably an accident, Hearst, with shrewd understanding of the potent sports–war equation, had "proposed recruiting a regiment of giant athletes—heavyweight boxers, football players, and baseball sluggers—to overawe the pitiful Spaniards."

The last man in Thomas' triumvirate is Teddy Roosevelt, whose devotion to manly sporting activities is too well known to require much amplification. As a young boy suffering from myopia and asthma, "Teedie" heaved himself into a regime of weightlifting, mountain climbing, and boxing, the bloody details of which he reported proudly to his father. Blood was an important aspect of Rooseveltian sport, hence the organization he founded in 1887, the Boone and Crockett Club, whose membership was limited to men who, in his words, "had killed with the rifle in fair chase." The club's purpose was "to promote manly sport with the rifle." The distance between "manly sport with the rifle" and the perceived sport of war was perilously short. Roosevelt's own ardently desired military blooding was achieved with his eventual command of the First U.S. Voluntary Cavalry, the eccentric "Rough Riders," whose exploits in the battle for San Juan Heights in Cuba were both significant and overplayed by the press and later by himself. The volunteer regiment was top heavy with sporting men, including an America's Cup yachtsman, reputedly the best quarterback who had ever played for Harvard, a steeplechase rider, a "crack" polo player, a tennis player, and a high jumper.

Informing Roosevelt's sporting ethos was the belief, widely prevalent at the time, that without physical strife America would lose her frontier spirit to effeteness. 5

In an 1896 speech that Thomas characterizes as a "paean to the ideal of sports as preparation for war," Lodge urged his Harvard classmates to consider that the "time given to athletic contests and the injuries incurred on the playing field are part of the price which the English-speaking race has paid for being world conquerors."

In England itself, whose shining empire seemed to testify to the imperial destiny of the Anglo-Saxon race, the fears for the inferiority of the nation's fighting men had some empirical basis. An inspection conducted during the Boer War of 1899–1902 — in which Britain had not performed particularly well — revealed the alarming fact that based upon measurements of chest size, height, and weight, a full 30 percent of its volunteer recruits were "unfit"; the average height of the British Tommy was only five foot six. In Britain as in America, sports were seen as an antidote to this racial degeneracy, and yet, for all their striking common ground, British and Rooseveltian sporting values were directed toward very different ideals of manhood. As befit the rough-riding frontier ethic, American athleticism was about being stronger, clobbering the competition, blood lust — in Roosevelt's words, letting "the wolf rise in the heart." The cult of British athleticism, on the other hand, was about playing games.

The fountainhead of this particular brand of the sports–war equation was undoubtedly the British public school, whose values and moral ethos prevailed throughout English society from the Victorian era well into the aftermath of the Great War. "The schools' secular trinity," according to one scholar, "was imperialism, militarism, and athleticism." The centrality of athletic games had not arisen naturally but was very much the product of a determined reformation of a failing educational system: the weak masters were often incapable of controlling their entitled and high-spirited charges. Riots, rebellions, strikes, mass displays of disobedience — and at Eton an attempt to blow up one of the school houses with gunpowder — were standing features of early Victorian public-school life. One future headmaster, who had been schooled through the reforming period of the late 1870s, while at Eton recalled the transition there from "open barbarism" to "something like decorum."

Games did more than keep boys too busy and too tired to cause trouble; they also fostered team tribalism and school pride. When an outstanding team or individual athlete won both the adulation of his schoolmates and the approving recognition of the master, a bond was formed between boys and authority. The first symptom of games mania, as one observer recalled, "was the taking over of games by the clergy as a proper theme for the pulpit": one sermon preached to boys at Exeter indicated that the performance of the school's cricket team had been displeasing to God.

Complementing a classically oriented curriculum that celebrated the imperial militarism of the revered ancient world, athletic games strengthened the British race, giving young boys the physical training to become hardy servants of the empire, as intrepid missionaries as well as soldiers. A good captain of the first eleven would undoubtedly make a good officer. Games taught a chap to play straight and not "offside." "[A] truly chivalrous football player," as it was put in Marlborough's school magazine, "was never yet guilty of lying, or deceit, or meanness whether of word or action." This insistence on the decency and "straightness" of the young athlete bolstered the attendant belief that just as the soldier-athlete was invariably decent, so too was his imperial cause. "In all this war there is nothing for us to be ashamed of," Sir James Yoxall, an MP and educational reformer declared at the outset of the First World War. "We fight for honor. You know what honor is among schoolboys — straight dealing, truth speaking, and 'playing the game.' Well, we are standing up for honor among nations, while Germany is playing the sneak and the bully in the big European school. Germany must be taught to 'play cricket.' "

That the apogee of this sporting faith would overlap the years of Europe's most catastrophic conflict is one of the many ironies that render the Great War so very pitiable and tragic. By 1914 it had been a long time since the English people as a whole had experienced warfare at first hand. Even the Boer War, in which 22,000 British troops died, had taken place safely out of sight, in faraway South Africa. As Richard van Emden points out in *Boy Soldiers of the Great War*, "Britain's colonial conflicts had been described but not seen, drawn but hardly photographed." At the same time, however, they were covered in the written press: the stories of thrilling conquests playing out in the exotic places of the empire — on the veld, in the East — that streamed in to fill British newspapers and, most particularly, *Boy's Own Paper*, portrayed war as a romantic and glorious adventure. By van Emden's estimate, the number of underage British boys who enlisted in the Great War was well in excess of a quarter of a million. Henry Newbolt's "Vitaï Lampada," with its relentless refrain of "Play up! Play up! And play the game," made clear the continuity between athlete and soldier. One youth recalled a picture that was hung in his nursery showing "a boy trumpeter with a bandaged head, galloping madly through bursting shells for reinforcements." Played "straight" and not "offside," war was the very best of games. "Dear Lord Kitchner," wrote one Irish boy of nine years of age, to the secretary of state for war, "I want to go to the front. I can ride jolley quick on my bycycle and would go as dispatch rider ... I am very strong and often win a fight with lads twice as big as myself." (He received a reply from Kitchener's private secretary. "Lord Kitchener asks me to thank you for your letter, but he is afraid that you are not quite old enough to go to the front.")

For applicants of every age, the recruiting process could draw on familiar schoolboy criteria, as van Emden quotes:

> "Where were you at school?" one seventeen-year-old applicant was asked by the recruiting officer.

10

"Eton, sir."

"In the Corps?"

"Yes sir, Sergeant."

"Play any games? Cricket?"

⚌⚌
⚌⚌

War was sport. Or so it must have seemed at first. The military exercises alone brought first-rate athletic benefits. "There's no doubt it did me good," one veteran recalled of his days of rifle drills and physical training. "What with the open air and exercise, I broadened out, gained confidence, and went in for boxing." Whole regiments of men, it was noted, with the benefit of good food and hardy exercise, added an inch to their height and a full stone, or fourteen pounds, of weight.

Beyond the training fields, the fiction that this was all a great game was maintained in the trenches. One young soldier recalled how as his battalion advanced, it was cheered, as if in a match, by the First Battalion Black Watch. "You feel like in a race, you're waiting to start," he recalled, "waiting for the signal, then the sergeant would shout, 'Right lads,' and you're over the top."

Of the 1,200,000 British men who joined the Army in 1914 as volunteers, almost half a million had done so through the influence of popular soccer organizations. "Join and be in at the final," one recruiting poster advertised, while a rugby poster exhorted men to "Play the Game!" And it was soccer that gave the war one of its most indelible and heartbreakingly pointless images: that of a soldier dribbling a soccer ball toward enemy lines. While this sporting feat was enacted in several campaigns, it was Captain "Billie" Nevill's exploit at the Somme that caught British imagination. As one veteran recalled, when "the gunfire died away I saw an infantry man climb onto the parapet of no man's land, beckoning others to follow. As he did so, he kicked off a football. A good kick." The stirring example of such sporting style, for the sentimental public, was made no less potent by the fact that enemy fire had at once cut Billie Nevill down.

When the war ended, Britain had far fewer sporting men. Some 885,000 had been killed outright, and another 1,700,000 soldiers grievously maimed and wounded. One woman recalled a scene toward the end of the war in Brighton, a seaside town to which the injured were sent for recuperation. "The sight of hundreds of men on crutches going about in groups, many having lost one leg, many others both legs, caused sickness and horror. The maiming of masses of strong young men thus brought home was appalling." Possibly it was these ubiquitous legions of disfigured men that, by their fearful, negative examples, kept the sporting ethic alive. The desire to see whole, healthy young men was painfully strong for a nation desperate to be healed, and sports held sway at public schools into the 1930s, by which time a new generation of chaps had arisen to shoulder the next war.

The association of war with sport is not likely to disappear, given the physicality and competitiveness embedded in the practice of both. More surprising are the enduring associations of sport with war, often occurring in ways that

15

rely on historic memory. Soccer matches played between England and Germany produce a flurry of admonitions for rowdy English fans—no impersonating Hitler, no shouting of "stand up if you won the war," no goose stepping. When in 2001 England defeated Germany in a preliminary World Cup match in Munich, the British tabloids commemorated the victory with the thundering headline: "Blitzed!"

Exploring the Text

1. Caroline Alexander's essay begins with a personal anecdote about her experience training for a pentathlon. What is the purpose of the anecdote? How does it lend credibility to her argument?
2. Alexander distinguishes between equating "sport with war" and, what she considers more dangerous, "war with sport" in paragraph 2. She comes back to that equation in the last paragraph of the essay. What do you think is the difference between the two?
3. Find at least three examples of appeals to pathos. Explain why they are or are not effective.
4. What type of sentence is this one in paragraph 4: "The volunteer regiment was top heavy with sporting men, including an America's Cup yachtsman, reputedly the best quarterback who had ever played for Harvard, a steeplechase rider, a 'crack' polo player, a tennis player, and a high jumper"? Why do you think Alexander chose that structure and language to describe the Rough Riders?
5. What argument is Alexander making about the connection between sports and war? What strategies does she use to develop it?
6. Alexander considers it ironic that faith in the positive aspects of sport was at its peak during the Great War (World War I). Explain why and whether you agree or disagree.
7. What do you think is the connection today between athletics and the armed forces?
8. How does Alexander characterize the differences between American and British athleticism?

Ex-Basketball Player

John Updike

John Updike (1932–2009) grew up in Pennsylvania and attended Harvard University on a full scholarship, before graduating summa cum laude. At Harvard, he was president of the *Harvard Lampoon*. Updike is known for his careful craftsmanship and for writing about the world of the Protestant middle class. In his novels and short stories he often explores the interrelationship of sex, faith, and death. His series of novels about Harry "Rabbit" Angstrom, a former high-school basketball star, defined the suburban experience. Two of these novels won the Pulitzer Prize. Updike is also known for his criticism and poetry.

Pearl Avenue runs past the high-school lot,
Bends with the trolley tracks, and stops, cut off
Before it has a chance to go two blocks,
At Colonel McComsky Plaza. Berth's Garage
Is on the corner facing west, and there,   5
Most days, you'll find Flick Webb, who helps Berth out.

Flick stands tall among the idiot pumps—
Five on a side, the old bubble-head style,
Their rubber elbows hanging loose and low.
One's nostrils are two S's, and his eyes   10
An E and O. And one is squat, without
A head at all—more of a football type.

Once Flick played for the high-school team, the Wizards.
He was good: in fact, the best. In '46
He bucketed three hundred ninety points,   15
A county record still. The ball loved Flick.
I saw him rack up thirty-eight or forty
In one home game. His hands were like wild birds.

He never learned a trade, he just sells gas,
Checks oil, and changes flats. Once in a while,   20
As a gag, he dribbles an inner tube,
But most of us remember anyway.
His hands are fine and nervous on the lug wrench.
It makes no difference to the lug wrench, though.

Off work, he hangs around Mae's Luncheonette.   25
Grease-gray and kind of coiled, he plays pinball,
Smokes those thin cigars, nurses lemon phosphates.
Flick seldom says a word to Mae, just nods
Beyond her face toward bright applauding tiers
Of Necco Wafers, Nibs, and Juju Beads.   30

Exploring the Text

1. In addition to creating a portrait of Flick Webb, the former basketball star, John Updike also creates a setting. What details does he use to set the scene?
2. Updike uses figurative language sparingly. Consider the effects of personification and simile in this poem.
3. What statement does the poem make about high school sports?
4. Compare the effect of the following excerpt about a pickup basketball game from Updike's novel *Rabbit, Run* (1960) with the effect of "Ex-Basketball Player" (1957).

> Yet in his time Rabbit was famous through the county; in basketball in his junior year he set a B-league scoring record that in his senior year he broke with a record that was not broken until four years later, that is, four years ago.
>
> He sinks shots one-handed, two-handed, underhanded, flat-footed, and out of the pivot, jump, and set. Flat and soft the ball lifts. That his touch still lives in his hands elates him. He feels liberated from long gloom.

The Twelfth Player in Every Football Game

New York World

The cartoon on the following page appeared in the *New York World* in 1897 as a comment on violence in football. It was reprinted in the *New Yorker* in 2011, accompanying an article by Ben McGrath entitled "Does Football Have a Future?" It is subtitled "The NFL and the Concussion Crisis."

Exploring the Text

1. Consider the words and the image separately. What is the relationship between them? Does the image support the words or vice versa?
2. What point does the cartoon make about the relationship between football and violence? Do you agree with the cartoon's thesis? Explain your response.
3. According to Ben McGrath, it was Yale football coach Walter Camp, the so-called Father of American Football, whose "preference for order over chaos led to the primary differentiating element between the new sport (football) and its parent, English rugby: a line of scrimmage, with discrete plays, or downs, instead of scrums," and who, in the 1890s, tried to present football as an upper-class training ground, not as a "middle class spectator sport." What do you suppose Walter Camp would think of the NFL now? Do you think this cartoon has resonance today? Explain your answer.
4. Read Malcolm Gladwell's essay "Offensive Play" in this chapter (p. 643). In what ways does this cartoon illustrate his thesis?

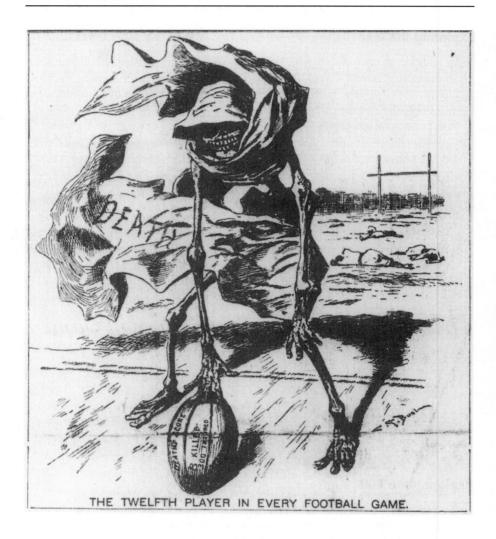

THE TWELFTH PLAYER IN EVERY FOOTBALL GAME.

5. A cartoon can be analyzed through the rhetorical triangle. Consider the cartoon's subject, the artist, and the audience separately; then analyze the relationships among those three elements. Also consider the context: the time and place of the work's creation, and how and where it is viewed. What do you think are differences and similarities between today's audience and the audience when the cartoon was originally published in 1897?

6. There is a tradition in football of the "12th Player," which supposedly began in 1921 when E. King Gill, a player on the Texas A&M football squad who had left the team to play basketball, came down from the stands and suited up for a game in which many of his former teammates had been injured. His willingness to do what he could for his team led to the idea that the fans within a stadium become the

"12th Player" on an eleven-player team; their support—and sometimes distract-ing noise—can be very influential. In this cartoon the twelfth player is Death. How does it contrast with the present-day tradition of the twelfth player? Might this cartoon have resonance today, despite the current meaning of the "12th Player"?

Yes!

Sports Illustrated

> Sports Illustrated ran this cover on July 19, 1999, after soccer player Brandi Chas-tain made the winning penalty kick in the 1999 World Cup.

Exploring the Text

1. What argument does this photo make? Why do you think *Sports Illustrated* chose to use it for a cover?

2. When this photo appeared, reactions ranged from appalled (a woman in a bra!) to ecstatic (a strong, athletic woman!). Do you think there is a double standard when it comes to images of women in sports? What is your response to the photo?

3. Consider the layout of the *Sports Illustrated* cover. How much space does the pho-tograph of Chastain take up? What is the effect of obscuring part of the title of the magazine? How is the cover's text balanced by the image of Chastain?

4. Chastain's take on the incident was this: "Momentary insanity, nothing more, nothing less. I wasn't thinking about anything. . . . This is the greatest moment of my life on the soccer field." In what ways does the photo communicate Chastain's explanation? Do you think a male athlete would be asked to explain his response? Why or why not?

5. Chastain has written a book entitled *It's Not about the Bra: Play Hard, Play Fair and Put the Fun Back into Competitive Sports* (2004). How does this photo help Chastain establish ethos? Do you think this iconic photo makes her more or less credible? Explain your response.

6. When asked about the popularity of her team—and their attractiveness—Chastain responded by saying, "There are those people who come purely for soccer. There are those people who come purely for the event. And there are those people who come because they like us, to look at us. Those are three great reasons to come." Which do you think is the most important reason people watch women's sports? Is it different for men's sports? Why or why not?

(See insert for color version.)

Conversation

Paying College Athletes

Following are seven selections that comment directly or indirectly on the issue of whether college athletes should be paid.

Sources

1. **Boris Drucker,** *"I'm Glad We Won . . ."* (cartoon)
2. **Frank Deford,** *Pay Dirt: College Athletes Deserve the Same Rights as Other Students*
3. **Michael Lewis,** *Serfs of the Turf*
4. **Bill Walton,** *My Priceless Opportunity*
5. **Michael Wilbon,** *As Colleges' Greed Grows, So Does the Hypocrisy*
6. **Steve Weiberg,** *Despite Criticism, NCAA Takes a Firm Stance on Professionalism*
7. **National Collegiate Athletic Association,** *Why Students Aren't Paid to Play*

After using the questions to discuss individual selections, synthesize the pieces through one of the suggested assignments on page 685.

1. "I'm Glad We Won . . ."

BORIS DRUCKER

In this cartoon, published in the *New Yorker* in 1997, a football coach responds to a reporter after a game.

"I'm glad we won, and I hope that someday we'll have a university that our football team can be proud of."

Questions

1. Characterize the cartoon's audience. What assumptions does Boris Drucker make about the people who will look at his cartoon?
2. Who are the characters in the cartoon? How does their placement help Drucker make his argument? What can you tell from their facial expressions?

3. Do you agree with Drucker's point, or do you think he is overstating his case? Explain your response.

2. *Pay Dirt: College Athletes Deserve the Same Rights as Other Students*

FRANK DEFORD

The following viewpoint piece was posted on SI.com in May 2003.

Last month at the Masters, a senior at the University of Arizona, Ricky Barnes, played with Tiger Woods and not only outshot Woods over the first 36 holes but also finished the tournament only three strokes over par. Barnes should have pocketed a nice paycheck, but instead he had to settle for a pat on the back.

That is, Barnes played the same course as Woods and all the other PGA players—he even beat most of them—but while they got paid, he didn't. That's because, of course, Ricky Barnes is something called an amateur—and while we have reached the 21st century, American sports still have these antiquated 19th century rules about amateurism.

Essentially, we can thank the British upper classes for amateurism. They wanted to keep sports to themselves, so as long as they made it so poor people couldn't afford to take time to play without reward, only the rich could practice and compete. Then, when we adopted Victorian amateurism in many of our sports, we covered it with the veil of the Olympics. Only it wasn't so. The old Greeks didn't waste their time running and jumping just to get a laurel wreath. The Greeks paid their Olympic champions handsomely. But the myth persists.

When the NCAA was established, amateur rules were ironclad, and it's awfully hard to break them because we in America have big-time sports tied up with academics. In most sports, American players have little chance to compete unless they go to college and play by the college rules.

I think good arguments can be made that Division I football and basketball players should be paid by their schools. I'll grant, though, it is an expensive and debatable proposition. But, pray tell, what are the arguments that say an athlete such as Ricky Barnes should be denied compensation when he is *not* competing for his college? If Barnes wants to accept a scholarship to Arizona and play for the Wildcats for free, fine, but why should Arizona deny him remuneration when he is *only* competing as Ricky Barnes? 5

The NCAA is, simply, a cartel when it disallows athletes that right. Why should a college student who happens to be a good athlete be denied the same rights as a college student who is a good musician or a good writer or a good actor? The kid who has those talents is, in fact, encouraged to get a paying summer job in his specialty to improve his skills. Why should a college basketball player be denied the same rights as a college piano player?

And the answer, of course, is because the NCAA adopted Victorian rules a century ago and maintains them today because it has the power to do so. The irony is, too, that if the NCAA lifted those old-fashioned regulations it would help college sports. The NBA, say, could draft a college player who is not yet quite good enough for the league, pay him and let him stay in college, where he would get good coaching and develop while boosting the popularity of his team and his sport.

Why should the NCAA care—or bear any authority—about where or how a college player makes money *outside* of college? Amateur is supposed to be about the love of the game. In truth, it's about how the NCAA loves the way it controls our athletes and denies them the same rights our other talented young people enjoy.

Questions

1. How does Frank Deford define "amateur"? How does his brief history of amateurism aid his argument?
2. Why is the example of Ricky Barnes an effective part of Deford's argument?
3. What is Deford's view of the NCAA? Do you agree or disagree with his assessment? Explain your answer.

3. *Serfs of the Turf*

Michael Lewis

The following op-ed piece appeared in the *New York Times* in November 2007.

The three most lucrative college football teams in 2005—Notre Dame, Ohio State and the University of Texas—each generated more than $60 million for their institutions. That number, which comes from the Department of Education, fails to account for the millions of dollars alumni donated to their alma maters because they were so proud of their football teams. But it still helps to explain why so many strangers to football success have reinvented themselves as football powerhouses (Rutgers?), and also why universities are spending huge sums on new football practice facilities, new football stadium skyboxes and new football coaches.

Back in 1958 the University of Alabama lured Bear Bryant with a promise of $18,000 a year, or the rough equivalent of $130,000 today; last year the university handed Nick Saban an eight-year deal worth roughly $32 million. Several dozen college football coaches now earn more than $1 million a year—and that's before the books, speeches, endorsement deals and who knows what else. Earlier this season the head coach at Texas A&M, Dennis Franchione, was caught topping up his $2.09 million salary by selling to Aggie alums, for $1,200 a pop, his private football-gossip newsletter.

The sports media treated that particular scheme as scandalous. Texas A&M made its coach apologize and promise to stop writing for a living. But really Dennis Franchione's foray into high-priced journalism was just an ingenious extension of the entrepreneurial spirit that's turned college football into a gold mine. The scandal wasn't what he did but how it was made to seem — unusually greedy.

College football's best trick play is its pretense that it has nothing to do with money, that it's simply an extension of the university's mission to educate its students. Were the public to view college football as mainly a business, it might start asking questions. For instance: why are these enterprises that have nothing to do with education and everything to do with profits exempt from paying taxes? Or why don't they pay their employees?

This is maybe the oddest aspect of the college football business. Everyone   5
associated with it is getting rich except the people whose labor creates the value. At this moment there are thousands of big-time college football players, many of whom are black and poor. They perform for the intense pleasure of millions of rabid college football fans, many of whom are rich and white. The world's most enthusiastic racially integrated marketplace is waiting to happen.

But between buyer and seller sits the National Collegiate Athletic Association, to ensure that the universities it polices keep all the money for themselves — to make sure that the rich white folk do not slip so much as a free chicken sandwich under the table to the poor black kids. The poor black kids put up with it because they find it all but impossible to pursue N.F.L. careers unless they play at least three years in college. Less than one percent actually sign professional football contracts and, of those, an infinitesimal fraction ever make serious money. But their hope is eternal, and their ignorance exploitable.

Put that way the arrangement sounds like simple theft; but up close, inside the university, it apparently feels like high principle. That principle, as stated by the N.C.A.A., is that college sports should never be commercialized. But it's too late for that. College football already is commercialized, for everyone except the people who play it. Were they businesses, several dozen of America's best-known universities would be snapped up by private equity tycoons, who would spin off just about everything but the football team. (The fraternities they might keep.)

If the N.C.A.A. genuinely wanted to take the money out of college football it'd make the tickets free and broadcast the games on public television and set limits on how much universities could pay head coaches. But the N.C.A.A. confines its anti-market strictures to the players — and God help the interior lineman who is caught breaking them. Each year some player who grew up with nothing is tempted by a booster's offer of a car, or some cash, and is never heard from again.

The lie at the bottom of the fantasy goes something like this: serious college football players go to college for some reason other than to play football. These marvelous athletes who take the field on Saturdays and generate millions for their colleges are students first, and football players second. They are like Franciscan monks set down in the gold mine. Yes, they play football, but they have no interest in the money. What they're really living for is that degree in criminology.

Of course, no honest person who has glimpsed the inside of a big-time college football program could actually believe this. Even from the outside the college end of things seems suspiciously secondary. If serious college football players are students first, why — even after a huge N.C.A.A. push to raise their graduation rates — do they so alarmingly fail to graduate? Why must the N.C.A.A. create incentives for football coaches to encourage their players even to attend classes? Why do we never hear of a great high school football player choosing a college for the quality of its professors? Why, when college football coaches sell their programs to high school studs, do they stress the smoothness of the path they offer to the N.F.L.?

It's not that football players are too stupid to learn. It's that they're too busy. Unlike the other students on campus, they have full-time jobs: playing football for nothing. Neglect the task at hand, and they may never get a chance to play football for money.

Last year the average N.F.L. team had revenue of about $200 million and ran payrolls of roughly $130 million: 60 percent to 70 percent of a team's revenues, therefore, go directly to the players. There's no reason those numbers would be any lower on a college football team — and there's some reason to think they'd be higher. It's easy to imagine the Universities of Alabama ($44 million in revenue), Michigan ($50 million), Georgia ($59 million) and many others paying the players even more than they take in directly from their football operations, just to keep school spirit flowing. (Go Dawgs!)

But let's keep it conservative. In 2005, the 121 Division 1-A football teams generated $1.8 billion for their colleges. If the colleges paid out 65 percent of their revenues to the players, the annual college football payroll would come to $1.17 billion. A college football team has 85 scholarship players while an N.F.L. roster has only 53, and so the money might be distributed a bit differently.

"You'd pay up for the most critical positions," one N.F.L. front office executive told me on the condition that I not use his name. "You'd pay more for quarterbacks and left tackles and pass rushing defensive ends. You'd pay less for linebackers because you'd have so many of them. You could just rotate them in and out."

A star quarterback, he thought, might command as much as 8 percent of his college team's revenues. For instance, in 2005 the Texas Longhorns would have paid Vince Young roughly $5 million for the season. In quarterbacking the Longhorns free of charge, Young, in effect, was making a donation to the university of $5 million a year — and also, by putting his health on the line, taking a huge career risk.

Perhaps he would have made this great gift on his own. The point is that Vince Young, as the creator of the economic value, should have had the power to choose what to do with it. Once the market is up and running players who want to go to enjoy the pure amateur experience can continue to play for free.

And you never know. The N.C.A.A. might one day be able to run an honest advertisement for the football-playing student-athlete: a young man who valued so highly what the University of Florida had to teach him about hospitality management that he ignored the money being thrown at him by Florida State.

Questions

1. How does Michael Lewis explain the growing number of college football "powerhouses"?
2. How does Lewis establish credibility? In what ways does he appeal to logos and pathos?
3. Explain what Lewis means when he says that the "world's most enthusiastic racially integrated marketplace is waiting to happen" (para. 5).
3. According to Lewis, what is the "lie at the bottom of the fantasy" (para. 9)?
4. How does Lewis explain the low graduation rate of college football players?
5. What is Lewis's solution? Do you think his idea is possible? Explain your response.

4. *My Priceless Opportunity*

BILL WALTON

The following selection, by Basketball Hall of Famer and sports commentator Bill Walton, was posted on the *New York Times* "Room for Debate" blog in March 2009.

College basketball players getting paid? What is this—the N.B.A.?

In a world that has changed beyond belief in the 39 years since I started playing N.C.A.A. basketball, we seem to have lost the sense of what is really valuable and built to last in our society. While the exponential growth in the business of sports across all spectrums, including collegiate athletics, is undeniable—for the student athlete it can't be all about the money, all the time. Getting paid to play ball is what professional sports are all about, and the N.C.A.A. and N.B.A. are two completely different sports, each glorious in their own way.

The young players entering the college game know the rules going in. They are being given a chance to make something of their lives in exchange for the privilege of being an N.C.A.A. student athlete. Most people would salivate at the opportunity to attend one of our nation's prestigious universities, and then to get in and have it cost you nothing. They house you, feed you, clothe you, educate you, give you a living stipend, and you get to travel the world. These opportunities are priceless.

What's most important is that these scholarships give students the opportunity to learn how to learn, think, analyze, and to gain some great life lessons—including humility and how to rebound from failure.

Paying the players more than what they are already receiving for their schol- 5
arship is a bad idea—how would it be managed? Would every student athlete
negotiate a separate deal?

When I left home in the fall of 1970 as a 17-year-old on my way to U.C.L.A.
on an N.C.A.A. basketball scholarship, I thought I was getting the greatest deal in
the world. And I did. I got an education, I got to meet and learn from the most
interesting people (including Coach Wooden), and I got to be a part of a most
remarkable team—the U.C.L.A. family. Outside of my health and family, they are
the most valuable possessions that I've ever had. While at U.C.L.A., I had summer
jobs and I was most fortunate that for the rest of my life I never had to go back to
my working-class parents for another dime.

Every one of our games was sold out; every one was on TV. I felt then, as I do
today, that I got the better end of the deal. (Considering our late career collapse
at U.C.L.A., they're probably still debating whether it was even worth it to offer
me the scholarship that I so desperately needed.)

If I hadn't gone to U.C.L.A., I shudder to think where and who I would be
today. I always counsel young dreamers who are searching for their own path to
happiness and success in sports, to use basketball to make a better life for yourself; don't let basketball use you.

I will be watching the N.C.A.A. tournament with great interest, as I do every
year. I love the passion, the excitement, the pride, the beaming alumni, the song
girls, the pageantry, and maybe mostly—the bands. I'm really hoping that this
year's playlist will include "Where Have All the Flowers Gone" and "Teach Your
Children."

Questions

1. In what ways does Bill Walton think college athletes are compensated?
2. How does Walton establish his credibility?
3. Walton says, "Paying the players more than what they are already receiving for
   their scholarship is a bad idea" (para. 5). What are his reasons? Are you convinced?
   Explain your response.

5. *As Colleges' Greed Grows, So Does the Hypocrisy*

MICHAEL WILBON

The following column by Michael Wilbon appeared in the *Washington Post* in
September 2010.

If you log on to the official online store of the University of Georgia Bulldogs
you'll be bombarded by images of a No. 8 football jersey. A wide receiver named
A.J. Green wears that particular jersey now. Mel Kiper rates him as the No. 4 pros-

pect in all of college football, which means he's a big deal in Georgia and so is his jersey.

There's a black replica that goes for $59.95; a red, a black and a white replica youth jersey, each of which goes for $43.95. Scroll down a bit and you'll see a red "twilled" jersey that sells for $74.95 and then there are preschool jerseys (black or white, take your pick) that sell for $41.95 apiece. And don't let me forget the "authentic" No. 8 jerseys, in black or red, that go for $150 each.

In all, counting the pink jerseys presumably for women, there are 17 options for sale.

Green is the biggest star in a state where the college football team matters more than anything except, possibly, one's place of worship. Thousands of those No. 8 jerseys, which Green wears on Saturdays, have been sold. And all proceeds, according to the official Web site, benefit Georgia athletics.

This has become enormously important the last couple of days, of course,   5 because the NCAA has suspended Green for the first four games for selling one of his game-worn jerseys. Probably got $500, $600 for it . . . we're told it was less than $1,000. But while the kid is sitting out the next three games the university can keep right on selling his jersey and reaping the financial rewards.

As a head coach of a major Division I program so accurately said to me recently on the subject of the behavior of big-time athletic leagues and their big-time programs, "They're now fully engaged in robbing the poor to give to the rich."

The person who most needs the money, Green, is prohibited from reaping a dime, even though he's the one who spends more than 40 hours a week working at being a college football player, even though he's the one who risks head injuries that could shorten his life. Not a dime for him, and all of it, 100 percent, for the school's athletic department.

The suspension of Green doesn't just point to the greed that permeates college athletics; it's shameful that the rules are set up to punish a kid this severely because he sees he's the only person not making any money off his labor and wants to sneak a few hundred bucks for himself.

We seem to have reached a point where kids who play revenue-producing college sports—and that means Division I men's basketball and football—are more determined than ever to get what's coming to them, whether that means associating with agents or taking some money to live better right now. Damn the consequences.

And they can better justify it because everywhere they look people are mak-   10 ing money off of them. I'd argue that university presidents and the people who run the biggest conferences have never been more openly greedy. Since the end of the last college football season, the dominant story in college sports has been to find a better conference deal and get more money. Your school gets $15 million for being on television? Try for $25 million.

Right now, the Pac-10 is trying to figure out how to realign its 12-team conference, and the whole affair is made more complex by television revenue sharing, which is how Colorado and Utah got into the Pac-10 in the first place. They wanted exposure to the Los Angeles area to recruit and take advantage of L.A.'s great capacity for television revenue.

The Big Ten's addition of Nebraska was done solely so that Nebraska and the Big Ten will make more money, largely through the Big Ten Network. But be certain that if a kid playing for Nebraska accepts $100 to fill his jalopy with gas and take his girlfriend to dinner after the game, the NCAA will take him down.

The hypocrisy is stunning, and nowhere more than Southern California, where the school wants to keep its 2004 national championship that Reggie Bush helped win, while the Heisman Trophy he earned on the field that season is being pried away.

Bush, as you know by now, reportedly might be stripped of the Heisman for accepting improper benefits . . . as if he's the first Heisman Trophy winner to take anything improper in 75 years. As my friend Bryan Burwell pointed out in the St. Louis Post-Dispatch, many Heisman winners have been tainted by scandal — and not just O.J. Simpson.

Paul Hornung, the 1956 winner, was later suspended by the NFL for gambling. Charles White, the 1979 winner, admitted being a cocaine abuser while playing in the NFL. Johnny Rodgers, the 1972 winner, was convicted of robbing a gas station while at Nebraska. Billy Cannon went to federal prison for counterfeiting. None has been asked to give back his prize.   15

The thread here that seems to connect Bush with Georgia's A.J. Green is that more and more often, at least anecdotally, talented athletes are willing to risk whatever the punishment to get something now, something more than tuition, room, board and books. For decades I went along with the folks who reasoned that was compensation enough, that the price of an education isn't "nothing."

But the constant pursuit of more money by the schools and conferences themselves is making me change my tune.

Sorry if the kids who play women's basketball or lacrosse or water polo don't stand to gain from any compensation plan; the kids whose jerseys produce tens of thousands of dollars for athletic departments need to see at least a fraction of that money themselves. (CNBC's Darren Rovell tweeted this week, "In 2005, Myles Brand told me the NCAA would look at compensating star players for sales of their jerseys. Guess they're still looking.")

If Green can't sell his jersey directly, then the NCAA or the University of Georgia ought to cut him a check. Please, don't cite me the NCAA rules. Change the damn rules to stop taking advantage of the poorest people in the equation.

If I'd been standing in front of A.J. Green when he whipped off his game-worn jersey and tried to sell it, I'd have paid him myself, and told the kid to keep his mouth shut.   20

Questions

1. What examples of hypocrisy does Michael Wilbon supply? What is your response to the examples?
2. Why does Wilbon differentiate between men's basketball and football and sports such as women's basketball, lacrosse, and water polo?
3. Explain what made Wilbon change his mind about compensation for college football players.

6. *Despite Criticism, NCAA Takes a Firm Stance on Professionalism*

STEVE WEIBERG

The following article appeared in *USA Today* in January 2011.

From the stiff penalties assessed Southern California in the Reggie Bush case to the pay-for-play soap opera surrounding Cam Newton to the pending suspensions of Ohio State football players for selling jerseys, rings and other trinkets, the last six months have underscored a key NCAA commandment:

College athletes are not to be paid, not to cash in on their prominence, never to cross any kind of line of professionalism.

The NCAA has largely stood firm on Bylaw 12—in which it spells out the dos and don'ts—as television, marketing and other revenue run ever deeper, spending on coaches and other personnel continues to climb and calls mount for those on the field to get something beyond a scholarship. The mother of one of the Ohio State offenders, receiver DeVier Posey, complained to the *Columbus (Ohio) Dispatch* last week that the association's strict, scholarships-only stand leaves many players and their families in unnecessary financial straits and invites violations.

"The NCAA has everybody's hands tied," Julie Posey said, "but they roll in dough."

USA TODAY briefly examines the issue: 5

Q. Why is the NCAA so hard-line?

Keep in mind that its 1,000-plus member schools and conferences draw up the regulations that fill a 419-page, almost inch-thick rules manual. They ostensibly agree with Bylaw 12's stipulation that "member institutions' athletics programs are designed to be an integral part of the educational program" and that athletes are "an integral part of the student body, thus maintaining a clear line of demarcation between college athletics and professional sports."

NCAA President Mark Emmert is intent on staying that course. "I feel adamantly that we can never move to a place where we are paying players to play," he said two weeks ago, echoing a sentiment he has expressed since taking office in October.

Q. How can he or anyone else defend that position given, for starters, the new 14-year, $10.8 billion contract the NCAA just struck with CBS and Turner Sports for media rights to the Division I men's basketball tournament?

College football's top-tier Bowl Championship Series pockets $125 million annually from ESPN. The games, and those who play them, are essential properties.

Players, or at least the vast majority of them, receive scholarships covering room, board, books and tuition. With that, Emmert says, they "benefit from the best coaching staff, the best facilities, the best trainers, the best educational environment that anybody can get in the world."

He adds, "OK, so the university generates some revenue to help support that effort. I don't have a problem with that." 10

Most major-college athletics programs aren't piling up money. Only 14 were operating in the black last year.

Q. Still . . .

Critics rail that keeping players amateur—i.e., unpaid—in an otherwise highly commercial enterprise is an injustice. Sales of replica jerseys are an oft-used example. Schools and marketers can profit; the performers who give them their cachet can't. Multiply that by millions when it comes to game revenue.

"The NCAA amateurism rules are a fictional, oppressive harness designed to protect a plantation-like economic model," sports attorney David Cornwell wrote recently in *SportsBusiness Journal*.

Q. Is change possible? Impossible?

Strip away all pretense and simply hand college players a paycheck? That not only won't fly philosophically in the NCAA, but it's also financially implausible, given the scores of programs that can't keep up with existing expenses.

Any proposal to limit salaries or bumped-up benefits to athletes in the revenue-generating sports of football and men's basketball almost certainly would meet legal resistance (and would scarcely be more affordable). 15

Emmert's predecessor, Myles Brand, briefly promoted the idea of adding $2,000–$3,000 to the value of scholarships to cover travel, laundry and other incidentals, which factor into the full cost of college attendance. But he was talked down by administrators and others in the trenches. A group of former athletes sought the same thing in a class-action suit that was settled in 2008, in part by widening access to supplemental funds.

The NCAA has moved on a few fronts, beefing up those supplemental funds—which athletes can tap for individual needs—and allowing them to borrow against future earnings for insurance against career-ending injury. In perhaps its most startling departure from tradition, athletes are allowed to compete as pros in one sport and maintain college eligibility in another. For example, North Carolina State quarterback Russell Wilson can be a minor league baseball player for the Colorado Rockies but still play for the Wolfpack football team.

Q. That's it, then?

Eyes are on another class-action suit, filed by former Arizona State and Nebraska quarterback Sam Keller and others claiming the NCAA and its video-game partner, EA Sports, have gone too far in using the likenesses of college players who are barred from sharing in the games' profits.

A court could award multimillion-dollar damages or, more likely, the sides could reach a settlement. The NCAA could be compelled to tighten the use of athletes' likenesses. But it's a good bet it won't move toward annually compensating them.

Interestingly, Emmert muses on change in another area. At a time when players' brushes with agents are drawing sanctions and attention, he questions the extent to which they're restricted from exploring pro careers.

"You want to be an accountant? Fine, we're going to introduce you to every accounting firm we can. We're going to bring in accountants to talk to you. You're going to get a summer internship," he said. "Say you want to be a Major League Baseball player, and you're toast. We don't let you talk to anybody.

"I think there's some part of that we've got to fix."

Questions

1. Does Steve Weiberg have a bias? If so, how can you tell? What do you think his view on compensation for college athletes is?
2. Why do you think Weiberg used a Q&A format? Do you think it's effective even though this isn't really an interview? Explain your response.
3. What is your opinion about the NCAA reforms, such as making funds available for players to buy insurance against a career-ending injury or allowing them to be professional in one sport and amateur in another?

7. *Why Students Aren't Paid to Play*

NATIONAL COLLEGIATE ATHLETIC ASSOCIATION

The following is from the NCAA's Web site, found under the heading "Key Issues."

Student-athletes are students first and athletes second. They are not university employees who are paid for their labor.

The benefits of the student-athlete experience are many. Student-athletes graduate at a higher rate than the general student body. Most do so while playing the sport they love and preparing for a future as a professional in something other than sports. Many receive athletics grants-in-aid that can be worth more than $100,000. NCAA studies show that student-athletes enjoy high levels of engagement in academics, athletics and community; have positive feelings about their overall athletics and academic experiences; attribute learning invaluable life skills to being a student-athlete; and are more likely to earn similar or higher wages after college than non-student-athletes.

Critics argue that student-athletes generate large amounts of money for the institution and therefore should be compensated. That argument ignores the fact that intercollegiate athletics programs are necessarily composed of many sports, many of which generate significant expenses over revenues. Only about two dozen programs nationally, all of them large Division I programs, actually yield revenues over expenses after the bills are paid. The remainder rely to varying degrees on institutional financial support.

Some pay-for-play advocates suggest eliminating nonrevenue sports and paying football and men's basketball players because of the perceived profitability of those sports. In fact, however, only 30 percent of Division I football and 26 percent of Division I men's basketball programs post revenues over expenses.

Likewise, almost all NCAA championships "lose money." However, overall   5
NCAA revenue, primarily derived from the Association's media agreements and the popularity of the Division I Men's Basketball Championship, helps 400,000 student-athletes at more than 1,000 member institutions learn and compete in 23 sports and 88 national championships.

Questions

1. What is the gist of the NCAA's policy?
2. What is the tone of this statement?
3. Are you convinced by the examples the statement provides? Explain your answer.

Making Connections

1. According to Steve Weiberg, the NCAA has begun to allow college athletes to compete in one sport as professionals and maintain college eligibility in another. What do you think Frank Deford, Michael Lewis, or Michael Wilbon would think of that reform?

2. Besides the basic issue of pay for college athletes, what underlying issues separate Wilbon and Bill Walton?

3. Do you think Lewis is one of the "pay-for-play advocates [who] suggest[s] eliminating nonrevenue sports and paying football and men's basketball players because of the perceived profitability of those sports" that the NCAA refers to in its statement? Explain your answer, citing evidence from Lewis's essay.

4. Wilbon reports that a head coach at a Division I school told him that "big-time athletic leagues and their big-time programs are '. . . fully engaged in robbing the poor to give to the rich'" (para. 6). How would Walton or the NCAA respond to that allegation?

5. Wilbon also reports on several Heisman Trophy winners who behaved badly after their careers ended, noting that none of them forfeited their titles as Reggie Bush was required to do after an NCAA investigation revealed that he had received improper benefits while playing football for the University of Southern California. How does that square with the NCAA's assertion about the benefits of sports for student athletes?

6. Jay Bilas, a lawyer and sports analyst for ESPN.com, says, "I don't believe college athletes should be paid as employees. Rather, I believe barriers should be removed that limit an athlete from receiving fair compensation for his or her image and likeness. There is no legitimate reason why a college athlete should be denied the opportunity to enter into legitimate, legally binding contracts to, among other things, hire an agent, do paid appearances, appear in advertisements, endorse shoes and apparel or otherwise profit from their [*sic*] names and likenesses. It would not sink college sports, substantially limit the NCAA's massive television profits or negatively affect the education of the athletes or any other student. It would simply be fair." How would the NCAA respond to Bilas? What might Walton say?

Entering the Conversation

As you respond to each of the following prompts, support your argument with references to at least three of the sources in this Conversation on paying college athletes. For help using sources, see Chapter 4.

1. Write an essay explaining why college athletes should or should not be paid. Be sure to consider athletes who participate in sports that are not revenue producing.

2. What is your solution? Write an essay in which you propose a system in which college athletes would be fairly compensated for the commitment they make to the athletic programs at their colleges and universities.

3. Dr. Boyce Watkins, a blogger on *Huffington Post*, wrote:

With March Madness upon us, perhaps it's time to think about what it means to be an American. We should also reconsider what it means to be a college student. As it stands, the 700-plus men and women signed on to play in the largest post-season extravaganza in professional sports (wait, did I say "professional"?) are treated neither as Americans nor as college students. Instead, they are expected to exist in a peculiar socio-economic purgatory created by March Madness that we might call pseudo-amateurism.

In pseudo-amateurism, you get to live the lifestyle of a professional: your schedule is rigorously controlled like an animal at the zoo. You are given massive amounts of media training so you can protect your brand in the public eye. You are expected to practice several times per day, and even on weekends. Oh, and that academic thing? You can do that too, as long as it doesn't interfere with your full-time job.

Write an essay in which you support, challenge, or qualify Watkins's definition of "pseudo-amateurism."

4. In a scene from the cartoon *South Park*, called "Stu-dent ATH-O-LEETS," Eric T. Cartman is a representative of a "prestigious institution." He asks a university president how he gets away with not paying his "slaves." Watch the clip online, and write an essay in which you imagine a roundtable discussion of it with the authors of the texts in this Conversation.

Student Writing
Rhetorical Analysis: Comparing Strategies

Following is a prompt that asks the writer to compare two passages describing similar events:

> Read William Faulkner's "An Innocent at Rinkside" (p. 619) and Lars Anderson's "The Sound and the Glory" from *Sports Illustrated*. Both recount the writers' first experiences at particular sporting events. Then write an essay in which you compare and contrast how each writer describes the event and conveys its effect on the writer as an observer.

Daniela Suarez, an eleventh-grade AP student, has written a response to this prompt. As you read her essay, consider the approach she takes in her comparison. Then answer the questions that follow about how she organized and developed it.

The following article appeared in *Sports Illustrated* on April 14, 2011.

The Sound and the Glory

Lars Anderson

You never forget your first time. Mine was in 2003, but it could have been five minutes ago, the way it still lives and rises in my memory. On that last Sunday in May eight years ago in Indianapolis, I drove my rental car through the predawn darkness to the corner of 16th and Georgetown, which, to the true race fan, is the nexus of the universe. By 7 A.M. a crush of humanity had already gathered in the shadow of the grandstands of the Brickyard, the sense of anticipation crackling in the cool morning air like an electrical current.

A few hours later I rolled through the tunnel between Turns 1 and 2, parked in the speedway's infield and made my way to pit road to cover the race for *SI*. Once the command to start your engines was issued, I immediately felt the roar of horsepower *thump, thump, thump* in my chest. This was a far different feeling than one experiences when the stock cars of NASCAR fire their engines. This was more penetrating, more powerful, more soul-rattling, like standing on an aircraft carrier next to a fighter jet that is about to blast off.

After three warmup laps the green flag waved. With 300,000 fans yelling in full throat — the Indy 500 is still the largest single-day sporting event every year in America — the field of open-wheel cars flew along the front-stretch at 225 mph, barreling through the canyon of fans, over the red bricks at the start-finish line, past the 153-foot-tall Pagoda tower. I always take a mental snapshot of this first-lap moment because it's the most picturesque scene in motor sports, the equivalent of a Van Gogh still life for those addicted to speed.

Just then, your senses are overwhelmed. There's the high pitch of the engines, the raw speed of the cars, the smell of burning rubber and — never forget — the specter of danger. The assault on your senses is all-encompassing, unmatched in motor sports, and it's precisely why the Indianapolis 500 is my favorite race of the year. Actually, it's more than that: Indy is my favorite *sporting event* of the year. "You have to come to the track and feel the power of the cars and smell the fuel to really appreciate what makes Indy so special," says Danica Patrick, who ran in her first Indy 500 in 2005. "I tell people, 'If you come, you'll be hooked for life.' And I've never been proven wrong."

Even NASCAR drivers such as Robby Gordon, Juan Pablo Montoya and Tony Stewart who have raced in the Indy 500 will say that it's the world's greatest race. Stewart is from Columbus, Ind., and he first

5

journeyed to the Brickyard at age five. Riding 45 minutes on a bus with his father, Nelson, before the sun had risen over the cornfields, Stewart slept in the luggage rack. When the bus got to the track, he was dazzled. "The speed and power . . . ," Stewart recalls. "It took me about a minute to realize I wanted to race there one day."

Stewart, like so many Indiana kids, can tell you the history of Indy by rote. The track was built in 1909 to serve as a testing facility for the automobile industry and given long straightaways and gradual turns to allow the vehicles to achieve and sustain top speeds. The surface was rough — too rough. In the first week of automobile races one driver, two riding mechanics and two spectators were killed; jagged rocks could puncture tires and cause drivers to lose control. The track was resurfaced with bricks, which were carried onto the grounds by horse and cart and would remain part of the speedway's surface until 1961, when it was repaved with asphalt over all but a three-foot strip at the start-finish line.

"It's the history that makes Indy so special," says Sam Hornish Jr., a native of Defiance, Ohio. "So many great stories."

The story of Indy, in a lot of ways, mirrors the story of America. For 100 years it has been a bastion of innovation, a place where the best and brightest in motor sports have tested new theories, new concepts. What has been developed at Indianapolis Motor Speedway? Turbo engines, energy-deflecting cockpits, aerodynamic downforce and, perhaps most significant, the SAFER barrier wall, which debuted at the speedway in 2002 and is now a fixture at every major racetrack. In short, the innovation that Indy has fostered has been the driving force behind the evolution of motor sports around the globe.

The Indy 500 has also become a cultural touchstone. To generations of fans it has been America's Roman Colosseum — with an infield so vast that Vatican City, Yankee Stadium, Churchill Downs, the Rose Bowl, the grounds at Wimbledon and the Colosseum could all fit inside at the same time. Indy is a track where danger and death lurk around every turn; a race where, if he or she has enough guts and guile, even the most unlikely underdog can walk away with the big trophy. Just ask Graham Hill, who in 1966 narrowly avoided a 16-car pileup on the first lap to win. Or ask Hornish Jr., who in 2006 made a dramatic late charge and on the last lap passed Marco Andretti to take the second-closest 500 ever (.0635 of a second). It's also where the greats have flourished, where A.J. Foyt, Al Unser and Rick Mears built and burnished their legacies. All of this is why after 100 years our eyes are still drawn to the Indy 500, truly the Greatest Spectacle in Racing.

Rituals have developed at Indy, from Jim Nabors singing *Back Home Again in Indiana* before each race, which he first did in 1972, to the winner

10

swigging milk in Victory Lane (thanks to Louis Meyer in the '30s). Indy's timelessness can make race weekend feel like a county fair. "It's not just the traditions that make the 500 the best race," Foyt told me a few years ago. "It's also that once the race starts, you have the best drivers in the planet going at it for 500 miles driving the best cars. As opposed to NASCAR, we can actually pass. On the last Sunday in May there's nowhere else in the world I'd rather be."

Me neither. Because once you head through the tunnel to the infield, you're overcome with one feeling, a feeling that sums up the allure of Indy: Anything is possible.

Rhetorical Analysis of Paired Texts

Daniela Suarez

In "An Innocent at Rinkside" and "The Sound and the Glory," William Faulkner and Lars Anderson recall their first time at a big sporting event as if it were a wondrous tale of mystic glory. They turn back the dial to the earlier days of their lives and take the reader on a voyage across a hockey rink and the Indy 500 race track so that we can almost feel the shrill of the wind and the excitement vibrating through every spectator's bones. These articles convey the significance of the two sporting events through the authors' creation of vivid images, their peculiar writing structure, and their ability to involve larger ideas.

Indeed, throughout both of these passages, Faulkner and Anderson manage to create a completely different universe in the mind of the reader. They both begin by using strong adjectives to describe seemingly pointless details. For instance, Faulkner refers to motion and speed as being "discorded and inconsequent, bizarre and paradoxical." Such terms are not what would usually come to mind when watching a hockey match and thus they contribute to the originality of the setting. Furthermore, he refers to the movements of players as "fluid [. . .] fast [. . .] effortless" and then even compares them to the "passionate glittering fatal alien quality of snakes." Such intense metaphors incite a feeling of fear or anxiety; therefore Faulkner seems to have accomplished his first initiative, which was to arouse emotions inside us readers as well. In the same way, Anderson characterizes the sound of the racecar's engine as "penetrating [. . .] powerful [. . .] soul-rattling," which may seem dramatic at first but ultimately succeeds in transferring his own feelings to the reader. Both authors also rely extensively on similes: for example, when Faulkner says that the player Geoffrion was "like an agile ruthless precocious boy" or when Anderson says that he could feel the horsepower of the cars' engines "like standing on an aircraft carrier next to a fighter jet that is about to blast off." By creating these comparisons the authors create a link between concrete elements, such as the ice or the cars, to something more abstract and more personal. Nonetheless, their language is also very precise and even scientific. For instance, Faulkner refers to the hockey puck as a "catalyst" and violence as a "byproduct," while Anderson states that his anticipation was "crackling in the cool morning air like an electrical current." Such descriptions are very concise and leave little room for interpretation, which leads us to believe that while Faulkner and Anderson wanted readers to feel emotions for themselves, they also wanted to establish their own very clear impressions.

On the other hand, Faulkner and Anderson also organize their pieces in a very unique manner. In fact, both of them begin by telling a story, and the narrative voice not only attracts the audience, but also creates a sense of proximity and trust. Both authors are also very precise in terms of timing. Faulkner, for instance, gives indications such as "a few minutes ago," "but not for long," and "then." Anderson also uses temporal cues such as "five minutes ago" and "a few hours later." In this way, the sequence of events appears almost like a movie before our eyes, with one event following the other chronologically with smooth transitions in between. In terms of syntax, these authors also have a similar style; they both begin their paragraphs with short declarative sentences. Indeed, every new idea is thrown directly at us and the authors waste no time perfecting their thoughts. On the contrary, their emotions are raw yet perfect, just like the simple beauty of a hockey match or a car race. Unlike Anderson, Faulkner also seems to ensure his sense of authority when he begins his fourth paragraph with "Excitement," thus putting himself in a position where he can define the term himself. In either case, these elements help create the authors' strong voices, which are proof not only of their utter passion for the subject, but also of their desire to utterly express their feelings.

Finally, Faulkner and Anderson both find a way to relate their personal experiences to the bigger picture of the whole world. Indeed, throughout these articles we witness a transition from personal and more intimate thoughts and feelings to a larger scope of importance. Faulkner begins by relating the ice to the "Christmas store window" or the "kaleidoscopic whirl like a child's toy," or even "the frantic darting of the weightless bugs," simple things we have all witnessed. Anderson deepens this personal side of the story, as he remembers driving his rental car "[o]n that last Sunday in May [. . .] through the predawn darkness to the corner of 16th and Georgetown." In Anderson's case, he mostly restates tiny details which show his relation to the events, but also uses terms such as "*that* last Sunday," just like Faulkner says "*the* innocent" in order to evoke a sense of mystery and vagueness; these imply that the author doesn't need to add more specifics since the facts remain purely alive in his mind. Nevertheless, both authors slowly begin to separate themselves from their own memories and enter the realm of the whole world. Indeed, Faulkner begins his appeal to a wider audience by stating, "We—Americans." He is no longer referring to his relatives or even people at the game but to any American like himself. In the same way, Anderson enlarges his scope by claiming, "The story of Indy, in a lot of ways, mirrors the story of America." Furthermore, both provide a light critique of society in the greater meaning of their own story. Faulkner criticizes this "new era" of sports, where they are no longer for fun, but have instead become like an artificial way for people to gain that "adrenalic discharge of vicarious excitement" in places "beneath lights" and with "spectator tobacco" trapped above their heads. On the contrary, Anderson highlights the more positive aspects of his sport by reminding us that the Indy race track has been a "bastion of innovation." Indeed, innovations such as "turbo engines, energy-deflecting cockpits, aerodynamic downforce and [. . .] the SAFER barrier wall" were born here. Therefore the track, just like the hockey ring, slowly switches from the authors' hearts to the screen of the world, available to us all.

William Faulkner and Lars Anderson both paint a canvas with their words as they look back into their memories and remember their first experiences at these different sporting events. Whether alongside an ice rink or in the midst of engine smoke, these authors manage to convince us of the importance of these seemingly simple events. They paint full landscapes, complete with sounds and smells, and pull us into their minds so we can feel what they felt on that one, special day.

Questions

1. What is your evaluation of Daniela Suarez's thesis statement? How might it be improved?
2. Would Daniela's essay have benefited from more examples? What other examples could she have used to highlight the differences between the two accounts? What examples would have highlighted the similarities?
3. Write a new conclusion to Daniela's essay that comments on the two pieces as examples of sportswriting.
4. What could Daniela have done by noting that the title of Anderson's piece — "The Sound and the Glory" — is an allusion to the title of one of Faulkner's novels, *The Sound and the Fury*?

Grammar as Rhetoric and Style
Direct, Precise, and Active Verbs

Direct, precise, active verbs energize writing. Consider this sentence with verbs in bold from "The Four Horsemen" by Grantland Rice (p. 610):

> Yesterday the cyclone **struck** again as Notre Dame **beat** the Army, 13 to 7, with a set of backfield stars that **ripped** and **crashed** though a strong Army defense with more speed and power than the warring cadets could **meet**.

The verbs in Rice's sentence re-create the high energy of the game. The rhetorical effect of the first three verbs is to move the sentence forward with such vigor and clarity that they vividly convey the force that overcame the strong Army defense. In addition, the verbs contribute to the highly energetic tone of the piece; in fact, they are a hallmark of Rice's extravagant, even hyperbolic, style.

Now consider another passage, this one from "The Silent Season of a Hero" by Gay Talese (p. 592), with its verbs, verb phrases, and verbals (adjectives made from verbs) in bold type:

> He **watched** until she **left**, **lost** in the crowd of the newly **arrived** tourists that **had** just **come** down the hill by cable car. Then he **sat** down again at the table in the restaurant, **finishing** his tea and **lighting** another cigarette, his fifth in the last half hour. It **was** 11:30 in the morning. None of the other tables **was occupied**, and the only sounds **came** from the bar, where a liquor salesman **was laughing** at something the headwaiter **had said**. But then the salesman, his briefcase under his arm, **headed** for the door, **stopping** briefly to **peek** into the dining room and **call** out, "See you later, Joe." Joe DiMaggio **turned** and **waved** at the salesman. Then the room **was** quiet again.

Talese uses the action verbs, verb phrases, and verbals to give you a sense of the scene's movement and drama. Yet the two shortest sentences — both emphasizing silence and stasis rather than movement — rely on the linking verb *was*.

Once you've learned to recognize effective verbs in your reading, you'll become more aware of them in your own writing. You may find yourself working on the verbs in revisions rather than first drafts, but here are some suggestions for making even your first draft active and precise.

Direct Verbs

Use forms of *to be* and other linking verbs sparingly and with a specific reason. Often you can change a form of *to be* followed by a predicate adjective or a predicate noun (also called nominalization, see p. 781) into an action verb. Consider how the second sentence in each pair below sports a stronger verb than the first:

> In England itself, whose shining empire seemed to be a testament to the imperial destiny of the Anglo-Saxon race, the fears for the inferiority of the nation's fighting men had some empirical basis.

> In England itself, whose shining empire seemed to testify to the imperial destiny of the Anglo-Saxon race, the fears for the inferiority of the nation's fighting men had some empirical basis.

> — CAROLINE ALEXANDER

If you're Henry Fonda's son and you want to be an actor, you get to be an actor.

If you're Henry Fonda's son and you want to act, you get to act.

— RICK REILLY

If you're Chelsea Clinton and want to be in government, you get to be in government.

If you're Chelsea Clinton and want to govern, you get to govern.

— RICK REILLY

Precise Verbs

While there is nothing wrong with the verbs walks and looks in the first sentence that follows, consider the precision of the verbs in the second sentence.

As Emily walks onto the floor in her green-and-gold uniform, she looks for me.

As Emily bounces onto the floor in her green-and-gold uniform, her eyes scan the crowd to meet mine.

— KRIS VERVAECKE

Similarly, in the first sentence that follows, looking forward to is a perfectly serviceable verb — until you compare it with the more precise verb that the writer selects.

There must have been little boys in that throng too, frantic with the slow excruciating passage of time, looking forward to the hour when they would be Richard or Geoffrion or Laparade. . . .

There must have been little boys in that throng too, frantic with the slow excruciating passage of time, panting for the hour when they would be Richard or Geoffrion or Laprade. . . .

— WILLIAM FAULKNER

Active Verbs

In addition to selecting a verb that is direct and creates a precise image, use verbs in the active voice — with an easy-to-picture subject doing something — unless you have a specific purpose for using the passive voice, where the subject is acted upon. Here, for example, in the final part of a sentence from "The Silent Season of a Hero," Gay Talese makes good use of the passive voice (p. 593, para. 10):

> Zio Pepe was among those who cheered when Joe DiMaggio returned to San Francisco after his first season with the New York Yankees and was carried along the wharf on the shoulders of the fishermen.

In this sentence, DiMaggio is acted upon by the fishermen. Why? Perhaps because Talese wanted *DiMaggio* to remain as the subject instead of switching away from *DiMaggio* and making *the fishermen* the subject.

By and large, though, strong writers stick with the active voice, as Talese does in the following passage (p. 598, para. 54):

> In the forty-first game [of 1941] . . . DiMaggio tied an American League record that George Sisler had set in 1922.

Talese could have cast that sentence in the passive voice, as follows:

> In the forty-first game . . . an American League record that had been set by George Sisler in 1922 was tied by DiMaggio.

As is often the case, the use of passive voice in this example makes for a wordy sentence that is hard to follow.

• EXERCISE 1 •

Improve the following sentences by replacing one or more verbs in each with a more effective verb — that is, a more vivid, precise, and active verb.

1. My first college visit will always be remembered by me.
2. There are many technological advances available to make our lives easier.
3. In the middle of the night, sirens could be heard.
4. It was not very long before she regretted buying the expensive handbag.
5. The Graham technique is little esteemed by modern dancers today.
6. The college advisor said she could not make a suggestion about which school to apply to because she didn't know his SAT scores.
7. The team captain is responsible for scheduling practices and communicating with team members.
8. A decision was reached by the arbitration panel.

9. The local sheriff gave a warning to the college students about walking around with open containers.

10. The chief of surgery took the opportunity to thank the volunteers.

11. Do your children have fears about going away to camp?

12. Antigone was very protective of Oedipus in *Oedipus at Colonus*.

• EXERCISE 2 •

Identify the verbs and verbals in the following passages. Discuss how these verbs affect the tone of the passages.

His vets warned us all along that the odds were against him, but we didn't really believe them. They had hope, too. How could a horse who appeared so full of life break his leg and be so suddenly close to death? His head was fine. His back was fine. His lungs and heart and chest were fine. In fact, after a while, his broken leg was fairly fine. It was another leg that was so worrisome, since the weight of his body constantly bearing down on the delicate structures inside his foot eventually damaged and destroyed them.

— JANE SMILEY, "Barbaro, The Heart in the Winner's Circle"

She maintains her composure until we get in the car, then crumples in humiliation. Once we're on the highway, forty miles to home, freezing rain coats our windows, but I can't see well enough to find a safe place to pull off. I drive with trepidation over the slippery road, through the foggy darkness, while Emily cries so hard it sounds as though she will break apart. "Mommy, I'm such a failure!" she weeps. At first my attempts to comfort her only increase her misery, so I shut up. I'm left to listen and worry about the road and think my resentful thoughts. I remember all the years in elementary school when she was "benched" in the classroom — left to do bulletin boards for the teacher — because she'd already mastered what was being taught. I think about the studies that suggest that girls who compete in athletics are far less likely to drink or take drugs or become pregnant.

— KRIS VERVAECKE, "A Spectator's Notebook"

• EXERCISE 3 •

Analyze the verbs in the opening paragraph of "The Cruelest Sport" (p. 622). How would you describe the verbs Joyce Carol Oates uses? How do they mirror the subject she is writing about? Do the verbs she uses tip you off that this is a piece that is more complex and academic than usual for sports-writing? Cite specific examples to support your view.

> Professional boxing is the only major American sport whose primary, and often murderous, energies are not coyly deflected by such artifacts as balls and pucks. Though highly ritualized, and as rigidly bound by rules, traditions, and taboos as any religious ceremony, it survives as the most primitive and terrifying of contests: two men, near-naked, fight each other in a brightly lit, elevated space roped in like an animal pen (though the ropes were originally to keep rowdy spectators out); two men climb into the ring from which only one, symbolically, will climb out. (Draws do occur in boxing, but are rare, and unpopular.)

• EXERCISE 4 •

Count the verbs in one of the passages in Exercise 2. Then categorize them into linking verbs and more vivid action verbs, and calculate the ratio. Do the same for several paragraphs of your own writing. Are you relying more on linking verbs, or are most of your verbs direct and precise action verbs?

Suggestions for Writing
Sports

Now that you have examined a number of texts that focus on sports, explore this topic yourself by synthesizing your own ideas and the readings. You might want to do additional research or use readings from other classes as you write.

1. Sportswriter Bill Simmons has named his Web site Grantland.com, the logo of which contains Grantland Rice's famous line: "For when the One Great Scorer comes to mark against your name, He writes — not that you won or lost — but how you played the Game." Do you agree with Rice's philosophy? Do you think Bill Simmons does? Write an essay in which you support, challenge, or qualify this assertion.

2. "The Proper Place for Sports" by Theodore Roosevelt appears on page 617. Kathleen Dalton, a historian and high-school history teacher, subtitled her 2002 biography of Theodore Roosevelt, *The Strenuous Life*. In an interview, she explained that Roosevelt used that phrase to summarize his philosophy of life.

> He urged Americans to turn their backs on the soft, easy indoor life they had been leading and embrace the challenges of the twentieth century with a spirit of

adventure and courage. He praised physical activity—sports, mountain climbing, exploring, and fighting if necessary—and strenuous endeavor of all kinds, including building an empire and making America a major moral force in the world. He criticized spectators and urged them to participate in sports rather than merely watch them. He also argued that you could lead a strenuous life by working politically to make your country a better place or by writing a book or a poem or by being a caring mother who raised good kids.

Dalton added that the subtitle has a direct connection to Roosevelt's own life. That is, Roosevelt

followed his own advice and lived his own kind of rugged strenuous life. He threw himself completely into each new endeavor—wrestling, bronco busting, mountain climbing, chopping trees, or exploring a dangerous uncharted river. He also led a strenuous life of struggle by making a new man of himself again and again: he resisted illness and built a stronger body, he proved himself a true man by holding his own among western ranch hands and cowboys, he made himself a writer and reformer, and he made himself a leader and a political prophet without losing his sense of ethics.

Write about your own philosophy of life. In your essay, explain your thoughts on how to improve humankind, and examine the ways you have practiced what you preach.

3. Write an essay in which you discuss the connection between sports and character. Do you think that athletes should be role models? Develop your response with at least three examples—pro or con—of athletes mentioned in the readings in this chapter.

4. Working in groups, research the ways in which sports such as boxing, football, car racing, and soccer have made reforms to preserve the health and safety of their participants. Create a visual, such as a timeline or graph, that indicates the timing of the changes as well as their effectiveness. Show for which sport the change has been most effective and/or most radical.

5. Write an essay comparing the ways the media projects images of male and female athletes. Which images create more pressure to conform—images of male athletes or images of female athletes?

6. Write a personal narrative in which you describe the effect sports has had on your connection to family, community, or school. Has the experience been positive or negative?

7. Do some research on Title IX, the law that bans sex discrimination at schools receiving federal funds. What effect has this legislation had on participation in high school, college, and professional sports? Develop a thesis and then write

about it, supporting it with your research sources. Be sure to consider the law's effect on male and female role models.

8. The following excerpt is from George Orwell's essay "The Sporting Spirit," published in 1945:

> I am always amazed when I hear people saying that sport creates goodwill between nations, and that if only the common peoples of the world could meet one another at football or cricket, they would have no inclination to meet on the battlefield. Even if one didn't know from concrete examples (the 1936 Olympics, for instance) that international sporting contests lead to orgies of hatred, one could deduce it from general principles. . . . At the international level sport is frankly mimic warfare.

In an essay, agree or disagree with Orwell's view of sports.

9. Read *The Old Man and the Sea* by Ernest Hemingway. Write an essay discussing whether you think Joe DiMaggio would have been a good fishing companion for the old man.

Language

How does the language we use reveal who we are?

In many people's opinion, to call the link between language and culture sacred would not be exaggeration. The language of our birth, the language of the first words we speak to our parents or those closest to us, creates a powerful bond and shapes our perception of the world. Yet few of us are fully aware of the way our language influences others or the extent to which language is used to manipulate our emotions, our politics, and our decisions.

Although the United States is closely associated with English, its citizens speak a myriad of other languages. In many American cities, Spanish is as common as English, and some urban school districts have students who, collectively, speak more than a hundred languages. The writers we study these days, often the children of immigrants, tell of parents who speak not standard written English but rather "broken English," a term author Amy Tan analyzes in her essay "Mother Tongue." The way a person speaks can lead to stereotyped judgments about him or her and assumptions about economic class and even IQ. The selections in this chapter examine these issues and more. Should English be the official language of the United States, sanctioned and enforced by legislation? What is it like being an immigrant and living and learning in a "foreign" language?

The power of language adds another dimension to our discussion. Language has deep connections to our thoughts and beliefs. Whether it's an advertising campaign or an election campaign, whether people are telling you what to think or what not to say, language is a potent and powerful tool. In this chapter's Conversation, we explore how language can be used to manipulate, motivate, and even stifle.

In his essay "If Black English Isn't a Language, Then Tell Me What Is," African American writer James Baldwin writes: "It goes without saying, then, that language is also a political instrument, means, and proof of power. It is the most vivid and crucial key to identity: it reveals the private identity, and connects one with, or divorces one from, the larger, public, or communal identity." In this chapter, you will explore language as both "political instrument, means, and proof of power" and "key to identity."

Mother Tongue

Amy Tan

Best-selling author Amy Tan (b. 1952) has written several novels, including *The Joy Luck Club* (1989), *The Kitchen God's Wife* (1991), *The Bonesetter's Daughter* (2001), and *Saving Fish from Drowning* (2005). Known for her portrayal of mother-daughter relationships, Tan draws on her Chinese heritage to depict the clash of traditional Chinese culture with modern-day American customs. Tan grew up in California, has an MA in linguistics, and worked as a business writer before turning to fiction. She is a member of the Rock Bottom Remainders, a band—including Dave Barry and Stephen King—that plays for charity events. Tan collected many of her nonfiction writings in *The Opposite of Fate: A Book of Musings* (2003). Among these is "Mother Tongue," an essay in which Tan explores "all the Englishes" that are part of her identity.

I am not a scholar of English or literature. I cannot give you much more than personal opinions on the English language and its variations in this country or others.

I am a writer. And by that definition, I am someone who has always loved language. I am fascinated by language in daily life. I spend a great deal of my time thinking about the power of language — the way it can evoke an emotion, a visual image, a complex idea, or a simple truth. Language is the tool of my trade. And I use them all — all the Englishes I grew up with.

Recently, I was made keenly aware of the different Englishes I do use. I was giving a talk to a large group of people, the same talk I had already given to half a dozen other groups. The nature of the talk was about my writing, my life, and my book, *The Joy Luck Club*. The talk was going along well enough, until I remembered one major difference that made the whole talk sound wrong. My mother was in the room. And it was perhaps the first time she had heard me give a lengthy speech, using the kind of English I have never used with her. I was saying things like "The intersection of memory upon imagination" and "There is an aspect of my fiction that relates to thus-and-thus" — a speech filled with carefully wrought grammatical phrases, burdened, it suddenly seemed to me, with nominalized forms, past perfect tenses, conditional phrases, all the forms of standard English that I had learned in school and through books, the forms of English I did not use at home with my mother.

Just last week, I was walking down the street with my mother, and I again found myself conscious of the English I was using, the English I do use with her. We were talking about the price of new and used furniture and I heard myself saying this: "Not waste money that way." My husband was with us as well, and he didn't notice any switch in my English. And then I realized why. It's because over the twenty years we've been together I've often used that same kind of English with him, and sometimes he even uses it with me. It has become our language of intimacy, a different sort of English that relates to family talk, the language I grew up with.

So you'll have some idea of what this family talk I heard sounds like, I'll quote what my mother said during a recent conversation which I videotaped and then transcribed. During this conversation, my mother was talking about a political gangster in Shanghai who had the same last name as her family's, Du, and how the gangster in his early years wanted to be adopted by her family, which was rich by comparison. Later, the gangster became more powerful, far richer than my mother's family, and one day showed up at my mother's wedding to pay his respects. Here's what she said in part:

"Du Yusong having business like fruit stand. Like off the street kind. He is Du like Du Zong—but not Tsung-ming Island people. The local people call putong, the river east side, he belong to that side local people. That man want to ask Du Zong father take him in like become own family. Du Zong father wasn't look down on him, but didn't take seriously, until that man big like become a mafia. Now important person, very hard to inviting him. Chinese way, came only to show respect, don't stay for dinner. Respect for making big celebration, he shows up. Mean gives lots of respect. Chinese custom. Chinese social life that way. If too important won't have to stay too long. He come to my wedding. I didn't see, I heard it. I gone to boy's side, they have YMCA dinner. Chinese age I was nineteen."

You should know that my mother's expressive command of English belies how much she actually understands. She reads the *Forbes* report, listens to *Wall Street Week*, converses daily with her stockbroker, reads all of Shirley MacLaine's books with ease—all kinds of things I can't begin to understand. Yet some of my friends tell me they understand 50 percent of what my mother says. Some say they understand 80 to 90 percent. Some say they understand none of it, as if she were speaking pure Chinese. But to me, my mother's English is perfectly clear, perfectly natural. It's my mother tongue. Her language, as I hear it, is vivid, direct, full of observation and imagery. That was the language that helped shape the way I saw things, expressed things, made sense of the world.

Lately, I've been giving more thought to the kind of English my mother speaks. Like others, I have described it to people as "broken" or "fractured" English. But I wince when I say that. It has always bothered me that I can think of no other way to describe it other than "broken," as if it were damaged and needed to be fixed, as if it lacked a certain wholeness and soundness. I've heard other terms used, "limited English," for example. But they seem just as bad, as if everything is limited, including people's perceptions of the limited English speaker.

I know this for a fact, because when I was growing up, my mother's "limited" English limited *my* perception of her. I was ashamed of her English. I believed that her English reflected the quality of what she had to say. That is, because she expressed them imperfectly her thoughts were imperfect. And I had plenty of empirical evidence to support me: the fact that people in department stores, at banks, and at restaurants did not take her seriously, did not give her good service, pretended not to understand her, or even acted as if they did not hear her.

My mother has long realized the limitations of her English as well. When I 10 was fifteen, she used to have me call people on the phone to pretend I was she. In this guise, I was forced to ask for information or even to complain and yell at people who had been rude to her. One time it was a call to her stockbroker in New York. She had cashed out her small portfolio and it just so happened we were going to go to New York the next week, our very first trip outside California. I had to get on the phone and say in an adolescent voice that was not very convincing, "This is Mrs. Tan."

And my mother was standing in the back whispering loudly, "Why he don't send me check, already two weeks late. So mad he lie to me, losing me money."

And then I said in perfect English, "Yes, I'm getting rather concerned. You had agreed to send the check two weeks ago, but it hasn't arrived."

Then she began to talk more loudly. "What he want, I come to New York tell him front of his boss, you cheating me." And I was trying to calm her down, make her be quiet, while telling the stockbroker, "I can't tolerate any more excuses. If I don't receive the check immediately, I am going to have to speak to your manager when I'm in New York next week." And sure enough, the following week there we were in front of this astonished stockbroker, and I was sitting there red-faced and quiet, and my mother, the real Mrs. Tan, was shouting at his boss in her impeccable broken English.

We used a similar routine just five days ago, for a situation that was far less humorous. My mother had gone to the hospital for an appointment, to find out about a benign brain tumor a CAT scan had revealed a month ago. She said she had spoken very good English, her best English, no mistakes. Still, she said, the hospital did not apologize when they said they had lost the CAT scan and she had come for nothing. She said they did not seem to have any sympathy when she told them she was anxious to know the exact diagnosis, since her husband and son had both died of brain tumors. She said they would not give her any more information until the next time and she would have to make another appointment for that. So she said she would not leave until the doctor called her daughter. She wouldn't budge. And when the doctor finally called her daughter, me, who spoke in perfect English—lo and behold—we had assurances the CAT scan would be found, promises that a conference call on Monday would be held, and apologies for any suffering my mother had gone through for a most regrettable mistake.

I think my mother's English almost had an effect on limiting my possibilities 15 in life as well. Sociologists and linguists probably will tell you that a person's developing language skills are more influenced by peers. But I do think that the language spoken in the family, especially in immigrant families which are more insular, plays a large role in shaping the language of the child. And I believe that it affected my results on achievement tests, IQ tests, and the SAT. While my English skills were never judged as poor, compared to math, English could not be considered my strong suit. In grade school I did moderately well, getting perhaps B's, sometimes B-pluses, in English and scoring perhaps in the sixtieth or seventieth percentile on achievement tests. But those scores were not good enough to override the opinion that my true abilities lay in math and science, because in those areas I achieved A's and scored in the ninetieth percentile or higher.

This was understandable. Math is precise; there is only one correct answer. Whereas, for me at least, the answers on English tests were always a judgment call, a matter of opinion and personal experience. Those tests were constructed around items like fill-in-the-blank sentence completion, such as "Even though Tom was _____, Mary thought he was _____." And the correct answer always seemed to be the most bland combinations of thoughts, for example, "Even though Tom was shy, Mary thought he was charming," with the grammatical structure "even though" limiting the correct answer to some sort of semantic opposites, so you wouldn't get answers like, "Even though Tom was foolish, Mary thought he was ridiculous." Well, according to my mother, there were very few limitations as to what Tom could have been and what Mary might have thought of him. So I never did well on tests like that.

The same was true with word analogies, pairs of words in which you were supposed to find some sort of logical, semantic relationship—for example, "*Sunset* is to *nightfall* as _____ is to _____." And here you would be presented with a list of four possible pairs, one of which showed the same kind of relationship: *red* is to *stoplight, bus* is to *arrival, chills* is to *fever, yawn* is to *boring*. Well, I could never think that way. I knew what the tests were asking, but I could not block out of my mind the images already created by the first pair, "*sunset* is to *nightfall*"— and I would see a burst of colors against a darkening sky, the moon rising, the lowering of a curtain of stars. And all the other pairs of words—red, bus, stoplight, boring—just threw up a mass of confusing images, making it impossible for me to sort out something as logical as saying: "A sunset precedes nightfall" is the same as "a chill precedes a fever." The only way I would have gotten that answer right would have been to imagine an associative situation, for example, my being disobedient and staying out past sunset, catching a chill at night, which turns into feverish pneumonia as punishment, which indeed did happen to me.

I have been thinking about all this lately, about my mother's English, about achievement tests. Because lately I've been asked, as a writer, why there are not more Asian Americans represented in American literature. Why are there few Asian Americans enrolled in creative writing programs? Why do so many Chinese students go into engineering? Well, these are broad sociological questions I can't begin to answer. But I have noticed in surveys—in fact, just last week—that

Asian students, as a whole, always do significantly better on math achievement tests than in English. And this makes me think that there are other Asian-American students whose English spoken in the home might also be described as "broken" or "limited." And perhaps they also have teachers who are steering them away from writing and into math and science, which is what happened to me.

Fortunately, I happen to be rebellious in nature and enjoy the challenge of disproving assumptions made about me. I became an English-major my first year in college, after being enrolled as pre-med. I started writing nonfiction as a free-lancer the week after I was told by my former boss that writing was my worst skill and I should hone my talents toward account management.

But it wasn't until 1985 that I finally began to write fiction. And at first I wrote using what I thought to be wittily crafted sentences, sentences that would finally prove I had mastery over the English language. Here's an example from the first draft of a story that later made its way into *The Joy Luck Club*, but without this line: "That was my mental quandary in its nascent state." A terrible line, which I can barely pronounce.

Fortunately, for reasons I won't get into today, I later decided I should envision a reader for the stories I would write. And the reader I decided upon was my mother, because these were stories about mothers. So with this reader in mind—and in fact she did read my early drafts—I began to write stories using all the Englishes I grew up with: the English I spoke to my mother, which for lack of a better term might be described as "simple"; the English she used with me, which for lack of a better term might be described as "broken"; my translation of her Chinese, which could certainly be described as "watered down"; and what I imagined to be her translation of her Chinese if she could speak in perfect English, her internal language, and for that I sought to preserve the essence, but neither an English nor a Chinese structure. I wanted to capture what language ability tests can never reveal: her intent, her passion, her imagery, the rhythms of her speech, and the nature of her thoughts.

Apart from what any critic had to say about my writing, I knew I had succeeded where it counted when my mother finished reading my book and gave me her verdict: "So easy to read."

Questions for Discussion

1. How is Amy Tan's use of the phrase "mother tongue" ambiguous?
2. What does Tan mean by "the power of language" (para. 2)? What does that phrase mean to you?
3. What are the "different Englishes" (para. 3) Tan describes in this essay? How does each have its own type of power?
4. How would you describe Tan's attitude toward her mother?
5. What does Tan mean when she says, "I think my mother's English almost had an effect on limiting my possibilities in life as well" (para. 15)? To what extent do you

think that speaking a non-standardized English (through grammatical differences or an accent) "limits . . . possibilities" for people in the United States today?

6. What is the "associative situation" (para. 17) that Tan claims accounts for her high performance on math tests but not on English tests—specifically, analogies?

7. Why does Tan believe that envisioning a reader—specifically, her mother— enabled her to write more authentically?

8. What are some of the class and cultural distinctions that people encounter because of their inability to use standardized English, according to Tan?

Questions on Rhetoric and Style

1. Why does Tan open her essay by stating, "I am not a scholar of English or litera-ture" but then state, in the next paragraph, "I am a writer"? What is the difference? How does she establish ethos by this juxtaposition?

2. At several points in her essay, Tan relates anecdotes. How do they further her argu-ment? Be sure to consider the anecdotes regarding Tan giving a speech, the stock-broker, the CAT scan, and Tan's experience with the SATs. What would be the impact of omitting one of them?

3. What is Tan's strategy behind including a lengthy, direct quotation from her mother (para. 6) rather than paraphrasing what she said?

4. Tan criticizes herself twice in this essay. In paragraph 3, she quotes a speech she gave "filled with carefully wrought grammatical phrases, burdened, it suddenly seemed to me, with nominalized forms, past perfect tenses, conditional phrases. . . ." What are "nominalized forms, past perfect tenses, conditional phrases," and why are they burdensome? At another point, Tan recalls a draft of *The Joy Luck Club* in which she wrote, "That was my mental quandary in its nascent state" (para. 20). Why does she call this "[a] terrible line"?

5. Although Tan clearly appeals to pathos through personal narration and character-ization, she makes some appeals to logos. Identify them and describe their effect.

6. Tan divides the essay into three sections. Why? How do these resemble chapters?

7. How does Tan avoid stereotyping Asian Americans in general and Chinese in particular in this essay? If you believe she is guilty of some stereotyping, discuss examples.

8. Discuss how Tan broadens the essay's relevance by going beyond just her personal experience and raising issues that would be germane to her audience.

9. This essay was first published in *Threepenny Review*, which the novelist Jonathan Franzen has described as one of the "few magazines left in this country which seem pitched at the general literary reader and which consistently publish such interest-ing, high-quality criticism, reflection, argument, fiction, and poetry." How does Tan appeal to this audience of "general literary reader[s]"?

Suggestions for Writing

1. Tan focuses in this essay on the influence her mother's "broken English" has had on her formation as a writer. Yet the essay has enjoyed a long-lasting popularity that suggests it holds meaning for readers beyond those interested in the life and times of Amy Tan. Write an essay analyzing the rhetorical strategies Tan uses to give this piece broad appeal.

2. At the end of the essay, Tan says that she "began to write stories using all the Englishes I grew up with" (para. 21). Read Tan's short story "Two Kinds" or her novel *The Joy Luck Club*, and analyze where and how she uses different "Englishes."

3. Tan argues that her novelist's perception made it difficult for her to do well on SAT-type questions because they were too limiting. Write an essay in which you describe some skills or kinds of knowledge that you have that could not be assessed by a standardized test.

4. In this essay, Tan makes the following assertion: "Sociologists and linguists probably will tell you that a person's developing language skills are more influenced by peers. But I do think that the language spoken in the family, especially in immigrant families which are more insular, plays a large role in shaping the language of the child" (para. 15). Write an essay in which you argue whether you believe that a person's language is more influenced by peers than by family. Use evidence from your reading, personal experience, or observations to support your position.

5. Keep an observational journal for several days, noting the judgments people make on the basis of how a person speaks or writes. Consider your peers, a business environment, or the media. Then write an essay explaining the relationship you have observed between power and language. Does someone's facility with a language (or, in some contexts, with bilingualism) confer power? Did you observe situations where one's position of authority makes his or her language acceptable? Did you note anyone who "code-switched," or shifted his or her way of speaking to accommodate a different audience or community? Work your analysis of these observations into your essay.

Politics and the English Language

GEORGE ORWELL

George Orwell (1903–1950) is the pseudonym of Eric Arthur Blair, a writer who was the son of an English civil servant during the Raj, the British rule of India. Orwell was educated in England, but when financial constraints prevented him from attending university, he joined the imperial police in Burma, an experience immortalized in his famous essay "Shooting an Elephant." He returned to England five years later, but in 1928 he moved to Paris. There he took on a series of menial jobs, which he described in his first book, *Down and Out in Paris and London* (1933). Later Orwell worked as a schoolteacher, fought on the side of the republicans in the Spanish civil war, and began writing for magazines, often speaking out against economic injustice. He finally gained recognition and considerable financial success with his novels *Animal Farm* (1945) and *Nineteen Eighty-four* (1949). The term *Orwellian* came to describe mechanisms used by totalitarian governments to manipulate the populace in order to enforce conformity. In the following essay, which first appeared in *Horizon* in 1946, Orwell explores the impact of totalitarian thinking on language.

Most people who bother with the matter at all would admit that the English language is in a bad way, but it is generally assumed that we cannot by conscious action do anything about it. Our civilization is decadent and our language—so the argument runs—must inevitably share in the general collapse. It follows that any struggle against the abuse of language is a sentimental archaism, like preferring candles to electric light or hansom cabs to aeroplanes. Underneath this lies the half-conscious belief that language is a natural growth and not an instrument which we shape for our own purposes.

Now, it is clear that the decline of a language must ultimately have political and economic causes: it is not due simply to the bad influence of this or that individual writer. But an effect can become a cause, reinforcing the original cause and producing the same effect in an intensified form, and so on indefinitely. A man may take to drink because he feels himself to be a failure, and then fail all the more completely because he drinks. It is rather the same thing that is happening to the English language. It becomes ugly and inaccurate because our thoughts are foolish, but the slovenliness of our language makes it easier for us to have foolish thoughts. The point is that the process is reversible. Modern English, especially written English, is full of bad habits which spread by imitation and which can be avoided if one is willing to take the necessary trouble. If one gets rid of these habits one can think more clearly, and to think clearly is a necessary first step towards political regeneration: so that the fight against bad English is not frivolous and is not the exclusive concern of professional writers. I will come back to this presently, and I hope that by that time the meaning of what I have said here will have become clearer. Meanwhile, here are five specimens of the English language as it is now habitually written.

These five passages have not been picked out because they are especially bad—I could have quoted far worse if I had chosen—but because they illustrate various of the mental vices from which we now suffer. They are a little below the average, but are fairly representative samples. I number them so that I can refer back to them when necessary:

(1) I am not, indeed, sure whether it is not true to say that the Milton who once seemed not unlike a seventeenth-century Shelley had not become, out of an experience ever more bitter in each year, more alien [*sic*] to the founder of that Jesuit sect which nothing could induce him to tolerate.

— Professor Harold Laski (Essay in *Freedom of Expression*)

(2) Above all, we cannot play ducks and drakes with a native battery of idioms which prescribes such egregious collocations of vocables as the Basic *put up with* for *tolerate* or *put at a loss* for *bewilder*.

— Professor Lancelot Hogben (*Interglossa*)

(3) On the one side we have the free personality: by definition it is not neurotic, for it has neither conflict nor dream. Its desires, such as they are, are transparent, for they are just what institutional approval keeps in the forefront of consciousness; another institutional pattern would alter their number and intensity; there is little in them that is natural, irreducible, or culturally dangerous. But *on the other side*, the social bond itself is nothing but the mutual reflection of these self-secure integrities. Recall the definition of love. Is not this the very picture of a small academic? Where is there a place in this hall of mirrors for either personality or fraternity?

— Essay on psychology in *Politics* (New York)

(4) All the "best people" from the gentlemen's clubs, and all the frantic fascist captains, united in common hatred of Socialism and bestial horror of the rising tide of the mass revolutionary movement, have turned to acts of provocation, to foul incendiarism, to medieval legends of poisoned wells, to legalize their own destruction of proletarian organizations, and rouse the agitated petty-bourgeoisie to chauvinistic fervor on behalf of the fight against the revolutionary way out of the crisis.

— Communist pamphlet

(5) If a new spirit *is* to be infused into this old country, there is one thorny and contentious reform which must be tackled, and that is the humanization and galvanization of the B.B.C. Timidity here will bespeak canker and atrophy of the soul. The heart of Britain may be sound and of strong beat, for instance, but the British lion's roar at present is like that of Bottom in Shakespeare's *Midsummer Night's Dream*— as gentle as any sucking dove. A virile new Britain cannot continue indefinitely to be traduced in the eyes, or rather ears, of the world by the effete languors of Langham Place, brazenly masquerading as "standard English." When the Voice of Britain is

heard at nine o'clock, better far and infinitely less ludicrous to hear aitches honestly dropped than the present priggish, inflated, inhibited, school-ma'amish arch braying of blameless bashful mewing maidens!

—Letter in *Tribune*

Each of these passages has faults of its own, but, quite apart from avoidable ugliness, two qualities are common to all of them. The first is staleness of imagery; the other is lack of precision. The writer either had a meaning and cannot express it, or he inadvertently says something else, or he is almost indifferent as to whether his words mean anything or not. This mixture of vagueness and sheer incompetence is the most marked characteristic of modern English prose, and especially of any kind of political writing. As soon as certain topics are raised, the concrete melts into the abstract and no one seems able to think of terms of speech that are not hackneyed: prose consists less and less of *words* chosen for the sake of their meaning, and more and more of *phrases* tacked together like the sections of a prefabricated henhouse. I list below, with notes and examples, various of the tricks by means of which the work of prose-construction is habitually dodged:

Dying Metaphors

A newly invented metaphor assists thought by evoking a visual image, while on   5 the other hand a metaphor which is technically "dead" (e.g., *iron resolution*) has in effect reverted to being an ordinary word and can generally be used without loss of vividness. But in between these two classes there is a huge dump of worn-out metaphors which have lost all evocative power and are merely used because they save people the trouble of inventing phrases for themselves. Examples are: *Ring the changes on, take up the cudgels for, toe the line, ride roughshod over, stand shoulder to shoulder with, play into the hands of, no axe to grind, grist to the mill, fishing in troubled waters, rift within the lute, on the order of the day, Achilles' heel, swan song, hotbed.* Many of these are used without knowledge of their meaning (what is a "rift," for instance?), and incompatible metaphors are frequently mixed, a sure sign that the writer is not interested in what he is saying. Some metaphors now current have been twisted out of their original meaning without those who use them even being aware of the fact. For example, *toe the line* is sometimes written *tow the line.* Another example is *the hammer and the anvil*, now always used with the implication that the anvil gets the worst of it. In real life it is always the anvil that breaks the hammer, never the other way about: a writer who stopped to think what he was saying would be aware of this, and would avoid perverting the original phrase.

Operators or Verbal False Limbs

These save the trouble of picking out appropriate verbs and nouns, and at the same time pad each sentence with extra syllables which give it an appearance of symmetry. Characteristic phrases are *render inoperative, militate against, make contact with, be subjected to, give rise to, give grounds for, have the effect of, play a leading part (role) in, make itself felt, take effect, exhibit a tendency to, serve the purpose of, etc., etc.* The keynote is, the elimination of simple verbs. Instead of being a single word, such as *break, stop, spoil, mend, kill,* a verb becomes a *phrase,* made up of a noun or adjective tacked on to some general-purposes verb such as *prove, serve, form, play, render.* In addition, the passive voice is wherever possible used in preference to the active, and noun constructions are used instead of gerunds (*by examination of* instead of *by examining*). The range of verbs is further cut down by means of the *-ize* and *de-* formations, and the banal statements are given an appearance of profundity by means of the *not un-* formation. Simple conjunctions and prepositions are replaced by such phrases as *with respect to, having regard to, the fact that, by dint of, in view of, in the interests of, on the hypothesis that;* and the ends of sentences are saved from anticlimax by such resounding commonplaces as *greatly to be desired, cannot be left out of account, a development to be expected in the near future, deserving of serious consideration, brought to a satisfactory conclusion,* and so on and so forth.

Pretentious Diction

Words like *phenomenon, element, individual* (as noun), *objective, categorical, effective, virtual, basic, primary, promote, constitute, exhibit, exploit, utilize, eliminate, liquidate* are used to dress up simple statements and give an air of scientific impartiality to biased judgments. Adjectives like *epoch-making, epic, historic, unforgettable, triumphant, age-old, inevitable, inexorable, veritable* are used to dignify the sordid processes of international politics, while writing that aims at glorifying war usually takes on an archaic color, its characteristic words being: *realm, throne, chariot, mailed fist, trident, sword, shield, buckler, banner, jackboot, clarion.* Foreign words and expressions such as *cul de sac, ancien régime, deus ex machina, mutatis mutandis, status quo, Gleichschaltung, Weltanschauung* are used to give an air of culture and elegance. Except for the useful abbreviations *i.e., e.g.,* and *etc.,* there is no real need for any of the hundreds of foreign phrases now current in English. Bad writers, and especially scientific, political and sociological writers, are nearly always haunted by the notion that Latin or Greek words are grander than Saxon ones, and unnecessary words like *expedite, ameliorate, predict, extraneous, deracinated, clandestine, subaqueous* and hundreds of others constantly gain ground from their Anglo-Saxon opposite numbers.[1] The jargon peculiar to

---

[1]An interesting illustration of this is the way in which the English flower names which were in use till very recently are being ousted by Greek ones, *snapdragon* becoming *antirrhinum, forget-me-not* becoming *myosotis,* etc. It is hard to see any practical reason for this change of fashion: it is probably due to an instinctive turning-away from the more homely word and a vague feeling that the Greek word is scientific.

Marxist writing (*hyena, hangman, cannibal, petty bourgeois, these gentry, lacquey, flunkey, mad dog, White Guard*, etc.) consists largely of words and phrases translated from Russian, German or French; but the normal way of coining a new word is to use a Latin or Greek root with the appropriate affix and, where necessary, the *-ize* formation. It is often easier to make up words of this kind (*deregionalize, impermissible, extramarital, non-fragmentary* and so forth) than to think up the English words that will cover one's meaning. The result, in general, is an increase in slovenliness and vagueness.

Meaningless Words

In certain kinds of writing, particularly in art criticism and literary criticism, it is normal to come across long passages which are almost completely lacking in meaning.[2] Words like *romantic, plastic, values, human, dead, sentimental, natural, vitality*, as used in art criticism, are strictly meaningless, in the sense that they not only do not point to any discoverable object, but are hardly ever expected to do so by the reader. When one critic writes, "The outstanding feature of Mr. X's work is its living quality," while another writes, "The immediately striking thing about Mr. X's work is its peculiar deadness," the reader accepts this as a simple difference of opinion. If words like *black* and *white* were involved, instead of the jargon words *dead* and *living*, he would see at once that language was being used in an improper way. Many political words are similarly abused. The word *Fascism* has now no meaning except in so far as it signifies "something not desirable." The words *democracy, socialism, freedom, patriotic, realistic, justice* have each of them several different meanings which cannot be reconciled with one another. In the case of a word like *democracy*, not only is there no agreed definition, but the attempt to make one is resisted from all sides. It is almost universally felt that when we call a country democratic we are praising it: consequently the defenders of every kind of régime claim that it is a democracy, and fear that they might have to stop using the word if it were tied down to any one meaning. Words of this kind are often used in a consciously dishonest way. That is, the person who uses them has his own private definition, but allows his hearer to think he means something quite different. Statements like *Marshal Pétain[3] was a true patriot, The Soviet Press is the freest in the world, The Catholic Church is opposed to persecution* are almost always made with intent to deceive. Other words used in variable

---

[2]Example: "Comfort's catholicity of perception and image, strangely Whitmanesque in range, almost the exact opposite in aesthetic compulsion, continues to evoke that trembling atmospheric accumulative hinting at a cruel, an inexorably serene timelessness. . . . Wrey Gardiner scores by aiming at simple bull's-eyes with precision. Only they are not so simple, and through this contented sadness runs more than the surface bitter-sweet of resignation."

[3]Henri Phillipe Pétain (1856–1951), head of the French government during the German occupation from 1940 to 1945, was convicted of treason in 1945. — Eds.

meanings, in most cases more or less dishonestly, are: *class, totalitarian, science, progressive, reactionary, bourgeois, equality.*

Now that I have made this catalogue of swindles and perversions, let me give another example of the kind of writing that they lead to. This time it must of its nature be an imaginary one. I am going to translate a passage of good English into modern English of the worst sort. Here is a well-known verse from Ecclesiastes:

> I returned and saw under the sun, that the race is not to the swift, nor the battle to the strong, neither yet bread to the wise, nor yet riches to men of understanding, nor yet favour to men of skill; but time and chance happeneth to them all.

Here it is in modern English:

> Objective consideration of contemporary phenomena compels the conclusion that success or failure in competitive activities exhibits no tendency to be commensurate with innate capacity, but that a considerable element of the unpredictable must invariably be taken into account.

This is a parody, but not a very gross one. Exhibit (3), above, for instance, contains several patches of the same kind of English. It will be seen that I have not made a full translation. The beginning and ending of the sentence follow the original meaning fairly closely, but in the middle the concrete illustrations—race, battle, bread—dissolve into the vague phrase "success or failure in competitive activities." This had to be so, because no modern writer of the kind I am discussing—no one capable of using phrases like "objective consideration of contemporary phenomena"—would ever tabulate his thoughts in that precise and detailed way. The whole tendency of modern prose is away from concreteness. Now analyse these two sentences a little more closely. The first contains forty-nine words but only sixty syllables, and all its words are those of everyday life. The second contains thirty-eight words of ninety syllables: eighteen of its words are from Latin roots, and one from Greek. The first sentence contains six vivid images, and only one phrase ("time and chance") that could be called vague. The second contains not a single fresh, arresting phrase, and in spite of its ninety syllables it gives only a shortened version of the meaning contained in the first. Yet without a doubt it is the second kind of sentence that is gaining ground in modern English. I do not want to exaggerate. This kind of writing is not yet universal, and outcrops of simplicity will occur here and there in the worst-written page. Still, if you or I were to write a few lines on the uncertainty of human fortunes, we should probably come much nearer to my imaginary sentence than to the one from Ecclesiastes.

As I have tried to show, modern writing at its worst does not consist in picking out words for the sake of their meaning and inventing images in order to make the meaning clearer. It consists in gumming together long strips of words which have already been set in order by someone else, and making the results presentable by sheer humbug. The attraction of this way of writing is that it is easy. It is easier — even quicker, once you have the habit — to say *In my opinion it is not an unjustifiable assumption that* than to say *I think.* If you use ready-made phrases, you not only don't have to hunt about for words; you also don't have to bother with the rhythms of your sentences, since these phrases are generally so arranged as to be more or less euphonious. When you are composing in a hurry — when you are dictating to a stenographer, for instance, or making a public speech — it is natural to fall into a pretentious, Latinized style. Tags like *a consideration which we should do well to bear in mind* or *a conclusion to which all of us would readily assent* will save many a sentence from coming down with a bump. By using stale metaphors, similes and idioms, you save much mental effort, at the cost of leaving your meaning vague, not only for your reader but for yourself. This is the significance of mixed metaphors. The sole aim of a metaphor is to call up a visual image. When these images clash — as in *The Fascist octopus has sung its swan song, the jackboot is thrown into the melting pot* — it can be taken as certain that the writer is not seeing a mental image of the objects he is naming; in other words he is not really thinking. Look again at the examples I gave at the beginning of this essay. Professor Laski (1) uses five negatives in fifty-three words. One of these is superfluous, making nonsense of the whole passage, and in addition there is the slip *alien* for akin, making further nonsense, and several avoidable pieces of clumsiness which increase the general vagueness. Professor Hogben (2) plays ducks and drakes with a battery which is able to write prescriptions, and, while disapproving of the everyday phrase *put up with*, is unwilling to look *egregious* up in the dictionary and see what it means; (3), if one takes an uncharitable attitude towards it, is simply meaningless: probably one could work out its intended meaning by reading the whole of the article in which it occurs. In (4), the writer knows more or less what he wants to say, but an accumulation of stale phrases chokes him like tea leaves blocking a sink. In (5), words and meaning have almost parted company. People who write in this manner usually have a general emotional meaning — they dislike one thing and want to express solidarity with another — but they are not interested in the detail of what they are saying. A scrupulous writer, in every sentence that he writes, will ask himself at least four questions, thus: What am I trying to say? What words will express it? What image or idiom will make it clearer? Is this image fresh enough to have an effect? And he will probably ask himself two more: Could I put it more shortly? Have I said anything that is avoidably ugly? But you are not obliged to go to all this trouble. You can shirk it by simply throwing your mind open and letting the ready-made phrases come crowding in. They will construct your sentences for you — even think your thoughts for you, to a certain extent — and at need they will perform the important service of partially concealing your meaning even from yourself. It is at this point that the special connection between politics and the debasement of language becomes clear.

In our time it is broadly true that political writing is bad writing. Where it is not true, it will generally be found that the writer is some kind of rebel, expressing his private opinions and not a "party line." Orthodoxy, of whatever color, seems to demand a lifeless, imitative style. The political dialects to be found in pamphlets, leading articles, manifestos, White Papers and the speeches of undersecretaries do, of course, vary from party to party, but they are all alike in that one almost never finds in them a fresh, vivid, homemade turn of speech. When one watches some tired hack on the platform mechanically repeating the familiar phrases — *bestial atrocities, iron heel, bloodstained tyranny, free peoples of the world, stand shoulder to shoulder* — one often has a curious feeling that one is not watching a live human being but some kind of dummy: a feeling which suddenly becomes stronger at moments when the light catches the speaker's spectacles and turns them into blank discs which seem to have no eyes behind them. And this is not altogether fanciful. A speaker who uses that kind of phraseology has gone some distance towards turning himself into a machine. The appropriate noises are coming out of his larynx, but his brain is not involved as it would be if he were choosing his words for himself. If the speech he is making is one that he is accustomed to make over and over again, he may be almost unconscious of what he is saying, as one is when one utters the responses in church. And this reduced state of consciousness, if not indispensable, is at any rate favorable to political conformity.

In our time, political speech and writing are largely the defence of the indefensible. Things like the continuance of British rule in India, the Russian purges and deportations, the dropping of the atom bombs on Japan, can indeed be defended, but only by arguments which are too brutal for most people to face, and which do not square with the professed aims of political parties. Thus political language has to consist largely of euphemism, question-begging and sheer cloudy vagueness. Defenceless villages are bombarded from the air, the inhabitants driven out into the countryside, the cattle machine-gunned, the huts set on fire with incendiary bullets: this is called *pacification*. Millions of peasants are robbed of their farms and sent trudging along the roads with no more than they can carry: this is called *transfer of population* or *rectification of frontiers*. People are imprisoned for years without trial, or shot in the back of the neck or sent to die of scurvy in Arctic lumber camps: this is called *elimination of unreliable elements*. Such phraseology is needed if one wants to name things without calling up mental pictures of them. Consider for instance some comfortable English professor defending Russian totalitarianism. He cannot say outright, "I believe in killing off your opponents when you can get good results by doing so." Probably, therefore, he will say something like this:

> While freely conceding that the Soviet régime exhibits certain features which the humanitarian may be inclined to deplore, we must, I think, agree that a certain curtailment of the right to political opposition is an unavoidable concomitant of transitional periods, and that the rigors which the Russian people have been called upon to undergo have been amply justified in the sphere of concrete achievement.

The inflated style is itself a kind of euphemism. A mass of Latin words falls   15
upon the facts like soft snow, blurring the outlines and covering up all the details.

The great enemy of clear language is insincerity. When there is a gap between one's real and one's declared aims, one turns as it were instinctively to long words and exhausted idioms, like a cuttlefish squirting out ink. In our age there is no such thing as "keeping out of politics." All issues are political issues, and politics itself is a mass of lies, evasions, folly, hatred and schizophrenia. When the general atmosphere is bad, language must suffer. I should expect to find — this is a guess which I have not sufficient knowledge to verify — that the German, Russian and Italian languages have all deteriorated in the last ten or fifteen years, as a result of dictatorship.

But if thought corrupts language, language can also corrupt thought. A bad usage can spread by tradition and imitation, even among people who should and do know better. The debased language that I have been discussing is in some ways very convenient. Phrases like *a not unjustifiable assumption, leaves much to be desired, would serve no good purpose, a consideration which we should do well to bear in mind*, are a continuous temptation, a packet of aspirins always at one's elbow. Look back through this essay, and for certain you will find that I have again and again committed the very faults I am protesting against. By this morning's post I have received a pamphlet dealing with conditions in Germany. The author tells me that he "felt impelled" to write it. I open it at random, and here is almost the first sentence that I see: "[The Allies] have an opportunity not only of achieving a radical transformation of Germany's social and political structure in such a way as to avoid a nationalistic reaction in Germany itself, but at the same time of laying the foundation of a cooperative and unified Europe." You see, he "feels impelled" to write — feels, presumably, that he has something new to say — and yet his words, like cavalry horses answering the bugle, group themselves automatically into the familiar dreary pattern. This invasion of one's mind by ready-made phrases (*lay the foundations, achieve a radical transformation*) can only be prevented if one is constantly on guard against them, and every such phrase anaesthetizes a portion of one's brain.

I said earlier that the decadence of our language is probably curable. Those who deny this would argue, if they produced an argument at all, that language merely reflects existing social conditions, and that we cannot influence its development by any direct tinkering with words and constructions. So far as the general tone or spirit of a language goes, this may be true, but it is not true in detail. Silly words and expressions have often disappeared, not through any evolutionary process but owing to the conscious action of a minority. Two recent examples were *explore every avenue* and *leave no stone unturned*, which were killed by the jeers of a few journalists. There is a long list of flyblown metaphors which could similarly be got rid of if enough people would interest themselves in the job; and it should also be possible to laugh the *not un-* formation out of existence,[4] to reduce the amount of Latin and Greek in the average sentence, to drive out foreign phrases

---

[4]One can cure oneself of the *not un-* formation by memorizing this sentence: *A not unblack dog was chasing a not unsmall rabbit across a not ungreen field.*

and strayed scientific words, and, in general, to make pretentiousness unfashionable. But all these are minor points. The defence of the English language implies more than this, and perhaps it is best to start by saying what it does *not* imply.

To begin with it has nothing to do with archaism, with the salvaging of obsolete words and turns of speech, or with the setting up of a "standard English" which must never be departed from. On the contrary, it is especially concerned with the scrapping of every word or idiom which has outworn its usefulness. It has nothing to do with correct grammar and syntax, which are of no importance so long as one makes one's meaning clear, or with the avoidance of Americanisms, or with having what is called a "good prose style." On the other hand it is not concerned with fake simplicity and the attempt to make written English colloquial. Nor does it even imply in every case preferring the Saxon word to the Latin one, though it does imply using the fewest and shortest words that will cover one's meaning. What is above all needed is to let the meaning choose the word, and not the other way about. In prose, the worst thing one can do with words is to surrender to them. When you think of a concrete object, you think wordlessly, and then, if you want to describe the thing you have been visualizing you probably hunt about till you find the exact words that seem to fit it. When you think of something abstract you are more inclined to use words from the start, and unless you make a conscious effort to prevent it, the existing dialect will come rushing in and do the job for you, at the expense of blurring or even changing your meaning. Probably it is better to put off using words as long as possible and get one's meaning as clear as one can through pictures or sensations. Afterwards one can choose — not simply *accept* — the phrases that will best cover the meaning, and then switch round and decide what impression one's words are likely to make on another person. This last effort of the mind cuts out all stale or mixed images, all prefabricated phrases, needless repetitions, and humbug and vagueness generally. But one can often be in doubt about the effect of a word or a phrase, and one needs rules that one can rely on when instinct fails. I think the following rules will cover most cases:

(i) Never use a metaphor, simile or other figure of speech which you are used to seeing in print.

(ii) Never use a long word where a short one will do.

(iii) If it is possible to cut a word out, always cut it out.

(iv) Never use the passive where you can use the active.

(v) Never use a foreign phrase, a scientific word or a jargon word if you can think of an everyday English equivalent.

(vi) Break any of these rules sooner than say anything outright barbarous.

These rules sound elementary, and so they are, but they demand a deep change of attitude in anyone who has grown used to writing in the style now fashionable. One could keep all of them and still write bad English, but one could not write the kind of stuff that I quoted in those five specimens at the beginning of this article.

I have not here been considering the literary use of language, but merely language as an instrument for expressing and not for concealing or preventing thought. Stuart Chase[5] and others have come near to claiming that all abstract words are meaningless, and have used this as a pretext for advocating a kind of political quietism. Since you don't know what Fascism is, how can you struggle against Fascism? One need not swallow such absurdities as this, but one ought to recognize that the present political chaos is connected with the decay of language, and that one can probably bring about some improvement by starting at the verbal end. If you simplify your English, you are freed from the worst follies of orthodoxy. You cannot speak any of the necessary dialects, and when you make a stupid remark its stupidity will be obvious, even to yourself. Political language—and with variations this is true of all political parties, from Conservatives to Anarchists—is designed to make lies sound truthful and murder respectable, and to give an appearance of solidity to pure wind. One cannot change this all in a moment, but one can at least change one's own habits, and from time to time one can even, if one jeers loudly enough, send some worn-out and useless phrase—some *jackboot, Achilles' heel, hotbed, melting pot, acid test, veritable inferno* or other lump of verbal refuse—into the dustbin where it belongs.

Questions for Discussion

1. George Orwell argues against the "belief that language is a natural growth and not an instrument which we shape for our own purposes" (para. 1). Explain why you do or do not agree with Orwell's position.
2. In speeches by contemporary politicians, find examples of each type of writing problem that Orwell discusses: dying metaphors, operators or verbal false limbs, pretentious diction, and meaningless words. Explain why the examples you've cited are "swindles and perversions," as Orwell calls them (para. 9).
3. Why does Orwell object to "ready-made phrases" and "mixed metaphors" (para. 12)?
4. In paragraph 12, Orwell says that every writer "ask[s] himself at least four questions, thus: What am I trying to say? What words will express it? What image or idiom will make it clearer? Is this image fresh enough to have an effect?" What do you think of these questions? Do you agree or disagree that they are the most essential questions for writers to ask themselves? Explain why.

---

[5]Stuart Chase (1888–1985) popularized the field of general semantics in his book *The Tyranny of Words* (1958). General semantics argued that words could never capture the entire essence of a thing; for instance, you can describe a smell, but you cannot directly share the experience with someone else. — Eds.

5. What does Orwell mean when he asserts, "But if thought corrupts language, language can also corrupt thought" (para. 16)?

6. Do you agree with Orwell that "correct grammar and syntax . . . are of no importance so long as one makes one's meaning clear" (para. 18)? Explain. If you do agree, cite examples from your own experience or reading that support your position.

Questions on Rhetoric and Style

1. What is Orwell's thesis? Does he actually state it, or is it implied?

2. How effective is Orwell's analogy of the cause and effect of alcohol abuse to the demise of language (para. 2)?

3. In each of the following paragraphs—paragraphs 4, 5, 12, 15, and 16—Orwell uses at least one metaphor or simile. Identify each figure of speech. Then explain how it works and whether you find it rhetorically effective.

4. Orwell develops his ideas through extensive use of examples. Try rewriting paragraph 5, 6, 7, or 8 without examples. How does the effect of the paragraph change?

5. What is the purpose of the additional information provided in Orwell's footnotes for paragraphs 7 and 8? Why do you think Orwell chose to put the information in footnotes rather than in the main text?

6. Orwell wrote this essay before he was well known for his novels. He uses the first person, yet he does not directly state his qualifications to speak on language. How does he establish ethos? Should he have been more direct?

7. How would you describe the overall organization of this essay? Examine its movement, from the examples in the opening to the rules near the ending.

8. What is Orwell's purpose in writing this essay? How might the historical context of post–World War II affect that purpose? Cite specific passages to support your response.

9. How would you describe the tone of Orwell's essay? Can you sum it up in one word, or does the essay range from one tone to another? Cite specific passages to support your response.

10. Find examples in the essay where Orwell is guilty of the four faults that characterize the writing he is criticizing.

Suggestions for Writing

1. Using examples from your own writing, observation of popular culture, or reading of contemporary texts, explain why you do or do not agree with Orwell's opening statement that "the English language is in a bad way."

2. Write an essay agreeing or disagreeing with the following assertion by Orwell in paragraph 13: "In our time it is broadly true that political writing is bad writing. Where it is not true, it will generally be found that the writer is some kind of rebel, expressing his private opinions and not a 'party line.' Orthodoxy, of whatever color, seems to demand a lifeless, imitative style." Support your position with

examples from political speeches, newspaper columns and articles, advertisements, and Web sites.

3. Compare and contrast paragraph 14 in Orwell's essay with the following paragraph from Toni Morrison's 1993 Nobel Prize speech.

> The systematic looting of language can be recognized by the tendency of its users to
> forgo its nuanced, complex, mid-wifery properties for menace and subjugation.
> Oppressive language does more than represent violence; it is violence; does more
> than represent the limits of knowledge; it limits knowledge. Whether it is obscuring
> state language or the faux-language of mindless media; whether it is the proud but
> calcified language of the academy or the commodity driven language of science;
> whether it is the malign language of law-without-ethics, or language designed for
> the estrangement of minorities, hiding its racist plunder in its literary cheek — it
> must be rejected, altered and exposed. It is the language that drinks blood, laps vul-
> nerabilities, tucks its fascist boots under crinolines of respectability and patriotism
> as it moves relentlessly toward the bottom line and the bottomed-out mind. Sexist
> language, racist language, theistic language — all are typical of the policing lan-
> guages of mastery, and cannot, do not permit new knowledge or encourage the
> mutual exchange of ideas.

4. Working in groups, find examples of writing in current newspapers or magazines
or a political speech that illustrate what Orwell calls "staleness of imagery" and
"lack of precision" (para. 11). Then revise the writing by applying one or more of
the six rules Orwell prescribes in the penultimate paragraph of his essay.

5. Orwell uses many terms that refer to language. Develop a glossary that has the following components: (1) the term as Orwell uses it, (2) a definition of the term, and
(3) an example from your own reading (including advertisements). Include the
following terms, along with any others you note: *mixed metaphor, pretentious diction, euphemism, parody, idiom, archaic language ("archaism"), dialect.*

6. Suppose "Politics and the English Language" were being reprinted in a specific
contemporary magazine. Redesign the essay by adding visual images and graphic
displays that will appeal to the magazine's audience. Do *not* change Orwell's language; simply download the essay from the Internet, and then redesign it by including graphs, charts, cartoon characters, icons, color, or different fonts. Explain the
rhetorical effect that you intend these changes to have.

Slang in America

WALT WHITMAN

Walt Whitman (1819–1892) was born on Long Island in New York. He worked as a teacher, a printer, and a journalist before making his name as a poet. Known widely for his free verse as well as his democratic spirit, Whitman is one of the most influential poets in the English language. His major work is *Leaves of Grass* (1855). Among the famous poems from that collection are "Facing West from California's Shores," "Crossing Brooklyn Ferry," and "When Lilacs Last in the Dooryard Bloom'd," about Abraham Lincoln. Whitman's essay "Slang in America" was first published in 1885 in the *North American Review* and later collected in *November Boughs* (1888), a volume of Whitman's prose and poetry.

View'd freely, the English language is the accretion and growth of every dialect, race, and range of time, and is both the free and compacted composition of all. From this point of view, it stands for Language in the largest sense, and is really the greatest of studies. It involves so much; is indeed a sort of universal absorber, combiner, and conqueror. The scope of its etymologies is the scope not only of man and civilization, but the history of Nature in all departments, and of the organic Universe, brought up to date; for all are comprehended in words, and their backgrounds. This is when words become vitaliz'd, and stand for things, as they unerringly and soon come to do, in the mind that enters on their study with fitting spirit, grasp, and appreciation.

Slang, profoundly consider'd, is the lawless germinal element, below all words and sentences, and behind all poetry, and proves a certain perennial rankness and protestantism in speech. As the United States inherit by far their most precious possession—the language they talk and write—from the Old World, under and out of its feudal institutes, I will allow myself to borrow a simile even of those forms farthest removed from American Democracy. Considering Language then as some mighty potentate, into the majestic audience-hall of the monarch ever enters a personage like one of Shakespere's clowns, and takes position there, and plays a part even in the stateliest ceremonies. Such is Slang, or indirection, an attempt of common humanity to escape from bald literalism, and express itself illimitably, which in highest walks produces poets and poems, and doubtless in pre-historic times gave the start to, and perfected, the whole immense tangle of the old mythologies. For, curious as it may appear, it is strictly the same impulse-source, the same thing. Slang, too, is the wholesome fermentation or eructation[1] of those processes eternally active in language, by which froth and specks are

---

[1]The act of belching. —Eds.

thrown up, mostly to pass away; though occasionally to settle and permanently chrystallize.

To make it plainer, it is certain that many of the oldest and solidest words we use, were originally generated from the daring and license of slang. In the processes of word-formation, myriads die, but here and there the attempt attracts superior meanings, becomes valuable and indispensable, and lives forever. Thus the term *right* means literally only straight. *Wrong* primarily meant twisted, distorted. *Integrity* meant oneness. *Spirit* meant breath, or flame. A *supercilious* person was one who rais'd his eyebrows. To *insult* was to leap against. If you *influenc'd* a man, you but flow'd into him. The Hebrew word which is translated *prophesy* meant to bubble up and pour forth as a fountain. The enthusiast bubbles up with the Spirit of God within him, and it pours forth from him like a fountain. The word prophecy is misunderstood. Many suppose that it is limited to mere prediction; that is but the lesser portion of prophecy. The greater work is to reveal God. Every true religious enthusiast is a prophet.

Language, be it remember'd, is not an abstract construction of the learn'd, or of dictionary-makers, but is something arising out of the work, needs, ties, joys, affections, tastes, of long generations of humanity, and has its bases broad and low, close to the ground. Its final decisions are made by the masses, people nearest the concrete, having most to do with actual land and sea. It impermeates all, the Past as well as the Present, and is the grandest triumph of the human intellect. "Those mighty works of art," says Addington Symonds, "which we call languages, in the construction of which whole peoples unconsciously co-operated, the forms of which were determin'd not by individual genius, but by the instincts of successive generations, acting to one end, inherent in the nature of the race—Those poems of pure thought and fancy, cadenced not in words, but in living imagery, fountainheads of inspiration, mirrors of the mind of nascent nations, which we call Mythologies—these surely are more marvellous in their infantine spontaneity than any more mature production of the races which evolv'd them. Yet we are utterly ignorant of their embryology; the true science of Origins is yet in its cradle."

Daring as it is to say so, in the growth of Language it is certain that the retrospect of slang from the start would be the recalling from their nebulous conditions of all that is poetical in the stores of human utterance. Moreover, the honest delving, as of late years, by the German and British workers in comparative philology, has pierc'd and dispers'd many of the falsest bubbles of centuries; and will disperse many more. It was long recorded that in Scandinavian mythology the heroes in the Norse Paradise drank out of the skulls of their slain enemies. Later investigation proves the word taken for skulls to mean *horns* of beasts slain in the hunt. And what reader had not been exercis'd over the traces of that feudal custom, by which *seigneurs* warm'd their feet in the bowels of serfs, the abdomen being open'd for the purpose? It now is made to appear that the serf was only required to submit his unharm'd abdomen as a foot cushion while his lord supp'd, and was required to chafe the legs of the seigneur with his hands.

5

It is curiously in embryons and childhood, and among the illiterate, we always find the groundwork and start, of this great science, and its noblest products. What a relief most people have in speaking of a man not by his true and formal name, with a "Mister" to it, but by some odd or homely appellative. The propensity to approach a meaning not directly and squarely, but by circuitous styles of expression, seems indeed a born quality of the common people everywhere, evidenced by nick-names, and the inveterate determination of the masses to bestow sub-titles, sometimes ridiculous, sometimes very apt. Always among the soldiers during the Secession War, one heard of "Little Mac" (Gen. McClellan), or of "Uncle Billy" (Gen. Sherman). "The old man" was, of course, very common. Among the rank and file, both armies, it was very general to speak of the different States they came from by their slang names. Those from Maine were call'd Foxes; New Hampshire, Granite Boys; Massachusetts, Bay Staters; Vermont, Green Mountain Boys; Rhode Island, Gun Flints; Connecticut, Wooden Nutmegs; New York, Knickerbockers; New Jersey, Clam Catchers; Pennsylvania, Logher Heads; Delaware, Muskrats; Maryland, Claw Thumpers; Virginia, Beagles; North Carolina, Tar Boilers; South Carolina, Weasels; Georgia, Buzzards; Louisiana, Creoles; Alabama, Lizzards; Kentucky, Corn Crackers; Ohio, Buckeyes; Michigan, Wolverines; Indiana, Hoosiers; Illinois, Suckers; Missouri, Pukes; Mississippi, Tad Poles; Florida, Fly up the Creeks; Wisconsin, Badgers; Iowa, Hawkeyes; Oregon, Hard Cases. Indeed I am not sure but slang names have more than once made Presidents. "Old Hickory" (Gen. Jackson) is one case in point. "Tippecanoe, and Tyler, too," another.

I find the same rule in the people's conversations everywhere. I heard this among the men of the city horse-cars, where the conductor is often call'd a "snatcher" (i.e., because his characteristic duty is to constantly pull or snatch the bell-strap, to stop or go on). Two young fellows are having a friendly talk, amid which, says 1st conductor, "What did you do before you was a snatcher?" Answer of 2d conductor, "Nail'd." (Translation of answer: "I work'd as carpenter.") What is a "boom"? says one editor to another. "Esteem'd contemporary," says the other, "a boom is a bulge." "Barefoot whiskey" is the Tennessee name for the undiluted stimulant. In the slang of the New York common restaurant waiters a plate of ham and beans is known as "stars and stripes," codfish balls as "sleeve-buttons," and hash as "mystery."

The Western States of the Union are, however, as may be supposed, the special areas of slang, not only in conversation, but in names of localities, towns, rivers, etc. A late Oregon traveller says:

On your way to Olympia by rail, you cross a river called the Shookum-Chuck; your train stops at places named Newaukum, Tumwater, and Toutle; and if you seek further you will hear of whole counties labell'd Wahkiakum, or Snohomish, or Kitsar, or Klikatat; and Cowlitz, Hookium, and Nenolelops greet and offend you. They complain in Olympia that Washington Territory gets but little immigration; but what wonder? What man, having the whole American continent to choose from, would willingly date his letters from the county of Snohomish or bring up his children in the city of Nenolelops? The village of Tumwater is, as I am ready to bear witness, very pretty indeed; but surely an emigrant would think twice before he establish'd himself either there or at Toutle. Seattle is sufficiently barbarous; Stelicoom is no better; and I suspect that the Northern Pacific Railroad terminus has been fixed at Tacoma because it is one of the few places on Puget Sound whose name does not inspire horror.

Then a Nevada paper chronicles the departure of a mining party from Reno: "The toughest set of roosters that ever shook the dust off any town left Reno yesterday for the new mining district of Cornucopia. They came here from Virginia. Among the crowd were four New York cock-fighters, two Chicago murderers, three Baltimore bruisers, one Philadelphia prize-fighter, four San Francisco hoodlums, three Virginia beats, two Union Pacific roughs, and two check guerrillas." Among the far-west newspapers, have been, or are, *The Fairplay* (Colorado) *Flume*, *The Solid Muldoon*, of Ouray, *The Tombstone Epitaph*, of Nevada, *The Jimplecute*, of Texas, and *The Bazoo*, of Missouri. Shirttail Bend, Whiskey Flat, Puppytown, Wild Yankee Ranch, Squaw Flat, Rawhide Ranch, Loafer's Ravine, Squitch Gulch, Toenail Lake, are a few of the names of places in Butte county, Cal.

Perhaps indeed no place or term gives more luxuriant illustrations of the fer- 10 mentation processes I have mention'd, and their froth and specks, than those Mississippi and Pacific coast regions, at the present day. Hasty and grotesque as are some of the names, others are of an appropriateness and originality unsurpassable. This applies to the Indian words, which are often perfect. Oklahoma is proposed in Congress for the name of one of our new Territories. Hog-eye, Lick-skillet, Rakepocket and Steal-easy are the names of some Texan towns. Miss Bremer found among the aborigines the following names: *Men's*, Horn-point; Round-Wind; Stand-and-look-out; The-Cloud-that-goes-aside; Iron-toe; Seek-the-sun; Iron-flash; Red-bottle; White-spindle; Black-dog; Two-feathers-of-honor; Gray-grass; Bushy-tail; Thunder-face; Go-on-the-burning-sod; Spirits-of-the-dead. *Women's*, Keep-the-fire; Spiritual-woman; Second-daughter-of-the-house; Blue-bird.

Certainly philologists have not given enough attention to this element and its results, which, I repeat, can probably be found working every where to-day, amid modern conditions, with as much life and activity as in far-back Greece or India, under prehistoric ones. Then the wit—the rich flashes of humor and genius and poetry—darting out often from a gang of laborers, railroad-men, miners, drivers or boatmen! How often have I hover'd at the edge of a crowd of them, to hear their repartees and impromptus! You get more real fun from half an hour with them than from the books of all "the American humorists."

The science of language has large and close analogies in geological science, with its ceaseless evolution, its fossils, and its numberless submerged layers and hidden strata, the infinite go-before of the present. Or, perhaps Language is more like some vast living body, or perennial body of bodies. And slang not only brings the first feeders of it, but is afterward the start of fancy, imagination and humor, breathing into its nostrils the breath of life.

Exploring the Text

1. Why is slang particularly American, according to Walt Whitman? Do you think this is still the case in twenty-first-century America?

2. Whitman opens his essay with a discussion of the English language. In what ways does this paragraph lay the foundation for the ideas that follow?

3. In paragraph 2, Whitman defines slang as "the lawless germinal element, below all words and sentences, and behind all poetry, and proves a certain perennial rankness and protestantism in speech." Divide that definition into specific parts, and analyze the meaning of each one. Thus, for instance, why is slang "lawless"? Use examples from today's slang to illustrate Whitman's definition.

4. In paragraph 2, Whitman uses two metaphors. What are they? Why is each one a fitting way to explore the meaning of slang? Is one more effective than the other? Explain.

5. Whitman opens paragraph 3 with the transitional phrase, "To make it plainer." What does he do in that paragraph to make his perspective on slang "plainer"?

6. What is the relationship between slang and mythology, according to Whitman?

7. In paragraphs 6–10, Whitman presents numerous examples as evidence. Do these illustrate a single point or several points? Explain what point(s) you believe they support.

8. What opinion of American humorists does Whitman imply in paragraph 11? Do you think that expressing this view undercuts his essay or strengthens it? Explain your response.

9. How would you describe the overall tone of this essay? How does the final paragraph, including the metaphors, contribute to the tone?

10. How does this essay reflect Whitman's poetry in terms of style and/or content? If you are familiar with his work, select your own examples; if you are not, you might consider "Song of Myself" or even the short poem "Mannahatta."

11. Apply the following definition of slang from Whitman's essay to examples that you know from your own experience or study: "an attempt of common humanity to escape from bald literalism, and express itself illimitably, which in highest walks produces poets and poems . . ." (para. 2).

12. A more current essay by Tom Dalzell, an expert on American slang, examines the impact of young people on its development:

> Whatever its source, youth slang is a core element of youth culture, as a defiant gesture of resistance and an emblem of tribe identity. Fashion and hair styles are other key manifestations of a generation's identity, but they can be easily regulated by adult authorities. With music and language, regulation and restriction are much more difficult. Even the most vigilant and repressive attempts by adult authority cannot completely eradicate slang and music with its slang lyrics.

Support, challenge, or qualify this view with evidence from your own generation or another with which you are familiar.

How to Tame a Wild Tongue

Gloria Anzaldúa

A poet, teacher, scholar, and political activist, Gloria Evangelina Anzaldúa (1942–2004) is known for her writings about the social and cultural marginalization of disenfranchised people. She grew up in the Rio Grande Valley of southern Texas, where her parents were sharecroppers. She received her BA from Pan American University and her MA from the University of Texas at Austin. Anzaldúa was completing her doctoral degree from the University of California–Santa Cruz at the time of her death; it was awarded posthumously in 2005. She coauthored with Cherríe Moraga *This Bridge Called My Back: Writings by Radical Women of Color* (1981). Her most well-known publication is *Borderlands/La Frontera* (1987), which is a combination of narrative, historical and linguistic analysis, and poetry about the concept of borders among classes, cultures, genders, and languages. The following essay from *Borderlands/La Frontera* explores the relationship of identity and language.

"We're going to have to control your tongue," the dentist says, pulling out all the metal from my mouth. Silver bits plop and tinkle into the basin. My mouth is a motherlode.

The dentist is cleaning out my roots. I get a whiff of the stench when I gasp. "I can't cap that tooth yet, you're still draining," he says.

"We're going to have to do something about your tongue," I hear the anger rising in his voice. My tongue keeps pushing out the wads of cotton, pushing back the drills, the long thin needles. "I've never seen anything as strong or as stubborn," he says. And I think, how do you tame a wild tongue, train it to be quiet, how do you bridle and saddle it? How do you make it lie down?

"Who is to say that robbing a people of its language is less violent than war?"

— Ray Gwyn Smith[1]

I remember being caught speaking Spanish at recess—that was good for three licks on the knuckles with a sharp ruler. I remember being sent to the corner of the classroom for "talking back" to the Anglo teacher when all I was trying to do was tell her how to pronounce my name. "If you want to be American, speak 'American.' If you don't like it, go back to Mexico where you belong."

"I want you to speak English. *Pa' hallar buen trabajo tienes que saber hablar el inglés bien. Qué vale toda tu educación si todavía hablas inglés con un* 'accent,'" my mother would say, mortified that I spoke English like a Mexican. At Pan American University, I and all Chicano students were required to take two speech classes. Their purpose: to get rid of our accents. 5

Attacks on one's form of expression with the intent to censor are a violation of the First Amendment. *El Anglo con cara de inocente nos arrancó la lengua.* Wild tongues can't be tamed, they can only be cut out.

Overcoming the Tradition of Silence

Ahogadas, escupimos el oscuro.
Peleando con nuestra propia sombra
el silencio nos sepulta.

En boca cerrada no entran moscas. "Flies don't enter a closed mouth" is a saying I kept hearing when I was a child. *Ser habladora* was to be a gossip and a liar, to talk too much. *Muchachitas bien criadas*, well-bred girls don't answer back. *Es una falta de respeto* to talk back to one's mother or father. I remember one of the sins I'd recite to the priest in the confession box the few times I went to confession: talking back to my mother, *hablar pa' 'tras, repelar. Hocicona, repelona, chismosa*, having a big mouth, questioning, carrying tales are all signs of being *mal criada*. In my culture they are all words that are derogatory if applied to women—I've never heard them applied to men.

The first time I heard two women, a Puerto Rican and a Cuban, say the word "*nosotras*," I was shocked. I had not known the word existed. Chicanas use *nosotros* whether we're male or female. We are robbed of our female being by the masculine plural. Language is a male discourse.

And our tongues have become
dry   the wilderness has
dried out our tongues   and
we have forgotten speech.

—Irena Klepfisz[2]

Even our own people, other Spanish speakers *nos quieren poner candados en la boca*. They would hold us back with their bag of *reglas de academia*.

Oyé como ladra: el lenguaje de la frontera

Quien tiene boca se equivoca.

—Mexican saying

"*Pocho*, cultural traitor, you're speaking the oppressor's language by speaking English, you're ruining the Spanish language," I have been accused by various Latinos and Latinas. Chicano Spanish is considered by the purist and by most Latinos deficient, a mutilation of Spanish.

But Chicano Spanish is a border tongue which developed naturally. Change, *evolución, enriquecimiento de palabras nuevas por invención o adopción* have created variants of Chicano Spanish, *un nuevo lenguaje. Un lenguaje que corresponde a un modo de vivir.* Chicano Spanish is not incorrect, it is a living language.

For a people who are neither Spanish nor live in a country in which Spanish is the first language; for a people who live in a country in which English is the reigning tongue but who are not Anglo; for a people who cannot entirely identify with either standard (formal, Castillian) Spanish nor standard English, what recourse is left to them but to create their own language? A language which they can connect their identity to, one capable of communicating the realities and values true to themselves—a language with terms that are neither *español ni inglés,* but both. We speak a patois, a forked tongue, a variation of two languages.

Chicano Spanish sprang out of the Chicanos' need to identify ourselves as a distinct people. We needed a language with which we could communicate with ourselves, a secret language. For some of us, language is a homeland closer than the Southwest—for many Chicanos today live in the Midwest and the East. And because we are a complex, heterogeneous people, we speak many languages. Some of the languages we speak are:

1. Standard English
2. Working class and slang English
3. Standard Spanish
4. Standard Mexican Spanish
5. North Mexican Spanish dialect
6. Chicano Spanish (Texas, New Mexico, Arizona, and California have regional variations)
7. Tex-Mex
8. *Pachuco* (called *caló*)

My "home" tongues are the languages I speak with my sister and brothers, with my friends. They are the last five listed, with 6 and 7 being closest to my heart. From school, the media, and job situations, I've picked up standard and working class English. From Mamagrande Locha and from reading Spanish and Mexican literature, I've picked up Standard Spanish and Standard Mexican Spanish. From *los recién llegados,* Mexican immigrants, and *braceros,* I learned the North Mexican dialect. With Mexicans I'll try to speak either Standard Mexican Spanish or the North Mexican dialect. From my parents and Chicanos living in the Valley, I picked up Chicano Texas Spanish, and I speak it with my mom, younger brother (who married a Mexican and who rarely mixes Spanish with English), aunts, and older relatives.

With Chicanas from *Nuevo México* or *Arizona* I will speak Chicano Spanish a little, but often they don't understand what I'm saying. With most California Chicanas I speak entirely in English (unless I forget). When I first moved to San Franciso, I'd rattle off something in Spanish, unintentionally embarrassing them. Often it is only with another Chicana *tejana* that I can talk freely.

Words distorted by English are known as anglicisms or *pochismos.* The *pocho* is an anglicized Mexican or American of Mexican origin who speaks Spanish with an accent characteristic of North Americans and who distorts and reconstructs the language according to the influence of English.[3] Tex-Mex, or Spanglish, comes most naturally to me. I may switch back and forth from English to Spanish in the same sentence or in the same word. With my sister and my brother Nune and with Chicano *tejano* contemporaries I speak in Tex-Mex.

From kids and people my own age I picked up *Pachuco*. *Pachuco* (the language of the zoot suiters) is a language of rebellion, both against Standard Spanish and Standard English. It is a secret language. Adults of the culture and outsiders cannot understand it. It is made up of slang words from both English and Spanish. *Ruca* means girl or woman, *vato* means guy or dude, *chale* means no, *simón* means yes, *churro* is sure, talk is *periquiar*, *pigionear* means petting, *que gacho* means how nerdy, *ponte águila* means watch out, death is called *la pelona*. Through lack of practice and not having others who can speak it, I've lost most of the *Pachuco* tongue.

Chicano Spanish

Chicanos, after 250 years of Spanish/Anglo colonization, have developed significant differences in the Spanish we speak. We collapse two adjacent vowels into a single syllable and sometimes shift the stress in certain words such as *maíz/maiz, cohete/cuete*. We leave out certain consonants when they appear between vowels: *lado/lao, mojado/mojao*. Chicanos from South Texas pronounce *f* as *j* as in *jue* (*fue*). Chicanos use "archaisms," words that are no longer in the Spanish language, words that have been evolved out. We say *semos, truje, haiga, ansina*, and *naiden*. We retain the "archaic" *j*, as in *jalar*, that derives from an earlier *h* (the French *halar* or the Germanic *halon* which was lost to standard Spanish in the 16th century), but which is still found in several regional dialects such as the one spoken in South Texas. (Due to geography, Chicanos from the Valley of South Texas were cut off linguistically from other Spanish speakers. We tend to use words that the Spaniards brought over from Medieval Spain. The majority of the Spanish colonizers in Mexico and the Southwest came from Extremadura—Hernán Cortés was one of them—and Andalucía. Andalucians pronounce *ll* like a *y*, and their *d*'s tend to be absorbed by adjacent vowels: *tirado* becomes *tirao*. They brought *el lenguaje popular, dialectors y regionalismos*.[4])

Chicanos and other Spanish speakers also shift *ll* to *y* and *z* to *s*.[5] We leave out initial syllables, saying *tar* for *estar, toy* for *estoy, hora* for *ahora* (*cubanos* and *puertorriqueños* also leave out initial letters of some words). We also leave out the final syllable such as *pa* for *para*. The intervocalic *y*, the *ll* as in *tortilla, ella, botella*, gets replaced by *tortia* or *tortiya, ea, botea*. We add an additional syllable at the beginning of certain words: *atocar* for *tocar, agastar* for *gastar*. Sometimes we'll say *lavaste las vacijas*, other times *lavates* (substituting the *ates* verb endings for the *aste*).

We use anglicisms, words borrowed from English: *bola* from ball, *carpeta* from carpet, *máchina de lavar* (instead of *lavadora*) from washing machine. Tex-Mex argot, created by adding a Spanish sound at the beginning or end of an

20

English word such as *cookiar* for cook, *watchar* for watch, *parkiar* for park, and *rapiar* for rape, is the result of the pressures on Spanish speakers to adapt to English.

We don't use the word *vosotros/as* or its accompanying verb form. We don't say *claro* (to mean yes), *imagínate*, or *me emociona*, unless we picked up Spanish from Latinas, out of a book, or in a classroom. Other Spanish-speaking groups are going through the same, or similar, development in their Spanish.

Linguistic Terrorism

> *Deslenguadas. Somos los del español deficiente.* We are your linguistic nightmare, your linguistic aberration, your linguistic *mestisaje*, the subject of your *burla*. Because we speak with tongues of fire we are culturally crucified. Racially, culturally, and linguistically *somos huérfanos*—we speak an orphan tongue.

Chicanas who grew up speaking Chicano Spanish have internalized the belief that we speak poor Spanish. It is illegitimate, a bastard language. And because we internalize how our language has been used against us by the dominant culture, we use our language differences against each other.

Chicana feminists often skirt around each other with suspicion and hesitation. For the longest time I couldn't figure it out. Then it dawned on me. To be close to another Chicana is like looking into the mirror. We are afraid of what we'll see there. *Pena.* Shame. Low estimation of self. In childhood we are told that our language is wrong. Repeated attacks on our native tongue diminish our sense of self. The attacks continue throughout our lives.

Chicanas feel uncomfortable talking in Spanish to Latinas, afraid of their censure. Their language was not outlawed in their countries. They had a whole lifetime of being immersed in their native tongue; generations, centuries in which Spanish was a first language, taught in school, heard on radio and TV, and read in the newspaper.

If a person, Chicana or Latina, has a low estimation of my native tongue, she 25 also has a low estimation of me. Often with *mexicanas y latinas* we'll speak English as a neutral language. Even among Chicanas we tend to speak English at parties or conferences. Yet, at the same time, we're afraid the other will think we're *agringadas* because we don't speak Chicano Spanish. We oppress each other trying to out-Chicano each other, vying to be the "real" Chicanas, to speak like Chicanos. There is no one Chicano language just as there is no one Chicano experience. A monolingual Chicana whose first language is English or Spanish is just as much a Chicana as one who speaks several variants of Spanish. A Chicana from Michigan or Chicago or Detroit is just as much a Chicana as one from the Southwest. Chicano Spanish is as diverse linguistically as it is regionally.

By the end of this century, Spanish speakers will comprise the biggest minority group in the U.S., a country where students in high schools and colleges are encouraged to take French classes because French is considered more "cultured."

But for a language to remain alive it must be used.[6] By the end of this century English, and not Spanish, will be the mother tongue of most Chicanos and Latinos.

So, if you want to really hurt me, talk badly about my language. Ethnic identity is twin skin to linguistic identity—I am my language. Until I can take pride in my language, I cannot take pride in myself. Until I can accept as legitimate Chicano Texas Spanish, Tex-Mex, and all the other languages I speak, I cannot accept the legitimacy of myself. Until I am free to write bilingually and to switch codes without having always to translate, while I still have to speak English or Spanish when I would rather speak Spanglish, and as long as I have to accommodate the English speakers rather than having them accommodate me, my tongue will be illegitimate.

I will no longer be made to feel ashamed of existing. I will have my voice: Indian, Spanish, white. I will have my serpent's tongue—my woman's voice, my sexual voice, my poet's voice. I will overcome the tradition of silence.

> My fingers
> move sly against your palm
> Like women everywhere, we speak in code. . . .
>
> —MELANIE KAYE/KANTROWITZ[7]

"Vistas," corridos, y comida: My Native Tongue   In the 1960s, I read my first Chicano novel. It was *City of Night* by John Rechy, a gay Texan, son of a Scottish father and a Mexican mother. For days I walked around in stunned amazement that a Chicano could write and get published. When I read *I Am Joaquín*[8] I was surprised to see a bilingual book by a Chicano in print. When I saw poetry written in Tex-Mex for the first time, a feeling of pure joy flashed through me. I felt like we really existed as a people. In 1971, when I started teaching High School English to Chicano students, I tried to supplement the required texts with works by Chicanos, only to be reprimanded and forbidden to do so by the principal. He claimed that I was supposed to teach "American" and English literature. At the risk of being fired, I swore my students to secrecy and slipped in Chicano short stories, poems, a play. In graduate school, while working toward a Ph.D., I had to "argue" with one advisor after the other, semester after semester, before I was allowed to make Chicano literature an area of focus.

Even before I read books by Chicanos or Mexicans, it was the Mexican movies I saw at the drive-in—the Thursday night special of $1.00 a carload—that gave me a sense of belonging. "*Vámonos a las vistas*," my mother would call out and we'd all—grandmother, brothers, sister, and cousins—squeeze into the car. We'd wolf down cheese and bologna white bread sandwiches while watching Pedro Infante in melodramatic tearjerkers like *Nosotros los pobres*, the first "real" Mexican movie (that was not an imitation of European movies). I remember seeing *Cuando los hijos se van* and surmising that all Mexican movies played up the

30

love a mother has for her children and what ungrateful sons and daughters suffer when they are not devoted to their mothers. I remember the singing-type "westerns" of Jorge Negrete and Miquel Aceves Mejía. When watching Mexican movies, I felt a sense of homecoming as well as alienation. People who were to amount to something didn't go to Mexican movies, or *bailes,* or tune their radios to *bolero, rancherita,* and *corrido* music.

The whole time I was growing up, there was *norteño* music sometimes called North Mexican border music, or Tex-Mex music, or Chicano music, or *cantina* (bar) music. I grew up listening to *conjuntos,* three- or four-piece bands made up of folk musicians playing guitar, *bajo sexto,* drums, and button accordion, which Chicanos had borrowed from the German immigrants who had come to Central Texas and Mexico to farm and build breweries. In the Rio Grande Valley, Steve Jordan and Little Joe Hernández were popular, and Flaco Jiménez was the accordion king. The rhythms of Tex-Mex music are those of the polka, also adapted from the Germans, who in turn had borrowed the polka from the Czechs and Bohemians.

I remember the hot, sultry evenings when *corridos*—songs of love and death on the Texas-Mexican borderlands—reverberated out of cheap amplifiers from the local *cantinas* and wafted in through my bedroom window.

Corridos first became widely used along the South Texas/Mexican border during the early conflict between Chicanos and Anglos. The *corridos* are usually about Mexican heroes who do valiant deeds against the Anglo oppressors. Pancho Villa's song, "*La cucaracha,*" is the most famous one. *Corridos* of John F. Kennedy and his death are still very popular in the Valley. Older Chicanos remember Lydia Mendoza, one of the great border *corrido* singers who was called *la Gloria de Tejas.* Her "*El tango negro,*" sung during the Great Depression, made her a singer of the people. The everpresent *corridos* narrated one hundred years of border history, bringing news of events as well as entertaining. These folk musicians and folk songs are our chief cultural myth-makers, and they make our hard lives seem bearable.

I grew up feeling ambivalent about our music. Country-western and rock-and-roll had more status. In the 50s and 60s, for the slightly educated and *agringado* Chicanos, there existed a sense of shame at being caught listening to our music. Yet I couldn't stop my feet from thumping to the music, could not stop humming the words, nor hide from myself the exhilaration I felt when I heard it.

There are more subtle ways that we internalize identification, especially in the 35 forms of images and emotions. For me food and certain smells are tied to my identity, to my homeland. Woodsmoke curling up to an immense blue sky; woodsmoke perfuming my grandmother's clothes, her skin. The stench of cow manure and the yellow patches on the ground; the crack of a .22 rifle and the reek of cordite. Homemade white cheese sizzling in a pan, melting inside a folded *tortilla.* My sister Hilda's hot, spicy *menudo, chile colorado* making it a deep red, pieces of *panza* and hominy floating on top. My brother Carito barbequing *fajitas* in the backyard. Even now and 3,000 miles away, I can see my mother spicing the ground beef, pork, and venison with *chile*. My mouth salivates at the thought of the hot steaming *tamales* I would be eating if I were home.

Si le preguntas a mi mamá, "¿Qué eres?"

> "Identity is the essential core of who we are as individuals, the conscious experience of the self inside."
>
> —GERSHEN KAUFMAN[9]

Nosotros los Chicanos straddle the borderlands. On one side of us, we are constantly exposed to the Spanish of the Mexicans, on the other side we hear the Anglos' incessant clamoring so that we forget our language. Among ourselves we don't say *nosotros los americanos, o nosotros los españoles, o nosotros los hispanos.* We say *nosotros los mexicanos* (by *mexicanos* we do not mean citizens of Mexico; we do not mean a national identity, but a racial one). We distinguish between *mexicanos del otro lado* and *mexicanos de este lado.* Deep in our hearts we believe that being Mexican has nothing to do with which country one lives in. Being Mexican is a state of soul — not one of mind, not one of citizenship. Neither eagle nor serpent, but both. And like the ocean, neither animal respects borders.

> *Dime con quien andas y te diré quien eres.* (Tell me who your friends are and I'll tell you who you are.)
>
> —MEXICAN SAYING

Si le preguntas a mi mamá, "¿Qué eres?" te dirá, "Soy mexicana." My brothers and sister say the same. I sometimes will answer "*soy mexicana*" and at others will say "*soy Chicana*" *o* "*soy tejana*." But I identified as "*Raza*" before I ever identified as "*mexicana*" or "Chicana."

As a culture, we call ourselves Spanish when referring to ourselves as a linguistic group and when copping out. It is then that we forget our predominant Indian genes. We are 70–80 percent Indian.[10] We call ourselves Hispanic[11] or Spanish-American or Latin American or Latin when linking ourselves to other Spanish-speaking peoples of the Western hemisphere and when copping out. We call ourselves Mexican-American[12] to signify we are neither Mexican nor American, but more the noun "American" than the adjective "Mexican" (and when copping out).

Chicanos and other people of color suffer economically for not acculturating. This voluntary (yet forced) alienation makes for psychological conflict, a kind of dual identity — we don't identify with the Anglo-American cultural values and we don't totally identify with the Mexican cultural values. We are a synergy of two cultures with various degrees of Mexicanness or Angloness. I have so internalized the borderland conflict that sometimes I feel like one cancels out the other and we are zero, nothing, no one. *A veces no soy nada ni nadie. Pero hasta cuando no lo soy, lo soy.*

When not copping out, when we know we are more than nothing, we call 40
ourselves Mexican, referring to race and ancestry; *mestizo* when affirming both our Indian and Spanish (but we hardly ever own our Black ancestry); Chicano when referring to a politically aware people born and/or raised in the U.S.; *Raza* when referring to Chicanos; *tejanos* when we are Chicanos from Texas.

Chicanos did not know we were a people until 1965 when Ceasar Chavez and the farmworkers united and *I Am Joaquín* was published and *la Raza Unida* party was formed in Texas. With that recognition, we became a distinct people. Something momentous happened to the Chicano soul — we became aware of our reality and acquired a name and a language (Chicano Spanish) that reflected that reality. Now that we had a name, some of the fragmented pieces began to fall together — who we were, what we were, how we had evolved. We began to get glimpses of what we might eventually become.

Yet the struggle of identities continues, the struggle of borders is our reality still. One day the inner struggle will cease and a true integration take place. In the meantime, *tenémos que hacer la lucha. ¿Quién está protegiendo los ranchos de mi gente? ¿Quién está tratando de cerrar la fisura entre la india y el blanco en nuestra sangre? El Chicano, si, el Chicano que anda como un ladrón en su propia casa.*

Los Chicanos, how patient we seem, how very patient. There is the quiet of the Indian about us.[13] We know how to survive. When other races have given up their tongue, we've kept ours. We know what it is to live under the hammer blow of the dominant *norte-americano* culture. But more than we count the blows, we count the days the weeks the years the centuries the eons until the white laws and commerce and customs will rot in the deserts they've created, lie bleached. *Humildes* yet proud, *quietos* yet wild, *nosotros los mexicanos-Chicanos* will walk by the crumbling ashes as we go about our business. Stubborn, persevering, impenetrable as stone, yet possessing a malleability that renders us unbreakable, we, the *mestizas* and *mestizos*, will remain.

Notes

1. Ray Gwyn Smith, *Moorland Is Cold Country*, unpublished book.
2. Irena Klepfisz, "*Di rayze aheym*/The Journey Home," in *The Tribe of Dina: A Jewish Women's Anthology*, Melanie Kaye/Kantrowitz and Irena Klepfisz, eds. (Montpelier, VT: Sinister Wisdom Books, 1986), 49.
3. R. C. Ortega, *Dialectología Del Barrio*, trans. Hortencia S. Alwan (Los Angeles, CA: R. C. Ortega Publisher & Bookseller, 1977), 132.
4. Eduardo Hernandéz-Chávez, Andrew D. Cohen, and Anthony F. Beltramo, *El Lenguaje de los Chicanos: Regional and Social Characteristics of Language Used by Mexican Americans* (Arlington, VA: Center for Applied Linguistics, 1975), 39.

5. Hernandéz-Chávez, xvii.

6. Irena Klepfisz, "Secular Jewish Identity: Yidishkayt in America," in *The Tribe Dina*, Kaye/Kantrowitz and Klepfisz, eds., 43.

7. Melanie Kaye/Kantrowitz, "Sign," in *We Speak in Code: Poems and Other Writings* (Pittsburgh, PA: Motheroot Publications, Inc., 1980), 85.

8. Rodolfo Gonzales, *I Am Joaquín/Yo Soy Joaquín* (New York, NY: Bantam Books, 1972). It was first published in 1967.

9. Gershen Kaufman, *Shame: The Power of Caring* (Cambridge, MA: Schenkman Books, Inc., 1980), 68.

10. John R. Chávez, *The Lost Land: The Chicano Images of the Southwest* (Albuquerque, NM: University of New Mexico Press, 1984), 88–90.

11. "Hispanic" is derived from *Hispanis* (*España*, a name given to the Iberian Peninsula in ancient times when it was a part of the Roman Empire) and is a term designated by the U.S. government to make it easier to handle us on paper.

12. The Treaty of Guadalupe Hidalgo created the Mexican-American in 1848.

13. Anglos, in order to alleviate their guilt for dispossessing the Chicano, stressed the Spanish part of us and perpetrated the myth of the Spanish Southwest. We have accepted the fiction that we are Hispanic, that is Spanish, in order to accommodate ourselves to the dominant culture and its abhorrence of Indians. Chávez, 88–91.

Exploring the Text

1. Much of this essay is written in Spanish or a variant of it. In some instances, Gloria Anzaldúa translates into English, though not all the time. As a reader, how do you react to the passages written in Spanish? How does your level of fluency with that language affect your response?

2. What is the purpose of the opening anecdote about the dentist (paras. 1–3)? What ethos is Anzaldúa establishing with her audience? When she writes, "My mouth is a motherlode," is she being facetious or aggressive? How can you tell?

3. In several instances (such as paras. 7 and 8), Anzaldúa points out the sexism inherent in the communities she is writing about. Explain whether you think this discussion is part of her overall point about the consequences of language bias and domination, or whether it is a separate point.

4. Examine the syntax of paragraph 12. What types of sentences does Anzaldúa use? How does the syntax reinforce the message she is conveying? Consider form, variety, and pacing in your response.

5. In paragraphs 14–17, Anzaldúa draws on her personal experiences to illustrate the eight languages she enumerates. Explain why you think that this focus makes readers feel excluded or included. Then discuss whether Anzaldúa's personal experience interwoven throughout the essay strengthens or weakens her argument. (See also paras. 31–34.)

6. Why is English a "neutral language" (para. 25), according to Anzaldúa? In what situations that you have observed or read does English become neutral ground for those who speak different languages?

7. What does Anzaldúa mean by her claim, "Ethnic identity is twin skin to linguistic identity—I am my language" (para. 27)? Is this her thesis, or primary claim, in the essay? Explain why you agree or disagree with her.

8. Anzaldúa claims, "I will overcome the tradition of silence" (para. 28). What does she mean? Explain to what extent you believe writing this essay contributes to her goal.

9. What strategies does Anzaldúa use to appeal to authority? Cite specific passages where these occur.

10. Anzaldúa divides her essay into four main sections: an introduction, "Overcoming the Tradition of Silence," "Chicano Spanish," and "Linguistic Terrorism." What is the progression and/or connection among these divisions?

11. The third section, "Chicano Spanish," is a fairly technical linguistic and historical analysis. What does it contribute to the essay? What would be lost if it were omitted or repositioned?

12. Some critics and readers of Anzaldúa's works have pointed out that while her anger about the issues she examines may be justified, her writing suffers as a result of overly strong emotions. Explain why you agree or disagree that her fiery tone detracts from her argument. Pay special attention to the final paragraph.

13. What similarities do you see among the sources that Anzaldúa has cited? What is the purpose of notes 11 and 13? Do you think it would have been more effective if Anzaldúa had incorporated these points within the text of her argument? Explain why or why not.

14. This essay was published in 1987, long before the day we now know as 9/11. Do you think that the new historical reality argues for changing the section heading entitled "Linguistic Terrorism," or does this reality make the heading even more powerful? Explain your viewpoint.

Always Living in Spanish

MARJORIE AGOSÍN

Human rights activist, author, and professor at Wellesley College, Marjorie Agosín (b. 1955) is a descendant of Russian and Austrian Jews. She was born in Maryland and raised in Chile, but she left for the United States with her parents when the dictator Augusto Pinochet overthrew the government of Salvador Allende. Agosín's writings reflect her heritage, especially the experience of Jewish refugees, and she has received international acclaim for her work on behalf of poor women in developing countries. Agosín has written many books of fiction, memoirs, poetry, and essays. These include the collection of bilingual poems entitled *Dear Anne*

Frank (1994); *A Cross and a Star: Memoirs of a Jewish Girl in Chile* (1995), about her mother; *At the Threshold of Memory: New and Selected Poems* (2003); and her latest, a long narrative poem called *The Light of Desire* (2010). In the following essay, written in 1999, Agosín explores the passionate connection she feels with Spanish, her first language.

In the evenings in the northern hemisphere, I repeat the ancient ritual that I observed as a child in the southern hemisphere: going out while the night is still warm and trying to recognize the stars as it begins to grow dark silently. In the sky of my country, Chile, that long and wide stretch of land that the poets blessed and dictators abused, I could easily name the stars: the three Marias, the Southern Cross, and the three Lilies, names of beloved and courageous women.

But here in the United States, where I have lived since I was a young girl, the solitude of exile makes me feel that so little is mine, that not even the sky has the same constellations, the trees and the fauna the same names or sounds, or the rubbish the same smell. How does one recover the familiar? How does one name the unfamiliar? How can one be another or live in a foreign language? These are the dilemmas of one who writes in Spanish and lives in translation.

Since my earliest childhood in Chile I lived with the tempos and the melodies of a multiplicity of tongues: German, Yiddish, Russian, Turkish, and many Latin songs. Because everyone was from somewhere else, my relatives laughed, sang, and fought in a Babylon of languages. Spanish was reserved for matters of extreme seriousness, for commercial transactions, or for illnesses, but everyone's mother tongue was always associated with the memory of spaces inhabited in the past: the shtetl,[1] the flowering and vast Vienna avenues, the minarets of Turkey, and the Ladino whispers of Toledo. When my paternal grandmother sang old songs in Turkish, her voice and body assumed the passion of one who was there in the city of Istanbul, gazing by turns toward the west and the east.

Destiny and the always ambiguous nature of history continued my family's enforced migration, and because of it I, too, became one who had to live and speak in translation. The disappearances, torture, and clandestine deaths in my country in the early seventies drove us to the United States, that other America that looked with suspicion at those who did not speak English and especially those who came from the supposedly uncivilized regions of Latin America. I had left a dangerous place that was my home, only to arrive in a dangerous place that was not: a high school in the small town of Athens, Georgia, where my poor English and my accent were the cause of ridicule and insult. The only way I could recover my usurped country and my Chilean childhood was by continuing to write in Spanish, the same way my grandparents had sung in their own tongues in diasporic sites.

---

[1]Yiddish: little town, specifically in Eastern Europe. — Eds.

The new and learned English language did not fit with the visceral emotions   5
and themes that my poetry contained, but by writing in Spanish I could recover
fragrances, spoken rhythms, and the passion of my own identity. Daily I felt the
need to translate myself for the strangers living all around me, to tell them why
we were in Georgia, why we ate differently, why we had fled, why my accent was so
thick, and why I did not look Hispanic. Only at night, writing poems in Spanish,
could I return to my senses, and soothe my own sorrow over what I had left behind.

This is how I became a Chilean poet who wrote in Spanish and lived in the
southern United States. And then, one day, a poem of mine was translated and
published in the English language. Finally, for the first time since I had left Chile,
I felt I didn't have to explain myself. My poem, expressed in another language,
spoke for itself . . . and for me.

Sometimes the austere sounds of English help me bear the solitude of knowing that I am foreign and so far away from those about whom I write. I must
admit I would like more opportunities to read in Spanish to people whose language and culture is also mine, to join in our common heritage and in the feast of
our sounds. I would also like readers of English to understand the beauty of the
spoken word in Spanish, that constant flow of oxytonic and paraoxytonic[2] syllables
(*Verde que te quiero verde*), the joy of writing — of dancing — in another language.
I believe that many exiles share the unresolvable torment of not being able to live
in the language of their childhood.

I miss that undulating and sensuous language of mine, those baroque descriptions, the sense of being and feeling that Spanish gives me. It is perhaps for this
reason that I have chosen and will always choose to write in Spanish. Nothing else
from my childhood world remains. My country seems to be frozen in gestures of
silence and oblivion. My relatives have died, and I have grown up not knowing a
young generation of cousins and nieces and nephews. Many of my friends disappeared, others were tortured, and the most fortunate, like me, became guardians of
memory. For us, to write in Spanish is to always be in active pursuit of memory. I
seek to recapture a world lost to me on that sorrowful afternoon when the blue
electric sky and the Andean cordillera[3] bade me farewell. On that, my last Chilean
day, I carried under my arm my innocence recorded in a little blue notebook I kept
even then. Gradually that diary filled with memoranda, poems written in free verse,
descriptions of dreams and of the thresholds of my house surrounded by cherry
trees and gardenias. To write in Spanish is for me a gesture of survival. And because
of translation, my memory has now become a part of the memory of many others.

Translators are not traitors, as the proverb says, but rather splendid friends in
this great human community of language.

. . . .

---

[2]Oxytonic words stress the last syllable, while paraoxytonics stress the next-to-last syllable.
— Eds.
[3]Coastal mountains. — Eds.

Exploring the Text

1. How would you describe Marjorie Agosín's opening strategy in the first two paragraphs? How effective are the two paragraphs in capturing the reader's attention and establishing the author's ethos?
2. What does Agosín mean by the allusion to "a Babylon of languages" (para. 3)?
3. What is the effect of the following statement, an example of antithesis, by Agosín: "I had left a dangerous place that was my home, only to arrive in a dangerous place that was not" (para. 4)?
4. Why is the first translation of a poem of Agosín's meaningful for her?
5. List the ways Agosín describes Spanish. How would you describe these descriptive terms? Contrast these descriptions with the way Agosín refers to English. How do the differences contribute to the effectiveness of her essay?
6. What is Agosín's thesis, or claim, in this essay? Find a sentence that seems closest to a directly stated thesis.
7. What does Agosín mean when she says, "To write in Spanish is for me a gesture of survival" (para. 8)?
8. How would you describe the tone of this essay? Cite specific passages to support your response.
9. This essay was published in *Poets & Writers*, a magazine for writers. Discuss why and how Agosín appeals to this audience.
10. Agosín alludes to the way her "grandparents had sung in their own tongues in diasporic sites" (para. 4). What does she mean by "diasporic sites"? Are they literal geographical places? Discuss the concept of diaspora as it applies to a group in the contemporary world (for example, the African diaspora, the Chinese diaspora).

The "F Word"

FIROOZEH DUMAS

Firoozeh Dumas was born in Iran in 1965 and moved to California when she was seven, returned with her family to Iran two years later, and then came back to the United States two years after that. She received her BA from the University of California, Berkeley. In 2001 she began writing her family's stories as a gift to her own children, and in 2003 they were published as *Funny in Farsi: A Memoir of Growing Up Iranian in America*. An immensely popular book, it has been selected by cities and campuses throughout the country as their community read and was nominated for the PEN/USA award in 2004. A finalist for the prestigious Thurber Prize for American Humor, Dumas was the first Middle Eastern woman ever nominated; she lost to Jon Stewart. She often writes commentaries for National Public Radio, the *New York Times*, and the *Los Angeles Times*, and in 2008 she published

Laughing without an Accent, a series of autobiographical essays. The following excerpt from *Funny in Farsi* depicts cultural clashes as manifested in language.

My cousin's name, Farbod, means "Greatness." When he moved to America, all the kids called him "Farthead." My brother Farshid ("He Who Enlightens") became "Fartshit." The name of my friend Neggar means "Beloved," although it can be more accurately translated as "She Whose Name Almost Incites Riots." Her brother Arash ("Giver") initially couldn't understand why every time he'd say his name, people would laugh and ask him if it itched.

All of us immigrants knew that moving to America would be fraught with challenges, but none of us thought that our names would be such an obstacle. How could our parents have ever imagined that someday we would end up in a country where monosyllabic names reign supreme, a land where "William" is shortened to "Bill," where "Susan" becomes "Sue," and "Richard" somehow evolves into "Dick"? America is a great country, but nobody without a mask and a cape has a *z* in his name. And have Americans ever realized the great scope of the guttural sounds they're missing? Okay, so it has to do with linguistic roots, but I do believe this would be a richer country if all Americans could do a little tongue aerobics and learn to pronounce "kh," a sound more commonly associated in this culture with phlegm, or "gh," the sound usually made by actors in the final moments of a choking scene. It's like adding a few new spices to the kitchen pantry. Move over, cinnamon and nutmeg, make way for cardamom and sumac.

Exotic analogies aside, having a foreign name in this land of Joes and Marys is a pain in the spice cabinet. When I was twelve, I decided to simplify my life by adding an American middle name. This decision serves as proof that sometimes simplifying one's life in the short run only complicates it in the long run.

My name, Firoozeh, chosen by my mother, means "Turquoise" in Farsi. In America, it means "Unpronounceable" or "I'm Not Going to Talk to You Because I Cannot Possibly Learn Your Name and I Just Don't Want to Have to Ask You Again and Again Because You'll Think I'm Dumb or You Might Get Upset or Something." My father, incidentally, had wanted to name me Sara. I do wish he had won that argument.

To strengthen my decision to add an American name, I had just finished fifth 5 grade in Whittier, where all the kids incessantly called me "Ferocious." That summer, my family moved to Newport Beach, where I looked forward to starting a new life. I wanted to be a kid with a name that didn't draw so much attention, a name that didn't come with a built-in inquisition as to when and why I had moved to America and how was it that I spoke English without an accent and was I planning on going back and what did I think of America?

My last name didn't help any. I can't mention my maiden name, because:

"Dad, I'm writing a memoir."

"Great! Just don't mention our name."

Suffice it to say that, with eight letters, including a *z*, and four syllables, my last name is as difficult and foreign as my first. My first and last name together generally served the same purpose as a high brick wall. There was one exception to this rule. In Berkeley, and only in Berkeley, my name drew people like flies to baklava. These were usually people named Amaryllis or Chrysanthemum, types who vacationed in Costa Rica and to whom lentils described a type of burger. These folks were probably not the pride of Poughkeepsie, but they were refreshingly nonjudgmental.

When I announced to my family that I wanted to add an American name, they reacted with their usual laughter. Never one to let mockery or good judgment stand in my way, I proceeded to ask for suggestions. My father suggested "Fifi." Had I a special affinity for French poodles or been considering a career in prostitution, I would've gone with that one. My mom suggested "Farah," a name easier than "Firoozeh" yet still Iranian. Her reasoning made sense, except that Farrah Fawcett was at the height of her popularity and I didn't want to be associated with somebody whose poster hung in every postpubescent boy's bedroom. We couldn't think of any American names beginning with *F*, so we moved on to *J*, the first letter of our last name. I don't know why we limited ourselves to names beginning with my initials, but it made sense at that moment, perhaps by the logic employed moments before bungee jumping. I finally chose the name "Julie" mainly for its simplicity. My brothers, Farid and Farshid, thought that adding an American name was totally stupid. They later became Fred and Sean.

That same afternoon, our doorbell rang. It was our new next-door neighbor, a friendly girl my age named Julie. She asked me my name and after a moment of hesitation, I introduced myself as Julie. "What a coincidence!" she said. I didn't mention that I had been Julie for only half an hour.

Thus I started sixth grade with my new, easy name and life became infinitely simpler. People actually remembered my name, which was an entirely refreshing new sensation. All was well until the Iranian Revolution, when I found myself with a new set of problems. Because I spoke English without an accent and was known as Julie, people assumed I was American. This meant that I was often privy to their real feelings about those "damn I-raynians." It was like having those X-ray glasses that let you see people undressed, except that what I was seeing was far uglier than people's underwear. It dawned on me that these people would have probably never invited me to their house had they known me as Firoozeh. I felt like a fake.

When I went to college, I eventually went back to using my real name. All was well until I graduated and started looking for a job. Even though I had graduated with honors from UC–Berkeley, I couldn't get a single interview. I was guilty of being a humanities major, but I began to suspect that there was more to my problems. After three months of rejections, I added "Julie" to my résumé. Call it coincidence, but the job offers started coming in. Perhaps it's the same kind of coincidence that keeps African Americans from getting cabs in New York.

10

Once I got married, my name became Julie Dumas. I went from having an identifiably "ethnic" name to having ancestors who wore clogs. My family and non-American friends continued calling me Firoozeh, while my coworkers and American friends called me Julie. My life became one big knot, especially when friends who knew me as Julie met friends who knew me as Firoozeh. I felt like those characters in soap operas who have an evil twin. The two, of course, can never be in the same room, since they're played by the same person, a struggling actress who wears a wig to play one of the twins and dreams of moving on to bigger and better roles. I couldn't blame my mess on a screenwriter; it was my own doing.

I decided to untangle the knot once and for all by going back to my real name. By then, I was a stay-at-home mom, so I really didn't care whether people remembered my name or gave me job interviews. Besides, most of the people I dealt with were in diapers and were in no position to judge. I was also living in Silicon Valley, an area filled with people named Rajeev, Avishai, and Insook.

Every once in a while, though, somebody comes up with a new permutation and I am once again reminded that I am an immigrant with a foreign name. I recently went to have blood drawn for a physical exam. The waiting room for blood work at our local medical clinic is in the basement of the building, and no matter how early one arrives for an appointment, forty coughing, wheezing people have gotten there first. Apart from reading *Golf Digest* and *Popular Mechanics*, there isn't much to do except guess the number of contagious diseases represented in the windowless room. Every ten minutes, a name is called and everyone looks to see which cough matches that name. As I waited patiently, the receptionist called out, "Fritzy, Fritzy!" Everyone looked around, but no one stood up. Usually, if I'm waiting to be called by someone who doesn't know me, I will respond to just about any name starting with an *F*. Having been called Froozy, Frizzy, Fiorucci, and Frooz and just plain "Uhhhh . . . ," I am highly accommodating. I did not, however, respond to "Fritzy" because there is, as far as I know, no *t* in my name. The receptionist tried again, "Fritzy, Fritzy DumbAss." As I stood up to this most linguistically original version of my name, I could feel all eyes upon me. The room was momentarily silent as all of these sick people sat united in a moment of gratitude for their own names.

Despite a few exceptions, I have found that Americans are now far more willing to learn new names, just as they're far more willing to try new ethnic foods. Of course, some people just don't like to learn. One mom at my children's school adamantly refused to learn my "impossible" name and instead settled on calling me "F Word." She was recently transferred to New York where, from what I've heard, she might meet an immigrant or two and, who knows, she just might have to make some room in her spice cabinet.

Exploring the Text

1. In the opening paragraph, Firoozeh Dumas gives several examples of names of her family members and friends, contrasting the meaning of each name and the version given by Americans. Is it funny? Is it inappropriate? What different perspectives is she asking her readers to see?

2. What rhetorical strategies does Dumas employ in paragraph 2 to establish a lively conversational tone? Where do you detect sarcasm?

3. At the end of paragraph 2, Dumas introduces the metaphor of "new spices [in] the kitchen pantry." How does she develop this metaphor as the essay continues? Do you find it an effective or ineffective way to talk about the issues she raises? Explain your response.

4. How does Dumas characterize the people she met in Berkeley, California (para. 9)? Do you think she is stereotyping them? Explain.

5. What points does the story of Dumas's decision to change her name allow her to make about both her own family and Americans? How does it prove the assertion that "sometimes simplifying one's life in the short run only complicates it in the long run" (para. 3)?

6. In paragraph 12, Dumas describes how having her American name Julie and speaking without an accent was like having "X-ray glasses that let you see people undressed." What other references to popular culture do you find, and why do you think Dumas includes them?

7. How does Dumas characterize Americans? Do you agree with her characterization? Given the fact that her audience is likely to be primarily Americans, to what extent do you think she risks antagonizing or offending them? Explain.

8. What is the argument Dumas is making? What is her claim? What evidence does she provide as support?

9. How does Dumas use humor to develop her argument? Identify specific examples, and discuss how each contributes to Dumas achieving her purpose(s). Are some more effective than others? Why?

10. Overall, how would you characterize her tone? Consider the role of humor in your response — that is, whether Dumas is amusing, sarcastic, playful, bitter, or a combination.

In Plain English: Let's Make It Official

Charles Krauthammer

Charles Krauthammer was born in New York City in 1950 and raised in Montreal. He studied political science and economics at McGill University and Oxford University before going to Harvard Medical School for his MD in psychiatry. After serving as a speechwriter for former vice president Walter Mondale, Krauthammer began his career in journalism with the *New Republic*. He went on to write regularly for *Time* magazine, the *Weekly Standard*, and the *Washington Post*. He is also a political analyst for Fox News. Krauthammer won the 1987 Pulitzer Prize for Commentary and has been called the most influential commentator in America by the *Financial Times*. The following piece appeared in *Time* magazine in 2006, shortly after the Senate passed two contradictory amendments to the Comprehensive Immigration Reform Act. One declared English the "common and unifying language of the United States," thus permitting government documents to be printed in other languages. The other declared English the "national language of the United States," thus ensuring that all government documents would be printed only in English.

Growing up (as I did) in the province of Québec, you learn not just the joys but also the perils of bilingualism. A separate national identity, revolving entirely around "Francophonie," became a raging issue that led to social unrest, terrorism, threats of separation and a referendum that came within a hair's breadth of breaking up Canada.

Canada, of course, had no choice about bilingualism. It is a country created of two nations at its birth, and has ever since been trying to cope with that inherently divisive fact. The U.S., by contrast blessed with a single common language for two centuries, seems blithely and gratuitously to be ready to import bilingualism with all its attendant divisiveness and antagonisms.

One of the major reasons for America's great success as the world's first "universal nation," for its astonishing and unmatched capacity for assimilating immigrants, has been that an automatic part of acculturation was the acquisition of English. And yet during the great immigration debate now raging in Congress, the people's representatives cannot make up their minds whether the current dominance of English should be declared a national asset, worthy of enshrinement in law.

The Senate could not bring itself to declare English the country's "official language." The best it could do was pass an amendment to the immigration bill tepidly declaring English the "national language." Yet even that was too much for Senate Democratic leader Harry Reid, who called that resolution "racist." Less hyperbolic opponents point out that granting special official status to English is simply unnecessary: America has been accepting foreign-language-speaking immigrants forever—Brooklyn is so polyglot it is a veritable Babel—and yet we've done just fine. What's the great worry about Spanish?

The worry is this. Polyglot is fine. When immigrants, like those in Brooklyn, are members of a myriad of linguistic communities, each tiny and discrete, there is no threat to the common culture. No immigrant presumes to make the demand that the state grant special status to his language. He may speak it in the street and proudly teach it to his children, but he knows that his future and certainly theirs lie inevitably in learning English as the gateway to American life.

But all of that changes when you have an enormous, linguistically monoclo-nal[1] immigration as we do today from Latin America. Then you get not Brook-lyn's successful Babel but Canada's restive Québec. Monoclonal immigration is new for the U.S., and it changes things radically. If at the turn of the 20th century, Ellis Island had greeted teeming masses speaking not 50 languages but just, say, German, America might not have enjoyed the same success at assimilation and national unity that it has.

Today's monoclonal linguistic culture is far from hypothetical. Growing rap-idly through immigration, it creates large communities — in some places already majorities — so overwhelmingly Spanish speaking that, in time, they may quite naturally demand the rights and official recognition for Spanish that French has in French-speaking Québec.

That would not be the end of the world — Canada is a decent place — but the beginning of a new one for the U.S., a world far more complicated and fraught with division. History has blessed us with all the freedom and advantages of multi-culturalism. But it has also blessed us, because of the accident of our origins, with a linguistic unity that brings a critically needed cohesion to a nation as diverse, multiracial and multiethnic as America. Why gratuitously throw away that price-less asset? How mindless to call the desire to retain it "racist."

I speak three languages. My late father spoke nine. When he became a natu-ralized American in midcentury, it never occurred to him to demand of his new and beneficent land that whenever its government had business with him — tax forms, court proceedings, ballot boxes — that it should be required to commu-nicate in French, his best language, rather than English, his last and relatively weakest.

English is the U.S.'s national and common language. But that may change over time unless we change our assimilation norms. Making English the official language is the first step toward establishing those norms. "Official" means the language of the government and its institutions. "Official" makes clear our expec-tations of acculturation. "Official" means that every citizen, upon entering Amer-ica's most sacred political space, the voting booth, should minimally be able to identify the words *President* and *Vice President* and *county commissioner* and *judge*. The immigrant, of course, has the right to speak whatever he wants. But he must understand that when he comes to the U.S., swears allegiance and accepts its bounty, he undertakes to join its civic culture. In English.

10

Exploring the Text

1. What is Charles Krauthammer's overall argument? State his claim (or identify it in the article), and cite the major points he makes to support it.

---

[1]Normally a biological term indicating a group of cells that can all trace their ancestry back to a single cell. Here it is used to mean a group of people with a single linguistic heritage. — Eds.

2. How does the writer establish ethos? Identify at least two passages within the essay that help him accomplish this.

3. What is the basis of the comparison Krauthammer makes between the United States and Canada? To what extent do you find this comparison an effective rhetorical strategy?

4. Which counterarguments does Krauthammer address? Cite at least two, and discuss how he concedes and refutes each.

5. What does he mean by the description of "an enormous, linguistically monoclonal immigration" (para. 6)? How does it connect to "Canada's restive Québec" (para. 6)?

6. Throughout the essay, Krauthammer employs diction with strong emotional connotations, such as the repeated use of the word "blessed." What other examples are there? Do you think these choices enhance or distract from his central argument? Explain why you hold this view.

7. What does Krauthammer suggest by putting the word "official" in quotation marks? Why does he do that in some instances but not in others? In the final paragraph, Krauthammer refers to "national," "common," and "official" language. What are the distinctions?

8. What does Krauthammer mean in the closing paragraph by "civic culture"? Do you think that the civic culture of the United States is or is not the same today as when he was writing in 2006? Explain your response.

9. Which part(s) of Krauthammer's argument do you agree with? Disagree with? Explain by citing examples drawn from your own observations or experience.

Words Don't Mean What They Mean

STEVEN PINKER

> Steven Pinker was born in Montreal, Canada, in 1954. He received a BA from McGill University and a PhD from Harvard. He taught for twenty-one years in the Department of Brain and Cognitive Sciences at the Massachusetts Institute of Technology and for two years at Stanford. Later, he moved to Harvard, where he is now a professor in the psychology department. Pinker writes about the nature of language and cognitive science; among his books are *The Language Instinct* (1994), *How the Mind Works* (1997), *The Blank Slate* (2002), and *The Better Angels of Our Nature* (2011). His essays have appeared in a variety of publications, including the *New York Times*, *Time* magazine, the *New Yorker*, *Technology Review*, and *Slate*. Taken from his 2007 book *The Stuff of Thought*, the essay included here appeared in *Time* in September of that year.

In the movie *Tootsie*, the character played by Dustin Hoffman is disguised as a woman and is speaking to a beautiful young actress played by Jessica Lange. During a session of late-night girl talk, Lange's character says, "You know what I wish? That a guy could be honest enough to walk up to me and say, 'I could lay a big line on you, but the simple truth is I find you very interesting, and I'd really like to make love to you.' Wouldn't that be a relief?"

Later in the movie, a twist of fate throws them together at a cocktail party, this time with Hoffman's character dressed as a man. The actress doesn't recognize him, and he tries out the speech on her. Before he can even finish, she throws a glass of wine in his face and storms away.

When people talk, they lay lines on each other, do a lot of role playing, side-step, shilly-shally and engage in all manner of vagueness and innuendo. We do this and expect others to do it, yet at the same time we profess to long for the plain truth, for people to say what they mean, simple as that. Such hypocrisy is a human universal.

Sexual come-ons are a classic example. "Would you like to come up and see my etchings?" has been recognized as a double entendre for so long that by 1939, James Thurber could draw a cartoon of a hapless man in an apartment lobby saying to his date, "You wait here, and I'll bring the etchings down."

The veiled threat also has a stereotype: the Mafia wiseguy offering protection 5 with the soft sell, "Nice store you got there. Would be a real shame if something happened to it." Traffic cops sometimes face not-so-innocent questions like, "Gee, Officer, is there some way I could pay the fine right here?" And anyone who has sat through a fund-raising dinner is familiar with euphemistic schnorring like, "We're counting on you to show leadership."

Why don't people just say what they mean? The reason is that conversational partners are not modems downloading information into each other's brains. People are very, very touchy about their relationships. Whenever you speak to someone, you are presuming the two of you have a certain degree of familiarity — which your words might alter. So every sentence has to do two things at once: convey a message and continue to negotiate that relationship.

The clearest example is ordinary politeness. When you are at a dinner party and want the salt, you don't blurt out, "Gimme the salt." Rather, you use what linguists call a whimperative, as in "Do you think you could pass the salt?" or "If you could pass the salt, that would be awesome."

Taken literally, these sentences are inane. The second is an overstatement, and the answer to the first is obvious. Fortunately, the hearer assumes that the speaker is rational and listens between the lines. Yes, your point is to request the salt, but you're doing it in such a way that first takes care to establish what linguists call "felicity conditions," or the prerequisites to making a sensible request. The underlying rationale is that the hearer not be given a command but simply be asked or advised about one of the necessary conditions for passing the salt. Your goal is to have your need satisfied without treating the listener as a flunky who can be bossed around at will.

Warm acquaintances go out of their way not to look as if they are presuming a dominant-subordinate relationship but rather one of equals. It works the other way too. When people are in a subordinate relationship (like a driver with police), they can't sound as if they are presuming anything more than that, so any bribe must be veiled. Fund raisers, simulating an atmosphere of warm friendship with their donors, also can't break the spell with a bald businesslike proposition.

It is in the arena of sexual relationships, however, that the linguistic dance can be its most elaborate. In an episode of *Seinfeld*, George is asked by his date if he would like to come up for coffee. He declines, explaining that caffeine keeps him up at night. Later he slaps his forehead: "'Coffee' doesn't mean coffee! 'Coffee' means sex!" The moment is funny, but it's also a reminder of just how carefully romantic partners must always tread. Make too blatant a request, as in *Tootsie*, and the hearer is offended; too subtle, as in *Seinfeld*, and it can go over the hearer's head.

In the political arena, miscalibrated speech can lead to more serious consequences than wine in the face or a slap on the forehead. In 1980, Wanda Brandstetter, a lobbyist for the National Organization for Women (NOW), tried to get an Illinois state representative to vote for the Equal Rights Amendment (ERA) by handing him a business card on which she had written, "Mr. Swanstrom, the offer for help in your election, plus $1,000 for your campaign for the pro-ERA vote." A prosecutor called the note a "contract for bribery," and the jury agreed.

So how do lobbyists in Gucci Gulch bribe legislators today? They do it with innuendo. If Brandstetter had said, "As you know, Mr. Swanstrom, NOW has a history of contributing to political campaigns. And it has contributed more to candidates with a voting record that is compatible with our goals. These days one of our goals is the ratification of the ERA," she would have avoided a fine, probation and community service.

Indirect speech has a long history in diplomacy too. In the wake of the Six-Day War in 1967, the U.N. Security Council passed its famous Resolution 242, which called for the "withdrawal of Israeli armed forces from territories occupied in the recent conflict." The wording is ambiguous. Does it mean "some of the territories" or "all of the territories"? In some ways it was best not to ask, since the phrasing was palatable to Israel and its allies only under the former interpretation and to concerned Arab states and their allies only under the latter. Unfortunately, for 40 years partisans have been debating the semantics of Resolution 242, and the Israeli-Arab conflict remains unresolved, to put it mildly.

That's not to say such calculated ambiguity never works for diplomats. After all, the language of an agreement has to be acceptable not just to leaders but to their citizens. Reasonable leaders might thus come to an understanding between themselves, while each exploits the ambiguities of the deal to sell it to their country's more bellicose factions. What's more, diplomats can gamble that times will change and circumstances will bring the two sides together, at which point they can resolve the vagueness amicably.

When all else fails, as it often does, nations can sort out their problems without any words at all — and often without fighting either. In these cases, they may fall back on communicating through what's known as authority ranking, also known as power, status, autonomy and dominance. The logic of authority ranking is "Don't mess with me." Its biological roots are in the dominance hierarchies that are widespread in the animal kingdom. One animal claims the right to a contested resource based on size, strength, seniority or allies, and the other animal cedes it when the outcome of the battle can be predicted and both sides have a stake in not getting bloodied in a fight whose winner is a forgone conclusion. Such sword-rattling gestures as a larger military power's conducting "naval exercises" in the waters off the coast of a weaker foe are based on just this kind of pre-emptive reminder of strength.

People often speak of indirect speech as a means of saving face. What we're referring to is not just a matter of hurt feelings but a social currency with real value. The expressive power of words helps us guard this prized asset, but only as long as we're careful. Words let us say the things we want to say and also things we would be better off not having said. They let us know the things we need to know, and also things we wish we didn't. Language is a window into human nature, but it is also a fistula, an open wound through which we're exposed to an infectious world. It's not surprising that we sheathe our words in politeness and innuendo and other forms of doublespeak.

Exploring the Text

1. Steven Pinker opens by describing a scene out of the movie *Tootsie*, which was made in 1982. Then, in paragraph 3, he explains how the scene illustrates the main point of his argument. Do you think it would have been more effective simply to begin with paragraph 3? Why or why not?

2. What does Pinker mean when he states, "Such hypocrisy is a human universal" (para. 3)? Is he being critical? Explain whether you agree or disagree with him.

3. How does the example of asking someone to pass the salt illustrate Pinker's claim that when we speak we are both conveying a message and negotiating a relationship? What is an example from your own experience that demonstrates these two functions of speech?

4. Pinker's essay appeared in *Time* magazine, which has a large general readership. How do the examples he has chosen explain specialized linguistic concepts to that audience?

5. Pinker ends his essay with a claim of value: "Language is a window into human nature, but it is also a fistula, an open wound through which we're exposed to an infectious world." What does he mean? How does this statement sum up his explanation of the way indirect speech functions? Would it have been more effective if he had stated it earlier in the essay? Why or why not?

6. Pinker describes a number of linguistic strategies, including double entendre, veiled threat, "whimperative," innuendo, calculated ambiguity, and authority ranking. Choose two of these and cite an example from your experience, observations, or reading that illustrates each.

7. Compare and contrast the argument Pinker makes with the argument George Orwell makes in "Politics and the English Language" (p. 707).

For Mohammed Zeid of Gaza, Age 15
and
Why I Could Not Accept Your Invitation

Naomi Shihab Nye

Poet, novelist, editor, and political activist Naomi Shihab Nye (b. 1952) is the daughter of a Palestinian father and American mother. Nye grew up in St. Louis, Missouri, visited Jerusalem for the first time when she was fourteen, and currently lives in San Antonio, Texas. Her works for children include the picture book *Sitti's Secret* (1994) and the novel *Habibi* (1996). Her poetry collections include *Different Ways to Pray* (1980), *19 Varieties of Gazelle: Poems of the Middle East* (2002), and *Transfer* (2011). She has won many awards and fellowships, including four Pushcart Prizes (for best work from small presses), the Jane Addams Children's Book Award, and the Isabella Gardner Poetry Award. Nye, who has been a visiting writer all over the world, describes herself as "a wandering poet." An advocate for peaceful solutions to conflict, she often writes about miscommunications caused by disregarding or misusing language, as in the following two poems from her collection *You and Yours* (2005).

For Mohammed Zeid of Gaza, Age 15

There is no *stray* bullet, sirs.
No bullet like a worried cat
crouching under a bush,
no half-hairless puppy bullet
dodging midnight streets.   5
The bullet could not be a pecan
plunking the tin roof,
not hardly, no fluff of pollen
on October's breath,
no humble pebble at our feet.   10

So don't gentle it, please.

We live among stray thoughts,
tasks abandoned midstream.

Our fickle hearts are fat
with stray devotions, we feel at home   15
among bits and pieces,
all the wandering ways of words.

But this bullet had no innocence, did not
wish anyone well, you can't tell us otherwise
by naming it mildly, this bullet was never the friend   20
of life, should not be granted immunity
by soft saying—friendly fire, straying death-eye,
why have we given the wrong weight to what we do?

Mohammed, Mohammed, deserves the truth.
This bullet had no secret happy hopes,   25
it was not singing to itself with eyes closed
under the bridge.

Exploring the Text

1. Who is the speaker in "For Mohammed Zeid of Gaza, Age 15"?
2. What is the setting of the poem? Why is it important?
3. Usually, what part of speech is the word *gentle*? What is the effect of using it in this poem as a verb (l. 11)?
4. The speaker objects to a certain use of "stray" (l. 1) yet accepts another (ll. 12 and 15). What distinction is being made?
5. What metaphors for the bullet does the speaker reject? Why are they inappropriate?
6. Why does the speaker believe our hearts are "fickle" and "fat with stray devotions" (ll. 14–15)?
7. What is the speaker's purpose in this poem? What does he or she want the audience to understand or feel?

Why I Could Not Accept Your Invitation

Besides the fact that your event
is coming up in three weeks
on the other side of the world
and you just invited me *now*,
your fax contained the following phrases: 5
action-research oriented initiative;
regionally based evaluation vehicles;
culture should impregnate all different sectors;

consumption of cultural products;
key flashpoints in thematic areas.   10
Don't get me wrong, I love what you are doing,
believing in art and culture,
there, in the country next to the country
my country has recently been devastating
in the name of democracy,   15
but that is not the language I live in
and so I cannot come.
I live in teaspoon, bucket, river, pain,
turtle sunning on a brick.
Forgive me. Culture is everything   20
right about now. But I cannot pretend
a scrap of investment in the language
that allows human beings to kill one another
systematically, abstractly, distantly.
The language wrapped around 37,000,   25
or whatever the number today,
dead and beautiful bodies thrown into holes
without any tiny, reasonable *goodbye.*

Exploring the Text

1. In "Why I Could Not Accept Your Invitation," what is wrong with the italicized phrases (ll. 6–10), according to the speaker?
2. Is it significant that the invitation — possibly an invitation to attend a conference or to give a poetry reading — arrived via fax? Why or why not?
3. What examples of irony do you see in "Why I Could Not Accept Your Invitation"?
4. What does the speaker mean by "I live in teaspoon, bucket, river, pain, / turtle sunning on a brick" (ll. 18–19)?
5. How would you describe the tone of this poem?
6. Discuss how these two poems by Naomi Shihab Nye might be interpreted as updated examples of George Orwell's points in "Politics and the English Language" (p. 707).

Language Use in the United States

U.S. Census Bureau

The following tables and figures are from the 2007 American Community Survey Reports, released by the U.S. Census Bureau in 2010.

Table 1.
Population 5 Years and Older Who Spoke a Language Other Than English at Home by Language Group and English-Speaking Ability: 2007

Characteristic		English-speaking ability			
	Total People	Very well	Well	Not well	Not at all
NUMBER					
Population 5 years and older	**280,950,438**	**(X)**	**(X)**	**(X)**	**(X)**
Spoke only English at home	225,505,953	(X)	(X)	(X)	(X)
Spoke a language other than English at home	55,444,485	30,975,474	10,962,722	9,011,298	4,494,991
Spoke a language other than English at home	**55,444,485**	**30,975,474**	**10,962,722**	**9,011,298**	**4,494,991**
Spanish or Spanish Creole	34,547,077	18,179,530	6,322,170	6,344,110	3,701,267
Other Indo-European languages	10,320,730	6,936,808	2,018,148	1,072,025	293,749
Asian and Pacific Island languages	8,316,426	4,274,794	2,176,180	1,412,264	453,188
Other languages	2,260,252	1,584,342	446,224	182,899	46,787
PERCENT					
Population 5 years and older	**100.0**	**(X)**	**(X)**	**(X)**	**(X)**
Spoke only English at home	80.3	(X)	(X)	(X)	(X)
Spoke a language other than English at home	19.7	55.9	19.8	16.3	8.1
Spoke a language other than English at home	**100.0**	**55.9**	**19.8**	**16.3**	**8.1**
Spanish or Spanish Creole	62.3	52.6	18.3	18.4	10.7
Other Indo-European languages	18.6	67.2	19.6	10.4	2.8
Asian and Pacific Island languages	15.0	51.4	26.2	17.0	5.4
Other languages	4.1	70.1	19.7	8.1	2.1

(X) Not applicable.
Source: U.S. Census Bureau, 2007 American Community Survey.

Table 2.
Languages Spoken at Home: 1980, 1990, 2000, and 2007

(For information on confidentiality protection, sampling error, nonsampling error, and definitions, see *www.census.gov/acs/www/*)

Characteristic	1980	1990	2000	2007	Percentage change 1980–2007
Population 5 years and older	**210,247,455**	**230,445,777**	**262,375,152**	**280,950,438**	**33.6**
Spoke only English at home	187,187,415	198,600,798	215,423,557	225,505,953	20.5
Spoke a language other than English at home	23,060,040	31,844,979	46,951,595	55,444,485	140.4
Spoke a language other than English at home	**23,060,040**	**31,844,979**	**46,951,595**	**55,444,485**	**140.4**
Spanish or Spanish Creole	11,116,194	17,345,064	28,101,052	34,547,077	210.8
French (incl. Patois, Cajun, Creole)	1,550,751	1,930,404	2,097,206	1,984,824	28.0
Italian	1,618,344	1,308,648	1,008,370	798,801	−50.6
Portuguese or Portuguese Creole	351,875	430,610	564,630	687,126	95.3
German	1,586,593	1,547,987	1,383,442	1,104,354	−30.4
Yiddish	315,953	213,064	178,945	158,991	−49.7
Greek	401,443	388,260	365,436	329,825	−17.8
Russian	173,226	241,798	706,242	851,174	391.4
Polish	820,647	723,483	667,414	638,059	−22.2
Serbo-Croatian	150,255	70,964	233,865	276,550	84.1
Armenian	100,634	149,694	202,708	221,865	120.5
Persian	106,992	201,865	312,085	349,686	226.8
Chinese	630,806	1,319,462	2,022,143	2,464,572	290.7
Japanese	336,318	427,657	477,997	458,717	36.4
Korean	266,280	626,478	894,063	1,062,337	299.0
Vietnamese	197,588	507,069	1,009,627	1,207,004	510.9
Tagalog	474,150	843,251	1,224,241	1,408,429	212.2

[1]The languages highlighted in this table are the languages for which data were available for the four time periods: 1980, 1990, 2000, and 2007.
[2]The total does not match the sum of the 17 languages listed in this table because the total includes all the other languages that are not highlighted here.
Source: U.S. Census Bureau, 1980 and 1990 Census, Census 2000, and 2007 American Community Survey.

Figure 2a.
Major Language Groups and English-Speaking Ability by Age: 2007
(Population 5 years and older, in millions.)

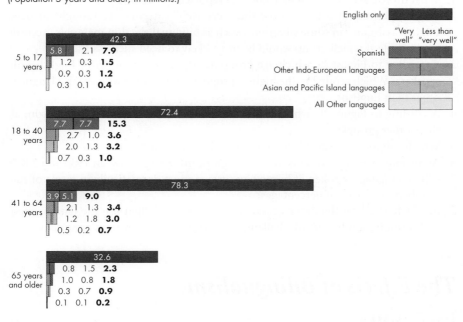

Source: U.S. Census Bureau, 2007 American Community Survey.

Figure 2b.
Major Language Groups and English-Speaking Ability by Nativity and Citizenship: 2007
(Population 5 years and older, in millions.)

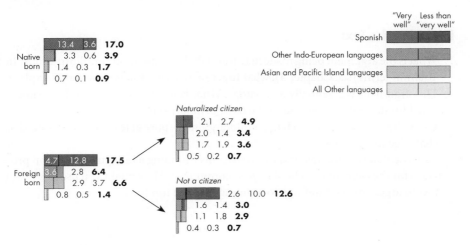

Source: U.S. Census Bureau, 2007 American Community Survey.

Exploring the Texts

1. What do you see as three major findings reported in Table 1?
2. People speaking at a level below the "very well" category are thought to need English assistance in some situations, such as bilingual election materials. According to Table 1, which group would be most likely to need such assistance?
3. According to Figure 2a, which age group has the largest number of English-only speakers? Which group has the highest proportion of people who speak a language other than English?
4. According to Figure 2b, which characteristic sets Spanish speakers apart from all three other groups?
5. Which subgroup is least likely to be naturalized citizens?
6. According to Table 2, what is the most significant change between 1980 and 2007?
7. Which languages spoken at home have grown most dramatically in terms of raw numbers? In terms of percentages?
8. Read Charles Krauthammer's essay on page 742, and then use the data in these tables and figures to defend, challenge, or qualify Krauthammer's argument.

The Effects of Bilingualism

Jim Cummins

> This illustration appeared in *Negotiating Identities: Education for Empowerment in a Diverse Society* (1996) by Jim Cummins, a professor at the University of Toronto. The book focuses on the social and educational barriers that limit academic success for culturally diverse students.

Exploring the Text

1. What is the argument being made here through the frame-by-frame illustrations? In Toulmin terms (see Chapter 3), what function does the final frame serve? Explain.
2. This argument is essentially an analogy. What is it? How effective is the analogy? What limitations do you find in the basic comparison?
3. Using the "yes, but" approach to counterargument, pose at least two questions that challenge this cartoon.
4. Suppose that you are involved in a debate over funding a bilingual education program for the elementary school in your community. How might you use this visual text to argue for the funding? To argue against the funding?

One
wheel
(one language)
can get you
places…

So can a
big wheel
and a
little wheel…

However, when your
wheels are nicely
balanced and fully
inflated you'll go farther…

Provided, of course,
the people who made
the wheels knew what
they were doing.

Conversation

American Politics and the English Language

The following eight texts comment directly or indirectly on the role of language in American politics.

Sources

1. **Institute for Propaganda Analysis,** *How to Detect Propaganda*
2. **Michiko Kakutani,** *The Word Police*
3. **North York Women Teachers' Association,** *Nonviolent Language* (table)
4. **Mike Lester,** *NCAA Native American Mascots* (cartoon)
5. **Geoffrey Nunberg,** *The -Ism Schism: How Much Wallop Can a Simple Word Pack?*
6. **Daniel Okrent,** *The War of the Words: A Dispatch from the Front Lines*
7. Letters to the Editor in Response to *The War of the Words*
8. **Frank Luntz,** from *Words That Work*

After you have read, studied and synthesized these pieces, enter the Conversation by responding to one of the prompts on page 778.

1. *How to Detect Propaganda*

Institute for Propaganda Analysis

The following essay appeared in the monthly newsletter of the Institute for Propaganda Analysis in 1937. The Institute's aim, as stated in one of its early publications, was "to conduct objective, non-partisan studies in the field of propaganda and public opinion . . . to help the intelligent citizen to detect and to analyze propaganda. . . ."

We are fooled by propaganda chiefly because we don't recognize it when we see it. It may be fun to be fooled but, as the cigarette ads used to say, it is more fun to know. We can more easily recognize propaganda when we see it if we are familiar with the seven common propaganda devices. These are:

1. The name-calling device.
2. The glittering-generalities device.
3. The transfer device.
4. The testimonial device.
5. The plain-folks device.

6. The card-stacking device.

7. The band-wagon device.

Why are we fooled by these devices? Because they appeal to our emotions rather than to our reason. They make us believe and do something we would not believe or do if we thought about it calmly, dispassionately. In examining these devices, note that they work most effectively at those times when we are too lazy to think for ourselves; also, they tie into emotions that sway us to be "for" or "against" nations, races, religions, ideals, economic and political policies and practices, and so on through automobiles, cigarettes, radios, toothpastes, presidents, and wars. With our emotions stirred, it may be fun to be fooled by these propaganda devices, but it is more fun and infinitely more in our own interests to know how they work.

Name Calling

"Name calling" is a device to make us form a judgment without examining the evidence upon which it should be based. Here the propagandist appeals to our hate and fear. He does this by giving "bad names" to those individuals, groups, nations, races, policies, practices, beliefs, and ideals that he would have us condemn and reject. For centuries the name "heretic" was bad. Thousands were oppressed, tortured, or put to death as heretics. Anybody who dissented from popular or group belief or practice was in danger of being called a heretic. In the light of today's knowledge, some heresies were bad and some were good. Many of the pioneers of modern science were called heretics; witness the cases of Copernicus, Galileo, Bruno. Today's bad names include: fascist, demagogue, dictator, red, financial oligarchy, communist, muck-raker, alien, outside agitator, economic royalist, utopian, rabble-rouser, trouble-maker, Tory, constitution wrecker.

"Al" Smith called Roosevelt a communist by implication when he said in his Liberty League speech, "There can be only one capital, Washington or Moscow." When Smith was running for the presidency many called him a tool of the pope, saying in effect, "We must choose between Washington and Rome." That implied that Smith, if elected president, would take his orders from the pope. Recently Justice Hugo Black has been associated with a bad name—Ku Klux Klan. In these cases propagandists have tried to make us form judgments without examining essential evidence and implications. "Al Smith is a Catholic. He must never be president." "Roosevelt is a red. Defeat his program." "Hugo Black is or was a Klansman. Take him out of the Supreme Court."

Use of bad names without presentation of their essential meaning, without all their pertinent implications, comprises perhaps the most common of all propaganda devices. Those who want to maintain the status quo apply bad names to those who would change it. For example, the Hearst press applies bad names to communists and socialists. Those who want to change the status quo apply bad names to those who would maintain it. For example, the *Daily Worker* and the *American Guardian* apply bad names to conservative Republicans and Democrats.

Glittering Generalities

"Glittering generalities" is a device by which the propagandist identifies his program with virtue by use of "virtue words." Here he appeals to our emotions of love, generosity, and brotherhood. He uses words such as truth, freedom, honor, liberty, social justice, public service, the right to work, loyalty, progress, democracy, the American way, constitution defender. These words suggest shining ideals. All persons of good will believe in these ideals. Hence the propagandist, by identifying his individual group, nation, race, policy, practice, or belief with such ideals, seeks to win us to his cause. As name-calling is a device to make us form a judgment to reject and condemn, without examining the evidence, glittering generalities is a device to make us accept and approve, without examining the evidence.

For example, use of the phrases "the right to work" and "social justice" may be a device to make us accept programs for meeting the labor–capital problem which, if we examined them critically, we would not accept at all.

In the name-calling and glittering-generalities devices, words are used to stir up our emotions and to befog our thinking. In one device "bad words" are used to make us mad; in the other "good words" are used to make us glad.

The propagandist is most effective in the use of these devices when his words make us create devils to fight or gods to adore. By his use of the bad words, we personify as a "devil" some nation, race, group, individual, policy, practice, or ideal; we are made fighting mad to destroy it. By use of good words, we personify as a god-like idol some nation, race, group, and so on. Words that are bad to some are good to others, or may be made so. Thus, to some the New Deal is "a prophecy of social salvation" while to others it is "an omen of social disaster."

From consideration of names, "bad" and "good," we pass to institutions and symbols, also "bad" and "good." We see these in the next device.

Transfer

"Transfer" is a device by which the propagandist carries over the authority, sanction, and prestige of something we respect and revere to something he would have us accept. For example, most of us respect and revere our church and our nation. If the propagandist succeeds in getting church or nation to approve a campaign on behalf of some program, he thereby transfers its authority, sanction, and prestige to that program. Thus we may accept something that otherwise we might reject.

In the transfer device symbols are constantly used. The cross represents the Christian Church. The flag represents the nation. Cartoons such as Uncle Sam represent a consensus of public opinion. Those symbols stir emotions. At their very sight, with the speed of light, is aroused the whole complex of feelings we have with respect to church or nation. A cartoonist, by having Uncle Sam disapprove a budget for unemployment relief, would have us feel that the whole United States disapproves relief costs. By drawing an Uncle Sam who approves the same budget, the cartoonist would have us feel that the American people approve it. Thus, the transfer device is used both for and against causes and ideas.

Testimonial

The "testimonial" is a device to make us accept anything from a patent medicine or a cigarette to a program of national policy. In this device the propagandist makes use of testimonials. "When I feel tired, I smoke a Camel and get the grandest 'lift.'" "We believe the John Lewis plan of labor organization is splendid; C. I. O. should be supported." This device works in reverse also; counter-testimonials may be employed. Seldom are these used against commercial products such as patent medicines and cigarettes, but they are constantly employed in social, economic, and political issues. "We believe that the John Lewis plan of labor organization is bad; C. I. O. should not be supported."

Plain Folks

"Plain folks" is a device used by politicians, labor leaders, business men, and even by ministers and educators to win our confidence by appearing to be people just like ourselves—"just plain folks among the neighbors." In election years especially candidates show their devotion to little children and the common, homey things of life. They have front-porch campaigns. For the newspaper men they raid the kitchen cupboard, finding there some of the good wife's apple pie. They go to country picnics; they attend service at the old frame church; they pitch hay and go fishing; they show their belief in home and mother. In short, they would win our votes by showing that they're just as ordinary as the rest of us—"just plain folks"—and, therefore, wise and good. Business men are often "plain folks" with the factory hands. Even distillers use the device, "It's our family's whiskey, neighbor; and neighbor, it's your price."

Card-Stacking

"Card-stacking" is a device in which the propagandist employs all the arts of deception to win our support for himself, his group, nation, race, policy, practice, belief, or ideal. He stacks the cards against the truth. He uses under-emphasis and over-emphasis to dodge issues and evade facts. He resorts to lies, censorship, and distortion. He omits facts. He offers false testimony. He creates a smoke-screen of clamor by raising a new issue when he wants an embarrassing matter forgotten. He draws a red herring across the trail to confuse and divert those in quest of facts he does not want revealed. He makes the unreal appear real and the real appear unreal. He lets half-truth masquerade as truth. By the card-stacking device, a mediocre candidate, through the "build-up," is made to appear an intellectual titan; an ordinary prize fighter a probable world champion; a worthless patent medicine a beneficent cure. By means of this device propagandists would convince us that a ruthless war of aggression is a crusade for righteousness. Some member nations of the Non-Intervention Committee send their troops to intervene in Spain. Card-stacking employs sham, hypocrisy, effrontery.

The Band Wagon

The "band wagon" is a device to make us follow the crowd, to accept the propagandist's program en masse. Here his theme is: "Everybody's doing it." His techniques range from those of medicine show to dramatic spectacle. He hires a hall, fills a great stadium, marches a million men in parade. He employs symbols, colors, music, movement, all the dramatic arts. He appeals to the desire, common to most of us, to "follow the crowd." Because he wants us to follow the crowd in masses, he directs his appeal to groups held together by common ties of nationality, religion, race, environment, sex, vocation. Thus propagandists campaigning for or against a program will appeal to us as Catholics, Protestants, or Jews; as members of the Nordic race or as Negroes; as farmers or as school teachers; as housewives or as miners. All the artifices of flattery are used to harness the fears and hatreds, prejudices and biases, convictions and ideals common to the group; thus emotion is made to push and pull the group on to the band wagon. In newspaper articles and in the spoken word this device is also found. "Don't throw your vote away. Vote for our candidate. He's sure to win." Nearly every candidate wins in every election — before the votes are in.

15

Propaganda and Emotion

Observe that in all these devices our emotion is the stuff with which propagandists work. Without it they are helpless; with it, harnessing it to their purposes, they can make us glow with pride or burn with hatred, they can make us zealots in behalf of the program they espouse. Propaganda as generally understood is expression of opinion or action by individuals or groups with reference to predetermined ends. Without the appeal to our emotion — to our fears and to our courage, to our selfishness and unselfishness, to our loves and to our hates — propagandists would influence few opinions and few actions.

To say this is not to condemn emotion, an essential part of life, or to assert that all predetermined ends of propagandists are "bad." What we mean is that the intelligent citizen does not want propagandists to utilize his emotions, even to the attainment of "good" ends, without knowing what is going on. He does not want to be "used" in the attainment of ends he may later consider "bad." He does not want to be gullible. He does not want to be fooled. He does not want to be duped, even in a "good" cause. He wants to know the facts and among these is included the fact of the utilization of his emotions.

Keeping in mind the seven common propaganda devices, turn to today's newspapers and almost immediately you can spot examples of them all. At election time or during any campaign, "plain folks" and "band wagon" are common. "Card-stacking" is hardest to detect because it is adroitly executed or because we lack the information necessary to nail the lie. A little practice with the daily newspapers in detecting these propaganda devices soon enables us to detect them elsewhere — in radio, newsreel, books, magazines, and in expressions of labor unions, business groups, churches, schools, political parties.

Questions

1. Considering the first and last sections of this piece, how would you express the Institute for Propaganda Analysis's attitude toward propaganda? Do you share its attitude? Explain.
2. Summarize each of the seven propaganda devices, and provide a contemporary example to illustrate each one.
3. In the final section of this essay, the authors define propaganda as "the expression of opinion or action by individuals or groups with reference to predetermined ends" (para. 16). Based on this definition, explain what propaganda is and what it is not. Use examples to illustrate your point.
4. Toward the end of this essay, the authors assert that their intent is "not to condemn emotion" (para. 17) but rather to help people understand how emotions are utilized in appeals made by advertisers, politicians, and others. Discuss a recent speech, public service announcement, or advertisement that appeals to emotions in a positive, not merely a manipulative, way.

2. *The Word Police*

Michiko Kakutani

Michiko Kakutani is a Pulitzer Prize–winning literary critic known for her book reviews in the *New York Times*. "The Word Police" appeared in the *New York Times* in January 1993.

This month's inaugural festivities, with their celebration, in Maya Angelou's words, of "humankind" — "the Asian, the Hispanic, the Jew / The African, the Native American, the Sioux, / The Catholic, the Muslim, the French, the Greek / The Irish, the Rabbi, the Priest, the Sheik, / The Gay, the Straight, the Preacher, / The privileged, the homeless, the Teacher" — constituted a kind of official embrace of multiculturalism and a new politics of inclusion.

The mood of political correctness, however, has already made firm inroads into popular culture. Washington boasts a store called Politically Correct that sells pro-whale, anti-meat, ban-the-bomb T-shirts, bumper stickers, and buttons, as well as a local cable television show called "Politically Correct Cooking" that features interviews in the kitchen with representatives from groups like People for the Ethical Treatment of Animals.

The Coppertone suntan lotion people are planning to give their longtime cover girl, Little Miss (Ms.?) Coppertone, a male equivalent, Little Mr. Coppertone. And even Superman (Superperson?) is rumored to be returning this spring, reincarnated as four ethnically diverse clones: an African-American, an Asian, a Caucasian and a Latino.

Nowhere is this P.C. mood more striking than in the increasingly noisy debate over language that has moved from university campuses to the country at large—a development that both underscores Americans' puritanical zeal for reform and their unwavering faith in the talismanic power of words.

Certainly no decent person can quarrel with the underlying impulse behind   5
political correctness: a vision of a more just, inclusive society in which racism, sexism, and prejudice of all sorts have been erased. But the methods and fervor of the self-appointed language police can lead to a rigid orthodoxy—and unintentional self-parody—opening the movement to the scorn of conservative opponents and the mockery of cartoonists and late-night television hosts.

It's hard to imagine women earning points for political correctness by saying "ovarimony" instead of "testimony"—as one participant at the recent Modern Language Association convention was overheard to suggest. It's equally hard to imagine people wanting to flaunt their lack of prejudice by giving up such words and phrases as "bull market," "kaiser roll," "Lazy Susan," and "charley horse."

Several books on bias-free language have already appeared, and the 1991 edition of the *Random House Webster's College Dictionary* boasts an appendix titled "Avoiding Sexist Language." The dictionary also includes such linguistic mutations as "womyn" (women, "used as an alternative spelling to avoid the suggestion of sexism perceived in the sequence m-e-n") and "waitron" (a gender-blind term for waiter or waitress).

Many of these dictionaries and guides not only warn the reader against offensive racial and sexual slurs, but also try to establish and enforce a whole new set of usage rules. Take, for instance, *The Bias-Free Word Finder, a Dictionary of Nondiscriminatory Language* by Rosalie Maggio (Beacon Press)—a volume often indistinguishable, in its meticulous solemnity, from the tongue-in-cheek *Official Politically Correct Dictionary and Handbook* put out last year by Henry Beard and Christopher Cerf (Villard Books). Ms. Maggio's book supplies the reader intent on using kinder, gentler language with writing guidelines as well as a detailed listing of more than 5,000 "biased words and phrases."

Whom are these guidelines for? Somehow one has a tough time picturing them replacing *Fowler's Modern English Usage* in the classroom, or being adopted by the average man (sorry, individual) in the street.

The "pseudogeneric 'he,'" we learn from Ms. Maggio, is to be avoided like the   10
plague, as is the use of the word "man" to refer to humanity. "Fellow," "king," "lord" and "master" are bad because they're "male-oriented words," and "king," "lord" and "master" are especially bad because they're also "hierarchical, dominator

society terms." The politically correct lion becomes the "monarch of the jungle," new-age children play "someone on the top of the heap," and the "Mona Lisa" goes down in history as Leonardo's "acme of perfection."

As for the word "black," Ms. Maggio says it should be excised from terms with a negative spin: she recommends substituting words like "mouse" for "black eye," "ostracize" for "blackball," "payola" for "blackmail" and "outcast" for "black sheep." Clearly, some of these substitutions work better than others: somehow the "sinister humor" of Kurt Vonnegut or *Saturday Night Live* doesn't quite make it; nor does the "denouncing" of the Hollywood 10.[1]

For the dedicated user of politically correct language, all these rules can make for some messy moral dilemmas. Whereas "battered wife" is a gender-biased term, the gender-free term "battered spouse," Ms. Maggio notes, incorrectly implies "that men and women are equally battered."

On one hand, say Francine Wattman Frank and Paula A. Treichler in their book *Language, Gender, and Professional Writing* (Modern Language Association), "he or she" is an appropriate construction for talking about an individual (like a jockey, say) who belongs to a profession that's predominantly male — it's a way of emphasizing "that such occupations are not barred to women or that women's concerns need to be kept in mind." On the other hand, they add, using masculine pronouns rhetorically can underscore ongoing male dominance in those fields, implying the need for change.

And what about the speech codes adopted by some universities in recent years? Although they were designed to prohibit students from uttering sexist and racist slurs, they would extend, by logic, to blacks who want to use the word "nigger" to strip the term of its racist connotations, or homosexuals who want to use the word "queer" to reclaim it from bigots.

In her book, Ms. Maggio recommends applying bias-free usage retroactively: 15
she suggests paraphrasing politically incorrect quotations, or replacing "the sexist words or phrases with ellipsis dots and/or bracketed substitutes," or using "*sic*" to show that the sexist words come from the original quotation and to call attention to the fact that they are incorrect."

Which leads the skeptical reader of *The Bias-Free Word Finder* to wonder whether "All the King's Men" should be retitled "All the Ruler's People"; "Pet Semetary," "Animal Companion Graves"; "Birdman of Alcatraz," "Birdperson of Alcatraz"; and "The Iceman Cometh," "The Ice Route Driver Cometh"?

Will making such changes remove the prejudice in people's minds? Should we really spend time trying to come up with non-male-based alternatives to "Midas touch," "Achilles' heel" and "Montezuma's revenge"? Will tossing out Santa Claus — whom Ms. Maggio accuses of reinforcing "the cultural male-as-norm system" — in favor of Belfana, his Italian female alter ego, truly help banish sexism? Can the avoidance of "violent expressions and metaphors" like "kill two

---

[1]Actors and filmmakers blacklisted from making movies in the 1940s because they were allegedly Communists. — Eds.

birds with one stone," "sock it to 'em" or "kick an idea around" actually promote a more harmonious world?

The point isn't that the excesses of the word police are comical. The point is that their intolerance (in the name of tolerance) has disturbing implications. In the first place, getting upset by phrases like "bullish on America" or "the City of Brotherly Love" tends to distract attention from the real problems of prejudice and injustice that exist in society at large, turning them into mere questions of semantics. Indeed, the emphasis currently put on politically correct usage has uncanny parallels with the academic movement of deconstruction—a method of textual analysis that focuses on language and linguistic pyrotechnics—which has become firmly established on university campuses.

In both cases, attention is focused on surfaces, on words and metaphors; in both cases, signs and symbols are accorded more importance than content. Hence, the attempt by some radical advocates to remove *The Adventures of Huckleberry Finn* from curriculums on the grounds that Twain's use of the word "nigger" makes the book a racist text—never mind the fact that this American classic (written in 1884) depicts the spiritual kinship achieved between a white boy and a runaway slave, never mind the fact that the "nigger" Jim emerges as the novel's most honorable, decent character.

Ironically enough, the P.C. movement's obsession with language is accompanied by a strange Orwellian willingness to warp the meaning of words by placing them under a high-powered ideological lens. For instance, the *Dictionary of Cautionary Words and Phrases*—a pamphlet issued by the University of Missouri's Multicultural Management Program to help turn "today's journalists into tomorrow's multicultural newsroom managers"—warns that using the word "articulate" to describe members of a minority group can suggest the opposite, "that 'those people' are not considered well educated, articulate and the like." 20

The pamphlet patronizes minority groups, by cautioning the reader against using the words "lazy" and "burly" to describe any member of such groups; and it issues a similar warning against using words like "gorgeous" and "petite" to describe women.

As euphemism proliferates with the rise of political correctness, there is a spread of the sort of sloppy, abstract language that Orwell said is "designed to make lies sound truthful and murder respectable, and to give an appearance of solidity to pure wind." "Fat" becomes "big boned" or "differently sized"; "stupid" becomes "exceptional"; "stoned" becomes "chemically inconvenienced."

Wait a minute here! Aren't such phrases eerily reminiscent of the euphemisms coined by the government during Vietnam and Watergate? Remember how the military used to speak of "pacification," or how President Richard M. Nixon's press secretary, Ronald L. Ziegler, tried to get away with calling a lie an "inoperative statement"?

Calling the homeless "the underhoused" doesn't give them a place to live; calling the poor "the economically marginalized" doesn't help them pay the bills.

Rather, by playing down their plight, such language might even make it easier to shrug off the seriousness of their situation.

Instead of allowing free discussion and debate to occur, many gung-ho advocates of politically correct language seem to think that simple suppression of a word or concept will magically make the problem disappear. In *The Bias-Free Word Finder*, Ms. Maggio entreats the reader not to perpetuate the negative stereotype of Eve. "Be extremely cautious in referring to the biblical Eve," she writes; "this story has profoundly contributed to negative attitudes toward women throughout history, largely because of misogynistic and patriarchal interpretations that labeled her evil, inferior, and seductive."

The story of Bluebeard, the rake (whoops! — the libertine) who killed his seven wives, she says, is also to be avoided, as is the biblical story of Jezebel. Of Jesus Christ, Ms. Maggio writes: "There have been few individuals in history as completely androgynous as Christ, and it does his message a disservice to overinsist on his maleness." She doesn't give the reader any hints on how this might be accomplished; presumably, one is supposed to avoid describing him as the Son of God.

Of course the P.C. police aren't the only ones who want to proscribe what people should say or give them guidelines for how they may use an idea; Jesse Helms and his supporters are up to exactly the same thing when they propose to patrol the boundaries of the permissible in art. In each case, the would-be censor aspires to suppress what he or she finds distasteful — all, of course, in the name of the public good.

In the case of the politically correct, the prohibition of certain words, phrases and ideas is advanced in the cause of building a brave new world free of racism and hate, but this vision of harmony clashes with the very ideals of diversity and inclusion that the multicultural movement holds dear, and it's purchased at the cost of freedom of expression and freedom of speech.

In fact, the utopian world envisioned by the language police would be bought at the expense of the ideas of individualism and democracy articulated in "The Gettysburg Address": "Fourscore and seven years ago our fathers brought forth on this continent a new nation, conceived in liberty and dedicated to the proposition that all men are created equal."

Of course, the P.C. police have already found Lincoln's words hopelessly "phallocentric." No doubt they would rewrite the passage: "Fourscore and seven years ago our foremothers and forefathers brought forth on this continent a new nation, formulated with liberty, and dedicated to the proposition that all humankind is created equal."

Questions

1. Michiko Kakutani opens with a reference to the poem "On the Pulse of Morning" that Maya Angelou read at the inauguration of President Bill Clinton. Why does she connect a poem and an event that illustrate the "politics of inclusion" (para. 1) to the "mood of political correctness" (para. 2)?

2. What does she mean by "the increasingly noisy debate over language" that "both underscores Americans' puritanical zeal for reform and their unwavering faith in the talismanic power of words" (para. 4)?

3. By using the term "language police" (para. 5), what attitude does Kakutani convey toward political correctness? Do you find the term appropriate? Explain why or why not.

4. Kakutani states her argument about language and political correctness most emphatically in the final paragraphs of the essay. What tension does she develop? To what extent do you agree with her?

3. *Nonviolent Language*

North York Women Teachers' Association

The following language guidelines appeared in a brochure written for elementary teachers in Ontario. The guidelines were reprinted in *Harper's* magazine in February 1995.

VIOLENT PHRASE	ALTERNATIVE
Kill two birds with one stone	Get two for the price of one
There's more than one way to skin a cat	There are different ways to solve a problem
Take a stab at it	Go for it!
Get away with murder	Avoid consequences
It's an uphill battle	It's next to impossible
You're dead meat	You're in serious trouble
Kick it around	Consider the options
That's a low blow	That's outside the rules
Hit them where it hurts	Find their vulnerability
Crash the party	Show up anyway
Shoot yourself in the foot	Undermine your own position
Hit the computer key	Press the computer key
Blown out of the water	Reduced to nothing

Questions

1. Which of these "violent phrase[s]" do you find offensive and thus in need of change? Which do you find foolish or silly?

2. Which of the alternatives would you say most change the meaning of the original phrase?
3. This list was suggested by a Canadian organization of teachers. Explain why you think it would or would not be taken seriously in the United States.
4. Most of these phrases are slang or clichés. What phrases in common parlance today might be considered "violent" and thus offensive?

4. *NCAA Native American Mascots*

MIKE LESTER

The following cartoon by Mike Lester, cartoonist for the *Rome News-Tribune* in Georgia, appeared in 2005. It refers to the National College Athletic Association's position on the use of Native American names for sports teams and their mascots.

(See insert for color version.)

Questions

1. What is the setting of Mike Lester's cartoon? Why is it important to his subject?
2. How does the written text contribute to the cartoon's message?
3. What point is Lester making? What role does irony play in making the point?

4. What are at least two different ways to interpret the point Lester is making in this cartoon?

5. Do you find this cartoon persuasive? Humorous? Insightful? Explain your response.

5. *The -Ism Schism: How Much Wallop Can a Simple Word Pack?*

Geoffrey Nunberg

In the following *New York Times* editorial, Geoffrey Nunberg, a senior researcher and linguistics professor at Stanford University, examines the history and use of the word *terror* and its derivatives.

"The long-term defeat of terror will happen when freedom takes hold in the broader Middle East," President Bush said on June 28, [2004], as he announced the early transfer of sovereignty to the Iraqis.

The "defeat of terror"—the working suggests that much has changed since Sept. 11, 2001. In his speech on that day, Mr. Bush said, "We stand together to win the war against terrorism," and over the following year in the White House described the enemy as terrorism twice as often as terror. But in White House speeches over the past year, those proportions have been reversed. And the shift from "terrorism" to "terror" has been equally dramatic in major newspapers, according to a search of several databases.

Broad linguistic shifts like those usually owe less to conscious decisions by editors or speechwriters than to often unnoticed changes in the way people perceive their world. Terrorism may itself be a vague term, as critics have argued. But terror is still more amorphous and elastic, and alters the understanding not just of the enemy but of the war against it.

True, phrases like "terror plots" or "terror threat level" can make terror seem merely a headline writer's shortening of the word terrorism. But even there, "terror" draws on a more complex set of meanings. It evokes both the actions of terrorists and the fear they are trying to engender.

"Do we cower in the face of terror?" Mr. Bush asked on Irish television a few days before the handover in Iraq, with terror doing double work. 5

And unlike "terrorism," "terror" can be applied to states as well as to insurgent groups, as in the President's frequent references to Saddam Hussein's "terror regime." Even if Mr. Hussein can't actually be linked to the attacks of Sept. 11, "terror" seems to connect them etymologically.

The modern senses of "terror" and "terrorism" reach back to a single historical moment: "la Terreur," Robespierre's Reign of Terror in 1793 and 1794.

"Terror," Robespierre said, "is nothing other than justice, prompt, severe, inflexible, it is therefore an emanation of virtue."

It was the ruthless severity of that emanation that moved Edmund Burke to decry "those hell-hounds called terrorists," in one of the first recorded uses of "terrorist" in English.

For Robespierre and his contemporaries, "terror" conveyed the exalted emo- 10
tion people may feel when face to face with the absolute. That was what led Albert Camus to describe terror as the urge that draws people to the violent certainties of totalitarianism, where rebellion hardens into ideology.

With time, though, the word's aura of sublimity faded. By 1880, "holy terror" was only a jocular name for an obstreperous child and "terrible" no longer suggested the sense of awe it had in "terrible swift sword." By the Jazz Age, "terrific" was just a wan superlative. Terror was still a name for intense fear, but it no longer connoted a social force.

"Terrorism," too, has drifted since its origin. By modern times, the word could refer only to the use of violence against a government, not on its behalf — though some still claimed the "terrorist" designation proudly, like the Russian revolutionaries who assassinated Czar Alexander II in 1881 and the Zionist Stern Gang (later the Lehi), which, in the 1940's used assassination and other violent means in hopes of driving the British occupiers out of Palestine.

It wasn't until the beginning of the post-colonial period that all groups rejected the terrorist label in favor of names like freedom fighters or mujahadeen. By then, "terrorism" was no longer a genuine -ism, but the name for a reprehensible strategy, often extended as a term of abuse for anyone whose methods seemed ruthless.

But the recent uses of "terror" seem to draw its disparate, superseded senses back together in a way that Burke might have found familiar. Today, it is again a name that encompasses both the dark forces that threaten "civilization" and the fears they arouse.

The new senses of the noun are signaled in another linguistic shift in the 15
press and in White House speeches. Just as "terrorism" has been replaced by "terror," so "war" is much more likely now to be followed by "on" rather than "against."

That "war on" pattern dates from the turn of the 20th century, when people adapted epidemiological metaphors like "the war on typhus" to describe campaigns against social evils like alcohol, crime and poverty — endemic conditions that could be mitigated but not eradicated. Society may declare a war on drugs or drunken driving, but no one expects total victory.

"The war on terror," too, suggests a campaign aimed not at human adversaries but at a pervasive social plague. At its most abstract, terror comes to seem as persistent and inexplicable as evil itself, without raising any inconvenient theological qualms. And in fact, the White House's use of "evil" has declined by 80 percent over the same period that its use of "terror" has been increasing.

Like wars on ignorance and crime, a "war on terror" suggests an enduring state of struggle — a "never ending fight against terror and its relentless onslaughts," as Camus put it in *The Plague*, his 1947 allegory on the rise and fall of Fascism. It is as if the language is girding itself for the long haul.

Questions

1. What is Geoffrey Nunberg's main point?
2. What is Nunberg's purpose in offering a historical perspective on the word *terror* and its derivatives?
3. What allusions does Nunberg make? What is the effect of these allusions?
4. Why does Nunberg include the analysis of "war *on*" versus "war *against*"? Do you see the analysis as peripheral or essential to his discussion of terror? Explain why.
5. Is Nunberg being critical of George W. Bush by using examples from his speeches? Cite specific passages to support your opinion.

6. *The War of the Words: A Dispatch from the Front Lines*

Daniel Okrent

In the following 2005 article, Daniel Okrent, then public editor of the *New York Times*, discusses the use of *terrorist* and *terrorism* in the *Times* and the language used to report news from the Middle East.

Nothing provokes as much rage as what many perceive to be the *Times*'s policy on the use of "terrorist," "terrorism" and "terror." There is no policy, actually, but except in the context of Al Qaeda, or in direct quotations, these words, as explosive as what they describe, show up very rarely.

Among pro-Israeli readers (and nonreaders urged to write to me by media watchdog organizations), the controversy over variants of the T-word has become the stand-in for the Israel-Palestine conflict itself. When Israel's targeted assassinations of suspected sponsors of terrorism provoke retaliation, some pro-Palestinian readers argue that any armed response against civilians by such groups as Hamas is morally equivalent. Critics on the other side say the *Times*'s general avoidance of the word "terrorism" is a political decision, and exactly what Hamas wants.

Here's what I want: A path out of this thicket, which is snarled with far more than "terror" and its derivative tendrils. I packed the preceding paragraph with enough verbal knots to secure the QE2, so I'll untangle them one by one.

"Pro-Israeli" and "pro-Palestinian": Adem Carroll of the Islamic Circle of North America has pointed out to me that both epithets represent value judgments. Are Ariel Sharon's policies pro-Israel? Not in the minds of his critics on the Israeli left. Is Mahmoud Abbas's negotiation policy pro-Palestinian? I doubt that supporters of Islamic jihad believe it is.

"Israel-Palestine conflict": I've heard from ardent Zionists who deplore this usage because, they say, "There is no Palestine."   5

"Targeted assassinations": The Israel Defense Forces use this term; Palestinians believe it implicitly exonerates Israel for the deaths of nearby innocents. The *Times* tries to avoid it, but an editor's attempt at a substitute on Jan. 27 [2005] — "pinpoint killings"—was even more accepting of the Israeli line.

"Settlers": Are they merely settlers when they carry out armed actions against Palestinians?

"Groups such as Hamas": According to the European Union and the United States government, which are both cited regularly by an army of readers, Hamas is a terrorist organization. According to *Times* deputy foreign editor Ethan Bronner: "We use 'terrorist' sparingly because it is a loaded word. Describing the goals or acts of a group often serves readers better than repeating the term 'terrorist.' We make clear that Hamas seeks the destruction of Israel through violence but that it is also a significant political and social force among Palestinians, fielding candidates and clinics and day care centers." According to many *Times* critics, that just won't do.

There was one more bugbear in that overloaded paragraph up top: "Media watchdog organizations." That's what you call the noble guardians on your side; the other guy's dishonest advocates are "pressure groups." Both are accurate characterizations, but trying to squeeze them into the same sentence can get awfully clumsy. It's also clumsy to befog clear prose by worrying over words so obsessively that strong sentences get ground into grits. But closing one's ears to the complaints of partisans would also entail closing one's mind to the substance of their arguments.

The Armed Conflict in the Area Between Lebanon and Egypt may yield the most linguistically volatile issues confronting *Times* editors, but I've encountered a ferocious tug-of-war between advocates of each of the following as well: Genital mutilation vs. genital cutting ("would you call ritual male circumcision 'genital mutilation'?"). Liberal vs. moderate ("you're simply trying to make liberalism look reasonable and inoffensive" as in calling Michael Bloomberg a "moderate Republican"). Abuse vs. torture ("if the Abu Ghraib victims had been American soldiers," the *Times* "would have described it as torture"). Partial birth vs. intact dilation and extraction (the use of the former demonstrates that the *Times* "has embraced the terminology of anti-abortion forces"). "Iraqi forces" vs. "American-backed forces" ("aren't the Sunni insurgents Iraqis?"). Don't get me started on "insurgents," much less homeless vs. vagrant, affirmative action vs. racial preferences, or loophole vs. tax incentive.

Now a rugby scrum has gathered around the Bush Social Security plan. Republicans tout "personal accounts"; Democrats trash "private accounts." In this atmosphere, I don't think reporters have much choice other than to use "private" and "personal" interchangeably, and to interchange them often. Once one side of an ideological conflict has seized control of a word, it no longer has a meaning of its own; opting for one or the other would be a declaration that doesn't belong in the news reports.

10

Hijacking the language proves especially pernicious when government officials deodorize their programs with near-Orwellian euphemism. (If Orwell were writing "Politics and the English Language" today, he'd need a telephone book to contain his "catalog of swindles and perversions.") The Bush administration has been especially good at this; just count the number of times self-anointing phrases like "Patriot Act," "Clear Skies Act" or "No Child Left Behind Act" appear in the *Times*, at each appearance sounding as wholesome as a hymn. Even the most committed Republicans must recognize that such phrases could apply to measures guaranteeing the opposite of what they claim to accomplish.

When the next Democratic administration rolls around, Republicans will likely discover how it feels to be on the losing side of a propaganda war. (The Clinton White House wasn't very good at this: somehow, the Personal Responsibility and Work Opportunity Reconciliation Act of 1996, which remade federal welfare policy, never hit the top of the charts.)

The *Times* shouldn't play along. If the sports section calls the Orange Bowl the Orange Bowl, even if its formal name is the Federal Express Orange Bowl, why can't the news pages refer to the Public Education Act of 2002, or the Industrial Emissions Act of 2005? Similarly, editors could ban the use of "reform" as a description of legislative action. It's even worse than "moderate," something so benign in tone and banal in substance that it can be used to camouflage any depredations its sponsors propose. Who could oppose health care reform, Social Security reform or welfare reform, and who could tell me what any of them means? You could call the rule barring (or at least radically limiting) the use of these shameless beards the Save the Language Act.

Of course, reform of the use of "reform," or a consistent assault on any of the linguistic cosmetics used by politicians and interest groups to disfigure public debate, could bring on charges of bias (a word which itself has almost come to mean "something I disagree with"). 15

But I think in some instances the *Times*'s earnest effort to avoid bias can desiccate language and dilute meaning. In a January memo to the foreign desk, former Jerusalem bureau chief James Bennet addressed the paper's gingerly use of the word "terrorism."

"The calculated bombing of students in a university cafeteria, or of families gathered in an ice cream parlor, cries out to be called what it is," he wrote. "I wanted to avoid the political meaning that comes with 'terrorism,' but I couldn't pretend that the word had no usage at all in plain English." Bennet came to believe that "not to use the term began to seem like a political act in itself."

I agree. While some Israelis and their supporters assert that any Palestinian holding a gun is a terrorist, there can be neither factual nor moral certainty that he is. But if the same man fires into a crowd of civilians, he has committed an act of terror, and he is a terrorist. My own definition is simple: an act of political violence committed against purely civilian targets is terrorism; attacks on military targets are not. The deadly October 2000 assault on the American destroyer

Cole or the devastating suicide bomb that killed 18 American soldiers and 4 Iraqis in Mosul last December may have been heinous, but these were acts of war, not terrorism. Beheading construction workers in Iraq and bombing a market in Jerusalem are terrorism pure and simple.

Given the word's history as a virtual battle flag over the past several years, it would be tendentious for the *Times* to require constant use of it, as some of the paper's critics are insisting. But there's something uncomfortably fearful, and inevitably self-defeating, about struggling so hard to avoid it.

7. *Letters to the Editor in Response to* The War of the Words

Following is a series of letters to Daniel Okrent in response to his article "The War of the Words."

Re "The War of the Words: A Dispatch from the Front Lines" (March 6):

The right definition of terrorism is "acts of war by nongovernmental organizations." But the fact that this is the only definition that matches both intent and usage is irrelevant. "Terrorism" has no agreed-upon definition. We should therefore drop the use of the term. Palestinian bus bombers should be called "bus bombers." Hamas should be called a "quasi-military group." The attack on New York and Washington by Al Qaeda should be called an "attack."

—WARREN SELTZER, *Jerusalem, March 6, 2005*

You write: "The deadly October 2000 assault on the American destroyer *Cole* or the devastating suicide bomb that killed 18 American soldiers and 4 Iraqis in Mosul last December may have been heinous, but these were acts of war, not terrorism."

The bombing of the *Cole* was an "act of war"? Isn't war a conflict between legitimate governments, adhering to certain universally agreed-upon "rules"? As far as I know, no government declared war against the United States by attacking the *Cole*, just as no government declared war by attacking the World Trade Center and the Pentagon.

—CATHLEEN MEDWICK, *Somers, N.Y., March 6, 2005*

Supporters of Israel's policies have long dominated this war of words in the American news media. Otherwise, you and your colleagues might be debating whether to use "settlers" or "colonists" for the inhabitants of Israeli enclaves in the occupied territories: the former implies that they moved into uninhabited territory; the latter that someone else might already have been living there. Use of "colonists" brings charges of anti-Semitism, however, while "settlers," which is at least equally partisan, is widely treated as a neutral descriptive term.

Journalists at the *New York Times* will never satisfy everyone when writing about the Middle East. But trying not to ruffle feathers should take a back seat to accuracy and clarity.

—ROBERT DIMIT, *New York, March 6, 2005*

Regarding the phrasing "Israel-Palestine conflict," you write, "I've heard from ardent Zionists who deplore this usage because they say, 'There is no Palestine.'" You failed to mention that most Palestinians, and other Arabs for that matter, say, "There is no Israel."

—SHLOMO SINGER, *New York, March 6, 2005*

You call terrorism "an act of political violence committed against purely civilian targets." By this definition the British and American bombing of Dresden was terrorism, as was the fire-bombing of Tokyo and the nuclear attacks on Hiroshima and Nagasaki. (Almost no one argues there was military value to these targets.) These were attacks meant to change people's minds by invoking fear. The same can be said for the German attacks on London, which were clearly aimed at the will of the British people. And, if you accept the argument that these attacks were military because they forced the diversion of military forces to stop them, then any civilian attack becomes a military one.

—JOHN A. KROLL, *Tarpon Springs, Fla., March 6, 2005*

Terrorism is the intentional harming of innocent civilians for political purposes. The *Times* should have the courage to use this term correctly, consistently and as often (or seldom) as the facts require. Let the political chips fall where they may.

—JOHN TOMASI, *Providence, March 6, 2005*
The writer is an associate professor of political science at Brown University.

Questions

1. In his article, how does Daniel Okrent fulfill his duty as a commentator on journalistic issues? Does he offer information and interpretation objectively? If so, how?
2. What is Okrent's main argument? Does it transcend the specific case of Israel and Palestine, or does it apply only to that conflict? Explain your response.
3. Okrent uses many metaphors and analogies. Identify three, and comment on their individual effectiveness. Then consider the overall effectiveness of Okrent's use of figurative language.
4. What does Okrent mean when he writes, "Hijacking the language proves especially pernicious when government officials deodorize their programs with near-Orwellian euphemism" (para. 12)? Try rewriting that sentence with entirely literal language—no metaphors and no allusions allowed.
5. What objections do the letters to the editor raise? Paraphrase at least three of them.

8. from *Words That Work*

Frank Luntz

Dr. Frank Luntz is a political consultant specializing in the use of polling and focus groups to effectively shape messages. The following selection comes from his 2007 book *Words That Work.*

Sometimes it is not what you say that matters but what you *don't* say. Other times, a single word or phrase can undermine or destroy the credibility of an otherwise successful pitch or presentation. Effective communication requires that you *stop* saying words and phrases that undermine your ability to educate the American people.

This memo is adopted from a document I originally prepared and presented to Republican congressional spouses in January 2005.

NEVER SAY	INSTEAD SAY
Global economy	Free market economy
Globalization	
Capitalism	

More Americans are afraid of "*globalization*" than even "*privatization.*" The reason? "*Globalization*" represents something big, something distant, and something foreign. We distrust "*globalization*" for the same reason we like our local government but dislike Washington—the closer you are, the more control you have. So instead of talking about the principles of "*globalization*," instead emphasize "*the value and benefits of a free market economy.*" True, blue collar and manufacturing audiences probably won't like any terminology you use—to them, anything global is a direct threat to their personal employment.

Similarly, "*capitalism*" reminds people of harsh economic competition that yields losers as well as winners, while "*the free market economy*" provides opportunity to all and allows everyone to succeed. And here's one more economic label: "*Small business owner*" is looked at more favorably than "*entrepreneur,*" even though people think the latter occupation is more financially successful. The difference? A "*small business owner*" is perceived to use her own money, her own skills, and her own sweat to build a business (the gender reference is correct— more women than men are small business owners), while "*entrepreneurs*" are more like speculators who benefit from other people's money and effort.

NEVER SAY	INSTEAD SAY
Foreign trade	International trade

For many reasons unrelated to this specific issue, the word "*foreign*" conjures up negative images in the minds of many Americans. We simply don't like "*foreign* 5 *oil"* or *"foreign products"* or *"foreign nationals."* Even though we are truly a nation of foreigners, we have grave concerns about the motives of foreigners—and that concern has only increased since 9/11. *"International"* is a more positive concept than either *"foreign"* or *"global"* not because of anything positive but because it doesn't come wrapped with all the negative connotations.

In the early days of CNN, network founder Ted Turner forbade anyone to say "foreign" on the air. After all, CNN was an international network and what was "foreign" to one person was likely home to another. The punishment for saying "foreign" rather than "international" was a $50 fine.

NEVER SAY	INSTEAD SAY
Undocumented workers/aliens	Illegal immigrants
	Border security

This linguistic distinction may prove to be the political battle of the decade. The label used to describe those who enter America illegally determines the attitudes people have toward them. Those supportive of a guest worker program that would allow illegal immigrants to remain in the country tend to label these people *"undocumented workers"* because it suggests legitimate employees who simply don't have the right paperwork, while those who want to deport these same individuals use the term *"illegal aliens"* because alien has the most negative connotations.

And instead of addressing *"immigration reform,"* which polarizes Americans, you should be talking about *"border security"* issues. Securing our borders and our people has universal support.

NEVER SAY	INSTEAD SAY
Drilling for oil	Exploring for energy

I have been involved in an entire language creation effort involving environmental issues, some of which is included in this book. But the one phrase that stands out more than any other is in some ways an energy issue rather than an environmental concern. *"Drilling for oil"* causes people to paint a picture in their minds of an old-fashioned oil rig that gushes up black goop. *"Exploring for energy"* conjures a picture of twenty-first-century technology and innovation that *"responsibly harvests energy"* and provides us the ability to heat our homes and drive our cars. When you talk about energy, use words such as *"efficient"* and *"balanced,"* and always express concern for the environment.

NEVER SAY	INSTEAD SAY
School choice	Parental choice
	Equal opportunity in education
Vouchers	Opportunity scholarships

Thanks to an effective advertising campaign by national and state teacher unions, Americans remain at best evenly split over whether they support *"school* 10 *choice.*" But they are heavily in favor of "*giving parents the right to choose the schools that are right for their children,*" and there is almost universal support for "*equal opportunity in education.*"

"*Vouchers,*" seen as depriving public schools of necessary dollars, have even less support than the principle of school choice. However, "*opportunity scholarships*" do have widespread backing, as they are perceived to be a reward for good students to get a good education. Here again, the words you use determine the support you will receive. . . .

NEVER SAY	INSTEAD SAY
Deny	Not give

Yes, the two phrases mean exactly the same thing and yield exactly the same result. But "*to deny*" implies that you are preventing someone from receiving something they are entitled to, while "*not to give*" suggests it was only a choice.

Questions

1. This memo was directed to the spouses of members of Congress — not the elected officials. What is the importance of this audience to the content Frank Luntz is explaining?
2. What is the difference between euphemisms and Luntz's recommendations?
3. Use the logic of Luntz. Imagine that a political client's staff has just hired you to help determine whether they should use the term "climate change" or "global warming" in their campaign. Depending on their political leanings, explain why they should choose one or the other.
4. Luntz writes: "The label used to describe those who enter America illegally determines the attitudes people have toward them" (para. 7). Do you think this statement about labels is true about any group, not just "those who enter America illegally"? Explain.
5. Develop your own list of at least three examples of what you should "never say" versus what you should "say instead" in a job application, on a date, or in a college essay.

Making Connections

1. How might the Institute for Propaganda Analysis respond to Daniel Okrent's assertion that "the *Times*'s earnest effort to avoid bias can desiccate language and dilute meaning" (para. 16)?

2. Is the main point made by Michiko Kakutani more like the one Okrent or Frank Luntz makes? Explain your response.

3. Which examples, if any, of the suggestions made in "Nonviolent Language" would Kakutani likely approve of? Why?

4. Which of the authors in this Conversation would probably *not* find Mike Lester's cartoon funny? Why?

5. Using what you learned in the piece by the Institute for Propaganda Analysis, select two examples from the pieces by Kakutani or Geoffrey Nunberg and discuss which propaganda devices you detect.

6. Which examples from "Words That Work" might Okrent cite to illustrate his claim that "hijacking the language proves especially pernicious when government officials deodorize their programs with near-Orwellian euphemism" (para. 12)?

Entering the Conversation

As you respond to the following prompts, support your argument with references to at least three of the sources in this Conversation on American Politics and the English Language. For help using sources, see Chapter 4.

1. Find an article related to terrorism in two different newspapers, magazines, or blogs, preferably two with different styles and political leanings. Using at least two sources from this Conversation as references, analyze the use of language in the articles you selected.

2. Write an essay explaining whether you believe that efforts to eliminate sexism, racism, and violence in language are effective, or whether such efforts simply mask these issues.

3. Choose a controversial local or national issue, and write an essay analyzing the language used in the debate. Use at least three sources from this Conversation to inform your analysis.

4. In *The Political Mind*, linguist George Lakoff makes the following statement about the importance of the language that politicians use to present ideas to us rather than the substance of the ideas alone:

   The political power of words lies not primarily in their form — that is, in speech — or even in the meanings they are directly linked to, but in the totality of brain circuitry that activation can spread to: the frames, metaphors, prototypes, metonymies, and the entire system of concepts. Words matter. They shape our politics — and our lives.

   Write an essay that supports, challenges, or qualifies Lakoff's assertion. Develop your position with evidence from your own experience along with at least three sources from this Conversation.

5. In 2011, *Washington Post* columnist Courtland Milloy urged the Washington Redskins football team to change its name. He wrote:

After a recent visit to the National Museum of the American Indian on the Mall, I'm wondering how much longer our city will tolerate having a football team known as "Redskins."

It's a racist name, patently offensive and the incongruence is simply ridiculous: a world-class institution devoted to showcasing Native American heritage in a city whose leading sports franchise makes a mockery of that heritage.

Write an essay agreeing or disagreeing with Milloy's assertion that the name "Washington Redskins" should be changed. Argue specifically about this team in the nation's capital, or broaden your argument to the use of Native American names in sports in general.

6. In his 1946 essay "Politics and the English Language" (p. 707), Orwell describes the English language by saying: "It becomes ugly and inaccurate because our thoughts are foolish, but the sloveliness of our language makes it easier for us to have foolish thoughts" (para. 2). Using at least three sources from this Conversation, explain whether you believe Orwell's statement is true today.

Student Writing

Narrative: Reflecting on Personal Experience

The following student essay was written in response to this prompt:

Write a narrative explaining the different "Englishes," as Amy Tan calls them, that you speak and write. If your home language is not English, consider the reasons and ways you switch from it to English and vice versa. But even if English is the only language you know, you "code switch" with different audiences as you speak formally, write informal e-mails, use jargon with peers, and so forth. After your narrative, discuss how these different "Englishes" create different personae for you.

As you read this essay, consider how Nazanin Nikaein develops a distinctive voice and tone. How does she draw her reader in?

My Three Englishes

Nazanin Nikaein

My life consists of three Englishes: the regular English I use for my friends, the English mixed with Farsi for my parents and family, and a type of Spanglish I use with my Spanish-speaking friends or friends who know some Spanish. Language can be a big barrier between people, and sometimes it's easier to create a blend of two languages so that both the people can talk to one another.

"Salaam, chobee?" "Hi, I'm doing well." This is the result of the various "Englishes" in my life. My parents speak to me in Farsi, and I respond in English. Farsi was originally my first language, but now it's just an afterthought for me. If I want to say anything in that language, I have to stop and think about it as if it's a mathematical problem and I have to use an equation to find the answer. I try to say something in Farsi, and it comes out in Spanish or Hebrew. There are too many ways of saying one phrase, and it eventually comes out wrong when I try to say anything. It may be a blessing to know multiple languages, but it can be rough on your mind. There are certain phrases in one language that don't exist in another language. There are foods and technology that don't exist in other languages, and to talk about them you have to adopt the original language's version of it. *Internet* in Hebrew is simply *Internet*. But, on the other hand, *cheeseburger* in Hebrew doesn't even exist. When my family came here and heard the term *cheeseburger*, they were astonished and never even thought it possible to eat a burger with cheese. So in many ways, culture does affect our languages.

Attitude and society also play a big role in affecting our languages. When a Persian person tries to say something in English, it sounds strong and forceful, almost pushy. But that is just how the power of the Persian attitude comes out in English. Often people ask me to translate something from Farsi to English, but the translation is never accurate. The translation sounds almost rude, and it is hard to explain to people that that is not the way it was intended. Word-for-word translating is not a good idea; instead I have to rearrange the entire sentence to get the point through correctly. It is hard to switch languages because you also have to switch mind-sets.

I have always wondered what it is like for people who speak multiple languages to switch languages around at a moment's notice. I asked my mother, who speaks three languages, what it's like, and she told me how at times she would have to think about it. She would have to stop and think because otherwise the wrong language would come out. I then asked her what language she thinks in, and she was stumped. I think in English, and if I try to think in Spanish or Farsi, it's hard, and oftentimes nothing comes out. Most likely, our main language is the one we are able to think in, and I wonder if we can change languages. What would be wonderful would be if we had a way of mixing languages so that both sides could understand. That is exactly what people have done with Spanish and English. Spanglish is an amazing version of English mixed with Spanish terms and verbs that English and Spanish speakers can understand. It involves none of the switching between verbs and tenses that would otherwise be called for if switching languages.

We are lucky to live in a time where we can read novels written in other languages because there are people out there willing to sit down and translate them. The only downside is that the meanings are not always accurate. Switching languages is difficult for me, but getting everything correct in tense and tone is on a completely different level of difficulty.

Questions

1. What do you find most appealing or effective about Nazanin's essay?
2. Are the personal examples the author uses more appropriate than ones from other sources? If you were making suggestions for a revision, would you recommend adding external sources? Why or why not?
3. Are there places in the essay that would benefit from the addition of another personal example? Explain where and why.
4. How would you describe Nazanin's tone? Cite passages to support your response.

Grammar as Rhetoric and Style
Concise Diction

At the start of her essay "Mother Tongue," Amy Tan (p. 700) criticizes herself for writing that is "burdened . . . with nominalized forms, past perfect tenses, conditional phrases." Similarly, George Orwell (p. 707) lambasts "the -*ize* and *de-* formations," preferring direct verbs. He also cautions against complex or unusual words that "dress up simple statements," preferring economy of language. Both writers argue for clear, authentic writing using the most straightforward language possible.

Nominalization

Nominalization is the process that changes a verb into its noun form. The verb *discuss* becomes *discussion*, for instance; the verb *depend* becomes *dependence*; *recognize* becomes *recognition*. The noun forms often result in wordiness, stiffness, or awkward constructions, as the following examples (with added color) show.

Marjorie Agosín could have written:

My poem, given expression in another language, spoke for itself . . . and for me.

Instead of its noun form *expression*, she chose the verb *express*:

My poem, expressed in another language, spoke for itself . . . and for me.

Notice that her choice results in two strong verbs that reinforce one another (i.e., *expressed* and *spoke*) and add force to the point she is making.

Similarly, Firoozeh Dumas writes:

When I was twelve, I decided to simplify my life by adding an American middle name.

If she used the nominalized version *decision*, her sentence would be more wordy and less clear:

> When I was twelve, I made the decision to simplify my life by adding an American middle name.

These changes might seem very minor, but often they have a cumulative effect. In paragraph 10 of Dumas's essay there are several other instances where she could have used the nominalized form but chose a strong verb instead. We've printed that paragraph below with the nominalized forms in brackets. Read the paragraph aloud and think about the effect of the strong clear verbs as opposed to the nominalized forms.

> When I announced [made the announcement] to my family that I wanted to add an American name, they reacted with their usual laughter.

> My mom suggested [gave the suggestion of] "Farah," a name easier than "Firoozeh" yet still Iranian.

> I don't know why we limited [imposed the limitation on] ourselves to names beginning with my initials. . . .

> I finally chose [made the choice of] the name "Julie" mainly for its simplicity.

Showy Vocabulary

Having a large and diverse vocabulary gives a writer many choices and usually results in more precise writing. Inexperienced writers, however, often believe that fancier is better and try to show off words they know. In "Mother Tongue," Amy Tan looks back on a first draft of a story containing this line:

> That was my mental quandary in its nascent state.

With a sense of humor about herself, she tells us that when she first wrote the questionable sentence she believed that a sentence with such elevated vocabulary "would finally prove I had mastery over the English language," but she realized it was "a terrible line" that needed revision. One such revision might read:

> That was my dilemma in its earliest state.

The key to figuring out if a word is too showy is to ask yourself if the fancy word — for example, *pernicious* — is more precise than the more ordinary word —

for example, *fatal*—or if you think the former is simply more impressive than the latter. *Pernicious* seems appropriate when Daniel Okrent (p. 770) says:

> Hijacking the language proves especially pernicious when government officials deodorize their programs with near-Orwellian euphemism.

On the other hand, *pernicious* is inappropriate in a sentence such as:

> We all heard the pernicious gunshots.

The only reason you might laugh when someone says to you, "Felicitations on your natal day!" is that that expression is so much more pompous than "Happy birthday!"—and much less authentic. Like Tan, you must make your own decisions because these choices are not a matter of hard-and-fast rules but rather of how you assess your audience's expectations and the effect your language will have.

Rhetorical and Stylistic Strategy

Writers who use nominalizations, *de-* and *-ize* verbs, and overly complex or unusual words may think these choices add elegance or complexity to their prose and the ideas they express. However, the opposite is true. A writer who relies on expressions that fall into these categories gives the impression of insecurity and perhaps even insincerity. Whenever possible, follow the aphorism "Less is more": less complexity, less length, and less obscurity will lead you toward clear and readable prose with an authentic voice.

• EXERCISE 1 •

Identify awkward or pretentious diction in the following sentences, and revise each sentence as necessary to improve clarity.

1. A person who has a dependence on constant approval from others is usually insecure.
2. Let's have a discussion of the essay you read for homework.
3. Khaya finally came to the realization that she preferred research to teaching.
4. A key step toward losing weight is to make a reduction in the amount of food you consume.
5. A supercilious manager rarely contributes to a felicitous workplace.
6. Recommendations are being made by the faculty for the honor society.
7. Colin filled out his application to work part-time during the holidays.

8. We should give serious consideration to the possibility of traveling to China this summer.

9. The president has every intention of hearing both viewpoints.

10. Before finalizing the meeting, the chair of the group offered a plethora of ideas.

11. Before Derrell made a serious purchase, such as a car, he made a study of the competition.

12. Many benefits accrue from residing in a heterogeneous community.

13. The press release gave an explanation for the senator's stance on homeland security.

14. A recalcitrant attitude has resulted from too many of our colleagues becoming mired in quotidian concerns.

15. Maya has a lot of sympathy for students who experience test anxiety.

• EXERCISE 2 •

In "Politics and the English Language," George Orwell cites the following paragraph as an example of "bad writing." Revise the paragraph by eliminating pretentious diction and improving clarity.

On the one side we have the free personality: by definition it is not neurotic, for it has neither conflict nor dream. Its desires, such as they are, are transparent, for they are just what institutional approval keeps in the forefront of consciousness; another institutional pattern would alter their number and intensity; there is little in them that is natural, irreducible, or culturally dangerous. But *on the other side*, the social bond itself is nothing but the mutual reflection of these self-secure integrities. Recall the definition of love. Is not this the very picture of a small academic? Where is there a place in this hall of mirrors for either personality or fraternity?

• EXERCISE 3 •

Find an article in a newspaper, a memo from an organization, or a speech that contains examples of pretentious and awkward diction. Identify the examples, and explain their effect. Suggest ways to revise that would make the writing clearer. Do you think the writer is intentionally keeping the language obscure? If so, why might that be the case?

Suggestions for Writing
Language

Now that you have examined a number of readings and other texts that focus on language, explore one dimension of this issue by synthesizing your own ideas and the texts. You might want to do more research or use readings from other classes as you prepare for the following projects.

1. The following assertion by Greg Lewis, a pioneer of computer-based technology and author of several books of political analysis, appeared in the *Washington Dispatch* in 2003:

   > To succeed in America—with a number of relatively minor although often highly visible exceptions—it's important to speak, read, and understand English as most Americans speak it. There's nothing cruel or unfair in that; it's just the way it is. And when liberals try to downplay that fact in the name of diversity or multiculturalism . . . they're cynically appealing to a kind of cultural vanity that almost every one of us possesses. . . . In this case, however, the appeal to cultural vanity is destructive.

   Is bilingual education or class instruction and discussion in African American vernacular English (or Ebonics, as it is often called) a viable alternative to conducting classes in standard American English? Write an essay explaining your position.

2. Should language be legislated? Congress has debated whether English should be declared the national language of the United States. What would be the implication of such a law? Do you believe that it is in the interest of national unity to pass a law making English the national language? Write an essay explaining your view.

3. Trace the history and derivation of terms used to describe one ethnic group. What do members of the ethnic group themselves prefer to be called? For instance, discuss the differences among the terms *Hispanic*, *Latino/Latina*, and *Chicano/Chicana*, both to the general public and to the people who identify themselves by these terms. Another option is to discuss the meanings of the terms *colored*, *Negro*, *black*, *Afro-American*, *African American*, and *person of color*—again to the general public and to members of the group itself. Your essay should examine why certain terms win favor over others, as well as the politics and values associated with those terms.

4. Write an essay in which you agree or disagree with the following assertion:

   > In classrooms and hallways and on the playground, young people are using inappropriate language more frequently than ever, teachers and principals say. Not

only is it coarsening the school climate and social discourse, they say, it is evidence of a decline in language skills. Popular culture has made ugly language acceptable and hip, and many teachers say they only expect things to get uglier.

—VALERIE STRAUSS, "More and More, Kids Say the Foulest Things"

5. Choose one of the following quotations, and explain why it speaks to you. Use examples from your own experience and reading to illustrate what the quotation means to you.

• Who does not know another language, does not know his own.

—JOHAN WOLFGANG VON GOETHE

• Languages are the pedigree of nations.

—SAMUEL JOHNSON

• Language is a city to the building of which every human being brought a stone.

—RALPH WALDO EMERSON

6. Some believe that the Internet is improving writing skills because everyone, especially younger people, spends so much time e-mailing, instant messaging, blogging, and chatting in forums. The very fact that young people are writing so frequently is bound to increase comfort level and may lead to the development of a creative style, they claim. Others argue that such activity only degrades writing skills because the language used is so informal, often a series of abbreviations, and the communication is usually a rapid-fire response rather than a sustained discussion. Write an essay explaining whether you think that writing online (in whatever form that might take) has a positive or negative impact on a person's writing. Feel free to use your own experience in your discussion.

7. Most professions—plumbers, lawyers, teachers, accountants, physicians—have their jargon, a language that practitioners use among themselves. In many ways, that language defines the user as a member of the community and sets him or her apart from others who do not "belong." Choose one profession or group (such as those who read graphic novels or listen to a particular type of music), describe key elements of that group's language, and analyze how the language defines the group as a community.

8. Advertisers are keenly aware of the importance of a product's name. Choose one specific type of product (for example, men's or women's cologne, cars, shampoos, lines of clothing, laundry detergents, medical remedies), and classify the names according to the connotations or images they suggest.

9. The idea of "voice" and "voicelessness" is a dominant theme in many novels written by immigrants to the United States. Choose one, and analyze the role of language use and acquisition in the formation of identity and the development of power relationships. Possibilities include *Monkey Bridge* by Lan Cao, *Native Speaker* by Chang-Rae Lee, *The Joy Luck Club* by Amy Tan, *How the Garcia Girls Lost Their Accents* by Julia Alvarez, and many others.

Popular Culture

To what extent does pop culture reflect our society's values?

Popular culture is a term that once characterized mass-produced or low-brow culture: pop music, potboilers and page-turners, movies, comics, advertising, radio, and television. Its audience was the masses. Opposite popular culture were highbrow forms of entertainment: opera, fine art, classical music, traditional theater, and literature. These were the realm of the wealthy and educated classes.

Today, the line between high and pop culture has blurred. Pop culture is often at the leading edge of what will become established culture. For example, the 1980s graffitist Jean-Michel Basquiat is considered a leading figure in contemporary art.

Popular culture moves through our world at warp speed. Rap music and mash-ups sample and remix current and past albums. Celebrity gossip in the morning is the talk-show host's monologue at night. Homemade videos are posted on the Internet, become cultural phenomena overnight, and are just as quickly forgotten. Albums and movies are exchanged on peer-to-peer networks months before they are officially released. What does this onslaught of entertainment and information mean?

These days, most people realize that pop culture asks many of the same questions that high culture does: Does it say something new? Does it tell us about ourselves? Popular culture also spawns new questions: What is pop? Should pop culture respect its roots? What is the relationship among pop culture, politics, and commerce? Do commercial interests control what is offered to the public, or does old-fashioned word of mouth still tell us what's hot and what's not?

The selections in this chapter are about media that you can access. Listen to the music, watch the films and TV shows, and look at the art. The connections made in this chapter prompt a conversation between the past and the present; enter the conversation, consider both, and imagine the future.

Hip Hop Planet

JAMES MCBRIDE

American writer and musician James McBride was born in 1957 in New York City. His father was an African American minister and his mother a Jewish immigrant from Poland who later converted to Christianity. His best-selling memoir, *The Color of Water* (1996), is about growing up in a large African American family and the influence of his Jewish mother, whose father was an orthodox rabbi. McBride is also a saxophonist and composer. His first novel, *Miracle at St. Anna* (2003), was made into a film by Spike Lee. His latest novel is *Song Yet Sung* (2008). McBride has written for the *Boston Globe*, *People* magazine, the *Washington Post*, and *Rolling Stone*. The essay that follows appeared in *National Geographic* in 2007.

This is my nightmare: *My daughter comes home with a guy and says, "Dad, we're getting married." And he's a rapper, with a mouthful of gold teeth, a do-rag on his head, muscles popping out his arms, and a thug attitude. And then the nightmare gets deeper, because before you know it, I'm hearing the pitter-patter of little feet, their offspring, cascading through my living room, cascading through my life, drowning me with the sound of my own hypocrisy, because when I was young, I was a knucklehead, too, hearing my own music, my own sounds. And so I curse the day I saw his face, which is a reflection of my own, and I rue the day I heard his name, because I realize to my horror that rap — music seemingly without melody, sensibility, instruments, verse, or harmony, music with no beginning, end, or middle, music that doesn't even seem to be music — rules the world. It is no longer my world. It is his world. And I live in it. I live on a hip hop planet.*

High-Stepping

I remember when I first heard rap. I was standing in the kitchen at a party in Harlem. It was 1980. A friend of mine named Bill had just gone on the blink. He slapped a guy, a total stranger, in the face right in front of me. I can't remember why. Bill was a fellow student. He was short-circuiting. Problem was, the guy he slapped was a big guy, a dude wearing a do-rag who'd crashed the party with three friends, and, judging by the fury on their faces, there would be no Martin Luther King moments in our immediate future.

There were no white people in the room, though I confess I wished there had been, if only to hide the paleness of my own frightened face. We were black and Latino students about to graduate from Columbia University's journalism school, having learned the whos, whats, wheres, whens, and whys of American reporting. But the real storytellers of the American experience came from the world of the guy that Bill had just slapped. They lived less than a mile from us in the South Bronx. They had no journalism degrees. No money. No credibility. What they did have, however, was talent.

Earlier that night, somebody tossed a record on the turntable, which sent my fellow students stumbling onto the dance floor, howling with delight, and made me, a jazz lover, cringe. It sounded like a broken record. It was a version of an old hit record called "Good Times," the same four bars looped over and over. And on top of this loop, a kid spouted a rhyme about how he was the best disc jockey in the world. It was called "Rapper's Delight." I thought it was the most ridiculous thing I'd ever heard. More ridiculous than Bill slapping that stranger.

Bill survived that evening, but in many ways, I did not. For the next 26 years, I high-stepped past that music the way you step over a crack in the sidewalk. I heard it pounding out of cars and alleyways from Paris to Abidjan, yet I never listened. It came rumbling out of boomboxes from Johannesburg to Osaka, yet I pretended not to hear. I must have strolled past the corner of St. James Place and Fulton Street in my native Brooklyn where a fat kid named Christopher Wallace, aka Biggie Smalls, stood amusing his friends with rhyme, a hundred times, yet I barely noticed. I high-stepped away from that music for 26 years because it was everything I thought it was, and more than I ever dreamed it would be, but mostly, because it held everything I wanted to leave behind.

In doing so, I missed the most important cultural event in my lifetime.

Not since the advent of swing jazz in the 1930s has an American music exploded across the world with such overwhelming force. Not since the Beatles invaded America and Elvis packed up his blue suede shoes has a music crashed against the world with such outrage. This defiant culture of song, graffiti, and dance, collectively known as hip hop, has ripped popular music from its moorings in every society it has permeated. In Brazil, rap rivals samba in popularity. In China, teens spray-paint graffiti on the Great Wall. In France it has been blamed, unfairly, for the worst civil unrest that country has seen in decades.

Its structure is unique, complex, and at times bewildering. Whatever music it eats becomes part of its vocabulary, and as the commercial world falls into place behind it to gobble up the powerful slop in its wake, it metamorphoses into the Next Big Thing. It is a music that defies definition, yet defines our collective societies in immeasurable ways. To many of my generation, despite all attempts to exploit it, belittle it, numb it, classify it, and analyze it, hip hop remains an enigma, a clarion call, a cry of "I am" from the youth of the world. We'd be wise, I suppose, to start paying attention.

Burning Man

Imagine a burning man. He is on fire. He runs into the room. You put out the flames. Then another burning man arrives. You put him out and go about your business. Then two, three, four, five, ten appear. You extinguish them all, send them to the hospital. Then imagine no one bothers to examine why the men caught fire in the first place. That is the story of hip hop.

It is a music dipped in the boiling cauldron of race and class, and for that reason it is clouded with mystics, snake oil salesmen, two-bit scholars, race-baiters, and sneaker salesmen, all professing to know the facts, to be "real," when the reality of race is like shifting sand, dependent on time, place, circumstance, and who's telling the history. Here's the real story: In the mid-1970s, New York City was nearly broke. The public school system cut funding for the arts drastically. Gone were the days when you could wander into the band room, rent a clarinet for a minimal fee, and march it home to squeal on it and drive your parents nuts.

The kids of the South Bronx and Harlem came up with something else. In the summer of 1973, at 1595 East 174th Street in the Bronx River Houses, a black teenager named Afrika Bambaataa stuck a speaker in his mother's first-floor living room window, ran a wire to the turntable in his bedroom, and set the housing project of 3,000 people alight with party music. At the same time, a Jamaican teenager named Kool DJ Herc was starting up the scene in the East Bronx, while a technical whiz named Grandmaster Flash was rising to prominence a couple of miles south. The Bronx became a music magnet for Puerto Ricans, Jamaicans, Dominicans, and black Americans from the surrounding areas. Fab 5 Freddy, Kurtis Blow, and Melle Mel were only a few of the pioneers. Grand Wizard Theodore, Kool DJ AJ, the Cold Crush Brothers, Spoony Gee, and the Rock Steady Crew of B-boys showed up to "battle"—dance, trade quips and rhymes, check out each other's records and equipment—not knowing as they strolled through the doors of the community center near Bambaataa's mother's apartment that they were writing musical history. Among them was an MC named Lovebug Starski, who was said to utter the phrase "hip hop" between breaks to keep time.

This is how it worked: One guy, the DJ, played records on two turntables. One guy—or girl—served as master of ceremonies, or MC. The DJs learned to move the record back and forth under the needle to create a "scratch," or to drop the needle on the record where the beat was the hottest, playing "the break" over and over to keep the folks dancing. The MCs "rapped" over the music to keep the party going. One MC sought to outchat the other. Dance styles were created — "locking" and "popping" and "breaking." Graffiti artists spread the word of the "I" because the music was all about identity: I am the best. I spread the most love in the Bronx, in Harlem, in Queens. The focus initially was not on the MCs, but on the dancers, or B-boys. Commercial radio ignored it. DJs sold mix tapes out of the back of station wagons. "Rapper's Delight" by the Sugarhill Gang—the song I first heard at that face-slapping party in Harlem—broke the music onto radio in 1979.

That is the short history.

The long history is that spoken-word music made its way here on slave ships

₁₀

from West Africa centuries ago: Ethnomusicologists trace hip hop's roots to the dance, drum, and song of West African griots, or storytellers, its pairing of word and music the manifestation of the painful journey of slaves who survived the middle passage. The ring shouts, field hollers, and spirituals of early slaves drew on common elements of African music, such as call and response and improvisation. "Speech-song has been part of black culture for a long, long time," says Samuel A. Floyd, director of the Center for Black Music Research at Columbia College in Chicago. The "dozens," "toasts," and "signifying" of black Americans — verbal dueling, rhyming, self-deprecating tales, and stories of blacks outsmarting whites — were defensive, empowering strategies.

You can point to jazz musicians such as Oscar Brown, Jr., Edgar "Eddie" Jefferson, and Louis Armstrong, and blues greats such as John Lee Hooker, and easily find the foreshadowing of rap music in the verbal play of their work. Black performers such as poet Nikki Giovanni and Gil Scott-Heron, a pianist and vocalist who put spoken political lyrics to music (most famously in "The Revolution Will Not Be Televised"), elevated spoken word to a new level. 15

But the artist whose work arguably laid the groundwork for rap as we know it was Amiri Baraka, a beat poet out of Allen Ginsberg's Greenwich Village scene. In the late 1950s and '60s, Baraka performed with shrieks, howls, cries, stomps, verse floating ahead of or behind the rhythm, sometimes in staccato syncopation. It was performance art, delivered in a dashiki and Afro, in step with the anger of a bold and sometimes frightening nationalistic black movement, and it inspired what might be considered the first rap group, the Last Poets.

I was 13 when I first heard the Last Poets in 1970. They scared me. To black America, they were like the relatives you hoped wouldn't show up at your barbecue because the boss was there — the old Aunt Clementine who would arrive, get drunk, and pull out her dentures. My parents refused to allow us to play their music in our house — so my siblings waited until my parents went to work and played it anyway. They were the first musical group I heard to use the N-word on a record, with songs like "N_____ Are Scared of Revolution." In a world where blacks were evolving from "Negroes" to "blacks," and the assassinations of civil rights leaders Malcolm X and Martin Luther King, Jr., still reverberated in the air like a shotgun blast, the Last Poets embodied black power. Their records consisted of percussion and spoken-word rhyme. They were wildly popular in my neighborhood. Their debut recording sold 400,000 records in three months, says Last Poet member Umar Bin Hassan. "No videos, no radio play, strictly word of mouth." The group's demise coincided with hip hop's birth in the 1970s.

It's unlikely that the Last Poets ever dreamed the revolution they sang of would take the form it has. "We were about the movement," Abiodun Oyewole, a founder of the group, says. "A lot of today's rappers have talent. But a lot of them are driving the car in the wrong direction."

The Crossover

Highways wrap around the city of Dayton, Ohio, like a ribbon bow-tied on a box of chocolates from the local Esther Price candy factory. They have six ladies at the plant who do just that: Tie ribbons around boxes all day. Henry Rosenkranz can tell you about it. "I love candy," says Henry, a slim white teenager in glasses and a hairnet, as he strolls the factory, bucket in hand. His full-time after-school job is mopping the floors.

Henry is a model American teenager — and the prototypical consumer at [20] which the hip hop industry is squarely aimed, which has his parents sitting up in their seats. The music that was once the purview of black America has gone white and gone commercial all at once. A sea of white faces now rises up to greet rap groups as they perform, many of them teenagers like Henry, a NASCAR fanatic and self-described redneck. "I live in Old North Dayton," he says. "It's a white, redneck area. But hip hop is so prominent with country people . . . if you put them behind a curtain and hear them talk, you won't know if they're black or white. There's a guy I work with, when Kanye West sings about a gold digger, he can relate because he's paying alimony and child support."

Obviously, it's not just working-class whites, but also affluent, suburban kids who identify with this music with African-American roots. A white 16-year-old hollering rap lyrics at the top of his lungs from the driver's seat of his dad's late-model Lexus may not have the same rationale to howl at the moon as a working-class kid whose parents can't pay for college, yet his own anguish is as real to him as it gets. What attracts white kids to this music is the same thing that prompted outraged congressmen to decry jazz during the 1920s and Tipper Gore to campaign decades later against violent and sexually explicit lyrics: life on the other side of the tracks; its "cool" or illicit factor, which black Americans, like it or not, are always perceived to possess.

Hip hop has continually changed form, evolving from party music to social commentary with the 1982 release of Grandmaster Flash and the Furious Five's "The Message." Today, alternative hip hop artists continue to produce socially conscious songs, but most commercial rappers spout violent lyrics that debase women and gays. Beginning with the so-called gangsta rap of the '90s, popularized by the still unsolved murders of rappers Biggie Smalls and Tupac Shakur, the genre has become dominated by rappers who brag about their lives of crime. 50 Cent, the hip hop star of the moment, trumpets his sexual exploits and boasts that he has been shot nine times.

"People call hip hop the MTV music now," scoffs Chuck D, of Public Enemy, known for its overtly political rap. "It's Big Brother controlling you. To slip something in there that's indigenous to the roots, that pays homage to the music that came before us, it's the Mount Everest of battles."

Most rap songs unabashedly function as walking advertisements for luxury cars, designer clothes, and liquor. Agenda Inc., a "pop culture brand strategy agency," listed Mercedes-Benz as the number one brand mentioned in *Billboard*'s top 20 singles in 2005. Hip hop sells so much Hennessy cognac, listed at number six, that the French makers, deader than yesterday's beer a decade ago, are now rolling in suds. The company even sponsored a contest to win a visit to its plant in France with a famous rapper.

In many ways, the music represents an old dream. It's the pot of gold to millions of kids like Henry, who quietly agonizes over how his father slaves 14 hours a day at two tool-and-die machine jobs to make ends meet. Like teenagers across the world, he fantasizes about working in the hip hop business and making millions himself.

"My parents hate hip hop," Henry says, motoring his 1994 Dodge Shadow through traffic on the way home from work on a hot October afternoon. "But I can listen to Snoop Dogg and hear him call women whores, and I know he has a wife and children at home. It's just a fantasy. Everyone has the urge deep down to be a bad guy or a bad girl. Everyone likes to talk the talk, but not everyone will walk the walk."

Full Circle

You breathe in and breathe out a few times and you are there. Eight hours and a wake-up shake on the flight from New York, and you are on the tarmac in Dakar, Senegal. Welcome to Africa. The assignment: Find the roots of hip hop. The music goes full circle. The music comes home to Africa. That whole bit. Instead it was the old reporter's joke: You go out to cover a story and the story covers you. The stench of poverty in my nostrils was so strong it pulled me to earth like a hundred-pound ring in my nose. Dakar's Sandaga market is full of "local color"—unless you live there. It was packed and filthy, stalls full of new merchandise surrounded by shattered pieces of life everywhere, broken pipes, bicycle handlebars, fruit flies, soda bottles, beggars, dogs, cell phones. A teenage beggar, his body malformed by polio, crawled by on hands and feet, like a spider. He said, "Hey brother, help me." When I looked into his eyes, they were a bottomless ocean.

The Hotel Teranga is a fortress, packed behind a concrete wall where beggars gather at the front gate. The French tourists march past them, the women in high heels and stonewashed jeans. They sidle through downtown Dakar like royalty, haggling in the market, swimming in the hotel pool with their children, a scene that resembles Birmingham, Alabama, in the 1950s—the blacks serving, the whites partying. Five hundred yards (460 meters) away, Africans eat off the sidewalk and sell peanuts for a pittance. There is a restlessness, a deep sense of something gone wrong in the air.

The French can't smell it, even though they've had a mouthful back home. A good amount of the torching of Paris suburbs in October 2005 was courtesy of the children of immigrants from former French African colonies, exhausted from being bottled up in housing projects for generations with no job prospects. They telegraphed the punch in their music—France is the second largest hip hop market in the world—but the message was ignored. Around the globe, rap music has become a universal expression of outrage, its macho pose borrowed from commercial hip hop in the U.S.

In Dakar, where every kid is a microphone and turntable away from squalor, 30 and American rapper Tupac Shakur's picture hangs in market stalls of folks who don't understand English, rap is king. There are hundreds of rap groups in Senegal today. French television crews troop in and out of Dakar's nightclubs filming the kora harp lute and tama talking drum with regularity. But beneath the drumming and the dance lessons and the jingling sound of tourist change, there is a quiet rage, a desperate fury among the Senegalese, some of whom seem to bear an intense dislike of their former colonial rulers.

"We know all about French history," says Abdou Ba, a Senegalese producer and musician. "We know about their kings, their castles, their art, their music. We know everything about them. But they don't know much about us."

Assane N'Diaye, 19, loves hip hop music. Before he left his Senegalese village to work as a DJ in Dakar, he was a fisherman, just like his father, like his father's father before him. Tall, lean, with a muscular build and a handsome chocolate face, Assane became a popular DJ, but the equipment he used was borrowed, and when his friend took it back, success eluded him. He has returned home to Toubab Dialaw, about 25 miles (40 kilometers) south of Dakar, a village marked by a huge boulder, perhaps 40 feet (12 meters) high, facing the Atlantic Ocean.

About a century and a half ago, a local ruler led a group of people fleeing slave traders to this place. He was told by a white trader to come here, to Toubab Dialaw. When he arrived, the slavers followed. A battle ensued. The ruler fought bravely but was killed. The villagers buried him by the sea and marked his grave with a small stone, and over the years it is said to have sprouted like a tree planted by God. It became a huge, arching boulder that stares out to sea, protecting the village behind it. When the fishermen went deep out to sea, the boulder was like a lighthouse that marked the way home. The Great Rock of Toubab Dialaw is said to hold a magic spirit, a spirit that Assane N'Diaye believes in.

In the shadow of the Great Rock, Assane has built a small restaurant, Chez Las, decorated with hundreds of seashells. It is where he lives his hip hop dream. At night, he and his brother and cousin stand by the Great Rock and face the sea. They meditate. They pray. Then they write rap lyrics that are worlds away from the bling-bling culture of today's commercial hip hoppers. They write about their lives as village fishermen, the scarcity of catch forcing them to fish in deeper and deeper waters, the hardship of fishing for 8, 10, 14 days at a time in an open pirogue in rainy season, the high fee they pay to rent the boat, and the paltry price their catches fetch on the market. They write about the humiliation of poverty, watching their town sprout up around them with rich Dakarians and richer French. And they write about the relatives who leave in the morning and never return, surrendered to the sea, sharks, and God.

The dream, of course, is to make a record. They have their own demo, their 35 own logo, and their own name, Salam T. D. (for Toubab Dialaw). But rap music represents a deeper dream: a better life. "We want money to help our parents," Assane says over dinner. "We watch our mothers boil water to cook and have nothing to put in the pot."

He fingers his food lightly. "Rap doesn't belong to American culture," he says. "It belongs here. It has always existed here, because of our pain and our hardships and our suffering."

On this cool evening in a restaurant above their village, these young men, clad in baseball caps and T-shirts, appear no different from their African-American counterparts, with one exception. After a dinner of chicken and rice, Assane says something in Wolof to the others. Silently and without ceremony, they take every bit of the leftover dinner — the half-eaten bread, rice, pieces of chicken, the chicken bones — and dump them into a plastic bag to give to the children in the village. They silently rise from the table and proceed outside. The last I see of them, their regal figures are outlined in the dim light of the doorway, heading out to the darkened village, holding on to that bag as though it held money.

The City of Gods

Some call the Bronx River Houses the City of Gods, though if God has been by lately, he must've slipped out for a chicken sandwich. The 10 drab, red-brick buildings spread out across 14 acres (5.7 hectares), coming into view as you drive east across the East 174th Street Bridge. The Bronx is the hallowed holy ground of hip hop, the place where it all began. Visitors take tours through this neighborhood now, care of a handful of fortyish "old-timers," who point out the high and low spots of hip hop's birthplace.

It is a telling metaphor for the state of America's racial landscape that you need a permit to hold a party in the same parks and playgrounds that produced the music that changed the world. The rap artists come and go, but the conditions that produced them linger. Forty percent of New York City's black males are jobless. One in three black males born in 2001 will end up in prison. The life expectancy of black men in the U.S. ranks below that of men in Sri Lanka and Colombia. It took a massive hurricane in New Orleans for the United States to wake up to its racial realities.

That is why, after 26 years, I have come to embrace this music I tried so hard 40 to ignore. Hip hop culture is not mine. Yet I own it. Much of it I hate. Yet I love it, the good of it. To confess a love for a music that, at least in part, embraces violence is no easy matter, but then again our national anthem talks about bombs bursting in air, and I love that song, too. At its best, hip hop lays bare the empty moral cupboard that is our generation's legacy. This music that once made visible the inner culture of America's greatest social problem, its legacy of slavery, has taken the dream deferred to a global scale. Today, 2 percent of the Earth's adult population owns more than 50 percent of its household wealth, and indigenous cultures are swallowed with the rapidity of a teenager gobbling a bag of potato chips. The music is calling. Over the years, the instruments change, but the message is the same. The drums are pounding out a warning. They are telling us something. Our children can hear it.

The question is: Can we?

Questions for Discussion

1. What do you consider James McBride's primary purpose in "Hip Hop Planet"? Do you think this is a personal essay or a cultural study? Explain your response.

2. "Hip Hop Planet" was included in the inaugural edition of *Best African-American Essays* (2009). In her review of the collection on the *Kenyon Review*'s Web site, Samantha Simpson notes that the collection "strains against the oversimplification of the African-American community's concerns. The collection does not only cull the voices concerned with the politics of race, but it also includes essays that deal with matters of the heart. That is, the collection is a far cry from the obligatory Black History Month lessons on important Black People." Do you consider McBride's essay to be about matters of the heart, or is it about the politics of race? Explain your answer.

3. McBride's lead (the opening paragraph of his essay) could be considered provocative, if not confrontational. Having read the whole essay, go back and reread the lead. Is it an effective introduction to the essay, or could it be considered misleading? Explain.

4. David Brooks, writing in the *New York Times* in 2005 about riots in French housing projects, says, "In a globalized age it's perhaps inevitable that the culture of resistance gets globalized, too. What we are seeing is what Mark Lilla of the University of Chicago calls a universal culture of the wretched of the earth. The images, modes and attitudes of hip hop and gangsta rap are so powerful they are having a hegemonic effect across the globe." How does that view of hip hop compare to McBride's? Do you think McBride would agree with Brooks? Explain why or why not.

5. In paragraph 23 McBride quotes Chuck D, of Public Enemy. What is your view of Chuck D's assertion? Are there ways in which rap music does pay "homage to the music that came before"? If so, what are they?

6. Read the description of the music composed by the would-be Senegalese rapper Assane N'Diaye (para. 34). Do you consider this to be a lesser form of rap or a truer form? Explain your answer.

7. In the next-to-last paragraph of McBride's essay, he justifies his acceptance of the violence that hip hop music embraces by saying that our national anthem is also about violence. What do you think of that comparison? In what ways does it help his argument? In what ways might it hinder it?

Questions on Rhetoric and Style

1. What rhetorical strategies does McBride use in his lead (the opening paragraph) to establish his persona and his credibility? Consider irony, hyperbole, metaphor, and colloquialisms.

2. Why do you think McBride calls the first section of his essay "High-Stepping"? In what ways does he play on the phrase? How do the rest of the essay's section names relate to their contents?

3. McBride transitions from the personal to the historical several times in "Hip Hop Planet." How does he achieve these transitions? What are some of the strategies he uses to make the transitions?

4. McBride names a dozen rappers in paragraph 11. What is the effect of mentioning all these names?

5. Find examples of figurative language in "Hip Hop Planet." How does McBride use them to connect to his audience and achieve his purpose?

6. How would you characterize Henry Rosenkranz, from Dayton, Ohio, whom we meet in "The Crossover"? How does Rosenkranz help McBride establish his own credibility? What about Assane N'Diaye, the young Senegalese man whom we meet in "Full Circle"?

7. What is McBride's central argument? What are his secondary arguments? How does he bring them together?

8. How does McBride use cause and effect to provide the reasons for hip hop's development?

9. Look carefully at paragraph 12. How does McBride's style mirror the paragraph's subject matter?

10. McBride is a novelist as well as a memoirist and essayist. What techniques of fiction does he employ in "Hip Hop Planet"? What are their effects?

11. McBride ends the essay with a question. Why do you think he gives that question its own paragraph?

12. Who is the likely audience for this essay? How does McBride consider audience throughout his essay?

Suggestions for Writing

1. McBride argues that hip hop music is a warning (para. 40). Write an essay in which you support, challenge, or qualify his assertion.

2. McBride quotes Abiodun Oyewole, a founder of what he considers the first rap group, the Last Poets (para. 18): "'A lot of today's rappers have talent. But a lot of them are driving the car in the wrong direction.'" Analyze Oyewole's statement, and write an essay in which you support, challenge, or qualify his assertion. Be sure to use examples of today's rappers who illustrate your argument.

3. Listen to the music and poetry of some of the old-school musicians and writers McBride cites, such as Louis Armstrong, Nikki Giovanni, and Amiri Baraka. Write an essay in which you examine their influence on specific hip hop musicians.

4. McBride suggests that the anger from the 2005 riots in the Paris suburbs found its way into hip hop music, its "macho pose borrowed from commercial hip hop in the U.S." (para. 29). Judy Rosen, writing in the online magazine *Slate*, argues that "France, the nation that enshrines conversational grandiloquence as a civic virtue right up there with *fraternité*, would take to the most blabbermouthed genre in music history," suggesting that it has remade hip hop in its own fashion. Research rap music in countries such as France, Brazil, and England; then write an essay in which you examine the influence of American hip hop on the music of these countries as well as the influence of foreign musicians on American rap and hip hop.

5. Imagine and write a conversation between Henry Rosenkranz and Assane N'Diaye in which they discuss the sources, messages, and benefits of hip hop music.

Corn-Pone Opinions

MARK TWAIN

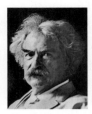 Mark Twain (1835–1910) is the pseudonym of Samuel Langhorne Clemens. Best known as a novelist—*The Adventures of Huckleberry Finn* (1884), *Tom Sawyer* (1876), and *A Connecticut Yankee in King Arthur's Court* (1889) are among Twain's most famous—Twain also worked as a typesetter, a riverboat pilot, a miner, a reporter, and an editor. His early writings reflect his pre–Civil War upbringing in their idyllic images as well as in their reminders of some of America's least acceptable social realities. Twain spent his life observing and reporting on his surroundings, and his work provides a glimpse into the mind-set of the late nineteenth century. "Corn-Pone Opinions," which was found in his papers after his death, was first published in 1923 in *Europe and Elsewhere*. In it, Twain comments—not always approvingly—on word of mouth as the spreader of popular opinion and culture.

Fifty years ago, when I was a boy of fifteen and helping to inhabit a Missourian village on the banks of the Mississippi, I had a friend whose society was very dear to me because I was forbidden by my mother to partake of it. He was a gay and impudent and satirical and delightful young black man—a slave—who daily preached sermons from the top of his master's woodpile, with me for sole audience. He imitated the pulpit style of the several clergymen of the village, and did it well, and with fine passion and energy. To me he was a wonder. I believed he was the greatest orator in the United States and would some day be heard from. But it did not happen; in the distribution of rewards he was overlooked. It is the way, in this world.

He interrupted his preaching, now and then, to saw a stick of wood; but the sawing was a pretense—he did it with his mouth; exactly imitating the sound the bucksaw makes in shrieking its way through the wood. But it served its purpose; it kept his master from coming out to see how the work was getting along. I listened to the sermons from the open window of a lumber room at the back of the house. One of his texts was this:

"You tell me whar a man gits his corn pone, en I'll tell you what his 'pinions is."

I can never forget it. It was deeply impressed upon me. By my mother. Not upon my memory, but elsewhere. She had slipped in upon me while I was absorbed and not watching. The black philosopher's idea was that a man is not independent, and cannot afford views which might interfere with his bread and butter. If he would prosper, he must train with the majority; in matters of large moment, like politics and religion, he must think and feel with the bulk of his

799

neighbors, or suffer damage in his social standing and in his business prosperi-
ties. He must restrict himself to corn-pone opinions—at least on the surface. He
must get his opinions from other people; he must reason out none for himself; he
must have no first-hand views.

I think Jerry was right, in the main, but I think he did not go far enough.   5

1. It was his idea that a man conforms to the majority view of his locality by
   calculation and intention. This happens, but I think it is not the rule.

2. It was his idea that there is such a thing as a first-hand opinion; an original
   opinion; an opinion which is coldly reasoned out in a man's head, by a
   searching analysis of the facts involved, with the heart unconsulted, and
   the jury room closed against outside influences. It may be that such an
   opinion has been born somewhere, at some time or other, but I suppose it
   got away before they could catch it and stuff it and put it in the museum.

I am persuaded that a coldly-thought-out and independent verdict upon a
fashion in clothes, or manners, or literature, or politics, or religion, or any other
matter that is projected into the field of our notice and interest, is a most rare
thing—if it has indeed ever existed.

A new thing in costume appears—the flaring hoopskirt, for example—and
the passers-by are shocked, and the irreverent laugh. Six months later everybody
is reconciled; the fashion has established itself; it is admired, now, and no one laughs.
Public opinion resented it before, public opinion accepts it now, and is happy in
it. Why? Was the resentment reasoned out? Was the acceptance reasoned out? No.
The instinct that moves to conformity did the work. It is our nature to conform;
it is a force which not many can successfully resist. What is its seat? The inborn
requirement of self-approval. We all have to bow to that; there are no exceptions.
Even the woman who refuses from first to last to wear the hoopskirt comes under
that law and is its slave; she could not wear the skirt and have her own approval;
and that she must have, she cannot help herself. But as a rule our self-approval
has its source in but one place and not elsewhere—the approval of other people.
A person of vast consequences can introduce any kind of novelty in dress and the
general world will presently adopt it—moved to do it, in the first place, by the
natural instinct to passively yield to that vague something recognized as authority, and in the second place by the human instinct to train with the multitude and
have its approval. An empress introduced the hoopskirt, and we know the result.
A nobody introduced the bloomer, and we know the result. If Eve should come
again, in her ripe renown, and reintroduce her quaint styles—well, we know
what would happen. And we should be cruelly embarrassed, along at first.

The hoopskirt runs its course and disappears. Nobody reasons about it. One
woman abandons the fashion; her neighbor notices this and follows her lead; this
influences the next woman; and so on and so on, and presently the skirt has vanished out of the world, no one knows how nor why, nor cares, for that matter. It
will come again, by and by and in due course will go again.

Twenty-five years ago, in England, six or eight wine glasses stood grouped by each person's plate at a dinner party, and they were used, not left idle and empty; to-day there are but three or four in the group, and the average guest sparingly uses about two of them. We have not adopted this new fashion yet, but we shall do it presently. We shall not think it out; we shall merely conform, and let it go at that. We get our notions and habits and opinions from outside influences; we do not have to study them out.

Our table manners, and company manners and street manners change from time to time, but the changes are not reasoned out; we merely notice and conform. We are creatures of outside influences; as a rule we do not think, we only imitate. We cannot invent standards that will stick; what we mistake for standards are only fashions, and perishable. We may continue to admire them, but we drop the use of them. We notice this in literature. Shakespeare is a standard, and fifty years ago we used to write tragedies which we couldn't tell from — from somebody else's; but we don't do it any more, now. Our prose standard, three quarters of a century ago, was ornate and diffuse; some authority or other changed it in the direction of compactness and simplicity, and conformity followed, without argument. The historical novel starts up suddenly, and sweeps the land. Everybody writes one, and the nation is glad. We had historical novels before; but nobody read them, and the rest of us conformed — without reasoning it out. We are conforming in the other way, now, because it is another case of everybody.

The outside influences are always pouring in upon us, and we are always obeying their orders and accepting their verdicts. The Smiths like the new play; the Joneses go to see it, and they copy the Smith verdict. Morals, religions, politics, get their following from surrounding influences and atmospheres, almost entirely; not from study, not from thinking. A man must and will have his own approval first of all, in each and every moment and circumstance of his life — even if he must repent of a self-approved act the moment after its commission, in order to get his self-approval again: but, speaking in general terms, a man's self-approval in the large concerns of life has its source in the approval of the peoples about him, and not in a searching personal examination of the matter. Mohammedans are Mohammedans because they are born and reared among that sect, not because they have thought it out and can furnish sound reasons for being Mohammedans; we know why Catholics are Catholics; why Presbyterians are Presbyterians; why Baptists are Baptists; why Mormons are Mormons; why thieves are thieves; why monarchists are monarchists; why Republicans are Republicans and Democrats, Democrats. We know it is a matter of association and sympathy, not reasoning and examination; that hardly a man in the world has an opinion upon morals, politics, or religion which he got otherwise than through his associations and sympathies. Broadly speaking, there are none but corn-pone opinions. And broadly speaking, corn-pone stands for self-approval. Self-approval is acquired mainly from the approval of other people. The result is conformity. Sometimes conformity has a sordid business interest—the bread-and-butter interest—but not in most cases, I think. I think that in the majority of cases it is unconscious and not calculated; that it's born of the human being's natural yearning to stand well with his fellows and have their inspiring approval and praise—a yearning which is commonly so strong and so insistent that it cannot be effectually resisted, and must have its way. A political emergency brings out the corn-pone opinion in fine force in its two chief variet-ies—the pocketbook variety, which has its origin in self-interest, and the bigger variety, the sentimental variety—the one which can't bear to be outside the pale; can't bear to be in disfavor; can't endure the averted face and the cold shoulder; wants to stand well with his friends, wants to be smiled upon, wants to be wel-come, wants to hear the precious words, "He's on the right track!" Uttered, per-haps by an ass, but still an ass of high degree, an ass whose approval is gold and diamonds to a smaller ass, and confers glory and honor and happiness, and mem-bership in the herd. For these gauds many a man will dump his life-long princi-ples into the street, and his conscience along with them. We have seen it happen. In some millions of instances.

Men think they think upon great political questions, and they do; but they think with their party, not independently; they read its literature, but not that of the other side; they arrive at convictions, but they are drawn from a partial view of the matter in hand and are of no particular value. They swarm with their party, they feel with their party, they are happy in their party's approval; and where the party leads they will follow, whether for right and honor, or through blood and dirt and a mush of mutilated morals.

In our late canvass half of the nation passionately believed that in silver lay salvation, the other half as passionately believed that that way lay destruction. Do you believe that a tenth part of the people, on either side, had any rational excuse for having an opinion about the matter at all? I studied that mighty question to the bottom—came out empty. Half of our people passionately believe in high tariff, the other half believe otherwise. Does this mean study and examination, or only feeling? The latter, I think. I have deeply studied that question, too—and didn't arrive. We all do no end of feeling, and we mistake it for thinking. And out of it we get an aggregation which we consider a boon. Its name is Public Opinion. It is held in reverence. It settles everything. Some think it the Voice of God.

Questions for Discussion

1. According to Mark Twain, "It is our nature to conform" (para. 7); he also says that we do so for self-approval. The two statements seem contradictory; how does Twain connect conformity and self-approval?

2. Twain makes a distinction between "standards" and "fashions" (para. 10). What is the difference? What examples does he provide for each? How does the distinction apply to the twenty-first century?

3. Twain's essay is ultimately a denunciation of cultural chauvinism. What consequences does he suggest are the result of "corn-pone opinions"? Which are explicit? Which are implicit?

4. The last paragraph begins with a reference to a "late canvass" in which "half the nation passionately believed" in one path and "the other half as passionately believed" in another. To what was Twain probably referring? Does he take sides? How does he distinguish between thinking and feeling?

5. In what two ways does a political emergency bring out corn-pone opinions? What does Twain mean by "an ass of high degree" (para. 11)?

Questions on Rhetoric and Style

1. What is Twain's purpose in "Corn-Pone Opinions"?

2. Trace Twain's use of the personal pronoun. What is the effect of changing from *I* to *we*?

3. Twain claims he got the idea of corn-pone opinions from a young slave with a talent for preaching. What does the anecdote add to his argument? Does it detract in any way? If so, how?

4. How does Twain expand Jerry's definition of corn-pone opinions? What is the effect of numbering the two items in which he begins to expand Jerry's definition (para. 5)?

5. Identify Twain's appeals to logos. Do the subjects of the appeals (hoopskirts, bloomers, wine glasses) strengthen the appeals or weaken them? Explain your response.

6. Explain the irony of Twain's qualification of Jerry's statement about calculation and intention in paragraph 5.

7. Why is paragraph 11 so long? Where, if anywhere, could Twain have broken it up? What is the effect of the series of subordinate clauses in the middle of the paragraph?

8. What is the effect of the parallelism in the two long sentences that make up paragraph 12?

9. What is the effect of capitalizing "Public Opinion" and "Voice of God" at the end of the essay?

10. How does a phrase such as "helping to inhabit" in the first paragraph contribute to the tone of the essay?

11. Find examples of understatement and hyperbole. Discuss their effects.

Suggestions for Writing

1. Do you agree or disagree with Twain's assertion that "[i]t is our nature to conform" (para. 7)? Explain why.

2. Refute Twain's view of Public Opinion by defending word of mouth as the most reliable communicator of cultural innovation.

3. In paragraph 10, Twain contrasts prose styles that are "ornate and diffuse" with those that are characterized by "compactness and simplicity." Find examples of each, and write an essay comparing and contrasting the effects of the two prose styles.

4. Twain says he believed that the slave Jerry was "the greatest orator in the United States" (para. 1) but that "in the distribution of rewards he was overlooked." Write about how Jerry might have viewed his situation.

5. Write your own version of "Corn-Pone Opinions," giving examples from contemporary culture and politics. Do you end up making the same argument as Twain, or do you think Americans are more independent thinkers now? Explain why.

from *Show and Tell*

SCOTT MCCLOUD

Scott McCloud (b. 1960) decided to become a comics artist when he was in tenth grade. After graduating from Syracuse University with a degree in illustration, McCloud worked in the production department of DC Comics until he began publishing his own comic series, "Zot!" and "Destroy!!" McCloud is the author of *Understanding Comics* (1993), *Reinventing Comics* (2000), and *Making Comics* (2006). In *Understanding Comics*, from which the accompanying excerpts are taken, a caricature of McCloud guides the reader through a study of "sequential art" by tracing the relationship between words and images.

Exploring the Text

1. Scott McCloud begins with a series of sixteen panels of a boy demonstrating how his toy robot turns into an airplane. Six of the panels have no words, yet the vignette manages to establish both pathos and ethos. How does McCloud accomplish this? Consider the drawings and the words separately, and then consider them together.

2. Why does McCloud use the show-and-tell vignette to open the piece? How does it support the piece's main idea?

3. On page 809, McCloud defines comics (although he says it isn't *his* definition) as "words and pictures in combination." He suggests that this is essentially show-and-tell. Trace how he uses classification to expand and refine his definition. How does he provide examples for each of his categories?

4. On page 813, McCloud uses dance as a metaphor to explain the relationship between words and images. Do you consider the words or the illustrations more powerful in illustrating that relationship? Can either stand alone? Explain.

5. What audience is McCloud addressing? In what ways does he acknowledge that audience? How does he establish ethos?

6. McCloud uses comic-book conventions such as exaggerated facial expressions to show emotion and a character walking left to right to create a sense of slowness and difficulty. Find other examples of these conventions, and compare them to the conventions of language he employs.

7. Charles McGrath, an editor of the *New York Times Book Review*, wrote in a 2004 essay, "Not Funnies," that comic books are "what novels used to be — an accessible, vernacular form with mass appeal." He says that if the "highbrows" are right, they are a "form perfectly suited to our dumbed-down culture and collective attention deficit." How might McCloud respond to McGrath and the "highbrows"? How does McCloud address the gap between high and low culture?

8. Describe the tone of "Show and Tell" on the following pages. How is it created? Are the words or images more instrumental in creating the tone? Are there places where the words and images create different tones? Please explain.

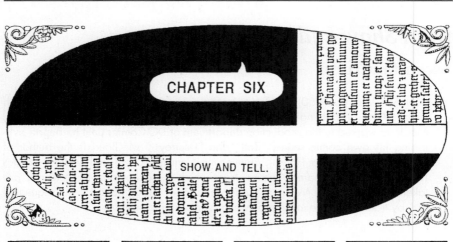

CHAPTER SIX

SHOW AND TELL.

THIS IS MY ROBOT.

WHAT CAN YOU *TELL* US ABOUT YOUR ROBOT, TOMMY?

WELL, UH... I LIKE IT 'CAUSE... 'CAUSE, UH...

IT'S GOT ONE OF *THESE* THINGS.

WHAT IS *THAT*, TOMMY?

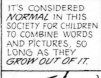

140

...

WORDS AND PICTURES IN COMBINATION MAY NOT BE MY *DEFINITION* OF COMICS, BUT THE COMBINATION HAS HAD *TREMENDOUS INFLUENCE* ON ITS *GROWTH*.

com·ics (kom'iks)**n.** p... e form, used with a singula... Juxtaposed pictori... er images in deliberate... ence, intended to conve... n and/or to prod... response in th... **2**.Superhe... costumes, figh... villains who want... ne world in violent s... ulse·

A HUGE RANGE OF HUMAN EXPERIENCES CAN BE *PORTRAYED* IN COMICS THROUGH EITHER WORDS OR PICTURES.

AS A RESULT--AND DESPITE ITS MANY *OTHER* POTENTIAL USES -- COMICS HAVE BECOME *FIRMLY IDENTIFIED* WITH THE ART OF *STORYTELLING*.

AND *INDEED*, WORDS AND PICTURES HAVE *GREAT* POWERS TO TELL STORIES WHEN CREATORS FULLY EXPLOIT THEM *BOTH*.

DADA
BIOGRAPHY · HORROR
ROMANCE · SURREALISM
BLANK VERSE · HISTORICAL FICTION
EPIC POETRY · FOLK TALES
SEQUENTIAL ART · EROTICA
SOCIAL ALLEGORY · MYSTERY
ADAPTATIONS · RELIGIOUS TOPICS
STREAM OF CONSCIOUSNESS
SATIRE

AND SO FAR, WE'VE ONLY SEEN THE *TIP OF THE ICEBERG!*

AS CHILDREN, WE "SHOW AND TELL" *INTERCHANGEABLY*, WORDS AND IMAGES COMBINING TO TRANSMIT A *CONNECTED SERIES OF IDEAS*.

IT'S GOT ONE OF *THESE* THINGS.

THE DIFFERENT WAYS IN WHICH WORDS AND PICTURES CAN *COMBINE* IN COMICS IS VIRTUALLY *UNLIMITED*.

BUT LET'S TRY TO BREAK IT DOWN INTO SOME DISTINCT *CATEGORIES*.

152

FIRST, WE HAVE THE *WORD SPECIFIC* COMBINATIONS, WHERE PICTURES *ILLUSTRATE*, BUT DON'T SIGNIFICANTLY *ADD* TO A LARGELY *COMPLETE* TEXT.

WE STUMBLED BACK TO THE APARTMENT SHORTLY BEFORE DAWN, *VOMITING* EVERY 20 YARDS.

JUDY GAVE ME HER KEYS AND SMILED.

THE *UNITED STATES CONSTITUTION* WAS ADOPTED BY THE *SECOND CONTINENTAL CONGRESS* IN 1787 AND PUT INTO EFFECT IN 1789.

THEN THERE ARE *PICTURE SPECIFIC* COMBINATIONS WHERE WORDS DO LITTLE MORE THAN ADD A *SOUNDTRACK* TO A VISUALLY TOLD SEQUENCE.

HE DID IT!

MMM... MMM...

AND, OF COURSE, *DUO-SPECIFIC* PANELS IN WHICH BOTH WORDS AND PICTURES SEND ESSENTIALLY THE *SAME* MESSAGE.

GRIM-FACED, GEORGE LIFTED HIS LOLLYPOP.

BUT THE CAPTAIN'S MIGHTY BLOW *MISSES* ITS INTENDED TARGET!

BLAST! HE *DODGED* MY PUNCH AND I STRUCK THIS *BRICK WALL!*

HA! I DODGED YOU!

I FEEL SO *SAD!*

...THOUGHT AMY.

153

ANOTHER TYPE IS THE **ADDITIVE** COMBINATION WHERE WORDS *AMPLIFY* OR *ELABORATE* ON AN IMAGE OR *VICE VERSA*.

MY HEAD FEELS LIKE A *SMASHED PUMPKIN!*

HOW D'YA LIKE MY *NEW THREADS*, BABE?

IS THIS THE SAME *JUPITER* OF MY YOUTH?

IN **PARALLEL** COMBINATIONS, WORDS AND PICTURES SEEM TO FOLLOW VERY DIFFERENT COURSES--WITHOUT *INTERSECTING.*

"TALKED TO *BILL* YET?"

"*SALLY* DID. *WHY?*"

"THE *TEST RESULTS* CAME BACK. ALL *NEGATIVE.*"

"*REALLY?* THAT'S *GREAT!*"

WELL...

PEPPER.

CEREAL.

MILK.   BUTTER.

LIGHT BULBS.

STILL ANOTHER OPTION IS THE **MONTAGE** WHERE WORDS ARE TREATED AS INTEGRAL *PARTS* OF THE PICTURE.

CASH
FLOW
PUB
BOTTO
LINE
ANNUA
REPORT

H
A
P
P
Y!

154

155

156

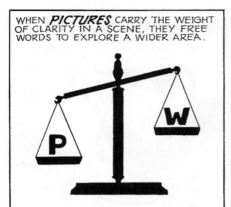

WHEN *PICTURES* CARRY THE WEIGHT OF CLARITY IN A SCENE, THEY FREE WORDS TO EXPLORE A WIDER AREA.

LET'S SAY I SHOW YOU A WOMAN WALKING ACROSS THE STREET IN THE RAIN, BUYING A PINT OF ICE CREAM AND EATING IT IN HER APARTMENT--

--ALL IN *PICTURES.*

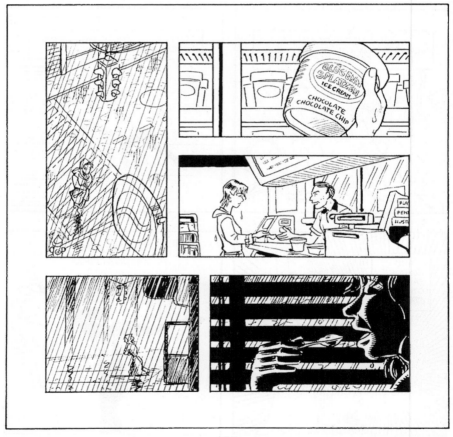

When a scene shows you all you *"NEED"* to know, like *THIS* one, the latitude for **SCRIPTING** grows *ENORMOUSLY.*

I MAY BE ALONE LIKE THIS FOR A VERY LONG TIME.

IT COULD BECOME AN *INTERNAL MONOLOGUE.*

(INTERDEPENDENT)

PERHAPS SOMETHING WILDLY *INCONGRUOUS*

"MISSION CONTROL, MISSION CONTROL, DO YOU READ ME?"

(PARALLEL)

MAYBE IT'S ALL JUST A BIG *ADVERTISEMENT!*

YOU'LL *Love* THE TASTE!

(INTERDEPENDENT)

OR A CHANCE TO RUMINATE ON *BROADER TOPICS:*

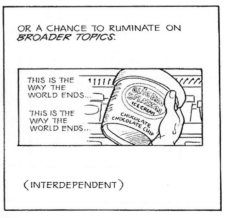

THIS IS THE WAY THE WORLD ENDS...

THIS IS THE WAY THE WORLD ENDS...

(INTERDEPENDENT)

158

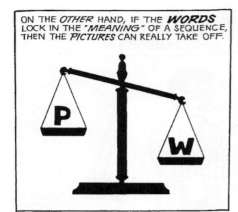

I CROSSED THE STREET TO THE CONVENIENCE STORE. THE RAIN SOAKED INTO MY BOOTS.

I FOUND THE LAST PINT OF CHOCOLATE CHOCOLATE CHIP IN THE FREEZER.

THE CLERK TRIED TO PICK ME UP. I SAID *NO THANKS.* HE GAVE ME THIS CREEPY LOOK...

I WENT BACK TO THE APARTMENT--

--AND FINISHED IT ALL IN AN HOUR.

ALONE AT LAST.

159

NOW, ONE COULD JUST *COMBINE* THE *PICTURES* FROM PAGE 157 WITH THE WORDS FROM PAGE 159--

--BUT WHAT ARE SOME *OTHER* OPTIONS?

IF THE ARTIST WANTS TO, HE/SHE CAN NOW SHOW ONLY *FRAGMENTS* OF A SCENE.

(WORD SPECIFIC)

OR MOVE TOWARD GREATER LEVELS OF *ABSTRACTION* OR *EXPRESSION.*

THE CLERK TRIED TO PICK ME UP. I SAID *NO THANKS.* HE GAVE ME THIS CREEPY LOOK...

(AMPLIFICATION)

PERHAPS THE ARTIST CAN GIVE US SOME IMPORTANT *EMOTIONAL* INFORMATION.

I WENT BACK TO THE APARTMENT--

(INTERDEPENDENT)

OR SHIFT AHEAD OR BACKWARDS IN TIME.

--AND FINISHED IT ALL IN AN HOUR.

ALONE AT LAST.

(WORD SPECIFIC)

HOWEVER MUCH WE MAY *CHART* THESE THINGS, THEY'RE ALL *ULTIMATELY* BEST LEFT TO THE CREATOR'S *INSTINCTS.*

THE MIXING OF WORDS AND PICTURES IS MORE *ALCHEMY* THAN SCIENCE.

SOME OF THE SECRETS OF THOSE *FIRST* ALCHEMISTS MAY HAVE BEEN LOST IN THE ANCIENT PAST.

BUT WE HAVE SOME POWERFUL MAGIC RIGHT HERE IN THE *20TH CENTURY, TOO!*

THE RICHNESS OF MODERN LANGUAGE IS AN *IRREPLACEABLE COMMODITY!*

THIS IS AN *EXCITING TIME* TO BE MAKING COMICS, AND IN MANY WAYS I FEEL VERY *LUCKY* TO HAVE BEEN BORN WHEN I WAS.

STILL, I DO FEEL A CERTAIN *VAGUE LONGING* FOR THAT TIME OVER *50 CENTURIES AGO* --

-- WHEN TO TELL WAS TO *SHOW* --

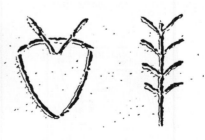

-- AND TO SHOW WAS TO *TELL*.

High-School Confidential

Notes on Teen Movies

DAVID DENBY

David Denby (b. 1943), who lives in New York City, is a staff writer and film critic for the *New Yorker* and the former film critic for *New York*. His writing has also appeared in the *Atlantic*, the *New York Review of Books*, and the *New Republic*. His first book, *Great Books: My Adventures with Homer, Rousseau, Woolf, and Other Indestructible Writers of the Western World* (1996), was a finalist for the National Book Critics Circle Award. Denby is also the editor of *Awake in the Dark: An Anthology of Film Criticism from 1915 to the Present* (1977), *American Sucker* (2004), and *Snark* (2009). The essay that follows was originally published in the *New Yorker* in May 1999.

The most hated young woman in America is a blonde—well, sometimes a redhead or a brunette, but usually a blonde. She has big hair flipped into a swirl of gold at one side of her face or arrayed in a sultry mane, like the magnificent pile of a forties movie star. She's tall and slender, with a waist as supple as a willow, but she's dressed in awful, spangled taste: her outfits could have been put together by warring catalogues. And she has a mouth on her, a low, slatternly tongue that devastates other kids with such insults as "You're vapor, you're Spam!" and "Do I look like Mother Teresa? If I did, I probably wouldn't mind talking to the geek squad." She has two or three friends exactly like her, and together they dominate their realm—the American high school as it appears in recent teen movies. They are like wicked princesses, who enjoy the misery of their subjects. Her coronation, of course, is the senior prom, when she expects to be voted "most popular" by her class. But, though she may be popular, she is certainly not liked, so her power is something of a mystery. She is beautiful and rich, yet in the end she is preeminent because . . . she is preeminent, a position she works to maintain with Joan Crawford–like tenacity. Everyone is afraid of her; that's why she's popular.

She has a male counterpart. He's usually a football player, muscular but dumb, with a face like a beer mug and only two ways of speaking—in a conspiratorial whisper, to a friend; or in a drill sergeant's sudden bellow. If her weapon is the snub, his is the lame but infuriating prank—the can of Sprite emptied into a knapsack, or something sticky, creamy, or adhesive deposited in a locker. Sprawling and dull in class, he comes alive in the halls and in the cafeteria. He hurls people against lockers; he spits, pours, and sprays; he has a projectile relationship with food. As the crown prince, he claims the best-looking girl for himself, though in a perverse display of power he may invite an outsider or an

awkward girl—a "dog"—to the prom, setting her up for some special humiliation. When we first see him, he is riding high, and virtually the entire school col-
ludes in his tyranny. No authority figure—no teacher or administrator—dares
correct him.

Thus the villains of the recent high-school movies. Not every American teen
movie has these two characters, and not every social queen or jock shares all the
attributes I've mentioned. (Occasionally, a handsome, dark-haired athlete can be
converted to sweetness and light.) But as genre figures these two types are hugely
familiar; that is, they are a common memory, a collective trauma, or at least a
social and erotic fantasy. Such movies . . . as *Disturbing Behavior, She's All That,
Ten Things I Hate about You,* and *Never Been Kissed* depend on them as stock
figures. And they may have been figures in the minds of the Littleton shooters,
Eric Harris and Dylan Klebold, who imagined they were living in a school like the
one in so many of these movies—a poisonous system of status, snobbery, and
exclusion.

Do genre films reflect reality? Or are they merely a set of conventions that refer to
other films? Obviously, they wouldn't survive if they didn't provide emotional
satisfaction to the people who make them and to the audiences who watch them.
A half century ago, we didn't need to see ten Westerns a year in order to learn that
the West got settled. We needed to see it settled ten times a year in order to provide ourselves with the emotional gratifications of righteous violence. By drawing his gun only when he was provoked, and in the service of the good, the classic
Western hero transformed the gross tangibles of the expansionist drive (land,
cattle, gold) into a principle of moral order. The gangster, by contrast, is a figure
of chaos, a modern, urban person, and in the critic Robert Warshow's formulation he functions as a discordant element in an American society devoted to a
compulsively "positive" outlook. When the gangster dies, he cleanses viewers of
their own negative feelings.

High-school movies are also full of unease and odd, mixed-up emotions. 5
They may be flimsy in conception; they may be shot in lollipop colors, garlanded
with mediocre pop scores, and cast with goofy young actors trying to make an
impression. Yet this most commercial and frivolous of genres harbors a grievance
against the world. It's a very specific grievance, quite different from the restless
anger of such fifties adolescent-rebellion movies as *The Wild One,* in which someone asks Marlon Brando's biker "What are you rebelling against?" and the biker
replies "What have you got?" The fifties teen outlaw was against anything that
adults considered sacred. But no movie teenager now revolts against adult authority, for the simple reason that adults have no authority. Teachers are rarely more
than a minimal, exasperated presence, administrators get turned into a joke, and
parents are either absent or distantly benevolent. It's a teen world bounded by
school, mall, and car, with occasional moments set in the fast-food outlets where
the kids work, or in the kids' upstairs bedrooms, with their pinups and rack stereo

systems. The enemy is not authority; the enemy is other teens and the social system that they impose on one another.

The bad feeling in these movies may strike grownups as peculiar. After all, from a distance American kids appear to be having it easy these days. The teen audience is facing a healthy job market; at home, their parents are stuffing the den with computers and the garage with a bulky S.U.V. But most teens aren't thinking about the future job market. Lost in the eternal swoon of late adolescence, they're thinking about their identity, their friends, and their clothes. Adolescence is the present-tense moment in American life. Identity and status are fluid: abrupt, devastating reversals are always possible. (In a teen movie, a guy who swallows a bucket of cafeteria coleslaw can make himself a hero in an instant.) In these movies, accordingly, the senior prom is the equivalent of the shoot-out at the O.K. Corral; it's the moment when one's worth as a human being is settled at last. In the rather pedestrian new comedy *Never Been Kissed*, Drew Barrymore, as a twenty-five-year-old newspaper reporter, goes back to high school pretending to be a student, and immediately falls into her old, humiliating pattern of trying to impress the good-looking rich kids. Helplessly, she pushes for approval, and even gets herself chosen prom queen before finally coming to her senses. She finds it nearly impossible to let go.

Genre films dramatize not what happens but how things feel — the emotional coloring of memory. They fix subjectivity into fable. At actual schools, there is no unitary system of status; there are many groups to be a part of, many places to excel (or fail to excel), many avenues of escape and self-definition. And often the movies, too, revel in the arcana of high-school cliques. In . . . *Disturbing Behavior*, a veteran student lays out the cafeteria ethnography for a newcomer: Motorheads, Blue Ribbons, Skaters, Micro-geeks ("drug of choice: Stephen Hawking's *A Brief History of Time* and a cup of jasmine tea on Saturday night"). Subjectively, though, the social system in *Disturbing Behavior* (a high-school version of *The Stepford Wives*) and in the other movies still feels coercive and claustrophobic: humiliation is the most vivid emotion of youth, so in memory it becomes the norm.

The movies try to turn the tables. The kids who cannot be the beautiful ones, or make out with them, or avoid being insulted by them — these are the heroes of the teen movies, the third in the trio of character types. The female outsider is usually an intellectual or an artist. (She scribbles in a diary, she draws or paints.) Physically awkward, she walks like a seal crossing a beach, and is prone to drop her books and dither in terror when she stands before a handsome boy. Her clothes, which ignore mall fashion, scandalize the social queens. Like them, she has a tongue, but she's tart and grammatical, tending toward feminist pungency and precise diction. She may mask her sense of vulnerability with sarcasm or with Plathian rue (she's stuck in the bell jar), but even when she lashes out she can't hide her craving for acceptance.

The male outsider, her friend, is usually a mass of stuttering or giggling sexual gloom: he wears shapeless clothes; he has an undeveloped body, either stringy or shrimpy; he's sometimes a Jew (in these movies, still the generic outsider). He's also brilliant, but in a morose, preoccupied way that suggests masturbatory absorption in some arcane system of knowledge. In a few special cases, the outsider is not a loser but a disengaged hipster, either saintly or satanic. (Christian Slater has played this role a couple of times.) This outsider wears black and keeps his hair long, and he knows how to please women. He sees through everything, so he's ironic by temperament and genuinely indifferent to the opinion of others — a natural aristocrat, who transcends the school's contemptible status system. There are whimsical variations on the outsider figure, too. In the recent *Rushmore*, an obnoxious teen hero, Max Fischer (Jason Schwartzman), runs the entire school: he can't pass his courses but he's a dynamo at extracurricular activities, with a knack for staging extraordinary events. He's a con man, a fund-raiser, an entrepreneur — in other words, a contemporary artist.

In fact, the entire genre, which combines self-pity and ultimate vindication, 10 might be called "Portrait of the Filmmaker as a Young Nerd." Who can doubt where Hollywood's twitchy, nearsighted writers and directors ranked — or feared they ranked — on the high-school totem pole? They are still angry, though occasionally the target of their resentment goes beyond the jocks and cheerleaders of their youth. Consider this anomaly: the young actors and models on the covers of half the magazines published in this country, the shirtless men with chests like burnished shields, the girls smiling, glowing, tweezed, full-lipped, full-breasted (but not too full), and with skin so honeyed that it seems lacquered — these are the physical ideals embodied by the villains of the teen movies. The social queens and jocks, using their looks to dominate others, represent an American barbarism of beauty. Isn't it possible that the detestation of them in teen movies is a veiled strike at the entire abs-hair advertising culture, with its unobtainable glories of perfection? A critic of consumerism might even see a spark of revolt in these movies. But only a spark.

My guess is that these films arise from remembered hurts which then get recast in symbolic form. For instance, a surprising number of the outsider heroes have no mother. Mom has died or run off with another man; her child, only half loved, is ill equipped for the emotional pressures of school. The motherless child, of course, is a shrewd commercial ploy that makes a direct appeal to the members of the audience, many of whom may feel like outsiders, too, and unloved, or not loved enough, or victims of some prejudice or exclusion. But the motherless child also has powers, and will someday be a success, an artist, a screenwriter. It's the wound and the bow all over again, in cargo pants.

As the female nerd attracts the attention of the handsomest boy in the senior class, the teen movie turns into a myth of social reversal — a Cinderella fantasy. Initially, his interest in her may be part of a stunt or a trick: he is leading her on, perhaps at the urging of his queenly girlfriend. But his gaze lights her up, and we see how attractive she really is. Will she fulfill the eternal specs? She wants her prince, and by degrees she wins him over, not just with her looks but with her superior nature, her essential goodness. In the male version of the Cinderella trip, a few years go by, and a pale little nerd (we see him at a reunion) has become rich. All that poking around with chemicals paid off. Max Fischer, of *Rushmore*, can't miss being richer than Warhol.

So the teen movie is wildly ambivalent. It may attack the consumerist ethos that produces winners and losers, but in the end it confirms what it is attacking. The girls need the seal of approval conferred by the converted jocks; the nerds need money and a girl. Perhaps it's no surprise that the outsiders can be validated only by the people who ostracized them. But let's not be too schematic: the outsider who joins the system also modifies it, opens it up to the creative power of social mobility, makes it bend and laugh, and perhaps this turn of events is not so different from the way things work in the real world, where merit and achievement stand a good chance of trumping appearance. The irony of the Littleton shootings is that Klebold and Harris, who were both proficient computer heads, seemed to have forgotten how the plot turns out. If they had held on for a few years they might have been working at a hip software company, or have started their own business, while the jocks who oppressed them would probably have wound up selling insurance or used cars. That's the one unquestionable social truth the teen movies reflect: geeks rule.

There is, of course, a menacing subgenre, in which the desire for revenge turns bloody. Thirty-one years ago, Lindsay Anderson's semi-surrealistic *If . . .* was set in an oppressive, class-ridden English boarding school, where a group of rebellious students drive the school population out into a courtyard and open fire on them with machine guns. In Brian De Palma's 1976 masterpiece *Carrie*, the pale, repressed heroine, played by Sissy Spacek, is courted at last by a handsome boy but gets violated—doused with pig's blood—just as she is named prom queen. Stunned but far from powerless, Carrie uses her telekinetic powers to set the room afire and burn down the school. *Carrie* is the primal school movie, so wildly lurid and funny that it exploded the clichés of the genre before the genre was quite set: the heroine may be a wrathful avenger, but the movie, based on a Stephen King book, was clearly a grinning-gargoyle fantasy. So, at first, was *Heathers*, in which Christian Slater's satanic outsider turns out to be a true devil. He and his girlfriend (played by a very young Winona Ryder) begin gleefully knocking off the rich, nasty girls and the jocks, in ways so patently absurd that their revenge seems a mere wicked dream. I think it's unlikely that these movies had a direct effect on the actions of the Littleton shooters, but the two boys would surely have recognized the emotional world of *Heathers* and *Disturbing Behavior* as their own. It's a place where feelings of victimization join fantasy, and you experience the social élites as so powerful that you must either become them or kill them.

But enough. It's possible to make teen movies that go beyond these fixed polarities—insider and outsider, blonde-bitch queen and hunch-shouldered nerd. In Amy Heckerling's 1995 comedy *Clueless*, the big blonde played by Alicia Silverstone is a Rodeo Drive clotheshorse who is nonetheless possessed of extraordinary virtue. Freely dispensing advice and help, she's almost ironically good—a designing goddess with a cell phone. The movie offers a sun-shiny satire of Beverly Hills affluence, which it sees as both absurdly swollen and generous in spirit. The most original of the teen comedies, *Clueless* casts away self-pity. So does *Romy and Michele's High School Reunion* (1997), in which two gabby, lovable friends, played by Mira Sorvino and Lisa Kudrow, review the banalities of their high-school experience so knowingly that they might be criticizing the teen-movie genre itself. And easily the best American film of the year so far is Alexander Payne's *Election*, a high-school movie that inhabits a different aesthetic and moral world altogether from the rest of these pictures. *Election* shreds everyone's fantasies and illusions in a vision of high school that is bleak but supremely just. The movie's villain, an over-achieving girl (Reese Witherspoon) who runs for class president, turns out to be its covert heroine, or, at least, its most poignant character. A cross between Pat and Dick Nixon, she's a lower-middle-class striver who works like crazy and never wins anyone's love. Even when she's on top, she feels excluded. Her loneliness is produced not by malicious cliques but by her own implacable will, a condition of the spirit that may be as comical and tragic as it is mysterious. *Election* escapes all the clichés; it graduates into art.

Exploring the Text

1. What is David Denby's opinion of teen movies? Does he find anything redeeming in them? Do you agree that it is the "most commercial and frivolous of genres" (para. 5)? Explain your response.
2. Denby mentions three movies that "go beyond [the] fixed polarities" (para. 15): *Clueless*, *Romy and Michele's High School Reunion*, and *Election*. Do you agree? Do any recent teen movies transcend the genre? Explain.
3. What rhetorical strategies does Denby use in the first paragraph to create a picture of the female villain of teen movies? Consider such strategies as irony, hyperbole, metaphor, colloquialisms, and opposition. What are their effects?
4. Where do you detect changes in Denby's tone? How does Denby achieve these changes?
5. The essay makes several appeals to ethos. Denby is a well-known film critic. How does he use the expertise of others—implicitly and explicitly—to support his argument?
6. What is Denby's central argument? What are his secondary arguments? How does he bring them together?
7. In paragraph 13, Denby argues that the two teenage boys who killed classmates, teachers, and then themselves at Columbine High School did not learn the lesson of teen movies: "geeks rule." How does he support this argument?
8. Who is the likely audience for this essay? How does Denby consider audience in his essay?

An Image a Little Too Carefully Coordinated

ROBIN GIVHAN

> Born in 1965 in Detroit, Robin Givhan was for many years the fashion editor at the *Washington Post*, where she won the 2006 Pulitzer Prize for Criticism—the first time a fashion writer was honored. Known for her bluntness, Givhan has commented in the press on, for example, Vice President Dick Cheney's dark green parka and First Lady Michelle Obama's shorts. She is now a special correspondent for style and culture at *Newsweek* and the *Daily Beast*. The piece presented here appeared in the *Washington Post* in July 2005 when President Bush named John Roberts as his choice for the Supreme Court.

It has been a long time since so much syrupy nostalgia has been in evidence at the White House. But Tuesday night, when President Bush announced his choice for the next associate justice of the Supreme Court, it was hard not to marvel at the 1950s-style *tableau vivant* that was John Roberts and his family.

There they were—John, Jane, Josie and Jack—standing with the president and before the entire country. The nominee was in a sober suit with the expected white shirt and red tie. His wife and children stood before the cameras, groomed and glossy in pastel hues—like a trio of Easter eggs, a handful of Jelly Bellies, three little Necco wafers. There was tow-headed Jack—having freed himself from the controlling grip of his mother—enjoying a moment in the spotlight dressed in a seersucker suit with short pants and saddle shoes. His sister, Josie, was half-hidden behind her mother's skirt. Her blond pageboy glistened. And she was wearing a yellow dress with a crisp white collar, lace-trimmed anklets and black patent-leather Mary Janes.

(Who among us did a double take? Two cute blond children with a boyish-looking father getting ready to take the lectern—Jack Edwards? Emma Claire? Is that you? Are *all* little boys now named Jack?)

The wife wore a strawberry-pink tweed suit with taupe pumps and pearls, which alone would not have been particularly remarkable, but alongside the nostalgic costuming of the children, the overall effect was of self-consciously crafted perfection. The children, of course, are innocents. They are dressed by their parents. And through their clothes choices, the parents have created the kind of honeyed faultlessness that jams mailboxes every December when personalized Christmas cards arrive bringing greetings "to you and yours" from the Blake family or the Joneses. Everyone looks freshly scrubbed and adorable, just like they have stepped from a Currier & Ives landscape.

In a time when most children are dressed in Gap Kids and retailers of similar price-point and modernity, the parents put young master Jack in an ensemble that calls to mind John F. "John-John" Kennedy Jr.

5

Separate the child from the clothes, which do not acknowledge trends, popular culture or the passing of time. They are not classic; they are old-fashioned. These clothes are Old World, old money and a cut above the light-up/shoe-buying hoi polloi.

The clothes also reflect a bit of the aesthetic havoc that often occurs when people visit the White House. (What should I wear? How do I look? Take my picture!) The usual advice is to *dress appropriately.* In this case, an addendum would have been helpful: Please select all attire from the commonly accepted styles of this century. (And someone should have given notice to the flip-flop-wearing women of Northwestern University's lacrosse team, who visited the White House on July 12 for a meet-and-greet with the president: proper footwear required. Flip-flops, modeled after shoes meant to be worn into a public shower or on the beach, have no business anywhere in the vicinity of the president and his place of residence.)

Dressing appropriately is a somewhat selfless act. It's not about catering to personal comfort. One can't give in fully to private aesthetic preferences. Instead, one asks what would make other people feel respected? What would mark the occasion as noteworthy? What signifies that the moment is bigger than the individual?

(See insert for color version.)

But the Roberts family went too far. In announcing John Roberts as his Supreme Court nominee, the president inextricably linked the individual—and his family—to the sweep of tradition. In their attire, there was nothing too informal; there was nothing immodest. There was only the feeling that, in the desire to be appropriate and respectful of history, the children had been costumed in it.

Exploring the Text

1. Do you think Robin Givhan makes a convincing argument? Explain why or why not.
2. Look at the photo of the Roberts family. Do you agree that they are "costumed in [history]," or are they just "appropriate and respectful of history" (para. 9)? Explain your answer.
3. What is the effect of the many proper names, including the names of products, that Givhan uses throughout the piece?
4. Who is Givhan's audience? What assumptions about audience bolster her argument? What are the ways in which Givhan shows she's open to other points of view?
5. How would you describe the tone of Givhan's piece? In what ways do you think her tone is a response to her audience and the subject matter?
6. What's your opinion on the subject of the flip-flop-wearing lacrosse team (para. 7)? What do you think they should have worn?
7. Consider the word *appropriately* in paragraph 7. Why do you think it is italicized? What do the italics add to the connotations of the word?

Watching TV Makes You Smarter

Steven Johnson

Steven Berlin Johnson (b. 1968) writes about science, technology, and personal experience. In addition to the best-selling *Everything Bad Is Good for You* (2005), Johnson has written *The Ghost Map* (2006), *The Invention of Air* (2008), and *Where Good Ideas Come From* (2010). He is a columnist at *Discover* magazine and a contributing editor at *Wired* magazine. The following excerpt from *Everything Bad Is Good for You* appeared in the *New York Times Magazine* in 2005.

The Sleeper Curve

Scientist A: Has he asked for anything special?

Scientist B: Yes, this morning for breakfast . . . he requested something called "wheat germ, organic honey and tiger's milk."

SCIENTIST A: Oh, yes. Those were the charmed substances that some years ago were felt to contain life-preserving properties.

SCIENTIST B: You mean there was no deep fat? No steak or cream pies or . . . hot fudge?

SCIENTIST A: Those were thought to be unhealthy.

—from Woody Allen's *Sleeper*

On Jan. 24, the Fox network showed an episode of its hit drama *24*, the real-time thriller known for its cliffhanger tension and often-gruesome violence. Over the preceding weeks, a number of public controversies had erupted around *24*, mostly focused on its portrait of Muslim terrorists and its penchant for torture scenes. The episode that was shown on the 24th only fanned the flames higher: in one scene, a terrorist enlists a hit man to kill his child for not fully supporting the jihadist cause; in another scene, the secretary of defense authorizes the torture of his son to uncover evidence of a terrorist plot.

But the explicit violence and the post-911 terrorist anxiety are not the only elements of *24* that would have been unthinkable on prime-time network television 20 years ago. Alongside the notable change in content lies an equally notable change in form. During its 44 minutes—a real-time hour, minus 16 minutes for commercials—the episode connects the lives of 21 distinct characters, each with a clearly defined "story arc," as the Hollywood jargon has it: a defined personality with motivations and obstacles and specific relationships with other characters. Nine primary narrative threads wind their way through those 44 minutes, each drawing extensively upon events and information revealed in earlier episodes. Draw a map of all those intersecting plots and personalities, and you get structure that—where formal complexity is concerned—more closely resembles *Middlemarch* than a hit TV drama of years past like *Bonanza*.

For decades, we've worked under the assumption that mass culture follows a path declining steadily toward lowest-common-denominator standards, presumably because the "masses" want dumb, simple pleasures and big media companies try to give the masses what they want. But as that *24* episode suggests, the exact opposite is happening: the culture is getting more cognitively demanding, not less. To make sense of an episode of *24*, you have to integrate far more information than you would have a few decades ago watching a comparable show. Beneath the violence and the ethnic stereotypes, another trend appears: to keep up with entertainment like *24*, you have to pay attention, make inferences, track shifting social relationships. This is what I call the Sleeper Curve: the most debased forms of mass diversion—video games and violent television dramas and juvenile sitcoms—turn out to be nutritional after all.

I believe that the Sleeper Curve is the single most important new force altering the mental development of young people today, and I believe it is largely a force for good: enhancing our cognitive faculties, not dumbing them down. And yet you almost never hear this story in popular accounts of today's media. Instead,   5 you hear dire tales of addiction, violence, mindless escapism. It's assumed that shows that promote smoking or gratuitous violence are bad for us, while those that thunder against teen pregnancy or intolerance have a positive role in society. Judged by that morality-play standard, the story of popular culture over the past 50 years—if not 500—is a story of decline: the morals of the stories have grown darker and more ambiguous, and the antiheroes have multiplied.

The usual counterargument here is that what media have lost in moral clarity, they have gained in realism. The real world doesn't come in nicely packaged public-service announcements, and we're better off with entertainment like *The Sopranos* that reflects our fallen state with all its ethical ambiguity. I happen to be sympathetic to that argument, but it's not the one I want to make here. I think there is another way to assess the social virtue of pop culture, one that looks at media as a kind of cognitive workout, not as a series of life lessons. There may indeed be more "negative messages" in the mediasphere today. But that's not the only way to evaluate whether our television shows or video games are having a positive impact. Just as important—if not more important—is the kind of thinking you have to do to make sense of a cultural experience. That is where the Sleeper Curve becomes visible.

Televised Intelligence

Consider the cognitive demands that televised narratives place on their viewers. With many shows that we associate with "quality" entertainment—*The Mary Tyler Moore Show, Murphy Brown, Frasier*—the intelligence arrives fully formed in the words and actions of the characters on-screen. They say witty things to one another and avoid lapsing into tired sitcom clichés, and we smile along in our living rooms, enjoying the company of these smart people. But assuming we're bright enough to understand the sentences they're saying, there's no intellectual labor involved in enjoying the show as a viewer. You no more challenge your mind by watching these intelligent shows than you challenge your body watching *Monday Night Football.* The intellectual work is happening on-screen, not off.

But another kind of televised intelligence is on the rise. Think of the cognitive benefits conventionally ascribed to reading: attention, patience, retention, the parsing of narrative threads. Over the last half-century, programming on TV has increased the demands it places on precisely these mental faculties. This growing complexity involves three primary elements: multiple threading, flashing arrows and social networks.

According to television lore, the age of multiple threads began with the arrival in 1981 of *Hill Street Blues,* the Steven Bochco police drama invariably praised for its "gritty realism." Watch an episode of *Hill Street Blues* side by side with any major drama from the preceding decades—*Starsky and Hutch*, for instance, or *Dragnet*—and the structural transformation will jump out at you. The earlier shows follow one or two lead characters, adhere to a single dominant plot and reach a decisive conclusion at the end of the episode. Draw an outline of the narrative threads in almost every *Dragnet* episode, and it will be a single line: from the initial crime scene, through the investigation, to the eventual cracking of the case. A typical *Starsky and Hutch* episode offers only the slightest variation on this linear formula: the introduction of a comic subplot that usually appears only at the tail ends of the episode, creating a structure that looks like the graph below. The vertical axis represents the number of individual threads, and the horizontal axis is time.

DRAGNET (ANY EPISODE)

STARSKY AND HUTCH (ANY EPISODE)

A *Hill Street Blues* episode complicates the picture in a number of profound   10
ways. The narrative weaves together a collection of distinct strands—sometimes as many as 10, though at least half of the threads involve only a few quick scenes scattered through the episode. The number of primary characters—and not just bit parts—swells significantly. And the episode has fuzzy borders: picking up one or two threads from previous episodes at the outset and leaving one or two threads open at the end. Charted graphically, an average episode looks like this:

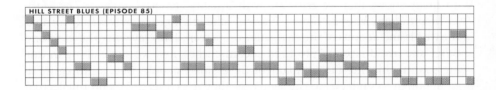

HILL STREET BLUES (EPISODE 85)

Critics generally cite *Hill Street Blues* as the beginning of "serious drama" narrative in the television medium—differentiating the series from the single-episode dramatic programs from the 50's, which were Broadway plays performed in front of a camera. But the *Hill Street* innovations weren't all that original; they'd long played a defining role in popular television, just not during the evening hours. The structure of a *Hill Street* episode—and indeed of all the critically acclaimed dramas that followed, from *thirtysomething* to *Six Feet Under*—is the structure of a soap opera. *Hill Street Blues* might have sparked a new golden age of television drama during its seven-year run, but it did so by using a few crucial tricks that *Guiding Light* and *General Hospital* mastered long before.

Bochco's genius with *Hill Street* was to marry complex narrative structure with complex subject matter. *Dallas* had already shown that the extended, interwoven threads of the soap-opera genre could survive the weeklong interruptions of a prime-time show, but the actual content of *Dallas* was fluff. (The most probing issue it addressed was the question, now folkloric, of who shot J.R.) *All in the Family* and *Rhoda* showed that you could tackle complex social issues, but they did their tackling in the comfort of the sitcom living room. *Hill Street* had richly drawn characters confronting difficult social issues and a narrative structure to match.

Since *Hill Street* appeared, the multi-threaded drama has become the most widespread fictional genre on prime time: *St. Elsewhere, L.A. Law, thirtysomething, Twin Peaks, N.Y.P.D. Blue, E.R., The West Wing, Alias, Lost.* (The only prominent holdouts in drama are shows like *Law and Order* that have essentially updated the venerable *Dragnet* format and thus remained anchored to a single narrative line.) Since the early 80's, however, there has been a noticeable increase in narrative complexity in these dramas. The most ambitious show on TV to date, *The Sopranos*, routinely follows up to a dozen distinct threads over the course of an episode, with more than 20 recurring characters. An episode from late in the first season looks like this:

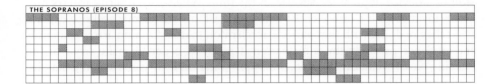

The total number of active threads equals the multiple plots of *Hill Street*, but here each thread is more substantial. The show doesn't offer a clear distinction between dominant and minor plots; each story line carries its weight in the mix. The episode also displays a chordal mode of storytelling entirely absent from *Hill Street*: a single scene in *The Sopranos* will often connect to three different threads at the same time, layering one plot atop another. And every single thread in this *Sopranos* episode builds on events from previous episodes and continues on through the rest of the season and beyond.

Put those charts together, and you have a portrait of the Sleeper Curve rising 15 over the past 30 years of popular television. In a sense, this is as much a map of cognitive changes in the popular mind as it is a map of on-screen developments, as if the media titans decided to condition our brains to follow ever-larger numbers of simultaneous threads. Before *Hill Street*, the conventional wisdom among television execs was that audiences wouldn't be comfortable following more than three plots in a single episode, and indeed, the *Hill Street* pilot, which was shown in January 1981, brought complaints from viewers that the show was too complicated. Fast-forward two decades, and shows like *The Sopranos* engage their audiences with narratives that make *Hill Street* look like *Three's Company*. Audiences happily embrace that complexity because they've been trained by two decades of multi-threaded dramas.

Multi-threading is the most celebrated structural feature of the modern television drama, and it certainly deserves some of the honor that has been doled out to it. And yet multi-threading is only part of the story.

The Case for Confusion

Shortly after the arrival of the first-generation slasher movies—*Halloween, Friday the 13th*—Paramount released a mock-slasher flick called *Student Bodies*, parodying the genre just as the *Scream* series would do 15 years later. In one scene, the obligatory nubile teenage baby sitter hears a noise outside a suburban house; she opens the door to investigate, finds nothing and then goes back inside. As the door shuts behind her, the camera swoops in on the doorknob, and we see that she has left the door unlocked. The camera pulls back and then swoops down again for emphasis. And then a flashing arrow appears on the screen, with text that helpfully explains: "Unlocked!"

That flashing arrow is parody, of course, but it's merely an exaggerated version of a device popular stories use all the time. When a sci-fi script inserts into some advanced lab a nonscientist who keeps asking the science geeks to explain what they're doing with that particle accelerator, that's a flashing arrow that gives the audience precisely the information it needs in order to make sense of the ensuing plot. ("Whatever you do, don't spill water on it, or you'll set off a massive explosion!") These hints serve as a kind of narrative hand-holding. Implicitly, they say to the audience, "We realize you have no idea what a particle accelerator is, but here's the deal: all you need to know is that it's a big fancy thing that explodes when wet." They focus the mind on relevant details: "Don't worry about whether the baby sitter is going to break up with her boyfriend. Worry about that guy lurking in the bushes." They reduce the amount of analytic work you need to do to make sense of a story. All you have to do is follow the arrows.

By this standard, popular television has never been harder to follow. If narrative threads have experienced a population explosion over the past 20 years, flashing arrows have grown correspondingly scarce. Watching our pinnacle of early 80's TV drama, *Hill Street Blues*, we find there's an informational wholeness to each scene that differs markedly from what you see on shows like *The West Wing* or *The Sopranos* or *Alias* or *E.R.*

Hill Street has ambiguities about future events: Will a convicted killer be executed? Will Furillo marry Joyce Davenport? Will Renko find it in himself to bust a favorite singer for cocaine possession? But the present-tense of each scene explains itself to the viewer with little ambiguity. There's an open question or a mystery driving each of these stories—how will it all turn out?—but there's no mystery about the immediate activity on the screen. A contemporary drama like *The West Wing*, on the other hand, constantly embeds mysteries into the present-tense events: you see characters performing actions or discussing events about which crucial information has been deliberately withheld. Anyone who has

20

watched more than a handful of *The West Wing* episodes closely will know the feeling: scene after scene refers to some clearly crucial but unexplained piece of information, and after the sixth reference, you'll find yourself wishing you could rewind the tape to figure out what they're talking about, assuming you've missed something. And then you realize that you're supposed to be confused. The open question posed by these sequences is not "How will this turn out in the end?" The question is "What's happening right now?"

The deliberate lack of hand-holding extends down to the microlevel of dialogue as well. Popular entertainment that addresses technical issues — whether they are the intricacies of passing legislation, or of performing a heart bypass, or of operating a particle accelerator — conventionally switches between two modes of information in dialogue: texture and substance. Texture is all the arcane verbiage provided to convince the viewer that they're watching Actual Doctors at Work; substance is the material planted amid the background texture that the viewer needs to make sense of the plot.

Conventionally, narratives demarcate the line between texture and substance by inserting cues that flag or translate the important data. There's an unintentionally comical moment in the 2004 blockbuster *The Day After Tomorrow* in which the beleaguered climatologist (played by Dennis Quaid) announces his theory about the imminent arrival of a new ice age to a gathering of government officials. In his speech, he warns that "we have hit a critical desalinization point!" At this moment, the writer-director Roland Emmerich — a master of brazen arrow-flashing — has an official follow with the obliging remark: "It would explain what's driving this extreme weather." They might as well have had a flashing "Unlocked!" arrow on the screen.

The dialogue on shows like *The West Wing* and *E.R.*, on the other hand, doesn't talk down to its audiences. It rushes by, the words accelerating in sync with the high-speed tracking shots that glide through the corridors and operating rooms. The characters talk faster in these shows, but the truly remarkable thing about the dialogue is not purely a matter of speed; it's the willingness to immerse the audience in information that most viewers won't understand. Here's a typical scene from *E.R.*:

> [WEAVER and WRIGHT push a gurney containing a 16-year-old girl. Her parents, Janna and Frank MIKAMI, follow close behind. CARTER and LUCY fall in.]
> WEAVER: 16-year-old, unconscious, history of biliary atresia.
> CARTER: Hepatic coma?
> WEAVER: Looks like it.
> MR. MIKAMI: She was doing fine until six months ago.
> CARTER: What medication is she on?
> MRS. MIKAMI: Ampicillin, tobramycin, vitamins A, D and K.
> LUCY: Skin's jaundiced.

WEAVER: Same with the sclera. Breath smells sweet.

CARTER: Fetor hepaticus?

WEAVER: Yep.

LUCY: What's that?

WEAVER: Her liver's shut down. Let's dip a urine. [To CARTER] Guys, it's getting a little crowded in here, why don't you deal with the parents? Start lactulose, 30 cc's per NG.

CARTER: We're giving medicine to clean her blood.

WEAVER: Blood in the urine, two-plus.

CARTER: The liver failure is causing her blood not to clot.

MRS. MIKAMI: Oh, God. . . .

CARTER: Is she on the transplant list?

MR. MIKAMI: She's been Status 2a for six months, but they haven't been able to find her a match.

CARTER: Why? What's her blood type?

MR. MIKAMI: AB.

[This hits CARTER like a lightning bolt. LUCY gets it, too. They share a look.]

There are flashing arrows here, of course — "The liver failure is causing her blood not to clot" — but the ratio of medical jargon to layperson translation is remarkably high. From a purely narrative point of view, the decisive line arrives at the very end: "AB." The 16-year-old's blood type connects her to an earlier plot line, involving a cerebral-hemorrhage victim who — after being dramatically revived in one of the opening scenes — ends up brain-dead. Far earlier, before the liver-failure scene above, Carter briefly discusses harvesting the hemorrhage victim's organs for transplants, and another doctor makes a passing reference to his blood type being the rare AB (thus making him an unlikely donor). The twist here revolves around a statistically unlikely event happening at the E.R. — an otherwise perfect liver donor showing up just in time to donate his liver to a recipient with the same rare blood type. But the show reveals this twist with remarkable subtlety. To make sense of that last "AB" line — and the look of disbelief on Carter's and Lucy's faces — you have to recall a passing remark uttered earlier regarding a character who belongs to a completely different thread. Shows like *E.R.* may have more blood and guts than popular TV had a generation ago, but when it comes to storytelling, they possess a quality that can only be described as subtlety and discretion. 25

Even Bad TV Is Better

Skeptics might argue that I have stacked the deck here by focusing on relatively highbrow titles like *The Sopranos* or *The West Wing*, when in fact the most significant change in the last five years of narrative entertainment involves reality TV. Does the contemporary pop cultural landscape look quite as promising if the representative show is *Joe Millionaire* instead of *The West Wing*?

I think it does, but to answer that question properly, you have to avoid the tendency to sentimentalize the past. When people talk about the golden age of television in the early 70's—invoking shows like *The Mary Tyler Moore Show* and *All in the Family*—they forget to mention how awful most television programming was during much of that decade. If you're going to look at pop culture trends, you have to compare apples to apples, or in this case, lemons to lemons. The relevant comparison is not between *Joe Millionaire* and *MASH*; it's between *Joe Millionaire* and *The Newlywed Game*, or between *Survivor* and *The Love Boat*.

What you see when you make these head-to-head comparisons is that a rising tide of complexity has been lifting programming at the bottom of the quality spectrum and at the top. *The Sopranos* is several times more demanding of its audiences than *Hill Street* was, and *Joe Millionaire* has made comparable advances over *Battle of the Network Stars*. This is the ultimate test of the Sleeper Curve theory: even the junk has improved.

If early television took its cues from the stage, today's reality programming is reliably structured like a video game: a series of competitive tests, growing more challenging over time. Many reality shows borrow a subtler device from gaming culture as well: the rules aren't fully established at the outset. You learn as you play.

On a show like *Survivor* or *The Apprentice*, the participants—and the audience—know the general objective of the series, but each episode involves new challenges that haven't been ordained in advance. The final round of the first season of *The Apprentice*, for instance, threw a monkey wrench into the strategy that governed the play up to that point, when Trump announced that the two remaining apprentices would have to assemble and manage a team of subordinates who had already been fired in earlier episodes of the show. All of a sudden the overarching objective of the game—do anything to avoid being fired—presented a potential conflict to the remaining two contenders: the structure of the final round favored the survivor who had maintained the best relationships with his comrades. Suddenly, it wasn't enough just to have clawed your way to the top; you had to have made friends while clawing. The original *Joe Millionaire* went so far as to undermine the most fundamental convention of all—that the show's creators don't openly lie to the contestants about the prizes—by inducing a construction worker to pose as a man of means while 20 women competed for his attention.

Reality programming borrowed another key ingredient from games: the intellectual labor of probing the system's rules for weak spots and opportunities. As each show discloses its conventions, and each participant reveals his or her personality traits and background, the intrigue in watching comes from figuring out how the participants should best navigate the environment that has been created for them. The pleasure in these shows comes not from watching other people being humiliated on national television; it comes from depositing other people in a complex, high-pressure environment where no established strategies exist and watching them find their bearings. That's why the water-cooler conversation about these shows invariably tracks in on the strategy displayed on the previous night's episode: Why did Kwame pick Omarosa in that final round? What devious strategy is Richard Hatch concocting now?

When we watch these shows, the part of our brain that monitors the emotional lives of the people around us—the part that tracks subtle shifts in intonation and gesture and facial expression—scrutinizes the action on the screen, looking for clues. We trust certain characters implicitly and vote others off the island in a heartbeat. Traditional narrative shows also trigger emotional connections to the characters, but those connections don't have the same participatory effect, because traditional narratives aren't explicitly about strategy. The phrase "Monday-morning quarterbacking" describes the engaged feeling that spectators have in relation to games as opposed to stories. We absorb stories, but we second-guess games. Reality programming has brought that second-guessing to prime time, only the game in question revolves around social dexterity rather than the physical kind.

The Rewards of Smart Culture

The quickest way to appreciate the Sleeper Curve's cognitive training is to sit down and watch a few hours of hit programming from the late 70's on Nick at Nite or the SOAPnet channel or on DVD. The modern viewer who watches a show like *Dallas* today will be bored by the content—not just because the show is less salacious than today's soap operas (which it is by a small margin) but also because the show contains far less information in each scene, despite the fact that its soap-opera structure made it one of the most complicated narratives on television in its prime. With *Dallas*, the modern viewer doesn't have to think to make sense of what's going on, and not having to think is boring. Many recent hit shows—*24, Survivor, The Sopranos, Alias, Lost, The Simpsons, E.R.*—take the opposite approach, layering each scene with a thick network of affiliations. You have to focus to follow the plot, and in focusing you're exercising the parts of your brain that map social networks, that fill in missing information, that connect multiple narrative threads.

Of course, the entertainment industry isn't increasing the cognitive complexity of its products for charitable reasons. The Sleeper Curve exists because there's money to be made by making culture smarter. The economics of television syndication and DVD sales mean that there's a tremendous financial pressure to make programs that can be watched multiple times, revealing new nuances and shadings on the third viewing. Meanwhile, the Web has created a forum for annotation and commentary that allows more complicated shows to prosper, thanks to the fan sites where each episode of shows like *Lost* or *Alias* is dissected with an intensity usually reserved for Talmud scholars. Finally, interactive games have trained a new generation of media consumers to probe complex environments and to think on their feet, and that gamer audience has now come to expect the same challenges from their television shows. In the end, the Sleeper Curve tells us something about the human mind. It may be drawn toward the sensational where content is concerned—sex does sell, after all. But the mind also likes to be challenged; there's real pleasure to be found in solving puzzles, detecting patterns or unpacking a complex narrative system.

In pointing out some of the ways that popular culture has improved our minds, I am not arguing that parents should stop paying attention to the way their children amuse themselves. What I am arguing for is a change in the criteria we use to determine what really is cognitive junk food and what is genuinely nourishing. Instead of a show's violent or tawdry content, instead of wardrobe malfunctions or the F-word, the true test should be whether a given show engages or sedates the mind. Is it a single thread strung together with predictable punch lines every 30 seconds? Or does it map a complex social network? Is your on-screen character running around shooting everything in sight, or is she trying to solve problems and manage resources? If your kids want to watch reality TV, encourage them to watch *Survivor* over *Fear Factor*. If they want to watch a mystery show, encourage *24* over *Law and Order*. If they want to play a violent game, encourage Grand Theft Auto over Quake. Indeed, it might be just as helpful to have a rating system that used mental labor and not obscenity and violence as its classification scheme for the world of mass culture.

Kids and grown-ups each can learn from their increasingly shared obsessions. Too often we imagine the blurring of kid and grown-up cultures as a series of violations: the 9-year-olds who have to have nipple broaches explained to them thanks to Janet Jackson; the middle-aged guy who can't wait to get home to his Xbox. But this demographic blur has a commendable side that we don't acknowledge enough. The kids are forced to think like grown-ups: analyzing complex social networks, managing resources, tracking subtle narrative intertwinings, recognizing long-term patterns. The grown-ups, in turn, get to learn from the kids: decoding each new technological wave, parsing the interfaces and discovering the intellectual rewards of play. Parents should see this as an opportunity, not a crisis. Smart culture is no longer something you force your kids to ingest, like green vegetables. It's something you share.

Exploring the Text

1. What audience is Steven Johnson addressing? How can you tell? How does he establish ethos?
2. How would you describe the tone of Johnson's piece? Why might it be particularly well suited to his subject matter?
3. Johnson calls his theory—that the "most debased forms of mass diversion" (para. 4) turn out to be good for us, after all—the "Sleeper Curve," after a scene in a Woody Allen movie. How does using one form of popular culture to examine

another form affect Johnson's argument? Find other examples of Johnson connecting different forms of popular culture to help develop his argument.

4. How do the charts accompanying the essay illustrate Johnson's points? How important is it to know the television programs to which the charts refer? Do the charts provide sufficient evidence that viewers are "cognitively engaged"? What other evidence might Johnson have used?

5. In the section "Televised Intelligence," Johnson equates the intellectual demands of television with those ascribed to reading. Do multiple threading, flashing arrows, and social networks match up with attention, patience, retention, and the need to follow several narrative threads? What qualities do they have in common? What are their differences?

6. Examine the ways that Johnson provides counterarguments and responds to them.

7. What economic explanation does Johnson offer for why television has become more intellectually demanding? What are the reasons that you watch your favorite television shows and movies multiple times?

8. Johnson says that "flashing arrows" (the way the audience is given the information it needs to follow the plot) have grown increasingly scarce as television narratives have grown more complicated. How does he connect that observation to the relationship between texture and substance (para. 21)? Based on your own television watching, do you agree or disagree? Explain your answer.

9. Create a chart that illustrates the "active threads" in a show you watch. How does it compare to the charts Johnson uses? How do your findings support or challenge Johnson's argument?

Celebrity Bodies

Daniel Harris

Cultural critic Daniel Harris (b. 1957) is the author of *The Rise and Fall of Gay Culture* (1999), *Cute, Quaint, Hungry and Romantic: The Aesthetics of Consumerism* (2001), *A Memoir of No One in Particular* (2002), and *Diary of a Drag Queen* (2005). His work has appeared in *Harper's*, *Newsday*, the *New York Times Magazine*, the *Los Angeles Times*, and the *Nation*, among other publications. His work was anthologized in *The Best American Essays 1993*. The essay presented here appeared in *Southwest Review* in 2008.

Just months after the fatal heart attacks of two Uruguayan fashion models, one of whom collapsed within seconds after stepping off the runway, having eaten nothing but lettuce leaves in the months before her death, *Titanic* star Kate Winslet announced that she is suing *Grazia* magazine for slander. The British tabloid accused her of undergoing a crash diet at a fat farm in Santa Monica, a claim that the 5'8", 119–130-pound actress categorically denies, and with good reason, since she is by most estimates, despite her well-founded reputation of having one of the healthier appetites in Hollywood, already between fifteen and twenty pounds underweight. She is famous for banning fashion magazines from her house lest her seven-year-old daughter fall prey to their anorexic aesthetic, a sentiment with which her countryman, the 5'9", 120-pound Mischa Barton, herself anywhere from twenty to forty pounds underweight, heartily agrees, stating that "the unhealthy look should be abandoned" and "it's wrong to try to stifle womanly curves." The rail-thin actress has, however, done a remarkable job in quelling her own and is considered by some to look sickly and malnourished, a charge she dismisses, summing up her philosophy of dieting in the reassuring assertion that "I don't not eat anything."

Others are more candid. Kate Bosworth was recently spotted at an expensive Hollywood restaurant openly dining on cigarettes, bottled water, and—the main course—a wedge of iceberg lettuce, a repast as frugal as former model Cleo Glyde's green grape diet: three for breakfast, two for snacks, and six for binges. The typical American woman is 5'4", weighs 140 pounds, and wears a size 14; the typical fashion model is seven inches taller, twenty-three pounds lighter, and twelve to fourteen sizes smaller. In an MSN photo essay about the fluctuating weights of Hollywood actors, an alarming shot of *Men in Black* star Lara Flynn Boyle is captioned with the snide but accurate comment "the jewelry she was wearing weighed more than she did," while a sickly photo of Selma Blair shows the *Legally Blonde* star looking "so slim she could seek cover behind the nearest swizzle stick." Teri Hatcher continues to flaunt the gams of a sub-Saharan famine victim while Calista Flockhart shocked the nation at the 1998 Emmys by wearing a backless gown that turned her spindly frame into a ghoulish anatomy lesson, an annotated diagram of frail scapulae and jutting vertebrae.

Few men are aroused by these stylishly accessorized carcasses, but their lack of sex appeal is what makes the new Hollywood aesthetic unique. It has been almost entirely detached from the biological function of beauty, that of attracting males. It is a man-made aesthetic, or, rather, a woman-made aesthetic, since the desire of men for voluptuous childbearing hips and pendulous breasts seems all but irrelevant to its look. Feminists have long complained that the so-called "beauty myth" consists entirely of male lust, of men looking at women as potential sex objects, subservient to their selfish demands. In fact, however, Hollywood is about women looking at women, not as sex objects, as a means for fulfilling the species's genetic mission, but as clothes hangers, as display mannequins for product lines. Men and their needs are entirely beside the point, which is why the aesthetic is so sterile, so sexless, because it has freed the female body from male desire, liberated it from its biological status as an organ of sex, which has given way to the commercial view of it as a wearer of commodities, a pretty face stuck on a stick. In many respects, the recent marriage of anorexia and glamour represents the final dehumanization of women who were once reduced to their bodies, objectified as tools for propagation, but have now been deprived of their corporeality altogether. A vision of the female body dictated by male desire would be far healthier and more attractive than one dictated by the imperatives of the closet, by manufacturers whose primary concern is showing off their goods to the best effect.

How much influence does this aesthetic have on the general public? Such well-known personalities as the withered Nicole Richie or the cadaverous Victoria "Posh" Beckham, a.k.a. "Skeletal Spice," are often cited as the chief culprits behind the endemic of eating disorders among the young but the fact remains that, while as many as one hundred thousand teenage girls suffer from excessive dieting, two out of three Americans are overweight and an estimated sixty million, or 20 percent of the population, are obese. Are Hollywood and the fashion world responsible for our ever-increasing girth or is the effect of our obsession with what many have dubbed "the rich and famished" as open to debate as the influence of television violence and the Xbox on actual crime statistics? Does Lindsay Lohan's waspish waistline make us skip meals and induce vomiting just as Mortal Kombat presumably makes us pick up assault rifles and open fire? How direct *is* the impact of Hollywood on our bodies, as direct as the *Daily Mirror* recently suggested when it ran a photograph of the emaciated Keira Knightley next to the headline "If Pictures Like This One of Keira Carried a Health Warning, My Darling Daughter Might Have Lived"? If many adolescents seek "thinspiration" from such desiccated waifs as Jessica Alba, who has admitted to being on a diet since age twelve, or Elisa Donovan, who dwindled to a mere 90 pounds after eating nothing but coffee, water, and toast for two years, the majority of Americans seem to be following the lead of reformed foodaholic Tom Arnold who, until he began taking the diet aid Xenical, regularly splurged on McDonald's and then hid his half-dozen Big Macs and Quarter Pounders from his equally gluttonous wife Roseanne, not out of shame, but because he didn't want to share.

What is dangerous about the influence of popular culture on our state of physical health is not how slavishly we imitate the stars, attempting to acquire Hilary Swank's lats, Jennifer Lopez's glutes, and Beyoncé's quads, but how little they affect us at all, how they have turned us into quiescent spectators who worship an unattainable ideal so remote from our daily affairs that its exemplars seem to belong to another species. Celebrities are like athletes, a class of surrogates who live vigorous, aerobic lives while we develop diabetes and arteriosclerosis on our sofas. Hollywood didn't create fat, anxious Americans; fat, anxious Americans created Hollywood, a vision of humanity that bears little resemblance to the typical dissipated physique, sagging from too many processed foods and sedentary hours watching lithe beauties cavort in haute couture. Fantasy worlds, like those inhabited by celebrities, are never fashioned in the image of the dreamer. The dreamer imagines an existence as unlike his own as possible and is content to admire this world from afar, not as a possible destination but as a wonderland all the more enticing the more unapproachable and exclusionary. Our fantasies engender a paralyzing awe that instills in us despair, a sense of hopelessness about maintaining our bodies, about achieving the buff perfections of stars spoon-fed by studio dieticians who force them to nibble on rice cakes and celery sticks and submit to grueling regimens of Pilates and kickboxing. In fact, we would almost certainly be healthier if we *did* imitate Hollywood, if we *did* work out and diet as compulsively as they do, if, like supermodel Dayle Haddon, we performed leg lifts while washing the dishes, side bends while standing in line at Starbucks, and thigh resistance exercises in the elevators of our four-star hotels.

We blame pop culture for turning us into diet-crazed bulimics, but how can celebrities be "role models," however derelict, when almost no one seems to imitate them, when we get fatter even as they get skinnier, exercise less even as they train like triathletes? Granted, we are preoccupied with celebrities, follow the evolution of their hair styles, take tours past the gates of their estates, make wild surmises about their sexual preferences, but obsession does not necessarily, or even usually, entail imitation. This does not keep us, however, from penalizing them with an unjust double standard, insisting that, in the name of public hygiene, they maintain scrupulously healthy diets, drink abstemiously, engage in unerringly faithful relations with their spouses, and indignantly turn down film roles in which they are asked to participate in such iniquitous activities as smoking. Never before have we demanded that popular culture be as virtuous as we have in the last forty years, that our stars, in the mistaken belief that they manufacture the moral templates of our lives, beat their breasts in remorse and enroll in rehab every time they fail a breathalyzer test, stumble on the red carpet, or light a cigarette in public. The anti-tobacco Web site Smokingsides.com provides exhaustive documentation of celebrated nicotine abusers; in its lengthy dossier on Nicole Kidman, for example, it cites no less than seventy-eight instances in which the actress was observed puffing away in full view of her fans, in particular at the infamous press conference at Cannes in 2003 in which, in an image broadcast around the world, she bummed a cigarette from a fellow actor, a faux pas that provoked such a vicious international backlash that an Australian senator threatened to slap parental advisories on films that depicted nicotine consumption favorably. We ourselves smoke like chimneys, drink like fish, swear like troopers, and copulate like rabbits, but those in Hollywood are expected to behave with unglamorous rectitude lest their misconduct deprave their malleable fans. We have moralized popular culture into one long tedious sermon, created a parallel universe far more chaste, more decorous, more modest and seemly than the one in which most of us live.

In the distant past, actors and artists occupied a seedy if alluring demimonde, a realm of license and nonconformity that flourished on the fringes of respectable society. Far from being role models, they were black sheep, bohemians high on cocaine and drunk on absinthe. Now, by contrast, we expect them to be the pillars of our society, moral leaders who scold us for the errors of our ways, elder statesmen who draft into the roles of goodwill ambassadors for the United

Nations, environmentalists, and spokesmen for such causes as gingivitis, erectile dysfunction, and irritable bowel syndrome. A paucity of conventional heroes has led to the invention of an implausible new set of mentors—a NASCAR mom, like race car driver Shawna Robinson, who feels that, behind the wheel of her souped-up Chevrolet Monte Carlo, she is able "to reach a lot of people," or even a golfer, such as Tiger Woods, whom Rolemodel.net singles out as an inspirational figure, a champion who triumphed over racial prejudice on the links and transformed his sport from a senile pastime for retirees in madras pants into "a vehicle . . . to influence people." Celebrities are rapidly filling the roles that priests, politicians, and wealthy philanthropists once served, perhaps because, as the church is rocked by molestation scandals and the government seems less and less capable of addressing the difficulties of our times, we are transferring moral authority to the only public servants that remain: pop singers, Hollywood stars, and the casts of our favorite sitcoms.

We admire them and yet at the same time distrust them. We are always ill at ease with beautiful people who, through no special effort of their own, get better jobs, more friends, and sexier lovers, but it is seldom that we encounter them in groups as large as we do on the idyllic Wisteria Lane in *Desperate Housewives*, a latter-day Peyton Place in which the entire cast—gardeners, pharmacists, plumbers, cable repairman—is gorgeous. Beautiful people in real life are scattered randomly throughout the population and it is statistically impossible that they should ever constitute more than a tiny, unthreatening minority. And yet with the international dissemination of American popular culture, they have triumphed over the statistical odds and done something they could never have done before the twentieth century: they have overcome their geographic dispersal, gravitated together, and emerged as a power elite, a physical aristocracy whose seat of government is one major U.S. city where they migrate at the invitation of directors, producers, talent scouts, and casting agents who scour the globe in search of the perfect photogenic face. For the first time in history, our daily lives are filled with images of a real live übermensch, a master race that flaunts the unfair privileges accorded to those whose talents are often little more than cheek bones and good genes. There have always been aristocracies, privileged classes whose social prestige derived from their material wealth or pedigree, but there has never been a Brahmin caste whose sole justification for power was its physical appeal. This unelected coalition of the sexually charismatic may not, like an actual government, regulate our daily affairs in any literal sense, but it does exercise autocratic authority over our imaginations, making us capitulate psychologically if not politically.

We seek to contain the influence of this new master race, to alleviate the sense of belittlement we experience from living in the shadow of its inconceivable affluence and glamour. Western culture affords us many ways of denigrating the beautiful, branding them stupid, egotistic, lonely, and unhappy, and our constant, self-abasing surveillance of their every move, our prurient eavesdropping on their private lives, from their sex tapes to the messages they leave on each other's answering machines, may itself be a method of diminishing their psychological power. Much as Louis XIV used Versailles as a glittering cage to imprison restive nobles, so we have surrounded our idols with an impregnable phalanx of flash-bulbs, herding them together in Hollywood, forcing them to live in a kind of internment camp, albeit one with all the amenities of a spa. The paparazzi, in turn, have become our watch dogs who never let them out of our sight, staking out their gyms, grocery stores, and nightclubs where they are forced to submit to our mean-spirited and yet, at the same time, obsequious espionage. We think of fame as a form of homage, the adulation we lavish on the gifted, but it may con-tain a large measure of resentment and vengefulness as well. Living in the lime-light, exposed to the scrutiny of anonymous multitudes, may be a method of punishment, a concerted campaign of ostracism, a discriminatory act that forces celebrities to live apart from us, immured in a gulag of tanning salons, acupunc-ture clinics, and trendy boutiques. Obviously, we are barred from entering their world, but so in many ways are they from ours.

Beauty is not democratic. It is unjust, distributed inequitably according to the luck of the draw. Our obsession with Hollywood celebrates this injustice, the irrationality with which fortune bestows its gifts. People cannot simply crash the gates and appropriate the privileges of the genetically blessed, creating faces dif-ferent from "the one [they] rode in on," as one blogger said of Nicole Kidman's suspiciously chiseled chin. When someone attempts to gain illegal entrance into the pantheon of the chosen few, manipulating Mother Nature through plastic surgery, we are both outraged and amused, angered that the inequalities we at once adore and fear are in fact phantasmal, and, at the same time, relieved that beauty is really just a con game, something we can control after all, an illusion fabricated through liposuction, collagen injections, and breast augmentations. Actors who submit to the knife are like athletes who inject steroids, fakes who should be disqualified from the race, interlopers who buy their way into the pub-lic's heart, who purchase their looks from any of the sixty-eight plastic surgeons in Beverly Hills, a number that translates into one surgeon for every 497 residents and compares astonishingly with the city's thirty-six pediatricians.

We are therefore thrilled when what Joan Rivers calls her "Simonizing," Dolly Parton her "fender work," and Demi Moore her "furniture" rearrangement goes hideously awry, as in the case of Tara Reid's left breast, which, mangled and mis-shapen, popped out of her dress at P-Diddy's thirty-fifth birthday party ("instead of a circle," Reid said of this scarred and lopsided protuberance, "it turned out to be a large square"); Sharon Osborne's tummy tuck, which chopped off so much loose skin as a result of her gastric bypass that they had to create a new belly but-ton; or Stevie Nicks's silicone implants, which caused such pain that, after their removal, she stored them in her freezer to remind herself of "the agony." "Scalpel slaves" — or "polysurgical patients," as they are known to industry insiders — are the butt of scathing Internet mockery: Mary Tyler Moore, whom doctors have

10

now placed on "an unofficial plastic surgery blacklist" and whose mouth has been stretched like taffy into a perpetual grin; model Alicia Douvall who, after her silicone implants ruptured, installed valves to pump saline solution in and out so she can vary the size of her breasts as the occasion warrants; or, the poster child of sloppy work, Michael Jackson, who may have had as many as thirty to forty rhinoplasties, including one that grafted cartilage from his ear to keep his nose from sinking back into his nasal cavity, leaving a gaping chasm in the middle of his face. If we are to believe in the beauty elite, to worship its exclusivity, its insuperable remoteness, we must be convinced that our idols acquired their physical assets the old-fashioned way, from Mom and Dad, not from Robert Rey, M.D., a.k.a. "Dr. 90210," perhaps the most famous plastic surgeon in the world. Our admiration of celebrities is much like our belief in God, and when our faith is tested by clear evidence of inauthenticity, by imposters who achieve illegal access to the inner sanctum through procedures we are increasingly able to spot, having become, as one reporter called it, "surgically literate," we are furious and vindictive. We mutiny against such swindlers in our gossip columns and Internet bulletin boards where we laugh hysterically when Britney Spears checks into a hospital for knee surgery and emerges several days later, according to many reports, two cup sizes larger or when Hollywood is stricken with crippling shortages of Botox just before the Academy Awards, which one Beverly Hills surgeon refers to as "tax season."

Our relationship with celebrities is so pathological in part because they are an absent presence in our lives: while they are physically absent and rarely seen in person, we are nonetheless nearer to their bodies, through close-ups, nude scenes, and simulated sex, than we are to anyone outside of our immediate families. We rarely examine even our lovers as meticulously as the Web site TMZ.com did in a recent exposé entitled "Heinous Extremities," an unsparing collection of photographs of celebrities' gnarly hands and stunted feet, appalling shots of Iman's twisted toes spilling painfully out of her stilettos and Jenna Jameson's arthritic claws clutching a soft drink can. In "Basic Instinct," Sharon Stone uncrosses her legs during a notorious police interrogation scene and gives us a clear shot of her pantyless crotch, bringing us closer to her genitalia than many men venture to those of their wives and girlfriends. The psychological mechanism of our obsession with celebrities lies in this deceptive intimacy, in the paradox that they are both present and absent, within reach and hidden behind wrought-iron gates, flashing their crotches at us in our living rooms and cowering behind ballistic-grade steel doors and closed-circuit surveillance systems. The camera is a tease, simulating an intimacy we do not have, a familiarity that incites us to narrow the physical distance that divides us from the stars, to eliminate the mediation of the lens, and press ourselves against them, flesh to flesh. Those who stalk celebrities, like the woman who left cookies in David Letterman's foyer and camped out on his tennis courts, or the man who slashes his wrists outside of the ABC studios where Andrea Evans was filming an episode of *One Life to Live*, are really just our ambassadors, envoys we send to do our investigative work for us, berserk enthusiasts whose actions are psychotic manifestations of a very normal impulse to ascertain the physical reality of bodies we know almost as well as our own, if only secondhand.

Not only do celebrities occupy a different space than their fans, they occupy a different, nonconsecutive time. They do not change as we do, gradually, imperceptibly. They exist only in photographs and films, outside of the passage of time, the chronology of their bodies scrambled by random encounters with images from various periods in their lives, one from the zenith of their careers, proudly cradling their Oscars, another decades later, unemployed has-beens, as in the notorious pair of photographs that many newspapers published side by side when Greta Garbo died in 1990—on the left, the young starlet in her twenties, untouchably beautiful; on the right, an aged crone with straggly white hair hobbling out of a health clinic just weeks before her death at the age of eighty-four. The descent of celebrities into infirmity, obesity, or even the terminal stages of an illness is telescoped by the very medium that at once celebrates their youth and beauty and, over time, renders them grotesque. Unlike the bodies of our friends and family, whom we see every day and who therefore do not age in any measurable way, stars seem to change in fits and starts. One minute, 5'4", 120-pound Janet Jackson has a six-pack and buns of steel, and the next she's 180 pounds wearing sweatpants and a baseball cap, a wardrobe malfunction far more troubling than that which occurred during so-called "Titgate" at the 2004 Super Bowl. Similarly, a famous photograph of her brother shows him when he is ten years old, sporting a huge Afro and an infectious smile, while his mug shot, taken some thirty-five years later after his arrest for child molestation, features the unforgettable image of a bleached mask, a macabre caricature of Caucasian features, a heartbreaking disavowal of his own blackness. Reruns and DVDs fast-forward the careers of the stars, allowing us to see them starting out fresh, exhilarated by their success, and then, with one flick of the remote control, sinking into the decrepitude of old age. We are shocked by the essay film and photography inadvertently write on physical dissolution, by the way they document the remorseless changes, the ebbing vitality, that celebrities take such unavailing pains to arrest. Art is long, life short, but in the case of Hollywood celebrities, art—their careers, their beauty—is short and life long—for most, too long.

Exploring the Text

1. How does the first paragraph of Daniel Harris's essay set up the reader's expectations? How are those expectations met? How are they upset?
2. How does Harris use examples to establish his credibility? How do his examples show his consideration of his audience?
3. Harris makes a few arguments here. What do you think is his primary argument? His secondary arguments? How does he bring them together?

4. What are some of the rhetorical strategies Harris uses to develop his argument? Find examples of strategies such as hyperbole, opposition, figurative language, and colloquialisms, and discuss their effects.

5. Look closely at Harris's topic sentences. What do you see as their strengths? Do you see any weaknesses? If so, identify them. How do the topic sentences set up each paragraph? What patterns can you see in the way Harris structures them?

6. How would you characterize Harris's tone? His attitude toward his subject matter?

7. In paragraph 7 Harris cites the Web site Rolemodel.net, whose mission statement says that it aims to inspire "the next generation towards an outward focus," as having named Tiger Woods an "inspirational figure." Rolemodel.net has now removed Tiger Woods as a role model, but not without a long explanation by its creator, Lamar Brantley. In what ways does the example of Tiger Woods still work for Harris? In what ways doesn't it?

8. Harris considers the way Americans relate to celebrities as being "pathological in part because they are an absent presence in our lives" (para. 12). What do you think about this paradox? Support, challenge, or qualify Harris's assertion.

9. What does Harris consider the effect of our fascination with celebrities on our daily lives? What point does he make about its effect on the dissemination of American culture throughout the world?

My Zombie, Myself

Why Modern Life Feels Rather Undead

CHUCK KLOSTERMAN

> Chuck Klosterman was born in Minnesota in 1972 and grew up in North Dakota. He has written for *Spin* magazine, *GQ*, the *New York Times Magazine*, and the *Washington Post*. A regularly featured columnist in *Esquire*, he is also a consulting editor on Grantland.com, a Web site for long-form writing on sports and popular culture. He is the author of several essay collections, including *Sex, Drugs, and Cocoa Puffs* (2003) and *Eating the Dinosaur* (2009), and two novels, *Downtown Owl* (2008), and *The Visible Man* (2011). The following essay appeared in the op-ed section of the *New York Times* in 2010.

Zombies are a value stock. They are wordless and oozing and brain dead, but they're an ever-expanding market with no glass ceiling. Zombies are a target-rich environment, literally and figuratively. The more you fill them with bullets, the more interesting they become. Roughly 5.3 million people watched the first episode of *The Walking Dead* on AMC, a stunning 83 percent more than the 2.9 million who watched the Season 4 premiere of *Mad Men*. This means there are at least 2.4 million cable-ready Americans who might prefer watching Christina Hendricks if she were an animated corpse.

Statistically and aesthetically that dissonance seems perverse. But it probably shouldn't. Mainstream interest in zombies has steadily risen over the past 40 years. Zombies are a commodity that has advanced slowly and without major evolution, much like the staggering creatures George Romero popularized in the 1968 film *Night of the Living Dead*. What makes that measured amplification curious is the inherent limitations of the zombie itself: You can't add much depth to a creature who can't talk, doesn't think and whose only motive is the consumption of flesh. You can't humanize a zombie, unless you make it less zombie-esque. There are slow zombies, and there are fast zombies — that's pretty much the spectrum of zombie diversity. It's not that zombies are changing to fit the world's condition; it's that the condition of the world seems more like a zombie offensive. Something about zombies is becoming more intriguing to us. And I think I know what that something is.

Zombies are just so easy to kill.

When we think critically about monsters, we tend to classify them as personifications of what we fear. Frankenstein's monster illustrated our trepidation about untethered science; Godzilla was spawned from the fear of the atomic age; werewolves feed into an instinctual panic over predation and man's detachment from nature. Vampires and zombies share an imbedded anxiety about disease. It's easy to project a symbolic relationship between zombies and rabies (or zombies and the pitfalls of consumerism), just as it's easy to project a symbolic relationship between vampirism and AIDS (or vampirism and the loss of purity). From a creative standpoint these fear projections are narrative linchpins; they turn creatures into ideas, and that's the point.

But what if the audience infers an entirely different metaphor?   5

What if contemporary people are less interested in seeing depictions of their unconscious fears and more attracted to allegories of how their day-to-day existence feels? That would explain why so many people watched that first episode of *The Walking Dead*: They knew they would be able to relate to it.

A lot of modern life is exactly like slaughtering zombies.

If there's one thing we all understand about zombie killing, it's that the act is uncomplicated: You blast one in the brain from point-blank range (preferably with a shotgun). That's Step 1. Step 2 is doing the same thing to the next zombie that takes its place. Step 3 is identical to Step 2, and Step 4 isn't any different from Step 3. Repeat this process until (a) you perish, or (b) you run out of zombies. That's really the only viable strategy.

Every zombie war is a war of attrition. It's always a numbers game. And it's more repetitive than complex. In other words, zombie killing is philosophically similar to reading and deleting 400 work e-mails on a Monday morning or filling out paperwork that only generates more paperwork, or following Twitter gossip out of obligation, or performing tedious tasks in which the only true risk is being consumed by the avalanche. The principal downside to any zombie attack is that the zombies will never stop coming; the principal downside to life is that you will never be finished with whatever it is you do.

The Internet reminds us of this every day.   10

Here's a passage from a youngish writer named Alice Gregory, taken from a recent essay on Gary Shteyngart's dystopic novel *Super Sad True Love Story* in the literary journal n+1: "It's hard not to think 'death drive' every time I go on the Internet," she writes. "Opening Safari is an actively destructive decision. I am asking that consciousness be taken away from me."

Ms. Gregory's self-directed fear is thematically similar to how the zombie brain is described by Max Brooks, author of the fictional oral history *World War Z* and its accompanying self-help manual, *The Zombie Survival Guide*: "Imagine a computer programmed to execute one function. This function cannot be paused, modified or erased. No new data can be stored. No new commands can be installed. This computer will perform that one function, over and over, until its power source eventually shuts down."

This is our collective fear projection: that we will be consumed. Zombies are like the Internet and the media and every conversation we don't want to have. All of it comes at us endlessly (and thoughtlessly), and — if we surrender — we will be overtaken and absorbed. Yet this war is manageable, if not necessarily winnable. As long as we keep deleting whatever's directly in front of us, we survive. We live to eliminate the zombies of tomorrow. We are able to remain human, at least for the time being. Our enemy is relentless and colossal, but also uncreative and stupid.

Battling zombies is like battling anything . . . or everything.

⚎

Because of the "Twilight" series it's easy to manufacture an argument in which   15
vampires are merely replacing zombies as the monster of the moment, a designation that is supposed to matter for metaphorical, nonmonstrous reasons. But that kind of thinking is deceptive. The recent five-year spike in vampire interest is only about the multiplatform success of "Twilight," a brand that isn't about vampirism anyway. It's mostly about nostalgia for teenage chastity, the attractiveness of its film cast and the fact that contemporary fiction consumers tend to prefer long serialized novels that can be read rapidly. But this has still created a domino effect. The 2008 Swedish vampire film *Let the Right One In* was fantastic, but it probably wouldn't have been remade in the United States if "Twilight" had never existed. *The Gates* was an overt attempt by ABC to tap into the housebound, preteen "Twilight" audience; HBO's *True Blood* is a camp reaction to Robert Pattinson's flat earnestness.

The difference with zombies, of course, is that it's possible to like a specific vampire temporarily, which isn't really an option with the undead. Characters like Mr. Pattinson's Edward Cullen in "Twilight" and Anne Rice's Lestat de

Lioncourt, and even boring old Count Dracula can be multidimensional and erotic; it's possible to learn who they are and who they once were. Vampire love can be singular. Zombie love, however, is always communal. If you dig zombies, you dig the entire zombie concept. It's never personal. You're interested in what zombies signify, you like the way they move, and you understand what's required to stop them. And this is a reassuring attraction, because those aspects don't really shift. They've become shared archetypal knowledge.

A few days before Halloween I was in upstate New York with three other people, and we somehow ended up at the Barn of Terror, outside a town called Lake Katrine. Entering the barn was mildly disturbing, although probably not as scary as going into an actual abandoned barn that didn't charge $20 and doesn't own its own domain name. Regardless, the best part was when we exited the terror barn and were promptly herded onto a school bus, which took us to a cornfield about a quarter of a mile away. The field was filled with amateur actors, some playing military personnel and others what they called the infected. We were told to run through the moonlit corn maze if we wanted to live; as we ran, armed soldiers yelled contradictory instructions while hissing zombies emerged from the corny darkness. It was designed to be fun, and it was. But just before we immersed ourselves in the corn, one of my companions sardonically critiqued the reality of our predicament.

"I know this is supposed to be scary," he said. "But I'm pretty confident about my ability to deal with a zombie apocalypse. I feel strangely informed about what to do in this kind of scenario."

I could not disagree. At this point who isn't? We all know how this goes: If you awake from a coma, and you don't immediately see a member of the hospital staff, assume a zombie takeover has transpired during your incapacitation. Don't travel at night and keep your drapes closed. Don't let zombies spit on you. If you knock a zombie down, direct a second bullet into its brain stem. But above all, do not assume that the war is over, because it never is. The zombies you kill today will merely be replaced by the zombies of tomorrow. But you can do this, my friend. It's disenchanting, but it's not difficult. Keep your finger on the trigger. Continue the termination. Don't stop believing. Don't stop deleting. Return your voice mails and nod your agreements. This is the zombies' world, and we just live in it. But we can live better.

Exploring the Text

1. Describe the tone of Chuck Klosterman's essay. How does the tone suit the essay's purpose?
2. How does Klosterman establish ethos? What effect does his tone have on his credibility?
3. In paragraph 4, Klosterman suggests that monsters personify our fears. What are other reasons that vampires, werewolves, and zombies might be so intriguing?

4. What is Klosterman's central argument? What kind of evidence does he use to develop it?
5. Paragraphs 3, 5, 7, 10, and 14 are one sentence each. What else do they have in common? Explain why they are or are not effective.
6. Why do you think Klosterman uses imperative sentences in the essay's last paragraph?

Emily Dickinson and Elvis Presley in Heaven

Hans Ostrom

Hans Ostrom (b. 1954) grew up in Sierra City, California. His grandfather, a Swedish immigrant, worked in gold mines in the Sierra Nevada range. Ostrom, Distinguished Professor of English at the University of Puget Sound, teaches composition, creative writing, rhetoric, and literature and is codirector of African American studies. He is the author of *Langston Hughes: A Study of the Short Fiction* (1993) and *A Langston Hughes Encyclopedia* (2001). Ostrom's articles, poems, and short stories have appeared in a variety of magazines and journals. He is also the author of the novels *Three to Get Ready* (1991) and *Honoring Juanita* (2010), as well as two poetry collections, *Subjects Apprehended* (2000) and *The Coast Starlight: Collected Poems, 1976–2006* (2006).

They call each other E. Elvis picks
wildflowers near the river and brings
them to Emily. She explains half-rhymes to him.

In heaven Emily wears her hair long, sports
Levis and western blouses with rhinestones.   5
Elvis is lean again, wears baggy trousers

and T-shirts, a letterman's jacket from Tupelo High.
They take long walks and often hold hands.
She prefers they remain just friends. Forever.

Emily's poems now contain naugahyde, Cadillacs,   10
Electricity, jets, TV, Little Richard and Richard
Nixon. The rock-a-billy rhythm makes her smile.

Elvis likes himself with style. This afternoon
he will play guitar and sing "I Taste a Liquor
Never Brewed" to the tune of "Love Me Tender."   15

Emily will clap and harmonize. Alone
in their cabins later, they'll listen to the river
and nap. They will not think of Amherst

or Las Vegas. They know why God made them
roommates. It's because America   20
was their hometown. It's because

God is a thing
without feathers. It's because
God wears blue suede shoes.

Exploring the Text

1. What does Hans Ostrom's pairing of Elvis Presley and Emily Dickinson suggest about the poem's idea of heaven?
2. The poem depends somewhat on the reader's familiarity with the works of Dickinson and Presley. Look up the references you don't recognize—such as Dickinson's poems "I taste a liquor never brewed" and "Hope is the thing with feathers," Presley's song "Love Me Tender," Little Richard, Amherst, and naugahyde. Then reconsider Ostrom's poem with all the blanks filled in.
3. What is the intention and effect of the period after "friends" in line 9?
4. In nearly every stanza, Ostrom uses enjambment—a stylistic device in which one line ends without a pause and continues into the next line for its meaning. What is the effect?
5. In the last two stanzas, Ostrom says God made Presley and Dickinson roommates for three reasons. What do these reasons suggest about the importance of pop culture in America?

Myths

Andy Warhol

Born in Pittsburgh, Andy Warhol (1928–1987) was an American artist who was as well known for his persona as he was for his work. He created paintings, prints, and films and was a leading figure in the pop art movement. Warhol is famous for his silkscreens and paintings of American manufactured products such as Campbell's Soup and Coca-Cola, as well as American celebrities such as Elizabeth Taylor and Marilyn Monroe. The painting presented here is part of the Emily Fisher Landau Collection, which was bequeathed to New York City's Whitney Museum. The ten figures in the painting, from left to right, are Superman, Santa Claus, Howdy Doody, Greta Garbo, Mickey Mouse, Uncle Sam, Aunt Jemima, Dracula, the Wicked Witch, and Warhol himself.

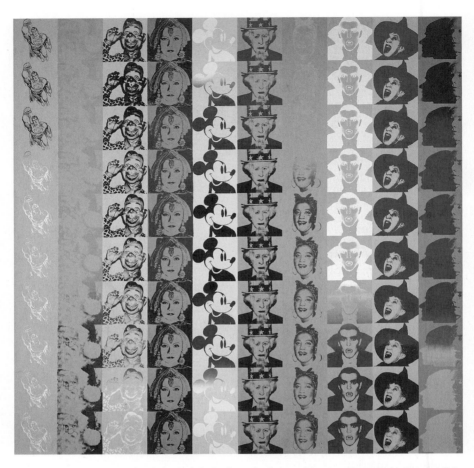

SOURCE: Copyright © 2011 The Andy Warhol Foundation for the Visual Arts, Inc./Artists Rights Society (ARS), New York. Collection of Emily Fisher Landau, New York, Andy Warhol, 1928–1987. *Myths*, 1981, Synthetic polymer and screenprint ink on canvas, 100 x 100 in. (254 x 254 cm); 102 x 102 x 3 in. (259.1 x 259.1 x 7.6 cm). Promised gift of the Fisher Landau Center for Art to Whitney Museum of American Art, New York; promised gift of the Fisher Landau Center for Art, P.2010.340

Exploring the Text

1. What do the strips of images remind you of? What might Andy Warhol have wanted the viewer to see in them?
2. The images in this piece were printed in black, in a process called silkscreening, onto a silver-painted canvas. The images were still shots from movies, and Warhol and his assistants printed them in an almost mechanical repetition. As they worked, however, they varied the pressure in squeezing the ink, sometimes allowing the screen to become clogged. Thus, no two images of the characters are exactly

the same. What statement does Warhol make about these pop culture icons with the variations in clarity? What patterns do you see? Why might he have used a silver background?

3. The title of the work is *Myths*, a name Warhol gave to many of his works depicting celebrities and icons. What is he saying here about myths and mythmaking? Where do the myths come from? Who creates them?

4. Uncle Sam is nearly at the center of the work. What might Warhol be saying about that American icon? Consider the figures on either side of Uncle Sam: a cartoon character and an image that is considered a racial stereotype.

5. Look carefully at the image of Warhol at the far right. Characterize him through his image here and through his role as "speaker" in this work. Hint: he portrays himself doubly—in one perspective as "The Shadow," a popular radio crime fighter from the 1930s, and in another perspective looking straight out at the viewer.

6. Warhol is credited with saying, "Art is what you can get away with." Using this work and other Warhols with which you are familiar, support, challenge, or qualify that assertion.

The Innocent Eye Test

Mark Tansey

A well-known New York City artist, Mark Tansey was born in California in 1949, the son of two art historians. His work has been described as surrealistic and postmodern; his subject matter is often ironic. He uses photographic images from popular culture, academia, and art history, relocating and recombining them in order to comment on humanity. *The Innocent Eye Test* (1981), a painting that hangs in New York's Metropolitan Museum of Art, comments on the relationship between the artist and the viewer, an important concern of Tansey's. The image shows a cow examining *Young Bull*, a 1647 oil painting by Paulus Potter that hangs in the Mauritshuis in The Hague. In the background is one of Monet's *Haystack* paintings from the early 1890s.

Exploring the Text

1. Who or what is being tested in *The Innocent Eye Test*? What does the painting say about art criticism? How do the details complicate the answer to who is testing whom?

2. Identify and analyze the visual and historical information in this painting.

3. Visual art can be analyzed through the rhetorical triangle (see Chapter 1). Consider the painting, the artist, and the audience separately, and then analyze the relationships among these three elements.

4. A hallmark of postmodern art is the appropriation—quoting or borrowing—of other art. What has Mark Tansey borrowed in this painting? What is the relationship between the old and the new? How does the appropriation create a conversation between the artist and the viewer? Between the past and the present?

5. American novelist William S. Burroughs (1914–1997) is credited with noting that there is no such thing as an innocent bystander. Does Tansey's painting make the same point, or does it refute it? Explain your response.

Exporting American Pop Culture

The following seven documents comment directly or indirectly on the effects of exporting American pop culture to the rest of the world.

Sources
1. **Thomas L. Friedman,** *The Revolution Is U.S.*
2. **Heather Havrilesky,** *Besieged by "Friends"*
3. **Deirdre Straughan,** *Cultural Hegemony: Who's Dominating Whom?*
4. **Kwame Anthony Appiah,** from *The Case for Contamination*
5. **Josef Joffe,** *The Perils of Soft Power*
6. **Joseph S. Nye Jr.,** *The U.S. Can Reclaim "Smart Power"*
7. **Hassan Ammar,** *Slovakian Soccer Fan at 2010 World Cup in South Africa* (photo)

After you have read, studied, and synthesized these pieces, enter the conversation by responding to one of the prompts on page 874.

1. *The Revolution Is U.S.*

Thomas L. Friedman

This reading is from journalist Thomas L. Friedman's 2000 book, *The Lexus and the Olive Tree*.

I believe in the five gas stations theory of the world.

That's right: I believe you can reduce the world's economies today to basically five different gas stations. First there is the Japanese gas station. Gas is $5 a gallon. Four men in uniforms and white gloves, with lifetime employment contracts, wait on you. They pump your gas. They change your oil. They wash your windows, and they wave at you with a friendly smile as you drive away in peace. Second is the American gas station. Gas costs only $1 a gallon, but you pump it yourself. You wash your own windows. You fill your own tires. And when you drive around the corner four homeless people try to steal your hubcaps. Third is the Western European gas station. Gas there also costs $5 a gallon. There is only one man on duty. He grudgingly pumps your gas and unsmilingly changes your oil, reminding you all the time that his union contract says he only has to pump gas and change oil. He doesn't do windows. He works only thirty-five hours a week, with ninety minutes off each day for lunch, during which time the gas

855

station is closed. He also has six weeks' vacation every summer in the south of France. Across the street, his two brothers and uncle, who have not worked in ten years because their state unemployment insurance pays more than their last job, are playing boccie ball. Fourth is the developing-country gas station. Fifteen people work there and they are all cousins. When you drive in, no one pays any attention to you because they are all too busy talking to each other. Gas is only 35 cents a gallon because it is subsidized by the government, but only one of the six pumps actually works. The others are broken and they are waiting for the replacement parts to be flown in from Europe. The gas station is rather run-down because the absentee owner lives in Zurich and takes all the profits out of the country. The owner doesn't know that half his employees actually sleep in the repair shop at night and use the car wash equipment to shower. Most of the customers at the developing-country gas station either drive the latest-model Mercedes or a motor scooter — nothing in between. The place is always busy, though, because so many people stop in to use the air pump to fill their bicycle tires. Lastly there is the communist gas station. Gas there is only 50 cents a gallon — but there is none, because the four guys working there have sold it all on the black market for $5 a gallon. Just one of the four guys who is employed at the communist gas station is actually there. The other three are working at second jobs in the underground economy and only come around once a week to collect their paychecks.

What is going on in the world today, in the very broadest sense, is that through the process of globalization everyone is being forced toward America's gas station. If you are not an American and don't know how to pump your own gas, I suggest you learn. With the end of the Cold War, globalization is globalizing Anglo-American-style capitalism and the Golden Straitjacket. It is globalizing American culture and cultural icons. It is globalizing the best of America and the worst of America. It is globalizing the American Revolution and it is globalizing the American gas station.

But not everyone likes the American gas station and what it stands for, and you can understand why. Embedded in the Japanese, Western European, and communist gas stations are social contracts very different from the American one, as well as very different attitudes about how markets should operate and be controlled. The Europeans and the Japanese believe in the state exercising power over the people and over markets, while Americans tend to believe more in empowering the people and letting markets be as free as possible to sort out who wins and who loses.

Because the Japanese, Western Europeans, and communists are uncomfortable with totally unfettered markets and the unequal benefits and punishments they distribute, their gas stations are designed to cushion such inequalities and equalize rewards. Their gas stations also pay more attention to the distinctive traditions and value preferences of their communities. The Western Europeans do this by employing fewer people, but paying them higher wages and collecting higher taxes to generously support the unemployed and to underwrite a goody bag

5

of other welfare-state handouts. The Japanese do it by paying people a little less but guaranteeing them lifetime employment, and then protecting those lifetime jobs and benefits by restricting foreign competitors from entering the Japanese market. The American gas station, by contrast, is a much more efficient place to drive through. The customer is king; the gas station has no social function; its only purpose is to provide the most gas at the cheapest price. If that can be done with no employees at all—well, all the better. A flexible labor market will find them work somewhere else. Too cruel, you say? Maybe so. But, ready or not, this is the model that the rest of the world is increasingly being pressured to emulate.

America is blamed for this because, in so many ways, globilization is us—or is at least perceived that way by a lot of the world. The three democratizations were mostly nurtured in America. The Golden Straitjacket was made in America and Great Britain. The Electronic Herd is led by American Wall Street bulls. The most powerful agent pressuring other countries to open their markets for free trade and free investment is Uncle Sam, and America's global armed forces keep these markets and sea lanes open for this era of globalization, just as the British navy did for the era of globalization in the nineteenth century. Joseph Nye Jr., dean of the Harvard University Kennedy School, summarized this reality well when he noted: "In its recent incarnation, globalization can be traced in part back to American strategy after World War II and the desire to create an open international economy to forestall another depression and to balance Soviet power and contain communism. The institutional framework and political pressures for opening markets were a product of American power and policy. But they were reinforced by developments in the technology of transportation and communications which made it increasingly costly for states to turn away from global market forces." In other words, even within the Cold War system America was hard at work building out a global economy for its own economic and strategic reasons. As a result, when the information revolution, and the three democratizations, came together at the end of the 1980s, there was a power structure already in place that was very receptive to these trends and technologies and greatly enhanced their spread around the world. As noted earlier, it was this combination of American power and strategic interests, combined with the made-in-America information revolution, that really made this second era of globalization possible, and gave it its distinctly American face.

Today, globalization often wears Mickey Mouse ears, eats Big Macs, drinks Coke or Pepsi, and does its computing on an IBM PC, using Windows 98, with an Intel Pentium II processor, and a network link from Cisco Systems. Therefore, while the distinction between what is globalization and what is Americanization may be clear to most Americans, it is not—unfortunately—to many others around the world. In most societies people cannot distinguish anymore among American power, American exports, American cultural assaults, American cultural exports, and plain vanilla globalization. They are now all wrapped into one.

I am not advocating that globalization should be Americanization—but pointing out that that is how it is perceived in many quarters. No wonder the Japanese newspaper *Nihon Keizai Shimbun* carried a headline on June 4, 1999, about a conference in Tokyo on globalization that referred to the phenomenon as "The American-Instigated Globalization." When many people in the developing world look out into this globalization system what they see first is a recruiting poster that reads: Uncle Sam wants you (for the Electronic Herd).

Martin Indyk, the former U.S. ambassador to Israel, told me a story that illustrates this point perfectly. As ambassador, he was called upon to open the first McDonald's in Jerusalem. I asked him what he said on the occasion of McDonald's opening in that holy city, and he said, "Fast food for a fast nation." But the best part, he told me later, was that McDonald's gave him a colorful baseball hat with the McDonald's logo on it to wear as he was invited to eat the first ceremonial Big Mac in Jerusalem's first McDonald's—with Israeli television filming every bite for the evening news. The restaurant was packed with young Israelis eager to be on hand for this historic event. While Ambassador Indyk was preparing to eat Jerusalem's first official Big Mac, a young Israeli teenager worked his way through the crowd and walked up to him. The teenager was carrying his own McDonald's hat and he handed it to Ambassador Indyk with a pen and asked, "Are you the ambassador? Can I have your autograph?"

Somewhat sheepishly, Ambassador Indyk replied, "Sure. I've never been asked for my autograph before."

As Ambassador Indyk took the hat and prepared to sign his name on the bill, the teenager said to him, "Wow, what's it like to be the ambassador from McDonald's, going around the world opening McDonald's restaurants everywhere?"   10

Stunned, Ambassador Indyk looked at the Israeli youth and said, "No, no. I'm the *American* ambassador—not the ambassador from McDonald's!"

The Israeli youth looked totally crestfallen. Ambassador Indyk described what happened next: "I said to him, 'Does this mean you don't want my autograph?' And the kid said, no, I don't want your autograph, and he took his hat back and walked away."

No wonder that the love-hate relationship that has long existed between America and the rest of the world seems to be taking on an even sharper edge these days. For some people Americanization-globalization feels more than ever like a highly attractive, empowering, incredibly tempting pathway to rising living standards. For many others, though, this Americanization-globalization can breed a deep sense of envy and resentment toward the United States—envy because America seems so much better at riding this tiger and resentment because Americanization-globalization so often feels like the United States whipping everyone else to speed up, Web up, downsize, standardize, and march to America's cultural tunes into the Fast World. While I am sure there are still more lovers of America than haters out there, this [essay] is about the haters. It is about the *other* backlash against globalization—the rising resentment of the United States that has been triggered as we move into a globalization system that is so heavily influenced today by American icons, markets, and military might.

As the historian Ronald Steel once pointed out: "It was never the Soviet Union but the United States itself that is the true revolutionary power. We believe that our institutions must confine all others to the ash heap of history. We lead an economic system that has effectively buried every other form of production and distribution—leaving great wealth and sometimes great ruin in its wake. The cultural messages we transmit through Hollywood and McDonald's go out across the world to capture and also undermine other societies. Unlike more traditional conquerors, we are not content merely to subdue others: We insist that they be like us. And of course for their own good. We are the world's most relentless proselytizers. The world must be democratic. It must be capitalistic. It must be tied into the subversive messages of the World Wide Web. No wonder many feel threatened by what we represent."

The classic American self-portrait is Grant Wood's *American Gothic*, the   15
straitlaced couple, pitchfork in hand, expressions controlled, stoically standing watch outside the barn. But to the rest of the world, American Gothic is actually two twentysomething American software engineers who come into your country wearing long hair, beads, and sandals, with rings in their noses and paint on their toes. They kick down your front door, overturn everything in the house, stick a Big Mac in your mouth, fill your kids' heads with ideas you've never had or can't understand, slam a cable box onto your television, lock the channel to MTV, plug an Internet connection into your computer, and tell you: "Download or die."

That's us. We Americans are the apostles of the Fast World, the enemies of tradition, the prophets of the free market, and the high priests of high tech. We want "enlargement" of both our values and our Pizza Huts. We want the world to follow our lead and become democratic, capitalistic, with a Web site in every pot, a Pepsi on every lip, Microsoft Windows in every computer and most of all— most of all—with everyone, everywhere, pumping their own gas.

Questions

1. How does Thomas Friedman use the "five gas stations theory of the world" (para. 1) to show the implicit values of five different cultures?
2. How does Friedman differentiate between globalization and Americanization?
3. What is the purpose of the anecdote about the U.S. ambassador to Israel at the opening of a new McDonald's?
4. Why does Friedman think that the "love-hate relationship" between America and the rest of the world has taken on an "even sharper edge" (para. 13)?

2. *Besieged by "Friends"*

HEATHER HAVRILESKY

Critic Heather Havrilesky posted this piece on Salon.com in 2003, as a review of a documentary entitled *Hollywood in the Muslim World.*

It must be tough living in the Middle East, what with all the dust and the camels and the angry terrorists running around, looking for stuff to blow up. I bet it's hard to get your coffee in the morning, with all those terrorists shouting that the line is too long, or threatening to level the joint because they specifically said "soy" or "no foam" and the little drummer boy behind the counter didn't hear them right the first time.

Despite the fact that most Arabs on the big screen have several sticks of dynamite packed into their BVDs, most of us aren't stupid enough to think that the Muslim world is filled with Wile E. Coyotes in robes. Still, when kids grow up watching *True Lies*, *The Siege* and *Rules of Engagement*, in which even a one-legged Yemeni girl totes a machine gun, it's not too hard to see how their perspectives get twisted beyond recognition. In his documentary "Hollywood in the Muslim World" Charles C. Stuart discovers a well of anger and frustration in the Middle East over American depictions of Arabs, anger that some believe stokes the flames of extremism.

As Stuart points out at the start of his film, by the year 2000, Arab television had grown into a half-billion dollar a year industry. With 100 satellite channels, Arab governments can no longer control the content of every broadcast. These days, people in Cairo, Egypt; Beirut, Lebanon; and Qatar are familiar with shows like *Friends*, *Sex and the City* and *Will & Grace*, as well as countless American movies. Two months before the war with Iraq began, Stuart visited the Middle East and talked with citizens in Egypt, Iraq, Lebanon and Qatar about the influence of Hollywood and American pop culture in the Middle East.

Many of those interviewed resented the pervasive influence of Hollywood, claiming that such "cultural pollution" is a threat to Muslim identity. One filmmaker in Beirut expressed regret at the way kids in Lebanon grow up with so many American influences. "I feel that Lebanon has lost part of its identity by imitating or having all the American things here. This winter I didn't go to any Starbucks cafe, I don't like Dunkin Donuts. . . . But the marketing of all these things is done in such a way that it reaches the children. I mean, who goes to McDonald's here? The children. Because at the same time, you have a McDonald's, a ticket to see a Disney film and you have a gadget. It's a market."

When Stuart interviewed a bunch of kids about their favorite American movies, a 19-year-old man interrupted them, fearing that the filmmaker was exploiting the children. When Stuart asked for the young man's point of view, he angrily railed off a list of Hollywood's stereotypes. "Do you see any camels around here?" he asked.

Others Stuart interviewed saw the influx of American culture as part of a U.S.

campaign to stereotype Arabs. "We know that there is a war, a war of propaganda, and a media war against the Arabs and the Muslims," said one network representative.

Whether or not they agreed with the assertion that American stereotypes are intentionally denigrating, many subjects feel certain that Americanization in the Muslim world is pushing some Arabs to embrace more extremist beliefs. Or, as professor Abdullah Schleifer of the American University in Cairo put it, "Radical fundamentalism is a reaction to radical Westernization or modernization."

As paranoid, oversensitive or wildly professorial as such remarks might seem, consider how American stereotypes conveniently mirror our government's foreign policy at any given time. While mid-century movies about World War II seem laughably dated in their depiction of psychotically evil Japanese soldiers, the trauma of Pearl Harbor stoked paranoia and hatred toward Japan in such a way that prejudices were absolutely taken for granted as holding some grain of truth. Meanwhile, in early Hollywood movies like *The Sheik* and *Lawrence of Arabia*, Arabs were depicted as exotic, wildly sexual beings. By the early '80s, with the Iran hostage crisis and rising turmoil in the Middle East, Hollywood's depictions of Arabs and Muslims became darker and more foreboding. Today, the trauma of Sept. 11 enables many to cast a blind eye on the way Hollywood perpetuates extreme prejudice against Arabs in America and in the Middle East.

Unfortunately, Stuart doesn't explore such points. As fascinating as it is to meet the writers of the Arab sitcom *Shabab Online*, which appears to be a badly blocked *Friends* with perpetually grinning actors, or to visit "The Friends Cafe," a coffee joint in Beirut modeled after "Central Perk," most of Stuart's interviews don't move past surface observations and he seems to touch on a wide range of subjects without delving too deep or pulling the threads together into a cohesive narrative.

Still, at a time when the "patriotic" view often simply means pervasive xenophobia, it's valuable to witness the resentment and anger welling up from those who feel their cultural identity has been taken hostage by Hollywood. And we can hardly blame them — if we were forced to watch reruns of *Shabab Online* on every channel, we'd be angry, too.

Questions

1. What assumptions about her audience does Heather Havrilesky make in paragraphs 1 and 2?
2. What stereotypes have you seen in American films that might fuel extremism? Do you think those stereotypes are more or less prevalent in the years since 9/11? Explain what you consider to be the sources and effects of those stereotypes.
3. Who does Havrilesky cite as making connections between radical fundamentalism and "the pervasive influence of Hollywood" (para. 4)? What connections do they comment on?
4. What does Havrilesky think is the most pervasive effect of post-9/11 xenophobia?

3. *Cultural Hegemony: Who's Dominating Whom?*

Deirdre Straughan

Deirdre Straughan posted this on her blog, Countries Beginning with I, in 2005.

A popular meme in American consciousness is cultural hegemony: the idea that American culture, as represented in widely exported American movies, TV shows, fast-food restaurants, and brands, is overwhelming the traditional cultures of other countries. The fear is that this will eventually result in a sadly homogenized world in which everyone abandons their own customary foods and entertainments to eat at McDonald's and listen to hip hop.

This theory seems to be popular on both sides of America's own cultural divide. The liberal left worries that we are teaching the rest of the world to be destructively, mindlessly capitalistic and individualistic. A more conservative viewpoint worries that we are "exporting the wrong picture" of America, an argument propounded by Martha Bayles of Boston College in a *Washington Post* editorial.

There are two problems with this theory.

The first is that it's arrogant. It is true that American popular culture is widely consumed worldwide. This is not simply because American media companies are good at selling their products—no one is forcing people to watch American shows. In many countries, local cinemas and TV stations show American stuff because their customers want to see it. Some governments work hard to censor what their people see, for political or religious/cultural reasons (or both). Nonetheless, their citizens often go to great lengths, sometimes breaking the law, to obtain and consume American media. It's not being forced on them by those evil capitalists in Hollywood.

The cultural hegemony argument is also a subtle put-down of other cultures: 5 it assumes that they are so weak or ignorant that they cannot be trusted to decide for themselves what they should see and hear. That these people should, "for their own good," be protected from invasive American culture, so that their "native" cultures will be preserved.

(Aside: Preserved for what? As a quaint playground for American tourists who want the "authentic" experience when they travel in other countries?)

The second problem with the theory of cultural hegemony is that it's simply not true. I've been in many parts of the world and, while you do see signs of American/Western culture everywhere, most people value their own cultures and work actively to preserve them, consuming local media, food, etc. alongside whatever foreign stuff they like.

India is a great example of a society which needs no special measures to preserve its traditional culture—unlike, say, France (said she mischievously). Indians love TV, and have plenty of it: at least two or three channels for every major language (of which India has 14 or 15, including English), and at least one each for Muslims, Christians, Jains, and Sikhs (probably Buddhists as well, though I didn't see this), plus one for each of the major branches of Hinduism. In addition to news and worship, there are channels dedicated to Indian-produced TV series and movies, and channels of Indian music videos. A few channels show imported TV, movies, and music, plus CNN International/Asia and BBC World, but these are vastly outnumbered by local fare—no case to be made there for Western culture overwhelming India! Which is hardly surprising: India has been absorbing and subsuming foreign cultures for 3000 years.

If there's any cultural invasion going on, it's occurring in the opposite direction. A number of Indian directors are doing well in Hollywood, some with films you can't tell apart from any other Hollywood product (M. Night Shyamalan), others bringing Indian or cross-cultural themes to Western audiences (Gurinder Chadha), and/or adding Indian spice to otherwise Hollywood-standard movies (Mira Nair's *Vanity Fair*).

There's a growing presence of American brands in India, but that doesn't 10 mean that Indians are adapting to American tastes. Reading a women's magazine in Mumbai, I saw an ad for a very familiar American brand, Pillsbury. Attempting to sell devil's food cake mix in India, you wonder? Nope. The ad was for a rice flour mix that could be used to make *dosas*, *idlis*, and *vadas*—distinctly south Indian treats. I'd be surprised if that product ever got to the U.S., and I didn't see any ads for Pillsbury brownie mix or refrigerator cookies in India. American companies, far from trying to foist American tastes on Indians, are studying the local market and adapting their products accordingly. You don't get to be a global brand by expecting everyone to like what Americans like—as most American multinationals are keenly aware, even if the American general public is not.

So, the next time you get worried about American culture taking over the world, look around you. If you can't get to a foreign country to see what's actually happening there, just look at your American hometown: how many "ethnic" restaurants do you have? And what is American culture itself, but a rich soup of the many cultures that Americans originally came from?

It's not just Americans who buy into the "American cultural behemoth" myth: UNESCO has recently passed a resolution supporting nations' rights to set a protected percentage of "local culture" to be shown in cinemas and aired on TV. Several nations have such laws, which Hollywood has been protesting as protectionist.

Questions

1. How does Deirdre Straughan define cultural hegemony? What are the two problems she sees with the "theory" of cultural hegemony?

2. How does Straughan use India as an example of a country that has preserved its heritage? Do you find it convincing? Explain your response.

3. How does Straughan argue that cultural hegemony is going "in the opposite direction" (para. 9)?

4. from *The Case for Contamination*

Kwame Anthony Appiah

The following is Part 1 of an article that appeared in the *New York Times Magazine* in 2006. Appiah is a professor of philosophy at Princeton.

I'm seated, with my mother, on a palace veranda, cooled by a breeze from the royal garden. Before us, on a dais, is an empty throne, its arms and legs embossed with polished brass, the back and seat covered in black-and-gold silk. In front of the steps to the dais, there are two columns of people, mostly men, facing one another, seated on carved wooden stools, the cloths they wear wrapped around their chests, leaving their shoulders bare. There is a quiet buzz of conversation. Outside in the garden, peacocks screech. At last, the blowing of a ram's horn announces the arrival of the king of Asante, its tones sounding his honorific, *kotokohene*, "porcupine chief." (Each quill of the porcupine, according to custom, signifies a warrior ready to kill and to die for the kingdom.) Everyone stands until the king has settled on the throne. Then, when we sit, a chorus sings songs in praise of him, which are interspersed with the playing of a flute. It is a Wednesday festival day in Kumasi, the town in Ghana where I grew up.

Unless you're one of a few million Ghanaians, this will probably seem a relatively unfamiliar world, perhaps even an exotic one. You might suppose that this Wednesday festival belongs quaintly to an African past. But before the king arrived, people were taking calls on cellphones, and among those passing the time in quiet conversation were a dozen men in suits, representatives of an insurance company. And the meetings in the office next to the veranda are about contemporary issues: H.I.V./AIDS, the educational needs of 21st-century children, the teaching of science and technology at the local university. When my turn comes to be formally presented, the king asks me about Princeton, where I teach. I ask him when he'll next be in the States. In a few weeks, he says cheerfully. He's got a meeting with the head of the World Bank.

Anywhere you travel in the world — today as always — you can find ceremonies like these, many of them rooted in centuries-old traditions. But you will also find everywhere — and this is something new — many intimate connections with places far away: Washington, Moscow, Mexico City, Beijing. Across the street from us, when we were growing up, there was a large house occupied by a number of families, among them a vast family of boys; one, about my age, was a good friend. He lives in London. His brother lives in Japan, where his wife is from. They have another brother who has been in Spain for a while and a couple more brothers who, last I heard, were in the United States. Some of them still live in Kumasi, one or two in Accra, Ghana's capital. Eddie, who lives in Japan, speaks his wife's language now. He has to. But he was never very comfortable in English, the language of our government and our schools. When he phones me from time to time, he prefers to speak Asante-Twi.

Over the years, the royal palace buildings in Kumasi have expanded. When I was a child, we used to visit the previous king, my great-uncle by marriage, in a small building that the British had allowed his predecessor to build when he returned from exile in the Seychelles to a restored but diminished Asante kingship. That building is now a museum, dwarfed by the enormous house next door—built by his successor, my uncle by marriage—where the current king lives. Next to it is the suite of offices abutting the veranda where we were sitting, recently finished by the present king, my uncle's successor. The British, my mother's people, conquered Asante at the turn of the 20th century; now, at the turn of the 21st, the palace feels as it must have felt in the 19th century: a center of power. The president of Ghana comes from this world, too. He was born across the street from the palace to a member of the royal Oyoko clan. But he belongs to other worlds as well: he went to Oxford University; he's a member of one of the Inns of Court in London; he's a Catholic, with a picture of himself greeting the pope in his sitting room.

What are we to make of this? On Kumasi's Wednesday festival day, I've seen   5
visitors from England and the United States wince at what they regard as the intrusion of modernity on timeless, traditional rituals—more evidence, they think, of a pressure in the modern world toward uniformity. They react like the assistant on the film set who's supposed to check that the extras in a sword-and-sandals movie aren't wearing wristwatches. And such purists are not alone. In the past couple of years, Unesco's members have spent a great deal of time trying to hammer out a convention on the "protection and promotion" of cultural diversity. (It was finally approved at the Unesco General Conference in October 2005.) The drafters worried that "the processes of globalization . . . represent a challenge for cultural diversity, namely in view of risks of imbalances between rich and poor countries." The fear is that the values and images of Western mass culture, like some invasive weed, are threatening to choke out the world's native flora.

The contradictions in this argument aren't hard to find. This same Unesco document is careful to affirm the importance of the free flow of ideas, the freedom of thought and expression and human rights—values that, we know, will become universal only if we make them so. What's really important, then, cultures or people? In a world where Kumasi and New York—and Cairo and Leeds and Istanbul—are being drawn ever closer together, an ethics of globalization has proved elusive.

The right approach, I think, starts by taking individuals—not nations, tribes or "peoples"—as the proper object of moral concern. It doesn't much matter what we call such a creed, but in homage to Diogenes, the fourth-century Greek Cynic and the first philosopher to call himself a "citizen of the world," we could call it cosmopolitan. Cosmopolitans take cultural difference seriously, because they take the choices individual people make seriously. But because cultural difference is not the only thing that concerns them, they suspect that many of globalization's cultural critics are aiming at the wrong targets.

Yes, globalization can produce homogeneity. But globalization is also a threat to homogeneity. You can see this as clearly in Kumasi as anywhere. One thing Kumasi isn't—simply because it's a city—is homogeneous. English, German, Chinese, Syrian, Lebanese, Burkinabe, Ivorian, Nigerian, Indian: I can find you families of each description. I can find you Asante people, whose ancestors have lived in this town for centuries, but also Hausa households that have been around for centuries, too. There are people there from every region of the country as well, speaking scores of languages. But if you travel just a little way outside Kumasi— 20 miles, say, in the right direction—and if you drive off the main road down one of the many potholed side roads of red laterite, you won't have difficulty finding villages that are fairly monocultural. The people have mostly been to Kumasi and seen the big, polyglot, diverse world of the city. Where they live, though, there is one everyday language (aside from the English in the government schools) and an agrarian way of life based on some old crops, like yams, and some newer ones, like cocoa, which arrived in the late 19th century as a product for export. They may or may not have electricity. (This close to Kumasi, they probably do.) When people talk of the homogeneity produced by globalization, what they are talking about is this: Even here, the villagers will have radios (though the language will be local); you will be able to get a discussion going about Ronaldo, Mike Tyson or Tupac; and you will probably be able to find a bottle of Guinness or Coca-Cola (as well as of Star or Club, Ghana's own fine lagers). But has access to these things made the place more homogeneous or less? And what can you tell about people's souls from the fact that they drink Coca-Cola?

It's true that the enclaves of homogeneity you find these days—in Asante as in Pennsylvania—are less distinctive than they were a century ago, but mostly in good ways. More of them have access to effective medicines. More of them have access to clean drinking water, and more of them have schools. Where, as is still too common, they don't have these things, it's something not to celebrate but to deplore. And whatever loss of difference there has been, they are constantly inventing new forms of difference: new hairstyles, new slang, even, from time to time, new religions. No one could say that the world's villages are becoming anything like the same.

So why do people in these places sometimes feel that their identities are threatened? Because the world, their world, is changing, and some of them don't like it. The pull of the global economy—witness those cocoa trees, whose chocolate is eaten all around the world—created some of the life they now live. If chocolate prices were to collapse again, as they did in the early 1990's, Asante farmers might have to find new crops or new forms of livelihood. That prospect is unsettling for some people (just as it is exciting for others). Missionaries came a while ago, so many of these villagers will be Christian, even if they have also kept some of the rites from earlier days. But new Pentecostal messengers are challenging the churches they know and condemning the old rites as idolatrous. Again, some like it; some don't.

Above all, relationships are changing. When my father was young, a man in a village would farm some land that a chief had granted him, and his maternal clan (including his younger brothers) would work it with him. When a new house needed building, he would organize it. He would also make sure his dependents were fed and clothed, the children educated, marriages and funerals arranged and paid for. He could expect to pass the farm and the responsibilities along to the next generation.

Nowadays, everything is different. Cocoa prices have not kept pace with the cost of living. Gas prices have made the transportation of the crop more expensive. And there are new possibilities for the young in the towns, in other parts of the country and in other parts of the world. Once, perhaps, you could have commanded the young ones to stay. Now they have the right to leave — perhaps to seek work at one of the new data-processing centers down south in the nation's capital — and, anyway, you may not make enough to feed and clothe and educate them all. So the time of the successful farming family is passing, and those who were settled in that way of life are as sad to see it go as American family farmers are whose lands are accumulated by giant agribusinesses. We can sympathize with them. But we cannot force their children to stay in the name of protecting their authentic culture, and we cannot afford to subsidize indefinitely thousands of distinct islands of homogeneity that no longer make economic sense.

Nor should we want to. Human variety matters, cosmopolitans think, because people are entitled to options. What John Stuart Mill said more than a century ago in "On Liberty" about diversity within a society serves just as well as an argument for variety across the globe: "If it were only that people have diversities of taste, that is reason enough for not attempting to shape them all after one model. But different persons also require different conditions for their spiritual development; and can no more exist healthily in the same moral, than all the variety of plants can exist in the same physical, atmosphere and climate. The same things which are helps to one person towards the cultivation of his higher nature, are hindrances to another. . . . Unless there is a corresponding diversity in their modes of life, they neither obtain their fair share of happiness, nor grow up to the mental, moral, and aesthetic stature of which their nature is capable." If we want to preserve a wide range of human conditions because it allows free people the best chance to make their own lives, we can't enforce diversity by trapping people within differences they long to escape.

Questions

1. What does Kwame Anthony Appiah's opening anecdote illustrate? How does it help him develop his argument?
2. What does Appiah think is the right approach to the ethics of globalization?
3. How does Appiah define "cosmopolitanism"? To what principles is the cosmopolitan committed?

4. Read the quote from John Stuart Mill in the last paragraph of this selection. Why does Appiah use it to characterize the way cosmopolitans think?

5. *The Perils of Soft Power*

JOSEF JOFFE

The following piece, by German newspaper publisher Josef Joffe, appeared in the *New York Times* in 2006.

In recent years, a number of American thinkers, led by Joseph S. Nye Jr. of Harvard, have argued that the United States should rely more on what he calls its "soft power"—the contagious appeal of its ideas, its culture and its way of life—and so rely less on the "hard power" of its stealth bombers and aircraft carriers. There is one problem with this argument: soft power does not necessarily increase the world's love for America. It is still power, and it can still make enemies.

America's soft power isn't just pop and schlock; its cultural clout is both high and low. It is grunge and Google, Madonna and MoMA, Hollywood and Harvard. If two-thirds of the movie marquees carry an American title in Europe (even in France), dominance is even greater when it comes to translated books. The figure for Germany in 2003 was 419 versus 3,732; that is, for every German book translated into English, nine English-language books were translated into German. It used to be the other way around. A hundred years ago, Humboldt University in Berlin was the model for the rest of the world. Tokyo, Johns Hopkins, Stanford and the University of Chicago were founded in conscious imitation of the German university and its novel fusion of teaching and research. Today Europe's universities have lost their luster, and as they talk reform, they talk American. Indeed, America is one huge global "demonstration effect," as the sociologists call it. The Soviet Union's cultural presence in Prague, Budapest and Warsaw vanished into thin air the moment the last Russian soldier departed. American culture, however, needs no gun to travel.

There may be little or no relationship between America's ubiquity and its actual influence. Hundreds of millions of people around the world wear, listen, eat, drink, watch and dance American, but they do not identify these accouterments of their daily lives with America. A Yankees cap is the epitome of things American, but it hardly signifies knowledge of, let alone affection for, the team from New York or America as such.

The same is true for American films, foods or songs. Of the 250 top-grossing movies around the world, only four are foreign-made: "The Full Monty" (U.K.), "Life Is Beautiful" (Italy) and "Spirited Away" and "Howl's Moving Castle" (Japan); the rest are American, including a number of co-productions. But these American products shape images, not sympathies, and there is little, if any, relationship between artifact and affection.

If the relationship is not neutral, it is one of repulsion rather than attrac- 5
tion—the dark side of the "soft power" coin. The European student movement
of the late 1960's took its cue from the Berkeley free-speech movement of 1964,
the inspiration for all post-1964 Western student revolts. But it quickly turned
anti-American; America was reviled while it was copied.

Now shift forward to the Cannes Film Festival of 2004, where hundreds of
protesters denounced America's intervention in Iraq until the police dispersed
them. The makers of the movie *Shrek 2* had placed large bags of green Shrek ears
along the Croisette, the main drag along the beach. As the demonstrators scattered, many of them put on free Shrek ears. "They were attracted," noted an
observer in this magazine, "by the ears' goofiness and sheer recognizability." And
so the enormous pull of American imagery went hand in hand with the country's,
or at least its government's, condemnation.

Between Vietnam and Iraq, America's cultural presence has expanded into
ubiquity, and so has the resentment of America's soft power. In some cases, like
the French one, these feelings harden into governmental policy. And so the French
have passed the Toubon law, which prohibits on pain of penalty the use of English
words—make that D.J. into a disque-tourneur. In 1993, the French coaxed the
European Union into adding a "cultural exception" clause to its commercial treaties exempting cultural products, high or low, from normal free-trade rules.
Other European nations impose informal quotas on American TV fare.

Nor is America's high culture more easily accepted than its pop—at least not
by the cultural elites. A fine example is how the art critics of two distinguished
German newspapers, *Süddeutsche Zeitung* (leftish) and *Frankfurter Allgemeine
Zeitung* (centrist), dealt with an exhibit of 200 pieces from the Museum of Modern Art in Berlin in 2004. More than a million visitors stood in line, many for up
to nine hours, to view the objets from across the Atlantic. Yet the fervor of the
hoi polloi mattered little to their betters, whose comments ran the gamut from
contempt to conspiracy.

The opening shots were fired by the *Süddeutsche Zeitung* of Munich. Without having seen the collection, its critic aimed his volley straight against imperial America. Regurgitating a standard piece of European ressentiment, the
author insinuated that what America has in the way of culture is not haute, and
what is haute is not American. (Or as Adolf Hitler is said to have declared, "A
single Beethoven symphony contains more culture than all that America has ever
created.")

After World War II, the critic contended, America had wrested "artistic hege- 10
mony" from Europe in two sleazy ways. One culprit was "a new abstract school of
painting"—Abstract Expressionism—"that had hyped itself into high heaven."
The other was American mammon: "Everything still available in old Europe was
bought up." And this "stolen idea of modern art will now be presented in Berlin."
Thus were pilferage and grand theft added to the oldest of indictments: America's
cultural inferiority.

The critic of *Frankfurter Allgemeine* went one worse. If his colleague claimed that America's art was either hyped or heisted, the man from Frankfurt thundered that MoMA's Berlin show was a mendacious ploy, indeed, an imperialist conspiracy. It was done by "concealment" and "censorship" in a game full of "marked cards," and its aim was not only to blank out Europe's greats but also to suppress their magnificent contribution to American art in the second half of the 20th century. This was an instance of the selective perception that suffuses anti-Americanism or any other "anti-ism," for the exhibit contained an impressive number of European works: Matisse, Picasso, Manet, Rousseau, Brancusi and Mondrian, plus assorted Expressionists and Surrealists.

That did not count. What about contemporary Germans like Beuys, Baselitz and Kiefer? the critic huffed. But even here, MoMA had done its duty, capping the progression with Gerhard Richter's "18 October 1977" cycle, which depicts dead members of the Baader-Meinhof terrorist gang. That MoMA would display these German works enraged the feuilletoniste from Frankfurt even more. That particular choice, he fumed, was the final proof of American perfidy. The terrorist motif was insidiously selected to finger Europe as a "creepy" place, as a messenger of "bad news."

There is a moral in this tale of two critics: the curse of soft power. In the affairs of nations, too much hard power ends up breeding not submission but resistance. Likewise, great soft power does not bend hearts; it twists minds in resentment and rage. And the target of Europe's cultural guardians is not just America, the Great Seductress. It is also all those "little people," a million in all, many of whom showed up in the wee hours to snag an admissions ticket to MoMA's Berlin exhibit. By yielding to America-the-beguiling, they committed cultural treason—and worse: they ignored the stern verdict of their own priesthood. So America's soft power is not only seductive but also subversive.

Hard power can be defanged by coalitions and alliances. But how do you balance against soft power? No confederation of European universities can dethrone Harvard and Stanford. Neither can all the subsidies fielded by European governments crack the hegemony of Hollywood. To breach the bastions of American soft power, the Europeans will first have to imitate, then improve on, the American model. Imitation and leapfrogging is the oldest game in the history of nations.

But competition has barely begun to drive the cultural contest. Europe, mourning the loss of its centuries-old supremacy, either resorts to insulation (by quotas and "cultural exception" clauses) or seeks solace in the disparagement of American culture as vulgar, inauthentic or stolen. If we could consult Dr. Freud, he would take a deep drag on his cigar and pontificate about inferiority feelings being compensated by hauteur and denigration.

Questions

1. According to Josef Joffe, what is the difference between "soft power" and "hard power" (para. 1)?
2. What does Joffe think is the "curse of soft power" (para. 13)?
3. How does Joffe think Europeans can "crack the hegemony of Hollywood" (para. 14)?

6. *The U.S. Can Reclaim "Smart Power"*

Joseph S. Nye Jr.

The following piece by political scientist Joseph S. Nye Jr. appeared in the op-ed section of the *Los Angeles Times* in 2009.

President Obama reminded us Tuesday that "our power grows through its prudent use; our security emanates from the justness of our cause, the force of our example, the tempering qualities of humility and restraint." A week ago, in her confirmation hearings to become Secretary of State, Hillary Rodham Clinton said: "America cannot solve the most pressing problems on our own, and the world cannot solve them without America. . . . We must use what has been called 'smart power,' the full range of tools at our disposal."

Smart power is the combination of hard and soft power. Soft power is the ability to get what you want through attraction rather than coercion or payments. Opinion polls show a serious decline in American attractiveness in Europe, Latin America and, most dramatically, the Muslim world.

The resources that produce soft power for a country include its culture (when it is attractive to others), its values (when they are attractive and not undercut by inconsistent practices) and policies (when they are seen as inclusive and legitimate).

When poll respondents are asked why they report a decline in American soft power, they cite American policies more than American culture or values. Because it is easier for a country to change its policies than its culture, this implies that Obama will be able to choose policies that could help to recover some of America's soft power.

Of course, soft power is not the solution to all problems. North Korean dictator Kim Jong Il likes to watch Hollywood movies, but that is unlikely to affect his nuclear weapons program. And soft power got nowhere in attracting the Taliban government away from its support for Al Qaeda in the 1990s. That took hard military power in 2001. But other goals, such as the promotion of democracy and human rights, are better achieved by soft power.

A little more than a year ago, the bipartisan Center for Strategic and International Studies' Commission on Smart Power concluded that America's image

5

and influence had declined in recent years, and that the U.S. had to move from exporting fear to inspiring optimism and hope.

The commission was not alone in this conclusion. Defense Secretary Robert M. Gates has called for the U.S. to commit more money and effort to soft-power tools, including diplomacy, economic assistance and communications, because the military alone cannot defend U.S. interests. He pointed out that military spending totals nearly half a trillion dollars annually—excluding Iraq and Afghanistan—compared with a State Department budget of $36 billion. In his words: "I am here to make the case for strengthening our capacity to use soft power and for better integrating it with hard power."

The Pentagon is the best resourced arm of the government, but there are limits to what hard power can achieve on its own. Promoting democracy, human rights and the development of civil society are not best handled with the barrel of a gun. The effects of the 9/11 terrorist attacks threw America off course. Terrorism is a real threat, but over-responding to the provocations of extremists does us more damage than the terrorists ever could. Success in the struggle against terrorism means finding a new central premise for U.S. foreign policy to replace the "war on terror." A commitment to providing for the global good can provide that premise.

America can become a smart America—a smart power—by again investing in global public goods, providing things people and governments of the world want but have not been able to get in the absence of leadership by the strongest country. Development, public health and coping with climate change are good examples. By complementing U.S. military and economic might with greater investments in soft power, and focusing on global public goods, the U.S. can rebuild the framework that it needs to tackle tough global challenges.

Style also matters. In 2001, columnist Charles Krauthammer argued for what he called "a new unilateralism," which recognized that the United States was the only superpower and was so strong that it could decide what was right and expect others to follow because they had little choice. But this style turned out to be counterproductive. Insensitivity to style and the perception of others can undercut soft-power efforts.   10

Obama faces a difficult international environment, but previous presidents have managed to employ hard, soft and smart power in equally difficult contexts. In 1970, during the Vietnam War, America was viewed as unattractive in many parts of the world, but with changed policies and the passage of time, the United States managed to recover its soft power. It can happen again.

Questions

1. How does Joseph Nye Jr. define "smart power"?
2. What recommendation does Nye offer President Obama?
3. What "global public goods" (para. 9) does Nye recommend investing in?

4. What additional recommendations does Nye offer for how the United States can recover its soft power?

7. *Slovakian Soccer Fan at 2010 World Cup in South Africa*

HASSAN AMMAR

This Associated Press photo taken by Hassan Ammar was posted on the *New York Daily News* Web site. Taken during the 2010 World Cup in South Africa, the photo shows a Slovakian fan in a Dracula mask blowing on the South African soccer horn, or vuvuzela.

(See insert for color version.)

Questions

1. How many different cultures can you account for in this photo?
2. Why might this photo have appeared on the Web site of a New York daily newspaper?
3. Do you think the image reinforces or challenges the notion that American pop culture is a dominant force in the world, supplanting traditional cultures? Explain your answer.

Making Connections

1. What would Kwame Anthony Appiah think of Thomas L. Friedman's five gas stations theory? What additional gas station scenarios might he imagine? Which ones might he eliminate?

2. How might Josef Joffe or Joseph Nye Jr. respond to the problem that Heather Havrilesky raises about the portrayal of the Muslim world in American media?

3. What would Deirdre Straughan make of the photo of the Slovakian fan in the Dracula mask? Does it support or challenge her argument? Explain.

4. Friedman says that in "most societies people cannot distinguish anymore among American power, American exports, American cultural assaults, American cultural exports, and plain vanilla globalization" (para. 7). How would Josef Joffe suggest distinguishing among them in order to give the United States the tools to lead?

5. Appiah says, "Yes, globalization can produce homogeneity. But globalization is also a threat to homogeneity" (para. 8). How might Friedman respond? What about Straughan?

Entering the Conversation

As you respond to the following prompts, support your argument with references to at least three sources in this Conversation on Exporting American Pop Culture. For help using sources, see Chapter 4.

1. Write an essay explaining why the export of American culture has either a positive or a negative effect on the cultures and societies that adopt it.

2. Access to the Internet is spreading throughout the world. What do you think America's role is in this medium? Write an essay in which you imagine the future of the Internet and its effects on "cosmopolitanism." Refer to at least three sources as you consider the effects of the possible spread of American popular culture through the Internet.

3. In the foreword to *Amusing Ourselves to Death*, media critic Neil Postman (1931–2003) suggests that the vision of Aldous Huxley's *Brave New World* (1932) turned out to be more terrifyingly true than the vision George Orwell created in *1984* (1949):

> What Orwell feared were those who would ban books. What Huxley feared was that there would be no reason to ban a book, for there would be no one who wanted to read one. Orwell feared those who would deprive us of information. Huxley feared

those who would give us so much that we would be reduced to passivity and egoism. Orwell feared that the truth would be concealed from us. Huxley feared the truth would be drowned in a sea of irrelevance. Orwell feared we would become a captive culture. Huxley feared we would become a trivial culture, preoccupied with some equivalent of the feelies, the orgy porgy, and the centrifugal bumblepuppy. As Huxley remarked in *Brave New World Revisited*, the civil libertarians and rationalists who are ever on the alert to oppose tyranny "failed to take into account man's almost infinite appetite for distractions." In *1984*, Huxley added, people are controlled by inflicting pain. In *Brave New World*, they are controlled by inflicting pleasure. In short, Orwell feared that what we hate will ruin us. Huxley feared that what we love will ruin us.

Write an essay explaining the extent to which you believe the export of American popular culture has proven Postman right or wrong. Refer to at least three sources.

4. Using the arguments and evidence in this Conversation, answer the following question in an essay: Should countries adopt policies that limit cultural imperialism in order to preserve cultures?

Student Writing
Rhetorical Analysis: Analyzing Satire

The following prompt asks students to comment on an article in the *Onion*, a satirical online magazine.

The following is a mock feature article from the *Onion*, a publication devoted to humor and satire. Read the piece carefully. Then write an essay in which you analyze the strategies used in the article to satirize common ideas about art and the Renaissance.

Four or Five Guys Pretty Much Carry Whole Renaissance

The Onion

Following 1,000 years of cultural decline and societal collapse known as the Dark Ages, the 15th century brought forth the Renaissance, an unprecedented resurgence in learning and the arts, which four or five guys pretty much just strapped onto their backs and carried the whole way.

"Our research indicates that da Vinci, Michelangelo, Shakespeare, and Galileo basically hoisted the entire intellectual transformation of mankind onto their shoulders while everyone else just sat around being superstitious nimrods," said Sue Viero of the Correr Museum of Art in Venice, Italy. "Here's da Vinci busting his ass to paint such masterpieces as *The Last Supper* and the *Mona Lisa*, while some loser like Albrecht Dürer is doing these dinky little woodcuts that are basically worthless.

"And how pathetic is it that Masaccio wasted so much time churning out his frescoes that barely revolutionized linear perspective or naturalism at all, when without Michelangelo's *David*, we wouldn't even have a Renaissance to begin with?" Viero added. "Honestly, it's not even friggin' close."

According to modern thought on the era, contributors to the Renaissance can be broken into two distinct groups: the brilliant few who, day in and day out, were thrusting society out of the depths of darkness and into the light of learning; and the rest of the so-called artists, mathematicians, and scientists, who were mostly all phoning it in.

Among those considered by historians not to have pulled their weight are Sandro Botticelli, Hugo van der Goes, Titian, and Italian humanist and total hanger-on Pico della Mirandola.

"So, Pico's most famous philosophical work was *Oration on the Dignity of Man*," scoffed Harvard philosophy professor Richard Nostrand. "I mean, come on. Compare that to Thomas More's *Utopia* for — actually, you know what? Don't bother. Because you can't."

While some claim the three-century-long movement would not have been possible without the contributions of lesser-known sculptors and thinkers, most scholars said they would challenge anyone to name an image by Jan van Eyck or Francesco Guicciardini that's more iconic than, say, Donatello's *Mary Magdalene*.

"It's a no-brainer, really," cultural anthropologist Diane Messinick said. "Mediocre talents like the playwright George Peele or renowned court painter Federico Brandani were pretty much the equivalent of the guy at work who brews a fresh pot of coffee while you're busy making sure there's still a company to come back to after everyone gets back from goddamn Christmas break."

Rhetorical Analysis

Camille LeMeur

The title of this mock feature article from the *Onion*, "Four or Five Guys Pretty Much Carry Whole Renaissance," speaks for itself. It's outrageous. But just in case such an absurd claim wasn't enough to tip us off on the fact that this article is, indeed, a satire, the author uses other means to convey the idea. A series of historical inaccuracies, added to the fact that the article pokes fun at even the most renowned artists, satirizes common ideas about the Renaissance and ultimately condemns the readers' ignorance.

This article is based on a plethora of historical inaccuracies, ranging from sweeping generalizations to erroneous details. It starts off by stating that the Middle Ages were a time of "cultural decline and societal collapse," which is a specious argument. Medieval schools of art or universities, like those we now know as Oxford and Cambridge, were clear precursors of the Renaissance. The article then states that all artists were "superstitious nimrods." Again, this is false. Putting aside the derogatory substitution of "religious" for "superstitious," the fact is that not all artists were imbued with religion. Raphael Sanzio, for instance, was an atheist, which was quite a revolutionary (not to mention worthy of persecution) notion for his time. Far from acting like "nimrods," these artists innovated and challenged social standards. The article then goes on to say that Masaccio "barely revolutionized linear perspective," when Masaccio was the first artist to use linear perspective in painting. Of course, he didn't revolutionize the technique in the sense that he *introduced* it. Likewise, Pico della Mirandola, one of the most sought-after philosophers of his time, is called a "hanger-on," a parasite, as if he hadn't been supported by Lorenzo de' Medici, one of the most significant patrons in the history of Italy. Through this deliberate accumulation of mistakes, the article satirizes common ideas about the Renaissance. Packing all of these stereotypes into a few neat paragraphs leads the readers to realize the absurdity of their oversimplified opinions.

Still, it's possible that ignorant people reading an article satirizing their ignorance may not detect the irony. This is why the article, in addition to making intentional historical errors, also pokes fun at the most renowned artists. The artists we supposedly owe the whole Renaissance to seemed to be making a huge physical effort. They "strapped onto their backs and carried the whole way," "hoisted (. . .) onto their shoulders," "[thrust] society," "pulled their weight." All of these metaphors suggest manual labor, physical effort, and a peasant's life rather than an intellectual's. This is a subtle way of ridiculing the "four or five" artists the article puts on a pedestal. See, I know Da Vinci conceptualized an Ornithopter, but I have yet to see him build it, let alone fly it. Here, the discrepancy between intellectualism and physical labor highlights the satire. One artist, Donatello, is specifically mocked. We see this because two pseudo-experts contradict themselves. While one debases Dürer's "dinky little woodcuts," another praises Donatello's *Mary Magdalene*, an equally drab-looking statue that is no less sculpted in wood. This paradox is another not-so-subtle hint to the readers. Who knows? If they can't figure out that the article is historically inaccurate, maybe they'll catch on to the fact that artists weren't peasants, or maybe even that the article is mocking the very people it is glorifying.

And ultimately, the article's goal is to criticize the readers' lack of knowledge. This is most obvious in the tone of the article. The disparity between the register we expect to find and the one the speaker uses is what first strikes us as readers. One wouldn't expect a curator to say that an artist "[isn't] even friggin' close," or that he's "phoning it in," and especially not in a scholarly article. Simplistic adverbs like "basically" and "pretty much" are repeated to show that the article is merely making things easier for its readers. This language discredits the contents of the article. In this way, the article denounces its readers' ignorance. You believe Renaissance stereotypes? Well, so do we! In fact, we're rounding this up for you and summarizing it in the most basic of terms so we're sure you'll understand. When using a term like "loser," the article is flat-out saying that its readers can't understand terms a bit more intricate than colloquial jargon. The fact that the readers are being addressed in this way is the final indication of satire.

This article satirizes common ideas about the Renaissance by giving deliberately inaccurate historical facts, and by mocking the very artists it praises. Above all, it does this to criticize its readers' ignorance. They are addressed as possibly dim-witted creatures in the hopes that, when faced with a satire of their beliefs, they become aware of how ignorant and ridiculous these beliefs are.

Questions

1. What are this essay's strengths? Explain.
2. How would you characterize Camille's tone? Do you think it's appropriate for the subject? Explain your reasons.
3. This essay is written in the third person. How would the use of *I* have strengthened or weakened the essay?
4. How did the use of independent research help Camille develop her argument?

Grammar as Rhetoric and Style
Modifiers

A modifier may be a one-word adverb or adjective; a phrase, such as a prepositional phrase or a participial phrase; or a clause, such as an adjective clause. At its best, a modifier describes, focuses, or qualifies the nouns, pronouns, and verbs it modifies. But when a writer overuses or incorrectly uses modifiers, the result may be verbose or even flowery writing.

Here is how David Denby describes the "most hated young woman in America" in "High-School Confidential: Notes on Teen Movies":

> a blonde—well, sometimes a redhead or a brunette, but usually a blonde. She has big hair flipped into a swirl of gold at one side of her face or arrayed in a sultry mane. . . .

> She's tall and slender, with a waist as supple as a willow, but she's dressed in awful, spangled taste.

These sentences include single-word adjectives (*sultry, tall, slender, supple, awful, spangled*), a participle followed by two prepositional phrases (*flipped into a swirl of gold*), and several other prepositional phrases (*at one side of her face; in a sultry mane; with a waist . . . ; in awful, spangled taste*). When we call attention to all of them like this, the modification may seem heavy, but in the passage itself, all the modifiers do *not* amount to overkill because Denby paces them.

Let's look more closely at another Denby sentence with a participial phrase as a modifier:

> Sprawling and dull in class, he comes alive in the halls and in the cafeteria.

Here Denby has essentially combined two sentences: "He is sprawling and dull in class. He comes alive in the halls and in the cafeteria." The result is a smoother, single sentence that focuses on the difference between the subject's behavior in and out of class.

In Chuck Klosterman's "My Zombie, Myself: Why Modern Life Feels Rather Undead," the author uses key single-word adverbs to create his distinctive voice. Look at *Rather* in the title, for example. Look also at this passage:

> In other words, zombie killing is philosophically similar to reading and deleting 400 work e-mails on a Monday morning or filling out paperwork that only generates more paperwork, or following Twitter gossip out of obligation, or performing tedious tasks in which the only true risk is being consumed by the avalanche.

The juxtaposition of *philosophically* and *zombie killing* is a good example of how Klosterman comments on an aspect of modern life through popular culture. The mock seriousness is a hallmark of his style.

Rhetorical and Stylistic Strategy

Modifiers can enliven, focus, and qualify ideas. The *placement* of modifiers can add to or detract from these effects. Note the following example by Denby.

> Physically awkward, she walks like a seal crossing a beach, and is prone to drop her books and dither in terror when she stands before a handsome boy.

The modifiers that describe the girl gather steam, and finally, in a prepositional phrase at the end of the sentence, they contrast her with the handsome boy. Note the different effect if the handsome boy comes into the sentence before the awkward girl drops her books and dithers:

> When she stands before the handsome boy, physically awkward, she walks like a seal crossing a beach, and is prone to drop her books and dither in terror.

Announcing the handsome boy early in the sentence undercuts the contrast between the girl and the boy that Denby wants to stress.

In the accompanying panel from page 140 in Scott McCloud's comic-book guide to reading comic books, note how the modifiers reinforce the changes in our reading habits that occur as we age. Note also the progression in the drawings: the very young boy in the first frame grows into the older man by the third; the narrator shows up in the fourth to finish his commentary. In addition to the drawings, McCloud has the advantage of the text's graphic flexibility: little punctuation besides dashes, and boldface and italics to stress certain words.

The first frame begins the progression with the modifier *as children* and describes picture books as having *pictures galore*. The second begins with *then*, showing time moving on, stressing text with *more* and minimizing pictures with *occasional*. The third places us *finally* as grown-ups, and our books have no pictures *at all*. Quite a switch from *galore*! In the last frame, McCloud's qualifier *perhaps* suggests further ruin in the future: *sadly . . . no **books** at all*.

Consider the effect of the modifier *now* in this sentence from Mark Twain:

> We are conforming in the other way, now, because it is another case of everybody.

The placement of *now* in the middle of the sentence reinforces *the other way* and reminds us that Twain is making a point about the mercurial nature of public opinion.

Cautions

Studying how accomplished writers use modifiers helps us understand how to use them effectively. Following are some cautions to keep in mind when using modifiers in your own writing.

1. *Do not use too many modifiers.* David Denby gives a clear visual image of the evil high school cheerleader by using a variety of modifiers. However, less experienced writers may overwrite by including too many adjectives, as shown in the following example:

   > The bright yellow compact car with the pun-laden, out-of-state vanity plates was like beautiful, warm sunshine on the gray, dreary Tuesday afternoon.

2. *Do not rely on adjectives when strong verbs are more effective.* Instead of writing, "Elani walked with a confident and quick stride," perhaps say, "Elani strutted" or "Elani strode."

3. *Beware of adding too many qualifiers.* Be especially careful about *really* and *very*.

   - "Troy felt really sad" might be expressed as "Troy felt discouraged" or "despondent." Or it might simply be stated as "Troy felt sad."
   - Similarly, "The mockingbird's song is very beautiful" is probably just as well stated as "The mockingbird's song is beautiful" or, introducing a strong verb, as "The mockingbird serenades."

You need not avoid qualifiers altogether, but if you find yourself using them over and over, it's time to check whether they're *really very* effective.

• EXERCISE 1 •

Rewrite each of the following sentences to make the modifiers more effective.

1. Dolores offered a rather unique view of the situation.
2. I had difficulty understanding my teacher because he talked so quickly and softly.
3. Michael was so very excited about the beginning of lacrosse season that he could barely sleep.
4. Susan talked with self-assurance about movies she hadn't even seen.
5. The skyline was amazing on the beautiful evening.

• EXERCISE 2 •

Discuss the following passage from Daniel Harris's "Celebrity Bodies." Focus on the writer's use of modifiers. Look carefully at the adjectives Harris uses to describe our fascination with celebrity. Look also at the qualifiers he uses — *albeit, in turn, yet, at the same time* — and consider how they suit the purpose of the essay.

Western culture affords us many ways of denigrating the beautiful, branding them stupid, egotistic, lonely, and unhappy, and our constant, self-abasing surveillance of their every move, our prurient eavesdropping on their private lives, from their sex tapes to the messages they leave on each other's answering machines, may itself be a method of diminishing their psychological power. Much as Louis XIV used Versailles as a glittering cage to imprison restive nobles, so we have surrounded our idols with an impregnable phalanx of flashbulbs, herding them together in Hollywood, forcing them to live in a kind of internment camp, albeit one with all the amenities of a spa. The paparazzi, in turn, have become our watch dogs who never let them out of our sight, staking out their gyms, grocery stores, and nightclubs where they are forced to submit to our mean-spirited and yet, at the same time, obsequious espionage.

• EXERCISE 3 •

Identify the modifiers, both words and phrases, in the following paragraph from "An Image a Little Too Carefully Coordinated" by Robin Givhan. Are the modifiers effective, or are they excessive? Cite specific examples to support your view.

There they were — John, Jane, Josie and Jack — standing with the president and before the entire country. The nominee was in a sober suit with the expected white shirt and red tie. His wife and children stood before the cameras, groomed and glossy in pastel hues — like a trio of Easter eggs, a handful of Jelly Bellies, three little Necco wafers. There was tow-headed Jack — having freed himself from the controlling grip of his mother — enjoying a moment in the spotlight dressed in a seersucker suit with short pants and saddle shoes. His sister, Josie, was half-hidden behind her mother's skirt. Her blond pageboy glistened. And she was wearing a yellow dress with a crisp white collar, lace-trimmed anklets and black patent-leather Mary Janes.

• EXERCISE 4 •

Most of the modifiers have been removed from the following passage from "Hip Hop Planet" by James McBride.

Not since the advent of jazz in the 1930s has an American music exploded across the world with force. Not since the Beatles invaded America and Elvis packed up his shoes has a music crashed against the world with outrage. The culture of song, graffiti, and dance, known as hip hop, has ripped music from its moorings in society it has permeated.

- Read the paragraph aloud, and listen to its cadence (the combination of the text's rhythm with the rise and fall in the inflection of the speaker's voice).
- Add the following modifiers: *blue, overwhelming, suede, swing, such, defiant, popular, every, collectively.* Use them to improve the paragraph's effectiveness.
- Compare your version to the original (see para. 7, p. 789).
- Discuss the rhetorical effect of the modifiers in this passage.

• EXERCISE 5 •

Following are examples of authors' skillful use of modifiers, both single words and phrases. In each, identify the modifier or modifiers, and discuss the effect they create. Then write a sentence or passage of your own, emulating the writer's technique.

1. . . . I realize to my horror that rap—music seemingly without melody, sensibility, instruments, verse, or harmony, music with no beginning, end, or middle, music that doesn't even seem to be music—rules the world.

   — JAMES MCBRIDE

2. He's usually a football player, muscular but dumb, with a face like a beer mug and only two ways of speaking—in a conspiratorial whisper, to a friend; or in a drill sergeant's sudden bellow.

   — DAVID DENBY

3. Broadly speaking, there are none but corn-pone opinions. And broadly speaking, corn-pone stands for self-approval.

   — MARK TWAIN

4. Outside in the garden, peacocks screech.

   — KWAME ANTHONY APPIAH

5. The difference with zombies, of course, is that it's possible to like a specific vampire temporarily, which isn't really an option with the undead.

   — CHUCK KLOSTERMAN

6. On Jan. 24, the Fox network showed an episode of its hit drama *24*, the real-time thriller known for its cliffhanger tension and often-gruesome violence.

   — STEVEN JOHNSON

7. The ad was for a rice flour mix that could be used to make *dosas, idlis,* and *vadas*—distinctly south Indian treats.

   — DEIRDRE STRAUGHAN

Suggestions for Writing
Popular Culture

Now that you have examined a number of readings and other texts that focus on popular culture, explore one dimension of the topic by synthesizing your own ideas and the texts. You might want to do more research or use readings from other classes as you prepare for the following projects.

1. Read this statement by Daniel Harris from "Celebrity Bodies," and write an essay in which you support, challenge, or qualify his assertion that we would be better off trying to be like the celebrities we admire.

> Our fantasies engender a paralyzing awe that instills in us despair, a sense of hopelessness about maintaining our bodies, about achieving the buff perfections of stars spoon-fed by studio dieticians who force them to nibble on rice cakes and celery sticks and submit to grueling regimens of Pilates and kickboxing. In fact, we would almost certainly be healthier if we *did* imitate Hollywood, if we *did* work out and diet as compulsively as they do, if, like supermodel Dayle Haddon, we performed leg lifts while washing the dishes, side bends while standing in line at Starbucks, and thigh resistance exercises in the elevators of our four-star hotels.

2. In a paper entitled "Moral Pluck: Ethics in Popular Culture," Columbia Law School professor William H. Simon writes about the portrayal of lawyers in film and television. He notes:

> While elite moralism is strongly authoritarian and categorical, popular culture exalts a quality that might be called Moral Pluck — a combination of resourcefulness and transgression in the service of basic but informal values.

Consider the portrayals of professionals — in law, in medicine, in education — in popular culture. Do you agree with Simon that the ethics of popular culture are sometimes in conflict with traditional ethics? Write an essay defending your position on this question.

3. Each of the following statements addresses the subject of media. Select one that interests you, and write an essay that defends or challenges its assertion. To support your argument, refer to your own experience with media and to the selections in this chapter.

> The one function TV news performs very well is that when there is no news, we give it to you with the same emphasis as if there were.
>
> — DAVID BRINKLEY, American TV network news anchor

> Whoever controls the media — the images — controls the culture.
>
> — ALLEN GINSBERG, poet

> If you want to use television to teach somebody something, you have first to teach somebody how to use television.
>
> — UMBERTO ECO, philosopher

> Visual chaos is not good for anyone. Billboard companies should not be allowed to sell what they don't own — our field of vision and our civic pride.
>
> — MEG MAGUIRE, president, Scenic America

4. In his essay "High-School Confidential: Notes on Teen Movies" (p. 819), David Denby suggests that the teen movies from the turn of this century reflect the secret wishes — and geekiness — of their screenwriters and directors. Watch a movie about teens from an earlier time — *Rebel without a Cause* (1955) or *Splendor in the Grass* (1961), for example — and discuss what the film said about the filmmakers of the era.

5. In "Corn-Pone Opinions," Mark Twain distinguishes between fashion and standards. Is it the same as the difference, discussed on page 787, between what was once considered popular culture and high culture? Write about what you see as the difference between fashion and standards.

6. Write an essay in which you apply Steven Johnson's arguments about television (p. 827) to another form of popular culture, such as video games, movies, or music.

7. "Hip Hop Planet" by James McBride (p. 788) refers to several different genres of popular music. Listen to an assortment of songs by the artists mentioned in his piece. Make a CD of the music, and write some liner notes in which you explain why you chose the songs and how you decided on the order in which they appear.

8. Consider a pairing in which one medium has been adapted into a new one — books and video games made into movies, or movies made into live theater, for example. Write about how the remake was changed to suit the new medium and how the new medium honors the old.

9. Write a sermon using "Emily Dickinson and Elvis Presley in Heaven" (p. 850) as a starting point.

10. Write a review of a concert, album, movie, or graphic novel. Keep in mind that reviews are arguments either applauding artists, criticizing them, or both.

The Environment

What is our responsibility to the natural environment?

Throughout history we have tried to conquer the wilderness, tame the jungles, and master the elements, and we are still trying to conquer space. But are nature and humankind necessarily in conflict? We created civilization to protect us from the undesirable features of the outdoors and, to some degree, from harm. But now our experience of the natural world is so mediated that many of us know it only as it is presented on television or online. Has our relationship with nature changed so drastically that nature now exists *within* civilization, as contemporary naturalist Bill McKibben suggests? Do we now contain nature rather than being contained by it? How does our perspective on Ralph Waldo Emerson's classic essay "Nature" change now that nature is threatened? Can we balance human progress and economic well-being with environmental protection?

In recent years, humankind's attitude toward the natural world has changed. Before Rachel Carson and others began to alert us to the dangers of pollution, most people simply didn't think about the environment. And looking back over the last half century, it is hard to imagine what may be in store for us over the next fifty years. Are we yet to see the consequences of what we have already done to alter the environment?

Once the environment becomes something we have to protect, our fundamental relationship with our world changes. We're still dwarfed by the awesome power of nature, but if we are creating conditions that may change nature itself, whether through pollution, development of open land, or global warming, then we need to consider our responsibility. Can we do enough right now to protect our world? Are we at risk of becoming an endangered species?

The selections in this chapter consider the environment from many perspectives. As you read, consider your responsibility to the natural world. What might we expect from it, and what might it expect from us?

from *Silent Spring*

Rachel Carson

 Rachel Carson (1907–1964) was educated at Johns Hopkins University and conducted research at the Marine Biological Laboratory in Woods Hole, Massachusetts. She worked as a biologist for the U.S. Fish and Wildlife Service and served as chief editor of publications from 1947 to 1952. She wrote many books and articles about the sea, including *Under the Sea-Wind* (1941); *The Sea around Us* (1951), which won a National Book Award; and *The Edge of the Sea* (1955). Carson was among the first scientists to raise environmental issues for the general public, and her views and insights have greatly influenced the environmental movement. The readings that follow—"A Fable for Tomorrow" and "The Obligation to Endure"—are the first two chapters of *Silent Spring* (1962), a book that "changed the course of history," according to former vice president Al Gore. It led to John F. Kennedy's presidential commission on the environment, as well as the banning of the use of the poison DDT in agriculture.

I. A Fable for Tomorrow

There was once a town in the heart of America where all life seemed to live in harmony with its surroundings. The town lay in the midst of a checkerboard of prosperous farms, with fields of grain and hillsides of orchards where, in spring, white clouds of bloom drifted above the green fields. In autumn, oak and maple and birch set up a blaze of color that flamed and flickered across a backdrop of pines. Then foxes barked in the hills and deer silently crossed the fields, half hidden in the mists of the fall mornings.

Along the roads, laurel, viburnum and alder, great ferns and wildflowers delighted the traveler's eye through much of the year. Even in winter the roadsides were places of beauty, where countless birds came to feed on the berries and on the seed heads of the dried weeds rising above the snow. The countryside was, in fact, famous for the abundance and variety of its bird life, and when the flood of migrants was pouring through in spring and fall people traveled from great distances to observe them. Others came to fish the streams, which flowed clear and cold out of the hills and contained shady pools where trout lay. So it had been from the days many years ago when the first settlers raised their houses, sank their wells, and built their barns.

Then a strange blight crept over the area and everything began to change. Some evil spell had settled on the community: mysterious maladies swept the flocks of chickens; the cattle and sheep sickened and died. Everywhere was a shadow of death. The farmers spoke of much illness among their families. In the town the doctors had become more and more puzzled by new kinds of sickness appearing among their patients. There had been several sudden and unexplained deaths, not only among adults but even among children, who would be stricken suddenly while at play and die within a few hours.

There was a strange stillness. The birds, for example—where had they gone? Many people spoke of them, puzzled and disturbed. The feeding stations in the backyards were deserted. The few birds seen anywhere were moribund; they trembled violently and could not fly. It was a spring without voices. On the mornings that had once throbbed with the dawn chorus of robins, catbirds, doves, jays, wrens, and scores of other bird voices there was now no sound; only silence lay over the fields and woods and marsh.

On the farms the hens brooded, but no chicks hatched. The farmers complained that they were unable to raise any pigs—the litters were small and the young survived only a few days. The apple trees were coming into bloom but no bees droned among the blossoms, so there was no pollination and there would be no fruit.

The roadsides, once so attractive, were now lined with browned and withered vegetation as though swept by fire. These, too, were silent, deserted by all living things. Even the streams were now lifeless. Anglers no longer visited them, for all the fish had died.

In the gutters under the eaves and between the shingles of the roofs, white granular powder still showed a few patches; some weeks before it had fallen like snow upon the roofs and the lawns, the fields and streams.

No witchcraft, no enemy action had silenced the rebirth of new life in this stricken world. The people had done it themselves.

This town does not actually exist, but it might easily have a thousand counterparts in America or elsewhere in the world. I know of no community that has experienced all the misfortunes I describe. Yet every one of these disasters has actually happened somewhere, and many real communities have already suffered a substantial number of them. A grim specter has crept upon us almost unnoticed, and this imagined tragedy may easily become a stark reality we all shall know.

What has already silenced the voices of spring in countless towns in America? This book is an attempt to explain.

II. The Obligation to Endure

The history of life on earth has been a history of interaction between living things and their surroundings. To a large extent, the physical form and the habits of the earth's vegetation and its animal life have been molded by the environment. Considering the whole span of earthly time, the opposite effect, in which life actually modifies its surroundings, has been relatively slight. Only within the moment of time represented by the present century has one species—man—acquired significant power to alter the nature of his world.

During the past quarter century this power has not only increased to one of disturbing magnitude but it has changed in character. The most alarming of all man's assaults upon the environment is the contamination of air, earth, rivers, and sea with dangerous and even lethal materials. This pollution is for the most part irrecoverable; the chain of evil it initiates not only in the world that must support life but in living tissues is for the most part irreversible. In this now universal contamination of the environment, chemicals are the sinister and little-recognized partners of radiation in changing the very nature of the world—the very nature of its life. Strontium 90, released through nuclear explosions into the air, comes to earth in rain or drifts down as fallout, lodges in soil, enters into the grass or corn or wheat grown there, and in time takes up its abode in the bones of a human being, there to remain until his death. Similarly, chemicals sprayed on croplands or forests or gardens lie long in soil, entering into living organisms, passing from one to another in a chain of poisoning and death. Or they pass mysteriously by underground streams until they emerge and, through the alchemy of air and sunlight, combine into new forms that kill vegetation, sicken cattle, and work unknown harm on those who drink from once pure wells. As Albert Schweitzer[1] has said, "Man can hardly even recognize the devils of his own creation."

It took hundreds of millions of years to produce the life that now inhabits the earth—eons of time in which that developing and evolving and diversifying life reached a state of adjustment and balance with its surroundings. The environment, rigorously shaping and directing the life it supported, contained elements that were hostile as well as supporting. Certain rocks gave out dangerous radiation; even within the light of the sun, from which all life draws its energy, there were short-wave radiations with power to injure. Given time—time not in years but in millennia—life adjusts, and a balance has been reached. For time is the essential ingredient; but in the modern world there is no time.

The rapidity of change and the speed with which new situations are created follow the impetuous and heedless pace of man rather than the deliberate pace of nature. Radiation is no longer merely the background radiation of rocks, the bombardment of cosmic rays, the ultraviolet of the sun that have existed before there was any life on earth; radiation is now the unnatural creation of man's tampering with the atom. The chemicals to which life is asked to make its adjustment are no longer merely the calcium and silica and copper and all the rest of the minerals washed out of the rocks and carried in rivers to the sea; they are the synthetic creations of man's inventive mind, brewed in his laboratories, and having no counterparts in nature.

---

[1]Albert Schweitzer (1875–1965), a French philosopher, musician, and medical missionary, spent much of his life in Africa. He won the 1952 Nobel Peace Prize. — Eds.

To adjust to these chemicals would require time on the scale that is nature's;   15
it would require not merely the years of a man's life but the life of generations.
And even this, were it by some miracle possible, would be futile, for the new
chemicals come from our laboratories in an endless stream; almost five hundred
annually find their way into actual use in the United States alone. The figure is
staggering and its implications are not easily grasped—500 new chemicals to
which the bodies of men and animals are required somehow to adapt each year,
chemicals totally outside the limits of biologic experience.

Among them are many that are used in man's war against nature. Since the
mid-1940s over 200 basic chemicals have been created for use in killing insects,
weeds, rodents, and other organisms described in the modern vernacular as
"pests"; and they are sold under several thousand different brand names.

These sprays, dusts, and aerosols are now applied almost universally to farms,
gardens, forests, and homes—nonselective chemicals that have the power to kill
every insect, the "good" and the "bad," to still the song of birds and the leaping of
fish in the streams, to coat the leaves with a deadly film, and to linger on in soil—
all this though the intended target may be only a few weeds or insects. Can anyone believe it is possible to lay down such a barrage of poisons on the surface of
the earth without making it unfit for all life? They should not be called "insecticides," but "biocides."

The whole process of spraying seems caught up in an endless spiral. Since
DDT was released for civilian use, a process of escalation has been going on in
which ever more toxic materials must be found. This has happened because
insects, in a triumphant vindication of Darwin's principle of the survival of the
fittest, have evolved super races immune to the particular insecticide used, hence
a deadlier one has always to be developed—and then a deadlier one than that. It
has happened also because, for reasons to be described later, destructive insects
often undergo a "flareback," or resurgence, after spraying, in numbers greater
than before. Thus the chemical war is never won, and all life is caught in its violent crossfire.

Along with the possibility of the extinction of mankind by nuclear war, the
central problem of our age has therefore become the contamination of man's total
environment with such substances of incredible potential for harm—substances
that accumulate in the tissues of plants and animals and even penetrate the germ
cells to shatter or alter the very material of heredity upon which the shape of the
future depends.

Some would-be architects of our future look toward a time when it will be   20
possible to alter the human germ plasm by design. But we may easily be doing so
now by inadvertence, for many chemicals, like radiation, bring about gene mutations. It is ironic to think that man might determine his own future by something
so seemingly trivial as the choice of an insect spray.

All this has been risked—for what? Future historians may well be amazed by
our distorted sense of proportion. How could intelligent beings seek to control a

few unwanted species by a method that contaminated the entire environment and brought the threat of disease and death even to their own kind? Yet this is precisely what we have done. We have done it, moreover, for reasons that collapse the moment we examine them. We are told that the enormous and expanding use of pesticides is necessary to maintain farm production. Yet is our real problem not one of *overproduction*? Our farms, despite measures to remove acreages from production and to pay farmers *not* to produce, have yielded such a staggering excess of crops that the American taxpayer in 1962 is paying out more than one billion dollars a year as the total carrying cost of the surplus-food storage program. And is the situation helped when one branch of the Agriculture Department tries to reduce production while another states, as it did in 1958, "It is believed generally that reduction of crop acreages under provisions of the Soil Bank will stimulate interest in use of chemicals to obtain maximum production on the land retained in crops."

All this is not to say there is no insect problem and no need of control. I am saying, rather, that control must be geared to realities, not to mythical situations, and that the methods employed must be such that they do not destroy us along with the insects.

The problem whose attempted solution has brought such a train of disaster in its wake is an accompaniment of our modern way of life. Long before the age of man, insects inhabited the earth—a group of extraordinarily varied and adaptable beings. Over the course of time since man's advent, a small percentage of the more than half a million species of insects have come into conflict with human welfare in two principal ways: as competitors for the food supply and as carriers of human disease.

Disease-carrying insects become important where human beings are crowded together, especially under conditions where sanitation is poor, as in time of natural disaster or war or in situations of extreme poverty and deprivation. Then control of some sort becomes necessary. It is a sobering fact, however, as we shall presently see, that the method of massive chemical control has had only limited success, and also threatens to worsen the very conditions it is intended to curb.

Under primitive agricultural conditions the farmer had few insect problems. These arose with the intensification of agriculture—the devotion of immense acreages to a single crop. Such a system set the stage for explosive increases in specific insect populations. Single-crop farming does not take advantage of the principles by which nature works; it is agriculture as an engineer might conceive it to be. Nature has introduced great variety into the landscape, but man has displayed a passion for simplifying it. Thus he undoes the built-in checks and balances by which nature holds the species within bounds. One important natural check is a limit on the amount of suitable habitat for each species. Obviously then, an insect that lives on wheat can build up its population to much higher levels on a farm devoted to wheat than on one in which wheat is intermingled with other crops to which the insect is not adapted.

The same thing happens in other situations. A generation or more ago, the towns of large areas of the United States lined their streets with the noble elm tree. Now the beauty they hopefully created is threatened with complete destruction as disease sweeps through the elms, carried by a beetle that would have only limited chance to build up large populations and to spread from tree to tree if the elms were only occasional trees in a richly diversified planting.

Another factor in the modern insect problem is one that must be viewed against a background of geologic and human history: the spreading of thousands of different kinds of organisms from their native homes to invade new territories. This worldwide migration has been studied and graphically described by the British ecologist Charles Elton in his recent book *The Ecology of Invasions*. During the Cretaceous Period, some hundred million years ago, flooding seas cut many land bridges between continents and living things found themselves confined in what Elton calls "colossal separate nature reserves." There, isolated from others of their kind, they developed many new species. When some of the land masses were joined again, about 15 million years ago, these species began to move out into new territories — a movement that is not only still in progress but is now receiving considerable assistance from man.

The importation of plants is the primary agent in the modern spread of species, for animals have almost invariably gone along with the plants, quarantine being a comparatively recent and not completely effective innovation. The United States Office of Plant Introduction alone has introduced almost 200,000 species and varieties of plants from all over the world. Nearly half of the 180 or so major insect enemies of plants in the United States are accidental imports from abroad, and most of them have come as hitchhikers on plants.

In new territory, out of reach of the restraining hand of the natural enemies that kept down its numbers in its native land, an invading plant or animal is able to become enormously abundant. Thus it is no accident that our most troublesome insects are introduced species.

These invasions, both the naturally occurring and those dependent on human assistance, are likely to continue indefinitely. Quarantine and massive chemical campaigns are only extremely expensive ways of buying time. We are faced, according to Dr. Elton, "with a life-and-death need not just to find new technological means of suppressing this plant or that animal"; instead we need the basic knowledge of animal populations and their relations to their surroundings that will "promote an even balance and damp down the explosive power of outbreaks and new invasions." 30

Much of the necessary knowledge is now available but we do not use it. We train ecologists in our universities and even employ them in our governmental agencies but we seldom take their advice. We allow the chemical death rain to fall as though there were no alternative, whereas in fact there are many, and our ingenuity could soon discover many more if given opportunity.

Have we fallen into a mesmerized state that makes us accept as inevitable that which is inferior or detrimental, as though having lost the will or the vision to demand that which is good? Such thinking, in the words of the ecologist Paul Shepard, "idealizes life with only its head out of water, inches above the limits of toleration of the corruption of its own environment. . . . Why should we tolerate a diet of weak poisons, a home in insipid surroundings, a circle of acquaintances who are not quite our enemies, the noise of motors with just enough relief to prevent insanity? Who would want to live in a world which is just not quite fatal?"

Yet such a world is pressed upon us. The crusade to create a chemically sterile, insect-free world seems to have engendered a fanatic zeal on the part of many specialists and most of the so-called control agencies. On every hand there is evidence that those engaged in spraying operations exercise a ruthless power. "The regulatory entomologists . . . function as prosecutor, judge and jury, tax assessor and collector and sheriff to enforce their own orders," said Connecticut entomologist Neely Turner. The most flagrant abuses go unchecked in both state and federal agencies.

It is not my contention that chemical insecticides must never be used. I do contend that we have put poisonous and biologically potent chemicals indiscriminately into the hands of persons largely or wholly ignorant of their potentials for harm. We have subjected enormous numbers of people to contact with these poisons, without their consent and often without their knowledge. If the Bill of Rights contains no guarantee that a citizen shall be secure against lethal poisons distributed either by private individuals or by public officials, it is surely only because our forefathers, despite their considerable wisdom and foresight, could conceive of no such problem.

I contend, furthermore, that we have allowed these chemicals to be used with   35
little or no advance investigation of their effect on soil, water, wildlife, and man himself. Future generations are unlikely to condone our lack of prudent concern for the integrity of the natural world that supports all life.

There is still very limited awareness of the nature of the threat. This is an era of specialists, each of whom sees his own problem and is unaware of or intolerant of the larger frame into which it fits. It is also an era dominated by industry, in which the right to make a dollar at whatever cost is seldom challenged. When the public protests, confronted with some obvious evidence of damaging results of pesticide applications, it is fed little tranquilizing pills of half truth. We urgently need an end to these false assurances, to the sugar coating of unpalatable facts. It is the public that is being asked to assume the risks that the insect controllers calculate. The public must decide whether it wishes to continue on the present road, and it can do so only when in full possession of the facts. In the words of Jean Rostand,[2] "The obligation to endure gives us the right to know."

. . . .

---

[2]Jean Rostand (1894–1977), a French biologist, science writer, and philosopher, spoke against nuclear proliferation. — Eds.

Questions for Discussion

1. Why does Rachel Carson begin with "There was once a town . . . ," as though she were writing a fairy tale? Is this a fairy tale of sorts? How does Carson present the town in paragraphs 1 and 2?

2. Carson claims in paragraph 12 that "[t]he most alarming of . . . assaults upon the environment is the contamination of air, earth, rivers, and sea with dangerous and even lethal materials." Is contamination still the most alarming assault on the environment, or has another problem taken its place? Explain your response.

3. In paragraph 16, Carson claims that humankind is engaged in a "war against nature" and describes the targets of that war. Do you agree that targeting certain things for destruction (or at least control) means we are at war with nature? Can we be at war with something that is not our intended target? Explain.

4. Carson says the products used to kill bugs should be called "biocides" instead of "insecticides" (para. 17). Why? What is the difference?

5. What has changed since Carson wrote *Silent Spring*? Has the natural environment improved? Has it declined? Since Carson's time, have we become more concerned with the effect we have on nature—or less concerned? Explain your response.

6. What does Jean Rostand mean by our "obligation to endure" (para. 36)? How is our "right to know" related to this obligation?

Questions on Rhetoric and Style

1. Why does Carson begin "A Fable for Tomorrow" with imagery rather than exposition? What is the effect?

2. How do Carson's tone, style, and purpose change in paragraphs 9 and 10? Why do they change? How does Carson's voice change from "A Fable for Tomorrow" to "The Obligation to Endure"? How does the difference serve the writer's rhetorical purpose?

3. Why does Carson call the insect problem a "train of disaster" (para. 23)? What is the effect of this metaphor?

4. How does Carson appeal to authority in paragraph 27? Where else in the selection does she appeal to authority? What is the effect of her use of statistics in paragraph 28?

5. What are the "agencies" to which Carson refers (para. 33)? Why are they reduced to "so-called control agencies"?

6. Why doesn't Carson mention her "contention" until she is nearly finished with the piece? Is her argument inductive or deductive? How do you know? Also, why does she tell the reader what her "contentions" *aren't* before stating what they *are*? What response from her readers might she anticipate at this point in their reading?

7. Carson says that the public "is fed little tranquilizing pills of half truth" when it contests the use of pesticides (para. 36). Why is this metaphor effective?

8. What do you think Carson's purpose was in ending the final paragraph (and the chapter) with someone else's words?

Suggestions for Writing

1. In imitation of Rachel Carson, write an update of "A Fable for Tomorrow."
2. In paragraph 19, Carson says, "Along with the possibility of the extinction of mankind by nuclear war, the central problem of our age has therefore become the contamination of man's total environment." Write an essay in which you defend, challenge, or qualify the validity of this statement.
3. Carson writes in paragraph 35, "Future generations are unlikely to condone our lack of prudent concern for the integrity of the natural world that supports all life." As a member of one of the generations after Carson's, write a letter to her, to someone of her generation, or to a polluter of today. In the letter, identify and explain your response to Carson's statement.
4. Carson concludes with the words of French biologist and philosopher Jean Rostand: "The obligation to endure gives us the right to know." Write an essay that defends or challenges Rostand's claim as it relates to our relationship to the natural world today.
5. Carson writes in paragraph 34, "If the Bill of Rights contains no guarantee that a citizen shall be secure against lethal poisons distributed either by private individuals or by public officials, it is surely only because our forefathers, despite their considerable wisdom and foresight, could conceive of no such problem." Imagine that the framers of the Constitution were here today, and write an essay explaining how they might use the Constitution to protect the environment.
6. Considering that *Silent Spring* was written fifty years ago, should we be optimistic or pessimistic in our attitude toward the preservation of the natural world? As you answer this question, consider what has changed since Carson's time in our approach toward the environment.

from *Nature*

RALPH WALDO EMERSON

Ralph Waldo Emerson (1803–1882), perhaps best known for his essay "Self-Reliance," was one of America's most influential thinkers and writers. After graduating from Harvard Divinity School, he followed nine generations of his family into the ministry but practiced for only a few years. Known as a great orator, Emerson made his living as a popular lecturer on a wide range of topics. From 1821 to 1826, he taught in city and country schools and later served on a number of school boards, including the Concord School Committee and the Board of Overseers of Harvard College. Central to Emerson's thought is recognizing the spiritual relationship between humans and the natural world. In 1836, he and other like-minded intellectuals, including Henry David Thoreau, founded the Transcendental Club, and that same year he published his influential essay "Nature," the first three chapters of which are included here.

I. Nature

To go into solitude, a man needs to retire as much from his chamber as from society. I am not solitary whilst I read and write, though nobody is with me. But if a man would be alone, let him look at the stars. The rays that come from those heavenly worlds, will separate between him and what he touches. One might think the atmosphere was made transparent with this design, to give man, in the heavenly bodies, the perpetual presence of the sublime. Seen in the streets of cities, how great they are! If the stars should appear one night in a thousand years, how would men believe and adore; and preserve for many generations the remembrance of the city of God which had been shown! But every night come out these envoys of beauty, and light the universe with their admonishing smile.

The stars awaken a certain reverence, because though always present, they are inaccessible; but all natural objects make a kindred impression, when the mind is open to their influence. Nature never wears a mean appearance. Neither does the wisest man extort her secret, and lose his curiosity by finding out all her perfection. Nature never became a toy to a wise spirit. The flowers, the animals, the mountains, reflected the wisdom of his best hour, as much as they had delighted the simplicity of his childhood.

When we speak of nature in this manner, we have a distinct but most poetical sense in the mind. We mean the integrity of impression made by manifold natural objects. It is this which distinguishes the stick of timber of the wood-cutter, from the tree of the poet. The charming landscape which I saw this morning, is indubitably made up of some twenty or thirty farms. Miller owns this field, Locke that, and Manning the woodland beyond. But none of them owns the landscape. There is a property in the horizon which no man has but he whose eye can integrate all the parts, that is, the poet. This is the best part of these men's farms, yet to this their warranty-deeds give no title.

To speak truly, few adult persons can see nature. Most persons do not see the sun. At least they have a very superficial seeing. The sun illuminates only the eye of the man, but shines into the eye and the heart of the child. The lover of nature is he whose inward and outward senses are still truly adjusted to each other; who has retained the spirit of infancy even into the era of manhood. His intercourse with heaven and earth, becomes part of his daily food. In the presence of nature, a wild delight runs through the man, in spite of real sorrows. Nature says,—he is my creature, and maugre[1] all his impertinent griefs, he shall be glad with me. Not the sun or the summer alone, but every hour and season yields its tribute of delight; for every hour and change corresponds to and authorizes a different state of the mind, from breathless noon to grimmest midnight. Nature is a setting that fits equally well a comic or a mourning piece. In good health, the air is a cordial of incredible virtue. Crossing a bare common, in snow puddles, at twilight, under a clouded sky, without having in my thoughts any occurrence of special good fortune, I have enjoyed a perfect exhilaration. I am glad to the brink of fear. In the woods too, a man casts off his years, as the snake his slough, and at what period soever of life, is always a child. In the woods, is perpetual youth. Within these plantations of God, a decorum and sanctity reign, a perennial festival is dressed, and the guest sees not how he should tire of them in a thousand years. In the woods, we return to reason and faith. There I feel that nothing can befall me in life,—no disgrace, no calamity, (leaving me my eyes,) which nature cannot repair. Standing on the bare ground,—my head bathed by the blithe air, and uplifted into infinite space,—all mean egotism vanishes. I become a transparent eye-ball; I am nothing; I see all; the currents of the Universal Being circulate through me; I am part or particle of God. The name of the nearest friend sounds then foreign and accidental: to be brothers, to be acquaintances,—master or servant, is then a trifle and a disturbance. I am the lover of uncontained and immortal beauty. In the wilderness, I find something more dear and connate[2] than in streets or villages. In the tranquil landscape, and especially in the distant line of the horizon, man beholds somewhat as beautiful as his own nature.

The greatest delight which the fields and woods minister, is the suggestion of an occult relation between man and the vegetable. I am not alone and unacknowledged. They nod to me, and I to them. The waving of the boughs in the storm, is new to me and old. It takes me by surprise, and yet is not unknown. Its effect is like that of a higher thought or a better emotion coming over me, when I deemed I was thinking justly or doing right.

5

---

[1]Despite. —Eds.

[2]Sympathetic. —Eds.

Yet it is certain that the power to produce this delight, does not reside in nature, but in man, or in a harmony of both. It is necessary to use these pleasures with great temperance. For, nature is not always tricked in holiday attire, but the same scene which yesterday breathed perfume and glittered as for the frolic of the nymphs, is overspread with melancholy today. Nature always wears the colors of the spirit. To a man laboring under calamity, the heat of his own fire hath sadness in it. Then, there is a kind of contempt of the landscape felt by him who has just lost by death a dear friend. The sky is less grand as it shuts down over less worth in the population.

II. Commodity

Whoever considers the final cause of the world, will discern a multitude of uses that enter as parts into that result. They all admit of being thrown into one of the following classes; Commodity; Beauty; Language; and Discipline.

Under the general name of Commodity, I rank all those advantages which our senses owe to nature. This, of course, is a benefit which is temporary and mediate, not ultimate, like its service to the soul. Yet although low, it is perfect in its kind, and is the only use of nature which all men apprehend. The misery of man appears like childish petulance, when we explore the steady and prodigal provision that has been made for his support and delight on this green ball which floats him through the heavens. What angels invented these splendid ornaments, these rich conveniences, this ocean of air above, this ocean of water beneath, this firmament of earth between? this zodiac of lights, this tent of dropping clouds, this striped coat of climates, this fourfold year? Beasts, fire, water, stones, and corn serve him. The field is at once his floor, his work-yard, his play-ground, his garden, and his bed.

> "More servants wait on man
> Than he 'll take notice of."—[3]

Nature, in its ministry to man, is not only the material, but is also the process and the result. All the parts incessantly work into each other's hands for the profit of man. The wind sows the seed; the sun evaporates the sea; the wind blows the vapor to the field; the ice, on the other side of the planet, condenses rain on this; the rain feeds the plant; the plant feeds the animal; and thus the endless circulations of the divine charity nourish man.

The useful arts are reproductions or new combinations by the wit of man, of 10 the same natural benefactors. He no longer waits for favoring gales, but by means of steam, he realizes the fable of Æolus's bag, and carries the two and thirty winds in the boiler of his boat. To diminish friction, he paves the road with iron bars,

---

[3]The quotation is from *Man* by English poet George Herbert (1593–1633). —Eds.

and, mounting a coach with a ship-load of men, animals, and merchandise behind him, he darts through the country, from town to town, like an eagle or a swallow through the air. By the aggregate of these aids, how is the face of the world changed, from the era of Noah to that of Napoleon! The private poor man hath cities, ships, canals, bridges, built for him. He goes to the post-office, and the human race run on his errands; to the book-shop, and the human race read and write of all that happens, for him; to the court-house, and nations repair his wrongs. He sets his house upon the road, and the human race go forth every morning, and shovel out the snow, and cut a path for him.

But there is no need of specifying particulars in this class of uses. The catalogue is endless, and the examples so obvious, that I shall leave them to the reader's reflection, with the general remark, that this mercenary benefit is one which has respect to a farther good. A man is fed, not that he may be fed, but that he may work.

III. Beauty

A nobler want of man is served by nature, namely, the love of Beauty.

The ancient Greeks called the world κόσμος,[4] beauty. Such is the constitution of all things, or such the plastic power of the human eye, that the primary forms, as the sky, the mountain, the tree, the animal, give us a delight *in and for themselves*; a pleasure arising from outline, color, motion, and grouping. This seems partly owing to the eye itself. The eye is the best of artists. By the mutual action of its structure and of the laws of light, perspective is produced, which integrates every mass of objects, of what character soever, into a well colored and shaded globe, so that where the particular objects are mean and unaffecting, the landscape which they compose, is round and symmetrical. And as the eye is the best composer, so light is the first of painters. There is no object so foul that intense light will not make beautiful. And the stimulus it affords to the sense, and a sort of infinitude which it hath, like space and time, make all matter gay. Even the corpse has its own beauty. But besides this general grace diffused over nature, almost all the individual forms are agreeable to the eye, as is proved by our endless imitations of some of them, as the acorn, the grape, the pine-cone, the wheat-ear, the egg, the wings and forms of most birds, the lion's claw, the serpent, the butterfly, sea-shells, flames, clouds, buds, leaves, and the forms of many trees, as the palm.

For better consideration, we may distribute the aspects of Beauty in a three-fold manner.

1. First, the simple perception of natural forms is a delight. The influence of the forms and actions in nature, is so needful to man, that, in its lowest functions, 15

---

[4]*Cosmos*, Greek for "universe" or "order." Emerson is equating *order* with *beauty*. —Eds.

it seems to lie on the confines of commodity and beauty. To the body and mind which have been cramped by noxious work or company, nature is medicinal and restores their tone. The tradesman, the attorney comes out of the din and craft of the street, and sees the sky and the woods, and is a man again. In their eternal calm, he finds himself. The health of the eye seems to demand a horizon. We are never tired, so long as we can see far enough.

But in other hours, Nature satisfies by its loveliness, and without any mixture of corporeal benefit. I see the spectacle of morning from the hill-top over against my house, from day-break to sun-rise, with emotions which an angel might share. The long slender bars of cloud float like fishes in the sea of crimson light. From the earth, as a shore, I look out into that silent sea. I seem to partake its rapid transformations: the active enchantment reaches my dust, and I dilate and con-spire with the morning wind. How does Nature deify us with a few and cheap ele-ments! Give me health and a day, and I will make the pomp of emperors ridiculous. The dawn is my Assyria; the sun-set and moon-rise my Paphos,[5] and unimagi-nable realms of faerie; broad noon shall be my England of the senses and the understanding; the night shall be my Germany of mystic philosophy and dreams.

Not less excellent, except for our less susceptibility in the afternoon, was the charm, last evening, of a January sunset. The western clouds divided and sub-divided themselves into pink flakes modulated with tints of unspeakable softness; and the air had so much life and sweetness, that it was a pain to come within doors. What was it that nature would say? Was there no meaning in the live repose of the valley behind the mill, and which Homer or Shakspeare could not re-form for me in words? The leafless trees become spires of flame in the sunset, with the blue east for their back-ground, and the stars of the dead calices of flowers, and every withered stem and stubble rimed with frost, contribute something to the mute music.

The inhabitants of cities suppose that the country landscape is pleasant only half the year. I please myself with the graces of the winter scenery, and believe that we are as much touched by it as by the genial influences of summer. To the atten-tive eye, each moment of the year has its own beauty, and in the same field, it beholds, every hour, a picture which was never seen before, and which shall never be seen again. The heavens change every moment, and reflect their glory or gloom on the plains beneath. The state of the crop in the surrounding farms alters the expression of the earth from week to week. The succession of native plants in the pastures and roadsides, which makes the silent clock by which time tells the sum-mer hours, will make even the divisions of the day sensible to a keen observer. The tribes of birds and insects, like the plants punctual to their time, follow each other, and the year has room for all. By water-courses, the variety is greater. In July, the blue pontederia or pickerel-weed blooms in large beds in the shallow

---

[5]City in Cyprus. At its height, in the ninth century b.c.e., the Assyrian empire controlled much of the Middle East, including Cyprus. — Eds.

parts of our pleasant river, and swarms with yellow butterflies in continual motion. Art cannot rival this pomp of purple and gold. Indeed the river is a perpetual gala, and boasts each month a new ornament.

But this beauty of Nature which is seen and felt as beauty, is the least part. The shows of day, the dewy morning, the rainbow, mountains, orchards in blossom, stars, moonlight, shadows in still water, and the like, if too eagerly hunted, become shows merely, and mock us with their unreality. Go out of the house to see the moon, and 't is mere tinsel; it will not please as when its light shines upon your necessary journey. The beauty that shimmers in the yellow afternoons of October, who ever could clutch it? Go forth to find it, and it is gone: 't is only a mirage as you look from the windows of diligence.

2. The presence of a higher, namely, of the spiritual element is essential to its 20 perfection. The high and divine beauty which can be loved without effeminacy, is that which is found in combination with the human will. Beauty is the mark God sets upon virtue. Every natural action is graceful. Every heroic act is also decent, and causes the place and the bystanders to shine. We are taught by great actions that the universe is the property of every individual in it. Every rational creature has all nature for his dowry and estate. It is his, if he will. He may divest himself of it; he may creep into a corner, and abdicate his kingdom, as most men do, but he is entitled to the world by his constitution. In proportion to the energy of his thought and will, he takes up the world into himself. "All those things for which men plough, build, or sail, obey virtue;" said Sallust.[6] "The winds and waves," said Gibbon,[7] "are always on the side of the ablest navigators." So are the sun and moon and all the stars of heaven. When a noble act is done—perchance in a scene of great natural beauty; when Leonidas and his three hundred martyrs consume one day in dying, and the sun and moon come each and look at them once in the steep defile of Thermopylæ; when Arnold Winkelried, in the high Alps, under the shadow of the avalanche, gathers in his side a sheaf of Austrian spears to break the line for his comrades, are not these heroes entitled to add the beauty of the scene to the beauty of the deed? When the bark of Columbus nears the shore of America;—before it, the beach lined with savages, fleeing out of all their huts of cane; the sea behind; and the purple mountains of the Indian Archipelago around, can we separate the man from the living picture? Does not the New World clothe his form with her palm-groves and savannahs as fit drapery? Ever does natural beauty steal in like air, and envelope great actions. When Sir Harry Vane was dragged up the Tower-hill, sitting on a sled, to suffer death, as the champion of the English laws, one of the multitude cried out to him, "You never sate on so glorious a seat." Charles II, to intimidate the citizens of London, caused the patriot Lord Russel to be drawn in an open coach, through the principal streets

---

[6]Sallust (86–34 B.C.E.), Roman historian. —Eds.
[7]Edward Gibbon (1737–1794), English historian and author of *The History of the Decline and Fall of the Roman Empire.* —Eds.

of the city, on his way to the scaffold. "But," his biographer says, "the multitude imagined they saw liberty and virtue sitting by his side." In private places, among sordid objects, an act of truth or heroism seems at once to draw to itself the sky as its temple, the sun as its candle. Nature stretcheth out her arms to embrace man, only let his thoughts be of equal greatness. Willingly does she follow his steps with the rose and the violet, and bend her lines of grandeur and grace to the decoration of her darling child. Only let his thoughts be of equal scope, and the frame will suit the picture. A virtuous man is in unison with her works, and makes the central figure of the visible sphere. Homer, Pindar, Socrates, Phocion, associate themselves fitly in our memory with the geography and climate of Greece. The visible heavens and earth sympathize with Jesus. And in common life, whosoever has seen a person of powerful character and happy genius, will have remarked how easily he took all things along with him,—the persons, the opinions, and the day, and nature became ancillary to a man.

3. There is still another aspect under which the beauty of the world may be viewed, namely, as it becomes an object of the intellect. Beside the relation of things to virtue, they have a relation to thought. The intellect searches out the absolute order of things as they stand in the mind of God, and without the colors of affection. The intellectual and the active powers seem to succeed each other, and the exclusive activity of the one, generates the exclusive activity of the other. There is something unfriendly in each to the other, but they are like the alternate periods of feeding and working in animals; each prepares and will be followed by the other. Therefore does beauty, which, in relation to actions, as we have seen, comes unsought, and comes because it is unsought, remain for the apprehension and pursuit of the intellect; and then again, in its turn, of the active power. Nothing divine dies. All good is eternally reproductive. The beauty of nature reforms itself in the mind, and not for barren contemplation, but for new creation.

All men are in some degree impressed by the face of the world; some men even to delight. This love of beauty is Taste. Others have the same love in such excess, that, not content with admiring, they seek to embody it in new forms. The creation of beauty is Art.

The production of a work of art throws a light upon the mystery of humanity. A work of art is an abstract or epitome of the world. It is the result or expression of nature, in miniature. For, although the works of nature are innumerable and all different, the result or the expression of them all is similar and single. Nature is a sea of forms radically alike and even unique. A leaf, a sun-beam, a landscape, the ocean, make an analogous impression on the mind. What is common to them all,—that perfectness and harmony, is beauty. The standard of beauty is the entire circuit of natural forms,—the totality of nature; which the Italians expressed by defining beauty "il piu nell' uno."[8] Nothing is quite beautiful

---

[8]Italian, "the many in one." —Eds.

alone: nothing but is beautiful in the whole. A single object is only so far beautiful as it suggests this universal grace. The poet, the painter, the sculptor, the musician, the architect, seek each to concentrate this radiance of the world on one point, and each in his several work to satisfy the love of beauty which stimulates him to produce. Thus is Art, a nature passed through the alembic[9] of man. Thus in art, does nature work through the will of a man filled with the beauty of her first works.

The world thus exists to the soul to satisfy the desire of beauty. This element I call an ultimate end. No reason can be asked or given why the soul seeks beauty. Beauty, in its largest and profoundest sense, is one expression for the universe. God is the all-fair. Truth, and goodness, and beauty, are but different faces of the same All. But beauty in nature is not ultimate. It is the herald of inward and eternal beauty, and is not alone a solid and satisfactory good. It must stand as a part, and not as yet the last or highest expression of the final cause of Nature.

Questions for Discussion

1. Explain Ralph Waldo Emerson's attitude toward nature in paragraphs 1 and 2.
2. In paragraph 4, Emerson writes, "I become a transparent eye-ball; I am nothing; I see all; the currents of the Universal Being circulate through me; I am part or particle of God." From those words, how would you describe Emerson's mental state here, and what has brought it about?
3. In paragraph 6, Emerson says, "Nature always wears the colors of the spirit." What does he mean? Do you agree? In paragraph 4, Emerson says, "Crossing a bare common, in snow puddles, at twilight, under a clouded sky . . . I have enjoyed a perfect exhilaration." Does this contradict his statement in paragraph 6? Explain how the relationship that Emerson describes between humans and nature works.
4. In paragraphs 7–9, what does Emerson suggest about the human condition?
5. In paragraph 10, what is Emerson's attitude toward the "useful arts"—what people now call technology? Would Emerson have the same attitude today? Why or why not?
6. In Part III of the selection, Emerson says that in regard to nature, loving its beauty is a nobler response than using it as a commodity. Do you agree or disagree? Explain why.
7. In paragraph 20, Emerson writes, "Nature stretcheth out her arms to embrace man, only let his thoughts be of equal greatness." What does he mean? What does this statement imply about the relationship between nature and humankind?

---

[9]A device that purifies or refines. —Eds.

Questions on Rhetoric and Style

1. What is the effect of the comparisons (including figurative language) and distinctions that Emerson makes in paragraphs 1 and 2? In the conclusion to the first paragraph, Emerson says the stars give an "admonishing smile." What does he mean by this phrase? How does Emerson characterize nature? What is the purpose of this characterization?

2. Identify the juxtapositions in paragraph 4. What is their effect? Is there a relationship among the juxtapositions that suggests a larger point? Explain.

3. In paragraph 8, Emerson speaks of "this green ball which floats him through the heavens." What is the effect of this metaphor? How does the repetition in the rest of the paragraph ("this ocean of air above, this ocean of water beneath, this . . . this . . .") contribute to this effect?

4. What three aspects of the beauty of nature does Emerson delineate in Part III? How does he use simile and metaphor to develop the first aspect? How do the rhetorical questions in paragraph 20 serve to develop the second aspect?

5. What is the relationship between paragraphs 18 and 19? What is the effect of the paradox that concludes paragraph 19?

6. In paragraph 21, what distinction does Emerson make between "barren contemplation" and "new creation"?

7. How does Emerson unite truth, goodness, and beauty in the final paragraph? Why is this a fitting conclusion for this section?

Suggestions for Writing

1. Write an essay in which you support, challenge, or qualify Emerson's main idea in Part I.

2. In Part II, Emerson presents an optimistic view of the "useful arts." In the voice of a modern-day environmentalist such as Rachel Carson (p. 888), discuss whether his view holds true today.

3. Write a letter to Emerson describing an experience you have had with nature. Explain how it was similar to or different from the experience he describes in Part II.

4. Select a powerful, challenging, or thought-provoking statement from Emerson — such as "The production of a work of art throws a light upon the mystery of humanity. A work of art is an abstract or epitome of the world" (para. 23). Write an essay that supports, qualifies, or refutes its assertion. Use evidence from your reading, as well as your own knowledge and experience, to defend your position.

5. Read the poem "Thanatopsis" by William Cullen Bryant, a contemporary of Emerson's, and write an essay comparing it with Emerson's essay "Nature."

from *The Land Ethic*

ALDO LEOPOLD

Aldo Leopold was born in Iowa in 1887. He attended the Sheffield Scientific School at Yale and subsequently enrolled in the Yale forestry school, the first graduate school of forestry in the United States. Graduating with a master's degree in 1909, he joined the U.S. Forest Service and stayed with that agency in various research and management positions until 1933, when he took a position at the University of Wisconsin. Throughout his life, Leopold was at the forefront of the conservation movement; many people acknowledge him as the father of wildlife conservation in America. He was also an internationally respected scientist who wrote over 350 articles, mostly on scientific and policy matters. In addition, he was an advisor on conservation to the United Nations. He died of a heart attack in 1948 while fighting a fire on a neighbor's farm. Leopold is best known for his book *A Sand County Almanac* (1949), which includes the chapter excerpted here, "The Land Ethic."

When god-like Odysseus returned from the wars in Troy, he hanged all on one rope a dozen slave-girls of his household whom he suspected of misbehavior during his absence.

This hanging involved no question of propriety. The girls were property. The disposal of property was then, as now, a matter of expediency, not of right and wrong.

Concepts of right and wrong were not lacking from Odysseus' Greece: witness the fidelity of his wife through the long years before at last his black-prowed galleys clove the wine-dark seas for home. The ethical structure of that day covered wives, but had not yet been extended to human chattels. During the three thousand years which have since elapsed, ethical criteria have been extended to many fields of conduct, with corresponding shrinkages in those judged by expediency only.

The Ethical Sequence

This extension of ethics, so far studied only by philosophers, is actually a process in ecological evolution. Its sequences may be described in ecological as well as in philosophical terms. An ethic, ecologically, is a limitation on freedom of action in the struggle for existence. An ethic, philosophically, is a differentiation of social from anti-social conduct. These are two definitions of one thing. The thing has its origin in the tendency of interdependent individuals or groups to evolve modes of co-operation. The ecologist calls these symbioses. Politics and economics are advanced symbioses in which the original free-for-all competition has been replaced, in part, by co-operative mechanisms with an ethical content.

The complexity of co-operative mechanisms has increased with population 5
density, and with the efficiency of tools. It was simpler, for example, to define the
anti-social uses of sticks and stones in the days of the mastodons than of bullets
and billboards in the age of motors.

The first ethics dealt with the relation between individuals; the Mosaic Decalogue[1] is an example. Later accretions dealt with the relation between the individual and society. The Golden Rule tries to integrate the individual to society;
democracy to integrate social organization to the individual.

There is as yet no ethic dealing with man's relation to land and to the animals
and plants which grow upon it. Land, like Odysseus' slave-girls, is still property.
The land relation is still strictly economic, entailing privileges but not obligations.

The extension of ethics to this third element in human environment is, if I
read the evidence correctly, an evolutionary possibility and an ecological necessity. It is the third step in a sequence. The first two have already been taken. Individual thinkers since the days of Ezekiel and Isaiah have asserted that the
despoliation of land is not only inexpedient but wrong. Society, however, has not
yet affirmed their belief. I regard the present conservation movement as the
embryo of such an affirmation.

An ethic may be regarded as a mode of guidance for meeting ecological situations so new or intricate, or involving such deferred reactions, that the path of
social expediency is not discernible to the average individual. Animal instincts
are modes of guidance for the individual in meeting such situations. Ethics are
possibly a kind of community instinct in-the-making.

The Community Concept

All ethics so far evolved rest upon a single premise: that the individual is a mem- 10
ber of a community of interdependent parts. His instincts prompt him to compete for his place in that community, but his ethics prompt him also to co-operate
(perhaps in order that there may be a place to compete for).

The land ethic simply enlarges the boundaries of the community to include
soils, waters, plants, and animals, or collectively: the land.

This sounds simple: do we not already sing our love for and obligation to the
land of the free and the home of the brave? Yes, but just what and whom do we
love? Certainly not the soil, which we are sending helter-skelter downriver. Certainly not the waters, which we assume have no function except to turn turbines,
float barges, and carry off sewage. Certainly not the plants, of which we exterminate whole communities without batting an eye. Certainly not the animals, of
which we have already extirpated many of the largest and most beautiful species.
A land ethic of course cannot prevent the alteration, management, and use of

---

[1]The Ten Commandments found in the book of Exodus in the Bible. —Eds.

these "resources," but it does affirm their right to continued existence, and, at least in spots, their continued existence in a natural state.

In short, a land ethic changes the role of *Homo sapiens* from conqueror of the land-community to plain member and citizen of it. It implies respect for his fellow-members, and also respect for the community as such.

In human history, we have learned (I hope) that the conqueror role is eventually self-defeating. Why? Because it is implicit in such a role that the conqueror knows, *ex cathedra*,[2] just what makes the community clock tick, and just what and who is valuable, and what and who is worthless, in community life. It always turns out that he knows neither, and this is why his conquests eventually defeat themselves.

In the biotic community, a parallel situation exists. Abraham knew exactly 15 what the land was for: it was to drip milk and honey into Abraham's mouth. At the present moment, the assurance with which we regard this assumption is inverse to the degree of our education.

The ordinary citizen today assumes that science knows what makes the community clock tick; the scientist is equally sure that he does not. He knows that the biotic mechanism is so complex that its workings may never be fully understood.

That man is, in fact, only a member of a biotic team is shown by an ecological interpretation of history. Many historical events, hitherto explained solely in terms of human enterprise, were actually biotic interactions between people and land. The characteristics of the land determined the facts quite as potently as the characteristics of the men who lived on it.

Consider, for example, the settlement of the Mississippi valley. In the years following the Revolution, three groups were contending for its control: the native Indian, the French and English traders, and the American settlers. Historians wonder what would have happened if the English at Detroit had thrown a little more weight into the Indian side of those tipsy scales which decided the outcome of the colonial migration into the cane-lands of Kentucky. It is time now to ponder the fact that the cane-lands, when subjected to the particular mixture of forces represented by the cow, plow, fire, and axe of the pioneer, became bluegrass. What if the plant succession inherent in this dark and bloody ground had, under the impact of these forces, given us some worthless sedge, shrub, or weed? Would Boone and Kenton[3] have held out? Would there have been any overflow into Ohio, Indiana, Illinois, and Missouri? Any Louisiana Purchase? Any transcontinental union of new states? Any Civil War?

Kentucky was one sentence in the drama of history. We are commonly told what the human actors in this drama tried to do, but we are seldom told that their

---

[2]Latin for "from the chair," here meaning from the seat of authority, often a reference to infallible papal decrees. —Eds.
[3]Daniel Boone (1734–1820) and Simon Kenton (1755–1836), famous American frontiersmen. —Eds.

success, or the lack of it, hung in large degree on the reaction of particular soils to the impact of the particular forces exerted by their occupancy. In the case of Kentucky, we do not even know where the bluegrass came from — whether it is a native species, or a stowaway from Europe.

Contrast the cane-lands with what hindsight tells us about the Southwest, 20 where the pioneers were equally brave, resourceful, and persevering. The impact of occupancy here brought no bluegrass, or other plant fitted to withstand the bumps and buffetings of hard use. This region, when grazed by livestock, reverted through a series of more and more worthless grasses, shrubs, and weeds to a condition of unstable equilibrium. Each recession of plant types bred erosion; each increment to erosion bred a further recession of plants. The result today is a progressive and mutual deterioration, not only of plants and soils, but of the animal community subsisting thereon. The early settlers did not expect this: on the ciénegas[4] of New Mexico some even cut ditches to hasten it. So subtle has been its progress that few residents of the region are aware of it. It is quite invisible to the tourist who finds this wrecked landscape colorful and charming (as indeed it is, but it bears scant resemblance to what it was in 1848).

This same landscape was "developed" once before, but with quite different results. The Pueblo Indians settled the Southwest in pre-Columbian times, but they happened *not* to be equipped with range livestock. Their civilization expired, but not because their land expired.

In India, regions devoid of any sod-forming grass have been settled, apparently without wrecking the land, by the simple expedient of carrying the grass to the cow, rather than vice versa. (Was this the result of some deep wisdom, or was it just good luck? I do not know.)

In short, the plant succession steered the course of history; the pioneer simply demonstrated, for good or ill, which successions inhered in the land. Is history taught in this spirit? It will be, once the concept of land as a community really penetrates our intellectual life.

The Ecological Conscience

Conservation is a state of harmony between men and land. Despite nearly a century of propaganda, conservation still proceeds at a snail's pace; progress still consists largely of letterhead pieties and convention oratory. On the back forty we still slip two steps backward for each forward stride.

The usual answer to this dilemma is "more conservation education." No one 25 will debate this, but is it certain that only the *volume* of education needs stepping up? Is something lacking in the *content* as well?

It is difficult to give a fair summary of its content in brief form, but, as I understand it, the content is substantially this: obey the law, vote right, join some

---

[4]Spring-fed marshes. — Eds.

organizations, and practice what conservation is profitable on your own land; the government will do the rest.

Is not this formula too easy to accomplish anything worth-while? It defines no right or wrong, assigns no obligation, calls for no sacrifice, implies no change in the current philosophy of values. In respect of land-use, it urges only enlightened self-interest. Just how far will such education take us? An example will perhaps yield a partial answer.

By 1930 it had become clear to all except the ecologically blind that southwestern Wisconsin's topsoil was slipping seaward. In 1933 the farmers were told that if they would adopt certain remedial practices for five years, the public would donate CCC labor to install them, plus the necessary machinery and materials. The offer was widely accepted, but the practices were widely forgotten when the five-year contract period was up. The farmers continued only those practices that yielded an immediate and visible economic gain for themselves.

This led to the idea that maybe farmers would learn more quickly if they themselves wrote the rules. Accordingly the Wisconsin Legislature in 1937 passed the Soil Conservation District Law. This said to farmers, in effect: *We, the public, will furnish you free technical service and loan you specialized machinery, if you will write your own rules for land-use. Each county may write its own rules, and these will have the force of law.* Nearly all the counties promptly organized to accept the proffered help, but after a decade of operation, *no county has yet written a single rule.* There has been visible progress in such practices as strip-cropping, pasture renovation, and soil liming, but none in fencing woodlots against grazing, and none in excluding plow and cow from steep slopes. The farmers, in short, have selected those remedial practices which were profitable anyhow, and ignored those which were profitable to the community, but not clearly profitable to themselves.

When one asks why no rules have been written, one is told that the community is not yet ready to support them; education must precede rules. But the education actually in progress makes no mention of obligations to land over and above those dictated by self-interest. The net result is that we have more education but less soil, fewer healthy woods, and as many floods as in 1937.

The puzzling aspect of such situations is that the existence of obligations over and above self-interest is taken for granted in such rural community enterprises as the betterment of roads, schools, churches, and baseball teams. Their existence is not taken for granted, nor as yet seriously discussed, in bettering the behavior of the water that falls on the land, or in the preserving of the beauty or diversity of the farm landscape. Land-use ethics are still governed wholly by economic self-interest, just as social ethics were a century ago.

To sum up: we asked the farmer to do what he conveniently could to save his soil, and he has done just that, and only that. The farmer who clears the woods off a 75 per cent slope, turns his cows into the clearing, and dumps its rainfall, rocks, and soil into the community creek, is still (if otherwise decent) a respected member of society. If he puts lime on his fields and plants his crops on contour, he is still entitled to all the privileges and emoluments of his Soil Conservation District. The District is a beautiful piece of social machinery, but it is coughing along on two cylinders because we have been too timid, and too anxious for quick success, to tell the farmer the true magnitude of his obligations. Obligations have no meaning without conscience, and the problem we face is the extension of social conscience from people to land.

No important change in ethics was ever accomplished without an internal change in our intellectual emphasis, loyalties, affections, and convictions. The proof that conservation has not yet touched these foundations of conduct lies in the fact that philosophy and religion have not yet heard of it. In our attempt to make conservation easy, we have made it trivial. . . .

Land Health and the A-B Cleavage

A land ethic, then, reflects the existence of an ecological conscience, and this in turn reflects a conviction of individual responsibility for the health of the land. Health is the capacity of the land for self-renewal. Conservation is our effort to understand and preserve this capacity.

Conservationists are notorious for their dissensions. Superficially these seem 35 to add up to mere confusion, but a more careful scrutiny reveals a single plane of cleavage common to many specialized fields. In each field one group (A) regards the land as soil, and its function as commodity-production; another group (B) regards the land as a biota, and its function as something broader. How much broader is admittedly in a state of doubt and confusion.

In my own field, forestry, Group A is quite content to grow trees like cabbages, with cellulose as the basic forest commodity. It feels no inhibition against violence; its ideology is agronomic. Group B, on the other hand, sees forestry as fundamentally different from agronomy because it employs natural species, and manages a natural environment rather than creating an artificial one. Group B prefers natural reproduction on principle. It worries on biotic as well as economic grounds about the loss of species like chestnut, and the threatened loss of the white pines. It worries about a whole series of secondary forest functions: wildlife, recreation, watersheds, wilderness areas. To my mind, Group B feels the stirrings of an ecological conscience.

In the wildlife field, a parallel cleavage exists. For Group A the basic commodities are sport and meat; the yardsticks of production are ciphers of take in pheasants and trout. Artificial propagation is acceptable as a permanent as well as a temporary recourse — if its unit costs permit. Group B, on the other hand, worries about a whole series of biotic side-issues. What is the cost in predators of producing a game crop? Should we have further recourse to exotics? How can management restore the shrinking species, like prairie grouse, already hopeless as shootable game? How can management restore the threatened rarities, like trumpeter swan and whooping crane? Can management principles be extended to wildflowers? Here again it is clear to me that we have the same A-B cleavage as in forestry.

In the larger field of agriculture I am less competent to speak, but there seem to be somewhat parallel cleavages. Scientific agriculture was actively developing before ecology was born, hence a slower penetration of ecological concepts might be expected. Moreover the farmer, by the very nature of his techniques, must modify the biota more radically than the forester or the wildlife manager. Nevertheless, there are many discontents in agriculture which seem to add up to a new vision of "biotic farming."

Perhaps the most important of these is the new evidence that poundage or tonnage is no measure of the food-value of farm crops; the products of fertile soil may be qualitatively as well as quantitatively superior. We can bolster poundage from depleted soils by pouring on imported fertility, but we are not necessarily bolstering food-value. The possible ultimate ramifications of this idea are so immense that I must leave their exposition to abler pens.

The discontent that labels itself "organic farming," while bearing some of the earmarks of a cult, is nevertheless biotic in its direction, particularly in its insistence on the importance of soil flora and fauna. 40

The ecological fundamentals of agriculture are just as poorly known to the public as in other fields of land-use. For example, few educated people realize that the marvelous advances in technique made during recent decades are improvements in the pump, rather than the well. Acre for acre, they have barely sufficed to offset the sinking level of fertility.

In all of these cleavages, we see repeated the same basic paradoxes: man the conqueror *versus* man the biotic citizen; science the sharpener of his sword *versus* science the searchlight on his universe; land the slave and servant *versus* land the collective organism. Robinson's injunction to Tristram may well be applied, at this juncture, to *Homo sapiens* as a species in geological time:

> Whether you will or not
> You are a King, Tristram, for you are one
> Of the time-tested few that leave the world,
> When they are gone, not the same place it was.
> Mark what you leave.

The Outlook

It is inconceivable to me that an ethical relation to land can exist without love, respect, and admiration for land, and a high regard for its value. By value, I of course mean something far broader than mere economic value; I mean value in the philosophical sense.

Perhaps the most serious obstacle impeding the evolution of a land ethic is the fact that our educational and economic system is headed away from, rather than toward, an intense consciousness of land. Your true modern is separated from the land by many middlemen, and by innumerable physical gadgets. He has no vital relation to it; to him it is the space between cities on which crops grow. Turn him loose for a day on the land, and if the spot does not happen to be a golf links or a "scenic" area, he is bored stiff. If crops could be raised by hydroponics instead of farming, it would suit him very well. Synthetic substitutes for wood, leather, wool, and other natural land products suit him better than the originals. In short, land is something he has "outgrown."

Almost equally serious as an obstacle to a land ethic is the attitude of the 45 farmer for whom the land is still an adversary, or a taskmaster that keeps him in slavery. Theoretically, the mechanization of farming ought to cut the farmer's chains, but whether it really does is debatable.

One of the requisites for an ecological comprehension of land is an understanding of ecology, and this is by no means co-extensive with "education"; in fact, much higher education seems deliberately to avoid ecological concepts. An understanding of ecology does not necessarily originate in courses bearing ecological labels; it is quite as likely to be labeled geography, botany, agronomy, history, or economics. This is as it should be, but whatever the label, ecological training is scarce.

The case for a land ethic would appear hopeless but for the minority which is in obvious revolt against these "modern" trends.

The "key-log" which must be moved to release the evolutionary process for an ethic is simply this: quit thinking about decent land-use as solely an economic problem. Examine each question in terms of what is ethically and esthetically right, as well as what is economically expedient. A thing is right when it tends to preserve the integrity, stability, and beauty of the biotic community. It is wrong when it tends otherwise.

It of course goes without saying that economic feasibility limits the tether of what can or cannot be done for land. It always has and it always will. The fallacy the economic determinists have tied around our collective neck, and which we now need to cast off, is the belief that economics determines *all* land-use. This is simply not true. An innumerable host of actions and attitudes, comprising perhaps the bulk of all land relations, is determined by the land-users' tastes and predilections, rather than by his purse. The bulk of all land relations hinges on investments of time, forethought, skill, and faith rather than on investments of cash. As a land-user thinketh, so is he.

I have purposely presented the land ethic as a product of social evolution 50 because nothing so important as an ethic is ever "written." Only the most superficial student of history supposes that Moses "wrote" the Decalogue; it evolved in the minds of a thinking community, and Moses wrote a tentative summary of it for a "seminar." I say tentative because evolution never stops.

The evolution of a land ethic is an intellectual as well as emotional process. Conservation is paved with good intentions which prove to be futile, or even dangerous, because they are devoid of critical understanding either of the land, or of economic land-use. I think it is a truism that as the ethical frontier advances from the individual to the community, its intellectual content increases.

The mechanism of operation is the same for any ethic: social approbation for right actions: social disapproval for wrong actions.

By and large, our present problem is one of attitudes and implements. We are remodeling the Alhambra[5] with a steam-shovel, and we are proud of our yardage. We shall hardly relinquish the shovel, which after all has many good points, but we are in need of gentler and more objective criteria for its successful use.

Exploring the Text

1. What is the effect of the story about Odysseus that begins Aldo Leopold's essay?
2. How would you describe Leopold's tone at the beginning of "The Ethical Sequence"?
3. What are the ecological and philosophical distinctions that Leopold makes regarding the land ethic? Think of two contemporary examples that illustrate how these are actually "two definitions of one thing" (para. 4).
4. Paragraph 15 ends: "At the present moment, the assurance with which we regard this assumption is inverse to the degree of our education." What is the assumption to which he refers? Who holds it? What is Leopold's attitude toward it? What can we infer from the allusion to Abraham that precedes this sentence?
5. How does Leopold use analogy, particularly in paragraph 31, as a rhetorical technique? Is the claim he develops in that paragraph still true today? Explain your response.
6. Identify the claim in paragraph 33. Do you agree with it? Explain.
7. In the section "Land Health and the A-B Cleavage," Leopold introduces two ways of looking at the land, which he labels A and B (para. 35). Which viewpoint is more prominent today?
8. How effective are Leopold's appeals to ethos in paragraphs 38 and 39? Do they make his argument more convincing? Explain.
9. Expressing a view widely held in 1949, Leopold writes of the "discontent that labels itself 'organic farming'" (para. 40). Do we still see organic farming as a discontent today? Explain.
10. At the beginning of "The Outlook," Leopold characterizes the "modern" (para. 44). Does that characterization hold true today? Explain your response.
11. How does Leopold's use of the "key-log" metaphor (para. 48) move his essay toward its conclusion?
12. Leopold wrote "The Land Ethic" over sixty years ago. To what extent do his ideas apply to our current environmental situation?

---

[5]A famous Spanish palace. —Eds.

Natural Man

Lewis Thomas

Lewis Thomas (1913–1993) was educated at Harvard Medical School and worked as a medical researcher. He served as president and chancellor of Memorial Sloan-Kettering Cancer Center in New York and as professor of pathology and medicine at Cornell University. Thomas published many scientific articles and books, and in 1971 he began writing regularly for the *New England Journal of Medicine*. His columns were collected in 1974 to form the best-selling book *Lives of a Cell*, which won the American Book Award and includes the essay presented here, "Natural Man." Thomas's other books include *The Medusa and the Snail* (1979) and *Late Night Thoughts on Listening to Mahler's Ninth Symphony* (1983). In honor of his stellar prose style as well as his engaging ideas, the Lewis Thomas Prize is awarded annually by the Rockefeller University to a scientist for artistic achievement. Thomas is widely known as one of the originators of the science-based personal essay.

The social scientists, especially the economists, are moving deeply into ecology and the environment these days, with disquieting results. It goes somehow against the grain to learn that cost-benefit analyses can be done neatly on lakes, meadows, nesting gannets, and even whole oceans. It is hard enough to confront the environmental options ahead, and the hard choices, but even harder when the price tags are so visible. Even the new jargon is disturbing: it hurts the spirit, somehow, to read the word "environments," when the plural means that there are so many alternatives there to be sorted through, as in a market, and voted on. Economists need cool heads and cold hearts for this sort of work, and they must write in icy, often skiddy, prose.

The degree to which we are all involved in the control of the earth's life is just beginning to dawn on most of us, and it means another revolution for human thought.

This will not come easily. We've just made our way through inconclusive revolutions on the same topic, trying to make up our minds how we feel about nature. As soon as we arrived at one kind of consensus, like an enormous committee, we found it was time to think it through all over, and now here we are, at it again.

The oldest, easiest to swallow idea was that the earth was man's personal property, a combination of garden, zoo, bank vault and energy source, placed at our disposal to be consumed, ornamented or pulled apart as we wished. The betterment of mankind was, as we understood it, the whole point of the thing. Mastery over nature, mystery and all, was a moral duty and social obligation.

In the last few years we were wrenched away from this way of looking at it, 5 and arrived at something like general agreement that we had it wrong. We still argue the details, but it is conceded almost everywhere that we are not the masters of nature that we thought ourselves; we are as dependent as the leaves or midges or fish on the rest of life. We are part of the system. One way to put it is that the earth is a loosely formed, spherical organism, with all its working parts linked in symbiosis. We are, in this view, neither owners nor operators; at best, we might see ourselves as motile tissue specialized for receiving information — perhaps, in the best of all possible worlds, functioning as a nervous system for the whole being.

There is, for some, too much dependency in this view, and they prefer to see us as a separate, qualitatively different, special species, unlike any other form of life, despite the sharing around of genes, enzymes and organelles. No matter, there is still the underlying idea that we cannot have a life of our own without concern for the ecosystem in which we live, whether in majesty or not. This idea has been strong enough to launch the new movements for the sustenance of wilderness, the protection of wild life, the turning off of insatiable technologies, the preservation of "whole earth."

But now, just when the new view seems to be taking hold, we may be in for another wrench, this time more dismaying and unsettling than anything we've come through. In a sense, we will be obliged to swing back again, still believing in the new way but constrained by the facts of life to live in the old. It may be too late, as things have turned out.

We are, in fact, the masters, like it or not.

It is a despairing prospect. Here we are, practically speaking 21st-century mankind, filled to exuberance with our new understanding of kinship to all the family of life, and here we are, still 19th-century man, walking bootshod over the open face of nature, subjugating and civilizing it. And we cannot stop this controlling, unless we vanish under the hill ourselves. If there were such a thing as a world mind, it should crack over this.

The truth is, we have become more deeply involved than we ever dreamed. 10 The fact that we sit around as we do, worrying seriously about how best to preserve the life of the earth, is itself the sharpest measure of our involvement. It is not human arrogance that has taken us in this direction, but the most natural of natural events. We developed this way, we grew this way, we are this kind of species.

We have become, in a painful, unwished-for way, nature itself. We have grown into everywhere, spreading like a new growth over the entire surface, touching and affecting every other kind of life, incorporating ourselves. The earth risks being eutrophied by us. We are now the dominant feature of our own environment. Human beings, large terrestrial metazoans, fired by energy from microbial symbionts lodged in their cells, instructed by tapes of nucleic acid stretching back to the earliest live membranes, informed by neurons essentially the same as all the other neurons on earth, sharing structures with mastodons and lichens, living off the sun, are now in charge, running the place, for better or worse.

Or is it really this way? It could be, you know, just the other way round. Perhaps we are the invaded ones, the subjugated, used.

Certain animals in the sea live by becoming part animal, part plant. They engulf algae, which then establish themselves as complex plant tissues, essential for the life of the whole company. I suppose the giant clam, if he had more of a mind, would have moments of dismay on seeing what he has done to the plant world, incorporating so much of it, enslaving green cells, living off the photosynthesis. But the plant cells would take a different view of it, having captured the clam on the most satisfactory of terms, including the small lenses in his tissues that focus sunlight for their benefit; perhaps algae have bad moments about what they may collectively be doing to the world of clams.

With luck, our own situation might be similar, on a larger scale. This might turn out to be a special phase in the morphogenesis of the earth when it is necessary to have something like us, for a time anyway, to fetch and carry energy, look after new symbiotic arrangements, store up information for some future season, do a certain amount of ornamenting, maybe even carry seeds around the solar system. That kind of thing. Handyman for the earth.

I would much prefer this useful role, if I had any say, to the essentially 15 unearthly creature we seem otherwise on the way to becoming. It would mean making some quite fundamental changes in our attitudes toward each other, if we were really to think of ourselves as indispensable elements of nature. We would surely become the environment to worry about the most. We would discover, in ourselves, the sources of wonderment and delight that we have discerned in all other manifestations of nature. Who knows, we might even acknowledge the fragility and vulnerability that always accompany high specialization in biology, and movements might start up for the protection of ourselves as a valuable, endangered species. We couldn't lose.

. . . .

Exploring the Text

1. What is Lewis Thomas's complaint in the first paragraph? What does he find "disquieting"? Do you see evidence today of the trend that Thomas bemoans? Do you find it disquieting, or do you have a different perspective? Explain your response.
2. The first "Earth Day" celebration was on April 22, 1970, and it became international in 1990. Considering the increased environmental awareness we have experienced since the 1970s, have we achieved the "revolution for human thought" (para. 2) that Thomas mentions?
3. What is Thomas's attitude toward the preference he alludes to in paragraph 6?
4. Why does Thomas regard the recognition that we are masters as a "despairing prospect" (para. 9)?
5. How many times does Thomas use the pronoun "we"? What is its effect?

6. Do you agree with Thomas that "the earth risks being eutrophied" (para. 11)? Explain your response.
7. Note the appositive for human beings that Thomas writes in paragraph 11. How does such a characterization affect the reader? How does it affect Thomas's argument?
8. What rhetorical relationship does paragraph 13 have with the preceding paragraph?
9. What are the implications of the analogy Thomas develops in paragraph 13? How effectively does it serve his purpose? Explain your response.

from *The End of Nature*

BILL MCKIBBEN

Author of a dozen books about the environment, Bill McKibben (b. 1960) grew up in Massachusetts and attended Harvard University, where he was president of the *Harvard Crimson* newspaper. After college he joined the *New Yorker*, where he was a staff writer until 1987. His first book, *The End of Nature*, was published in 1989 after being serialized in the *New Yorker*. It is regarded as the first book about climate change for a general audience and has been printed in more than twenty languages. Among McKibben's other books are *Long Distance: A Year of Living Strenuously* (2000), *Enough* (2003), and *Wandering Home* (2005). In 2010, he published another national best seller, *Eaarth: Making a Life on a Tough New Planet*, an account of the rapid onset of climate change. It was excerpted in *Scientific American. Time* magazine has called McKibben "the planet's best green journalist," and the *Boston Globe* has said that he is "probably the country's most important environmentalist." He is currently a scholar-in-residence at Middlebury College in Vermont. The excerpt included here is from the conclusion of *The End of Nature*.

The inertia of affluence, the push of poverty, the soaring population— these and the other reasons . . . make me pessimistic about the chances that we will dramatically alter our ways of thinking and living, that we will turn humble in the face of our troubles.

A purely personal effort is, of course, just a gesture—a good gesture, but a gesture. The greenhouse effect is the first environmental problem we can't escape by moving to the woods. There are no personal solutions. There is no time to just decide we'll raise enlightened children and they'll slowly change the world. (When the problem was that someone might drop the Bomb, it perhaps made sense to bear and raise sane, well-adjusted children in the hope that they'd help prevent the Bomb from being dropped. But the problem now is precisely too many children, well adjusted or otherwise.) We have to be the ones to do it, and simply driving less won't matter, except as a statement, a way to get other people—many other people—to drive less. *Most* people have to be persuaded, and persuaded quickly, to change.

But saying that something is difficult is not the same as saying it is impossible. After all, George Bush decided in the wake of the 1988 heat that he was an environmentalist. Margaret Thatcher, who in 1985 had linked environmental groups with other "subversives" as "the enemy within," found the religion at about the same time, after the death of the North Sea seals and the odyssey of the *Karin B*, the wandering toxic-waste barge. "Protecting the balance of nature," she said, is "one of the great challenges of the twentieth century."

I've been using the analogy of slavery throughout this discussion: we feel it our privilege (and we feel it a necessity) to dominate nature to our advantage, as whites once dominated blacks. When one method of domination seems to be ending—the reliance on fossil fuels, say—we cast about for another, like genetic tinkering, much as Americans replaced slavery with Jim Crow segregation. However, in my lifetime that official segregation ended. Through their courage, men and women like Martin Luther King and Fannie Lou Hamer managed to harness the majority's better qualities—idealism, love for one's neighbor—to transform the face of American society. Racism, it is true, remains virulent, but the majority of Americans have voted for legislators who passed laws—radical laws—mandating affirmative action programs. Out of some higher motive (and, of course, some base motives, such as the fear of black revolt), whites have sacrificed at least a little potential wealth and power. It would be wrong to say categorically that such a shift couldn't happen with regard to the environment—that a mixture of fear and the love for nature buried in most of us couldn't rise to the surface. Some small but significant steps have been taken. Los Angeles, for instance, recently enacted a series of laws to improve air quality that will change at least the edges of the lives of every resident. Los Angelenos will drive different cars, turn in their gas-powered lawn mowers, start their barbecues without lighter fluid.

Most of my hope, however, fades in the face of the uniqueness of the situation. As we have seen, nature is already ending, its passing quiet and accidental. And not only does its ending prevent us from returning to the world we previously knew, but it also, for two powerful reasons, makes any of the fundamental changes we've discussed even more unlikely than they might be in easier times. If the end of nature were still in the future, a preventable possibility, the equation might be different. But it isn't in the future—it's in the recent past, and the present.

⁂

The end of nature is a plunge into the unknown, fearful as much because it is unknown as because it might be hot or dry or whipped by hurricanes. This lack of security is the first reason that fundamental change will be much harder, for the changes we've been discussing—the deep ecology alternative, for instance—would make life even more unpredictable. One would have to begin to forgo the traditional methods of securing one's future—many children, many possessions, and so on. Jeremy Rifkin, in his book on genetic engineering, said there was still a chance we would choose to sacrifice "a measure of our own future security in order to represent the interests of the rest of the cosmos. . . . If we have been saving that spirit up for a propitious moment, then certainly now is the time for it to pour forth."

But now isn't the time—now, as the familiar world around us starts to change, is the moment when every threatened instinct will push us to scramble to preserve at least our familiar style of life. We can—and we may well—make the adjustments necessary for our survival. For instance, much of the early work in agricultural biotechnology has focused on inventing plants able to survive heat and drought. It seems the sensible thing to do—the way to keep life as "normal" as possible in the face of change. It leads, though, as I have said, to the second death of nature: the imposition of our artificial world in place of the broken natural one.

The rivers of the American Southwest, in particular the Colorado, provide a perfect example of this phenomenon. Though Ed Abbey wrote about the entire Southwest, the one spot he kept returning to, the navel of his universe, was Glen Canyon dam. The dam, built a couple of decades ago near the Utah-Arizona line, is just upstream of the Grand Canyon. It backs up the waters of the Colorado into Lake Powell, a reservoir that rises and falls with the demand for hydroelectric power. The water covers Glen Canyon, a place so sweet Abbey called it "paradise"—and the description of his raft trip through the gorge shortly before the dam was finished makes the term sound weak, understated.

Since the degradation of this canyon stood in his mind for all human arrogance, its salvation would be the sign that man had turned the corner, begun the long trek back toward his proper station. (Blowing up the dam is the great aim of [Abbey's] Monkey Wrench Gang.) If we decide to take out the dam, it would signal many things, among them that perhaps the desert should not house huge numbers of people—that some should move, and others take steps to ensure smaller future generations. True, if we decide to take out the dam and the lake flowed away toward Mexico, it would "no doubt expose a drear and hideous scene: immense mud flats and whole plateaus of sodden garbage strewn with dead trees, sunken boats, the skeletons of long-forgotten, decomposing waterskiers," Abbey writes. "But to those who find the prospect too appalling, I say give nature a little time. In five years, at most in ten, the sun and wind and storms will cleanse and sterilize the repellent mess. The inevitable floods will soon remove all that does not belong within the canyons. Fresh green willow, box elder, and redbud will reappear; and the ancient drowned cottonwoods (noble monuments to themselves) will be replaced by young of their own kind. . . . Within a generation—thirty years—I predict the river and canyons will bear a decent resemblance to their former selves. Within the lifetime of our children Glen Canyon and the living river, heart of the canyonlands, will be restored to us. The wilderness will again belong to God, the people, and the wild things that call it home."

Such a vision is, of course, romantically unlikely under any circumstances. But the new insecurity that accompanies the end of nature makes it even more far-fetched. As we have seen, the projected increases in evaporation and decreases in rainfall in the Colorado watershed could cut flows along the river nearly in half. As a result, noted an EPA report, the reluctance in recent years to build big dams, for fear of environmental opposition, "may be re-evaluated in light of possible new demands for developed water under warm-dry climate change scenarios." Specifically, "climate change may create pressure to build the Animas-LaPlata and Narrows projects proposed for Colorado." In other words, where Abbey hoped for box elder and redbud more dams will bloom. The authors of *Gaia: An Atlas of Planet Management* are quite explicit about dam building. In a section on water conservation they put forth a lot of good ideas for fixing leaky mains and such, but they also sing the praises of damming rivers, a process that "can help satisfy a number of needs at once: it helps control flooding, provides the potential for generating hydropower, and stores water for a variety of purposes, including irrigation. The resulting reservoirs represent a multi-purpose resource, with potential for aquaculture and leisure activities." A flood-washed paradise of cottonwood or a "multi-purpose resource"—that is the choice, and it is not hard to guess, if the heat is on, what the voters of Arizona will demand.

I got a glimpse of this particular future a few years ago when I spent some time along the La Grande River, in sub-Arctic Quebec. It is barren land but beautiful—a tundra of tiny ponds and hummocks stretching to the horizon, carpeted in light-green caribou moss. There are trees—almost all black spruce, and all spindly, sparse. A number of Indians and Eskimos lived there—about the number the area could support. Then, a decade or so ago, Hydro-Quebec, the provincial utility, decided to exploit the power of the La Grande by building three huge dams along the river's 350-mile length. The largest, said the Hydro-Quebec spokesman, is the size of fifty-four thousand two-story houses or sixty-seven billion peas. Its spillway could carry the combined flow of all the rivers of Europe, and erecting it was a Bunyanesque task: eighteen thousand men carved the roads north through the tundra and poured the concrete. (Photos show the cooks stirring spaghetti sauce with canoe paddles.) On the one hand, this is a perfect example of "environmentally sound" energy generation; it produces an enormous amount of power without giving off so much as a whiff of any greenhouse gas. This is the sort of structure we'll be clamoring to build as the warming progresses.

But environmentally sound is not the same as natural. The dams have altered an area larger than Switzerland—the flow of the Caniapiscau River, for instance, has been partly reversed to provide more water for the turbines. In September 1984, at least ten thousand caribou drowned trying to cross the river during their annual migration. They were crossing at their usual spot, but the river was not its usual size; it was so swollen that many of the animals were swept forty-five miles downstream. Every good argument—the argument that fossil fuels cause the greenhouse effect; the argument that in a drier, hotter world we'll need more water; the argument that as our margin of security dwindles we must act to restore it—will lead us to more La Grande projects, more dams on the Colorado, more "management." Every argument—that the warmer weather and increased ultraviolet is killing plants and causing cancer; that the new weather is causing food shortages—will have us looking to genetic engineering for salvation. And with each such step we will move farther from nature.

※

At the same time—and this is the second kicker—the only real counterargument, the argument for an independent, eternal, ever-sweet nature, will grow ever fainter and harder to make. Why? Because nature, independent nature, is already ending. Fighting for it is like fighting for an independent Latvia except that it's harder, since the end of nature may be permanent. Take out Glen Canyon dam and let the Colorado run free, let the "inevitable floods" wash away the debris? But floods may be a thing of the past on the Colorado; the river may, in effect, be dammed at the source—in the clouds that no longer dump their freight on its upper reaches, and in the heat that evaporates the water that does fall.

If nature were about to end, we might muster endless energy to stave it off; but if nature has already ended, what are we fighting for? Before any redwoods had been cloned or genetically improved, one could understand clearly what the fight against such tinkering was about. It was about the idea that a redwood was somehow sacred, that its fundamental identity should remain beyond our control. But once that barrier has been broken, what is the fight about then? It's not like opposing nuclear reactors or toxic waste dumps, each one of which poses new risks to new areas. This damage is to an idea, the idea of nature, and all the ideas that descend from it. It is not cumulative. Wendell Berry once argued that without a "fascination" with the wonder of the natural world "the energy needed for its preservation will never be developed"—that "there must be a mystique of the rain if we are ever to restore the purity of the rainfall." This makes sense when the problem is transitory—sulfur from a smokestack drifting over the Adirondacks. But how can there be a mystique of the rain now that every drop—even the drops that fall as snow on the Arctic, even the drops that fall deep in the remaining forest primeval—bears the permanent stamp of man? Having lost its separateness, it loses its special power. Instead of being a category like God— something beyond our control—it is now a category like the defense budget or the minimum wage, a problem we must work out. This in itself changes its meaning completely, and changes our reaction to it.

A few weeks ago, on the hill behind my house, I almost kicked the biggest rabbit I had ever seen. She had nearly finished turning white for the winter, and we stood there watching each other for a pleasant while, two creatures linked by curiosity. What will it mean to come across a rabbit in the woods once genetically engineered "rabbits" are widespread? Why would we have any more reverence or affection for such a rabbit than we would for a Coke bottle? 15

The end of nature probably also makes us reluctant to attach ourselves to its remnants, for the same reason that we usually don't choose friends from among the terminally ill. I love the mountain outside my back door — the stream that runs along its flank, and the smaller stream that slides down a quarter-mile mossy chute, and the place where the slope flattens into an open plain of birch and oak. But I know that some part of me resists getting to know it better — for fear, weak-kneed as it sounds, of getting hurt. If I knew as well as a forester what sick trees looked like, I fear I would see them everywhere. I find now that I like the woods best in winter, when it is harder to tell what might be dying. The winter woods might be perfectly healthy come spring, just as the sick friend, when she's sleeping peacefully, might wake up without the wheeze in her lungs.

Writing on a different subject, the bonds between men and women, Allan Bloom describes the difficulty of maintaining a committed relationship in an age when divorce — the end of that relationship — is so widely accepted: "The possibility of separation is already the fact of separation, inasmuch as people today must plan to be whole and self-sufficient and cannot risk interdependence." Instead of working to strengthen our attachments, our energies "are exhausted in preparation for independence." How much more so if that possible separation is definite, if that hurt and confusion is certain. I love winter best now, but I try not to love it too much, for fear of the January perhaps not so distant when the snow will fall as warm rain. There is no future in loving nature.

And there may not even be much past. Though Thoreau's writings grew in value and importance the closer we drew to the end of nature, the time fast approaches when he will be inexplicable, his notions less sensible to future men than the cave paintings are to us. Thoreau writes, on his climb up Katahdin, that the mountain "was vast, Titanic, and such as man never inhabits. Some part of the beholder, even some vital part, seems to escape through the loose grating of his ribs. . . . Nature has got him at a disadvantage, caught him alone, and pilfers him of some of his divine faculty. She does not smile on him as in the plains. She seems to say sternly, why came ye here before your time? This ground is not prepared for you." This sentiment describes perfectly the last stage of the relationship of man to nature — though we had subdued her in the low places, the peaks, the poles, the jungles still rang with her pure message. But what sense will this passage make in the years to come, when Katahdin, the "cloud factory," is ringed by clouds of man's own making? When the massive pines that ring its base have been genetically improved for straightness of trunk and "proper branch drop," or, more likely, have sprung from the cones of genetically improved trees that began a few miles and a few generations distant on some timber plantation? When the moose that ambles by is part of a herd whose rancher is committed to the enlightened, Gaian notion that "conservation and profit go hand in hand"?

Thoreau describes an afternoon of fishing at the mouth of Murch Brook, a dozen miles from the summit of Katahdin. Speckled trout "swallowed the bait as fast as we could throw in; and the finest specimens . . . that I have ever seen, the largest one weighing three pounds, were heaved upon the shore." He stood there to catch them as "they fell in a perfect shower" around him. "While yet alive, before their tints had faded, they glistened like the fairest flowers, the product of primitive rivers; and he could hardly trust his senses, as he stood over them, that these jewels should have swam away in that Aboljacknagesic water for so long, some many dark ages—these bright fluviatile flowers, seen of Indians only, made beautiful, the Lord only knows why, to swim there!" But through biotechnology we have already synthesized growth hormone for trout. Soon pulling them from the water will mean no more than pulling cars from an assembly line. We won't have to wonder why the Lord made them beautiful and put them there; we will have created them to increase protein supplies or fish-farm profits. If we want to make them pretty, we may. Soon Thoreau will make no sense. And when that happens, the end of nature—which began with our alteration of the atmosphere, and continued with the responses to our precarious situation of the "planetary managers" and the "genetic engineers"—will be final. The loss of memory will be the eternal loss of meaning.

In the end, I understand perfectly well that defiance may mean prosperity and a sort of security—that more dams will help the people of Phoenix, and that genetic engineering will help the sick, and that there is so much progress that can still be made against human misery. And I have no great desire to limit my way of life. If I thought we could put off the decision, foist it on our grandchildren, I'd be willing. As it is, I have no plans to live in a cave, or even an unheated cabin. If it took ten thousand years to get where we are, it will take a few generations to climb back down. But this could be the epoch when people decide at least to go no farther down the path we've been following—when we make not only the necessary technological adjustments to preserve the world from overheating but also the necessary mental adjustments to ensure that we'll never again put our good ahead of everything else's. This is the path I choose, for it offers at least a shred of hope for a living, eternal, meaningful world. 20

The reasons for my choice are as numerous as the trees on the hill outside my window, but they crystallized in my mind when I read a passage from one of the brave optimists of our managed future. "The existential philosophers—particularly Sartre—used to lament that man lacked an essential purpose," writes Walter Truett Anderson. "We find now that the human predicament is not quite so devoid of inherent purpose after all. To be caretakers of a planet, custodians of all its life forms and shapers of its (and our own) future is certainly purpose enough." This intended rallying cry depresses me more deeply than I can say. That is our destiny? To be "caretakers" of a managed world, "custodians" of all life? For that job security we will trade the mystery of the natural world, the pungent mystery of our own lives and of a world bursting with exuberant creation? Much better, Sartre's neutral purposelessness. But much better than that, another vision, of man actually living up to his potential.

As birds have flight, our special gift is reason. Part of that reason drives the intelligence that allows us, say, to figure out and master DNA, or to build big power plants. But our reason could also keep us from following blindly the biological imperatives toward endless growth in numbers and territory. Our reason allows us to conceive of our species as a species, and to recognize the danger that our growth poses to it, and to feel something for the other species we threaten. Should we so choose, we could exercise our reason to do what no other animal can do: we could limit ourselves voluntarily, *choose* to remain God's creatures instead of making ourselves gods. What a towering achievement that would be, so much more impressive than the largest dam (beavers can build dams) because so much harder. Such restraint — not genetic engineering or planetary management — is the real challenge, the hard thing. Of course we can splice genes. But can we *not* splice genes?

The momentum behind our impulse to control nature may be too strong to stop. But the likelihood of defeat is not an excuse to avoid trying. In one sense it's an aesthetic choice we face, much like Thoreau's, though what is at stake is less the shape of our lives than the very practical question of the lives of all the other species and the creation they together constitute. But it is, of course, for our benefit, too. Jeffers wrote, "Integrity is wholeness, the greatest beauty is / organic wholeness of life and things, the divine beauty of the universe. Love that, not man / Apart from that, or else you will share man's pitiful confusions, or drown in despair when his days darken." The day has come when we choose between that wholeness and man in it or man apart, between that old clarity or new darkness.

The strongest reason for choosing man apart is, as I have said, the idea that nature has ended. And I think it has. But I cannot stand the clanging finality of the argument I've made, any more than people have ever been able to stand the clanging finality of their own deaths. So I hope against hope. Though not in our time, and not in the time of our children, or their children, if we now, *today*, limited our numbers and our desires and our ambitions, perhaps nature could someday resume its independent working. Perhaps the temperature could someday adjust itself to its own setting, and the rain fall of its own accord.

Time, as I said at the start of this essay, is elusive, odd. Perhaps the ten thousand years of our encroaching, defiant civilization, an eternity to us and a yawn to the rocks around us, could give way to ten thousand years of humble civilization when we choose to pay more for the benefits of nature, when we rebuild the sense of wonder and sanctity that could protect the natural world. At the end of that span we would still be so young, and perhaps ready to revel in the timelessness that surrounds us. I said, much earlier, that one of the possible meanings of the end of nature is that God is dead. But another, if there was or is any such thing as God, is that he has granted us free will and now looks on, with great concern and love, to see how we exercise it: to see if we take the chance offered by this crisis to bow down and humble ourselves, or if we compound original sin with terminal sin.

25

And if what I fear indeed happens? If the next twenty years sees us pump ever more gas into the sky, and if it sees us take irrevocable steps into the genetically engineered future, what solace then? The only ones in need of consolation will be those of us who were born in the transitional decades, too early to adapt completely to a brave new ethos.

I've never paid more than the usual attention to the night sky, perhaps because I grew up around cities, on suburban blocks lined with streetlights. But last August, on a warm Thursday afternoon, my wife and I hauled sleeping bags high into the mountains and laid them out on a rocky summit and waited for night to fall and the annual Perseid meteor shower to begin. After midnight, it finally started in earnest—every minute, every thirty seconds, another spear of light shot across some corner of the sky, so fast that unless you were looking right at it you had only the sense of a flash. Our bed was literally rock-hard, and when, toward dawn, an unforecast rain soaked our tentless clearing, it was cold—but the night was glorious, and I've since gotten a telescope. When, in *Paradise Lost*, Adam asks about the movements of the heavens, Raphael refuses to answer. "Let it speak," he says, "the Maker's high magnificence, who built / so spacious, and his line stretcht out so far; / That man may know he dwells not in his own; / An edifice too large for him to fill, / Lodg'd in a small partition, and the rest / Ordain'd for uses to his Lord best known." We may be creating microscopic nature; we may have altered the middle nature all around us; but this vast nature above our atmosphere still holds mystery and wonder. The occasional satellite does blip across, but it is almost a self-parody. Someday, man may figure out a method of conquering the stars, but at least for now when we look into the night sky, it is as Burroughs[1] said: "We do not see ourselves reflected there—we are swept away from ourselves, and impressed with our own insignificance."

As I lay on the mountaintop that August night I tried to pick out the few constellations I could identify—Orion's Belt, the Dippers. The ancients, surrounded by wild and even hostile nature, took comfort in seeing the familiar above them—spoons and swords and nets. But we will need to train ourselves not to see those patterns. The comfort we need is inhuman.

Exploring the Text

1. At the beginning of the first section, Bill McKibben confesses that he is pessimistic. How does such a remark affect your reading of the selection?
2. He says in paragraph 5 that there are two reasons for pessimism. What are they? Paraphrase each. Do you agree? Explain why or why not.
3. What does McKibben mean by "the second death of nature" (para. 7)?

---

[1]John Burroughs (1837–1921), Amerian naturalist and nature writer. —Eds.

4. What is significant about the quotation marks around such words and phrases as "multi-purpose resource" (para. 10), "environmentally sound" (para. 11), "management" (para. 12), "conservation and profit go hand in hand" (para. 18), and "planetary managers" and "genetic engineers" (para. 19)?

5. In paragraph 12, McKibben delineates where "[e]very good argument" will lead us. Do you think each of the arguments that McKibben presents is "good," as he states? Do you think that the public at large would agree? Explain why or why not.

6. What is the nature of the argument McKibben advances in paragraph 14? Explain it according to the Toulmin model (see Chapter 3).

7. Identify the analogies McKibben develops in paragraphs 16 and 17. How effectively do they contribute to his position?

8. Do you think that the choice McKibben discusses in paragraph 22 is a likely one for humanity to take? Why or why not? Does McKibben think it likely? Explain.

9. McKibben confesses that perhaps there is room for hope if we take action now, casting *today* in italics (para. 24) in 1989. He then writes, "And if what I fear indeed happens? If the next twenty years sees us pump ever more gas into the sky, and if it sees us take irrevocable steps into the genetically engineered future, what solace then?" (para. 26). We now know what those twenty years (and more) have seen. Do you think that we can still "hope against hope," as McKibben puts it? Explain.

10. What is the "brave new ethos" (para. 26) that McKibben suggests will arrive?

11. Why is our environmental problem unique when compared to the threats posed by the human cruelty associated with slavery or atomic warfare? Do you agree with McKibben that nature has ended? Why or why not?

The Clan of One-Breasted Women

Terry Tempest Williams

Terry Tempest Williams was born in Nevada in 1955. She studied at the University of Utah, where she became a professor of English. She has also been naturalist-in-residence at the Utah Museum of Natural History. Williams's work has appeared in the *New Yorker, Orion,* the *New York Times,* the *Nation,* and *The Best American Essays* (2000). Williams has won a Guggenheim Fellowship and a Lannan Literary Fellowship. Among her books are the essay collections *An Unspoken Hunger: Stories from the Field* (1995), *Finding Beauty in a Broken World* (2008), and *Refuge: An Unnatural History of Family and Place* (1989), from which the following selection is taken. The essay is based on her family's experience in Utah, where she lives and writes on social and environmental issues.

I belong to a Clan of One-breasted Women. My mother, my grandmothers, and six aunts have all had mastectomies. Seven are dead. The two who survive have just completed rounds of chemotherapy and radiation.

I've had my own problems: two biopsies for breast cancer and a small tumor between my ribs diagnosed as "a border-line malignancy."

This is my family history.

Most statistics tell us breast cancer is genetic, hereditary, with rising percentages attached to fatty diets, childlessness, or becoming pregnant after thirty. What they don't say is living in Utah may be the greatest hazard of all.

We are a Mormon family with roots in Utah since 1847. The word-of-wisdom, a religious doctrine of health, kept the women in my family aligned with good foods: no coffee, no tea, tobacco, or alcohol. For the most part, these women were finished having their babies by the time they were thirty. And only one faced breast cancer prior to 1960. Traditionally, as a group of people, Mormons have a low rate of cancer.

Is our family a cultural anomaly? The truth is we didn't think about it. Those who did, usually the men, simply said, "bad genes." The women's attitude was stoic. Cancer was part of life. On February 16, 1971, the eve before my mother's surgery, I accidently picked up the telephone and overheard her ask my grandmother what she could expect.

"Diane, it is one of the most spiritual experiences you will ever encounter."

I quietly put down the receiver.

Two days later, my father took my three brothers and me to the hospital to visit her. She met us in the lobby in a wheelchair. No bandages were visible. I'll never forget her radiance, the way she held herself in a purple velour robe and how she gathered us around her.

"Children, I am fine. I want you to know I felt the arms of God around me." 10

We believed her. My father cried. Our mother, his wife, was thirty-eight years old.

Two years ago, after my mother's death from cancer, my father and I were having dinner together. He had just returned from St. George where his construction company was putting in natural gas lines for towns in southern Utah. He spoke of his love for the country: the sandstoned landscape, bare-boned and beautiful. He had just finished hiking the Kolob trail in Zion National Park. We got caught up in reminiscing, recalling with fondness our walk up Angel's Landing on his fiftieth birthday and the years our family had vacationed there. This was a remembered landscape where we had been raised.

Over dessert, I shared a recurring dream of mine. I told my father that for years, as long as I could remember, I saw this flash of light in the night in the desert. That this image had so permeated my being, I could not venture south without seeing it again, on the horizon, illuminating buttes and mesas.

"You did see it," he said.

"Saw what?" I asked, a bit tentative. 15

"The bomb. The cloud. We were driving home from Riverside, California. You were sitting on your mother's lap. She was pregnant. In fact, I remember the date, September 7, 1957. We had just gotten out of the Service. We were driving north, past Las Vegas. It was an hour or so before dawn, when this explosion went off. We not only heard it, but felt it. I thought the oil tanker in front of us had blown up. We pulled over and suddenly, rising from the desert floor, we saw it, clearly, this golden-stemmed cloud, the mushroom. The sky seemed to vibrate with an eerie pink glow. Within a few minutes, a light ash was raining on the car."

I stared at my father. This was new information to me.

"I thought you knew that," my father said. "It was a common occurrence in the fifties."

It was at this moment I realized the deceit I had been living under. Children growing up in the American Southwest, drinking contaminated milk from contaminated cows, even from the contaminated breasts of their mother, my mother—members, years later, of the Clan of One-breasted Women.

It is a well-known story in the Desert West, "The Day We Bombed Utah," or per- 20 haps, "The Years We Bombed Utah."[1] Above ground atomic testing in Nevada took place from January 27, 1951, through July 11, 1962. Not only were the winds blowing north, covering "low use segments of the population" with fallout and leaving sheep dead in their tracks, but the climate was right. The United States of the 1950s was red, white, and blue. The Korean War was raging. McCarthyism was rampant. Ike was it and the Cold War was hot. If you were against nuclear testing, you were for a Communist regime.

Much has been written about this "American nuclear tragedy." Public health was secondary to national security. The Atomic Energy Commissioner, Thomas Murray said, "Gentlemen, we must not let anything interfere with this series of tests, nothing."[2]

Again and again, the American public was told by its government, in spite of burns, blisters, and nausea, "It has been found that the tests may be conducted with adequate assurance of safety under conditions prevailing at the bombing reservations."[3] Assuaging public fears was simply a matter of public relations. "Your best action," an Atomic Energy Commission booklet read, "is not to be worried about fallout." A news release typical of the times stated, "We find no basis for concluding that harm to any individual has resulted from radioactive fallout."[4]

On August 30, 1979, during Jimmy Carter's presidency, a suit was filed entitled "Irene Allen vs. the United States of America." Mrs. Allen was the first to be alphabetically listed with twenty-four test cases, representative of nearly 1200 plaintiffs seeking compensation from the United States government for cancers caused from nuclear testing in Nevada.

---

[1]Fuller, John G., *The Day We Bombed Utah* (New York: New American Library, 1984).
[2]Szasz, Ferenc M., "Downwind from the Bomb," *Nevada Historical Society Quarterly*, Fall 1987, Vol. XXX, No. 3, p. 185.
[3]Fradkin, Philip L., *Fallout* (Tucson: University of Arizona Press, 1989), 98.
[4]Ibid., 109.

Irene Allen lived in Hurricane, Utah. She was the mother of five children and had been widowed twice. Her first husband with their two oldest boys had watched the tests from the roof of the local high school. He died of leukemia in 1956. Her second husband died of pancreatic cancer in 1978.

In a town meeting conducted by Utah Senator Orrin Hatch, shortly before the suit was filed, Mrs. Allen said, "I am not blaming the government, I want you to know that, Senator Hatch. But I thought if my testimony could help in any way so this wouldn't happen again to any of the generations coming up after us . . . I am really happy to be here this day to bear testimony of this."[5]

God-fearing people. This is just one story in an anthology of thousands.

On May 10, 1984, Judge Bruce S. Jenkins handed down his opinion. Ten of the plaintiffs were awarded damages. It was the first time a federal court had determined that nuclear tests had been the cause of cancers. For the remaining fourteen test cases, the proof of causation was not sufficient. In spite of the split decision, it was considered a landmark ruling.[6] It was not to remain so for long.

In April, 1987, the 10th Circuit Court of Appeals overturned Judge Jenkins' ruling on the basis that the United States was protected from suit by the legal doctrine of sovereign immunity, the centuries-old idea from England in the days of absolute monarchs.[7]

In January, 1988, the Supreme Court refused to review the Appeals Court decision. To our court system, it does not matter whether the United States Government was irresponsible, whether it lied to its citizens or even that citizens died from the fallout of nuclear testing. What matters is that our government is immune. "The King can do no wrong."

In Mormon culture, authority is respected, obedience is revered, and independent thinking is not. I was taught as a young girl not to "make waves" or "rock the boat."

"Just let it go —" my mother would say. "You know how you feel, that's what counts."

For many years, I did just that — listened, observed, and quietly formed my own opinions within a culture that rarely asked questions because they had all the answers. But one by one, I watched the women in my family die common, heroic deaths. We sat in waiting rooms hoping for good news, always receiving the bad. I cared for them, bathed their scarred bodies and kept their secrets. I watched beautiful women become bald as cytoxan, cisplatin and adriamycin were injected

---

[5]Town meeting held by Senator Orrin Hatch in St. George, Utah, April 17, 1979, transcript, 26–28.

[6]Fradkin, op. cit., 228.

[7]U.S. vs. Allen, 816 Federal Reporter, 2d/1417 (10th Circuit Court 1987), cert. denied, 108 S. Ct. 694 (1988).

into their veins. I held their foreheads as they vomited green-black bile and I shot them with morphine when the pain became inhuman. In the end, I witnessed their last peaceful breaths, becoming a midwife to the rebirth of their souls. But the price of obedience became too high.

The fear and inability to question authority that ultimately killed rural communities in Utah during atmospheric testing of atomic weapons was the same fear I saw being held in my mother's body. Sheep. Dead sheep. The evidence is buried.

I cannot prove that my mother, Diane Dixon Tempest, or my grandmothers, Lettie Romney Dixon and Kathryn Blackett Tempest, along with my aunts contracted cancer from nuclear fallout in Utah. But I can't prove they didn't.

My father's memory was correct, the September blast we drove through in 1957 was part of Operation Plumbbob, one of the most intensive series of bomb tests to be initiated. The flash of light in the night in the desert I had always thought was a dream developed into a family nightmare. It took fourteen years, from 1957 to 1971, for cancer to show up in my mother—the same time, Howard L. Andrews, an authority on radioactive fallout at the National Institutes of Health, says radiation cancer requires to become evident.[8] The more I learn about what it means to be a "downwinder," the more questions I drown in. 35

What I do know, however, is that as a Mormon woman of the fifth generation of "Latter-Day-Saints," I must question everything, even if it means losing my faith, even if it means becoming a member of a border tribe among my own people. Tolerating blind obedience in the name of patriotism or religion ultimately takes our lives.

When the Atomic Energy Commission described the country north of the Nevada Test Site as "virtually uninhabited desert terrain," my family members were some of the "virtual uninhabitants."

One night, I dreamed women from all over the world were circling a blazing fire in the desert. They spoke of change, of how they hold the moon in their bellies and wax and wane with its phases. They mocked at the presumption of even-tempered beings and made promises that they would never fear the witch inside themselves. The women danced wildly as sparks broke away from the flames and entered the night sky as stars.

And they sang a song given to them by Shoshoni grandmothers:

Ah ne nah, nah
nin nah nah—
Ah ne nah, nah
nin nah nah—
Nyaga mutzi

---

[8]Fradkin, op. cit., 116.

oh ne nay—
Nyaga mutzi
oh ne nay—[9]

The women danced and drummed and sang for weeks, preparing themselves   40
for what was to come. They would reclaim the desert for the sake of their children, for the sake of the land.

A few miles downwind from the fire circle, bombs were being tested. Rabbits felt the tremors. Their soft leather pads on paws and feet recognized the shaking sands while the roots of mesquite and sage were smoldering. Rocks were hot from the inside out and dust devils hummed unnaturally. And each time there was another nuclear test, ravens watched the desert heave. Stretch marks appeared. The land was losing its muscle.

The women couldn't bear it any longer. They were mothers. They had suffered labor pains but always under the promise of birth. The red hot pains beneath the desert promised death only as each bomb became a stillborn. A contract had been broken between human beings and the land. A new contract was being drawn by the women who understood the fate of the earth as their own.

Under the cover of darkness, ten women slipped under the barbed wire fence and entered the contaminated country. They were trespassing. They walked toward the town of Mercury in moonlight, taking their cues from coyote, kit fox, antelope squirrel, and quail. They moved quietly and deliberately through the maze of Joshua trees. When a hint of daylight appeared they rested, drinking tea and sharing their rations of food. The women closed their eyes. The time had come to protest with the heart, that to deny one's genealogy with the earth was to commit treason against one's soul.

At dawn, the women draped themselves in mylar, wrapping long streamers of silver plastic around their arms to blow in the breeze. They wore clear masks that became the faces of humanity. And when they arrived on the edge of Mercury, they carried all the butterflies of a summer day in their wombs. They paused to allow their courage to settle.

The town which forbids pregnant women and children to enter because of   45
radiation risks to their health was asleep. The women moved through the streets as winged messengers, twirling around each other in slow motion, peeking inside homes and watching the easy sleep of men and women. They were astonished by such stillness and periodically would utter a shrill note or low cry just to verify life.

---

[9]This song was sung by the Western Shoshone women as they crossed the line at the Nevada Test Site on March 18, 1988, as part of their "Reclaim the Land" action. The translation they gave was: "Consider the rabbits how gently they walk on the earth. Consider the rabbits how gently they walk on the earth. We remember them. We can walk gently also. We remember them. We can walk gently also."

The residents finally awoke to what appeared as strange apparitions. Some simply stared. Others called authorities, and in time, the women were apprehended by wary soldiers dressed in desert fatigues. They were taken to a white, square building on the other edge of Mercury. When asked who they were and why they were there, the women replied, "We are mothers and we have come to reclaim the desert for our children."

The soldiers arrested them. As the ten women were blindfolded and handcuffed, they began singing:

> *You can't forbid us everything*
> *You can't forbid us to think —*
> *You can't forbid our tears to flow*
> *And you can't stop the songs that we sing.*

The women continued to sing louder and louder, until they heard the voices of their sisters moving across the mesa.

> *Ah ne nah, nah*
> *nin nah nah —*
> *Ah ne nah, nah*
> *nin nah nah —*
> *Nyaga mutzi*
> *oh ne nay —*
> *Nyaga mutzi*
> *oh ne nay —*

"Call for re-enforcement," one soldier said.

"We have," interrupted one woman. "We have — and you have no idea of our numbers." 50

On March 18, 1988, I crossed the line at the Nevada Test Site and was arrested with nine other Utahns for trespassing on military lands. They are still conducting nuclear tests in the desert. Ours was an act of civil disobedience. But as I walked toward the town of Mercury, it was more than a gesture of peace. It was a gesture on behalf of the Clan of One-breasted Women.

As one officer cinched the handcuffs around my wrists, another frisked my body. She found a pen and a pad of paper tucked inside my left boot.

"And these?" she asked sternly.

"Weapons," I replied.

Our eyes met. I smiled. She pulled the leg of my trousers back over my boot. 55

"Step forward, please," she said as she took my arm.

We were booked under an afternoon sun and bused to Tonapah, Nevada. It was a two-hour ride. This was familiar country to me. The Joshua trees standing their ground had been named by my ancestors who believed they looked like prophets pointing west to the promised land. These were the same trees that bloomed each spring, flowers appearing like white flames in the Mojave. And I recalled a full moon in May when my mother and I had walked among them, flushing out mourning doves and owls.

The bus stopped short of town. We were released. The officials thought it was a cruel joke to leave us stranded in the desert with no way to get home. What they didn't realize is that we were home, soul-centered and strong, women who recognized the sweet smell of sage as fuel for our spirits.

Exploring the Text

1. The first section of the essay (paras. 1–19) begins and ends with a reference to the title. Why do you think Terry Tempest Williams frames this section this way? How does it affect the tone?

2. Williams claims that "[t]raditionally, as a group of people, Mormons have a low rate of cancer" (para. 5). What are some of the possible reasons for this?

3. Research the story that a group of women warriors called the Amazons each slashed off one breast to get better leverage when using bow and arrow. How effectively does Williams use the reference to this legend?

4. What is the effect of repeating the word *contaminated* three times in paragraph 19?

5. At paragraph 20, why does Williams interrupt the story of her own family's illness to begin to tell the story of Irene Allen and her family?

6. Williams says in paragraph 22, "Assuaging public fears was simply a matter of public relations" by the government. What does she mean? Is she being ironic, or is she giving a matter-of-fact description of public policy at the time? Explain your response.

7. Why does Williams put a section break between paragraphs 29 and 30? Why is there no smooth transition from the Supreme Court case to Mormon culture?

8. How does footnote 9 differ from the others?

9. What is the effect of the footnotes Williams includes and of the reference to the National Institutes of Health in paragraph 35?

10. In paragraph 43, Williams writes, "The time had come to protest with the heart, that to deny one's genealogy with the earth was to commit treason against one's soul." What underlying assumption connects her support to this claim?

11. In paragraphs 43 and 58, how does Williams give the impression of a spiritual presence in nature?

12. What is the rhetorical effect of shifting among narration, exposition, and argument in this essay?

Save the Whales, Screw the Shrimp

Joy Williams

Joy Williams was born in Chelmsford, Massachusetts, in 1944 and presently lives in Key West, Florida, and Tucson, Arizona. She received a BA from Marietta College and an MFA from the University of Iowa. She has taught creative writing at the University of Houston, the University of Florida, the University of Iowa, the University of Arizona, and the University of Wyoming. Williams is the author of four novels. Her first, *State of Grace* (1973), was nominated for a National Book Award for Fiction. Her most recent novel, *The Quick and the Dead* (2000), was a finalist for the Pulitzer Prize for Fiction. She has also written works of nonfiction, including *The Florida Keys: A History & Guide*, illustrated by Robert Carawan (2003). "Save the Whales, Screw the Shrimp" is from the essay collection *Ill Nature: Rants and Reflections on Humanity and Other Animals* (2001), a finalist for the National Book Critics Circle Award for Criticism.

I don't want to talk about *me*, of course, but it seems as though far too much attention has been lavished on *you* lately—that your greed and vanities and quest for self-fulfillment have been catered to far too much. You just want and want and want. You believe in yourself excessively. You don't believe in Nature anymore. It's too isolated from you. You've abstracted it. It's so messy and damaged and sad. Your eyes glaze as you travel life's highway past all the crushed animals and the Big Gulp cups. You don't even take pleasure in looking at nature photographs these days. Oh, they can be just as pretty as always, but don't they make you feel increasingly . . . anxious? Filled with more trepidation than peace? So what's the point? You see the picture of the baby condor or the panda munching on a bamboo shoot, and your heart just sinks, doesn't it? A picture of a poor old sea turtle with barnacles on her back, all ancient and exhausted, depositing her five gallons of doomed eggs in the sand hardly fills you with joy, because you realize, quite rightly, that just outside the frame falls the shadow of the condo. What's cropped from the shot of ocean waves crashing on a pristine shore is the plastics plant, and just beyond the dunes lies a parking lot. Hidden from immediate view in the butterfly-bright meadow, in the dusky thicket, in the oak and holly wood, are the surveyors' stakes, for someone wants to build a mall exactly there— some gas stations and supermarkets, some pizza and video shops, a health club, maybe a bulimia treatment center. Those lovely pictures of leopards and herons and wild rivers—well, you just know they're going to be accompanied by a text that will serve only to bring you down. You don't want to think about it! It's all so uncool. And you don't want to feel guilty either. Guilt is uncool. Regret maybe you'll consider. *Maybe.* Regret is a possibility, but don't push me, you say. Nature photographs have become something of a problem, along with almost everything else. Even though they leave the bad stuff out—maybe because you *know* they're leaving all the bad stuff out—such pictures are making you increasingly aware that you're a little too late for Nature. Do you feel that? Twenty years too late? Well, it appears that you are. And since you are, you've decided you're just not going to attend this particular party.

※※

Pascal said that it is easier to endure death without thinking about it than to endure the thought of death without dying. This is how you manage to dance the strange dance with that grim partner, nuclear annihilation. When the U.S. Army notified Winston Churchill that the first A-bomb had been detonated in New Mexico, it chose the code phrase BABIES SATISFACTORILY BORN. So you entered the age of irony, and the strange double life you've been leading with the world ever since. Joyce Carol Oates suggests that the reason writers—*real* writers, one assumes—don't write about Nature is that it lacks a sense of humor and registers no irony. It just doesn't seem to be of the times—these slick, sleek, knowing, objective, indulgent times. And the word *environment*. Such a bloodless word. A flat-footed word with a shrunken heart. A word increasingly disengaged from its association with the natural world. Urban planners, industrialists, economists, developers use it. It's a lost word, really. A cold word, mechanistic, suited strangely to the coldness generally felt toward Nature. It's their word now. You don't mind giving it up. As for *environmentalist*, that's one that can really bring on the yawns, for you've tamed and tidied it, neutered it quite nicely. An environmentalist must be calm, rational, reasonable, and willing to compromise; otherwise, you won't listen to him. Still, his beliefs are *opinions* only, for this is the age of radical subjectivism. Some people might prefer a Just for Feet store to open space, and they shouldn't be castigated for it. All beliefs and desires and needs are pretty much equally valid. The speculator has just as much right to that open space as the swallow, and the consumer has the most rights of all. Experts and computer models, to say nothing of lawsuits, can hold up environmental checks and reform for decades. The Environmental Protection Agency protects us by finding "acceptable levels of harm" from pollutants and then issuing rules allowing industry to pollute to those levels. Any other approach would place limits on economic growth. Limits on economic growth! What a witchy notion! The EPA can't keep abreast of progress and its unintended consequences. They're drowning in science. Whenever they do lumber into action and ban a weed killer, say (and you do love your weed killers—you particularly hate to see the more popular ones singled out), they have to pay all disposal costs and compensate the manufacturers for the market value of the chemicals they still have in stock.

That seems . . . that seems only fair, you say. *Financial loss is a serious matter. And think of the farmers when a particular effective herbicide or pesticide is banned. They could be driven right out of business.*

Farmers grow way too much stuff anyway. Federal farm policy, which subsidizes overproduction, encourages bigger and bigger farms and fewer and fewer farmers. The largest farms don't produce food at all, they grow feed. One third of the wheat, three quarters of the corn, and almost all of the soybeans are used for feed. You get cheap hamburgers; the agribusiness moguls get immense profits. Subsidized crops are grown with subsidized water created by turning rivers great and small into a plumbing system of dams and irrigation ditches. Rivers have become conduits. Wetlands are increasingly being referred to as *filtering systems*— things deigned *useful* because of their ability to absorb urban runoff, oil from roads, et cetera.

We know that. We've known that for years about farmers. We know a lot these 5 *days. We're very well informed. If farmers aren't allowed to make a profit by growing surplus crops, they'll have to sell their land to developers, who'll turn all that arable land into office parks. Arable land isn't Nature anyway, and besides, we like those office parks and shopping plazas, with their monster supermarkets open twenty-four hours a day and aisle after aisle after aisle of products. It's fun. Products are fun.*

Farmers like their poisons, but ranchers like them even more. There are well-funded federal programs like the Agriculture Department's "Animal Damage Control Unit," which, responding to public discomfort about its agenda, decided recently to change its name to the euphemistic Wildlife Services. Wildlife Services poisons, shoots, and traps thousands of animals each year. Servicing diligently, it kills bobcats, foxes, black bears, mountain lions, rabbits, badgers, countless birds—all to make this great land safe for the string bean and the corn, the sheep and the cow, even though you're not consuming as much cow these days. A burger now and then, but burgers are hardly cows at all, you feel. They're not all *our* cows, in any case, for some burger matter is imported. There's a bit of Central American burger matter in your bun. Which is contributing to the conversion of tropial rain forest into cow pasture. Even so, you're getting away from meat these days. You're eschewing cow. It's seafood you love, shrimp most of all. And when you love something, it had better watch out, because you have a tendency to love it to death. Shrimp, shrimp, shrimp. It's more common on menus than chicken. In the wilds of Ohio, far, far from watery shores, four out of the six entrees on a menu will be shrimp something-or-other, available for a modest sum. Every-where, it's all the shrimp you can eat or all you *care* to eat, for sometimes you just don't feel like eating all you *can*. You are intensively *harvesting* shrimp. Soon there won't be any left, and then you can stop. Shrimpers put out these big nets, and in these nets, for each pound of shrimp, they catch more than ten times that amount of fish, turtles, and dolphins. These, quite the worse for wear, are dumped back in. There is an object called TED (Turtle Excluder Device) that would save thou-sands of turtles and some dolphins from dying in the net, but shrimpers are loath to use TEDs, as they argue it would cut the size of their shrimp catch.

We've heard about TED, you say.

At Kiawah Island, off the coast of South Carolina, visitors go out on Jeep "safaris" through the part of the island that hasn't been developed yet. ("Wher-ever you see trees," the guide says, "it's actually a lot.") The visitors (i.e., potential buyers) drive their own Jeeps, and the guide talks to them by radio. Kiawah has nice beaches, and the guide talks about turtles. When he mentions the shrimpers' role in the decline of the turtle, the shrimpers, who share the same frequency, scream at him. Shrimpers and most commercial fishermen (many of them working with drift and gill nets anywhere from six to thirty miles long) think of themselves as an *endangered species*. A recent newspaper headline said, "SHRIMPERS SPARED ANTI-TURTLE DEVICES." Even so, with the continuing wanton depletion of shrimp beds, they will undoubtedly have to find some other means of employment soon. They might, for instance, become part of that vast throng laboring in the *tourist industry*.

⠿

Tourism has become an industry as destructive as any other. You are no longer benign in traveling somewhere to look at the scenery. You never thought there was much gain in just looking anyway; you've always preferred to *use* the scenery in some manner. In your desire to get away from what you've got, you've caused there to be no place to get away *to*. You're just all bumpered up out there. Sewage and dumps have become prime indicators of America's lifestyle. In resort towns in New England and the Adirondacks, measuring the flow into the sewage plants serves as a business barometer. Tourism is a growth industry. You believe in growth. *Controlled* growth, of course. Controlled exponential growth is what you'd really like to see. You certainly don't want to put a moratorium or a cap on anything. That's illegal, isn't it? Retro you're not. You don't want to go back or anything. Forward. Maybe ask directions later. Growth is *desirable* as well as being *inevitable*. Growth is the one thing you seem to be powerless before, so you try to be realistic about it. Growth — it's weird — it's like cancer or something.

As a tourist you have long ago discovered your national parks and are quickly *overburdening* them. All that spare land, and it belongs to you! It's exotic land too, not looking like all the stuff around it that looks like everything else. You want to take advantage of this land, of course, and use it in every way you can. Thus the managers — or *stewards*, as they like to be called — have developed *wise* and *multiple-use* plans, keeping in mind exploiters' interests (for they have their needs, too), as well as the desires of the backpackers. Thus mining, timbering, and ranching activities take place in the national forest, where the Forest Service maintains a system of logging roads eight times greater than the interstate highway system. Snowmobilers demand that their trails be *groomed*. The national parks are more of a public playground and are becoming increasingly Europeanized in their look and management. Lots of concessions and motels. Paths paved to accommodate strollers. You deserve a clean bed and a hot meal when you go into the wilderness. At least, your stewards think that you do. You keep your stewards busy. Not only must they cater to your multiple and conflicting desires, they have to manage your wildlife *resources*. They have managed wildfowl to such an extent that, the reasoning has become, if it weren't for hunters, ducks would disappear. Duck stamps and licensing fees support the whole rickety duck manage-

10

ment system. Yes! If it weren't for the people who kill them, wild ducks wouldn't exist! Many a manager believes that better wildlife *protection* is provided when wildlife is allowed to be shot. Conservation commissions can only oversee hunting when hunting is allowed. But wild creatures are managed in other ways as well. Managers track and tape and tag and band. They relocate, restock, and reintroduce. They cull and control. It's hard to keep it straight. Protect or poison? Extirpate or just mostly eliminate? Sometimes even the stewards get mixed up.

This is the time of machines and models, hands-on management and master plans. Don't you ever wonder as you pass that billboard advertising another MASTER PLANNED COMMUNITY just what master they are actually talking about? Not the Big Master, certainly. Something brought to you by one of the tiny masters, of which there are many. But you like these tiny masters and have even come to expect and require them. In Florida they're well into building a ten-thousand-acre city in the Everglades. It's a *megaproject*, one of the largest ever in the state. Yes, they must have thought you wanted it. No, what you thought of as the Everglades, the park, is only a little bitty part of the Everglades. Developers have been gnawing at this irreplaceable, strange land for years. It's like they just *hate* this ancient sea of grass. Maybe you could ask them about this sometime. Every tree and bush and inch of sidewalk in the project has been planned, of course. Nevertheless, because the whole thing will take twenty-five years to complete, the plan is going to be constantly changed. You can understand this. The important thing is that there be a blueprint. You trust a blueprint. The tiny masters know what you like. You like a *secure landscape* and *access to services*. You like grass — that is, lawns. The ultimate lawn is the golf course, which you've been told has "some ecological value." You believe this! Not that it really matters — you just like to play golf. These golf courses require a lot of watering. So much that the more inspired of the masters have taken to watering them with effluent, *treated* effluent, but yours, from all the condos and villas built around the stocked artificial lakes you fancy.

I really don't want to think about sewage, you say, but it sounds like progress.

It is true that the masters are struggling with the problems of your incessant flushing. Cuisine is also one of their concerns. Great advances have been made in sorbets — sorbet intermezzos — in their clubs and fine restaurants. They know what you want. You want A HAVEN FROM THE ORDINARY WORLD. If you're a NATURE LOVER in the West, you want to live in a WILD ANIMAL HABITAT. If you're eastern and consider yourself more hip, you want to live in a new town — a brand-new reconstructed-from-scratch town — in a house of NINETEENTH-CENTURY DESIGN. But in these new towns the masters are building, getting around can be confusing. There is an abundance of curves and an infrequency of through streets. It's the new wilderness without any trees. You can get lost, even with all the "mental bread crumbs" the masters scatter about as visual landmarks — the windmill, the water views, the various groupings of landscape "material." You *are* lost, you know. But you trust a Realtor will show you the way.

There are many more Realtors than tiny masters, and many of them have to make do with less than a loaf — that is, trying to sell stuff that's already been built in an environment already "enhanced" rather than something being planned — but they're everywhere, willing to show you the path. If Dante returned to Hell today, he'd probably be escorted down by a Realtor talking all the while about how it was just another level of Paradise.

> When have you last watched a sunset? Do you remember where you were? With whom? At Loews Ventana Canyon Resort, the Grand Foyer will provide you with the opportunity through lighting that is computerized to diminish with the approaching sunset!

The tiny masters are willing to arrange Nature for you. They will compose it into a picture that you can look at at your leisure, when you're not doing work or something like that. Nature becomes scenery, a prop. At some golf courses in the Southwest, the saguaro cactuses are reported to be repaired with green paste when balls blast into their skin. The saguaro can attempt to heal themselves by growing over the balls, but this takes time, and the effect can be somewhat . . . baroque. It's better to get out the pastepot. Nature has become simply a visual form of entertainment, and it had better look snappy.

Listen, you say, we've been at Ventana Canyon. It's in the desert, right? It's very, very nice, a world-class resort. A totally self-contained environment with everything that a person could possibly want, on more than a thousand acres in the middle of zip. It sprawls but nestles, like. And they've maintained the integrity of as much of the desert ecosystem as possible. Give them credit for that. Great *restaurant, too. We had baby bay scallops there. Coming into the lobby there are these two big hand-carved coyotes, mutely howling. And that's the way we like them,* mute. *God, why do those things howl like that?* 15

Wildlife is a personal matter, you think. The attitude is up to you. You can prefer to see it dead or not dead. You might want to let it mosey about its business or blow it away. Wild things exist only if you have the graciousness to allow them to. Just outside Tucson, Arizona, there is a structure modeled after a French foreign legion outpost. It's the *International Wildlife Museum*, and it's full of dead animals. Three hundred species are there, at least a third of them — the rarest ones — killed and collected by one C. J. McElroy, who enjoyed doing it and now shares what's left with you. The museum claims to be educational because you can watch a taxidermist at work or touch a lion's tooth. You can get real close to these dead animals, closer than you can in a zoo. Some of you prefer zoos, however, which are becoming bigger, better, and bioclimatic. New-age zoo designers want the animals to *flow right out into your space*. In Dallas there's a Wilds of Africa exhibit; in San Diego there's a simulated rain forest, where you can thread your way "down the side of a lush canyon, the air filled with a fine mist from 300 high-pressure nozzles . . ."; in New Orleans you've constructed a swamp, the real swamp not far away being on the verge of disappearing. Animals in these places are abstractions — wandering relics of their true selves, but that doesn't matter. Animal behavior in a zoo is nothing like natural behavior, but that doesn't matter, either. Zoos are pretty, contained, and accessible. These new habitats can contain one hundred different species—not more than one or two of each thing, of course—on seven acres, three, one. You don't want to see *too much* of anything, certainly. An *example* will suffice. Sort of like a biological Crabtree & Evelyn basket selected with *you* in mind. You like things reduced, simplified. It's easier to take it all in, park it in your mind. You like things inside better than outside anyway. You are increasingly looking at and living in proxy environments created by substitution and simulation. *Resource economists* are a wee branch in the tree of tiny masters, and one, Martin Krieger, wrote, "Artificial prairies and wildernesses have been created, and there is no reason to believe that these artificial environments need be unsatisfactory for those who experience them. . . . We will have to realize that the way in which we experience nature is conditioned by our society—which more and more is seen to be receptive to responsible intervention."

Fiddle, fiddle, fiddle. You support fiddling, as well as meddling. This is how you learn. Though it's quite apparent that the environment has been grossly polluted and the natural world abused and defiled, you seem to prefer to continue pondering effects rather than preventing causes. You want proof, you insist on proof. A Dr. Lave from Carnegie-Mellon—and he's an expert, an economist and an environmental *expert*—says that scientists will have to prove to you that you will suffer if you don't become less of a "throw-away society." *If you really want me to give up my car or my air conditioner, you'd better prove to me first that the earth would otherwise be uninhabitable*, Dr. Lave says. *Me* is *you*, I presume, whereas *you* refers to them. You as in me—that is, *me, me, me*—certainly strike a hard bargain. Uninhabitable the world has to get before you rein in your requirements. You're a consumer after all, *the* consumer upon whom so much attention is lavished, the ultimate user of a commodity that has become, these days, everything. To try to appease your appetite for proof, for example, scientists have been leasing for experimentation forty-six pristine lakes in Canada.

They don't want to *keep* them, they just want to *borrow* them.

They've been intentionally contaminating many of the lakes with a variety of pollutants dribbled into the propeller wash of research boats. It's *one of the boldest experiments in lake ecology ever conducted.* They've turned these remote lakes into huge *real-world test tubes.* They've been doing this since 1976! And what they've found so far in these *preliminary* studies is that pollutants are really destructive. The lakes get gross. Life in them ceases. It took about eight years to make this happen in one of them, everything carefully measured and controlled all the while. Now the scientists are slowly reversing the process. But it will take hundreds of years for the lakes to recover. They think.

Remember when you used to like rain, the sound of it, the feel of it, the way it   20
made the plants and trees all glisten? We needed that rain, you would say. It
looked pretty too, you thought, particularly in the movies. Now it rains and you
go, Oh-oh. A nice walloping rain these days means *overtaxing our sewage treatment plants.* It means *untreated waste discharged directly into our waterways.* It
means . . .

   Okay. Okay.

   Acid rain! And we all know what this is. Or most of us do. People of power
in government and industry still don't seem to know what it is. Whatever it is,
they say, they don't want to curb it, but they're willing to study it some more.
Economists call air and water pollution "externalities" anyway. Oh, acid rain.
You do get so sick of hearing about it. The words have already become a white-
noise kind of thing. But you think in terms of *mitigating* it maybe. As for *the
greenhouse effect,* you think in terms of *countering* that. One way that's been discussed is the planting of new forests, not for the sake of the forests alone, oh my
heavens, no. Not for the sake of majesty and mystery or of Thumper and Bambi,
are you kidding me, but because, as every schoolchild knows, trees absorb carbon dioxide. They just soak it up and store it. They just love it. So this is the plan:
you can plant millions of acres of trees, and you go on doing pretty much whatever you're doing—driving around, using staggering amounts of energy, keeping those power plants fired to the max. Isn't Nature remarkable? So willing to
serve? You wouldn't think it had anything more to offer, but it seems it does. Of
course, these "forests" wouldn't exactly be forests. They would be more like trees.
Managed trees. The Forest Service, which now manages our forests by cutting
them down, might be called upon to evolve in its thinking and allow these trees
to grow. They would probably be patented trees after a time. Fast-growing, uniform, genetically created toxin-eating *machines.* They would be *new-age* trees,
because the problem with planting the old-fashioned variety to *combat* the greenhouse effect, which is caused by pollution, is that they're already dying from it. All
along the crest of the Appalachians from Maine to Georgia, forests struggle to
survive in a toxic soup of poisons. They can't *help* us if we've killed them, now can
they?

All right, you say, *wow, lighten up, will you? Relax. Tell about yourself.*

   Well, I say, I live in Florida . . .

   Oh my god, you say. *Florida! Florida is a joke! How do you expect us to take you*   25
*seriously if you still live there! Florida is crazy, it's pink concrete. It's paved, it's over.
And a little girl just got eaten by an alligator down there. It came out of some swamp
next to a subdivision and carried her off. That set your Endangered Species Act back
fifty years, you can bet.*

   I . . .

   *Listen, we don't want to hear any more about Florida. We don't want to hear
about Phoenix or California's Central Valley. If our wetlands—our vanishing wetlands—are mentioned one more time, we'll scream. And the talk about condors and*

grizzlies and wolves is becoming too de trop.[1] *We had just managed to get whales out of our minds. Now there are butterflies,* frogs *even that you want us to worry about. And those manatees. Don't they know what a boat propeller can do to them by now? They're not too smart. And those last condors are* pathetic. *Can't we just get this over with?*

Aristotle said that all living beings are ensouled and strive to participate in eternity.

Oh, I just bet he said that, you say. *That doesn't sound like Aristotle. He was a humanist. We're all humanists here. This is the age of humanism. Militant humanism. And it has been for a long time.*

You are driving with a stranger in the car, and it is the stranger who is behind the wheel. In the backseat are your pals for many years now—DO WHAT YOU LIKE and his swilling sidekick, WHY NOT. A deer, or some emblematic animal—something from that myriad natural world you've come from that you now treat with such indifference and scorn—steps from the dimming woods and tentatively upon the highway. The stranger does not decelerate or brake, not yet, maybe not at all. The feeling is that whatever it is *will get out of the way.* Oh, it's a fine car you've got, a fine machine, and oddly you don't mind the stranger driving it, because in a way, everything has gotten too complicated, way, way out of your control. You've given the wheel to the masters, the managers, the comptrollers. Something is wrong, *maybe*, you feel a little sick, *actually*, but the car is luxurious and fast and you're *moving*, which is the most important thing by far.

Why make a fuss when you're so comfortable? Don't make a fuss, make a baby. Go out and get something to eat, build something. Make *another* baby. Babies are cute. Babies show you have faith in the future. Although faith is perhaps too strong a word. They're everywhere these days; in all the crowds and traffic jams, there are the babies too. You don't seem to associate them with the problems of population increase. They're just babies! And you've come to believe in them again. They're a lot more tangible than the afterlife, which, of course, you haven't believed in in ages. At least not for yourself. The afterlife now belongs to plastics and poisons. Yes, plastics and poisons will have a far more extensive afterlife than you, that's known. A disposable diaper, for example, which is all plastic and wood pulp, will take around four centuries to degrade. But you like disposables—so easy to use and toss—and now that marketing is urging you not to rush the potty training by making diapers for four-year-olds available and socially acceptable, there will be more and more dumped diapers around, each taking, like most plastics, centuries and centuries to deteriorate. In the sea, many marine animals die from ingesting or being entangled in discarded plastic. In the dumps, plastic squats on more than 25 percent of dump space. But your heart is disposed toward plastic. Someone, no doubt the plastics industry, told you it was convenient. This same industry avidly promotes recycling in an attempt to get the critics

[1]French; "excessive." —Eds.

of their nefarious, multifarious products off their backs. That should make you feel better, because *recycling* has become an honorable word, no longer merely the hobby of Volvo owners.The fact is that people in plastics are born obscurants. Recycling won't solve the plastic glut, only reduction of production will, and the plastics industry isn't looking into that, you can be sure. Waste is not just the stuff you throw away, of course, it's also the stuff you use to excess. With the exception of *hazardous waste*, which you do worry about from time to time, it's even thought that you have a declining sense of emergency about the problem. Builders are building bigger houses because you want bigger. You're trading up. Utility companies are beginning to worry about your constantly rising consumption. Utility companies! You haven't entered a new age at all but one of upscale nihilism, deluxe nihilism.

With each election there is the possibility that the environment will become a political issue. But it never does. You don't want it to be, preferring instead to continue in your politics of subsidizing and advancing avarice. The issues are the same as always — jobs, defense, the economy the economy the economy, maintaining the standard of living in this greedy, selfish, expansionistic, industrialized society.

You're getting a little shrill here, you say.

You're pretty well off. And you expect to become even better off. You do. What does this mean? More software, more scampi, more square footage, more communication towers to keep you in touch and amused and informed? You want to count birds? Go to the bases of communication towers being built across the country. Three million migratory songbirds perish each year by slamming into towers and their attendant guy wires. The building of thousands of new digital television towers one thousand feet and taller is being expedited by the FCC, which proposes to preempt all local and state environmental laws. You have created an ecological crisis. The earth is infinitely variable and alive, and you are moderating it, simplifying it, killing it. It seems safer this way. But you are not safe. You want to find wholeness and happiness in a land increasingly damaged and betrayed, and you never will. More than material matters. You must change your ways.

What is this? Sinners in the Hands of an Angry God?   35

The ecological crisis cannot be resolved by politics. It cannot be resolved by science or technology. It is a crisis caused by culture and character, and a deep change in personal consciousness is needed. Your fundamental attitudes toward the earth have become twisted. You have made only brutal contact with Nature; you cannot comprehend its grace. You must change. Have few desires and simple pleasures. Honor nonhuman life. Control yourself, become more authentic. Live lightly upon the earth and treat it with respect. Redefine the word *progress* and dismiss the managers and masters. Grow inwardly and with knowledge become truly wiser. Think differently, behave differently. For this is essentially a moral issue we face, and moral decisions must be made.

A moral issue! *Okay, this discussion is now over. A moral issue . . . And who's this we now? Who are you, is what I'd like to know. You're not me, anyway. I admit someone's to blame and something should be done. But I've got to go. It's getting late. Take care of yourself.*

. . . .

Exploring the Text

1. You will doubtless notice that Joy Williams speaks in the second person through-out the essay. Count the instances of the word *you* and its forms (*your*, *yours*, *yourself*, etc.). What tone does she achieve through this repetition? How do you feel reading the essay, considering the fact that it addresses you directly? Do you sympathize with her perspective? Explain.

2. Note the details Williams chooses to use at the beginning — such places as a plastics plant, gas stations, video shops, and the like. Identify all of the "place" references. What is their cumulative effect?

3. Williams writes, "So you entered the age of irony, and the strange double life you've been leading with the world ever since" (para. 2). What does she mean by "age of irony" and "strange double life"?

4. Why does Williams cast *environment* in italics in paragraph 2?

5. In paragraph 5, Williams writes a response from "you" saying, "We know a lot these days." What is her intended purpose here? What is the supposed source of the knowledge?

6. Select what you think is Williams's most ironic or most humorous statement. What are its tone and purpose?

7. Consider the difference between verbal irony and sarcasm. Where in the essay does Williams's irony become sarcasm? Is it effective? Why or why not?

8. Of the concerns and issues that Williams mentions, which is the most serious, which the most difficult to address? Why?

9. Williams employs italics, quotation marks, and capital letters liberally, and for different purposes. Identify three examples of each, and analyze their rhetorical effect.

10. Williams uses quite a few inverted sentences in this piece. Identify a few, and discuss their rhetorical effect.

11. Effective humorists and satirists usually have a very serious point. What is Williams's serious point? Do you agree with her overall idea? Explain your response.

from *The Future of Life*

E. O. WILSON

Edward O. Wilson was born in Birmingham, Alabama, in 1929. As a boy he found companionship in nature and was determined early on to become an entomologist. Wilson received his PhD from Harvard University and is recognized as the world's leading authority on ants — he discovered their use of pheromones for communication. In 1975, he published his first major book, *Sociobiology*. In *On Human Nature*, which was awarded the Pulitzer Prize in 1978, he examined the scientific arguments surrounding the role of biology in the evolution of human culture. Officially retired from teaching at Harvard in 1996, he continues to hold the posts of Professor Emeritus and Honorary Curator in Entomology. Wilson's most recent books include *Creation: An Appeal to Save Life on Earth* (2006); *Nature Revealed: Selected Writings, 1949–2006*; and a novel, *Anthill* (2010). The selection included here is from the final chapter of his 2002 book *The Future of Life*, called "The Solution."

The human species is like the mythical giant Antaeus, who drew strength from contact with his mother, Gaea, the goddess Earth, and used it to challenge and defeat all comers. Hercules, learning his secret, lifted and held Antaeus above the ground until the giant weakened—then crushed him. Mortal humans are also handicapped by our separation from Earth, but our impairment is self-administered, and it has this added twist: our exertions also weaken Earth.

What humanity is inflicting on itself and Earth is, to use a modern metaphor, the result of a mistake in capital investment. Having appropriated the planet's natural resources, we chose to annuitize them with a short-term maturity reached by progressively increasing payouts. At the time it seemed a wise decision. To many it still does. The result is rising per-capita production and consumption, markets awash in consumer goods and grain, and a surplus of optimistic economists. But there is a problem: the key elements of natural capital, Earth's arable land, ground water, forests, marine fisheries, and petroleum, are ultimately finite, and not subject to proportionate capital growth. Moreover, they are being decapitalized by overharvesting and environmental destruction. With population and consumption continuing to grow, the per-capita resources left to be harvested are shrinking. The long-term prospects are not promising. Awakened at last to this approaching difficulty, we have begun a frantic search for substitutes.

Meanwhile, two collateral results of the annuitization of nature, as opposed to its stewardship, and settling in to beg our attention. The first is economic disparity: in relative terms the rich grow richer and the poor poorer. According to the United Nations Human Development Report 1999, the income differential between the fifth of the world's population in the wealthiest countries and the fifth in the poorest was 30 to 1 in 1960, 60 to 1 in 1990, and 74 to 1 in 1995. Wealthy people are also by and large profligate consumers, and as a result the income differential has this disturbing consequence: for the rest of the world to reach United States levels of consumption with existing technology would require four more planet Earths.

Europe is only slightly behind, while the Asian economic tigers appear to be pulling up at maximum possible speed. The income gap is the setting for resentment and fanaticism that causes even the strongest nations, led by the American colossus, to conduct their affairs with an uneasy conscience and a growing fear of heaven-bound suicide bombers.

The second collateral result, and the principal concern of the present work, is 5
the accelerating extinction of natural ecosystems and species. The damage already
done cannot be repaired within any period of time that has meaning for the
human mind. The fossil record shows that new faunas and floras take millions of
years to evolve to the richness of the prehuman world. The more the losses are
allowed to accumulate, the more future generations will suffer for it, in some
ways already felt and in others no doubt waiting to be painfully learned.

Why, our descendants will ask, by needlessly extinguishing the lives of other
species, did we permanently impoverish our own? That hypothetical question is
not the rhetoric of radical environmentalism. It expresses a growing concern
among leaders in science, religion, business, and government as well as the educated public.

What is the solution to biological impoverishment? The answer I will now
pose is guardedly optmistic. In essence, it is that the problem is now well understood, we have a grip on its dimensions and magnitude, and a workable strategy
has begun to take shape.

The new strategy to save the world's fauna and flora begins, as in all human
affairs, with ethics. Moral reasoning is not a cultural artifact invented for convenience. It is and always has been the vital glue of society, the means by which
transactions are made and honored to ensure survival. Every society is guided by
ethical precepts, and every one of its members is expected to follow moral leadership and ethics-based tribal law. The propensity does not have to be beaten into
us. Evidence exists instead of an instinct to behave ethically, or at least to insist on
ethical behavior in others. Psychologists, for example, have discovered a hereditary tendency to detect cheaters and to respond to them with intense moral outrage. People by and large are natural geniuses at spotting deception in others, and
equally brilliant in constructing deceptions of their own. We are daily soaked in
self-righteous gossip. We pummel others with expostulation, and we hunger for
sincerity in all our relationships. Even the tyrant is sterling in pose, invoking
patriotism and economic necessity to justify his misdeeds. At the next level down,
the convicted criminal is expected to show remorse, in the course of which he
explains he was either insane at the time or redressing personal injustice.

And everyone has some kind of environmental ethic, even if it somehow
makes a virtue of cutting the last ancient forests and damming the last wild rivers.
Done, it is said, to grow the economy and save jobs. Done because we are running
short of space and fuel. *Hey, listen, people come first!*—and most certainly before
beach mice and louseworts. I recall vividly the conversation I had with a cab
driver in Key West in 1968 when we touched on the Everglades burning to the
north. Too bad, he said. The Everglades are a wonderful place. But wilderness
always gives way to civilization, doesn't it? That is progress and the way of the
world, and we can't do much about it.

Everyone is also an avowed environmentalist. No one says flatly, "To hell with 10
nature." On the other hand, no one says, "Let's give it all back to nature." Rather,
when invoking the social contract by which we all live, the typical people-first

ethicist thinks about the environment short-term and the typical environmental ethicist thinks about it long-term. Both are sincere and have something true and important to say. The people-first thinker says we need to take a little cut here and there; the environmentalist says nature is dying the death of a thousand cuts. So how do we combine the best of short-term and long-term goals? Perhaps, despite decades of bitter philosophical dispute, an optimum mix of goals might result in a consensus more satisfactory than either side thought possible from total victory. The people-firster likes parks, and the environmentalist rides petroleum-powered vehicles to get there.

The first step is to turn away from claims of inherent moral superiority based on political ideology and religious dogma. The problems of the environment have become too complicated to be solved by piety and an unyielding clash of good intentions.

The next step is to disarm. The most destructive weapons to be stacked are the stereotypes, the total-war portraits crafted for public consumption by extremists on both sides. I know them very well from years of experience on the boards of conservation organizations, as a participant in policy conferences, and during service on government advisory committees. To tell the truth, I am a little battle-fatigued. The stereotypes cannot be simply dismissed, since they are so often voiced and contain elements of real substance, like rocks in snowballs. But they can be understood clearly and sidestepped in the search for common ground. Let me illustrate a stereotype skirmish with imaginary opponents engaging in typical denunciations.

The People-First Critic Stereotypes the Environmentalists

Environmentalists or conservationists is what they usually call themselves. Depending on how angry we are, we call them greens, enviros, environmental extremists, or environmental wackos. Mark my word, conservation pushed by these people always goes too far, because it is an instrument for gaining political power. The wackos have a broad and mostly hidden agenda that always comes from the left, usually far left. How to get power? is what they're thinking. Their aim is to expand government, especially the federal government. They want environmental laws and regulatory surveillance to create government-supported jobs for their kind of bureaucrats, lawyers, and consultants. The New Class, these professionals have been called. What's at stake as they busy themselves are your tax dollars and mine, and ultimately our freedom too. Relax your guard when these people are in power and your property rights go down the tube. Some Bennington College student with a summer job will find an endangered red spider on your property, and before you know what happened the Endangered Species Act will be used to shut you down. Can't sell to a developer, can't even harvest your woodlot. Business investors can't get at the oil and gas on federal lands this country badly needs. Mind you, I'm all for the environment, and I agree that species extinction is a bad thing, but conservation should be kept in perspective. It is best put in private hands. Property owners know what's good for their own land. They care about the plants and animals living there. Let them work out conservation. They are the real grass roots in this country. Let them be the stewards and handle conservation. A strong, growing free-market economy, not creeping socialism, is what's best for America — and it's best for the environment too.

The Environmentalist Stereotypes the People-First Critics

"Critics" of the environmental movement? That may be what they call themselves, but we know them more accurately as anti-environmentalists and brown lashers or, more locally out west, wise users (their own term, not intended to be ironic) and sagebrush rebels. In claiming concern of any kind for the natural environment, these people are the worst bunch of hypocrites you'll ever not want to find. What they are really after, especially the corporate heads and big-time landowners, is unrestrained capitalism with land development über alles. They keep their right-wing political agenda mostly hidden when downgrading climate change and species extinction, but for them economic growth is always the ultimate, and maybe the only, good. Their idea of conservation is stocking trout streams and planting trees around golf courses. Their conception of the public trust is a strong military establishment and subsidies for loggers and ranchers. The anti-environmentalists would be laughed out of court if they weren't tied so closely to the corporate power structure. And notice how rarely international policy makers pay attention to the environment. At the big conferences of the World Trade Organization and other such gatherings of the rich and powerful, conservation almost never gets so much as a hearing. The only recourse we have is to protest at their meetings. We hope to attract the attention of the media and at least get our unelected rulers to look out the window. In America the right-wingers have made the word "conservative" a mockery. What exactly are they trying to conserve? Their own selfish interests, for sure, not the natural environment.

There are partisans on both sides who actually state their case in this manner, either in pieces or in entirety. And the accusations sting, because so many people on either side believe them. The suspicion and anger they express paralyze further discussion. Worse, in an era when journalism feeds on controversy, its widely used gladiatorial approach divides people and pushes them away from the center toward opposite extremes. 15

It is a contest that will not be settled by partisan victory. The truth is that everyone wants a highly productive economy and lots of well-paying jobs. People almost all agree that private property is a sacred right. On the other hand, everyone treasures a clean environment. In the United States at least, the preservation of nature has almost the status of a sacred trust. In a 1996 survey conducted by Belden & Russonello for the U.S. Consultative Group on Biological Diversity, 79 percent rated a healthy and pleasant environment of the greatest importance, giving it a 10 on a scale of 1 to 10. Seventy-one percent agreed at the same high level with the statement "Nature is God's creation and humans should respect God's work." Only when these two obvious and admirable goals, prosperity and saving the creation, are cast in opposition does the issue become confused. And when the apparent conflict is in addition reinforced by opposing political ideologies, as it frequently is, the problem becomes intractable.

The ethical solution is to diagnose and disconnect extraneous political ideology, then shed it in order to move toward the common ground where economic progress and conservation are treated as one and the same goal.

The guiding principles of a united environmental movement must be, and eventually will be, chiefly long-term. If two hundred years of history of environmentalism have taught us anything, it is that a change of heart occurs when people look beyond themselves to others, and then to the rest of life. It is strengthened when they also expand their view of landscape, from parish to nation and beyond, and their sweep of time from their own life spans to multiple generations and finally to the extended future history of humankind. . . .

The precepts of the people-firsters are foundationally just as ethical as those of the traditional environmentalists, but their arguments are more about method and short-term results. Further, their values are not, as often assumed, merely a reflection of capitalist philosophy. Corporate CEOs are people too, with families and the same desire for a healthy, biodiverse world. Many are leaders in the environmental movement. It is time to recognize that their commitment is vital to success. The world economy is now propelled by venture capital and technical innovation; it cannot be returned to a pastoral civilization. Nor will socialism return in a second attempt to rescue us, at least in any form resembling the Soviet model. Quite the contrary, its demise was a good thing all around for nature. In most places the socialist experiment was tried, its record was even worse than in capitalist countries. Totalitarianism, left or right, is a devil's bargain: slavery purchased at the price of a ruined environment.

The juggernaut of technology-based capitalism will not be stopped. Its [20] momentum is reinforced by the billions of poor people in developing countries anxious to participate in order to share the material wealth of the industrialized nations. But its direction can be changed by mandate of a generally shared long-term environmental ethic. The choice is clear: the juggernaut will very soon either chew up what remains of the living world, or it will be redirected to save it.

Notes (by paragraph)

3 The **income disparities** of the richest and poorest countries are cited from the United Nations' *Human Development Report 1999* and discussed by Fouad Ajami in *Foreign Policy* 119: 30–4 (summer 2000). The consequences of the disparity are explored by Geoffrey D. Dabelko in the *Wilson Quarterly* 23 (4): 14–19 (autumn 1999) and by Thomas F. Homer-Dixon in *Environment, Scarcity, and Violence* (Princeton: Princeton Univ. Press, 1999) and *The Ingenuity Gap* (New York: Knopf, 2000).

3 On the **difference in consumption** by rich and poor nations: William E. Rees and Mathis Wackernagel in AnnMari Jansson et al., eds., *Investing in Natural Capital: The Ecological Economics Approach to Sustainability* (Washington, D.C.: Island Press, 1994), pp. 362–90. The four-worlds estimate is from a personal communication from Mathis Wackernagel (January 24, 2000) (Redefining Progress, 1 Kearny St., San Fran-

cisco, CA); see the explanation of the concept of the ecological footprint in chapter 2 of the present book.

16 The poll of **American attitudes toward the natural world** and the values that shape them was conducted by the research firm Belden & Russonello and Research/Strategy/Management (R/S/M), commissioned by the Communications Consortium Media Center on behalf of the Consultative Group on Biodiversity, and published as a report, "Human Values and Nature's Future: American Attitudes on Biological Diversity" (October 1996). The results are cited here by permission of the CCMC.

Exploring the Text

1. Why does E. O. Wilson begin with an allusion to Antaeus? How effectively does the allusion serve to introduce the author's ideas? Explain your response.

2. Explain the problem that Wilson identifies in paragraph 2. Why does he use economic language to criticize an economic approach to the environment?

3. What are the assumptions underlying the rhetorical question that begins paragraph 6?

4. In paragraph 8, Wilson writes: "We pummel others with expostulation, and we hunger for sincerity in all our relationships. Even the tyrant is sterling in pose, invoking patriotism and economic necessity to justify his misdeeds." How would you explain the relationship between those two sentences?

5. Wilson claims that "when invoking the social contract by which we all live, the typical people-first ethicist thinks about the environment short-term and the typical environmental ethicist thinks about it long-term. Both are sincere and have something true and important to say" (para. 10). Do you agree? Explain your position with examples.

6. In paragraph 12, Wilson uses metaphor and simile to describe the nature of stereotypes. How effectively do these communicate his attitude and meaning?

7. How does Wilson use rhetorical strategies to satirize the "people-first critic" (para. 13)? How does he do so for "the environmentalist" (para. 14)?

8. Are there reasonable statements in either of the stereotyped characterizations? What are they? How could they be more reasonably expressed so as to be rhetorically effective?

9. After presenting the two stereotypes, Wilson writes: "The suspicion and anger they express paralyze further discussion" (para. 15). Do you agree?

10. How effectively does Wilson characterize the precepts of the opposing groups in paragraphs 19 and 20? Do you think his solution is possible? Why or why not?

11. How does the information in the endnotes contribute to the effectiveness of Wilson's argument? Does it appeal more to ethos, logos, or pathos? Explain.

Inversnaid

GERARD MANLEY HOPKINS

Torn between his obligations as a Jesuit priest and his love for poetry, Gerard Manley Hopkins (1844–1889) declined to seek an audience for his work during his lifetime; the bulk of his poems were published posthumously in 1916. Hopkins was born in Stratford, England, to a wealthy family. After converting to Catholicism near the end of his studies at Oxford, Hopkins entered the priesthood and, adhering to one of his vows, burned nearly all of his accumulated poems. He began to write again in 1875, when he was asked to commemorate the death of five Franciscan nuns who drowned in a shipwreck off the coast of England as they fled oppression in Germany. In the poem he wrote, entitled "Wreck of the Deutschland," Hopkins introduced what he called "sprung rhythm," a meter designed to imitate the rhythm of natural speech; this meter anticipated free verse and would influence new generations of poets. Inversnaid is a village near Loch Lomond in Scotland.

This darksome burn,[1] horseback brown,
His rollrock highroad roaring down,
In coop[2] and in comb[3] the fleece of his foam
Flutes and low to the lake falls home.

A windpuff-bonnet of fawn-froth   5
Turns and twindles[4] over the broth
Of a pool so pitchblack, fell-frowning,
It rounds and rounds Despair to drowning.

Degged[5] with dew, dappled with dew,
Are the groins of the braes[6] that the brook treads through,   10
Wiry heathpacks, flitches[7] of fern,
And the beadbonny ash that sits over the burn.

What would the world be, once bereft
Of wet and wildness? Let them be left,

---

[1] A brook or stream. —Eds.
[2] A hollow. —Eds.
[3] A crest. —Eds.
[4] Hopkins's own invention: both *twist* and *dwindle*. —Eds.
[5] Dappled or sprinkled. —Eds.
[6] Hills. —Eds.
[7] Clumps or clusters. —Eds.

O let them be left, wildness and wet; 15
Long live the weeds and the wilderness yet.

Exploring the Text

1. How would you characterize the speaker of this poem?
2. What is the effect of the images presented in the first three quatrains?
3. What is the effect of such diction as "burn," "rollrock," "coop," "comb," "fawn-froth," "twindles," "degged," "braes," and "flitches"?
4. How does line 8 stand out among the first 12 lines of the poem? What does Hopkins suggest that nature is capable of?
5. What might be the value of "the weeds and the wilderness" in the last line?
6. How would Rachel Carson answer the rhetorical question that Hopkins poses at the beginning of the fourth stanza? Lewis Thomas? Bill McKibben? Joy Williams? What would your answer be? Write a brief response from each, and then your own.
7. Would you call Hopkins an environmentalist? Explain why or why not.

A Short History of America

ROBERT CRUMB

Born in 1943, Robert Crumb was one of the originators of "underground" comics, creating such characters as Mr. Natural and Fritz the Cat. The comic strip included here first appeared in *CoEvolution Quarterly* in 1979.

Exploring the Text

1. How would you paraphrase the narrative sequence depicted in the twelve frames?
2. Imagine that you are living in the time that one of the frames presents. In a letter to someone living in an earlier frame, write about the progress the country has made. Or, write a warning to future generations who might occupy later frames.
3. What can you infer about Robert Crumb's attitude toward the progress depicted in the cartoon? Do you agree with his perspective? Why or why not?
4. Write an answer to the question posed at the end of the final frame. Then create your own visual that supports your response. You can create your visual in one of three ways: draw the next frame or sequence of frames, take photos that depict the next frame or sequence, or find images online or in magazines that do so.

(See insert for color version.)

Let's Go

ROYAL DUTCH/SHELL

The following advertisement for the major oil company Royal Dutch/Shell has appeared in several national magazines.

Exploring the Text

1. Based on your reading of this ad, how would you define Shell's position on fuel efficiency and energy conservation?
2. What is the relationship between the graphic and the text in this ad? Explain how each complements the other.
3. The text begins with the inclusive "we." Notice also the repetition of "Let's go" (i.e., let *us* go) in the caption and the text. How does such a hortatory approach influence the effectiveness of the ad?
4. Shell makes much of its living selling gasoline. If we convert kilometers to miles and litres to gallons, the car featured could get as much as 8,700 miles per gallon. Why would such a company extol the efficiency of such a vehicle? What is the rhetorical effect of such an advertisement?
5. What is the primary appeal of the ad? To ethos, logos, or pathos? Explain.
6. Considering its claims, assumptions, and evidence, how would you analyze this ad according to the Toulmin model that you learned about in Chapter 3?
7. After reading and thinking about the ad, how do you feel about the Shell oil company? How do you feel about the issues raised by the ad?

(See insert for color version.)

LET'S GO FURTHER ON ONE LITRE OF FUEL.

We must learn to use energy more efficiently. For over 25 years, the Shell Eco-marathon has supported teams worldwide who explore ways to maximise fuel economy. The current record holder is capable of travelling 3,771km on the equivalent of one litre of fuel. This spirit epitomises our relationship with car manufacturers, finding ways to make cars more efficient. And is typical of our ambition to help build a better energy future. www.shell.com/letsgo

LET'S GO.

Conversation

Sustainable Eating

The following texts each present a view on the issue of eating in an environmentally sustainable way.

Sources

1. **Peter Menzel,** from *Hungry Planet* (photo essay)
2. **Michael Pollan,** *A Naturalist in the Supermarket*
3. **James McWilliams,** *The Locavore Myth*
4. **Jonathan Safran Foer,** *The American Table* and *The Global Table*
5. **Nicolette Hahn Niman,** *The Carnivore's Dilemma*
6. **Will Allen,** *A Good Food Manifesto for America*
7. **A. J. Jacobs,** *Farm to Table: How Our Restaurant Gets Its Food to Your Plate*
8. **Michael Specter,** from *Test-Tube Burgers*

After you have read, studied, and synthesized these pieces, enter the Conversation by responding to one of the writing prompts on page 987.

1. from *Hungry Planet*

PETER MENZEL

The photos on the following pages appeared in the book *Hungry Planet: What the World Eats* (2005). Each photo is a portrait of a family posing with one week's worth of groceries, accompanied by geographical location, food expenditure for one week, and favorite foods or family recipe. See the color insert for color versions of the photos.

United States: The Caven family of California
Food expenditure for one week: $159.18
Favorite foods: beef stew, berry yogurt sundae, clam chowder, ice cream

Kuwait: The Al Haggan family of Kuwait City
Food expenditure for one week: 63.63 dinar or $221.45
Family recipe: Chicken biryani with basmati rice

Bhutan: The Namgay family of Shingkhey Village
Food expenditure for one week: 224.93 ngultrum or $5.03
Family recipe: Mushroom, cheese and pork

Ecuador: The Ayme family of Tingo
Food expenditure for one week: $31.55
Family recipe: Potato soup with cabbage

Chad: The Aboubakar family of Breidjing Camp
Food expenditure for one week: 685 CFA francs or $1.23
Favorite foods: soup with fresh sheep meat

Germany: The Melander family of Bargteheide
Food expenditure for one week: 375.39 euros or $500.07
Favorite foods: fried potatoes with onions, bacon and herring, fried noodles with eggs and cheese, pizza, vanilla pudding

Questions

1. Which of the photos resemble each other the most regarding the food represented?
2. Which are most similar in terms of the setting?
3. Consider the number of family members, or "mouths to feed," in each photo. Compute the cost of food per person per week. What does your answer suggest about the global economy?
4. From your analysis of the photos, what inferences do you make about the countries depicted? Overall, what does the photo sequence suggest about sustainable eating worldwide?

2. *A Naturalist in the Supermarket*

MICHAEL POLLAN

The following selection is from the first chapter of *The Omnivore's Dilemma* (2006), a best-selling book about sustainable eating.

Air-conditioned, odorless, illuminated by buzzing fluorescent tubes, the American supermarket doesn't present itself as having very much to do with Nature. And yet what is this place if not a landscape (man-made, it's true) teeming with plants and animals?

I'm not just talking about the produce section or the meat counter, either — the supermarket's flora and fauna. Ecologically speaking, these are this landscape's most legible zones, the places where it doesn't take a field guide to identify the resident species. Over there's your eggplant, onion, potato, and leek; here your apple, banana, and orange. Spritzed with morning dew every few minutes, Produce is the only corner of the supermarket where we're apt to think "Ah, yes, the bounty of Nature!" Which probably explains why such a garden of fruits and vegetables (sometimes flowers, too) is what usually greets the shopper coming through the automatic doors.

Keep rolling, back to the mirrored rear wall behind which the butchers toil, and you encounter a set of species only slightly harder to identify — there's chicken and turkey, lamb and cow and pig. Though in Meat the creaturely character of the species on display does seem to be fading, as the cows and pigs increasingly come subdivided into boneless and bloodless geometrical cuts. In recent years some of this supermarket euphemism has seeped into Produce, where you'll now find formerly soil-encrusted potatoes cubed pristine white, and "baby" carrots machine-lathed into neatly tapered torpedoes. But in general here in flora and fauna you don't need to be a naturalist, much less a food scientist, to know what species you're tossing into your cart.

Venture farther, though, and you come to regions of the supermarket where the very notion of species seems increasingly obscure: the canyons of breakfast cereals and condiments; the freezer cases stacked with "home meal replacements" and bagged platonic peas; the broad expanses of soft drinks and towering cliffs of snacks; the unclassifiable Pop-Tarts and Lunchables; the frankly synthetic coffee whiteners and the Linnaeus-defying Twinkie. Plants? Animals?! Though it might not always seem that way, even the deathless Twinkie is constructed out of . . . well, precisely *what* I don't know offhand, but ultimately some sort of formerly living creature, i.e., a *species.* We haven't yet begun to synthesize our foods from petroleum, at least not directly.

If you do manage to regard the supermarket through the eyes of a naturalist, your first impression is apt to be of its astounding biodiversity. Look how many different plants and animals (and fungi) are represented on this single acre of land! What forest or prairie could hope to match it? There must be a hundred different species in the produce section alone, a handful more in the meat counter. And this diversity appears only to be increasing: When I was a kid, you never saw radicchio in the produce section, or a half dozen different kinds of mushrooms, or kiwis and passion fruit and durians and mangoes. Indeed, in the last few years a whole catalog of exotic species from the tropics has colonized, and considerably enlivened, the produce department. Over in fauna, on a good day you're apt to find—beyond beef—ostrich and quail and even bison, while in Fish you can catch not just salmon and shrimp but catfish and tilapia, too. Naturalists regard biodiversity as a measure of a landscape's health, and the modern supermarket's devotion to variety and choice would seem to reflect, perhaps even promote, precisely that sort of ecological vigor.

Except for the salt and a handful of synthetic food additives, every edible item in the supermarket is a link in a food chain that begins with a particular plant growing in a specific patch of soil (or, more seldom, stretch of sea) somewhere on earth. Sometimes, as in the produce section, that chain is fairly short and easy to follow: As the netted bag says, this potato was grown in Idaho, that onion came from a farm in Texas. Move over to Meat, though, and the chain grows longer and less comprehensible: The label doesn't mention that that ribeye steak came from a steer born in South Dakota and fattened in a Kansas feedlot on grain grown in Iowa. Once you get into the processed foods you have to be a fairly determined ecological detective to follow the intricate and increasingly obscure lines of connection linking the Twinkie, or the nondairy creamer, to a plant growing in the earth someplace, but it can be done.

So what exactly would an ecological detective set loose in an American supermarket discover, were he to trace the items in his shopping cart all the way back to the soil? The notion began to occupy me a few years ago, after I realized that the straightforward question "What should I eat?" could no longer be answered without first addressing two other even more straightforward questions: "What *am* I eating? And where in the world did it come from?" Not very long ago an eater didn't need a journalist to answer these questions. The fact that today one so often does suggests a pretty good start on a working definition of industrial food: Any food whose provenance is so complex or obscure that it requires expert help to ascertain.

When I started trying to follow the industrial food chain—the one that now feeds most of us most of the time and typically culminates either in a supermarket or fast-food meal—I expected that my investigations would lead me to a wide variety of places. And though my journeys did take me to a great many states, and covered a great many miles, at the very end of these food chains (which is to say, at the very beginning), I invariably found myself in almost exactly the same place: a farm field in the American Corn Belt. The great edifice of variety and choice that is an American supermarket turns out to rest on a remarkably narrow biological foundation comprised of a tiny group of plants that is dominated by a single species: *Zea mays*, the giant tropical grass most Americans know as corn.

Corn is what feeds the steer that becomes the steak. Corn feeds the chicken and the pig, the turkey and the lamb, the catfish and the tilapia and, increasingly, even the salmon, a carnivore by nature that the fish farmers are reengineering to tolerate corn. The eggs are made of corn. The milk and cheese and yogurt, which once came from dairy cows that grazed on grass, now typically come from Holsteins that spend their working lives indoors tethered to machines, eating corn.

Head over to the processed foods and you find ever more intricate manifestations of corn. A chicken nugget, for example, piles corn upon corn: what chicken it contains consists of corn, of course, but so do most of a nugget's other constituents, including the modified corn starch that glues the thing together, the corn flour in the batter that coats it, and the corn oil in which it gets fried. Much less obviously, the leavenings and lecithin, the mono-, di-, and triglycerides, the attractive golden coloring, and even the citric acid that keeps the nugget "fresh" can all be derived from corn.

To wash down your chicken nuggets with virtually any soft drink in the supermarket is to have some corn with your corn. Since the 1980s virtually all the sodas and most of the fruit drinks sold in the supermarket have been sweetened with high-fructose corn syrup (HFCS)—after water, corn sweetener is their principal ingredient. Grab a beer for your beverage instead and you'd still be drinking corn, in the form of alcohol fermented from glucose refined from corn. Read the ingredients on the label of any processed food and, provided you know the chemical names it travels under, corn is what you will find. For modified or unmodified starch, for glucose syrup and maltodextrin, for crystalline fructose and ascorbic acid, for lecithin and dextrose, lactic acid and lysine, for maltose and HFCS, for MSG and polyols, for the caramel color and xanthan gum, read: corn. Corn is in the coffee whitener and Cheez Whiz, the frozen yogurt and TV dinner, the canned fruit and ketchup and candies, the soups and snacks and cake mixes, the frosting and gravy and frozen waffles, the syrups and hot sauces, the mayonnaise and mustard, the hot dogs and the bologna, the margarine and shortening, the salad dressings and the relishes and even the vitamins. (Yes, it's in the Twinkie, too.) There are some forty-five thousand items in the average American supermarket and more than a quarter of them now contain corn. This goes for the nonfood items as well—everything from the toothpaste and cosmetics to the disposable diapers, trash bags, cleansers, charcoal briquettes, matches, and batteries, right down to the shine on the cover of the magazine that catches your eye by the checkout: corn. Even in Produce on a day when there's ostensibly no corn for sale you'll nevertheless find plenty of corn: in the vegetable wax that gives the cucumbers their sheen, in the pesticide responsible for the produce's perfection, even in the coating on the cardboard it was shipped in. Indeed, the supermarket itself—the wallboard and joint compound, the linoleum and fiberglass and adhesives out of which the building itself has been built—is in no small measure a manifestation of corn.

And us?

Questions

1. Does Michael Pollan's humor contibute to the effectiveness of his argument? Provide a few examples in support of your response.
2. In paragraph 3, why does Pollan use the term "cow" rather than "beef," and "pig" rather than "pork"? What does this language suggest about our attitude toward eating these animals?
3. Pollan writes, "When I was a kid, you never saw radicchio in the produce section, or a half dozen different kinds of mushrooms, or kiwis and passion fruit and durians and mangoes" (para. 5). What is his point? Have things changed in the supermarket since you were "a kid" as well? Is this a good thing, or not? Explain your response.
4. In paragraph 7, Pollan asks three questions and writes, "Not very long ago an eater didn't need a journalist to answer these questions." Do you see those questions as important? Do you share his concerns? Why or why not?
5. Pollan's piece is based largely on observation and reporting. How does this method serve to advance his argument?
6. What is the most surprising thing that you learned from Pollan's piece? How does it affect your attitude toward food? Toward eating?

3. *The Locavore Myth*

James McWilliams

The following article challenging the locavore movement appeared in *Forbes*, a business magazine, in 2009. McWilliams is a professor of history at Texas State University.

Buy local, shrink the distance food travels, save the planet. The locavore movement has captured a lot of fans. To their credit, they are highlighting the problems with industrialized food. But a lot of them are making a big mistake. By focusing on transportation, they overlook other energy-hogging factors in food production.

Take lamb. A 2006 academic study (funded by the New Zealand government) discovered that it made more environmental sense for a Londoner to buy lamb shipped from New Zealand than to buy lamb raised in the U.K. This finding is counterintuitive—if you're only counting food miles. But New Zealand lamb is raised on pastures with a small carbon footprint, whereas most English lamb is produced under intensive factory-like conditions with a big carbon footprint. This disparity overwhelms domestic lamb's advantage in transportation energy.

New Zealand lamb is not exceptional. Take a close look at water usage, fertilizer types, processing methods and packaging techniques and you discover that factors other than shipping far outweigh the energy it takes to transport food. One analysis, by Rich Pirog of the Leopold Center for Sustainable Agriculture, showed that transportation accounts for only 11% of food's carbon footprint. A fourth of the energy required to produce food is expended in the consumer's kitchen. Still more energy is consumed per meal in a restaurant, since restaurants throw away most of their leftovers.

Locavores argue that buying local food supports an area's farmers and, in turn, strengthens the community. Fair enough. Left unacknowledged, however, is the fact that it also hurts farmers in other parts of the world. The U.K. buys most of its green beans from Kenya. While it's true that the beans almost always arrive in airplanes—the form of transportation that consumes the most energy—it's also true that a campaign to shame English consumers with small airplane stickers affixed to flown-in produce threatens the livelihood of 1.5 million sub-Saharan farmers.

Another chink in the locavores' armor involves the way food miles are calculated. To choose a locally grown apple over an apple trucked in from across the country might seem easy. But this decision ignores economies of scale. To take an extreme example, a shipper sending a truck with 2,000 apples over 2,000 miles would consume the same amount of fuel per apple as a local farmer who takes a pickup 50 miles to sell 50 apples at his stall at the green market. The critical measure here is not food miles but apples per gallon.

The one big problem with thinking beyond food miles is that it's hard to get the information you need. Ethically concerned consumers know very little about processing practices, water availability, packaging waste and fertilizer application. This is an opportunity for watchdog groups. They should make life-cycle carbon counts available to shoppers.

Until our food system becomes more transparent, there is one thing you can do to shrink the carbon footprint of your dinner: Take the meat off your plate. No matter how you slice it, it takes more energy to bring meat, as opposed to plants, to the table. It takes 6 pounds of grain to make a pound of chicken and 10 to 16 pounds to make a pound of beef. That difference translates into big differences in inputs. It requires 2,400 liters of water to make a burger and only 13 liters to grow a tomato. A majority of the water in the American West goes toward the production of pigs, chickens and cattle.

The average American eats 273 pounds of meat a year. Give up red meat once a week and you'll save as much energy as if the only food miles in your diet were the distance to the nearest truck farmer.

If you want to make a statement, ride your bike to the farmer's market. If you want to reduce greenhouse gases, become a vegetarian.

Questions

1. According to James McWilliams, locavores point to what serious problems? What are some of the unexpected disadvantages of the locavore movement?
2. Do you find McWilliams's use of lamb as an example to be convincing? Why or why not?
3. In paragraph 4, McWilliams writes, "Fair enough." What is the rhetorical effect of this sentence fragment? How does it contribute to his argument?
4. McWilliams writes, "To take an extreme example, a shipper sending a truck with 2,000 apples over 2,000 miles would consume the same amount of fuel per apple as a local farmer who takes a pickup 50 miles to sell 50 apples at his stall at the green market" (para. 5). Do you find the example of the local farmer to be realistic? Is McWilliams's "extreme example" perhaps too extreme? Is it a "straw man"? How does it affect the persuasiveness of his argument? Explain your response.
5. Go back and read the title of the article. Which features of the locavore movement does McWilliams regard as "myth"? Which does he regard as real?
6. In paragraph 7, McWilliams shifts his attention to the topic of meat. Do you think this shift in focus is effective, or is it an unnecessary tangent? What is the rhetorical effect of the final sentence? Explain.

4. *The American Table* and *The Global Table*

JONATHAN SAFRAN FOER

The following piece is excerpted from the final chapter of *Eating Animals* (2009), a book by novelist Jonathan Safran Foer that reflects on the ethics of eating meat.

The American Table

We shouldn't kid ourselves about the number of ethical eating options available to most of us. There isn't enough nonfactory chicken produced in America to feed the population of Staten Island and not enough nonfactory pork to serve New York City, let alone the country. Ethical meat is a promissory note, not a reality. Any ethical-meat advocate who is serious is going to be eating a lot of vegetarian fare.

A good number of people seem to be tempted to continue supporting factory farms while also buying meat outside that system when it is available. That's nice. But if it is as far as our moral imaginations can stretch, then it's hard to be optimistic about the future. Any plan that involves funneling money to the factory farm won't end factory farming. How effective would the Montgomery bus boycott have been if the protesters had used the bus when it became inconvenient not to? How effective would a strike be if workers announced they would go back to work as soon as it became difficult to strike? If anyone finds in this book encouragement to buy some meat from alternative sources while buying factory farm meat as well, they have found something that isn't here.

If we are at all serious about ending factory farming, then the absolute least we can do is stop sending checks to the absolute worst abusers. For some, the decision to eschew factory-farmed products will be easy. For others, the decision will be a hard one. To those for whom it sounds like a hard decision (I would have counted myself in this group), the ultimate question is whether it is worth the inconvenience. We *know*, at least, that this decision will help prevent deforestation, curb global warming, reduce pollution, save oil reserves, lessen the burden on rural America, decrease human rights abuses, improve public health, and help eliminate the most systematic animal abuse in world history. What we don't know, though, may be just as important. How would making such a decision change *us*?

Setting aside the direct material changes initiated by opting out of the factory farm system, the decision to eat with such deliberateness would itself be a force with enormous potential. What kind of world would we create if three times a day we activated our compassion and reason as we sat down to eat, if we had the moral imagination and the pragmatic will to change our most fundamental act of consumption? Tolstoy famously argued that the existence of slaughterhouses and battlefields is linked. Okay, we don't fight wars because we eat meat, and some wars should be fought—which is not to mention that Hitler was a vegetarian. But compassion is a muscle that gets stronger with use, and the regular exercise of choosing kindness over cruelty would change us.

It might sound naive to suggest that whether you order a chicken patty or a veggie burger is a profoundly important decision. Then again, it certainly would have sounded fantastic if in the 1950s you were told that where you sat in a restaurant or on a bus could begin to uproot racism. It would have sounded equally fantastic if you were told in the early 1970s, before César Chávez's workers' rights campaigns, that refusing to eat grapes could begin to free farmworkers from slave-like conditions. It might sound fantastic, but when we bother to look, it's hard to deny that our day-to-day choices shape the world. When America's early settlers decided to throw a tea party in Boston, forces powerful enough to create a nation were released. Deciding what to eat (and what to toss overboard) is the founding act of production and consumption that shapes all others. Choosing leaf or flesh, factory farm or family farm, does not in itself change the world, but

5

teaching ourselves, our children, our local communities, and our nation to choose conscience over ease can. One of the greatest opportunities to live our values — or betray them — lies in the food we put on our plates. And we will live or betray our values not only as individuals, but as nations.

We have grander legacies than the quest for cheap products. Martin Luther King Jr. wrote passionately about the time when "one must take a position that is neither safe, nor politic, nor popular." Sometimes we simply have to make a decision because "one's conscience tells one that it is right." These famous words of King's, and the efforts of Chávez's United Farm Workers, are also our legacy. We might want to say that these social-justice movements have nothing to do with the situation of the factory farm. Human oppression is not animal abuse. King and Chávez were moved by a concern for suffering humanity, not suffering chickens or global warming. Fair enough. One can certainly quibble with, or even become enraged by, the comparison implicit in invoking them here, but it is worth noting that César Chávez and King's wife, Coretta Scott King, were vegans, as is King's son Dexter. We interpret the Chávez and King legacies — we interpret America's legacy — too narrowly if we assume in advance that they cannot speak against the oppression of the factory farm.

The Global Table

Next time you sit down for a meal, imagine that there are nine other people sitting with you at the table, and that together you represent all the people on the planet. Organized by nations, two of your tablemates are Chinese, two Indian, and a fifth respresents all the other countries in Northeast, South, and Central Asia. A sixth represents the nations of Southeast Asia and Oceana. A seventh represents sub-Saharan Africa, and an eighth represents the remainder of Africa and the Middle East. A ninth represents Europe. The remaining seat, representing the countries of South, Central, and North America, is for you.

If we allocate seats by native language, only Chinese speakers would get their own representative. All English and Spanish speakers together would have to share a chair.

Organized by religion, three people are Christian, two are Muslim, and three practice Buddhism, traditional Chinese religions, or Hinduism. Another two belong to other religious traditions or identify as nonreligious. (My own Jewish community, which is smaller than the margin of error in the Chinese census, can't even squeeze half of a tuches onto a chair.)

If seated by nourishment, one person is hungry and two are obese. More than half eat a mostly vegetarian diet, but that number is shrinking. The stricter vegetarians and vegans have one seat at the table, but barely. And more than half of the time any one of you reaches for eggs, chicken, or pork, they will have come from a factory farm. If current trends continue for another twenty years, the beef and mutton you reach for also will.

The United States is not even close to getting its own seat when the table is organized by population, but it would have somewhere between two and three seats when people are seated by how much food they consume. No one loves to eat as much as we do, and when we change what we eat, the world changes.

I've restricted myself to mostly discussing how our food choices affect the ecology of our planet and the lives of its animals, but I could have just as easily made the entire book about public health, workers' rights, decaying rural communities, or global poverty—all of which are profoundly affected by factory farming. Factory farming, of course, does not cause all the world's problems, but it is remarkable just how many of them intersect there. And it is equally remarkable, and completely improbable, that the likes of you and me would have real influence over factory farming. But no one can seriously doubt the influence of U.S. consumers on global farm practices.

I realize that I'm coming dangerously close to suggesting that quaint notion that every person can make a difference. The reality is more complicated, of course. As a "solitary eater," your decisions will, in and of themselves, do nothing to alter the industry. That said, unless you obtain your food in secret and eat it in the closet, you don't eat alone. We eat as sons and daughters, as families, as communities, as generations, as nations, and increasingly as a globe. We can't stop our eating from radiating influence even if we want to.

As anyone who has been a vegetarian for a number of years might tell you, the influence that this simple dietary choice has on what others around you eat can be surprising. The body that represents restaurants in America, the National Restaurant Association, has advised every restaurant in the nation to have at least one vegetarian entrée. Why? It's simple: their own polling data indicates that more than a third of restaurant operators have observed an uptick in demand for vegetarian meals. A leading restaurant industry periodical, *Nation's Restaurant News*, advises restaurants to "add vegetarian or vegan dishes to the mix. Vegetarian dishes, aside from being less expensive . . . also mitigate the veto vote. Usually, if you have a vegan in your party, that will dictate where the party eats."

Millions upon millions of advertising dollars are spent to make sure that we see people drinking milk or eating beef in movies, and millions more are spent to make sure that when I have a soda in my hand, you can tell (probably from some distance) whether it is Coke or Pepsi. The National Restaurant Association doesn't make these recommendations, and multinational corporations don't spend millions on product placement, to make us feel good about the influence we have on others around us. They simply recognize the fact that eating is a social act. 15

When we lift our forks, we hang our hats somewhere. We set ourselves in one relationship or another to farmed animals, farmworkers, national economies, and global markets. Not making a decision—eating "like everyone else"—is to make the easiest decision, a decision that is increasingly problematic. Without question, in most places and in most times, to decide one's diet by not deciding—to eat like everyone else—was probably a fine idea. Today, to eat like everyone else is to add another straw to the camel's back. Our straw may not be the backbreaker, but the act will be repeated—every day of our lives, and perhaps every day of the lives of our children and our children's children. . . .

The seating arrangements and servings at the global table we all eat from change. The two Chinese at our table have four times the amount of meat on their plates as they did a few decades ago—and the pile keeps getting higher. Meanwhile, the two people at the table without clean drinking water are eyeballing China. Today, animal products still account for only 16 percent of the Chinese diet, but farmed animals account for more than 60 percent of China's water consumption—and at a time when Chinese water shortages are already cause for global concern. The desperate person at our table, who is struggling to find enough food to eat, might reasonably worry even more at how much of the world's march toward U.S.-style meat eating will make the basic grains he or she relies on for life even less available. More meat means more demand for grains and more hands fighting over them. By 2050, the world's livestock will consume as much food as four billion people. Trends suggest that the one hungry person at our table could easily become two (270,000 more people become hungry each day). This will almost certainly happen as the obese also gain another seat. It's too easy to imagine a near future in which most of the seats at the global table are filled by either obese or malnourished people.

But it doesn't have to be this way. The best reason to think that there could be a better future is the fact that we know just how bad the future could be.

Rationally, factory farming is so obviously wrong, in so many ways. In all of my reading and conversations, I've yet to find a credible defense of it. But food is not rational. Food is culture, habit, and identity. For some, that irrationality leads to a kind of resignation. Food choices are likened to fashion choices or life-style preferences—they do not respond to judgments about how we should live. And I would agree that the messiness of food, the almost infinite meanings it proliferates, does make the question of eating—and eating animals especially—surprisingly fraught. Activists I spoke with were endlessly puzzled and frustrated by the disconnect between clear thinking and people's food choices. I sympathize, but I also wonder if it is precisely the irrationality of food that holds the most promise.

Food is never simply a calculation about which diet uses the least water or causes the least suffering. And it is in this, perhaps, that our greatest hope for actually motivating ourselves to change lies. In part, the factory farm requires us to suppress conscience in favor of craving. But at another level, the ability to reject the factory farm can be exactly what we most desire.

The debacle of the factory farm is not, I've come to feel, just a problem about ignorance—it's not, as activists often say, a problem that arose because "people don't know the facts." Clearly that is one cause. I've filled this book with an awful lot of facts because they are a necessary starting point. And I've presented what we know scientifically about the legacy we are creating with our daily food choices because that also matters a great deal. I'm not suggesting our reason should not guide us in many important ways, but simply that being human, being humane, is more than an exercise of reason. Responding to the factory farm calls for a capacity to care that dwells beyond information, and beyond the oppositions of desire and reason, fact and myth, and even human and animal.

The factory farm will come to an end because of its absurd economics someday. It is radically unsustainable. The earth will eventually shake off factory farming like a dog shakes off fleas; the only question is whether we will get shaken off along with it.

Thinking about eating animals, especially publicly, releases unexpected forces into the world. The questions are charged like few others. From one angle of vision, meat is just another thing we consume, and matters in the same way as the consumption of paper napkins or SUVs — if to a greater degree. Try changing napkins at Thanksgiving, though — even do it bombastically, with a lecture on the immorality of such and such a napkin maker — and you'll have a hard time getting anyone worked up. Raise the question of a vegetarian Thanksgiving, though, and you'll have no problem eliciting strong opinions — *at least* strong opinions. The question of eating animals hits chords that resonate deeply with our sense of self — our memories, desires, and values. Those resonances are potentially controversial, potentially threatening, potentially inspiring, but always filled with meaning. Food matters and animals matter and eating animals matters even more. The question of eating animals is ultimately driven by our intuitions about what it means to reach an ideal we have named, perhaps incorrectly, "being human."

Questions

1. Jonathan Safran Foer writes of the things "[w]e *know*" (para. 3). Would most people agree that we know the things that he indicates? Would most of his readers? Do you? Why or why not?
2. Safran Foer writes: "One of the greatest opportunities to live our values — or betray them — lies in the food we put on our plates" (para. 5). Do you agree? Why or why not? Do you find the extended analogy between civil rights and ethical eating persuasive? Explain.
3. What is the most surprising fact that you've learned through the analogy of the ten people sitting at the global table? How does it affect your attitude toward eating?
4. The writer, in paragraph 16, suggests that things *today* are not like before. Why is that? What has changed?
5. Safran Foer writes, "In part, the factory farm requires us to suppress conscience in favor of craving" (para. 20). What does the author imply with that statement? Do you agree? Explain.
6. Safran Foer says that the factory farm is "radically unsustainable" and that it will end because of its "absurd economics" (para. 22). Do you think that is true? Why or why not?

5. *The Carnivore's Dilemma*

NICOLETTE HAHN NIMAN

In the following selection, published in the *New York Times* in 2009, Nicolette Hahn Niman, who is a lawyer and rancher, argues the case for eating meat.

Is eating a hamburger the global warming equivalent of driving a Hummer? This week an article in the *Times* of London carried a headline that blared: "Give Up Meat to Save the Planet." Former Vice President Al Gore, who has made climate change his signature issue, has even been assailed for omnivorous eating by animal rights activists.

It's true that food production is an important contributor to climate change. And the claim that meat (especially beef) is closely linked to global warming has received some credible backing, including by the United Nations and University of Chicago. Both institutions have issued reports that have been widely summarized as condemning meat-eating.

But that's an overly simplistic conclusion to draw from the research. To a rancher like me, who raises cattle, goats and turkeys the traditional way (on grass), the studies show only that the prevailing methods of producing meat — that is, crowding animals together in factory farms, storing their waste in giant lagoons and cutting down forests to grow crops to feed them — cause substantial greenhouse gases. It could be, in fact, that a conscientious meat eater may have a more environmentally friendly diet than your average vegetarian.

So what is the real story of meat's connection to global warming? Answering the question requires examining the individual greenhouse gases involved: carbon dioxide, methane and nitrous oxides.

Carbon dioxide makes up the majority of agriculture-related greenhouse   5
emissions. In American farming, most carbon dioxide emissions come from fuel burned to operate vehicles and equipment. World agricultural carbon emissions, on the other hand, result primarily from the clearing of woods for crop growing and livestock grazing. During the 1990s, tropical deforestation in Brazil, India, Indonesia, Sudan and other developing countries caused 15 percent to 35 percent of annual global fossil fuel emissions.

Much Brazilian deforestation is connected to soybean cultivation. As much as 70 percent of areas newly cleared for agriculture in Mato Grosso State in Brazil is being used to grow soybeans. Over half of Brazil's soy harvest is controlled by a handful of international agribusiness companies, which ship it all over the world for animal feed and food products, causing emissions in the process.

Meat and dairy eaters need not be part of this. Many smaller, traditional farms and ranches in the United States have scant connection to carbon dioxide emissions because they keep their animals outdoors on pasture and make little use of machinery. Moreover, those farmers generally use less soy than industrial operations do, and those who do often grow their own, so there are no emissions from long-distance transport and zero chance their farms contributed to deforestation in the developing world.

In contrast to traditional farms, industrial livestock and poultry facilities keep animals in buildings with mechanized systems for feeding, lighting, sewage flushing, ventilation, heating and cooling, all of which generate emissions. These factory farms are also soy guzzlers and acquire much of their feed overseas. You can reduce your contribution to carbon dioxide emissions by avoiding industrially produced meat and dairy products.

Unfortunately for vegetarians who rely on it for protein, avoiding soy from deforested croplands may be more difficult: as the Organic Consumers Association notes, Brazilian soy is common (and unlabeled) in tofu and soymilk sold in American supermarkets.

Methane is agriculture's second-largest greenhouse gas. Wetland rice fields   10
alone account for as much as 29 percent of the world's human-generated methane. In animal farming, much of the methane comes from lagoons of liquefied manure at industrial facilities, which are as nauseating as they sound.

This isn't a problem at traditional farms. "Before the 1970s, methane emissions from manure were minimal because the majority of livestock farms in the U.S. were small operations where animals deposited manure in pastures and corrals," the Environmental Protection Agency says. The E.P.A. found that with the rapid rise of factory farms, liquefied manure systems became the norm and methane emissions skyrocketed. You can reduce your methane emissions by seeking out meat from animals raised outdoors on traditional farms.

Critics of meat-eating often point out that cattle are prime culprits in methane production. Fortunately, the cause of these methane emissions is understood, and their production can be reduced.

Much of the problem arises when livestock eat poor quality forages, throwing their digestive systems out of balance. Livestock nutrition experts have demonstrated that by making minor improvements in animal diets (like providing nutrient-laden salt licks) they can cut enteric methane by half. Other practices, like adding certain proteins to ruminant diets, can reduce methane production per unit of milk or meat by a factor of six, according to research at Australia's University of New England. Enteric methane emissions can also be substantially reduced when cattle are regularly rotated onto fresh pastures, researchers at University of Louisiana have confirmed.

Finally, livestock farming plays a role in nitrous oxide emissions, which make up around 5 percent of this country's total greenhouse gases. More than three-quarters of farming's nitrous oxide emissions result from man-made fertilizers. Thus, you can reduce nitrous oxide emissions by buying meat and dairy products from animals that were not fed fertilized crops—in other words, from animals raised on grass or raised organically.

In contrast to factory farming, well-managed, non-industrialized animal farming minimizes greenhouse gases and can even benefit the environment. For example, properly timed cattle grazing can increase vegetation by as much as 45 percent, North Dakota State University researchers have found. And grazing by large herbivores (including cattle) is essential for well-functioning prairie ecosystems, research at Kansas State University has determined. 15

Additionally, several recent studies show that pasture and grassland areas used for livestock reduce global warming by acting as carbon sinks. Converting croplands to pasture, which reduces erosion, effectively sequesters significant amounts of carbon. One analysis published in the journal *Global Change Biology* showed a 19 percent increase in soil carbon after land changed from cropland to pasture. What's more, animal grazing reduces the need for the fertilizers and fuel used by farm machinery in crop cultivation, things that aggravate climate change.

Livestock grazing has other noteworthy environmental benefits as well. Compared to cropland, perennial pastures used for grazing can decrease soil erosion by 80 percent and markedly improve water quality, Minnesota's Land Stewardship Project research has found. Even the United Nations report acknowledges, "There is growing evidence that both cattle ranching and pastoralism can have positive impacts on biodiversity."

As the contrast between the environmental impact of traditional farming and industrial farming shows, efforts to minimize greenhouse gases need to be much more sophisticated than just making blanket condemnations of certain foods. Farming methods vary tremendously, leading to widely variable global warming contributions for every food we eat. Recent research in Sweden shows that, depending on how and where a food is produced, its carbon dioxide emissions vary by a factor of 10.

And it should also be noted that farmers bear only a portion of the blame for greenhouse gas emissions in the food system. Only about one-fifth of the food system's energy use is farm-related, according to University of Wisconsin research. And the Soil Association in Britain estimates that only half of food's total greenhouse impact has any connection to farms. The rest comes from processing, transportation, storage, retailing and food preparation. The seemingly innocent potato chip, for instance, turns out to be a dreadfully climate-hostile food. Foods that are minimally processed, in season and locally grown, like those available at farmers' markets and backyard gardens, are generally the most climate-friendly.

Rampant waste at the processing, retail and household stages compounds the problem. About half of the food produced in the United States is thrown away, according to University of Arizona research. Thus, a consumer could measurably reduce personal global warming impact simply by more judicious grocery purchasing and use. 20

None of us, whether we are vegan or omnivore, can entirely avoid foods that play a role in global warming. Singling out meat is misleading and unhelpful, especially since few people are likely to entirely abandon animal-based foods.

Mr. Gore, for one, apparently has no intention of going vegan. The 90 percent of Americans who eat meat and dairy are likely to respond the same way.

Still, there are numerous reasonable ways to reduce our individual contributions to climate change through our food choices. Because it takes more resources to produce meat and dairy than, say, fresh locally grown carrots, it's sensible to cut back on consumption of animal-based foods. More important, all eaters can lower their global warming contribution by following these simple rules: avoid processed foods and those from industrialized farms; reduce food waste; and buy local and in season.

Questions

1. What is the "overly simplistic conclusion" that Nicolette Hahn Niman challenges? Why is it "overly simplistic" (para. 3)?
2. How successfully does Hahn Niman use sources and statistics to help support her argument? Do you find them convincing? Why or why not?
3. According to this article, what are the chief differences between factory farms and traditional farms? How compelling is the argument for traditional farming methods?
4. How has reading this piece affected your view of sustainable eating?
5. What is your view of the three rules with which the selection concludes? Are they good rules to follow? Why or why not?

6. *A Good Food Manifesto for America*

Will Allen

The following blog post from growingpower.org is a plea for sustainable agricultural practices. It was written in 2010 by Will Allen, an urban farmer and former professional basketball player.

I am a farmer. While I find that this has come to mean many other things to other people — that I have become also a trainer and teacher, and to some a sort of food philosopher — I do like nothing better than to get my hands into good rich soil and sow the seeds of hope.

So, spring always enlivens me and gives me the energy to make haste, to feel confidence, to take full advantage of another all-too-short Wisconsin summer. This spring, however, much more so than in past springs, I feel my hope and confidence mixed with a sense of greater urgency. This spring, I know that my work will be all the more important, for the simple but profound reason that more people are hungry.

For years I have argued that our food system is broken, and I have tried to teach what I believe must be done to fix it. This year, and last, we have begun seeing the unfortunate results of systemic breakdown. We have seen it in higher prices for those who can less afford to pay, in lines at local food pantries, churches, and missions, and in the anxious eyes of people who have suddenly become unemployed. We have seen it, too, in nationwide outbreaks of food-borne illness in products as unlikely as spinach and peanuts.

Severe economic recession certainly has not helped matters, but the current economy is not alone to blame. This situation has been spinning toward this day for decades. And while many of my acquaintances tend to point the finger at the big agro-chemical conglomerates as villains, the fault really is with all of us who casually, willingly, even happily surrendered our rights to safe, wholesome, affordable, and plentiful food in exchange for over-processed and pre-packaged convenience.

Over the past century, we allowed our agriculture to become more and more   5
industrialized, more and more reliant on unsustainable practices, and much more distant from the source to the consumer. We have allowed corn and soybeans, grown on the finest farmland in the world, to become industrial commodities rather than foodstuffs. We have encouraged a system by which most of the green vegetables we eat come from a few hundred square miles of irrigated semi-desert in California.

When fuel prices skyrocket, as they did last year, things go awry. When a bubble like ethanol builds and then bursts, things go haywire. When drought strikes that valley in California, as is happening right now, things start to topple. And when the whole economy shatters, the security of a nation's food supply teeters on the brink of failure.

To many people, this might sound a bit hysterical. There is still food in the suburban supermarket aisles, yes. The shelves are not empty; there are no bread lines. We haven't read of any number of Americans actually starving to death.

No, and were any of those things to happen, you can rest assured that there would be swift and vigorous action. What is happening is that many vulnerable people, especially in the large cities where most of us live, in vast urban tracts where there are in fact no supermarkets, are being forced to buy cheaper and lower-quality foods, to forgo fresh fruits and vegetables, or are relying on food programs—including our children's school food programs—that by necessity are obliged to distribute any kind of food they can afford, good for you or not. And this is coming to haunt us in health care and social costs. No, we are not suddenly starving to death; we are slowly but surely malnourishing ourselves to death. And this fate is falling ever more heavily on those who were already stressed: the poor. Yet there is little action.

Many astute and well-informed people beside myself, most notably Michael Pollan, in a highly persuasive treatise last fall in the *New York Times*, have issued these same warnings and laid out the case for reform of our national food policy. I need not go on repeating what Pollan and others have already said so well, and I do not wish merely to add my voice to a chorus.

I am writing to demand action.   10

It is time and past time for this nation, this government, to react to the dangers inherent in its flawed farm and food policies and to reverse course from subsidizing wealth to subsidizing health.

We have to stop paying the largest farm subsidies to large growers of unsustainable and inedible crops like cotton. We have to stop paying huge subsidies to Big Corn, Big Soy, and Big Chem to use prime farmland to grow fuel, plastics, and fructose. We have to stop using federal and state agencies and institutions as taxpayer-funded research arms for the very practices that got us into this mess.

We have to start subsidizing health and well-being by rewarding sustainable practices in agriculture and assuring a safe, adequate, and wholesome food supply to all our citizens. And we need to start this reform process now, as part of the national stimulus toward economic recovery.

In my organization, Growing Power Inc. of Milwaukee, we have always before tried to be as self-sustaining as possible and to rely on the market for our success. Typically, I would not want to lean on government support, because part of the lesson we teach is to be self-reliant.

But these are not typical times, as we are now all too well aware.   15

As soon as it became clear that Congress would pass the National Recovery Act, I and members of my staff brainstormed ideas for a meaningful stimulus package aimed at creating green jobs, shoring up the security of our urban food systems, and promoting sound food policies of national scope. The outcome needed to be both "shovel-ready" for immediate impact and sustainable for future growth.

We produced a proposal for the creation of a public-private enabling institution called the Centers for Urban Agriculture. It would incorporate a national training and outreach center, a large working urban farmstead, a research and development center, a policy institute, and a state-of-the-future urban agriculture demonstration center into which all of these elements would be combined in a functioning community food system scaled to the needs of a large city.

We proposed that this working institution—not a "think tank" but a "do tank"—be based in Milwaukee, where Growing Power has already created an operating model on just two acres. But ultimately, satellite centers would become established in urban areas across the nation. Each would be the hub of a local or regional farm-to-market community food system that would provide sustainable jobs, job training, food production, and food distribution to those most in need of nutritional support and security.

This proposal was forwarded in February to our highest officials at the city, state, and federal level, and it was greeted with considerable approval. Unfortunately, however, it soon became clear that the way Congress had structured the stimulus package, with funds earmarked for only particular sectors of the economy, chiefly infrastructure, afforded neither our Congressional representatives nor our local leaders with the discretion to direct any significant funds to this innovative plan. It simply had not occurred to anyone that immediate and lasting job creation was plausible in a field such as community-based agriculture.

I am asking Congress today to rectify that oversight, whether by modifying the current guidelines of the Recovery Act or by designating new and dedicated funds to the development of community food systems through the creation of this national Centers for Urban Agriculture.

Our proposal budgeted the initial creation of this CUA at a minimum of $63 million over two years—a droplet compared to the billions being invested in other programs both in the stimulus plan and from year-to-year in the federal budget.

Consider that the government will fund the Centers for Disease Control at about $8.8 billion this year, and that is above the hundreds of millions more in research grants to other bio-medical institutions, public and private. This is money well spent for important work to ensure Americans the best knowledge in protecting health by fighting disease; but surely by now we ought to recognize that the best offense against many diseases is the defense provided by a healthy and adequate diet. Yet barely a pittance of CDC money goes for any kind of preventive care research.

In 2008, the Department of Homeland Security approved spending $450 million for a new National Bio and Agro-Defense Facility at Kansas State University, in addition to the existing Biosecurity Research Institute already there. Again, money well spent to protect our food supply from the potential of a terrorist attack. But note that these hundreds of millions are being spent to protect us from a threat that may never materialize, while we seem to trivialize the very real and material threat that is upon us right now: the threat of malnourishment and undernourishment of very significant numbers of our citizens.

Government programs under the overwhelmed and overburdened departments of Agriculture and of Health and Human Services do their best to serve their many masters, but in the end, government farm and food policies are most often at odds between the needs of the young, the old, the sick, and the poor versus the wants of the super-industry that agriculture has become.

By and large, the government's funding of nutritional health comes down to spending millions on studies to tell us what we ought to eat without in any way guaranteeing that many people will be able to find or afford the foods they recommend. For instance, food stamps ensure only that poor people can buy food; they cannot ensure that, in the food deserts that America's inner cities have become, there will be any good food to buy.

We need a national nutrition plan that is not just another entitlement, that is not a matter of shipping surplus calories to schools, senior centers, and veterans' homes. We need a plan that encourages a return to the best practices of both farming and marketing, that rewards the grower who protects the environment and his customers by nourishing his soil with compost instead of chemicals and who ships his goods the shortest distance, not the longest.

If the main purpose of government is to provide for the common security of its citizens, surely ensuring the security of their food system must be among its paramount duties. And if among our rights are life, liberty, and the pursuit of happiness, we are denied all those rights if our cities become prisons of poverty and malnutrition.

As an African-American farmer, I am calling on the first African-American president of the United States to lead us quickly away from this deepening crisis. Demand, President Obama, that Congress and your own Administration begin without delay the process of reforming our farm and food policies. Start now by correcting the omission in your economic stimulus and recovery act that prevented significant spending on creating new and sustainable jobs for the poor in our urban centers as well as rural farm communities.

It will be an irony, certainly, but a sweet one, if millions of African-Americans whose grandparents left the farms of the South for the factories of the North, only to see those factories close, should now find fulfillment in learning once again to live close to the soil and to the food it gives to all of us.

I would hope that we can move along a continuum to make sure that all our 30 citizens have access to the same fresh, safe, affordable good food regardless of their cultural, social, or economic situation.

Questions

1. Where does Will Allen lay blame for the conditions that he describes in paragraph 4?
2. What does Allen suggest are "unsustainable practices" (para. 5)?
3. Allen writes, "To many people, this might sound a bit hysterical" (para. 7). Does it to you? Why or why not?
4. What does Allen mean by "subsidizing health" (para. 11)? What current practices does he identify as unhealthy? Do you agree with him? Explain your response.
5. Allen suggests that access to "fresh, safe, affordable good food" (para. 30) is a right that all Americans should have. Do you agree? How can we work to bring such a condition about?

7. *Farm to Table*

How Our Restaurant Gets Its Food to Your Plate

A. J. JACOBS

The following piece appeared in the men's magazine *Esquire* in March 2011.

In the spring, the asparagus is planted in a field just three hundred yards down the road. It is allowed to grow without interference from pesticide, fungicide, herbicide, cell-phone radiation, traffic noises, or human eye contact.

———————

We wait.

———————

At just the right time, the asparagus spear is gently handpicked by a well-compensated Latin American earth worker, but only after it has been subjected to Ericksonian hypnosis to minimize the pain.

———————

A short bereavement service follows, incorporating Jewish, Christian, and Shinto textual elements, acknowledging the asparagus is sacrificing its life for our consumption.

———————

The asparagus spear is transported directly and swiftly to the kitchen by an Ivy League–educated barefoot runner trained by Mexico's Tarahumara tribe.

———————

It is washed in the morning dew that gathers on the staff's yurts.

———————

The asparagus spear then rests in silence.

———————

Our executive chef cooks the asparagus for thirty seconds by holding it ten feet from a fire of recycled cypress chips.

———————

The asparagus is served to you, the diner, by hormone-free, locally grown waiters. Instead of plates, we use hardened clumps of dirt from the restaurant's backyard, inspired by the ancient menarche ceremony of the local Chippewa tribe.

———————

After the meal, it is customary for diners to walk to the asparagus field, squat, and fertilize the vegetables with their own organic matter, starting the whole beautiful process anew!

Questions

1. What stereotypes about restaurants and food does A. J. Jacobs address?
2. What contribution do the visuals make to the piece?
3. How does Jacobs's tone affect your response to the piece?
4. How would you paraphrase the serious argument that Jacobs delivers? How persuasive is it?

8. from *Test-Tube Burgers*

MICHAEL SPECTER

In the following essay published in May 2011 in the *New Yorker,* author Michael Specter discusses the developing science of meat production.

Meat supplies a variety of nutrients—among them iron, zinc, and Vitamin B_{12}—that are not readily found in plants. We can survive without it; millions of vegetarians choose to do so, and billions of others have that choice imposed upon them by poverty. But for at least two million years animals have provided our most consistent source of protein. For most of that time, the economic, social, and health benefits of raising and eating livestock were hard to dispute. The evolutionary biologist Richard Wrangham argues, in his book *Catching Fire: How Cooking Made Us Human,* that the development of a brain that could conceive of cooking meat—a singularly efficient way to consume protein—has defined our species more clearly than any other characteristic. Animals have always been essential to human development. Sir Albert Howard, who is often viewed as the founder of the modern organic-farming movement, put it succinctly in his 1940 mission statement, *An Agricultural Testament*: "Mother earth never attempts to farm without livestock."

For many people, the idea of divorcing beef from a cow or pork from a pig will seem even more unsettling than the controversial yet utterly routine practice of modifying crops with the tools of molecular biology. The Food and Drug Administration currently has before it an application, which has already caused rancorous debate, to engineer salmon with a hormone that will force the fish to grow twice as fast as normal. Clearly, making meat without animals would be a more fundamental departure. How we grow, prepare, and eat our food is a deeply emotional issue, and lab-grown meat raises powerful questions about what most people see as the boundaries of nature and the basic definitions of life. Can something be called chicken or pork if it was born in a flask and produced in a vat? Questions like that have rarely been asked and have never been answered.

Still, the idea itself is not new. On January 17, 1912, the Nobel Prize–winning biologist Alexis Carrel placed tissue from an embryonic chicken heart in a bath of nutrients. He kept it beating in his laboratory, at the Rockefeller Institute, for more than twenty years, demonstrating that it was possible to keep muscle tissue alive outside the body for an extended period. Laboratory meat has also long been the subject of dystopian fantasy and literary imagination. In 1931, Winston Churchill published an essay, "Fifty Years Hence," in which he described what he saw as the inevitable future of food: "We shall escape the absurdity of growing a whole chicken in order to eat the breast or wing." He added, "Synthetic food will, of course, also be used in the future. Nor need the pleasure of the table be banished. . . . The new foods will from the outset be practically indistinguishable from the natural products." The idea has often been touched on in science fiction. In *Neuromancer*, William Gibson's 1984 novel, artificial meat—called vat-grown flesh—is sold at lower prices than the meat from living animals. In Margaret Atwood's *Oryx and Crake*, published in 2003, "Chickie-Nobs" are engineered to have many breasts and no brains.

Past discussions have largely been theoretical, but our patterns of meat consumption have become increasingly dangerous for both individuals and the planet. According to the United Nations Food and Agriculture Organization, the global livestock industry is responsible for nearly twenty per cent of humanity's greenhouse-gas emissions. That is more than all cars, trains, ships, and planes combined. Cattle consume nearly ten per cent of the world's freshwater resources, and eighty per cent of all farmland is devoted to the production of meat. By 2030, the world will likely consume seventy percent more meat than it did in 2000. The ecological implications are daunting, and so are the implications for animal welfare: billions of cows, pigs, and chickens spend their entire lives crated, boxed, or force-fed grain in repulsive conditions on factory farms. These animals are born solely to be killed, and between the two events they are treated like interchangeable parts in a machine, as if a chicken were a sparkplug, and a cow a drill bit.

The consequences of eating meat, and our increasing reliance on factory farms, are almost as disturbing for human health. According to a report issued recently by the American Public Health Association, animal waste from industrial farms "often contains pathogens, including antibiotic-resistant bacteria, dust, arsenic, dioxin and other persistent organic pollutants." Seventy per cent of all antibiotics and related drugs consumed in the United States are fed to hogs, poultry, and beef. In most cases, they are used solely to promote growth, and not for any therapeutic reason. By eating animals, humans have exposed themselves to SARS, avian influenza, and AIDS, among many other viruses. The World Health Organization has attributed a third of the world's deaths to the twin epidemics of diabetes and cardiovascular disease, both greatly influenced by excessive consumption of animal fats.

"We have an opportunity to reverse the terribly damaging impact that eating animals has had on our lives and on this planet," Mark Post, a professor in the physiology department at Maastricht University, in the Netherlands, told me. "The goal is to take the meat from one animal and create the volume previously provided by a million animals." Post, who is a vascular biologist and a surgeon,

5

also has a doctorate in pulmonary pharmacology. His area of expertise is angio-genesis—the growth of new blood vessels. Until recently, he had dedicated him-self to creating arteries that could replace and repair those in a diseased human heart. Like many of his colleagues, he was reluctant to shift from biomedicine to the meat project. "I am a scientist, and my family always respected me for that," he said. "When I started basically spending my time trying to make the beginning of a hamburger, they would give me a pitiful look, as if to say, You have completely degraded yourself."

We met recently at the Eindhoven University of Technology, where he served on the faculty for years and remains a vice-dean. "First, people ask, 'Why would anyone want to do this?'" he said. "The initial position often seems to be a reflex: nobody will ever eat this meat. But in the end I don't think that will be true. If people visited a slaughterhouse, then visited a lab, they would realize this approach is so much healthier." He added, "I have noticed that when people are exposed to the facts, to the state of the science, and why we need to look for alternatives to what we have now, the opposition is not so intense."

Post, a trim fifty-three-year-old man in rimless glasses and a polo shirt, stressed, too, that scientific advances have been robust. "If what you want is to grow muscle cells and produce a useful source of animal protein in a lab, well, we can do that today," he said—an assertion echoed by Mironov, in South Carolina, and by many other scientists in the field. To grow ground meat—which accounts for half the meat sold in the United States—one needs essentially to roll sheets of two-dimensional muscle cells together and mold them into food. A steak would be much harder. That's because before scientists can manufacture meat that looks as if it came from a butcher, they will have to design the network of blood vessels and arteries required to ferry nutrients to the cells. Even then, no producer with a label that said "Born in cell culture, raised in a vat" would be commercially viable until the costs fall.

Scientific advances necessarily predate the broad adoption of any technology—often by years. Post points to the first general-purpose computer, Eniac. Built during the Second World War, and designed to calculate artillery-firing ranges, the computer cost millions of dollars and occupied a giant room in the U.S. Army's Ballistic Research Laboratory. "Today, any cell phone or five-dollar watch has a more powerful computer," Post noted. In the late nineteen-eighties, as the Human Genome Project got under way, researchers estimated that sequencing the genome of a single individual would take fifteen years and cost three billion dollars. The same work can now be done in twenty-four hours for about a thou-sand dollars.

Those numbers will continue to fall as personal genomics becomes more 10 relevant, and, as would be the case with laboratory meat, it will become more relevant if the price keeps falling. "The first hamburger will be incredibly expen-sive," Post said. "Somebody calculated five thousand dollars. The skills you need to grow a small amount of meat in a laboratory are not necessarily those that would permit you to churn out ground beef by the ton. To do that will require money and public interest. We don't have enough of either right now. That I do not understand, because, while I am no businessman, there certainly seems to be a market out there."

Meat and poultry dominate American agriculture, with sales that exceeded a hundred and fifty billion dollars in 2009. It is unlikely that the industry would cheer on competitors who could directly challenge its profits. Yet, if even a small percentage of customers switched their allegiance from animals to vats, the market would be huge. After all, the world consumes two hundred and eighty-five million tons of meat every year—ninety pounds per person. The global population is expected to rise from seven billion to more than nine billion by the year 2050. This increase will be accompanied by a doubling of the demand for meat and a steep climb in the greenhouse-gas emissions for which animals are responsible. Owing to higher incomes, urbanization, and growing populations—particularly in emerging economies—demand for meat is stronger than it has ever been. In countries like China and India, moving from a heavily plant-based diet to one dominated by meat has become an essential symbol of a middle-class life.

Cultured meat, if it were cheap and plentiful, could dispense with many of these liabilities by providing new sources of protein without inflicting harm on animals or posing health risks to humans. One study, completed last year by researchers at Oxford and the University of Amsterdam, reported that the production of cultured meat could consume roughly half the energy and occupy just two per cent of the land now devoted to the world's meat industry. The greenhouse gases emitted by livestock, now so punishing, would be negligible. The possible health benefits would also be considerable. Eating meat that was engineered rather than taken from an animal might even be good for you. Instead of committing slow suicide by overdosing on saturated fat, we could begin to consume meat infused with omega-3 fatty acids—which have been demonstrated to prevent the type of heart disease caused by animal fats. "I can well envision a scenario where your doctor would prescribe hamburgers rather than prohibit them," Post said. "The science is not simple and there are hurdles that remain. But I have no doubt we will get there."

Questions

1. Michael Specter writes, "For many people, the idea of divorcing beef from a cow or pork from a pig will seem even more unsettling than the controversial yet utterly routine practice of modifying crops with the tools of molecular biology" (para. 2). Why do you think that would be the case? Do you think this is a valid comparison? Explain your response.

2. In paragraph 2, Specter asks, "Can something be called chicken or pork if it was born in a flask and produced in a vat?" What is your answer to that question?

3. Specter reports that ground meat accounts for half the meat sold in the United States (para. 8). How does this surprising fact influence your perspective regarding sustainable eating?

4. In paragraph 7, Specter quotes scientist Mark Post: "'The initial position often seems to be a reflex: nobody will ever eat this meat. But in the end I don't think that will be true. If people visited a slaughterhouse, then visited a lab, they would realize this approach is so much healthier.'" Do you find Post's argument convincing? Is there another argument that you think people would find more convincing, or do you think people would never accept lab-grown meat? Explain.

5. How persuasive is the case that Specter makes in paragraph 12 for lab-grown meat as a partial solution to the sustainable eating issue?

6. Specter interviewed Princeton philosopher Peter Singer, author of "The Singer Solution to World Poverty" (p. 369), who is considered by many to be the father of the animal rights movement. Speaking of in-vitro meat, Singer said, "It seems all pluses and no minuses to me." What are some pluses in your view? And minuses? Do you think that one outweighs the other? Explain.

Making Connections

1. How might the supermarket described by Michael Pollan be different if we followed the three rules suggested by Nicolette Hahn Niman?

2. How might Jonathan Safran Foer's "global table" be affected by in-vitro meat production as Michael Specter describes it?

3. Compare Hahn Niman's perspective on factory farms with that of Safran Foer. Then compare her position on the eating of meat with that of Safran Foer and James McWilliams. How would Safran Foer respond to Hahn Niman? How would Hahn Niman respond to McWilliams? Refer to their texts in your answers.

4. Several of the writers in the Conversation support the locavore movement. How effectively does McWilliams refute their positions? Support your response with examples.

5. Which writer develops the most persuasive argument regarding factory farms? Safran Foer? Hahn Niman? Specter? Will Allen? Choose two or three, and compare them with one another.

6. Do you think that Safran Foer's position on eating meat would change if we were to grow in-vitro meat successfully? Why or why not?

7. In "A Good Food Manifesto for America," Will Allen writes, "For years I have argued that our food system is broken . . ." (para. 3). Which two writers in the Conversation present the most convincing arguments concerning how to "fix" the system Allen discusses? Explain with reference to their texts.

8. Which of the writers in the Conversation would most likely find "Farm to Table" funny? Which of them might find Jacobs's piece offensive? Explain your answers.

9. Which of the arguments presented in the Conversation are supported by the visual and textual information in the photo essay by Peter Menzel?

Entering the Conversation

As you respond to the following prompts, support your argument with references to at least three of the sources in this Conversation on Sustainable Eating. For help using sources, see Chapter 4.

1. Write a letter about sustainable eating to your local school board regarding the food offered in school cafeterias. Consider the factors that the board should consider before making dietary decisions for students.

2. Each of the writers in this Conversation is a contemporary, living writer. Write a letter addressed to one of them in which you defend, challenge, or qualify his or her position regarding sustainable eating. Refer to three of the other sources to support your position.

3. Imagine that your school's environmental club wants to place posters of animals in a factory farm in the hallways of the elementary, middle, and high schools in your district. Compose a speech that you would deliver to your school board in order to defend or challenge that practice. Refer to three of the sources in the Conversation to support your position.

4. Go back to E. O. Wilson's essay from *The Future of Life* (p. 945). Following his lead, write two opposing arguments in which you stereotype the extreme positions that might be taken by vegetarians and carnivores regarding sustainable eating.

5. Imagine that there is a grassroots campaign developing that wants Congress to legislate against in-vitro meat production. Write an editorial for your school newspaper that supports or challenges this proposed ban. Refer to three of the sources in the Conversation as you support your argument.

6. Imagine that the largest employer in your town is what many of these writers would call a "factory farm." In the voice of the owner of the farm, write a defense of your business, addressed to one of the writers in the Conversation. Refer to three of the other sources in your letter.

Student Writing
Visual Rhetoric: Analyzing a Photo Essay

Ali Hazel, an eleventh-grade AP English Language student, analyzed the visual texts on pages 958–61 and wrote the essay below in response to this prompt:

> Look carefully at the series of photos from *Hungry Planet*, a photo essay by Peter Menzel, and carefully consider the information that accompanies each photo. What is Menzel suggesting about food consumption by combining visual and textual information? Write an essay that analyzes how effectively the photo sequence conveys an important point about global food consumption and sustainable eating, and develops a position on those issues. Refer to the perspectives conveyed by the photos as you develop your position.

As you read Ali's essay, consider the techniques that she uses to do a close reading of the visual texts. Then answer the questions about how she conducts her analysis and develops her argument.

Hard to Swallow
Ali Hazel

Life, especially family life, revolves around food, Earth's most precious and indispensable resource. For many of us, including myself (a middle-class American), food is easy to come by, always accessible, and always on-hand. Unfortunately, this accessibility allows us consumers to take food for granted, to misuse and mistreat the life-sustaining gift of our planet. We often assume our right to have food; we grumble until it's ours, we take more than is necessary, and we throw the remains and the packaging into the trash. This frivolous consumption can only last so long; how much more can the human race afford to waste before we completely devour all of Earth's resources? These six pictures offer an answer to this grisly question, but the suggestion may be hard for consumers to swallow. The series of images shocks its audience with an effective combination of realism and indisputable facts. Each of the six families, representing diverse cultures and countries, displays the food they consume in one week. Accompanying each image are two brief statements, describing the total weekly food expenditure, as well as the family's favorite foods or favorite recipes. Clearly, the quantity of food displayed in several images suggests a dire need to change our attitude toward consumption. Moreover, images of the types of food and of the family members themselves, and the juxtaposition of textual information all combine to convey a sense of urgency to the audience; the images offer a wakeup call for consumers who are willing to stop, listen, and act.

With its factories of mass-production and its hoards of processed food, America breeds consumers of packaged and plastic-wrapped goodies. If an American family wants to eat nutritiously, aiming for an organic and sustainable lifestyle, they must have money. Eating fresh is expensive; the recent "locavore" movement caters to the well off. Unfortunately, the processed and packaged foodstuffs available at any grocery store are significantly cheaper than the fare at your local farm-stand. Perhaps this explains why the Caven family's kitchen is filled with familiar, shiny, synthetic packaging: vanilla wafers, raisin bran, frozen pizza, and pretzels. Perhaps, also, this image provokes the audience, causing them to consider the eventual fate of the colorful packaging. A significant factor of the current environmental crisis is the sheer amount of waste that packaged goods produce. In the forefront of the Cavens' kitchen, three dull, unhappy pieces of broccoli represent the family's greens. For this California family, who typically spends about $40 a person per week, fresh veggies may be expensive to come by. Whether the Caven family simply chooses to omit vegetables from their diet or not, the expense of fresh fare is undeniable. Ironically, on the other end of the spectrum, the Namgay family of Bhutan and the Ayme family of Ecuador spend about $0.40 and $3.51 per person on food per week, respectively. Their diet consists almost exclusively of unpackaged fresh vegetables and fruits; in fact, the greens displayed by the Namgays are much more appetizing than the Cavens' broccoli. These images suggest that in commercialized countries, eating fresh from the Earth requires excessive amounts of income; in less-developed, non-commercialized countries, a family can sustain itself on harvested food for next to nothing. The Cavens feed themselves for $160 a week, producing an enormous amount of waste in the process. If one California family can use *that* much packaging in one week, consider the amount of trash generated in one year. Now multiply that pile of waste by ten families, by twenty, by a million.

A common thread that connects families who spend more on food, like those in Kuwait, Germany, and the United States, is the consumption of animal products. The Melander family of Germany spends weekly an astounding $125 per person on food; featured prominently in their diet are meats and cheese, seen in the center left and the bottom of the picture. Although in Kuwait the family members spend significantly less than their German counterparts — $28 per person each week — the Al Haggan family also consumes a large amount of animal products, especially eggs (left, center). The images suggest that the more resources consumed from animals, the higher the weekly food expenditure. The series of pictures begs an important question: if the family in Bhutan can feed thirteen members with the products of the Earth, then why can't the family in Germany feed their family of four for less than $100 per person? Animals represent a precious and endangered aspect of our food supply; these images indicate that, regarding animal-product consumption, humans need to exercise moderation. This practice will prove to be healthy, economical, and environmentally sound.

The quantity and type of food consumed by each family reinforce the images' foreboding message of wastefulness; however, the pictures not only depict the resources a family consumes, but also the family members themselves. The individuals, their age, expression, and demeanor, are critical rhetorical devices. We can connect a body with the food it consumes. Take, for instance, the family of six in the Breidjing Camp in Chad. The appalling scarcity of food for this close-knit family is evident at first glance; however, consider the body language of the six individuals. The family, leaning, grasping, and supporting one another, clearly shares a close and dependent relationship. Consider also the age of the members, another significant aspect of the image. Excluding the woman to the far left, holding the small baby girl, the family is made up of children. The family in Bhutan houses several generations. At first glance, one might even miss the child hiding next to the eggplant. Similarly, the family in Ecuador is composed of a mother and father, and seven small children. The countenances of these kids sharply contrast with the faces of the two children from the family of four in Germany; clearly, more meat, dairy, and microwavable pizza do not guarantee one's happiness. Is it a coincidence that the children of the Caven family look equally unenthused and disjoined from their parents? Is this disparity a result of the consumerism that marks these two societies? Clearly, the food that each family displays is not the only aspect of the images that tells a story.

The textual information that accompanies each image acts as rhetorical pathos, catalyzing an emotional reaction from the audience. Besides providing the viewer with a clear number for food expenditure, the foods and recipes give the audience a personal insight into each highlighted family; we understand more about the solemn German children through their favorite meals (you are what you eat, right?). Through this information, the image becomes more real, and the message of the series truly hits home. For example, consider the image of the Namgay family of Bhutan. The additional information describes a special family recipe, comprised of mushroom, cheese, and pork. The viewer again returns to the image. Where is the cheese? Where is the pork? Unlike the favorite foods of the Caven and Melander families, the information suggests that this Bhutanese family does not always have the resources necessary to make their prized meals. The Namgay family has no freezer for ice cream, berry yogurt sundaes, or vanilla pudding. In a global context, the favorite foods of the well-off German and American families seem shamefully extravagant compared to "potato soup with cabbage" and "soup with fresh sheep meat."

This particular series of images encompasses a global crisis in six illustrations. The images successfully catalyze an emotional reaction from the viewer; they describe the wasteful excesses of processed foods and the dire need for an even distribution of resources. Don Delillo's postmodern novel *White Noise* addresses similar concerns. An analysis of contemporary consumer society, *White Noise* describes the responses and reactions of American Jack Gladney to a complex, industrial world. In one particularly vivid scene, Jack digs through his family's garbage bin, considers the waste, and questions, "Was this ours? Did it belong to us? Had we created it?" (Delillo 247). Jack is disgusted by his own trash, humiliated and slightly overwhelmed at the garbage that contains the "shameful secrets" of humanity. Waste, like the waste that the Gladney household produces, is a universal problem. Consider the enormous amounts of packaging needed to supply the Al Haggan, Melander, and Caven families their weekly amount of food; besides produce, every item is carefully wrapped in precious material. The beverages alone (water, liquor, and soda) require copious amounts of glass and plastic. The images send a critical message to an audience who may be too full to hear: we, as consumers and stewards of the Earth, must respect and revere the food our planet produces. Keeping in mind the families that have so little, we must discard our excessive habits and grow into a global community, a modern society where no child is left without his or her meal. We must acknowledge the gifts that Earth gives us and decrease our consumption of wasteful, processed, and packaged items.

Works Cited

Delillo, Don. *White Noise*. New York: Viking, 1985. Print.

Menzel, Peter. "Hungry Planet: What the World Eats." *The Language of Composition*. 2nd ed. Ed. Shea, Renée H., Lawrence Scanlon, and Robin Dissin Aufses. Boston: Bedford, 2013. Print.

Questions

1. How effectively does Ali analyze the presentation of food in the series of photos? What rhetorical techniques does she use to do so?
2. How effectively does she analyze the presentation of the families themselves? What rhetorical techniques does she use to do so?
3. List several examples of specific details that Ali uses to support her argument. How does each of the specific details contribute to the development of the essay?
4. Note references to the text that accompanies the photos. How does Ali use the combination of visual and textual information to support her argument?
5. Select three examples of Ali's vivid writing. Explain their effect on the essay as a whole.
6. How effective is the argument that Ali develops? Do you find it convincing? Explain your response.
7. Imagine that you are Ali's editor and that you have to trim this essay by 20 percent. Revise the essay so that it is still clear and cogent, while cutting one-fifth. Explain the reasons for your edits.

Grammar as Rhetoric and Style
Cumulative, Periodic, and Inverted Sentences

Most of the time, writers of English use the following standard sentence patterns:

Subject/Verb (SV)

My father cried. — TERRY TEMPEST WILLIAMS

Subject/Verb/Subject complement (SVC)

> Even the streams were now lifeless.   —Rachel Carson

Subject/Verb/Direct object (SVO)

> We believed her.   —Terry Tempest Williams

To make longer sentences, writers often coordinate two or more of the standard sentence patterns or subordinate one sentence pattern to another. (See the grammar lesson about subordination on p. 1124.) Here are examples of both techniques.

Coordinating patterns

> S   V   C
> Yet every one of these disasters has actually happened somewhere, and many
> S   V   O
> real communities have already suffered a substantial number of them.
>   —Rachel Carson

Subordinating one pattern to another

> S   V   S   V   O
> And when they arrived on the edge of Mercury, they carried all the butter-
>   I
> flies of a summer day in their wombs.
>   —Terry Tempest Williams

The downside to sticking with standard sentence patterns, coordinating them, or subordinating them is that too many standard sentences in a row become monotonous. So writers break out of the standard patterns now and then by using a more unusual pattern, such as the cumulative sentence, the periodic sentence, or the inverted sentence.

When you use one of these sentence patterns, you call attention to that sentence because its pattern contrasts significantly with the pattern of the sentences surrounding it. You can use unusual sentence patterns to emphasize a point, as well as to control sentence rhythm, increase tension, or create a dramatic impact. In other words, using the unusual pattern helps you avoid monotony in your writing.

Cumulative Sentence

The cumulative, or so-called loose, sentence begins with a standard sentence pattern (shown here in blue) and adds multiple details *after* it. The details can take the form of subordinate clauses or different kinds of phrases. These details accumulate, or pile up—hence, the name *cumulative*.

The women moved through the streets as winged messengers, twirling around each other in slow motion, peeking inside homes and watching the easy sleep of men and women.   —Terry Tempest Williams

Here's another cumulative sentence, this one from Michael Pollan.

Venture farther, though, and you come to regions of the supermarket where the very notion of species seems increasingly obscure: the canyons of breakfast cereals and condiments; the freezer cases stacked with "home meal replacements" and bagged platonic peas; the broad expanses of soft drinks and towering cliffs of snacks; the unclassifiable Pop-Tarts and Lunchables; the frankly synthetic coffee whiteners and the Linnaeus-defying Twinkie.

Look closely at this cumulative sentence by Lewis Thomas:

We have grown into everywhere, spreading like a new growth over the entire surface, touching and affecting every other kind of life, incorporating ourselves.

The independent clause in the sentence focuses on the *growth* of humanity. Then the sentence accumulates a string of modifiers about the extent of that growth. Using a cumulative sentence allows Thomas to include all of these modifiers in one smooth sentence, rather than using a series of shorter sentences that repeat *grown*. Furthermore, this accumulation of modifiers takes the reader into the scene just as the writer experiences it, one detail at a time.

Periodic Sentence

The periodic sentence *begins* with multiple details and holds off a standard sentence pattern — or at least its predicate (shown here in blue) — until the end. The following periodic sentence by Lewis Thomas presents its subject, *human beings*, followed by an accumulation of modifiers, with the predicate coming at the end.

Human beings, large terrestrial metazoans, fired by energy from microbial symbionts lodged in their cells, instructed by tapes of nucleic acid stretching back to the earliest live membranes, informed by neurons essentially the same as all the other neurons on earth, sharing structures with mastodons and lichens, living off the sun, are now in charge, running the place, for better or worse.

In the following periodic sentence, Ralph Waldo Emerson packs the front of the sentence with phrases providing elaborate detail:

Crossing a bare common, in snow puddles, at twilight, under a clouded sky, without having in my thoughts any occurrence of special good fortune, I have enjoyed a perfect exhilaration.

The vivid descriptions engage us, so that by the end of the sentence we can feel (or at least imagine) the exhilaration Emerson feels. By placing the descriptions at the beginning of the sentence, Emerson demonstrates how nature can ascend from the physical ("snow puddles," "clouded sky") to the psychological ("without ... thoughts of ... good fortune"), and finally to the spiritual ("perfect exhilaration").

Could Emerson have written this as a cumulative sentence? He probably could have by moving things around—"I have enjoyed a perfect exhilaration as I was crossing ..."—and then providing the details. In some ways, the impact of the descriptive detail would be similar.

Whether you choose to place detail at the beginning or end of a sentence often depends on the surrounding sentences. Unless you have a good reason, though, you probably should not put one cumulative sentence after another or one periodic sentence after another. Instead, by shifting sentence patterns, you can vary sentence length and change the rhythm of your sentences.

Finally, perhaps the most famous example of the periodic sentence in modern English prose is the fourth sentence in paragraph 14 of Martin Luther King Jr.'s "Letter from Birmingham Jail" (p. 280):

> But when you have seen vicious mobs lynch your mothers and fathers at will and drown your sisters and brothers at whim; when you have seen hate-filled policemen curse, kick, and even kill your black brothers and sisters; when you see the vast majority of your twenty million Negro brothers smothering in an airtight cage of poverty in the midst of an affluent society; when you suddenly find your tongue twisted and your speech stammering as you seek to explain to your six-year-old daughter why she can't go to the public amusement park that has just been advertised on television, and see tears welling up in her eyes when she is told that Funtown is closed to colored children, and see ominous clouds of inferiority beginning to form in her little mental sky, and see her beginning to distort her personality by developing an unconscious bitterness toward white people; when you have to concoct an answer for a five-year-old son who is asking, "Daddy, why do white people treat colored people so mean?"; when you take a cross-country drive and find it necessary to sleep night after night in the uncomfortable corners of your automobile because no motel will accept you; when you are humiliated day in and day out by nagging signs reading "white" and "colored"; when your first name becomes "nigger," your middle name becomes "boy" (however old you are) and your last name becomes "John," and your wife and mother are never given the respected title "Mrs."; when you are harried by day and haunted by night by the fact that you are a Negro, living constantly at tiptoe stance, never quite knowing what to expect next, and are plagued with inner fears and outer resentments; when you are forever fighting a degenerating sense of "nobodiness"—then you will understand why we find it difficult to wait.

Inverted Sentence

In every standard English sentence pattern, the subject comes before the verb (SV). But if a writer chooses, he or she can invert the standard sentence pattern and put the verb before the subject (VS). This is called an inverted sentence. Here is an example:

> Everywhere was a shadow of death. —RACHEL CARSON

> Controlled exponential growth is what you'd really like to see. —JOY WILLIAMS

> What's at stake as they busy themselves are your tax dollars and mine, and ultimately our freedom too. —E. O. WILSON

The inverted sentence pattern slows the reader down, because it is simply more difficult to comprehend inverted word order. Take this example from Emerson's "Nature":

V   S

In the woods, is perpetual youth.

In this example, Emerson calls attention to "woods" and "youth," minimizing the verb "is" and juxtaposing a place ("woods") with a state of being ("youth"). Consider the difference if he had written:

S V

Perpetual youth is in the woods.

This "revised" version is easier to read quickly, and even though the meaning is essentially the same, the emphasis is different. In fact, to understand the full impact, we need to consider the sentence in its context. If you look back at Emerson's essay "Nature," you'll see that his sentence is a short one among longer, more complex sentences. That combination of inversion and contrasting length makes the sentence—and the idea it conveys—stand out.

A Word about Punctuation

It is important to follow the normal rules of comma usage when punctuating unusual sentence patterns. In a cumulative sentence, the descriptors that follow the main clause need to be set off from it and from one another with commas, as in the example from Terry Tempest Williams on page 927. Likewise, in a periodic sentence, the series of clauses or phrases that precede the subject should be set off from the subject and from one another by commas, as in the Emerson example on page 897. When writing an inverted sentence, you may be tempted to insert a comma between the verb and the subject because of the unusual order—but don't.

• EXERCISE 1 •

For each of the following, craft a periodic, cumulative, or inverted sentence by filling in the blanks.

1. Among the tangle of weeds and brush were _____.
2. Hoping, knowing _____, but realizing _____, the candidate _____.
3. All his life he would remember that fateful moment when the fish _____, _____, _____.
4. If you _____ and if you _____, then _____.
5. Into the clouds soared _____.
6. Only when _____ will _____.

• EXERCISE 2 •

In the following paragraph from *The End of Nature* by Bill McKibben, the cumulative sentences are in blue. Rewrite them as periodic sentences. How does the sentence structure affect the focus, tone, and meaning of each of the three sentences? Discuss the rhetorical effectiveness of the way that McKibben decided to write them.

In the end, I understand perfectly well that defiance may mean prosperity and a sort of security—that more dams will help the people of Phoenix, and that genetic engineering will help the sick, and that there is so much progress that can still be made against human misery. And I have no great desire to limit my way of life. If I thought we could put off the decision, foist it on our grandchildren, I'd be willing. As it is, I have no plans to live in a cave, or even an unheated cabin. If it took ten thousand years to get where we are, it will take a few generations to climb back down. But this could be the epoch when people decide at least to go no farther down the path we've been following—when we make not only the necessary technological adjustments to preserve the world from overheating but also the necessary mental adjustments to ensure that we'll never again put our good ahead of everything else's. This is the path I choose, for it offers at least a shred of hope for a living, eternal, meaningful world. (para. 20)

• EXERCISE 3 •

The following paragraph from *The Future of Life* by E. O. Wilson consists of three sentences: a simple declarative sentence, then a periodic sentence, and finally a cumulative sentence. Keep the first one as it is; then rewrite the periodic sentence as cumulative and the cumulative as periodic. Compare the two paragraphs. Discuss the relationship among the sentences in each paragraph and the rhetorical effect of syntax on meaning and tone.

The guiding principles of a united environmental movement must be, and eventually will be, chiefly long-term. If two hundred years of history of environmentalism have taught us anything, it is that a change of heart occurs when people look beyond themselves to others, and then to the rest of life. It is strengthened when they also expand their view of landscape, from parish to nation and beyond, and their sweep of time from their own life spans to multiple generations and finally to the extended future history of humankind. (para. 18)

• EXERCISE 4 •

Identify each of the following sentences as periodic, cumulative, or inverted, and discuss the impact of using that pattern. (Each sentence is a direct quotation from essays in this chapter, so you might want to check the context of the sentence to appreciate its impact more fully. Note that some sentences use more than one unusual pattern.)

1. Similarly, chemicals sprayed on croplands or forests or gardens lie long in soil, entering into living organisms, passing from one to another in a chain of poisoning and death.

   —RACHEL CARSON, para. 12

2. Among them are many that are used in man's war against nature.

   —RACHEL CARSON, para. 16

3. I see the spectacle of morning from the hill-top over against my house, from day-break to sun-rise, with emotions which an angel might share.

   —RALPH WALDO EMERSON, para. 16

4. Not less excellent, except for our less susceptibility in the afternoon, was the charm, last evening, of a January sunset.

   —RALPH WALDO EMERSON, para. 17

5. When a noble act is done,—perchance in a scene of great natural beauty; when Leonidas and his three hundred martyrs consume one

day in dying, and the sun and moon come each and look at them once in the steep defile of Thermopylæ; when Arnold Winkelried, in the high Alps, under the shadow of the avalanche, gathers in his side a sheaf of Austrian spears to break the line for his comrades, are not these heroes entitled to add the beauty of the scene to the beauty of the deed?

— RALPH WALDO EMERSON, para. 20

6. Regret maybe you'll consider.

— JOY WILLIAMS, para. 1

7. The oldest, easiest to swallow idea was that the earth was man's personal property, a combination of garden, zoo, bank vault and energy source, placed at our disposal to be consumed, ornamented or pulled apart as we wished.

— LEWIS THOMAS, para. 4

8. How to get power? is what they're thinking.

— E. O. WILSON, para. 13

9. This might turn out to be a special phase in the morphogenesis of the earth when it is necessary to have something like us, for a time anyway, to fetch and carry energy, look after new symbiotic arrangements, store up information for some future season, do a certain amount of ornamenting, maybe even carry seeds around the solar system.

— LEWIS THOMAS, para. 14

10. Though not in our time, and not in the time of our children, or their children, if we now, *today*, limited our numbers and our desires and our ambitions, perhaps nature could someday resume its independent working.

— BILL MCKIBBEN, para. 24

11. Every good argument — the argument that fossil fuels cause the greenhouse effect; the argument that in a drier, hotter world we'll need more water; the argument that as our margin of security dwindles we must act to restore it — will lead us to more La Grande projects, more dams on the Colorado, more "management." Every argument — that the warmer weather and increased ultraviolet is killing plants and causing cancer; that the new weather is causing food shortages — will have us looking to genetic engineering for salvation.

— BILL MCKIBBEN, para. 12

12. What's at stake as they busy themselves are your tax dollars and mine, and ultimately our freedom too.

— E. O. WILSON, para. 13

13. When I started trying to follow the industrial food chain — the one that now feeds most of us most of the time and typically culminates either in a supermarket or fast-food meal — I expected that my investigations would lead me to a wide variety of places.

—MICHAEL POLLAN, para. 8

14. Hidden from immediate view in the butterfly-bright meadow, in the dusky thicket, in the oak and holly wood, are the surveyors' stakes, for someone wants to build a mall exactly there — some gas stations and supermarkets, some pizza and video shops, a health club, maybe a bulimia treatment center.

—JOY WILLIAMS, para. 1

• EXERCISE 5 •

The following selection is from paragraph 11 of "A Naturalist in the Supermarket" by Michael Pollan. Read the paragraph carefully, and identify whether the underlined sentences are cumulative or periodic. Discuss the effect of the syntax in each case. Then, imitating the structure of each, write a sentence of your own on an environmental issue.

To wash down your chicken nuggets with virtually any soft drink in the supermarket is to have some corn with your corn. Since the 1980s virtually all the sodas and most of the fruit drinks sold in the supermarket have been sweetened with high-fructose corn syrup (HFCS) — after water, corn sweetener is their principal ingredient. Grab a beer for your beverage instead and you'd still be drinking corn, in the form of alcohol fermented from glucose refined from corn. Read the ingredients on the label of any processed food and, provided you know the chemical names it travels under, corn is what you will find. For modified or unmodified starch, for glucose syrup and maltodextrin, for crystalline fructose and ascorbic acid, for lecithin and dextrose, lactic acid and lysine, for maltose and HFCS, for MSG and polyols, for the caramel color and xanthan gum, read: corn. Corn is in the coffee whitener and Cheez Whiz, the frozen yogurt and TV dinner, the canned fruit and ketchup and candies, the soups and snacks and cake mixes, the frosting and gravy and frozen waffles, the syrups and hot sauces, the mayonnaise and mustard, the hot dogs and the bologna, the margarine and shortening, the salad dressings and the relishes and even the vitamins. (Yes, it's in the Twinkie, too.) There are some forty-five thousand items in the average American supermarket and more than a quarter of them now contain corn. This goes for the nonfood items as well — everything from thetoothpaste and cosmetics to the disposable diapers, trash bags, cleansers, charcoal briquettes, matches, and batteries, right down to the shine on the cover of the magazine that catches your eye by the checkout: corn. Even in Produce on a day when there's ostensibly no corn for sale you'll nevertheless find plenty of corn: in the vegetable wax that gives the cucumbers their sheen, in the pesticide responsible for the produce's perfection, even in the coating on the cardboard it was shipped in. Indeed, the supermarket itself—the wallboard and joint compound, the linoleum and fiberglass and adhesives out of which the building itself has been built—is in no small measure a manifestation of corn.

• EXERCISE 6 •

Following are five examples of unusual sentence patterns. Choose two or three; then write your own sentences, using each example as a model.

1. Neither in its clearness, its colour, its fantasy of motion, its calmness of space, depth, and reflection or its wrath, can water be conceived by a low-lander, out of sight of sea.

   —JOHN RUSKIN, *Modern Painters*

2. There are hills, rounded, blunt, burned, squeezed up out of chaos, chrome and vermilion painted, aspiring to the snow-line.

   —MARY AUSTIN, "The Land of Little Rain"

3. The yucca bristles with bayonet-pointed leaves, dull green, growing shaggy with age, tipped with panicles of fetid, greenish bloom.

   —MARY AUSTIN, "The Land of Little Rain"

4. Scores of millions of years before man had risen from the shores of the ocean to perceive its grandeur and to venture forth upon its turbulent waves, this eternal sea existed, larger than any other of the earth's features, vaster than the sister oceans combined, wild, terrifying in its immensity and imperative in its universal role.

   —JAMES MICHENER, *Hawaii*

5. Something will have gone out of us as a people if we ever let the remaining wilderness be destroyed; if we permit the last virgin forests to be turned into comic books and plastic cigarette cases; if we drive the few remaining members of the wild species into zoos or to extinction; if we pollute the last clear air and dirty the last clean streams and push our paved roads through the last of the silence, so that never again will Americans be free in their own country from the noise, the exhausts, the stinks of human and automotive waste. And so that never again can we have the chance to see ourselves single, separate, vertical and individual in the world, part of the environment of trees and rocks and soil,

> brother to the other animals, part of the natural world and competent to belong in it.
>
> —WALLACE STEGNER, "Wilderness Letter"

Suggestions for Writing
The Environment

Now that you have examined a number of readings and other texts focusing on nature, explore one dimension of this topic by synthesizing your own ideas and the selections. You might want to do more research or use readings from other classes as you prepare for the following projects.

1. Take a walk in a favorite natural place close to where you live—in the woods, or out on the prairie, or along the beach, or in the desert. Then write to one of the authors in this chapter, comparing your impressions of nature with those he or she presents.

2. Research a local environmental issue—the development of open land, hunting or fishing regulations, wildlife protection, auto emissions, or another important concern. Then write a letter to the editor of your local newspaper in which you take a position on the issue. Refer to at least three sources from the chapter to support your position.

3. Write an essay in which you compare the ways in which two authors in this chapter use research to support their arguments.

4. Write a personal essay that answers this chapter's essential question: What is our responsibility to the natural environment? Refer in your essay to at least three sources from the chapter for support.

5. Write an essay evaluating and comparing the classic appeals to ethos, pathos, and logos used by two or more of the authors in this chapter.

6. Write an essay explaining how one of the visual texts illustrates a major idea espoused by one of the authors in the chapter.

7. Imagine what a person living fifty years in the future might say to us now about the effect we have had on the environment. Employing both exposition and argument, write a "report from the future" warning our society about the consequences of our treatment of the natural world.

8. Select one of the following statements about nature and the environment, and write an essay that explores its validity. To support your essay, refer to your personal experience and to the selections in this chapter.

- The West of which I speak is but another name for the Wild; and what I have been preparing to say is, that in Wildness is the preservation of the World.

  —HENRY DAVID THOREAU

- Sometimes we forget that nature also means us. Termites build mounds; we build cities. All of our being—juices, flesh and spirit—is nature.

  —DIANE ACKERMAN

- A true conservationist is a man who knows that the world is not given by his fathers but borrowed from his children.

  —JOHN JAMES AUDUBON

- To waste, to destroy our natural resources, to skin and exhaust the land instead of using it so as to increase its usefulness, will result in undermining in the days of our children the very prosperity which we ought by right to hand down to them amplified and developed.

  —THEODORE ROOSEVELT

- We seem to be in a period in which the conservation of anything is disparaged—the conservation of books, the conservation of ideas, the conservation of time, the conservation of darkness, the conservation of love, the conservation of intelligence—it all gets very short shrift in contemporary society. And I think that in the environmental movement, in the curious way in which it overlaps the women's movement and other social movements of the late twentieth century, what we are really seeing is an insistence on the moral dimension of life. When I say the moral dimension, I mean issues of integrity and dignity and responsibility.

  —BARRY LOPEZ

9. View former vice president Al Gore's documentary film *An Inconvenient Truth*. Write a review of the film in the voice of one of the writers you've read in this chapter.

10. View one of the following three films—*Fast Food Nation*; *Supersize Me*; or *Food, Inc.*—and compare it with the voices you have read in the Conversation on Sustainable Eating.

11. View the documentary film *No Impact Man*. Do you find its argument persuasive? How does it address this chapter's essential question?

12. In 1977, artist Andy Warhol said, "I'm a city boy. In the big cities, they've set it up so you can go to a park and be in a miniature countryside; but in the countryside they don't have any patches of big city, so I get very homesick." Write an essay on "the end of nature" in which you consider Warhol's perspective in relation to those of Bill McKibben, Aldo Leopold, and others included in this chapter.

13. Writers Aldo Leopold, Lewis Thomas, Bill McKibben, and E. O. Wilson all discuss a "choice" that confronts humanity regarding the environment. Indicate each of the choices they discuss, and evaluate which one makes the most sense and offers the best solution.

14. "The ethical solution is to diagnose and disconnect extraneous political ideology, then shed it in order to move toward the common ground where economic progress and conservation are treated as one and the same goal," writes E. O. Wilson in *The Future of Life* (para. 12). Having read the selections included in this chapter, how likely do you think it is that we will achieve the ethical solution that Wilson suggests? Refer specifically to at least three of the texts to support your answer.

15. ExxonMobil, self-described as "the world's largest publicly traded international oil and gas company, providing energy that helps underpin growing economies and improve living standards around the world," makes the following statements on its Web site:

    Managing long-term climate risks

    Rising greenhouse-gas emissions pose significant risks to society and ecosystems. Since most of these emissions are energy-related, any integrated approach to meeting the world's growing energy needs over the coming decades must incorporate strategies to address the risk of climate change.

    Managing climate change risks

    Our strategy to reduce greenhouse-gas emissions is focused on increasing energy efficiency in the short term, implementing proven emission-reducing technologies in the near and medium term, and developing breakthrough, game-changing technologies for the long term. Technological innovation will play a central role in our ability to increase supply, improve efficiency, and reduce emissions. Approximately 90 percent of the greenhouse-gas emissions generated by petroleum products are released when customers use our products, and the remaining 10 percent are generated by industry operations. Therefore, technology is also needed to reduce energy-related emissions by end users.

    In a time when we still hear many people—even some public officials—questioning the reality of climate change and global warming, it might seem surprising to discover the perspective above coming from a large energy company. What do these statements suggest about climate change? About global warming? About the relationship between economic concerns and environmental protection? Finally, what do they suggest about the essential question posed at the beginning of this chapter: What is our responsibility to the natural environment? Refer to several texts from this chapter as you answer these questions.

Politics

What is the relationship between the citizen and the state?

Politics, the process by which groups make decisions, plays a part in all human interactions. When we study history, the social sciences, religion, or business, we learn about politics; whenever we read the newspaper or watch the news on television, we see politics in action; and when we discuss issues with our classmates and friends or involve ourselves in our community, we engage in politics. Politics is as much the context for our daily lives as it is for government legislation and international affairs. Thus, one could argue that politics is the cause of all social change.

Democratic governments, such as the one under which we live, exercise power through the will of the people. With that power comes responsibility, even the responsibility to dissent if necessary. So what is the nature of patriotism in a democracy? Is it loyalty to the government or loyalty to the ideals of the nation? How is American patriotism colored by the fact that our country was born out of a revolution? In this chapter, writers on American politics ranging from Henry David Thoreau to Tim O'Brien examine the rights of citizens to resist and remind us of the connection between political action and social change.

In America, a former subject of colonial power, colonialism is an especially interesting subject. Looking at the effects of colonialism elsewhere gives us a more informed view of our own nation's experience as well as that of other nations and peoples. Is our view of colonialism affected by our nation's origin? Does colonialism ever have positive benefits? And how does patriotism work when the government is a foreign power? The selections in this chapter raise those questions and also remind us of the effects of both colonialism and postcolonialism on language, culture, social change, and global politics.

Educated citizens — the root of the word *politics* is the Greek word for *citizen* — must know about the politics of the world as well as the politics of their own country. This chapter presents a variety of voices and perspectives on national and world politics. The selections examine the interrelationships among citizens, their states, and the world. Here you will read classic voices delivering sardonic criticism and lofty idealism; you will encounter the immediacy of personal reflections on the nature and experience of war; and you will read contemporary reflections on the lingering effects of colonialism in the modern world.

1005

On Seeing England for the First Time

Jamaica Kincaid

Jamaica Kincaid was born in 1949 on the Caribbean island of Antigua, then a British colony. She came to the United States as a teenager to work as an au pair in New York City, where she then attended the New School for Social Research. Kincaid became a staff writer for the *New Yorker* in 1975 and published much of her short work there. Perhaps her most widely known works are "Girl" from *At the Bottom of the River* (1985), a collection of short stories, and *Annie John* (1985), a novel. *A Small Place* (1988), her book-length essay on the tensions between tourists and the native people of the Caribbean, followed. Among her later books are *My Garden* (1999), the novel *Mr. Potter* (2002), and the nonfiction *Among Flowers: A Walk in the Himalaya* (2005). The autobiographical essay included here originally appeared in *Transition* in 1991 and later that year was excerpted in *Harper's*.

When I saw England for the first time, I was a child in school sitting at a desk. The England I was looking at was laid out on a map gently, beautifully, delicately, a very special jewel: it lay on a bed of sky blue—the background of the map—its yellow form mysterious, because though it looked like a leg of mutton, it could not really look like anything so familiar as a leg of mutton because it was England—with shadings of pink and green, unlike any shadings of pink and green I had seen before, squiggly veins of red running in every direction. England was a special jewel all right, and only special people got to wear it. The people who got to wear England were English people. They wore it well and they wore it everywhere: in jungles, in deserts, on plains, on top of the highest mountains, on all the oceans, on all the seas, in places where they were not welcome, in places they should not have been. When my teacher had pinned this map up on the blackboard, she said, "This is England"—and she said it with authority, seriousness, and adoration, and we all sat up. It was as if she had said, "This is Jerusalem, the place you will go to when you die but only if you have been good." We understood then—we were meant to understand then—that England was to be our source of myth and the source from which we got our sense of reality, our sense of what was meaningful, our sense of what was meaningless— and much about our own lives and much about the very idea of us headed that last list.

At the time I was a child sitting at my desk seeing England for the first time, I was already very familiar with the greatness of it. Each morning before I left for school, I ate a breakfast of half a grapefruit, an egg, bread and butter and a slice of cheese, and a cup of cocoa; or half a grapefruit, a bowl of oat porridge, bread and butter and a slice of cheese, and a cup of cocoa. The can of cocoa was often left on the table in front of me. It had written on it the name of the company, the year the company was established, and the words "Made in England." Those words, "Made in England," were written on the box the oats came in too. They would also have been written on the box the shoes I was wearing came in; a bolt of gray linen cloth lying on the shelf of a store from which my mother had bought three yards to make the uniform that I was wearing had written along its edge those three words. The shoes I wore were made in England; so were my socks and cotton under-garments and the satin ribbons I wore tied at the end of two plaits of my hair. My father, who might have sat next to me at breakfast, was a carpenter and cabinet maker. The shoes he wore to work would have been made in England, as were his khaki shirt and trousers, his underpants and undershirt, his socks and brown felt hat. Felt was not the proper material from which a hat that was expected to pro-vide shade from the hot sun should be made, but my father must have seen and admired a picture of an Englishman wearing such a hat in England, and this pic-ture that he saw must have been so compelling that it caused him to wear the wrong hat for a hot climate most of his long life. And this hat—a brown felt hat—became so central to his character that it was the first thing he put on in the morning as he stepped out of bed and the last thing he took off before he stepped back into bed at night. As we sat at breakfast a car might go by. The car, a Hillman or a Zephyr, was made in England. The very idea of the meal itself, breakfast, and its substantial quality and quantity was an idea from England; we somehow knew that in England they began the day with this meal called breakfast and a proper breakfast was a big breakfast. No one I knew liked eating so much food so early in the day; it made us feel sleepy, tired. But this breakfast business was Made in England like almost everything else that surrounded us, the exceptions being the sea, the sky, and the air we breathed.

At the time I saw this map—seeing England for the first time—I did not say to myself, "Ah, so that's what it looks like," because there was no longing in me to put a shape to those three words that ran through every part of my life, no matter how small; for me to have had such a longing would have meant that I lived in a certain atmosphere, an atmosphere in which those three words were felt as a bur-den. But I did not live in such an atmosphere. My father's brown felt hat would develop a hole in its crown, the lining would separate from the hat itself, and six weeks before he thought that he could not be seen wearing it—he was a very vain man—he would order another hat from England. And my mother taught me to eat my food in the English way: the knife in the right hand, the fork in the left, my elbows held still close to my side, the food carefully balanced on my fork and then brought up to my mouth. When I had finally mastered it, I overheard her saying to a friend, "Did you see how nicely she can eat?" But I knew then that I enjoyed my food more when I ate it with my bare hands, and I continued to do so when she wasn't looking. And when my teacher showed us the map, she asked us to study it carefully, because no test we would ever take would be complete without this statement: "Draw a map of England."

I did not know then that the statement "Draw a map of England" was something far worse than a declaration of war, for in fact a flat-out declaration of war would have put me on alert, and again in fact, there was no need for war — I had long ago been conquered. I did not know then that this statement was part of a process that would result in my erasure, not my physical erasure, but my erasure all the same. I did not know then that this statement was meant to make me feel in awe and small whenever I heard the word "England": awe at its existence, small because I was not from it. I did not know very much of anything then — certainly not what a blessing it was that I was unable to draw a map of England correctly.

After that there were many times of seeing England for the first time. I saw   5
England in history. I knew the names of all the kings of England. I knew the names of their children, their wives, their disappointments, their triumphs, the names of people who betrayed them; I knew the dates on which they were born and the dates they died. I knew their conquests and was made to feel glad if I figured in them; I knew their defeats. I knew the details of the year 1066 (the Battle of Hastings, the end of the reign of the Anglo-Saxon kings) before I knew the details of the year 1832 (the year slavery was abolished). It wasn't as bad as I make it sound now; it was worse. I did like so much hearing again and again how Alfred the Great, traveling in disguise, had been left to watch cakes, and because he wasn't used to this the cakes got burned, and Alfred burned his hands pulling them out of the fire, and the woman who had left him to watch the cakes screamed at him. I loved King Alfred. My grandfather was named after him; his son, my uncle, was named after King Alfred; my brother is named after King Alfred. And so there are three people in my family named after a man they have never met, a man who died over ten centuries ago. The first view I got of England then was not unlike the first view received by the person who named my grandfather.

This view, though — the naming of the kings, their deeds, their disappointments — was the vivid view, the forceful view. There were other views, subtler ones, softer, almost not there — but these were the ones that made the most lasting impression on me, these were the ones that made me really feel like nothing. "When morning touched the sky" was one phrase, for no morning touched the sky where I lived. The mornings where I lived came on abruptly, with a shock of heat and loud noises. "Evening approaches" was another, but the evenings where I lived did not approach; in fact, I had no evening — I had night and I had day and they came and went in a mechanical way: on, off; on, off. And then there were gentle mountains and low blue skies and moors over which people took walks for nothing but pleasure, when where I lived a walk was an act of labor, a burden, something only death or the automobile could relieve. And there were things that a small turn of a head could convey — entire worlds, whole lives would depend on this thing, a certain turn of a head. Everyday life could be quite tiring, more tiring than anything I was told not to do. I was told not to gossip, but they did that all the time. And they ate so much food, violating another of those rules they taught me: do not indulge in gluttony. And the foods they ate actually: if only sometime I could eat cold cuts after theater, cold cuts of lamb and mint sauce, and Yorkshire pudding and scones, and clotted cream, and sausages that came from up-country (imagine, "up-country"). And having troubling thoughts at twilight, a good time to have troubling thoughts, apparently; and servants who stole and left in the middle of a crisis, who were born with a limp or some other kind of deformity, not nourished properly in their mother's womb (that last part I figured out for myself; the point was, oh to have an untrustworthy servant); and wonderful cobbled streets onto which solid front doors opened; and people whose eyes were blue and who had fair skins and who smelled only of lavender, or sometimes sweet pea or primrose. And those flowers with those names: delphiniums, foxgloves, tulips, daffodils, floribunda, peonies; in bloom, a striking display, being cut and placed in large glass bowls, crystal, decorating rooms so large twenty families the size of mine could fit in comfortably but used only for passing through. And the weather was so remarkable because the rain fell gently always, only occasionally in deep gusts, and it colored the air various shades of gray, each an appealing shade for a dress to be worn when a portrait was being painted; and when it rained at twilight, wonderful things happened: people bumped into each other unexpectedly and that would lead to all sorts of turns of events—a plot, the mere weather caused plots. I saw that people rushed: they rushed to catch trains, they rushed toward each other and away from each other; they rushed and rushed and rushed. That word: rushed! I did not know what it was to do that. It was too hot to do that, and so I came to envy people who would rush, even though it had no meaning to me to do such a thing. But there they are again. They loved their children; their children were sent to their own rooms as a punishment, rooms larger than my entire house. They were special, everything about them said so, even their clothes; their clothes rustled, swished, soothed. The world was theirs, not mine; everything told me so.

If now as I speak of all this I give the impression of someone on the outside looking in, nose pressed up against a glass window, that is wrong. My nose was pressed up against a glass window all right, but there was an iron vise at the back of my neck forcing my head to stay in place. To avert my gaze was to fall back into something from which I had been rescued, a hole filled with nothing, and that was the word for everything about me, nothing. The reality of my life was conquests, subjugation, humiliation, enforced amnesia. I was forced to forget. Just for instance, this: I lived in a part of St. John's, Antigua, called Ovals. Ovals was made up of five streets, each of them named after a famous English seaman—to be quite frank, an officially sanctioned criminal: Rodney Street (after George Rodney), Nelson Street (after Horatio Nelson), Drake Street (after Francis Drake), Hood Street, and Hawkins Street (after John Hawkins). But John Hawkins was knighted after a trip he made to Africa, opening up a new trade, the slave trade. He was then entitled to wear as his crest a Negro bound with a cord. Every single person living on Hawkins Street was descended from a slave. John Hawkins's ship, the one in which he transported the people he had bought and kidnapped, was called *The Jesus*. He later became the treasurer of the Royal Navy and rear admiral.

Again, the reality of my life, the life I led at the time I was being shown these views of England for the first time, for the second time, for the one-hundred-millionth time, was this: the sun shone with what sometimes seemed to be a deliberate cruelty; we must have done something to deserve that. My dresses did not rustle in the evening air as I strolled to the theater (I had no evening, I had no theater; my dresses were made of a cheap cotton, the weave of which would give way after not too many washings). I got up in the morning, I did my chores (fetched water from the public pipe for my mother, swept the yard), I washed myself, I went to a woman to have my hair combed freshly every day (because before we were allowed into our classroom our teachers would inspect us, and children who had not bathed that day, or had dirt under their fingernails, or whose hair had not been combed anew that day, might not be allowed to attend class). I ate that breakfast. I walked to school. At school we gathered in an auditorium and sang a hymn, "All Things Bright and Beautiful," and looking down on us as we sang were portraits of the Queen of England and her husband; they wore jewels and medals and they smiled. I was a Brownie. At each meeting we would form a little group around a flagpole, and after raising the Union Jack, we would say, "I promise to do my best, to do my duty to God and the Queen; to help other people every day and obey the scouts' law."

Who were these people and why had I never seen them, I mean really seen them, in the place where they lived? I had never been to England. No one I knew had ever been to England, or I should say, no one I knew had ever been and returned to tell me about it. All the people I knew who had gone to England had stayed there. Sometimes they left behind them their small children, never to see them again. England! I had seen England's representatives. I had seen the governor general at the public grounds at a ceremony celebrating the Queen's birthday. I had seen an old princess and I had seen a young princess. They had both been extremely not beautiful, but who of us would have told them that? I had never seen England, really seen it, I had only met a representative, seen a picture, read books, memorized its history. I had never set foot, my own foot, in it.

The space between the idea of something and its reality is always wide and deep and dark. The longer they are kept apart—idea of thing, reality of thing—the wider the width, the deeper the depth, the thicker and darker the darkness. This space starts out empty, there is nothing in it, but it rapidly becomes filled up with obsession or desire or hatred or love—sometimes all of these things, sometimes some of these things, sometimes only one of these things. The existence of the world as I came to know it was a result of this: idea of thing over here, reality of thing way, way over there. There was Christopher Columbus, an unlikable man, an unpleasant man, a liar (and so, of course, a thief) surrounded by maps and schemes and plans, and there was the reality on the other side of that width, that depth, that darkness. He became obsessed, he became filled with desire, the hatred came later, love was never a part of it. Eventually, his idea met the longed-for reality. That the idea of something and its reality are often two completely different things is something no one ever remembers; and so when they meet and find that they are not compatible, the weaker of the two, idea or reality, dies. That idea Christopher Columbus had was more powerful than the reality he met, and so the reality he met died.

And so finally, when I was a grown-up woman, the mother of two children, the wife of someone, a person who resides in a powerful country that takes up more than its fair share of a continent, the owner of a house with many rooms in it and of two automobiles, with the desire and will (which I very much act upon) to take from the world more than I give back to it, more than I deserve, more than I need, finally then, I saw England, the real England, not a picture, not a painting, not through a story in a book, but England, for the first time. In me, the space between the idea of it and its reality had become filled with hatred, and so when at last I saw it I wanted to take it into my hands and tear it into little pieces and then crumble it up as if it were clay, child's clay. That was impossible, and so I could only indulge in not-favorable opinions.

There were monuments everywhere; they commemorated victories, battles fought between them and the people who lived across the sea from them, all vile people, fought over which of them would have dominion over the people who looked like me. The monuments were useless to them now, people sat on them and ate their lunch. They were like markers on an old useless trail, like a piece of old string tied to a finger to jog the memory, like old decoration in an old house, dirty, useless, in the way. Their skins were so pale, it made them look so fragile, so weak, so ugly. What if I had the power to simply banish them from their land, send boat after boatload of them on a voyage that in fact had no destination, force them to live in a place where the sun's presence was a constant? This would rid them of their pale complexion and make them look more like me, make them look more like the people I love and treasure and hold dear, and more like the people who occupy the near and far reaches of my imagination, my history, my geography, and reduce them and everything they have ever known to figurines as evidence that I was in divine favor, what if all this was in my power? Could I resist it? No one ever has.

And they were rude, they were rude to each other. They didn't like each other very much. They didn't like each other in the way they didn't like me, and it occurred to me that their dislike for me was one of the few things they agreed on.

I was on a train in England with a friend, an English woman. Before we were in England she liked me very much. In England she didn't like me at all. She didn't like the claim I said I had on England, she didn't like the views I had of England.

I didn't like England, she didn't like England, but she didn't like me not liking it too. She said, "I want to show you my England, I want to show you the England that I know and love." I had told her many times before that I knew England and I didn't want to love it anyway. She no longer lived in England; it was her own country, but it had not been kind to her, so she left. On the train, the conductor was rude to her; she asked something, and he responded in a rude way. She became ashamed. She was ashamed at the way he treated her; she was ashamed at the way he behaved. "This is the new England," she said. But I liked the conductor being rude; his behavior seemed quite appropriate. Earlier this had happened: we had gone to a store to buy a shirt for my husband; it was meant to be a special present, a special shirt to wear on special occasions. This was a store where the Prince of Wales has his shirts made, but the shirts sold in this store are beautiful all the same. I found a shirt I thought my husband would like and I wanted to buy him a tie to go with it. When I couldn't decide which one to choose, the salesman showed me a new set. He was very pleased with these, he said, because they bore the crest of the Prince of Wales, and the Prince of Wales had never allowed his crest to decorate an article of clothing before. There was something in the way he said it; his tone was slavish, reverential, awed. It made me feel angry; I wanted to hit him. I didn't do that. I said, my husband and I hate princes, my husband would never wear anything that had a prince's anything on it. My friend stiffened. The salesman stiffened. They both drew themselves in, away from me. My friend told me that the prince was a symbol of her Englishness, and I could see that I had caused offense. I looked at her. She was an English person, the sort of English person I used to know at home, the sort who was nobody in England but somebody when they came to live among the people like me. There were many people I could have seen England with; that I was seeing it with this particular person, a person who reminded me of the people who showed me England long ago as I sat in church or at my desk, made me feel silent and afraid, for I wondered if, all these years of our friendship, I had had a friend or had been in the thrall of a racial memory.

I went to Bath—we, my friend and I, did this, but though we were together, I was no longer with her. The landscape was almost as familiar as my own hand, but I had never been in this place before, so how could that be again? And the streets of Bath were familiar, too, but I had never walked on them before. It was all those years of reading, starting with Roman Britain. Why did I have to know about Roman Britain? It was of no real use to me, a person living on a hot, drought-ridden island, and it is of no use to me now, and yet my head is filled with this nonsense, Roman Britain. In Bath, I drank tea in a room I had read about in a novel written in the eighteenth century. In this very same room, young women wearing those dresses that rustled and so on danced and flirted and sometimes disgraced themselves with young men, soldiers, sailors, who were on their way to Bristol or someplace like that, so many places like that where so many adventures, the outcome of which was not good for me, began. Bristol, England.

A sentence that began "That night the ship sailed from Bristol, England" would end not so good for me. And then I was driving through the countryside in an English motorcar, on narrow winding roads, and they were so familiar, though I had never been on them before; and through little villages the names of which I somehow knew so well though I had never been there before. And the country-side did have all those hedges and hedges, fields hedged in. I was marveling at all the toil of it, the planting of the hedges to begin with and then the care of it, all that clipping, year after year of clipping, and I wondered at the lives of the people who would have to do this, because wherever I see and feel the hands that hold up the world, I see and feel myself and all the people who look like me. And I said, "Those hedges" and my friend said that someone, a woman named Mrs. Rothchild, worried that the hedges weren't being taken care of properly; the farmers couldn't afford or find the help to keep up the hedges, and often they replaced them with wire fencing. I might have said to that, well if Mrs. Rothchild doesn't like the wire fencing, why doesn't she take care of the hedges herself, but I didn't. And then in those fields that were now hemmed in by wire fencing that a privileged woman didn't like was planted a vile yellow flowering bush that produced an oil, and my friend said that Mrs. Rothchild didn't like this either; it ruined the English coun-tryside, it ruined the traditional look of the English countryside.

It was not at that moment that I wished every sentence, everything I knew, that began with England would end with "and then it all died; we don't know how, it just all died." At that moment, I was thinking, who are these people who forced me to think of them all the time, who forced me to think that the world I knew was incomplete, or without substance, or did not measure up because it was not England; that I was incomplete, or without substance, and did not measure up because I was not English. Who were these people? The person sitting next to me couldn't give me a clue; no one person could. In any case, if I had said to her, I find England ugly, I hate England; the weather is like a jail sentence, the English are a very ugly people, the food in England is like a jail sentence, the hair of English people is so straight, so dead looking, the English have an unbearable smell so different from the smell of people I know, real people of course, she would have said that I was a person full of prejudice. Apart from the fact that it is I — that is, the people who look like me — who made her aware of the unpleas-antness of such a thing, the idea of such a thing, prejudice, she would have been only partly right, sort of right: I may be capable of prejudice, but my prejudices have no weight to them, my prejudices have no force behind them, my prejudices remain opinions, my prejudices remain my personal opinion. And a great feeling of rage and disappointment came over me as I looked at England, my head full of personal opinions that could not have public, my public, approval. The people I come from are powerless to do evil on grand scale.

The moment I wished every sentence, everything I knew, that began with England would end with "and then it all died; we don't know how, it just all died" was when I saw the white cliffs of Dover. I had sung hymns and recited poems that were about a longing to see the white cliffs of Dover again. At the time I sang the hymns and recited the poems, I could really long to see them again because I had never seen them at all, nor had anyone around me at the time. But there we were, groups of people longing for something we had never seen. And so there they were, the white cliffs, but they were not that pearly majestic thing I used to sing about, that thing that created such a feeling in these people that when they died in the place where I lived they had themselves buried facing a direction that would allow them to see the white cliffs of Dover when they were resurrected, as surely they would be. The white cliffs of Dover, when finally I saw them, were cliffs, but they were not white; you would only call them that if the word "white" meant something special to you; they were dirty and they were steep; they were so steep, the correct height from which all my views of England, starting with the map before me in my classroom and ending with the trip I had just taken, should jump and die and disappear forever.

Questions for Discussion

1. What is ironic about the essay's title, "On Seeing England for the First Time"?
2. In paragraph 4, Jamaica Kincaid says, "I had long ago been conquered." What does she mean?
3. How does Kincaid regard the British influence under which she was raised? Refer to specific passages.
4. How do Kincaid's childhood memories of school compare with your own?
5. In paragraph 10, Kincaid writes, "The space between the idea of something and its reality is always wide and deep and dark." What does she mean?
6. At the end of paragraph 12, Kincaid says, in reference to power, "No one ever has [resisted it]." Do you think this is true? Explain.
7. What is the effect of the shirt-shopping example Kincaid provides (para. 14)? What does it contribute to your understanding of Kincaid's attitude toward England?
8. Where in the essay does Kincaid's epiphany occur? Support your claim with evidence from the text.
9. Having read the essay, how do you regard Kincaid?

Questions on Rhetoric and Style

1. In the opening paragraph, how does Kincaid build up detail to develop a clearly ironic tone?
2. How does the use of parallelism serve Kincaid's rhetorical purpose in the first paragraph?
3. What is the effect of the mutton simile that Kincaid uses in paragraph 1? What is the effect of retracting that simile within the same clause?

4. In paragraphs 1 and 2, Kincaid uses listing as a technique. What is the effect? How does this effect serve her purpose?

5. Kincaid writes in paragraph 5 that "there were many times of seeing England for the first time." What is her purpose for developing this paradox?

6. Kincaid uses the phrases "extremely not beautiful" (para. 9) and "not-favorable" (para. 11). Why not simply say "ugly" or "homely" or "unfavorable"? How does Kincaid's diction contribute to her purpose?

7. In paragraph 11, Kincaid says she has "the desire and will . . . to take from the world more than I give back to it, more than I deserve, more than I need." What effect does such a statement have on the reader?

8. Kincaid uses repetition in paragraph 16. She mentions "my prejudices" four times. What is the effect of the repetition as she confesses to the reader?

9. What is the rhetorical effect of the phrase "as surely they would be" in paragraph 17?

10. What is the effect of Kincaid's attitude toward her friend? How does her description of this relationship affect her ethos?

11. Throughout the essay Kincaid conveys her anger and her sense of injustice with various appeals to pathos. How does she also appeal to logos? Identify specific examples.

Suggestions for Writing

1. Reread paragraph 10, which begins, "The space between the idea of something and its reality is always wide and deep and dark." Has there ever been a time in your life when an idea and reality have come into conflict? Write an essay explaining how your experience supports Kincaid's observation.

2. Many readers note the bitter voice in this essay. Does Kincaid present a narrator who becomes bitter as the piece develops, or is the speaker's voice consistently bitter from the beginning? Use specific references to support your answer.

3. We consider education as a liberating process, a "leading out," according to its etymology. This essay presents a different view. Explain how Kincaid uses her youthful experience to present education as an oppressive rather than a generative force.

4. Has there ever been a time in your life when you saw something "for the first time" many times? Write an essay explaining that experience.

5. Read carefully paragraphs 12 and 16, noting particularly where Kincaid comments on the universality of power and prejudice as she concludes each paragraph. Write an essay supporting or challenging her analysis.

6. Some readers may consider Kincaid's criticism of England and its people as extreme and may characterize her essay as polemical. Write an essay that discusses Kincaid's views of England, and evaluate the success of her argument.

On the Duty of Civil Disobedience

HENRY DAVID THOREAU

 Henry David Thoreau (1817–1862) was a philosopher, poet, essayist, and naturalist as well as an outspoken social critic. Born in Concord, Massachusetts, he was educated at Harvard and worked at a variety of professions, from land surveyor to teacher to pencil maker. Strongly influenced by his neighbor and friend Ralph Waldo Emerson, Thoreau considered himself a fierce patriot who honored his country and its ideals, if not always its government. He spoke out against the war with Mexico and criticized the Fugitive Slave Act, and he defended the abolitionist John Brown. Thoreau is best known for *Walden, or Life in the Woods* (p. 296), published in 1854, which presents his account of living in a cabin on Walden Pond for two years. Originally delivered as a lecture, "On the Duty of Civil Disobedience" is Thoreau's response to his arrest and incarceration for not paying a poll tax. Its influence has been enormous, deeply affecting such twentieth-century figures as Gandhi and Martin Luther King Jr.

I heartily accept the motto,—"That government is best which governs least"; and I should like to see it acted up to more rapidly and systematically. Carried out, it finally amounts to this, which I also believe,—"That government is best which governs not at all"; and when men are prepared for it, that will be the kind of government which they will have. Government is at best but an expedient; but most governments are usually, and all governments are sometimes, inexpedient. The objections which have been brought against a standing army, and they are many and weighty, and deserve to prevail, may also at last be brought against a standing government. The standing army is only an arm of the standing government. The government itself, which is only the mode which the people have chosen to execute their will, is equally liable to be abused and perverted before the people can act through it. Witness the present Mexican war, the work of comparatively a few individuals using the standing government as their tool; for, in the outset, the people would not have consented to this measure.

This American government,—what is it but a tradition, though a recent one, endeavoring to transmit itself unimpaired to posterity, but each instant losing some of its integrity? It has not the vitality and force of a single living man; for a single man can bend it to his will. It is a sort of wooden gun to the people themselves. But it is not the less necessary for this; for the people must have some complicated machinery or other, and hear its din, to satisfy that idea of government which they have. Governments show thus how successfully men can be imposed on, even impose on themselves, for their own advantage. It is excellent, we must all allow. Yet this government never of itself furthered any enterprise, but by the alacrity with which it got out of its way. *It* does not keep the country free. *It* does not settle the West. *It* does not educate. The character inherent in the American people has done all that has been accomplished; and it would have done somewhat more, if the government had not sometimes got in its way. For government is an expedient by which men would fain succeed in letting one another alone; and, as has been said, when it is most expedient, the governed are most let alone by it. Trade and commerce, if they were not made of India-rubber, would never manage to bounce over the obstacles which legislators are continually putting in their way; and, if one were to judge these men wholly by the effects of their actions and not partly by their intentions, they would deserve to be classed and punished with those mischievous persons who put obstructions on railroads.

But, to speak practically and as a citizen, unlike those who call themselves no-government men, I ask for, not at once no government, but *at once* a better government. Let every man make known what kind of government would command his respect, and that will be one step toward obtaining it.

After all, the practical reason why, when the power is once in the hands of the people, a majority are permitted, and for a long period continue, to rule, is not because they are most likely to be in the right, nor because this seems fairest to the minority, but because they are physically the strongest. But a government in which the majority rule in all cases cannot be based on justice, even as far as men understand it. Can there not be a government in which majorities do not virtually decide right and wrong, but conscience? — in which majorities decide only those questions to which the rule of expediency is applicable? Must the citizen ever for a moment, or in the least degree, resign his conscience to the legislator? Why has every man a conscience, then? I think that we should be men first, and subjects afterward. It is not desirable to cultivate a respect for the law, so much as for the right. The only obligation which I have the right to assume, is to do at any time what I think right. It is truly enough said, that a corporation has no conscience; but a corporation of conscientious men is a corporation *with* a conscience. Law never made men a whit more just; and, by means of their respect for it, even the well-disposed are daily made the agents of injustice. A common and natural result of an undue respect for law is, that you may see a file of soldiers, colonel, captain, corporal, privates, powder-monkeys, and all, marching in admirable order over hill and dale to the wars, against their wills, ay, against their common sense and consciences, which makes it very steep marching indeed, and produces a palpitation of the heart. They have no doubt that it is a damnable business in which they are concerned; they are all peaceably inclined. Now, what are they? Men at all? or small movable forts and magazines, at the service of some unscrupulous man in power? Visit the Navy-Yard, and behold a marine, such a man as an American government can make, or such as it can make a man with its black arts, — a mere shadow and reminiscence of humanity, a man laid out alive and standing, and already, as one may say, buried under arms with funeral accompaniments, though it may be, —

Not a drum was heard, not a funeral note.
As his corse to the rampart we hurried;
Not a soldier discharged his farewell shot
O'er the grave where our hero we buried.[1]

The mass of men serve the state thus, not as men mainly, but as machines,   5
with their bodies. They are the standing army, and the militia, jailers, constables,
posse comitatus, &c. In most cases there is no free exercise whatever of the judgment or of the moral sense; but they put themselves on a level with wood and
earth and stones; and wooden men can perhaps be manufactured that will serve
the purpose as well. Such command no more respect than men of straw or a lump
of dirt. They have the same sort of worth only as horses and dogs. Yet such as
these even are commonly esteemed good citizens. Others,—as most legislators,
politicians, lawyers, ministers, and office-holders,—serve the state chiefly with
their heads; and, as they rarely make any moral distinctions, they are as likely to
serve the Devil, without *intending* it, as God. A very few, as heroes, patriots, martyrs, reformers in the great sense, and *men*, serve the state with their consciences
also, and so necessarily resist it for the most part; and they are commonly treated
as enemies by it. A wise man will only be useful as a man, and will not submit to
be "clay," and "stop a hole to keep the wind away,"[2] but leave that office to his dust
at least:—

I am too high-born to be propertied,
To be a secondary at control,
Or useful serving-man and instrument
To any sovereign state throughout the world.[3]

He who gives himself entirely to his fellow-men appears to them useless and
selfish; but he who gives himself partially to them is pronounced a benefactor and
philanthropist.

How does it become a man to behave toward this American government
today? I answer, that he cannot without disgrace be associated with it. I cannot for
an instant recognize that political organization as *my* government which is the
slave's government also.

All men recognize the right of revolution; that is, the right to refuse allegiance to, and to resist, the government, when its tyranny or its inefficiency are
great and unendurable. But almost all say that such is not the case now. But such
was the case, they think, in the Revolution of '75. If one were to tell me that this
was a bad government because it taxed certain foreign commodities brought to
its ports, it is most probable that I should not make an ado about it, for I can do
without them. All machines have their friction; and possibly this does enough

---

[1]From an early nineteenth-century song.—Eds.
[2]*Hamlet* 5.1.236–237.—Eds.
[3]*King John* 5.1.79–82.—Eds.

good to counterbalance the evil. At any rate, it is a great evil to make a stir about it. But when the friction comes to have its machine, and oppression and robbery are organized, I say, let us not have such a machine any longer. In other words, when a sixth of the population of a nation which has undertaken to be the refuge of liberty are slaves, and a whole country is unjustly overrun and conquered by a foreign army, and subjected to military law, I think that it is not too soon for honest men to rebel and revolutionize. What makes this duty the more urgent is the fact, that the country so overrun is not our own, but ours is the invading army.

[William] Paley, a common authority with many on moral questions, in his chapter on the "Duty of Submission to Civil Government," resolves all civil obligation into expediency; and he proceeds to say, "that so long as the interest of the whole society requires it, that is, so long as the established government cannot be resisted or changed without public inconveniency, it is the will of God that the established government be obeyed, and no longer."——"This principle being admitted, the justice of every particular case of resistance is reduced to a computation of the quantity of the danger and grievance on the one side, and of the probability and expense of redressing it on the other." Of this, he says, every man shall judge for himself. But Paley appears never to have contemplated those cases to which the rule of expediency does not apply, in which a people, as well as an individual, must do justice, cost what it may. If I have unjustly wrested a plank from a drowning man, I must restore it to him though I drown myself. This, according to Paley, would be inconvenient. But he that would save his life, in such a case, shall lose it. This people must cease to hold slaves, and to make war on Mexico, though it cost them their existence as a people.

In their practice, nations agree with Paley; but does any one think that Massachusetts does exactly what is right at the present crisis?

> A drab of state, a cloth-'o-silver slut,
> To have her train borne up, and her soul trail in the dirt.[4]

Practically speaking, the opponents to a reform in Massachusetts are not a hundred thousand politicians at the South, but a hundred thousand merchants and farmers here, who are more interested in commerce and agriculture than they are in humanity, and are not prepared to do justice to the slave and to Mexico, *cost what it may.* I quarrel not with far-off foes, but with those who, near at home, cooperate with, and do the bidding of, those far away, and without whom the latter would be harmless. We are accustomed to say, that the mass of men are unprepared; but improvement is slow, because the few are not materially wiser or better than the many. It is not so important that many should be as good as you, as that there be some absolute goodness somewhere; for that will leaven the whole lump. There are thousands who are *in opinion* opposed to slavery and to the war, who yet in effect do nothing to put an end to them; who, esteeming themselves children

10

---

[4]From a work by Cyril Tourneur (c. 1575–1626).—Eds.

of Washington and Franklin, sit down with their hands in their pockets, and say that they know not what to do, and do nothing; who even postpone the question of freedom to the question of free-trade, and quietly read the prices-current along with the latest advices from Mexico, after dinner, and, it may be, fall asleep over them both. What is the price-current of an honest man and a patriot today? They hesitate, and they regret, and sometimes they petition; but they do nothing in earnest and with effect. They will wait, well disposed, for others to remedy the evil, that they may no longer have it to regret. At most, they give only a cheap vote, and a feeble countenance and God-speed, to the right, as it goes by them. There are nine hundred and ninety-nine patrons of virtue to one virtuous man. But it is easier to deal with the real possessor of a thing than with the temporary guardian of it.

All voting is a sort of gaming, like checkers or backgammon, with a slight moral tinge to it, a playing with right and wrong, with moral questions; and betting naturally accompanies it. The character of the voters is not staked. I cast my vote, perchance, as I think right; but I am not vitally concerned that that right should prevail. I am willing to leave it to the majority. Its obligation, therefore, never exceeds that of expediency. Even voting *for the right* is *doing* nothing for it. It is only expressing to men feebly your desire that it should prevail. A wise man will not leave the right to the mercy of chance, nor wish it to prevail through the power of the majority. There is but little virtue in the action of masses of men. When the majority shall at length vote for the abolition of slavery, it will be because they are indifferent to slavery, or because there is but little slavery left to be abolished by their vote. *They* will then be the only slaves. Only *his* vote can hasten the abolition of slavery who asserts his own freedom by his vote.

I hear of a convention to be held at Baltimore, or elsewhere, for the selection of a candidate for the Presidency, made up chiefly of editors, and men who are politicans by profession; but I think, what is it to any independent, intelligent, and respectable man what decision they may come to? Shall we not have the advantage of his wisdom and honesty, nevertheless? Can we not count upon some independent votes? Are there not many individuals in the country who do not attend conventions? But no: I find that the respectable man, so called, has immediately drifted from his position, and despairs of his country, when his country has more reason to despair of him. He forthwith adopts one of the candidates thus selected as the only *available* one, thus proving that he is himself *available* for any purposes of the demagogue. His vote is of no more worth than that of any unprincipled foreigner or hireling native, who may have been bought. O for a man who is *a man*, and, as my neighbor says, has a bone in his back which you cannot pass your hand through! Our statistics are at fault: The population has been returned too large. How many *men* are there to a square thousand miles in this country? Hardly one. Does not America offer any inducement for men to settle here? The American has dwindled into an Odd Fellow,—one who may be known by the development of his organ of gregariousness, and a manifest lack of intellect and cheerful self-reliance; whose first and chief concern, on coming into the world, is to see that the Almshouses are in good repair; and, before yet he has lawfully donned the virile garb, to collect a fund for the support of the widows and orphans that may be; who, in short, ventures to live only by the aid of the Mutual Insurance company, which has promised to bury him decently.

It is not a man's duty, as a matter of course, to devote himself to the eradication of any, even the most enormous wrong; he may still properly have other concerns to engage him; but it is his duty, at least, to wash his hands of it, and, if he gives it no thought longer, not to give it practically his support. If I devote myself to other pursuits and contemplations, I must first see, at least, that I do not pursue them sitting upon another man's shoulders. I must get off him first, that he may pursue his contemplations too. See what gross inconsistency is tolerated. I have heard some of my townsmen say, "I should like to have them order me out to help put down an insurrection of the slaves, or to march to Mexico;—see if I would go"; and yet these very men have each, directly by their allegiance, and so indirectly, at least, by their money, furnished a substitute. The soldier is applauded who refuses to serve in an unjust war by those who do not refuse to sustain the unjust government which makes the war; is applauded by those whose own act and authority he disregards and sets at naught; as if the State were penitent to that degree that it hired one to scourge it while it sinned, but not to that degree that it left off sinning for a moment. Thus, under the name of Order and Civil Government, we are all made at last to pay homage to and support our own meanness. After the first blush of sin comes its indifference; and from immoral it becomes, as it were, *un*moral, and not quite unnecessary to that life which we have made.

The broadest and most prevalent error requires the most disinterested virtue to sustain it. The slight reproach to which the virtue of patriotism is commonly liable, the noble are most likely to incur. Those who, while they disapprove of the character and measures of a government, yield to it their allegiance and support, are undoubtedly its most conscientious supporters, and so frequently the most serious obstacles to reform. Some are petitioning the State to dissolve the Union, to disregard the requisitions of the President. Why do they not dissolve it themselves,— the union between themselves and the States,—and refuse to pay their quota into its treasury? Do not they stand in the same relation to the State, that the State does to the Union? And have not the same reasons prevented the State from resisting the Union, which have prevented them from resisting the State?

How can a man be satisfied to entertain an opinion merely, and enjoy *it*? Is there any enjoyment in it, if his opinion is that he is aggrieved? If you are cheated out of a single dollar by your neighbor, you do not rest satisfied with knowing that you are cheated, or with saying that you are cheated, or even with petitioning him to pay you your due; but you take effectual steps at once to obtain the full amount, and see that you are never cheated again. Action from principle, the perception and the performance of right, changes things and relations; it is essentially revolutionary, and does not consist wholly with anything which was. It not

15

only divides states and churches, it divides families; ay, it divides the *individual*, separating the diabolical in him from the divine.

Unjust laws exist: Shall we be content to obey them, or shall we endeavor to amend them, and obey them until we have succeeded, or shall we transgress them at once? Men generally, under such a government as this, think that they ought to wait until they have persuaded the majority to alter them. They think that, if they should resist, the remedy would be worse than the evil. But it is the fault of the government itself that the remedy *is* worse than the evil. *It* makes it worse. Why is it not more apt to anticipate and provide for reform? Why does it not cherish its wise minority? Why does it cry and resist before it is hurt? Why does it not encourage its citizens to be on the alert to point out its faults, and *do* better than it would have them? Why does it always crucify Christ, and excommunicate Copernicus and Luther, and pronounce Washington and Franklin rebels?

One would think, that a deliberate and practical denial of its authority was the only offence never contemplated by government; else, why has it not assigned its definite, its suitable and proportionate penalty? If a man who has no property refuses but once to earn nine shillings for the State, he is put in prison for a period unlimited by any law that I know, and determined only by the discretion of those who placed him there; but if he should steal ninety times nine shillings from the State, he is soon permitted to go at large again.

If the injustice is part of the necessary friction of the machine of government, let it go, let it go: Perchance it will wear smooth,—certainly the machine will wear out. If the injustice has a spring, or a pulley, or a rope, or a crank, exclusively for itself, then perhaps you may consider whether the remedy will not be worse than the evil; but if it is of such a nature that it requires you to be the agent of injustice to another, then, I say, break the law. Let your life be a counter friction to stop the machine. What I have to do is to see, at any rate, that I do not lend myself to the wrong which I condemn.

As for adopting the ways which the State has provided for remedying the evil, I know not of such ways. They take too much time, and a man's life will be gone. I have other affairs to attend to. I came into this world, not chiefly to make this a good place to live in, but to live in it, be it good or bad. A man has not everything to do, but something; and because he cannot do *everything*, it is not necessary that he should do *something* wrong. It is not my business to be petitioning the Governor or the Legislature any more than it is theirs to petition me; and, if they should not hear my petition, what should I do then? But in this case the State has provided no way: Its very Constitution is the evil. This may seem to be harsh and stubborn and unconciliatory; but it is to treat with the utmost kindness and consideration the only spirit that can appreciate or deserves it. So is all change for the better, like birth and death, which convulse the body.

I do not hesitate to say, that those who call themselves Abolitionists should at once effectually withdraw their support, both in person and property, from the government of Massachusetts, and not wait till they constitute a majority of one, 20 before they suffer the right to prevail through them. I think that it is enough if they have God on their side, without waiting for that other one. Moreover, any man more right than his neighbors constitutes a majority of one already.[5]

I meet this American government, or its representative, the State government, directly, and face to face, once a year — no more — in the person of its tax-gatherer; this is the only mode in which a man situated as I am necessarily meets it; and it then says distinctly, Recognize me; and the simplest, the most effectual, and, in the present posture of affairs, the indispensablest mode of treating with it on this head, of expressing your little satisfaction with and love for it, is to deny it then. My civil neighbor, the tax-gatherer, is the very man I have to deal with, — for it is, after all, with men and not with parchment that I quarrel, — and he has voluntarily chosen to be an agent of the government. How shall he ever know well what he is and does as an officer of the government, or as a man, until he is obliged to consider whether he shall treat me, his neighbor, for whom he has respect, as a neighbor and well-disposed man, or as a maniac and disturber of the peace, and see if he can get over this obstruction to his neighborliness without a ruder and more impetuous thought or speech corresponding with his action. I know this well, that if one thousand, if one hundred, if ten men whom I could name, — if ten *honest* men only, — ay, if *one* HONEST man, in this State of Massachusetts, *ceasing to hold slaves*, were actually to withdraw from this copartnership, and be locked upon the county jail therefor, it would be the abolition of slavery in America. For it matters not how small the beginning may seem to be: What is once well done is done forever. But we love better to talk about it. That we say is our mission. Reform keeps many scores of newspapers in its service, but not one man. If my esteemed neighbor, the State's ambassador, who will devote his days to the settlement of the question of human rights in the Council Chamber, instead of being threatened with the prisons of Carolina, were to sit down the prisoner of Massachusetts, that State which is so anxious to foist the sin of slavery upon her sister, — though at present she can discover only an act of inhospitality to be the ground of a quarrel with her, — the Legislature would not wholly waive the subject the following winter.

Under a government which imprisons any unjustly, the true place for a just man is also a prison. The proper place today, the only place which Massachusetts has provided for her freer and less desponding spirits, is in her prisons, to be put out and locked out of the State by her own act, as they have already put themselves out by their principles. It is there that the fugitive slave, and the Mexican prisoner on parole, and the Indian come to plead the wrongs of his race, should find them; on that separate, but more free and honorable ground, where the State places those who are not *with* her, but *against* her, — the only house in a slave State in which a free man can abide with honor. If any think that their influence

---

[5]An allusion to a statement by John Knox (1505?–1572), a religious reformer, who said, "A man with God is always in the majority." — Eds.

would be lost there, and their voices no longer afflict the ear of the State, that they would not be as an enemy within its walls, they do not know by how much truth is stronger than error, nor how much more eloquently and effectively he can combat injustice who has experienced a little in his own person. Cast your whole vote, not a strip of paper merely, but your whole influence. A minority is power-less while it conforms to the majority; it is not even a minority then; but it is irresistible when it clogs by its whole weight. If the alternative is to keep all just men in prison, or give up war and slavery, the State will not hesitate which to choose. If a thousand men were not to pay their tax-bills this year, that would not be a violent and bloody measure, as it would be to pay them, and enable the State to commit violence and shed innocent blood. This is, in fact, the definition of a peaceable revolution, if any such is possible. If the tax-gatherer, or any other pub-lic officer, asks me, as one has done, "But what shall I do?" my answer is, "If you really wish to do anything, resign your office." When the subject has refused alle-giance, and the officer has resigned his office, then the revolution is accomplished. But even suppose blood should flow. Is there not a sort of blood shed when the conscience is wounded? Through this wound a man's real manhood and immor-tality flow out, and he bleeds to an everlasting death. I see this blood flowing now.

I have contemplated the imprisonment of the offender, rather than the seizure of his goods,—though both will serve the same purpose,—because they who assert the purest right, and consequently are most dangerous to a corrupt State, commonly have not spent much time in accumulating property. To such the State renders comparatively small service, and a slight tax is wont to appear exorbi-tant, particularly if they are obliged to earn it by special labor with their hands. If there were one who lived wholly without the use of money, the State itself would hesitate to demand it of him. But the rich man,—not to make any invidious comparison,—is always sold to the institution which makes him rich. Absolutely speaking, the more money, the less virtue; for money comes between a man and his objects, and obtains them for him; and it was certainly no great virtue to obtain it. It puts to rest many questions which he would otherwise be taxed to answer; while the only new question which it puts is the hard but superfluous one, how to spend it. Thus his moral ground is taken from under his feet. The oppor-tunities of living are diminished in proportion as what are called the "means" are increased. The best thing a man can do for his culture when he is rich is to endeavor to carry out those schemes which he entertained when he was poor. Christ answered the Herodians according to their condition. "Show me the tribute-money," said he;—and one took a penny out of his pocket;—if you use money which has the image of Caesar on it, and which he has made current and valuable, that is, *if you are men of the State*, and gladly enjoy the advantages of Caesar's government, then pay him back some of his own when he demands it; "Render therefore to Caesar that which is Caesar's, and to God those things which are God's,"[6]—leaving them no wiser than before as to which was which; for they did not wish to know.

---

[6]Matt. 22:16–21.—Eds.

When I converse with the freest of my neighbors, I perceive that, whatever they may say about the magnitude and seriousness of the question, and their regard for the public tranquility, the long and the short of the matter is, that they cannot spare the protection of the existing government, and they dread the consequences to their property and families of disobedience to it. For my own part, I should not like to think that I ever rely on the protection of the State. But, if I deny the authority of the State when it presents its tax-bill, it will soon take and waste all my property, and so harass me and my children without end. This is hard. This makes it impossible for a man to live honestly, and at the same time comfortably, in outward respects. It will not be worth the while to accumulate property; that would be sure to go again. You must hire or squat somewhere, and raise but a small crop, and eat that soon. You must live within yourself, and depend upon yourself always tucked up and ready for a start, and not have many affairs. A man may grow rich in Turkey even, if he will be in all respects a good subject of the Turkish government. Confucius said: "If a state is governed by the principles of reason, poverty and misery are subjects of shame; if a state is not governed by the principles of reason, riches and honors are the subjects of shame." No: Until I want the protection of Massachusetts to be extended to me in some distant Southern port, where my liberty is endangered, or until I am bent solely on building up an estate at home by peaceful enterprise, I can afford to refuse allegiance to Massachusetts, and her right to my property and life. It costs me less in every sense to incur the penalty of disobedience to the State, than it would to obey. I should feel as if I were worth less in that case.

Some years ago, the State met me in behalf of the Church and commanded   25
me to pay a certain sum toward the support of a clergyman whose preaching my father attended, but never I myself. "Pay," it said, "or be locked up in the jail." I declined to pay. But, unfortunately, another man saw fit to pay it. I did not see why the schoolmaster should be taxed to support the priest, and not the priest the schoolmaster; for I was not the State's schoolmaster, but I supported myself by voluntary subscription. I did not see why the lyceum should not present its tax-bill, and have the State to back its demand, as well as the Church. However, at the request of the selectmen, I condescended to make some such statement as this in writing: — "Know all men by these presents, that I, Henry Thoreau, do not wish to be regarded as a member of any incorporated society which I have not joined." This I gave to the town clerk; and he has it. The State, having thus learned that I did not wish to be regarded as a member of that church, has never made a like demand on me since; though it said that it must adhere to its original presumption that time. If I had known how to name them, I should then have signed off in detail from all the societies which I never signed on to; but I did not know where to find a complete list.

I have paid no poll-tax for six years. I was put into a jail once on this account, for one night; and, as I stood considering the walls of solid stone, two or three feet thick, the door of wood and iron, a foot thick, and the iron grating which strained the light, I could not help being struck with the foolishness of that institution which treated me as if I were mere flesh and blood and bones, to be locked up. I wondered that it should have concluded at length that this was the best use it could put me to, and had never thought to avail itself of my services in some way. I saw that, if there was a wall of stone between me and my townsmen, there was a still more difficult one to climb or break through, before they could get to be as free as I was. I did not for a moment feel confined, and the walls seemed a great waste of stone and mortar. I felt as if I alone of all my townsmen had paid my tax. They plainly did not know how to treat me, but behaved like persons who are underbred. In every threat and in every compliment there was a blunder; for they thought that my chief desire was to stand the other side of that stone wall, I could not but smile to see how industriously they locked the door on my meditations, which followed them out again without let or hindrance, and *they* were really all that was dangerous. As they could not reach me, they had resolved to punish my body; just as boys, if they cannot come at some person against whom they have a spite, will abuse his dog. I saw that the State was half-witted, that it was timid as a lone woman with her silver spoons, and that it did not know its friends from its foes, and I lost all my remaining respect for it, and pitied it.

Thus the State never intentionally confronts a man's sense, intellectual or moral, but only his body, his senses. It is not armed with superior wit or honesty, but with superior physical strength. I was not born to be forced. I will breathe after my own fashion. Let us see who is the strongest. What force has a multitude? They only can force me who obey a higher law than I. They force me to become like themselves. I do not hear of *men* being *forced* to live this way or that by masses of men. What sort of life were that to live? When I meet a government which says to me, "Your money or your life," why should I be in haste to give it my money? It may be in a great strait, and not know what to do: I cannot help that. It must help itself; do as I do. It is not worth the while to snivel about it. I am not responsible for the successful working of the machinery of society. I am not the son of the engineer. I perceive that, when an acorn and a chestnut fall side by side, the one does not remain inert to make way for the other, but both obey their own laws, and spring and grow and flourish as best they can, till one, perchance, over-shadows and destroys the other. If a plant cannot live according to its nature, it dies; and so a man.

The night in prison was novel and interesting enough. The prisoners in their shirt-sleeves were enjoying a chat and the evening air in the doorway, when I entered. But the jailer said, "Come, boys, it is time to lock up"; and so they dispersed, and I heard the sound of their steps returning into the hollow apartments. My roommate was introduced to me by the jailer, as "a first-rate fellow and a clever man." When the door was locked, he showed me where to hang my hat, and how he managed matters there. The rooms were white-washed once a month; and this one, at least, was the whitest, most simply furnished, and probably the neatest apartment in the town. He naturally wanted to know where I came from, and what brought me there; and, when I had told him, I asked him in my turn how he came there, presuming him to be an honest man, of course; and, as the world goes, I believe he was. "Why," said he, "they accuse me of burning a barn; but I never did it." As near as I could discover, he had probably gone to bed in a barn when drunk, and smoked his pipe there; and so a barn was burnt. He had the reputation of being a clever man, had been there some three months waiting for his trial to come on, and would have to wait as much longer; but he was quite domesticated and contented, since he got his board for nothing, and thought that he was well-treated.

He occupied one window, and I the other; and I saw, that, if one stayed there long, his principal business would be to look out the window. I had soon read all the tracts that were left there, and examined where former prisoners had broken out, and where a grate had been sawed off, and heard the history of the various occupants of that room; for I found that even here there was a history and a gossip which never circulated beyond the walls of the jail. Probably this is the only house in the town where verses are composed, which are afterward printed in a circular form, but not published. I was shown quite a long list of verses which were composed by some young men who had been detected in an attempt to escape, who avenged themselves by singing them.

I pumped my fellow-prisoner as dry as I could, for fear I should never see him again; but at length he showed me which was my bed, and left me to blow out the lamp. 30

It was like travelling into a far country, such as I had never expected to behold, to lie there for one night. It seemed to me that I never had heard the town-clock strike before, nor the evening sounds of the village; for we slept with the windows open, which were inside the grating. It was to see my native village in the light of the Middle Ages, and our Concord was turned into a Rhine stream, and visions of knights and castles passed before me. They were the voices of old burghers that I heard in the streets. I was an involuntary spectator and auditor of whatever was done and said in the kitchen of the adjacent village-inn, — a wholly new and rare experience to me. It was a closer view of my native town. I was fairly inside of it. I never had seen its institutions before. This is one of its peculiar institutions; for it is a shire town. I began to comprehend what its inhabitants were about.

In the morning, our breakfasts were put through the hole in the door, in small oblong-square tin pans, made to fit, and holding a pint of chocolate, with brown bread, and an iron spoon. When they called for the vessels again, I was green enough to return what bread I had left; but my comrade seized it, and said that I should lay that up for lunch or dinner. Soon after he was let out to work at haying in a neighboring field, whither he went every day, and would not be back till noon; so he bade me good-day, saying that he doubted if he should see me again.

When I came out of prison, — for some one interfered, and paid that tax, — I did not perceive that great changes had taken place on the common, such as he observed who went in a youth, and emerged a tottering and gray-headed man; and yet a change had to my eyes come over the scene,—the town, a State, and country,—greater than any mere time could effect. I saw yet more distinctly the State in which I lived. I saw to what extent the people among whom I lived could be trusted as good neighbors and friends; that their friendship was for summer weather only; that they did not greatly propose to do right; that they were a distinct race from me by their prejudices and superstitions, as the Chinamen and Malays are; that, in their sacrifices to humanity, they ran no risks, not even to their property; that, after all, they were not so noble but they treated the thief as he had treated them, and hoped, by a certain outward observance and a few prayers, and by walking in a particular straight though useless path from time to time, to save their souls. This may be to judge my neighbors harshly; for I believe that many of them are not aware that they have such an institution as the jail in their village.

It was formerly the custom in our village, when a poor debtor came out of jail, for his acquaintances to salute him, looking through their fingers, which were crossed to represent the grating of a jail window. "How do ye do?" My neighbors did not thus salute me, but first looked at me, and then at one another, as if I had returned from a long journey. I was put into jail as I was going to the shoemaker's to get a shoe which was mended. When I was let out the next morning, I proceeded to finish my errand, and having put on my mended shoe, joined a huckleberry party, who were impatient to put themselves under my conduct; and in half an hour,—for the horse was soon tackled,—was in the midst of a huckleberry field, on one of our highest hills, two miles off, and then the State was nowhere to be seen.

This is the whole history of "My Prisons."   35

I have never declined paying the highway tax, because I am as desirous of being a good neighbor as I am of being a bad subject; and, as for supporting schools, I am doing my part to educate my fellow-countrymen now. It is for no particular item in the tax-bill that I refuse to pay it. I simply wish to refuse allegiance to the State, to withdraw and stand aloof from it effectually. I do not care to trace the course of my dollar, if I could, till it buys a man or a musket to shoot one with,—the dollar is innocent,—but I am concerned to trace the effects of my allegiance. In fact, I quietly declare war with the State, after my fashion, though I will still make what use and get what advantage of her I can, as is usual in such cases.

If others pay the tax which is demanded of me, from a sympathy with the State, they do but what they have already done in their own case, or rather they abet injustice to a greater extent than the State requires. If they pay the tax from a mistaken interest in the individual taxed, to save his property, or prevent his going to jail, it is because they have not considered wisely how far they let their private feelings interfere with the public good.

This, then, is my position at present. But one cannot be too much on his guard in such a case, lest his action be biased by obstinacy, or an undue regard for the opinions of men. Let him see that he does only what belongs to himself and to the hour.

I think sometimes, Why, this people mean well; they are only ignorant; they would do better if they knew how; why give your neighbors this pain to treat you as they are not inclined to? But I think again, this is no reason why I should do as they do, or permit others to suffer much greater pain of a different kind. Again, I sometimes say to myself, When many millions of men, without heat, without ill will, without personal feeling of any kind, demand of you a few shillings only, without the possibility, such is their constitution, of retracing or altering their present demand, and without the possibility, on your side, of appeal to any other millions, why expose yourself to this overwhelming brute force? You do not resist cold and hunger, the winds and the waves, thus obstinately; you quietly submit to a thousand similar necessities. You do not put your head into the fire. But just in proportion as I regard this as not wholly a brute force, partly a human force, and consider that I have relations to those millions as to so many millions of men, and not of mere brute or inanimate things, I see that appeal is possible, first and instantaneously, from them to the Maker of them, and, secondly, from them to themselves. But, if I put my head deliberately into the fire, there is no appeal to fire or to the Maker of fire, and I have only myself to blame. If I could convince myself that I have any right to be satisfied with men as they are, and to treat them according, and not according, in some respects, to my requisitions and expectations of what they and I ought to be, then, like a good Mussulman[7] and fatalist, I should endeavor to be satisfied with things as they are, and say it is the will of God. And, above all, there is this difference between resisting this and a purely brute or natural force, that I can resist this with some effect; but I cannot expect, like Orpheus, to change the nature of the rocks and trees and beasts.

I do not wish to quarrel with any man or nation. I do not wish to split hairs, to make fine distinctions, or set myself up as better than my neighbors. I seek rather, I may say, even an excuse for conforming to the laws of the land. I am but too ready to conform to them. Indeed, I have reason to suspect myself on this head; and each year, as the tax-gatherer comes round, I find myself disposed to review the acts and position of the general and State governments, and the spirit of the people, to discover a pretext for conformity.

> We must affect our country as our parents;
> And if at any time we alienate
> Our love or industry from doing it honor,
> We must respect effects and teach the soul
> Matter of conscience and religion,
> And not desire of rule or benefit.

40

---

[7]Muslim. — Eds.

I believe that the State will soon be able to take all my work of this sort out of my hands, and then I shall be no better a patriot than my fellow-countrymen. Seen from a lower point of view, the Constitution, with all its faults, is very good; the law and the courts are very respectable; even this State and this American government are, in many respects, very admirable and rare things, to be thankful for, such as a great many have described them; but seen from a point of view a little higher, they are what I have described them; seen from a higher still, and the highest, who shall say what they are, or that they are worth looking at or thinking of at all?

However, the government does not concern me much, and I shall bestow the fewest possible thoughts on it. It is not many moments that I live under a government, even in this world. If a man is thought-free, fancy-free, imagination-free, that which *is not* never for a long time appearing *to be* to him, unwise rulers or reformers cannot fatally interrupt him.

I know that most men think differently from myself; but those whose lives are by profession devoted to the study of these or kindred subjects, content me as little as any. Statesmen and legislators, standing so completely within the institution, never distinctly and nakedly behold it. They speak of moving society, but have no resting-place without it. They may be men of a certain experience and discrimination, and have no doubt invented ingenious and even useful systems, for which we sincerely thank them; but all their wit and usefulness lie within certain not very wide limits. They are wont to forget that the world is not governed by policy and expediency. Webster never goes behind government, and so cannot speak with authority about it. His words are wisdoms to those legislators who contemplate no essential reform in the existing government; but for thinkers, and those who legislate for all time, he never once glances at the subject. I know of those whose serene and wise speculations on this theme would soon reveal the limits of his mind's range and hospitality. Yet, compared with the cheap professions of most reformers, and the still cheaper wisdom and eloquence of politicians in general, his are almost the only sensible and valuable words, and we thank Heaven for him. Comparatively, he is always strong, original, and, above all, practical. Still his quality is not wisdom, but prudence. The lawyer's truth is not Truth, but consistency, or a consistent expediency. Truth is always in harmony with herself, and is not concerned chiefly to reveal the justice that may consist with wrong-doing. He well deserves to be called, as he has been called, the Defender of the Constitution. There are really no blows to be given by him but defensive ones. He is not a leader, but a follower. His leaders are the men of '87. "I have never made an effort," he says, "and never propose to make an effort; I have never countenanced an effort, and never mean to countenance an effort, to disturb the arrangement as originally made, by which the various States came into the Union."[8] Still thinking of the sanction which the Constitution gives to slavery,

---

[8]From an 1845 speech given by Daniel Webster about the admission of Texas to the United States. — Eds.

he says, "Because it was a part of the original compact,—let it stand." Notwith-standing his special acuteness and ability, he is unable to take a fact out of its merely political relations, and behold it as it lies absolutely to be disposed of by the intellect,—what, for instance, it behooves a man to do here in America today with regard to slavery, but ventures, or is driven, to make some such desperate answer as the following, while professing to speak absolutely, and as a private man,—from which what new and singular code of social duties might be in-ferred? "The manner," says he, "in which the governments of those States where slavery exists are to regulate it, is for their own consideration, under their respon-sibility to their constituents, to the general laws of propriety, humanity, and jus-tice, and to God. Associations formed elsewhere, springing from a feeling of humanity, or any other cause, have nothing whatever to do with it. They have never received any encouragement from me, and they never will."

They who know of no purer sources of truth, who have traced up its stream no higher, stand, and wisely stand, by the Bible and the Constitution, and drink at it there with reverence and humility; but they who behold where it comes trickling into this lake or that pool, gird up their loins once more, and continue their pilgrimage toward its fountain-head.

No man with a genius for legislation has appeared in America. They are rare in the history of the world. There are orators, politicians, and eloquent men, by the thousand; but the speaker has not yet opened his mouth to speak, who is capable of settling the much-vexed questions of the day. We love eloquence for its own sake, and not for any truth which it may utter, or any heroism it may inspire. Our legislators have not yet learned the comparative value of free-trade and of freedom, of union, and of rectitude, to a nation. They have no genius or talent for comparatively humble questions of taxation and finance, commerce and manu-factures and agriculture. If we were left solely to the wordy wit of legislators in Congress for our guidance, uncorrected by the seasonable experience and the effectual complaints of the people, America would not long retain her rank among the nations. For eighteen hundred years, though perchance I have no right to say it, the New Testament has been written; yet where is the legislator who has wisdom and practical talent enough to avail himself of the light which it sheds on the science of legislation?

The authority of government, even such as I am willing to submit to,—for I will cheerfully obey those who know and can do better than I, and in many things even those who neither know nor can do so well,—is still an impure one: To be strictly just, it must have the sanction and consent of the governed. It can have no pure right over my person and property but what I concede to it. The progress from an absolute to a limited monarchy, from a limited monarchy to a democ-racy, is a progress toward a true respect for the individual. Even the Chinese phi-losopher was wise enough to regard the individual as the basis of the empire. Is a democracy, such as we know it, the last improvement possible in government? Is it not possible to take a step further towards recognizing and organizing the

45

rights of man? There will never be a really free and enlightened State, until the State comes to recognize the individual as a higher and independent power, from which all its own power and authority are derived, and treats him accordingly. I please myself with imagining a State at last which can afford to be just to all men, and to treat the individual with respect as a neighbor; which even would not think it inconsistent with its own repose, if a few were to live aloof from it, not meddling with it, nor embraced by it, who fulfilled all the duties of neighbors and fellowmen. A State which bore this kind of fruit, and suffered it to drop off as fast as it ripened, would prepare the way for a still more perfect and glorious State, which also I have imagined, but not yet anywhere seen.

Questions for Discussion

1. In paragraph 1, what distinction does Henry David Thoreau make between the government and the people? Why does he begin the essay this way? Why does Thoreau not begin the essay with his stay in jail?
2. Why does Thoreau refer to civil disobedience not merely as a right but as a duty?
3. What are the two government policies Thoreau most objects to? Explain his objection.
4. Thoreau writes, "When the majority shall at length vote for the abolition of slavery, it will be because they are indifferent to slavery, or because there is but little slavery left to be abolished by their vote" (para. 11). What does this statement imply about the voting populace? Do you think that Thoreau is accurate in his characterization of the populace? Why or why not?
5. In paragraph 20, Thoreau states that "any man more right than his neighbors constitutes a majority of one already." What does he mean by this? How does this statement support his thesis?
6. In paragraph 23, Thoreau discusses the effects of wealth on character. Paraphrase that discussion. Do you agree with his analysis? Why or why not?
7. What did Thoreau learn from his night in jail (paras. 26–35)? Explain using specific reference to the text.
8. In paragraph 36, Thoreau distinguishes among different types of taxes. Why? In the same paragraph he says, "I do not care to trace the course of my dollar, if I could, till it buys a man or a musket to shoot one with,—the dollar is innocent,—but I am concerned to trace the effects of my allegiance." What might our dollars buy today that would cause such a reflection and response?
9. Under the circumstances Thoreau describes, do you believe civil disobedience is a duty, as he says? What circumstances in our own society would justify civil disobedience? Explain how Thoreau's essay speaks to our own time. Is the essay dated? Is it still relevant?

Questions on Rhetoric and Style

1. Describe the tone Thoreau establishes in paragraph 2. How does it contribute to the rhetorical effect of the paragraph?
2. What is the effect of the metaphor about friction in paragraphs 8 and 18?
3. Thoreau develops many analogies to support his arguments (e.g., in paras. 8 and 9). Select three, and explain whether you find them convincing. How effectively does each one support the claim Thoreau is using it to support?
4. One characteristic of Thoreau's style is the use of aphorism. For example, in paragraph 4, he writes, "It is not desirable to cultivate a respect for the law, so much as for the right." Find other examples of Thoreau's aphorisms. You might find some in paragraphs 9–10 and 20–22. What is the rhetorical effect of such statements?
5. How would you describe Thoreau's tone in paragraph 12? How does it contribute to his position?
6. Thoreau uses several rhetorical questions in the essay. Identify three, and explain how each one contributes to the paragraph in which it is found.
7. Which of the three classic rhetorical appeals dominates in paragraph 21, where Thoreau gives the government a human face? Defend your answer.
8. Note how Thoreau qualifies his argument in paragraph 40. How does using this strategy serve his rhetorical purpose?

Suggestions for Writing

1. "There are nine hundred and ninety-nine patrons of virtue to one virtuous man," states Thoreau (para. 10). Do you agree? Can you think of a "virtuous man" in American public life today? Write an essay about someone you regard as a virtuous man or woman according to Thoreau's characterization of such a person. Refer specifically to the text of Thoreau's essay.
2. Compare and contrast Thoreau's "On the Duty of Civil Disobedience" with Martin Luther King Jr.'s "Letter from Birmingham Jail" (p. 280) by focusing on one of the following: purpose, definition of a just law, or figurative language.
3. Thoreau writes, "We love eloquence for its own sake, and not for any truth which it may utter, or any heroism it may inspire" (para. 44). Do you believe that is true? Defend, challenge, or qualify the accuracy of that statement as it applies to contemporary society. Use examples of public voices from such institutions as the schools, government, religion, industry, or finance to support your position.
4. Thoreau says, "No man with a genius for legislation has appeared in America. They are rare in the history of the world. There are orators, politicians, and eloquent men, by the thousand; but the speaker has not opened his mouth to speak, who is capable of settling the much-vexed questions of the day" (para. 44). Surely there are many who would disagree. Write an essay that defends, challenges, or qualifies Thoreau's statement as it applies to his time or our own.

5. Think of a contemporary issue that would justify the kind of civil disobedience that Thoreau discusses. Write a letter to your local newspaper making the case for civil disobedience in protest of what you regard as injustice in our society. Be sure to explain the gravity of the situation and the justification for your recommended actions.

6. Think of a contemporary issue that some people in our society regard as justification for civil disobedience. Write an editorial piece that explains why civil disobedience would be wrong and offers alternative solutions.

The Gettysburg Address

ABRAHAM LINCOLN

Abraham Lincoln (1809–1865) was the sixteenth president of the United States of America. He was born in rural Kentucky, was raised in rural Indiana, and settled in Illinois, where he held various jobs before becoming a self-taught lawyer and a member of the state legislature. He was elected president in 1860 and re-elected in 1864 in the midst of the Civil War, which broke out in 1861. On January 1, 1863, Lincoln signed the Emancipation Proclamation, proclaiming the freeing of slaves in America—something he would not live to see. He was assassinated in 1865. Shortly before his death Lincoln delivered the Gettysburg Address, a speech that many people regard as the most powerful and most significant one by an American, to commemorate the dead and wounded soldiers at the site of the battle in Gettysburg, Pennsylvania. In addition to being one of the greatest American presidents, Lincoln also was a skilled writer and rhetorician.

Four score and seven years ago our fathers brought forth on this continent a new nation, conceived in liberty, and dedicated to the proposition that all men are created equal.

Now we are engaged in a great civil war, testing whether that nation, or any nation, so conceived and so dedicated, can long endure. We are met on a great battle-field of that war. We have come to dedicate a portion of that field, as a final resting place for those who here gave their lives that that nation might live. It is altogether fitting and proper that we should do this.

But, in a larger sense, we can not dedicate, we can not consecrate, we can not hallow this ground. The brave men, living and dead, who struggled here, have consecrated it, far above our poor power to add or detract. The world will little note, nor long remember what we say here, but it can never forget what they did here. It is for us the living, rather, to be dedicated here to the unfinished work which they who fought here have thus far so nobly advanced. It is rather for us to be here dedicated to the great task remaining before us — that from these honored dead we take increased devotion to that cause for which they gave the last full measure of devotion — that we here highly resolve that these dead shall not have died in vain — that this nation, under God, shall have a new birth of freedom — and that government of the people, by the people, for the people, shall not perish from the earth.

Exploring the Text

1. What does Abraham Lincoln refer to in the first sentence? Explain the effect of this reference.

2. How would you describe the tone of this speech?

3. When Lincoln delivered the Gettysburg Address, the audience was quite surprised by how short it was: a mere 272 words. Do you think it should have been longer? Why or why not? Notice what he does not mention; for instance, there is no mention of the enemy. Discuss the rhetorical effect of such brevity.

4. Indicate examples of repeated diction. What is the purpose and effect of these repetitions?

5. Identify examples of diction that relate to life and to death. What is the effect of such language?

6. Indicate as many examples of parallel structures, juxtapositions, and antitheses that you can find. Explain their effect.

7. Note the rhetorical shift indicated by "But . . ." in sentence 6. What is its purpose and effect?

8. What is the "great task remaining before us" that Lincoln mentions in sentence 10?

9. In such a short speech, the final sentence is notable for its length (eighty-two words, roughly 30 percent of the total) and complexity. How do the style and rhetoric of the final sentence contribute to the speech as a whole?

10. Considering the importance of the speech, note how ironic it is that Lincoln said, "The world will little note, nor long remember what we say here" (sentence 8). Why do you think this speech has endured?

11. The historian Gary Wills titled his historical and rhetorical analysis of the Gettysburg Address *Lincoln at Gettysburg: The Words That Remade America* (1992). That title, and the book as a whole, makes a mighty strong claim about the speech. Do you think that it is a reasonable claim? Drawing on your knowledge of U.S. history, discuss the extent to which Wills's title accurately characterizes the importance of the speech.

12. Read "The Gettysburg PowerPoint Presentation" by Peter Norvig. It can be found online. What is the object of Norvig's satire? Do you find it effective? Refer to Lincoln's speech as well as your own experience with PowerPoint demonstrations to support your answer.

Thoughts on Peace in an Air Raid

VIRGINIA WOOLF

A prolific novelist, critic, and essayist, Virginia Woolf (1882–1941) was born in London. Her novels, particularly *Mrs. Dalloway* (1925) and *To the Lighthouse* (1927), are renowned for their penetrating psychological insight. Woolf's works are noted for the interior monologue, or stream of consciousness. She is also known for her nonfiction, especially for such major works as *The Common Reader* (1925), *A Room of One's Own* (1929), and *Three Guineas* (1938). Severely depressed over the war in Europe and anxious about her own sanity, she drowned herself in 1941. Woolf wrote the following essay in 1940 and published it in her *Collected Essays*, Volume Four. It also appears in *The Death of a Moth and Other Essays* (1942).

The Germans were over this house last night and the night before that. Here they are again. It is a queer experience, lying in the dark and listening to the zoom of a hornet, which may at any moment sting you to death. It is a sound that interrupts cool and consecutive thinking about peace. Yet it is a sound — far more than prayers and anthems — that should compel one to think about peace. Unless we can think peace into existence we — not this one body in this one bed but millions of bodies yet to be born — will lie in the same darkness and hear the same death rattle overhead. Let us think what we can do to create the only efficient air-raid shelter while the guns on the hill go pop pop pop and the searchlights finger the clouds and now and then, sometimes close at hand, sometimes far away, a bomb drops.

Up there in the sky young Englishmen and young German men are fighting each other. The defenders are men, the attackers men. Arms are not given to Englishwomen either to fight the enemy or to defend herself. She must lie weaponless tonight. Yet if she believes that the fight going on up in the sky is a fight by the English to protect freedom, by the Germans to destroy freedom, she must fight, so far as she can, on the side of the English. How far can she fight for freedom without firearms? By making arms, or clothes or food. But there is another way of fighting for freedom without arms: we can fight with the mind. We can make ideas that will help the young Englishman who is fighting up in the sky to defeat the enemy.

But to make ideas effective, we must be able to fire them off. We must put them into action. And the hornet in the sky rouses another hornet in the mind. There was one zooming in *The Times* this morning — a woman's voice saying, "Women have not a word to say in politics." There is no woman in the Cabinet; nor in any responsible post. All the idea-makers who are in a position to make ideas effective are men. That is a thought that damps thinking, and encourages irresponsibility. Why not bury the head in the pillow, plug the ears, and cease this futile activity of idea-making? Because there are other tables besides officer tables and conference tables. Are we not leaving the young Englishman without a weapon that might be of value to him if we give up private thinking, tea-table thinking, because it seems useless? Are we not stressing our disability because our ability exposes us perhaps to abuse, perhaps to contempt? "I will not cease from mental fight," Blake wrote. Mental fight means thinking against the current, not with it.

That current flows fast and furious. It issues in a spate of words from the loudspeakers and the politicians. Every day they tell us that we are a free people, fighting to defend freedom. That is the current that has whirled the young airman up into the sky and keeps him circling there among the clouds. Down here, with a roof to cover us and a gas-mask handy, it is our business to puncture gas-bags and discover seeds of truth. It is not true that we are free. We are both prisoners tonight — he boxed up in his machine with a gun handy; we lying in the dark with a gas-mask handy. If we were free we should be out in the open, dancing, at the play, or sitting at the window talking together. What is it that prevents us? "Hitler!" the loudspeakers cry with one voice. Who is Hitler? What is he? Aggressiveness, tyranny, the insane love of power made manifest, they reply. Destroy that, and you will be free.

The drone of the planes is now like the sawing of a branch overhead. Round and round it goes, sawing and sawing at a branch directly above the house. Another sound begins sawing its way in the brain. "Women of ability"— it was Lady Astor[1] speaking in *The Times* this morning—"are held down because of a subconscious Hitlerism in the hearts of men." Certainly we are held down. We are equally prisoners tonight — the Englishmen in their planes, the Englishwomen in their beds. But if he stops to think he may be killed; and we too. So let us think for him. Let us try to drag up into consciousness the subconscious Hitlerism that holds us down. It is the desire for aggression; the desire to dominate and enslave. Even in the darkness we can see that made visible. We can see shop windows blazing; and women gazing; painted women; dressed-up women; women with crimson lips and crimson fingernails. They are slaves who are trying to enslave. If we could free ourselves from slavery we should free men from tyranny. Hitlers are bred by slaves.

A bomb drops. All the windows rattle. The anti-aircraft guns are getting active. Up there on the hill under a net tagged with strips of green and brown stuff to imitate the hues of autumn leaves guns are concealed. Now they all fire at once. On the nine o'clock radio we shall be told "Forty-four enemy planes were shot down during the night, ten of them by anti-aircraft fire." And one of the terms of peace, the loudspeakers say, is to be disarmament. There are to be no more guns, no army, no navy, no air force in the future. No more young men will be trained to fight with arms. That rouses another mind-hornet in the chambers of the brain — another quotation. "To fight against a real enemy, to earn undying honour and glory by shooting total strangers, and to come home with my breast covered with medals and decorations, that was the summit of my hope. . . . It was for this that my whole life so far had been dedicated, my education, training, everything. . . ."

Those were the words of a young Englishman who fought in the last war. In the face of them, do the current thinkers honestly believe that by writing "Disarmament" on a sheet of paper at a conference table they will have done all that

[1]Nancy Witcher Astor (1879–1964), Viscountess Astor, first woman to serve in the British House of Commons.—Eds.

is needful? Othello's occupation will be gone; but he will remain Othello.[2] The young airman up in the sky is driven not only by the voices of loudspeakers; he is driven by voices in himself—ancient instincts, instincts fostered and cherished by education and tradition. Is he to be blamed for those instincts? Could we switch off the maternal instinct at the command of a table full of politicians? Suppose that imperative among the peace terms was: "Child-bearing is to be restricted to a very small class of specially selected women," would we submit? Should we not say, "The maternal instinct is a woman's glory. It was for this that my whole life has been dedicated, my education, training, everything. . . ." But if it were necessary, for the sake of humanity, for the peace of the world, that child-bearing should be restricted, the maternal instinct subdued; women would attempt it. Men would help them. They would honour them for their refusal to bear children. They would give them other openings for their creative power. That too must make part of our fight for freedom. We must help the young Englishmen to root out from themselves the love of medals and decorations. We must create more honourable activities for those who try to conquer in themselves their fighting instinct, their subconscious Hitlerism. We must compensate the man for the loss of his gun.

The sound of sawing overhead has increased. All the searchlights are erect. They point at a spot exactly above this roof. At any moment a bomb may fall on this very room. One, two, three, four, five, six . . . the seconds pass. The bomb did not fall. But during those seconds of suspense all thinking stopped. All feeling, save one dull dread, ceased. A nail fixed the whole being to one hard board. The emotion of fear and of hate is therefore sterile, unfertile. Directly that fear passes, the mind reaches out and instinctively revives itself by trying to create. Since the room is dark it can create only from memory. It reaches out to the memory of other Augusts—in Bayreuth, listening to Wagner; in Rome, walking over the Campagna; in London. Friends' voices come back. Scraps of poetry return. Each of those thoughts, even in memory, was far more positive, reviving, healing, and creative than the dull dread made of fear and hate. Therefore if we are to compensate the young man for the loss of his glory and of his gun, we must give him access to the creative feelings. We must make happiness. We must free him from the machine. We must bring him out of his prison into the open air. But what is the use of freeing the young Englishman if the young German and the young Italian remain slaves?

The searchlights, wavering across the flat, have picked up the plane now. From this window one can see a little silver insect turning and twisting in the light. The guns go pop pop pop. Then they cease. Probably the raider was brought down behind the hill. One of the pilots landed safe in a field near here the other day. He said to his captors, speaking fairly good English, "How glad I am that the

---

[2]Venetian general, title character in *Othello* by William Shakespeare.—Eds.

fight is over!" Then an Englishman gave him a cigarette, and an Englishwoman made him a cup of tea. That would seem to show that if you can free the man from the machine, the seed does not fall upon altogether stony ground. The seed may be fertile.

At last all the guns have stopped firing. All the searchlights have been extin- 10 guished. The natural darkness of a summer's night returns. The innocent sounds of the country are heard again. An apple thuds to the ground. An owl hoots, winging its way from tree to tree. And some half-forgotten words of an old English writer come to mind: "The huntsmen are up in America. . . ."[3] Let us send these fragmentary notes to the huntsmen who are up in America, to the men and women whose sleep has not yet been broken by machine-gun fire, and in the belief that they will rethink them generously and charitably, perhaps shape them into something serviceable. And now, in the shadowed half of the world, to sleep.

Exploring the Text

1. What is the effect of beginning the essay in the first-person plural, present tense?
2. In paragraph 2, what kind of fighting does Virginia Woolf call on women to do?
3. How do the hornet metaphor (para. 3) and the sawing simile (para. 5) serve Woolf's purpose as she argues for women to fight against the war?
4. Woolf includes a quotation from the *Times* in paragraph 3 and offers examples to support its validity. How would the change in women's social and political status in England since 1940 affect Woolf's thesis today?
5. In paragraph 5, Woolf writes, "Hitlers are bred by slaves." How can such a paradoxical statement be accurate? What is the effect of following that short sentence with the abrupt three-word sentence in paragraph 6?
6. What are the purpose and effect of the rhetorical questions in paragraph 7? Woolf concludes paragraph 7 with the aphoristic statement "We must compensate the man for the loss of his gun." What does she mean?
7. In paragraph 8, Woolf refers to "this roof" and "this very room" and counts the seconds. What is the effect of such details?
8. What is Woolf's attitude toward war and peace as revealed in the last two paragraphs? How does Woolf try to appeal to Americans?
9. Woolf writes of the English fighters. Does her essay speak to the American fighters as well? And even to the German fighters?
10. Explain whether you believe that Woolf's suggestions about the relationship between gender and warfare, between gender and aggression, are still relevant.

---

[3]"The huntsmen are up in America, and they are already past their first sleep in Persia." — Sir Thomas Browne (1605–1682), from "The Garden of Cyrus." — Eds.

The Destruction of Culture

CHRIS HEDGES

Educated at Colgate University and at the Harvard Divinity School, Chris Hedges (b. 1956) has worked as a foreign correspondent for over two decades, witnessing wars in the Balkans, Central America, and the Middle East. In 2002, he shared the Pulitzer Prize for coverage of global terrorism. His most recent books include *The World as It Is* (2011) and *Death of the Liberal Class* (2011). The selection included here is taken from the chapter entitled "The Destruction of Culture" in his book *War Is a Force That Gives Us Meaning* (2002). Referring to the book, General Wesley K. Clark—former NATO Supreme Allied Commander in Europe—says, "War is a culture of its own, [Hedges] warns, and it can undercut and ultimately destroy the civil societies that engage in it."

The first casualty when war comes is truth.

—SENATOR HIRAM JOHNSON, 1917

In wartime the state seeks to destroy its own culture. It is only when this destruction has been completed that the state can begin to exterminate the culture of its opponents. In times of conflict authentic culture is subversive. As the cause championed by the state comes to define national identity, as the myth of war entices a nation to glory and sacrifice, those who question the value of the cause and the veracity of the myths are branded internal enemies.

Art takes on a whole new significance in wartime. War and the nationalist myth that fuels it are the purveyors of low culture—folklore, quasi-historical dramas, kitsch, sentimental doggerel, and theater and film that portray the glory of soldiers in past wars or current wars dying nobly for the homeland. This is why so little of what moves us during wartime has any currency once war is over. The songs, books, poems, and films that arouse us in war are awkward and embarrassing when the conflict ends, useful only to summon up the nostalgia of war's comradeship.

States at war silence their own authentic and humane culture. When this destruction is well advanced they find the lack of critical and moral restraint useful in the campaign to exterminate the culture of their opponents. By destroying authentic culture—that which allows us to question and examine ourselves and our society—the state erodes the moral fabric. It is replaced with a warped version of reality. The enemy is dehumanized; the universe starkly divided between the forces of light and the forces of darkness. The cause is celebrated, often in overt religious forms, as a manifestation of divine or historical will. All is dedicated to promoting and glorifying the myth, the nation, the cause.

The works of the writers in Serbia, such as Danilo Kis and Milovan Djilas, were mostly unavailable during the war. It remains hard even now to find their books. In Croatia the biting satires of Miroslav Krleža, who wrote one of the most searing portraits of Balkan despots, were forgotten. Writers and artists were inconvenient. They wrote about social undercurrents that were ignored by a new crop of self-appointed nationalist historians, political scientists, and economists.

National symbols—flags, patriotic songs, sentimental dedications—invade   5
and take over cultural space. Art becomes infected with the platitudes of patriotism. More important, the use of a nation's cultural resources to back up the war effort is essential to mask the contradictions and lies that mount over time in the drive to sustain war. Cultural or national symbols that do not support the crusade are often ruthlessly removed.

In Bosnia the ethnic warlords worked hard to wipe out all the records of cohabitation between ethnic groups. The symbols of the old communist regime—one whose slogan was "Brotherhood and Unity"—were defaced or torn down. The monuments to partisan fighters who died fighting the Germans in World War II, the lists of names clearly showing a mix of ethnic groups, were blown up in Croatia. The works of Ivo Andrić, who wrote some of the most lyrical passages about a multiethnic Bosnia, were edited by the Bosnian Serbs and selectively quoted to support ethnic cleansing.

All groups looked at themselves as victims—the Croats, the Muslims, and the Serbs. They ignored the excesses of their own and highlighted the excesses of the other in gross distortions that fueled the war. The cultivation of victimhood is essential fodder for any conflict. It is studiously crafted by the state. All cultural life is directed to broadcast the injustices carried out against us. Cultural life soon becomes little more than the drivel of agitprop. The message that the nation is good, the cause just, and the war noble is pounded into the heads of citizens in everything from late-night talk shows to morning news programs to films and popular novels. The nation is soon thrown into a trance from which it does not awake until the conflict ends. In parts of the world where the conflict remains unresolved, this trance can last for generations.

I walked one morning a few years ago down the deserted asphalt tract that slices through the center of the world's last divided capital, Nicosia, on the island of Cyprus. At one spot on the asphalt dividing line was a small painted triangle. For fifteen minutes each hour, Turkish troops, who control the northern part of the island, were allowed to move from their border posts and stand inside the white triangular lines. The arrangement was part of a deal laboriously negotiated by the United Nations to give Greek Cypriots and Turkish Cypriots access to several disputed areas along the 110-mile border that separates the north from the south. The triangle was a potent reminder that once the folly of war is over, folly itself is often all that remains. . . .

War, just as it tears down old monuments, demands new ones. These new monuments glorify the state's uniform and unwavering call for self-sacrifice and ultimately self-annihilation. Those who find meaning in the particular, who embrace affirmation not through the collective of the nation but through the love of another individual regardless of ethnic or national identity, are dangerous to the emotional and physical domination demanded by the state. Only one message is acceptable.

A soldier who is able to see the humanity of the enemy makes a troubled and ineffective killer. To achieve corporate action, self-awareness and especially self-criticism must be obliterated. We must be transformed into agents of a divinely inspired will, as defined by the state, just as those we fight must be transformed into the personification of unmitigated evil. There is little room for individuality in war.

The effectiveness of the myths peddled in war is powerful. We often come to doubt our own perceptions. We hide these doubts, like troubled believers, sure that no one else feels them. We feel guilty. The myths have determined not only how we should speak but how we should think. The doubts we carry, the scenes we see that do not conform to the myth are hazy, difficult to express, unsettling. And as the atrocities mount, as civil liberties are stripped away (something, with the "War on Terror," already happening to hundreds of thousands of immigrants in the United States), we struggle uncomfortably with the jargon and clichés. But we have trouble expressing our discomfort because the collective shout has made it hard for us to give words to our thoughts.

This self-doubt is aided by the monstrosity of war. We gape and wonder at the collapsing towers of the World Trade Center. They crumble before us, and yet we cannot quite comprehend it. What, really, did we see? In wartime an attack on a village where women and children are killed, an attack that does not conform to the myth peddled by our side, is hard to fathom and articulate. We live in wartime with a permanent discomfort, for in wartime we see things so grotesque and fantastic that they seem beyond human comprehension. War turns human reality into a bizarre carnival that does not seem part of our experience. It knocks us off balance.

On a chilly, rainy day in March 1998 I was in a small Albanian village in Kosovo, twenty-five miles west of the provincial capital of Pristina. I was waiting with a few thousand Kosovar Albanian mourners for a red Mercedes truck to rumble down the dirt road and unload a cargo of fourteen bodies. A group of distraught women, seated on wooden planks set up on concrete blocks, was in the dirt yard.

When the truck pulled into the yard I climbed into the back. Before each corpse, wrapped in bloodstained blankets and rugs, was lifted out for washing and burial I checked to see if the body was mutilated. I pulled back the cloth to uncover the faces. The gouged-out eyes, the shattered skulls, the gaping rows of broken teeth, and the sinewy strands of flayed flesh greeted me. When I could not see clearly in the fading light I flicked on my Maglite. I jotted each disfigurement in my notebook.

The bodies were passed silently out of the truck. They were laid on crude wooden coffin lids placed on the floor of the shed. The corpses were wound in white shrouds by a Muslim cleric in a red turban. The shed was lit by a lone kerosene lamp. It threw out a ghastly, uneven, yellowish light. In the hasty effort to confer some dignity on the dead, family members, often weeping, tried to wash away the bloodstains from the faces. Most could not do it and had to be helped away.

It was not an uncommon event for me. I have seen many such dead. Several weeks later it would be worse. I would be in a warehouse with fifty-one bodies, including children, even infants, women, and the elderly from the town of Prekaz. I had spent time with many of them. I stared into their lifeless faces. I was again in the twilight zone of war. I could not wholly believe what I saw in front of me.

This sense that we cannot trust what we see in wartime spreads throughout the society. The lies about the past, the eradication of cultural, historical, and religious monuments that have been part of a landscape for centuries, all serve to shift the ground under which we stand. We lose our grip. Whole worlds vanish or change in ways we cannot fully comprehend. A catastrophic terrorist strike will have the same effect.

In Bosnia the Serbs, desperately trying to deny the Muslim character of Bosnia, dynamited or plowed over libraries, museums, universities, historic monuments, and cemeteries, but most of all mosques. The Serbs, like the Croats, also got rid of monuments built to honor their own Serb or Croat heroes during the Communist era. These monuments championed another narrative, a narrative of unity among ethnic groups that ran contrary to the notion of ancient ethnic hatreds. The partisan monuments that honored Serb and Croat fighters against the Nazis honored, in the new narrative, the wrong Serbs and Croats. For this they had to be erased.

This physical eradication, coupled with intolerance toward any artistic endeavor that does not champion the myth, formed a new identity. The Serbs, standing in flattened mud fields, were able to deny that there were ever churches or mosques on the spot because they had been removed. The town of Zvornik in Serb-held Bosnia once had a dozen mosques. The 1991 census listed 60 percent of its residents as Muslim Slavs. By the end of the war the town was 100 percent Serb. Branko Grujic, the Serb-appointed mayor, informed us: "There never were any mosques in Zvornik."

No doubt he did not believe it. He knew that there had been mosques in Zvornik. But his children and grandchildren would come to be taught the lie. Serb leaders would turn it into accepted historical fact. There are no shortage of villages in Russia or Germany or Poland where all memory of the Jewish community is gone because the physical culture has been destroyed. And, when mixed with the strange nightmarish quality of war, it is hard to be completely sure of your own memories.

The destruction of culture sees the state or the group prosecuting the war take control of the two most important mediums that transmit information to the nation—the media and the schools. The alleged "war crimes" of the enemy, real and imagined, are played and replayed night after night, rousing a nation to

20

fury. In the Middle East and the Balkans, along with many other parts of the world, children are taught to hate. In Egypt pupils are told Jews are interlopers on Arab land. Israel does not appear on schoolroom maps. In Jordan, children learn that Christians are "infidels" who "must be forced into submission," that the Jewish Torah is "perverted," and that Jews have only "their own evil practices" to blame for the Holocaust. Syrian schoolbooks exhort students to "holy war" and paint pictures of Israelis "perpetrating beastly crimes and horrendous massacres," burying people alive in battle and dancing drunk in Islamic holy places in Jerusalem. And Israel, despite efforts in secular state schools to present a more balanced view of Arab history, allows state-funded religious schools to preach that Jewish rule should extend from the Nile in Egypt to the Euphrates in Iraq and that the kingdom of Jordan is occupied Jewish land.

The reinterpretation of history and culture is dizzying and dangerous. But it is the bedrock of the hatred and intolerance that leads to war.

On June 28, 1914, Gavrilo Princip shot and killed Archduke Franz Ferdinand of Austria in a Sarajevo street, an act that set off World War I. But what that makes him in Bosnia depends on which lesson plan you pick up.

"A hero and a poet," says a textbook handed to high school students in the Serb-controlled region of this divided country. An "assassin trained and instructed by the Serbs to commit this act of terrorism," says a text written for Croatian students. "A nationalist whose deed sparked anti-Serbian rioting that was only stopped by the police from all three ethnic groups," reads the Muslim version of the event.

In communist Yugoslavia, Princip was a hero. But with the partition of Bosnia along ethnic lines, huge swathes of history are reinterpreted. The Muslim books, for example, portray the Ottoman Empire's rule over Bosnia, which lasted 500 years, as a golden age of enlightenment; the Serbs and Croats condemn it as an age of "brutal occupation."

These texts have at least one thing in common: a distaste for [Marshal] Tito, the Communist leader who ruled the country from 1945 to 1980 and was a staunch opponent of the nationalist movements that now hold power. And Tito's state pioneered the replacement of history with myth, forcing schoolchildren to memorize mythical stories about Tito's life and aphorisms.

By the time today's books in the Balkans reach recent history, the divergence takes on ludicrous proportions; each side blames the others for the Bosnian war and makes no reference to crimes or mistakes committed by its own leaders or fighters.

The Muslims are taught that the Serbs "attacked our country" and started the war. The Serbs are told that "Muslims, with the help of mujahadeen fighters from Pakistan, Iraq and Iran, launched a campaign of genocide against the Serbs that almost succeeded."

The Croatian students learn that Croatian forces in "the homeland war" fought off "Serbian and Muslim aggressors."

Even the classics get twisted into a political diatribe. I saw a pro-Milošević 30
production of *Hamlet* in Belgrade that was scripted to convey the message that
usurping authority, even illegitimate authority, only brings chaos and ruin. Hamlet was portrayed as a bold and decisive man, constantly training for battle. He
was not consumed by questions about the meaning of existence or a desire to
withdraw from society, but the steely drive to seize power, even if it plunged the
kingdom into chaos. Horatio, usually portrayed as a thoughtful and humane
scholar, was the incarnation of evil.

Hamlet's treachery was illustrated at the conclusion of the play when Prince
Fortinbras of Norway entered Elsinore to view the carnage. Fortinbras, dressed
to look like the chief European representative at the time in Bosnia, Carl Bildt,
walked onstage with a Nazi marching song as his entrance music. He unfolded
maps showing how, with the collapse of authority, he had now carved up Serbian
territory among foreign powers.

"Here is a *Hamlet* for our time," the director, Dejan Krstović, told me. "We
want to show audiences what happens when individuals tamper with power and
refuse to sublimate their own ambitions for the benefit of the community.

"Because of Hamlet, the bodies pile up on the altar of authority and the system collapses. Because of Hamlet, the foreign prince, Fortinbras, who for us represents the new world order, comes in from the outside and seizes control, as has
happened to the Serbs throughout their history."

Every reporter struggles with how malleable and inaccurate memory can be
when faced with trauma or stress. Witnesses to war, even moments after a killing
or an atrocity, often cannot remember what took place in front of them. They
struggle to connect disparate images. And those who see events with some coher-
ency find there is an irreversible pull to twist the facts to conform to the myth.
Truth, in such moments, is too nuanced and contradictory for most to swallow. It
is best left untouched.

I went one rainy afternoon to the Imperial War Museum in Vienna, mostly to 35
see the rooms dedicated to the 1878 Bosnian rebellion and the assassination of
Archduke Franz Ferdinand. His car, peppered with bullet holes, and the bloodstained couch on which he died are on display. But I also wandered through the
other rooms designed to honor the bloodlust and forgotten skirmishes of the
Austro-Hungarian Empire. When I finished with the World War I exhibit I looked
for the room dedicated to World War II. There wasn't one. And when I inquired
at the desk, I was told there was no such exhibit in the city. World War II, at least
in terms of the collective memory of the Austrian nation, unlike in Germany,
might as well have not existed. Indeed, in one of the great European perversions of
memory, many Austrians had come to think of themselves as victims of that war.

The destruction of culture plays a crucial role in the solidification of a wartime narrative. When the visible and tangible symbols of one's past are destroyed
or denied, the past can be recreated to fit the myth. It is left only to those on the
margins to keep the flame of introspection alive, although the destruction of cul-

ture is often so great that full recovery is impossible. Yugoslavia, a country that had a vibrant theater and cinema, has seen its cultural life wither, with many of its best talents living in exile or drinking themselves to death in bars in Belgrade or Vienna.

Most societies never recover from the self-inflicted wounds made to their own culture during wartime. War leaves behind not memory but amnesia. Once wars end, people reach back to the time before the catastrophe. The books, plays, cinema take up the established cultural topics; authors and themes are often based on issues and ideas that predated the war. In post-war Germany it was as if Weimar had never ended, as if the war was just some bad, horrible dream from which everyone had just awoken and no one wanted to discuss.

This is why the wall of names that is the Vietnam Veterans Memorial is so important. It was not a project funded or organized by the state but by those who survived and insisted we not forget. It was part of America's battle back to truth, part of our desire for forgiveness. It ultimately held out to us as a nation the opportunity for redemption, although the state has prodded us back towards the triumphalism that led us into Vietnam.

But just as the oppressors engage in selective memory and myth, so do the victims, building unassailable monuments to their own suffering. It becomes impossible to examine, to dispute, or to criticize the myths that have grown up around past suffering of nearly all in war. The oppressors are painted by the survivors as monsters, the victims paint themselves as holy innocents. The oppressors work hard to bury inconvenient facts and brand all in wartime with the pitch of atrocity. They strive to reduce victims to their moral level. Each side creates its own narrative. Neither is fully true.

Until there is a common vocabulary and a shared historical memory there is   40
no peace in any society, only an absence of war. The fighting may have stopped in Bosnia or Cyprus but this does not mean the war is over. The search for a common narrative must, at times, be forced upon a society. Few societies seem able to do this willingly. The temptation, as with the Turks and the Armenian genocide, is to forget or ignore, to wallow in the lie. But reconciliation, self-awareness, and finally the humility that makes peace possible come only when culture no longer serves a cause or a myth but the most precious and elusive of all human narratives—truth.

Exploring the Text

1. Why do you suppose Chris Hedges opens his essay with both exposition and argument? Where in the text does he shift among exposition, narration, and argument? What is the effect of shifting modes of discourse in this way?

2. Note how Hedges uses transitions. For example, what is the relationship between paragraphs 12 and 13? Between 15 and 16?

3. What is the effect of the highly descriptive details in paragraphs 14 and 15? Do they detract from his argument or strengthen it?
4. Do you agree with Hedges's claim that "the two most important mediums that transmit information to the nation [are] the media and the schools" (para. 21)? Please explain.
5. How do paragraphs 23–29 support the assertion Hedges makes in paragraph 22?
6. What does Hedges mean by *culture*? Provide examples to support what you think he means. What does Hedges think the purpose of culture is? Do you agree? Explain your response.
7. In paragraph 38, Hedges claims that the Vietnam Veterans Memorial is important because it was funded and organized "by those who survived," rather than by the government. Visit the National Park Service Web site for more information about the memorial. Do you agree that it offers our nation an "opportunity for redemption"? Please explain. Do you agree with Hedges's claim that "the state has prodded us back towards the triumphalism that led us into Vietnam"? Why or why not?
8. Reread the final paragraph, and then reread the quotation from Senator Hiram Johnson with which Hedges begins the chapter. How effectively has Hedges illustrated the meaning of Johnson's assertion?
9. What do you think is Hedges's most interesting or provocative statement? Why?
10. Has reading this essay affected your thinking regarding culture? Regarding war? Explain your response.

The Apology

Letters from a Terrorist

LAURA BLUMENFELD

> Laura Blumenfeld (b. 1964) is a journalist who covers homeland security and presidential politics. Her work has appeared in the *New York Times, Elle,* and the *Los Angeles Times.* She holds an MA in international affairs from Columbia University. Since 1992 she has been a staff writer for the *Washington Post.* In 1986, her father was shot and wounded by a terrorist. Later she wrote about the incident and its aftermath in the book *Revenge: A Story of Hope* (2002), and in "The Apology: Letters from a Terrorist," which appeared in the *New Yorker* on March 4, 2002.

The gunman was not at home. "Come in," his mother said. "Would you like some orange soda?" My knocking must have shaken her out of a nap; she was wearing slippers and a pink embroidered bathrobe. Inside, the living room was full of family members, young and old.

"That's him," the woman said, pointing over her grandchildren's heads to the gunman's photograph. "He tried to kill someone," she said in an easy voice.

"Who?" I asked.

"Some Jew," said a boy, who appeared to be about twelve years old. He smiled crookedly, and added, "I don't know who—a Mossad agent."

"I'm not sure he was a Mossad agent," a man who introduced himself as Saed, the gunman's older brother, said. "He was a person from the outside—a leader from New York. We heard he was doing something against Palestinians. Why else would they choose him to be shot?"

"Why did he fire only once?" I asked.

"It was in the marketplace," Saed said.

"After the shooting, he threw the gun in the air, and it fell to the ground," his mother said. She began to chuckle and the others joined in.

The attack had taken place in the early spring of 1986. It had been a quiet time in Jerusalem: people could walk through the Old City without fear. In March, all that changed when Palestinian terrorists began gunning down foreign tourists—Americans, British, Germans. Their first target was an American man; he had been shot as he strolled through the Arab market shortly after sundown. The gunman had aimed a little too high, and the bullet had grazed his scalp.

Twelve years later, I arrived in Israel for an extended honeymoon with my husband. While he did part-time legal work, I took a leave of absence from my job at the *Washington Post* to do research for a book about the culture of vengeance— the thirst for settling scores which has created so much turmoil in the Middle East and throughout the world. My research took me to Albania, Sicily, Iran, and other countries; between trips I looked for the gunman who had shot the American in the market. From records in the Jerusalem District Attorney's office, I learned that several Palestinians in a pro-Syria breakaway faction of the Palestine Liberation Organization had been convicted in 1986 for the shooting of foreigners. The man who had shot the American was named Omar Khatib. He had been tried and convicted in an Israeli court, and was now serving a sentence of twenty-five years in Shikma Prison, in Ashkelon.

The Khatibs lived in the West Bank, in the last house on a narrow, rutted lane, which ended at a limestone quarry. Trash and rusty appliances spilled over the precipice. Their house, which was behind a red gate, was really a number of buildings joined together— cement improvisations with raw concrete steps and half-stacked cinder blocks. In rudimentary Arabic, I introduced myself as an American journalist.

"Why did he do it?" I asked the gunman's father, a tall, bony man in a gray robe.

The father's response was terse. "He did his duty," he said. "Every Palestinian must do it. Then there will be justice."

Another brother of the gunman came into the room. He introduced himself as Imad. His mustache and goatee were dyed burnt orange, and he was wearing a silky red-and-black shirt. He told me that he had been a member of the Popular Front for the Liberation of Palestine, a radical faction of the P.L.O., and that he had returned to Palestine, after twenty-five years of exile in Jordan, in 1994, the summer after the Israelis and the Palestinians signed the Oslo peace accords. "Anybody would do what my brother did under those circumstances," he said. "If you pretend to be a Palestinian for five minutes, you'll feel what we feel."

"And what about the man he tried to kill?" I asked.

"It wasn't a personal vendetta," Imad replied. "It was public relations. It was like telling the media to pay attention to us."

"Won't someone from the victim's family kill one of your people?" I asked.

"My brother never met the man," Imad said. "Nothing personal, so no revenge."

For me, however, the shooting was personal. The man whom Imad's brother had tried to kill was my father.

In March of 1986, when I was an undergraduate at Harvard, my father, in his capacity as executive director of the New York Holocaust Memorial Commission, went to Israel to look at the country's various Holocaust museums. One evening, after a visit to the Western Wall, in Jerusalem, one of the Holy Land's most sacred sites, he was walking back to his hotel when he was shot by an unseen assailant. He was treated for the head wound in an Israeli hospital, and the story of the shooting made front-page news.

"Did you ever wonder who the gunman was or what he looked like?" I later asked my father. "I never thought about it," he replied. But, for me, putting the incident out of my mind wasn't so easy. I understood that people who commit acts of terrorism are less concerned with what happens to their victims than with advancing their cause, but I had resolved to find a way to make my father human in the gunman's eyes. And I wanted him to see that what he had done was horrible. I thought about introducing myself as the daughter of his victim but discarded the idea, because I did not want him to regard me as "a Jew" or as an adversary. Given the Palestinians' eagerness to get their views out to the world, I reasoned that the best way to gain access to him would be to identify myself to him and his family simply as an American journalist who was interested in hearing his story.

Several weeks after I met Omar's family, I went back to their house to return some clippings about the shooting which they had given me to photocopy. I was greeted by Omar's mother and his brother Imad, and led to an upstairs bedroom. We sat down on the couch where Omar had slept before his imprisonment.

"His head was here, his feet were here," his mother said, brushing the upholstery with her fingers. She brought out a black attaché case and opened it. Inside was a karate manual, a picture of Omar in martial-arts dress, executing a kick, and a black-belt certificate that he had won in 1979. The picture showed a slim young man with an angry expression on his face. There was also a copy of the Koran, a book entitled *Theories About Revolution and National Liberation*, and a copy of *Measure for Measure*.

"He was at Bethlehem University, studying English," Imad pointed out.

"And business, too," his mother said. "He got a ninety-five in public relations." 25
I was shown Omar's report cards, his birth certificate from a hospital on the Mount of Olives, and a high-school certificate of graduation that read, "The school administration certifies that Mr. Omar Kamel Said Al Khatib was a student in 1980–81. His conduct was very good." Before saying goodbye, Imad offered to take a letter from me to his brother in prison. Only immediate relatives were allowed contact with such prisoners, but Imad agreed to deliver whatever I wanted to write.

In my first letter to Omar, I explained that I was an American journalist who was writing a book about the region, and that I was curious about his life in an Israeli prison. I asked him about his hobbies and his plans for the future. At the end of the letter, I wrote, "And finally, I would like to hear about the events that led to your arrest. What happened? When you think back on it, what were your feelings then? How do you feel about it today?"

Six weeks later, Omar wrote back, in an intricate light-blue scrawl, on eight sheets of tissue paper:

> Dear Laura,
>
> I would like first to extend my appreciation and regard for your message, which I have read with interest and care. This is not a dream, but a real fact we are seeking to incarnate on land through the long march of our revolution and in accordance with rules of justice and equality and the right of people to liberate their lands, this sacred right which was secured by international law. We, as sons to this people, and part of its past and present, have on our shoulders the burden of holding the difficulty of the liberation road; it's our mission to let the rifles live.
>
> I would like you to know that our choice in the military struggle is a legitimate choice on a historical basis that takes into account the fact that the enemy we are facing is one who stands on a Zionist ideology that is racist in its basis and fascist in its aims and means. It is an enemy with a huge military destructive machine higher in its ability than any other superpower state. It's an enemy that can be faced and defeated only by force. . . .
>
> There is a huge difference, my dear, between "terror" and the right of self-determination, between a criminal and a revolutionary. . . . It is hard for us, as prisoners, to accept a peace process which does not answer all the questions that the Israeli/Palestinian conflict has raised. We continue in our efforts to affect what is going on outside the walls of our prisons.
>
> Sincerely,
> Omar Kamel Al Khatib

The letter read more like a manifesto than like an exchange between two people. I wanted to know Omar as he really was, beneath the layers of ideology, and the next day I wrote to him again and inquired about what he was currently reading, what he could tell me about his family's history, and what, in particular, had inflamed his feelings against Israel.

A month later, he replied: 30

> I love English literature, and have been reading it from the first years of my imprison-
> ment; lately I have dedicated my time to the reading of theoretical and philosophical
> books. . . . I have read the works of Tolstoy and Dostoevsky. I do suggest that you read
> Dostoevsky's *Memoirs from the House of the Dead*; it will help you in the work you are
> conducting.
>
> My chances of being released now are big because of my deteriorating health
> conditions. I suffer from asthma, an illness which puts me very near death. I'm living
> in unhealthy conditions, with ten of my friends in a small, cold cell very full of
> humidity. They smoke, cook, and do all their daily activities, which brings me a hard
> time. You can't imagine how it feels when you find yourself being chased even by the
> breath you breathe.
>
> I don't know if the Israelis consider me as "having blood on my hands," but I do
> know that there is no meaning in keeping me in prison after more than 13 years. The
> term "blood on their hands" is a bad term I do not like to hear. It is a racist term used
> to fulfill some political purpose aimed to distort our identity as freedom fighters.

He went on to say that he had been "chosen" to join the rebel Abu Musa faction of
the Palestine Liberation Organization in 1985, with orders to "create a state of
unrest," whose objective was to put an end to Israel's occupation of Palestine.

> I was young at that time, but since then I have discovered that violence is not in my
> personality. Maybe this is the answer to your question of why I shot just one shot at
> that man, despite the fact that my pistol was very full of bullets.

When Israel became a state, in 1948, Omar said, his mother's family had been
forced to leave their home in Jaffa and migrate to Lebanon. Omar's father was
born in the West Bank, but after his marriage to Omar's mother he had gone to
live in Jerusalem, where the couple had brought up their children.

He continued:

> This city has shaped my identity; she planted in my mind unforgettable memories. I
> witnessed the Israeli aggression of the Six-Day War. I was four years old then, but
> enough aware to understand what was going on. I remember when my mother used
> to hide us with the rest of our neighbors who came to have shelter in our small room.
> We were so frightened by the darkness and the sound of guns. Six days, and the his-
> tory entered into a new stage, the stage of the occupation.
>
> The resistance movement began, and at the end of the '60s my brother was
> arrested and sent to prison. . . . I saw the painful time that my family went through,
> searching to know the fate of my brother. I remember visiting him with my mother
> once or twice, but after that he was expelled to Jordan. . . . There he was sent to prison
> for no reason but under the pretext of crossing the borders illegally.
>
> We were such a poor family at the time, we didn't have enough money to eat. . . .
> I will never forget the exhaustion and pain of the journey when I accompanied my
> mother to visit my brother. . . . Do you know when I saw [my brother] next?! It was
> 25 years later. This time I was the prisoner, and he was the visitor. After the signing of

the Oslo agreement he got the chance to return to his home land. He came to visit me at Ashkelon prison. It was a very sad meeting, we both couldn't stop crying. I had no words to say, I had forgotten everything, but felt the need of touching him, and kissing him.

For all its self-justifying tone, the letter was more candid on a personal level, and in my reply I asked Omar to describe how he had felt when he shot the man in the marketplace. I also asked him what he would say to the man if the two of them were to meet again. In his next two letters, he dwelled on the hardships of prison life and the satisfaction he felt in taking a college correspondence course. He said that he had learned French and Hebrew, and that he had written a book of grammar for his fellow-prisoners entitled *The Practical Use of English Structure*. He said that he had six more courses to complete before earning his B.A.

In my next letter, I again asked Omar why he had shot the American tourist. Omar wrote back:

> With regard to David Blumenfeld—I hope he can understand the reasons behind my act. If I were him I would. I have thought a lot about meeting him one day. We have been in a state of war, and now we are passing through a new stage of historical reconciliation where there is no place for hatred and detestation. In this new era and atmosphere, he is welcome to be my guest in Jerusalem.

The letter hinted that Omar was capable of remorse, though an earlier reference to my father as a "chosen military site" had made me wince. And Omar's lofty talk about "historical reconciliation" made me wonder whether we were both involved in an elaborate game of manipulation, each for a different purpose. To give him a better sense of David Blumenfeld, I replied that I had contacted David, and discovered that his grandparents had been killed in the Holocaust, and that he had come to Israel to gather material for building a Holocaust museum in New York. I told him that David was not hostile to the Palestinian cause but that he was concerned about whether Omar would ever again resort to violence against anyone, innocent or not. Omar began his next letter with an account of an examination that he had undergone for his asthma, in the hope of winning a release from prison on medical grounds: 35

> When the van stopped in front of Ramallah hospital, it was as if I were an alien from another world. Each of the guards took his place around my vehicle. Guns were ready for use. The door was opened, and all around me I saw people looking at me strangely. I touched the ground with slow steps because my hands and legs were tied. I took a deep breath and looked at the sky, feeling the need to fly. . . . And all the people looked at me with pity and wonder because of my weak appearance.
>
> They led me to an elevator to the main section of the testing area. We waited till a very beautiful Moroccan girl came to lead us to the examination room. I introduced myself to her and spoke with her a little about the prison while she conducted the test three times. She was shocked to see the bad test results.

In his next letter, he wrote:

Back to David, I do admire his talking to you and I appreciate his understanding, his support for my people. If these feelings are really from the depth of his heart, this may contribute a lot to our friendship. Of course, my answer to his question [about committing an act of violence again] is NO.

A few weeks later, I learned that the parole board had rejected Omar's petition for release. Two months later, his petition came up again, on appeal to a higher court. I asked Imad if I could attend the hearing, and he agreed.

The courtroom was packed with defendants and their families—Israelis and Palestinians together on the benches. Omar's mother and his brother Imad were there, along with nine other relatives. I took a seat directly in front of them. Three judges filed into the room, and finally Omar arrived. Although he was in ankle chains, his entrance was triumphant. He greeted the other prisoners effusively, shaking their hands and clapping them on the back. And yet the effects of his incarceration were visible: the skin on his face was so taut that his cheekbones cast a skeletal shadow under his eyes; there was a noticeable swelling around his mouth. His mother rushed over to him and kissed him. Imad ruffled his hair. Then Imad pointed to me. "Laura is here," he said.

"Laura!" Omar said, smiling. "I hoped to meet you one day, but not in this setting." I couldn't keep my hands from shaking as I smiled back.

"I need to know if you're sorry," I said.

"I will write David a long letter," he said.

"No, I need to know now," I said. For a moment our eyes met, and then a court officer led him away.

Several hours passed before Omar's lawyer, an energetic Israeli woman, presented the case to the judges. They listened to the details of Omar's asthma, and then gave orders for the petition to be sent back to the medical-parole committee for further review. As Omar and his family got up to leave, I realized that this was my last chance to confront him. I stood up and said, "I am David Blumenfeld's daughter, Laura Blumenfeld." For a moment, Omar and his family stared at me. Then Omar's mother, Imad, and several other relatives began to weep. I tried to explain why I had concealed my identity for so long. "I did it for one reason," I said. "This conflict is between human beings, and not between disembodied Arabs and Jews. And we're people. Not military targets. We're people with families." I turned to Omar. He looked stunned. "You promised me you would never hurt anyone again," I said. He looked at me and said nothing. As he was led away, his family rushed over to embrace me.

A few weeks later, I received another letter from Omar:

A week has passed since the day of the hearing, and all that is in my mind and imagination is the picture of you standing in front of the court, and the echo of your voice.
    You made me feel so stupid that once I was the cause of your and your kind mother's pain. Sorry and please understand.

40

Of course I was shocked to learn that you are David's daughter. I didn't sleep for almost two days. I reread all your precious letters trying to rearrange the whole puzzle again.

My stay in Israel was nearly over. Before leaving for America, I visited Omar's family one last time. The house was full of people, and in honor of my departure Omar's mother had laid out plates of vegetables, bread, and cheese. Arabic music was coming from a tape player, and several of the women and children invited me to dance with them. Imad presented me with gifts from Omar—two gold necklaces, one for me and one for my father, with Omar's name inscribed on it. I felt unsure of this display of warmth: only a short while ago, these same people had condoned the attempted killing of my father, as they might condone other attacks on innocent bystanders in their struggle with Israel, if the fragile peace process broke down.

45

A few weeks after I had returned to America, my father received a letter from Omar that I have read many times since, in the hope that its sentiments are genuine:

> Dear David,
>
> Thirteen years have passed. Yes, it's so late to come and ask you about your injuries, but I would like you to know that I've prayed a lot for you. I hope you are well today.
>
> I admit to having some good feeling toward you from the beginning, a feeling that made me hope to meet you one day. It seems to me that this good feeling is coming to be a reality. . . . I would like first to express to you my deep pain and sorrow for what I caused you. I've learned many things about you. You are supposed to be a very close friend to my people. I hope you believe that we both were victims of this long historical conflict. . . . Laura was the mirror that made me see your face as a human person deserving to be admired and respected. I apologize for not understanding her message from the beginning.
>
> If God helps and I get to be released, I hope you accept my invitation to be my guest in the holy city of peace, Jerusalem.

Exploring the Text

1. Notice how Laura Blumenfeld begins her essay, first with the arresting opening sentence "The gunman was not at home" and then with ordinary details such as "orange soda," "slippers," and "a pink embroidered bathrobe." What is the effect of this juxtaposition of the suspenseful with the mundane in the first paragraph?

2. What is similar in the father's and brother's responses to Blumenfeld's question, "Why did he do it?" (para. 12)? Why do they claim it was "nothing personal," as Imad says (para. 18)?

3. The author keeps her identity as the victim's daughter secret from the Khatibs, identifying herself "as an American journalist who was interested in hearing his [Omar's] story" (para. 21) and who was also "writing a book about the region" (para. 27). These claims are broadly true, of course, but do you think she was

wrong to deceive them? How would the family have reacted had she told the full truth from the beginning?

4. How would you characterize the style and tone of Omar Khatib's first letter (para. 28)? What does Blumenfeld mean by saying that it "read more like a manifesto than like an exchange between two people" (para. 29)? Do you agree with her? Why or why not? How does that statement connect to Blumenfeld's purpose in this essay?

5. Why do you think Omar doesn't answer Blumenfeld's questions directly in his next letter (para. 30), discussing literature and the conditions of his imprisonment instead?

6. In Omar's second letter (para. 30), he talks about "freedom fighters." In his first he had written, "There is a huge difference, my dear, between 'terror' and the right of self-determination, between a criminal and a revolutionary." Read "The War of Words: A Dispatch from the Front Lines" (p. 770), an editorial by Daniel Okrent. Evaluate Omar's position in terms of what Okrent says in his piece.

7. Toward the end of paragraph 30, Blumenfeld uses both paraphrase and direct quotation to deliver Omar's communication. Which of the two presents the more political message? Which the more personal? Why do you suppose the author chose to present this information in this way?

8. In the letter quoted in paragraph 34, Omar writes, "With regard to David Blumenfeld—I hope he can understand the reasons behind my act. If I were him I would." What leads him to say that? Do you think Omar is right—would David Blumenfeld indeed understand if their positions were reversed? Explain your response.

9. Laura Blumenfeld writes, "And Omar's lofty talk about 'historical reconciliation' made me wonder whether we were both involved in an elaborate game of manipulation, each for a different purpose" (para. 35). What causes her to wonder that? Do you think that is the case? Why or why not?

10. Were you surprised by the warm reception that the author received from the Khatibs after she revealed her identity to them (para. 43)? Why or why not? Why were the Khatibs so gracious? Explain your response.

11. In one of his letters (para. 36), Omar refers to "our friendship," and the essay concludes with Omar's words addressed to his victim, David Blumenfeld: "If God helps and I get to be released, I hope you accept my invitation to be my guest in the holy city of peace, Jerusalem." Do you think that the author's father would accept? Why or why not? Write a letter from him in response to Omar's invitation.

12. Early in the essay, the author reveals her purpose: "I had resolved to find a way to make my father human in the gunman's eyes" (para. 21). Referring specifically to the text of the essay, evaluate the extent to which she has achieved her purpose.

The Partly Cloudy Patriot

Sarah Vowell

Sarah Vowell was born in 1969 in Muskogee, Oklahoma. She received a BA from Montana State University in 1993 and an MA in art history from the Art Institute of Chicago in 1996. She has published several books about U.S. history and culture, including *Assassination Vacation* (2005), about a road trip to presidential assassination sites; *The Wordy Shipmates* (2008), about the New England Puritans; and *Unfamiliar Fishes* (2011), about the history of Hawaii. A performer as well as a writer, she was the voice of Violet Parr in the Pixar animated film *The Incredibles* (2004). She has been noted by the *New York Times* for her "funny querulous voice and shrewd comic delivery" and by *Newsweek* as "a cranky stylist with talent to burn." Both assessments are validated by the selection included here, the title essay from *The Partly Cloudy Patriot* (2002).

In the summer of 2000, I went to see the Mel Gibson blockbuster *The Patriot*. I enjoyed that movie. Watching a story line like that is always a relief. Of course the British must be expelled, just as the Confederates must surrender, Hitler must be crushed, and yee-haw when the Red Sea swallows those slave-mongering Egyptians. There were editorials about *The Patriot*, the kind that always accompany any historical film, written by professors who insist things nobody cares about, like Salieri wasn't that bad a sort or the fact that Roman gladiators maybe didn't have Australian accents. A little anachronism is part of the fun, and I don't mind if in real life General Cornwallis never lost a battle in the South as he does rather gloriously in the film. Isn't art supposed to improve on life?

Personally, I think there was more than enough historical accuracy in *The Patriot* to keep the spoilsports happy. Because I'm part spoilsport on my father's side, and I felt nagged with quandaries every few minutes during the nearly three-hour film. American history is a quagmire, and the more one knows, the quaggier the mire gets. If you're paying attention during *The Patriot* and you know your history and you have a stake in that history, not to mention a conscience, the movie is not an entirely cartoonish march to glory. For example, Mel Gibson's character, Benjamin Martin, is conflicted. He doesn't want to fight the British because he still feels bad about chopping up some Cherokee into little pieces during the French and Indian War. Since I'm a part-Cherokee person myself, Gibson lost a little of the sympathy I'd stored up for him because he'd been underrated in *Conspiracy Theory*. And did I mention his character lives in South Carolina? So by the end of the movie, you look at the youngest Mel junior bundled in his mother's arms and think, Mel just risked his life so that that kid's kids can rape their slaves and vote to be the first state to secede from the Union.

The Patriot did confirm that I owe George Washington an apology. I always liked George fine, though I dismissed him as a mere soldier. I prefer the pen to the sword, so I've always been more of a Jeffersonhead. The words of the Declaration of Independence are so right and true that it seems like its poetry alone would have knocked King George III in the head. Like, he would have read this beloved passage, "We hold these Truths to be self-evident, that all Men are created equal, that they are endowed by their Creator with certain unalienable Rights— that among these are Life, Liberty, and the pursuit of Happiness," and thought the notion so just, and yet still so wonderfully whimsical, that he would have dethroned himself on the spot. But no, it took a grueling, six-year-long war to make independence a fact.

I rarely remember this. In my ninety-five-cent copy of the Declaration of Independence and the Constitution, the two documents are separated by only a blank half page. I forget that there are eleven years between them, eleven years of war and the whole Articles of Confederation debacle. In my head, the two documents are like the A side and B side of the greatest single ever released that was recorded in one great drunken night, but no, there's a lot of bleeding life between them. Dead boys and dead Indians and Valley Forge.

Anyway, *The Patriot*. The best part of seeing it was standing in line for tickets. I remember how jarring it was to hear my fellow moviegoers say that word. "Two for *The Patriot* please." "One for *The Patriot* at 5:30." For years, I called it the *P* word, because it tended to make nice people flinch. For the better part of the 1990s, it seemed like the only Americans who publicly described themselves as patriots were scary militia types hiding out in the backwoods of Michigan and Montana, cleaning their guns. One of the few Americans still celebrating Patriot's Day—a nearly forgotten holiday on April 19 commemorating the Revolutionary War's first shots at Lexington and Concord—did so in 1995 by murdering 168 people in the federal building in Oklahoma City. In fact, the same week I saw *The Patriot*, I was out with some friends for dessert. When I asked a fellow named Andy why he had chosen a cupcake with a little American flag stuck in the frosting, I expected him to say that he was in a patriotic mood, but he didn't. He said that he was "feeling jingoistic."

Well, that was a long time ago. As I write this, it's December 2001 in New York City. The only words one hears more often than variations on *patriot* are "in the wake of," "in the aftermath of," and "since the events of September 11." We also use the word *we* more. Patriotism as a word and deed has made a comeback. At Halloween, costume shops did a brisk business in Uncle Sam and Betsy Ross getups. Teen pop bombshell Britney Spears took a breather during her live telecast from Vegas's MGM Grand to sit on a piano bench with her belly ring glinting in the spotlight and talk about "how proud I am of our nation right now." Chinese textile factories are working overtime to fill the consumer demand for American flags.

Immediately after the attack, seeing the flag all over the place was moving, endearing. So when the newspaper I subscribe to published a full-page, full-color

5

flag to clip out and hang in the window, how come I couldn't? It took me a while to figure out why I guiltily slid the flag into the recycling bin instead of taping it up. The meaning had changed; or let's say it changed back. In the first day or two the flags were plastered everywhere, seeing them was heartening because they indicated that we're all in this sorrow together. The flags were purely emotional. Once we went to war, once the president announced that we were going to retaliate against the "evildoers," then the flag again represented what it usually represents, the government. I think that's when the flags started making me nervous. The true American patriot is by definition skeptical of the government. Skepticism of the government was actually one of the platforms the current figurehead of the government ran on. How many times in the campaign did President Bush proclaim of his opponent, the then vice president, "He trusts the federal government and I trust the people"? This deep suspicion of Washington is one of the most American emotions an American can have. So by the beginning of October, the ubiquity of the flag came to feel like peer pressure to always stand behind policies one might not necessarily agree with. And, like any normal citizen, I prefer to make up my mind about the issues of the day on a case by case basis at 3:00 A.M. when I wake up from my *Nightline*-inspired nightmares.

One Independence Day, when I was in college, I was living in a house with other students on a street that happened to be one of the main roads leading to the football stadium where the town's official Fourth of July fireworks festivities would be held. I looked out the window and noticed a little American flag stabbed into my yard. Then I walked outside and saw that all the yards in front of all the houses on the street had little flags waving above the grass. The flags, according to a tag, were underwritten by a local real estate agency and the Veterans of Foreign Wars. I marched into the house, yanked out the phone book, found the real estate office in the yellow pages, and phoned them up immediately, demanding that they come and take their fucking flag off my lawn, screaming into the phone, "The whole point of that goddamn flag is that people don't stick flags in my yard without asking me!" I felt like Jimmy Stewart in *Mr. Smith Goes to Washington*, but with profanity. A few minutes later, an elderly gentleman in a VFW cap, who probably lost his best friend liberating France or something, pulled up in a big car, grabbed the flag, and rolled his eyes as I stared at him through the window. Then I felt dramatic and dumb. Still, sometimes I think the true American flag has always been that one with the snake hissing "Don't Tread on Me."

The week of the attack on the World Trade Center and the Pentagon, I watched TV news all day and slept with the radio on. I found myself flipping channels hoping to see the FBI handcuff a terrorist on camera. What did happen, a lot, was that citizens or politicians or journalists would mention that they wonder what it will be like for Americans now to live with the constant threat of random, sudden death. I know a little bit about what that's like. I did grow up during the Cold War. Maybe it says something about my level of cheer that I found this notion comforting, to remember that all those years I was sure the world might blow up at any second, I somehow managed to graduate from high school and do my laundry and see Smokey Robinson live.

Things were bad in New York. I stopped being able to tell whether my eyes were teary all the time from grief or from the dirty, smoky wind. Just when it seemed as if the dust had started to settle, then came the anthrax. I was on the phone with a friend who works in Rockefeller Center, and he had to hang up to be evacuated because a contaminated envelope had infected a person in the building; an hour later, another friend in another building was sitting at his desk eating his lunch and men in sealed plastic disease-control space suits walked through his office, taking samples. Once delivering the mail became life-threatening, pedestrians trudging past the main post office on Eighth Avenue bowed their heads a little as they read the credo chiseled on the façade, "Neither snow, nor rain, nor heat, nor gloom of night stays these couriers from the swift completion of their appointed rounds."

During another war, across the river, in Newark, a writer turned soldier named Thomas Paine sat down by a campfire in September 1776 and wrote, "These are the times that try men's souls. The summer soldier and the sunshine patriot will, in this crisis, shrink from the service of their country; but he that stands it now, deserves the love and thanks of man and woman." In September and October, I liked to read that before I pulled the rubber band off the newspaper to find out what was being done to my country and what my country was doing back. I like the black and white of Paine's words. I know I'm no sunshine patriot. I wasn't shrinking, though, honestly; the most important service we mere mortal citizens were called upon to perform was to spend money, so I dutifully paid for Korean dinners and a new living room lamp. But still I longed for the morning when I could open up the paper and the only people in it who would irk me would be dead suicide bombers and retreating totalitarians on the other side of the world. Because that would be the morning I pulled that flag out of the recycling bin and taped it up in the window. And while I could shake my fists for sure at the terrorists on page one, buried domestic items could still make my stomach hurt—school prayer partisans taking advantage of the grief of children to circumvent the separation of church and state; the White House press secretary condemning a late-night talk show host for making a questionable remark about the U.S. military: "The reminder is to all Americans, that they need to watch what they say, watch what they do, and that this is not a time for remarks like that." Those are the sorts of never-ending qualms that have turned me into the partly cloudy patriot I long not to be.

When Paine wrote his pamphlet, which came to be called *The American Crisis*, winter was coming, Washington's armies were in retreat, the Revolution was floundering. His words inspired soldiers and civilians alike to buck up and endure the war so that someday "not a place upon earth might be so happy as America."

Thing is, it worked. The British got kicked out. The trees got cleared. Time passed, laws passed and, five student loans later, I made a nice little life for myself.

I can feel it with every passing year, how I'm that much farther away from the sacrifices of the cast-off Indians and Okie farmers I descend from. As recently as fifty years ago my grandmother was picking cotton with bleeding fingers. I think about her all the time while I'm getting overpaid to sit at a computer, eat Chinese takeout, and think things up in my pajamas. The half century separating my fingers, which are moisturized with cucumber lotion and type eighty words per minute, and her bloody digits is an ordinary Land of Opportunity parable, and don't think I don't appreciate it. I'm keenly aware of all the ways my life is easier and lighter, how lucky I am to have the time and energy to contemplate the truly important things—Bill Murray in *Groundhog Day*, the baked Alaska at Sardi's, the Dean Martin Christmas record, my growing collection of souvenir snow globes. After all, what is happiness without cheap thrills? Reminds me of that passage in Philip Roth's novel *American Pastoral* when the middle-aged, prosperous grandson of immigrants marvels that his own daughter loathes the country enough to try to blow it up:

> Hate America? Why, he lived in America the way he lived inside his own skin. All the pleasures of his younger years were American pleasures, all that success and happiness had been American, and he need no longer keep his mouth shut about it just to defuse her ignorant hatred. The loneliness he would feel if he had to live in another country. Yes, everything that gave meaning to his accomplishments had been American. Everything he loved was here.

A few weeks after the United States started bombing Afghanistan and the Taliban were in retreat, I turned on the TV news and watched grinning Afghans in the streets of Kabul, allowed to play music for the first time in years. I pull a brain muscle when I try to fathom the rationale for outlawing all music all the time—not certain genres of music, not music with offensive lyrics played by the corrupters of youth, but any form of organized sound. Under Taliban rule, my whole life as an educated (well, at a state school), working woman with CD storage problems would have been null and void. I don't know what's more ridiculous, that people like that would deny a person like me the ability to earn a living using skills and knowledge I learned in school, or that they would deny me my unalienable right to chop garlic in time with the B-52's "Rock Lobster" as I cook dinner.

A few years back, a war correspondent friend of mine gave a speech about Bosnia to an international relations department at a famous midwestern university. I went with him. After he finished, a group of hangers-on, all men except for me, stuck around to debate the finer points of the former Yugoslavia. The conversation was very detailed, including references to specific mayors of specific Croatian villages. It was like record collector geek talk, only about Bosnia. They were the record collectors of Bosnia. So they went on denouncing the various idiotic nationalist causes of various splinter groups, blaming nationalism itself for the genocidal war. And of course a racist nationalism is to blame. But the more they ranted, the more uncomfortable I became. They, many of them immigrants themselves, considered patriotic allegiance to be a sin, a divisive, villainous drive leading to exclusion, hate, and murder. I, theretofore silent, spoke up. This is what I said. I said that I had recently flown over Memphis, Tennessee. I said that the idea of Memphis, Tennessee, not to mention looking down at it, made me go all soft. Because I looked down at Memphis, Tennessee, and thought of all my heroes who had walked its streets. I thought of Sun Records, of the producer Sam Phillips. Sam Phillips, who once described the sort of person he recorded as "a person who had dreamed, and dreamed, and dreamed." A person like Elvis Presley, his funny bass player Bill Black, his guitarist Scotty Moore (we have the same birthday he and I). Jerry Lee Lewis. Carl Perkins. Hello, I'm Johnny Cash. I told the Bosnian record collectors that when I thought of the records of these Memphis men, when I looked out the window at the Mississippi mud and felt their names moistening my tongue what I felt, what I was proud to feel, was patriotic. I noticed one man staring at me. He said he was born in some something-istan I hadn't heard of. Now that my globe is permanently turned to that part of the world, I realize he was talking about Tajikistan, the country bordering Afghanistan. The man from Tajikistan looked me in the eye and delivered the following warning.

"Those," he said, of my accolades for Elvis and friends, "are the seeds of war."

I laughed and told him not to step on my blue suede shoes, but I got the feeling he wasn't joking.

Before September 11, the national events that have made the deepest impressions on me are, in chronological order: the 1976 Bicentennial, the Iran hostage crisis, Iran-Contra, the Los Angeles riots, the impeachment trial of President Clinton, and the 2000 presidential election. From those events, I learned the following: that the Declaration of Independence is full of truth and beauty; that some people in other parts of the world hate us because we're Americans; what a shredder is; that the rage for justice is so fierce people will set fire to their own neighborhoods when they don't get it; that Republicans hate Bill Clinton; and that the ideal of one man, one vote doesn't always come true. (In the U.S. Commission on Civil Rights's report *Voting Irregularities in Florida During the 2000 Presidential Election*, the testimony of Dr. Frederick Shotz of Broward County especially sticks out. A handicapped voter in a wheelchair, Dr. Shotz "had to use his upper body to lift himself up to get up the steps in order for him to access his polling place. Once he was inside the polling place, he was not given a wheelchair accessible polling booth. Once again, he had to use his arms to lift himself up to see the ballot and, while balancing on his arms, simultaneously attempt to cast his ballot.")

Looking over my list, I can't help but notice that only one of my formative experiences, the Bicentennial, came with balloons and cake. Being a little kid that year, visiting the Freedom Train with its dramatically lit facsimile of the Declaration, learning that I lived in the greatest, most fair and wise and lovely place on earth, made a big impression on me. I think it's one of the reasons I'm so fond of

President Lincoln. Because he stared down the crap. More than anyone in the history of the country, he faced up to our most troubling contradiction—that a nation born in freedom would permit the enslavement of human beings—and never once stopped believing in the Declaration of Independence's ideals, never stopped trying to make them come true.

On a Sunday in November, I walked up to the New York Public Library to see   20
the Emancipation Proclamation. On loan from the National Archives, the document was in town for three days. They put it in a glass case in a small, dark room. Being alone with old pieces of paper and one guard in an alcove at the library was nice and quiet. I stared at Abraham Lincoln's signature for a long time. I stood there, thinking what one is supposed to think: This is the paper he held in his hands and there is the ink that came from his pen, and when the ink dried the slaves were freed. Except look at the date, January 1, 1863. The words wouldn't come true for a couple of years, which, I'm guessing, is a long time when another person owns your body. But I love how Lincoln dated the document, noting that it was signed "in the year of our Lord one thousand eight hundred and sixty-three, and of the Independence of the United States of America the eighty-seventh." Four score and seven years before, is the wonderfully arrogant implication, something as miraculous as the virgin birth happened on this earth, and the calendar should reflect that.

The Emancipation Proclamation is a perfect American artifact to me—a good deed that made a lot of other Americans mad enough to kill. I think that's why the Civil War is my favorite American metaphor. I'm so much more comfortable when we're bickering with each other than when we have to link arms and fight a common enemy. But right after September 11, the TV was full of unity. Congressmen, political enemies from both houses of Congress, from both sides of the aisle, stood together on the Capitol steps and sang "God Bless America." At the memorial service at the National Cathedral, President and Mrs. Carter chatted like old friends with President and Mrs. Ford. Rudolph Giuliani, the mayor of New York, kissed his former opponent Senator Hillary Clinton on the cheek as the New York congressional delegation toured the World Trade Center disaster area.

In September, people across the country and all over the world—including, bless them, the Canadians, and they are born sick of us—were singing the American national anthem. And when I heard their voices I couldn't help but remember the last time I had sung that song. I was one of hundreds of people standing in the mud on the Washington Mall on January 20 at the inauguration of George W. Bush. Everyone standing there in the cold rain had very strong feelings. It was either/or. Either you beamed through the ceremony with smiles of joy, or you wept through it all with tears of rage. I admit, I was one of the people there who needed a hankie when it was over. At the end of the ceremony, it was time to sing the national anthem. Some of the dissenters refused to join in. Such was their anger at the country at that moment they couldn't find it in their hearts to sing.

But I was standing there next to my friend Jack, and Jack and I put our hands over our hearts and sang that song loud. Because we love our country too. Because we wouldn't have been standing there, wouldn't have driven down to Washington just to burst into tears if we didn't care so very, very much about how this country is run.

When the anthem ended — land of the free, home of the brave — Jack and I walked to the other end of the Mall to the Lincoln Memorial to read Lincoln's Second Inaugural Address, the speech Lincoln gave at the end of the Civil War about how "we must bind up the nation's wounds." It seems so quaint to me now, after September, after CNN started doing hourly live remotes from St. Vincent's, my neighborhood hospital, that I would conceive of a wound as being peeved about who got to be president.

My ideal picture of citizenship will always be an argument, not a sing-along. I did not get it out of a civics textbook either. I got it from my parents. My mom and dad disagree with me about almost everything. I do not share their religion or their political affiliation. I get on their nerves sometimes. But, and this is the most important thing they taught me, so what? We love each other. My parents and I have been through so much and known each other for so long, share so many in-jokes and memories, our differences of opinion on everything from gun control to Robin Williams movies hardly matter at all. Plus, our disagreements make us appreciate the things we have in common all the more. When I call Republican Senator Orrin Hatch's office to say that I admire something he said about stem cell research, I am my parents' daughter. Because they have always enjoyed playing up things we do have in common, like Dolly Parton or ibuprofen. Maybe sometimes, in quiet moments of reflection, my mom would prefer that I not burn eternally in the flames of hell when I die, but otherwise she wants me to follow my own heart.

I will say that, in September, atheism was a lonely creed. Not because atheists have no god to turn to, but because everyone else forgot about us. At a televised interfaith memorial service at Yankee Stadium on September 23, Muslim, Christian, Jewish, Sikh, and Hindu clerics spoke to their fellow worshipers. Placido Domingo sang "Ave Maria" for the mayor. I waited in vain for someone like me to stand up and say that the only thing those of us who don't believe in god have to believe in is other people and that New York City is the best place there ever was for a godless person to practice her moral code. I think it has something to do with the crowded sidewalks and subways. Walking to and from the hardware store requires the push and pull of selfishness and selflessness, taking turns between getting out of someone's way and them getting out of yours, waiting for a dog to move, helping a stroller up steps, protecting the eyes from runaway umbrellas. Walking in New York is a battle of the wills, a balance of aggression and kindness. I'm not saying it's always easy. The occasional "Watch where you're going, bitch" can, I admit, put a crimp in one's day. But I believe all that choreography has made me a better person. The other day, in the subway at 5:30, I was crammed into my sweaty, crabby fellow citizens, and I kept whispering under my breath "we the people, we the people," over and over again, reminding myself we're all in this together and they had as much right — exactly as much right — as I to be in the muggy underground on their way to wherever they were on their way to.

Once, headed uptown on the 9 train, I noticed a sign posted by the Metropolitan Transit Authority advising subway riders who might become ill in the train. The sign asked that the suddenly infirm inform another passenger or get out at the next stop and approach the stationmaster. Do not, repeat, do not pull the emergency brake, the sign said, as this will only delay aid. Which was all very logical, but for the following proclamation at the bottom of the sign, something along the lines of "If you are sick, you will not be left alone." This strikes me as not only kind, not only comforting, but the very epitome of civilization, good government, i.e., the crux of the societal impulse. Banding together, pooling our taxes, not just making trains, not just making trains that move underground, not just making trains that move underground with surprising efficiency at a fair price — but posting on said trains a notification of such surprising compassion and thoughtfulness, I found myself scanning the faces of my fellow passengers, hoping for fainting, obvious fevers, at the very least a sneeze so that I might offer a tissue.

Exploring the Text

1. In paragraph 2, Sarah Vowell purposely confuses Mel Gibson, the actor, with his character, Benjamin Martin. How does this strategy support her contention that "American history is a quagmire"?
2. Vowell writes, "I've always been more of a Jeffersonhead" (para. 3). What is the effect of such diction?
3. What is the primary implication of paragraph 4?
4. What is the definition of "patriotic"? What is the definition of "jingoistic" (para. 5)? What are Vowell's definitions of the terms? How does knowing the difference affect your understanding of her essay?
5. How does the addition of the word "Chinese" contribute to the tone and meaning of paragraph 6?
6. In discussing the American flag, Vowell writes, "The meaning had changed; or let's say it changed back" (para. 7). What does she mean?
7. In paragraph 11, Vowell writes, "I like the black and white of Paine's words." And she concludes the paragraph with the phrase, "the partly cloudy patriot I long not to be." What has caused her to be a "partly cloudy patriot"? How effectively does this phrase serve as the title of the essay?
8. Choose either paragraphs 1 and 2 or 13 and 14, and rewrite them in what you imagine would be Vowell's sincere voice, meaning without irony or sarcasm.

Compare the two. Why has Vowell chosen to write with an ironic persona in the voice of a "cranky stylist," as *Newsweek* has said?

9. What is the effect of the narrative portion of the essay that runs from paragraph 15 through 17?

10. In paragraph 18, Vowell lists "the national events that have made the deepest impressions" on her and explains what she learned from them. What historical events have made the deepest impressions on you? What have you learned from them?

11. How does the section on Abraham Lincoln (paras. 19–21) contribute to the essay as a whole?

12. Moving toward her conclusion, Vowell begins a discussion of her parents and her personal beliefs (para. 24). What is the rhetorical effect of this shift? How does it prepare the reader for the conclusion of the essay?

13. Read the headnote above the opening paragraph, and find several examples in the essay that support Vowell's characterization by the *New York Times*. How do those examples contribute to the essay as a whole?

The Veil

Marjane Satrapi

Like the heroine of *Persepolis*, Marjane Satrapi was born in Iran in 1969 into a modern, progressive family. Her great-grandfather was the last emperor of Iran before he was overthrown in 1925. Satrapi attended the Lycée Français (French-language high school) in Tehran before being sent to Austria at age fourteen during the Iran-Iraq war. After returning, she earned a degree in art before moving to France, where her popular book, *Persepolis*, was published in French in 2000. *Persepolis* is a graphic memoir that blends the personal and the political. It's the story of a child growing up in Iran during a tumultuous time in the nation's history that included a war with Iraq, the overthrow of the shah, and the Islamic revolution. "The Veil," included here, is the first chapter of the book.

THE VEIL

THIS IS ME WHEN I WAS 10 YEARS OLD. THIS WAS IN 1980.

AND THIS IS A CLASS PHOTO. I'M SITTING ON THE FAR LEFT SO YOU DON'T SEE ME. FROM LEFT TO RIGHT: GOLNAZ, MAHSHID, NARINE, MINNA.

IN 1979 A REVOLUTION TOOK PLACE. IT WAS LATER CALLED "THE ISLAMIC REVOLUTION".

THEN CAME 1980: THE YEAR IT BECAME OBLIGATORY TO WEAR THE VEIL AT SCHOOL.

WEAR THIS!

WE DIDN'T REALLY LIKE TO WEAR THE VEIL, ESPECIALLY SINCE WE DIDN'T UNDERSTAND WHY WE HAD TO.

IT'S TOO HOT OUT!

EXECUTION IN THE NAME OF FREEDOM.

GIVE ME MY VEIL BACK!

YOU'LL HAVE TO LICK MY FEET!

OOH! I'M THE MONSTER OF DARKNESS.

GIDDYAP!

AND ALSO BECAUSE THE YEAR BEFORE, IN 1979, WE WERE IN A FRENCH NON-RELIGIOUS SCHOOL.

WHERE BOYS AND GIRLS WERE TOGETHER.

AND THEN SUDDENLY IN 1980...

ALL BILINGUAL SCHOOLS MUST BE CLOSED DOWN.

THEY ARE SYMBOLS OF CAPITALISM.

BRAVO!

WHAT WISDOM!

OF DECADENCE.

THIS IS CALLED A "CULTURAL REVOLUTION."

WE FOUND OURSELVES VEILED AND SEPARATED FROM OUR FRIENDS.

AND THAT WAS THAT...

EVERYWHERE IN THE STREETS THERE WERE DEMONSTRATIONS FOR AND AGAINST THE VEIL.

the veil! the veil! the veil! the veil! the veil!

freedom! freedom! freedom! freedom! freedom!

AT ONE OF THE DEMONSTRATIONS, A GERMAN JOURNALIST TOOK A PHOTO OF MY MOTHER.

I WAS REALLY PROUD OF HER. HER PHOTO WAS PUBLISHED IN ALL THE EUROPEAN NEWSPAPERS.

AND EVEN IN ONE MAGAZINE IN IRAN. MY MOTHER WAS REALLY SCARED.

HAVE YOU SEEN THIS?

DON'T WORRY, DARLING.

SHE DYED HER HAIR,

AND WORE DARK GLASSES FOR A LONG TIME.

I REALLY DIDN'T KNOW WHAT TO THINK ABOUT THE VEIL. DEEP DOWN I WAS VERY RELIGIOUS BUT AS A FAMILY WE WERE VERY MODERN AND AVANT-GARDE.

I WAS BORN WITH RELIGION.

AT THE AGE OF SIX I WAS ALREADY SURE I WAS THE LAST PROPHET. THIS WAS A FEW YEARS BEFORE THE REVOLUTION.

O' Celestial light!

BEFORE ME THERE HAD BEEN A FEW OTHERS.

A WOMAN?

I AM THE LAST PROPHET.

I WANTED TO BE A PROPHET...

BECAUSE OUR MAID DID NOT EAT WITH US.

BECAUSE MY FATHER HAD A CADILLAC.

AND, ABOVE ALL, BECAUSE MY GRANDMOTHER'S KNEES ALWAYS ACHED.

COME HERE MARJI! HELP ME TO STAND UP.

DON'T WORRY, SOON YOU WON'T HAVE ANY MORE PAIN. YOU'LL SEE.

LIKE ALL MY PREDECESSORS I HAD MY HOLY BOOK.

THE FIRST THREE RULES CAME FROM ZARATHUSTRA. HE WAS THE FIRST PROPHET IN MY COUNTRY BEFORE THE ARAB INVASION.

YOU MUST BASE EVERYTHING ON THESE THREE RULES: BEHAVE WELL, SPEAK WELL, ACT WELL.

I ALSO WANTED US TO CELEBRATE THE TRADITIONAL ZARATHUSTRIAN HOLIDAYS. LIKE THE FIRE CEREMONY,

BEFORE THE PERSIAN NEW YEAR, NOROUZ, ON MARCH 21ST, THE FIRST DAY OF SPRING.

ONLY MY GRANDMOTHER KNEW ABOUT MY BOOK.

RULE NUMBER SIX: EVERYBODY SHOULD HAVE A CAR.

RULE NUMBER SEVEN: ALL MAIDS SHOULD EAT AT THE TABLE WITH THE OTHERS.

RULE NUMBER EIGHT: NO OLD PERSON SHOULD HAVE TO SUFFER.

IN THAT CASE, I'LL BE YOUR FIRST DISCIPLE.

REALLY?

BUT TELL ME HOW YOU'LL ARRANGE FOR OLD PEOPLE NOT TO SUFFER?

IT WILL SIMPLY BE FORBIDDEN.

EVERY NIGHT I HAD A BIG DISCUSSION WITH GOD.

GOD, GIVE ME SOME MORE TIME. I AM NOT QUITE READY YET.

YES YOU ARE, CELESTIAL LIGHT, YOU ARE MY CHOICE, MY LAST AND MY BEST CHOICE.

EXCEPT FOR MY GRANDMOTHER I WAS OBVIOUSLY THE ONLY ONE WHO BELIEVED IN MYSELF.

WHAT DO YOU WANT TO BE WHEN YOU GROW UP?

I'LL BE A PROPHET.

HAHA! HAHA! HAHA!

SHE'S CRAZY.

MY PARENTS WERE CALLED IN BY THE TEACHER.

YOUR CHILD IS DISTURBED. SHE WANTS TO BECOME A PROPHET.

WHAT ABOUT IT?

DOESN'T THIS WORRY YOU?

NO! NOT AT ALL!

?

Exploring the Text

1. Why has Marjane Satrapi left the protagonist out of page 1067, panel 2? What rhetorical purpose does the omission serve?
2. How would you characterize the way the children are presented in the last panel on page 1067 and the first two on page 1068?
3. What is Satrapi's attitude toward the responses of the people depicted on page 1068, panel 4? Explain your response.
4. What cultural values are being criticized on page 1070, panels 6 and 7? Explain.
5. Read carefully the exchange depicted on page 1071, panel 5. What is Satrapi suggesting in this exchange?
6. What can you infer about Satrapi's attitude toward religion? Refer to specific content to explain your answer.
7. How does the process of reading differ when visuals are included, as they are in graphic novels and memoirs? Do you read the text first? Do you look at the pictures first? Which is primary? Which serves the other? Explain your response.
8. Are the illustrations humorous? Objective? Argumentative? Select one that illustrates each of these descriptions, and explain how it does so.
9. Does "The Veil" appeal more to ethos or to logos? Explain.
10. About the writing of *Persepolis*, Satrapi says, "I had the advantage of being cute, because I am just a small girl, it's not me who makes any decisions, it's not me who does anything. So the world around me changed, I am a witness of this big change around me." Why does Satrapi see such an approach as "an advantage"? How would the piece differ if it were presented in the third person? Or by an adult?
11. Is "The Veil" an appropriate title for this chapter? Explain why or why not.

On the Rainy River

TIM O'BRIEN

Tim O'Brien (b. 1946) grew up in a small town in Minnesota. In 1968, he received a BA from Macalester College and, soon thereafter, a draft notice. He served as a soldier in the Vietnam War and wrote about his experiences in his memoir, *If I Die in a Combat Zone* (1973). O'Brien won the National Book Award in 1979 for a novel about the war, *Going after Cacciato*. "On the Rainy River," the story that follows, is from *The Things They Carried* (1990), a work of fiction that O'Brien based on his war experiences and in which he placed himself as the protagonist.

This is one story I've never told before. Not to anyone. Not to my parents, not to my brother or sister, not even to my wife. To go into it, I've always thought, would only cause embarrassment for all of us, a sudden need to be elsewhere, which is the natural response to a confession. Even now, I'll admit, the story makes me squirm. For more than twenty years I've had to live with it, feeling the shame, trying to push it away, and so by this act of remembrance, by putting the facts down on paper, I'm hoping to relieve at least some of the pressure on my dreams. Still, it's a hard story to tell. All of us, I suppose, like to believe that in a moral emergency we will behave like the heroes of our youth, bravely and forthrightly, without thought of personal loss or discredit. Certainly that was my conviction back in the summer of 1968. Tim O'Brien: a secret hero. The Lone Ranger. If the stakes ever became high enough — if the evil were evil enough, if the good were good enough — I would simply tap a secret reservoir of courage that had been accumulating inside me over the years. Courage, I seemed to think, comes to us in finite quantities, like an inheritance, and by being frugal and stashing it away and letting it earn interest, we steadily increase our moral capital in preparation for that day when the account must be drawn down. It was a comforting theory. It dispensed with all those bothersome little acts of daily courage; it offered hope and grace to the repetitive coward; it justified the past while amortizing the future.

In June of 1968, a month after graduating from Macalester College, I was drafted to fight a war I hated. I was twenty-one years old. Young, yes, and politically naive, but even so the American war in Vietnam seemed to me wrong. Certain blood was being shed for uncertain reasons. I saw no unity of purpose, no consensus on matters of philosophy or history or law. The very facts were shrouded in uncertainty: Was it a civil war? A war of national liberation or simple aggression? Who started it, and when, and why? What really happened to the USS *Maddox* on that dark night in the Gulf of Tonkin? Was Ho Chi Minh a Communist stooge, or a nationalist savior, or both, or neither? What about the Geneva Accords? What about SEATO and the Cold War? What about dominoes? America was divided on these and a thousand other issues, and the debate had spilled out across the floor of the United States Senate and into the streets, and smart men in pinstripes could not agree on even the most fundamental matters of public policy. The only certainty that summer was moral confusion. It was my view then, and still is, that you don't make war without knowing why. Knowledge, of course, is always imperfect, but it seemed to me that when a nation goes to war it must have reasonable confidence in the justice and imperative of its cause. You can't fix your mistakes. Once people are dead, you can't make them undead.

In any case those were my convictions, and back in college I had taken a modest stand against the war. Nothing radical, no hothead stuff, just ringing a few doorbells for Gene McCarthy, composing a few tedious, uninspired editorials for the campus newspaper. Oddly, though, it was almost entirely an intellectual activity. I brought some energy to it, of course, but it was the energy that accompanies almost any abstract endeavor; I felt no personal danger; I felt no sense of an impending crisis in my life. Stupidly, with a kind of smug removal that I can't begin to fathom, I assumed that the problems of killing and dying did not fall within my special province.

The draft notice arrived on June 17, 1968. It was a humid afternoon, I remember, cloudy and very quiet, and I'd just come in from a round of golf. My mother and father were having lunch out in the kitchen. I remember opening up the letter, scanning the first few lines, feeling the blood go thick behind my eyes. I remember a sound in my head. It wasn't thinking, just a silent howl. A million things all at once—I was too *good* for this war. Too smart, too compassionate, too everything. It couldn't happen. I was above it. I had the world . . . [licked]—Phi Beta Kappa and summa cum laude and president of the student body and a full-ride scholarship for grad studies at Harvard. A mistake maybe—a foul-up in the paperwork. I was no soldier. I hated Boy Scouts. I hated camping out. I hated dirt and tents and mosquitoes. The sight of blood made me queasy, and I couldn't tolerate authority, and I didn't know a rifle from a slingshot. I was a *liberal*, for Christ sake: If they needed fresh bodies, why not draft some back-to-the-stone-age hawk? Or some dumb jingo in his hard hat and Bomb Hanoi button, or one of LBJ's pretty daughters, or [General William] Westmoreland's whole handsome family—nephews and nieces and baby grandson. There should be a law, I thought. If you support a war, if you think it's worth the price, that's fine, but you have to put your own precious fluids on the line. You have to head for the front and hook up with an infantry unit and help spill the blood. And you have to bring along your wife, or your kids, or your lover. A *law*, I thought.

I remember the rage in my stomach. Later it burned down to a smoldering self-pity, then to numbness. At dinner that night my father asked what my plans were. "Nothing," I said. "Wait."   5

I spent the summer of 1968 working in an Armour meatpacking plant in my hometown of Worthington, Minnesota. The plant specialized in pork products, and for eight hours a day I stood on a quarter-mile assembly line—more properly, a disassembly line—removing blood clots from the necks of dead pigs. My job title, I believe, was Declotter. After slaughter, the hogs were decapitated, split down the length of the belly, pried open, eviscerated, and strung up by the hind hocks on a high conveyer belt. Then gravity took over. By the time a carcass reached my spot on the line, the fluids had mostly drained out, everything except for thick clots of blood in the neck and upper chest cavity. To remove the stuff, I used a kind of water gun. The machine was heavy, maybe eighty pounds, and was suspended from the ceiling by a heavy rubber cord. There was some bounce to it, an elastic up-and-down give, and the trick was to maneuver the gun with your whole body, not lifting with the arms, just letting the rubber cord do the work for you. At one end was a trigger; at the muzzle end was a small nozzle and a steel roller brush. As a carcass passed by, you'd lean forward and swing the gun up against the clots and squeeze the trigger, all in one motion, and the brush would whirl and water would come shooting out and you'd hear a quick splattering sound as the clots dissolved into a fine red mist. It was not pleasant work. Goggles were a necessity, and a rubber apron, but even so it was like standing for eight hours a day under a lukewarm blood-shower. At night I'd go home smelling of pig. It wouldn't go away. Even after a hot bath, scrubbing hard, the stink was always there—like old bacon, or sausage, a dense greasy pig-stink that soaked deep into my skin and hair. Among other things, I remember, it was tough getting dates that summer. I felt isolated; I spent a lot of time alone. And there was also that draft notice tucked away in my wallet.

In the evenings I'd sometimes borrow my father's car and drive aimlessly around town, feeling sorry for myself, thinking about the war and the pig factory and how my life seemed to be collapsing toward slaughter. I felt paralyzed. All around me the options seemed to be narrowing, as if I were hurtling down a huge black funnel, the whole world squeezing in tight. There was no happy way out. The government had ended most graduate school deferments; the waiting lists for the National Guard and Reserves were impossibly long; my health was solid; I didn't qualify for CO [conscientious objector] status—no religious grounds, no history as a pacifist. Moreover, I could not claim to be opposed to war as a matter of general principle. There were occasions, I believed, when a nation was justified in using military force to achieve its ends, to stop a Hitler or some comparable evil, and I told myself that in such circumstances I would've willingly marched off to the battle. The problem, though, was that a draft board did not let you choose your war.

Beyond all this, or at the very center, was the raw fact of terror. I did not want to die. Not ever. But certainly not then, not there, not in a wrong war. Driving up Main Street, past the courthouse and the Ben Franklin store, I sometimes felt the fear spreading inside me like weeds. I imagined myself dead. I imagined myself doing things I could not do—charging an enemy position, taking aim at another human being.

At some point in mid-July I began thinking seriously about Canada. The border lay a few hundred miles north, an eight-hour drive. Both my conscience and my instincts were telling me to make a break for it, just take off and run like hell and never stop. In the beginning the idea seemed purely abstract, the word Canada printing itself out in my head; but after a time I could see particular shapes and images, the sorry details of my own future—a hotel room in Winnipeg, a battered old suitcase, my father's eyes as I tried to explain myself over the telephone. I could almost hear his voice, and my mother's. Run, I'd think. Then I'd think, Impossible. Then a second later I'd think, *Run*.

It was a kind of schizophrenia. A moral split. I couldn't make up my mind. I feared the war, yes, but I also feared exile. I was afraid of walking away from my own life, my friends and my family, my whole history, everything that mattered to me. I feared losing the respect of my parents. I feared the law. I feared ridicule and censure. My hometown was a conservative little spot on the prairie, a place where tradition counted, and it was easy to imagine people sitting around a table down

10

at the old Gobbler Café on Main Street, coffee cups poised, the conversation slowly zeroing in on the young O'Brien kid, how the damned sissy had taken off for Canada. At night, when I couldn't sleep, I'd sometimes carry on fierce arguments with those people. I'd be screaming at them, telling them how much I detested their blind, thoughtless, automatic acquiescence to it all, their simple-minded patriotism, their prideful ignorance, their love-it-or-leave-it platitudes, how they were sending me off to fight a war they didn't understand and didn't want to understand. I held them responsible. By God, yes, I *did*. All of them—I held them personally and individually responsible—the polyestered Kiwanis boys, the merchants and farmers, the pious churchgoers, the chatty housewives, the PTA and the Lions club and the Veterans of Foreign Wars and the fine upstanding gentry out at the country club. They didn't know Bao Dai from the man in the moon. They didn't know history. They didn't know the first thing about Diem's tyranny, or the nature of Vietnamese nationalism, or the long colonialism of the French—this was all too damned complicated, it required some reading—but no matter, it was a war to stop the Communists, plain and simple, which was how they liked things, and you were a . . . [traitor] if you had second thoughts about killing or dying for plain and simple reasons.

I was bitter, sure. But it was so much more than that. The emotions went from outrage to terror to bewilderment to guilt to sorrow and then back again to outrage. I felt a sickness inside me. Real disease.

Most of this I've told before, or at least hinted at, but what I have never told is the full truth. How I cracked. How at work one morning, standing on the pig line, I felt something break open in my chest. I don't know what it was. I'll never know. But it was real, I know that much, it was a physical rupture—a cracking-leaking-popping feeling. I remember dropping my water gun. Quickly, almost without thought, I took off my apron and walked out of the plant and drove home. It was midmorning, I remember, and the house was empty. Down in my chest there was still that leaking sensation, something very warm and precious spilling out, and I was covered with blood and hog-stink, and for a long while I just concentrated on holding myself together. I remember taking a hot shower. I remember packing a suitcase and carrying it out to the kitchen, standing very still for a few minutes, looking carefully at the familiar objects all around me. The old chrome toaster, the telephone, the pink and white Formica on the kitchen counters. The room was full of bright sunshine. Everything sparkled. My house, I thought. My life. I'm not sure how long I stood there, but later I scribbled out a short note to my parents.

What it said, exactly, I don't recall now. Something vague. Taking off, will call, love Tim.

⁜

I drove north.

It's a blur now, as it was then, and all I remember is a sense of high velocity   15
and the feel of the steering wheel in my hands. I was riding on adrenaline. A giddy

feeling, in a way, except there was the dreamy edge of impossibility to it—like running a dead-end maze—no way out—it couldn't come to a happy conclusion and yet I was doing it anyway because it was all I could think of to do. It was pure light, fast and mindless. I had no plan. Just hit the border at high speed and crash through and keep on running. Near dusk I passed through Bemidji, then turned northeast toward International Falls. I spent the night in the car behind a closed-down gas station a half mile from the border. In the morning, after gassing up, I headed straight west along the Rainy River, which separates Minnesota from Canada, and which for me separated one life from another. The land was mostly wilderness. Here and there I passed a motel or bait shop, but otherwise the country unfolded in great sweeps of pine and birch and sumac. Though it was still August, the air already had the smell of October, football season, piles of yellow-red leaves, everything crisp and clean. I remember a huge blue sky. Off to my right was the Rainy River, wide as a lake in places, and beyond the Rainy River was Canada.

For a while I just drove, not aiming at anything, then in the late morning I began looking for a place to lie low for a day or two. I was exhausted, and scared sick, and around noon I pulled into an old fishing resort called the Tip Top Lodge. Actually it was not a lodge at all, just eight or nine tiny yellow cabins clustered on a peninsula that jutted northward into the Rainy River. The place was in sorry shape. There was a dangerous wooden dock, an old minnow tank, a flimsy tar paper boathouse along the shore. The main building, which stood in a cluster of pines on high ground, seemed to lean heavily to one side, like a cripple, the roof sagging toward Canada. Briefly, I thought about turning around, just giving up, but then I got out of the car and walked up to the front porch.

The man who opened the door that day is the hero of my life. How do I say this without sounding sappy? Blurt it out—the man saved me. He offered exactly what I needed, without questions, without any words at all. He took me in. He was there at the critical time—a silent, watchful presence. Six days later, when it ended, I was unable to find a proper way to thank him, and I never have, and so, if nothing else, this story represents a small gesture of gratitude twenty years overdue.

Even after two decades I can close my eyes and return to that porch at the Tip Top Lodge. I can see the old guy staring at me. Elroy Berdahl: eighty-one years old, skinny and shrunken and mostly bald. He wore a flannel shirt and brown work pants. In one hand, I remember, he carried a green apple, a small paring knife in the other. His eyes had the bluish gray color of a razor blade, the same polished shine, and as he peered up at me I felt a strange sharpness, almost painful, a cutting sensation, as if his gaze were somehow slicing me open. In part, no doubt, it was my own sense of guilt, but even so I'm absolutely certain that the old man took one look and went right to the heart of things—a kid in trouble. When I asked for a room, Elroy made a little clicking sound with his tongue. He nodded, led me out to one of the cabins, and dropped a key in my hand. I remember smiling at him. I also remember wishing I hadn't. The old man shook his head as if to tell me it wasn't worth the bother.

"Dinner at five-thirty," he said. "You eat fish?"

"Anything," I said.

Elroy grunted and said, "I'll bet."

⠿⠿

We spent six days together at the Tip Top Lodge. Just the two of us. Tourist season was over, and there were no boats on the river, and the wilderness seemed to withdraw into a great permanent stillness. Over those six days Elroy Berdahl and I took most of our meals together. In the mornings we sometimes went out on long hikes into the woods, and at night we played Scrabble or listened to records or sat reading in front of his big stone fireplace. At times I felt the awkwardness of an intruder, but Elroy accepted me into his quiet routine without fuss or ceremony. He took my presence for granted, the same way he might've sheltered a stray cat—no wasted sighs or pity—and there was never any talk about it. Just the opposite. What I remember more than anything is the man's willful, almost ferocious silence. In all that time together, all those hours, he never asked the obvious questions: Why was I there? Why alone? Why so preoccupied? If Elroy was curious about any of this, he was careful never to put it into words.

My hunch, though, is that he already knew. At least the basics. After all, it was 1968, and guys were burning draft cards, and Canada was just a boat ride away. Elroy Berdahl was no hick. His bedroom, I remember, was cluttered with books and newspapers. He killed me at the Scrabble board, barely concentrating, and on those occasions when speech was necessary he had a way of compressing large thoughts into small, cryptic packets of language. One evening, just at sunset, he pointed up at an owl circling over the violet-lighted forest to the west.

"Hey, O'Brien," he said. "There's Jesus."

The man was sharp—he didn't miss much. Those razor eyes. Now and then he'd catch me staring out at the river, at the far shore, and I could almost hear the tumblers clicking in his head. Maybe I'm wrong, but I doubt it.

One thing for certain, he knew I was in desperate trouble. And he knew I couldn't talk about it. The wrong word—or even the right word—and I would've disappeared. I was wired and jittery. My skin felt too tight. After supper one evening I vomited and went back to my cabin and lay down for a few moments and then vomited again; another time, in the middle of the afternoon, I began sweating and couldn't shut it off. I went through whole days feeling dizzy with sorrow. I couldn't sleep; I couldn't lie still. At night I'd toss around in bed, half awake, half dreaming, imagining how I'd sneak down to the beach and quietly push one of the old man's boats out into the river and start paddling my way toward Canada. There were times when I thought I'd gone off the psychic edge. I couldn't tell up from down, I was just falling, and late in the night I'd lie there watching weird pictures spin through my head. Getting chased by the Border Patrol—helicopters and searchlights and barking dogs—I'd be crashing through the woods, I'd be down on my hands and knees—people shouting out my name—the law closing in on all sides—my hometown draft board and the FBI and the Royal Canadian Mounted Police. It all seemed crazy and impossible. Twenty-one years old, an ordinary kid with all the ordinary dreams and ambitions, and all I wanted was to live the life I was born to—a mainstream life—I loved baseball and hamburgers and cherry Cokes—and now I was off on the margins of exile, leaving my country forever, and it seemed so impossible and terrible and sad.

I'm not sure how I made it through those six days. Most of it I can't remember. On two or three afternoons, to pass some time, I helped Elroy get the place ready for winter, sweeping down the cabins and hauling in the boats, little chores that kept my body moving. The days were cool and bright. The nights were very dark. One morning the old man showed me how to split and stack firewood, and for several hours we just worked in silence out behind his house. At one point, I remember, Elroy put down his maul and looked at me for a long time, his lips drawn as if framing a difficult question, but then he shook his head and went back to work. The man's self-control was amazing. He never pried. He never put me in a position that required lies or denials. To an extent, I suppose, his reticence was typical of that part of Minnesota, where privacy still held value, and even if I'd been walking around with some horrible deformity—four arms and three heads—I'm sure the old man would've talked about everything except those extra arms and heads. Simple politeness was part of it. But even more than that, I think, the man understood that words were insufficient. The problem had gone beyond discussion. During that long summer I'd been over and over the various arguments, all the pros and cons, and it was no longer a question that could be decided by an act of pure reason. Intellect had come up against emotion. My conscience told me to run, but some irrational and powerful force was resisting, like a weight pushing me toward the war. What it came down to, stupidly, was a sense of shame. Hot, stupid shame. I did not want people to think badly of me. Not my parents, not my brother and sister, not even the folks down at the Gobbler Café. I was ashamed to be there at the Tip Top Lodge. I was ashamed of my conscience, ashamed to be doing the right thing.

Some of this Elroy must've understood. Not the details, of course, but the plain fact of crisis.

Although the old man never confronted me about it, there was one occasion when he came close to forcing the whole thing out into the open. It was early evening, and we'd just finished supper, and over coffee and dessert I asked him about my bill, how much I owed so far. For a long while the old man squinted down at the tablecloth.

"Well, the basic rate," he said, "is fifty bucks a night. Not counting meals. This makes four nights, right?" 30

I nodded. I had three hundred and twelve dollars in my wallet.

Elroy kept his eyes on the tablecloth. "Now that's an on-season price. To be fair, I suppose we should knock it down a peg or two." He leaned back in his chair. "What's a reasonable number, you figure?"

"I don't know," I said. "Forty?"

"Forty's good. Forty a night. Then we tack on food—say another hundred? Two hundred sixty total?"

"I guess." 35

He raised his eyebrows. "Too much?"

"No, that's fair. It's fine. Tomorrow, though . . . I think I'd better take off tomorrow."

Elroy shrugged and began clearing the table. For a time he fussed with the dishes, whistling to himself as if the subject had been settled. After a second he slapped his hands together.

"You know what we forgot?" he said. "We forgot wages. Those odd jobs you done. What we have to do, we have to figure out what your time's worth. Your last job—how much did you pull in an hour?"

"Not enough," I said. 40

"A bad one?"

"Yes. Pretty bad."

Slowly then, without intending any long sermon, I told him about my days at the pig plant. It began as a straight recitation of the facts, but before I could stop myself I was talking about the blood clots and the water gun and how the smell had soaked into my skin and how I couldn't wash it away. I went on for a long time. I told him about wild hogs squealing in my dreams, the sounds of butchery, slaughterhouse sounds, and how I'd sometimes wake up with that greasy pig-stink in my throat.

When I was finished, Elroy nodded at me.

"Well, to be honest," he said, "when you first showed up here, I wondered 45 about all that. The aroma, I mean. Smelled like you was awful damned fond of pork chops." The old man almost smiled. He made a snuffling sound, then sat down with a pencil and a piece of paper. "So what'd this crud job pay? Ten bucks an hour? Fifteen?"

"Less."

Elroy shook his head. "Let's make it fifteen. You put in twenty-five hours here, easy. That's three hundred seventy-five bucks total wages. We subtract the two hundred sixty for food and lodging, I still owe you a hundred and fifteen."

He took four fifties out of his shirt pocket and laid them on the table.

"Call it even," he said.

"No." 50

"Pick it up. Get yourself a haircut."

The money lay on the table for the rest of the evening. It was still there when I went back to my cabin. In the morning, though, I found an envelope tacked to my door. Inside were the four fifties and a two-word note that said EMERGENCY FUND.

The man knew.

Looking back after twenty years, I sometimes wonder if the events of that summer didn't happen in some other dimension, a place where your life exists before you've lived it, and where it goes afterward. None of it ever seemed real. During my time at the Tip Top Lodge I had the feeling that I'd slipped out of my own skin, hovering a few feet away while some poor yo-yo with my name and face tried to make his way toward a future he didn't understand and didn't want. Even now I can see myself as I was then. It's like watching an old home movie: I'm young and tan and fit. I've got hair — lots of it. I don't smoke or drink. I'm wearing faded blue jeans and a white polo shirt. I can see myself sitting on Elroy Berdahl's dock near dusk one evening, the sky a bright shimmering pink, and I'm finishing up a letter to my parents that tells what I'm about to do and why I'm doing it and how sorry I am that I'd never found the courage to talk to them about it. I ask them not to be angry. I try to explain some of my feelings, but there aren't enough words, and so I just say that it's a thing that has to be done. At the end of the letter I talk about the vacations we used to take up in this north country, at a place called Whitefish Lake, and how the scenery here reminds me of those good times. I tell them I'm fine. I tell them I'll write again from Winnipeg or Montreal or wherever I end up.

❊

On my last full day, the sixth day, the old man took me out fishing on the Rainy 55 River. The afternoon was sunny and cold. A stiff breeze came in from the north, and I remember how the little fourteen-foot boat made sharp rocking motions as we pushed off from the dock. The current was fast. All around us, I remember, there was a vastness to the world, an unpeopled rawness, just the trees and the sky and the water reaching out toward nowhere. The air had the brittle scent of October.

For ten or fifteen minutes Elroy held a course upstream, the river choppy and silver-gray, then he turned straight north and put the engine on full throttle. I felt the bow lift beneath me. I remember the wind in my ears, the sound of the old outboard Evinrude. For a time I didn't pay attention to anything, just feeling the cold spray against my face, but then it occurred to me that at some point we must've passed into Canadian waters, across that dotted line between two different worlds, and I remember a sudden tightness in my chest as I looked up and watched the far shore come at me. This wasn't a daydream. It was tangible and real. As we came in toward land, Elroy cut the engine, letting the boat fishtail lightly about twenty yards off shore. The old man didn't look at me or speak. Bending down, he opened up his tackle box and busied himself with a bobber and a piece of wire leader, humming to himself, his eyes down.

It struck me then that he must've planned it. I'll never be certain, of course, but I think he meant to bring me up against the realities, to guide me across the river and to take me to the edge and to stand a kind of vigil as I chose a life for myself.

I remember staring at the old man, then at my hands, then at Canada. The shoreline was dense with brush and timber. I could see tiny red berries on the bushes. I could see a squirrel up in one of the birch trees, a big crow looking at me from a boulder along the river. That close—twenty yards—and I could see the delicate latticework of the leaves, the texture of the soil, the browned needles beneath the pines, the configurations of geology and human history. Twenty yards. I could've done it. I could've jumped and started swimming for my life. Inside me, in my chest, I felt a terrible squeezing pressure. Even now, as I write this, I can still feel that tightness. And I want you to feel it—the wind coming off the river, the waves, the silence, the wooded frontier. You're at the bow of a boat on the Rainy River. You're twenty-one years old, you're scared, and there's a hard squeezing pressure in your chest.

What would you do?

Would you jump? Would you feel pity for yourself? Would you think about   60 your family and your childhood and your dreams and all you're leaving behind? Would it hurt? Would it feel like dying? Would you cry, as I did?

I tried to swallow it back. I tried to smile, except I was crying.

Now, perhaps, you can understand why I've never told this story before. It's not just the embarrassment of tears. That's part of it, no doubt, but what embarrasses me much more, and always will, is the paralysis that took my heart. A moral freeze: I couldn't decide, I couldn't act, I couldn't comport myself with even a pretense of modest human dignity.

All I could do was cry. Quietly, not bawling, just the chest-chokes.

At the rear of the boat Elroy Berdahl pretended not to notice. He held a fishing rod in his hands, his head bowed to hide his eyes. He kept humming a soft, monotonous little tune. Everywhere, it seemed, in the trees and water and sky, a great worldwide sadness came pressing down on me, a crushing sorrow, sorrow like I had never known it before. And what was so sad, I realized, was that Canada had become a pitiful fantasy. Silly and hopeless. It was no longer a possibility. Right then, with the shore so close, I understood that I would not do what I should do. I would not swim away from my hometown and my country and my life. I would not be brave. That old image of myself as a hero, as a man of conscience and courage, all that was just a threadbare pipe dream. Bobbing there on the Rainy River, looking back at the Minnesota shore, I felt a sudden swell of helplessness come over me, a drowning sensation, as if I had toppled overboard and was being swept away by the silver waves. Chunks of my own history flashed by. I saw a seven-year-old boy in a white cowboy hat and a Lone Ranger mask and a pair of holstered six-shooters; I saw a twelve-year-old Little League shortstop pivoting to turn a double play; I saw a sixteen-year-old kid decked out for his first prom, looking spiffy in a white tux and a black bow tie, his hair cut short and flat, his shoes freshly polished. My whole life seemed to spill out into the river, swirling away from me, everything I had ever been or ever wanted to be. I couldn't get my breath; I couldn't stay afloat; I couldn't tell which way to swim. A hallucination, I suppose, but it was as real as anything I would ever feel. I saw my parents calling to me from the far shoreline. I saw my brother and sister, all the townsfolk, the mayor and the entire Chamber of Commerce and all my old teachers and girlfriends and high school buddies. Like some weird sporting event: everybody screaming from the sidelines, rooting me on — a loud stadium roar. Hotdogs and popcorn — stadium smells, stadium heat. A squad of cheerleaders did cartwheels along the banks of the Rainy River; they had megaphones and pompoms and smooth brown thighs. The crowd swayed left and right. A marching band played fight songs. All my aunts and uncles were there, and Abraham Lincoln, and Saint George, and a nine-year-old girl named Linda who had died of a brain tumor back in fifth grade, and several members of the United States Senate, and a blind poet scribbling notes, and LBJ, and Huck Finn, and Abbie Hoffman, and all the dead soldiers back from the grave, and the many thousands who were later to die — villagers with terrible burns, little kids without arms or legs — yes, and the Joint Chiefs of Staff were there, and a couple of popes, and a first lieutenant named Jimmy Cross, and the last surviving veteran of the American Civil War, and Jane Fonda dressed up as Barbarella, and an old man sprawled beside a pigpen, and my grandfather, and Gary Cooper, and a kind-faced woman carrying an umbrella and a copy of Plato's *Republic*, and a million ferocious citizens waving flags of all shapes and colors — people in hard hats, people in headbands — they were all whooping and chanting and urging me toward one shore or the other. I saw faces from my distant past and distant future. My wife was there. My unborn daughter waved at me, and my two sons hopped up and down, and a drill sergeant named Blyton sneered and shot up a finger and shook his head. There was a choir in bright purple robes. There was a cabbie from the Bronx. There was a slim young man I would one day kill with a hand grenade along a red clay trail outside the village of My Khe.

The little aluminum boat rocked softly beneath me. There was the wind and the sky. 65

I tried to will myself overboard.

I gripped the edge of the boat and leaned forward and thought, *Now.*

I did try. It just wasn't possible.

All those eyes on me — the town, the whole universe — and I couldn't risk the embarrassment. It was as if there were an audience to my life, that swirl of faces along the river, and in my head I could hear people screaming at me. Traitor! they yelled. Turncoat! . . . I felt myself blush. I couldn't tolerate it. I couldn't endure the mockery, or the disgrace, or the patriotic ridicule. Even in my imagination, the shore just twenty yards away, I couldn't make myself be brave. It had nothing to do with morality. Embarrassment, that's all it was.

And right then I submitted. 70

I would go to the war — I would kill and maybe die — because I was embarrassed not to.

That was the sad thing. And so I sat in the bow of the boat and cried.

It was loud now. Loud, hard crying.

Elroy Berdahl remained quiet. He kept fishing. He worked his line with the tips of his fingers, patiently, squinting out at his red and white bobber on the Rainy River. His eyes were flat and impassive. He didn't speak. He was simply there, like the river and the late-summer sun. And yet by his presence, his mute watchfulness, he made it real. He was the true audience. He was a witness, like God, or like the gods, who look on in absolute silence as we live our lives, as we make our choices or fail to make them.

"Ain't biting," he said. 75

Then after a time the old man pulled in his line and turned the boat back toward Minnesota.

⌗⌗

I don't remember saying goodbye. That last night we had dinner together, and I went to bed early, and in the morning Elroy fixed breakfast for me. When I told him I'd be leaving, the old man nodded as if he already knew. He looked down at the table and smiled.

At some point later in the morning it's possible that we shook hands—I just don't remember—but I do know that by the time I'd finished packing the old man had disappeared. Around noon, when I took my suitcase out to the car, I noticed that his old black pickup truck was no longer parked in front of the house. I went inside and waited for a while, but I felt a bone certainty that he wouldn't be back. In a way, I thought, it was appropriate. I washed up the breakfast dishes, left his two hundred dollars on the kitchen counter, got into the car, and drove south toward home.

The day was cloudy. I passed through towns with familiar names, through the pine forests and down to the prairie, and then to Vietnam, where I was a soldier, and then home again. I survived, but it's not a happy ending. I was a coward. I went to the war.

Exploring the Text

1. What is the rhetorical effect of the first seven sentences? Based on the opening, what were your expectations of the story to follow?

2. This is a fictional story in which Tim O'Brien has used himself—or a character by the same name—as the protagonist. Describe how you determine which details are factual and which are imaginative. What is the effect of mixing fact and fiction?

3. Reread the questions in paragraph 2. Are they rhetorical? What purpose do they serve? Could we ask similar questions about events today? Explain your response.

4. What is the narrator's conflict (para. 9)? How does this conflict relate to the theme of this chapter?

5. Why does O'Brien address the reader directly in paragraphs 58–60? How would you answer his questions?

6. Identify the rhetorical strategies O'Brien uses in paragraph 64. What are the effects of these strategies in this long paragraph?
7. What is the effect of collapsing time in the final paragraph? What is the rhetorical effect of the irony in this paragraph?
8. If you have read *The Adventures of Huckleberry Finn* by Mark Twain, compare Huck's conflict about doing what he has been taught is "the right thing"—turning Jim in—with O'Brien's statement at the end of paragraph 27. How are the situations of the two protagonists similar?

Guernica

PABLO PICASSO

Widely regarded as the twentieth century's most respected and influential painter, Pablo Picasso (1881–1973) painted *Guernica*, an eleven-foot-tall, twenty-six-foot-wide mural, in 1937. It was his response to the bombing of the Basque capital in the Spanish civil war. The bombing had been carried out by Nazis at the behest of Francisco Franco, who went on to rule Spain as dictator from 1939 to 1975. Thousands of people in Guernica were killed or wounded, and the town was destroyed. The painting is housed in the Museo Nacional Centro de Arte Reina Sofía in Madrid.

(See insert for color version.)

Exploring the Text

1. Look carefully at the elements of *Guernica*, specifically the burning woman, the horse, the warrior with the broken sword, the crying woman with the child, and the bull. How does each element contribute to the painting's theme — the apocalyptic horrors of war?

2. Discuss the style of *Guernica*. If you have studied art history, you may know that Picasso was a prime practitioner of Cubist fragmentation. How does such a method serve the meaning of this painting?

3. In the painting, Pablo Picasso uses only black, white, and gray. What is the effect of the absence of color?

4. Picasso once said, "Painting is not made to decorate apartments. It is an instrument for offensive and defensive war against the enemy." How does *Guernica* exemplify this statement? What, if anything, has replaced fine art as a political statement in the post-Picasso world?

5. How does the painting appeal to ethos, logos, and pathos?

6. A tapestry of *Guernica* hangs at the United Nations building in New York City. What is its rhetorical effect as a mural in this setting?

Depictions of Guernica

In February 2003, Colin Powell, then U.S. secretary of state, delivered a speech at the United Nations making the case for the invasion of Iraq. During Powell's talk, a tapestry depicting Pablo Picasso's *Guernica* was covered so that the audience would not see it. U.N. officials claim they covered the image to provide a neutral backdrop for television camera crews. Two national magazines that address political and cultural issues, the *New Yorker* and *Harper's*, responded to that event with their covers, shown on the following pages.

Exploring the Text

1. Why would authorities at the United Nations decide to cover *Guernica* during a political speech? What rhetorical purpose would covering it serve?

2. Which of the classic appeals do both the *New Yorker* and *Harper's* use in their covers?

3. What assumptions about their audiences — their readers' familiarity with history and art, their awareness of current events — do both publications evidently hold?

4. From these two covers, what inferences can you make about the political attitudes of each magazine? Explain.

5. Considering these covers as examples of visual rhetoric, what claim do they make?

6. Compare and contrast the two covers. How does each cover depict the draping? What images from the original does each cover show? Is one more powerful than the other? Explain.

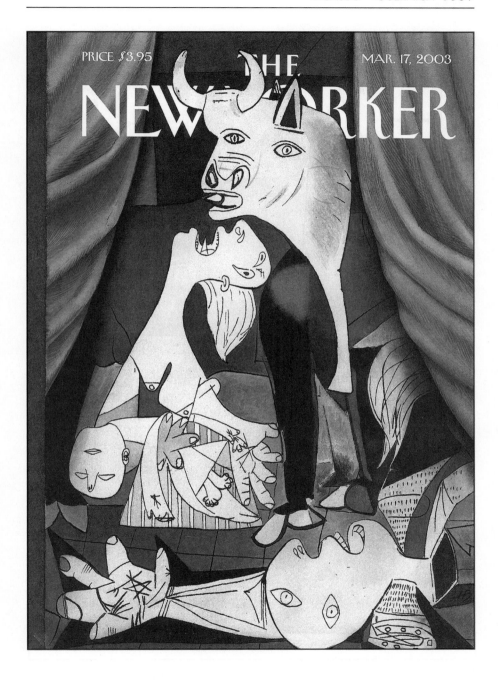

BILL MCKIBBEN: THE POSTHUMAN CONDITION

HARPER'S

HARPER'S MAGAZINE/APRIL 2003 $5.95

CAUSE FOR DISSENT
Ten Questions for the Bush Regime
By Lewis H. Lapham

❖

NO MORE UNTO THE BREACH
Part II: The Unconquerable World
By Jonathan Schell

A HOUSE UNDIVIDED
Andrea Palladio and the Science of Happiness
By Dave Hickey

AJAX IS ALL ABOUT ATTACK
A story by Jim Shepard

Also: Francine Prose, Daniel Lazare

❖

Conversation

The following eight texts comment directly or indirectly on colonialism:

Sources

1. **Christopher Columbus,** *Letter to King Ferdinand of Spain*
2. **King Ferdinand,** *The Requerimiento*
3. **Red Jacket,** *Defense of Native American Religion*
4. **George Orwell,** *Shooting an Elephant*
5. **Frantz Fanon,** from *Concerning Violence*
6. **Eavan Boland,** *In Which the Ancient History I Learn Is Not My Own* (poem)
7. **Chinua Achebe,** from *The Empire Fights Back*
8. **National Park Service,** *Christiansted: Official Map and Guide*

After you have read, studied, and synthesized these pieces, enter the Conversation by responding to one of the suggested prompts on pages 1118–19.

1. *Letter to King Ferdinand of Spain*

Christopher Columbus

The following is Christopher Columbus's 1493 letter addressed to the Spanish finance minister, but ultimately intended for King Ferdinand of Spain, in which Columbus describes the results of his first voyage to the New World.

Sir:

As I know you will be rejoiced at the glorious success that our Lord has given me in my voyage, I write this to tell you how in thirty-three days I sailed to the Indies with the fleet that the illustrious King and Queen, our Sovereigns, gave me, where I discovered a great many islands, inhabited by numberless people; and of all I have taken possession for their Highnesses by proclamation and display of the Royal Standard without opposition.

To the first island I discovered I gave the name of San Salvador, in commemoration of His Divine Majesty, who has wonderfully granted all this. The Indians call it Guanaham. The second I named the Island of Santa Maria de Concepción; the third, Fernandina; the fourth, Isabella; the fifth, Juana; and thus to each one I gave a new name.

When I came to Juana, I followed the coast of that isle toward the west, and found it so extensive that I thought it might be the mainland, the province of

Cathay;[1] and as I found no towns nor villages on the seacoast, except a few small settlements, where it was impossible to speak to the people, because they fled at once, I continued the said route, thinking I could not fail to see some great cities or towns; and finding at the end of many leagues that nothing new appeared, and that the coast led northward, contrary to my wish, because the winter had already set in, I decided to make for the south, and as the wind also was against my proceeding, I determined not to wait there longer, and turned back to a certain harbor whence I sent two men to find out whether there was any king or large city. They explored for three days, and found countless small communities and people, without number, but with no kind of government, so they returned. I heard from other Indians I had already taken that this land was an island, and thus followed the eastern coast for 107 leagues, until I came to the end of it. From that point I saw another isle to the eastward, at eighteen leagues' distance, to which I gave the name of Hispaniola. I went thither and followed its northern coast to the east, as I had done in Juana, 178 leagues eastward, as in Juana. This island, like all the others, is most extensive. It has many ports along the seacoast excelling any in Christendom — and many fine, large, flowing rivers. The land there is elevated, with many mountains and peaks incomparably higher than in the centre isle. They are most beautiful, of a thousand varied forms, accessible, and full of trees of endless varieties, so high that they seem to touch the sky, and I have been told that they never lose their foliage. I saw them as green and lovely as trees are in Spain in the month of May. Some of them were covered with blossoms, some with fruit, and some in other conditions, according to their kind. The nightingale and other small birds of a thousand kinds were singing in the month of November when I was there. There were palm trees of six or eight varieties, the graceful peculiarities of each one of them being worthy of admiration as are the other trees, fruits, and grasses. There are wonderful pine woods, and very extensive ranges of meadow land. There is honey, and there are many kinds of birds, and a great variety of fruits. Inland there are numerous mines of metals and innumerable people.

Hispaniola is a marvel. Its hills and mountains, fine plains and open country, are rich and fertile for planting and for pasturage, and for building towns and villages. The seaports there are incredibly fine, as also the magnificent rivers, most of which bear gold. The trees, fruits, and grasses differ widely from those in Juana. There are many spices and vast mines of gold and other metals in this island.

The people of this island and of all the other islands which I have found, and of which I have information, all go naked, men and women, as their mothers bore them, although some of the women cover a single place with the leaf of a plant or with a net of cotton which they make for the purpose. They have no iron, nor steel, nor weapons, nor are they fit for them, because although they are well-made men of commanding stature, they appear extraordinarily timid. The only arms

5

---

[1] China. — Eds.

they have are sticks of cane, cut when in seed, with a sharpened stick at the end, and they are afraid to use these. Often I have sent two or three men ashore to some town to converse with them, and the natives came out in great numbers, and as soon as they saw our men arrive, fled without a moment's delay although I protected them from all injury. At every point where I landed, and succeeded in talking to them, I gave them some of everything I had — cloth and many other things — without receiving anything in return, but they are a hopelessly timid people. It is true that since they have gained more confidence and are losing this fear, they are so unsuspicious and so generous with what they possess, that no one who had not seen it would believe it. They never refuse anything that is asked for. They even offer it themselves, and show so much love that they would give their very hearts. Whether it be anything of great or small value, with any trifle of whatever kind, they are satisfied. I forbade worthless things being given to them, such as bits of broken bowls, pieces of glass, and old straps, although they were as much pleased to get them as if they were the finest jewels in the world. One sailor was found to have got for a leathern strap, gold of the weight of two and a half castellanos, and others for even more worthless things much more; while for a new *blancas* they would give all they had, were it two or three castellanos of pure gold or an arroba or two of spun cotton. Even bits of the broken hoops of wine casks they accepted, and gave in return what they had, like fools, and it seemed wrong to me. I forbade it, and gave a thousand good and pretty things that I had to win their love, and to induce them to become Christians, and to love and serve their Highnesses and the whole Castilian nation, and help to get for us things they have in abundance, which are necessary to us.

They have no religion, nor idolatry, except that they all believe power and goodness to be in heaven. They firmly believed that I, with my ships and men, came from heaven, and with this idea I have been received everywhere, since they lost fear of me. They are, however, far from being ignorant. They are most ingenious men, and navigate these seas in a wonderful way, and describe everything well, but they never before saw people wearing clothes, nor vessels like ours.

As soon as I reached the Indies, in the first isle I discovered, I took by force some of the natives, that from them we might gain some information of what there was in these parts; and so it was that we immediately understood each other, either by words or signs. They are still with me and still believe that I come from heaven. They were the first to declare this wherever I went, and the others ran from house to house, and to the towns around, crying out, "Come! come! and see the men from heaven!" Then all, both men and women, as soon as they were re-assured about us, came, both small and great, all bringing something to eat and to drink, which they presented with marvellous kindness.

In these isles there are a great many canoes, something like rowing boats, of all sizes, and most of them are larger than an eighteen-oared galley. They are not so broad, as they are made of a single plank, but a galley could not keep up with them in rowing, because they go with incredible speed, and with these they row about among all these islands, which are innumerable, and carry on their commerce. I have seen some of these canoes with seventy and eighty men in them, and each had an oar.

In all the islands I observed little difference in the appearance of the people, or in their habits and language, except that they understand each other, which is remarkable. Therefore I hope that their Highnesses will decide upon the conversion of these people to our holy faith, to which they seem much inclined.

I have already stated how I sailed 107 leagues along the seacoast of Juana, in a straight line from west to east. I can therefore assert that this island is larger than England and Scotland together, since beyond these 107 leagues there remained at the west point two provinces where I did not go, one of which they call Avan, the home of men with tails. These provinces are computed to be fifty or sixty leagues in length, as far as can be gathered from the Indians with me who are acquainted with all these islands.

The other, Hispaniola, is larger in circumference than all Spain from Catalonia to Fuenterrabia in Biscay, since upon one of its four sides I sailed 188 leagues from west to east. This is worth having, and must on no account be given up. I have taken possession of all these islands, for their Highnesses, and all may be more extensive than I know, or can say, and I hold them for their Highnesses, who can command them as absolutely as the kingdoms of Castile. In Hispaniola, in the most convenient place, most accessible for the gold mines and all commerce with the mainland on this side or with that of the Great Khan, on the other, with which there would be great trade and profit, I have taken possession of a large town, which I have named the City of Navidad. I began fortifications there which should be completed by this time, and I have left in it men enough to hold it, with arms, artillery, and provisions for more than a year; and a boat with a master seaman skilled in the arts necessary to make others; I am so friendly with the king of that country that he was proud to call me his brother and hold me as such. Even should he change his mind and wish to quarrel with my men, neither he nor his subjects know what arms are, nor wear clothes, as I have said. They are the most timid people in the world, so that only the men remaining there could destroy the whole region, and run no risk if they know how to behave themselves properly.

In all these islands the men seem to be satisfied with one wife, except they allow as many as twenty to their chief or king.

The women appear to me to work harder than the men, and so far I can hear they have nothing of their own, for I think I perceived that what one had others shared, especially food.

In the islands so far, I have found no monsters, as some expected, but, on the contrary, they are people of very handsome appearance. They are not black as in Guinea, though their hair is straight and coarse, as it does not grow where the sun's rays are too ardent. And in truth the sun has extreme power here, since it is within twenty-six degrees of the equinoctial line. In these islands there are mountains where the cold this winter was very severe, but the people endure it from habit, and with the aid of the meat they eat with very hot spices. As for monsters, I have found no trace of them except at the point in the second isle as one enters the Indies, which is inhabited by a people considered in all the isles as most ferocious, who eat human flesh. They possess many canoes, with which they overrun all the isles of India, stealing and seizing all they can. They are not worse looking than the others, except that they wear their hair long like women, and use bows and arrows of the same cane, with sharp stick at the end for want of iron, of which they have none. They are ferocious compared to these other races, who are extremely cowardly; but I only hear this from the others. They are said to make treaties of marriage with the women in the first isle to be met with coming from Spain to the Indies, where there are no men. These women have no feminine occupation, but use bows and arrows of cane like those before mentioned, and cover and arm themselves with plates of copper, of which they have a great quantity. Another island, I am told, is larger than Hispaniola, where the natives have no hair, and where there is countless gold; and from them all I bring Indians to testify to this.

To speak, in conclusion, only of what has been done during this hurried voyage, their Highnesses will see that I can give them as much gold as they desire, if they will give me a little assistance, spices, cotton, as much as their Highnesses may command to be shipped, and mastic, as much as their Highnesses choose to send for, which until now has only been found in Greece, in the isle of Chios, and the Signoria can get its own price for it; as much aloe as they command to be shipped, and as many slaves as they choose to send for, all heathens. I think I have found rhubarb and cinnamon. Many other things of value will be discovered by the men I left behind me, as I stayed nowhere when the wind allowed me to pursue my voyage, except in the City of Navidad, which I left fortified and safe. Indeed, I might have accomplished much more, had the crews served me as they ought to have done.

The eternal and almighty God, our Lord, it is Who gives to all who walk in His way, victory over things apparently impossible, and in this case signally so, because although these lands had been imagined and talked of before they were seen, most men listened incredulously to what was thought to be but an idle tale. But our Redeemer has given victory to our most illustrious King and Queen, and to their Kingdoms rendered famous by this glorious event, at which all Christendom should rejoice, celebrating it with great festivities and solemn thanksgivings to the Holy Trinity, with fervent prayers for the high distinction that will accrue to them from turning so many peoples to our holy faith; and also from the temporal benefits that not only Spain but all Christian nations will obtain.

Thus I record. What has happened in a brief note written on board the *Caravel*, off the Canary Isles, on the 15th of February, 1493.

Yours to command,

THE ADMIRAL

Questions

1. Why do you suppose Columbus is surprised by the lack of diversity among the natives? How do his first-hand impressions differ from what he has heard? Offer specific examples to support your answer.
2. Look closely at Columbus's diction — for example, at "taken possession" (para. 1) and "command them" (para. 11). What do these phrases suggest about the attitude of both Columbus and King Ferdinand toward the native people?
3. Columbus states that he has established a fort where he has left some men for a year. He writes, "I am so friendly with the king of that country that he was proud to call me his brother and hold me as such. Even should he change his mind and wish to quarrel with my men, neither he nor his subjects know what arms are" (para. 11), and that the few men he left behind could destroy the whole region. Given this language, what is the nature of the "friendship" that has been established?
4. In paragraph 15, Columbus enumerates the things that he will give to King Ferdinand, and he promises that he will find "many other things of value." What are the eight things that he mentions? What do they have in common? Are you surprised at anything about the list? Explain your response.
5. What assumptions concerning authority, ownership, and faith underlie the statements Columbus makes in paragraph 16? What are the "temporal benefits" Columbus refers to? Are they secondary to religious ones, as he suggests? Explain your response.

2. *The Requerimiento*

KING FERDINAND

The following letter — a *requerimiento*, or demand — was sent with Spanish conquistadors on their voyages to the New World. It explained to the natives that Pope Alexander VI had given King Ferdinand the right to take possession of any lands that the conquistadors discovered.

On the part of the King, Don Fernando, and of Doña Juana, his daughter, Queen of Castile and León, subduers of the barbarous nations, we their servants notify and make known to you, as best we can, that the Lord our God, living and eternal, created the heaven and the earth, and one man and one woman, of whom you and we, and all the men of the world, were and are all descendants, and all those who come after us.

Of all these nations God our Lord gave charge to one man, called St. Peter, that he should be lord and superior of all the men in the world, that all should obey him, and that he should be the head of the whole human race, wherever men should live, and under whatever law, sect, or belief they should be; and he gave him the world for his kingdom and jurisdiction.

One of these pontiffs, who succeeded St. Peter as lord of the world in the dignity and seat which I have before mentioned, made donation of these isles and Terra-firma to the aforesaid King and Queen and to their successors, our lords, with all that there are in these territories,

Wherefore, as best we can, we ask and require you that you consider what we have said to you, and that you take the time that shall be necessary to understand and deliberate upon it, and that you acknowledge the Church as the ruler and superior of the whole world,

But if you do not do this, and maliciously make delay in it, I certify to you   5
that, with the help of God, we shall powerfully enter into your country, and shall make war against you in all ways and manners that we can, and shall subject you to the yoke and obedience of the Church and of their highnesses; we shall take you, and your wives, and your children, and shall make slaves of them, and as such shall sell and dispose of them as their highnesses may command; and we shall take away your goods, and shall do you all the mischief and damage that we can, as to vassals who do not obey, and refuse to receive their lord, and resist and contradict him: and we protest that the deaths and losses which shall accrue from this are your fault, and not that of their highnesses, or ours, nor of these cavaliers who come with us.

Questions

1. In paragraphs 1 and 2, what assumptions about the world underlie the contents of the letter? What does the speaker evidently assume about the audience?
2. Read carefully the long sentence that comprises paragraph 2 and submit it to the Toulmin model of argument analysis as described in Chapter 3. What does that analysis reveal about the Requerimiento's argument?
3. Make a list of the unwarranted assumptions and unsupported claims made in paragraph 3. Why do you think King Ferdinand does not make a more cogent argument?
4. Considering the threat that begins paragraph 5, what is ironic about the text that precedes it?
5. Which of the statements in the letter do you find most surprising or shocking? Explain why.
6. In this letter, the king makes what might be called an "offer they can't refuse." Imagine that you are the intended audience. What would you say in response to this letter?

3. *Defense of Native American Religion*

Red Jacket

Chief Sagoyewatha of the Senecas, who were members of the Iroquois federation, was known as Red Jacket from his habit of wearing red coats given to him by the British, on whose side the Senecas fought in the American Revolution.

After the war, Red Jacket led a delegation that met with George Washington, acting as a mediator between the U.S. government and the Senecas. The text below is his 1805 response to a Boston missionary society that wanted to proselytize among the Iroquois.

Friend and brother; it was the will of the Great Spirit that we should meet together this day. He orders all things, and he has given us a fine day for our council. He has taken his garment from before the sun, and caused it to shine with brightness upon us; our eyes are opened, that we see clearly; our ears are unstopped, that we have been able to hear distinctly the words that you have spoken; for all these favors we thank the Great Spirit, and him only.

Brother, this council fire was kindled by you; it was at your request that we came together at this time; we have listened with attention to what you have said. You requested us to speak our minds freely; this gives us great joy, for we now consider that we stand upright before you, and can speak what we think; all have heard your voice, and all speak to you as one man; our minds are agreed.

Brother, you say you want an answer to your talk before you leave this place. It is right you should have one, as you are a great distance from home, and we do not wish to detain you; but we will first look back a little, and tell you what our fathers have told us, and what we have heard from the white people.

Brother, listen to what we say. There was a time when our forefathers owned this great island. Their seats extended from the rising to the setting sun. The Great Spirit had made it for the use of Indians. He had created the buffalo, the deer, and other animals for food. He made the bear and the beaver, and their skins served us for clothing. He had scattered them over the country, and taught us how to take them. He had caused the earth to produce corn for bread. All this he had done for his red children because he loved them. If we had any disputes about hunting grounds, they were generally settled without the shedding of much blood. But an evil day came upon us; your forefathers crossed the great waters, and landed on this island. Their numbers were small; they found friends, and not enemies; they told us they had fled from their own country for fear of wicked men, and come here to enjoy their religion. They asked for a small seat; we took pity on them, granted their request, and they sat down amongst us; we gave them corn and meat; they gave us poison in return. The white people had now found our country; tidings were carried back, and more came amongst us; yet we did not fear them, we took them to be friends; they called us brothers; we believed them, and gave them a larger seat. At length, their numbers had greatly increased; they wanted more land; they wanted our country. Our eyes were opened, and our minds became uneasy. Wars took place; Indians were hired to fight against Indians, and many of our people were destroyed. They also brought strong liquor among us; it was strong and powerful, and has slain thousands.

Brother, our seats were once large, and yours were very small; you have now become a great people, and we have scarecely a place left to spread our blankets; 5

you have got our country, but are not satisfied; you want to force your religion upon us.

Brother, continue to listen. You say you are sent to instruct us how to worship the Great Spirit agreeably to his mind, and if we do not take hold of the religion which you white people teach, we shall be unhappy hereafter. You say that you are right, and we are lost; how do we know this to be true? We understand that your religion is written in a book; if it was intended for us as well as you, why has not the Great Spirit given it to us, and not only to us, but why did he not give to our forefathers the knowledge of that book, with the means of understanding it rightly? We only know what you tell us about it. How shall we know when to believe, being so often deceived by the white people?

Brother, you say there is but one way to worship and serve the Great Spirit; if there is but one religion, why do you white people differ so much about it? Why not all agree, as you can all read the book?

Brother, we do not understand these things. We are told that your religion was given to your forefathers, and has been handed down from father to son. We also have a religion which was given to our forefathers, and has been handed down to us their children. We worship that way. It teacheth us to be thankful for all the favors we receive; to love each other, and to be united. We never quarrel about religion.

Brother, the Great Spirit has made us all; but he has made a great difference between his white and red children; he has given us a different complexion, and different customs; to you he has given the arts; to these he has not opened our eyes; we know these things to be true. Since he has made so great a difference between us in other things, why may we not conclude that he has given us a different religion according to our understanding. The Great Spirit does right; he knows what is best for his children; we are satisfied.

Brother, we do not wish to destroy your religion, or take it from you; we only want to enjoy our own. 10

Brother, you say you have not come to get our land or our money, but to enlighten our minds. I will now tell you that I have been at your meetings, and saw you collecting money from the meeting. I cannot tell what this money was intended for, but suppose it was for your minister; and if we should conform to your way of thinking, perhaps you may want some from us.

Brother, we are told that you have been preaching to the white people in this place. These people are our neighbors; we are acquainted with them; we will wait a little while and see what effect your preaching has upon them. If we find it does them good, makes them honest and less disposed to cheat Indians, we will then consider again what you have said.

Brother, you have now heard our answer to your talk, and this is all we have to say at present. As we are going to part, we will come and take you by the hand, and hope the Great Spirit will protect you on your journey, and return you safe to your friends.

Questions

1. Notice how Red Jacket begins each paragraph. How does this approach appeal to both ethos and pathos?
2. What is the significance of ending the first paragraph with the phrase "and him only"?
3. How would you characterize Red Jacket's tone in paragraphs 2 and 3?
4. What is Red Jacket's rhetorical purpose in paragraphs 4 and 5? Elsewhere in the text, Red Jacket repeats the phrases "we are told" and "you say" several times. How does this repetition serve his purpose?
5. Red Jacket says, "Brother, we do not understand these things" (para. 8). Is he being disingenuous? Explain your response.
6. How effectively does Red Jacket use rhetorical questions? Imagine and describe the audience's probable response to each of them.
7. In paragraph 12, Red Jacket makes a promise. Is it a sincere one? Is it similar to a rhetorical question, in that Red Jacket already knows the result of what he suggests? Explain your response.

4. *Shooting an Elephant*

George Orwell

In the following autobiographical essay written in 1936, George Orwell talks about his experience as a British officer in British-occupied Burma in the 1920s.

In Moulmein, in Lower Burma, I was hated by large numbers of people — the only time in my life that I have been important enough for this to happen to me. I was sub-divisional police officer of the town, and in an aimless, petty kind of way anti-European feeling was very bitter. No one had the guts to raise a riot, but if a European woman went through the bazaars alone somebody would probably spit betel juice over her dress. As a police officer I was an obvious target and was baited whenever it seemed safe to do so. When a nimble Burman tripped me up on the football field and the referee (another Burman) looked the other way, the crowd yelled with hideous laughter. This happened more than once. In the end the sneering yellow faces of young men that met me everywhere, the insults hooted after me when I was at a safe distance, got badly on my nerves. The young Buddhist priests were the worst of all. There were several thousands of them in the town and none of them seemed to have anything to do except stand on street corners and jeer at Europeans.

All this was perplexing and upsetting. For at that time I had already made up my mind that imperialism was an evil thing and the sooner I chucked up my job and got out of it the better. Theoretically — and secretly, of course — I was all for the Burmese and all against their oppressors, the British. As for the job I was doing, I hated it more bitterly than I can perhaps make clear. In a job like that you see the dirty work of Empire at close quarters. The wretched prisoners huddling in the stinking cages of the lock-ups, the grey, cowed faces of the long-term convicts, the scarred buttocks of the men who had been flogged with bamboos—all these oppressed me with an intolerable sense of guilt. But I could get nothing into perspective. I was young and ill-educated and I had had to think out my problems in the utter silence that is imposed on every Englishman in the East. I did not even know that the British Empire is dying, still less did I know that it is a great deal better than the younger empires that are going to supplant it. All I knew was that I was stuck between my hatred of the empire I served and my rage against the evil-spirited little beasts who tried to make my job impossible. With one part of my mind I thought of the British Raj as an unbreakable tyranny, as something clamped down, *in saecula saeculorum*[1] upon the will of prostrate peoples; with another part I thought that the greatest joy in the world would be to drive a bayonet into a Buddhist priest's guts. Feelings like these are the normal by-products of imperialism; ask any Anglo-Indian official, if you can catch him off duty.

One day something happened which in a roundabout way was enlightening. It was a tiny incident in itself, but it gave me a better glimpse than I had had before of the real nature of imperialism—the real motives for which despotic governments act. Early one morning the sub-inspector at a police station the other end of the town rang me up on the phone and said that an elephant was ravaging the bazaar. Would I please come and do something about it? I did not know what I could do, but I wanted to see what was happening and I got on to a pony and started out. I took my rifle, an old .44 Winchester and much too small to kill an elephant, but I thought the noise might be useful *in terrorem*.[2] Various Burmans stopped me on the way and told me about the elephant's doings. It was not, of course, a wild elephant, but a tame one which had gone "must." It had been chained up, as tame elephants always are when their attack of "must" is due, but on the previous night it had broken its chain and escaped. Its mahout, the only person who could manage it when it was in that state, had set out in pursuit, but had taken the wrong direction and was now twelve hours' journey away, and in the morning the elephant had suddenly reappeared in the town. The Burmese population had no weapons and were quite helpless against it. It had already destroyed somebody's bamboo hut, killed a cow and raided some fruit-stalls and devoured the stock; also it had met the municipal rubbish van and, when the driver jumped out and took to his heels, had turned the van over and inflicted violences upon it.

The Burmese sub-inspector and some Indian constables were waiting for me in the quarter where the elephant had been seen. It was a very poor quarter, a

---

[1] Latin, "for ever and ever."—Eds.
[2] A legal term meaning "to scare a person into complying with terms."—Eds.

labyrinth of squalid bamboo huts, thatched with palm-leaf, winding all over a steep hillside. I remember that it was a cloudy, stuffy morning at the beginning of the rains. We began questioning the people as to where the elephant had gone and, as usual, failed to get any definite information. That is invariably the case in the East; a story always sounds clear enough at a distance, but the nearer you get to the scene of events the vaguer it becomes. Some of the people said that the elephant had gone in one direction, some said that he had gone in another, some professed not even to have heard of any elephant. I had almost made up my mind that the whole story was a pack of lies, when we heard yells a little distance away. There was a loud, scandalized cry of "Go away, child! Go away this instant!" and an old woman with a switch in her hand came round the corner of a hut, violently shooing away a crowd of naked children. Some more women followed, clicking their tongues and exclaiming; evidently there was something that the children ought not to have seen. I rounded the hut and saw a man's dead body sprawling in the mud. He was an Indian, a black Dravidian coolie,[3] almost naked, and he could not have been dead many minutes. The people said that the elephant had come suddenly upon him round the corner of the hut, caught him with its trunk, put its foot on his back and ground him into the earth. This was the rainy season and the ground was soft, and his face had scored a trench a foot deep and a couple of yards long. He was lying on his belly with arms crucified and head sharply twisted to one side. His face was coated with mud, the eyes wide open, the teeth bared and grinning with an expression of unendurable agony. (Never tell me, by the way, that the dead look peaceful. Most of the corpses I have seen looked devilish.) The friction of the great beast's foot had stripped the skin from his back as neatly as one skins a rabbit. As soon as I saw the dead man I sent an orderly to a friend's house nearby to borrow an elephant rifle. I had already sent back the pony, not wanting it to go mad with fright and throw me if it smelt the elephant.

The orderly came back in a few minutes with a rifle and five cartridges, and   5
meanwhile some Burmans had arrived and told us that the elephant was in the paddy fields below, only a few hundred yards away. As I started forward practically the whole population of the quarter flocked out of the houses and followed me. They had seen the rifle and were all shouting excitedly that I was going to shoot the elephant. They had not shown much interest in the elephant when he was merely ravaging their homes, but it was different now that he was going to be shot. It was a bit of fun to them, as it would be to an English crowd; besides they wanted the meat. It made me vaguely uneasy. I had no intention of shooting the elephant—I had merely sent for the rifle to defend myself if necessary—and it is always unnerving to have a crowd following you. I marched down the hill, looking and feeling a fool, with the rifle over my shoulder and an ever-growing army of people jostling at my heels. At the bottom, when you got away from the huts,

---

[3] An unskilled Indian laborer.—Eds.

there was a metalled road and beyond that a miry waste of paddy fields a thousand yards across, not yet ploughed but soggy from the first rains and dotted with coarse grass. The elephant was standing eight yards from the road, his left side towards us. He took not the slightest notice of the crowd's approach. He was tearing up bunches of grass, beating them against his knees to clean them and stuffing them into his mouth.

I had halted on the road. As soon as I saw the elephant I knew with perfect certainty that I ought not to shoot him. It is a serious matter to shoot a working elephant—it is comparable to destroying a huge and costly piece of machinery—and obviously one ought not to do it if it can possibly be avoided. And at that distance, peacefully eating, the elephant looked no more dangerous than a cow. I thought then and I think now that his attack of "must" was already passing off; in which case he would merely wander harmlessly about until the mahout came back and caught him. Moreover, I did not in the least want to shoot him. I decided that I would watch him for a little while to make sure that he did not turn savage again, and then go home.

But at that moment I glanced round at the crowd that had followed me. It was an immense crowd, two thousand at the least and growing every minute. It blocked the road for a long distance on either side. I looked at the sea of yellow faces above the garish clothes—faces all happy and excited over this bit of fun, all certain that the elephant was going to be shot. They were watching me as they would watch a conjurer about to perform a trick. They did not like me, but with the magical rifle in my hands I was momentarily worth watching. And suddenly I realized that I should have to shoot the elephant after all. The people expected it of me and I had got to do it; I could feel their two thousand wills pressing me forward, irresistibly. And it was at this moment, as I stood there with the rifle in my hands, that I first grasped the hollowness, the futility of the white man's dominion in the East. Here was I, the white man with his gun, standing in front of the unarmed native crowd—seemingly the leading actor of the piece; but in reality I was only an absurd puppet pushed to and fro by the will of those yellow faces behind. I perceived in this moment that when the white man turns tyrant it is his own freedom that he destroys. He becomes a sort of hollow, posing dummy, the conventionalized figure of a sahib.[4] For it is the condition of his rule that he shall spend his life in trying to impress the "natives," and so in every crisis he has got to do what the "natives" expect of him. He wears a mask, and his face grows to fit it. I had got to shoot the elephant. I had committed myself to doing it when I sent for the rifle. A sahib has got to act like a sahib; he has got to appear resolute, to know his own mind and do definite things. To come all that way, rifle in hand, with two thousand people marching at my heels, and then to trail feebly away, having done nothing—no, that was impossible. The crowd would laugh at me.

---

[4]In colonial India, the title used to address a European.—Eds.

And my whole life, every white man's life in the East, was one long struggle not to be laughed at.

But I did not want to shoot the elephant. I watched him beating his bunch of grass against his knees, with that preoccupied grandmotherly air that elephants have. It seemed to me that it would be murder to shoot him. At that age I was not squeamish about killing animals, but I had never shot an elephant and never wanted to. (Somehow it always seems worse to kill a *large* animal.) Besides, there was the beast's owner to be considered. Alive, the elephant was worth at least a hundred pounds; dead, he would only be worth the value of his tusks, five pounds, possibly. But I had got to act quickly. I turned to some experienced-looking Burmans who had been there when we arrived, and asked them how the elephant had been behaving. They all said the same thing: he took no notice of you if you left him alone, but he might charge if you went too close to him.

It was perfectly clear to me what I ought to do. I ought to walk up to within, say, twenty-five yards of the elephant and test his behavior. If he charged, I could shoot; if he took no notice of me, it would be safe to leave him until the mahout came back. But also I knew that I was going to do no such thing. I was a poor shot with a rifle and the ground was soft mud into which one would sink at every step. If the elephant charged and I missed him, I should have about as much chance as a toad under a steam-roller. But even then I was not thinking particularly of my own skin, only of the watchful yellow faces behind. For at that moment, with the crowd watching me, I was not afraid in the ordinary sense, as I would have been if I had been alone. A white man mustn't be frightened in front of "natives"; and so, in general, he isn't frightened. The sole thought in my mind was that if anything went wrong those two thousand Burmans would see me pursued, caught, trampled on and reduced to a grinning corpse like that Indian up the hill. And if that happened it was quite probable that some of them would laugh. That would never do. There was only one alternative. I shoved the cartridges into the magazine and lay down on the road to get a better aim.

The crowd grew very still, and a deep, low, happy sigh, as of people who see the theatre curtain go up at last, breathed from innumerable throats. They were going to have their bit of fun after all. The rifle was a beautiful German thing with cross-hair sights. I did not then know that in shooting an elephant one would shoot to cut an imaginary bar running from ear-hole to ear-hole. I ought, therefore, as the elephant was sideways on, to have aimed straight at his ear-hole; actually I aimed several inches in front of this, thinking the brain would be further forward.

When I pulled the trigger I did not hear the bang or feel the kick — one never does when a shot goes home — but I heard the devilish roar of glee that went up from the crowd. In that instant, in too short a time, one would have thought, even for the bullet to get there, a mysterious, terrible change had come over the elephant. He neither stirred nor fell, but every line of his body had altered. He looked suddenly stricken, shrunken, immensely old, as though the frightful impact of

10

the bullet had paralysed him without knocking him down. At last, after what seemed a long time—it might have been five seconds, I dare say—he sagged flabbily to his knees. His mouth slobbered. An enormous senility seemed to have settled upon him. One could have imagined him thousands of years old. I fired again into the same spot. At the second shot he did not collapse but climbed with desperate slowness to his feet and stood weakly upright, with legs sagging and head drooping. I fired a third time. That was the shot that did for him. You could see the agony of it jolt his whole body and knock the last remnant of strength from his legs. But in falling he seemed for a moment to rise, for as his hind legs collapsed beneath him he seemed to tower upward like a huge rock toppling, his trunk reaching skywards like a tree. He trumpeted, for the first and only time. And then down he came, his belly towards me, with a crash that seemed to shake the ground even where I lay.

I got up. The Burmans were already racing past me across the mud. It was obvious that the elephant would never rise again, but he was not dead. He was breathing very rhythmically with long rattling gasps, his great mound of a side painfully rising and falling. His mouth was wide open—I could see far down into caverns of pale pink throat. I waited a long time for him to die, but his breathing did not weaken. Finally I fired my two remaining shots into the spot where I thought his heart must be. The thick blood welled out of him like red velvet, but still he did not die. His body did not even jerk when the shots hit him, the tortured breathing continued without a pause. He was dying, very slowly and in great agony, but in some world remote from me where not even a bullet could damage him further. I felt that I had got to put an end to that dreadful noise. It seemed dreadful to see the great beast lying there, powerless to move and yet powerless to die, and not even to be able to finish him. I sent back for my small rifle and poured shot after shot into his heart and down his throat. They seemed to make no impression. The tortured gasps continued as steadily as the ticking of a clock.

In the end I could not stand it any longer and went away. I heard later that it took him half an hour to die. Burmans were bringing dahs and baskets even before I left, and I was told they had stripped his body almost to the bones by the afternoon.

Afterwards, of course, there were endless discussions about the shooting of the elephant. The owner was furious, but he was only an Indian and could do nothing. Besides, legally I had done the right thing, for a mad elephant has to be killed, like a mad dog, if its owner fails to control it. Among the Europeans opinion was divided. The older men said I was right, the younger men said it was a damn shame to shoot an elephant for killing a coolie, because an elephant was worth more than any damn Coringhee coolie. And afterwards I was very glad that the coolie had been killed; it put me legally in the right and it gave me a sufficient pretext for shooting the elephant. I often wondered whether any of the others grasped that I had done it solely to avoid looking a fool.

Questions

1. What is George Orwell's attitude toward imperialism, toward the native peoples, and toward his own position in Burma? Give evidence supporting your claim.
2. In paragraph 3, the narrator says that the incident of shooting the elephant "in a roundabout way was enlightening. It was a tiny incident in itself, but it gave me a better glimpse than I had had before of the real nature of imperialism—the real motives for which despotic governments act." What does he see as "the real nature of imperialism," and how does this incident reveal that nature?
3. In paragraph 6, the narrator says, "As soon as I saw the elephant I knew with perfect certainty that I ought not to shoot him." Why, then, does he decide to shoot it? Cite specific factors that influence his decision.
4. Explain the opinions of the Europeans about the killing of the elephant, as presented in the final paragraph. At the conclusion of the essay, how do you feel toward Orwell?
5. Describe Orwell's position concerning human motives. Support or challenge his position using evidence drawn from your readings, observations, and experiences.

5. from *Concerning Violence*

Frantz Fanon

In the following excerpt from the first chapter of his book *The Wretched of the Earth* (1963), Algerian psychiatrist and philosopher Frantz Fanon discusses colonialism.

The colonial world is a world cut in two. The dividing line, the frontiers are shown by barracks and police stations. In the colonies it is the policeman and the soldier who are the official, instituted go-betweens, the spokesmen of the settler and his rule of oppression. In capitalist societies the educational system, whether lay or clerical, the structure of moral reflexes handed down from father to son, the exemplary honesty of workers who are given a medal after fifty years of good and loyal service, and the affection which springs from harmonious relations and good behavior—all these aesthetic expressions of respect for the established order serve to create around the exploited person an atmosphere of submission and of inhibition which lightens the task of policing considerably. In the capitalist countries a multitude of moral teachers, counselors and "bewilderers" separate the exploited from those in power. In the colonial countries, on the contrary, the policeman and the soldier, by their immediate presence and their frequent and direct action, maintain contact with the native and advise him by means of rifle butts and napalm not to budge. It is obvious here that the agents of government speak the language of pure force. The intermediary does not lighten the oppression, nor seek to hide the domination; he shows them up and puts them into practice with the clear conscience of an upholder of the peace; yet he is the bringer of violence into the home and into the mind of the native.

The zone where the natives live is not complementary to the zone inhabited by the settlers. The two zones are opposed, but not in the service of a higher unity. Obedient to the rules of pure Aristotelian logic, they both follow the principle of reciprocal exclusivity. No conciliation is possible, for of the two terms, one is superfluous. The settlers' town is a strongly built town, all made of stone and steel. It is a brightly lit town; the streets are covered with asphalt, and the garbage cans swallow all the leavings, unseen, unknown and hardly thought about. The settler's feet are never visible, except perhaps in the sea; but there you're never close enough to see them. His feet are protected by strong shoes although the streets of his town are clean and even, with no holes or stones. The settler's town is a well-fed town, an easygoing town; its belly is always full of good things. The settlers' town is a town of white people, of foreigners.

The town belonging to the colonized people, or at least the native town, the Negro village, the medina, the reservation, is a place of ill fame, peopled by men of evil repute. They are born there, it matters little where or how; they die there, it matters not where, nor how. It is a world without spaciousness; men live there on top of each other, and their huts are built one on top of the other. The native town is a hungry town, starved of bread, of meat, of shoes, of coal, of light. The native town is a crouching village, a town on its knees, a town wallowing in the mire. It is a town of niggers and dirty Arabs. The look that the native turns on the settler's town is a look of lust, a look of envy; it expresses his dreams of possession — all manner of possession: to sit at the settler's table, to sleep in the settler's bed, with his wife if possible. The colonized man is an envious man. And this the settler knows very well; when their glances meet he ascertains bitterly, always on the defensive, "They want to take our place." It is true, for there is no native who does not dream at least once a day of setting himself up in the settler's place.

This world divided into compartments, this world cut in two is inhabited by two different species. The originality of the colonial context is that economic reality, inequality, and the immense difference of ways of life never come to mask the human realities. When you examine at close quarters the colonial context, it is evident that what parcels out the world is to begin with the fact of belonging to or not belonging to a given race, a given species. In the colonies the economic substructure is also a superstructure. The cause is the consequence; you are rich because you are white, you are white because you are rich. This is why Marxist analysis should always be slightly stretched every time we have to do with the colonial problem.

Everything up to and including the very nature of precapitalist society, so well explained by Marx, must here be thought out again. The serf is in essence different from the knight, but a reference to divine right is necessary to legitimize this statutory difference. In the colonies, the foreigner coming from another country imposed his rule by means of guns and machines. In defiance of his successful transplantation, in spite of his appropriation, the settler still remains a foreigner. It is neither the act of owning factories, nor estates, nor a bank balance which distinguishes the governing classes. The governing race is first and foremost those who come from elsewhere, those who are unlike the original inhabitants, "the others."

Questions

1. In paragraph 1, Frantz Fanon makes distinctions between colonial and capitalist countries. According to his analysis, how are they different? How are they alike?
2. Who do you suppose the "bewilderers" (para. 1) are? What is their role, according to Fanon?
3. What does Fanon mean by "reciprocal exclusivity" (para. 2)? How does that principle affect both the natives and the settlers?
4. What are the implications suggested by the observations Fanon makes in paragraph 4?
5. Fanon writes, "The cause is the consequence; you are rich because you are white, you are white because you are rich" (para. 4). Such a statement seems at first to be a logical fallacy. How does this circular reasoning illustrate Fanon's ideas? Do you agree with them? Explain your response.
6. In the final paragraph, Fanon draws an analogy to medieval times and then questions its applicability. What, according to Fanon, makes the analogy inapplicable today?

6. *In Which the Ancient History I Learn Is Not My Own*

Eavan Boland

In the following 1993 poem, Irish poet Eavan Boland examines national history and identity.

The linen map
hung from the wall.
The linen was shiny
and cracked in places.
The cracks were darkened by grime.   5
It was fastened to the classroom wall with
a wooden batten on
a triangle of knotted cotton.

The colours
were faded out   10

so the red of Empire —
the stain of absolute possession —
the mark once made from Kashmir
to the oast-barns[1] of the Kent
coast south of us was   15
underwater coral.

Ireland was far away
and farther away
every year.
I was nearly an English child.   20
I could list the English kings.
I could name the famous battles.
I was learning to recognize
God's grace in history.

And the waters   25
of the Irish Sea,
their shallow weave
and cross-grained blue green
had drained away
to the pale gaze   30
of a doll's china eyes —
a stare without recognition or memory.

We have no oracles,
no rocks or olive trees,
no sacred path to the temple   35
and no priestesses.
The teacher's voice had a London accent.
This was London. 1952.
It was Ancient History Class.
She put the tip   40

of the wooden
pointer on the map.
She tapped over ridges and dried-
out rivers and cities buried in
the sea and seascapes which   45
had once been land.
And stopped.
Remember this, children.

---

[1]A kiln for drying hops or malt. — Eds.

The Roman Empire was
the greatest Empire   50
ever known —
until our time of course —
while the Delphic Oracle
was reckoned to be
the exact centre   55
of the earth.

Suddenly
I wanted
to stand in front of it.
I wanted to trace over   60
and over the weave of my own country.
To read out names
I was close to forgetting.
Wicklow. Kilruddery. Dublin.

To ask   65
where exactly
was my old house?
Its brass One and Seven.
Its flight of granite steps.
Its lilac tree whose scent   70
stayed under your fingernails
for days.

For days —
she was saying — *even months,*
the ancients traveled   75
to the Oracle.
They brought sheep and killed them.
They brought questions about tillage and war.
They rarely left with more
than an ambiguous answer.   80

Questions

1. The Romans conquered Britain but did not conquer Ireland. How does knowing this affect your reading of "In Which the Ancient History I Learn Is Not My Own"?
2. In lines 17–19, the speaker says, "Ireland was far away / and farther away / every year." What does the speaker mean?
3. What does the speaker mean by "God's grace in history" (l. 24)?

4. What is ironic in line 39, "It was Ancient History Class"?
5. What is significant about the qualifier "until our time of course" in line 52?
6. What are the implications of the final stanza?
7. What point does Eavan Boland's poem make about imperialism?

7. from *The Empire Fights Back*

CHINUA ACHEBE

In the following excerpt from the second chapter of his book *Home and Exile* (2000), Nigerian writer Chinua Achebe looks at British impressions of Africa as delivered in literature.

I will begin . . . with a question: what did I do with my experience of classroom rebellion over *Mister Johnson*?[1] Anyone familiar with the gossip in African literature may have heard that it was that book that made me decide to write. I am not even sure that I have not said it somewhere myself, in one of those occasional seizures of expansive ambition we have to sum up the whole world in a single, neat metaphor. Of course we need such moments now and again to stir things up in our lives. But other times we must be content to stay modest and level-headed, more factual. What *Mister Johnson* did do for me was not to change my course in life and turn me from something else into a writer; I was born that way. But it did open my eyes to the fact that my home was under attack and that my home was not merely a house or a town but, more importantly, an awakening story in whose ambience my own existence had first begun to assemble its fragments into a coherence and meaning; the story I had begun to learn consciously the moment I descended from the lorry that brought me to my father's house in Ogidi, the story that, seventeen years later at the university, I still had only a sketchy, tantalizing knowledge of, and over which even today, decades later, I still do not have sufficient mastery, but about which I can say one thing: that it is not the same story Joyce Cary intended me to have.

For me there are three reasons for becoming a writer. The first is that you have an overpowering urge to tell a story. The second, that you have intimations of a unique story waiting to come out. And the third, which you learn in the process of becoming, is that you consider the whole project worth the considerable trouble — I have sometimes called it terms of imprisonment — you will have to endure to bring it to fruition. For me, those three factors were present, and would have been present had Joyce Cary never been born, or set foot in Nigeria. History, however, had contrived a crossing of our paths, and such crossings may sometimes

---

[1]A 1939 novel by the writer Joyce Cary, who had served as an administrator and soldier in Nigeria, Achebe's country. — Eds.

leave their footmarks, faint or loud, on memory. And if they do, they should be acknowledged.

Another question. Was there any way Joyce Cary could have written a Nigerian novel that we Nigerian students could have accepted as our story? My answer, in retrospect, must be: not likely. And my reason would not be the obvious fact that Cary was a European, but rather because he was the product of a tradition of presenting Africa that he had absorbed at school and Sunday school, in magazines and in British society in general, at the end of the nineteenth century. In theory, a good writer might outgrow these influences, but Cary did not.

In their Introduction to *The Africa That Never Was*, Hammond and Jablow tell us that the large number of writers they studied "were not, and could not be, selected for literary merit" and that there were many more "bad" writers than "good" ones in their sample. (Which, I dare say, is hardly surprising.) They then identify [Joseph] Conrad, Cary, [Graham] Greene and Huxley (not Aldous but Elspeth) among the better writers (which is still OK by me — it only tells us how bad the bad ones must be). But when they proceed to praise these four for their handling of Africa in their books, I don't quite know what to make of it:

> The better writers, such as Conrad, Cary, Greene and Huxley . . . use the conventions of the tradition with skill and subtlety. Each of them has an unmistakably individual style in which he or she selectively exploits the conventions, without allowing the writing to become overwhelmed by them. They all have more to say about Africa than the merely conventional clichés, along with the talent to say it well.[2]

I suppose we can all differ as to the exact point where good writing becomes overwhelmed by racial cliché. But overwhelmed or merely undermined, literature is always badly served when an author's artistic insight yields place to stereotype and malice. And it becomes doubly offensive when such a work is arrogantly proffered to you as your story. Some people may wonder if, perhaps, we were not too touchy, if we were not oversensitive. We really were not. And I have a somewhat unusual reason for saying so.

Although my classmates and I would not have known it at the time, the London publishing house of Methuen had brought out the year before, in 1951, a little book titled simply *West Africa*. Its author, F. J. Pedler, was a highly respected public servant in Britain, with considerable experience of West Africa. Although the book was not entirely free of the stereotypes of contemporary British colonial writing, it was in some ways remarkably advanced for its time, and even for today. One small example will suffice. "It is misleading," Mr. Pedler wrote, "when Europeans talk of Africans buying a wife."[3] Although he did not mention Joyce Cary by name it is inconceivable that he would not have been aware of him or of his

---

[2]Dorothy Hammond and Alta Jablow, *The Africa That Never Was* (Prospect Heights, Ill.: Waveland Press, 1992), p. 9.
[3]F. J. Pedler, *West Africa* (London: Methuen & Co., 1951), p. 32.

much celebrated novel *Mister Johnson*, in which that very stereotype was exploited for all it was worth in the episode in which Johnson, after much haggling, buys himself a local girl, Bamu, as wife.

But what I find truly remarkable about Pedler's book is the prominence he gave to, and the faith he had in, African literature that was not even in existence yet: "A country's novels reveal its social condition. West Africa has no full-length novels, but a few short stories may serve the purpose. We quote from two recent publications which show how educated West Africans themselves describe some of the features of social life in their own country." Pedler then proceeded to summarize for his reader two short stories published in a magazine in 1945 in the British colony of the Gold Coast. He devoted almost three pages of his short book to this matter and then concluded as follows: "Here is a dramatic treatment of a contemporary social phenomenon which leaves one with the hope that more West Africans may enter the field of authorship and give us authentic stories of the lives of their own people."[4]

These brief quotations speak volumes to us on the issue of peoples and their stories. We should note Pedler's phrases: West Africans themselves; their own country; authentic stories; of their own people. Without calling any names this extraordinary Englishman seemed to be engaged in a running argument against an age-old practice: the colonization of one people's story by another. In sidestepping Joyce Cary and all the other high-profile practitioners of this brand of writing and going, in search of authenticity, to two unpretentious short stories written by two completely unknown West African authors whose names did not ring any bell at all, Pedler was putting himself decisively and prophetically on the side of the right of a people to take back their own narrative. And because he was British, and because we, the students at Ibadan, did not even know of him, nor he presumably of us, our little rebellion in class one year after his book can, in retrospect, assume the status of a genuine, disinterested service to literature, and transcend the troubling impression it might otherwise easily create, of a white/black, British/Nigerian divide.

Incidentally Pedler's prayer for West African novels was instantly answered. There was already in the works, as we now know, a startling literary concoction from the pen of a Nigerian coppersmith, Amos Tutuola, which Faber would publish in 1952. It may not have been the social realism which F. J. Pedler had presumably hoped for but an odyssey in peculiar English, which roamed about from realism to magic and back again, as in old Africa. But no matter, *The Palm-Wine Drinkard* opened the floodgates to modern West African writing. Hot on its heels came another Nigerian, Cyprian Ekwensi, with *People of the City*; Camara Laye of Guinea with *L'Enfant Noir*; my *Things Fall Apart*; Mongo Beti of Cameroon and his countryman, Ferdinand Oyono, with *Poor Christ of Bomba* and *Houseboy*, respectively; Cheikh Hamidou Kane of Senegal with *Ambiguous Adventure*.

[4]Both quotes from Pedler, *West Africa*, pp. 49, 50.

Looking back now on that incredible 1950s decade and all the intersecting   10
events I have been describing, each of which seemed at first sight to be about its
own separate little errand but then chanced upon these others on a large, open
space such as is used to hold a big market once in eight days and abandoned
again to a profound and watchful emptiness till another market-day—looking
back on all this, it does become easy to indulge a temptation to see History as
mindful, purposeful; and to see the design behind this particular summons and
rendezvous as the signal at long last to end Europe's imposition of a derogatory narrative upon Africa, a narrative designed to call African humanity into
question.

As we have seen, Captain John Lok's voyage to West Africa in 1561 provided
an early model of what would become a powerful and enduring tradition. One of
his men had described the Negroes as "a people of beastly living, without a God,
laws, religion."[5] Three hundred and fifty years later we find that this model, like
the Energizer Bunny, is still running strong, beating away on its tin drum. "Unhu-
man" was how Joyce Cary, in the early part of our own century, saw his African
dancers. One generation before him, Joseph Conrad had created a memorable
actor/narrator who could be greatly troubled by the mere thought of his Africans
being human, like himself: "Well, you know, that was the worst of it—this suspicion of their not being inhuman."[6]

Questions

1. What did Chinua Achebe learn from *Mister Johnson*?
2. According to Achebe, what are the three reasons for becoming a writer? Which one
   do you think is most important? Why?
3. In paragraph 3, Achebe analyzes the sources of Joyce Cary's impressions of Africa.
   What are they? Achebe says in paragraph 3 that "a good writer might outgrow
   [the] influences" of prejudice. Do you agree? Explain your response.
4. How does Achebe's attitude toward *The Africa That Never Was* differ from his attitude toward the contemporaneous *West Africa*?
5. Among the books he lists in paragraph 9, Achebe includes one of his own, *Things
   Fall Apart*. Achebe took the title from a line in a poem by the Irish poet W. B. Yeats.
   Explain the significance of this.
6. Read paragraph 10 carefully, noting that it is one sentence. What statement does
   Achebe make there about the "derogatory narrative"? Paraphrase his thesis.

---

[5]Hammond and Jablow, p. 20.
[6]Joseph Conrad, *Heart of Darkness* (New York: W. W. Norton, 1988), p. 37.

8. *Christiansted: Official Map and Guide*

NATIONAL PARK SERVICE

The following U.S. National Park Service travel brochure for tourists in St. Croix, Virgin Islands, discusses the history of the island's capital, Christiansted.

Denmark was a latecomer in the race for colonies in the New World. Columbus' voyages to the Caribbean gave Spain a monopoly in the region for well over a century. But after the English planted a colony in the Lesser Antilles in 1624, the French, the Dutch, and eventually Danes joined the scramble for empire. Seeking islands on which to cultivate sugar as well as an outlet for trade, the Danish West India & Guinea Company (a group of nobles and merchants chartered by the Crown) took possession of St. Thomas in 1672 and its neighbor St. John in 1717. Because neither island was well suited to agriculture, the company in 1733 purchased St. Croix—a larger, flatter, and more fertile island, 40 miles south—from France. Colonization of St. Croix began the next year, after troops put down a slave revolt on St. John.

For their first settlement, the Danes chose a good harbor on the northeast coast, the site of an earlier French village named Bassin. Their leader Frederick Moth was a man of some vision. Among his accomplishments were a plan for a new town, which he named Christiansted in honor of the reigning monarch, King Christian VI, and a survey of the island into plantations of 150 acres, which were offered at bargain prices to new settlers. The best land came under cultivation and dozens of sugar factories began operating. Population approached 10,000, of which nearly 9,000 were slaves imported from West Africa to work in the fields.

Even with this growth St. Croix's economy did not flourish. The planters chaffed under the restrictive trading practices of the DWI&G Company. This monopoly so burdened planters with regulations that they persuaded the king to take over the islands in 1755. Crown administration coincided with the beginning of a long period of growth for the cane sugar industry. St. Croix became the capital of the "Danish Islands of America," as they were then called, and royal governors took up residence in Christiansted. For the next century and a half, the town's fortunes were tied to St. Croix's sugar industry. Between 1760 and 1820 the economy boomed. Population rose dramatically, in part because free-trade policies and neutrality attracted settlers from other islands—hence the prevalence of English culture on this Danish island with a French name—and exports of sugar and rum soared. Capital was available, sugar prices were high, labor cheap. Planters, merchants, and traders—most of them—reaped great profits, which were reflected in the fine architecture of town and country. This golden age was, within a few decades, eclipsed by the rise of the beet sugar industry in Europe and North America. A drop in the price of cane sugar, an increase in planters' debts, drought, hurricanes, and the rising cost of labor after slavery was abolished in 1848 all

Christiansted

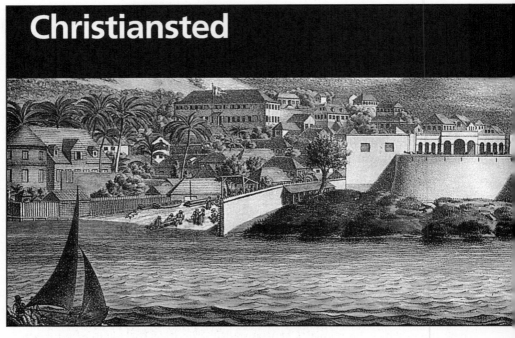

(See insert for color version.)

contributed to economic decline. As the 19th century wore on, St. Croix became little more than a marginal sugar producer, her era of fabulous wealth now a thing of the past. When the United States purchased the Danish West Indies in 1917, it was for the islands' strategic harbors, not their agriculture. The lovely town of Christiansted is a link to the old way of life here, with all its elegance, complexity, and contradiction.

Questions

1. The second paragraph concludes, "Population approached 10,000, of which nearly 9,000 were slaves imported from West Africa to work in the fields." Consider the diction in that sentence. What is the effect of the word *imported*? What is the effect of calling those 9,000 people *slaves* rather than "people who had been enslaved"?
2. Paragraph 3 describes St. Croix as a "Danish island with a French name." Find out about St. Croix, noting its distance from France and Denmark. What was it about this island that attracted the interest of the French and the Danes?
3. Look carefully at the portrait of Christiansted by the Danish artist Theodore C. Sabroe. What is the effect of the painting's pastoral and idyllic images?

**Christiansted National Historic Site
St. Croix, Virgin Islands**

**National Park Service
U.S. Department of the Interior**

4. Are there unintended ironies in the brochure? Identify any that you can find. What does the text reveal about the attitude and purpose of the government department that generated the brochure?

Making Connections

1. In "Shooting an Elephant," George Orwell observes, "In a job like that you see the dirty work of Empire at close quarters. The wretched prisoners huddling in the stinking cages of the lock-ups, the grey, cowed faces of the long-term convicts, the scarred buttocks of the men who had been flogged with bamboos—all these oppressed me with an intolerable sense of guilt" (para. 2). In "The Wretched of the Earth," Frantz Fanon writes, "When you examine at close quarters the colonial context, it is evident that what parcels out the world is to begin with the fact of belonging to or not belonging to a given race, a given species" (para. 4). A reader cannot help noticing these writers' common subject and even common language. Compare the ways that Orwell and Fanon respond to the wretched of the earth seen at close quarters.

2. You have read Red Jacket's defense of Native American religion in his response to a Boston missionary society. Imagine what Red Jacket's response might have been to King Ferdinand's letter if it had been addressed to him. Write a paragraph of Red Jacket's likely response.

3. A writer's diction can reveal a great deal about his or her perspective and attitude toward the subject. Consider the way that four writers in the Conversation — Christopher Columbus, King Ferdinand, Eavan Boland, and the author of the Christiansted tourist brochure — use the word *possession*. For each of the four selections, explain what the word means in context and how it reveals the author's attitudes. Then, recognizing the vast differences in periods represented, discuss the similarities among the four.

4. Imagine that George Orwell, Chinua Achebe, Eavan Boland, or Frantz Fanon were to visit the Virgin Islands and come upon the Christiansted tourist brochure. How might each writer react? How might each one respond? In the voice of one of them, write a brief letter to the U.S. Department of the Interior, explaining the writer's view regarding the brochure.

5. Achebe's essay concludes with the words of Marlow, the narrator of Joseph Conrad's famous novel, *Heart of Darkness*: "Well, you know, that was the worst of it — this suspicion of their not being inhuman." Which selections in the Conversation address this "suspicion"? Explain how they do so.

Entering the Conversation

As you respond to the following prompts, support your argument with references to the sources in this Conversation on colonialism. For help using sources, see Chapter 4.

1. Assume you want to teach an audience of middle school students about colonialism. In words and sentences middle school students can understand, explain what colonialism is, and discuss its effects in the modern world. Consider the effects on the governing nations and on the people living in the colonies. Use your knowledge of history and current events, and refer to at least two texts in this Conversation on colonialism.

2. What factual information could someone glean about colonialism from the texts in this chapter? Refer to all of the sources as you enumerate the facts.

3. Write an essay in which you discuss the individual's struggle against the power of the colonizer.

4. Dwight David Eisenhower, president of the United States from 1953 to 1961, once said, "We are so proud of our guarantees of freedom in thought and

speech and worship, that, unconsciously, we are guilty of one of the greatest errors that ignorance can make—we assume our standard of values is shared by all other humans in the world." Write an essay that evaluates the truth of this statement. For evidence to support your position, refer specifically to the selections in the Conversation.

5. George Orwell says of the imperialist, "He wears a mask, and his face grows to fit it" (para. 7). Write an essay exploring the implications of this statement.

6. Having read the modern selections by George Orwell, Frantz Fanon, Eavan Boland, the U.S. Department of the Interior, and Chinua Achebe, consider the perspectives presented in the older selections from Christopher Columbus, King Ferdinand, and Red Jacket. Examine the extent to which issues and attitudes from these older pieces are still relevant in the modern pieces and in the world today.

Student Writing

Synthesis: Responding to a Quotation

The following prompt invites the student to enter this chapter's Conversation.

> In "Shooting an Elephant" (p. 1100), George Orwell observes that "when the white man turns tyrant it is his own freedom that he destroys," and that this man "wears a mask, and his face grows to fit it." Consider the implications of Orwell's observations about human nature in political situations. Then write an essay in which you defend, challenge, or qualify the paradoxes that Orwell presents. To support your argument, refer to the selections in this chapter as well as to your knowledge of history and current events.

Consider this essay by Sarah Berlinger, an eleventh-grade student, and analyze the rhetorical strategies that she employs.

The Paradox of Power

Sarah Berlinger

The archetypal tyrant rules his empire from behind the closed walls of a sumptuous palace, meting out unilateral pronouncements with a heavy, jewel-encrusted hand. Yet beneath the gaudy façade, the expectations of his people and the reputation he must uphold shackle him to conformity. In his 1936 essay "Shooting an Elephant," George Orwell articulates this paradox: "When the white man turns tyrant it is his own freedom that he destroys. . . . He wears a mask, and his face grows to fit it." As a policeman in Burma, Orwell was the closest link that the townspeople had to an authority figure. As a result, they brought him under their will and expected him to ward off any dangers. An elephant once threatened the safety of the village. The townspeople wanted Orwell to kill the elephant — against his own wishes. In reality, the powerful and absolute possess the least amount of control, as they have no choice but to do everything possible to hold on to their dominion; ultimately, the authority lies in the calloused hands of the common man.

Imperialism counterintuitively empowers the oppressed; in the end, the people emerge victorious, while the imperialists remain trapped by their follies. The definition of tyranny can extend to any situation in which one government controls a separate people. In this sense, imperialism and tyranny are synonymous — yet by overpowering another group, tyrants unwittingly surrender their freedom, bound to their role as oppressor, much as their new subjects are bound to them. The most familiar example of the imperialistic paradox within our own history can be found in the American Revolution. The Stamp Act was the tipping point in the colonists' tolerance of British rule. After this, organized resistance movements sprang up and gained both support and momentum. The subjugated retain the power of rebellion, masters of their own future, whereas those in charge have no choice but to fruitlessly follow the mission to which they have condemned themselves — or risk losing face. King George III had no option but to retaliate against his subjects, which served only to further fuel their fury. His reputation and the expectations of his subjects forced the king to reject the Olive Branch Petition, the colonists' last attempt for a peaceful resolution. Too deeply involved, the king had to barrel blindly along his one-way path, dooming himself and his country to failure. Imperialism binds oppressors to precedent and conformity much more tightly than rulers can bind their subjects to them.

Similarly, when a government professes its complete superiority, the regime goads the rest of the world to prove it wrong; often, the world does just that. King Ferdinand of Spain sent a letter with the conquistadors on their voyages to the New World. The king demanded that the natives "acknowledge the Church as the ruler and superior of the whole world." He warned that if they

> do not do this and maliciously make delay in it, I certify to you that, with the help of God, we shall powerfully enter into your country, and shall make war against you in all ways and manners that we can, and shall subject you to the yoke and obedience of the Church and of their highnesses; we shall take you, and your wives, and your children, and shall make slaves of them.

The list of enumerable threats incited the natives to resist. Upon their arrival, however, the Spanish were forced to carry out what they had promised. Yet, as history can attest, the Spanish no longer control the Carribean, nor any other former colonies in Central and South America. Political might engenders greed and corruption, yet it also encourages the common man to rebel — when he does so, he dooms the tyrant's rule: the determination of many usually overpowers the greed of a few.

In contrast to an imperialistic society, only in a governmental system where a Big Brother authority is absent does Orwell's power paradox fade into the background:

5

a government President Abraham Lincoln proclaimed in the Gettysburg Address as a "government of the people, by the people" that "shall not perish from this earth." Henry David Thoreau, an American author and philosopher, states in "On the Duty of Civil Disobedience" that a government "is only the mode which the people have chosen to execute their will." People, however, can corrupt and be corrupted. The government itself "is equally liable to be abused and perverted before the people can act through it." Act they will, though, for as Thoreau observed during the Mexican-American War, "the people would not have consented to this measure." For this reason, in order to hinder a power-hungry tyrant from taking over, it is advantageous to weaken a government's authority from the beginning by placing the might in the hands of the many, instead of entrusting it to the whims of a few. In this way, one person cannot subsume all the power, tethering himself to his own precarious might. As Thoreau proclaims, "That government is best which governs least. . . . For government is an expedient by which men would fain succeed in letting one another alone; and . . . when it is most expedient, the governed are most let alone by it." This form of authority ensures that Orwell's political paradoxes — the inseparable relationship between power and weakness — cannot develop to stifle the advancement of individual societies.

However, despite all these preventative measures that attempt to thwart a political power imbalance, when one country declares war on another, Orwell's paradox eventually surfaces. Countries enter war for a variety of reasons. Often, however, they do so out of self-interest: territorial expansion, monetary gain, or trade development and protection. In short, greed — however nobly disguised — usually prompts war. In much the same way that imperialism represses the independence of colonists, an entire country loses its freedom when it enters into combat. This is because in a war, countries become tyrants, concentrating power in the hands of the few — the government — and restricting it from the many — the world. Even though a country may dominate the globe, its strength impedes the freedom of its citizens. John Adams's Alien and Sedition Acts, the 1917 Espionage Act, and the 1944 Supreme Court decision *Korematsu v. United States* all proclaimed that in times of war the government could limit the average citizen's civil liberties, overriding existing democratic principles. Moreover, even though the country has dominance, and a person within it retains the ability to choose, the impetus of going to war binds many emotionally and physically. Tim O'Brien wrote about such a situation in *The Things They Carried*, a fictionalized account of his own experiences in Vietnam. In one scene, O'Brien receives a draft notice during the Vietnam War era; morally lost and confused, he runs away toward the Canadian border. O'Brien laments: "All those eyes on me — the town, the whole universe — and I couldn't risk the embarrassment. . . . I couldn't endure the mockery, or the disgrace, or the patriotic ridicule." Because of this he "submitted. . . . [He] would go to the war — [he] would kill and maybe die — because [he] was embarrassed not to." Even though he was less than twenty yards from freedom and the border, O'Brien could not leave because the force of war held him in place. War suppresses the freedom of the nation and its citizens, rather than expanding it.

Furthermore, governments and their people each wear Orwell's "mask" during times of war. Armed conflict, both a by-product and a cause of Orwell's paradox, causes a state to "[seek] to destroy its own culture." This idea is mirrored in "The Destruction of Culture," in *War Is a Force That Gives Us Meaning*, written by Chris Hedges, a contemporary American writer and war correspondent specializing in the socio-political environments of the United States and the Middle East. Hedges explains that "only when this destruction has been completed" can the government "begin to exterminate the culture of its opponents." The regime destroys "authentic culture — that which allows us to question and examine ourselves and our society" — and replaces it "with a warped version of reality" where "[t]he enemy is dehumanized" and "[a]ll is dedicated to promoting and glorifying the myth, the nation, the cause." These myths cause us to "doubt our own perceptions." The "mask" then arises: people are transformed into what the government wants them to resemble and to think. Hedges points out the horrific results of this practice: "[w]hen the visible and tangible symbols of one's past are destroyed or denied, the past can be recreated to fit the myth." In wartime, all forms of government brainwash their respective citizens into believing the "mask" and "myth" that will further promote the war — and the unilateral desires of the country. Hedges describes how on a trip to a war museum in Vienna, he couldn't find a single room dedicated to World War II. Asking around, he discovered that in Austria World War II might as well have not existed — the "mask" of society had wiped the war from the collective consciousness of the country's citizenry. History itself has disparate interpretations based on which side of the war a country has pledged its allegiance. One Serbian textbook describes Gavrilo Princip, a Bosnian Serb who assassinated Archduke Franz Ferdinand, as a "hero and a poet." A Croatian textbook, however, castigates him as an "assassin trained and instructed by the Serbs to commit this act of terrorism," whose actions sparked the onset of World War I. Similarly, Jamaica Kincaid reflects Hedges's and Orwell's ideas in "On Seeing England for the First Time," an essay in which she examines her life growing up in colonized British Antigua. Kincaid comments that colonization, in some cases, is a result of war. As such, she had "long ago been conquered" — forced to believe in England's superiority, and her inferiority, because she "was not from it." Her whole country wore a "mask," throwing away their culture, cloaking themselves in all things "Made in England." These "masks" divide the world across wartime alliance lines, cementing the hatreds of opposing sides during times of peace and colonization. The antagonistic views that arise irrevocably alter the entire globe's history, with no two groups agreeing on the same series of events. History, one of the only definite aspects of time on this planet, is rendered indefinable and inconstant because of this process, rewritten to fit the needs of each society. Whole communities wear a "mask," wishing to conform to the "myths" of their country preceding, during, and following times of war. Orwell's lens redefines power as a distortion of truth.

Excessive power consumption makes a person — or a government — considerably weakened and restricted; might and politics are extremely corrosive to the freedom and advancement of society. In times of war, all governments descend into tyranny and wear respective Orwellian "masks." These render a united community shattered. This social phenomenon holds true in contemporary times. A vast number of Americans view the U.S. occupation of Iraq in a positive light, thinking themselves liberators of the Iraqi people and crusaders of democracy. However, the majority of Iraqis think of Americans not as liberators, but as oppressors. Similarly, Libyan dictator Muammar el Qaddafi imposed a brutal regime on his people for forty-two years. Eventually, his subjects revolted against him. They gained both national and international support: world leaders across the globe called for Qaddafi's resignation. Nevertheless, the Libyan leader stubbornly and fruitlessly clung to his power, in the same restrictive way that his power clung to him, binding him to his demise. Our world is drunk on and dripping in power. Even in the alleged democratic nations, democracy has transformed into something ostensible: existing governmental regimes endanger and circumvent core principles of egalitarianism; economic collapse threatens the global markets; citizen unrest is both pervasive and destabilizing. The current fragile state of the world is a result of an unequal distribution of power and is a plea for greater transparency, truth, change, and equality in government and politics. Ironically, only the common man, whose vision remains unobstructed by tyrannical tendencies, can break this cycle of degeneracy and distorted reality that increasingly characterizes the world today.

Questions

1. What is Sarah's central position in this essay? Paraphrase her thesis in a sentence or two.
2. How does she establish ethos?
3. Discuss two appeals to pathos and two to logos in the essay. How do these appeals contribute to the effectiveness of the essay?
4. Identify and explain the effects of five rhetorical strategies in this student essay, including allusion, organization, vivid imagery, and figurative language.
5. Discuss Sarah's use of sources. Does she use them effectively? Would using fewer have weakened or strengthened her argument? Explain your response.
6. Sarah supplements her essay with historical information drawn from outside the sources. How effectively does this information support her position and contribute to the essay as a whole?
7. If you were Sarah's editor, what might you suggest for revision? Would you have any suggestions regarding organization? Would you ask her to develop any points further? Would you suggest cutting anything from the essay so as to shorten it? Explain your suggestions with specific reference to the text of the essay.

Grammar as Rhetoric and Style
Subordination in the Complex Sentence

One way that writers build longer sentences that are logical and clear is through subordination. **Subordination** is the use of a subordinating conjunction to make the meaning of one clause dependent on another clause. Although there are different types of subordination, involving both clauses and phrases, we are focusing here on the **complex sentence** — that is, a sentence formed by an **independent clause** and a **dependent clause** that begins with a subordinating conjunction.

Just because a clause is subordinate does not mean that what it says is unimportant. The ideas in both clauses contribute to the meaning of the sentence. It is the job of subordination to tell us how those ideas are related. This ability to connect ideas is the reason subordination is so effective; by using *because*, you tell your reader that one thing causes another; by using *when*, you indicate that two things are related chronologically. Thus, you can show the logical relationships in a rather lengthy sentence so that the length in no way impedes clarity.

Note the relationship between the dependent and independent clauses in the following sentence:

> When a nimble Burman tripped me up on the football field and the referee (another Burman) looked the other way, the crowd yelled with hideous laughter.
>
> — George Orwell

In this example, Orwell uses the subordinate clause to establish the chronology of events that lead to the main action of the sentence — that is, his being laughed at by the crowd.

Subordinating conjunctions can be classified by the relationships they indicate:

Contrast or Concession: although, even though, though, while, whereas

> Although the book was not entirely free of the stereotypes of contemporary British colonial writing, it was in some ways remarkably advanced for its time . . .
>
> — Chinua Achebe

Cause and Effect or Reason: because, since, so that

> Because neither island was well suited to agriculture, the company in 1733 purchased St. Croix — a larger, flatter, and more fertile island, 40 miles south — from France.
>
> — National Park Service

Condition: if, once, unless, should

> If God helps and I get to be released, I hope you accept my invitation to be my guest in the holy city of peace, Jerusalem.
>
> —LAURA BLUMENFELD

Time: when, whenever, after, before, as, once, since, while, until

> When the United States purchased the Danish West Indies in 1917, it was for the islands' strategic harbors, not their agriculture.
>
> —NATIONAL PARK SERVICE

> Until there is a common vocabulary and a shared historical memory there is no peace in any society, only an absence of war.
>
> —CHRIS HEDGES

Punctuation

Correct punctuation adds clarity to longer sentences. The rule of thumb is: use a comma to set off a subordinate clause that opens a sentence unless that sentence is very short. Notice that each of the opening clauses in the preceding examples from Achebe, Blumenfeld, and the National Park Service is set off with a comma. Note that the comma comes not after the subordinating conjunction but after the entire clause. If you read the examples aloud, you'll probably find yourself naturally pausing at the end of the subordinate clause. Of course, these rules are not rigid; they are matters of style. Notice that Chris Hedges in the last example above has decided not to interrupt the rhythm of the sentence with the pause of a comma.

When the subordinate clause follows the independent clause, it gets a little trickier. Most of the time there is no comma at all because the dependent clause is necessary to the meaning of the sentence; this is called a *restrictive clause*. The sentence you just read is an example: the clause "because the dependent clause is necessary . . ." is essential to the meaning of the sentence. In some cases, however, the dependent clause adds information but is not necessary to the meaning of the sentence. For example:

> It is left only to those on the margins to keep the flame of introspection alive, although the destruction of culture is often so great that full recovery is impossible.
>
> —CHRIS HEDGES

Here the subordinate clause is not essential to the meaning of the sentence, so it is set off with a comma; this is called a *nonrestrictive clause*. This all may sound a bit familiar to you. You may remember that in the discussion of appositives in Chapter 5 (p. 269) we also talked about using commas with essential and non-essential elements. Here the rule is the same: essential information must be included and thus should not be set off with a comma; non-essential information that can be excluded should be set off with a comma.

Keep in mind that a dependent clause cannot stand alone. When you're using a dependent clause, be careful not to end up with a *sentence fragment*—that is, a dependent clause followed by a period. To correct a sentence fragment, simply attach it to the independent clause.

Rhetorical and Stylistic Strategy

One strategy is to use subordination to blend short sentences into more graceful, longer sentences. Consider the following two sentences:

> It was still August. The air already had the smell of October, football season, piles of yellow-red leaves, everything crisp and clean.

Both are complete sentences. As readers, we understand them easily. The relationship between the two is temporal. But consider the difference with the addition of a subordinating conjunction:

> Though it was still August, the air already had the smell of October, football season, piles of yellow-red leaves, everything crisp and clean.
>
> —TIM O'BRIEN

Here the conjunction *though* indicates a contrast between the summer months and the smell of the air. Combining the two short sentences does not make the resulting sentence more difficult to understand; on the contrary, the longer sentence is easier to understand because it leaves nothing to chance.

A writer has to determine which clause should be dependent and which should be independent in a complex sentence. Although one clause is just as important as the other, the independent clause usually carries the most force, so you should put the idea you want to emphasize in an independent clause. Sometimes, the choice is obvious because the relationship is chronological or cause and effect, but other times either clause could be independent. Consider the following example:

> Although my classmates and I would not have known it at the time, the London publishing house of Methuen had brought out the year before, in 1951, a little book titled simply *West Africa*.
>
> —CHINUA ACHEBE

What would the difference in effect have been if Achebe had written the following?

> Although the London publishing house of Methuen had brought out the year before, in 1951, a little book titled simply *West Africa*, my classmates and I would not have known it at the time.

Both examples indicate that the relationship between the two clauses is one of contrast. But the second example puts the emphasis on Achebe and his classmates when, in fact, the publication of *West Africa* is the main event in the sentence and deserves more emphasis; the publication of the book affected Achebe and his friends, not vice versa.

Where to place the subordinate clause is another choice a writer must make. For instance, examine once again the dependent clause in the following example:

> Though it was still August, the air already had the smell of October, football season, piles of yellow-red leaves, everything crisp and clean.
>
> —TIM O'BRIEN

The dependent clause ("Though it was still August") could have been put at the end of the sentence or even in the middle. Why do you think O'Brien placed it at the beginning? Perhaps placing the dependent clause in the middle of all those descriptive phrases would have muddled the sentence, making it difficult to decipher. As for putting it at the end, consider this example:

> The air already had the smell of October, football season, piles of yellow-red leaves, everything crisp and clean, though it was still August.

The effect is different. In the original sentence, O'Brien signals at the outset that something is unusual: "Though it was still August." However, if this clause appears at the end of the sentence, it gets buried. By the time we've read about the smell of things associated with autumn, the fact that "it was still August" seems beside the point.

• EXERCISE 1 •

Combine each of the following pairs of sentences into one sentence, using subordination. You might shift the order of the sentences, and in some cases you may have to change the wording slightly. Be sure to punctuate correctly.

1. The investigators have gathered and analyzed all the evidence. We may expect a full report.
2. Tom had listened to the music of Bruce Springsteen for years. He had no idea a live performance could be so exciting.
3. The team has suffered its share of injuries this year. It could have improved its performance by giving Flynn more time on the field.
4. We will not be able to resolve this situation amicably. We must be willing to leave our prejudices at the door.
5. The crime rate has escalated near the mall. Many people have stopped shopping at the mall.

6. Rose Henderson has the qualifications to become a first-rate senator. Most of us knew she did not have a good chance to be elected. We worked hard on her campaign.

7. Lan Cao is a law professor at the College of William and Mary. She is also the author of the novel *Monkey Bridge.*

8. I'm not feeling well today. I plan to leave the office early.

9. Apple offered a free iPod with every MacBook. Sales of the MacBook improved dramatically.

10. The affluent population of Dallas, Texas, is increasing steadily. Housing prices are rising beyond what someone with a middle-class salary can afford.

11. We all realize the necessity for increased security. We need to protect our civil liberties.

12. Thousands of vacationers travel to our national parks in search of solitude and fresh air. Other people prefer the excitement of casinos and amusement parks.

• EXERCISE 2 •

Identify each subordinate clause in the following sentences, and explain its effect. All are direct quotations from the readings in this chapter.

1. When I saw England for the first time, I was a child in school sitting at a desk. —JAMAICA KINCAID

2. If now as I speak of all this I give the impression of someone on the outside looking in, nose pressed up against a glass window, that is wrong. —JAMAICA KINCAID

3. Although the old man never confronted me about it, there was one occasion when he came close to forcing the whole thing out into the open. —TIM O'BRIEN

4. Once people are dead, you can't make them undead. —TIM O'BRIEN

5. If he charged, I could shoot; if he took no notice of me, it would be safe to leave him until the mahout came back. —GEORGE ORWELL

6. I perceived in this moment that when the white man turns tyrant it is his own freedom that he destroys. —GEORGE ORWELL

7. As the 19th century wore on, St. Croix became little more than a marginal sugar producer . . . —NATIONAL PARK SERVICE

8. It is true, for there is no native who does not dream at least once a day of setting himself up in the settler's place. —FRANTZ FANON

9. If I have unjustly wrestled a plank from a drowning man, I must restore it to him though I drown myself. —HENRY DAVID THOREAU

10. A minority is powerless while it conforms to the majority.
—HENRY DAVID THOREAU

11. There will never be a really free and enlightened State, until the State comes to recognize the individual as a higher and independent power, from which all its own power and authority are derived, and treats him accordingly. —HENRY DAVID THOREAU

• EXERCISE 3 •

Analyze the use of subordinate clauses in the following passages. Pay particular attention to how the writer varies sentence patterns.

1. I suppose we can all differ as to the exact point where good writing becomes overwhelmed by racial cliché. But overwhelmed or undermined, literature is always badly served when an author's artistic insight yields place to stereotype and malice. And it becomes doubly offensive when such a work is arrogantly proffered to you as your story. Some people may wonder if, perhaps, we were not too touchy, if we were not oversensitive. We really were not. And I have a somewhat unusual reason for saying so. —CHINUA ACHEBE

2. All this was perplexing and upsetting. For at that time I had already made up my mind that imperialism was an evil thing and the sooner I chucked up my job and got out of it the better. Theoretically—and secretly, of course—I was all for the Burmese and all against their oppressors, the British. . . . Feelings like these are the normal by-products of imperialism; ask any Anglo-Indian official, if you can catch him off duty. . . .

   Afterwards, of course, there were endless discussions about the shooting of the elephant. The owner was furious, but he was only an Indian and could do nothing. Besides, legally I had done the right thing, for a mad elephant has to be killed, like a mad dog, if its owner fails to control it. Among the Europeans opinion was divided. The older men said I was right, the younger men said it was a damn shame to shoot an elephant for killing a coolie, because an elephant was worth more than any damn Coringhee coolie. And afterwards I was very glad that the coolie had been killed; it put me legally in the right and it gave me a sufficient pretext for shooting the elephant. I often wondered whether any of the others grasped that I had done it solely to avoid looking a fool.
—GEORGE ORWELL

3. In wartime the state seeks to destroy its own culture. It is only when this destruction has been completed that the state can begin to exterminate

the culture of its opponents. In times of conflict authentic culture is subversive. As the cause championed by the state comes to define national identity, as the myth of war entices a nation to glory and sacrifice, those who question the value of the cause and the veracity of the myths are branded internal enemies. —CHRIS HEDGES

4. A minority is powerless while it conforms to the majority; it is not even a minority then; but it is irresistible when it clogs by its whole weight. If the alternative is to keep all just men in prison, or give up war and slavery, the State will not hesitate which to choose. If a thousand men were not to pay their tax-bills this year, that would not be a violent and bloody measure, as it would be to pay them, and enable the State to commit violence and shed innocent blood. This is, in fact, the definition of a peaceable revolution, if any such is possible. If the tax-gatherer, or any other public officer, asks me, as one has done, "But what shall I do?" my answer is, "If you really wish to do anything, resign your office." When the subject has refused allegiance and the officer has resigned his office, then the revolution is accomplished.

—HENRY DAVID THOREAU

• **EXERCISE 4** •

In a national magazine that features writing on cultural and political subjects, find a passage that is effective in its use of subordination. Discuss how each subordinate clause works to support the speaker's rhetorical purpose.

Suggestions for Writing

Politics

Now that you have examined a number of texts that focus on politics, explore one dimension of this topic by synthesizing your own ideas and the readings. You might want to do more research or use readings from other classes as you discuss and prepare for the following projects.

1. Read the following section from a translation of an ancient text, the *Tao Te Ching* by Lao-tzu, a Chinese philosopher who lived in the sixth century B.C. Then write an essay in which you support or refute Lao-tzu's claims about political leadership. Use your knowledge of history and current events, and refer to the texts in this chapter to support your argument.

When the Master governs, the people
are hardly aware that he exists.
Next best is a leader who is loved.
Next, one who is feared.
The worst is one who is despised.

If you don't trust the people,
you make them untrustworthy.

The Master doesn't talk, he acts.
When his work is done,
the people say, "Amazing:
we did it, all by ourselves!"

2. Henry David Thoreau's objections to slavery and to what he saw as unjustified war prompted the writing of the essay "On the Duty of Civil Disobedience" (p. 1016), which strongly influenced both Gandhi and Martin Luther King Jr. as they opposed injustice. In "On the Rainy River" (p. 1074), Tim O'Brien considers civil disobedience as a response to what he also considers an unjust war. Reflect on the state of our society today, and write an essay in which you apply Thoreau's ideas to our time. Is civil disobedience an appropriate response to perceived injustice today? Why or why not?

3. Assuming the voice of one of the contemporary writers in this chapter, or in your own informed voice, write a letter to one of the earlier writers (for example, Red Jacket, Henry David Thoreau, Abraham Lincoln, Virginia Woolf) about political issues. In your letter, refer to current political problems that would interest the earlier writer. Your letter may take the form of a request for information or guidance, a complaint or polemic defending or challenging the writer's views, or a complimentary letter telling the writer how prescient he or she was.

4. In paragraph 3 of "Shooting an Elephant" (p. 1101), George Orwell says that the incident of shooting the elephant "in a roundabout way was enlightening. It was a tiny incident in itself, but it gave me a better glimpse than I had had before of the real nature of imperialism—the real motives for which despotic governments act." He implies that governments act from the same petty impulses that drive human beings in response to pressures. Write an essay in which you support, refute, or qualify Orwell's position concerning despotic governments. Use evidence from your knowledge of history and from other readings in this chapter to support your position.

5. Consider the importance of appealing to ethos in political writing. To take four examples, Virginia Woolf, Chris Hedges, Laura Blumenfeld, and Tim O'Brien all write from personal experience. How important is that experience

to the relationships established among the speaker, the text, and the reader, as illustrated by Aristotle's rhetorical triangle? Would ethos be equally served if these four writers had not personally experienced what they report but instead had based their writings on research or on the accounts of others? Referring to at least two of the texts, write an argument about the importance of personal experience as support for an argument.

6. Write a thoughtful essay on the relationship between the citizen and the state in our time. Refer to at least three of the texts in this chapter to support your position.

7. About the legacy of George Orwell, political commentator Christopher Hitchens writes:

> His importance to the century just past, and therefore his status as a figure in history as well as literature, derives from the extraordinary salience of the subjects he "took on," and stayed with, and never abandoned. As a consequence, we commonly use the term "Orwellian" in one of two ways. To describe a state of affairs as "Orwellian" is to imply crushing tyranny and fear and conformism. To describe a piece of writing as "Orwellian" is to recognize that human resistance to these terrors is unquenchable.

Write an essay in which you apply Hitchens's second definition of *Orwellian* to "Shooting an Elephant" and to at least two other texts in this chapter.

8. From one of the texts in the chapter (a piece by Kincaid, Thoreau, Blumenfeld, Vowell, O'Brien, or Orwell, for instance), select a narrative section. Then create a graphic novelization of the events in the passage you select, writing captions and dialogue to accompany the illustrations.

9. Compare Kincaid's characterization of Christopher Columbus in "On Seeing England for the First Time" (para. 10) with the Christopher Columbus revealed in his letter to the Spanish monarchy.

10. This chapter, which includes an image of *Guernica* along with the magazine covers from *Harper's* and the *New Yorker*, "The Veil" from *Persepolis*, and the Christiansted travel brochure, is particularly rich in visual material. Write an essay that explains how the visual texts have helped you to gain an understanding of political issues raised in this chapter. Refer to at least three of the visual selections as well as to other texts in the chapter.

11. Go online and watch the TED Talk by Nigerian writer Chimamanda Adiche called "The Danger of a Single Story." Then write an essay about the danger of the "single story" as Adiche characterizes it. In your essay, refer to several of the pieces in this chapter for support and illustration.

12. Each of the following statements addresses the nature of politics. Select one that interests you, and write an essay defending or challenging its assertion.

To support your argument, refer to your knowledge of history and to the selections in this chapter.

> No cause is left but the most ancient of all, the one, in fact, that from the beginning of our history has determined the very existence of politics, the cause of freedom versus tyranny. —HANNAH ARENDT

> We are not afraid to entrust the American people with unpleasant facts, foreign ideas, alien philosophies, and competitive values. For a nation that is afraid to let its people judge the truth and falsehood in an open market is a nation that is afraid of its people. —JOHN F. KENNEDY

> In our age there is no such thing as "keeping out of politics." All issues are political issues, and politics itself is a mass of lies, evasions, folly, hatred and schizophrenia. —GEORGE ORWELL

> Injustice anywhere is a threat to justice everywhere. —MARTIN LUTHER KING JR.

> Nobody made a greater mistake than he who did nothing because he could do only a little. —EDMUND BURKE

> Do not put such unlimited power into the hands of husbands. Remember all men would be tyrants if they could. —ABIGAIL ADAMS

> What we think, or what we know, or what we believe is, in the end, of little consequence. The only consequence is what we do. —JOHN RUSKIN

> If we are to survive, we are to have ideas, vision, and courage. These things are rarely produced by communities. Everything that matters in our intellectual and moral life begins with an individual confronting his own mind and conscience in a room by himself. —ARTHUR SCHLESINGER JR.

MLA Guidelines for a List of Works Cited

Print Resources

1. A Book with One Author

A book with one author serves as a general model for most MLA citations. Include author, title, city of publication, publisher, date of publication, and medium.

> Beavan, Colin. *No Impact Man*. New York: Farrar, 2009. Print.

2. A Book with Multiple Authors

> Kasarda, John D., and Greg Lindsay. *Aerotropolis: The Way We'll Live Next*. New York: Farrar, 2011. Print.

3. Two or More Works by the Same Author

Multiple entries should be arranged alphabetically by title. The author's name appears at the beginning of the first entry but is replaced by three hyphens and a period in all subsequent entries.

> Gladwell, Malcolm. *Outliers: The Story of Success*. New York: Little, Brown, 2008. Print.

> ---. *What the Dog Saw, and Other Adventures*. New York: Little, Brown, 2009. Print.

4. Author and Editor Both Named

> Vidal, Gore. *The Selected Essays of Gore Vidal*. Ed. Jay Parini. New York: Vintage, 2009. Print.

Alternatively, to cite the editor's contribution, start with the editor's name.

> Parini, Jay, ed. *The Selected Essays of Gore Vidal*. By Gore Vidal. New York: Vintage, 2009. Print.

5. Anthology

> Oates, Joyce Carol, ed. *Telling Stories: An Anthology for Writers*. New York: Norton, 1997. Print.

6. Translation

> Wiesel, Elie. *Night*. Trans. Marion Wiesel. New York: Hill-Farrar, 2006. Print.

7. Entry in a Reference Work

Because most reference works are alphabetized, you should omit page numbers.

> Lounsberry, Barbara. "Joan Didion." *Encyclopedia of the Essay*. Ed. Tracy Chandler. Chicago: Fitzroy Dearborn, 1997. Print.

For a well-known encyclopedia, use only the edition and year of publication. When an article is not attributed to an author, begin the entry with the article title.

> "Gilgamesh." *The Columbia Encyclopedia*. 5th ed. 1993. Print.

8. Sacred Text

Unless a specific published edition is being cited, sacred texts should be omitted from the Works Cited list.

> *The New Testament*. Trans. Richmond Lattimore. New York: North Point-Farrar, 1997. Print.

9. Article in a Journal

The title of the journal should be followed by the volume, issue, and year of the journal's publication.

> de Botton, Alain. "Treasure Hunt." *Lapham's Quarterly* 4.2 (2011): 205–10. Print.

10. Article in a Magazine

In a weekly:

> Menand, Louis. "The Unpolitical Animal: How Political Science Understands Voters." *New Yorker* 30 Aug. 2004: 92–96. Print.

In a monthly:

> Baker, Kevin. "Barack Hoover Obama: The Best and the Brightest Blow It Again." *Harper's* July 2009: 29–37. Print.

11. Article in a Newspaper

If you are citing a local paper that does not contain the city name in its title, add the city name in brackets after the title.

> Edge, John T. "Fast Food Even before Fast Food." *New York Times* 30 Sept. 2009, late ed.: D1+. Print.

12. Review

In a weekly:

> Davis, Jordan. "Happy Thoughts!" Rev. of *The Golden Age of Paraphernalia*, by Kevin
>   Davies. *Nation* 23 Feb. 2009: 31–34. Print.

In a monthly:

> Simpson, Mona. "Imperfect Union." Rev. of *Mrs. Woolf and the Servants*, by Alison
>   Light. *Atlantic Monthly* Jan.–Feb. 2009: 93–101. Print.

Electronic Resources

13. Article from a Database Accessed through a Subscription Service

Apply the normal rules for citing a journal article, but follow this with the name
of the subscription service in italics, the medium used, and the date of access.

> Morano, Michele. "Boy Eats World." *Fourth Genre: Explorations in Nonfiction* 13.2
>   (2011): 31–35. *Project MUSE*. Web. 11 Nov. 2011.

14. Article in an Online Magazine

Follow the author name and article title with the name of the magazine in italics,
the organization hosting the Web page (usually found at the very bottom of the
site), the date published, the medium, and the date accessed. If there is no host or
sponsor of the site, write *N.p.*, for "no publisher."

> Yoffe, Emily. "Full Metal Racket: Metal Detecting Is the World's Worst Hobby."
>   *Slate*. Washington Post. Newsweek Interactive, 25 Sept. 2009. Web. 30 Sept.
>   2009.

15. Article in an Online Newspaper

> Sisario, Ben. "Record Stores: Out of Sight, Not Obsolete." *New York Times*. New York
>   Times, 29 Sept. 2009. Web. 30 Sept. 2009.

16. Online Review

> Stevens, Dana. "Catcher in the MRI." Rev. of *50/50*, dir. Adam Levine. *Slate*.
>   Washington Post, 30 Sept. 2011. Web. 8 Oct. 2011.

17. Entry in an Online Reference Work

> "John Ruskin." *Encyclopædia Britannica Online*. Encyclopædia Britannica, 2009.
>   Web. 5 Oct. 2009

18. Work from a Web Site

> "Wallace Stevens (1879–1955)." *Poetryfoundation.org*. Poetry Foundation, 2009. Web. 30 Sept. 2009.

19. Entire Web Site

Web site with editor:

> Dutton, Dennis, ed. *Arts and Letters Daily*. Chronicle of Higher Education, 2009. Web. 2 Oct. 2009.

Web site without editor:

> *Poets.org*. Academy of American Poets, 2009. Web. 2 Oct. 2009.

For a personal Web site, use the following model:

> Mendelson, Edward. Home page. Columbia U, 2009. Web. 2 Oct. 2009.

20. Entire Web Log (Blog)

If there is no host or sponsor of the site, write *N.p.*, for "no publisher."

> Holbo, John, ed. *The Valve*. N.p., 2 Oct. 2009. Web. 2 Oct. 2009.

21. Entry in a Wiki

> "Pre-Raphaelite Brotherhood." *Wikipedia*. Wikimedia Foundation, 1 Oct. 2009. Web. 2 Oct. 2009.

Other

22. Film, Video, or DVD

Follow the title with the director, notable performers, the distribution company, the date of release, and the medium. For films viewed on the Web, follow this with the name of the Web site used to view the film, the medium (*Web*), and the date viewed. If citing the editor's contribution, begin the entry with his or her name before the title.

Viewed in theaters:

> *The Hurt Locker*. Dir. Kathryn Bigelow. Summit, 2009. Film.

Viewed on DVD or videocassette (follow original release date with distributor and release date of DVD or video):

> *Dead Poets Society*. Dir. Peter Weir. Perf. Robin Williams. 1989. Buena Vista Home Entertainment, 2006. DVD.

Viewed on the Web (use original distributor and release date):

> Lynch, David, dir. *The Elephant Man*. Perf. Anthony Hopkins and John Hurt.
> Paramount, 1980. *Netflix*. Web. 2 Oct. 2009.

23. Broadcast Interview

On the radio:

> Gioia, Dana. Interview with Leonard Lopate. *The Leonard Lopate Show*. NPR. WNYC,
> New York, 19 July 2004. Radio.

On the Web:

> Gioia, Dana. Interview with Leonard Lopate. *The Leonard Lopate Show*. *NPR.org*. NPR,
> 19 July 2004. Web. 2 Oct. 2009.

24. Lecture or Speech

Viewed in person:

> Kass, Leon. "Looking for an Honest Man: Reflections of an Unlicensed Humanist."
> Jefferson Lecture in the Humanities. NEH. Warner Theatre, Washington, D.C.
> 22 May 2009. Lecture.

Viewed on the Web:

> Batuman, Elif. Lowell Humanities Series. Boston College. *Boston College Front Row*.
> Trustees of Boston College, 13 Oct. 2010. Web. 2 Oct. 2011.

25. Podcast

> "The Consequences to Come." Moderator Robert Silvers. Participants Darryl Pinckney,
> Ronald Dworkin, Joan Didion, and Mark Danner. *New York Review of Books*.
> NYREV, Inc., 24 Sept. 2008. MP3 File.

26. Work of Art or Photograph

In a museum:

> Hopper, Edward. *Nighthawks*. 1942. Oil on canvas. Art Institute, Chicago.

On the Web:

> Thiebaud, Wayne. *Three Machines*. 1963. De Young Museum, San Francisco. *Famsf.org*.
> Web. 2 Oct. 2009.

In print:

> Clark, Edward. *Navy CPO Graham Jackson Plays "Goin' Home."* 1945. Life Gallery of
> Photography. *The Great LIFE Photographers*. Eds. of *Life*. New York: Bulfinch,
> 2004. 78–79. Print.

27. Map or Chart

In print:

> "U.S. Personal Savings Rate, 1929–1999." Chart. *Credit Card Nation: The Consequences of America's Addiction to Credit*. By Robert D. Manning. New York: Basic, 2000. 100. Print.

On the Web:

> "1914 New Balkan States and Central Europe Map." Map. *National Geographic*. National Geographic Society, 2009. Web. 5 Oct. 2009.

28. Cartoon or Comic Strip

In print:

> Vey, P. C. Cartoon. *New Yorker* 10 Nov. 2008: 54. Print.

On the Web:

> Davis, Jim. "Garfield." Comic strip. *Garfield.com*. Paws, 24 July 2001. Web. 2 Oct. 2009.

29. Advertisement

In print:

> Rosetta Stone. Advertisement. *Harper's* Aug. 2008: 21. Print.

On the Web:

> Zurich. Advertisement. *Wall Street Journal*. Dow Jones, Inc., 2 Oct. 2009. Web. 2 Oct. 2009.

Glossary

ad hominem   Latin for "to the man," this fallacy refers to the specific diversionary tactic of switching the argument from the issue at hand to the character of the other speaker. If you argue that a park in your community should not be renovated because the person supporting it was arrested during a domestic dispute, then you are guilty of *ad hominem.*

ad populum (bandwagon appeal)   This fallacy occurs when evidence boils down to "everybody's doing it, so it must be a good thing to do."

You should vote to elect Rachel Johnson—she has a strong lead in the polls.

Polling higher does not necessarily make Senator Johnson the "best" candidate, only the most popular.

alliteration   Repetition of the same sound beginning several words or syllables in sequence.

[L]et us go forth to lead the land we love . . .

—JOHN F. KENNEDY

allusion   Brief reference to a person, event, or place (real or fictitious) or to a work of art.

Let both sides unite to heed in all corners of the earth the command of Isaiah . . .

—JOHN F. KENNEDY

analogy   A comparison between two seemingly dissimilar things. Often, an analogy uses something simple or familiar to explain something unfamiliar or complex.

As birds have flight, our special gift is reason.

—BILL MCKIBBEN

If I have unjustly wrested a plank from a drowning man, I must restore it to him though I drown myself. . . . But he that would save his life, in such a case, shall lose it. This people must cease to hold slaves and to make war on Mexico, though it cost them their existence as a people.

—HENRY DAVID THOREAU

anaphora   Repetition of a word or phrase at the beginning of successive phrases, clauses, or lines.

> . . . *not as a call to bear arms, though arms we need—not as a call to battle, though embattled we are . . .*
>
> —JOHN F. KENNEDY

anecdote   A brief story used to illustrate a point or claim.

annotation   The taking of notes directly on a text.

antimetabole   Repetition of words in reverse order.

> *[A]sk not what your country can do for you—ask what you can do for your country.*
>
> —JOHN F. KENNEDY

antithesis   Opposition, or contrast, of ideas or words in a parallel construction.

> *[W]e shall . . . support any friend, oppose any foe . . .*
>
> —JOHN F. KENNEDY

appeal to false authority   This fallacy occurs when someone who has no expertise to speak on an issue is cited as an authority. A TV star, for instance, is not a medical expert, though pharmaceutical advertisements often use celebrity endorsements.

> *According to former congressional leader Ari Miller, the Himalayas have an estimated Yeti population of between 300 and 500 individuals.*

archaic diction   Old-fashioned or outdated choice of words.

> . . . *beliefs for which our forebears fought . . .*
>
> —JOHN F. KENNEDY

argument   A process of reasoned inquiry. A persuasive discourse resulting in a coherent and considered movement from a claim to a conclusion.

Aristotelian triangle   See **rhetorical triangle**.

assertion   A statement that presents a claim or thesis.

assumption   See **warrant**.

asyndeton   Omission of conjunctions between coordinate phrases, clauses, or words.

> *[W]e shall pay any price, bear any burden, meet any hardship, support any friend, oppose any foe to assure the survival and the success of liberty.*
>
> —JOHN F. KENNEDY

audience   The listener, viewer, or reader of a text. Most texts are likely to have multiple audiences.

> *Gehrig's audience was his teammates and fans in the stadium that day, but it was also the teams he played against, the fans listening on the radio, and posterity—us.*

backing   In the Toulmin model, backing consists of further assurances or data without which the assumption lacks authority. For an example, see **Toulmin model**.

bandwagon appeal   See *ad populum* **fallacy.**

begging the question   A fallacy in which a claim is based on evidence or support that is in doubt. It "begs" a question whether the support itself is sound.
> *Giving students easy access to a wealth of facts and resources online allows them to develop critical thinking skills.*

circular reasoning   A fallacy in which the argument repeats the claim as a way to provide evidence.
> *You can't give me a C; I'm an A student!*

claim   Also called an assertion or proposition, a claim states the argument's main idea or position. A claim differs from a topic or subject in that a claim has to be arguable.

claim of fact   A claim of fact asserts that something is true or not true.
> *The number of suicides and homicides committed by teenagers, most often young men, has exploded in the last three decades . . .*
> —ANNA QUINDLEN

claim of policy   A claim of policy proposes a change.
> *Yet one solution continues to elude us, and that is ending the ignorance about mental health, and moving it from the margins of care and into the mainstream where it belongs.*
> —ANNA QUINDLEN

claim of value   A claim of value argues that something is good or bad, right or wrong.
> *There's a plague on all our houses, and since it doesn't announce itself with lumps or spots or protest marches, it has gone unremarked in the quiet suburbs and busy cities where it has been laying waste.*
> —ANNA QUINDLEN

classical oration, the   Five-part argument structure used by classical rhetoricians. The five parts are:

> **introduction (*exordium*)**   Introduces the reader to the subject under discussion.

> **narration (*narratio*)**   Provides factual information and background material on the subject at hand or establishes why the subject is a problem that needs addressing.

> **confirmation (*confirmatio*)**   Usually the major part of the text, the confirmation includes the proof needed to make the writer's case.

> **refutation (*refutatio*)**   Addresses the counterargument. It is a bridge between the writer's proof and conclusion.

> **conclusion (*peroratio*)**   Brings the essay to a satisfying close.

closed thesis   A closed thesis is a statement of the main idea of the argument that also previews the major points the writer intends to make.

The three-dimensional characters, exciting plot, and complex themes of the Harry Potter series make them not only legendary children's books but enduring literary classics.

complex sentence   A sentence that includes one independent clause and at least one dependent clause.

If a free society cannot help the many who are poor, it cannot save the few who are rich.
—JOHN F. KENNEDY

compound sentence   A sentence that includes at least two independent clauses.

The energy, the faith, the devotion which we bring to this endeavor will light our country and all who serve it and the glow from that fire can truly light the world.
—JOHN F. KENNEDY

concession   An acknowledgment that an opposing argument may be true or reasonable. In a strong argument, a concession is usually accompanied by a refutation challenging the validity of the opposing argument.

Lou Gehrig concedes what some of his listeners may think—that his bad break is a cause for discouragement or despair.

confirmation   In classical oration, this major part of an argument comes between the narration and refutation; it provides the development of proof through evidence that supports the claims made by the speaker.

connotation   Meanings or associations that readers have with a word beyond its dictionary definition, or denotation. Connotations are often positive or negative, and they often greatly affect the author's tone. Consider the connotations of the words below, all of which mean "overweight."

That cat is plump. *That cat is* fat. *That cat is* obese.

context   The circumstances, atmosphere, attitudes, and events surrounding a text.

The context for Lou Gehrig's speech is the recent announcement of his illness and his subsequent retirement, but also the poignant contrast between his potent career and his debilitating disease.

counterargument   An opposing argument to the one a writer is putting forward. Rather than ignoring a counterargument, a strong writer will usually address it through the process of concession and refutation.

Some of Lou Gehrig's listeners might have argued that his bad break was a cause for discouragement or despair.

cumulative sentence   Sentence that completes the main idea at the beginning of the sentence and then builds and adds on.

But neither can two great and powerful groups of nations take comfort from our present course—both sides overburdened by the cost of modern weapons, both rightly alarmed by the steady spread of the deadly atom, yet both racing to alter that uncertain balance of terror that stays the hand of mankind's final war.
—JOHN F. KENNEDY

deduction   Deduction is a logical process wherein you reach a conclusion by starting with a general principle or universal truth (a major premise) and applying it to a specific case (a minor premise). The process of deduction is usually demonstrated in the form of a syllogism:

MAJOR PREMISE: Exercise contributes to better health.

MINOR PREMISE: Yoga is a type of exercise.

CONCLUSION: Yoga contributes to better health.

diction   A speaker's choice of words. Analysis of diction looks at these choices and what they add to the speaker's message.

either/or (false dilemma)   In this fallacy, the speaker presents two extreme options as the only possible choices.

Either we agree to higher taxes, or our grandchildren will be mired in debt.

enthymeme   Essentially a syllogism with one of the premises implied, and taken for granted as understood.

You should take her class because I learned so much from her last year.

(Implied premise: If you take her class, you will learn a lot too.)

equivocation   A fallacy that uses a term with two or more meanings in an attempt to misrepresent or deceive.

We will bring our enemies to justice, or we will bring justice to them.

ethos   Greek for "character." Speakers appeal to ethos to demonstrate that they are credible and trustworthy to speak on a given topic. Ethos is established by both who you are and what you say.

Lou Gehrig brings the ethos of being a legendary athlete to his speech, yet in it he establishes a different kind of ethos — that of a regular guy and a good sport who shares the audience's love of baseball and family. And like them, he has known good luck and bad breaks.

exordium   In classical oration, the introduction to an argument, in which the speaker announces the subject and purpose, and appeals to ethos in order to establish credibility.

fallacy   See **logical fallacy**.

false dilemma   See **either/or**.

faulty analogy   A fallacy that occurs when an analogy compares two things that are not comparable. For instance, to argue that because we put animals who are in irreversible pain out of their misery, so we should do the same for people, asks the reader to ignore significant and profound differences between animals and people.

figurative language (figure of speech)   Nonliteral language, sometimes referred to as tropes or metaphorical language, often evoking strong imagery, figures of speech often compare one thing to another either explicitly (simile) or implicitly (metaphor). Other forms of figurative language include personification, paradox, overstatement (hyperbole), understatement, metonymy, synecdoche, and irony.

first-hand evidence   Evidence based on something the writer *knows*, whether it's from personal experience, observations, or general knowledge of events.

hasty generalization   A fallacy in which a faulty conclusion is reached because of inadequate evidence.

> Smoking isn't bad for you; my great aunt smoked a pack a day and lived to be 90.

hortative sentence   Sentence that exhorts, urges, entreats, implores, or calls to action.

> Let both sides explore what problems unite us instead of belaboring those problems which divide us.
>
> —John F. Kennedy

hyperbole   Deliberate exaggeration used for emphasis or to produce a comic or ironic effect; an overstatement to make a point.

> My first and last name together generally served the same purpose as a high brick wall.
>
> —Firoozeh Dumas

imagery   A description of how something looks, feels, tastes, smells, or sounds. Imagery may use literal or figurative language to appeal to the senses.

> Your eyes glaze as you travel life's highway past all the crushed animals and the Big Gulp cups.
>
> —Joy Williams

imperative sentence   Sentence used to command or enjoin.

> My fellow citizens of the world: ask not what America will do for you, but what together we can do for the freedom of man.
>
> —John F. Kennedy

induction   From the Latin *inducere*, "to lead into," induction is a logical process wherein you reason from particulars to universals, using specific cases in order to draw a conclusion, which is also called a generalization.

> Regular exercise promotes weight loss.
>
> Exercise lowers stress levels.
>
> Exercise improves mood and outlook.
>
> GENERALIZATION: Exercise contributes to better health.

inversion   Inverted order of words in a sentence (variation of the subject-verb-object order).

> United there is little we cannot do in a host of cooperative ventures. Divided there is little we can do.
>
> —John F. Kennedy

irony   A figure of speech that occurs when a speaker or character says one thing but means something else, or when what is said is the opposite of what is expected, creating a noticeable incongruity.

> *Nature has become simply a visual form of entertainment, and it had better look snappy.*
>
> — JOY WILLIAMS

juxtaposition   Placement of two things closely together to emphasize similarities or differences.

> *The nations of Asia and Africa are moving at jet-like speed toward gaining political independence, but we still creep at horse-and-buggy pace toward gaining a cup of coffee at a lunch counter.*
>
> — MARTIN LUTHER KING

logical fallacies   Logical fallacies are potential vulnerabilities or weaknesses in an argument. They often arise from a failure to make a logical connection between the claim and the evidence used to support it.

logos   Greek for "embodied thought." Speakers appeal to logos, or reason, by offering clear, rational ideas and using specific details, examples, facts, statistics, or expert testimony to back them up.

> *Gehrig starts with the thesis that he is "the luckiest man on the face of the earth" and supports it with two points: (1) the love and kindness he's received in his seventeen years of playing baseball, and (2) a list of great people who have been his friends, family, and teammates.*

metaphor   Figure of speech that compares two things without using *like* or *as*.

> *And if a beachhead of cooperation may push back the jungle of suspicion . . .*
>
> — JOHN F. KENNEDY

metonymy   Figure of speech in which something is represented by another thing that is related to it or emblematic of it.

> *The pen is mightier than the sword.*

modifier   An adjective, adverb, phrase, or clause that modifies a noun, pronoun, or verb. The purpose of a modifier is usually to describe, focus, or qualify.

> <u>*Sprawling and dull in class,*</u> *he comes alive in the halls and in the cafeteria.*
>
> — DAVID DENBY

mood   The feeling or atmosphere created by a text.

narration   In classical oration, the factual and background information, establishing why a subject or problem needs addressing; it precedes the confirmation, or laying out of evidence to support claims made in the argument.

nominalization   The process of changing a verb into a noun.

> Discuss *becomes* discussion. Depend *becomes* dependence.

occasion   The time and place a speech is given or a piece is written.

> *In the case of Gehrig's speech, the occasion is Lou Gehrig Appreciation Day. More specifically, his moment came at home plate between games of a doubleheader.*

open thesis An open thesis is one that does not list all of the points the writer intends to cover in an essay.

The popularity of the Harry Potter series demonstrates that simplicity trumps complexity when it comes to the taste of readers, both young and old.

oxymoron A paradox made up of two seemingly contradictory words.

But this peaceful revolution . . .

—JOHN F. KENNEDY

paradox A statement or situation that is seemingly contradictory on the surface, but delivers an ironic truth.

There is that scattereth, yet increaseth.

—THE BIBLE

To live outside the law you must be honest.

—BOB DYLAN

parallelism Similarity of structure in a pair or series of related words, phrases, or clauses.

Let both sides explore. . . . Let both sides, for the first time, formulate serious and precise proposals. . . . Let both sides seek to invoke. . . . Let both sides unite to heed . . .

—JOHN F. KENNEDY

pathos Greek for "suffering" or "experience." Speakers appeal to pathos to emotionally motivate their audience. More specific appeals to pathos might play on the audience's values, desires, and hopes, on the one hand, or fears and prejudices, on the other.

The most striking appeal to pathos is the poignant contrast between Gehrig's horrible diagnosis and his public display of courage.

periodic sentence Sentence whose main clause is withheld until the end.

To that world assembly of sovereign states, the United Nations, our last best hope in an age where the instruments of war have far outpaced the instruments of peace, we renew our pledge of support . . .

—JOHN F. KENNEDY

peroration In classical oration, the final part of an argument. It follows the refutation and typically appeals to pathos as it moves the audience toward the conclusion.

persona Greek for "mask." The face or character that a speaker shows to his or her audience.

Lou Gehrig is a famous baseball hero, but in his speech he presents himself as a common man who is modest and thankful for the opportunities he's had.

personification Attribution of a lifelike quality to an inanimate object or an idea.

. . . with history the final judge of our deeds . . .

—JOHN F. KENNEDY

polemic   Greek for "hostile." An aggressive argument that tries to establish the superiority of one opinion over all others. Polemics generally do not concede that opposing opinions have any merit.

polysyndeton   The deliberate use of multiple conjunctions between coordinate phrases, clauses, or words.

> *I paid for my plane ticket, and the taxes, and the fees, and the charge for the checked bag, and five dollars for a bottle of water.*

post hoc ergo propter hoc   This fallacy is Latin for "after which therefore because of which," meaning that it is incorrect to always claim that something is a cause just because it happened earlier. One may loosely summarize this fallacy by saying that correlation does not imply causation.

> *We elected Johnson as president and look where it got us: hurricanes, floods, stock market crashes.*

propaganda   The spread of ideas and information to further a cause. In its negative sense, propaganda is the use of rumors, lies, disinformation, and scare tactics in order to damage or promote a cause. For more information, see *How to Detect Propaganda* on p. 756.

purpose   The goal the speaker wants to achieve.

> *One of Gehrig's chief purposes in delivering his Farewell Address is to thank his fans and his teammates, but he also wants to demonstrate that he remains positive: he emphasizes his past luck and present optimism and downplays his illness.*

qualified argument   An argument that is not absolute. It acknowledges the merits of an opposing view, but develops a stronger case for its own position.

qualifier   In the Toulmin model, the qualifier uses words like *usually*, *probably*, *maybe*, *in most cases*, and *most likely* to temper the claim a bit, making it less absolute. For an example, see **Toulmin model**.

qualitative evidence   Evidence supported by reason, tradition, or precedent.

quantitative evidence   Quantitative evidence includes things that can be measured, cited, counted, or otherwise represented in numbers—for instance, statistics, surveys, polls, census information.

rebuttal   In the Toulmin model, a rebuttal gives voice to possible objections. For an example, see **Toulmin model**.

refutation   A denial of the validity of an opposing argument. In order to sound reasonable, a refutation often follows a concession that acknowledges that an opposing argument may be true or reasonable. One of the stages in classical oration, usually following the confirmation, or proof, and preceding the conclusion, or peroration.

> *Lou Gehrig refutes that his bad break is a cause for discouragement by saying that he has "an awful lot to live for!"*

reservation   In the Toulmin model, a reservation explains the terms and conditions necessitated by the qualifier. For an example, see **Toulmin model**.

rhetoric   Aristotle defined rhetoric as "the faculty of observing in any given case the available means of persuasion." In other words, it is the art of finding ways of persuading an audience.

rhetorical appeals   Rhetorical techniques used to persuade an audience by emphasizing what they find most important or compelling. The three major appeals are to ethos (character), logos (reason), and pathos (emotion).

rhetorical question   Figure of speech in the form of a question posed for rhetorical effect rather than for the purpose of getting an answer.
Will you join in that historic effort?
—JOHN F. KENNEDY

rhetorical triangle (Aristotelian triangle)   A diagram that illustrates the interrelationship among the speaker, audience, and subject in determining a text. See p. 4.

Rogerian arguments   Developed by psychiatrist Carl Rogers, Rogerian arguments are based on the assumption that fully understanding an opposing position is essential to responding to it persuasively and refuting it in a way that is accommodating rather than alienating.

satire   The use of irony or sarcasm to critique society or an individual.

scheme   Artful syntax; a deviation from the normal order of words. Common schemes include parallelism, juxtaposition, antithesis, and antimetabole.

second-hand evidence   Evidence that is accessed through research, reading, and investigation. It includes factual and historical information, expert opinion, and quantitative data.

simile   A figure of speech used to explain or clarify an idea by comparing it explicitly to something else, using the words *like*, *as*, or *as though*.
Zoos are pretty, contained, and accessible. . . . Sort of like a biological Crabtree & Evelyn basket selected with you in mind.
—JOY WILLIAMS

SOAPS   A mnemonic device that stands for Subject, Occasion, Audience, Purpose, and Speaker. It is a handy way to remember the various elements that make up the rhetorical situation.

speaker   The person or group who creates a text. This might be a politician who delivers a speech, a commentator who writes an article, an artist who draws a political cartoon, or even a company that commissions an advertisement.
In his Farewell Address, the speaker is not just Lou Gehrig, but baseball hero and ALS victim Lou Gehrig, a common man who is modest and thankful for the opportunities he's had.

stance   A speaker's attitude toward the audience (differing from tone, the speaker's attitude toward the subject).

straw man   A fallacy that occurs when a speaker chooses a deliberately poor or oversimplified example in order to ridicule and refute an idea.

> *Politician X proposes that we put astronauts on Mars in the next four years. Politician Y ridicules this proposal by saying that his opponent is looking for "little green men in outer space."*

subject   The topic of a text. What the text is *about*.

> *Lou Gehrig's subject in his speech is his illness, but it is also an expression of his gratitude for all of the lucky breaks that preceded his diagnosis.*

syllogism   A logical structure that uses the major premise and minor premise to reach a necessary conclusion.

> MAJOR PREMISE: Exercise contributes to better health.
>
> MINOR PREMISE: Yoga is a type of exercise.
>
> CONCLUSION: Yoga contributes to better health.

synecdoche   Figure of speech that uses a part to represent the whole.

> *In your hands, my fellow citizens, more than mine, will rest the final success or failure of our course.*
>
> —JOHN F. KENNEDY

syntax   The arrangement of words into phrases, clauses, and sentences. This includes word order (subject-verb-object, for instance, or an inverted structure); the length and structure of sentences (simple, compound, complex, or compound-complex); and such schemes as parallelism, juxtaposition, antithesis, and antimetabole.

synthesize   Combining two or more ideas in order to create something more complex in support of a new idea.

text   While this term generally means the written word, in the humanities it has come to mean any cultural product that can be "read"—meaning not just consumed and comprehended, but investigated. This includes fiction, nonfiction, poetry, political cartoons, fine art, photography, performances, fashion, cultural trends, and much more.

tone   A speaker's attitude toward the subject conveyed by the speaker's stylistic and rhetorical choices.

Toulmin model   An approach to analyzing and constructing arguments created by British philosopher Stephen Toulmin in his book *The Uses of Argument* (1958). The Toulmin model can be stated as a template:

> Because (evidence as support), therefore (claim), since (warrant or assumption), on account of (backing), unless (reservation).

Because it is raining, therefore I should probably take my umbrella, since it will keep me dry on account of its waterproof material, unless, of course, there is a hole in it.

trope   Artful diction; from the Greek word for "turning," a figure of speech such as metaphor, simile, hyperbole, metonymy, or synecdoche.

understatement   A figure of speech in which something is presented as less important, dire, urgent, good, and so on, than it actually is, often for satiric or comical effect. Also called *litotes*, it is the opposite of hyperbole.

You might want to write clearly and cogently in your English class.

The night in prison was novel and interesting enough.

—Henry David Thoreau

warrant   In the Toulmin model, the warrant expresses the assumption necessarily shared by the speaker and the audience.

wit   In rhetoric, the use of laughter, humor, irony, and satire in the confirmation or refutation of an argument.

zeugma   Use of two different words in a grammatically similar way that produces different, often incongruous, meanings.

When you open a book, you open your mind.

Now the trumpet summons us again — not as a call to bear arms, though arms we need — not as a call to battle, though embattled we are — but a call to bear the burden . . .

—John F. Kennedy

Text Credits

Chinua Achebe. From "The Empire Fights Back." Excerpt from pages 37–46, from *Home and Exile* by Chinua Achebe. Copyright © 2001 by Chinua Achebe. Reprinted with permission of Oxford University Press UK.

Marjorie Agosín. "Always Living in Spanish." First published in *Poets & Writers* (March/April 1999). Copyright © 1999 by Marjorie Agosín. Translated by Celeste Kostopulos-Cooperman. Reprinted by permission of the author.

Caroline Alexander. "The Great Game." Copyright © 2010 by Caroline Alexander. This essay was originally published in the Summer 2010 issue of *Lapham's Quarterly: Sports & Games*. Reprinted by permission of Aitken Alexander Associates, Ltd.

Sherman Alexie. "Superman and Me." Published in the *Los Angeles Times,* April 19, 1998. Copyright © 1997 by Sherman Alexie. Reprinted with permission of the author. All rights reserved.

Will Allen. "A Good Food Manifesto for America." Copyright © 2008 Growing Power, Inc. Reprinted with permission of the author.

Lori Arviso Alvord, M.D., and Elizabeth Cohen Van Pelt. "Walking the Path between Worlds." From *The Scalpel and the Silver Bear*. Copyright © 1999 by Lori Arviso Alvord and Elizabeth Cohen Van Pelt. Used by permission of Bantam Books, a division of Random House, Inc.

Lars Anderson. "The Sound and Glory: Beyond the Excitement of Race Day, the Story of the Indy 500 Mirrors the Story of America." From *Sports Illustrated* (sportsillustrated.cnn.com/vault/), April 14, 2011. Used with permission.

Gloria Anzaldúa. "How to Tame a Wild Tongue." From *Borderlands/La Frontera: The New Mestiza*. Copyright © 1987, 1999, 2007 by Gloria Anzaldúa. Reprinted by permission of Aunt Lute Books. www.auntlute.com

Kwame Anthony Appiah. From "The Case for Contamination." From *Cosmopolitanism: Ethics in a World of Strangers*. Copyright © 2006 by Kwame Anthony Appiah. Used by permission of W. W. Norton & Company, Inc.

Anne Applebaum. "If the Japanese Can't Build a Safe Reactor, Who Can?" *washingtonpost.com/opinions*, March 14, 2011. Copyright © 2011 by The Washington Post. All rights reserved. Used by permission and protected by the Copyright Laws of the United States. The printing, copying, redistribution, or retransmission of this Content without express written permission is prohibited.

The Associated Press. "Volunteering Opens Teen's Eyes to Nursing." From the *Detroit News*, November 22, 2008. Reprinted with permission of the YGS Group on behalf of The Associated Press Permissions.

James Baldwin. "A Talk to Teachers." Originally published in the *Saturday Review*. Collected in *The Price of the Ticket*, published by St. Martin's Press. Copyright © 1963 by James Baldwin. Used by arrangement with the James Baldwin Estate.

David Barboza. "Shanghai Schools' Approach Pushes Students to Top of Tests." From the *New York Times*, December 29, 2010. Copyright © 2010 the New York Times Company. Used by permission and protected by the Copyright Laws of the United States. The printing, copying, redistribution, or retransmission of the Material without express written permission is prohibited.

Mark Bauerlein and Sandra Stotsky. "Why Johnny Won't Read." Originally published in the *Washington Post*, January 25, 2005. Copyright © 2005 by Mark Bauerlein and Sandra Stotsky. Reprinted by permission of the authors.

Sharon Begley. "The Dumbest Generation? Don't Be Dumb." From *Newsweek*, May 24, 2008. [www.newsweek.com]. Reprinted with permission of Harman Newsweek LLC and protected by the Copyright Laws of the United States.

Wendell Berry. "Waste." From *What Are People For?* Copyright © 2010 by Wendell Berry. Reprinted by permission of Counterpoint.

Michael Binyon. "Absurd Decision on Obama Makes a Mockery of the Nobel Peace Prize." From the *London Times*, October 1, 2009. Reprinted with permission of News International Syndication Ltd.

Laura Blumenfeld. "The Apology: Letters from a Terrorist." From the *New Yorker*, March 4, 2002. Used with permission of William Morris Entertainment Endeavor.

Eavan Boland. "In which the Ancient History I Learn Is Not My Own." From *In a Time of Violence* by Eavan Boland. Copyright © 1994 by Eavan Boland. Used by permission of W. W. Norton & Company, Inc.

Leon Botstein. "Let Teenagers Try Adulthood." From the *New York Times*, May 17, 1999. Copyright © 1999 by Leon Botstein. Reprinted by permission of the author.

Lars Eighner. "On Dumpster Diving." From *Travels with Lizbeth* by Lars Eighner. Copyright © 1993 by Lars Eighner. Reprinted by permission of St. Martin's Press, LLC, and by Steven Saylor as agent for the author.

Albert Einstein. *Letter to Phyllis Wright*, January 24, 1936. Reprinted with permission of the Albert Einstein Archives, The Hebrew University of Jerusalem.

Ralph Ellison. "On Bird, Bird-Watching, and Jazz" from *Shadow and Act* by Ralph Ellison, copyright © 1953, 1964 by Ralph Ellison. Used by permission of Random House, Inc. Electronic rights granted by The Wylie Agency.

Frantz Fanon. From "Concerning Violence." Pages 37–39 from *The Wretched of the Earth.* Copyright © 1963 by *Presence Africaine.* Used by permission of Grove/Atlantic, Inc.

William Faulkner. "An Innocent at Rinkside." From *Sports Illustrated*, January 24, 1955. Copyright © 1955 by Estelle Faulkner and Jill Faulkner Summers. Renewed 1965, 2004 by Random House, Inc. Collected in *Essays, Speeches, and Public Letters* by William Faulkner, James B. Meriwether, ed. Used by permission of Random House, Inc. Electronic rights by permission of W. W. Norton & Co., Inc.

Jonathan Safran Foer. "The American Table" and "The Global Table." From *Eating Animals* by Jonathan Safran Foer. Copyright © 2009 by Jonathan Safran Foer. Used with permission of Little, Brown and Company.

Thomas L. Friedman. "The Revolution Is U.S." From *The Lexus and the Olive Tree* by Thomas L. Friedman. Copyright © 2000 by Thomas L. Friedman. Used with permission of Farrar, Straus & Giroux, LLC, and International Creative Management, Inc.

John Kenneth Galbraith. From "The Dependence Effect." From *The Affluent Society,* 4th edition, by John Kenneth Galbraith. Copyright © 1958, 1969, 1976, 1984 by John Kenneth Galbraith. Reprinted by permission of Houghton Mifflin Harcourt Publishing Company. All rights reserved.

Lou Gehrig. "The Luckiest Man on the Face of the Earth." Speech given on July 4, 1939. Lou Gehrig™ is a trademark of Rip van Winkle Foundation. Licensed by CMG Worldwide, Inc. www.LouGehrig.com.

"German Millionaire Criticizes Gates' 'Giving Pledge.'" *Spiegel International Online*, September 10, 2010. www.spiegel.de/international/. Copyright © 2010. Reprinted by permission of SPIEGEL-Verlag.

Todd Gitlin. "The Liberal Arts in an Age of Info-Glut." From the *Chronicle of Higher Education*, 1998. Copyright © 1998 by Todd Gitlin. Reprinted by permission of Trident Media Group.

Robin Givhan. "An Image a Little Too Carefully Coordinated." The *Washington Post*, July 22, 2005. Copyright © 2005 by The Washington Post. All rights reserved. Used by permission and protected by the Copyright Laws of the United States. The printing, copying, redistribution, or retransmission of this Content without express written permission is prohibited.

Malcolm Gladwell. From *Outliers.* Copyright © 2008 by Malcolm Gladwell. Used by permission of Little, Brown, and Company. "Small Change." The *New Yorker*, October 4, 2010, and "Offensive Play," the *New Yorker*, October 19, 2009. Copyright © Malcolm Gladwell. Used with permission of the author.

Ellen Goodman. "The Family That Stretches (Together)." From the *Washington Post.* Copyright © 1983 by The Washington Post. All rights reserved. Used by permission and protected by the Copyright Laws of the United States. The printing, copying, redistribution, or retransmission of this Content without express written permission is prohibited.

Stephen Jay Gould. "Women's Brains." Copyright © 1980 by Stephen Jay Gould. Reprinted with permission of the Art Science Research Laboratory.

Garrett Hardin. From "Lifeboat Ethics: The Case Against Helping the Poor." Originally published in *Psychology Today*, September 1974. Reprinted by permission of Sussex Publishers, LLC.

Daniel Harris. "Celebrity Bodies." First appeared in *Southwest Review*, Vol. 93, No. 1, 2008. Copyright © 2008 Daniel Harris. Used with permission of the Malaga Baldi Agency on behalf of the author.

Heather Havrilesky. "Besieged by 'Friends.'" Copyright © 2003. This article first appeared on http://www.salon.com. An online version remains in the Salon archives. Reprinted by permission.

Christopher Hedges. "The Destruction of Culture." From *War Is a Force That Gives Us Meaning.* Copyright © 2002 by Chris Hedges. Reprinted by permission of *Public Affairs,* a member of Perseus Books, LLC.

A. J. Jacobs. "Farm to Table." From *Esquire*, March 2011. Used with permission of the author.

Josef Joffe. "The Perils of Soft Power." From the *New York Times*, May 14, 2006. Copyright © 2006 by Dr. Josef Joffe. Reprinted by permission of the author.

Steven Johnson. "Watching TV Makes You Smarter." From *Everything Bad Is Good for You.* Copyright © 2005 by Steven Johnson. Used by permission of Riverhead Books, an imprint of Penguin Group (USA) Inc. and the Lydia Wills Literary Agency.

Diane Ravitch. "Stop the Madness." From *The Death and the Life of the Great American School System* by Diane Ravitch. Copyright © 2010 by Diane Ravitch. Reprinted by permission of Basic Books, a member of the Perseus Books Group.

Rick Reilly. "Why I Love My Job." From *ESPN the Magazine*. December 2, 2009.

Richard Rodriguez. "Aria." From *Hunger of Memory: The Education of Richard Rodriguez* by Richard Rodriguez. Copyright ©1982 by Richard Rodriguez. Reprinted with permission of David R. Godine, Publisher, Inc.

Phyllis Rose. "Shopping and Other Spiritual Adventures in America Today." Copyright © 1984 by Phyllis Rose. Used by permission of The Wylie Agency, LLC.

Bertrand Russell. "The Happy Man" excerpted from *The Conquest of Happiness*. Copyright © 1930 by Horace Liveright, Inc. Renewed © 1958 by Bertrand Russell. Used by permission of Liveright Publishing Corporation and The Bertrand Russell Peace Foundation.

Fabiola Santiago. "In College, These American Citizens Are Not Created Equal." From the *Miami Herald*, October 25, 2011. Copyright © 2011 by McClatchy. All rights reserved. Used by permission and protected by the Copyright Laws of the United States. The printing, copyright, redistribution, or retransmission of this Content without express written permission is prohibited.

Marjane Satrapi. "The Veil," from *Persepolis: The Story of a Childhood*. Translation by Mattias Ripa & Blake Ferris, copyright © 2003 by L'Association, Paris, France. Used by permission of Pantheon Books, a division of Random House, Inc.

Eric Schlosser. Excerpt from *Reefer Madness: Sex, Drugs, and Cheap Labor in the American Black Market*. Copyright © 2003 by Eric Schlosser. Reprinted by permission of Houghton Mifflin Harcourt Publishing Company. All rights reserved.

Juliet Schor. "The New Politics of Consumption: Why Americans Want So Much More Than They Need." Originally published in the Summer 1999 issue of *Boston Review*. Copyright © 1999 by Juliet Schor. Reprinted by permission of the author.

David Sedaris. "Me Talk Pretty One Day." From *Me Talk Pretty One Day* by David Sedaris. Copyright © 2000 by David Sedaris. Used with permission of Little, Brown & Company and Don Congdon Associates, Inc.

Peter Singer. From "The Singer Solution to World Poverty." From the *New York Times* magazine section, September 5, 1999. Copyright © 1999 Peter Singer. Reprinted by permission of the author.

Jane Smiley. "Barbaro, The Heart in the Winner's Circle." From the *Washington Post*. Copyright © 2007 by The Washington Post Writers Group. Used by permission of The Washington Post.

Joan Smith. "Shop-happy." This article first appeared in Salon.com, at http://www.Salon.com, May 11, 2000. An online version remains in the Salon archives. Reprinted with permission.

Michael Specter. Excerpts from "Test-Tube Burgers." The *New Yorker*, May 23, 2011. Copyright © 2001 by Michael Specter. Reprinted by permission of the author.

Brent Staples. "Just Walk on By: A Black Man Ponders His Power to Alter Public Space." Copyright © 1986 by Brent Staples. Reprinted by permission of the author.

Deirdre Straughan. "Cultural Hegemony: Who's Dominating Whom?" Copyright © 2005 by Deirdre Straughan. Reprinted by permission of the author.

Margaret Talbot. "Best in Class: Students Are Suing Their Way to the Top." From the *New Yorker*, June 6, 2005, pages 32–43. Used with permission of The Wylie Agency, LLC.

Gay Talese. "The Silent Season of a Hero." Copyright © 1966 by Gay Talese. Originally published in *Esquire Magazine*. Reprinted by permission of the Janklow & Nesbitt Associates as agents for the author.

Amy Tan. "Mother Tongue." Copyright © 1990 by Amy Tan. First appeared in *The Threepenny Review*. Reprinted by permission of the author and the Sandra Dijkstra Literary Agency.

Deborah Tannen. "Wears Jumpsuits, Sensible Shoes. Uses Husband's Last Name." Original title, "Marked Women, Unmarked Men" from the *New York Times Magazine*, June 20, 1993. Copyright © 1993 Deborah Tannen. Adapted from the book *Talking from Nine to Five*. Used with permission of the author.

Paul Theroux. "Being a Man." From *Sunrise with Seamonsters* by Paul Theroux. Copyright © 1985 by Cape Cod Scriveners Co. Reprinted by permission of Houghton Mifflin Harcourt Publishing Company and The Wylie Agency. All rights reserved.

Dana Thomas. "Terror's Purse Strings." From the *New York Times*, August 30, 2007. All rights reserved. Used by permission and protected by the Copyright Laws of the United States. The printing, copying, redistribution, or retransmission of the Material without express written permission is prohibited.

Picture Credits

reserved; **133,** www.polyp.org.uk; **136,** Digital Image © The Museum of Modern Art/Licensed by SCALA/ Art Resource, NY; **137,** Getty Images/Photo courtesy of the *Bergen Record*; **138,** TOLES © 2005 The Washington Post. Reprinted with permission of UNIVERSAL UCLICK. All rights reserved; **159,** CIRCLE (Center for Information & Research on Civic Learning & Engagement); **174,** © Roz Chast/The New Yorker Collection/www.cartoonbank.com; **176,** Ulf Andersen/Getty Images; **189,** Mary Evans Picture Library/The Image Works; **242,** Works by Norman Rockwell. Printed by permission of the Norman Rockwell Family Agency Book Rights, Copyright © 2012 The Norman Family Entities. Photo: Norman Rockwell Museum Collections; **244–246,** © Roz Chast/The New Yorker Collection/www.cartoonbank.com; **256,** © Edward Koren/The New Yorker Collection/www.cartoonbank.com; **261,** Source: Eric A. Hanushek, Paul E. Peterson, and Ludger Woessmann, 2010. "U.S. Math Performance in Global Perspective: How well does each state do at producing high-achieving students?" PEPG 10-19 (2010), modification of graph presented on pp. 16–17 (the original is available at http://www.hks.harvard.edu/pepg/PDF/Papers/PEPG10-19_ HanushekPetersonWoessmann.pdf); **280,** Arty Pomerantz/The Image Works; **296,** Bettmann/Corbis; **357,** Works by Norman Rockwell. Printed by permission of the Norman Rockwell Family Agency Book Rights Copyright © 2012 The Norman Family Entities. Photo: Norman Rockwell Museum Collections; **358,** © Roz Chast/The New Yorker Collection/www.cartoonbank.com; **359,** Photography by Gustavo di Mario, © 2010 Nissan. Nissan, Nissan model names, and the Nissan logo are registered trademarks of Nissan; **375,** © 2003–2011 Zapiro (All rights reserved). Originally published in Sunday *Times* on 2nd Feb 2003; **394,** Andrew Shurtleff/AP Images; **404,** Ann Ronan Picture Library/HIP/The Image Works; **471,** Jeff Parker/Florida Today/Cagle Cartoons; **473,** © Tom Tomorrow; **518,** Richard Howard Photography; **525,** Ann Ronan Picture Library/HIP/The Image Works; **563,** Reunion des Musees Nationaux/Art Resource, NY; **564,** *The Chancellor Seguier on Horseback* © Kehinde Wiley. Used by permission. Courtesy Sean Kelly Gallery, New York, Roberts & Tilton, Culver City, California, and Rhona Hoffman Gallery, Chicago; **567,** Time Life Pictures/Getty Images; **592,** Elisabetta A. Villa/Getty Images; **610,** The Granger Collection, New York; **615,** Notre Dame University/Getty Images; **668,** Courtesy of the University of North Carolina Press; **670,** Robert Beck/Sports Illustrated/Getty Images; **672,** © Boris Drucker/The New Yorker Collection/ www.cartoonbank.com; **700,** Will Ragozzino/Getty Images; **707,** Bettmann/Corbis; **752,** United States Census Bureau; **755,** Reprinted with permission from Cummins, J. (2001). Negotiating Identities: Education for Empowerment in a Diverse Society (p. 171). Los Angeles: California Association for Bilingual Education; **767,** Mike Lester, www.mikelester.com; **788,** Tiziana Fabi/AFP/Getty Images; **799,** Roger Viollet/ TOPHAM/The Image Works; **826,** REUTERS/Kevin Lamarque KL/JJ; **852,** © 2011 The Andy Warhol Foundation for the Visual Arts, Inc./Artists Rights Society (ARS), New York. Collection of Emily Fisher Landau, New York. Andy Warhol, 1928–1987. Myths, 1981. Synthetic polymer and screenprint ink on canvas, 100 x 100 in. (254 x 254 cm); 102 x 102 x 3 in. (259.1 x 259.1 x 7.6 cm) Promised gift of the Fisher Landau Center for Art to Whitney Museum of American Art, New York; promised gift of the Fisher Landau Center for Art P.2010.340; **854,** *The Innocent Eye Test* (1981), Mark Tansey. Oil on canvas, 78 x 120 in. (198.1 x 304.8 cm). Partial and promised gift of Jan Cowles and Charles Cowles, in honor of William S. Lieberman, 1988 (1988.183), Metropolitan Museum, New York. Copyright © 1981 Mark Tansey/Gagosian Gallery, New York/Image copyright © Metropolitan Museum of Art. Image source: Art Resource, NY; **873,** AP/Wide World Photos; **888,** Bettmann/Corbis; **897,** Mary Evans Picture Library/The Image Works; **954,** © Robert Crumb; **956–957,** Courtesy of Royal Dutch Shell; **959–961,** © Peter Menzel/www.menzelphoto .com; **981,** © Joe McKendry; **1006,** Ulf Andersen/Getty Images; **1016,** Bettmann/Corbis; **1087,** *Guernica* (1937) (Detail), Pablo Picasso. Oil on canvas, 350 x 782 cm. Museo Reina Sofia, Madrid. Photo by John Bigelow Taylor/Art Resource, New York/Copyright © 2008 Estate of Pablo Picasso/Artists Rights Society (ARS), New York; **1089,** *Guernica* (1937) (Detail), Pablo Picasso. Oil on canvas, 350 x 782 cm. Museo Reina Sofia, Madrid. Photo by John Bigelow Taylor/Art Resource, New York/Copyright © 2008 Estate of Pablo Picasso/Artists Rights Society (ARS), New York/The New Yorker cover art by Harry Bliss/Copyright © 2003 Condé Nast Publications, Inc.; **1090,** *Guernica* (1937) (Detail), Pablo Picasso. Oil on canvas, 350 x 782 cm. Museo Reina Sofia, Madrid. Photo by John Bigelow Taylor/Art Resource, New York/Copyright © 2008 Estate of Pablo Picasso/Artists Rights Society (ARS), New York/Photomontage by Penny Gentieu/ Copyright © 2003 by Harper's Magazine. All rights reserved. Reproduction from the April issue by special permission; **1122–1123,** Christiansted brochure courtesy of the National Park Service/Detail of lithograph by J. F. Fritz from a drawing by Theodore C. Sabroe courtesy of the Danish Royal Library.

Index